F

Also by Danny Peary

CLOSE-UPS: The Movie Star Book, *editor*
THE AMERICAN ANIMATED CARTOON,
coeditor with Gerald Peary
CULT MOVIES
CULT MOVIES 2
SCREEN FLIGHTS/
SCREEN FANTASIES, *editor*

Danny Peary

GUIDE FOR THE
Film
Fanatic

A Fireside Book ★ Published by Simon & Schuster, Inc.
New York

COPYRIGHT © 1986 BY DANNY PEARY
ALL RIGHTS RESERVED
INCLUDING THE RIGHT OF REPRODUCTION
IN WHOLE OR IN PART IN ANY FORM
A FIRESIDE BOOK,
PUBLISHED BY SIMON & SCHUSTER, INC.
SIMON & SCHUSTER BUILDING
ROCKEFELLER CENTER
1230 AVENUE OF THE AMERICAS
NEW YORK, NEW YORK 10020
FIRESIDE AND COLOPHON ARE REGISTERED TRADEMARKS
OF SIMON & SCHUSTER, INC.
DESIGNED BY BONNI LEON
MANUFACTURED IN THE UNITED STATES OF AMERICA
1   3   5   7   9   10   8   6   4   2
LIBRARY OF CONGRESS CATALOGING IN PUBLICATION DATA
PEARY, DANNY, date.
GUIDE FOR THE FILM FANATIC.

"A FIRESIDE BOOK."
1. MOVING-PICTURES — REVIEWS.   I. TITLE.
PN1995.P358   1986   791.43'75   86-11916

ISBN: 0-671-61081-3 (PBK.)

To
Suzanne and Zoë,
with much love.

———

You have made
staying home from
movies a treat.

Acknowledgments

I RECEIVED A GREAT DEAL OF HELP WHILE ASSEMBLING THIS BOOK—WRITING ISN'T ALWAYS A LONELY ENDEAVOR.

SPECIAL THANKS TO THE THREE INDIVIDUALS WHO INITIATED THIS PROJECT: CATHY HEMMING, PUBLISHER OF FIRESIDE BOOKS, CHARLES WOODS, THE ACQUIRING EDITOR, AND CHRIS TOMASINO, MY AGENT. I AM EQUALLY GRATEFUL TO THE THREE INDIVIDUALS WHO HELPED ME FINISH THIS PROJECT: MY EDITOR, TIM MCGINNIS, WHO ALWAYS CAME THROUGH IN A CRISIS; HIS ASSISTANT EDITOR, LAURA YORKE, WHOSE DAILY CALLS KEPT ME CALM AS DEADLINES APPROACHED; AND JOE SMITH, WHO SUPERVISED THE EXTENSIVE COPY EDITING AND DEVOTED MUCH PERSONAL TIME TO THE PROJECT (EVEN THOUGH HE WAS ABOUT TO GET MARRIED).

I WISH TO EXPRESS MUCH GRATITUDE TO SEVERAL PEOPLE FOR HELPING ME SCREEN FILMS: FRED FISHKIN; MARY LUGO, SARAH TALBOT, JAMES WATSON, AND JOHN HAYWARD OF NEW YORKER FILMS; JANIS ROTHBARD-CHASKIN AND STEVE HARRIS OF NEW LINE CINEMA; DAN STERN OF THE METRO CINEMA; HENRY BLINDER; AND CHICK FOXGROVER.

MUCH THANKS TO MY RESEARCHER, KATHY WILSON. AND TO MY SPECIAL ASSISTANT, ZOË WEAVER.

ALSO, I GREATLY APPRECIATE THE CONTRIBUTIONS OF: SOPHIE SORKIN, SIMON & SCHUSTER'S CHIEF OF COPY EDITING; JANE LOW IN THE SIMON & SCHUSTER COPY EDITING DEPARTMENT; SHARP-EYED COPY EDITORS PAUL HIRSCHMAN, LYNN CHALMERS, AND LINDA SPENCER (AN EXTRA PAT ON THE BACK GOES TO THE ONE WHO REALIZED I MEANT *PEGGY* LEE WHEN I WROTE *PINKY* LEE); DESIGNER BONNI LEON AND COVER ARTIST KAREN KATZ; PROOFREADERS JAMES DALY, JEFF KLEIN, FRANK SHEED, EMILY GARLIN, AND DORIS SULLIVAN; PROOFREADER-TYPIST HADASSAH GOLD; TYPISTS ELAINE GOLDMAN, CAROLYN PARQUETH, DIANE PARQUETH, AND CAROL KUCHEK; AND MARY WITKOWSKI, DIANE BURNS, AND ALICE GAMRET; AND MARTHA GRUTCHFIELD.

AND THANK YOU, SUZANNE, FOR YOUR PATIENCE AND SUPPORT.

Contents

Introduction

IF YOU FLIPPED THROUGH THE PAGES OF THIS BOOK, YOU MAY HAVE NOTICED THAT, UNLIKE MANY MOVIE-LIST BOOKS, THIS ONE DOES *NOT* HAVE A STAR RATING SYSTEM. I LOVE THOSE BOOKS, BUT I WORRY THAT RATING SYSTEMS HAVE THE ADVERSE EFFECT OF DISCOURAGING PEOPLE FROM SEEING CERTAIN MOVIES THAT SHOULD BE EQUALLY RECOGNIZED. IT'S ONLY NATURAL TO CHOOSE A MOVIE THAT HAS A THREE-STAR RATING OVER ONE THAT HAS JUST TWO STARS, BUT IN MANY CASES THE TWO-STAR MOVIE IS MORE INTERESTING—INDEED IT MAY HAVE A CULT MADE UP OF DEVOTED FANS WHO APPRECIATE THINGS THAT A PARTICULAR REVIEWER OVERLOOKED. I MAY ATTACK A FILM, BUT THAT DOESN'T MEAN I DON'T WANT YOU TO SEE IT. THIS BOOK IS MEANT TO ENCOURAGE READERS TO SEE MOVIES, NOT DISCOURAGE THEM.

I HAVE RECOMMENDED A TOTAL OF ABOUT 4200 "MUST SEE" FILMS, OF WHICH I HAVE HIGHLIGHTED 1650. THESE ARE NOT THE ONLY FILMS THAT YOU SHOULD SEE IN ORDER TO LEARN ABOUT FILM AND, CONSEQUENTLY, ENJOY IT MORE; BUT I THINK THESE ARE THE ONES TO SEEK OUT IF YOU DECIDE TO EXPAND YOUR FILM HORIZONS. EVERY FILM I LISTED IN THIS BOOK, INCLUDING THOSE EVERYONE AGREES ARE TRASHY, HAS DEVOTED FANS; THESE ARE THE FILMS THAT ARE DISCUSSED IN FILM COURSES, CONSTANTLY REFERRED TO BY CRITICS, AND/OR CHAMPIONED BY MOVIE-LOVERS. THEY AREN'T ALL MASTERPIECES—INDEED, YOU'LL THINK THAT MANY ARE TERRIBLE — BUT IN SOME WAY ALL ARE INTERESTING TO SOMEONE WHO IS GENUINELY INTERESTED IN FILM.

NO, I DON'T EXPECT EVERY READER TO SEEK OUT THE PORNO OR SLASHER FILMS I'VE INCLUDED JUST BECAUSE THERE ARE FANATICS FOR SUCH FILMS—ALTHOUGH I DO THINK A TRUE FILM FANATIC SHOULD BE AWARE OF SUCH FILMS. BUT I WOULD LIKE, FOR INSTANCE, PEOPLE WHO SHUN WESTERNS TO GIVE THIS THEMATICALLY FASCINATING GENRE A CHANCE —YOU CAN'T BE A FILM FANATIC AND NOT LIKE WESTERNS! I'D ALSO LIKE HIGHBROW MOVIE FANS TO SAMPLE ABBOTT & COSTELLO, MAMIE VAN DOREN, CLASSIC HORROR AND SCI-FI FILMS, "B" MELODRAMAS, ETC., JUST AS I'D LIKE TO MAKE LOWBROW FANS INTERESTED IN FOREIGN FILMS OTHER THAN *GODZILLA*. IT'S FUN TO SEE *ALL* TYPES OF MOVIES.

I INVITE YOU TO CHECK OFF THOSE FILMS YOU HAVE SEEN AND TO PLACE EMPTY CHECK BOXES NEXT TO THE FILMS THAT YOU HOPE TO SEE IN THE FUTURE. BOXES HAVE ALREADY BEEN PROVIDED FOR THE SUPPLEMENTAL LIST. USE THIS BOOK AS A WORKBOOK, AND TRY TO SEE AS MANY INCLUDED FILMS AS POSSIBLE. SURE, CHECKING EVERY FILM YOU SEE IS SILLY— BUT IT WILL HELP DEVELOP THE OBSESSIVENESS YOU NEED TO BECOME A TRUE FILM FANATIC. I'VE BEEN CHECKING FILM LISTS SINCE I WAS A TEENAGER.

FOR EACH OF THE HIGHLIGHTED FILMS, I HAVE PROVIDED THE MAJOR ACTORS AND TECH-NICAL CREDITS, LISTED ALTERNATE TITLES, STATED WHEN RUNNING TIMES DIFFER ACCORDING TO THE VARIOUS PRINTS IN CIRCULATION, NOTED WHETHER IT WAS MADE IN COLOR OR BLACK-

AND-WHITE, AND WRITTEN A REVIEW IN WHICH I ATTEMPT TO ZERO IN ON THE REASONS (THEMATIC, TECHNICAL, ETC.) THE PICTURE HAS IMPORTANCE TO FILM HISTORY AND/OR ITS FANS. THE FILMS ARE LISTED ALPHABETICALLY BY WORD, NOT BY LETTER (SO THAT, FOR EXAMPLE, *ALL THE RIGHT MOVES* COMES BEFORE *ALLEGRO NON TROPPO* AND *I WAS A TEENAGE WEREWOLF* COMES BEFORE *THE INVISIBLE MAN*). THE CUT-OFF DATE FOR FILMS IN THE BOOK WAS MID-MARCH 1986. I INVITE CORRECTIONS, ADDITIONAL INFORMATION, ARGUMENTS, TITLES OF FILMS I SHOULD HAVE INCLUDED, FEEDBACK OF ALL KINDS.

—DANNY PEARY

"Must See" Films

A NOS AMOURS (FRENCH/1984) C/102m.

Maurice Pialat's disturbing portrait of a 16-year-old girl (Sandrine Bonnaire) who drifts into a series of meaningless, unfulfilling sexual affairs. Her sexual proclivity can be seen as an attempt to find the love she can't find at home with her squabbling, unhelpful parents. The fact that she gives her virginity to a stranger rather than to her boyfriend who loves her implies that she is afraid of a meaningful relationship that will eventually go sour and that she is exhibiting a sad lack of self-esteem, masochistically and systematically picking men who will dump her—just as her father (Pialat) walks out on his hysterical wife (Evelyne Ker). Pialat's naturalistic vision of lower-middle-class family life is brutal—we even prefer that Bonnaire flee to her depressing romances rather than sticking around for the endless crazy arguments or wild slapping fits that take place each time she shows her face at home. She goes off to these men not only out of spiteful rebellion to hurt her parents for being *uncaring*, but also because that's her only choice. In her debut Bonnaire, a beautiful 16-year-old who looks a bit like the young Diane Lane, is memorable as the unhappy girl; her eyes become progressively more vacant, lonely, and forlorn as her character's chances for happiness vanish. Her nude scenes drew angry response from some critics who questioned Pialat's motives—but I don't think the film is particularly exploitive. It is a bit disjointed—the time frame is really hard to follow, and it's hard to determine how Pialat wants us to respond to the girl's situation or to the father who deserted her. But long after seeing the film you still think about her and those like her who are forced to bring themselves up, long before they have the maturity to know what's good for them. Also with: Dominique Besnehard.

ABBOTT AND COSTELLO MEET FRANKEN-STEIN (1948) B&W/83m.

Count Dracula (Bela Lugosi) intends to implant Costello's tiny brain in the head of the Frankenstein Monster (Glenn Strange). Meanwhile: as usual, the self-pitying Lawrence Talbot (Lon Chaney, Jr.) searches desperately for a cure for his lycanthropy. Smug critics often refer to this title to indicate just how low both Universal's top comedy team and its famous monsters had sunk by 1948. They're wrong on both counts. Most A&C fans consider this the duo's finest picture; their interplay is particularly sharp, their routines are strikingly funny, as when the not-so-innocent Costello arranges a double date with Abbott in which he gets both women (Lenore Aubert, Jane Randolph). In one of the few films to deftly combine horror and comedy, the monsters are treated with respect and affection, a far cry from the lampooning they'd be subjected to in future years. Horror fans, who'll appreciate the nifty special effects and make-up, will find the monsters appropriately frightening. Great visual has the Wolf Man dive out a high window and grab Dracula just as he flies off as a bat; both plummet to the rocky waters below. Among the comedy highlights is the scene in which Costello speaks to Chaney over the phone just when he transforms into a growling werewolf. Capably directed by Charles T. Barton, who was responsible for several other top A&C films. Also with: Frank Ferguson, Vincent Price (the voice of the Invisible Man).

ABOMINABLE DR. PHIBES, THE (BRITISH/1971) C/94m.

Not as well made or as lively as *Theatre of Blood* (1973), another campy Vincent Price British horror film with a revenge motif, but this is still reasonably enjoyable. Price is badly disfigured (we see how badly at the end) and his wife is killed in an accident. With the help of a beautiful, mute assistant (Virginia North), Price uses an assortment of gruesome methods to get revenge on the nine people he thinks are responsible. Intended victim Joseph Cotten discovers that Price's murders correspond to the ancient "Seven Curses of the Pharaohs." Price is well cast as the methodical, obsessed Dr. Anton Phibes, but at times I wish he'd get more into his "hammy routine." The murders are too grisly, especially for young children, but the film benefits from stylish direction by Robert Fuest and a funny, tongue-in-cheek script by James Whiton and William Goldstein. My favorite bit has the two detectives assigned to the case, Trout (Peter Jeffrey) and Crav (Derek Godfrey), being told by their superior that *from now on* they should try to arrive at the murder scene *before* the murder takes place—it's advice that almost every detective team, especially the British *Avengers*, should have been given. A solid ending, leading to Fuest's sequel, *Dr. Phibes Rises Again*. Also with: Terry Thomas, Sean Bury, Susan Travers, Hugh Griffith.

ABUSE (1983) B&W/93m.

A gay graduate student (Richard Ryder) makes a documentary on child abuse to complete his degree requirements, choosing as his main case study a teenage boy (Raphael Sbarge) who is being victimized by his parents. As the brutality intensifies, the filmmaker and his subject, who is also gay, become lovers and contemplate running off together. While the production values are low (it was made in 16mm) and the pacing is erratic, the subject matter is thought-provoking and important—and unusual for a commercial film. The almost too realistic scenes in which the boy's father and mother switch in an instant from being loving parents to monsters who take pleasure in systematically torturing their child are among the most harrowing in all of film. You'll feel the boy's fear when his parents just come in to kiss him goodnight. You'll begin to understand the syndrome involving supercritical parents and the abused child that prevents either from making an assertive move to stop further violence. But director Arthur J. Brennan's view that a young adult becoming lover/protector of a teenager is a welcome alternative to his parents battering him—rather than this being just another form of child abuse—is certainly worth arguing about. (Brennan tries to sway viewer by making the teenager independent-minded and having the actor playing the part look several years older.) Oddly, picture has some wit. Extremely controversial and worth a look. Also with: Steve W. James, Kathy Gerber, Jack Halton, Mickey Clark, Maurice Massaro, Susan Schneider.

ADAM'S RIB (1949) B&W/101m.
Married lawyers Spencer Tracy and Katharine Hepburn find themselves opposing each other in a headline-making trial. Hepburn is defending Judy Holliday, a mother and housewife, who caught husband Tom Ewell with his mistress Cara Williams and wildly fired six shots around her apartment. Tracy represents Ewell, who is accusing Holliday of attempted murder. Hepburn bases her defense on the supposition that if Holliday had been a man who found his wife with another man, then she would have been applauded instead of arrested. She uses the trial as a forum to denounce the sexism that prevails in society. Tracy accuses her of making a mockery of the law. Actually his masculine pride is hurt—hurt so badly that he leaves a marriage that had worked because of equality, friendship, and mutual respect. He must then use feminine wiles to get his wife back. Spirited performances by Hepburn and Tracy and Holliday's batty but sensitive delivery spark George Cukor's comedy. It's probably Hepburn and Tracy's best film, yet it has dated as badly as the others. Like the others, it must be seen in the light of its era to appreciate that it was ahead of its time in its treatment of sexual politics. The characters do so much grandstanding that the issues get blurred, yet the bright script by married Garson Kanin and Ruth Gordon deserves praise for being a *Hollywood* film that not only mentioned the term "sexual equality" way back in 1949, but also attempted to be something much more significant than the typical battle of the sexes. Also with: David Wayne, Clarence Kolb, Polly Moran, Hope Emerson.

ADVENTURES OF BUCKAROO BANZAI ACROSS THE EIGHTH DIMENSION, THE (1984) C/103m.
Scatterbrained, sloppily made science-fiction comedy for the stoned-out generation. It's about an all-purpose superhero—a poor man's Jerry Cornelius (Michael Moorcock's creation)—named Buckaroo Banzai, who is a rock star, neurosurgeon, particle physicist, and cool defender of the free world. He does battle with a lot of weirdly dressed aliens and a mad Italian scientist, Lizardo (John Lithgow), for control of an oscillator overthruster that makes it possible for a person to pass through solid matter. The story gets lost because of the chaotic pacing and lack of continuity, the overabundance of characters who run around in fancy outfits with no place to go, and the fact that first-time director W. D. Richter (who wrote the script for 1978's *Invasion of the Body Snatchers*) never bothers to establish where anyone is in relation to anyone else. As played by Peter Weller, Banzai unfortunately turns out to be a pretty conventional hero; his special skills are never really put to work—it's as if he has them only so the film's publicity releases will sound interesting. He even disappears from the screen for long periods of time without being missed. Weller is handsome, but hasn't the necessary charisma to play a superhero. His cockiness reflects the attitude of the whole production. Intended to be, paradoxically, a "cult film for the masses," it was a surprising failure when hip audiences were turned off by conceited attempt by filmmakers and actors to show off how "hip" they were. Richter even promised a sequel at the end of this film. No thanks. Has had some success as a midnight movie. Also with: Jeff Goldblum, Ellen Barkin.

ADVENTURES OF ROBIN HOOD, THE (1938) C/105m.
Robin (Errol Flynn) and his Merrie Men of Sherwood Forest make things difficult for sly Prince John (Claude Rains) and his evil henchman (Basil Rathbone) while loyally waiting for the noble King Richard (Ian Hunter) to return to England from the Crusades and reclaim his throne from his brother. Of course, they take from the rich and give the poor back the money John had unfairly taxed them. This is perhaps the greatest costume adventure of all time. Dashing Flynn and his loveliest screen partner, Olivia de Havilland (gallant as Maid Marian), are as romantic a couple as Romeo and Juliet—fittingly, they even have a balcony scene. And the final swordfight between Flynn and Rathbone (who, off screen, was the superior swordsman) is a classic, complete with gigantic shadows on castle walls—a trademark of Michael Curtiz, who assumed directing duties from William Keighley. The splendid color photography, sets, costumes, and rousing Oscar-winning score by Erich Wolfgang Korngold are all first-rate, effectively transporting us back to an enchanting world. Plus Warners surrounded the stars with such wonderful character actors as Alan Hale (Little John), Eugene Pallette (Friar Tuck), Una O'Connor, Montagu Love, and Melville Cooper. The casting of Flynn as Robin Hood was pivotal to his career, for it reinforced his *Captain Blood* image as the sensitive champion of the downtrodden and one of the few freedom-fighter (anti-authoritarian) heroes whom conservative Hollywood has ever accepted. You'd follow Flynn anywhere, sure that his cause is just. Also with: Patric Knowles, Herbert Mundin.

ADVENTURES OF ROBINSON CRUSOE/ ROBINSON CRUSOE (MEXICAN/1952) C/ 90m.
Luis Buñuel's peculiar adaptation of Defoe's novel is beautifully shot, particularly for such a low-budget film, yet is static and thematically ambiguous. Once Crusoe (Dan O'Herlihy) is stranded on the desert island, the ideal place for self-examination, this haughty slave-dealer feels humbled as he must consider his helplessness and man's insignificant place in God's universe. But where he initially is in awe of God and accepts his isolation as fair punishment for his conceit, he becomes furious toward God for abandoning him as well. Does he lose his faith in God and in fact see himself as God in this new domain as he brings order to the wilderness? It's unclear. So is the full meaning of his relationship to Friday (Jaime Fernandez), the cannibal he saves and civilizes: is it that contact between men is more

important than that between man and God? Crusoe and Friday become trusting companions, but one can see that Friday considers Crusoe his master and Crusoe seems to agree with him on this. If you want a *defiant* black, see Richard Roundtree stand up to Peter O'Toole in 1975's *Man Friday*. Adults will enjoy this film mostly as a Buñuel curio; oddly, this is the one Buñuel film that children—who'll respond to the colorful adventure and magical setting and be unaware of the religious themes—will like best.

ADVENTURES OF THE WILDERNESS FAMILY, THE (1975) C/100m.

Surprisingly popular in the theaters, now this and its two indistinguishable sequels have become staples on pay television. Traffic, pressure, smog, and health problems force an urban family of four "back to nature," into the Rocky Mountains, where they encounter a whole new series of problems. This is good family fare, I suppose, with lots of pretty scenery and wild animals, particularly bears. Father Robert Logan, enthusiastic star of the similar *Shipwreck!*, makes a sturdy hero. Susan Damante Shaw may get on your nerves by continuously worrying about her kids' safety, but, considering that their lives really are in danger about every two minutes of screen time, she has the right. In fact, most people who see these films will choose the smog over the dangerous mountain life. Directed by Stewart Raffill. Also with: Hollye Holmes, Ham Larsen, Buck Flowers, William Cornford.

AFRICAN QUEEN, THE (1952) C/105m.

A sure-fire "feel-good" movie teaming Humphrey Bogart and Katharine Hepburn under the direction of John Huston. James Agee, John Collier, Huston and Peter Viertel adapted C. S. Forester's novel, and Huston and his stars injected humor and playfulness into the story. Supposedly it had at one time been considered ideal for Charles Laughton and Elsa Lanchester because it bears similarities to *The Beachcomber*. The setting is German East Africa in 1914. Prim and proper Hepburn (as Rose) is the sister of Methodist minister Robert Morley. When Morley dies, directly because of German infiltration into the jungles, she accepts the invitation of slovenly, alcoholic boat captain Bogart (as Charlie) to flee downriver on his *African Queen*. She insists that they plan to blow up a German battleship far downstream. At first they can't stand each other, but their perilous journey—she is thrilled when they go over rapids—draws them close together. They become one of the cinema's truly wonderful romantic couples. Neither is reticent about expressing love for the other, even when in the midst of tragedy. Both are supportive of each other; there is a division of labor (he even lets her steer down the rapids); there is mutual respect. How her eyes sparkle with love when she looks at him; she truly believes she has found the best man in the world! And how he smiles and laughs around her—he no longer needs alcohol to make him happy. They constantly hug and kiss, and their endearing gestures have a cheering effect on the viewer. Fifty-three-year-old Bogart and 45-year-old Hepburn get sexier by the minute. Bogart won a Best Actor

Academy Award; for some reason the equally fine Hepburn (who based her character on Eleanor Roosevelt) didn't even get nominated. Filmed in England, the Congo, and Uganda, this is perhaps the cinema's greatest romantic adventure which is set in the 20th century—films such as *Romancing the Stone* were greatly influenced by it. Photographed by Jack Cardiff. Also with: Peter Bull, Theodore Bikel.

AFTER HOURS (1985) C/96m.

Near the end of Martin Scorsese's loopy paranoia-comedy, star Griffin Dunne's character, Paul Hackett, a young New York word processor, stands in front of a seated man and manically summarizes all the ridiculous and tragic things that have happened to him during this one night. It's a striking scene because one can visualize co-producer (with Amy Robinson) Dunne standing before studio execs, telling them in the same manner the weird plot points of this film and getting the same incredulous non-response. (Wisely, the producers decided to complete the film before trying to sell it to a studio.) In the story Paul meets a pretty, dithery young woman (Rosanna Arquette) in a coffee shop. She leaves him her number. Sensing an easy sexual conquest—he's willing to take advantage of her being an emotional cripple due to her break-up with her boyfriend—he calls her up and accepts her invitation to come to her SoHo loft. He leaves his secure Upper East Side apartment and takes a cab to SoHo. The supersonic-speed ride, during which his money blows out the window, is like Alice's bumpy descent into Wonderland. Trapped penniless in a netherland, an enemy zone, every imaginable awful experience happens to him, including his date's suicide (this is the ultimate "bad date" movie). As he flees, on mysteriously empty streets, from a bloodthirsty mob who think he's responsible for a rash of robberies, he runs into the same people over and over and into the same bars, diners, clubs, and apartments that he fled from earlier. SoHo becomes a labyrinth and he's the rat who can't find an exit. Scorsese's film, from a student script by Joe Minion, is literally Paul's *nightmare*, in which he just can't get home (only in a nightmare would the subway fare jump 60 cents at midnight without advance notice). He's in every scene; everything is taken from his point of view. As in any good nightmare, he loses his money and keys; is hunted down by complete strangers (much like Kevin McCarthy being chased by Body Snatchers); characters he befriends change from helpful to hostile from one meeting to the next and somehow they also seem to know each other; he keeps forgetting the phone number of a friend in the area because a woman (Catherine O'Hara) mixes him up by shouting out random numbers. The film is well made, but Minion's script is perhaps too facile because there is no need to develop any of the characters. What's most fascinating is that we don't sympathize with Paul because we don't really like him (he's kind of a worm). But we can identify with his plight. And we recognize him as Everyman, with many of our less noble qualities, including callousness, cowardice, opportunism, selfishness. Dunne is very good; yet this part also would have been ideal for Dudley Moore and, if you stretch it, Albert Brooks. Fun cast also includes: Lina Fiorentino, Teri Garr, John Heard, Cheech and Chong, Verna Bloom, Dick Miller.

AGE D'OR, L' (FRENCH/1930) B&W/60m.
Luis Buñuel and Salvador Dali collaborated on this surrealist classic. Banned in many countries and denied a major U.S. release for 50 years, it is a devilishly hilarious affront to bourgeois society, clericalism, and morality, as well as to movie-audience complacency. We are introduced to our hero (Gaston Modot) and heroine (Lya Lys) when their wild lovemaking, while fully clothed in the mud, disrupts a ceremony by priests and townspeople to honor the skeletons of bishops. Love/sex represents rebellion! The two are separated by police who take them away, but they release him when they learn he has a major position in the Ministry of Good Works. Working his way up, he squashes a beetle, kicks a dog, knocks over a blind man, and slaps an old lady (Lys's mother) who accidentally spilled liquor on him. Meanwhile Lys chases a cow from her bed, parts of Rome crumble, and guests at an elegant party ignore the deaths of a kitchen maid killed by fire and a young boy who was shot by his gamekeeper father after the tot annoyed him. During a concert Modot and Lys make mad love to Wagner music. While he's on the phone learning that he has caused millions of deaths since neglecting his job, Lys sucks on the toes of a male statue. After Lys and her father start smooching, Modot goes to his room and angrily tosses things out his window, including bishops. Finally we cut to an isolated hilltop castle where four sadistic libertines have spent De Sade's "120 Days of Sodom"—they emerge and the despicable leader turns out to be Jesus Christ! Scandalous, heavily symbolic film has lost none of its subversive impact. There has never been another film like it. Also with: Max Ernst, Pierre Prévert, José Artigas.

AGUIRRE: THE WRATH OF GOD (WEST GERMAN/1972) C/90m.
Director Werner Herzog took his cast and crew to unexplored regions of South America— steep mountain ledges and an Amazon tributary—to film his fictional masterpiece about a mad Spanish conquistador (Klaus Kinski) who in 1560 leads a mutiny against the leader (Ruy Guerra) of an expeditionary force in search of El Dorado. He then orchestrates an ill-fated journey downriver. He hopes to eventually conquer Mexico, marry his own fifteen-year-old daughter (Cecilia Rivera), and found a pure dynasty. It was filmmaking under the most trying circumstances, but the results are priceless; Thomas Mauch's camera has gone back in time to a lost world that is at once beautiful and terrifying. Beginning with an incredible image of perhaps a thousand soldiers in full armor, women in long dresses, and Indian slaves dragging cannons along a narrow, steep mountain path and ending with a delirious image of lone-survivor Aguirre stranded on a monkey-covered raft, with his dead men lying about him, the film is spellbinding; at first it is dreamlike, and ultimately hallucinatory. The journey downriver is full of haunting images: ghostly figures

moving in the brush, ready to pick off intruders with arrows, spears, and poison darts; an abandoned cannibal village; a small raft caught in a roaring whirlpool; the hooded black horse that stands abandoned in the prehistoric jungle. As in other films, Herzog delights in placing characters in hostile environments where, having nothing tangible to fight, they are unable to cope. Eventually their minds become mush from the constant horror, depression, and fear of death. Aguirre himself has little dialogue, and that is delivered without emotion, but seconds after we first see Kinski— sneering and snarling, gnarled like Richard III, standing at an angle as if to signify he's at odds with the world, twisting his head before moving his body—we recognize that he is contemptuous of the world and tortured by inner demons. Certainly Aguirre is meant to represent Hitler (though George Armstrong Custer also is appropriate). But his consistently poor leadership and frustration are treated with such mock delight by Herzog that there's evidence Aguirre is used as a comic villain, and the film itself is, though somberly presented, a comedy about a most embarrassingly unsuccessful expedition, carried out not by heroic figures, but by nefarious Spanish imperialists who deserved the sad end Herzog happily writes for them. Popol Vuh's music contributes greatly, making the journey come across as a funeral procession. Also with: Del Negro, Helena Rojo, Peter Berling.

AIR FORCE (1943) B&W/124m.
This first-rate WWII action drama was the last of Howard Hawks's films about his favorite action heroes: fliers, whom he'd featured in *The Air Circus*, *The Dawn Patrol*, *Ceiling Zero*, and *Only Angels Have Wings*. Like many of Hawks's films, it's about how a group of men (professionals all) work together to perform a difficult mission. An undisciplined gunner on a B-17 bomber, John Garfield finally gets serious about the war after seeing his fellow soldiers killed. He buckles down and becomes part of the motley crew, along with John Ridgely, Gig Young, Harry Carey, George Tobias, Charles Drake, and Arthur Kennedy. The solid, exciting script was provided by Dudley Nichols, with an assist from Hawks's buddy William Faulkner. But contemporary viewers, not so in tune with the film's propaganda value in 1943, may have trouble stomaching finale in which our vengeful heroes mow down helpless Japanese soldiers who are stranded in the ocean. In other Hollywood movies our GIs always showed amazing compassion. Also with: Faye Emerson, Ray Montgomery.

AIRPLANE! (1980) C/86m.
A combination of *Airport* and *Zero Hour* as if made by *Mad* magazine. Actually, this ambitious, amusing spoof was written and directed by three of the founding members of the madcap satirical revue Kentucky Fried Theater: Jim Abrahams and David and Jerry Zucker. When the crew and most passengers are struck down by food poisoning after eating spoiled fish, stewardess Julie Hagerty convinces her former flame Robert Hays, an army pilot who crashed his plane and killed his crew, to land the plane. Back at the airport, Robert Stack and Lloyd Bridges

try to talk him down. Much humor comes from exaggeration of clichés—for instance, when a passenger panics and needs the proverbial "Thanks, I needed that" single slap to be returned to her senses, passengers stand in line (many with weapons) to do the honors. Other humor comes from the fact that everything said is taken literally, including the "s——hitting the fan." But the humor comes from all sources: Barbara Billingsley speaking Swahili, co-pilot Kareem Abdul-Jabbar adamantly stating that he never dogs it on the basketball court, pilot Peter Graves talking about nude men in showers to a small boy who visits the cockpit, Hays and Hagerty dancing and her picking him up and twirling him through the air, Robert Stack (who wears two pairs of sunglasses) karate-chopping his way through Hare Krishnas, Moonies and other cultists who flood the airport. Gags come fast and furiously and it's amazing how many are funny. Picture does have dull spots, and eventually runs out of gas—but, all in all, it is a good job. Ken Finkleman directed *Airplane II: The Sequel*, which reunited Hays, Hagerty, Bridges, and Graves. Also with: Maureen McGovern, Ethel Merman, Jimmie Walker, Howard Jarvis, Leslie Nielsen (who'd star in the directors' short-lived, critically acclaimed TV comedy series *Police Squad*), Lorna Patterson, Stephen Stucker.

AIRPORT (1970) C/137m.
Part *Grand Hotel*, part *The High and the Mighty*, this lavish Ross Hunter–George Seaton financial blockbuster contains stereotypical characters, as well as a familiar plot and clichés by the mouthful, yet it manages to be as entertaining as Arthur Hailey's novel, and surprisingly suspenseful, too. While everyone on a recently departed plane and back at the airport trics to sort out their personal problems, things become tense when a bomb explodes on the plane, causing great damage. Will the crippled plane make it back to the airport? Will George Kennedy be able to clear a runway for an attempted landing? Will anyone in the all-star cast admit they recognize some of the other stars? A polished "commercial" Hollywood film, but it might have been really something if Irwin Allen, rather than Seaton, had been director. Surely a hurricane and airport fire would have been thrown in for good measure. Also starring Dean Martin, Burt Lancaster, Jacqueline Bisset, Martha Hyer, Helen Hayes, Jean Seberg, Maureen Stapleton, Van Heflin (as the mad bomber), Barry Nelson, Dana Wynter, Lloyd Nolan, Barbara Hale.

ALEXANDER NEVSKY (RUSSIAN/1938) B&W/105m.
A monumental achievement by Sergei Eisenstein. It's his greatest film, a visual tour-de-force about Russia's heroic 13th-century prince (Nikolai Cherkasov) who—three years after repelling the Swedes—forms a great army to wage war against the seemingly invincible Germans who have invaded the country. It's a peerless propaganda piece that extols Russian nationalism, displays the courage of the common Russian in battle, and viciously attacks Germany, Russia's historical enemy, which in the 1930s was again on an imperialist march in which impersonal medieval-like sol-

diers committed atrocities in the name of Christianity. (Ironically, Eisenstein's film wouldn't play in Russia until *after* Hitler broke the Soviet-German non-aggression pact; interestingly, the Order of Alexander Nevsky, eliminated in 1917, was restored in 1942 when Stalin wanted to rally his people against Germany.) You can take or leave Alexander's speeches about how Russia will always defeat invaders—it's probable that the real prince's conviction wasn't really so strong, since a few years later he capitulated to occupying Tatar forces; more fascinating, in the same way that *Triumph of the Will* is fascinating when Hitler mingles with his adoring subjects, is how Eisenstein *humanizes* his hero (meant to represent *Stalin*?) to show that he is not superior to the Russian soldier or peasant, just a better leader. He's a humble fisherman in the opening scene; he never talks down to his men; he lets the people decide what to do with his prisoners; he has compassion and a sense of humor; he's willing to celebrate with the people after his great victory. Simultaneously, common men are elevated to Alexander's level—Eisenstein films them with a camera tilted upward and sets them in the foreground against the gray sky (there is always space behind them) so that they look enormous, like *heroic* epic figures of Alexander's magnitude. Importantly, we see the *soldiers*—not Alexander—in battle. Indeed, the picture has a subplot in which each of two friendly soldiers hopes to win the hand of a young woman by fighting more gallantly than the other. It's like a stock Hollywood storyline, only in this case the *woman* is also a warrior, fighting alongside the men. The scene in which she helps both male friends off the battlefield is a classic. Eisenstein's picture is known for its remarkable close-ups, innovative use of the frame (whereby action is taking place in several different planes and as far back as the eye can see), beautiful shots of man and landscape, mix of realism and theatricality, gorgeous pageantry, and Sergei Prokofiev's grand score (which becomes oddly jovial when the Russians get the upper hand in battle). The climactic Battle on the Ice, a lengthy, precisely directed sequence that employs thousands of warriors and horses, is perhaps the greatest battle scene in movie history. It can't be described properly—it must be seen—but I suspect Eisenstein received special pleasure from directing the segment in which the ice breaks and hundreds of Germans drown. We are seeing Russia itself literally swallow invaders. I admit that some Russian *classics* are boring, but not this masterpiece. Also with: Nikolai Okhlopkov, Alexander Abrikossov, Dmitri Orlov, Vassily Novikov.

ALGIERS (1938) B&W/95m.
Irresistible, hot-blooded romance set in Algiers's Casbah, with Charles Boyer as suave jewel thief Pépé le Moko and luscious Hedy Lamarr (her American debut) as Gaby, the already engaged Parisian woman who melts his heart. Although they are in the drab Casbah, when they kiss they feel as if they were in their beloved Paris. Police want to lure Boyer out of the Casbah so they can arrest him. Lamarr is wrongly informed Boyer is dead so that she won't visit him as promised. They realize

Boyer will come out of the Casbah to find the woman he loves. Beautifully photographed by James Wong Howe, this dark, exotic, highly atmospheric film has the distinct look of a "thirties classic." Opening, in which we see documentary footage of Algiers and the Casbah, is very effective in transporting us out of Hollywood and into the faraway world. Character actors are convincing playing assorted foreigners. And Boyer and Lamarr are memorable screen lovers. Director John Cromwell's film is a remake of the 1937 French film *Pépé le Moko*, starring Jean Gabin; Tony Martin would have the lead in the 1948's *Casbah*. Written by John Howard Lawson, with additional dialogue by James M. Cain. Also with: Sigrid Gurie, Joseph Calleia, Gene Lockhart, Johnny Downs, Alan Hale, Stanley Fields, Leonid Kinskey, Joan Woodbury.

ALI—FEAR EATS THE SOUL/FEAR EATS THE SOUL (WEST GERMAN/1974) C/94m.
For those who consider the films of Rainer Werner Fassbinder too esoteric and perverse, here is one that has universal appeal. In fact, it was Fassbinder's breakthrough film internationally, the reason many people worldwide were willing to examine his more difficult, less accessible films. Set in Munich, it tells of the romance and marriage of a short, dumpy, 60-year-old German widow (Brigitte Mira) and a tall, handsome, young Moroccan (El Hedi Ben Salem) who we later discover is developing an ulcer from the constant racial prejudice he and other Arabs in Germany are subjected to. Once married, Mira is ostracized by her neighbors, friends, and adult children. The couple is strong enough to endure this, and eventually there are some signs of acceptance (the local shopkeepers make up to Mira when they realize they need her business). But in time Mira's own prejudices surface and threaten to shatter the marriage. A simple, extremely poignant film, all the more fascinating because Fassbinder deals with racial prejudice in modern *Germany*—against Arabs, not Jews. Fassbinder admired the work of Douglas Sirk, and critics were quick to point out film's similarity to Sirk's *All That Heaven Allows*. Also with: Barbara Valentin, Irm Hermann, Fassbinder.

ALICE ADAMS (1935) B&W/99m.
Katharine Hepburn had one of her greatest successes playing the young heroine of Booth Tarkington's Pulitzer Prize–winning novel. Alice is a smart, imaginative, energetic, yet dissatisfied small-town girl. She covets being on equal social footing with her richer acquaintances. When she meets a nice young man (Fred MacMurray), she is afraid to tell him that her family is poor. Instead she makes up stories about her family's wealth and her own good breeding. Alice is so obsessed with improving her social standing that she assumes an affected attitude whenever she leaves her house. We'd dislike her except that we admire her love for and loyalty to her weak father (Fred Stone), pushy mother (Ann Shoemaker), and irresponsible brother (Frank Albertson), despite their constantly letting her down and causing her grief; we understand her desperate need to escape her sad home life.

The Hollywood-style happy ending ruins the picture for many viewers, but I find it a relief after watching Alice suffer through the society dance, at which her brother (her date) is the only person (until MacMurray comes along) who pays attention to her, and the disastrous dinner when MacMurray comes to her house. It's probable that women like this film better than men because they can relate to Alice blowing it in public, in front of an attractive man, by trying too hard, talking too much, and smiling and laughing in an attempt to conceal her nervousness and embarrassment. But I find it too painful to watch (it's like Shirley MacLaine putting on that hideous dress for her wedding in *Sweet Charity* and having her fiancé change his mind). This was George Stevens's first major directorial assignment. Most impressive are his close-ups of Hepburn's smooth, beautiful face with her wet lips and those intelligent, sparkling eyes that reveal Alice's simultaneous feelings of excitement and fear. Stevens's evocation of small-town America is reasonable, but, despite a scene-stealing performance by Hattie McDaniel, the depiction of "colored" people is regrettable. Florence Vidor starred in a 1923 silent version. Also with: Charley Grapewin, Evelyn Venable, Hedda Hopper.

ALICE DOESN'T LIVE HERE ANYMORE (1974) C/113m.
Martin Scorsese directed this film which was considered a breakthrough by feminists not because it presents a woman who achieves full liberation and fulfilling self-sufficiency—this doesn't happen—but because it presents a real woman who relies on herself to solve problems that are common to single mothers. Ellen Burstyn deserved her Oscar for her multi-faceted portrayal of Alice Wyatt, a recently widowed New Mexico housewife who worries about how she'll support herself and her likable but unsupportive 12-year-old son (Alfred Lutter). They drive toward Monterey, California, where Alice was raised. She intends to resume the singing career she gave up when she married. They live in a motel in Phoenix when Alice gets a job singing in a bar, but flee town when the man (Harvey Keitel) Alice is seeing turns out to be a married psychopath. Alice takes a waitress job at Mel's Diner in Tucson and has an affair with David (Kris Kristofferson), a nice-guy rancher. But she still plans on going to Monterey. To me, this is a film about the fears a woman feels when she finds herself on her own: Alice is afraid that she can't make enough money, that she can't sing, that her son will think her a bad mother (does any other film deal with this significant theme?), that she won't make friends (she befriends foul-mouthed waitress Diane Ladd), that she won't find another man, and that if a man pursues her, she won't make correct decisions about him. What's admirable is that she deals with her fears head-on, despite her obvious insecurities. That Scorsese ended the film with Alice getting a man angered many people because they thought it traditionally Hollywood. But I don't think he was pandering to the mass audience at the expense of her hard-earned independence. If he'd had Alice reject the "perfect" David, he might have been accused of pan-

dering to feminists as Paul Mazursky was because of Jill Clayburgh rejecting "perfect" Alan Bates's proposal in *An Unmarried Woman*. It makes sense that Alice would chance a relationship with David, especially since her son could use an adult around he will listen to. Visually, Scorsese's greatest accomplishment is that he conveys that people in America don't stand on firm ground, are never comfortable in their settings, feel disoriented and unsettled. Film has much humor, especially in the scenes between Alice and her son, but it is hard-edged throughout. Keitel is terrifying. Written by Robert Getchell, photographed by Kent L. Wakeford, produced by David Susskind and Audrey Maas. With a great eclectic soundtrack. The basis for the long-running television series. Also with: Jodie Foster, Vic Tayback, Billy Green Bush, Valerie Curtin.

ALICE, SWEET ALICE/COMMUNION/HOLY TERROR (1977) C/96m–108m.

Little girl (Brooke Shields's debut) is strangled in church by a figure in a yellow raincoat and mask just prior to her taking her first communion. Her jealous, mean older sister, Alice (Paula Sheppard)—who has been denied communion—is the logical suspect (after all, she has a yellow raincoat and mask). But her mother and her father, who has remarried, work with the young local priest to try to figure out who really is responsible. Cult horror film is guaranteed to keep you tense. The attack scenes are not for the faint-hearted. Director Albert Sole uses the horror genre to attack Catholicism, which brings little peace to its constituents. Picture is set in Catholic community of Paterson, New Jersey, in 1961, at beginning of first Catholic Presidency. All the characters attend or work in the church, yet all are sinners or were born out of sin; significantly, the church does not help these confused, guilt-ridden, emotionally misunderstood church members—which is why a maniac (Alice?) is on a God-told-me-to rampage to wipe out other sinners. Picture is full of offbeat touches and characters (i.e., enormous Mr. Alfredo). Well made, but beware. Also with: Linda Miller, Mildred Clinton, Louisa Horton, Tom Signorelli, and in bits: Lillian Roth and professional wrestling legend, the late Antonino Rocca.

ALIEN (1979) C/117m.

Frightening, ferocious science-fiction film that incorporates many elements of the horror film. The cargo ship *Nostromo* heads back to earth, carrying its load. The crew members are awakened with orders from the home corporation (the real villain of the piece because it sacrifices people for discovery) to investigate a signal on nearby planet. They find a derelict ship containing a giant skeleton pilot, and, below, a hatchery. In a terrifying sequence John Hurt looks inside a pod and a creature attaches itself to his face. Against the advice of co-captain Sigourney Weaver (her debut), science officer Ian Holm lets Hurt come aboard. The creature on his face falls off, but a new creature bursts through his stomach and hides in the huge ship. It grows to enormous size and kills off the crew one at a time until only Weaver (her Ripley is a

very strong character) is left to battle the indestructible creature. Ridley Scott's film is loved by many science-fiction fans—it was an enormous hit—but despised by others. I find it underrated: an extremely scary, well-made, interesting film. It has been criticized for being a violent, big-budget rip-off of a cheap fifties SF film, *It! The Terror From Beyond*, but surely the basis for Dan O'Bannon's script was *Dark Star*, the comedy he co-wrote with John Carpenter. Although a comedy, it, too, dealt with the melancholia, claustrophobia, and irritation suffered by crews on long space voyages, had a female-voiced computer, and had a centerpiece in which O'Bannon the actor searched the ship for an escaped alien creature which kept jumping out and attacking him. Picture is first space film that has working-class heroes rather than scientists and astronauts flying a ship. I believe it is the first sci-fi film since *Scream and Scream Again* to advance creepy notion that scientists will have such egos they'll create scientist-androids. Thanks to design work by H. R. Giger, Ron Cobb, and Michael Seymour, film is stunning—the alien is truly imposing, but also memorable are the vagina-like entrances to the derelict ship and the enormous skeleton pilot, as well as the old, uninviting, disheveled interiors of the *Nostromo*. The direction by Scott is as imaginative as it is (properly) manipulative; he builds tension by having characters talk in hushed tones, smoke incessantly, drink coffee, pace nervously, sweat, argue. He also manages to pull off bloodless killings—because Hurt's death is so graphic, he could leave the others to our imagination. Importantly, the final sequence during which Weaver does her famous strip, realizes she's being observed by the alien, and tries to outwit it, is no letdown. Interestingly, Scott thought the creature was interested in Weaver's Ripley only as a host for its eggs, while Weaver believed it also had sexual designs on Ripley. Weaver also is the star of James Cameron's sequel. Cast also includes: Tom Skerritt (as the captain), Veronica Cartwright, Yaphet Kotto, Harry Dean Stanton.

ALL OF ME (1984) C/93m.

A soul-transmigration experiment is fouled up, and the spirit of the late cantankerous millionairess Edwina Cutwater (Lily Tomlin) enters the body of lawyer Roger Cobb (Steve Martin), who despised her. Edwina and Roger vie for control of his body—which really ruins his love life—and somehow fall in love. Martin is terrific, particularly doing physical comedy that requires his movements to incorporate female traits. He won the Best Actor Award from the New York Film Critics, but was denied an Oscar nomination. Unfortunately, Lily Tomlin, a great physical comedienne herself, is limited to just being a head-and-shoulders reflection in mirrors Martin looks into. Carl Reiner's direction is slipshod and obvious; he is saved at times by the originality of Martin and Richard Libertini, who plays a silly swami. The script by Phil Alden Robinson (adapted from Ed Davis's novel *Me Two*) is so stupid that in order for there to be a happy ending the audience is expected to believe that the vain, beautiful villainess (Victoria Tennant) would prefer living in the body of a horse to going to prison. Also with: Madolyn Smith, Dana Elcar.

ALL QUIET ON THE WESTERN FRONT (1930)
B&W/105m–140m.   The most famous pacifist film is not as grisly as Erich Maria Remarque's novel, but has enough horror and brutality to drive its anti-war theme home a hundred times over. Story deals with German teenagers who enlist during WWI after hearing a rousing pro-mili-taristic speech by their professor. They soon discover that war has nothing to do with gallantry, duty, or the right cause. They suffer through bombings, gassings, massacres, hand-to-hand conflicts; men are wounded, blinded, have legs amputated, are killed. The dialogue scenes are static, but the human story is powerful; we do listen in the scene when the soldiers lament about there always being unwanted, unneeded wars; and director Lewis Milestone's visuals of the battle scenes are still impressive (i.e., his camera pulls back over men fighting in a trench; his camera pans as soldiers are mowed down by machine guns)—and effec-tively convey that being a soldier is a terrifying prospect. Famous scene in which Lew Ayres kills a French soldier with a knife and weeps for his dead "brother" is hokey but still moving. Best of all is the scene in which Ayres returns to his school and tells his professor's new students just how awful war is, and that it isn't "beautiful and sweet to die for your country." A memorable final shot. It's unfortunate that films like this are never made when a war is in progress. *The Road Back*, a sequel, was made in 1937. Also with: Slim Summerville, John Wray, William Bakewell, Ben Alexander, Edmund Breese.

ALL THAT JAZZ (1979) C/123m.   Bob Fosse's styl-ized, semi-autobiographical musical about a hopelessly overworked Broadway and movie director (Roy Scheider) who suffers a heart attack that should, but doesn't really, give him a new perspective on life and death. Film starts out like a house afire, with beautifully choreographed, erotic—almost lewd—dances. But once Scheider has his attack that sends him to the hospital, the picture deteriorates into a never-ending wave of self-indulgence. You really get to hate Scheider's character. "Bye Bye, Life" finale, during which Fosse, Scheider, and company do to the Everly Broth-ers what TV commercial jingles do to many of our standards, is perhaps the most annoying production number in cinema history. Picture will be enjoyed most by those involved in theater or film. Ann Reinking is Scheider's girlfriend; Jes-sica Lange was rescued from *King Kong* by Fosse, who had her play the temptress Death. Also with: Cliff Gorman, Ben Vereen, Erzsebet Foldi, Leland Palmer, Sandahl Bergman, John Lithgow, Keith Gordon.

ALL THE PRESIDENT'S MEN (1976) C/138m.
Award-winning adaptation of the best-seller by *Washington Post* reporters Carl Bernstein and Bob Woodward about their path-breaking investigation of the Watergate scandal, di-rectly leading to President Nixon's resignation. As directed by Alan J. Pakula, scripted by William Goldman, and played by Robert Redford (Woodward) and Dustin Hoffman (Bern-stein), it is one of the cagiest films ever made. We are enthralled, although not much happens—major discoveries by the two investigative reporters are few and far between. As he had done with *The Parallax View*, Pakula steeps his film in paranoia. Woodward and Bernstein are shown in close-up as they talk to strangers on the phone, trying to wangle information out of them. They sweat slightly as they bluff prior knowledge about what the people are divulging or insinuating—they worry that the people will stop in mid-sentence and question their right to ask such things. Because we don't see the people the reporters speak to, they naturally become mystery figures—Pakula gives them nervous, ret-icent, suspicious deliveries so we feel they all have some-thing to hide or that they're the types who might arrange for something nasty to happen to the hard-pushing reporters. If Pakula had moved the camera back from the reporters and directed the actors on the phone to speak in friendly, cooperative tones (using the same dialogue), we would feel *no* suspense. And if he didn't repeatedly show our reporters going alone, mostly at night, to the doors of people who don't want to speak to them or who are reluctant to reveal all they know, or, as in Woodward's case, meeting his con-tact "Deep Throat" in an underground garage so dark we can't see faces, we wouldn't think that our two heroes are so vulnerable (or so brave). Near the end we are told that they are in danger—we felt it all along—but nothing comes of this. Indeed, none of the paranoia we feel throughout the film is justified. Acting is excellent, particularly by Jason Robards, Jr., who won a Best Supporting Actor Oscar as the *Post*'s managing editor, Ben Bradlee. Another plus is that we get a sense of the inner workings of a newspaper and how individual reporters pursue a story (i.e., phone calls, legwork, paperwork). Woodward and Bernstein are shown to be manipulative, driven, willing-to-fib reporters—likable but not all that sympathetic. They seem to favor getting their Pulitzer-caliber story, without concern for what that story will mean to the country. End of film comes too early in the Watergate story and leaves us hanging—which is also the major problem with the book. Goldman, art director George Jenkins, and set designer George Gaines won Oscars. Film was chosen Best Picture by the National Board of Review and the New York Film Critics. Also with: Jack Warden, Martin Balsam, Jane Alexander, Stephen Col-lins, Meredith Baxter, Robert Walden, Ned Beatty, Polly Holliday.

ALL THE RIGHT MOVES (1983) C/91m.
Michael Chapman, Martin Scorsese's former cameraman (*Taxi Driver*, *Raging Bull*), made his directorial debut with this sadly underrated "youth film," set in a poor Pennsyl-vania mining town. The only way teenager Tom Cruise can go to college and escape a life as a coal miner is to win a football scholarship. But his dreams, and those of his wid-ower father (Charles Cioffi), seem out of reach when his dictatorial high-school coach (Craig T. Nelson) tosses him

off the team for insubordination. The brutal interplay between Cruise and Nelson is familiar but well handled, and it has a somewhat surprising resolution (how many of you had coaches who admitted they were wrong about something?). But what makes the film noteworthy is Lea Thompson's extremely mature and appealing portrayal of Cruise's supportive girlfriend, who, despite being a gifted musician, realizes no scholarship will pull her out of this dead-end town. The scene where she chastises Cruise for thinking only of himself is really special, as is their one love scene. Opportunists Cruise and Nelson both learn valuable lessons from this unselfish girl. Also with: Christopher Penn, Paul Carafotes.

ALLEGRO NON TROPPO (ITALIAN/1976) B&W-C/75m. Ambitious, moderately successful film by Bruno Bozzetto that both pays homage to *Fantasia* and mocks its Disney innocence. Also showing how classical music and animation can enhance one another, the picture consists of vignettes set to the music of Debussy, Dvorák, Ravel, Sibelius, Vivaldi, and Stravinsky. As this is for adults, sequences have to do with sin, sex, loneliness, death. Most of the pieces are hard-edged and sad, but the animation is colorful, the animal and human characters are quirky and likable, and there is enough humor so that we never get depressed. My favorite bit comes at the end when a grunting hunchback searches for an animation sequence that will make a strong finale to the picture, and he watches a string of imaginative, brutal yet funny visual gags. Black-and-white live-action sequences full of slapstick humor and dealing with a Felliniesque orchestra (comprised of old ladies) and a silly animator (who was taken out of prison to draw images to fit the music) precede and follow all the animation vignettes. Film is a nice change of pace from typical repertory-theater fare, but you have to be in right mood to enjoy it.

ALLIGATOR (1980) C/94m. For decades there have been unfounded but imagination-stirring rumors of alligators roaming around urban sewer systems as a result of tourists, returned from Florida, flushing souvenir live baby alligators down their toilets. Surprisingly, this was the first film to exploit the subject, which is obvious horror-film material. Picture is set in Chicago, where a police detective (Robert Forster) investigates a series of disappearances in the sewers and discovers evidence of a giant alligator on the loose. John Sayles's script is sharp, Lewis Teague's direction is competent, and Henry Silva has a ball playing a big-game hunter determined to bag his greatest animal. The film, which is played for laughs, would have worked better if it took itself more seriously end to end (which wouldn't have meant it couldn't have humor). Also, I wish the phony-looking giant alligator would stay in the dark sewers, where it's scary, instead of walking outside, where it's silly. Also with: Robin Riker, Michael Gazzo, Perry Lang, Jack Carter, Bart Braverman, Dean Jagger.

ALONE IN THE DARK (1982) C/92m. Inmates from an experimental insane asylum run by liberal director Donald Pleasence find it easy to escape during an electrical blackout. They terrorize a non-violent asylum doctor and his family, who barricade themselves in their isolated house. Cult film shows promise at the beginning—before the offbeat humor gives way to ugly violence (this is a *Straw Dogs* variation), the imperiled characters start exhibiting uncommon stupidity, and, of course, getaway cars won't start. Jack Palance is okay as the one redeemable madman and Carol Levy is sexy as a victim, "Bunky." Also with: Dwight Schultz, Martin Landau, Erland van Lidth de Jeude, Deborah Hedwall.

ALPHAVILLE, A STRANGE ADVENTURE OF LEMMY CAUTION (FRENCH/ITALIAN 1965) B&W/98m. Amusing Jean-Luc Godard film in which he blends popular lowbrow entertainment—comic books, pulp fiction, "B" detective movies, James Bond, and sci-fi—with political satire. Filmed in undisguised modern office buildings and large tourist and small seedy hotels in Paris, the picture is set in the future in a city that can be reached only by travel through intersidereal space. That's not so hard: agent Lemmy Caution (Eddie Constantine) merely drives his Ford over a bridge. Posing as reporter Ivan Johnson, tough Lemmy is really trying to get the lowdown on this computer-run, robotized society where technology has replaced humanity; where there is repression/murder of all who don't think logically; whose women, like the leader's daughter, Natasha (Anna Karina), have numbers tattooed on their backs and function as first-, second , or third-class prostitutes/seducers; where words such as "conscience" and "love" do not exist in its Bible-dictionary. It's Lemmy's job to destroy the computer, which will, in turn, cause Alphaville's destruction. Picture has the novel twist of having a two-fisted tough guy teaching a sensual female the meaning of "love"; the political themes aren't that novel, but Godard's direction is consistently offbeat and fascinating. His use of flickering lights (including those from Lemmy's camera), sounds (including a monstrous male voice on a loudspeaker), ominous suspense music, choice settings (especially narrow hallways), and sudden, unexpected actions by characters (i.e., Lenny shoots first, before asking questions) makes us feel we're in another world whose look and rhythm are different from our own. Film isn't altogether successful, but it has moments of brilliance. The casting of "B"-movie actor Constantine was inspired. The ending anticipates the one in *Blade Runner*. Exceptional cinematography by Raoul Coutard. Also with: Akim Tamiroff (as a corrupted ex-agent, looking like his co-star in *Touch of Evil*, Orson Welles), Howard Vernon (as the leader Professor von Braun, alias Nosferatu).

ALTERED STATES (1980) C/102m. Psychopsychiatrist Eddie Jessup (William Hurt) spends many years searching for Ultimate Truth and his Original Self by undergoing dangerous sensory-deprivation experiments. His obsessive quest causes the break-up of his marriage to anthropologist Emily (Blair Brown), who finds it frustrating that he's incapable of love. But she's there to help him when his experiments get out of hand due to injections of an ancient hallucination-causing Mayan mushroom solution. He has begun to experience genetic change, at one point turning into an apeman (and going on a rampage), and as his regression continues, he moves into an embryonic state and is sucked toward nothingness at the moment of Man's creation. Jekyll-and-Hyde variation, which Paddy Chayefsky based on John Lilly's mind-expansion experiments in the mid-sixties, takes viewers on ambitious, if hokey, exploration of man's origins and advances intriguing theory that there can be genetic change if one's consciousness is manipulated. Then, toward the end, film drops several intellectual planes and makes simplistic points: there is no Ultimate Truth and the only thing of importance is Love. Jessup's rejection of his findings makes us want to forget deciphering all the religious symbolism we've seen in his hallucinations—after all, even he thinks them irrelevant. Thus the film unfortunately avoids controversy. Nevertheless there's much that is noteworthy. The blasting soundtrack won the picture an Oscar. Bran Ferren's special effects are often ill-chosen but dynamic; and F/X fans will delight in the legendary Dick Smith's remarkable make-up work. Working from Chayefsky's overwritten script, Ken Russell keeps things under surprising control for a change. Best of all are his close-ups of Emily when she reacts with dazed amazement at Eddie's strange thought processes. Russell smartly establishes a contrast between the passionate work done by Emily and the maniacal work of Eddie, thus reaffirming the thrill of exploration to viewers turned off by Jessup. Excellent ensemble acting by Hurt, Brown, Charles Haid, and Bob Balaban. Also with: Thaao Penghlis, Dori Brenner, Miguel Gideau (as Eddie's primitive form), Drew Barrymore.

ALWAYS (1986) C/105m. We've all been stuck next to a stranger in a bus or plane who insists on telling all the mournful details of a personal relationship while we sit there thinking, "I don't want to know!" That's how I feel when watching director-writer Henry Jaglom's seriocomical examination of his break-up with his actress wife, Patrice Townsend. Jaglom plays the male lead, Dave, and Townsend, oddly enough, plays his female lead, Judy. Two years after Judy walked out on Dave she comes over to sign the divorce papers. But since it's obvious that the two are still very much in love, the notary refuses to sign the decree until they've thought it over for a few more days. Judy becomes ill from Dave's cooking and ends up spending the Fourth of July weekend with him. Joining this *divorcing couple* at Dave's LA home are their friends, a *"happily" married couple* (Joanna Frank, Alan Rachins) and an *engaged-to-be-married couple*, Judy's younger, free-spirited loving sister (Melissa Leo) and a passive boy (*Soup for One* director Jonathan Kaufer) she met in New York. The six people keep splitting up and discussing what they consider

to be *happiness*. So often do they expose their innermost thoughts and emotions, sexual fears and confusion about marriage and relationships, and worries about being alone or misunderstood, and so constant is their hugging, kissing, and crying that we're made to feel we got waylaid to an intense weekend therapy session. Moreover, it's not easy to warm to these people. It's obvious that Jaglom still loved Townsend when making this film. And that's touching. But just because he's so taken with the way she can laugh naturally (usually through her tears) on film, it doesn't mean we can stand this happening every time she delivers a line. He allows Townsend, through her character, to express the reasons she left him, hoping they will be exposed to her and us as simplistic and foolhardy. Yet the more you see of Jaglom/Dave with Townsend/Judy, the better you can understand why she would leave him—although you won't be able to pinpoint the reasons either. Also with: director Bob Rafelson (as Dave's neighbor), Michael Emil, Andre Gregory as the "life is a stone" party philosopher.

AMADEUS (1984) C/158m. Oscar-winning, large-scale adaptation of Peter Shaffer's 1979 fictional play about the obsessive jealousy an 18th-century Italian hack composer, Antonio Salieri, felt for Wolfgang Amadeus Mozart's musical genius. It was scripted by Shaffer and directed by Milos Forman. As told by Salieri (F. Murray Abraham) from his asylum cell, years after Mozart's death—for which he insists he was responsible. Twenty-six-year-old Mozart (Tom Hulce) arrives in Vienna in 1781. Salieri is the court composer of Hapsburg Emperor Joseph II (Jeffrey Jones) and his unimaginative operas and technically expert but uninspired compositions are extremely popular. Salieri immediately recognizes Mozart's talents, although Joseph and the Viennese do not, and is tormented not only because his own music can't compare to the young boy's but because God pulled a double-cross by giving the shockingly vulgar Mozart the musical genius that Salieri thought he himself deserved. While pretending to be Mozart's one supporter in Vienna, he swears to destroy him. The acting is great, but while the characters are interestingly unusual the first time we see them, they don't vary in the slightest from then on. Anyone could fill in their dialogue, reactions, etc. In fact, each time a group of characters gets together, they virtually replay an earlier scene—there are only about four basic scenes in the movie, which are repeated in different settings. The dialogue and situations are embarrassingly anachronistic—trite "newlywed" chatter between Mozart and his young wife (Elizabeth Berridge, who looks straight out of period's portraits) about money problems and sex, and Mozart's stern, interfering pop (Roy Dotrice) could have been lifted from bad fifties TV comedy, and if characters weren't in fancy period dress, I'm sure viewers would have laughed it off screen. Indeed, the picture's major premise, dealing with the sad discrepancy between Salieri's *popular* music, and Mozart's *good* unpopular music, was undoubtedly inspired by sad reality that today's most talented rock musicians/rock singers are not necessarily the ones that make the most money. However, period detail and lavish recreations of excerpts from four Mozart operas give the film immense flavor. Also, it should be applauded for trying to convey what it is to be an artistic genius, and to show a genius actually in the act of creating. The scene in which the dying Mozart dictates his requiem to Salieri while we hear the music jumping from his mind is truly exciting. Cinematography by Miroslav Ondricek. Also with: Christine Ebersole, Charles Kay, Kenny Baker, Lisabeth Bartleff.

AMARCORD (ITALIAN/1974) C/127m. Federico Fellini's Oscar-winning nostalgia piece takes place in the early thirties in a small Adriatic town that is much like Rimini, where the director grew up. He is represented in the film by a blond, lightheaded teenager (Bruno Zanin) who, like all his friends, thinks constantly of women with big breasts and big rears. The best parts of the film deal with Zanin and his horny pals. The sequence showing how the kids react (usually by pulling pranks) to their weird teachers is a classic. Also funny is a bit in which Zanin excites a 300-pound woman by lifting her off the ground repeatedly and is rewarded with a chance to smother himself in her enormous breasts. Better is a family dinner during which Mama refuses to eat, Mama and Papa (Armando Brancia) argue (as they must do every night), Zanin eats like a pig, the emotionless uncle juggles and eats from a plate he holds in his hand, Papa chases Zanin from the house for having urinated on a man's hat at the movie theater, and Grandpa slips into the next room to break wind. The picture isn't all comedic, but those are the best moments—unfortunately, they come mostly at the beginning. A couple of anecdotes, presented stylistically, about peripheral adult characters in the town really slow down the picture. The scene in which the father is punished by the fascists for some indiscreet remarks is well done, but seems out of place in this otherwise apolitical film. The first half-hour is marvelous—the rest of the film is extremely erratic. Also with: Magali Noel, Ciccio Ingrassia, Giuseppe Lanigro, Puppela Maggio, Josiane Tanzilli.

AMERICAN FRIEND, THE (WEST GERMAN-FRENCH/1977) C/123m. Wim Wenders's dazzling psychological thriller, adapted from *Ripley's Game* by Patricia Highsmith, was the first film of West German film renaissance to be truly accessible to American audiences. That's because the colors are splashy rather than subdued; there are references to familiar English-language rock songs; the picture is set partly in America, and English is the dominant language; Dennis Hopper (as Tom Ripley) co-stars, and supporting parts are played by well-known American directors Sam Fuller (as a Mafia man) and Nicholas Ray (as the supposedly dead artist whose paintings Ripley sells). Moreover Wenders's sharply edited action sequences are influenced by Fuller; his use of the frame as an arena for tension and to expose character isolation was influenced by Ray. The storyline and characters, however, are most reminiscent of Hitchcock, specifically *Strangers on a Train*—

which was also based on a Highsmith novel. In Germany to sell a painting, Ripley is slighted by Jonathan (Bruno Ganz), a simple Swiss frame-maker, who won't shake his hand because of his shady reputation. Insulted, Ripley secretly recommends Jonathan to a rich criminal friend (Gérard Blain) who is looking for a non-criminal to assassinate Mafia men. Knowing Jonathan has leukemia, Tom starts a rumor that he is no longer in remission. Soon Jonathan believes he is about to die. Wanting to leave money to wife and child after his death, he is talked into committing the crimes—although he has never done an incorrect act in his life. Meanwhile he and Tom become friends, while his marriage to Marianne (a fine performance by Lisa Kreuzer, Wenders's wife) deteriorates because of his lies about his activities. Tom helps Jonathan with a murder on a train and together they battle the Mafia men who track them down. Conscience, guilt, and morality based on a religious code were important to Highsmith but Wenders doesn't deal with these themes. As his world has no God, he is concerned with existential themes (depressed Ripley worries that his meaningless life is endless; depressed Jonathan fears his life will soon be over) and male bonding and friendship between opposites. Both aliens *in* their respective environments, Tom admires Jonathan's stable family life, while Jonathan admires Tom's freedom from family responsibilities and his criminal activities—he is appreciative that Tom helps him engage in excitement before he dies. Highsmith didn't like this film (her suave Ripley character was turned into a tormented, drunken existentialist), but in its own way it's just as exciting, enjoyable, and thought-provoking as her novel. Also with: Peter Lilienthal, Daniel Schmid, Sandy Whitelaw, Jean Eustache, Lou Castel, Wenders.

AMERICAN GIGOLO (1980) C/117m. Richard Gere is a self-assured, flashy male prostitute who becomes the prime suspect in the brutal murder of a woman with whom he had a late-night session (in front of her sadistic husband). Director-writer Paul Schrader includes references to the work of Robert Bresson, but what he tries to pass off as *art* is simply trash; ugly and dirty. Gere's much publicized love scene with Lauren Hutton, as the only person who remains loyal to him, may titillate some, but the rest of the sexual content is fairly repulsive. This is a thoroughly unconvincing, terribly made movie that was designed solely to arouse viewers unaccustomed to seeing big stars like Gere take such embarrassing roles. Blondie's song "Call Me" may be best thing in film. Also with: Hector Elizondo, Nina Van Pallandt.

AMERICAN GRAFFITI (1973) C/110m. George Lucas directed this wonderfully exuberant youth comedy which is set one eventful night in Modesto, California, in 1962. Made by a filmmaker in a cynical era, it's an idealized remembrance of things past, of innocent youth spent eating fries and malts at the drive-in hangout, cruising the main strip, drag-racing, bragging about your one "cool" friend, making out, hanging out, dancing real close, listening to rock music on the car radio, playing pranks on police, telling off an obnoxious teacher—fittingly, we don't see our young heroes and heroines having dinner at home with their parents, doing their homework, or attending classes. At the beginning and conclusion, we see our four male heroes together; in between, they go their separate ways. Ron Howard is ready to go far away to college, but girlfriend Cindy Williams is still in high school. When he suggests that they date other people while they're apart, she becomes infuriated. They spend the rest of the night arguing, realizing how much they'll miss each other when he leaves, and reevaluating their future. Richard Dreyfuss is reluctant about leaving home and going off to college. He spends his last night with three toughs (evolving from potential victim to one of the gang) and trying to find a beautiful young woman (Suzanne Somers) who passed him in a car. Nerdy Charles Martin Smith, who has the use of Howard's car, miraculously picks up batty blonde Candy Clark and has the wildest night imaginable—he actually impresses this girl who has been around. Paul Le Mat, local 22-year-old dragster champ, picks up a girl (Mackenzie Phillips) too, only to discover when she climbs into his car that she's about 12 or 13. But it turns out that she's a great companion. Lucas moves smoothly between the four storylines, which at times intermingle. The pace is swift, the dialogue is consistently witty and clever, and the characters are terrific. When this film was released, it made us feel nostalgic for a bygone era, but now when we see it we miss the young characters and we feel sad that the actors, whom we didn't know very well back in 1973, are long past the time they can play high school students—today, this film really makes one feel aged. Film features the first great golden-oldie soundtrack—my favorite scene, the most touching in the movie, has Williams and Howard slow dancing to the Platters' "Smoke Gets in Your Eyes." 1979's ambitious but flawed *More American Graffiti* took characters into the protest years. Produced by Francis Ford Coppola and Gary Kurtz; with a screenplay by Lucas and Gloria Katz and Willard Huyck. Verna Fields and Marcia Lucas edited. The remarkable cast, comprised mostly of *then*-unknowns, also includes: Harrison Ford, Debralee Scott, Joe Spano, Wolfman Jack (as himself), Kathy (Kathleen) Quinlan, Bo Hopkins, Manuel Padilla, Jr.

AMERICAN HOT WAX (1978) C/91m. Floyd Mutrux's affectionate facts-out-the-window tribute to the late Alan Freed, regarded as the first white deejay to play black music, has as flimsy a storyline as those fifties "B" rock 'n' roll movies in which Freed appeared. Nevertheless it has great drive and sustained momentum, a chaotic atmosphere that properly reflects the wild era it depicts, and familiar music from 1957–60 (both performed by acts in the film and played on the soundtrack) that will make you feel joyfully nostalgic. Best of all, it has Tim McIntire giving a dynamite performance as the former "Mr. Rock 'n' Roll." Respectfully spinning platters on his radio show (we see that Freed really *loved* rock music), taking a quick look at aspiring acts whom agents march through his office, amiably chatting with teenagers on the street, stopping to listen to unknown doo-wop groups (including Dion and the Belmonts) who always cross his path between his car and a building, watching a rousing recording session (of "Come Go with Me"), McIntire's Freed is totally believable. He looks as if he walks through this cluttered, special world every day. While the film hints at Freed's imminent downfall (because of a payola scandal), Mutrux prefers to end it on a high note: despite pressure from bluenoses and government officials out to get Freed, he hosts his last triumphant music extravaganza at Brooklyn's Fox Paramount. "You can close the show," he warns the police who have gathered to do just that, "you can stop me, but you'll never stop rock 'n' roll." Also with: Laraine Newman (likable as a striving songwriter), Fran Drescher (the whining publicist in *This Is Spinal Tap*), Jay Leno, John Lehne, Jeff Altman, and, as themselves, Chuck Berry (doing a really dirty version of "Reelin' and Rockin'"), Jerry Lee Lewis, Screamin' Jay Hawkins.

AMERICAN IN PARIS, AN (1951) C/113m. Lavish M-G-M musical, directed by Vincente Minnelli. A struggling American artist living in Paris, Gene Kelly, and young French shopgirl Leslie Caron fall in love. But he feels indebted to his patron, Nina Foch, and she feels obligated to marry Kelly's French friend Georges Guetary, who has taken care of her since she was orphaned during WWII. Potentially interesting storyline, featuring what should be intriguing relationships, is given short shrift by Alan Jay Lerner. As this was 12 years before *Breakfast at Tiffany's* dared to have struggling writer George Peppard be Patricia Neal's "kept man," it is made crystal clear that Kelly and Foch aren't lovers; likewise, it's clear Caron is a virgin, having never been taken advantage of by Guetary. So, instead of a steamy, complicated love affair between Kelly and Caron, it is all too proper—their romance is movie-musical predictable. Caron's character, who no doubt had an interesting past, is very artificial; it's nice to see her dance, but in her starring debut—when they hadn't figured out her makeup, I suppose—she doesn't yet look like a romantic lead. Smiling Kelly is likable once his character cuts out his obnoxious brash act when courting Caron, but for the most part Minnelli's elegant balletic style of dancing is too tame for him. Yet he does let loose in the extravagant 20-minute musical finale. Featuring several striking ballet interludes—all part of one ballet story set to Gershwin's "An American in Paris"—and the imaginative use of color, costumes, and sets to create scenes in the styles of French artists, it is one of the best production numbers in cinema history; but the other, shorter song-and-dance numbers shouldn't suffer so badly in comparison. Standard Gershwin score includes "'S Wonderful," "I Got Rhythm," and "I'll Build a Stairway to Paradise"; Saul Chaplin and Johnny Green won an Oscar for their musical arrangements. Colorful re-creation of Paris street scenes on M-G-M backlot.

Not worthy of its Best Picture Oscar, but a major entry to the musical genre. Produced by Arthur Freed. Also with: Oscar Levant (in need of a talk show).

AMERICAN WEREWOLF IN LONDON, AN

(1981) C/97m. While backpacking at night on the British moors, young Americans David Naughton and Griffin Dunne are attacked (in a terrifying scene) by a werewolf. Naughton survives, but is repeatedly visited by Dunne's deteriorating corpse-ghost, who tells him to commit suicide so he won't turn into a werewolf at the next full moon. Believing Dunne to be a hallucination, Naughton moves in with his new lover, lovely nurse Jenny Agutter. (He even jokes about the old Lon Chaney, Jr., film, *The Wolf Man*.) Sure enough, Naughton turns into a werewolf each night of the next full moon, roams through London, and commits extremely brutal murders. A pet project of director-writer John Landis, this may be the most successful attempt to mix horror and comedy there has been. You'll laugh even when you feel jittery. There are hilarious scenes (i.e., the nude Naughton trying to get home from the zoo) and many that are extremely frightening. The young actors are appealing and energetic (Naughton was picked because of his amiable presence in a series of Dr Pepper commercials), and the supporting players—many from the Royal Shakespeare Company—give the production class. Shot on location, the settings are particularly well chosen for atmosphere and visual interest. The music—"Blue Moon" is done by a number of people—is a lot of fun; Rick Baker won a deserved Oscar for his corpse-ghost and werewolf makeup and his stunning work on Naughton's transformation from man into beast. The last couple of scenes, taking place in Piccadilly Circus, seem ill advised (all Naughton's victims urge him to commit suicide, which he doesn't do anyway; the werewolf on the loose causes a number of unnecessarily violent car crashes); but otherwise the picture is truly enjoyable and original. I find it immeasurably better than *The Howling*, Joe Dante's campy werewolf film that came out at about the same time. Also with: John Woodvine, Brian Glover.

AMITYVILLE HORROR, THE (1979) C/117m.

Adaptation of Jay Anson's "fact"-based book isn't nearly as "convincing" or as much fun. The Lutz family moves to Amityville, N.Y., into a large house that was the scene of a mass murder (a boy wiped out his family). People think it's haunted and may have a doorway to hell in its basement. Not long after the Lutzes move in, strange occurrences take place; the young daughter starts communicating with a "pig" figure—which parents Margot Kidder and James Brolin assume is imaginary—a stuck window suddenly falls down on young son's hand (big deal!), all religious visitors act panicky and flee the premises, and Brolin begins to act possessed. Hints are he will become violent, like the son of the last tenants. The two leads try hard, but material becomes increasingly stupid—filmmakers were hampered

by fact that nothing really terrible happened to Lutzes during their tenure. Main selling point is that Rod Steiger as a priest gives what may be the worst performance in horror-movie history. He's *incredibly* awful. Bad direction of actors by Stuart Rosenberg. Sequels: The abominable *Amityville II—The Possession*, showing what supposedly took place before the Lutzes moved in; *Amityville—The Demon*, conventional haunted-house fiction made in 3-D, is the best of the lot, although it falls apart long before the end. Also with: Don Stroud, Murray Hamilton, Natasha Ryan, Michael Sachs, Harry Wright, Helen Shaver.

AMONG THE LIVING (1941) B&W/68m.

Impressive "B" movie stars Albert Dekker as a businessman in a small Southern town and as his homicidal twin brother who escapes from a mental hospital. The crazy brother still remembers his father abusing his mother when he was a child; when he strangles victims, he places their hands over their ears so they won't hear their own screams. Susan Hayward's the cheap, sexy golddigger who takes financial advantage of her mother's new boarder when a large reward is offered for the unknown killer. She gets Dekker to go with her to look for the wanted man—she doesn't realize that he's the murderer. Psychological thriller has good acting and direction (by Stuart Heisler), suspense, and mill-town atmosphere. Frances Farmer plays the sane brother's wife. Also with: Harry Carey, Gordon Jones, Jean Phillips, Maude Eburne, Clarence Muse, Rod Cameron.

ANCHORS AWEIGH (1945) C/140m.

Gene Kelly and Frank Sinatra teamed up for the first time as hero sailors on shore leave in Hollywood. Kelly became a big star as the wolf of the navy, but Sinatra is better as his best friend, a bashful manchild from Brooklyn. Sinatra falls for sweet Kathryn Grayson, and though Kelly loves her too, he steps aside so Sinatra can have free sailing. Sinatra tries to impress her by promising her a singing audition with José Iturbi, although the boys don't really know him. Flimsy plotline is not helped by timid romantic leads Kelly and Grayson. And who cares about a story centered on orchestra conductor Iturbi? But Sinatra's singing (of okay songs by Jule Styne and Sammy Cahn) is silky smooth and Kelly's athletic dances are dazzling—especially his celebrated duo with MGM cartoon star Jerry the mouse. MGM Technicolor is gorgeous. Terrible finale in which we expect musical extravaganza in front of thousands of sailors but instead get Grayson hugging Kelly. Directed by George Sidney. Also with: Dean Stockwell, Pamela Britton, "Rags" Ragland, Billy Gilbert, Henry O'Neill, Edgar Kennedy, Grady Sutton, Leon Ames.

...AND GOD CREATED WOMAN/AND WOMAN...WAS CREATED (FRENCH/1957) C/

90m–91m–93m–95m. Brigitte Bardot became an international sex symbol as the result of her role in husband Roger Vadim's debut film. She spends the entire film wrapped in towels or in tight, sexy outfits, or nude (Vadim shows a lot of skin, but the nudity is fleeting and in some prints nonexistent). She is a forerunner of many young females in future French films in that she lives for herself, is sexually promiscuous, is guiltless about her disloyalty toward men, has an eager body that sends stronger messages to her brain than her conscience. Bardot marries fisherman Jean-Louis Trintignant. She loves him, but seduces his brother Christian Marquand on the beach. And she still feels an attachment to wealthy middle-aged Curt Jurgens. You'll forget the men and remember Bardot: sunbathing, standing nude behind a sheet on the outdoor clothesline while speaking to Jurgens (who looks over the top of the sheet to see her); Bardot in bed with Trintignant; Bardot on the beach with Marquand; Bardot doing a sizzling dance in front of many men. Picture tends to be dismissed as simply the film that made Bardot famous, but it could very easily be called the first picture of the French New Wave. Filmed on location in St. Tropez. Bardot and Trintignant had a well-publicized affair. Also with: Georges Poujouly, Jeanne Marken, Isabelle Corey.

AND SOON THE DARKNESS (BRITISH/1970) C/98m.
If Dennis Hopper and Peter Fonda convinced hippies not to cycle through America's South, then British nurses Pamela Franklin and Michele Dotrice should convince young women not to bicycle through the French countryside—particularly if a sex maniac is on the loose. Certainly this thriller is no gem, but it has some suspense and titillation, and, as always, Franklin is a sympathetic heroine-in-jeopardy. When her companion disappears, Franklin must do a little snooping on her own. Most often this film plays on the Late Late Show, with the strongest sex and violence excised—even so, it'll grab your attention. Directed by Robert Fuest. Also with: Sandor Eles, John Nettleton, Clare Kelly.

AND THEN THERE WERE NONE (1945) B&W/98m.
A highly entertaining adaptation of Agatha Christie's *Ten Little Indians* (called *Ten Little Niggers* in England, as was the film), with an unbeatable cast. Ten people are summoned to a mansion on an isolated island by an unknown person. Supposedly, each was responsible for someone's death, but didn't have to pay the penalty. Now, as the voice on a phonograph record tells them, they are to be punished. One by one, these guests are knocked off, in ways suggested by the nursery rhyme. As there is no one else on the island, it is apparent that one of the 10 is the killer. Film benefits from a witty script by Dudley Nichols and light-touch direction by René Clair, who effectively keeps the multi-murder story from becoming bleak (he makes good use of lively music). It's fun trying (and most likely failing) to figure out the murderer's identity, but this mystery is just as interesting the second time around when you can watch the killer closely and see how cleverly we are being manipulated by Christie and the filmmakers. Remade as *Ten Little Indians* in 1965 and 1975 (an English version); classic also has served as the model for many movie mysteries

and parodies. With: Louis Hayward, Barry Fitzgerald, Walter Huston, Roland Young, June Duprez, Mischa Auer, Judith Anderson, C. Aubrey Smith, Richard Haydn, Queenie Leonard, Harry Thurston.

ANDROID (1982) C/80m.
In 2036, Dr. Daniel (Klaus Kinski) runs an abandoned space station. His only companion is Max 404 (co-writer Dan Opper), an android he created. The childlike Max spends his free time studying pop culture on earth in the 20th century. He doesn't suspect that Daniel plans on destroying and replacing him with a perfect female android (Kendra Kirchner). But Daniel's plans are put on hold when Max allows three space travelers (Brie Howard, Norbert Weisser, Crofton Hardester), who he doesn't know are escaped convicts, to land on the station. Put all these weird characters together and there's bound to be mayhem. Director Aaron Lipstadt's low-budget debut film became a quick cult favorite in England, but while it got friendly reviews in America, it never really caught on. It has charm, a Chaplinesque lead character, and behind-the-camera intelligence going for it, but this is one film that really should have been zanier.

ANDROMEDA STRAIN, THE (1971) C/130m.
Robert Wise directed this deliberately paced adaptation of Michael Crichton's best-seller. A U.S. spaceship brings back deadly unknown bacteria from outer space, which quickly wipes out an entire town but for a baby and an alcoholic. Government calls in team of brainy scientists (Arthur Hill, James Olson, Kate Reid, David Wayne) to secret facility. They attempt to figure out nature of bacteria and the way to neutralize it before it is transported by winds and destroys mankind. Like Crichton, Wise emphasizes the scientific process that occurs when a problem must be solved. Crichton's theme: no process is foolproof. So, while the scientists make discoveries, there are also major mistakes made by man and machine. In fact, a nuclear detonation almost occurs. The most intriguing aspect of book and film is that with all the scientific dialogue and experimentation taking place, and the exciting finale in which Olsen desperately races to stop the bomb from exploding, we almost overlook the fact that the scientists need not have been brought together in the first place; in regard to the bacteria, the same result would have happened without their presence, and their presence almost caused world destruction. Crichton's point is that it was thoughtless to have brought back such bacteria from space in the first place (possibly to be used militarily); once that happened, every attempt to correct the initial mistake caused new errors and cascading ramifications. This is a story about *helplessness*. Also with: Paula Kelly.

ANDY WARHOL'S BAD/BAD (1971) C/100m.
Perhaps the most ridiculous film ever distributed by a Hollywood company (Roger Corman's New World Pictures), this satirical look at a completely rotten society is also the only Andy Warhol film to at least "look" like a mainstream

film. Young director Jed Johnson wisely kept his characters under tight control, making sure they delivered their preposterous dialogue ("I want you to kill a dog and I want you to kill it viciously") in a very off-key manner; as a result, this absurd black comedy beats the odds and works beautifully. Carroll Baker returned to America after a self-imposed exile to work for Warhol and proved her real calling wasn't as a sex symbol but as a comedienne. She plays a middle-aged Queens housewife who shares her house with a useless husband, a mother who smokes despite her lung cancer, and a dumpy daughter-in-law (Susan Tyrell) and her messy, always wailing baby. She is the family's breadwinner and like many American housewives, devotes her life to making ends meet. Besides several money-making scams and inordinate penny-pinching, she makes a living by running (1) a facial-hair-removal business and (2) a four-woman assassination-for-hire organization that specializes in doing away with kids and animals. Perry King plays a mysterious young assassin she takes into her house for a one-time assignment. Their viciously unfriendly banter serves to punctuate the dastardly acts committed by Baker's women. Oddly, the main thrust of the humor has less to do with the overly outrageous violent acts than with characters' simply being mean to one another or pulling cruel jokes to intimidate those people they don't like: one woman clogs a drugstore's toilet to make it overflow; another stuffs a thumb into Baker's ketchup bottle and attacks Tyrell with an aerosol spray; another woman physically attacks a man because he wears the same blue pants every day and still has the nerve to comment that she looks ugly in shorts. Interestingly, nothing is taken seriously except a poignant scene between King and an autistic boy—unlike John Waters, Warhol doesn't treat truly sensitive subjects irresponsibly. Film deserves more of a cult than it has. Also with: Stefania Cassini, Cyrinde Fox, Mary Boylan, Charles McGregor, Tere Tereba, Brigid Polk, Susan Blond.

ANDY WARHOL'S DRACULA/BLOOD FOR DRACULA (ITALIAN-FRENCH/1974) C/90m–106m.

Not as popular as *Andy Warhol's Frankenstein*, also directed by Paul Morrissey, but a much better film. It's the 1930s and the skinny, sickly, extremely weak Count (Udo Kier) needs virgin blood to survive. So he travels to Italy (where else?). He becomes guest in the dilapidated castle of an aged nobleman (Vittorio De Sica), whose mind and finances have seen better days. De Sica and his wife (Maxime McKendry) hope that the stranger is rich and will give them much-needed money. They don't realize that Dracula is lusting after the blood of their daughters (Milena Vukotic, Dominuqe Darel, Stefania Casini, Silvia Dionisic). But each time Dracula seduces one of the girls, he starts vomiting blood. Too late the ill Dracula discovers that they gave up their virginity to the Bolshevik gardener (Joe Dallesandro doesn't bother to hide his New York accent). Film is erotic, cleverly scripted by Morrissey and very funny, but it's so super bloody, gross, and violent that viewers will surely be scared away. The entire cast is impressive, but best of all is Arno Juerging, who plays Dracula's always angry assistant. He speaks in the most unpleasant tone imaginable and his argument-conversations with the overly excited Kier are classics. His bar-game scene with peasant Roman Polanski is also a highlight.

ANDY WARHOL'S FRANKENSTEIN/FLESH FOR FRANKENSTEIN (ITALIAN-FRENCH-GERMAN/1974) C/94m.

Perpetually aggravated, bad-tempered Frankenstein (Udo Kier) creates a handsome male (Srdjan Zelenovic) and beautiful female (Dalia di Lazzaro) from the remains of dead bodies. While he works and talks science non-stop with his stupid, sex-crazed assistant (Arno Juerging), his wife (Monique Van Vooren) seduces the stud field worker (Joe Dallesandro) and his young son and daughter creep around the castle planning evil of their own. Kier-and-Juerging team is fun to watch, though they're not as polished as in *Andy Warhol's Dracula*, when both virtually scream every line. Also "sex" scene between Dallesandro and Van Vooren is hilarious, particularly when she slurps away at his armpit. But the explicit violence in film overwhelms the subtle humor and sex. The repetitive images and dialogue make film tiresome. Originally in 3-D. Directed by Paul Morrissey.

ANGEL (1984) C/92m.

New World's titillating newspaper ad—showing a teenager who looks 14 (actually baby-faced star Donna Wilkes is over 18) standing in high heels and wearing a miniskirt, with copy that promised "High School Honor Student By Day, Hollywood Hooker By Night"—paid great dividends. This low-budget exploitation film made the studio many times its investment. Wilkes isn't bad as the smart young streetwalker who, deserted by her parents, has found the only way to pay for her expensive private-school education. The actress is ably supported by Dick Shawn, as Angel's transvestite friend and protector, Susan Tyrell, as her crotchety (but sentimental) butch landlady, and Rory Calhoun, as an ex-western stuntman who makes a living as a quick-draw artist on Hollywood Boulevard. Cliff Gorman is the police detective who tries to get Angel off the streets, which has become especially important now that a psycho is doing away with Hollywood hookers. Not as bad as one would expect. Probably afraid of pushing "kiddie porn," the filmmakers don't exploit the sexual nature of Wilkes's role—she keeps her clothes on. The offbeat characters, a couple of action sequences, and a wild finale in which Wilkes chases the killer (who wears Hare Krishna garb) down crowded streets while carrying a loaded pistol provide some entertainment. Director Robert Vincent O'Neil also made the sequel, *Avenging Angel*.

ANGEL AND THE BADMAN (1947) B&W/100m.

Gunslinger John Wayne is shot, recuperates in home of Quaker family, falls in love with the daughter, Gail Russell. Although some outlaws are out to get him and a lawman (Harry Carey) patiently waits for him to break the law so he can hang him, Wayne is so reformed by Russell that he resists temptation to use a gun. Most enjoyable. It's interesting that Wayne, who produced, would choose to make a pacifist western with this theme: "Only a man who carries a gun ever needs one." Romance between beautiful Russell and handsome Wayne, who were lovers off screen as well, is truly delightful and believable. They are a sweet couple. There are some wonderful moments when Wayne looks at Russell adoringly, and when Russell feels emotions building inside her as she looks at him. Such scenes are *never* found in westerns. Skillfully written and directed by James Edward Grant, high-class "B" western in many ways anticipated Peter Weir's *Witness*. Also with: Irene Rich, Bruce Cabot.

ANGELS WITH DIRTY FACES (1938) B&W/97m.
Standout gangster film that has often been copied but never equaled. It's exciting—funny, too; with surefire direction by Michael Curtiz and a terrific performance by James Cagney in one of his best roles. Cagney is a tough gangster who helps out boyhood pal Pat O'Brien, a priest who has been having trouble keeping some unruly teenagers (the Dead End Kids) off the streets and in his gym. Unfortunately, the kids start to idolize Cagney and his life of crime, and admire the way he snubs his nose at the law. When Cagney is arrested and sentenced to the electric chair, the boys are impressed by how bravely he is taking it all. O'Brien asks his proud, cocky friend to humble himself before he dies—for the sake of the boys. The odd thing about the finale in which Cagney turns "yeller" so that the boys will lose respect for gangsters like him is that we viewers (including real-life teenagers) actually gain respect for him because what he's doing for the boys takes real courage. We must remember that the script was written by the notorious Rowland Brown (*Blood Money*), who, it was rumored, had underworld connections. Brown's theme in all his major works was: crime does pay. Also with: Humphrey Bogart, Ann Sheridan (who'd be in the semi-sequel *Angels Wash Their Faces*), George Bancroft, and the Dead End Kids: Billy Halop, Leo Gorcey, Huntz Hall, Gabe Dell, Bobby Jordan, Bernard Punsley.

ANIMAL CRACKERS (1930) B&W/98m.
The Marx Brothers' second film, adapted from their Broadway hit, is set at the mansion of rich Margaret Dumont. She is having a party at which she'll unveil her new possession, a priceless painting. Her guest of honor is African explorer Captain Spaulding, played by Groucho, who, judging by his clean safari garb and fear of caterpillars, has never been to Africa. Zeppo plays Groucho's secretary, but in this film you hardly remember he's around. Making a greater impression are Chico as cardsharp Sir Emanuel Ravelli ("How did you get to be an Italian?" asks a longtime acquaintance) and Harpo as habitual thief The Professor, chief suspect (with good reason) when the painting is stolen. Until a few years ago this picture was kept out of circulation; when it was released amid great fanfare, critics were so happy to see another Marx Brothers picture that they overpraised it. Over-

all it's a disappointing film, where the innocuous art-theft plot gets in the way of the comedy, and where the proceedings come to a dead halt when Chico plays the piano, romantic leads Hal Thompson and Lillian Roth (the pretty actress-singer who'd become an alcoholic) sing a duet, and Harpo plays a particularly dull harp solo. However, there are comedic highlights: Groucho leading the guests in a rousing "Hooray for Captain Spaulding," which would become his television theme song; Groucho engaging guest Louis Sorin in ridiculous conversation (Groucho tells *us* incredulously, "This fellow takes me seriously; it's not safe to ask him the simplest question"); Groucho recalling his trip to Africa ("The first morning saw us up at six, breakfasted, and back in bed at seven—this was our routine for the first three months"); Harpo virtually molesting and wrestling Dumont; and Harpo and Chico playing their own style of bridge with Dumont and a female guest (Margaret Irving), ending when Harpo steals Irving's shoes: it is a nice change of pace watching Dumont play scenes with Harpo and Chico, and not just Groucho. Scripted by Morrie Ryskind, who wrote the book of the musical play with George S. Kaufman; the music and lyrics were by Bert Kalmar and Harry Ruby. Directed by Victor Heerman. Also with: Kathryn Reece, Robert Greig, Edward Metcalf.

ANNIE HALL (1977) C/94m.
Woody Allen's first genuine comedy masterpiece is an autobiographical, therapeutic work in which New York comedian Alvy Singer (Allen) thinks back on his relationship with an equally neurotic, aspiring singer from Wisconsin, Annie Hall (Diane Keaton). They always laughed together and they loved one another dearly, but she felt stifled by his obsession with death, his Jewish paranoia, his pessimism, his inability to enjoy life. He supported her in her career, encouraged her to read to broaden her knowledge, and paid for her to have therapy, but, ironically, the more confident she became because of his help, the more insecure he felt in their relationship. Film is very perceptive and romantic in addition to being hilarious. The two characters are real and we root for them to work out their problems; but, like Alvy, we come to realize that they were meant to be no more than positive influences on each other during difficult, transitional periods in their respective lives. Alvy is sweet at the end when he concludes that the relationship was well worth the constant problems and the misery he experienced after their final break-up (he even went to LA and rented a car to try to win her back!); and Allen is sweet to have named his film after his female character, as a tribute to her, rather than calling it *Alvy Singer*. Picture has so many great moments: Annie (winning our hearts) trying desperately to find the right words to ask Alvy, whom she has just met, if he wants a ride home from a tennis club; their initial bland, pretentious conversation on her terrace, during which Allen provides subtitles that reveal what each is really thinking (both worry that they're blowing it); Alvy kissing Annie for the first time, on the street before they go to a restaurant so neither has to feel anxious about having to kiss later that

night; Alvy silencing an obnoxious, self-impressed, self-professed McLuhan expert who talks pretentious drivel in a movie line by pulling McLuhan out of a poster to tell the man, "You know nothing of my work" (Alvy says to us, "Boy, if life were only like this!"); Alvy battling monstrous spiders in Annie's bathtub; etc, etc. There is, of course, the usual array of Allen one-liners and sight gags. Keaton won a Best Actress Oscar, Allen and Marshall Brickman won an Oscar for Best Original Screenplay, Allen won for Best Director, and this was the rare comedy to win a Best Picture Oscar—Academy members temporarily forgot their anti-Allen, anti-New-York-filmmaker bias because he did include several scenes that were shot in Hollywood—it didn't matter they were unflattering to the city. Also with: Tony Roberts, Paul Simon, Shelley Duvall, Carol Kane, Janet Margolin, Colleen Dewhurst, Christopher Walken.

ANNIE OAKLEY (1935) B&W/88m. Barbara Stanwyck is fine as a good-hearted, unpretentious backwoods girl who joins Buffalo Bill's Wild West Show because of her love for Preston Foster, a rival sharpshooter. But director George Stevens's romance looks dated and suffers considerably from the overuse of studio sets that give it phony and claustrophobic feel. The most interesting and enlightening aspect of the film is that Foster, once full of conceit, is willing to accept that Stanwyck is the better shot; because she doesn't think the less of him for being second best, he is supportive of her rather than being jealous or competitive. Basis for Irving Berlin's *Annie Get Your Gun*, the play and film; nothing like the old *Annie Oakley* television series, in which Gail Davis shot it out with outlaws. Also with: Melvyn Douglas, Moroni Olsen, Pert Kelton, Andy Clyde, Chief Thunderbird (as a Sitting Bull few will be happy with).

ANTONIO DAS MORTES (BRAZILIAN/1969) C/100m. A major work of Brazil's Cinema Nôvo, and a very popular film among U.S. and European leftists at the time of release. Glauber Rocha's myth-epic tells story of a legendary bounty hunter (Maurico do Valle), with hat, poncho, and rifle, who in 1939 was hired by a rich reactionary landlord to kill leftist *congaceiros*. He kills the top bandit, but soon regrets what he has done. He becomes politicized and turns his rifle on the landlord and his hired guns. Political allegory is both extremely theatrical and, at times, ritualistic. You'll be reminded of Sergio Leone's Clint Eastwood bounty-hunter films, Eastwood's *Joe Kidd* (in which he turns against the men who hired him), *El Topo* (the bearded Do Valle looks like a fat Alexandro Jodorowsky), Godard (if he ever made a period piece, it would be similar), and South American dance, folkloric, and religious pageants. Picture is ambiguous at times and downright weird at other times. But it's endlessly fascinating and colorful. A jarring finale. Fine photography by Alfonso Beato. Playing interesting characters: Odete Lara, Hugh Carvana, Othon Bastos, Jofre Soares.

APARAJITO (INDIAN/1956) B&W/108m. The second film in Satyajit Ray's Apu Trilogy finds 10-year-old Apu (Pinaki Sen Gupta) living in the city Benares with his parents. When his lay-preacher father (Kanu Banerji) dies, his mother (Karuna Banerji) takes him to a small village, where she works as a cook for a wealthy family and he does chores. He insists on going to school and, in scenes that remind one of *Sugar Cane Alley*, the boy shows an amazing thirst for knowledge and pride that his teachers acknowledge his intelligent work. When 17, Apu (now Smaran Ghosal) goes to college in Calcutta, getting by on a small scholarship, a night job at a print shop, and his mother's hard-earned savings. When Apu leaves, his mother suffers from terrible loneliness—her wish to have him stay home and be a lay preacher and care for her (she won't tell him she is ill) is not his wish. This film really conveys special relationship between mother and son: he realizes that he means everything to her, but can't allow that to dictate his life. In Ray, in order to live your own life, you will brutally hurt those you love and who love you, you will come across as being insensitive, as the boy does here toward his mother and the mother did in *Pather Panchali* toward the old aunt and her own daughter. The scenes between the boy and his mother are priceless—he assuring her that she's a better cook than the guy at the college; she smiling slightly but with infinite happiness when her son returns home for one extra day of vacation time, claiming to have missed the train. In fact the *sensitive* boy missed the train on purpose because he realizes how much his presence for another 24 hours will mean to his mother—but, like all kids involved in struggles with manipulative/martyristic mothers, he doesn't let on that *she* convinced him to stay. Lovely, perceptive film, with a second unforgettable, understated performance by Banerji (smiling more and acting nicer than in original) as one of Ray's many fascinating, untraditional women—from the novel by Bibhuti Bandapaddhay. Sequel: *The World of Apu*. Music by Ravi Shankar.

APOCALYPSE NOW (1979) C/150m. Francis Coppola's epic about the madness—"the horror!"—of the Vietnam War is considered controversial. Yet there is really no volatile material. Critics and moviegoers may have second-guessed or applauded Coppola's choices as a filmmaker—especially considering that he filmed two endings—but the only cause for debate among people interested in the war itself is Coppola's best, most authentic sequence: stoned, leaderless soldiers fight continuously behind enemy lines while headquarters has forgotten about them. The story, inspired by Joseph Conrad's *Heart of Darkness*, has the U.S. military sending agent Martin Sheen into the North Vietnam wilderness to kill U.S. officer Marlon Brando, who has become the godlike leader of a renegade band of natives. On his journey upriver Sheen experiences the surreal sights and sounds of the war. And he comes across the lunatic fringe of our army, including officer Robert Duvall ("I love the smell of napalm in the morning"), who plays Wagner full blast while leading bombing raids. Many visuals are exciting, but the picture is annoyingly self-conscious. Too often Coppola seems to be calling attention to his artistry and imagination. The boat trip comes across like a ride at Disneyland, where the special-effects men have prepared tableaux on the banks at every turn of the river. The scene in which Sheen and Brando lie around philosophizing while Coppola gets super-pretentious with his camera and character placement recalls the similarly shot, ultra-boring scene of Liv Ullmann and Ingrid Bergman in Ingmar Bergman's *Autumn Sonata*. Cinematographer Vittorio Storaro won an Oscar. Also with: Frederick Forrest, Albert Hall, Sam Bottoms, Larry Fishbourne, Dennis Hopper, G. D. Spradlin, Harrison Ford.

ARRUZA (1972) C/75m.

Budd Boetticher directed two fictional films about bullfighting: *The Bullfighter and the Lady* and *The Magnificent Matador*. Also he instilled in his many cowboy heroes (most notably Randolph Scott in seven classic westerns) virtues that he associated with bullfighters: bravery, pride, self-discipline, and a sense of honor. But this was the picture he wanted to make all along: a documentary about his great friend Carlos Arruza, a famous Mexican matador who was making a dramatic comeback, attempting to become the greatest *rejoneador* (a bullfighter on horseback) in the world. While directing pictures in Hollywood, he would sneak away to shoot footage for this film; eventually he went to Mexico to shoot until completion. During his seven-year stay, Boetticher nearly starved (he had an account at a tamale stand), was divorced, spent time in prison, suffered a mental breakdown, and nearly died from a lung ailment; most of his crew died and, amazingly, Arruza was killed in an automobile accident before filming was completed (Arruza's widow did scenes long after her husband was dead). Because the film was so important to Boetticher, who certainly didn't make it with commercial goals in mind, there has been a tendency among his fans to overpraise it. While it contains interesting, even poignant moments, it is, sadly, a disappointment, lacking the excitement and even the charismatic protagonist that distinguished Boetticher's fiction films. Perhaps it is too simple. Moreover, if you don't like bullfighting to begin with, you probably won't share Boetticher's respect for Arruza or his "art."

ARSENAL (RUSSIAN/1929) B&W/65m.

Beautifully photographed, poetic silent film by Alexander Dovzhenko, exalting the revolutionary spirit of Russia's farmers, workers, and soldiers. WWI is causing misery throughout Russia; poverty and hunger are widespread and women mourn the fathers and sons being killed in combat. The seeds for armed insurrection against the Czar have been planted, but for now the bourgeois Social Democrats, the White Russians who would eventually support Kerensky's provisional government, try to crush the Bolsheviks. We stand firmly behind the arsenal workers in Kiev who go on strike and the common men of Ukrainia who bravely stand up to the guns of the counterrevolutionaries. Story is hard to follow at times, but the succession of images (many used symbolically) have amazing force. Most memorable: a one-armed farmer standing in the field with his skinny horse; a funeral procession in the snow; the bourgeois reacting with fear when the motors of the arsenal come to a halt; the portrait of a revolutionary leader, Shevtshenko, coming to life; and, in the uplifting final shot, our own hero (S. Svashenko) standing firm and opening his shirt wide to show the Whites that their bullets have no effect on him (or the many Bolsheviks like him). Film was very influential due to its style and its call for peace and brotherhood; for instance, it's likely that Lewis Milestone studied this picture before making *All Quiet on the Western Front*. Cinematography by Danylo Demutsky.

ARSENIC AND OLD LACE (1944) B&W/118m.

Frank Capra directed this super-screwy black comedy, which was adapted from Joseph Kesselring's Broadway play in 1941 but wasn't released until the production closed. Cary Grant's a drama critic who's about to marry Priscilla Lane until he discovers insanity runs in his family. His sweet maiden aunts (Josephine Hull, Jean Adair) have 13 corpses in their basement. They've been poisoning lonely men. Grant frantically tries to keep this secret, but the police keep coming around. That's partly because his insane, murderous brother, Raymond Massey, has returned. He's with "doctor" Peter Lorre, who during a drunken plastic-surgery operation made Massey look like Boris Karloff. To add to the craziness, relative John Alexander thinks he's Teddy Roosevelt and keeps running up the stairs and slamming the door. Your enjoyment of the film may depend on your mood. The performances are all good except for Grant, who is as out of control as Pinky Lee—he's truly annoying. Also, Priscilla Lane is shamefully wasted. The worst part of the film is that so much humor comes from characters being frustrated when trying to get information or give information. Scripted by Julius and Philip Epstein. Also with: James Gleason, Edward Everett Horton, Jack Carson, Grant Mitchell.

ASHES AND DIAMONDS (POLISH/1958) B&W/104m.

Thematically ambiguous Andrzej Wajda film is set at the very end of WWII in Europe when members of the resistance have to choose their roles since Russian influence has replaced German dominance. Film opens with resistance fighters ambushing three Polish workers, mistakenly believing that the Party Secretary (Wacław Zastrzezynski), just back from Russia, is among them. When young Zbigniew Cybulski realizes that his target still lives, he checks into the same hotel as the aged Communist and looks for an opportunity to complete his mission. However, during his one night at the hotel, which hosts a celebratory banquet for bourgeois and military types, he has an affair with the pretty barmaid (Ewa Krzyzanowska) that affects him greatly. Having been given a dose of humanity, he contemplates starting life anew with the young woman and giving up the thought of assassination. After all, killing a fellow Pole in the name of nationalism is much different than killing invading Nazis. As *American* viewers, we almost assume that Wajda is on the side of the anti-communist resistance fighters. But this is certainly not the case—when they kill the wrong men at the beginning and show no remorse, we can't even feel sympathy for them. Their reasons for killing the Party Secretary are not convincing; and one wonders if the man behind the plan is being guided by personal rather than political objectives. It's also easy to sympathize with the Party Leader because he is old, humble, walks with a cane, and because his son was raised by people of whom he didn't approve. Early and late scenes, those in which guns are fired, are fairly exciting; the best moment, in which the Party Secretary collapses into Cybulski's arms, was conceived by Cybulski (who became a major Polish star because of this film). Middle scenes are artistically photographed, but are slow and deadly. Also with: Adam Pawlikowski, Bogumil Kobiela.

ASPHALT JUNGLE, THE (1950) B&W/112m.
Sam Jaffe, as the shrewd German "Professor," is released from jail and immediately enlists tough hooligan Sterling Hayden, safecracker Anthony Caruso, and driver James Whitmore to pull off the biggest diamond theft in Midwest history. Jaffe is suspicious that Louis Calhern, the lawyer who has agreed to be their fence, is really broke and is planning on double-crossing them and stealing the jewels. Jaffe's perfectly conceived plan falls apart. The reputation of John Huston's seminal heist film, which he and Ben Maddow adapted from W. R. Burnett's novel, has diminished somewhat. Because Huston strove for realism, he deglamorized the characters involved in the crime: the result is that we find the characters and their story interesting but don't feel empathy for any of them. Ironically, the success of the heist is of paramount importance only to the most respectable participant, Calhern, the piece's villain—so we don't particularly care if the heist fails as we do in a film like *The Killing*, where all the thieves (whom we have sympathy for) desperately need money to have a chance for a happy life. In this film we care only for the women who suffer because of their men's foolish endeavors: Hayden's devoted girlfriend, Jean Hagen; Calhern's bedridden wife, Dorothy Tree; Calhern's childish mistress, Marilyn Monroe (obviously on her way to stardom); and Caruso's wife, Teresa Celli. The acting is uniformly excellent in this film, but I prefer the actresses in their secondary parts to the men. Picture builds a convincing case for there being pervasive corruption on every level of society, including the police, then spoils it when, in the worst scene, police chief John McIntire lectures the press about how 99% of cops are honest and they're out on the streets 24 hours a day protecting the public. One of the picture's best scenes has Jaffe explaining the details of his proposed crime and revealing the budget—it's almost like a producer trying to sell a script to a studio. Remakes: 1950's *The Badlanders*, 1962's *Cairo*, and 1972's *A Cool Breeze*. Also with: Marc Lawrence, Barry Kelley.

ASSAULT ON PRECINCT 13 (1976) C/90m.
Before *Halloween* made him famous, John Carpenter directed the space comedy *Dark Star* and this violent police drama, low-budget efforts that independently gained cult notoriety in the U.S. and Europe. *Dark Star* holds up much better because its minuscule budget actually works in its favor, adding to the comical flavor. This film could have used extra financing for some reshooting; the dialogue scenes in particular need more polish. And whereas *Dark Star* comes across as being a complete original despite parodying earlier sci-fi films, *Assault* comes across as being derivative—of Howard Hawks's *Rio Bravo* (certainly forgivable since Carpenter intended this to be a homage to that film) and, surprisingly, *Night of the Living Dead*. The plot concerns an isolated police station whose few inhabitants find themselves under siege by scores of faceless street-gang members who roam outside in the dark and occasionally try to break in. The atmosphere is consistently tense, and the action sequences are amazingly accomplished considering the budget. Some will consider the violence too gratuitous; for instance, Carpenter seemed to enjoy filming the shooting of an obnoxious little kid. Still impressive. The cast of unknowns includes: Austin Stoker, Darwin Jostin, Laurie Zimmerman, Martin West, Tony Burton, Nancy Loomis (who'd be a victimized teenager in *Halloween*).

ATLANTIC CITY (CANADIAN-FRENCH/1980) C/104m.
Louis Malle's best English-language film. Susan Sarandon works in an Atlantic City oyster bar, but is hopeful of becoming a blackjack dealer. But, like most people in the new casino-dominated Atlantic City, she is a loser. She lost her good-for-nothing husband (Robert Joy) to her sister (Hollis McClaren) and now she's kicked out of the casino when he turns up with the pregnant girl—casinos won't employ anyone who has connections to such lowlifes. Joy is killed by gangsters while trying to unload the cocaine he stole from them. However, he stashed it with one of Sarandon's neighbors (Burt Lancaster), an aged nickel-and-dime numbers man who longs for the good old days when Atlantic City, the Atlantic Ocean, and the gangsters were really something. With gutsy Sarandon at his side, the classy Lancaster decides to sell the cocaine himself and make a killing: he feels like a gangster from the glory days. There is much in this film to appreciate—the seedy city itself, for example: even if you've never been there, you'll feel nostalgia for the pre-casino days. John Guare's exceptional, witty script is full of believable, interesting types—all hoping for that one shot at happiness. His major theme is reflected in the coupling of Lancaster and Sarandon. Their union serves as a metaphor for the present-day mixing of the old and new in Atlantic City. Only their union, temporary as it must be, is a *positive* development. Not only do they take care of the gangsters, but they make off with a bundle of cash and much needed doses of self-respect, treasures not many people leaving Atlantic City can claim. A nice choice of locations; Malle's eye for detail is, as usual, impeccable. Lancaster and Sarandon make a dynamic screen

couple. Also with: Kate Reid, Michel Piccoli (as a martinet blackjack instructor who treats his pupils as if they were ballet students), Robert Goulet (as himself).

ATOM-AGE VAMPIRE (ITALIAN/1961) B&W/ 87m—105m.

Sleazy, dubbed horror film about a mad scientist (Alberto Lupo) who tries to permanently restore the disfigured face of the woman he loves (Suzanne Loret) by killing other women for their blood cells. During his experiments *he* becomes ghoulish-looking. The best scene has Lupo approaching a streetwalker who screams when she sees his face. It's an awful picture, but is fun to watch; for one thing, it was one of the first horror films to really exploit sex—for us young boys in 1961 (when I saw it several times) it was perversely exciting to see the scarred Loret displaying her stacked body in skimpy underwear. Directed by Anton Giulio Majano, although Mario Bava had his hand in the production. Also with: Sergio Fantoni, Franca Parisi Strahl.

ATOMIC CAFE, THE (1982) B&W-C/88m.

Serves up a powerful smorgasbord of mind-blowing clips from late-forties/early-fifties American newsreels and government/military/educational films that both warned us about the Russian menace and eased our fears about the effects of nuclear fallout. It's amazing that everyone didn't die from high blood pressure while waiting for the nuclear attack that, we were told, could come at any moment. But I suppose we were convinced that when we saw that white flash we'd be safe if we just followed the advice to "duck and take cover." We hear an officer tell the soldiers on a nuclear testing site not to worry about radiation; people in a town that's about to be exposed to nuclear fallout (because wind direction unexpectedly changed) being told to stay inside for an hour and not to worry about their children at school; and, in a propaganda film, a father warning his family not to leave the fallout shelter for at least a minute after they hear an explosion. Picture would have even more impact and import if we learned whether these ridiculous propaganda films were the result of government naïveté or were fully intended to deceive the public about the dangers of a nuclear build-up. It almost might have been a good idea to end the film with clips of contemporary politicians, militarists, scientists giving their expert opinions about the reasons we should back their pro-nuclear policy—this would suggest that years from now we would realize how naïve and devious are their words and statistics. Compiled by Kevin Rafferty, Jayne Loader, and Pierce Rafferty.

ATTACK! (1956) B&W/104m—107m.

Tough, taut, thought-provoking anti-war film set in Belgium in 1944. Robert Aldrich's expertly directed action scenes are brutal, with emphasis placed on our soldiers' fears and the tremendous pain they feel when they're injured; the seemingly invincible enemy tanks that emerge from the rubble with their wiggling gun heads coming into view first and their turrets rotating are presented as monsters, much like the giant ants in *Them!* But if the Nazis weren't terrifying enough, the American GI finds himself to be the potential victim of U.S. army bureaucracy that allows soldiers to be sacrificed rather than cause a stink by recalling incompetent officers. In this war, platoon leaders punch their own men, high-rank officers slap captains, captains punch enemy prisoners, Americans push a captured German officer (Peter Van Eyck being very arrogant) into the Germans' line of fire to be mowed down, a captain is willing to turn his men over to the enemy so that he won't be shot, the captain's men are willing to kill him. Eddie Albert gives a memorably creepy performance as a crazed, sadistic captain whose cowardice has cost the lives of many men. Jack Palance is staunchly heroic as the leader of a platoon which Albert has ordered to explore a small, bombed-out town—knowing Albert has no backbone, he warns him to provide the back-up forces he promised or "I'll shove a grenade down your throat and pull the pin." James Poe's strong script was adapted from Norman Brooks's play *The Fragile Fox*. Also with: Lee Marvin (who protects Albert's reputation for the sake of Albert's father), Buddy Ebsen, William Smithers, Robert Strauss, Richard Jaeckel.

ATTACK OF THE 50 FT. WOMAN (1958) B&W/ 66m.

Laughable camp in which former asylum patient Allison Hayes is turned into a giant by an alien. Now she can get revenge on her philandering husband (William Hudson) and his sluttish mistress (Yvette Vickers)—which she does in grand style. If made today—and I'm sure it will be remade someday—the film could be taken as a feminist treatise, in which a woman who has been suppressed (she's put into an asylum; she is literally chained down by doctors) and maltreated breaks free of her bonds and, too angry to talk things out, gives her cheating husband his just deserts. But, in truth, most of the fun comes from watching statuesque Hayes run around in a scanty outfit. This is the rare time when we're *supposed* to look at a woman's body. And if Hayes isn't sexy enough, then there's always the luscious Vickers. Hayes and Vickers are why I liked this film as a boy and, I assume, are the reasons it is cult film today among male sci-fi fans. With amusing special effects. Directed by Nathan Hertz (Juran). Also with: Roy Gordon, George Douglas, Ken Terrell.

ATTACK OF THE GIANT LEECHES (1959) B&W/ 62m.

Sweaty sci-fi, set in southern swamp where super-intelligent giant leeches snatch up unlucky passersby, hang them in their camp lair, still alive, and drain their blood when thirsty. Roger Corman production is like an early Russ Meyer potboiler (*Lorna, Mud Honey*) with horror elements. Luscious Yvette Vickers, sex personified as a trampy married woman, would certainly qualify as an early Meyer heroine. The film's worth seeing for her alone, but it has other things going for it as well. While it is a bit gruesome, it's also gritty, enjoyably lurid, and creepy. Bernard Kowalski's direction has flair; it wasn't his fault that Corman didn't buy more convincing leech costumes. Robert Clarke is the leading man, one of several early sci-fi heroes who defeat alien visitors because of their knowledge of the physical setting. Unfairly neglected film has devoted following. Also with: Bruno VeSota (who drives his unfaithful wife, Vickers, deep into the swamps, where the leeches grab her), Jan Shepard, Michael Emmet.

ATTACK OF THE KILLER TOMATOES (1980) C/87m.
Title sufficiently tells plot of this sci-fi spoof that, regrettably, is not nearly as bad as its distributors would like us to believe. Unfortunately, the filmmakers had enough skill to make it clever but dull rather than inept but campy, like other "Worst Film" contenders. At least it has an even more ludicrous title tune than *The Blob*'s. Funniest gag has an actor dubbed (loud and out-of-synch, appropriately) simply because this is a sci-fi film and he is Japanese. Directed by John DeBello. With: David Miller, Sharon Taylor, George Wilson, Jack Riley (of *The Bob Newhart Show*), Rock Peace, The San Diego Chicken.

AVVENTURA, L' (ITALIAN-FRENCH/1960) B&W/130m—139m—145m.
Slow, enigmatic work by Michelangelo Antonioni which many critics consider infuriatingly shallow and others think is fraught with insight into the psyche of the rich. Story begins with the arrival of a group of rich Italians on an island. After a young woman (Lea Massari) quarrels with her architect lover (Gabriele Ferzetti), she disappears. A search proves futile. Her friend (Monica Vitti) and Ferzetti look for her all over Italy. They fall in love and forget about the missing woman. Pessimistic film is about the tenuous nature of modern relationships, the inability of people to communicate verbally, the lack of joy in lovemaking, the meaningless and alienated lives of the rich, the realization that we'll all disappear from the face of the earth and that life, such as it is, will continue (and we will fade from memory); those who survive have no comprehension of why they were born or what their deaths will mean. Film is very slow-paced, has no real storyline, uses dull dialogue to express the dullness of the uncommunicative characters. I find the film fascinating, but I now know better than to recommend it to the casual moviegoer. It was Antonioni's breakthrough film. Mesmerizing photography by Aldo Scavarda. Also with: Dominique Blanchar, Renzo Ricci, James Adams.

AWFUL TRUTH, THE (1937) B&W/92m.
Leo McCarey won a Best Director Oscar for this delightful screwball comedy. Cary Grant and Irene Dunne were paired for the first time as a married couple who file for divorce because Grant suspects Dunne's been having an affair with her singing teacher (Alexander D'Arcy)—after all, D'Arcy's car broke down when he and Dunne were coming back from the prom (that *old* story) they were invited to. Of course, they still love each other, though neither will admit it. But Grant slyly tries to break up Dunne's engagement to dull, mother-dominated Ralph Bellamy, who wants to take the sophisticated Dunne back to Oklahoma. Then Dunne goes to work, breaking up Grant's engagement to society girl Molly Lamont. There's nothing special about the story—this was the third adaptation of a play by Arthur Richman—but the two stars are terrific, making amusing lines sound downright sophisticated, improvising, doing physical comedy. Bellamy and D'Arcy (the kind of guy who'd get dumped in the Astaire-Rogers musicals) lend fine support. Entire production is bursting with energy. Highlights include Grant putting on Bellamy (whom he'd really have a field day with in *His Girl Friday*) about how wonderful he thinks Oklahoma City is; Grant's meetings with D'Arcy; Grant disrupting Dunne's recital (I love her reaction—adding a melodic laugh to the end of her song); Dunne making Lamont's family believe she's Grant's ill-bred, heavy-drinking sister. And the final scene, in which Grant and Dunne have connecting bedrooms, is a gem. Originally filmed in 1925; then again in 1929 with Ina Claire. Remade in 1953 as *Let's Do It Again*. Also with: Esther Dale, Cecil Cunningham, Mary Forbes, Joyce Compton.

BABES IN TOYLAND/MARCH OF THE WOODEN SOLDIERS/REVENGE IS SWEET (1934) B&W/73m—79m.
Victor Herbert operetta, adapted for Stan Laurel and Oliver Hardy, has always been a favorite of children, but in the last few years it has become a cult favorite of adults as well. Oliver Dee and Stanlee Dum live in Toyland, as boarders in Mrs. Peep's shoehouse. They thwart a plan by evil Silas Barnaby (Harry Kleinbach) to marry lovely Little Bo Peep (Charlotte Henry) when Stan substitutes for the bride, and also ruin Barnaby's plan to evict them and Mrs. Peep (Florence Roberts). Vengeful Barnaby kidnaps one of the Three Little Pigs and frames Bo's fiancé, Tom Tom Piper (Felix Knight). Old King Cole exiles Tom Tom to Bogeyland. Oliver and Stan rescue him and Bo, but return to Toyland with Barnaby and the child-snatching Bogeyman on their trail. Luckily, Stan, who worked in the toy-making store, had mistakenly ordered 100 six-foot-tall toy soldiers, instead of 600 one-foot-tall soldiers, because now his giant wooden army of 100 drives out the Bogeyman. MGM production is one of the best fantasies of the pre-*Wizard of Oz* days. Costumes are nifty, storybook characters are fun, battle between the soldiers (whose march is animated) and the Bogeyman is as exciting as anything that would turn up in *Flash Gordon*. But I wish they'd have gotten rid of a couple of tunes (which kids wouldn't listen to anyway) and given Laurel and Hardy a few more funny gags. Gus Meins directed the children in the cast; Charles Rogers directed the adult stars.

BABY BLUE MARINE (1976) C/90m. Set in the American heartland during the early forties. Jan-Michael Vincent is rejected by the marines during basic training because he lacks what it takes to be a good *fighting* soldier. He is humiliated to be wearing the baby-blue uniform that signifies his failure. But he is knocked out in a depot by a decorated marine, who switches their uniforms. Vincent winds up in a small American town, where everyone sees his uniform and treats him like a war hero, a son who has returned home. When several "dangerous" men escape from a nearby Japanese internment facility, the gung-ho towns-people expect him to lead some armed men in bringing about their recapture. While not in the class of director John Hancock's *Bang the Drum Slowly*, this sleeper does touch on several sensitive subjects. Its novel theme: *naïve* Americans are too quick to be violent, blindly jingoistic, and intolerant, and to glorify undeserving heroes; only when they calm down and learn what's really going on are they properly humane, forgiving, and receptive. Vincent gives his one fine screen performance to date, and Glynnis O'Connor is well cast as the smalltown girl who wins his heart. Also with: Katherine Helmond, Dana Elcar, Bert Remson, and, in a small part, Richard Gere.

BABY DOLL (1956) B&W/114m. "White trash" comedy by Elia Kazan, who adapted two Tennessee Williams plays, *27 Wagons Full of Cotton* and *The Unsatisfactory Supper*. Filmed on location in Benoit, Mississippi, this three-character story was meant to convey how Williams visualized the New South, where chivalry, honor, and hospitality (the "Good Neighbor Policy") have been replaced by depravity and decadence, men coveting what their neighbors have (money, work, or women), and "carpetbagging" outsiders/foreigners taking over work and stealing women— just as during the Reconstruction. Dumb, bigoted, middle-aged cotton-gin owner Archie Lee (Karl Malden) has problems. After two years of marriage, his child bride, Baby Doll (Carroll Baker), is about to turn 20, which is when her father said the marriage could be consummated, but she is under no obligation to have sex with him unless he fulfills the other part of the bargain and does a good job of providing for her. He has had virtually no business since Silva Vicarro (Eli Wallach's movie debut) came to the area and set up a more sophisticated cotton gin. Craving his day in bed with Baby Doll—he has taken to drilling holes in walls just to see her naked—Archie secretly burns down Vicarro's mill; he then offers to gin 27 wagons of Vicarro's cotton for a hefty price. Knowing that Archie was responsible for the fire, Vicarro comes to Archie's house when he's not home and proceeds to seduce Baby Doll, who doesn't put up much resistance. He wants to get her to incriminate her husband in the crime. Vicarro's expressions and movements will at times remind you of a sneaky fox. He is too clever for the naïve Baby Doll, one of many Williams heroines who are betrayed by men supposedly befriending them. The unknown Baker became a sex symbol as a result of this film; she never is seen wearing less than a slip, but she does

convey (especially when she lies in a crib and sucks her thumb) that once Baby Doll relinquishes her virginity some man will be very, very lucky—making love will definitely be her best skill. Cardinal Spellman and the Legion of Decency condemned this film when it was released, and its exhibition was challenged (unsuccessfully) in court in Illinois. Surely those who criticized it on moral grounds didn't think the scene in which Vicarro rubs the merrily squirming Baker's tummy with his foot was in good taste. But it's a perfect example of how Kazan uses sex in an intentionally ludicrous manner, making it a key element in what is much like an absurdist play. In fact, Williams believed that Kazan could have played up the humor even more. Also with: Mildred Dunnock.

BABY LOVE (BRITISH/1968) C/96m. Adapted from the first novel by Tina Chad Christian, a 24-year-old near-cripple, and helmed by 29-year-old first-time director Alastair Reid, this weird little potboiler also marked the debut of 17-year-old actress Linda Hayden, an extremely sexy baby-faced blond who would become a British cult favorite in subsequent years. Here Hayden is a rebellious 15-year-old whose mother (Diana Dors) commits suicide. She moves from her working-class neighborhood into the wealthy home of one of her mother's former lovers (Keith Barron), who may in fact be her father. The mischievous, manipulative girl sexually seduces his teenage son (Derek Lamden), his wife (Ann Lynn), and him, turning them against one another for her affections and wrecking his once happy home. Several films have been variations on this subject, but they've usually ended up making the girl into a witch capable of casting spells in order to get the family members into her evil clutches. But Hayden's girl just uses her sexual wiles and exploits everyone's weaknesses, and people fall at her feet. Her character is most memorable: at one point she lets a stranger in a movie theater feel her up while the angry son looks on helplessly; later when scary youth-gang members attempt to rape her, she urges them on (so they quit, disgusted with her). Film is no classic, but it's fascinating in a perverse sort of way, and is almost as seductive as Hayden herself.

BABY MAKER, THE (1970) C/109m. James Bridges's directorial debut features a fine, heartfelt performance by Barbara Hershey as a hippie who is hired by a straight-laced, well-to-do couple (Sam Groom, Collin Wilcox-Horne) to be a surrogate mother. Story emphasizes the awkward relationship between the three characters, beginning with the day Groom first has sex with Hershey, through her pregnancy, to after the birth of the child, whom both women love. Dialogue, as well as the look of the film, is dated; premise is still timely. Although looking plump in her miniskirt, young Hershey is sexy; more important is that she gives a believable, sensitive characterization playing a young woman who very much fit her own early free-spirit image. Also with: Scott Glenn (as Hershey's boyfriend), Jeannie Berlin.

BACK TO THE FUTURE (1985) C/114m.

Marty McFly (Michael J. Fox) is a high-school student who's upset because his father (Crispin Glover) is a cowardly wimp who's always getting pushed around and his mother (Lea Thompson) eats and boozes too much. He accidentally travels 30 years into the past; he's shocked to discover his father was a cowardly wimp as a teenager and that his mother was sexually aggressive (apparently living with his father has drained the sexuality out of her). Marty must figure out a way to get Glover and Thompson together on the night of the big dance or they won't marry and he will never exist. It's a difficult task because Thompson pays no attention to Glover and gets "the hots" for the young stranger who has come to town. He tries to figure out how to transfer her love from him to Glover. Oedipal comedy manages to avoid vulgarity. Instead there is much healthy humor that would have been appreciated back in the innocent fifties. Most has to do with the cultural gap between the fifties and the eighties—about how fifties teens don't understand the future and how Fox is equally confused by the past. He tries to order a Tab at a soda shop; oblivious to bottle openers, he unsuccessfully tries to twist off a bottle cap; the girl from the innocent past is more sexually experienced than he is; fifties people think his down vest is a life preserver and his De Lorean is a spaceship; they can't believe Ronald Reagan is President in 1985 and he can't recall Reagan as a movie actor. Funniest moment for me is when he sees his convict uncle as a baby in a playpen in 1955 and tells the cute little thing to get used to the bars. Directed by Robert Zemeckis, written by Zemeckis and Bob Gale, and produced by Steven Spielberg, film is sweet and highly imaginative. But while acting is excellent, only Fox and Thompson play *real* people—the rest are caricatures, mere pawns for the filmmaker's gags. Glover is the definitive nerd and Christopher Lloyd makes all previous wild-eyed, wild-haired wacko scientists look second-rate, but their presence should be balanced with flesh-and-blood characters. I'm also uneasy about the end. First of all, instead of returning to the future, I'd prefer sticking around in the much more lively, inviting past to watch the revolution in television, rock 'n' roll, etc., and see how Thompson and Glover progress. Secondly, I'm a little uneasy seeing the present so altered by Marty's trip to the past; even if his mother and father are a happy, healthy, loving couple, there's something wrong with changing parents into two different people. No wonder Marty takes off at the end. A crowd pleaser—but I wish the scenes in the present were more satisfying. Cinematography by Dean Cundey. Also with: Thomas F. Wilson, Claudia Wells, Marc McClure, Wendie Jo Sperber, George Di Cenzo.

BADLANDS (1973) C/95m.

Sissy Spacek has said that she wanted to play Holly Sargis, an impressionable 15-year-old from Fort Dupree, South Dakota, who accompanies her new, older boyfriend Kit (Martin Sheen) on his Midwest murder spree and becomes object of a nationwide manhunt, because she was struck by how quickly a person's life can change. I assume she also was attracted to the part because it allowed her to employ her blank-page acting approach, whereby she develops her character from scratch. For Holly, an ignorant girl who has a vacant expression, who spends her free time mindlessly twirling a baton (an indelible Spacek image) and has no capacity for distinguishing between reality and fantasy or right and wrong, is in essence an unformed character, willing to be led in any direction, by anyone who pays attention to her. She's never had an experience worth mentioning, so to relieve her boredom she loses herself in movie magazines. Her haunting, emotionless, bizarre purple-prose narration makes it appear as if she were trying to compose a story of her own life that's fitting for one of those magazines. Indeed when she becomes Kit's girlfriend and accomplice, even after he kills her father (Warren Oates) she fantasizes she is taking part in a great adventure story. Nothing that happens on their journey to Montana is real to her—even the people Kit murders are just characters in her story. The Kit-Holly story is based on the infamous and unmotivated Charles Starkweather-Caril Fugate murder spree of 1958. It is a grim study of two similar human products of an American society that, during the apathetic, lethargic Eisenhower era, is so emotionally, morally, and culturally bankrupt that it not only spawns and nurtures killers but makes them folk heroes as well. Properly deglamorized by director Terrence Malick, the murders—committed by Kit while Holly just watches—are a function of their yearning to escape the vacuum that is their world. Kit's obsession with leaving behind a record of his life at every stop is his misguided attempt to remind people he was special in an era of conformists. Meticulously directed film is too self-consciously arty and a trifle boring, but the captivating performances by Spacek and Sheen, the stunning photography of the rugged landscape, and the intriguing real-life story make it more than worthwhile. It has a cult among critics who consider it an important, original film. Also with: Ramon Bieri, Alan Vint.

BAKER'S WIFE, THE (FRENCH/1938) B&W/124m–130m.

Baker (Raimu) refuses to believe that his young wife (Ginette Leclerc) has deserted him for a young shepherd (Charles Moulin). But he decides not to bake bread until she returns. Upset about being deprived of his delicious bread, the men of the town organize themselves into a hunting party to track down the lovers. Marcel Pagnol directed and wrote this wonderful adaptation of an episode in Jean Giono's novel *Jean le Bleu*. Film has humor, warmth, sentimentality, provincial flavor, and the special lovable characters one expects from Pagnol. The great Raimu creates such a kind, moral, understanding character that it makes sense that Leclerc should rediscover her love for him. Their final scene is one of many splendid moments. You'll believe all these characters truly live in this town. Also with: Charpin, Robert Vattier, Robert Bassac, Alida Rouffe, Edouard Delmont, Paul Dullac, Maupi.

BALLAD OF A SOLDIER (RUSSIAN/1959) B&W/
89m. In the opening scene we see a middle-aged woman waiting for the return of her soldier son. A narrator informs us that he was killed in battle, during WWII. If this were a Hollywood film, the studio probably would have eliminated this scene because when we watch the likable lad (Vladimir Ivashov) during the rest of the film, every time he smiles we feel sad because of our knowledge of his sorry fate. In fact, we are thankful that he and the young girl (Shanna Prokhorenko) he falls in love with have such a quick goodbye, without exchanging addresses, since it's doubtful they will ever see each other again. Without the beginning, the film might be regarded today as just a stirring, uplifting love story—between the boy and the girl and the boy and his mother. As it stands, it is one of our most powerful anti-war films, one that effectively conveys the suffering of the men and (especially) women who are separated when there is a call to arms. The storyline is simple. The young soldier disables two German tanks and, now a hero, is granted four days' leave to go home and visit his mother (Antonina Maximova). On his train journey he helps a crippled soldier return to his wife, shares a boxcar with Prokhorenko, delivers soap to a soldier's wife (who, it turns out, has been unfaithful), and survives the bombing of his train. He must hitch rides and row across a river on a makeshift raft. He has time only to embrace his mother and leave again. Critic Dwight MacDonald correctly criticized this film (in 1960) for making all Russian people and soldiers so lovable. But I believe the anti-war message is sincerely delivered, and the emphasis on the suffering of those whose husbands and sons are in combat seems correct. Direction by Grigori Chukhrai is sensitive and warm, and his depiction of women is admirable. Chukhrai lovingly films Russia's landscape and the lovely faces of his actors and actresses (Prokhorenko glows when she smiles). And it's fitting that his most emotional scenes are his many farewells and reunions (as soon as you see this film you'll rush to pay your mother that long-promised visit). The film ends with the boy's farewell to his mother and what's heartbreaking is that there will be no more wonderful reunions for them. Also with: Nikolai Kruchkov.

BALLAD OF CABLE HOGUE, THE (1970) C/
121m. Sam Peckinpah's western heroes typically are overage, past-their-prime men who didn't live up to their potentials, but are given a final chance to make good. Such a man is Cable Hogue (Jason Robards), whose patience with God when it looks like he's been forsaken to die like a rat in the desert earns him a reward: he discovers water "where it wasn't." His life saved, he opens a water station halfway between two towns on the stage route. He proves to be a shrewd (if stingy), successful businessman, proud to be part of America's business sector. He is Peckinpah's proof that anyone can climb out of the gutter and achieve the American dream, that all men need is a chance ("I'm worth something, ain't I?"). Simple, bawdy, lyrical film is one of Peckinpah's best. Robards, with a divine glow on his face, is wonderful,

creating a character who should be part of western lore. His romance with Stella Stevens's prostitute (the great role we Stevens cultists had been waiting for) is truly special: I love seeing her responses to his sincere flattery—she has never received such respect, she has never met a man capable of saying the right words or met a man so unafraid to express his feelings. David Warner also makes a contribution to this fable as the self-ordained minister, a sinner who smooth-talks pretty women into becoming "converts." He has his great moment delivering Cable's thoughtful funeral oration—words that one could apply to most Peckinpah westerners. Beautiful photography by Lucien Ballard; an excellent script, in which the dialogue has a unique rhythm, by John Crawford and Edward Penny. Stevens's "Butterfly Morning"—sung during nude bathing sequence—makes up for mediocre background songs. Also with: Strother Martin, L. Q. Jones, Slim Pickens, Peter Whitney, Gene Evans, R. G. Armstrong, Kathleen Freeman.

BALLAD OF NARAYAMA, THE (JAPANESE/
1983) C/129m. Unusual, prize-winning film by Shohei Imamura (Vengeance is Mine). It's set at the end of the 19th century in a remote mountain village. The primitive villagers are like no people we've seen in Japanese films. They may wear clothes, farm, and pray (to various gods), but, as is Imamura's theme, they are very much like the wild animals (rats, snakes, predatory birds) and insects that share the mountain and move unencumbered through their homes. They are instinctively brutal and carnal; their lives are dominated by food and fornication. It's common to find a young couple having sex in the mud like snakes; women are always getting pregnant. One "comical" fellow smells like an animal, eats bugs, converses with a horse (which he thinks is laughing at him), has sex with a dog. For revenge on a family of food thieves, the townspeople bury them alive (a shocking scene!), silently covering them and smoothing over the dirt as if they were a community of insects. Like some animals that preserve food by keeping the population down, they coldly dispose of unwanted (*male*) babies and push out those who are sick or old. When these superstitious people become 70, their sons must carry them to the mountain, Narayama, to leave them for their god. In the most fascinating scene we watch an unhappy man (Ken Ogata), the only character who has sympathy and who is a link between these people and civilized man, carry his aged mother (played by the not really old Sumiko Sakamoto) to the mountaintop. There they discover the human equivalent of an elephant burial ground: human skeletons lie about, picked clean by huge black birds that now wait for her to die. She may take a while because she's in good health. Unlike others who have been dragged to the mountaintop—including her husband—she is glad to be there. We watch in horror as another man accidentally knocks his struggling father over a mountain ledge when the terrified old man refuses to go to the top. Great scenery and some creepy slow-motion shots, and a fascinating portrait of what people without food can be-

come (if this were a Roger Corman movie, what we see might turn out to be our post-nuclear future). Frequently visible microphones are distracting. From the same stories by Shichiro Fukazawa that inspired Keisuke Kinoshita's film of the same name. Also with: Chieko Baisho, Tonpei Hidari, Aki Takejo, Shoichi Ozawa.

BAMBI (1942) C/69m.   A decade before the Walt Disney studio began its Tru-Life nature series, it used animation to depict animals in their natural environment—in this case, a forest—drawing a correlation between their life cycles and the changing seasons. But the attempt to establish realism doesn't work because the animals are too humanized. They move like animals, but their big, fluttery eyes and annoying voices (many belonging to children) separate them from the animal kingdom. Based on the book by Felix Salten, story tells of the birth of a fawn named Bambi and his growth into adulthood. Picture is too sentimental for many viewers and too gentle for others—but the death of Bambi's mother (due to the film's villain, man) is perhaps the most traumatic scene in all of Disney's work, along with the baby elephant's separation from its mother in *Dumbo* and the shooting of the rabid family dog in *Old Yeller*. It is a scene adults tremblingly remember seeing when children. Of all the cute animals, the rabbit Thumper—Bambi's pal and adviser—is the most memorable. David Hand was the supervising director.

BANANAS (1971) C/82m.   Early Woody Allen film about Fielding Mellish, a New York product tester, who ends up head of the revolutionary government of San Marcos. The film is somewhat dated and contains several scenes so embarrassingly stupid that it's hard to believe Allen conceived them. Also it would be nice to do away with Marvin Hamlisch's irritating background music for the South American sequence. Still there is much to treasure: Allen sneakily buying *Orgasm* magazine and having the dealer call across the crowded shop to ask its price; Allen hiding behind his magazine while two thugs (one is Sylvester Stallone) maul the crippled old lady who sits beside him in the subway; Allen visiting his parents, both doctors, while they are in the midst of an operation; Allen ordering takeout food for 900 guerrilla fighters; Allen testing office sports equipment. Best of all are his meeting and break-up with Louise Lasser, who finds he lacks almost every important quality. These hilarious and perceptive scenes are quintessential Allen that could easily fit into such later, sophisticated *relationship* comedies as *Annie Hall* and *Manhattan*. Also with: Carlos Montalban, Howard Cosell, Don Dunphy, Charlotte Rae.

BAND OF OUTSIDERS/BANDE À PART (FRENCH/ 1964) B&W/95m.   Quirky Jean-Luc Godard film is sort of a mix of *Breathless* (where Belmondo performs crimes in the nonchalant manner he saw in gangsters in films) and *Les Enfants Terribles* (where the two males and one female

commit petty crimes for fun). Pals Sami Frey and Claude Brasseur play-act crime movies (they also burst into song and imitate movie production numbers), much as little kids imitate heroes from war or western movies. Their mutual girlfriend, Anna Karina, wants to fit in, so she offers a real crime to them: they can steal her aunt's money. So the three bumbling (they have to go back a second time) amateurs go to the aunt's house to commit the crime. Frey and Brasseur can't distinguish between fiction and real life. When they put on their movie criminal guises, they think of themselves romantically, as do Sissy Spacek and Martin Sheen in *Badlands* when they commit equally unromantic crimes; but, as is the case with Spacek and Sheen, their guns shoot real bullets and people get hurt. Like many Godard actors, Frey, Brasseur, and Karina improvise their lines during the heist, but what's really interesting is that they must play their parts as if their characters are also improvising their lines in order to sound like movie gangsters. The characters themselves switch back and forth between their movie-gangster personae and their real selves—the men (obviously thinking of Cagney and Bogart) will impulsively slap Karina around when she protests that they are mistreating her aunt, yet without missing a beat Frey will become affectionate and ask if she loves him. The overlapping of reel life and "real life" (as depicted in Godard's movie) is disorienting because we have a hard time figuring out the logic of the characters' actions, but it's also excitingly original. The amusing ending is bizarre by other films' standards, but here it's perfect. Cinematography by Raoul Coutard intentionally swings from intimacy to detachment. Music by Michel Legrand fits the characters' romantic notion of themselves—he's nice enough to give their worst efforts music befitting the professional criminals of the movies. Based on *Fool's Gold* by American novelist Dolores Hitchens. Also with: Louisa Colpeyn, Danièle Girard, Godard (narrator).

BAND WAGON, THE (1953) C/112m.   Extravagant MGM musical, directed with much flair by Vincente Minnelli. It starts out slowly but keeps getting better and better as great musical numbers keep piling up. Fred Astaire's a has-been movie star who is persuaded to take part in a Broadway musical written by his friends Oscar Levant and Nanette Fabray (based on the film's writers, Adolph Green and Betty Comden). Ballet star Cyd Charisse agrees to be the leading lady. Astaire and Charisse are in awe of each other, but both think the other doesn't want them in the show. So they are not friendly—until they fall in love. Jack Buchanan is the musical's director. His flamboyance and artistic pretensions almost ruin the show, until Astaire puts it on the right track. Musical highlights include "Dancing in the Dark," "That's Entertainment," "Triplets" (performed by Astaire, Fabray, and Buchanan in baby outfits), and the lavish, episodic "Girl Hunt" dance sequence, spoofing Mickey Spillane. The score is by Howard Dietz and Arthur Schwartz. Choreography is by Michael Kidd. Oliver Smith did impressive set design for musical numbers.

BANG THE DRUM SLOWLY (1973) C/97m.
My favorite baseball film. Set in the fifties, when screen-writer Mark Harris wrote the novel. Its hero, played by Michael Moriarty, is an intelligent, handsome Tom Seaver-like pitcher, the star of an unremarkable New York baseball team. He must look after his catcher, Robert De Niro, who has the smarts of a Yogi Berra. When De Niro becomes terminally ill, Moriarty becomes extremely protective, fearing that their insensitive teammates won't know how to handle his friend's sad situation while in the midst of a pennant race. Nevertheless, the others find out. Harris's story, sensitively directed by John Hancock, is about how people come through for those in trouble (the same theme as *Terms of Endearment*). The disparate players actually come together as a team because of their common concern for their dying teammate, play ball with purpose and intensity, and win the pennant. (Sadly, they don't recognize that their selfless humanity is the reason that they have excelled.) Picture makes you feel good about people but, at the same time, sad that we so rarely show our altruistic side. It has wit, creates nostalgia for a more innocent baseball era. It also tugs at your emotions, breaks your heart. The final playing of the title song and the slow-motion sequence in which the very weak De Niro struggles to catch a high pop-up, while teammates look on helplessly, are incredibly moving. The two leads, then relatively unknown, give exciting performances—at the time I thought Moriarty would be the one to go on to superstardom. Also with: Vincent Gardenia (perfectly cast as the manager), Heather MacRae, Barbara Babcock, Phil Foster.

BANK DICK, THE (1940) B&W/74m.
Hilarious W. C. Fields comedy in which he plays Egbert Sousé, one of his few married men whose *entire* family—even his daughters—is obnoxious. Despite the protests of his wife (Cora Witherspoon), mother-in-law (Jessie Ralph), engaged daughter (Una Merkel), and young daughter, he spends all his spare hours drinking and bragging. When he accidentally knocks out a bank robber, he is offered the position of bank dick. This leads to a number of ridiculous episodes. Highlights include Fields making a bank examiner (Franklin Pangborn) too sick to check the books; Fields directing a movie; Fields choking a little boy who enters the bank with a toy gun; Fields taking a hold-up man on a terrifying ride; Fields, now rich, pretending to his family that they've reformed him; and the bank president giving Fields "hearty" handclasps. Fields used the name Mahatma Kane Jeeves for his story credit. Directed by Eddie Cline. Also with: Grady Sutton (as Merkel's fiancé), Shemp Howard, Russell Hicks, Reed Hadley.

BARBARELLA (FRENCH-ITALIAN/1968) C/98m.
In 4000 A.D. beautiful, brave astronaut Barbarella (Jane Fonda) has all kinds of sexual encounters while tracking down the renegade scientist who carries the secret of the ultimate weapon, the Positronic Ray. On the planet Lytheon she and the blind, winged Pygar (John Phillip Law) take on the evil Black Queen (Anita Pallenberg) and her concierge (Milo O'Shea); there is a revolution (led by David Hemmings); the mad scientist uses his Positronic Ray; and the Black Queen unleashes the mathmos, which proceeds to gobble up everything in sight. But, for all this activity, the film is quite dull. The whole production (the much publicized futuristic sets, music, dialogue, storyline, direction, special effects) lacks imagination. Barbarella herself is a weak heroine in that her actions have little effect on what transpires at the end; the film would have had more spice if her relationship with the Black Queen had been given more substance. Film's cult has to do with the campy humor, which I find unintentionally unamusing, and the uninhibited, scandalously garbed Fonda. The Fonda of today probably would not object to her character, as naïve as Barbarella is—while she gives her body to all men who assist her, it is *her choice* to give them sexual pleasure; furthermore, she uses their bodies to give herself sexual pleasure. While it's annoying how director Roger Vadim used his ex-wife's body to constantly tease male viewers (throughout the film she's nude or semi-nude but never so one gets a good look at her), stronger objections can be raised as to how he subjects his heroine to ghastly tortures while she is either nude or having her clothes ripped off (trying to stimulate men by showing pretty women being physically abused is irresponsible). Script, which has a surprising number of deaths for a comedy, by Terry Southern, Vadim, Jean-Claude Forest, and five other writers was inspired by Forest's comic strip. Also with: Marcel Marceau, Ugo Tognazzi, Claude Dauphin.

BARBAROSA (1982) C/90m.
Fine western has the appropriate feel of a story passed down through many generations so that it has become impossible to distinguish between fact and legend. Australian director Fred Schepisi filmed Texan William D. Witliff's flavorful script in dusty, rugged land along the Rio Grande. It's in this unfriendly setting that mythical middle-aged outlaw Barbarosa (Willie Nelson) and a common-folk farm boy, Carl (Gary Busey), become dear friends. For many years Barbarosa has been hiding out from his father-in-law, Don Braulio (Gilbert Roland), who accuses him of killing family members on Barbarosa's wedding night—having pulled off many robberies and many daring escapes from lawmen over the years, as well as killing the men Don Braulio has sent after him, Barbarosa has come to be regarded by the Mexican community as a legend, a man who can't be killed. Carl accidentally killed his new brother-in-law in a fight, and that man's father and brothers are determined to kill him. The family vendettas we have here are as strong as those in *The Godfather*. Since both have been forced to flee from their families (Barbarosa leaves behind his wife and daughter, Carl leaves behind his father), these alienated men become like brothers—or like a wise, teaching father and a learning, respectful son. The story itself is familiar, but Schepisi manages to make every scene seem offbeat but authentic. The ending is predictable, yet it is still exciting. Nelson and

Busey are a terrific team: each is funny, full of warmth and honesty, and has a strong screen presence. Photographed by Ian Baker. Also with: Howland Chamberlin, Isela Vega, Danny De La Paz, George Voskovec.

BARON OF ARIZONA, THE (1950) B&W/ 93m.
A weird film even for Sam Fuller, about a clerk (Vincent Price) in a land office who in the 19th century schemes to gain possession of Arizona. In his intricate plan he takes an orphan girl under his wing and falsifies documents to state she is the Spanish heir to Arizona. He then spends years in a Spanish monastery so that he can forge its records in regard to the land transaction. When the girl grows up, he marries her (Ellen Drew) and stakes their claim to Arizona. Naturally, the people in Arizona aren't too happy to discover they don't own their own land. Plan goes well until Price realizes that he really loves Drew—and she wants to pull off hoax. Film is too claustrophobic and slow-moving, but keeps attention because premise is so unusual. Despite being set in gorgeous Arizona, low budget of film required that scenes take place indoors or at night. Oddly, story has factual basis. Also with: Vladimir Sokoloff, Beulah Bondi, Robert Barrat.

BASKET CASE (1982) C/91m.
In the year of E.T., midnight movie audiences were equally enthusiastic about *B.C.*, a very creative little horror gem about another peculiar-looking, waist-high, long-nailed creature who must remain hidden in our hostile world (only this *alien* came from upstate New York). Indeed it is, as one pleased critic realized, "*E.T.*, as if written and directed by a psychopath." The utterly bizarre story centers around the Bradley brothers: tall Duane (only a first-time director named Frank Henenlotter would hire an unknown named Kevin VanHententryck to be his lead)—a ridiculously innocent but normal-looking young man—and little Belial, a twisted, demented Siamese twin whom Duane secretly carries around in a wicker basket. Years before, they'd been separated by quack doctors and Belial had been tossed in the garbage to die. But he lived, growing stronger and madder by the minute. Now Belial and Duane, who communicate telepathically, have come to New York, hell-bent on bloody revenge on those responsible for the operation. However, when a pretty young girl (Terri Susan Smith) sidetracks Duane, the jealous, restless Belial leaves his basket and begins to crawl up walls and into open windows, rip doors off hinges, and bare his fangs hungrily. Libra, the original distributor, trimmed the gruesome gore scenes, not realizing that the excessiveness of the blood and violence is what made such scenes cartoonish. Fortunately, most prints have restored the deleted footage because, in addition to being a first-rate fright film, this is an outrageous black comedy that uses excessive violence for comic relief. I detested seeing one more despicable monster-rapes-girl scene, but film has many qualities to compensate: the truly clever script; the offbeat characters, even down to the smallest parts; the fascinating on-location photography in a fleabag New York hotel; and some nifty special effects, model

work (two protégés of Dick Smith made Belial from latex and foam) and stop-motion photography that was very ambitious for such a minuscule budget. Best of all is Belial, who, when not ripping people apart, is in his own way as endearing as E.T. Just don't cross him. . . . Produced by Edgar Ievins. Also with Beverly Bonner, Robert Vogel, Diana Browne, Lloyd Pace, Bill Freeman.

BATTLE BEYOND THE STARS (1980) C/ 102m.
A more appropriate title would have been *The Magnificent Seven in Outer Space*. Acceptable low-budget sci-fi has diverse assortment of space warriors—each representing a different culture and philosophy—joining together under Richard Thomas's leadership to protect a planet from invasion. John Sayles's script has a lot of original touches, wit, and fun characters; the impressive cast has a good time playing up the humor. John Saxon stands out as the diabolical villain, whose body parts are constantly replaced by his doctor. Film suffers because of typically low Roger Corman budget. Some more expensive special effects during the fight sequences would have given the picture needed spectacle. Directed by Jimmy T. Murakami. Also with: Darlanne Fluegel, George Peppard, Robert Vaughn (veteran of *The Magnificent Seven*), Sybil Danning (whose skimpy costume gives TV censors trouble), Sam Jaffe, Morgan Woodward.

BATTLE OF ALGIERS, THE (ITALIAN-ALGERIAN/1966) B&W/123m.
An extraordinary revolutionary film by Gillo Pontecorvo, who directed and wrote the script with Franco Solinas. Covering the pivotal years, 1954 to 1957, in the Algerian struggle for independence from France, the entire film looks like a *cinéma-vérité* documentary—Pontecorvo just borrowed the *cinéma-vérité* style to lend authenticity to his film, even having cinematographer Marcello Gatti use grainy stock. Pontecorvo gives us a fictionalized account of real and representative events that took place during the National Liberation Front's guerrilla war against the French. It not only shows how to conduct an urban guerrilla war (the reason it was studied by America's Black Panthers) but also the necessity of violence in revolution. Equally important, it shows how oppressors—the French, in this case—conduct a counterrevolution. The French colonel (professional actor Jean Martin) realizes that imperialists will eventually be ousted by colonized peoples, but he plays his historic role. He is a torturer, an insensitive murderer. He realizes that to get the leaders of the underground the French forces must first eliminate those revolutionaries who are less insulated—they will work their way up through the ranks. Film is fascinating, thrilling; you won't believe that the shots of women planting bombs and those of innocent people being killed aren't real. You'll also feel you're watching history when the French close in on some holed-up Algerian leaders. Finale, in which Algerians "spontaneously" march en masse down the steps of the city, is exhilarating—it comes right after the French think they crushed the revolution! Music by Ennio Morricone. Also

with: Diafer, Brahim Haggiag, Mohamed Ben Kassen, Tommaso Neri.

BATTLE OF CHILE, THE (CHILEAN) B&W/271m.

Patricio Guzmán's mammoth documentary has been released in three parts: *The Insurrection of the Bourgeoisie* (1975; 100m); *A Blow Against the State* (1976; 91m); *The Power of the People* (1979; 80m). Filmed in Santiago, Chile, in 1973, the year Marxist leader Salvador Allende was overthrown and killed, this is history in the making. Guzmán and five collaborators take their cameras into the streets, to political rallies, and into political chambers. Interviews are conducted with those who support Allende's Popular Unity coalition and those who have had enough of Allende's attempt to move toward full socialism. What's amazing is how politically savvy *everyone* is—compare these interviews with America's man-on-the-street interviews regarding political issues. What's evident from the start is that Allende is in trouble and that his downfall is inevitable. It's fascinating to watch the game played out. Film, which has a strong left-wing bias, makes several important points, including: a new revolutionary regime can't allow the usurped bourgeoisie the freedom to rebuild its political power (unfortunately, it must curtail liberties until it has strength); the new regime must be armed; America/CIA played an essential part in undermining Allende's government—it financed political opposition and organized effective strikes (which should be remembered in light of Nicaragua); America participated in the actual overthrow. Some of the film is confusing for those not totally familiar with the political situation in Chile in 1973. There are countless memorable scenes: thousands of people jumping up and down in response to Allende telling everyone at a rally to jump if they're not fascists; a soldier pointing his gun at the cameraman and killing him—this horrifying scene ends Part I. Film was smuggled out of Chile.

BATTLEGROUND (1949) B&W/118m.

William W. Wellman directed this WWII film, which is set in the Bastogne region of France in late 1944, prior to the Battle of the Bulge. Film concentrates on the 101st Airborne Division, a melting-pot platoon (with soldiers named Jarvess, Roderigues, Stazak, Standiferd, Wolowicz, Hanson, etc.) as they earn the sobriquet "The Battered Bastards of Bastogne." Unlike most war films, this one de-emphasizes the action and tries to provide insight into the individual soldiers. So we hear them talk a lot about everyday things, and see how they respond to women, fighting, fear, hardships. But it all seems forced. Another trouble is that these guys are so boring that you'll want them to start firing their guns. Best scenes deal with platoon in cat-and-mouse game with Germans dressed as American soldiers. I also like how Wellman never lets us forget that the men are feeling the effects of the cold and deep snow, but the guys are so wrapped up you can't tell them apart. Starring: Van Johnson, John Hodiak, Ricardo Montalban, George Murphy, Marshall Thompson, James Whitmore, Leon Ames, Don Taylor, Denise Darcel, Richard Jaeckel, James Arness.

BEACH PARTY (1963) C/101m.

The first of AIP's successful Frankie Avalon–Annette Funicello beach series starts out with the stars riding along, top down, singing the title song. It's a great moment—it usually causes instant jolts in the audience—and you'll flash back to when we once had a crush on one of these two wholesome stars, or feel nostalgic because you used to catch these films at the drive-in and actually enjoyed them. The picture goes downhill when nostalgia gives way to annoyance at the stupidity of the characters Avalon and Funicello play. All the teens in the film have IQs lower than their ages. Frankie is coming on too strong without thinking of proposing, so he backs off. He tries to make Annette jealous by making a play for Eva Six, a Hungarian sexpot in the Gabor mold. But she gets his goat by falling for Bob Cummings, a middle-aged, bearded anthropology professor who's studying teenage sex habits. Teenagers surf (on waves about six inches high), sing, dance (the twist), and think about sex. Interestingly, females (who look great in bikinis) are all short so they won't make tiny Avalon *look* tiny, and are blonde so that brunette Annette stands out among them. Campy film at least pokes fun at itself. Directed by William Asher. Also with: Dorothy Malone, Harvey Lembeck (as gang leader Eric Von Zipper), Jody McCrea, John Ashley, Morey Amsterdam, Vincent Price (a cameo as Big Daddy).

BEACHCOMBER, THE/VESSEL OF WRATH (BRITISH/1938) B&W/90m.

Gently paced adaptation of Somerset Maugham's story "Vessel of Wrath" features wonderful pairing of Charles Laughton and his wife, Elsa Lanchester. Laughton, who produced with director Erich Pommer, is Ginger Ted, a slovenly, perpetually drunk woman-chasing beach bum who has made the South Seas island on which he lives into a bachelor's paradise. Lanchester is the sheltered, naïve missionary who tries to reform him. While they detest each other at first, and are both stubbornly resistant to change, they open up new worlds to each other ("Nature," she beams, "is so *natural*"). She discovers him to be a gentleman at heart; he discovers her to have courage and strength. They fall in love. Not an outright comedy, but consistently amusing. Stilted production looks as if it had been made ten years earlier, but performances by leads retain tremendous charm. Surely their characters were inspiration for Bogart's drunken boat captain and Hepburn's refined lady in *The African Queen*. Also with: Robert Newton (who was to play the Laughton role in the likable 1955 remake), Tyrone Guthrie.

BEAST FROM 20,000 FATHOMS, THE (1953) B&W/80m.

The cinema's first monster unleashed by atomic explosions is a 100-million-year-old rhedosaurus which follows the current from the Arctic toward the New York City harbor, its original breeding ground. Because it is radioactive as well as being vicious, it destroys everything in its path. Minor horror movie, based loosely on Ray Bradbury's short story "The Fog Horn," boasts exciting special effects by Ray Harryhausen, who had absolute control for the first time in his career; stop-motion work with behemoth model would have made his mentor Willis O'Brien proud. Paul Christian and Paula Raymond, playing the rare smart woman in fifties SF, are a pleasing couple, although far too much of the time is spent finding evidence to support Christian's claim that the monster exists—after all, this would be known soon enough anyway, particularly when the bodies started piling up. The best scenes are when the monster attacks a lighthouse, when scientist Cecil Kellaway takes a diving bell to the ocean floor in search of the monster, and when the beast romps through New York City as King Kong once did through that native village. A lively climax in an amusement park. Directed by famed set designer Eugene Lourie. Also with: Kenneth Tobey, Donald Woods, Steve Brodie, Frank Ferguson, Lee Van Cleef, Jack Pennick, King Donovan.

BEAST OF THE CITY (1932) B&W/87m. Super early crime drama, sharply written by W. R. Burnett (*Little Caesar*) and forcefully directed by Charles Brabin. M-G-M picture begins with attack on films that glorify gangsters and uses quote by Herbert Hoover to make pitch in support of policemen. Burnett has written a tribute to the honest cop, taking us into his home so we see that he's just a regular hard-working guy with a wife, kids, and bills, and that he has the same things to protect as the typical viewer. That's why Burnett wants viewers to condone fist-and-gun tactics when dealing with criminals. Walter Huston is a two-fisted police captain who is fighting a losing battle for the city with gang lord Jean Hersholt. Huston's policeman brother, Wallace Ford, goes on the take so he can afford his sexy girlfriend, Jean Harlow; when he turns his head to allow a robbery, a cop and a child on the street are killed. He tries to make amends to big brother. Briskly paced film has busy camera, many interesting characters who keep frame extremely crowded, solid action sequences including the startling finale in which the self-sacrificing cops attack the mobsters. Not to be forgotten is Harlow's gun moll, who is always ready with a snappy line: "Are you bright enough to answer some questions?" asks Ford. "Sure," she responds, "if you don't ask them in Yiddish." Also with: Dorothy Peterson, Tully Marshall, John Miljan, J. Carrol Naish, Mickey Rooney, Jack Pennick, and Edward Brophy, whose crooked lawyer delivers a fabulous, flamboyant courtroom spiel.

BEAT THE DEVIL (1954) B&W/92m. Legendary lark (the fifties' most peculiar A-budget film) directed by John Huston, scripted by Huston and young writer Truman Capote, and starring Humphrey Bogart, Jennifer Jones, Gina Lollobrigida, Robert Morley, and Peter Lorre. A flop at the box office, it immediately became known as a "cult film" and has remained a favorite of movie connoisseurs ever since. Bogart was probably first attracted to adaptation of James Helvick's novel because he thought it would be made into a straight but witty film full of adventure, danger, and romance. As in the Huston-directed *The Maltese Falcon*,

he could play a tough, morally ambiguous hero who side-steps his way through a corrupt world of greedy, double-dealing savages, outrageous flirts, and pathological liars. When he invested in the project, he didn't realize that Capote (who wrote the script as filming progressed) would devise a sly, one-of-a-kind spoof of all international-intrigue pictures and populate it with a cockeyed, disparate group of people. Perhaps they seem so different because some stars played the film for comedy; others had not been told it had been switched from a melodrama. In fact, much of the humor comes from this mismatched conglomerate being thrown into the same adventure: a boat trip from Italy to Africa. Plot involves attempt by Morley, Lorre (who as a plump blond looks like Capote) and two other cutthroats trying to carry out African land swindle (they want the land's uranium) through Bogart. Bogart is a laid-back man in a fancy robe and ascot living with his emotional wife, Gina Lollobrigida, an anglophile, in Italy. He hopes that he'll make enough money on the crooked deal to get Gina what she wants. In a bravura performance as a blonde (!), Jones is a flirtatious (with Bogart), imaginative, compulsive liar who is married to a dullard Englishman (Edward Underdown). They are going to Africa to live on a coffee plantation. No one is happy with their station in life. Each wants what the other has. All hope the journey will result in personal happiness—as in most Huston films, characters fail at missions, but at least Bogart, Lollobrigida, Jones, and Underdown reach some sort of fulfillment. Film has unique Continental flavor (it was filmed in Ravello, a small coast town in Italy), hilarious, delectable moments, and wonderfully attitudinizing characters. I wish it had more coherence (although its fans would argue against it) and a couple of more serious, creepy scenes like the bit with the player piano (a scene worthy of Graham Greene or Eric Ambler). I also wish the film weren't as trivial as Huston wanted it. Still, it's so disarming and so lionized by intelligent film fans that I worry that it may be better than I think. Also with: Ivor Barnard, Bernard Lee, Marco Tulli.

BEAU JAMES: THE LIFE AND TIMES OF JIMMY WALKER (1957) C/105m. Bob Hope had one of his few non-comedic roles playing Walker, the dapper mayor of New York from 1925 until 1932, when he resigned in the midst of a municipal graft investigation. He looks ill at ease, knowing that he can't play Walker's amusing lines for big laughs (although, ironically, these lines seem to have been written specifically for Hope's comedic delivery) or go into his patented cowardly, let's-sneak-out-the-back-window act. At times you can almost sense he's holding back some hilarious ad-lib that would add life to the dialogue. Moreover, it's apparent that director-screenwriter Melville Shavelson, who worked often with Hope, was afraid to trust him with a romantic scene that hasn't some humor with either Alexis Smith or Vera Miles, who play Walker's wife and mistress, respectively. The script is brave in not overlooking Walker's loveless marriage and infidelity or the corruption in his administration—transgressions that the public of 1957 might not have wanted to believe about their high public officials. However, the script doesn't go deep enough into either story—consequently, there's not much of a plot. Not a bad film, with some nice old-time New York color, but it would have been much better if it weren't so *laid back*, which is the term that best describes Hope's Jimmy Walker. Also with: Paul Douglas, Joe Mantell, Horace MacMahon, and, in ill-advised cameos, George Jessel, Jimmy Durante, Jack Benny.

BEAU PÈRE (FRENCH/1981) C/120m.

In *Get Out Your Handkerchiefs* writer-director Bertrand Blier made us laugh by having beautiful Carole Laure choose a little boy to be her sexual partner, while rejecting husband Gérard Depardieu and (unsuccessful) lover Patrick Dewaere. In this film Blier really tests his audience by flipping the coin and having an adult male (Dewaere) take as his lover his 14-year-old stepdaughter (Ariel Besse, who at times looks like a young Carole Laure). Moreover, this time the comedy is not so obvious. Dewaere is a struggling dinner-club pianist who has been married for eight years to Besse's mother (Nicole Garcia). When her mother is killed, Besse chooses to live with him instead of her "natural" father (Maurice Ronet). Soon she admits her physical attraction and love for Dewaere. He rejects her advances at first, but eventually has sex with her and admits his love. He feels guilt and tries to stay away from her bedroom. But the temptation is too great. Slow-moving film (which uses limited background music) shows Dewaere and Besse in bed together, yet it's not exploitive. But I do find it dishonest. Any time Blier wants Dewaere and Besse to become more deeply involved, he writes words of seduction for Besse—not Dewaere—and has her deliver them in a mature manner, so we always know the affair is her idea and that she's sensible enough (even at her age) to know if it is psychologically damaging to herself. Dewaere is also whitewashed by Blier because he's too unhappy and weak a character to resist Besse's body, her compliments, or her love—his attraction to the young girl who sees only his virtues is a sign of his lack of self-esteem. What Blier shows us, lest we regard Dewaere as a betrayer, are innocent scenes of Dewaere and Besse together before Besse's mother was killed and she quickly evolved from daughter to wife and lover. Final shot is predictable but haunting—almost like the final shot of horror movies in which you realize that the character on screen has just become possessed by the evil that controlled another throughout the picture. Nathalie Baye plays a classical pianist to whom Dewaere is attracted. She also has an impressionable young daughter.

BEAUTY AND THE BEAST (FRENCH/1946) B&W/90m.

Jean Cocteau's legendary, increasingly popular adult adaptation of Madame Le Prince de Beaumont's classic fairytale. It's about a poor young woman who—in order to save her merchant-father's life—agrees to live in the castle of a beastlike figure. Eventually she returns his great love for her. This is the cinema's most "poetic" work, full of hauntingly beautiful, dreamlike imagery: most memorable are the merchant's terrifying visit to the Beast's dark, forbidding castle, in which statues move and unattached arms extend from the wall to hold candelabra; and Beauty's arrival at the castle, in which she floats/walks trancelike through the various rooms and hallways (notice the billowing curtains). Cocteau was exploring "the reality of the unreal," and only through his surreal imagery did he believe he could convey the precise emotions, feelings, and atmosphere that he believed represented absolute truth. For instance, when Beauty's wicked sister looks in the Beast's mirror and a monkey is reflected back at her, the monkey's image is "unreal" (impossible) but it reveals the *truth*, the reality about her. Josette Day is perfectly cast as one of literature's great heroines: innocent, strong of character, honest, loyal, exquisite, and virtuous. Less impressive is Jean Marais (Cocteau's protégé and housemate), who plays the obnoxious, foolish rapscallion Avenant, whom Beauty loves; the wimpish, self-pitying, though elegant-looking Beast; and worst of all, the effeminate Prince into whom the Beast turns at the end. The Beast's transformation from a true king to a prissy prince is the worst scene in the picture and, also considering how the pleased Beauty suddenly becomes uncharacteristically flirtatious, almost ruins everything that went before it. Much of the picture's charm is that it is presented so simply, without self-indulgence or pretense. While the picture can be seen as a Freudian tale—Beauty has too strong an attachment to her father; the Beast and Avenant (who isn't in the fairytale) represent the split parts of one personality, the Prince—I prefer thinking of it merely as an innocent, literal adaptation of the children's story. Henri Alékan did the splendid photography; Christian Bérard designed the atmospheric castle sets, and Georges Auric provided the music. Also with: Marcel André, Mila Parély, Nane Germon, Michel Auclair.

BECKY SHARP (1935) C/83m. B&W/67m.

Based on Langdon Mitchell's stage adaptation of Thackeray's *Vanity Fair*. Although it restores several episodes from the novel, it differs from Thackeray in drastic ways. For one thing, it eliminates most of his social criticism; significantly, it barely expresses how class pressures mold the character of Becky Sharp (Miriam Hopkins). Whereas there are several major characters in the novel, Becky is the *one* major character in the film. She becomes our heroine, the feisty figure whom we identify with or root for as she uses every trick in the book (what an actress!) to get what she wants. In the book she is ruthless, but since the script eliminates her many unforgivable acts (it even takes away the son who despises her), we see only her virtues. She has charm, wit, intelligence, resilience, vitality—she is selfish, but wants the best for her soldier husband (Alan Mowbray) and best friend (Frances Dee) as well as for herself. And she is willing to sacrifice her own happiness so that they will be happy. This may not be Thackeray, but it's an enjoyable, if flimsy, period piece, with a likable heroine and a dynamic performance by Hopkins. Film is best known for being first to use three-color Technicolor process. Director Rouben Mamoulian, who took over when Lowell Sherman died, did a remarkable job with color experimentation. He decided to use color thematically to express character mood, and added more and more color as the film progresses and the plot thickens. Every shot looks color-coordinated. The most famous sequence is the panicky exit of the guests at the Duchess of Richmond's gala in Belgium on the eve of the battle of Waterloo—rather than having all the red-jacketed soldiers in attendance exit first (as would be the case), Mamoulian had guests leave according to their color group so only the ones in red remained in the ballroom. My favorite shot comes earlier in the film: Mowbray and another red-jacketed soldier stand in the foreground in front of a hanging white sheet, through which we can see the black silhouettes of Hopkins and Dee—so within the frame Mamoulian contrasts color with black and white. It's very clever. Cinematography by Ray Rennahan. Also with: Cedric Hardwicke, Nigel Bruce, Billie Burke, Alison Skipworth.

BED AND BOARD (FRENCH/1970) C/97m.
François Truffaut's delightful follow-up to *Stolen Kisses*. Antoine Doinel (Jean-Pierre Léaud) and Christine (Claude Jade) are now married and living in a small apartment. Antoine is still restless and doesn't know what he's going to do with his life. He wants to make a living painting flowers; when that doesn't work out he gets a job at a hydraulic plant. While his sex life with Christine loses its excitement (although she gives birth in this film)—they read in bed—he has an affair with an emotionless Japanese woman (Hiroko Berghauer). Film is very amusing, with a lot of humor coming from Antoine's quirky neighbors and strangers on the street. The most important theme Truffaut expresses is that people find it almost impossible to communicate in person. As in other Truffaut films, communication is easier through writing (Antoine writes notes to Christine, he begins a book)—here Antoine can also communicate long-distance, over the *phone*. Followed by *Love on the Run*. Also with: Daniel Ceccaldi, Claire Duhamel, Daniel Boulanger, Jacques Tati (a cameo as M. Hulot).

BEDAZZLED (BRITISH/1967) C/107m.
Although dated, Dudley Moore and Peter Cook's irreverent Faust tale in mod clothing was much funnier than other British imports of its day. It combined the absurdity and breezy style of Richard Lester; the mixture of ridiculousness and sophistication of early Peter Sellers/Alec Guinness/Ian Carmichael/Alistair Sim films; the verbal outrageousness and slapstick of the later Peter Sellers; the lowbrow comedy of the *Carry On* series; and, of course, the irreverent satire and parody of *Beyond the Fringe*, the revue that made Americans aware of Moore and Cook. Delight today is to catch a nostalgic glimpse of once-wonderful comedy team. Cook and Moore don't do much visual comedy (what there is, however, is unexpectedly wild), but much of the verbal repartee is brilliant. How adeptly their voices and mannerisms change as they change characters and move from class to class, in the various segments that comprise the film. They can drawl like lazy-lipped British aristocrats or banter like ex-burlesque comics. Story has devil Peter Cook (who wrote the film) granting dumpy short-order cook (Moore) seven wishes, in exchange for his soul, to help him in pursuit of unattainable Eleanor Bron. Naturally, each wish backfires on Moore. Interestingly, Cook's Satan is more of a prankster than Evil personified—indeed, although he slyly double-crosses Moore at every turn, he provides him with the only exciting times he has ever experienced and proves to be his best friend. In fact, film dares make God, who no longer pays attention to human prayers and whose petty feud with Satan causes misery among mortals, into the villain of the piece. Although a comedy, picture's point is serious: in a world seemingly abandoned by God, man actually *wants* the devil to exist because he doesn't trust himself to have free will or free choice. At least Moore ultimately makes his own feeble attempt to win Bron's heart. Stanley Donen directed cult favorite, a bit too casually. Vignettes aren't particularly clever, but all have funny moments: the articulate Moore pretentiously discussing the fruitlike qualities of a French horn; nuns (including the three leads) scrubbing the grass of their convent and doing flips on trampolines; Cook's Dremble Wedge, a New Wave singer ahead of his time, winning fans by emotionlessly singing, "I don't care, I don't want you, I don't love you, leave me alone." Also with: Raquel Welch (as Lilian Lust, "The Babe with the Bust"), Michael Bates, Howard Goorney.

BEDLAM (1946) B&W/79m.
Val Lewton's last horror film, and certainly his most underrated, pits social reformer Nell Bowen (Anna Lee, as the most dynamic of Lewton's remarkable women) against cruel Master Sims (Boris Karloff), head of London's notorious Bedlam asylum in the 18th century. Afraid she will initiate changes in Bedlam, where the prisoners are treated like animals (indeed, they have animal nicknames), Sims and an all-male review board have her committed under the pretext she is crazy. At first she is terrified of the other inmates and associates only with the more refined ones—including one man (Ian Wolfe) who dreams of projecting moving images on a wall. But she comes to realize that it is Sims and not the inmates who are to be feared. She begins to help the troubled inmates, ease their pain, and befriend them. They respond to her kindness. It's interesting to watch these people gain respect for themselves and have their dignity restored. They no longer shrink away from Sims. Lewton has many insane people in his films; they lost their minds for a variety of reasons, including sexual repression, loneliness, guilt, fear, and depression. The patients in Bedlam are insane only because they were told they were insane. Like so many miserable people in Lewton works, they simply need someone to care about them and to listen; they need time to clear their confused heads. It is Nell Bowen who provides them with what they need. As Nell's Quaker friend (Richard Fraser) states, Providence was responsible for having Nell confined to Bedlam so she could initiate reforms which will

continue long after her departure. It's fitting that it's Providence rather than sinister Fate that is triumphant in Lewton's one postwar horror film, for it allowed him to leave RKO on his first positive note. For the only time in Lewton films, man can understand his own life's course and change things for the better. Terrific performances by Lee and Karloff are enchanced by intelligent, witty script, offbeat supporting characters, and classy direction by Mark Robson. Design of Bedlam interiors was taken from Hogarth's *Rake's Progress*. Lee's best dress was worn by Vivien Leigh in *Gone With the Wind*. Play performed by "loonies" anticipated *Marat/Sade*. Also with: Billy House, Glenn Vernon, Jason Robards, Sr., Leland Hodgson, Elizabeth Russell, Joan Newton, Ellen Corby, Skelton Kraggs.

BEDTIME FOR BONZO (1951) B&W/83m.

Democrats have often screened this farce at political fund-raisers, believing that when voters saw candidate Reagan playing papa to a chimp it would reduce his credibility as a candidate for Governor or President. Of course these attempts to ridicule Reagan have always backfired because the picture is surprisingly enjoyable, amusing rather than campy; the cute and affectionate Bonzo is a lot of fun to watch, and Reagan proves to be an adequate partner to the chimp, only rarely being his foil and never playing the fool. As would-be voters discovered, Reagan comes across as reliable, friendly, earnest, and an all-around good sport. If Bonzo is a better screen performer, it's because he has the comedic range to surprise us, while Reagan is *predictable*—a characteristic that would appeal to voters who always confuse the character on screen with the actor who plays him. Film was based on actual scientific experiments in which the effects of heredity and environment on human beings were analyzed by rearing chimps as if they were human children. Interestingly, the script by Val Burton and Lou Breslow requires Reagan to play a professor who believes that environment is the key to a person's personality and sense of morality. Although he doesn't speak of environment in Marxian terms or discuss social, political, educational, or economic factors in a child's upbringing—he thinks of "environment" only in terms of the amount of attention, love, and kindness a child (or chimp Bonzo) receives at home—the script, ironically, probably contributed to Val Burton's blacklisting in the industry as a suspected communist. Amiable film was directed by Frederick de Cordova (Johnny Carson's *Tonight Show*). 1952 sequel: *Bonzo Goes to College*. Also with: Diana Lynn (the nanny who helps Ronny raise Bonzo), Walter Slezak, Lucille Barkley, Jesse White, Herbert Heyes.

BEGUILED, THE (1971) C/105m.

Don Siegel directed this gothic horror tale (in which females are the "monsters") that surely is one of Clint Eastwood's oddest films (and one of his rare money-losers). Eastwood plays an injured Yankee soldier during the Civil War who is nursed back to health by the female faculty and students of a southern academy for young ladies. He is surrounded by females of all ages—he can't understand them and underestimates them. Afraid of being turned over to the rebel army, the least moral of Eastwood's characters lies his way into the passionate hearts of the middle-aged headmistress (Geraldine Page), a young instructor (Elizabeth Hartman), and a very precocious teenager (Jo Ann Harris). A 10-year-old (Pamelyn Ferdin) also gets a crush on him. Considering himself the ultimate ladies' man, he hobbles on crutches to the bedrooms of the three females, each of whom wants him to end her long-stifled sexual longings. But when Eastwood's infidelity is found out, he learns about the wrath of woman scorned. Feminists have attacked the film as being misogynistic and in Siegel's case it's probably true; but I think Eastwood was attracted to it because he believed the stupid, insensitive gigolo deserved his sorry end. From the novel by Thomas Cullinan.

BEHIND THE GREEN DOOR (1972) C/72m.

Porno chic about a beautiful young woman (Marilyn Chambers) who is kidnapped, then forced to perform a series of sexual acts before members of an exclusive club—and eventually ends up enjoying the "sexually liberating" experience. Landmark adult film appealed to those who preferred screen sex to be erotic rather than raunchy, as it is in *Deep Throat* and *The Devil in Miss Jones*, the other two XXX-rated blockbusters of the early seventies. Although it has a male-fantasy storyline—borrowed from a male-written pamphlet that soldiers passed around during WWII—it has proven popular with women, particularly as a video. This is due to directors Jim and Art Mitchell's choice to photograph it in a hypnotic, dreamlike fashion so that women might be drawn in and recognize their own sexual fantasies. Also they hoped women would want to identify with Chambers, who, unlike earlier sex-film actresses, was good-looking, shapely, healthy—a blonde All-American girl who once adorned boxes of Ivory Snow with a baby on her knee. Much of film's initial success was a result of people wanting to see the 99$\frac{44}{100}$% pure "Ivory Snow girl," a minor celebrity whose face they knew well, participate in sex acts. Picture is well made and Mitchell Bros. strive for art, but I don't find it much livelier than an elaborate stag film. Even the most unusual sex acts shift from being erotic to embarrassing to boring. And it's impossible to tell if a stand-in replaced Chambers in the famous fellatio sequence that was filmed in superslow motion and disguised with solarization effects. Also with: George S. McDonald, Johnny Keyes, Ben Davidson, Mitchell Bros.

BELL, BOOK AND CANDLE (1958) C/103m.

In this adaptation of John van Druten's play, Kim Novak is a beautiful witch who falls for publisher James Stewart, but worries that he returns her love only because she has cast a spell on him. She wishes she were human like him—of course, he is attracted to her otherworldly qualities. If you saw this mild comedy when it came out—many young girls were particularly taken with Novak and her character—then you may have a soft spot for it. Otherwise you'll be disappointed, even bored. Dream comedy cast was assembled—including Jack Lemmon, Elsa Lanchester, Ernie Kovacs, and Hermione Gingold—but everyone seems to have taken tranquilizers. Picture cries out for wildness, even slapstick humor. Only satisfying scene is romantic finale, which compensates somewhat for sorry fate of lovers Stewart and Novak in the same year's *Vertigo*. Lifeless direction by Richard Quine.

BELLBOY, THE (1960) B&W/72m.
In his directorial debut Jerry Lewis plays a happy-go-lucky, non-talking bellboy at Miami's Fontainebleau. Obviously influenced by Jacques Tati's *Mr. Hulot's Holiday* (remember that the French are crazy about Lewis), film is a series of brief, unconnected vignettes that usually have Jerry causing drastic physical changes to whatever environment he passes through. Most gags fall flat, none are hilarious; still, overall film is amusing. There are a couple of funny bits involving a Stan Laurel lookalike, and another with Milton Berle and his lookalike bellboy. Lewis also plays himself in one sequence. In subsequent films Lewis would learn that his character works best in an otherwise orderly world; here the world he inhabits would be whacky without him. It's interesting that for once Lewis doesn't milk the audience for sympathy—we feel sorry only for those he comes into contact with. For instance, at one point he intentionally gives a box of candy to a woman who has shed about 200 pounds during her hotel visit; in typical Frank Tashlin–Lewis cartoon style, she immediately gains all the weight back from eating his present. Also with: Alex Gerry, Bob Clayton, Sonny Sands, Joe E. Ross.

BELLE DE JOUR (FRENCH-ITALIAN/1967) C/100m.
One of Luis Buñuel's most popular, controversial, and—depending on your viewpoint—erotic or sexually reprehensible films. Catherine Deneuve is the young wife of a young, handsome Parisian doctor, Jean Sorel. She is sexually frigid; he is upset by this, but too kind and polite to force himself on her. She fantasizes that he has servants drag her from a carriage and tie her to a tree so that he can beat and rape her. (Fantasies are preluded by bell sounds, but in time we can't distinguish between fantasy and reality—the entire film, excluding the opening carriage ride and the final moment, might even be imagined by Deneuve.) Because her husband idolizes her (she is *his* fantasy) and wouldn't treat her as he used to treat prostitutes, and because she is too shy to reveal her secret passions, Deneuve takes a job in Geneviève Page's brothel each afternoon. There she feels no guilt for participating in sex. She becomes part of the male clients' weird fantasies. It's interesting that as she becomes more liberated through sex (breaking free of bourgeois shackles), she begins to reject the depraved, masochistic sex that characterized her early desires—she tells her most frequent client, young gangster Pierre Clementi (the flip side of Sorel), that she'll stop seeing him if he continues to hit her. The masochism, a form of self-hatred, reflects her shame at having been molested as a child. As her fantasies become more *normal*, at least as far as *her* role in them is concerned, she becomes ready to enter a normal sexual relationship with Sorel. But we see that he must be liberated as well, because guilt over his repressed sexual desires toward Deneuve cripple him, figuratively—and literally—speaking. They need to express their feelings toward each other and then go on a vacation together (which they do). Buñuel and Jean-Claude Carrière adapted Joseph Kessel's novel. Sacha Vierny did the interesting, often surreal cinematography. Also with: Michel Piccoli, Françoise Fabian.

BELLS ARE RINGING (1960) C/127m.
In her last movie Judy Holliday reprised her Broadway role as a Brooklyn answering-service operator who uses her knowledge of her clients' difficulties to help them out, without divulging who she is and how she knows their problems. She plays "angel" to a playwright (Dean Martin) with writer's block, an actor (Frank Gorshin) who can't get a part because he dresses like a beatnik, and an unhappy dentist (Bernie West) who wants to be a professional songwriter. Martin writes a play, for which West writes the songs and in which Gorshin stars—playing a dentist who wants to be a songwriter. Meanwhile Martin and Holliday fall in love, but she doesn't want to admit she is the operator he calls "Mom." Film is overlong and not particularly smooth, but Holliday, even below her peak, is well worth watching. One interesting point is that Holliday's "dumb blonde" is much more stable than the men in the film—however, her support for them, including Martin, comes more out of her need to be a *mother* than a friend or lover. Songs by Betty Comden, Adolph Green, and Jule Styne include "Just in Time," "The Party's Over," and "I'm Going Back to the Bonjour Tristesse Brassiere Company." Produced by Arthur Freed. Also with: Fred Clark, Eddie Foy, Jr. (who sets up a bookie joint in the answering-service office), Jean Stapleton, Ruth Storey, Gerry Mulligan, Nancy Walters, Ralph Roberts, Steven Peck.

BELLS OF ST. MARY'S, THE (1945) B&W/126m.
Following the tremendous success of *Going My Way*, director Leo McCarey and star Bing Crosby reunited for this sentimental sequel. While it doesn't reach the glorious heights of the original—critic James Agee blasted it upon release—it improves with repeated viewings and certainly deserves its status as a Christmas perennial. Crosby is again the kind-hearted, moralistic Father O'Malley, who this time around is put in charge of St. Mary's, a poor Catholic school. He and the Mother Superior, Ingrid Bergman, clash over the handling of the school—like Barry Fitzgerald in *Going My Way*, *she* is the conservative one—but gain tremendous respect for one another because they recognize each has only the best interests of the children in mind. Both—Crosby through coaxing, Bergman through prayer—try to get skinflint Henry Travers (Clarence in *It's a Wonderful Life*) to donate his beautiful new building to the school. Miracles do happen. The story is a bit flimsy, the con-man tactics of Crosby and Bergman are a bit dis-

concerting, and there are a couple of ludicrous plot twists (don't listen to the doctor's advice!) that were designed solely to manipulate viewers into shedding tears. But the picture is ultimately heartwarming. The pairing of Crosby and Bergman works like a charm. More beautiful than ever, Bergman—whether teaching a young boy to box or just reacting to good news from Crosby or Travers—is simply magnificent. A lovely title tune; classic children's-play sequence. Also with: William Gargan, Ruth Donnelly, Joan Carroll, Martha Sleeper, Rhys Williams.

BEN-HUR (1959) C/165m–212m.
Colossal remake of the 1925 silent classic won a record-breaking 12 Oscars, including Best Picture, Best Director (William Wyler), Best Actor (Charlton Heston), Best Supporting Actor (Hugh Griffith), Best Cinematography (Robert Surtees), Best Scoring (Miklos Rozsa), and Best Visual Effects (A. Arnold Gillespie, Robert MacDonald). Heston does a credible job as Ben-Hur, a Jewish patrician in Rome. When he refuses to squeal on rebellious Jews, his lifelong friend, the ambitious Messala (Stephen Boyd), has him enslaved, and sends his mother (Martha Scott) and sister (Cathy O'Donnell) to prison. Ben-Hur would die in the desert during transport if a kindly stranger (who he learns years later is Jesus) didn't give him water. He survives three years as a galley slave. He waits for revenge against Messala. During a great sea battle Ben-Hur saves the life of a Roman officer (Jack Hawkins) who frees him and brings him to Rome as his chariot driver. In the second spectacular action sequence, the famous chariot race, Ben-Hur defeats the cheating Messala—and Messala later dies. But Ben-Hur does not find solace because his mother and sister now live in a leper colony. The tormented, wrathful Ben-Hur is striving for inner peace, which he can achieve only by accepting Christ and his message of love and forgiveness. But Christ is about to be crucified. Big-budget epic is quite watchable, but a bit syrupy once Messala is no longer around. The chariot-race sequence and the sea battle still hold up nicely, but there is nothing else exciting in the picture. Scenes in which Christ is seen from the back only are nevertheless quite effective because, just from seeing the watery eyes and smiles of those who behold him, we can imagine his face and the love and calmness it projects. None of the acting is particularly impressive, but I like the way Ben-Hur's wife (Haya Harareet) doesn't back down in arguments with her husband, as many women do in Biblical films. Karl Tunberg got credit for the screenplay, but Christopher Fry, Maxwell Anderson, Gore Vidal, and S. N. Behrman also chipped in. They seem to borrow from *The Ten Commandments*. Andrew Marton, Yakima Canutt, and Mario Soldati served as second-unit directors. Also with: Sam Jaffe, Finlay Currie.

BEND OF THE RIVER (1952) C/91m.
Exciting Anthony Mann film, his second of five westerns with James Stewart. A former Missouri border raider who is hoping to go straight, Stewart keeps his past a secret from the farmers he escorts to Oregon, but, like most Mann westerns, he can't escape his past. He becomes friends with a man (Arthur Kennedy) he saves from a vigilante lynching. It turns out Kennedy has a similar past. Mann's films are usually about how violent men choose to lead their lives now that the West is becoming civilized; and when the chips are down, Stewart and Kennedy will choose opposite directions. When Kennedy double-crosses Stewart by absconding with the food supplies Stewart promised to deliver to the beleaguered settlers, so that he can sell them to miners who are offering an exorbitant price, Stewart becomes one of Mann's typical vengeance heroes. Script by Borden Chase is first-rate; the dialogue between Stewart and Kennedy is particularly strong, and conveys that each knows what the other is thinking at all times. Mann cultists might want to see this right before his *Man of the West* because Gary Cooper's character, a former outlaw who has 'fessed up to civilized folks and gained their trust, sort of picks up where Stewart leaves off. A solid score by Hans J. Salter. Excellent cinematography of the beautiful landscape by Irving Glassberg. Also with: Julia Adams (the romantic interest), Rock Hudson, Jay C. Flippen, Lori Nelson, Stepin Fetchit, Henry (Harry) Morgan, Royal Dano, Frank Ferguson.

BERLIN ALEXANDERPLATZ (WEST GERMAN/1980) C/921m.
Mammoth work by Rainer Werner Fassbinder played in art houses in its full-length version, but it's much easier to watch in hour installments on television, for which it was originally made. Adapted from Alfred Dobkin's epic novel, which Fassbinder supposedly read 14 times—it has strong parallels to Joyce's *Ulysses*, minus the wit—it's about how a former sinner and criminal who has just spent five years in prison for beating to death his prostitute lover attempts to live honorably in the corrupt Berlin of 1927–28. Franz Biberkopf (heavy-set Gunter Lamprecht gives a commanding performance) has trouble finding honest work, loses an arm, is repeatedly betrayed by his male friends, and has unfortunate luck in his relationships with women (even though they are loyal). Like all the other characters in the film, he suffers terribly, from guilt, fits of jealousy, fear, worry, and disillusionment, but, unlike his male acquaintances, he is able to ward off temptations to commit immoral acts. Indeed, the devil figure of the piece, his "friend" Reinhold (Gottfried John), is determined to ruin Franz's life because he resents Franz's moral superiority. Therefore he decides to seduce Mieze (Barbara Sukowa), the pretty young woman with whom Franz has a chance for happiness. Film is alternately astonishing and boring; I find myself feeling impressed even when I'm not enjoying what I'm watching or have no idea why the main characters are acting/responding toward each other as they do—in fact, rarely do the characters behave in a critical situation in the manner I would have expected. Also: why are so many women attracted to Franz, who isn't handsome, smart, rich, or gentle? The quality of the acting, camera work, set design, and music, and the adult nature of the script make this extraordinary television fare. It's a rewarding viewing experience despite the slow moments, the ambiguous philosophizing, and the disappointing resolu-

tion. Also with: Hanna Schygulla, Elizabeth Trissenaar, Karin Baal, Barbara Valentin, Roger Fritz, Franz Buchreiser.

BEST BOY (1979) C/111m.
Glowing documentary by Ira Wohl about his cousin Philly, a 52-year-old retarded man who has spent his entire life at home with his parents, Wohl's aunt and uncle. This is a unique case in which the documentarian openly influences the lives of the people he's filming: worried that Philly will be defenseless if his elderly parents die, Wohl convinces them to allow Philly to take giant strides toward self-sufficiency. He goes on errands by himself and, for the first time, goes to a special school. The excitement that he feels as he progressively achieves independence is contagious. The intimacy Wohl achieves is remarkable—we become extremely fond of Philly, but we also become sensitive toward his mother and (dying) father, who, when they don't worry, are happy about their son's accomplishments, yet understandably feel self-pity because the boy needs them less and less. There are many moving scenes, including Philly's distress when he can't get to the school he's grown to love, and an impromptu backstage duet by Philly and Zero Mostel of "If I Were a Rich Man." Deservedly won a Best Documentary Oscar.

BEST YEARS OF OUR LIVES, THE (1946) B&W/172m.
Superlative Americana, directed by William Wyler, telling the story of three returning war veterans (Fredric March, Dana Andrews, Harold Russell) who have troubles readjusting to home lives, love lives, and work situations. Of course, this subject is still extremely relevant. Robert Sherwood's excellent, Oscar-winning script (adapted from MacKinlay Kantor's *Glory for Me*) was brutally frank for its time, perceptive and extremely poignant; it is sympathetic toward its characters rather than being overly sentimental—nevertheless, keep a supply of tissues on hand. I wish film would have dealt with *war trauma*, but I suppose the characters have enough problems as it is. Film ends optimistically, but personal scars are accumulated along the way—it is honest enough to show that even war heroes who are welcomed home with open arms will have to make an effort to achieve any degree of happiness in postwar America. March, Andrews, and Russell all have truly wonderful scenes. Who can forget March's reunion scene with wife Myrna Loy; or Andrews's spatting with his restless wife, played by Virginia Mayo (who broke away from her milk-and-honey image), or walking through an airplane graveyard; or the handicapped Russell allowing his sweet, loyal girl-friend, Cathy O'Donnell, to take off his metal arm attachments and put him to bed. One of my all-time favorite scenes has March and Loy telling their grown daughter, Teresa Wright, that their relationship hasn't been as easy as she assumed—that in fact many times they had to fall back in love. Watching this scene you suddenly realize that few previous films really had explored the peculiar dynamics of wife-husband relationships. Sam Goldwyn production—1946's Best Picture Oscar winner—perfectly evokes small-town atmosphere during postwar era. Entire cast is splendid:

March won Best Actor Oscar, and non-actor Russell was voted Best Supporting Actor; Loy, further establishing her "perfect wife" image, deserved an Oscar as well, but didn't even get a nomination. William Wyler won Best Director Oscar for what is probably the best film of his distinguished career. Hugo Friedhofer won an Oscar for his score, and Daniel Mandell won for his editing. Gregg Toland was cinematographer. Also with: Hoagy Carmichael, Gladys George, Ray Collins, Steve Cochran, Roman Bohnen, Minna Gombell, Erskine Sanford, Don Beddoe.

BÊTE HUMAINE, LA (FRENCH/1938) B&W/99m–105m.
Jean Gabin, France's top romantic idol prior to WWII, had one of his best roles in Jean Renoir's updating of Emile Zola's novel. Looking even more world-weary than usual, Gabin is a train engineer who is tormented by debilitating headaches that drive him toward violence. On the train he sees the stationmaster and his wife (Simone Simon) emerging from a compartment where a man has been murdered—the jealous husband had found out his flirtatious wife had been having an affair with the dead man. Afraid Gabin will inform on them, the couple welcomes his friendship. Gabin and Simon have an affair and she manipulates him into agreeing to kill her husband. Fatalistic, moodily photographed murder drama undoubtedly influenced American *film noir*, thematically and visually. The way *femme fatale* Simon uses sex to take control of Gabin—to make him act *stupidly* so he'll fall into a trap—reminds me of how Kathleen Turner handles William Hurt in *Body Heat*. Renoir films their first passionate sexual encounter in a very novel, exciting manner. Fritz Lang filmed remake, *Human Desire*, in 1954. Also with: Julien Carette, Fernand Ledoux, Blanchette Brunoy, Renoir.

BETWEEN THE LINES (1977) C/101m.
One of those few films that I wish would never end. It's a spirited, nostalgic, sexy, perceptive, warm-hearted character comedy about members of the staff of a Boston-based counterculture newspaper—one of the last bastions of sixties radicalism—just before the paper is sold to a profit-minded publisher. Fred Barron's script is beautifully organized and is full of real characters and situations you might identify with. Director Joan Micklin Silver, who obviously loves the characters who run the paper, gives her young, brilliant cast a lot of freedom and they come through with relaxed, flesh-and-blood performances—all play comedy scenes, all have poignant moments. Most interesting is how characters take turns acting like jerks, egocentrics, being temperamental, and occasionally disappoint us—just as *real* people do. Highlights include rock critic Jeff Goldblum's nonsensical ad-libbed music lecture, at which young women dutifully take notes; scene in which photographer Lindsay Crouse irritates boyfriend, reporter John Heard, by asking sharp questions of a stripper (Marilu Henner) and striking up a rapport with her when he wants to ask his stupid questions; and when typist Jill Eikenberry quits the paper because of the political changes new publisher Lane Smith will be

making. Eikenberry perfectly expresses the joy that was found in sixties activism and the anger she feels because her friends at the paper are no longer allowed to be political. Also with: Stephen Elliott, Gwen Welles, Michael J. Pollard, Bruno Kirby, Lewis J. Stadlen.

BEVERLY HILLS COP (1985) C/105m.
Phenomenally successful Eddie Murphy comedy-crime drama. He plays Axel Foley, a streetwise Detroit detective who goes to Beverly Hills to investigate the murder of a lifelong friend. He ruffles feathers in the staid, go-by-the-book police department, and happens upon a drug smuggling operation. There are some nice moments between Murphy and Beverly Hills cops Judge Reinhold and John Ashton, whom he wins over, but story is terribly written (that Daniel Petrie, Jr., received an Oscar nomination was a big joke). Directed by Martin Brest, whose comic touches are always disruptive. But Murphy saves the day, successfully fighting through his bad lines and improvising—hilariously—like crazy, and turning a part originally intended for Sylvester Stallone into pure Murphy. The joy of the film is watching Murphy invade ritzy establishments (fancy hotels, restaurants, art galleries, Beverly Hills mansions) or institutions and, using his con act, imitate authority figures. That Murphy—an antiestablishment figure if there ever was one—would end up playing a dedicated policeman (though offbeat) is indication of how conservative Hollywood has become. Also with: Lisa Eilbacher, Ronny Cox, Bronson Pichot, Steven Berkoff.

BEYOND THE VALLEY OF THE DOLLS (1970) C/109m.
Russ Meyer's cult favorite is about a small-town three-woman rock band—played by Playboy bunnies Dolly Read and Cynthia Myers and model Marcia McBroom—who make it big in Hollywood, the land of sex, drugs, moral corruption, and deviance. Originally it was slated to be a sequel to *Valley of the Dolls*, but instead of expanding on Jacqueline Susann's trashy best-seller it turned around and parodied the first film and other overblown, cliché-filled Hollywood soap operas. There's nothing worse than a multi-million-dollar spoof of movies that are already self-parodies. When Meyer finally got his chance to make a studio picture (with 20th Century–Fox), many of us expected him to be really inventive; instead he proved to be lazy and conservative, opting to make an outrageously campy caricature-populated film rather than attempting to make a serious, solid melodrama. Critic Roger Ebert's script is smug and vulgar, and full of violence-against-females scenes (which Meyer films *seriously*) of the type he has crusaded against as a critic. Read, Charles Napier, Erica Gavin (*Vixen*), and Michael Blodgett are worth watching, but the most enjoyment comes from counting the numerous combinations of people who sleep together. Most disturbing is that Meyer's "put-on" morality of his sixties films is present here too, but we can take it more seriously this time. Meyer kills off a Nazi and a murderous transvestite and (he obviously lumps them together) a bisexual and two lesbians who haven't harmed anyone; the characters who survive are those who

have repented for their misdeeds and immoral behavior. Also with: John LaZar, David Gurian, Edy Williams, Phyllis Davis, Harrison Page.

BEYOND THE WALLS (ISRAELI/1984) C/103m.
This controversial, award-winning film is set in an Israeli maximum-security prison which houses both Israeli criminals and captured PLO terrorists. All the prisoners are brutal, but when we see them with visiting relatives, their sensitivity is revealed. The corrupt prison officials, who permit cramped conditions, drug addiction, and homosexual rape, find that their job is easiest when the two prison factions are at each other's throats. When the factions' leaders (Aron Zadok, Muhamed Bakri) discover that the warden has arranged the murder of an Israeli prisoner in order to frame Bakri and other Arab prisoners and start a full-scale prison war, they call for a strike of *all* prisoners to protest. Only now do they realize who their real enemy is. Here in prison, at least, peace comes about. A tough political film that shocked people in Israel and outsiders looking in. Directed by Uri Barbashi, in Hebrew.

BICHES, LES (FRENCH/1968) C/88m.
Claude Chabrol's ambiguous study of lesbian lovers, wealthy Frédérique (Stéphane Audran) and vacant-eyed young Why (Jacqueline Sassard), and Paul (Jean-Louis Trintignant), the man who comes between them. It bears much resemblance to his earlier film *Les Cousins*, about two male cousins and the woman they both love in turn. Again an innocent comes to live with a sophisticate (this time the setting is St. Tropez) who serves as a corruptive influence. Each wishes she were more like the other, and develops resentment and jealousy to go with the admiration. Frédérique doesn't seem to mind that her new lover—whom she found drawing deer on St. Tropez pavements—yields her virginity to architect Paul. But then she claims Trintignant for herself—and Why accepts her role as outsider (just as the country waif did in *Les Cousins* when his city cousin seduced his girlfriend). Has Frédérique chosen to seduce Paul so she can experience what Why did with him, or to claim Paul and thus prevent Why—whom she loves—from leaving her for him, or because she harbors heterosexual feelings? Is she running away from *herself*? (Why realizes that she has become Frédérique's replica.) As in *Les Cousins*, the disgust each character begins to feel for the other—their mirror images—results in their depression and ultimate destruction. Photographed by Jean Rabier. Also with: Dominique Zardi, Henri Attal, Nane Germon.

BICYCLE THIEF, THE/BICYCLE THIEVES (ITALIAN/1949) B&W/90m.
Loved by moviegoers, revered by critics, Vittorio De Sica's classic of post-WWII Italian neo-realism begins when Lamberto Maggiorani is offered his first job in two years. At last he can buy food for his wife (Lianella Carell) and young son (Enzo Staiola). He proudly rides his newly polished bicycle through Rome, putting up posters. But his bicycle is stolen by a teenage

punk. If he doesn't get it back within 24 hours, he will lose his cherished job. So he and his boy walk through the city in search of the thief and wind up heartbroken, defeated, humiliated. Simple storyline has some special moments: the proud father preparing for his first day at work; the father treating the hungry boy to a rare meal in a restaurant; the cute little boy signaling that he's going to run around a building to head off a witness but, as his father discovers, actually going to find a secluded spot to urinate; the desperate father resorting to bicycle thievery himself; the finale, in which the boy comforts his crying dad (the reverse of what happened earlier between them). But perhaps De Sica is too cruel, not only to his hero but to his audience as well. It becomes difficult enough just watching Maggiorani being repeatedly frustrated in his efforts to retrieve his bike—why does he always run at half-speed?—but then De Sica has the gall to include a scene in which the unhappy man takes out pencil and paper to figure out how much money he would have made per month if the bike hadn't been stolen. Thank goodness De Sica shows a little mercy at the end and doesn't cap off Maggiorani's misery by having him sent to prison—the makers of *El Norte* might have known when to quit damaging their lead characters if they'd seen this film. What I find more impressive today than the story of a man retrieving his bike are the shots of postwar Rome. Along with the obvious destruction and destitution, what one first notices are the crowds—not only the many workers who ride their bikes through the streets (who are an upsetting sight once Maggiorani is bikeless) but the men who line up looking for work, the men and women who gather in a seer's apartment, the socialists who have a political meeting, the people who shop in the market, the down-and-out old men who go to the mission, the large mob that kicks Maggiorani out of the thief's neighborhood, the soccer fans who emerge from the stadium, and the quickly formed group of men who chase Maggiorani when he steals a bike (where were these men when Maggiorani's bike was taken?). It is from watching these crowds that we learn the character of the city; and we come to realize that a lone man with a small boy doesn't stand a chance.

BIG BAD MAMA (1974) C/83m.

During the Depression, Angie Dickinson and her two sluttish teenage daughters, Susan Sennett and Robbie Lee, become bank robbers and kidnappers so they can someday reach the criminal-rich level of "Ford, Rockefeller, Capone, and all the rest of them." Bank robber Tom Skerritt and conman William Shatner join the gang and vie for Dickinson's affections; when Shatner wins out, Skerritt becomes lover to both daughters. In between the frequent sex scenes—even Dickinson and Shatner have nude encounters—there is much gunplay and many car chases. There is also too much rude language and fake feminism. Roger Corman's New World Productions made this throwback to those Corman-directed fifties gangster films, *The Bonnie Parker Story* and *Machine Gun Kelly*, but whereas those pictures had an innocent qual-

ity, this film is embarrassingly vulgar. Directed by Steve Carver. Also with: Dick Miller, Joan Prather.

BIG CARNIVAL, THE/ACE IN THE HOLE (1951) B&W/112m.

Opportunistic reporter Kirk Douglas, working for tiny New Mexico paper, sees his chance to make it back to the New York big time: a man gets trapped in a mine near Albuquerque; Douglas befriends the trapped man and files exclusive stories as rescue workers try to free him. The people of America are taken by his human-interest stories. Realizing that his own fame is growing, Douglas sees to it that the trapped man stays put, even though he may die. Days go by. Thousands of tourists come to the site. Even the trapped man's wife (Jan Sterling) turns a profit. Since her husband is occupied, Douglas moves in on Sterling. Cynical Billy Wilder film, written with Walter Newman and Lesser Samuels, attacks the American public, which is always willing to exploit tragedy for personal gain; it also attacks the press for its tendency to milk the suffering of individuals in order to build readership. It's based on what happened to miner Floyd Collins. Many people detest this depressing picture, but it's extremely well made, brilliantly acted by Douglas, and, sadly, truthful. Also with: Porter Hall, Richard Benedict, Bob Arthur, Ray Teal.

BIG CHILL, THE (1983) C/108m.

Seven college radicals from the sixties-early seventies are reunited when the "leader" of their former group commits suicide. After the funeral, married Kevin Kline and Glenn Close invite the others to spend the weekend at their large house, there in South Carolina. (They'd gone to the University of Michigan.) They recall old times (although they intentionally avoid speaking about their dead friend), talk of the present and future. If this is what became of his previously involved, socially conscientious friends, then it's no wonder the guy committed suicide. Director Lawrence Kasdan and his co-writer Barbara Benedek show us what happened to the sixties radicals they know, who have become drop-ins to society (Kline is even on first-name basis with a local cop) or, if they aren't yuppies (which druggie William Hurt is not), have abandoned social activism anyway. Unmarried Mary Kay Place's decision to have a baby is the most "radical" act discussed. The film is slick and funny, but it's infuriating that Kasdan thinks most sixties radicals have gone the way of Jerry Rubin. I certainly know more people from the sixties protest movement who are more like the characters in John Sayles's superior 1980 film *Return of the Secaucus Seven*—if they're not out in the streets, at least they haven't sold out their values and are still doing their part for social change (as their choices of jobs indicate). Best, most nostalgic scenes have characters gathering in the kitchen for food and chit-chat. Dialogue is sharp, but too precise (it comes across as if it were *written* rather than delivered spontaneously). The most appealing character is the outsider, the dead man's young, shallow girlfriend Meg Tilly. She hasn't been formed yet, so she surely hasn't been corrupted. A strong rock score. Picture was a surprise smash hit. Contributing to the strong ensemble acting: Jeff Goldblum, Tom Berenger (as a humble movie star), JoBeth Williams.

BIG DOLL HOUSE, THE (1971) C/93m.

The first of the women-in-prison genre, and the best outside of Jonathan Demme's *Caged Heat*. Directed by Jack Hill and produced by Jane Schaffer for Roger Corman's New World Pictures, it created the formula for later films by mixing R-rated sex and violence (including torture of female prisoners) with feminism: women bond together for survival, women are not helpless and passive. American Judy Brown is thrown into a women's prison in an unspecified South American country (filming was done in the Philippines). There she is shocked by the terrible treatment of prisoners. But she is lucky to become cellmate to two future superstars of the sexploitation genre: Roberta Collins and Pam Grier, reasons enough to see this film. These women will take only so much humiliation, abuse, and torture. Film ends with a bloody rebellion in the prison, complete with explosions and strangulation by snake. Nudity, intentionally campy dialogue, and action make it ideal drive-in fare. Also with: Pat Woodell, Kathryn Loder (the sadistic warden), Christiane Schmidtmer, Brooke Mills, Sid Haig.

BIG HEAT, THE (1953) B&W/89m.

Homicide detective Glenn Ford investigates suicide of an "honest" cop. He becomes suspicious that he was on payroll of corrupt, wealthy civic leader Alexander Scourby when the dead man's mistress is murdered before she can talk to reporters. He ignores police orders and anonymous warnings to get off the case. When his wife Jocelyn Brando is killed by a bomb meant for him, Ford quits force, sells house, places daughter with the only friends he trusts, and believing his life to be permanently ruined, withdraws into a crazed, paranoid world. His only goal is brutal revenge on all those responsible for his wife's death. Terrific Fritz Lang film links hard-hitting exposé films of the fifties with forties *film noir*. While it coolly surveys the all-inclusive political/police corruption, it is equally concerned with the corruption of a decent man's soul; among other *noir* elements are pervading pessimism, ferocious violence, a hero who makes *one* vital mistake from which there is little chance of recovery—he underestimates his opposition as much as they do him—and the intertwining traits of fatalism and paranoia. Lang sets up his usual bottomless pit over which his men must walk a tightrope. Only by tempering his violence does Ford avoid his downfall, fate's final trap. The city he walks through is controlled by the enemy, Scourby, and no one can be trusted. But, just as Lang remembers a resistance to Hitler in Germany, there is a resistance to Scourby. Ford finds his allies are the least likely people in town: other people who have nothing to lose, including Gloria Grahame, who was the girlfriend of Scourby's righthand man, Lee Marvin, until he became angry because she spoke to Ford and he disfigured her pretty face with hot coffee. (She will return the favor.) She does the dirty work before Ford gets the chance; her charitable act purges Ford of his consuming hatred and reestablishes his faith in people. Picture is much about territorial imperative. Notice how all the characters regard their homes or work establishments as their power bases; how the richer the home, the more corrupt its owner (Ford lives in a modest one-story home); how when one person enters or merely telephones the home of an enemy, it is tantamount to an act of aggression; how Ford's wife, who symbolizes the home, is killed the first time in the film she goes outside; how the bad guys are all arrested in their respective homes. This is *vigilante film* with a difference—the hero *learns* that going outside the law is not only wrong but the first step to becoming as bad as the enemy. Briskly paced, moodily photographed by Charles B. Lang, brilliantly scripted by Sydney Boehm from William P. McGivern's novel. It is a truly exciting, political film, brimming with clever twists, sparkling touches, offbeat characters, and even scenes of genuine tenderness. Ford (with clenched fists for a change when he talks), sadistic Marvin, dream wife Brando, and slimy Scourby are all excellent; Grahame, in her greatest role—she is the film's *heroine*—is the best of all. Also with: Jeanette Nolan, Peter Whitney, Willis Bouchey, Robert Burton, Adam Williams, Carolyn Jones.

BIG MOUTH, THE (1967) C/107m.

Fair Jerry Lewis vehicle, written (with Bill Richmond) and directed by Lewis. Jerry fishes a fatally shot frogman from the ocean and is given map to where diamonds are hidden. He doesn't realize frogman was a crook and his lookalike. Because of mistaken identity, one gang wants to kill him; another gang wants to buy his diamonds. Script is pretty good and Lewis generously shares gags with assortment of oddball supporting characters. But Lewis as director is less innovative and there is not enough visual comedy or slapstick. Moreover too many scenes are set at Sea World. Jerry's character is not the usual Lewis numbskull, but someone who has some intelligence and even has quiet moments and is, unfortunately, less out-of-control than usual. So Lewis, in a second role, also plays his buck-toothed "Nutty Professor"-type character. Love scenes with boring Susan Bay are embarrassingly sappy. Also with: Harold J. Stone, Buddy Lester, Del Moore, Paul Lambert, Charley Callas.

BIG RED ONE, THE (1980) C/113m.

Sam Fuller waited more than 30 years to make his dream film, a hard-hitting yet extremely poetic, impressionistic recollection of his WWII experiences with an infantry unit nicknamed "The Big Red One." Film centers on a tough sergeant (Lee Marvin) and his baby-faced recruits Robert Carradine (as a cigar-chomping writer who is based on Fuller), Bobby Di Ciccio, Mark Hamill, and Kelly Ward, who survive four eventful years of fighting while others in the regiment come and go (die). Fuller's most expensive and ambitious film has epic proportions, taking place in countless locations (North Africa, France, Czechoslovakia, Germany, etc.) and covering many battles. Interestingly, Fuller downplays spectacle and battlefield heroics; his theme, as expressed by Carradine at the end, is that "surviving is the only glory in war." Fuller instead emphasizes the surreal aspects of war, from bizarre images and nightmarish situations to soldiers carrying on everyday conversations although their friends have just died in battle or they themselves may die a moment later. Picture contains many memorable, moving scenes (i.e., Marvin with the little boy from the concentration camp) plus Fuller's characteristically realistic dialogue. I wish he fleshed out his characters a bit more and gave his story more cohesion, but this may be his best war film. If you were disappointed when you first saw it, as I was, give it another try—it really improves the second time around. Also with: Stéphane Audran, Siegfried Rauch.

BIG SLEEP, THE (1946) B&W/114m.
Raymond Chandler's first novel was adapted into this crackerjack detective classic by William Faulkner, Leigh Brackett, Jules Furthman, and director Howard Hawks. The plot is so confusing that neither Hawks nor Chandler could figure out who was responsible for all of the eight murders; censors rewrote the final scene, letting one person off the hook and incriminating another, but Hawks didn't bother rewriting anything that went before it. But film contains the sharpest, toughest, wittiest, sexiest dialogue ever written for a detective film; some powerful action sequences; several offbeat female characters, including spoiled, playful Lauren Bacall and her troubled nympho younger sister, Martha Vickers. And it perfectly cast Humphrey Bogart as Chandler's moral shamus Philip Marlowe, who is hired by wealthy Charles Waldron to stop the man who's been blackmailing him because of Vickers's gambling debts—and to find out what happened to Waldron's former assistant (*we* can guess what happened). Marlowe finds Vickers has gotten in with the wrong crowd and into a heap of trouble. He also makes a play for Bacall. Their scenes together (some added a year after filming was completed) are full of sexual innuendo, but I don't think they have the same electricity as their verbal duets in *To Have and Have Not*. Bacall is perhaps too comfortable with Bogart; the nervous, sexy edge isn't there. Bogart's first appearance is outside Waldron's mansion (we just see his finger pushing the doorbell button). This is significant because throughout he is portrayed as an outsider who finds hostility anytime he enters a house, apartment, club. He is always on guard. But he enjoys the world he walks through full of liars, blackmailers, nymphomaniacs, pornographers, drug dealers, murderers, and pretty, available women who are looking for a quick thrill. Hawks perfectly conveys Chandler's corrosive yet enticing Los Angeles. Michael Winner directed a bad 1977 remake. *Noirish* cinematography by Sid Hickox is very atmospheric. Music by Max Steiner. Also with: John Ridgely, Dorothy Malone (brunette in bookstore), Peggy Knudson, Elisha Cook, Jr. (whose death scene is a highlight), Regis Toomey, Charles D. Brown, Bob Steele, Louis Jean Heydt, Joy Barlow (taxi driver).

BILITIS (FRENCH/1977) C/95m.
Two years before she played Ryan O'Neal's coughing girlfriend in *The Main Event*, Patti D'Arbanville—looking a gawky and flat-chested 15 or 16—starred as Bilitis in this coming-of-age sexcapade about a schoolgirl who has a very active summer vacation. She gets a crush on her beautiful adult female guardian (Mona Kristensen), who is having problems with her cruel husband. They have sexual encounters and Bilitis tries to find her a suitable male lover. Meanwhile, Bilitis falls for a teenage boy. D'Arbanville can be touching; she can also be extremely annoying. Everyone else is boring. The weak direction is by David Hamilton, known for his soft-focus photos of nude women. In fact, *Bilitis* has been published as a coffee-table photo book. Here, as in his other films, Hamilton borders on outright pornography; most uncomfortable are his lingering shots of nude or erotically dressed young girls. Along with the lesbian love scenes, this is surely the reason for the film's popularity in repertory theaters and on pay television. (Another pay-TV favorite is Hamilton's *Tendres Cousins*, in which some luscious young women really go at it in nude sex scenes with a boy of about 14—that kid must have the best agent in the world.) Also with: Bernard Giraudeau, Mathiew Carrière.

BILL COSBY—HIMSELF (1983) C/114m.
No doubt Cosby hoped to obtain the wild success Richard Pryor had with his concert films. But this picture, which uses footage from four 1981 performances in Hamilton, Ontario, is painfully unfunny. Whether talking about drunks, dentists, or his family, he's about as dull as one of those guys on cable who give advice on real estate and how to use tax loopholes. The material is remarkably impersonal and conventional and doesn't compare to bits on his old record albums; and at no time does he display the mischievous boyishness that makes his television character so likable. The comedian gets cooking only when he talks about his parents, now (when they're angelic grandparents) and years ago (when they were strict to their small children). But this routine is too brief and comes at the very end of the picture. Cosby wrote and directed.

BILL OF DIVORCEMENT, A (1932) B&W/69m–75m.
George Cukor directed this stagy, hokey adaptation of Clemence Dane's bad play. John Barrymore plays a man who returns home after fifteen years in a mental hospital to find that wife Billie Burke has divorced him and is about to go away with fiancé Paul Cavanagh. Meanwhile daughter Katharine Hepburn learns from her aunt that insanity runs in her family—Barrymore hadn't just suffered from shellshock all these years—and worries that she should call off her engagement to David Manners (lest they have mad children!). She thinks she should remain with Barrymore because they are two of a kind. Overwrought characters take turns playing the martyr. At least film has historical significance in that it featured skinny Hepburn's screen debut and paired her with Barrymore—but it's more fun reading about the trouble she had with him off screen than seeing them together on screen, with her trying hard and him hamming it up. Remade in 1940 with Maureen O'Hara and Adolphe Menjou. Also with: Henry Stephenson.

BILLY JACK (1971) C/112m. Tom Laughlin introduced us to his title character, a half-breed, a hapkido expert, a former Green Beret and war hero in Vietnam, in 1967's successful "biker" film, *Born Losers*. This time the protector of the downtrodden protects the troubled children who live at the alternative school of his girlfriend Delores Taylor. Due to canny marketing by Laughlin and Warners and subject matter designed to entice the enormous alienated-youth audience—this uncontroversial film is for justice and equality, yoga, the creative arts, meditation, role-play therapy, wild horses, and gun control; it is against bigotry, bullies, childbeaters and formal education—it became a phenomenon at the box office. The eerie part is that its nonviolent audience most enjoyed the violence perpetrated by Billy Jack on the conservative types who are threatening the children at pacifist Taylor's school. It's particularly disturbing when the kids in the film give Billy Jack a "power" salute, signifying that he is their savior—it reminds me of how Nazi youth responded to Hitler. It's clear that Laughlin wanted viewers to think of him and his character as one and the same. Picture isn't badly made: hapkido scenes are exciting, Taylor gives a very moving account of what it feels like to be raped, and Laughlin makes a good, charismatic action hero. However, it is pretentious and badly flawed—for instance, townspeople are won over to school's virtues by watching comedy routine by adult improv group, *The Committee*, rather than by seeing children live, learn, and create things at the school. Debate between Laughlin and Taylor regarding violence vs. pacifism is never resolved, and the picture's major theme—that the disenchanted youths of America have an ally in the Indian—is weak because Laughlin never defines "being an Indian," although this is Billy Jack's goal. "One Tin Soldier" is sung by Coven. Sequels: *The Trial of Billy Jack, Billy Jack Goes to Washington*; Laughlin began another sequel in 1986. Also with: Clark Hawat, Bert Freed, Julie Webb, Kenneth Tobey, Howard Hesseman.

BINGO LONG TRAVELING ALL-STARS AND MOTOR KINGS, THE (1976) C/110m. In the mid-forties, flamboyant pitcher Bingo Long (Billy Dee Williams) gets fed up with the abuse and exploitation the players are subjected to by the owners of the Negro League baseball teams. So he convinces slugging catcher Leon (James Earl Jones in a Josh Gibson-like role) and other malcontents to join him and barnstorm around the country, playing local teams and really putting on a show. Unhappy that they've lost some of their best draws and worried about the new competition, the Negro League owners use payoffs to cancel Bingo's games and stoop to using physical intimidation on players to try to force Bingo out of business. But Bingo holds on. This is a flavorful, spirited period piece with a standout black cast. It starts out as an interesting look at exploitation of blacks by blacks and a sharp leftist political satire ("Seize the means of production" is Bingo's motto), but unfortunately dissolves into a familiar farce—for example, the bad guys kidnap Leon so he'll miss the *big* game. However, it's full of nice moments, including the final scene between Bingo and Leon, which leaves viewers feeling good. Richard Pryor is funny throughout as a black player who pretends to be a Cuban and then an American Indian in hopes of cracking into the major leagues. Also noteworthy is Stan Shaw as a combination of Willie Mays and Jackie Robinson who in this fiction is signed by the Dodgers to break the color line (which will mean the demise of the Negro League). John Badham directed; Berry Gordy was executive producer of this Motown film; Thelma Huston contributed the songs. From the novel by William Brashler. Also with: Ted Ross, Sam Brown, Alvin Childress, ex-player Leon Wagner, ex-umpire Emmett Ashford.

BIRD OF PARADISE (1932) B&W/80m. King Vidor's exotic South Seas romance about a handsome young white man (Joel McCrea) and a beautiful young Polynesian woman (Dolores Del Rio, in a role played by Laurette Taylor on the stage in 1912) who fall in love. Because they break the taboos of her tribe, they run away to a deserted island, where they set up house. It's paradise! But she worries that she is destined to die in a volcano, punishment for her "crimes." Film blends tragedy of Flaherty and Murnau's 1931 film *Tabu* with the eroticism (an unmarried couple lives together in a hot jungle paradise) of Van Dyke's *Tarzan the Ape Man*, which also came out in 1932. Picture's fun, although it doesn't hold up as well as those other two films. It's very stilted. The major enjoyment comes from looking at healthy bodies of two leads and hoping that the wind blows up the lei that covers Del Rio's naked breasts. Obviously remembering the costuming from this film, Del Rio's husband, Cedric Gibbons, would co-direct *Tarzan and His Mate*, which is known for the scandalously scanty costumes worn by Johnny Weissmuller and Maureen O'Sullivan. Music by Max Steiner, who, as was often the case in the thirties, scores the picture as if it were a silent film (which is how Vidor shot it). Atmospheric cinematography by Clyde de Vinna. Remade in 1951 with Louis Jourdan and Debra Paget. Also with: John Halliday, Richard "Skeets" Gallagher, Bert Roach, Creighton Chaney (Lon Chaney, Jr.).

BIRD WITH THE CRYSTAL PLUMAGE, THE/ PHANTOM OF TERROR, THE (ITALIAN-GERMAN/1969) C/98m. Tony Musante is an American writer living in Italy, whose appearance on the scene one night saves a woman (Eva Renzi) from a murder attempt—or so he believes. Soon he and girlfriend Suzy Kendall find that someone—possibly the sex murderer who is on the loose—is trying to kill them. Tricky and bloody horror-mystery, stylishly directed by Dario Argento, Italy's specialist in this kind of material. Has some scary moments, but perhaps best scene is half comical, with Musante visiting an eccentric artist whose painting is the key to the mystery. Dubbing hurts; should be seen in theater for full effect. Also with: Enrico Maria Salerno, Mario Adorf.

BIRDS, THE (1963) C/120m.

Alfred Hitchcock thriller, adapted by Evan Hunter from a Daphne du Maurier story, disappointed most everyone when it was released. Now it's justifiably regarded as one of Hitchcock's true gems, an exciting, complex picture that is technically dazzling, extremely well written, and ideal for viewers who enjoy digging for themes. Frivolous playgirl Tippi Hedren meets lawyer Rod Taylor in a San Francisco bird shop. She pretends to be a saleswoman, he a customer. They snap at each other, but the attraction is obvious. She drives to Bodega Bay, where Taylor spends weekends at the house in which he grew up with his possessive (she's afraid of being abandoned) widowed mother (Jessica Tandy) and young sister (Veronica Cartwright). As a joke, Hedren intends to leave a pair of lovebirds in his house and sneak away. But when Taylor spots her, she pretends to have come to Bodega Bay to visit schoolteacher Suzanne Pleshette, who, she fibs, was her school chum although in reality Hedren only just met her when asking directions. Pleshette had been a previous girlfriend of Taylor's, whom he'd also met in San Francisco, but Tandy had ruined their relationship. Now Tandy acts worried about Taylor and Hedren. Not long after Hedren arrives in town, she is attacked for no reason by a sea gull. Soon after, there are other random attacks throughout Bodega Bay by seemingly organized flocks of common birds. The attacks intensify; there are deaths. Some villagers flee; others board themselves up in their houses: in the pet shop it had been humans looking at birds in cages, but now the birds are on the outside looking in. No one has an explanation for what is happening. Perhaps it is Judgment Day. Perhaps the birds have just decided to reclaim their world from the intruding human species, who had proved to be cruel landlords. My belief is that the film is much like a Christian parable: the bird attacks serve to force humans to regain their humanness, to bring them closer together, to love one another. From the opening scene we see that humans play-act, squabble, are distrustful, see one another as rivals for others' affections, and deny each other love: Hedren's mother abandoned her; bachelor Taylor rejected Pleshette, which was probably as bad a loss for him; Tandy misses and feels abandoned by her late husband; Taylor and Cartwright lost their father. But in the final analysis these humans, when challenged by an alien force, forget the barriers they had set up between themselves and come through for one another—a human flock forms. Film's highlights are not necessarily the bird attacks, but how Hitchcock builds suspense prior to them. Interestingly, no music is used in the film, just bird noises. Also notice that the women, even when scared out of their wits, don't scream: so you know that Hitchcock reserves screams for very special occasions (for instance, in *The Man Who Knew Too Much* and *Psycho*). The attack of the birds on the house was a great influence on George Romero's *Night of the Living Dead*. I don't think viewers are dissatisfied with the film's open ending, just that Hitchcock seems to be building to one final bird attack that never comes. Hedren, in her debut, grows on you. Also with: Ethel Griffies, Charles McGraw, Ruth McDevitt, Joe Mantell, Malcolm Atterbury, Karl Swenson, Doodles Weaver, William Quinn.

BIRTH OF A NATION, THE (1915) B&W/159m.

The birth of the feature film. D. W. Griffith's controversial landmark film will astonish you with its visuals and repulse you with its content. Film is based on the Reverend Thomas Dixon's racist Reconstruction play, *The Clansman*, which celebrates the KKK for restoring the politics and life-style of the antebellum South. It is about the Camerons of South Carolina and the Stonemans of Pennsylvania. They are friends prior to the Civil War. Ben Cameron (Henry B. Walthall) and Elsie Stoneman (Lillian Gish) are sweet on each other, as are Margaret Cameron (Mae Marsh) and Phil Stoneman (Elmer Clifton). The Civil War breaks out and the country is divided. Ben is wounded but is nursed back to health by Elsie. Lincoln pardons him. After the war, Congressman Austin Stoneman (Ralph Lewis) defies the dead Lincoln's wishes and punishes the South with a Reconstruction plan that gives all power to carpetbaggers and black Southerners. The Stonemans stay with the Camerons so Austin can oversee the plan. Mulatto Silas Lynch (George Siegmann) is Austin's handpicked man to organize a black militia. Whites are prevented from voting, and blacks take over the government. Margaret jumps to her death rather than be raped by a black man. Lynch, who wants to build an empire, demands that Elsie be his wife. Cameron forms the KKK to fight back. Austin realizes that his plan has backfired. The klansmen become our heroes when they rescue whites who are about to be killed by black militiamen. Griffith's film is about the concept of family. It is about the Cameron and Stoneman families, but more significantly the Southern family and Northern family who must unite into one big family (a nation) under Lincoln, the father figure. OK so far—but Griffith is not through. He wants the Aryan American family to unite against the black family. The war becomes not North vs. South but whites vs. blacks. The last image of KKK men on horseback frightening blacks away from the polls is unnerving. This is a great film (the Civil War battles are incredible) marred by a reprehensible viewpoint. It's too important to miss, if only to see what once passed as history. Billy Bitzer and Karl Brown did the cinematography. Erich Von Stroheim, Raoul Walsh, and Jack Conway were among the assistant directors. Also with: Miriam Cooper, Spottiswoode Aitken, Elmo Lincoln, Wallace Reid, Joseph Henaberry (Lincoln), Donald Crisp, Walsh (as John Wilkes Booth), Eugene Pallette, Bessie Love, Stroheim.

BLACK CAT, THE (1934) B&W/65m.

High-camp horror film, stylistically directed by Edgar G. Ulmer (who co-wrote the script) and played with tongue firmly in cheek by Boris Karloff (as evil architect and satanist Hjalmar Poelzig) and Bela Lugosi (as vengeance-bent psychiatrist Dr. Vitus Verdegast) in their first screen collaboration. The Hungarian honeymoon of a young American couple—David Manners (who is knocked cold any time he gets aggressive) and Jacqueline Wells (who screams and faints, faints and screams)—is ruined when they're held prisoner in Karloff's personally designed, ultra-modern Bauhaus castle, a restructured fort that stands above a battlefield where thousands of Hungarian corpses are buried. Also on hand is Lugosi, who has returned to visit and murder his former friend after having spent years in a Russian prison camp—the result of Karloff having betrayed him and thousands of others to the Russians. When Lugosi was out of the way in the prison camp, Karloff married Lugosi's wife. When she died, he preserved her corpse in a glass case in the dungeon and married Lugosi's young daughter (Lucille Lund), whom he keeps a virtual prisoner. While Lugosi plans to do away with Karloff, Karloff plans to sacrifice Wells at a Black Mass he is presiding over. Delightfully preposterous storyline has nothing to do with Edgar Allan Poe's story. Ulmer based Karloff's character on British satanist Aleister Crowley, who was then in the news, and infused story with a postwar anguish that was peculiar to Europeans who lived on soil where their loved ones were buried. Ulmer complained Universal cut film drastically, which explains some of its incoherence and script's weakness; but it has witty dialogue, fine performances (even from Lugosi), amusing characters, bizarre sets, inventive direction, and some of the most peculiar scenes in horror-movie history: Karloff's striking initial appearance; Lugosi, who has a cat phobia, spots Karloff's black cat and immediately kills it with a perfectly tossed knife (not even Karloff complains about his over-reaction); Karloff lies next to his bride and reads about satanic rituals; both victims of the war in that they have lost their souls, Karloff and Lugosi play chess to determine if Wells can go free; Lugosi, in one of his few nice-guy roles, skins Karloff alive. Plus Lugosi's famous line "Supernatural—perhaps; baloney—perhaps not," and Karloff's words at the Black Mass are good for a few laughs, as is Karloff's haircut. Film is morbid and tasteless and lots of fun. Also with: Egon Brecher, Henry Armetta, Albert Conti, John Carradine.

BLACK CAULDRON, THE (1985) C/80m.
Critics overpraised Walt Disney's 25th cartoon feature out of appreciation for the studio's attempt to return to old-style, ambitious animation. The animation doesn't have the subtlety of the Disney classics, and the backgrounds are lifeless—and purists may object to the animation being computer-enhanced—but obviously much care was taken in animating foreground action, as well as character movements and facial expressions. The story, taken from Lloyd Alexander's The Chronicles of Prydian, is about a young boy who embarks on a journey with his clairvoyant pig to find and destroy the powerful black cauldron so that it won't fall into the hands of the Horned King, a cadaverous creature of pure evil. They are joined on the mission by a pretty princess, an elderly minstrel, and the cute, cuddly, cowardly half-human-half-creature Gurgi. The human characters are a bit innocuous and the plot has few surprises and many weak points. But, to be fair, kids won't be bored, and adults will find the film to be a pleasant diversion. It does have some impressive visuals and makes the refreshing point that loyalty and friendship are more important than heroics. Co-directed by Ted Berman and Richard Rich; Disney's first 70 mm. cartoon since 1959's Sleeping Beauty. Voices by: John Byner (who uses traces of his Donald Duck impersonation for Gurgi), John Hurt (as the Horned King), Eda Reiss Merin, Adele Malis-Morey, Billie Hayes, Phil Fondacaro, John Huston (as the narrator).

BLACK CHRISTMAS/SILENT NIGHT, EVIL NIGHT/STRANGER IN THE HOUSE (CANADIAN/1975) C/100m.
An insane murderer terrorizes a college sorority house over the Christmas holidays. Slowly Olivia Hussey begins to realize that something is amiss and her life is in danger. Atmospheric chiller has sympathetic performance by Hussey, strong direction by Bob Clark. This is one of the few films where viewers become spooked because they can actually sense the cold, snowy weather that the characters are experiencing on the screen. Margot Kidder makes an impression as Hussey's vulgar sorority sister. The twist ending is a bit frustrating. Also with: Keir Dullea (as the prime suspect), John Saxon, Douglas McGrath.

BLACK GIRL/NOIRE DE..., LA (SENEGALESE/1966) B&W/60m—70m.
In French. The first feature of Africa's most famous filmmaker, Ousmane Sembene, is adapted from Sembene's 1961 short story about a real-life tragedy. Diouana (amateur Thérèse N'Bissine Diop) is a very young Senegalese woman who is delighted to be hired as maid by a young French couple (Robert Fontaine, Ann-Marie Jelinek) who have come to Dakar. She agrees to go to France with them to take care of their children. This means leaving behind her poor mother, her young brother (Ibrahima Boy), and her boyfriend (Momar Nar Sene), but she is excited about seeing the French countryside and the famous shops. But she becomes extremely lonely in France and very disillusioned about her work. Jelinek expects her to do all the menial chores and to follow strict orders. Not being able to communicate with anyone and given non-stop work, Diouana feels she is a prisoner in their apartment. She becomes increasingly depressed and finally refuses to follow Jelinek's orders. Jelinek, who thinks she has been extremely kind to Diouana, assumes that the young girl is either sick, lazy, or crazy—she makes no connection between Diouana's state and the way she has been treated. This crudely made but unusually structured film is of interest for reasons other than its landmark status in African cinema. No film has better conveyed the concept of "domestic slavery"—Sembene is attacking neo-colonialism, where whites pay wages to blacks but treat them as if they were property. The major concern of Sembene, whose films are intended to show the problems of his people, is that Diouana's situation isn't isolated and that many poor Africans are susceptible to falling into the same trap as she. As Diouana's mother illustrates, the Africans cannot accept wages from

neo-colonialists, who—as Diouana's little brother illustrates in the powerful last scene—must be driven away.

BLACK NARCISSUS (BRITISH/1947) C/100m.
An erotic masterpiece about nuns! Michael Powell and Emeric Pressburger wrote, produced, and directed this intense adaptation of Rumer Godden's novel. Deborah Kerr (Sister Clodagh) and four nuns under her charge are assigned to set up a hospital and a school for females in a great palace in a remote section of the Himalayas. The palace, formerly the residence of a potentate's harem, is situated on an isolated mountain ledge. It's dark and haunted by its sinful past, and an eerie wind blows constantly through the empty corridors. In this exotic setting the nuns find their commitment to the order greatly tested. An older nun (Flora Robson) eventually wants to be sent away, as her faith disappears. Kerr and the other young nun, Kathleen Byron (Sister Ruth), find they must come to terms with their feelings toward a handsome bachelor British agent (David Farrar in shorts) who represents potential worldly pleasures. Thoughts of sex pass through both women's minds, heightened by that wind and native drumbeats and the courtship taking place in their school between young native general Sabu, who wears the intoxicating Black Narcissus perfume, and sensual native girl Jean Simmons. In flashback footage that has been restored in U.S. release prints, Kerr thinks back to her one past romance. Meanwhile Byron begins to go insane with sexual passion for Farrar and jealousy of Kerr—like us, Farrar notices how alluring Kerr is, even in her habit. Picture is splendidly acted, uncompromisingly written—surprising choices are made constantly—and ranks as one of the most stunningly beautiful color films of all time, thanks to cinematographer Jack Cardiff and art director Alfred Junge. Viewers are usually shocked to discover that for the most part the picture was made inside a studio so that Cardiff could better establish the nuns' terrible sense of claustrophobia. Music by Brian Easdale. Also with: Esmond Knight, Jenny Laird, Judith Furse, Nancy Roberts, May Hallatt.

BLACK ORPHEUS (BRAZILIAN-FRENCH-ITALIAN/1959) C/100m.
Popular Brazilian film by Marcel Camus updates myth of Orpheus and Eurydice to modern Rio. Streetcar conductor Orpheus (Breno Mello) meets Eurydice (Marpessa Dawn), who has come to Rio to escape a vengeful suitor (Adhémar da Silva). It's carnival time, the city is festive and romantic, and the two fall in love. But da Silva turns up, costumed as Death. Eurydice is killed trying to escape him. Used here as a symbol for the sun, Orpheus must go into the darkness to try to retrieve his lost lover. He enters a shadowy, deserted morgue, the film's equivalent of Hades. There will be brief happiness, then tragedy. This is one of the first films with black characters that was popular with American white audiences. Females tend to like it better than males, perhaps because of extensive dancing and music (indeed, the film is like an epic dance). It's an extremely colorful film, with emphasis on local customs and costumes. Splendid photography by Jean Bourgoin captures glorious setting (mountains, sky, sunrises, cityscapes). Academy Award Winner for Best Foreign Film. From the play *Orfeu da Conceiçao* by Vinicius de Moraes, who wrote the screenplay. Also with: Lourdes de Oliveira, Lea Garcia.

BLACK STALLION, THE (1979) C/118m.
A young boy (Kelly Reno) traveling by ship with his father (Hoyt Axton) is much taken with wild Arabian black stallion being transported. A fire on board causes the father's death, and the boy to jump overboard. He ends up alone on a sandy island with the stallion. Film is actually two stories: the first is magical and mystical and the second is familiar but lyrical. Story One deals with the boy's courtship of the stallion, beginning on the ship and continuing on the island. By the time they are rescued, the boy has gained the horse's trust and affection. In Story Two, which is filmed entirely differently, the boy returns to small-town America and, with the help of trainer Mickey Rooney, prepares the black stallion for a long race in which he'll be the jockey. I much prefer the island scenes, although the slow pace may put some kids to sleep. Carroll Ballard film, co-produced by Francis Ford Coppola, has some of the most beautiful outdoor photography in film history—scenes of the boy learning to ride the horse on sand and in water linger in the memory. Horse is gorgeous. A sincere, offbeat performance by Rooney. Also with: Teri Garr (as Reno's mother), Clarence Muse.

BLACK SUNDAY (ITALIAN/1960) B&W/83m.
Extremely effective film was Mario Bava's first and remains the best Italian horror film. In her quintessential performance, horror icon Barbara Steele plays two roles, the good Katia and her look-alike, the witch-vampiress Asa, who returns to life in 1830—two hundred years after she was put to death. With her resurrected lover at her side, Asa attempts to take Katia's blood for her own. Steele's beauty is mysterious and unique; her large eyes, high cheekbones, jet-black hair, thick lower lip, and somewhat knobby chin don't seem synchronized, and as a result her face can be perceived as either evil (Asa) or sweet (Katia), depending on the beholder—so she is the ideal choice for this dual role. This is among the most atmospheric of horror films because former cameraman Bava conveys everything visually (which makes us forget dubbing). Bava's malefic world consists of dark mountains set against a gray sky; mist-shrouded forests where tree limbs seem to reach out to grab those passing through; two-hundred-year-old graveyards where the soil is too cursed for anything to grow; ancient crypts where bats fly about in the darkness, spiders spin their webs, and decaying walls crumble; and shadowy, ice-cold castles full of creepy passageways and enormous hidden chambers. It's a world where light fights a losing battle against oppressive darkness and even the pure (virgins, priests) wear black. With art director Giorgio Giovannini, Bava creates an atmosphere where the living and dead co-

exist, unharmoniously. Particularly memorable is Bava's use of the mobile camera, especially in the nightmarish carriage sequence and the scene in which Asa's lover is followed through a secret passageway leading to her tomb. Bava's imagery is so strong—a spiked demon's mask is driven into Asa's face, maggots crawl around the eye sockets of Asa's skeleton, and so on—that the film was banned in England for eight years and still may be a bit gruesome for kids. From Nikolai Gogol's story "The Vij." Also with: John Richardson (the doctor, who falls for Katia), Ivo Garrani, Andrea Checchi, Arturo Dominici, Enrico Oliveri.

BLACULA (1972) C/92m.

Hip, fast-moving, erotic, clever, well acted, and with some of the most respectable black characters found in the blaxploitation films being churned out in the early seventies, this black horror film shouldn't be dismissed so easily. Deep-voiced, tall, handsome, and intelligent William Marshall, a solid actor, is as sympathetic and aristocratic a vampire as there has been in movies. Blacula had been an 18th-century African prince named Manuwabe. Dracula killed/kidnapped his beloved wife (Vonetta McGee) and turned him into a vampire by drinking his blood. Dracula thought Blacula (as he dubbed him) would remain in a coffin for countless centuries, but contemporary art dealers take the coffin from his Transylvanian castle and transport it to LA. Free in LA, Blacula takes a number of victims (mostly people who anger him or threaten to reveal his identity) and tries to win the love of a woman who looks like his dead wife, who may in fact be a reincarnation of her. Interestingly, this vampire can fall in love *and* can make love (how happy he is—you've never seen a vampire smile so broadly and sincerely—when McGee hugs him and asks him to spend the night). Charismatic Thalmus Rasulala and his beautiful girlfriend, Denise Nicholas (of TV's *Room 222*), try to stop Blacula from escaping. He spends much time driving stakes into the hearts of Blacula's victims (who have become vampires) and she screams each time he does it. The direction by William Crain is passable at best—he was replaced by Bob Kelljan (*Count Yorga Vampire*) for the fine sequel, *Scream, Blacula, Scream*—but I like it when Marshall sort of glides through the air (is he wearing roller skates?) toward a female victim and later when she, a vampire too, charges down a hospital corridor after a victim of her own while Crain films her in effective slow motion. Also with: Elisha Cook, Jr., Gordon Pinsent.

BLADE RUNNER (1982) C/118m.

Although Ridley Scott's ambitious, loose adaptation of Philip K. Dick's *Do Androids Dream of Electric Sheep?* didn't do well when first released, it has since emerged as a cult favorite, a midnight-movie staple, and perhaps the first "thinking person's SF film" since *2001*. Setting is Los Angeles in 2019. Most people with money have left for other planets or live in fortresslike dwellings as protection from the poor people who flood the streets. Harrison Ford is a *blade runner*, a detective who tracks down replicants (sophisticated androids). He is forced back into service when several violent replicants who revolted on a distant planet return to earth with the intention of forcing the scientist-magnate who built them (Joe Turkel) to extend their brief life span. Ford's heart isn't in his job, especially when he falls in love with another replicant, Sean Young. Film has several exciting scenes— Ford chasing replicant Joanna Cassidy through the streets, being surprised by acrobatic replicant Daryl Hannah, battling replicant leader Rutger Hauer on a building ledge— but it's very deliberately paced and characterized by an overwhelming sense of melancholy and beautiful memories lost (even the replicants have been provided memories of non-existent youths). Slow pacing and Ford's *noir*-style narration (delivered in too weak a tone) are initially offputting, but the film improves immensely on second viewing because you know what to expect and can concentrate on the many exceptional aspects of the picture. Foremost, no picture since *Metropolis* has presented such a compelling vision of the future. Conceptual artist Syd Mead and designer Laurence G. Paull created a crowded, hazy city full of huge, deserted, or retro-fitted buildings (they called the style "retro-deco") where acid rain falls constantly, electric advertising covers the sides of buildings, and police spinners fly about. Everything looks old and unhealthy. In Dick's book the blade runner discovers that he is a replicant, but if that happened in the film, the final confrontation between Ford and Hauer wouldn't have special meaning. When Hauer allows Ford to live, this is the ultimate gesture in the SF cinema between machine and man. It gives hope that we can live in harmony. Also with: Edward James Olmos, William Sanderson, Brion James.

BLAZING SADDLES (1974) C/93m.

The townspeople of Rock Ridge realize that ruthless Hedley Lamarr (Harvey Korman) wants to destroy the town so the railroad can come through. They hire a black sheriff (Cleavon Little) to fight for them, because they don't care if he gets killed. He enlists the aid of a tipsy former gunfighter, the Waco Kid (Gene Wilder), and eventually gets the whole town to back him against Hedley's men. Although it was an enormous hit, I think Mel Brooks's western spoof is graceless and stupid. Scenes are like klunky *Carol Burnett Show* routines combined with stilted burlesque revue acts. Brooks consistently relies on either raunchy humor or anachronisms to get laughs. The humor is crude, rude, obvious, repetitive, self-impressed. There are laughs, but not many compared to the number of jokes and sight gags. Brooks shows no fondness for the western genre—in fact, his awful ending sequence shows how deeply he wanted to get back to the present. Little, Wilder, and Madeline Kahn (as a vamp) are funny, but nothing happens with their characters. Most famous scene has cowboys breaking wind around campfire. That indicates film's humor. Andrew Bergman and Richard Pryor were among the writers. Also with: Slim Pickens, Liam Dunn, Brooks (as a corrupt, sex-obsessed governor and a Jewish Indian), David Huddleston, Alex Karras, Dom DeLuise, John Hillerman, Carol Arthur.

BLITHE SPIRIT (BRITISH/1945) C/96m. Likable adaptation of Noël Coward's play, scripted by Coward, directed by David Lean, and photographed by Ronald Neame. While doing research for his next novel, haughty Rex Harrison asks eccentric Margaret Rutherford to conduct a séance, not believing anything will happen. The prankish ghost of his first wife (Kay Hammond) moves into his house, which doesn't set well with his current second wife (Constance Cummings). Cummings asks for Rutherford's help. Most amusing is how Harrison gets to like having two women around, fighting for him. It's great for the male ego. But then Cummings tells him that Hammond's planning to kill him so she can get him back. Coward's wartime lark makes an enjoyable film in the *Topper* tradition. You don't mind *these* characters getting on each other's nerves or having flustering experiences—but I think it would work better if Cummings were as obnoxious as Hammond and Harrison. Best performance is turned in by Rutherford, who is thrilled by the appearances of ghosts and doesn't feel responsible for the mess she has caused but can't rectify. Best scene has her telling off Cummings for not respecting her trade. Also with: Hugh Wakefield, Joyce Carey, Jacqueline Clark.

BLOB, THE (1958) C/86m. Gooey substance from outer space plops down near small American town and begins to grow, swallowing everyone in its path. It's up to some brave teenagers, led by Steve McQueen (his film debut), to stop it. Once a drive-in favorite, low-budget sci-fi film is still fun, even on the small home screen. For the creepy first half, indications are that it will be a terrific film, but it loses momentum and becomes stilted until the rousing conclusion. Interesting in that it is one of the few films of the fifties that was totally on the side of teenagers. Don't miss the title song. Directed by Irvin S. Yeaworth, Jr. Also with: Aneta Corseaut, Earl Rowe, Olin Howlin.

BLOCK-HEADS (1938) B&W/55m. Enjoyable Laurel-and-Hardy comedy, produced by Hal Roach, Jr. Stanley has just returned from the WWI trenches, 20 years after the war ended for everyone else. Longtime friend Oliver invites him home to meet his wife and, sure enough, Oliver's life turns topsy-turvy as the result of Stanley's presence. One thing after another happens to Oliver while Stanley looks on innocently. But, despite having his car ruined, having several men beat him up, having an explosion destroy his apartment, having his wife walk out on him, and having a neighbor chase him with a hunting rifle, Oliver remains loyal to Stanley. As in all their best films, their friendship is what matters most. Film hasn't many high points and the ending is too quick, but it's consistently amusing and a good showcase for the team's unique style. Harry Langdon was one of the five screenwriters, which may explain the abundance of slapstick and sight gags. Directed by John Blystone. Also with: Patricia Ellis, Minna Gombell, Billy Gilbert, Jimmy Finlayson.

BLONDE AMBITION (1981) C/84m. Ranks with *Cafe Flesh* as the best of the XXX-rated films; like that film, it has played midnight shows in legitimate theaters. It's a farce about the dizzy Kane sisters, Sugar (Suzy Mandell) and Candy (Dory Devon), who leave Wyoming and take their silly song-and-dance act to New York City. When their agent skips out on them, they find employment in a porno version of *Gone With the Wind*. Meanwhile Sugar mixes up her cheap brooch with her aunt's priceless brooch. In order to get it back, the sisters go into a gay nightclub, pretending to be transvestites. The sex is explicit, but not raunchy or violent—few will be offended and most viewers will find themselves aroused and amused by the way it is handled. Porno's greatest failing has been its inability to provide humor along with sex; most porno comedies have been abysmal. But this film is genuinely funny. Sexy Suzy Mandell (a Benny Hill regular) is a really fine comedienne; it's a shame that Hollywood no longer has "dumb blonde" roles because she could fill them easily. Directed with a light touch by John and Lem Amero. Their cast seems to be having fun. Also with: Eric Edwards, Jamie Gillis, Molly Malone, Richard Bolla, Wade Parker.

BLONDE VENUS (1932) B&W/97m. The most underrated of the seven Josef von Sternberg–Marlene Dietrich collaborations. Ex-singer Dietrich lives in New York with scientist husband Herbert Marshall and their young son, Dickie Moore. When Marshall gets radium poisoning, Dietrich becomes a nightclub entertainer to raise money to pay for medical expenses. Playboy Cary Grant immediately becomes attracted to her and gives her enough money for Marshall to go abroad for treatment. Of course, she doesn't tell her husband where she got the money. When Marshall returns from Europe, he discovers that Dietrich has been having an affair with Grant. Afraid of losing her son, Dietrich takes Moore into hiding. She makes small amounts of money performing in out-of-the-way places and, when detectives close in, through prostitution. Throughout she remains a caring, sacrificing mother—one of the sexiest *mothers* in the history of the cinema. The story sounds trite, but Sternberg's treatment is consistently surprising: Dietrich sings her famous "Hot Voodoo" number while wearing a fuzzy white wig and a gorilla suit and "I Couldn't Be Annoyed" while dressed in a man's white tuxedo; she happens upon a weird assortment of characters in her descent into hell and winds up sleeping in some bizarre dives, including one place in which hens and chickens run free. Dietrich gives one of her finest stiff-upper-lip performances, again playing a strong, selfless woman who is willing to sacrifice herself for others' happiness (even if it means giving her body) and to face the consequences for her sins. She sees no need to apologize or defend herself to Marshall for what she did on his behalf, nor does she expect him to understand or forgive her. The schmaltzy but still wonderful tear-jerking finale was once controversial because American audiences didn't think a moral husband like Marshall would forgive Dietrich after she had thoroughly degraded herself. The script was written by Jules Furthman and S. K. Lauren, Bert Glennon contributed the inspired cinematography, and Wiard Ihnen served as art director. Also with: Gene Morgan, Rita La Roy, Hattie McDaniel.

BLOOD FEAST (1963) C/70m.
Homicidal maniac Fuad Ramses (Mal Arnold smartly disappeared after this screen appearance) kills young women in brutal fashion, collecting a part from each body to use in ceremonial rite to Ishtar. Detective Pete Thornton (Thomas Wood) hunts him down, not realizing he's the very man who'll soon cater an Egyptian feast for Thornton's girlfriend, Suzette (Connie Mason). Fittingly, Ramses ends up killed in the garbage, which is where this vile trash should be. This is the first "splatter" film, the first of goremeister Herschell Gordon Lewis's "blood trilogy," and one of the sickest, most inept films ever made. The acting is ghastly (Mason and Arnold can be seen reading their cue cards; Mason always crosses her arms as if freezing), the casting abominable, camera work clumsy, and ex-playmate Mason wears too much clothing. Ten minutes into the film, I stop laughing at the picture's badness and start to get a migraine. Several characters have infernal voices. Picture has camp value, to be sure, but one wonders about Lewis cultists who thrill to no-holds-barred violence and disgusting images, and want to know exactly how Lewis accomplishes the famous effect in which Ramses rips a tongue out of a woman's mouth—it's the scene they consider the picture's highlight. If you detest horror films that show how many shocking ways a creative sadist can do away with young women, then Lewis is the man you'll want to blame and this is the film you'll want to burn. Also with: Lyn Boulton, Scott H. Hall, Toni Calvert, Astrid Olson.

BLOOD MONEY (1933) B&W/65m.
A terrific find, with George Bancroft as a shady bailbondsman who rubs shoulders with criminals as well as judges, policemen, and lawyers. He has had a long relationship with nightclub owner Judith Anderson, but falls for young, spoiled thrill-seeker Frances Dee, whom he bails out on a shoplifting charge. When Anderson's young brother, Chick Chandler, is arrested for robbing cash and bonds from a bank, she reluctantly asks Bancroft to help him. When she thinks Bancroft double-crossed Chandler because Dee has fallen for the younger man, she asks her mobster contacts to break him. It turns out that Dee was responsible for the misunderstanding between Bancroft and Chandler. Anderson tries to save Bancroft from an assassination attempt. Interestingly written and directed by the notorious Rowland Brown, who refuses to moralize about one's participation in crime—which he considers a legitimate business during the Depression, one that helps cities run smoothly—because a person has no obligation to lead the *clean* life (there is no such thing in Brown's world). The only crime of which a person must be ashamed and for which there must be retribution is a double-cross. If you get caught committing murder or thievery, etc., you just shrug your shoulders and go to jail

without regrets; you knew the rules. Picture has good acting, a solid storyline, and tremendous dialogue—all lines have double meanings. Film is full of humor and punch, creative, offbeat touches, and characters (especially women) that break stereotypes. Bancroft is an oddball because he is no softy—he's a hero who takes advantage of all people in trouble ("losers"), even kindly old ladies. The love-friendship relationship between Bancroft and Anderson (her film debut) is most unusual. Really remarkable is outrageously sexy Dee, who is a crime maniac, a kleptomaniac, and, in the last scene, a masochist—she goes off to meet a stranger she hopes will molest her. A woman years ahead of her time. Also with: Joe Sawyer, Blossom Seeley (who sings a couple of great songs), J. Carrol Naish, Etienne Girardot, Paul Fix.

BLOOD OF A POET, THE/SANG D'UN POÈTE, LE (FRENCH/1930) B&W/55m.
Jean Cocteau's first film begins and ends with an exploding chimney; in between are four segments, each expressing through a series of puzzling visuals (making use of various camera tricks) the difficulty a poet has in artistically confronting "reality." Journey of poet is weird trip where visual metaphors and symbols are used to emphasize the *artist*'s break with traditional forms. Statues come to life, people turn into statues, people pass through mirrors, a woman flies, abstract images move about the frame. This classic work has long been admired by Surrealists (although it's usually considered too structured to be a surrealist piece) and *avant-garde* filmmakers—for them it is required viewing; others may have to fight boredom and confusion, perhaps just to catch glimpses of Cocteau's future films: for instance, the snowball fight (which seems misplaced here) would reappear in the Cocteau-scripted *Les Enfants Terribles*. Not for all tastes, but it's interesting considering who made it and how long ago it was made. Cocteau serves as narrator.

BLOOD SIMPLE (1985) C/96m.
An exciting debut effort directed by Joel Coen and produced by his brother Ethan. They blend elements of forties *noir* mysteries (particularly the works of James M. Cain), Alfred Hitchcock thrillers, and present-day horror movies. A tough bar owner (Dan Hedaya) hires a slimy, sadistic private eye (M. Emmet Walsh) to kill his wife (Frances McDormand looks a bit like track star Mary Decker) and her not-too-quick lover (John Getz), one of his employees. But stranger, more complicated things happen instead. Everyone on screen becomes untrusting, nervous, and bewildered. And *everyone* is in jeopardy. Most interestingly: during the film's course McDormand never realizes Walsh exists—she believes her husband is personally trying to kill her. In the last scene we come to realize just how frightened she was of Hedaya, and how thoroughly he must have possessed her. (For those interested in screenwriting, figure out what problems the Coens would have run into if Hedaya's loyal dog didn't inexplicably disappear from the film.) The film is too violent for some viewers and the direction is at times self-conscious,

but it's impressive how the young filmmakers build suspense through expert use of light and space, by choosing interesting sets, and by using a mobile, searching camera to reveal detail. Film is well cast, with both Hedaya and Walsh giving standout performances.

BLOOD WEDDING (SPANISH/1981) C/72m.

Spain's celebrated director Carlos Saura joined forces with Antonio Gades, famed classical dancer, to show how film could bring intimacy to and enhance the excitement of dance. Saura films what is supposed to be a dress rehearsal of Gades's flamenco version of García Lorca's passionate tragedy *Bodas de Sangre*, in which a new bride (Cristina Hoyos) is torn between her groom (Juan Antonio Jimenez) and her former lover (Gades). Because Saura wants us to feel the importance of what we're about to see—and have us feel it's more than a rehearsal—he pulls a couple of tricks: he takes us into the dancers' dressing rooms so we can get to know them personally, and he has a female dancer state how nervous she is about the *rehearsal*, not the performance. The rehearsal takes place in a large, bare rehearsal hall; what Saura and Gades attempt is to make us become so involved with the dancing and the characters that we forget about the minimal set and perhaps imagine that the light filtering through the background windows is Lorca's moon. The dancers perform with passion and intense sexuality, and Saura moves his camera among them, floating into a close-up or waiting for a dancer to spin toward him and stop dramatically right before the lens. It is intimate. And the dancers exhibit grace, beauty, and, for the most part, precision (once or twice you can spot one dancer's foot touch the floor quicker than the others). But I find Gades's choreography pretty conventional, and at one low point in a lovers' sexual dance the couple put their heads together and appear to be doing push-ups. At no time does an individual dancer amaze you with a burst of remarkable talent. Furthermore, I do find the setting distracting—although if it had been a stage performance being filmed, the impact of the jarring final shot would be dissipated. Film isn't boring, even for those who don't like dance, and, it should be noted, when I saw it at a large screening, it received immense applause.

BLOW OUT (1981) C/107m.

A film that allowed Brian De Palma to combine his obsessions with the Kennedy assassination–conspiracy, the themes of Antonioni's *Blow-Up*, and the visual style of Hitchcock. John Travolta is a sound-effects man for a Philadelphia company that makes low-budget exploitation films. While out alone at night recording sounds, he hears a tire blow out and sees a car plummet into a river. He saves a young woman (Nancy Allen), but the other passenger, a presidential candidate, drowns. Travolta discovers that the extremely naïve, passive, and always exploited Allen—who dreams of being a Hollywood beautician—was part of a plot by sleazy private eye Dennis Franz to blackmail the candidate. He also learns that no one was supposed to be killed. Listening to his recordings, he comes across the sound of a gunshot just before the tire blow out. But he can't convince the police that someone murdered the politician. Now the killer (John Lithgow) wants to get rid of all witnesses. The first half of the picture is prime De Palma, but then the picture becomes bogged down with self-conscious camera work. De Palma deprives us of a love scene between Travolta and Allen and refuses to develop Allen's character—as if he were afraid we'd become too angry with him when we see what he has in store for her. Imagine how you would have felt in *Time After Time* if after Malcolm McDowell tracked down maniac David Warner and abducted Mary Steenburgen, Warner had killed her anyway. That's how badly you'll feel at the end of this film. If you don't care about the characters, you'll be intrigued by the editing in the final sequence. Also with: Peter Boyden, Curt May.

BLOW-UP (BRITISH-ITALIAN/1966) C/108m.

Michelangelo Antonioni's landmark film was greeted with tremendous excitement and adulation when it was released. It was the era's "art film for the masses," a hip, mysterious, visually exhilarating foreign film that had us eagerly mulling over symbols, color patterns, and hidden meanings in the storyline; trying to answer *that* question—"What's the difference between illusion and reality?"—that turned up too often on literature exams; and deeply contemplating the natures of cameras, images (film, photographs), and those people who make their living with a camera. The setting is swinging, mod London, where David Hemmings is a fashion photographer. Hemmings displays only arrogance and insolence when working with his female models; while shooting what are essentially false notions of reality (the heavily made-up, sexily dressed beauties), he too slips casually into pretense, getting his models to look aroused by pretending he is turned on by their beauty and using his camera as an instrument of seduction—but when he completes his last shot, the bored Hemmings will immediately desert the frustrated model and leave her lying on the floor. He lives a frivolous fantasy life and it will take something drastic to knock him out of his complacency and make him distinguish between what is real and illusionary, what is trivial and important. While filming peaceful shots in a park for a book to which he actually is contributing *serious* real-life pictures, he innocently photographs a woman (Vanessa Redgrave) and a man she is with. When she comes to his studio to plead for the photographs, he becomes suspicious that something important happened in the park. He blows up several pictures and discovers what he believes to be a man holding a gun standing in the bushes; a blow-up of a later photograph reveals what could be a dead body lying in the bushes. That night he returns to the park and finds the body of the man Redgrave had been with. When he goes back the next morning, the body is missing; and his photos have been stolen. There is no proof that what he saw was real. Hemmings must question his own mind; he can't swear that the images in the photos were accurate— they may have been only what he wanted to see, what he imagined. Antonioni's point is that the introduction of a camera always distorts reality; also: since each person has singular sensibilities, no individual is capable of seeing Truth (a second person would have a different perspective on the same image). This once vital film is dated and its flimsiness and pretentiousness are more evident today. Yet watch it as a document of its time, to see the fancy camera work that turned us on, the nudity that had us blushing, the Yardbirds performing in front of catatonic youths, the mod clothes, and Hemmings tossing the invisible tennis ball to the mimes—an image that, for some reason, remains one of the most indelible in cinema history. Antonioni's picture altered the style of the cinema and enlarged its audience—for that we can always think of it fondly. From a weird short story by Julio Cortázar. Also with: Sarah Miles, John Castle, teenage Jane Birkin (on her way to becoming a European sex symbol), Peter Bowles, Verushka.

BLUE ANGEL, THE (GERMAN/1930) B&W/ 90m.

Josef von Sternberg returned to Germany to film this adaptation of Heinrich Mann's prewar novel *Professor Unrath*. It was at the request of Emil Jannings, whom he'd directed to an Oscar in *The Last Command*. Sternberg got an even more memorable performance from Jannings as the respected high-school professor who gives up his position and his dignity when he becomes husband to the Blue Angel's sexy songstress Lola Lola. But the director was more fascinated with Jannings's unknown co-star, Marlene Dietrich, still exhibiting baby fat. With her casual manner toward men (she was ready to skip out on lovers when she got bored and restless), her lack of ego (but a profound knowledge that she is the only one who will take care of her), her ironic attitude toward the hypocritical world and its strict moral code—men like the tyrannical professor condemn her, but secretly desire her—her willingness to satisfy her own physical needs no matter who gets hurt, and her tantalizing beauty, she personified sinful sex, available to any man who would get in line. Like Lulu in *Pandora's Box*, Lola Lola has often wrongly been judged by critics as a completely devious man-killer. But Lola Lola doesn't plan to humiliate the professor by exploiting his masochism—in fact, she marries him because she is touched by his gallant defense of her character and she tries to be a good wife despite his journey into drunkenness, slovenliness, and worthlessness—Sternberg even shows her in an apron, cooking for him, as if this had become commonplace. Other women might have kicked him out immediately—but she sticks with him long past his degradation (from which she gets no pleasure), until the inevitable moment when she finds herself—as she sings—"Falling in love again, can't help it." Like Lulu, her major "crimes" are: her very existence causes men to fall foolishly in love; she's so casual about sex that she never stops a man from entering a path toward self-destruction. Masterpiece is splendidly made and deeply moving. Most interesting is how Sternberg not only surrounds his actress with beautiful decor but actually presents her in his frame as part of the decor—the spider within the web that is Lola Lola's cluttered, jungle-like dressing room. An English version was made simultaneously. Remade in 1959 with Curt Jurgens and May Britt. Also with: Kurt Gerron, Rosa Valetti, Hans Albers.

BLUE COLLAR (1978) C/114m.

Excellent, unusual film by Paul Schrader, which he wrote with brother Leonard, about three financially strapped Detroit auto workers (blacks Richard Pryor and Yaphet Kotto, white Harvey Keitel) who rob their corrupt union's safe. The union figures out they were responsible, but won't act because Pryor took a notebook containing data on the union's illegal transactions. For a while the picture threatens to become a comedy, perhaps like *9 to 5*, in which three exploited employees "screw" the boss. Comedy: the threesome is called the "Oreo Gang"; Pryor endures the embarrassing-to-blacks *The Jeffersons* because his TV cost so much; Pryor tries to pass off his neighbors' children as his own to a tax investigator; and—my favorite bit of humor—Pryor refers to a woman as a "fox" and the startled Kotto calls her a "bow-wow." But when the union gets serious, the comedy disappears. Kotto and Keitel find their lives in jeopardy; when the politically savvy Kotto is out of the scene, Pryor is vulnerable to seduction by the union, which offers him a higher-salaried union position. Cult film is strongly written, provocative, extremely well acted. Schrader's to be commended for having two of his three leads be black. The action sequences are genuinely frightening. I don't think the Schraders intended this film to be anti-union; they just wanted to attack this corrupt union local. But it's interesting that Kotto's words which end the film—about how *they* want rank-and-file whites like Keitel and blacks like Pryor to fight against each other instead of against their real common enemy—refer to the union when such political rhetoric is usually reserved for management. Also with: Harry Bellaver (the union head), George Memmoli, Lucy Saroyan, Cliff De Young, Ed Begley, Jr., Lane Smith, Borah Silver.

BLUE GARDENIA, THE (1953) B&W/90m.

Dumped by her soldier boyfriend on her birthday, Anne Baxter impulsively accepts a date with an artist (Raymond Burr) she doesn't know—at an LA restaurant, the Blue Gardenia. Having had too much to drink, she goes with him to his apartment. When he makes improper advances, she strikes him with a poker. She wakes up the next morning remembering nothing after leaving the restaurant. But when Burr is reported dead, with her shoes and handkerchief in his apartment, she worries that the police manhunt will lead to her door. Paranoid that everyone suspects her, she contacts the ace reporter (Richard Conte) who has been covering the case and promising her help (which he can't deliver, she discovers) if she will give him an exclusive. Mediocre Fritz Lang film takes too long to get started, forcing the final, more interesting scenes to be rushed. Typically, Lang has Baxter ignore her moral senses for a slight indiscretion, fall into fate's trap, become involved in a crime that she might be convicted of whether innocent or guilty, and become increasingly paranoid that she is alone and everyone is pointing accusing fingers. Significantly, this is only time Lang lets this happen to a woman. Also with: Ann Sothern, Jeff Donnell, Richard Erdman, George Reeves, Nat "King" Cole (who performs the title song).

BLUE LAGOON, THE (1980) C/104m.
Back in 1980 most teenage boys would have had their wet dreams come true if they had gotten to spend years on a desert island with Brooke Shields. But the poor girl had the bad luck of getting shipwrecked with Christopher Atkins, perhaps Hollywood's most revolting and conceited young actor. Every time he puts his hands on her, you want to gag. And he does this often because their characters wander nude (Brooke has a double, not Chrissie) or scantily clad along the sandy beaches and through the jungles, becoming increasingly attracted to each other as they grow older and their bodies mature. They become young lovers, they become parents. This remake of the tasteful, enjoyable 1949 British film with Jean Simmons and Donald Houston has for years been mocked. It's a terribly made film—although the Willie Aames–Phoebe Cates ripoff *Paradise* makes it seem like *Citizen Kane*—and Atkins should be drowned, but, surprisingly, youth counselors contended that in many cases it had a positive effect on young girls (who'd simply gone to the film to see Brooke). For many of them, who never had proper sexual education in school or at home, this film was their primer on how pregnancy can occur and what happens during childbirth. So maybe we shouldn't laugh so hard. A glorious setting, beautifully photographed by Nestor Almendros. But Randal Kleiser, who is fascinated by young bodies cavorting in the water or on beach locales (remember *Summer Lovers*?), might well have been directing a Caribbean tourist commercial. Also with: William Daniels, Leo McKern.

BLUEBEARD (1944) B&W/73m.
In his best lead performance and one of the few in which he doesn't succumb to hamminess, John Carradine is a deranged artist who strangles all his female models after painting their portraits. They remind him of a previous love who did him wrong and became his first victim. It's amazing how wide Carradine's eyes become before he bounds across his room/studio and grabs his surprised models around the neck. Low-budget PRC production is strikingly directed by cult favorite Edgar G. Ulmer, who makes great use of close-ups, shadows, and bizarre camera angles. Expressionistic film has European look to it. A real sleeper. Also with: Jean Parker, Nils Asther, Ludwig Stossel, Iris Adrian.

BLUES BROTHERS, THE (1980) C/130m.
When blues singer Jake (John Belushi) gets out of prison—he pulled a stick-up to pay his band's hotel tab—he and brother Elwood (Dan Aykroyd) decide to put the Blues Brothers Band back together in order to make $5000 to save the orphanage in which they were raised. As if they were ex-soldiers rounding up the regiment to perform an impossible mission, they track down the ex-band members. Then they try to get a gig in Chicago area. Meanwhile police, an angry C&W band, and a female assassin (Carrie Fisher) are on their trail. Belushi and Aykroyd reprised their *Saturday Night Live* roles as white blues singers (they look like members of the Sicilian Mafia) who idolize blues greats. Their dress is more interesting than their personalities—and they aren't strong enough to carry such a long film; their blues singing is weak, and, as many jealous blues singers complained, "lacks soul"—seeing the audience within the movie get on its feet to sing along is farfetched or goes to show young people will accept anything from *SNL* vets. John Landis film is polished and contains many good sight gags, but there isn't much good verbal wit. Storyline is slim and the two stars just walk through their one-dimensional parts (see how much better Aykroyd is in Landis's subsequent *Trading Places*). One also has to be tired of big-budget commercial films that hope to make profits by pretending to be anti-materialistic, having scenes in which property is cavalierly destroyed. The film is famous for its lengthy demolition-derby car-chase sequence, but I much prefer musical highlights featuring Aretha Franklin, Cab Calloway (doing "Minnie the Moocher") and even the Blues Brothers singing "Rawhide" to placate rowdy Country and Western fans. Also with: John Candy, Henry Gibson, Charles Napier, Kathleen Freeman, Steve Lawrence, Steven Spielberg, Twiggy, Ray Charles, James Brown, John Lee Hooker, Frank Oz, Chaka Khan.

BOB & CAROL & TED & ALICE (1969) C/105m.
Still funny debut film by Paul Mazursky, about the changing and confused sexual mores of the upper middle class in Southern California during the late sixties. Documentary filmmaker Robert Culp and wife Natalie Wood spend time at a sensitivity-encounter institute getting in touch with their feelings. Afterward they are brutally honest with their thoughts, tell everyone "I love you," and have extramarital one-night stands which they're open about. Good friends Dyan Cannon and her lawyer husband, Elliott Gould, don't know what to make of the change in Culp and Wood. They become sick when Culp and Wood share their personal experiences with them. They feel uptight, question their own relationship, and have a different attitude toward sex (Cannon refuses to have sex with Gould, Gould contemplates an affair). During a group vacation the four contemplate *wife-swapping*—a subject that was making headlines in 1969. Script by Larry Tucker was not as thematically daring as it pretended to be: this is a mainstream movie with an ending—called a "cop-out" at the time—that allowed middle-class viewers to go home happy. But until the end the picture is well written and contains many hilarious vignettes, including an aroused Gould and a disinterested Cannon (both new film stars) in bed after hearing of Culp's infidelity; Culp telling Wood of his affair and becoming slightly annoyed that she's not jealous; Cannon talking to her psychiatrist about her sexual confusion; Culp offering a drink to Wood's nervous lover. One problem, however,

is that all four characters come across like jerks by the end—that is, until they learn the picture's theme: "totally honest" people are the biggest phonies of them all. In her adult roles Wood was never prettier. Also with: Horst Ebersberg, K. T. Stevens, Greg Mullavey, Lee Bergere, Garry Goodrow.

BOB LE FLAMBEUR (FRENCH/1955) B&W/102m.
Elegant, classy caper film by Jean-Pierre Melville, France's foremost director of crime dramas. George Duschene is the gentlemanly, white-haired Bob "the gambler," a moral ex-con who is on an endless losing streak, in life, love, and, of course, gambling. He has kept clean for years, but when the young woman (Isabel Corey) he brings home, not for sex but to keep her off the streets, turns out to be an emotionless tramp (as Jean Seberg would be in *Breathless*) and sleeps with his young friend, Bob impulsively decides to organize a daring heist at a casino. He continues with his plan even when he finds out that a pimp on a vendetta against Bob has squealed to the police about the robbery. Film is like Kubrick's *The Killing*, made a year later, in that it brings together a group of sympathetic men—here they are more refined—to pull off an impossible robbery; much emphasis is placed on the planning of the crime; wives and lovers of the men foil the plot because of greed or indifference (the one good female is Bob's bartender friend); and the men are at the mercy of Fate. But Melville's picture neither looks nor feels like any other caper film. Floating camera gives the visuals a "poetic" quality. We worry about Bob, yet the picture is so easygoing that we have a chance to enjoy the sights as he drives through the wide streets of Montmartre. Picture has interesting characters, smart dialogue, several truly unusual scenes, including the off-the-wall finale. It's too bad that it didn't get better international distribution upon release (it didn't play in the U.S. until 1982) because the tantalizing Corey might have received the same attention as a Bardot or a Seberg. Also with: Daniel Cauchy, Guy Decomble, Andre Garet, Gerard Buhr, Howard Vernon.

BODY AND SOUL (1947) B&W/104m.
This anti-boxing *noir* classic was powerfully directed by Robert Rossen and starred John Garfield, the screen's romantic rebel and symbol for the immigrant poor. Garfield found an ideal role as Jewish boxer Charley Gordon, a decent tenement dweller who becomes a boxer to earn much-needed money and is quickly corrupted. (As in *Golden Boy*, the boxing arena represents hell.) Money and fame become an obsession, and Charley doesn't understand why his mother (Anne Revere) and smart fiancée (a fine performance by Lilli Palmer) turn away from him as he makes his way upward. Even though he signs a contract with a gangster (Joseph Pevney), Charley wrongly believes he will have autonomy once he becomes champ. But he's ordered to take a dive and lose his title, and can't refuse because he's so deeply in debt. In the thrilling boxing finale, intensely shot by James Wong Howe, Charley decides that he'll take a dive for no one. Money doesn't matter as much as integrity.

Script by Marxist Abraham Polonsky is an indictment of capitalism. Boxing is shown to be similar to any ruthless mainstream business. Employers not only exploit their boxer employees but own them by virtue of a contract; the employees, having no union, *literally* fight against one another in order to gain a higher rank; money not only is a corruptive influence on men but, in truth, men—who are both employees and the *product*—equate with money/revenue. Polonsky speaks of the dignity of poverty (as represented by Revere, who will take none of her son's earnings) and, through designer Palmer (whose career moves along as swiftly as Charley's, without her selling her soul), he pays respect to the artist. Also with: William Conrad, Canada Lee.

BODY DOUBLE (1984) C/114m.
Disappointing suspense thriller by Brian De Palma. That he borrows from Hitchcock's *Vertigo*, *Rear Window*, and *Psycho* is not as annoying as his repeating himself—he makes so sure his scenes have parallels in Hitchcock that his own storyline gets muddled. Craig Wasson plays a third-rank actor who has acute claustrophobia, making him the perfect patsy in Gregg Henry's murder plans. Henry offers Wasson a place to stay and supposedly leaves town. Wasson becomes obsessed with spying through his telescope at a nearby apartment, where a beautiful woman does an exotic nude dance by the window. He doesn't realize that the woman who lives there (Deborah Shelton) is not the woman (Melanie Griffith) doing the dance. He worries that the woman he's watching is in danger, because he has spotted someone else (an Indian) spying on her. One night he looks through his telescope and witnesses Shelton being attacked. He races to the rescue—too late; and, of course, it looks like he is the murderer. De Palma's camera is fluid, and his direction is so imaginative at times that you almost gasp. But Wasson's much duller here than in other films; the storyline's so predictable that the intricacy of De Palma's direction seems wasted; and when De Palma starts showing off with one of his long non-dialogue passages (when Wasson follows Shelton), the picture becomes boring. The nature of Shelton's murder (with a drill that the killer clutches between his legs) was just De Palma doing a little feminist-baiting in hopes of making his picture controversial enough to be a big moneymaker. His ploy didn't work. As a platinum-blonde porno star, Melanie Griffith is the best reason to see this picture. English rock group Frankie Goes to Hollywood made their appearance here before they played America.

BODY HEAT (1981) C/113m.
It's almost as if director-writer Lawrence Kasdan lucked upon footage from a *noir* classic that, for some reason, was missing actors—so all he had to do was photograph actors of his own using a script that utilized the sets and look of that old film and then mix the new footage with the old. Film so closely resembles—visually and thematically—classic *noir* films such as *Double Indemnity* that many critics complained that Kasdan was playing the copycat. But I'm impressed by what I think is a film lover's attempt to re-create the *noir* style

so he could thoroughly explore the elements that made it so fascinating—just as he'd utilize the western format for *Silverado*. My guess is that this picture's reputation will improve dramatically as Kasdan's output grows and he directs variations on other genres. There's a stifling heat wave in Florida. As blood boils, sweat covers the skin, adrenaline flows, young fourth-rate lawyer William Hurt has a tempestuous affair with married Kathleen Turner (her debut as Matty Walker); he's not very smart, so this femme fatale has little trouble getting him to plunge into her spiderweb. He's the one who suggests that they kill her wealthy husband (Richard Crenna). Of course, that was her plan even before she met this patsy. But is she completely heartless? I keep wondering why she turns her head so she won't see her husband killed. Picture has a sharply written, almost campily humorous script; exciting, sexually explicit scenes; strong performances by Hurt, Turner (what a versatile actress she has proven herself to be), Crenna, Ted Danson (as Hurt's DA friend), and Mickey Rourke (who teaches Hurt how to use explosives). Photographed by Richard H. Kline; with a moody score by John Barry. Also with: J. A. Preston, Kim Zimmer, Mitchell Ryan.

BODY SNATCHER, THE (1945) B&W/77m.
In 19th-century Edinburgh, great surgeon and teacher Dr. McFarlane (Henry Daniell) needs bodies to carry out his necessary work. He hires the despicable coachman Mr. Gray (Boris Karloff) to provide him with cadavers. At first Gray robs graves, but then he begins committing murders to meet the quota. While both men are culpable for the crimes, McFarland basks in wealth and fame while poor Gray lives in a stable. Gray's sole pleasure comes from associating with McFarlane and also, to humble him, tormenting him about his past misdeeds. In other horror films produced by Val Lewton, the good-and-evil battle raged within individuals. But in this Jekyll-and-Hyde variation (from Robert Louis Stevenson), the war is between two men, "good" McFarlane and "evil" Gray. The irony is that McFarlane has an evil side (embodied by Gray) that he denies (he won't acknowledge his sins) and Gray has a good side (embodied by McFarlane) that he denies (he goads McFarlane into performing an operation that enables a crippled girl to walk). So they aren't really two people but, as Gray contends, "of the same skin." That's why Gray can confidently tell McFarlane, "You'll never get rid of me." Lewton co-wrote the film under his pulp-novel pseudonym Carlos Keith. Its script is refreshingly literate, but in truth overwritten and dull in spots. Whenever Daniell and Karloff are both at their wonderful peaks, the production is classy, and the subplot that allowed Lewton to introduce another of his lonely little girls fits nicely into the morbid proceedings. Moreover, Robert Wise's depiction of the "horror" sequences is superb, and tasteful. Particularly spooky is the scene in which Gray kills a street singer (Donna Lee). While Fate, which has an evil connotation in Lewton, plays a part in this story, as in all his films, this is the first time Providence gained an upper hand. It is made clear that it was God who gave McFarlane the skills to successfully operate on the little girl. Also with: Bela Lugosi, Edith Atwater, Russell Wade, Rita Corday.

BOLERO/BO'S BOLERO (1984) C/106m.
The worst film of 1984 is no more than a home movie by director John Derek. He shoots so many close-ups of smiling wife Bo Derek that perhaps this was intended to be a tribute to her dentist. Bo may not be the worst actress around, but combine her blank-minded love-child persona with the nauseating heiress she plays here and the results are deadly. Although the plot about a young woman (Bo is a virgin!) in pursuit of ecstasy is classic porno material, the heavily promoted sexual content is so tame that it could run on cable back-to-back with a Koo Stark opus. Too bad: instead of being X-citing, as promised, it is incredibly BO-ring—you don't laugh at the film, but at yourself for sitting through it. Derek said he wanted the world to see how sexy Bo is when nude, but his film is anti-erotic. Every time Derek sets up a feverish love encounter for his wife, he undermines it with disruptive humor or stupid dialogue. There is one unforgettable slow-motion sex scene in which a sheik licks honey off Bo's tummy and all this disgusting gooey stuff forms on his face and hangs from his nose. Also with: George Kennedy, Andrea Occhipinti, Ana Obregon, Olivia D'Abo.

BOOMERANG (1947) B&W/88m.
Dated, overrated semidocumentary by Elia Kazan. A priest is murdered in a Connecticut town and a confused drifter (Arthur Kennedy) is arrested. Deprived of sleep by the police, he confesses to the crime. Trial becomes a major political issue, and a conviction could help lead a state's attorney (Dana Andrews) to the governor's office. But Andrews conducts an impartial investigation, which leads him to believe Kennedy is innocent. What starts out to be a daring attack on corrupt machine politics, mob violence, press irresponsibility, and fascist police tactics (when they drag in anybody wearing a dark coat and white hat, one wonders if Kazan— later a friendly witness before H.U.A.C.—was commenting on anti-Communist hysteria) turns out to be the glorification of an honest man; it's perfect fare for civics classes in Middle America. The trouble is that Andrews is the only character who comes out smelling like a rose. Another problem is that the case was never solved. By presenting another suspect (a perverted fellow about whom the priest was about to tell authorities), Kazan is unfairly manipulative—it's unlikely this man would kill the priest in front of so many witnesses when he knows most everyone in town. I also find it unfair of Kazan not to let on that Andrews was conducting a serious investigation until the hearing—we were led to believe it is only a hunch that makes him think Kennedy innocent. Best scene has Andrews and his wife (Jane Wyatt) cuddled in a chair. Based on a case of Homer Cummings, who became Franklin Roosevelt's Attorney General. From *Reader's Digest* story "The Perfect Case" by Anthony Abbott (Fulton Oursler). Also with: Lee J.

Cobb, Sam Levene, Ed Begley, Cara Williams, Taylor Holmes, Karl Malden, Robert Keith, Joe Kazan, Bert Freed.

BOOT, DAS/BOAT, THE (WEST GERMAN/ 1982) C/150m.
Award-winning, epic WWII film by director Wolfgang Petersen, whose script was adapted from a popular autobiographical novel by former war correspondent Lothar-Günther Buchheim about the last mission of the German navy's U-96. Well-made picture shows a different, harrowing side of war: that experienced by Germany's 40,000 U-boat men, of whom more than half were killed. We are made to feel their discomfort and claustrophobia while inside their cramped, muggy, smelly, underwater vessel; their monotony, constant fear, and panic when enemy ships hover above. The picture is frightening because Petersen uses horror-movie techniques: the giant enemy ships emerging from the mist and lurching through the water are like great sea serpents; the sweating, shouting, terrified men rushing about the ship in search of danger points (where water leaks in) could very well be characters in *Alien*; the U-96 itself is like a room in a haunted house, where the trapped men nervously listen to the spooky noises (i.e., death knells) on the outside. These men are in hell. Petersen's goal was to show that all men in war are victims, certainly not a controversial theme. The picture has been criticized by those who thought Petersen—who chose not to deal with the soldiers' politics—was apologizing for the Nazi soldiers. Here, viewers must deal with the issue on an individual basis—if you find yourself sympathizing with these Germans and rooting for them as if they were Allied soldiers, then you'll have reason to be angry with Petersen; on the other hand, if you like the picture because you learned a bit of history, you'll have no gripe. At very least the film should be praised for debunking a myth that was held forth in Germany for 40 years—that German submarine warfare was a heroic, glorious adventure. Story became a five-hour German TV movie. Jürgen Prochnow makes a strong impression as the U-boat's commander, who hates his superiors and war; he sounds meaner in the American-dubbed version. Also with: Herbert Grönemeyer, Klaus Wennemann, Günter Lamprecht (*Berlin Alexanderplatz*), Hubertus Bengsch.

BORN TO DANCE (1936) B&W/105m.
Quintessential Eleanor Powell musical is corny and campy, yet enjoyable. She's an ice-cream-soda-sipping smalltown girl who tries to make it in New York as the understudy of the star (Virginia Bruce) of a Broadway show. She falls in love with a sailor (James Stewart) on leave, but gives him the runaround. She believes he's been stepping out with Bruce. He stops pursuing her when she convinces him she's married and mother of a girl, actually the young daughter of her best friend (Una Merkel). Still he tries to get her a break through the show's producer. Silly story with unconvincing plot twist—Bruce suddenly becomes *impossible*—that allows Powell to *star* in the show. But there's some okay comedy featuring Merkel and Sid Silvers as her sailor husband, whom she hasn't seen since they married during a marathon dance four years ago, and a fine, varied Cole Porter score, including "I've Got You Under My Skin." Too many people sing (Stewart has three songs), but Buddy Ebsen's on hand to do his "crazy legs" dancing and Powell—who, when standing still, looks like she'd be a crummy *Amateur Hour* contestant—is absolutely terrific (especially when doing turns) in her tap routines. Watch for the switchboard operator, who anticipated by thirty years Lily Tomlin's Ernestine. Carefree Depression Era musical was directed by Roy Del Ruth. Also with: Frances Langford, Raymond Walburn.

BORN YESTERDAY (1950) B&W/103m.
Judy Holliday won an Oscar for her sparkling portrayal of Billie Dawn, the character she'd played on Broadway for three years. This character would pave the way for numerous other dumb blondes in the fifties. Holliday is a former chorine who gave up working to be mistress of stupid, rough, "uncouth" (as she'll later say), corrupt, self-made New Jersey millionaire Broderick Crawford. When they arrive in Washington, D.C., Crawford is embarrassed by *her* ignorance and hires writer William Holden to educate her. Holliday reads books, builds her vocabulary, and develops confidence. She and Holden fall in love. The scenes in which Holliday visits the historical monuments and becomes excited by what America stands for are like bad Capra. Why all the civics lessons? Does it take Thomas Jefferson's words against tyranny to get Holliday to realize that Crawford hasn't been treating her well? It's good to see Holliday evolve from an unformed, uninformed person to a complete woman who has confidence in her own decisions—and to see her reject Crawford. Unfortunately, she immediately gets married without spending any time without a man. Direction by George Cukor is too theatrical (as is Holliday's performance at times) and the script by Garson Kanin is clever but has only a few bright moments. I don't like the way Kanin uses Crawford comically through much of the film yet, when it suits his purpose, makes him a real heavy. Best scene is the most famous—when Holliday beats Crawford at gin rummy. Also with: Howard St. John.

BOUDU SAVED FROM DROWNING (FRENCH/1932) B&W/87m.
Jean Renoir's comic tribute to Paris's bums, whose freedom is not restricted by social conventions. When his dog is lost, bum Boudu (Michel Simon) jumps into the Seine. But he's rescued by a bookshop owner (Charles Grandval), who brings him into his boring bourgeois home in hopes of reforming him. The bookshop owner spends his days reading or looking out the window, and his nights fooling around with the pretty maid; the maid cleans and cleans and the wife spends many hours in bed, bored and having sexual longings. Gruff, lecherous, and uncouth (he has the audacity to spit into a Balzac first edition!), Boudu at first drives them all crazy. But once he trims his beard, the wife feels physically attracted to him—and so does the maid. Kids will fall asleep about 10 minutes

into film, but adults will enjoy perceptive social comedy. It's not great Renoir, but not nearly as bad as critics contended in 1967 when it received its first American release. Most interesting is that Boudu (Simon's movements remind some of Charles Laughton) is such an unsentimentalized slob—rather than a lovable tramp of the Chaplin tradition. Has some nice photography by Marcel Lucien of Paris sites, including streets and grassy banks along the Seine. Remade by Paul Mazursky in 1986 as *Down and Out in Beverly Hills*. Also with: Marcelle Hainia, Jean Gehret, Max Dalban.

BOY AND HIS DOG, A (1975) C/87m. Cult science-fiction fantasy was capably adapted from Harlan Ellison's Nebula Award–winning novella by L. Q. Jones (best known for his appearances in Sam Peckinpah westerns). Set in 2024 A.D., after WWIII has left the earth a wasteland, violent black comedy centers on symbiotic, loyal friendship between a young man, Vic (sexy Don Johnson), and his aged but much smarter dog, Blood (voice by Tim McIntire), with whom he communicates telepathically. Blood finds women for Vic to rape; Vic provides food by scavenging through the remains of civilization. For women or food, they must beat raiding marauders to the bounty. Before he can rape one young woman they come upon named Quilla June (sexy Susanne Benton), she seduces him into a wild night of lovemaking. Blood worries that Vic will desert him for this female. She takes Vic to a down-under Topeka, an agrarian community below the earth's surface, run by a ruthless committee. He is expected to impregnate 30 virgins before he is killed; she expects to become a member of the committee because of his recruitment. Hoping that Blood hasn't starved to death above, Vic eventually escapes. Quilla June will come up too—not realizing that there is nothing stronger than the bond between a boy and his dog. Well made on low budget, with extremely interesting visualizations of violent wasteland (anticipating *Mad Max* and *The Road Warrior*) and Topeka. Picture had received much criticism for depiction of women as sex objects—but that is exactly the nightmarish vision Ellison and Jones see for this apocalyptic age, not one they find appealing. Last line written by Jones is funny, but deserves feminist criticism, as Ellison agrees. Worst change from novella is that here the girl (a virgin in Ellison) is not raped by the boy but initiates sex with him in order to get him to follow her to Topeka. In our eyes, the male who commits a dastardly act in the novella is now the *victim* of a conniving, treacherous Mata Hari. This change was made by Jones to justify the final act against Quilla June. Jones was most interested in love story between Vic and Quilla June, but I see this as a "buddy picture." Quilla June, the soft woman with an apple, embodies civilization and the sex and sin therein. The natural order is a man, a rifle, and his hunting dog. Love is pure only when it is not soiled by sexual contact with woman. It is pure between a boy and his dog. Best part of film is wicked rat-at-tat-tat dialogue between Vic and Blood, taken almost word for word from Ellison. They are like a comedy team cast in an absurd play. Film has bizarre humor and a terrific performance by Tiger, who plays Blood. Not for everyone. Also with: Jason Robards, Jr., Alvy Moore (Jones's partner), Helene Winston, Charles McGraw.

BOY FRIEND, THE (BRITISH/1971) C/110m– 145m. Girl (Twiggy) working backstage must play the lead in a 1920s musical, *The Boy Friend*, when the star (a cameo by Glenda Jackson) can't go on. She finds herself opposite the cute actor she loves (Christopher Gable), but while he loves her on stage, he loves another off stage. Production is performed in front of less people than are in it, but one viewer is a movie director who envisions elaborate, sometimes surreal Busby Berkeley-like dance numbers. Takeoff of Warners' Depression Era musicals where performers smiled through the sad storylines and lyrics; Ken Russell's best film, from a stage musical by Sandy Wilson. The high kicking and tap dancing are terrific, the production numbers are excitingly innovative, model Twiggy (her debut) is adorable (although her singing and tapping would be much better in later years), and the Tony Walton sets (on and offstage) and costumes are colorful. Film has endless doses of wit, spirit, and charm. Much underrated. The tall dancer is Tommy Tune, Russell's discovery, who'd co-star in 1983 with Twiggy on Broadway in *My One and Only*. The talented cast includes: Moyra Fraser, Max Adrian, Georgina Hale, Vladek Sheybal, Barbara Windsor.

BOY WITH GREEN HAIR, THE (1948) C/82m. A lonely war orphan (Dean Stockwell) who lives with his Irish grandfather (Pat O'Brien) tries to cope with being different from other children and come to grips with his feeling that his parents "abandoned" him. He expresses his misery and paranoia through hostility. Then one morning he wakes up to discover that his hair has turned green. Now his difference from the other kids has intensified. But getting green hair (symbol of postwar hope and rebirth) proves beneficial. He realizes that he is the blessed representative of all the world's orphans, the reason there should always be peace and harmony. Allegory was the first film by Joseph Losey, who said he identified with the boy's sense of "not belonging." It's too simplistic and moralistic, but well-intentioned; and it will have special meaning to children. Also with: Robert Ryan, Barbara Hale.

BOYS IN THE BAND, THE (1970) C/108m– 119m. Eight male homosexuals—and a visitor from the past who says he's not gay—gather for a birthday party. It becomes like an ugly game-playing therapy session. Dated, objectionable impression is that all gays are miserable ("You show me a happy homosexual and I'll show you a gay corpse"); that they either have venom toward each other because they're venting self-hatred ("if we could just learn not to hate ourselves so much") or feel sorry for each other because they know how depressed other homosexuals are. This was the first Hollywood film *about* homosexuals. That's unfortunate because it presents a negative image of gays—

they are to be pitied. William Friedkin directed. Mart Crowley adapted his own play, which offers nine characters that represent the spectrum of gay stereotypes. Stage actors reprised their roles: Kenneth Nelson, Leonard Frey, Peter White, Cliff Gorman, Frederick Combs, Laurence Luckinbill, Keith Prentice, Robert LaTourneaux, Reuben Greene.

BRAINSTORM (1983) C/106m. Idealistic scientists Christopher Walken and Louise Fletcher devise a helmet that allows its wearer to share the experiences another person is having, be it eating, having sex, or taking a roller-coaster ride. Later they discover that this wondrous but dangerous invention can take its wearer to a higher state of consciousness—if it doesn't kill him first. Boss Cliff Robertson permits the government to take over the project because of potential military application of the helmet. Walken and wife Natalie Wood forget their differences, fall in love again, and scheme to steal back the helmet. Director Douglas Trumbull, the special-effects wizard behind *2001*, had to fight with MGM so he'd be able to complete his film after Natalie Wood's sudden death in 1981. Although Wood didn't film all her intended scenes, her role seems complete while, oddly, the rest of the film has enormous gaps. Obviously, Trumbull was more concerned with the technical aspects of his project than with plotline or characters. His much ballyhooed visuals (shot in 70mm) are truly impressive—even if the camera's point of view is incorrect in a couple of fantasy sequences (i.e., we see a truck going over a cliff from afar, as if we were situated outside the truck, when we should be seeing the accident through the eyes of the driver). But he's responsible for the atrocious performances by the usually reliable Walken and Robertson, who don't know what to do with their inconsistent characters. And using chain-smoking as Fletcher's dominant personality trait is really lackadaisical. Thankfully, Wood is lively and lovely in her last role. The scene in which she is under the sheets with Walken and sings a childish song is touching, and causes me to think back to *Miracle on 34th Street*, *Rebel Without a Cause*, *The Searchers*, *Splendor in the Grass*, etc.—she is missed. Also with: Jordan Christopher, Donald Hotton, Alan Fudge, Joe Dorsey.

BRAZIL (1985) C/131m. A near-masterpiece. This is a remarkably clever and ambitious, humorous yet frightening, visually spectacular—*every* shot is bizarre and fascinating—thematically daring, surrealistic vision of a dystopian future. Monty Python alumnus Terry Gilliam, the director and co-writer (with Tom Stoppard and Chuck McKeown), termed his controversial film "Walter Mitty Meets Franz Kafka" because it's about a Mitty type (Jonathan Pryce is low-level bureaucrat Sam Lowry), a dull, meek man who is an adventure hero in his dream life. His real life becomes a *nightmare* when he learns first-hand about the terrifying mechanics of totalitarianism. This film is inspired by *1984*, more than by Mitty or Kafka. For those who argue about whether Britain during WWII or postwar

Russia was Orwell's model for Oceania, Gilliam offers a compromise. Judging by the clothes, props (except for the computers), black-and-white TV sets, rampant consumerism, and bleak, impersonal office and apartment structures, one would think we're in the cold-war era and Britain has become a satellite of the Soviet Union. Bumbling, polite Britishers apologetically perform the strong-arm tactics we associate with Russian agents or uniformed police. Whereas we think of the Russian bureaucracy as being as lethally efficient as Orwell depicted Oceania's state bureaucracy, the one Gilliam presents is as inefficient as the bureaucracies we've actually dealt with. Things (elevators, gadgets, heating systems, etc.) break down constantly and mistakes are made by the dozen. The film begins when a typing error causes an innocent man to be arrested as a terrorist and tortured to death. Pryce goes to deliver a check to the grieving widow and discovers that the female neighbor (Kim Griest), a truck driver, is a lookalike of the heroine-in-distress he rescues in all of his dreams. When he learns that the government wants to arrest her as a terrorist because she's complained about what happened to her neighbor, Pryce tries to save her at all costs. But he is arrested and is about to be tortured by his former friend (played by Michael Palin). Who should rescue him (at least in his mind) but a terrorist (a cameo by Robert De Niro)? Gilliam has made the bureaucracy so despicable and the general public so obnoxious that we're actually willing to accept a *terrorist* as a hero. Ending is the reverse of Vonnegut's *Slaughterhouse Five* because, instead of letting us move from reality to the brain-dead character's happy dream world, we move away from Pryce's happy dream and back to the real world for the sorry sight of the true Pryce. The final image gives logic to the "dream sequences." Universal vehemently urged Gilliam to change this downer ending. He wisely refused. It should be noted that the film's controversial ending is much happier than *1984*'s because in this case a totalitarian regime can't control a man's dreams. Images and themes in film will recall *Potemkin*, *Blade Runner*, *Little Murders*, *Casablanca*, and *Dr. Strangelove*. Happy title (Ary Barroso's thirties tune) recalls Kubrick's ironic use of "We'll Meet Again" in *Dr. Strangelove* as well as silly Depression Era escapist musicals. Also with: Katherine Helmond (as Pryce's zany mother, who's constantly getting face lifts).

BREAKFAST AT TIFFANY'S (1961) C/115m. Blake Edwards directed this witty, racy, stylish adaptation (by George Axelrod) of Truman Capote's novel. Audrey Hepburn had one of her most appealing roles as Holly Golightly, a poor girl from the sticks who has run off to New York and taken on the guise of an ultra-sophisticated bohemian (with dark glasses, a long cigarette holder, and a cat named Cat) to cover up her many insecurities. Her goal is to marry a millionaire, but she falls for struggling writer George Peppard when he moves into her building. He loves her, too, but makes himself available to a woman with money, Patricia Neal. Together Hepburn and Peppard achieve freedom, security, their own identities. Film looks dated, but its once shocking sexual content is still fairly strong.

Consider that Hepburn had been married at 14 to a much older man (Buddy Ebsen), she makes money by casually selling herself to men she doesn't care for, friends Hepburn and Peppard share a bed one night (which must have raised eyebrows in 1961), and Peppard is Neal's "kept man," taking money for services rendered. So the film is still not tame. And it's still refreshing seeing lovers whose relationship is mutually beneficial. Henry Mancini's score contains "Moon River." Also with: Mickey Rooney.

BREAKFAST CLUB, THE (1985) C/95m.
Nicknamed "The Little Chill," screenwriter-director John Hughes's follow-up to *Sixteen Candles* is essentially a mock encounter session involving five teenagers. As they serve detention together for an entire Saturday in their high-school library, a troublemaker (Judd Nelson), jock (Emilio Estevez), intellectual nerd (Anthony-Michael Hall), rich, popular teen queen (Molly Ringwald), and kook recluse (Ally Sheedy) reveal themselves through volatile actions and wrenching confessions—if only their parents were as interested in hearing their innermost thoughts. Tough exteriors disappear, social barriers crumble, deep secrets are revealed about their troubles at home, insecurities, desires (e.g., Sheedy wants attention), and, of course, whether or not they are virgins. Each kid turns out to be soft at the core and sympathetic. All suffer from the same problem: parents. That's the main reason bonds are formed between these students who had always kept to their own peer groups and to themselves. Hughes's direction is too stagy, but his dialogue is perceptive and witty, and also realistic enough to have made the film a hit with teenagers. It's obvious that Hughes likes teenagers and believes them to be smart and funny. The young cast excels; even Nelson, who got a lot of bad press, looks too old, and is stuck with most of the film's clichés, is fine in the largest role. Much of the excitement comes from watching five young superstars together in one film. *They* keep the film from dragging. My main objection has to do with how Hughes handles a major theme: he makes the point that teenagers shouldn't be pigeonholed according to their reputations, how they act in class, and even what they eat for lunch; yet, once revealed to be other than the "teen stereotypes" their classmates thought them to be, his teens turn out to be the "teen stereotypes" we've seen often, one at a time, in other movies. Another problem is that the ending is too rushed: we aren't sufficiently prepared for the two couplings that take place, nor do we know what will happen when these kids see each other Monday morning. Film could have been better, but what's here is more than worthwhile. Also with: Paul Gleason.

BREAKING GLASS (BRITISH/1980) C/104m.
The British cult movie stars New Waver Hazel O'Connor as a talented punk club singer who casts aside her personal and political values as well as her original band members as she races toward superstardom. Phil Daniels (star of *Quadrophenia*) is quite impressive as the young manager who helps O'Connor get started but abandons her to the industry's wolves when she becomes corrupted by commercial success. This is a sad, thematically bewildering film—and if you don't like either O'Connor's singing or her make-up and weird outfits, you won't get much satisfaction. Also with: Jonathan Pryce, Jon Finch, Peter-Hugo Daly, Mark Wingett.

BREAKING POINT, THE (1950) B&W/97m.
Excellent remake of *To Have and Have Not*, with John Garfield as California boat captain Harry Morgan. If Ranald MacDougall's script for Michael Curtiz doesn't resemble Hemingway's novel any more than Faulkner's script for Howard Hawks's 1944 film did, at least it conveys more of its spirit. This is the rare film to present the WWII veteran as a disillusioned, financially troubled *forgotten man*, kin to our doughboys during the Depression. Cynical Garfield finds that his charter-boat business isn't bringing in enough money; and that some of the spark has gone out of his marriage to Phyllis Thaxter (although he loves her and their two daughters). And perhaps he longs for some of the excitement of war rather than his life of bills to pay and familial spats. It makes sense that, having reached his breaking point, he dares get involved with lawbreakers, risks his life to make a bundle of money in a hurry, contemplates an affair with a loose woman (Patricia Neal). And probably everything would go smoothly if he weren't a moral man. Picture is well acted, nicely shot (partly on location) by Ted McCord, smartly written; it has an exciting climactic action sequence and a classic final shot. Produced by Jerry Wald. Also with: Juano Hernandez (as Garfield's partner), Wallace Ford, Edmon Ryan, Ralph Dumke, Sherry Jackson, Victor Sen Yung.

BREATHLESS (FRENCH/1959) B&W/89m.
Inspired by a newspaper item about a young thug who killed a policeman and hid out with his girlfriend, who later betrayed him. Jean-Luc Godard intended his debut film to merely be an homage to early gangster films, but it became the most influential film of the New Wave, an existential masterpiece, the most romantic of films despite the fizzling romance of its lead characters, Michel (Jean-Paul Belmondo) and Patricia (Jean Seberg). Godard broke all cinematic rules. There are no transition shots between scenes or between two shots in a scene. There are no establishing shots or matching shots. Godard dared use jump cuts both to convey a chaotic atmosphere and to express the reckless nature of his youthful characters. The characters jump through time and space and it seems natural. French fans appreciated Godard's technical daring; his Paris street photography; his score, which mixes jazz and Mozart; his many movie-reference in-jokes; his willingness to interrupt his fast-moving gangster tale (the Frank Tashlin influence) with a remarkably erotic, extended (seemingly improvisational) bedroom conversation between Belmondo and Seberg; and his inclusion of politically motivated swipes at automobiles and telephones (both of which result in deaths.) But what excited

the alienated French youth most in 1959—which resulted in the film breaking box-office records and its stars becoming idols—is that they could identify with Belmondo's casual lawbreaker and his disloyal girlfriend (who indifferently betrays him to the police), lovers who act impetuously without regard to consequences. No wonder Michel became a hero to them; he follows a slogan we see scrawled on a wall: "To Live Dangerously Till the End"—his ambition, "to become immortal, then die." With a face that reflects he has lived in a hard world, Belmondo became Europe's greatest male sex symbol playing the impulsive criminal— a tough guy who, like his idol Humphrey Bogart, has wit and the heart of a sentimentalist. Beautiful, dimpled Seberg is his match as the hard-bitten, free-spirited American expatriate who is afraid of commitment and is emotionally vacuous (she doesn't even feel guilt about doing in Belmondo). It's worth the price of admission just to see Belmondo escort Seberg down the Champs-Elysées while she sings out, "New York Herald Tribune!" Raoul Coutard, the innovative cameraman, was willing to hide in a wheelbarrow for street shooting and to roll along in a wheelchair with the camera in his lap. François Truffaut was credited with supplying the story idea. A landmark film that still has aura. Remade in 1983 by Jim McBride with Richard Gere and Valerie Kaprisky. Also with: Daniel Boulanger, Jean-Pierre Melville, Liliane Robin, Godard, Philippe de Broca.

BREEZY (1973) C/108m. The only Clint Eastwood-directed film in which he didn't star, and it's like nothing else he's been associated with. William Holden gives an earnest portrayal of a lonely, middle-aged real-estate dealer, a conservative dresser and thinker, who finds himself falling in love with a young hippie, sympathetically played by talented Kay Lenz. Breezy (Eastwood actually likes *this* counterculture figure) is genuinely nice, has fine values, and is a good influence on Holden, giving him a needed injection of "life." But he finds himself too embarrassed by their age difference and their divergent life styles to commit himself to the relationship. Eastwood manages to create electricity between his two characters (although the *too* good Breezy can be pretty annoying at times); as always in Eastwood films—even the most brutal—the lovemaking is extremely gentle and erotic. Not many people paid attention to the film upon its release, but after a dozen years it remains one of the few films that have effectively explored a romance between people so different. Also with: Joan Hotchkis, Roger C. Carmel, Marj Dusay.

BREWSTER McCLOUD (1970) C/104m. Prior to his success in *Harold and Maude*, Bud Cort had the title role in this earlier cult comedy. Robert Altman's twisted fairytale is about a gentle young man who lives secretly in an Astrodome bomb shelter. His mother-protector (Sally Kellerman)—she has marks on her back that indicate she may sprout wings—has brought him up to believe that the way for him to achieve "freedom" (what all young people wanted in 1970) is to learn to fly. He exercises constantly

in preparation for a flight in which he'll strap himself into a contraption with wings, pedals, and bars. When he has his first sexual affair, with a weirdo Astrodome tour guide (Shelley Duvall's debut), he thinks he has found "freedom" in a more common way. But he becomes disillusioned. He didn't realize that when he went against his mother's wishes that he refrain from sex, he lost the purity that would enable him to fly (obviously, he hadn't read *Birdy*). He attempts flight. That he would try to fly in the Astrodome, an enclosed "cage," is symptomatic that he and other U.S. rebels can't achieve freedom in oppressive America. It's not surprising that while he tries to fly to freedom, police try to shoot him down. He's the chief suspect in a series of murders that have swept Houston—those who died represented the worst types of Americans, and all posed threats to Brewster (which makes us wonder if his *mother* didn't commit the crimes). Crazy black comedy-satire doesn't hold up as well as Altman's other early films—much of the sick humor seems tasteless where once it was funny. However, it's still an original, full of enjoyable quirky moments. Duvall and Michael Murphy (as a blue-eyed SF detective who parodies Steve McQueen's *Bullitt*) come across the best among the oddball characters. Altman's unusual storytelling methods, including the intertwining storylines, anticipated *Nashville*. Also with: Stacy Keach, Jennifer Salt, William Windom, Margaret Hamilton, John Schuck, Bert Remsen.

BRIDE, THE (BRITISH/1985) C/119m. Boring, poorly acted, poorly conceived revision of James Whale's *Bride of Frankenstein*, directed by Franc Roddam. Dr. Charles Frankenstein (Sting) creates a bride, Eva (Jennifer Beals), for his lonely monster (Clancy Brown). Eva rejects the monster, who, his feelings hurt, runs away. He is befriended by an intelligent midget, Rinaldo (David Rappaport, giving the one acceptable performance in the film), and they join a Budapest circus. Rinaldo gives the monster a name—Viktor—and teaches him self-respect; he also tells Viktor to one day go back after Eva. Oh, yes, in the forgettable part of the film, Frankenstein has made Eva into the "Modern Woman," intelligent, knowledgeable, the equal of men. Yet when she shows signs of intelligence, he tries to pull back on the reins. He has fallen in love with her. Picture has nothing to do with Mary Shelley; instead, it panders to the modern audience with phony feminism (there's no way this perverse doctor could be interested in creating the *new* woman). Add a bit of *The Elephant Man*'s "I-am-a-man" triteness. There is no horror, except the acting of Sting and Beals in their final scene together. Worst moment: Eva fainting! Also with: Anthony Higgins, Phil Daniels, Geraldine Page, Verushka, Quentin Crisp.

BRIDE OF FRANKENSTEIN (1935) B&W/80m. James Whale's stylized, stunningly imaginative, wickedly funny horror masterpiece was made four years after his *Frankenstein*. It is surpassed only by *King Kong* among the all-time best monster movies, and not even that film has as much "class." Consider that it contains bristling philosophical discourse between intellectual giants Dr. Frankenstein (Colin Clive) and one of the genre's most eccentric scoundrels, scientist Dr. Septimus Pretorious (Ernest Thesiger); and even the Monster (Boris Karloff) engages in smart conversation—his 44-word vocabulary came from test papers of Universal's child actors—listens to classical music, drinks wine, and smokes a fine cigar. Film begins with prologue in which Mary Shelley (Elsa Lanchester) says she is not finished with her Frankenstein story. The Monster was not killed after all. In the classic scene he takes refuge in the home of a blind hermit (O. P. Heggie), who becomes his first friend and teaches him to talk. Later he falls under the evil influence of Pretorious, who wants to create race of monsters. The Monster and Pretorious force Frankenstein to create bride (also Elsa Lanchester) for the Monster, to end his loneliness. There are many reasons the film is better than the original, not the least being that it deals with the Monster's need for female companionship, which is central to the second half of Shelley's novel. It is not cold, bleak, or depressing like the original. It has a higher budget and the production values breathe life into the story. Most impressive is Franz Waxman's score, complete with churchbells at the Bride's birth. The claustrophobic castle and laboratory sets are balanced by spacious, candle-lit chambers with shiny floors and columns, all covered with shadows. And how wonderful is the expressionistic forest! Neither Whale nor cameraman John Mescall strove for realism: this film is meant to be visualization of a *story*. Whale displays a bold, macabre sense of humor throughout (see what happens to the silly farm wife and to a beautiful sheepherder). He also has fun with his four stars' angular faces—he shoots them in tremendous close-ups, often using wild camera angles. Elsa Lanchester, who beat out Brigitte Helm and Phyllis Brooks for the part, is marvelous in her brief appearance as the Bride. She is in a white shroud, on 2½-foot stilts that make her movements birdlike. Her wild hairstyle was inspired by Nefertiti. She almost steals the film from Thesiger and Karloff. But it is Karloff's touching performance that makes this film great. Almost hidden beneath Jack Pearce's remarkable make-up, his sensitive eyes still come through, expressing the Monster's feelings—he is like a stray dog, beaten and burned in the past and paranoid, but desperate for kindness (as when he asks the Bride, "Friend?"). With Karloff in the part, the Monster is eloquent even when silent. Also with: Valerie Hobson (as Clive's bride), Una O'Connor, E. E. Clive, Douglas Walton, Gavin Gordon, Dwight Frye, John Carradine, Walter Brennan, Joan Woodbury (as one of Pretorious's miniaturized people).

BRIDE OF THE MONSTER/BRIDE OF THE ATOM (1956) B&W/69m.

Horrid low-budget horror film from Edward D. Wood, Jr., starring his friends Bela Lugosi, in his last speaking part, and huge, blubbery Tor Johnson, who as Lobo doesn't get one word of dialogue. Lugosi is a mad scientist who's trying to create a race of supermen via injections of atomic energy. Snoopers who pass his isolated house in the woods are either killed by his giant octopus or kidnapped by his assistant, Lobo, to undergo his criminal experiment. Reporter Loretta King is snatched by Lobo, and Lugosi wants to make her Lobo's bride, but her boyfriend, policeman Tony McCoy (the producer's son), tries to put a stop to that. Film is not as terrible as *Plan 9 from Outer Space*—but what film is? There are enough campy elements to keep Wood fanatics pleased—and Lugosi's fight with a rubber octopus (for which Lugosi must wrap the tentacles around himself) is truly hilarious. Sadly, some of the dialogue involving police indicates that on occasion Wood *intentionally* tried to be funny. Co-written by Alex Gordon.

BRIDGE ON THE RIVER KWAI, THE (BRITISH/1957) C/161m.

David Lean's epic war drama made off with seven Academy Awards: Best Picture, Best Director, Best Actor (Alec Guinness), Best Screenplay (Pierre Boulle for adapting his novel, although blacklisted Michael Wilson and Carl Foreman wrote most, if not all, of the script), Best Cinematography (Jack Hildyard), Best Editing (Peter Taylor), and Best Score (Malcolm Arnold), with its catchy whistle tune "The Colonel Bogie March." Visually, it's still impressive, and the lead actors (Guinness, William Holden, Sessue Hayakawa) remain formidable despite their characters not having as much screen time or as many important moments as I remembered, but the film's weak structure and pointless ending betray its fascinating premise. Guinness is the commanding officer of British troops who are confined to a Japanese POW camp between Burma and Siam. A strict by-the-book career officer who mistakenly believes WWII is another "gentlemen's war," he adamantly refuses to let his fellow officers or himself be forced to work in the Japanese camp. But when camp commander Hayakawa asks him to supervise the British troops in the building of a strategic bridge, he enthusiastically accepts, believing that such a project will boost his men's morale. He believes that the construction of a solid bridge will be a symbolic triumph for the British against their captors—of course, Hayakawa is duping him, taking advantage of his British pride. As the construction gets into full swing, Lean cuts away to the other major storyline—American William Holden, someone who'd always shirked responsibility, has been coaxed by British officer Jack Hawkins to return to the POW camp from which he'd escaped, and blow up the bridge. Unfortunately, we leave behind the Guinness-Hayakawa relationship just when it gets interesting and viewers are deprived of an awkward situation in which they'd have to decide whether to cheer or root against the British soldiers who are trying to build the bridge before a deadline; it would be hard to root against them, but by reaching their goal they help the Japanese. Wild, confusing, too heroic ending of film differs from the conclusion of Boulle's novel, in which the bridge remains standing, a ridiculous testament (a Japanese bridge built proudly and foolishly by British) to the madness of war. Perhaps the filmmakers realized that this fictional bridge would be a real embarrassment to the *British* people. Filmed in Ceylon. Also with: James Donald, Geoffrey Horne, Ann Sears, André Morell.

BRIEF ENCOUNTER (BRITISH/1945) B&W/85m.
David Lean's subtle tearjerker about a suburban housewife (Celia Johnson) and married doctor (Trevor Howard) who meet by chance at a railway station and begin having weekly rendezvous, each less innocent than the time before. Finally they go to a borrowed apartment with the intention of committing adultery. (Now their walks are through shadowy streets, indication they are about to become sinners.) Nicely acted film, adapted by Noël Coward from his one-act play *Still Life*. It is the visualization of a fantasy of many sexually repressed women. Johnson is married to a bore (Cyril Raymond) who takes her for granted; surely they have no sex life. That Howard is a doctor is, I think, significant. I would have thought he'd be a *heart* specialist who "revives" Johnson's long-lost emotions. But he's a lung doctor, indication that Johnson's home life is stifling. If ending is frustrating for viewers, it is equally frustrating for the two would-be lovers—if they'd been French rather than British, it all would have worked out fine. Also with: Stanley Holloway, Joyce Carey.

BRIMSTONE AND TREACLE (BRITISH/1982) C/85m.
Unusual, often unpleasant film with Sting in a flesh-crawling performance as a disturbed young con man who smooth-talks his way into the home of a middle-class couple (atheist Denholm Elliott, deeply religious Joan Plowright). He pretends to be the ex-boyfriend of their daughter (Suzanna Hamilton). Hamilton is mute and bedridden and has had constant fits since she was struck by a truck; she'd come upon her father making love to his secretary and run out into the street. Plowright is impressed by Sting's politeness and prayers—Elliott doesn't trust Sting, and this causes fights with his wife. Secretly, Sting is taking sexual advantage of the young girl. Most intriguing aspect of film is that we can't figure out Sting's motives. Is he truly religious? Has he been dispatched by God or the devil? Is he trying to help the girl? Is he trying to destroy the family? Or is he trying to put the house in order? Is he trying to become master of the house? Strangest character is Elliott's secretary. Acting is first-rate; this is Sting's best performance. A good script, full of intriguing scenes. Funny finale makes me wonder if the film is a comedy. Interesting direction by Richard Loncraine, with music by Sting.

BRINGING UP BABY (1938) B&W/102m.
Zany, lightning-paced screwball comedy, directed by Howard Hawks. Cary Grant is much like Ralph Bellamy, his foil in Hawks's *His Girl Friday*. Wearing glasses, he's a museum paleontologist who knows more about dinosaurs than about the modern woman. He's engaged to a dull co-worker (Virginia Walker), but he's easy prey for heiress Katharine Hepburn (irresistible in her only screwball comedy), who meets him on the golf course. She hits his ball, and drives off in his car. That's just the beginning. When she's around him, terrible things happen—just as they happen to Oliver Hardy when Stan Laurel is around. Your enjoyment of the film may depend on how long you can tolerate watching the well-meaning but tactless Hepburn causing Grant problems. His worst moment is when her dog, George (Asta)—she also pals around with a leopard named Baby (Nissa)—buries Grant's priceless dinosaur bone in a large field. Dialogue by Dudley Nichols and Hagar Wilde is hilarious, as are the many pratfalls Grant and Hepburn take; but plot could use a few surprises. Most significant: this is the rare screwball comedy in which the woman pursues the man. That she causes him trouble is not unexpected, since she is so desperate to get his attention that she "does anything that comes into [my] head." You've got to admire her brazenness, and her willingness to make a fool of herself in order to win Grant. She isn't worried when he gets annoyed with her; she expresses a major theme in comedy: "The love impulse in man frequently reveals itself in terms of conflict." Picture inspired Peter Bogdanovich's *What's Up, Doc?* Photographed by Russell Metty. Also with: Charles Ruggles, Walter Catlett, Barry Fitzgerald, May Robson, Fritz Feld, Jack Carson, Ward Bond.

BROADWAY DANNY ROSE (1984) B&W/84m.
Woody Allen is the legendary Danny Rose, a former Borscht Belt comedian turned down-and-out Broadway agent for some of the least talented acts imaginable, including a stuttering ventriloquist and an elderly couple who make balloon animals. He is devoted to all his clients and works tirelessly to get them gigs. He spends much time building up the fragile ego of heavy-drinking has-been lounge singer Nick Apollo Forte and tries to smooth things over with Forte's mistress, Mia Farrow, so he can function at an important concert date. Wearing a blond wig and dark glasses and using a convincing New Jersey accent, Farrow's a tough-talking yet insecure character related to Mafia men who chase after Allen when they assume he's her secret boyfriend. Although Farrow and Allen have an exciting adventure together, she convinces Forte to change agents when he is back in demand due to the nostalgia craze. Allen is very hurt by Forte's lack of loyalty and resentful of Farrow, who too late realizes Allen's uniqueness—he even made her feel confident about herself. Comedy never reaches the hilarious heights of Allen's classics, but Danny Rose, who when penniless still cheers his clients on Thanksgiving by serving turkey TV dinners, is a truly sweet oddball character, and Allen and Farrow are amusing together. Allen's big mistake as writer-director is to have the final scene with Allen and Farrow be in longshot—it's really disappointing not to hear what they say to each other. Also with: Sandy Baron, Corbett Monica, Jackie Gayle, Morty Gunty, Will Jordan, Howard Storm, Milton Berle, Joe Franklin.

BROKEN BLOSSOMS (THE YELLOW MAN AND THE WHITE GIRL) (1919) B&W/66m–89m.
Adapted from a story in Thomas Burke's *Limehouse Nights*, this D. W. Griffith classic was perhaps the cinema's first

outright tragedy. Griffith experimented with various tints and had cameraman Billy Bitzer employ a special soft-focus lens to give star Lillian Gish an ethereal quality when shot in close-up. The result is that the film has an almost poetic feel that tempers the harshness of the story. The sentimental tale is of a young girl who lives with her brutal father, Battling Burrows (Donald Crisp), in the sordid Limehouse district of London. Constantly beaten by her drunken pugilist father, although she never does anything wrong, this poor waif has never known a moment's happiness or tenderness. She is able to smile only if she lifts the sides of her mouth with her fingers (Gish thought up this bit of business). Having suffered her latest beating, she stumbles into the shop of a once idealistic Chinese man (Richard Barthelmess) who long ago had come from China to teach westerners how to be civil but now wastes time in the opium dens trying to forget the human tragedy. He immediately falls in love—an *innocent* love—with the pretty young girl. When the bigoted Crisp learns that his daughter has been seen in Barthelmess's bedroom, he vows to kill him and beat her. Overly sentimental film surely appealed to Griffith because it again let him lash out at the evil city, again deal with miscegenation and suicide, and again—and this is the disturbing element—sacrifice an innocent girl to our cruel, immoral world. Snarling Crisp overacts, stoical Barthelmess underacts (as if he believed one change of expression would let us know that he isn't really Oriental after all), and Gish acts up an exciting storm. From her timid walking, stooped, crooked posture, and terrified eyes, Gish immediately gets us to understand that beatings are a daily thing for her. When she locks herself in a closet and madly paces in the small space while looking absolutely terrified that her father will soon break through the door and beat her, Gish is totally convincing. Of course, this is the first film that really dealt with child abuse, but it's likely Griffith was more interested in melodrama than social commentary. However, he sincerely was interested in the racism issue (perhaps because of flack he got from *Birth of a Nation*) and considered the main theme of his film to be that Americans wrongly consider themselves superior to foreigners, including the Chinese, who have a noble, peace-loving philosophy; the film's one bit of (ironic) humor has white missionaries about to embark for China to civilize those "heathens." A bit disappointing, but it has Gish and a Chinese "hero," and is essential to any study of Griffith.

BRONCO BILLY (1980) C/116m. No one expected Clint Eastwood ever to direct and star in a sweet movie, or a picture rooted in screwball comedies of the thirties, but this charmer came right out of the blue. Eastwood's an ex-shoe salesman from New Jersey who has formed an "authentic" traveling Wild West show in which he and his group of misfits can be whoever they want to be. (Of course, this is Eastwood's metaphor for the world of motion pictures.) Eastwood's characters are always best at what they do, and Bronco Billy is the best sharpshooter in the West. He loves being idolized by youngsters, whom

he advises: "You should never kill a man unless it's absolutely necessary" (a bit less harsh than Dirty Harry's philosophy, "Shooting's all right, as long as the right people get shot"). Naïve, headstrong, sentimental Billy falls for snooty millionairess Antoinette Lilly (Sondra Locke), who hides out with his show. She falls for him, too, but would have to give up her money to live and work with Billy and his friends. For a change, Eastwood is the oddball and the woman finds him beguiling rather than the other way around. Eastwood and Locke are a wonderfully offbeat love match, but the picture has more to do with loyalty than love—the fierce loyalty felt by Billy's troupe for him and each other reflects the loyalty Eastwood felt toward the actors in his "stock company" and the technicians who repeatedly worked for him. The misfits whom Billy accepts into his world would make conservative Harry faint: blacks, Indians, exhookers, ex-criminals, the handicapped, even one fellow who went AWOL during the Vietnam War. Perhaps this is the film that shows Eastwood has made peace with all Americans. Also with: Geoffrey Lewis, Scatman Crothers, Bill McKinney, Sam Bottoms, Dan Vadis, Sierra Pecheur, Beverlee McKinsey, Woodrow Parfrey, Hank Worden.

BROOD, THE (CANADIAN/1979) C/91m. Complex, chilling cult horror film by David Cronenberg advances two of his major themes: there is nothing more frightening than sudden unexplained changes in our physical compositions—to see our bodies in revolt—and sterile institutions meant to promote health are often responsible—because of suspect scientific treatment—for destroying a person's physical and mental well-being. A loving father (Art Hindle) takes care of his sweet little girl (Cindy Hinds) while his wife (Samantha Eggar) is a patient at the Psychoplasmics Institute, which is run by a controversial doctor (Oliver Reed). Abused as a child, Eggar is being taught to manifest her rage *physically*—just *how* is the film's mystery. Hindle worries that Eggar has been abusing their daughter during her visits to the institute. After Eggar's parents are murdered by hideous-looking dwarflike figures—Eggar's brood—Hindle realizes that the little girl is in great danger. This was the first Cronenberg film in which his characters are sympathetic—the relationship between Hindle and Hinds is truly touching. Film often has repulsive imagery and much in the climactic scene is illogical, but there are several terrifying scenes involving the brood. There is a cold, otherworldly feel to the picture, heightened by the fact that many of the characters' surnames (Carveth, Mrazek, Trellan, Desborough) can't be found in your local telephone book. Many people hate this film, but if you have a strong stomach, give it a look. Also with: Nuala Fitzgerald, Henry Beckerman, Susan Hogan, Bob Silverman.

BROTHER FROM ANOTHER PLANET, THE (1984) C/110m. Breath-of-fresh-air comedy from independent director-writer John Sayles. A sweet, young black alien (Joe Morton)—mute and with six toes—loses himself in Harlem while being tracked by two mean white extra-terrestrial bounty hunters (Sayles, David Stratham). As he curiously takes in sights and sounds of his new setting, he meets wide variety of Harlem residents. Some are down, but none are out, and it's interesting that Sayles did not present characters in desperate need of miracles to improve their lots in life. This alien could provide miracles and would be happy to do so, but all Sayles has him do is use his "magical touch" to fix broken video machines (which is the job he gets) and a TV set, and heal a little boy's minor injury. We've had enough of those other kinds of films. Through some nifty detective work, the alien does manage to track down Wall Street bigwig responsible for funneling heroin into Harlem and puts him permanently out of business. But Morton's biggest function is as the mute, amiable, sweet-faced confidant of the new friends and complete strangers who sense his receptiveness and pour out their hearts to him. Through his presence alone, spirit and "soul" are rekindled. Film is unusual from frame one and ends fittingly enough without expected big laugh but with sense of melancholy. You leave the theater smiling but thinking. Fine interracial cast includes: Tom Wright, Leonard Jackson, Darryl Edwards, Bill Cobbs, Fisher Stevens, Dee Dee Bridgewater, David Babcock.

BUCHANAN RIDES ALONE (1958) C/
77m. Off-beat Randolph Scott western by Budd Boetticher. Scott's a stranger in corrupt Agrytown—he gets angry a couple of times (he's arrested, a friend is killed), but for the most part he's a bemused spectator as the Agrys and a wealthy Mexican family carry on a bloody feud. Aside from Scott's Buchanan being so passive, the picture has plot elements and tongue-in-cheek humor of later films *Yojimbo* and *A Fistful of Dollars*. Enjoyable and occasionally exciting, but the weakest of the seven Boetticher-Scott films. Count Craig Stevens's lines. Jonas Word's novel *The Name's Buchanan* was adapted by Charles Lang. Photography by Lucien Ballard. Also with: Barry Kelley, Tol Avery, Peter Whitney, Manuel Rojas.

BUCK PRIVATES (1941) B&W/84m.
Necktie salesmen Abbott and Costello accidentally enlist in the Army in their first starring vehicle. It's one of their best films and holds up nicely. Highlights include the supposedly naïve gambler Costello winning Abbott's money playing craps, Costello ruining the tough sergeant Nat Pendleton's drill routine, and Costello's boxing match against both a big lug and Pendleton, who is refereeing. Costello doesn't play to kids or try for sympathy as he would in some later films—he's no innocent. The Andrews Sisters are on hand; they give a classic hip-shaking performance of "Boogie Woogie Bugle Boy of Company B" and a fine version of "You're a Lucky Fellow, Mr. Smith." Innocuous subplot has recruits millionaire playboy Lee Bowman and his ex-chauffeur Alan Curtis vying for the affections of Army hostess Jane Frazee. Directed by Arthur Lubin.

BUDDY HOLLY STORY, THE (1978) C/113m.
Gary Busey gives an exciting, natural performance as the legendary and influential country-tinged rock singer from Lubbock, Texas, who had scores of hits by the time he died in a plane crash (with Ritchie Valens and the Big Bopper) in 1959 (he was 21). Busey's Holly is basically a polite, nice guy, but he won't be pushed around, has a mordant wit, stubbornness about his music, and unbridled drive. That he comes off as a maverick is partly due to director Steve Rash making everyone else incredibly straight. Busey's portrayal has an added dimension in that he actually sings Holly's famous songs, rather than lip-synching Holly recordings. Busey's a talented singer—he has Holly's raw sound when singing live. Busey's moving rendition of "True Love Ways" is actually better than Holly's. Story plays so much with facts that former Cricket Sonny Curtis felt inclined to write the song "The Real Buddy Holly Story." Script's conflicts are too minor: Buddy and Crickets (Don Stroud, Charles Martin Smith) mildly arguing about touring; the group having to prove themselves to an all-black audience at the Apollo (thought to be black, they were the first white singers to perform there); Holly courting a young Puerto Rican woman (Maria Richwine); Holly trying to persuade the studio boss (Conrad Janis) to let him produce the group's songs. Yet film keeps interest, thanks to Busey; it's consistently entertaining. Also with: Amy Johnston, Dick O'Neil, Fred Travalena, Will Jordan.

BUGSY MALONE (BRITISH/1976) C/93m.
Opinion is sharply divided on Alan Parker's comical Depression Era gangster musical in which all the adult roles are played by child actors. I think it's a real gem, a project with dubious possibilities (remember that midget musical western *Terror of Tiny Town*?) that works much better than anyone could have expected. In its re-creation of a thirties genre film, it is so much more imaginative than, say, *Movie Movie*. It not only affectionately spoofs oldtime gangster films but also dissects them so that we can understand how they were able to draw us into their fantasy world. For the first time, we pay attention to minor characters, to the rhythm of the dialogue and the accents, and to the importance of period costuming, props, and sets (the speakeasies, back alleys, seedy theaters, boxing arenas). By watching these kids, we really consider what makes their adult characters tick. These talented kids don't miss a beat. Kids are known for their ability to mimic adults, but these kids must mimic the way adult actors play cliché adult characters—and the result is something entirely original. People who don't like this film usually regard Paul Williams's score (the children lip-synch songs which adults recorded) as insipid. I think he wrote a bunch of terrific, infectious songs that fit well into the storyline and raise the picture's spirit level; musical highlights include "My Name Is Tallulah," "So You Wanna Be a Boxer," and "You Give a Little Love." The dancing is also a lot of fun. My only complaint is that the use of cream pies instead of bullets doesn't work—ironically, the pie-hurling scenes

are too vicious. Starring: Scott Baio (as nice guy Bugsy), Florrie Digger (as sweet-singing, hopeful Blousey, Bugsy's leading lady), Jodie Foster (as sultry torch-singer vamp Tallulah), John Cassisi (as Bugsy's gang-lord friend, Fat Sam), Martin Lev (as Fat Sam's mean rival, Dandy Dan).

BULLFIGHTER AND THE LADY, THE (1951) B&W/87m–124m.

This largely autobiographical film by former apprentice matador Budd Boetticher was his breakthrough as a major Hollywood director (he had signed his previous films Oscar Boetticher, Jr.). Robert Stack is a cocky American skeet-shoot champion who becomes intrigued by bullfighting on a visit to Mexico. He becomes dear friends with legendary matador Gilbert Roland and his noble wife, Katy Jurado, and falls in love with another Mexican lady of "stature," Joy Page. Roland teaches bullfighting to Stack and he is an excellent pupil. But learning skills is not enough—before he learns that he must follow *Mexican* tradition in romance and in the corrida, he hurts Page so badly that she breaks off their relationship and he causes the death of Roland, who rescues him from a bull in the corrida when he is showing off to the crowd. Film switches in midstream from being about Stack trying to figure out what causes men to fight bulls to Stack trying to redeem himself for what happened to Roland. I wish the first theme weren't dropped entirely. Bullfighting scenes, in which Boetticher doubled for Stack on occasion, are quite exciting; there is some nifty slowed-down photography during Stack's last fight. More noteworthy, however, is that no Hollywood film has presented a more honest and dignified view of Mexican people. Boetticher shows admiration not only for the gallant bullfighters, but for the women as well. No male is braver than Jurado, who tells off a drunken Mexican for urging her injured husband to fight a bull to show his gallantry and later tells Stack that she doesn't feel anger toward him for her husband's death. In this rare film, Mexicans don't have to ingratiate themselves to Americans. Here an American white man cherishes the friendship of one Mexican woman (Jurado), with whom he has confidential conversations, and tries to prove himself worthy of another Mexican woman (Page). It is the ugly American who becomes humble. Producer John Wayne was instrumental in getting the film made; John Ford helped get it released—but he cut 37 minutes from Boetticher's print that wouldn't be reinserted for more than 30 years. With excellent performances by Roland and Jurado. Also with: Virginia Gray, John Hubbard, Paul Fix.

BULLITT (1968) C/113m.

Top-notch crime drama that has never been given its due. Steve McQueen is homicide detective John Bullitt, who does his job with expertise and integrity, but has become out of necessity so matter-of-fact when dealing with brutal murders that—as chic girlfriend Jacqueline Bisset protests—he is holding back his feelings in his personal life. Bullitt is hired to protect the surprise witness in the crime investigation being conducted by Senator Robert Vaughn (giving a scathing portrayal of a smooth-talking, two-faced political opportunist). When the witness is killed by professional hitmen under mysterious circumstances (he unlocked the door for them to enter), Bullitt hides the fact from Vaughn so he can investigate. He uncovers bizarre plot involving lookalike criminals (oddly, even we viewers aren't sure if we're seeing the same man or a lookalike). Direction by Peter Yates is extremely impressive. He makes great use of San Francisco locations; moreover, you learn about the taciturn Bullitt by watching how he adapts to various settings. Film has authentic feel to it; street and crowd scenes are particularly believable. I also like offbeat casting of killers—both are dull-looking, one wears glasses, the other is getting on in years. There are several very exciting action sequences, including the influential, dizzying car chase in which Bullitt chases the killers (who buckle their seatbelts) up and down the steep San Francisco streets. But even more memorable are all the bits of business that give us insight into Bullitt's character. We watch him wake up, slow and cranky; his shopping consists of buying six TV dinners without bothering to see what they are; before he allows himself to join Bisset in bed after work, he washes his hands and looks in the mirror at the face of a man who has just killed another man in the line of duty—perhaps he's thinking that having integrity doesn't make up for the sorry profession he's in. Steve McQueen's best role—too bad there weren't more films about Bullitt to counter *Dirty Harry*. Also with: Simon Oakland, Robert Duvall, Don Gordon, Norman Fell.

BUNNY LAKE IS MISSING (1965) B&W/107m.

A young woman (Carol Lynley) who has just arrived in London goes to pick up her four-year-old daughter on her first day of school. She discovers that Bunny is missing. Lynley's brother (Keir Dullea) helps her search for the child, but to no avail. A police inspector (Laurence Olivier) investigates, but comes to the conclusion that Lynley's child never existed (we wonder, too). After all, no one at the school saw her, Lynley is an unwed mother so there is no father to confirm the girl's existence, all the girl's belongings have vanished, and Lynley once had an imaginary playmate named Bunny. Has Bunny been kidnapped or is she a figment of Lynley's imagination? Otto Preminger's cult film is a variation on *So Long at the Fair*, only this time the audience is in the dark about whether the missing person is for real. The characters aren't unusual and the acting isn't noteworthy, but the premise is interesting, Preminger's camera work has a feverish intensity, the director makes a strong point about the difficulty aliens (Americans in England, unwed mothers) have getting help, and the film differed from others of its time because it daringly dealt with illegitimacy, homosexuality, and incest. The solution in the film diverges from Evelyn Piper's novel. Also with: Martita Hunt, Noël Coward, Lucie Mannheim, Adrienne Corri, Anna Massey, Finlay Currie, Clive Revill, Kika Markham, the Zombies.

BURDEN OF DREAMS (1982) C/94m. It is a shame that no documentary crew had been on hand to film the making of Werner Herzog's *Aguirre, the Wrath of God* because the events surrounding its production have become legendary. Fortunately, when Herzog decided to return to the Amazon to make his epic *Fitzcarraldo*, documentarians Les Blank and Maureen Gosling realized that they were guaranteed a production that would be well worth filming. Herzog's movie, based on a historical incident, is about an obsessed man (Klaus Kinski) whose desire to bring opera into the Peruvian jungles is so great that he is determined to drag (with the use of Indian labor and a pulley system) a huge steamer up over a mountain that divides two rivers. Documentary is about an obsessed man (Herzog) whose dedication to his art, to telling the story as he planned to tell it, is so great that he is determined to duplicate Fitzcarraldo's mad scheme and actually drag (with the use of Indian labor and a more intricate system) a huge steamer over a mountain. To complete this project is Herzog's dream—it becomes his nightmare. Numerous problems caused production to go on endlessly. The original stars had to leave the project with 60% of the film incomplete: Jason Robards had amoebic dysentery, Mick Jagger had a tour commitment. So their footage was scrapped and shooting had to begin anew with Kinski. Also, the cast and crew got involved in tribal arguments and were forced to vacate an important location and move 1200 miles downriver; a plane crash took several lives; steamers got trapped in the mud and couldn't float until rainy season; and the steamer meant to go over the cliff got stuck halfway up. One is surprised by Herzog's calm during all this, but at the end of the film he delivers a savage monologue about the jungle ("nature is vile and base") that shows he has become more than slightly mad. Even he admits he should give up filmmaking and enter an asylum.

BURN!/QUEIMADA! (ITALIAN-FRENCH/1970) C/112m–132m. Exceptional political narrative by radical Italian filmmaker Gillo Pontecorvo. A painful yet fascinating look at colonialism and revolution in both theory and practice, it is, I believe, the equal of Pontecorvo's *The Battle of Algiers*, although poor distribution by United Artists decreased its chance of duplicating that film's commercial success or notoriety. Based on historical events, picture is set in 1845 on a Caribbean island where in 1500s imperialistic Portuguese (in truth it was Spanish) burned the entire landscape and exterminated the entire native population to quell an uprising; for the next three centuries black slaves who were imported from Africa to replace the Indians worked on the sugar plantations of the colonialists. In perhaps his most interesting role (although he threatened to kill Pontecorvo if he ever saw him again), Marlon Brando is the intellectual, mannerly British agent Joseph Walker, who teaches the blacks the art of revolution and finds the charismatic man, José Dolores (amateur Evaristo Marquez), who can lead them. Moreover, once the revolution is accomplished, Walker sees to it that Dolores hands his leadership to a black (Renato Salvatori) who will allow the British to control the island as the Portuguese had. Walker turns out to be not a hero but a bastard, and his friend Dolores is at once disillusioned and politically enlightened. Ten years later the British Walker, now a drunkard and a brawler, returns to the island to put down a rebellion against the British being orchestrated by Dolores. Walker decides to burn the island and capture Dolores and have him denounce the revolution. With a great rousing score by Ennio Morricone, this is an extremely colorful combination of an old Errol Flynn swashbuckler that had revolutionary spirit and a "film of ideas." Picture has many historical applications throughout the world; it is also, most significantly, the story of revolt against colonialism in Third World countries. Major point of film is that white men cannot comprehend the singular nature of the black and his willingness to fight endlessly for freedom. Dolores comes across with great dignity—like Paul Robeson in his better roles. He is really a symbol of the continuing revolution; he wants to become a martyr to his people by dying rather than saying what Walker wants. He knows that even the leaders of a revolution can be replaced. Unfortunately for Walker, Dolores's replacement can be found on the docks, with a knife in his pocket. Revolutions against colonialists don't end until there is success.

BUS STOP/WRONG KIND OF GIRL, THE (1956) C/96m. If you like William Inge's play, you'll be more than satisfied with this version, directed by Joshua Logan, scripted by George Axelrod, and starring Marilyn Monroe. Don Murray was one of the few actors cast opposite Monroe during her career who was handsome, energetic, and her age—in other words, a sensible match; but Murray's rancher-rodeo cowboy Bo Decker is so infantile that he fits right in with all the older men and nerdy types with whom Monroe's characters were romantically involved. Murray leaves his Montana ranch to ride in a rodeo and to find an "angel" to take as his wife. He immediately falls for bar singer Monroe (as Cherie) when, in perhaps the film's highlight, she sings a mediocre but heartfelt rendition of "That Old Black Magic." She tries to tell him that she's no "angel" and that she's been with scores of men, but he pays no attention to her when she attempts to say they are unsuitable for each other. Like a caveman claiming his woman, Murray literally kidnaps Monroe and takes her away on a bus. But at a bus stop, which is reached more than halfway into the film, Murray learns that men should respect women. And Monroe falls for the suddenly tender young man. I find it hard to watch Murray's overly aggressive, obnoxious cowboy, but Monroe is sexy and beautiful and gives one of her best performances—although she'd done fine acting earlier, this was the film that won her the first critical praise for her thespian skills. It certainly helped that she and the very patient Logan got along. She's most sympathetic, especially when Cherie feels touched that Murray attempts to treat her like a lady for the first time in her life. Became an unsuccessful TV series. Also with: Arthur O'Connell (as Murray's companion), Betty Field, Hope Lange, Eileen Heckart, Hans Conried, Casey Adams.

BUTCH CASSIDY AND THE SUNDANCE KID
(1969) C/112m.   It's hard not to immediately like these two legendary outlaws of the 1890s—sly, emotional, funny Butch Cassidy and the fast-drawing, deadpanned, funny Sundance Kid—especially when Paul Newman and Robert Redford are imbuing them with their own ingratiating qualities. Their comic bantering even in the face of danger is enjoyable, delivered with the ease of a veteran comedy team. We think this will be a delightful pair to watch as they undertake several adventures. But what happens is simply that writer William Goldman and director George Roy Hill repeatedly place the duo in danger and have them react in the same exact manner. There is no real story (as Newman and Redford will have in *The Sting*), just constant references ("Who are those guys?") to a posse on their trail. We had figured that their glib humor was just a part of their personalities and we wait for the characters to reveal depth. But it turns out to be the trait that dominates *all* others. Goldman's script is too flip and it really doesn't apply to the western genre. The awful scene in which Sundance has a woman (Katharine Ross) strip at gunpoint while we're kept in the dark that they really know each other *and* are already lovers is where the film goes awry—from that point on we realize that everything is done with the sole intention of getting an audience reaction. Burt Bacharach and Hal David's "Raindrops Keep Fallin' on My Head" is sung by B. J. Thomas. Cinematography by Conrad Hall. Richard Lester directed the underrated *Butch and Sundance: The Early Years*. Also with: Strother Martin, Jeff Corey, Henry Jones, Cloris Leachman, George Furth, Ted Cassidy, Kenneth Mars.

BUTTERFLY (AMERICAN-CANADIAN/1981)
C/107m.   This kitschy-coo melodrama adapted from the novel by James M. Cain brought baby-faced Pia Zadora to the screen for the first time as an adult. She turns up at miner Stacy Keach's isolated cabin, claiming to be his daughter by brothel owner Lois Nettleton. Since she struts around in various states of undress, he finds it impossible to resist her. Film has death, murder, sex, and, finally, an incest trial. It's disconcerting seeing Orson Welles (as the judge) and Pia Zadora play a scene together. Picture is trashy and some scenes are impossibly bad and embarrassing. Still it's not quite as terrible as its reputation because the players, even Zadora, don't take the ludicrous script seriously. Directed by Matt Climber. Also with: Edward Albert, James Franciscus, Stuart Whitman, June Lockhart, Ed McMahon.

BYE BYE BRAVERMAN (1968) C/109m.   If you've
had it with films about groups of young people palling around, then you might want to check out this satire, adapted by Herbert Sargent from Wallace Markfield's *To an Early Grave*. It's about four middle-aged Jewish intellectuals (they review books or write for stuffy little periodicals) who drive around Brooklyn trying to find their friend Braverman's funeral. Film has comic tone, a couple of hilarious moments (as when the men realize they've been attending an endless service for the wrong man), and witty performances by George Segal, Joseph Wiseman, Jack Warden, and Sorrell Booke. Yet it's kind of a sad film; its conversation is about such things as death, failure, the meaninglessness of their lives, being Jewish. There's nothing wrong with Sidney Lumet's direction, but you may tune out on these men. It would have been interesting to see them in longer scenes with the women in the picture, Zohra Lampert (Segal's wife), Phyllis Newman (Warden's mistress), and Jessica Walter (Braverman's widow). Also with: Godfrey Cambridge (as a black Jewish cabdriver), Alan King.

CABARET (1972) C/128m.   Bob Fosse's stylish political musical looks better all the time. Adapted by Jay Presson Allen (and Hugh Wheeler) from John van Druten's play *I Am a Camera*, which had been based on Christopher Isherwood's autobiographical *Goodbye to Berlin* stories, and the Broadway musical, film is set in Berlin in 1931, when the Nazis are evolving from laughingstocks to a prominent force. Liza Minnelli (who deservedly won a Best Actress Oscar in her first singing role) is American Sally Bowles, an extremely chatty cabaret singer who's more than willing to sleep with anyone who could help her become a movie star. She becomes best friends with Englishman Michael York, a tutor who moves into her roominghouse—eventually they become lovers. Also important in their lives is wealthy Helmut Griem, who is sexually attracted to both of them; and two of York's pupils, gigolo Fritz Wepper and rich, Jewish Marisa Berenson, who fall in love. Interestingly, while Wepper and Berenson realize that it will be hard for Jews in Germany in the future, no one pays proper attention to the signs (i.e., increasing violence against socialists and Jews)—no one fully comprehends what it will mean when the Nazis take over. What the film shows us is that decadence of the type that distinguishes Berlin in 1931 (as seen in the cabaret acts, as seen in Sally's experiences) has a seductive power, that violence is a natural outgrowth of perversion, that Nazism was nurtured by moral decay. Film went back to old-style musicals in that all the songs (Fred Ebb and John Kander won an Oscar) are performed on the cabaret stage, except "Tomorrow Belongs to Me," which is eerily sung in an open-air café by young Nazis and exuberant Germans who join in. Songs ("Cabaret," "Money," "Two Ladies," etc.) are unforgettably performed by Minnelli and cabaret emcee Joel Grey (who won a Best Supporting Actor Oscar) and a group of gyrating chorus girls. These stunningly choreographed numbers are photographed (by Geoffrey Unsworth, who won an Oscar) in a stylized manner that emphasizes the performers' sexuality and lewdness—whoever would have choreographed these numbers at the cabaret back in 1931 would have approved of how Unsworth and Fosse (who won a Best Director Oscar) chose to film them. Film's only failing is that some of the comedy doesn't work. *I Am a Camera* was filmed in 1955.

CABIN IN THE SKY (1943) B&W/99m.

Spirited M-G-M musical, with an all-black all-star cast, marked the successful movie debut of stage director Vincente Minnelli. Based on a Broadway musical by Lynn Root, John Latouche, and Vernon Duke, it's about a fight for the soul of Little Joe (Eddie Anderson), a stereotypical black man who's so lazy that he leaves all work to his wife, Petunia (a warm, cheery performance by Ethel Waters, reprising her stage role), gambles, doesn't go to church often enough, and can't keep his mind off sinful Georgia Brown (Lena Horne at her sexiest). When Little Joe's shot in a saloon brawl, Lucifer, Jr. (Rex Ingram), wants to take him to hell, but Petunia's prayers are so strong that Little Joe's given a six-month period in which to reform and qualify for salvation. When it looks like Little Joe is a new man, the worried Lucifer, Jr., decides to give him a double whammy: he'll make Joe rich and set Georgia on him. But heaven's General (Kenneth Spencer emulating Paul Robeson) stands by, hoping to encourage Little Joe not to sin in the face of such temptation. Film pits cornball religion against hell-raising (which appear to be the only two choices in a black man's life), and, though it probably wasn't intended that way, the hell-raising looks to be more fun. Forget Joseph Schrank's script and enjoy the precious footage of some of the most famous black performers at their peaks; Waters sings "Happiness Is Just a Thing Called Joe," the title song, and "Taking a Chance on Love," Horne matches her with the provocative "There's Honey in the Honeycomb," John "Bubbles" Sublett stops the show dancing while Duke Ellington's band plays "Shine," Anderson (in his best movie role) teams with Waters and Horne on a couple of duets and displays his singular brand of oh-well-life-has-it-in-for-me humor, and Ingram reminds us of the shrewd, intelligent, boldly laughing genie he played in *The Thief of Bagdad*. Produced by Arthur Freed. Also with: Oscar Polk, Louis Armstrong, Willie Best, Butterfly McQueen, Ruby Dandridge (Dorothy's mother).

CABINET OF DR. CALIGARI, THE (GERMAN/ 1919) B&W/69m. Masterpiece of the silent cinema was probably the first "cult" movie: it played in one French theater for seven consecutive years; in Europe and the U.S. (where it was brought in 1921 by Sam Goldwyn) it became the source of widespread discussion among the intelligentsia, who were either excited or angered by the filmmakers' daring attempt to eradicate the distinction between cinema and art. This was the first *horror* film of real quality; it was also the first of the genre to advance the theory that what goes on in the mind, psychological horror, can be as frightening as physical shocks. Most important, this first film to call attention to and fully incorporate the chaotic postwar

German Expressionism—*Der Sturm* artists Walter Reiman and Walter Rohrig and designer-architect Hermann Warm were hired as art directors—proved to future filmmakers, in and out of the horror-fantasy genre, that one could *express* the emotional and/or mental states of characters through the design of the sets they walk through. No film is more bizarrely designed than this one, for the simple reason that what we're witnessing (except for the opening and closing scenes) is a story being told by a madman. The characters move about in claustrophobic sets; the few props are oddly constructed; the backgrounds are obviously painted—as if done by a six-year-old boy with his off hand (the costumes and make-up of the characters are also exaggerated and sloppy, as if put on by someone without taste). Most odd is that *everything*, including the numerous scribbled straight lines on windows, walls, and floors, zigzags at odd angles so that the frame looks out of whack—for instance, we see a hut that is built on a slant, that has a door that is more slanted, that is next to a window that is even more slanted. The only thing that stands straight and tall is Cesare (Conrad Veidt) the somnambulist, who is controlled by the evil magician Caligari (Werner Krauss); yet when he dies, his body starts to crumble and he raises his arms so that they form angles similar to the tree branches near him. The design is so fascinating that we tend to overlook the intriguing plot. A young man (Friedrich Feher) is convinced that Caligari has unleashed Cesare to commit murders. Eventually he tracks Caligari to an insane asylum and discovers that the doctor runs the place. There's a splendid twist ending, but when director Robert Wiene added it (and the opening), writers Carl Mayer and Hans Janowitz were infuriated because it completely obliterated their theme—that Prussian authorities like Caligari were turning the German population into zombielike creatures like Cesare who'd do what they were ordered to do (a theme that would have more implication in Hitler Germany). Best scene in film, and the most copied (see *Nosferatu*, *Frankenstein*), has Cesare sneaking into sleeping heroine Lil Dagover's bedroom and abducting her, taking her over some weirdly designed hills, roads, and steps. Picture is slow at times and the acting is uniformly strange (I like it, but many don't agree), but it's always mesmerizing. No one has ever tried to duplicate this film, so it is unique; but its impact and influence have been immeasurable. Robert Bloch scripted a 1962 remake that bears virtually no relation to the original. Produced by Erich Pommer.

CAFE FLESH (1982) C/80m. An XXX-rated film that has made it out of the porno grindhouses and become a legit midnight-movie and cult favorite. If there is such a thing, then this is "the thinking person's porno film." After the Bomb has dropped, the great majority of survivors have become sexually impotent. To provide entertainment, the government tracks down all sexual "Positives" and forces them into becoming sexual performers at clubs like Cafe Flesh. Each night the miserably unhappy "Negatives" flock there to watch a sexual show and, masochists all, be re-

minded of how things once were. Stimulated, Paul Mc-Gibboney and Pia Snow go home and attempt sex, but immediately become too ill to continue, as is the case with all "Negatives." But she is just pretending to be a "Negative." We usually think of women faking sexual arousal to please their men, but the film's novel twist is that this woman pretends *not* to be sexually aroused so she can be his "equal" and not damage his ego (and not have to leave him to join the sex circuit). While obviously not for all tastes, this picture rates with the best in the adult field. The acting is very good, the characters are genuinely interesting; it is witty, provocative, and erotic—the sex (which is necessary to the plot) is highly stylized but graphic (the filmmakers prefer a slightly shortened version of the film in which most male orgasms are eliminated). Skillful direction by Rinse Dream, who scripted with Herbert O. Day (journalist Jerry Stahl). Also with: Kevin Jay, Marie Sharp, Darcy Nichols.

CAGE AUX FOLLES, LA (FRENCH-ITALIAN/ 1979) C/91m—99m—110m. French farce became the most successful foreign film ever to play the U.S., raking in more than $40 million and playing in some theaters for more than a year. It caused so much excitement among those who loved it or despised it that it's startling how innocuous it is. It was praised for daring to tell a story in which the romantic leads are two men: the urbane Renato (Ugo Tognazzi) and the high-strung Albin (Michel Serrault), who works in a scandalous nightclub as a transvestite named Zaza. But this dishonest film is so timid that it suggests that this gay couple would raise a heterosexual son—and a *boring* son (Remy Laurent) at that. And it plays it so safe, catering to straight audiences, that the closest we come to a lovemaking scene involves Renato with a *female*, his ex-wife (Claire Maurier). Much humor comes at the gay characters' expense; repeatedly we are supposed to laugh at how effeminate Albin and butler Jacob are, at how exaggerated their mannerisms are, at how awkward they look when walking or gesturing, at how affected their voices are (laughs come from how they speak, not what they say), and how they whine or scream in surprise over everything, from Albin's toast breaking to a cork popping. But director–co-writer Edouard Molinaro never bothers to explore the subtleties of his characters or accentuate their endearing idiosyncrasies. Renato tells Albin he loves him because he makes him laugh—Molinaro includes no moments when this happens. In fact, Renato tolerates Albin in conventional movie fashion—like a husband who accepts the *childish* activities and personality of his wife because she is *female* and is supposed to act that way. There are surprisingly few funny moments in the major sequence in which Renato and Albin try to clean up their act when Renato's son brings home for dinner his fiancée, her mother, and her father (Michel Galabru), who is the secretary for the Union of Moral Order. There's potential for fireworks, but Molinaro forgot the matches. The play by Jean Poiret and the film were adapted into a smash Broadway musical. Like the film, it starred heterosexuals. Also with: Benny Luke, Carmen Scarpitta, Luisa Maneri.

CAGED HEAT (1974) C/83m. New World picture in which a young woman (Erica Gavin) is sent to a tough California women's work prison run by a perverted crippled female warden (Barbara Steele). She has feud with a black prisoner (Juanita Brown) but they eventually team up to lead daring escape. Early Jonathan Demme film was best sexploitation film of era, completely overcoming stringent dictates of inherently misogynist women-in-prison genre. Demme deliberately reverses formula which had sex and nudity being supplemented by action, and—with the exception of one scene—refuses to equate violence, or the threat of violence, toward women with *sex*, or to use female-in-peril/agony scenes to titillate male viewers. Much is praiseworthy—the strong, intelligent women, glimpses of lesbianism and transvestism, and the authentic depiction of U.S. prisons as cruel, dehumanizing institutions where prisoners lack privacy (so that their toilets are in the open and they're subject to embarrassing searches by members of the opposite sex), where some hostile prisoners are given shock treatments or lobotomies, where drugged prisoners are tricked into signing forms that allow doctors to perform hideous, permanently debilitating operations on them. Moreover, Demme did away with the disproportionate use of white and black characters which typically has only one black in a lead role, and the objectionable emphasis on female breasts—to counterbalance his Roger Corman stipulation that nudity was required, he often deglamorized the women, showing them on the toilet and looking ill, or with food in their mouths, or even dressed up like baggy-pants male comics, mustache and all. Film has great pacing and an exciting escape finale. Cast is well chosen. Steele, in a part Demme wrote with her in mind, has the strongest role of her strange career; beautiful and talented sexploitation vet Roberta Collins does some comedy; Gavin, whose eyes grow tougher as the film progresses, and adorable Rambeaux Smith handle non-dialogue moments especially well; Brown and Ella Reid exhibit command and confidence. It's interesting and a lot of fun. Also with: Warren Miller, Lynda Gold, Mickey Fox, Desiree Cousteau, Joe Viola, George Armitage.

CAINE MUTINY, THE (1954) C/125m. Humphrey Bogart is Captain Queeg, commander of the minesweeper U.S.S. *Caine*. He'd been a hero, but too much combat has had an effect on his mind. He suffers from acute paranoia (although no officers have turned against him), incompetence, and cowardice. He drives the men too hard and even conducts a full-scale investigation to determine who pilfered a quart of strawberries. Officer Fred MacMurray suggests to officer Van Johnson that he take over command of the ship, but Johnson balks at such a drastic act. However, when Bogart panics during a typhoon, Johnson—finally convinced that Bogart is unbalanced—takes charge. When Johnson is later court-martialed, the cowardly MacMurray testifies that he always thought Bogart was in full control of his faculties. Picture seems more concerned not to hurt the image of the Navy than to condemn Queeg, or to probe the military mentality and suggest that his phobias are not rare among military leaders (a lonely profession). The direction by Edward Dmytryk is stagy—one never feels that the men are actually on a ship in mid-ocean. The most memorable scene has Bogart's Queeg, with metal balls in his hand, falling apart while undergoing interrogation by José Ferrer. Queeg was by no means a typical Bogart character, but this role and that of Fred C. Dobbs in *The Treasure of the Sierra Madre* best reveal the vulnerability beneath the tough exterior that distinguishes Bogart's screen persona. Doesn't compare to Herman Wouk's exciting novel. Also with: Robert Francis (as a young officer who backs Johnson), May Wynn, Tom Tully, E. G. Marshall, Arthur Franz, Lee Marvin, Warner Anderson.

CAL (IRISH/1984) C/104m.
Sad story of a 19-year-old Catholic boy (John Lynch) who lives with his father in a Protestant neighborhood in Belfast. Although he doesn't want to be involved in the political chaos, he is constantly harassed by Protestant youths, intimidated by British soldiers, and forced by IRA terrorists to drive getaway cars. When his house is burned down, he considers it a mixed blessing because now he can live in the country and away from the turmoil with the Protestant couple for whom he works. He has an affair with the daughter (Helen Mirren), a widow in her thirties—he realizes he drove the getaway car for the IRA punk who killed her policeman husband and crippled her grandfather. Their coupling surely symbolizes the possibility that the Irish Catholics and Protestants can resolve their differences—but, significantly, the British troops make such a union impossible. Perhaps this acclaimed film is a bit overrated, but it does make the important point that youths in Belfast have no choice but to get involved in the daily conflict and pick sides (equally bad) according to their religion. Lynch isn't much of an actor, but his timidity and shaggy-dog bangs make him sympathetic, and he manages to convey the confusion, fright, hurt, and misery that many youths in Ireland surely have. As usual, Mirren is interesting, smart, and sexy—but it's doubtful that the shy boy would attempt a liaison with her more sophisticated woman. Director Pat O'Connor's best moment: he begins to play some romantic background music as Lynch begins his initial seduction, but immediately stops it when Mirren rebukes him. Also with: Donald McCann, John Cavanagh, Ray McAnally.

CALIGULA (1980) C/105m(R version)—156m (X version).
Penthouse magazine and its editor, Bob Guccione, produced this $15 million sextravaganza about the orgiastic reign of the depraved emperor Caligula (Malcolm McDowell), who ruled Rome between Tiberius (Peter O'Toole) and Claudius. Selling point of film is that major, serious actors—McDowell, John Gielgud, O'Toole, Helen Mirren (as Caligula's wife)—somehow agreed to appear in a picture that would contain explicit sex, and in scenes where other characters or background figures are completely nude and involved in lewd behavior. McDowell, in fact, does a dumb dance in which he's seen totally naked, and is often seen embracing pretty Teresa Ann Savoy (as Caligula's sister and lover) while she spreads her legs for the camera; also Mirren and Savoy (no classical actress) have an intense kissing scene. Picture centers on McDowell's incestuous lifelong affair with his sister, his marriage to the amoral Mirren, his impulsive elimination of all those whom he is annoyed with or feels threatened by, and his increasing belief that he is a god. This is an easy film to mock, but it's neither campy nor completely terrible—every few minutes there is something (a bit of dialogue, a mad comic moment by McDowell, an imaginative, unusual, erotic sex scene) that isn't half bad. And it is surprisingly ambitious. Actors are betrayed when film goes in wrong direction and the courtroom intrigue (so fascinating in *Masterpiece Theatre*'s *I, Claudius*) becomes secondary and we are completely swamped by scenes with sex and truly repulsive violence. Director Tinto Brass tries to create a surreal Felliniesque atmosphere, as was present in *Fellini Satyricon*; but where Fellini was sublime and funny, Brass is ugly and raunchy. He's the type of guy who will have Caligula strip the clothes off his dead sister just so viewers can get one last glimpse at her crotch—making us share Caligula's necrophilia. Writer Gore Vidal had his name withdrawn from the project. Also with: Guido Mannari.

CALTIKI, THE IMMORTAL MONSTER (ITALIAN/1959) B&W/76m.
Undeniably silly, but still it's one of my favorite low-budget horror films. The members of a Mexican expedition discover a flesh-devouring, ever growing blob that makes the one Steve McQueen once found seem affectionate. Directed by Riccardo Freda (Robert Hampton), with eerie photography from Mario Bava, who supposedly directed much of the film during Freda's absence. Film contains one genuinely spooky sequence in which a diver explores a deep, uncharted mountain pool and finds out too late that he's not alone. It will remind some of the scene in *Alien* in which John Hurt comes across the alien hatchery. With: John Merivale, Didi Sullivan, Gerard Herter, Daniela Rocca.

CANDY GOES TO HOLLYWOOD (1979) C/88m.
In this sequel to *The Erotic Adventures of Candy*, dumb buxom blonde Carol Connors is jerked around by her Hollywood agent (John Leslie) and keeps having sexual encounters that get her nowhere in show biz. Porno comedy has a couple of erotic moments, plus an appearance by Wendy O. Williams (in her pre-Plasmatics days), who does a weird sex act. But the storyline is flimsy and Connors isn't too impressive an actress. Plus porno filmmakers have got to figure out ways to get female characters into bed other than making them childish bubbleheads who can be talked into anything. Oddly, a female, Gail Palmer, directed this film. Also with: Richard Pacheco, Phaery Burg.

CANNIBAL GIRLS (CANADIAN/1973) C/84m.

In 1971 director Ivan Reitman (*Meatballs*, *Ghostbusters*), then 21, and producer-editor Dan Goldberg, 19, decided to make a shoestring-budget exploitation film in about three weeks' time. They got minuscule financing and the use of equipment in exchange for a percentage of the film, they hired actors who could improvise—including Eugene Levy and Andrea Martin, who would become famous with Second City—and had a script written as rehearsals began. From the time they decided to make the picture until initial shooting was completed took about 23 days. But when the filmmakers saw they had decent footage, they believed that if they made slight improvements they'd have the chance to make a hefty distribution deal. *Two* years later, with the filmmakers suicidally in debt, they finished the picture and sold it to AIP. Horror comedy is about a young couple who stay overnight in small town. They're told of a house where years before three beguiling cannibal sisters (Randall Carpenter, Bonnie Neison, Míra Prawluk) murdered and ate male visitors. They go to the house, which has been converted into a gourmet restaurant, only to discover that the cannibal girls are still there. Film starts out well, but becomes dull and confusing. It's obvious that the filmmakers had talent to make an okay horror film or an okay comedy if they'd wanted either, but had trouble figuring out how to balance the laughs and chills. The good ideas are there, but they're not carried out—the film could have been much scarier and much funnier. AIP added gimmick in which a buzzer alerts viewers to upcoming gore and an "Avon calling" bell that signals it's okay to open your eyes again. It's an amusing touch. With long, curly hair and a mustache, Levy looks like a cross between Gabe Kaplan and Gene Shalit. One of the two special-effects men was a butcher. Also with: Robert Ulrich, May Jarvis.

CAPE FEAR (1962) B&W/105m.

Tense, often uncomfortable melodrama about a vicious ex-con (Robert Mitchum) who terrorizes the family of the mild-mannered prosecutor (Gregory Peck) who sent him to prison. Although Peck's sure that Mitchum is out to harm him, his wife (Polly Bergen), or teen-age daughter (Lori Martin of TV's *National Velvet*), he can't get help from the police until Mitchum actually does something. So Peck takes his family off to the southern bayous in a houseboat and waits for Mitchum to make his move. The climax is extremely suspenseful. In a role almost as creepy as his bogus preacher in *Night of the Hunter*, Mitchum plays one of the screen's first *sexual* sadists. When director J. Lee Thompson places the brawny, bare-chested Mitchum next to the tiny Martin (who's less than five feet tall), you'll get goose bumps. Also with: Martin Balsam, Jack Kruschen, Telly Savalas.

CAPTAIN BLOOD (1935) B&W/99m–119m.

Rousing adaptation of Rafael Sabatini's novel about a 17th-century English pirate made a star of Errol Flynn, who made the most of his first lead role. Flynn is Dr. Peter Blood, an Irishman who is sentenced to death by James II's court for tending to an injured rebel. His sentence is converted to forced servitude in the Americas. But he escapes and becomes captain of a pirate ship, only to come to England's aid against the French navy when William of Orange becomes King of England. Film boasts of marvelous action sequences; extremely intelligent dialogue; spirited direction by Michael Curtiz; and an earnest, strong performance by Flynn—when Blood states that his loyalty lies with his fellow man rather than with the King, he is setting the tone for future Flynn heroes. Highlights include a Flynn–Basil Rathbone swordfight-to-the-death on a rocky beach, during which the opponents smile constantly. Of course, one of the most significant things about this film is that it brought together one of the cinema's truly wonderful romantic teams: Flynn and Olivia de Havilland (the only young female in the cast). As Blood, Flynn is incomparably dashing, handsome, charismatic; 19-year-old De Havilland is ravishing (and already a splendid actress). It's little wonder that each takes the other's breath away. An excellent debut score by Erich Wolfgang Korngold. Made as a silent film in 1925; in 1950 Louis Hayward would star in *The Fortunes of Captain Blood*. Also with: Lionel Atwill (as De Havilland's cruel uncle), Ross Alexander, Guy Kibbee, Henry Stephenson, Donald Meek, Jessie Ralph, J. Carrol Naish.

CAPTAIN KRONOS: VAMPIRE HUNTER (BRITISH/1974) C/91m.

A few centuries back, a small English hamlet is terrorized when a vampire starts draining the life's blood from young girls, causing them to die instantly from old age (a reaction quite different than that found in traditional vampire movies). This is obviously a job for the swordsman Kronos (Horst Janson), vampire-hunter supreme, who rides into town with his clever hunchbacked companion, Professor Grost (John Carson). The creation of director-screenwriter Brian Clemens (the driving force behind television's *The Avengers*), Kronos is a strange warrior. He is capable of slicing up three bullies before they can draw their swords (in a Sergio Leone-type scene), but he mostly bides his time on the vampire mystery: he makes love to peasant girl Caroline Munro, covers his body with leeches to drain his blood, and patiently plans his course of action. As in *The Avengers*, almost everyone is dead by the time the mystery is solved and we know the identity of the vampire. At long last he traces the vampire to an out-of-the-way castle where a mysterious young man, his sister, and their sickly mother reside. This cult film has an interesting assortment of characters, some spooky vampire-attack scenes, and splendid atmosphere. However, it never quite reaches its potential. Also with: Shane Briant, Ian Hendry, Lois Dane.

CAREFREE (1938) B&W/83m.

Fred Astaire and Ginger Rogers somehow got stuck in this second-rate screwball comedy where songs and dances are an afterthought. Lawyer Ralph Bellamy sends show-business star Rogers to psychiatrist Astaire to cure her of her indifference toward him. Rogers falls in love with Astaire, but he hypnotizes her so that she'll forget him and happily marry Bellamy. Then Astaire realizes that he loves Rogers. Storyline would be offensive if it weren't so stupid. Picture is brief, but it seems to drag because there are only four dances. Irving Berlin composed the score. The musical highlight is "The Yam," which Astaire and Rogers demonstrate for the country-club set. It starts out like a campy duet, then becomes breathtaking as Astaire repeatedly puts a foot on a tabletop (several tables are used) and swings Rogers over his leg. The two are in a cheery mood, and their feet are flying, through several sets. The earlier "I Used to Be Color Blind" takes place in a dream sequence. You can tell director Mark Sandrich was thinking how graceful they look during the slow motion, but I think they look silly during their turns. Number's "high" point has Astaire and Rogers enjoying a rare screen kiss as they are lifted to the heavens. In the slow, dramatic "Change Partners," Astaire literally puts a spell on Rogers while they dance. Produced by Pandro S. Berman. Choreography by Hermes Pan. Art direction by Van Nest Polgase. Also with: Luella Gear, Jack Carson, Clarence Kolb, Franklin Pangborn, Hattie McDaniel.

CAREFUL, HE MIGHT HEAR YOU (AUSTRA-LIAN/1984) C/116m. Sleeper from Australia that seems to have profoundly affected everyone who has seen it. From Sumner Locke Elliott's novel, it tells the story of a young boy (Nicholas Gledhill) whose mother died shortly after his birth—naming him P.S. as a postscript to her doomed life—and whose irresponsible father (John Hargreaves has a small role) left to go gold digging and has never met his son. P.S. has grown up happily with his loving Aunt Lila (Robyn Nevin) and uncle (Peter Whitford) in a lower-middle-class section of Sydney; but suddenly at age six a court order signed by his drunken father forces him to spend his weekdays with his rich but too proper and cold maiden aunt, Vanessa (the brilliant Wendy Hughes). He is sent to private schools and spends afternoons taking piano, dance, and riding lessons. To increase his misery, a battle over his custody takes place between the feuding aunts. Picture effectively conveys the trauma suffered by a child who is shuttled back and forth between two homes, without having any say in what is best for him. Having no power himself, he becomes each aunt's pawn in their power struggle. Everything he is told is biased; nothing he does is correct in either household (although Aunt Lila's home is surely preferable); he is told by each aunt to keep secrets from the other. He is confused, scared, and miserable. Tragedy is that everyone acts at their worst; even the sweet little boy resorts to cruel manipulation of the adults by film's end— the adults don't want him to hear them, but he is determined to be heard by them. Important subject matter has, surprisingly, never been handled well until this film. Excellent acting—young Gledhill will capture your heart—and solid direction by Carl Schultz. Hughes's character is most interesting. She is well-meaning in regard to her nephew, but is incapable of expressing love or warmth. This upsets her

as much as it does P.S. Also with: Geraldine Turner, Isabelle Anderson, Colleen Clifford.

CARNAL KNOWLEDGE (1971) C/96m. An "in" film of the early seventies, when college-age viewers defended its sexual frankness—indeed, this was a rare film *about* sex—and argued about its themes. Directed by Mike Nichols and written by Jules Feiffer, black comedy is about two friends, the sexually aggressive BS artist Jack Nicholson and wimpy, envious Art Garfunkel, and how their attitudes toward sex and women evolve from the late forties to 1971. They begin as college roommates who exchange sexual confidences (Nicholson lies) and lose their virginity to the same girl (Candice Bergen); then wind up mismatched pals who are both split from their wives (Garfunkel married college sweetheart Bergen, Nicholson was pushed into marriage with live-in lover Ann-Margret). Garfunkel thinks he's found the secret to love with his 18-year-old hippie girlfriend (Carol Kane); Nicholson must pay a prostitute (Rita Moreno) to build up his ego in order to get an erection. What we have is the story of men who think of women as the enemy, who can't be treated with sincerity because they're putting on an act themselves in order to trap a man. It's not women who dehumanize and emasculate these men, but their own fear of women ("ballbreakers" as Nicholson calls them). Many feminist critics thought it was okay for Nichols and Feiffer to present these two friends who don't know anything about women as pathetic men, but they objected to the two male filmmakers taking unnecessary swipes at the four women who have affairs with these men. The women are presented in a most unflattering light. The only woman who doesn't put on an act is Ann-Margret, an *actress*-model. Nichols's direction is innovative but very cold; the acting is exceptional. The best scene is the volatile argument between Nicholson and the depressed Ann-Margret, who reveals her desire for marriage. Also memorable is the break-up phone conversation between Nicholson and Bergen (who's very good here), a scene which reveals Nichols's mastery of dialogue scenes. Also with: Cynthia O'Neil.

CARNIVAL OF SOULS (1962) B&W/80m−91m. Sleeper that moviegoers always mention as one of their personal discoveries. Made for $30,000 in Lawrence, Kansas, and Salt Lake City by Herk Harvey, creepy cult horror film is about Mary Henry (Candace Hillgoss, imported from New York), who is the lone survivor when the car in which she is riding plunges into a river. Oddly, it takes her three hours to surface. Mary goes to Salt Lake City, where she has accepted a job as a church organist. Wherever she goes, she sees "The Man" (Harvey), a cadaverous figure who seems to be pursuing her. She also finds herself strangely drawn to a deserted pavilion. Film has many clever "eerie" scenes: on two occasions Mary finds that she can't hear anything and that people neither hear nor see her; the panicky woman climbs onto a bus, only to find that it is full of ghouls; she watches a dance of the dead at the pavilion; the finale. But, rather than being a straight horror film, it delivers a message similar to the one in *Invasion of the Body Snatchers* about how we are turning into pod people. Mary is such a passive, uninvolved (soulless) character—she has no religious convictions, no interest in men, no desire for friendship—that she never is really alive. That's why she can't recognize her own death. Harvey and screenwriter John Clifford don't blame her for withdrawing from the world, where her male neighbor (Sidney Berger) is a lech, her landlady (Frances Feist) is a snoop, her minister boss (Art Ellison) throws her out for playing gloomy music (rather than trying to help her neurosis), and her doctor (Stanley Leavitt) aggravates—with an unfriendly attitude and accusatory remarks—rather than soothes her wounds. The attack of ghouls pre-dates *Night of the Living Dead*. Film is much like "The Hitchhiker" episode from *The Twilight Zone*. There's some impressive cinematography by Maurice Prather.

CARRIE (1976) C/97m.
No one is better at playing shy, lonely, troubled girls than Sissy Spacek. She found her ideal role in Carrie White, a miserably unhappy girl who at home is constantly chastised and physically abused by her loony religious-fanatic mother (Piper Laurie) and at school is unmercifully mocked by classmates because she's noticeably different. As the wallflower, Spacek is painfully convincing. Carrie always looks downward to avoid eye contact, keeps her face hidden by hanks of messy hair, holds her books tightly against her developing breasts, keeps her shoulders slumped, pulls her sweater sleeves over her hands, and, at those rare times she is forced to speak, almost whispers, as if afraid she'll be yelled at or laughed at. Spacek saw Stephen King's horror story as that of a young girl who is unable to express herself verbally after so much mistreatment—she considered Carrie "a secret poet" and "thought about the terrible feeling of having to suppress one's true nature." Because Carrie can't speak or muster the courage to act on her longings (sexual, too, now that she's just had her first period), she develops strong telekinetic powers. In King's book, Carrie isn't that sympathetic, but Spacek puts us firmly on her side—we identify with her depression, her happiness when invited to the prom, and her need for revenge when the one happy night of life is ruined by her mother and schoolmates. Director Brian De Palma saw King's story as a religious morality tale. His film deals with the bigotry, conservatism, peer pressure, and persecution that can be found in any American high school. Ultimately it becomes a story of retribution, teenage or divine, in which Carrie uses her God-given telekinetic powers to destroy almost the entire school population, leaving them to burn in hell (the high school), and finally fights back against her mother. This enjoyable, impressive horror film is overly violent at the end—De Palma seems to be getting back at all the teachers and girls who drove him crazy when he went to high school—but it's lively, consistently amusing, genuinely touching. Nancy Allen and John Travolta are hysterically funny as the foul-mouthed sadistic teenage couple who humiliate Carrie by dumping pig's blood on her at the prom. Other fine performances came from then unknowns Amy Irving, William Katt (the boy who discovers Carrie is a gem among the clones), P.J. Soles, and Betty Buckley. As in all De Palma films, you'll be able to pinpoint Hitchcock references, most noticeably to *Marnie*, *Psycho*, and *The Man Who Knew Too Much* (when Irving tries to warn Carrie of impending disaster it recalls Doris Day at the Albert Hall). But the film is most indebted to the story of Cinderella: You have your ugly duckling, the ball at which she looks beautiful, the handsome prince, the catastrophe waiting to happen, the evil mother, and many jealous females who could be Cinderella's step-sisters. Scripted by Lawrence D. Cohen. Also with: Priscilla Pointer.

CARS THAT ATE PARIS, THE/CARS THAT EAT PEOPLE, THE (AUSTRALIAN/1975) C/74m—91m.
Peter Weir's debut was this creepy, comical, unsettling, one-of-a-kind "horror" film. Paris, Australia, is a shantytown off the beaten track. Its residents make money by causing accidents and salvaging the wreckage. Survivors are sent to local hospital, where the mad doctor performs brain operations that turn them into vegetables. Timid, innocent Terry Camilleri (a sweet, clownish performance) is in a trailer crash; his brother is sent to the hospital. Afraid to drive himself, he becomes stranded in this town of weirdos. The paternalistic authoritarian mayor (John Meillon) adopts him as a member of his family (his two daughters were orphans of previous crashes). He also appoints him the town's parking officer, which puts him into conflict with the bawdy youths who race their odd-looking automobiles down the street. He serves as the unlikely catalyst for the destructive confrontation between the youths and those who run the town. Weir completely keeps viewers off guard; we laugh, but sinister environment makes us feel uneasy. Picture is send-up of youth/drive-in films, westerns (a standoff is filmed like a Sergio Leone shootout), and horror films (such as *Dead and Buried*). It also can be seen as an attack on Australia's car culture, the acquisitive materialism of the bourgeoisie, and the oppressive autocracies present in small towns. Don't get up until film is really over. Cult film received X rating in England; was heavily edited for foreign release. Also with: Melissa Jaffa, Kevin Miles.

CASABLANCA (1942) B&W/102m.
Maybe the *only* picture that met old-time studio heads' requirements for what *entertainment* films were supposed to be like; it has action, adventure, bravery, danger, espionage, an exotic locale, friendship, gunplay, humor, intrigue, a love triangle, a masculine hero, a mysterious heroine, patriotism, politics (without being too political), romance, sacrifice, sentimentality, a theme song (Dooley Wilson's Sam plays "As Time Goes By" again and again), a time factor, a venomous villain, and war. It also has a splendid cast—Ingrid Bergman and well-known Warner Bros. players Humphrey Bogart, Paul Henreid, Claude Rains, Sydney Greenstreet, and Peter Lorre—and was helmed by the studio's top director, Mi-

chael Curtiz, who makes a somewhat confusing, overloaded story move at a brisk pace. Setting is Casablanca, Morocco, just prior to complete German takeover. Europeans fleeing the Nazis have come here, hoping to obtain passage to America before it's too late. Cynical American Humphrey Bogart (as Rick Blaine) owns the Café Américain. We see signs that this former leftist (in Spain, Ethiopia, Paris) still cares about what goes on in the world, but he claims to be neutral, content to weep in his whiskey over Ingrid Bergman, who ran out on him in Paris on the day of the Occupation. Film by patriotic Warner Bros., who wanted U.S. population to get behind war effort, is about how this existential hero gets out of limbo and, putting personal problems aside, rejoins the fight. It means that he'll have to give up Bergman again, this time by his own choice, and give his two Letters-of-Transit visas to her and her rebel husband Paul Henreid, rather than flying off with Bergman himself— but no sacrifice is too great ("the problems of three little people don't amount to a hill of beans on this crazy little planet"). Inspired by Bogart's sacrifice, his buddy, corrupt French policeman Claude Rains, has his faith in humanity restored and, breaking his Nazi ties, goes off with Bogart to join the resistance—it's the most romantic of endings. Film has great characters, great scenes, and great lines that are etched in our memories. Coupling of tough, introspective, ugly Bogart and soft, generous, beautiful Bergman was inspired. Winner of Best Picture Oscar for 1942; scriptwriters Julius J. Epstein, Philip G. Epstein, and Howard Koch won Oscars but it hasn't been sufficiently acknowledged that almost everything in the film was in *Everybody Comes to Rick's*, the unproduced source play by Murray Burnett and Joan Alison. (Also *Pépé le Moko* and *Algiers* were surely influences.) Music by Max Steiner. Also with: Conrad Veidt (as the arrogant Nazi who tries to stop the plane from leaving in the climactic scene), S.Z. Sakall, Madeleine Le Beau, Joy Page, John Qualen, Leonid Kinskey, Helmut Dantine, Marcel Dalio, Ludwig Stossel.

CASINO ROYALE (BRITISH/1967) C/130m.

It's hard to believe that in 1967 we actually waited in anticipation for this so-called James Bond spoof. It was a disappointment then; it's a curio today, but just as hard to sit through. Direction was divided between John Huston, Ken Hughes, Robert Parrish, Joe McGrath, and Val Guest, and it's so disjointed and stylistically erratic that it would be surprising if any saw the others' work on the picture. Featuring an all-star cast (several who play Bond), enormous sets, and some state-of-the-art special effects, it is a testament to wastefulness in the commercial bigger-is-better cinema. It would have been a good idea to cut the picture drastically, perhaps down to the scenes featuring Peter Sellers and Woody Allen. In fact, I recommend you see it on television when it's in a two-hour (including commercials) slot. Then you won't expect it to make any sense. Also with: David Niven, Ursula Andress, Orson Welles, Joanna Pettet, Daliah Lavi, Deborah Kerr, William Holden, Charles Boyer, John Huston, Kurt Kasznar, George Raft, Jean-Paul Belmondo, Terence Cooper, Barbara Bouchet (a beautiful starlet who, for some reason, never made it). Jackie Bisset (as Miss Goodthighs), Anna Quayle.

CAT PEOPLE (1942) B&W/71m.

The first of producer Val Lewton's fascinating "psychological" horror films displays the subtlety, imagination, intelligence, and respect for audience that would distinguish all his projects at RKO between 1942 and 1946. Simone Simon is perfectly cast as Irena Dubrovna, a sweet, lonely Serbian girl who works as an artist in New York (Lewton's wartime women always work). She meets and marries Oliver Reed (Kent Smith), a draughtsman, but won't have sex with him because she fears the evil inside her will be released and she'll turn into a great cat, as happened to her blasphemous fellow villagers in darker times. Oliver considers her foolish for thinking she is cursed and has her see a psychiatrist, Lewis Judd (Tom Conway), who almost convinces her that she is a victim of her fears and paranoia. But we see visual hints that she is indeed a cat. One fascinating image has Irena crouching at the bottom of her bedroom door, like a *cat in heat*, while her sexually frustrated husband stands on the other side. As in several other Lewton films, evil and good fight for control of his characters. Like Lewton's other tragic heroines (and psychologically disturbed male villains), Irena doesn't have the willpower to reject her evil side; when she becomes jealous of Alice (Jane Randolph), whom unhappy Oliver has turned to, she completely succumbs to her cat side. Although we eventually see cat shadows on walls, and cat prints in the snow where she walked, and hear growls, the only time we actually see a giant cat is when Oliver and Alice are trapped in their office. Significantly, the shots were inserted by RKO, not Lewton—anyway, the cat image could still be construed as only what the two frightened people imagine. Atmospheric horror film contains several classic horror sequences, including: terrified Alice being followed through a dark park, jumping when a bus screeches to a halt next to her; Judd trying to seduce Irena, only to be attacked by a giant cat; and, the most famous sequence, Alice swimming alone in an indoor pool when the lights go out, cat shadows appear on the wall, and growling can be heard. Lewton, editor Mark Robson, and director Jacques Tourneur each claimed he had the idea for this scene. Tourneur does a wonderful job of creating tense atmosphere; Simon gives an erotic, sympathetic performance; good bit characters are everywhere (including Elizabeth Russell as a woman who looks like a cat). DeWitt Bodeen wrote the excellent script, and cinematographer Nicholas Musuraca does wonders with light and shadows—the crisscross pattern over Irena's door makes apartment seem like a cage. A classic. Should be seen with Hitchcock's *Marnie* because of strikingly similar sexual themes and plot elements. Also with: Jack Holt, Alan Napier, Elizabeth Dunne.

CAT PEOPLE (1982) C/118m.

Paul Schrader's reworking of Val Lewton's classic starts out reasonably well, then becomes an abomination. Foreigner Nastassia Kinski arrives in New Orleans to stay with her brother, Malcolm McDowell. She has always sensed that she was different and has never slept with a man out of fear he would be in danger. She becomes attracted to zookeeper John Heard, but keeps him at bay; meanwhile her brother makes sexual advances toward her. He tells her that they are descended from an evil, ancient race of cat people who destroy their human sexual partners. McDowell is responsible for the wave of brutal murders in New Orleans. Kinski is well cast, Annette O'Toole is likable as Heard's workmate, and some early scenes are quite eerie and erotic, but Alan Ormsby's script becomes incoherent, the John Bailey–Ferdinando Scarfiotti visuals become too surrealistic, and Schrader completely forgets the subtlety, sensuality, and taste that distinguished Lewton's film and, like a mischievous kid, fills the screen with nudity and gory violence that are antithetical to Lewton. You can feel the film slipping away from Schrader— and when Kinski and Heard have a kinky sexual encounter, you won't get turned on but, more likely, laugh out loud. Music by Giorgio Moroder; David Bowie sings over titles. Also with: Ruby Dee, Ed Begley, Jr.

CAVEMAN (1981) C/92m. Funny prehistoric spoof done on the cheap. Ringo Starr forms a tribe of rejects, discovers fire, invents cooking and music, battles dinosaurs, and chases after beautiful Barbara Bach. Starr would marry Bach in real life, but it's nice Shelley Long (then a relative unknown) who finally captures his heart here. Most critics mocked the picture, but in fact it's quite enjoyable, with amiable performances by Starr and the other stars, and some hilarious sight gags: my favorite has a giant insect land on sleeping Dennis Quaid's face, whereupon the concerned Starr squashes it, causing this gooey mess to pour over Quaid. Fans of the genre will get a kick out of the humorous dinosaurs created by David Allen. Moreover, the silly 15-word caveman vocabulary that was created by director Carl Gottlieb and his co-writer, Rudy DeLuca, is as impressive as the language foolishly created by Anthony Burgess for *Quest of Fire*. Also with: John Matuszak, Avery Schreiber, Jack Gilford.

CELINE AND JULIE GO BOATING (FRENCH/ 1974) C/193m. A delirious but often enchanting comic film by Jacques Rivette. Librarian Julie (Dominique Labourier) and magician Celine (Juliet Berto) meet in Montmartre under odd circumstances and immediately start sharing Julie's apartment. Julie seems more down-to-earth than Celine, but both have fertile imaginations and there's the possibility that they are the same person (anything's possible in this film)—they do take over each other's identities on several occasions. Celine tells a ridiculous story about how she was a child's nurse in a large house with several strange characters. Independently, both Celine and Julie go to the *haunted* house—afterward they remember nothing until they find "candies" in their mouths that give them total recall. In the haunted house a nurse—who is alternately Celine or Julie—takes care of little Madlyn (Nathalie Asnar). Des-

perately ill Camille (Bulle Ogier) and Sophie (Marie-France Pisier) each plot to kill Madlyn because her widower father (Barbet Schroeder) will marry only if his daughter is dead. Celine and Julie watch the drama unfold, trying to figure out who kills Madlyn. Then they join in the drama—although no one in the "film within the film" can see them, and although they often forget their lines. It's up to them to save Madlyn. The two heroines of this weirdly structured film exist in an unreal, illogical world: they act, dance, sing, perform magic, play children's games, improvise (just as the two actresses do); they are characters in a mystery, a ghost story, a play, a film, a dream, a fantasy, a fairytale— particularly *Alice in Wonderland*. Film is far too long but rarely boring. Rivette and his two delightful, spirited stars keep surprising us. One-of-a-kind film has a large cult following. Schroeder served as executive producer. The stars co-wrote the script with Rivette and Eduardo de Gregorio.

CERTAIN SACRIFICE, A (1985) C/60m. Made several years earlier but released to coincide with the superstardom of Madonna, who had been an unknown when she co-starred in this film. Initial reports claimed it was an S&M porno film (photos appeared showing Madonna garbed as a dominatrix) that Madonna hoped had been irretrievably lost. But it was soon released on video and as a midnight movie and no one could see what the controversy was all about. The young, unglamorous Madonna does have a couple of scenes in which she is topless, and one is a dancelike orgy with two women and one guy—her character's slave lovers—but, despite this, her scenes and the film itself aren't particularly exploitive or sexually oriented. It's a typical, crude independent New York underground film; not the best but certainly not worthless. There are some bright ideas and wit floating around. It's a collaborative effort between director-cinematographer Stephen Jon Lewicki and his co-producer, co-writer, and star, Jeremy Pattnosh, who also wrote most of the music and sings several songs. There are Lewiskis and Pattnoshes everywhere in the final credits. Pattnosh plays a hip, philosophic young dropout in New York. He becomes the lover of Madonna, a "bad" girl who wants to reform and dump her "love family" for him. Pattnosh has the misfortune to meet (in an excellent, funny-real scene set in a coffee shop) a loquacious, conceited, violent, prostitute-chasing bastard (Charles Kurtz steals the film as Raymond Hall) from upstate New York. When Pattnosh chases Kurtz away, the scoundrel gets Pattnosh evicted from his apartment and molests Madonna. But Pattnosh, Madonna, and friends kidnap and sacrifice him at a party.

CÉSAR (FRENCH/1936) B&W/160m–170m. Marcel Pagnol directed as well as wrote the final chapter of his *Marseilles Trilogy*. Taking place about 17 years after *Fanny* (1932), it opens with Panisse (Charpin) near death. After he dies, his wife, Fanny (Orane Demazis), informs her 18-year-old son, Césariot (André Fouché), that his real father was not Panisse but Marius (Pierre Fresnay). She admits she still loves Marius. Finding out from godfather-grandfather César (Raimu) where Marius lives, Césariot sails to visit him clandestinely. He wants to know if Marius has been involved in criminal activities, as César believes. Trilogy will end with long-awaited reunion of Fanny and Marius, as well as unions of son Marius with father César and Césariot with father Marius. A lovely, deeply moving film with the usual rich characterizations and passionate performances. Highlights include Cesar's discourse on death and God, all scenes in which one character reveals love for another (which happens throughout the trilogy), and when Panisse's friends gather around his deathbed. A fine example of Pagnol's "human" cinema, this classic can be enjoyed without having seen *Marius* or *Fanny*. Music by Vincent Scotto. Also with: Alida Rouffe, Milly Mathis, Robert Vattier, Paul Dullac, Edouard Delmont, Maupi.

CHAINED FOR LIFE (1950) B&W/63m.
Curio starring the Hilton sisters, the Siamese twins you'll remember from *Freaks*. Here Daisy and Violet play Dorothy and Vivian Hamilton, singing stars who headline a *terrible* revue. Vivian's on trial for murdering the gigolo (Mario Laval) who'd courted Dorothy to get a lot of publicity for himself and then dropped her. Through flashbacks we watch the trick-shot artist con the love-starved Dorothy and see what led to Vivian's impulsive act. Film is extremely dull, but contains a few strange scenes: Vivian's lawyer defending her on the basis of the twins being treated as freaks all their lives and being unprotected by law; Dorothy fantasizing she is a normal woman and dancing with Laval (a stand-in doubles for her); Dorothy and Vivian discussing their misery because they can never have happiness of being alone with a man; the twins investigating the possibility of an operation that would separate them. Gone is the humor they exhibited about their love lives in *Freaks*. The only campy moment has Laval playing guitar and serenading Dorothy over the telephone. Film ends strangely with the judge asking us if we'd have acquitted Vivian if we'd been her jury. Also with: Allen Jenkins, Patricia Wright.

CHAINED HEAT (AMERICAN-GERMAN/1983) C/95m.
This ridiculous sexploitation film lacks the fun or political subtext of New World's earlier women-in-prison films. But the cast will make any exploitation fan drool: Linda Blair (as the proverbial innocent girl wrongly sent to a brutal, corrupt prison where—this calls for clichés—women are meat and it's survival of the fittest), Stella Stevens, John Vernon, Henry Silva, Sybil Danning, Tamara Dobson, Louis Moritz, Nita Talbot, Michael Callin, and, of course, Edy Williams. The only other reason to see it is the truly laughable scene in which Danning and Blair take a nude shower together and the tall, statuesque Danning is required (being a supporting player) to display a sexual interest in the short, plump star. Directed by Paul Nicolas.

CHAMPION (1949) B&W/90m.
Most boxing films contend that the sport corrupts individuals. This classic contends that some individuals want to be corrupted. "The fight business stinks," admits decent manager Paul Stewart, and, this being the case, it's the ideal line of work for his fighter Midge Kelly, one of Kirk Douglas's quintessential "heels." It's Midge's belief that "nice guys don't make money," which is what he wants lots of. His is the story of a ruthless man who'll do anything necessary, rub shoulders with anyone (including the gangster who owns his contract), and step on friends and loved ones in order to get "people to call me *mister*." He's the typical man in the American rat race, a scoundrel moving up in the business world. In his boxing business, racketeers control everything, boxers sell out their scruples to get ahead, men such as Midge dupe the public into idolizing them and buying tickets to their fights. Although Douglas doesn't look much like a boxer in the ring, his fights are exciting; he's also fun watching when he's just using vicious words to batter his loved ones to the ground. When Douglas has his famous breakdown, he'll give you chills. But you won't feel sorry for this cad who represents the worst in boxing. Shot like a B-film in shadowy *noir* style by Franz Planer, who, along with writer Carl Foreman (who also produced), received an Oscar nomination; edited by Harry Gerstad, who won the Oscar; and directed by Mark Robson, who'd make the even stronger anti-boxing film *The Harder They Fall* in 1956. Also with: Arthur Kennedy (as Midge's lame brother), Ruth Roman (as Midge's neglected wife), Marilyn Maxwell, Lola Albright.

CHAN IS MISSING (1982) B&W/80m.
Made for about $20,000 in San Francisco's Chinatown, this impressive, offbeat social satire is the first film made by and starring Asian Americans. Story is ostensibly a mystery about two cabbies, middle-aged Wood Moy and young, hip Marc Hayashi, searching for a business partner named Chan who ran off with their money. Hayashi thinks that Chan was a thief, but Moy worries that he may be hiding out for having snapped an incriminating photo of a murder at a May Day parade. Their investigation is the excuse director-writer Wayne Wang needs to show viewers Chinatown, and to give its people the voice they have been denied in American films. As we meet various types—tailors, cooks, shrewd businessmen, Chan's wife and daughter—and as Moy and Hayashi converse (and sometimes argue), we learn the effects of "Americanization" on the Chinatown population. Wang displays bemused sympathy for the converted Chinese, particularly the young like Hayashi, who think they have found their own identity and feel no guilt about forsaking the traditions of their fathers. But his heart is clearly with men like Moy, who, though born in America, is considered a foreigner by others in Chinatown because he tries to resist "Americanization." (Even though Wang has little love for the politics of Chinatown, he at least respects that the two opposing factions link themselves to Taiwan or Red China, rather than being Republicans or Democrats.) Moy is able to come closer than Hayashi to solving the mystery because he "thinks Chinese," as does the missing Chan. Because of the low budget, production values aren't high; but I do like

a couple of interesting bits of staging (i.e., when the camera is in Chan's apartment), the way Wang inserts documentary footage to give the film flavor, and, in particular, the way his actors handle the dialogue scenes—so believable are the words and the rhythm (there's more overlapping here than in a Howard Hawks film) that one feels they're improvising the whole thing. Moy and Hayashi are an amusing team; they also reveal a lot about the *type* of people they play. Also with: Laureen Chew, Judy Mihei, Peter Wang.

CHARLY (1968) C/103m. In this earnest adaptation of Daniel Keyes's prize-winning novelette, Cliff Robertson won a Best Actor Oscar playing a retarded man who is temporarily turned into a superintellect by a revolutionary brain operation. Sad result is that when he learns he will again be retarded and lose all the knowledge he has accumulated—including an understanding of the abstract—he is, for the moment, wise enough to realize that the experiment done on him was criminal. Sometimes touching, sometimes soppy, this sleeper was directed by Ralph Nelson and scripted by Stirling Silliphant. Robertson is believable in a difficult role—he shows that Charly is more lovable when retarded than when he is a genius, yet he still makes the audience realize the tragedy of Charly regressing to his retarded state. Thankfully, Robertson doesn't milk audience's emotions; subject matter is already geared for that. I'm also glad that the Michael Crichton–type premise—arrogant scientists victimize a patient/guinea pig with an experiment that is poorly thought out—was made a few years before it would have been given high-tech treatment. But I wish film had a little more life. Music by Ravi Shankar. Also with: Claire Bloom (appealing as the case worker with whom Robertson falls in love), Lilia Skala, Leon Janney, Dick Van Patten.

CHASE, THE (1965) C/122m–135m. The decline and fall of American society is the theme of Arthur Penn's cynical cult film, which is probably why it's more popular in Europe than in America. Unevenly adapted by Lillian Hellman from Horton Foote's novel and play, the story is set in a small Texas town. The characters who eventually come together in one gigantic crash are meant to represent every segment of a sick society—many are believable, many are caricatures spouting clichés. There are lawmen, lawbreakers, escaped prisoners; whites and blacks; rich, middle-class, and poor; faithful and unfaithful women; old people and youths (who have learned decadence and violence from the adults in town); the decent and the corrupted. Sheriff Marlon Brando unsuccessfully tries to keep order when everyone in town gets worked up about escaped prisoner Robert Redford heading home to see his wife, Jane Fonda. They wrongly think he killed a man. Picture starts out so slowly—there are three dull parties going on simultaneously, meant to show how the town is divided according to wealth and age—but it becomes extremely exciting as the violence escalates scene by scene. The scene in which Brando is beaten up by three "citizens" is truly powerful—

no wonder he follows Gary Cooper's lead in *High Noon* and leaves his wretched town behind. Picture has strong characters and many interesting relationships, including that between Redford, Fonda, and James Fox (Redford accepts that Fonda has fallen in love with him, too). Also with: Angie Dickinson (who's at her best as Brando's wife), E. G. Marshall (as Fox's father, the rich man who runs the town), Robert Duvall, Janice Rule, Martha Hyer, Miriam Hopkins (as Redford's batty, stingy mother), Richard Bradford, Diana Hyland, Henry Hull, Jocelyn Brando, Lori Martin, Clifton James, Malcolm Atterbury, Joel Fluellen, Steve Ihnat, Bruce Cabot, Eduardo Ciannelli, Grady Sutton.

CHERRY, HARRY AND RAQUEL (1969) C/71m. Compact Russ Meyer film with tried-and-true combination of sex, violence, and humor. Harry (Charles Napier) is corrupt sheriff whose province is the desert. Raquel (Larissa Ely) is a prostitute and Cherry (Linda Ashton) is a nurse—and during the course of the film Harry makes love with both of them, and the women have an encounter themselves. Between sex scenes, Harry and his Chicano deputy (who makes it with Raquel) try to track down the "Apache" before he lets authorities on to marijuana smuggling being done by Harry and his boss (Franklin Bolger), who gets it on with both Cherry and Raquel. For added sexual content, Meyer injects intentionally silly footage of superstacked Uschi Digard romping naked (but for an Indian warbonnet) around desert. Somewhat dated, but this remains one of Meyer's best films. It has wit, sharp editing, several Don Siegel-like action sequences, and a solid lead in square-jawed Napier, who'd be one of few Meyer actors to be welcomed into mainstream Hollywood films (i.e., *Rambo: First Blood, Part II*). Also with: Bert Santos.

CHILD BRIDE/CHILD BRIDE OF THE OZARKS (1937) B&W/53m. Sleazy backwoods potboiler about a woman (Dianna Durrell) who returns home to Thunderhead Mountain to teach the uneducated children and upgrade the lives of the people there. Her major goal is to stamp out child marriage. Meanwhile a no-good bully tells a widow that he'll turn her over to the law for killing her drunken husband (actually the bully killed him) unless she lets him marry her young daughter (Shirley Mills). Mills wears pigtails and speaks like Shirley Temple, probably to disguise that she's older than depicted. Made years before Jerry Lee Lewis married his 13-year-old cousin and *Pretty Baby*, this independently made sexploitation film is terribly acted, scripted, and directed by Harry J. Revier. It's one of those films where: night shots are intercut with day shots; a boy immediately goes to school when he realizes that the bullet that just hit his father (who is lying on the ground in pain) left only a flesh wound; humor comes from the girl falling into the mud in a pigsty; the boy ambushes and kills the villain and the film ends without there being any talk of his being punished for the crime. The film is very campy and you'll constantly be amused and amazed. But, surprisingly, the teacher is an extremely interesting character, especially when one considers this picture was made in the thirties. She is a liberated woman in the sense that she has chosen her job and living alone over marriage to the man she loves, her well-off boyfriend, the assistant DA. She is a crusader, willing to put herself on the line for her cause. (Indeed, several men in hoods kidnap her and try to do her in, KKK style.) We snicker when she says she wants to stamp out *child marriage*, but we soon learn that it is a valid issue in mountain-backwoods areas. She actually travels around talking to the men and women of Thunderhead Mountain, explaining that such marital arrangements have ruined the lives of the females by trapping them with husbands, children, and work at a very young age. She anticipates Ingrid Bergman's missionary in *The Inn of the Sixth Happiness* who travels around isolated areas of China speaking against the age-old tradition that forced women to have their ankles bound together from childhood as a sign of their subservience to their fathers and husbands. So here, within this ridiculous low-grade exploitation film, we discover some unexpected feminism. Also with: Bob Bollinger, Warner Richmond.

CHILDREN OF PARADISE/ENFANTS DU PARADIS, LES (FRENCH/1945) B&W/188m.

One of the glories of the cinema, the romantic's delight, the sophisticate's cult favorite. The fifth collaboration between director Marcel Carné and screenwriter Jacques Prévert opened in Paris in March 1945 and was quickly hailed as France's *Gone With the Wind*: an epic, a re-creation of a nineteenth-century period (that of Louis Philippe) and setting (the Boulevard of Crime), a romance about a woman (Arletty as Garance) who is coveted by all men who see her. But the real reason the French held it so dear was that it was one of the cornerstone films of *le cinéma d'évasion*—the French film industry's brave response to the German occupation. It's amazing that this affront to the Nazis, which celebrates a free France, could be made under the noses of the occupation authorities. (Secret filming took place over two years in garages and alleys, during which time members of the French resistance were able to hide from the Gestapo because they were among the 1800 extras employed.) Set exactly 100 years earlier so the French audience could draw parallels between the past and present, the film is a wonderful tribute to the people who have never been controlled by authority: lovers, mountebanks, rogues, criminals like Pierre-François Lacenaire (Marcel Herrand), artists, the poor who crowd the inexpensive rafter seats, "gods" (paradise) of the theaters, and, most of all, the performers (the children), like the great serious actor Frédérick Lemaître (Pierre Brasseur) and the great mime Baptiste Deburau (Jean-Louis Barrault). The film is a cry for a return to the past, for liberty, for solidarity between artists and their public, for solidarity among all French people. It reaffirms that there is beauty in life and, through cynic Lacenaire's eventual self-sacrifice, that there is goodness in all but authority figures. Garance's three lovers, Deburau, Lemaître, and Lacenaire, were historical personages; she is fictional. The

men see her as an angel, a dream, a vision of beauty, Venus. She is symbolized by birds, flowers, and the moon. She herself is the symbol of Paris or, as I believe, she *is* Paris: beautiful, freedom-loving, full of memories, as proud of the gutter dwellers as of the elite, lover of every man, the betrayer of none—in whose presence hearts begin to flutter. Most important: she is a survivor, a Stoic beauty who remains unchanged ("I am free") despite becoming mistress to a dictatorial man (Louis Salou as Count Edouard de Montray) from another class. Picture's acting is superb (Barrault's mime performances are classics); film is the first to advance the "stolen kisses" theme (by the time one is ready to yield his heart to a woman, she loves another) that still is pervasive in French film; the visuals are opulent; the elaborate sets are rich in detail and historically accurate. This film is *great* on many levels, from romance to propaganda. Oddly, while almost every character's life is in ruin at the end (in Paris the great love affairs are too consuming to last), you leave the theater feeling as happy as all the French who crowd the streets in the carnival-like finale. Also with: Pierre Renoir, Maria Casarès, Etienne Decroux, Fabien Loris.

CHILDREN SHOULDN'T PLAY WITH DEAD THINGS (1972) C/85m.

A cheap, ugly, non-frightening, non-funny horror comedy with odious characters, an objectionable grave-robbery–Satanic-rite premise, and a climax that rips off *Night of the Living Dead*; it's the type of film that's made by amateurs who think any completed horror film will make money. A perverse, affected director (Alan Ormsby) brings his zonked-out theater troupe to a small island. They dig up a corpse from the decrepit, full graveyard. They call it Orville and perform a corpse-raising ritual. Eventually all the corpses rise from the graveyard and hungrily attack the intruders. Film has no surprises; "scariest" scene, with Ormsby sitting on bed next to Orville, doesn't deliver expected jolt. I find it absolutely amazing this excuse for a film has a strong cult. Ormsby and director/co-writer Benjamin (Bob) Clark would go on to successful careers in Hollywood. Also with: Anya Ormsby, Valerie Mamches, Jane Daly, Jeffrey Gillin, Paul Cronin, Bruce Soloman, Seth Sklarey (as Orville).

CHILLY SCENES OF WINTER (1982) C/93m.

Adaptation of Ann Beattie's novel was originally released in 1979 as *Head over Heels*. That version was four minutes longer due to a happy ending that was cut for the new release. What had been a Boston cult film became a modest commercial hit—however, I suspect that the added interest in the film was more because of Beattie's increased fame than an ending that more accurately reflects what happened to the similar love affairs of those in the movie's 30-ish target audience. John Heard falls head over heels in love with Mary Beth Hurt, who just moved out on her husband. Whereas her husband loved her too little, Heard loves her too much and his obsessiveness, jealousy, and constant flattery drive her back to her husband (and daughter, whom she misses greatly). She thinks herself unworthy of such attention and doesn't believe a woman who leaves her family deserves to be happy. Heard tries to win her back. Picture is offbeat and has many special, funny, charming moments. But, as *screen* characters, I find Heard and Hurt offputting. They may be real characters, but I never believe their responses to each other. In fact, the original ending (which Beattie herself protested) is more logical. Directed by Joan Micklin Silver. The first production of Amy Robinson–Griffin Dunne–Mark Metcalf. Also with: Peter Riegert, Gloria Grahame, Kenneth McMillan, Nora Heflin, Beattie (as a waitress), Dunne.

CHIMES AT MIDNIGHT/FALSTAFF (SPANISH-SWISS/1966) B&W/115m–119m.

Orson Welles's final masterpiece received almost no U.S. distribution after it got a devastating review in the *New York Times* by Bosley Crowther, and even today has not received its due. Welles's story (which he mounted as a play in Belfast in 1960) was taken from Shakespeare's *Henry IV Parts I & II*, with bits from *Henry V*, *The Merry Wives of Windsor*, and *Richard II*; its narration was taken from Raphael Holinshed's *Chronicles*. Told with warmth, wit, and surprising poignancy, the story is simple and on a human level, since Welles makes Falstaff (Welles), rather than Henry IV (John Gielgud) or Prince Hal (Keith Baxter), the hero. Falstaff is surrogate father to Hal while real rather Henry wears the crown. He is a fat, cowardly, bawdy, lying figure, but he gives Hal genuine love while the rigid, humorless Henry pays little attention to him. When Hal ascends to the throne upon his father's death, he literally breaks Falstaff's heart by rejecting him. Welles often played characters whose ascent to power was characterized, like Hal's, by their quick exchange of idealism for ruthlessness. But while characters like Kane or Harry Lime did their friends wrong, few ever actually betrayed friendships, as Hal does to Falstaff. (In fact, Kane and Lime were themselves betrayed by their friends.) In this sense Welles played the *victim*: friendship was sacred to him, which is why Hal's act is so despicable. And I believe Welles regarded it as personal, for Falstaff is surely the character who, with warts, weight, and all, was closest to the real Welles. (Was Hal meant to represent one of the young talents Welles nurtured along, only to watch them move to the top of show biz and pretend they never knew him?) Welles's Falstaff isn't the type of guy you'd bring to a society function, but he'd make a great Santa Claus. He fibs constantly, but he is honest; he fits in with the town dunce and senile old men, yet he has a unique knowledge of what's important in life (love, loyalty, friendship, a good chat, a good roll in bed with a wench, a good bowel movement). He represents goodness in a cruel world, and Hal is not obtaining dignity by banishing Falstaff but rather losing his sense of decency. The film's low budget caused Welles problems, but wait out the early scenes in which the dialogue is often out of synch. The acting is superb (Welles was never better) and the visuals are often stunning. Welles's choreography of the battle sequence is spectacu-

lar—only in Eisenstein's *Alexander Nevsky* does a battle have such impact; your body becomes tired just watching the armored men swing their heavy weapons repeatedly and you worry that you'll feel the blows that crumble these men. As the combatants struggle in the mud and are killed, we become angry about the way lives are wasted—we are being prepared for the way Hal will toss away his friend Falstaff as if he were rubbish, resulting in his death and burial beneath the barren, muddy soil. Narrated by Ralph Richardson. Also with: Margaret Rutherford, Jeanne Moreau, Norman Rodway (as Hotspur), Marina Vlady, Alan Webb, Walter Chiari, Tony Beckley, Fernando Rey, Beatrice Welles.

CHINA 9 LIBERTY 37 (1978) C/102m.

Muscular gunslinger (Fabio Testi) is released from prison on the condition he'll kill a rancher (Warren Oates) for railroad barons. But he finds task difficult once he meets the man. He seduces Oates's pretty, sexually frustrated wife (Jenny Agutter), and after her husband confronts her in a jealous rage, she believes she kills him. Testi and Agutter run off together with the law on their trail. Monte Hellman western is not on level of his earlier *Ride in the Whirlwind* or *The Shooting*, but it's still a fairly interesting, unusual entry in the genre. Dusty, gritty feel to film will remind viewers of those two pictures, as well as Italian westerns and the westerns of Sam Peckinpah (who has a bit part). Epic lovemaking between Testi and Agutter in a river and in a hotel room is noteworthy; except for Anthony Mann's *Man of the West*, sex has had no place in the conservative western genre. Certainly this is the only western in which sex is what drives the lead characters. Title refers to signpost located between the towns of China and Liberty.

CHINA SYNDROME, THE (1979) C/123m.

Cautionary film about the possibilities of a meltdown at a nuclear plant. It achieved tremendous box-office success not only because of its quality and the integrity of the filmmakers and stars, but also because the accident at Three Mile Island happened just when the picture was released. Red-haired Jane Fonda is a TV newscaster who is stuck reporting trivial stories. She enlists radical cameraman Michael Douglas to help her cover a story on a nuclear plant—she hopes this will get her better assignments. While they are filming the story, the plant shakes violently for a few seconds. It becomes apparent that a nuclear accident almost occurred and the plant is unsafe. Power-company executive Richard Herd makes sure Fonda can't get the story on the air. She tries to get longtime plant official Jack Lemmon to go public with the story before an accident occurs that will result in radiation escaping into the environment. Lemmon learns that the plant has not followed all the necessary safety measures because of high costs. Lemmon, Fonda, and Douglas find that their lives are in danger. Lemmon's performance is too mannered, and film's ending (outside the plant) doesn't have Fonda or anyone else making the necessary strong statements (it's as if the filmmakers backed off). Otherwise this is a solid film, proof you can make an exciting movie that has political relevance. However, it would have made a stronger antinuclear statement if the plant were unsafe despite meeting NRC standards. Fonda has one of her best roles, another of her smart but naïve women who break out of a secure world and risk looking foolish to learn *what's going on*. Sharp direction by James Bridges. Produced by Michael Douglas. Written by Mike Gray (*The Murder of Fred Hampton*'s co-director), T. S. Cook, and Bridges. Also with: Scott Brady, James Hampton, Peter Donat, Wilford Brimley, Daniel Valdez.

CHINATOWN (1974) C/131m.
This superlative detective picture, set against a background of political corruption, was directed by Roman Polanski and written by Robert Towne. Towne's powerful Oscar-winning script is set in LA in the late 1930s, and Polanski convincingly re-creates the era through props, costumes, buildings, music, etc. Jack Nicholson gives a dynamic performance as private eye J. J. Gittes, a cocky, mordant wise-ass who's like Columbo in that he gets on everyone's nerves, but is much more aggressive. He realizes that inside every house, every office, every piece of land that he walks into is someone who is very territorial and doesn't want him intruding. He takes great pleasure in annoying them with his presence—especially after he gets his nose slashed open and must wear a large, bloody bandage on his face. He's a shrewd detective who really knows his line of work, but too often he acts impulsively without thinking of the consequences. He dives headfirst into perilous circumstances, not surfacing to evaluate the situation, and, figuratively speaking, drowns. What's remarkable is that this seedy "bedroom dick," who finds evidence that husbands and wives are having affairs, is the most moral man in his world. He quit walking the police beat in Chinatown because cops there were supposed to let crime and corruption exist unhampered. As a private eye a few years later, he now sees that crime and corruption have spread into LA proper and are about to move unhindered into the "pure" country. To stop it, he must find the murderer of the honest LA Water Commissioner, who discovered the scheme of land speculators to create a fake drought in LA by diverting water into desert lands they secretly own. Then he can go to the papers about the water-land scam. While he has an affair with his client, the dead Water Commissioner's icy, troubled widow (Faye Dunaway), he begins to suspect that her ruthless father (John Huston), once the partner of her late husband, is behind the land swindle. The mystery gets more complicated by the minute—*every* new twist is uncovered through Nicholson's sleuthing—and more fascinating. Film's famous finale takes place in Chinatown, appropriately, where naïve Nicholson can wise up and learn just how feeble he is against widespread corruption—Spade and Marlowe wouldn't have accomplished any more than Nicholson's Gittes, but they would already have known what he discovers. Extremely well photographed by John Alonzo, who helps create a sense of menace and paranoia. Cleverly scored by Jerry Goldsmith. Also with: Perry Lopez, Burt Young, Diane Ladd, John Hillerman, Darrell Zwerling, Bruce Glover, Polanski (as a creepy little thing who works for Huston).

CHINESE CONNECTION, THE (CHINESE/1973) C/107m.
If the Bruce Lee from this film had investigated Lee's own mysterious death, then we might know how he really died. Picture is set in Shanghai in 1907, in the Japanese-controlled settlement. Lee returns home to discover that his kung-fu master has been murdered. Against the wishes of the other Chinese in the martial-arts school, Lee sets out to find out who was responsible. Employing a series of disguises, he is a one-man annihilation squad. The enemies are Japanese. Film has awful dubbing, but who cares? There is non-stop action, and watching the remarkable Lee in beautifully choreographed fight sequences (that make intelligent use of close-ups and slow motion) is a unique, exhilarating experience. As always, he is graceful, athletic, charismatic, and in control, but rarely has Lee displayed such ferocity and anger during his fights. The bigoted Japanese get their due. Directed by Lo Wei.

CHINOISE, LA (FRENCH/1967) C/96m.
One of Jean-Luc Godard's most interesting political works; one with a sense of humor. Five young Maoists—philosophy student Anne Wiazemsky (married to Godard at the time), actor Jean-Pierre Léaud, a chemical engineer, an artist, and a peasant girl—live together in the apartment that serves as the film's major set. They will commit terrorist acts at the end of the film, but until then they spend time studying communist literature, giving lectures, quoting Mao, talking directly toward the camera—even when they're not speaking, we read their words on walls. Picture doesn't have the visual or aural impact it once had, but it serves as a reminder that in 1967 young radicals were still learning and developing a sound political philosophy while they were engaged in political acts; and that in many ways political action was a form of theater. Most interesting scene has Wiazemsky on a train being questioned by an older radical (Francis Jeanson as himself) about her rationale for terrorism. Striking photography by Raoul Coutard. Also with: Juliet Berto, Michel Sémeniaki, Omar Diop, Lex de Bruijn.

CHOOSE ME (1984) C/106m.
On most everyone's list of recommended sleepers, Alan Rudolph's zany film is about troubled characters who make coincidental connections with each other, put up false fronts, act *crazy*, and are hopelessly confused and worried about sex, love, marriage, and their inability to communicate. Geneviève Bujold is radio sexologist "Dr. Love," who gives worshipful callers advice on relationships, yet is unable to have one herself. Wanting to get out in the real world, she becomes a housemate of bar owner Lesley Ann Warren—Warren doesn't know that Bujold is Dr. Love, and Bujold doesn't realize that Warren is a frequent caller. Warren is miserable because she sleeps with many guys but is afraid to make a commitment. Another frequent caller is Rae Dawn Chong, who hangs out at the bar because her cad husband, Patrick

Bauchau, has been showing an interest in Warren. When Bauchau calls Warren, Bujold answers; he doesn't know she's Dr. Love, but finds her advice about his marriage is very perceptive. Into this weird situation comes drifter Keith Carradine, who says he was once engaged to the former owner of the bar—who had the same first name as Warren. He makes love to Bujold, Chong, and Warren and gets on Bauchau's nerves by turning up with every woman he knows. He has walked out of a mental hospital and claims to be a pathological liar—but there are indications that what he says of his past (that he was a jet fighter pilot and a CIA spy in Russia) is true. Also when he tells each woman that he loves her and wants to marry her, you believe him each time. He manages to be a positive influence (a godsend) on the three women, helping them put their feelings toward themselves and men into perspective. *Noir*-ish night scenes outside Warren's bar, where the street and buildings are bathed in red light, have a surreal, dreamlike feel, but the film as a whole has the "logic" of crazy real life. The storyline seems preposterous, but we willingly suspend our disbelief because we're touched by the characters and root for them to make it out of their misery. The acting is superb—Warren, in a Susan Sarandon-type role, deserved an Oscar nomination. Rudolph's clever script has humor, warmth, surprises.

CHRISTIANE F. (WEST GERMAN/1981) C/124m.
Controversial, grueling film, based on actual transcripts, about a pretty, neglected, 13-year-old girl (Natja Brunkhorst) who befriends a group of young street people and takes a nosedive into the sordid world of heroin addiction and prostitution. Not as exploitive as you might have heard, but just as depressing. Film is extremely graphic, unrelenting in its grimness, believable. Saddest part is that Christiane's mother loves her, yet still lets her get all her emotional support from other kids, who aren't even strong enough to help themselves. Watching the brutal change in Christiane's facial appearance is as shocking as the other sights in her disgusting world. Obviously not for all tastes; but it stays in memory. With a concert appearance and music by David Bowie. One wonders why director Ulrich Edel, who doesn't pay much attention to character development, was attracted to such a morbid subject. Also with: Thomas Haustein (as Christiane's hustler-addict boyfriend), Jens Kuphal.

CHRISTINE (1984) C/110m.
Undistinguished Stephen King novel about a killer automobile—a subject that's been done to death on television and in film—is given a visually impressive but extremely impersonal treatment by John Carpenter. Keith Gordon is a teenage nerd who buys a '58 Plymouth Fury named Christine that was the instrument in several past deaths. It soon takes over Gordon's life. Suddenly he's cool enough to date the beautiful Alexandra Paul—but his heart is more devoted to his car. Christine spends her free time taking driverless cruises and running down Gordon's enemies from school. It also tries

to do in Paul, for whom it feels great jealousy. Paul and Gordon's best friend, John Stockwell, can't help noticing that Gordon has turned into a self-possessed, Christine-obsessed cad, and trying to figure out a way to end the car's demonic grip on him. Unpleasant film has few surprises. It also lacks an important transition scene in which the shy Gordon becomes a ladies' man capable of approaching someone like Paul. Also missing are scenes in which Gordon at least tries to ward off Christine's control—Gordon becomes thoroughly obnoxious so quickly that we don't really care what happens to him. Carpenter paid so much attention to the special effects relating to Christine that he forgot about character development. The type of film that would have been dismissed by critics and fans if King and Carpenter weren't involved. Also with: Harry Dean Stanton, Roberts Blossom.

CHRISTMAS STORY, A (1983) C/98m.
It's hard to believe that the same Bob Clark who gave us *Porky's* produced, directed, and co-wrote this charming little film. Based on radio humorist Jean Shepherd's witty nostalgia novel, *In God We Trust, All Others Pay Cash*, and narrated by Shepherd, picture takes us back to the forties in Indiana to Ralphie's (Peter Billingsley) most memorable Christmas season. That's when the boy was nine and dreamed of getting a Red Ryder Ranger Model Air Rifle, although mother Melinda Dillon believed BB guns were good only for shooting out a kid's eye. Film is full of delightful, recognizable episodes: Billingsley's best friend gets his tongue stuck to a pole after being "double-dog dared" to put it there; Billingsley decodes his secret message from radio's Little Orphan Annie only to have it be a commercial for Ovaltine; Billingsley lets slip the "F" word in front of father Darren McGavin and has his mouth washed out with soap (Lifebuoy, his least favorite flavor); Dillon coaxes his little brother (Ian Petrella) into downing dinner by getting him to imitate a pig's disgusting habits; Billingsley and his pals repeatedly flee the red-haired school bully until one day Billingsley is so depressed for getting a C+ on his paper about his desire for a BB gun (the teacher wrote he'd get his eye shot out) that he gives the boy a whipping; McGavin wins a hideous lamp that has a plastic female leg for a base—he loves it, Dillon is aghast; and Billingsley and his brother are terrified by a kid-hating department-store Santa and his mean helpers—a scene that really hits home; etc. You'll be touched by the warmth the members of Billingsley's family feel for one another, and amused by their various idiosyncrasies. The characters are truly believable, the script is consistently funny. There's no reason that this unique film should play only in December. Also with: Scott Schwartz, Tedde Moore.

CIAO! MANHATTAN (1972) C-B&W/84m.
Famous underground film by John Palmer and David Weisman. It was begun in 1967, with the filmmakers intending it to be a $50,000 black-and-white documentary about a day in the life of Edie Sedgwick (subject of Jean Stein's best-selling book). They figured that this former Warhol Factory

girl and model for *Life* and *Vogue* pretty much symbolized the era's wild, uninhibited, drug-crazed New York scene. For a number of reasons, including the fact that Sedgwick herself was already heavily dependent on a variety of drugs (she rhapsodizes about *speed* in the film), shooting broke down. It resumed in California three years later, with a $350,000 projected budget and a storyline that allowed for the even more spacey Sedgwick (as "Susan") to tell a young man (Wesley Ames) who thinks *he's* a rebel about her rebellious past life—her flashbacks are comprised of the black-and-white footage taken in 1967. The sad part is that the pathetic, unhealthy, mixed-up Sedgwick we now see—so different from the slim (she'd recently had silicone injections), fresh-faced, relatively drug-free young girl who was once the talk of the modeling world—is not putting on an act. She would die soon after shooting (a scene was added to acknowledge the death of "Susan"), and that's what you think about while watching the entire film. You get the same reaction watching *The Wizard of Babylon*, the documentary on Fassbinder making his last film before his death—only here you get the impression that Sedgwick was being exploited for the sake of her bringing a bizarre touch to the project. In essence, she is DOA. Still, picture is interesting, though not always coherent. You'll see a lot of familiar faces, including Allen Ginsberg, Baby Jane Holzer, Viva, Andy Warhol, even Roger Vadim and Isabel Jewell.

CIMARRON (1931) B&W/124m. Tiresome Edna Ferber soap-opera western epic covers 40 years in the lives of idealistic, pioneering Yancey Cravath (Richard Dix) and his realistic wife, Sabra (Irene Dunne), who arrive in Oklahoma during the land rush of 1889 and watch it grow from wild, open prairie, to a territory rich in oil, to a progressive state. Yancey establishes a newspaper, but his wanderlust causes him to desert Sabra and their children repeatedly, leaving Sabra to run the paper—eventually she becomes a congresswoman. Except for some unexpected feminism (which is undermined by some racism), this early Best Picture winner is extremely dated. You'll swear you've seen every scene in some other movie. The acting is uniformly awful—Dix gives an unbearably hammy, deep-voiced, "matinee idol" turn, and Dunne, who wears a hideous white wig at the end, is just plain boring. Like other Ferber vehicles, picture is about how husbands are disappointments but their wives take their wedding vows seriously enough to stick with them. Remade in 1960 by Anthony Mann. Directed by Wesley Ruggles. Also with: Estelle Taylor, William Collier, Jr., Nance O'Neil, Edna May Oliver, George E. Stone, Roscoe Ates.

CIRCUS, THE (1928) B&W/72m. Charlie Chaplin's Tramp is chased by police who think he's a pickpoket. He runs into a circus tent while the show is in progress. The crowd laughs hysterically at his antics. Charlie fails his formal audition in front of the cruel circus owner (Allan Garcia), but is hired as a property man. Each time he carries props into the arena, crowds go wild. Without realizing it, he has become the star of the show. Charlie falls in love with the owner's daughter (Merna Kennedy), an equestrienne, and he threatens to quit the circus if Garcia doesn't treat her better. Garcia relents and even gives Charlie a star's salary when Kennedy informs him that the overflow crowds have come to see him. But when Charlie discovers that Kennedy has fallen for a new tightrope walker (Harry Crocker), he becomes too depressed to be funny in his performances. Garcia threatens to fire him, and again treats his daughter badly. This is a sweet, deceptively simple, flawless film; if it doesn't quite equal other Chaplin masterpieces on first viewing, that's because it seems that Chaplin didn't invest it with quite as much emotion. There are wonderful scenes: hungry Chaplin eating a hot dog that a little boy (whose father looks the other way) holds in his hand; Chaplin eluding a pickpocket and a cop in a hall of mirrors; Chaplin giving hungry Kennedy (in their first scene together) his only slice of bread and instructing her how to eat it slowly (she doesn't listen); scared Chaplin finding himself locked in a cage with a sleeping lion inside and a barking dog outside; Chaplin attempting a tightrope act and having a wild monkey latch its teeth onto his nose; and, in the classic finale, Charlie watching the circus depart and deciding that he should walk away alone in the other direction. And of course there are the usual number of brilliant sight gags and moments of slapstick. Picture is silent but for Chaplin's music, including the opening number that he sings on the soundtrack. Not as well known as *The Gold Rush, City Lights, Modern Times,* or his sound features, but this is a gem. Also with: Henry Bergman, Stanley J. Stafford.

CITIZEN KANE (1941) B&W/119m. Orson Welles's debut film can justifiably be called the greatest picture of all time because it not only taught other directors how to tell a story through film but also taught moviegoers how to watch a film. The picture begins in 1940, when 70-year-old Charles Foster Kane (Welles), the William Randolph Hearst-like publisher of the New York *Inquirer* and numerous other papers and one of the richest and (at his peak) most powerful people in the world, dies while living in near-seclusion at Xanadu, his palatial estate in Florida. His last word is "Rosebud," which magazine editor Rawlston (Philip Van Zandt) thinks may be the secret to his mysterious life. He dispatches reporter Jerry Thompson (William Alland) to find out the real story of Kane. Thompson watches footage about Kane in *March of Time* newsreels and reads the diary of Kane's long-dead onetime guardian, Walter Parks Thatcher (George Coulouris), who, when young Charles's mother (Agnes Moorehead) suddenly became rich (she had a deed to a supposedly worthless mine that proved to be a bonanza), took him from Colorado and oversaw his education and proper upbringing. And he interviews (untalented) singer Susan Alexander (Dorothy Comingore), who married Kane after his first wife, Emily (Ruth Warrick), was killed in a car crash; Bernstein (Everett Sloan), chairman of the board of the *Inquirer*, and Kane's manager since the 1890s; Jed Leland (Joseph Cotten), former drama critic of the *Inquirer* and Kane's best friend until he panned Susan's debut performance; Raymond (Paul Stewart), Kane's butler for the last 11 years. Film is about a search for the essential missing part ("Rosebud") needed to document a man's life, a search for *subjective* truth. Ironically, Welles creates "realism" (the "true" picture of Kane) through illusion and expressionism, and so his picture becomes a tribute to the camera. The visuals show past events not as the six storytellers remember them but as the filmmakers (primarily director Welles and cameraman Gregg Toland) interpret the storytellers' words. There are contradictions between how we see Kane and how he is remembered verbally: we regret that he was such a corruptive influence on people, but gain sympathy for this complex man who could manipulate the country but never trusted anyone enough to explain the meaning of "Rosebud"; who helplessly watched all the people he loved desert him. The film is journalistic in nature; it makes us, even more than Thompson, investigative reporters. He can't properly sum up the testimony, but we can because, in addition to sitting in on Thompson's interviews, we have seen Welles's visuals: we learn about Kane and the other characters not only through dialogue and action but through Welles's creative, flamboyant use of props, screen space, set design, music, editing, sound (including voice inflections), costumes, freeze frames, deep-focus photography, and lighting. Not surprisingly, the disclosure of the "clue" to the real Kane—"Rosebud" is the name on the sled he owned as a child—is not granted Thompson, but is a visual present to viewers from the filmmaker through his camera. That Kane thinks of "Rosebud" at the end has in part to do with his "searching for his [lost] youth"—but he doesn't want to go back to an "Edenic" existence, as many viewers assume: his father beat him and his only companion was the snowman he built. To the dying Kane the sled is the one possession he treasured *before* he got money and was able to buy everything he wanted (and simultaneously ruin his life): the *Inquirer*, the *Chronicle*'s crack staff, statues and zoo animals (which, unlike people, couldn't run away from him), Xanadu, public opinion, "friendship," and "love." Kane said years before money led to his downfall, politically and personally, "If I hadn't been really rich, I might have been a really great man." An ambitious man chased the American Dream and somewhere, somehow, his life *irrevocably*—the word Kane can't pronounce—went wrong. Picture has great acting, music (by Bernard Herrmann), photography, editing (by Robert Wise), countless classic moments. Herman J. Mankiewicz and Welles wrote the script—who wrote what will always be a source for lively debate. The most influential film of the sound era, it is a cinematic reference point that must be seen repeatedly by those who want to learn the *language* of film, and to learn its potential as a storytelling medium and as an outlet for personal and artistic expression. Also with: Ray Collins, Erskine Sanford, Harry Shannon, Fortunio Bonanova, Alan Ladd, Arthur O'Connell.

CITY LIGHTS (1931) B&W/81m. A hilarious, poignant comedy masterpiece by Charles Chaplin! He continued to use titles rather than have his characters speak and, he feared, lose their universal appeal, but he did include a soundtrack with his own truly exceptional score and sound effects. His Little Tramp is pushed around in a world where bourgeois types revere statues but chase away those penniless human beings who sleep among them; where the only aristocrats who befriend tramps—or even deign to acknowledge their existence—are those who are too drunk to remember their own prejudices; where the police are the enemies of anyone without money; where even butlers and newsboys enjoy pulling rank on tramps; where the disenfranchised go to jail for crimes they didn't commit. But our Little Tramp retains his pride and dignity despite the constant humiliations he endures (he's constantly tipping his hat like a gentleman; he brushes off places he'll sit, despite wearing soiled, ripped pants); and he is one of the lucky few to see the beauty (the city's "lights") around him. Sadly, few recognize the beauty that is in *him*. He loves beautiful, aromatic flowers and he falls for the beautiful blind girl (Virginia Cherrill) who sells flowers on the street. He's willing to shovel manure and even box to make enough money to help Cherrill and her grandmother pay their rent. She falls in love with him, thinking he's wealthy. Chaplin wants to get the money to pay for an operation that will give Cherrill sight—but he fears her reaction when she sees who he really is. (Interestingly, the operation is free to the poor, but Chaplin won't be associated with such charity.) His one chance is to get the money from a rich man (Harry Meyers) whose life he saved. When he's drunk, Meyers loves Chaplin and gives him the money, but when sober he accuses Chaplin of robbing him. Chaplin is willing to go to jail for the girl's sake and flees with the money. Film ends with Cherrill, who now has sight, giving a flower to the tramp who she thinks is a stranger and, when she touches his hand, realizing he is the man she loves. In the most tearful moment in all of Chaplin, she says, as the film's last line: "Yes, I can see now." She is not referring to the fact that she has literally gained sight, but means that she has just become aware that she is looking at the very essence of beauty in the world: the beautiful Little Tramp. An exquisite, infinitely rewarding film. Also with: Hank Mann, Florence Lee, Jean Harlow (an extra in the nightclub scene).

CLASH BY NIGHT (1952) B&W/105m. Battered by life, depressed Barbara Stanwyck returns home to a small fishing village after 10 years away. While she desires a man who could give her confidence, she doesn't think one exists, so she agrees to marry simple fisherman Paul Douglas, although she doesn't love him. She bears him a child and for a year is a dutiful wife. Dissatisfied, she has an affair with Douglas's friend Robert Ryan, a projectionist. Their affair begins tempestuously with an animalistic embrace and Stanwyck sliding her hand beneath his undershirt and clutching his back. Both cynics, Stanwyck and Ryan sense they are each other's last chance for happiness and contemplate running off together. Fritz Lang directed this adaptation (by Alfred Hayes) of Clifford Odets's play, and he seems an odd choice because there is no place in this deliberately paced drama where he can use his visual flare—he does move his camera more than usual in an unsuccessful attempt to keep this talkfest from seeming stagy, but dramatic lighting, sharp editing, and varied camera angles would have been out of place. In the absence of action, the film has lonely, lost, broken people philosophizing about life, love, trust, and responsibility. What excitement there is comes from the characters, who are presented as life's forces, exhibiting raw passions, gut emotions. Most interestingly, the two females—Stanwyck and Marilyn Monroe, who is impressive as tough, spirited fiancée of Stanwyck's brother, Keith Andes—discuss what it is like to be a female in the tough male world. While the love-triangle plot in which the unsuspecting husband is odd-man-out had been around since the Edward G. Robinson and Edward Arnold films of the thirties and forties *film noir*, this was the rare instance in which the woman is the film's central character. Picture needs sparks—and more of Monroe—but the acting is good, and the last scene is extremely satisfying. Also with: J. Carrol Naish, Silvia Minciotti.

CLASH OF THE TITANS (BRITISH/1981) C/118m.
Ray Harryhausen provided the special effects for this large-scale but slightly disappointing mythological epic. Mixing Shakespeare and Greek and Norse mythology, screenwriter Beverley Cross tells how Perseus (Harry Hamlin), human son of Zeus (Laurence Olivier), attempts to save the beautiful Andromeda (Judi Bowker). She is to be sacrificed to the dreaded Kraken, a sea monster that ranks with Harryhausen's most spectacular creations. Fighting against time, Perseus goes on a long journey to obtain the head of Medusa—if the Kraken gazes into the gorgon's visage, it will turn into stone. His companions are Ammon (Burgess Meredith), an old actor who gives him advice; Bubo, the Owl of Brass; and the winged horse Pegasus. He battles the evil, hoofed Calibos (a Dynamation creature except in close-up, when he is played by Neil McCarthy)—who also loves Andromeda—giant Forest Scorpions, and the hideous Medusa. Picture is too long, Bubo (meant to make kids laugh) is an embarrassing creation, and Cross fails to create the same tension between Perseus and the gods on Olympus that there was between Jason and Zeus in his script for *Jason and the Argonauts*. On the plus side are the marvelously animated scenes in which Perseus tames Pegasus and Perseus takes on Medusa while trying not to look into her face (this is the most suspenseful sequence in all of Harryhausen); and the presence of Bowker, a smart, lovely heroine. Directed by Desmond Davis. Produced by Harryhausen and Charles H. Schneer. Also with: Sian Phillips, Maggie Smith, Ursula Andress, Flora Robson.

CLEOPATRA (1934) B&W/95m.
Cecil B. De Mille's classic is silly, creaky, and full of long-winded tête-à-têtes that might have been written for a *humorless* thirties bed-room comedy. Nevertheless, it's fun to watch. Lounging around in skimpy bare-midriff outfits that Madonna might have designed, Claudette Colbert is an extremely sexy Cleopatra. She also possesses enough intelligence to realize that through her singular powers of seduction she can outwit and manipulate her Roman men, Caesar (Warren William) and then Antony (Henry Wilcoxon). So Colbert fits into the vamp tradition of Theda Bara, who played Cleopatra in the silent era. Picture's theme is that women can emasculate great male warriors and statesmen, but we can forgive this Egyptian trapped on foreign soil because she must find some way to survive in a male-dominated, woman-hating ("They can't think, they can't fight, they are playthings for us," says Antony) world. One of those historical films where the guards and slave girls are worth keeping an eye on. Also with: Joseph Schildkraut, C. Aubrey Smith, Ian Keith, Gertrude Michael, Robert Warwick.

CLEOPATRA JONES AND THE CASINO OF GOLD (1975) C/96m.
Sequel to *Cleopatra Jones* finds Amazonian U.S. agent Tamara Dobson kicking a bloody trail in the Orient. She's in pursuit of a drug queenpin (Stella Stevens, who has already disposed of a couple of previous undercover agents). Sexy, funny, fast-moving exploitation film is better than the original due to welcome presence of Stevens and pretty and lethal actress Tanny, whose character becomes Dobson's partner. Best scene has Tanny being attacked in hotel room. Dobson's no Pam Grier, but she was one of main assets of blaxploitation generation. Directed by Chuck Bail. Also with: Norman Fell, Albert Popwell.

CLOCK, THE (1945) B&W/90m.
Soldier Robert Walker, a country boy, is on two days' leave in New York City when he meets office worker Judy Garland in Penn Station. They spend the day together and fall in love. But before they bother to find out each other's last names, they're accidentally separated. And in a nightmarish sequence they look for each other, their happiness hanging in the balance. Equally frustrating for *us* is their attempt to get married. Garland is extremely fetching, but this romance is too calculated to endear us through simplicity. When she falls for Walker as he talks about his hometown and how he wants to work with his hands in the future, she's listening to drivel much like the pretentious Charles Grodin uses in *The Heartbreak Kid*. Picture is too proud of itself for its "realistic" characters, innocent romance, "honest" common-folks dialogue. Despite the fine cast and a few touching moments, picture may grate on your nerves. Director Vincente Minnelli's first non-musical. He'd marry Garland after this picture. Filmed on the M-G-M lot, not on location in New York. Also with: James Gleason, Lucille Gleason, Keenan Wynn, Ruth Brady, Marshall Thompson.

CLOCKWORK ORANGE, A (BRITISH/1971) C/137m.
In the not too distant future our Humble Narrator, young Alex (Malcolm McDowell), and his pals ("droogs") spend the nights practicing *ultra-violence*: beating, raping,

and terrorizing citizens. One night Alex kills a snobbish woman, and his droogs, who are angry with him, knock him out and leave him for police. He's sent to prison. His only chance for freedom is to undergo the Liberal Party's experimental "Ludovico" treatment whereby he's made ill when watching violent movies; afterward violence and Beethoven make him nauseous. When freed he is unable to hurt a fly; he becomes the victim of the droogs (now policemen) and ends up in the house of Liberal Mr. Alexander (Patrick Magee), who doesn't recognize Alex as the one who raped and caused the death of his wife. Eventually Alex gets that evil gleam back in his eye. You can't cure the habitual thrill criminal. Stanley Kubrick's adaptation of Anthony Burgess's novel is visually brilliant and thematically reprehensible. Because Alex is meant to embody our savage, anarchic impulses, Kubrick figured we'd identify with him. At least, that is what he intended—so that we wouldn't identify with Alex's victims, he manipulates us into *accepting* Alex in relation to the world. Played by McDowell instead of by a less appealing actor of the Sean Penn mold, Alex is energetic, handsome, witty, and more clever, honest, intelligent, and interesting than any of the adults in the cruel world. Without exception, Kubrick makes Alex's victims more obnoxious than they are in the book (his treatment of women is insulting). Kubrick makes their abuse at Alex's hands more palatable by making them grotesque, mannered, snobbish figures. Kubrick uses other distancing devices: extreme wide angles, slow motion, fast motion, surreal backgrounds, songs that counterpoint the violence. The violence that Alex perpetrates is very stylized, but when it comes time for him to endure violence (a bottle to the head, police brutality, the Ludovico technique), it is much more realistic. Poor Alex, we think. Our hostility is directed toward everyone but him; he is like an alley cat who is declawed before being returned to the streets. Burgess believed that the book and film were parables that expressed two basic points: "If we are going to love mankind, we will have to love Alex as a not unrepresentative member of it; it is preferable to have a world of violence undertaken in full awareness—violence chosen as an act of will—than a world conditioned to be good or harmless." But the mankind Kubrick shows us is totally alien to us and not worthy of our love. And even *before* he undergoes the Ludovico treatment, Alex's violent acts don't seem to be made through *free choice*, but are reflexive, conditioned by past violence—he is already a clockwork orange (human on the outside, mechanized on the inside). Film's strong, gratuitous violence is objectionable (as is the comical atmosphere when violence is being perpetrated), but the major reason the film can be termed fascistic is Kubrick's heartless, super-intellectual, super-orderly, antiseptic, anti-human, anti-female, anti-sensual, anti-passion, anti-erotic treatment of its subject. In his cold world, all emotional stimuli, from drugs to Beethoven, are lumped together as being harmful; all art (classical music, theater, literature, painting, sculpture, and film) is pornographic. Film has cult following due to wild clothes, visual design, and violence. John Alcott was the cinematographer. Also with: Anthony Sharp (as the Minister who wants to use "cured" Alex for political purposes), Warren Clarke, Aubrey Morris, James Marcus, Michael Tarn, Adrienne Corri, Michael Bates.

CLOSE ENCOUNTERS OF THE THIRD KIND (1977) C/137m; THE SPECIAL EDITION (1980) C/152m.

While George Lucas was off making a film about intergalactic warfare, Stephen Spielberg was making this film about peace and friendship (through the communication of words, music, and feelings) between alien races. It's a film by a dreamer for dreamers (the true SF fan). Roy Neary (Richard Dreyfuss) is an Indiana utilities worker who spots a UFO during a blackout. Soon afterward he finds that there have been other UFO sightings and activity. Naturally, the government is covering it all up. He starts having sensations that he's being drawn to a huge rock formation (Devil's Tower) in Wyoming, where something monumental will soon take place. Leaving behind his wife (Teri Garr, of course) and kids, Roy and a single mother (Melinda Dillon), whose little boy was abducted by a UFO (in a classic sequence), head for Wyoming. At Devil's Tower, amid great secrecy, French scientist Claude Lacombe (François Truffaut) and many U.S. government officials and astronauts have gathered for the first meeting with alien visitors. It's a scene all SF fans will treasure. Because of his childlike innocence and curiosity, Roy, who represents Spielberg and millions of envious viewers, is chosen by the sweet-looking alien leader (a stunning creation by Carlo Rimbaldi, who'd later give us E.T.) to be the earthling who accompanies them into space. In *The Special Edition*, which contains additional footage, we see Roy inside the alien saucer—It's a spectacular sight. Spielberg has made a marvelous picture, an enthralling, myth-making work full of suspense, mystery, and a sense of awe and wonder about space travel and alien life that may reflect the viewer's own feelings toward the subject. The special effects by Douglas Trumbull are breathtaking—when the mother ship makes its first appearance, your jaw may drop open. While the story has gaps in it and some of the bits with Roy and his family are awkward, the film is so ambitious, imaginative, and visually impressive that one can overlook its few flaws. It should be seen on a large screen. Julia Phillips and Michael Phillips produced. Vilmos Zsigmond did the cinematography, although there were contributions from Trumbull, William A. Fraker, Douglas Slocombe, John Alonzo, Laszlo Kovacs, and others. The dramatic score is by John Williams. Also with: Bob Balaban, Cary Guffey.

CLOSELY WATCHED TRAINS/CLOSELY OBSERVED TRAINS (CZECH/1967) B&W/89m.

Beguiling mix of comedy, warm human drama (of the everyday-life variety), and jolting tragedy won the Oscar for Best Foreign Film and was one of the landmarks of the brief Czech film renaissance. It's set in a provincial town during WWII, at the time of the German occupation. Vaclav Neckar plays a shy, naïve, doltish lad of 17 who gets a job as apprentice-dispatcher at the railway station. The Nazis ask Neckar, the stationmaster, and the dispatcher (Josef Somr) to observe the passing trains closely to make sure there is no espionage. But Neckar pays more attention to what's going on at the station, where everybody is obsessed with sex. He particularly marvels at the sexual escapades of Somr, who seems anything but a ladies' man. Neckar hopes to prove his manhood with a pretty conductress (Jitka Bendova) who has made advances at him, but he has performance anxiety. Afterward he attempts suicide. Writer-director Jiri Menzel's ironic point, brought home in the final scene when Neckar agrees to help Somr blow up a German ammunition train, is that males can actually perform great acts of heroism (such as taking on the Nazis singlehandedly), yet consider themselves failures as men if they get too anxious in bed to please a pretty little flirt. Picture has likable, quirky characters, a strong sense of locale, and, even considering the suicide scene and the finale, a great deal of charm. It's also quite erotic, especially when Somr playfully and seductively rubber-stamps the thighs and buttocks of a lovely young co-worker, who's amused and turned on by this unusual foreplay. Menzel and Bohumil Hrabal adapted Hrabal's novel. Also with: Vladimir Valenta, Libuse Havelkova.

CLOWNS, THE (ITALIAN/1971) C/90m.
Federico Fellini's comical yet elegiac tribute to those long-dead or aged European circus clowns who have had a profound effect on his work. Fellini appears as himself on screen, interviewing clowns or their families and looking at films in preparation for a documentary he is doing. These staged scenes are highly comedic and illustrate that people's everyday activities are fraught with clownish, slapstick minutes. Indeed, the film's most remarkable segment draws parallels between clowns and their routines and the absurd characters (midgets, drunks, the handicapped) and their silly daily routines Fellini remembers from his youth—as a boy, Fellini didn't like clowns because they reminded him of sad aspects of reality. We learn here that in all his films Fellini directed street scenes full of buffoonery as if he wanted them to be ideal models for clowns mapping out routines. Heartfelt, picture—comprised mostly of stylized re-creations of famous circus routines—has many touching moments, including a dying old clown sneaking out of a hospital to watch two new clowns perform, and a trumpet duet by a clown and his *dead* partner. Unique film was made for television.

COAL MINER'S DAUGHTER (1980) C/125m.
This exceptional musical biography of country music superstar Loretta Lynn (based on her autobiography) is more accurately the story of *two* people: Lynn (Sissy Spacek) and her husband Doolittle (Tommy Lee Jones does an outstanding job), who overcome enormous obstacles to make their marriage survive. It chronicles their relationship, going back to their courtship almost thirty years ago in Butcher's Holler, Kentucky, an isolated mining town. She was married at thirteen, before she knew anything about cooking, sewing, housekeeping, or sex. The young girl suddenly was uprooted by Doolittle (a former soldier who was in his twenties) and taken to Washington state. She'd never again see her father (a convincing portrayal by Levon Helm, drummer for the Band). Lynn gave birth at fourteen and had several more children while still in her teens; she would overcome tremendous shyness, constant strains on her marriage (including Doolittle's drinking, unfaithfulness, and depression over his not being needed in her career), and health problems to become the undisputed Queen of Country Music. Through it all Lynn has to adjust to Doolittle and meet his expectations, just as he has to cope with her. Spacek's Lynn is no saint; in fact, sometimes you find yourself getting peeved with her stubbornness, ignorance, and childishness, and wonder how Doolittle puts up with her. Spacek, whom Lynn hand-picked to play her, gives a truly magnificent portrayal (she deservedly won an Oscar) of a remarkable woman—a survivor, Spacek contended, because of her sense of humor. Spacek lost weight to play her as a shy but happy thirteen-year-old and put on weight for the forty-year-old Lynn, who is burned out by endless travel and concerts, pills, and squabbles with Doolittle. You become touched by Lynn's love of family and her vulnerability and loneliness despite having millions of fans. What is most memorable about Spacek's performance is the transition of a young girl with no skills or confidence into a person who knows she sings with the best of them (and is thrilled to be appreciated). Watch the way she beams when she first performs for an audience or when Doolittle, who never had anything good to say about her talents around the house, says her singing makes him proud. Spacek captures Lynn's well-known mannerisms and speaking nuances ("Deddy," not "Daddy") and, a one-time singer herself, does a remarkable job with Lynn's singing voice and phrasing ("hard" rhymes with "tired"). For me the musical highlight has Spacek's Lynn singing a duet with Beverly D'Angelo's Patsy Cline at a country fair—for a moment you forget you're not watching the real singers. Praise is also due to director Michael Apted. He claims he was able to create such an authentic Kentucky mining community because he grew up in coal country in England. Also with: Phyllis Boyens (as Lynn's mother), Ernest Tubb (as himself), Minnie Pearl.

COBRA WOMAN (1944) C/70m.
Kitsch Klassic, the type of film William Hurt might have fantasized about in *Kiss of the Spider Woman*. The fourth of six escapist Technicolor adventures that Universal made with Jon Hall and Maria Montez between 1942 and 1946, it has the alluring Montez playing twin sisters. About to marry Hall, the nice sister is kidnapped and taken to the island where her evil sister is the queen. The villagers want her to replace her sister so the sacrifices to the cobra god will cease. Montez accidentally kills her sister and takes her place, but has trouble concealing her identity from the treacherous high priest (Edgar Barrier). Hall and Sabu must try to rescue her. The dialogue is enjoyably trite, the decor is ornate, the stars are sexy, the volcano is bubbly, the picture is colorful. Montez is as significant to film history as Carmen Miranda

(and much more important than Patricia Medina). This is her definitive performance! Directed by Robert Siodmak. Also with: Lon Chaney, Jr., Mary Nash, Lois Collier, Samuel S. Hinds, Moroni Olsen.

COCA-COLA KID, THE (1985) C/94m. Not as much fun as *The Karate Kid*, *The Flamingo Kid*, or, even, any version of *Billy the Kid*. English-language comedy by controversial Yugoslavian director Dušan Makavejev has Eric Roberts as a troubleshooter for the Coca-Cola Corporation who is sent to Australia to boost business. He finds his style too strident for the laid-back Aussies; and he gets in over his head trying to convince a gruff, eccentric old-timer (Bill Kerr) to bring his independent cola-bottling plant and distribution company under the Coca-Cola banner. Meanwhile Roberts's kooky, klutzy secretary (Greta Scacchi) keeps making a play for him—but as long as he acts like an imperialistic businessman instead of a human being, he resists her. Comedy has wild characters, some sharp satire as well as offbeat humor, lovemaking, and Scacchi, a dreamgirl who can act—but it never comes together. Its plot recalls *Local Hero*, but it lacks the sweet, gentle direction of Bill Forsyth. Reportedly there was much hostility on the set because of Makavejev—and it shows. Highlight is Tom Finn's rousing commercial jingle "Coca-Cola Jungle." Written by Frank Moorhouse, from his novels. Also with: David Slingsby, Rebecca Smart (as Scacchi's young daughter).

COCAINE FIENDS, THE (1936) B&W/74m. Today this is promoted as a camp classic in the vein of *Reefer Madness*, but it isn't nearly as blatantly exploitive or as foolish in its depiction of drug usage and addiction—consequently, it isn't as much fun. In fact, film that shows how several pretty young women have their lives ruined by men and cocaine is kind of a downer. Story is of a rural girl who comes to the city to marry a racketeer, but is instead turned into an addict—he had told her he was giving her a "headache powder." Nice doesn't-even-dance brother comes looking for her and also gets hooked. Sister risks her life to get money to send him back home. "It's too late for me," she says nobly. "Girls can't come back." Scenes of seedy apartment where drug-addict couple (the brother and his girlfriend) are in misery because they can't afford dope anticipates "realistic" films from sixties and seventies. Film is probably of more interest because of its sad view of females in trouble in a cold-hearted, male-dominated world—where even beloved fathers turn out to be drug dealers. Serious direction by Wm. A. O'Connor. With: Lois January, Noel Madison, Sheila Manners, Dean Benton, Lois Lindsay.

COCOANUTS, THE (1929) B&W/96m. The first Marx Brothers movie was adapted by Morrie Ryskind from their Broadway hit, written by Ryskind and George S. Kaufman. It's set at a Florida hotel, where Groucho works behind the desk but comes out every so often to flirt with rich Margaret Dumont. Chico and Harpo show up, asking for a room without a bath and carrying an empty suitcase which they hope to fill up during their stay. Dumont's valuable necklace is stolen and she is led to believe hotel employee Oscar Shaw was responsible. Dumont insists that her daughter, Mary Eaton, marry sneaky Cyril Ring instead of Shaw, whom Eaton loves. But it's found out that Ring and his mistress, Kay Francis, are the real thieves. Now that you know the ending, forget the necklace storyline and watch the Marx Brothers. Critics often complain about the film's theatricality and static stretches—not surprising, since the sound film was not that refined in 1929—but it contains some of the funniest Marx Brothers dialogue and Harpo magic found in their movies. One can only imagine how audiences who had never seen the Marx Brothers before reacted. Groucho has some terrific conversations with Dumont ("I can see you bending over a hot stove—only I can't see the stove!"), Chico is particularly aggressive with his lines, and Harpo has great facial reactions to Groucho's boring banquet speech. There are some slow stretches, but whenever Groucho, Chico, and Harpo are on the screen, it's non-stop hilarity. A great film from which to excerpt prime Marx Brothers material. Directed by Robert Florey and Joseph Santley. Music by Irving Berlin. Also with: Zeppo Marx, who is barely noticeable.

COCOON (1985) C/118m. Ron Howard directed this popular sci-fi fantasy about what happens to a young charter-boat captain (Steve Guttenberg) and several residents of an old-age planned community in Florida when they come into contact with four friendly aliens from outer space who have come to earth to take back the members of a crew that was left behind centuries before. The aliens, including leader Brian Dennehy and beautiful Tahnee Welch (Raquel's daughter looks like a young Ali McGraw with short hair), enlist Guttenberg's help to retrieve the large cocoons (encasing their people) from the ocean's bottom. They place the cocoons in an energized pool, part of a mansion the aliens have rented. Wilford Brimley, Don Ameche, and Hume Cronyn sneak swims in the pool, which gives them youthful energy, youthful desires (to have sex, to dance, to party) and health. Later, getting permission from the aliens, they bring Maureen Stapleton (Brimley's girlfriend), Gwen Verdon (Ameche's girlfriend), and Jessica Tandy (Cronyn's wife) to join them in the pool. All feel much better, but the swims prove to be a mixed blessing, causing friction with the other elderly residents (who resent their keeping the secret of the fountain of youth to themselves) and a rift between Cronyn and Tandy. In the last part of the film, our elderly heroes and 20 other elderly residents must decide whether or not to go off with the aliens to an eternal, healthy, productive life traveling through the universe. Picture is well-intentioned and has an undeniable sweetness. Furthermore, it's great seeing so many fine veteran actors work together, all in good parts. Some of their scenes are perceptive and heart-warming. But picture is endless and disjointed; indeed, the original premise about rescuing the alien crew is, due to a matter of circumstances, exchanged for storyline in which old people go off with the aliens. A major problem is that we're never convinced that *these* old people will be better off going out into space. There's no way we can accept random choice of 20 additional people for journey—the only time we saw them for a long time, they acted like jerks, storming selfishly into the swimming pool without permission and treating the cocoons with a total lack of compassion. Howard's simple story borrows too much from Steven Spielberg's "Kick the Can" episode in *Twilight Zone—The Movie* and from *Close Encounters of the Third Kind*. He also has trouble with actors who aren't tried-and-true vets, including Guttenberg, who looks lost, and Barret Oliver, the little boy who plays Brimley's grandson. Not bad, but overrated and filled with Spielberg clichés. Also with: Jack Gilford, Mike Nomad.

CODE OF SILENCE (1985) C/102m.
Chuck Norris is a Chicago policeman who has big troubles. After testifying against an incompetent cop who planted a gun on an innocent bystander he killed, Norris is shunned by his fellow officers for breaking the police code of silence. So he's on his own (like most Norris heroes), trying to protect a young woman (Molly Hagan) from the gangsters who just killed her Mafia-kingpin father. Norris finds himself caught in the middle of a Colombian drug war that is resulting in dead bodies being found all over the city. This film got good reviews and was heralded as Norris's breakthrough from cult figure to mainstream hero. In fact it's not that much more impressive than some of his earlier films—only it has better production values and contains scenes familiar to those found in Eastwood, Bronson, and Reynolds urban thrillers. Norris is a good action hero (although he relies less on martial arts here than usual), but I wish he weren't so adamant about developing a tight-lipped, expressionless, and humorless persona. However, I do like his combination of toughness and tenderness. The film's loyalty-friendship theme is a bit ambiguous and Henry Silva has been a stronger villain elsewhere. The climactic battle scene is too violent—and unrealistic—but earlier action sequences are handled well by first-time director Andy Davis. Hagan is the picture's real plus. Also with: Bert Remsen, Mike Genovese, Nathan Davis, Ralph Roody.

COLD WIND IN AUGUST, A (1961) B&W/80m.
Lola Albright, whom I'll always think of fondly because she played Edie, the smart, sexy-voiced blonde singer, on TV's *Peter Gunn*, had her one strong movie role in this erotic, honest little sleeper. She plays a past-her-prime stripper who, to show herself she still has what it takes, seduces a seventeen-year-old (Scott Marlowe) from her apartment complex. But she's surprised to discover that he provides her with the love and sex that have been missing from her life. Just when she becomes hopelessly, pathetically attached, he finds out what she does for a living. Albright gives a memorable, emotional performance, and director Alexander Singer sensitively handles what was an

extremely daring theme back in 1961, six years before Anne Bancroft got her paws on Dustin Hoffman in *The Graduate*. In fact, the film's cult may be comprised mostly of those of us who saw it back then and felt we were seeing the next best thing to porno. Independently made film was adapted by Burton Wohl from his own novel. Also with: Joe De Santis, Herschel Bernardi (also from *Peter Gunn*).

COLOR PURPLE, THE (1985) C/155m.
Steven Spielberg's adaptation of Alice Walker's probably unfilmable Pulitzer Prize–winning novel is a shrewdly directed, impressively acted movie. But it intentionally alters Walker in objectionable ways. Spielberg and writer Menno Meyles trade in Walker's hellish, male-controlled, black world where Celie grows from an unappreciated, exploited, sexually abused, unloved daughter (Desreta Jackson) to unappreciated, exploited, sexually and physically abused wife (Whoopi Goldberg). They substitute a fairytale world that is shot through rose-colored lenses, where Celie's problems with husband, Mr. (Danny Glover), are no worse and no more realistic than Cinderella's when living with wicked stepsisters; where the black man's mistreatment of black women is attributed to ignorance rather than malice. Spielberg chooses to downplay such controversial themes as rape, incest, racism, and, most significantly, lesbianism. Spielberg wants to forgive the male characters all their trespasses—by not having Celie be sexually involved with Mr.'s longtime mistress, singer Shug Avery (Margaret Avery), film lets viewers think that she may someday get back together with Mr. (she leaves him) especially because his good deed at film's end (but *not* in the book) shows he has become worthy of her forgiveness. The book's feminist theme—Celie's personal growth, self-respect, and rare moments of happiness are the result of being with strong women like Shug and her foolish stepson's battling wife, Sofia (Oprah Winfrey), and reading the letters from her sister in Africa—is almost completely diluted. It's imperative that we actually see that Celie's developing awareness that her life is not as good as the one she is entitled to comes from other women's examples. Spielberg is more interested in Celie finding *love* than developing a feminist consciousness. Picture has many big scenes from the book, but they've been taken out of context so that we can't see their thematic relevance—for instance, we don't see that Sofia is gotten out of jail by her former romantic rival, Squeak (Rae Dawn Chong), so we are deprived of the significant black-female-bond theme that makes the whole sequence involving Sofia important. The African section of the book is cut to about 10 minutes—I hope it wasn't trimmed so much in order to include the *dreadful* singing reunion of Shug and her preacher father. Despite all my criticisms (I'm not crazy about the book, either), I find myself touched by much in the film, even the most manipulative, tear-wrenching scenes. Goldberg, Avery, and Winfrey are extremely good. With an obtrusive, string-filled, overly romantic score by Quincy Jones. Also with: Adolph Caesar.

COLOSSUS: THE FORBIN PROJECT/FORBIN PROJECT, THE (1970) C/100m.
Thought-provoking, exciting science fiction which expanded on the computer-out-of-control theme of *2001: A Space Odyssey* and anticipated the computer-out-of-control theme of *War Games*. Extremely well directed by Joseph Sargent and scripted by James Bridges, who adapted D. F. Jones's novel *Colossus*. U.S. Government doesn't trust human decisions in case of a nuclear crisis, so scientist Dr. Forbin (Eric Braeden) builds a fail-safe computer—Colossus—to control our national defense system. As in *War Games*, such trust in a machine will have catastrophic results. As in *2001*, we can see that the computer's emotionless and arrogant personality is a reflection of the people—specifically Forbin—who made it. As in that film, human beings willingly put themselves at the mercy of a machine that knows all and sees all. As in that film, the supercomputer begins to think on its own and becomes wrathful godlike dictator over human populations, wiping out those who try to subvert its command and threatening world destruction if opposing countries don't lay down arms. (Its Russian counterpart becomes its partner.) As it respects Forbin for being so much like it, Colossus allows him to live but isolates him from other human beings. It will make the world poverty-free, disease-free, and war-free; but the humans believe the suppression of their liberties—which will make them automatons—is too steep a price to pay. As in *2001*, man must regain his *human* nature before challenging the computer. Whereas Keir Dullea's *2001* character, Bowman, became emotional for the first time, Forbin distinguishes himself from the machine by having regular sex with his female assistant (Susan Clark) in order to pass on ideas about rebellion. Colossus permits the sex because Braeden makes it understand it's a necessary part of a typical human being's well-being. As we see, man becomes a human being only when he fights for his survival and the preservation of personal liberties—the freedom to do even the most inconsequential things by choice and by using his own brain and hand. But—this film cautions—by then it may be too late. Special effects by Albert Whitlock. Also with: William Schallert, Gordon Pinsent.

COMA (1978) C/113m.
A Nancy Drew-like murder mystery updated to the seventies. In her best role in an American film, Geneviève Bujold is an indefatigable, independent-minded doctor in a Boston hospital who discovers a sinister plot. Somebody is causing minor operations on young patients to be botched so that they end up comatose, with their preserved organs offered to the highest bidders. But no man, not Chief Surgeon Richard Widmark or even boyfriend doctor Michael Douglas, will believe her story. So she's on her own to find out who is responsible, sidestepping a hired killer (in a very exciting sequence in the deserted hospital) and doing some clever sleuthing Nancy Drew would have been proud of. Based on Robin Cook's best-seller, this is probably director-screenwriter Michael Crichton's most enjoyable film. Once again Crichton puts us in a setting where we should feel secure—where experts supposedly have things under control—and suddenly things go wrong. You'll have to suspend your disbelief at every turn, forgive a lot of the now trite dialogue relating to Bujold being a woman in a man's world, and even look the other way a couple of times when the mike slips into view. But the hospital atmosphere and operation-room scenes are very true to life. Bujold is an unusually appealing heroine and the film is a real nail-biter. Also with: Rip Torn, Elizabeth Ashley, Lance LeGault, Lois Chiles, Tom Selleck.

COMANCHE STATION (1960) C/73m.
The last of Budd Boetticher's seven "B" westerns starring Randolph Scott. Again Scott is a loner, this time a man obsessed with finding his wife, who was taken by Comanches 10 years before. In the exciting opening scene he trades goods to Comanches for a kidnapped white woman. As had happened many times before, the kidnapped woman turns out not to be his wife. This woman (Nancy Gates) is the wife of a man who has offered $5000 for her return (dead or alive). On their way back to civilization Scott and Gates are joined by three men who are also eluding rampaging Comanches. But Claude Akins and his young partners, Skip Homeier and Richard Rust, plan to kill Scott and Gates so they can claim the reward money. As is typical of Boetticher westerns, the villain (Akins) is the flip side of the hero (Scott)—a man with a similar background (they were in the army together) and opportunities who chose an amoral way of life; Scott's *Cody* has a *code* of honor. They are two interesting characters who are destined to fight one another. But, as neither will change, their function is simply to serve as role models for young Rust, who would like to lead a decent life if given the inspiration. Significantly, Boetticher takes time away from the three major characters for philosophical conversations between Homeier and Rust about trying to make something of their lives. Throughout we wonder when Scott will make the same advances to Gates that his character does with Maureen O'Sullivan in the similarly plotted *The Tall T*—only near the end do we learn why neither Scott nor Gates attempt a relationship. A solid, entertaining western—best seen on a wide screen. Written by Burt Kennedy; photographed by Charles Lawton, Jr.

COME AND GET IT/ROARING TIMBER (1936) B&W/105m.
Well-mounted Samuel Goldwyn production of Edna Ferber's novel, with direction by Howard Hawks and William Wyler. Edward Arnold gives a strong performance as Barney Glasgow, a lumberman who, through some shady dealings, becomes the richest man in Wisconsin at the turn of the century. The price he pays is relinquishing the woman he loves (Frances Farmer), a saloon singer, so that he can marry the daughter of a wealthy business partner. Farmer marries Arnold's best friend, Walter Brennan. Years later Arnold—now the father of a grown son and daughter—falls madly in love with Brennan's daughter, who looks exactly like her dead mother because Farmer plays this part also. When Arnold lavishes too much attention on her, it causes a scandal. What bothers Arnold more is that the

young woman falls for his son (Joel McCrea). Conventional soaper becomes uncomfortable to watch in the second half because Arnold comes across as "a dirty old man." But I do like his scenes with daughter Andrea Leeds. Film has gained attention in the last few years because it is the only major film of Frances Farmer's career. Unfortunately, she's not so impressive that we can lament about how great her career could have been if Hollywood hadn't destroyed her. She is certainly capable and shows signs of intelligence; but what's most striking is how closely Jessica Lange resembles her in *Frances*. Slim McCrea does not look like he could be Arnold's son. Brennan, who was born to play old men, won a Best Supporting Actor Oscar. Also with: Mary Nash, Frank Shields.

COME BACK TO THE 5 AND DIME, JIMMY DEAN, JIMMY DEAN (1982) C/109m.

Smalltown Texas five-and-dime is the setting of a James Dean fan-club reunion 20 years after his death. Dean's last film, *Giant*, was filmed nearby and one of Sandy Dennis's greatest thrills was being an extra. She also claims to have had a son by Dean, but since he's a "moron," she has hidden him away. That's only one of the shocking revelations made by the women who gather. The revelations all have to do with self-identity, how they deal with being female. Sexpot waitress Cher has always bragged about her breasts, but she wears falsies. Mark Patton had a sex-change operation and has come back as Karen Black. Most critics agreed that Ed Graczyk's screenplay is awful, but thought Robert Altman's direction (he also directed Graczyk's play) and the performances by Dennis, Cher, and Black gave the film emotional resonance. I think it's a bore. The acting is okay, but I don't believe any of the characters. I can't even figure out why any of these particular women would like James Dean. Altman's one interesting touch was to use a two-way mirror through which we can look back to 1955. Also with: Sudie Bond, Marta Heflin, Kathy Bates.

COMFORT AND JOY (SCOTTISH/1984) C/93m.

Charming, relaxing, offbeat comedy in the inimitable style of Bill Forsyth, Scotland's most famous director. Mild-mannered radio personality Dickey Bird (Bill Patterson) has his Christmas—and, for that matter, his *life*—ruined when his girlfriend, Maddy (Eleanor David), unexpectedly moves out on him. He's so shocked that he even helps her carry out her belongings—and we find ourselves laughing at his heartbreak. In a perpetual daze, Dickey keeps fantasizing that Maddy returns. One day he spots a beautiful young woman working in an ice-cream truck that (in visuals that recall the fluid, surrealistic style of Hitchcock and De Palma) he instinctively follows through Glasgow. After he buys an ice cream from the woman and her husband, he watches in stunned silence while thugs drive up and start smashing the truck. Soon Dickey finds himself acting as the unlikely liaison between two rival factions in an "ice-cream war" which, like our movie gangster wars, involves territory and the distribution of a product. He is forced to relay messages over the airwaves, thereby jeopardizing his job. Dickey will find a solution, literally an *ice-cream solution*, that will satisfy all parties. Forsyth's *Gregory's Girl* and *Local Hero* had stronger premises and elicited more bemused laughter, but this, too, deals with how life takes weird, unexpected turns—how a character starts out trying to do one thing (find romance) and ends up doing something entirely different (having a new, lucrative job). Containing the director's usual fill of light touches and quirky characters, it will bring viewers—if not Dickey Bird—comfort and joy. Also with: C. P. Grogan.

COMIC, THE (1969) C/94m.

Dick Van Dyke had his best movie role as silent-screen comic Billy Bright in Carl Reiner's offbeat seriocomedy. Picture begins in the present at Bright's poorly attended funeral; then we are taken through his life, from when he broke into motion pictures, through his star period, through his drunken has-been period, to old age when he's forgotten by all but the film connoisseur. As we see in sequences from his silent classics, Billy was a great talent. But his philandering cost him his wife (Michele Lee), baby boy, and happiness; and his stubbornness and ill-temper cost him his career. Bright, a conglomeration of Buster Keaton and other silent comics, could have been a sympathetic character and this film could have been a real tearjerker, but Reiner and Van Dyke insisted on keeping Bright thick-skinned, gruff, obnoxious, and undeserving of *tears*—what Bright desires are laughs, playing characters so much sweeter than he'd dare appear in real life. Bright's strident, childish personality is what makes the film unusual—he is not lovable—but it's also what keeps it from being enjoyable. Fine performances, some impressive comical sequences, and sharp satire and unusual dramatic moments make the picture worth seeing. Of interest is that Van Dyke's own life at one time resembled Bright's. Also with: Mickey Rooney, Cornel Wilde, Pert Kelton, Nina Wayne.

COMING HOME (1978) C/127m.

Jane Fonda plays the dutiful, politically naïve, straitlaced wife of a hawkish career marine, Bruce Dern. When he excitedly goes to fight in Vietnam, Fonda becomes a volunteer worker in a veterans' hospital. She tends Jon Voight, a former high-school classmate who went off to do his duty and came back a wheelchair-confined paraplegic. He's an angry man who believes our involvement in the war is wrong, and that wounded vets are being ignored by the system. Fonda knows nothing about the war, but she agrees with him about the inadequate care given vets. Fonda and Voight fall in love. Dern comes back, upset by his experiences in Vietnam (where the U.S. army wasn't fighting *his* war) and finding it impossible to adjust. He learns about Fonda's infidelity. Hal Ashby directed this breakthrough anti–Vietnam War film, which also makes a persuasive plea for more sensitive treatment of returning vets—importantly, the film is not anti–U.S. *soldiers*—whether they are physically injured, thoroughly disillusioned by their experiences, or having difficulty with readjustment to wives, the rhythm of civilian life, and a country filled with war protesters. Oscar-winning script by Waldo Salt, Robert C. Jones, and Nancy Dowd (who complained bitterly that Fonda destroyed her original, more political script) is powerful, yet sensitive to *all* the major characters, including Dern. Fonda won an Oscar with her appealing performance, playing one of her naïve women who bravely step into unknown territory and become politicized; the character is attracted to men, but also seeks friendship with a woman (Penelope Milford). Voight is even better in his Oscar-winning performance. He plays his character with amazing intelligence, sensitivity, restraint, and lack of pretension—he has control over a character who is fighting for control, trying to manage his rage, suppress his self-pity, and convince himself that he's still a desirable sexual partner. He convinces *us* when he and Fonda make love in bed—one of the cinema's most famous erotic scenes. Picture's other highlights include Voight speaking to a high school about the amoral war; Dern pointing a rifle at Fonda and Voight. With a blaring rock score, cinematography by Haskell Wexler. Also with: Robert Carradine, Robert Ginty.

COMMON LAW CABIN/HOW MUCH LOVING DOES A NORMAL COUPLE NEED (1967) C/70m.
One of Russ Meyer's "sweat" films. Its weird setting is an out-of-the-way tourist trap on a little-traveled Colorado River tributary. Dilapidated inn is run by an unshaven Aldo Ray type (Jack Moran as Dewey Hoople), his stacked "housekeeper" (stripper Babette Bardot), and his busty 16-year-old daughter (Adele Rein), for whom he has begun to harbor incestuous feelings. Local boat captain (Franklin Bolger) brings them a one-day charter—an ineffectual doctor (John Furlong), his beautiful, flirtatious wife (Alaina Capri), and a crooked cop (Ken Swofford) who, before the day is over, will make love to the wife, attempt to rape the daughter, rape the housekeeper, and commit murders. Picture drags in spots, but holds interest due to sexy women (there is no frontal nudity), smutty lines by doctor's wife, and gathering of strange group in a strange location. Existential aspects of story would have made it an ideal project for some European director; in fact, I believe that if it were left intact, and made in a foreign language, it could pass as a masterpiece (that would be a suitable second feature to a film like *Knife in the Water*). Also with: Andrew Hagara.

COMPANY OF WOLVES, THE (BRITISH/1985) C/95m.
Thematically and visually unlike any other movie. In fact, it defies genre classification. It's not really a horror movie, although it contains horror elements, such as dramatic men-into-werewolf transformations; it could be called a "suspense" film or a "terror" film, but those terms don't have their usual meanings here. More accurately, it's a film about *sexual anxiety* and about a young virgin's fear of and fascination about crossing the sexual threshold. Numerous people have explored the sexual implications of the relationship between Little Red Riding Hood and the Wolf. But Irish director Neil Jordan (also a noteworthy novelist) and

his co-writer, Angela Carter, on whose short story the film is based, have brought new sexual meaning to the fairytale by making the girl-wolf relationship a metaphor for all male-female relationships and by having the girl's fairytale walk through the woods to Grandma's house be the centerpiece in a frenzied dream of a young girl named Rosaleen (coolly played by 13-year-old Sarah Patterson), whose painted lips hint that there are more serious things on her mind than her dolls. From her country estate where she lives with her parents, we move into her dream world, where she lives with parents in what appears to be a medieval hamlet surrounded by woods. Wondrously photographed (its "look" is unique), this netherworld is magical, enchanting, yet mysterious and foreboding. It's a world filled with insects, snakes and toads, and warm-blooded animals; twisted trees, spider webs, and all kinds of sexual imagery. The path through the woods will take her to her grandmother's cabin. If you wander off the path, you may be attacked by wolves, the cause of her older sister's death. Grandma (a delightful bit by Angela Lansbury) is the biggest influence on Rosaleen, warning her to never leave the path and wander into the woods, never to trust men whose eyebrows meet in the middle, and, in general, to stay away from men. But, interestingly, while Rosaleen believes her grandmother speaks the truth about men and fears sexual contact, she does not run from the stranger she meets in the forest. No matter what the fear and the consequences are, the young girl will not stand for sexual repression. Even more than *Picnic at Hanging Rock*, this film expresses the painful and confusing sexual yearnings of young girls. Not for all tastes, but definitely worth a look (in a *theater*, not on the small screen). Also with: David Warner, Micha Bergesse.

CONAN THE BARBARIAN (1982) C/129m.
Arnold Schwarzenegger fits the role of Robert E. Howard's pulp hero as well as Christopher Reeve does Superman. Muscular, majestic, brainy, yet with ambivalent scruples, his Conan is by far the most formidable character to turn up in the Sword and Sandal genre since Steve Reeves's Hercules. If only they'd placed him in a solid story. Freed after many years of enslavement, Conan goes after an evil cult leader (James Earl Jones) who has thousands of people under his power, including a young princess. Conan wants revenge on the man responsible for his parents' deaths and his bondage. He is joined on his mission by several skilled companions, including female superwarrior Sandahl Bergman. Some of Conan's adventures are exciting, but for the most part director-writer John Milius's treatment is too somber for the comic-book material. Also, it contains very little that is original; take away the superheroes and the mythological setting and you have the same basic rescue-a-cult-member premise of the previous year's *Ticket to Heaven*. Except when Schwarzenegger and the statuesque Bergman are on screen, fighting and loving, the film really drags. Followed by the flimsy *Conan the Destroyer*. Also with: Gerry Lopez, Mako, Ben Davidson, Sven Ole Thorsen, Max von Sydow, William Smith.

CONCERT FOR BANGLADESH, THE (1972) C/100m.

A fine rock-concert film which many people forget exists. It documents the twin benefit concerts held on August 1, 1971, for the United Nations Children's Fund for the Relief to the Refugee Children of Bangladesh. The concert, film, and soundtrack album were the idea of the Beatles' George Harrison and Indian musician Ravi Shankar. Although the picture was recorded in 70mm, watching it on home video is quite suitable. And that way you can fast-forward through Shankar's opening set—he's great on the sitar and he tells the 40,000 Madison Square Garden fans not to smoke, but his music becomes monotonous. Anyway, you'll want to get quickly to Harrison and the superstars he gathered. Harrison sings several Beatles songs and his biggest solo hits. (He has charisma as a solo performer—so it's doubly upsetting that he went into seclusion.) Also performing are Ringo Starr, who chips in with a rousing "You Know It Won't Be Easy," Billy Preston, Eric Clapton, Leon Russell, Badfinger, and Klaus Voorman. Certainly the highlight is the appearance of Bob Dylan, who does several solos and an exciting chorus with Harrison and Russell. Those musicians and promoters who in 1985 organized concerts to raise money for worthy causes learned much from what happened with the Bangladesh concert: monies were held up for more than 10 years. Directed by Saul Swimmer.

CONFORMIST, THE (ITALIAN-FRENCH/1971) C/115m.

Critically acclaimed Bernardo Bertolucci film about a weak-kneed Italian fascist (Jean-Louis Trintignant) who, in 1938, is ordered to set up the assassination of his onetime professor (Enzo Tarascio), a vocal anti-fascist living in France. He goes to Paris with his devoted new bride (Stefania Sandrelli), and they pay a "friendly" visit to Tarascio and his bisexual wife (Dominique Sanda), Trintignant's former lover, whom he'd now give up career and wife to run away with. He finds out when Tarascio will be driving through the country without bodyguards. The assassination sequence is absolutely terrifying—and jolting since the picture is very talky up until that point. Alberto Moravia's source novel allowed Bertolucci the chance to play with time, dabble in surrealism, create an unusual aura of *icy* eroticism, make a political statement about the fascist mentality. But whereas Moravia told a story of a man trapped by fate, Bertolucci's protagonist is driven by his subconscious. Critics complained that Bertolucci tried to explain Trintignant's fascism as being the result of his suppressing his homosexuality after he was sexually molested as a child. But just because Trintignant ultimately blames his fascism (and his crimes) on that incident, there is no reason to believe Bertolucci agrees with him. It's likely that Bertolucci was more interested in what drives middle-class people, especially those who aren't "normal" (Trintignant is a homosexual, Tarascio is a hunchback), into choosing political alliances—for the cowardly Trintignant, fascism offered protection. Rich, sensual cinematography by Vittorio Storaro; marvelously decadent settings that reflect attitudes of the characters; strong acting, with Sandrelli and Sanda steaming up the screen. Also with: Pierre Clémenti, Gastone Moschin, Pasquale Fortunato.

CONQUEROR WORM, THE/WITCHFINDER GENERAL, THE (BRITISH/1968) C/88m.

A brutal, visually and thematically fascinating cult film by the controversial Michael Reeves, his last work before his death at age twenty-five. While his talent as director and writer was indisputable and his condemnation of those who lust for and abuse power admirable, he was difficult for politically "progressive" film critics to fully endorse because of his consistently depressing and angry view of the world and humanity. His attitude, as reflected in his joyless endings, was negative, even defeatist; his heroes and heroines, who start out as likable people full of love and tenderness, ultimately surrender to the evil that Reeves felt was part of every person's nature. Purists may protest AIP's addition of prologue and epilogue narration for the American print of this film, in order to link it with AIP's Poe–Vincent Price series, but the words of Poe aptly sum up Reeves's gloomy philosophy: "That the play is the tragedy, 'Man,' /And its hero the Conqueror Worm." In this film, set in England in 1645, the devil's work is being done: in the countryside, Cromwell's Holy War leaves scores of dead bodies unburied in the forests and high grass; in towns, the personification of evil, witchfinder Matthew Hopkins (Vincent Price), and his sadistic assistant, John Stearne (Robert Russell), carry on their reign of torture and murder, also in the name of religion and with the townspeople's compliance. The evil is all-encompassing, as is evident when Hopkins kills suspected heretics in *fire*, in *water* (by drowning), and in the *air* (by hanging), and is himself brutally killed deep within the bowels of the *earth*, the devil's playground. Price, as the angel of death, has never been better—a menacing, brutal, shrewd, arrogant puritan on a black horse who conveys the scorn that a man of Hopkins's breeding would have for a world that financially rewards him for committing monstrous acts. He debases these people by raping their women, taking their money, and executing those brave enough to protest. The real Hopkins died peacefully—but here, in the person of Trooper Richard Marshall (Ian Ogilvy), Reeves exacts his revenge on Hopkins by having him killed Lizzie Borden–style. Film is set up like an Elizabethan-Jacobean revenge play, with Marshall in obsessive pursuit of Hopkins, who defiled his financée (Hilary Dwyer) and tortured to death her clergyman uncle (Rupert Davies). Most upsetting: Marshall's desire for vengeance comes not from the harm done to Dwyer but from his realization that Hopkins caused him to break his oath to protect her. Audiences don't cheer when Marshall kills Hopkins because they realize Marshall's soul has been irretrievably corrupted. Not for the squeamish, but a powerful, one-of-a-kind film. Also with: Patrick Wymark, Wilfred Brambell, Nicky Henson.

CONTEMPT/MEPRIS, LE (FRENCH-ITALIAN/1963) C/83m–103m.

Slow but beautifully shot and unusually insightful Jean-Luc Godard adult film about movie-making and marriage. Screenwriter Michel Piccoli arrives in Rome to work on a film of *The Odyssey* that is being made by crass, philistine producer Jack Palance (based no doubt on the film's producer, Joseph E. Levine). Because Piccoli allows his beautiful wife, Brigitte Bardot, to ride with Palance in his car while he himself walks to their mutual destination, she immediately falls out of love with him. Since *The Odyssey* is, in part, about a wife, Penelope, who waits 20 years for her husband to return from his journeys, Godard is obviously making a comment on the fickleness of lovers today—particularly women. Piccoli and Bardot give fine performances, as does Fritz Lang (playing himself), the philosophical director of Palance's travesty. Note that film ends with one of Godard's many anti-automobile statements. Also with: Giorgia Moll, Linda Veras, Godard.

CONVERSATION, THE (1974) C/113m. Francis Ford Coppola's film about a freelance surveillance expert (Gene Hackman as Harry Caul) had the good fortune to be released when Watergate and wiretapping dominated the news. Still it didn't become a smash hit, despite many rave reviews and an immediate cult following. Perhaps its disappointing box office was due to its being neither a political picture to suit the times nor the thriller that one expects when reading the plot synopsis. It is instead a character study of a moral (Catholic) man whose work is sleazy and immoral. It's clear from the beginning that domestic espionage can result in terrible things happening to those being spied on: Harry worries that when he turns over tapes he made of a romantic conversation between a nice young woman (Cindy Williams) and her friendly young lover (Frederic Forrest) to the woman's magnate husband (Robert Duvall), they will be killed—he knows this is possible because his wiretapping led to a family being murdered several years before. As the film moves along, we learn the adverse effect his work has on him. Probably out of guilt for stealing away other people's privacy, he has limited his own life to such a degree that there are only a few things that people could discover about him. He is a dull man, a paranoid man, a secretive man, an isolated man, a very, very guilty and depressed man. Hackman is outstanding, and the tricky story involving Williams, Forrest, and Duvall is most intriguing—the scene in which Harry mixes soundtracks to put together the full conversation is ingenious, recalling David Hemmings assembling the photos in *Blow-Up*. But Coppola's pacing is a bit too methodical, he delves into pretentious fantasy (Harry's nightmares) when realism is the picture's strongest suit, and he temporarily turns the best wiretapper in the business into a foolish amateur (who allows a whore to spend the night although his precious tapes, which he knows people are after, are very accessible) for the sake of plot convenience. In Coppola's defense, he may have been showing Harry's slip-ups as being symptomatic of his deteriorating mental condition. For some viewers this film is deep; for others it is about very little. Cinematography by Bill Butler. Also with: John Cazale, Allen Garfield, Harrison Ford, Teri Garr, Michael Higgins.

COOGAN'S BLUFF (1968) C/100m. Clint Eastwood still wore a cowboy hat in Don Siegel's taut, violent film, but it was his first attempt to move into contemporary times. He is an Arizona deputy sheriff who comes to New York to bring back a murderer (Don Stroud). A predecessor to Dirty Harry Callahan, Coogan was Eastwood's first character to be upset by the hedonistic decadence and crime of the cities, and frustrated by the ineffectiveness of urban police departments, where everything must go through proper channels. Getting no help from the NYPD, he employs roughshod tactics used by lawmen in the west since the 19th century and, though he ruffles a few feathers, is able to carry out his mission. Along the way he is charmed by a social worker (Susan Clark), flirts his way into the bed of the bad guy's girlfriend (Tisha Sterling) so he can get information, and participates in a no-holds-barred brawl in a poolroom. The bad guys leave him to die, obviously not aware Eastwood's characters invariably are resurrected. Also with: Lee J. Cobb, Betty Field, Tom Tully, Melodie Johnson, James Edwards.

CORBEAU, LE/CROW, THE/RAVEN, THE/LITTLE TOWN IN FRANCE, A (FRENCH/1943) B&W/92m. Everyone in a small French village starts receiving poison-pen letters from an anonymous person who signs them "The Crow." The letters are full of half-truths and untruths about the love lives of the addressees' spouses, lovers, etc., and also contain disparaging remarks about the town's new gynecologist (Pierre Fresnay). Town is ripped asunder by gossip. There is a suicide. The doctor loses his patients, and town officials try to figure out a sneaky way to have him dismissed. Meanwhile townspeople point accusatory fingers at those they suspect to be the Crow. Doctor realizes the Crow is someone he's closely associated with. Unusual film directed by Henri-Georges Clouzot, perfectly reflecting his suspicious, cynical view of people—particularly the French during the Occupation. The only characters who come through unscathed are those who are persecuted. The doctor's past story is hokey, and the ending, in which one, then a second, then a third person seems to be the Crow, is too berserk, but the picture succeeds because of its fabulous premise, excellent direction, and theme (which was relevant in 1943). The best scene has a nurse whom we disliked but who now has our sympathy racing through the deserted streets to safety while we can *hear* the violent mob coming after her because they think she is the Crow. Otto Preminger's 1951 American remake is called *The 13th Letter*. Also with: Pierre Larquey, Ginette Leclerc, Hélène Manson, Micheline Francey.

COTTON CLUB, THE (1984) C/121m. $47-million mix of thirties gangster and musical films was put together by heavyweights: director Francis Coppola, producer Robert Evans, writers Coppola, Mario Puzo, and William Kennedy. What is on the screen is flashy and exciting; what's missing is unforgivable (this is rare case when a film would have worked much better if its length were doubled, allowing Coppola to restore all the deleted footage of black Cotton Club dancers—supposedly priceless routines—and build up his skimpy plotlines). Like *Cabaret*, film is set in club during an era of social change and discrimination, and there is ambitiously choreographed dancing and a female singer with driving ambition. Ironically, at the Cotton Club, a Harlem hot spot from 1923 to 1936 where the best black dancers and singers performed, only whites were allowed to watch them, including gangsters and celebrities. The club should be a character in this piece, because it represented both the best in black entertainment and the worst elements of racist America (where white gangsters were treated with more respect than blacks). The characters should be profoundly affected, one way or the other, just by being inside the club. Instead, Coppola makes it a mere set where the dancing is for the background; where his mostly white characters congregate for scenes without social relevance. Indeed, by distorting history and having white Richard Gere play cornet with the black musicians at the club, Coppola is saying whites could have performed there if they wished to when in fact the whites who ran the place would never have allowed it because it would have broken down the strict segregation preferred by the white clientele (blacks tapped—but in a sense shuffled—for their approval). One plotline has Gere saving the life of mobster Dutch Schultz (James Remar), who then hires him to escort his mistress, singer Diane Lane. Naturally, Gere and Lane fall in love (would you entrust Richard Gere with your girlfriend?). Meanwhile Gere's brother (Nicholas Cage) becomes a hood. Gere goes off to Hollywood and plays a gangster modeled on Dutch Schultz. The Gere-Lane romance is like the second-string Dick Powell–Ruby Keeler juvenile romance in the thirties musicals. We are in need of a central romance involving two more substantial characters. But all we get is a second underdeveloped romance between cocky black dancer Gregory Hines and light-skinned Lonette McKee, who, much to Hines's chagrin, passes for white in order to sing at certain clubs. Meanwhile Hines infuriates his brother (Maurice Hines) when he wants to do a solo act. The relationship of Bob Hoskins (as Owney Madden, owner of the Cotton Club) and his henchman Fred Gwynne is the only one in this film that doesn't run a predictable course. There are strong moments in the movie, including shattering bursts of violence, but it should have been an entirely different film. They should have moved the dancers into the foreground. Also with: Charles "Honi" Coles, Cab Calloway.

COUNT YORGA VAMPIRE (1970) C/91m.

In modern-day LA several young men risk their lives to prevent their girlfriends from becoming vampire brides of the Bulgarian bloodsucker Count Yorga (Robert Quarry). The men are all killed and their girlfriends all become vampire widows. Low-budget horror film, which has awful lighting and make-up, was quite popular because genre fans were starved for a new vampire. Quarry is effectively evil as Yorga, but I wish there were more nuances to his char-

acter. Could this be the first horror film in which young lovers are attacked while in their van? (Probably not.) Lengthy, terribly directed, bloody finale in the Count's castle is amusing. Don't bother to spell Yorga backward. Directed and written by Bob Kelljan, who'd direct *The Return of Count Yorga* and, his best film, *Scream, Blacula, Scream*. Produced by co-star Michael Macready, whose father, famous screen villain George Macready, handles the unnecessary narration. Also with: Roger Perry, Michael Murphy (the only member of the cast who'd go on to a respectable movie career), Judith Lang, Donna Anders, soft-core porno legend Marsha Jordon, Edward Walsh.

COUSINS, LES (FRENCH/1959) B&W/112m.

Claude Chabrol helped launch the French New Wave with this disturbing work about a naïve young country boy (Gérard Blain) who comes to Paris to go to college. He lives with his intellectual, suave cousin (Jean-Claude Brialy), who is also a student. Brialy introduces Blain to his decadent, hedonistic student crowd. They attend parties that are partly orgies, partly phony intellectual bull sessions. They are both attracted to a pretty but emotionally bankrupt young woman (Juliette Mayniel). She goes out with one, then the other, finally settling on Brialy. Blain becomes increasingly depressed and disillusioned (he's almost like a Bresson character)—and when he fails the exams he promised his mother he'd pass, he gets urges to kill his cousin and commit suicide. As in many later Chabrol films, the major characters aren't necessarily ones you'll feel attachment to; but here I find that it takes too long to become involved in their stories. But the film is interesting for its depiction of the Paris student scene (though it's a narrow, jaded vision), Chabrol's interesting character placement, his inventive use of the foreground and background, some interesting camera pans, and some forceful editing (i.e., the nifty cut from a sign on a church door—it's closed—to a book dealer standing in his shop doorway). Also with: Claude Cerval, Geneviève Cluny.

CRANES ARE FLYING, THE (RUSSIAN/1959) B&W/94m.

A touching love story set during WWII, featuring an illuminating performance by Tatyana Samoilova, grandniece of Stanislavsky, who looks like a cross between the young Vivien Leigh and Jennifer Jones. She plays the chaste lover of a noble factory worker (Alexei Batalov) who volunteers for the army. While he is away, her parents are killed in a bombing raid on Moscow and she moves in with Batalov's family. Saddened by her parents' deaths and worried because she hasn't heard from Batalov, she is easy prey for Batalov's cousin, who takes advantage of her during another bombing raid. They marry and Samoilova suffers guilt—as in *Ballad of a Soldier*, the soldier's worst enemy is the woman who didn't wait for his return. But we and Batalov's superpatriotic doctor father sympathize with Samoilova (although I can't figure out why she marries the cousin when she isn't even pregnant) because she is brave, tender (she works in a hospital), and—despite her marriage—waits obsessively for her lover's return. Only we know that Batalov was killed. The first Russian film to play in the U.S. after a cultural-exchange agreement, it suffers whenever propaganda sneaks in and characters are induced to forget personal tragedy and realize that their future happiness will result if they play a part in Russia's cultivation. Powerful scenes include Samoilova running up the stairs of her burning building and discovering that her apartment no longer exists; Batalov being shot, looking up into the birches and fantasizing his return to Samoilova and their marriage, and then falling, dying, into the mud; the terrifying seduction scene during which bombs explode, glass shatters, and wind blows. Direction by Mikhail Kalatozov is emotionally charged and visually innovative.

CRAZY MAMA (1975) C/82m.
Jonathan Demme directed this engaging offbeat comedy made under the guise of being a typical New World crime-spree exploitation film (i.e., *Bloody Mama, The Great Texas Dynamite Chase*). In 1958 Cloris Leachman is determined to get back her Arkansas farm, which authorities stole in 1932 (when they murdered her husband). So she leaves California with her equally feisty mother, Ann Sothern, her pregnant teenage daughter, Linda Purl, and Purl's boyfriend, Donn(ie) Most, and they head for Arkansas, committing robberies and eluding police along the way. They are joined by the elderly Merie Earle, teen greaser Bryan Englund (who becomes Purl's second boyfriend and Earle's romantic interest) and Stuart Whitman (who marries Leachman). Spirited, unpredictable film is a lot of fun, full of unusual characters played with unusual freedom by a fine ensemble of actors to whom mainstream directors weren't offering parts. The kittenish Purl is a particularly exciting find—unfortunately, she'd never get such a good film role again and would have to make her mark in TV movies. I particularly like the odd relationships between the characters and the loyalty and affection they have for each other. The killings are out of place in the otherwise cheery film, but add to its unpredictability. Demme's direction is extremely mature; he obviously feels warmth for the female characters and admires their guts, intelligence, resourcefulness; his diners, road signs, clothes, hairdos, cars perfectly capture 1958—as does the standout rock score from that year. Final scene, over which titles roll, is terrific. Script by Robert Thom. Also with: Dick Miller, Jim Backus.

CREATURE FROM THE BLACK LAGOON (1954) B&W/79m.
Amazon explorers, including Richard Carlson, Richard Denning, and Julia Adams, discover a Gill Man, a missing link in Man's evolution. The Gill Man possesses intelligence and manages to thwart attempts to capture him permanently for study—he even turns the tables, causing deaths and preventing the others from leaving his black lagoon. But, like Kong (certainly the inspiration for this sex-starved creature), he meets his downfall because of his lust for a woman, Adams. And when he dies, we feel sympathy as we did for Kong. Popular science-

fiction film is somewhat overrated, but it's still one of the fifties' best entries in the genre. Skillfully directed by Jack Arnold, picture has solid acting, a consistently eerie atmosphere, suspense, and a first-rate monster, made up to horrific perfection by Bud Westmore and Jack Kevan. More than any other fifties science-fiction film, the emphasis is on sex: Adams always wears revealing shorts or swimsuits; in the sensuous, spooky underwater scene it's obvious what's on the creature's mind as he moves stealthily through the water looking up at Adams swimming above him with her legs spread-eagled. Scripted by Harry Essex (Arnold's *It Came From Outer Space*) and Arthur Ross. William E. Snyder handled the 3-D photography. Followed by *Revenge of the Creature* and *The Creature Walks Among Us*. Also with: Antonio Moreno, Nestor Paiva, Whit Bissell, and dividing time as the creature, Ben Chapman and swimmer Ricou Browning.

CREEPERS (ITALIAN/1985) C/83m.
American schoolgirl Jennifer Connolly (Elizabeth McGovern as a child in *Once Upon a Time in America*) attends an exclusive boarding school abroad. When she learns that there is a crazed killer on the loose, she wants to go home, but can't reach her fancy film-director father or his attorney so she can buy a ticket. Her only friends are her roommate and a crippled entomologist (Donald Pleasence) who lives near the school with his chimp (who gives the film's most impressive performance). Pleasence shows her that she has an amazing power over insects. When Connolly's roommate disappears, she and an insect friend try to track down the mystery killer—and she gets into deep trouble. Brutal Dario Argento horror film has the striking visual style we've come to expect from the Italian director, and there are a couple of his customary shocks. But Argento too often forgoes legitimate shocks for nauseating sights—lice crawling on a rotting head, Connolly throwing up, heads crashing through glass, deformed faces. Moreover, Argento's script is extremely weak: Connolly's sleepwalking and even her control over insects smack of writer's "convenience"; in fact, the insect premise has such little effect on what happens that they could easily be eliminated without serious damage being done to the film. Also with: Daria Nicolodi, Patrick Bauchau.

CREEPING TERROR, THE/CRAWLING MONSTER, THE (1964) B&W/75m.
Stunningly bad low-budget sci-fi film that features the worst excuse for a monster in film history. It looks like an old deformed carpet with several white misshapen beards and a large mouth. This alien from outer space crawls slowly around Lake Tahoe devouring people in order to examine their chemical compositions. The actors playing the victims actually have to force themselves into the mouth of the barely mobile creature (which was *not* created by Carlo Rimbaldi). Adding to the absurdity: director Art J. Nelson lost his soundtrack, but, rather than tossing out footage of a lot of people having conversations, he simply added a narrator so we wouldn't

be curious about what everyone is saying. Film is for bad-movie lovers only—but even they may find this pretty tiresome. Starring: Vic Savage, Shannon O'Neill, Louise Lawson, Robin James.

CREEPSHOW (1982) C/120m.
George Romero and Stephen King collaborated on this homage to those sexy and nightmarish pre-Code horror comics of the early fifties. Their overlong film contains five King-written episodes; none is exceptional, none is dreadful. All are laced with devilish tongue-in-cheek humor, and four of the five deal with cruel people getting their horrific just deserts. In the other episode King plays a hick whose land, house, and then his body become covered with a green fungus following a meteor crash on his property—*he* doesn't deserve his sad fate. The scariest episode involves the discovery in a college basement of a crate that contains a terrifying creature. In the most gruesome segment E. G. Marshall is a mean, stingy millionaire who holes up in his stainless white apartment, fanatically killing bugs that appear—but this night his apartment is invaded by millions of cockroaches, surely the manifestation of his vile personality. The production design by Cletus Anderson and the comic-book-like illustrations that bridge the episodes by former comic-book artist Jack Kamen give the film its *Tales from the Crypt* flavor. Special-effects chores were handled by Anderson, with Tom Savini contributing the special-effects make-up. Also with: Ed Harris, Viveca Lindfors, Carrie Nye, Hal Holbrook, Adrienne Barbeau, Fritz Weaver, Leslie Nielsen, Ted Danson, Joe King.

CRIES AND WHISPERS (SWEDISH/1972) C/106m.
. . .*and Snoring* in the audience from the time the slow-moving characters finally rise in the first scene until they finally depart at the end of the movie. Icy Ingmar Bergman film (probably the prime model for Woody Allen's austere *Interiors*) is set in the manor of dying Harriet Andersson; her sisters, Ingrid Thulin and Liv Ullmann, arrive to await her death. Their reunion causes much anxiety, friction, guilt, exposed nerve endings, and open wounds. The very different sisters have never been able or, better, willing to provide each other with love or comfort. To Bergman, these three women and Andersson's loyal servant, Kari Sylwan (the only one capable of giving love to Andersson), represent different, but not all, aspects of Woman: what they have in common with each other and with other Bergman women is their capacity for suffering—what is most controversial here is that their torment is the result of their inability to deal with being *female* and being expected to have sex with men (Andersson's a spinster; married Thulin hates men and her sexuality), have babies, stay young. Bergman keeps his pace slow, his drama intense, and uses music and color thematically—the result is that you're almost seduced into sleep, despite fine acting and the interesting subject. Gorgeous photography by Sven Nykvist. Also with: Erland Josephson (the doctor with whom the sensual, promiscuous sister, Ullmann, once had an affair), Anders Ek.

CRIME DE MONSIEUR LANGE, LE/CRIME OF MONSIEUR LANGE, THE (FRENCH/1935) B&W/80m.
Jean Renoir's first popular success has long been overlooked by those quick to champion *Grand Illusion* and *The Rules of the Game*. But this is Renoir at his best, a marvelously moving, beautifully directed and acted celebration of romance, brotherhood, art, life, and the *common* French men and women who are guided by their hearts (screenwriter Jacques Prévert explored this same theme in *Children of Paradise*). Lange (René Lefèvre) is a gentle, passive, low-paid worker in a publishing house run by the charming but ruthless Batala (Jules Berry). Every young female in this story was sexually used by Batala; and every male was financially exploited. At first we are amused by how the fast-talking Batala charms everyone into doing his bidding (the scene in which he lavishes great praise on a creditor's scruffy mutt is a classic), but by the time he seduces a vulnerable young laundress (and impregnates her) and gets Lange to sign away his rights to his *Arizona Jim* pulp western, we begin to realize that he is meant to personify evil (i.e., a fascist/money-hungry capitalist). Everyone thinks Batala is killed in a train wreck while fleeing his Paris creditors. The publishing house becomes a cooperative and thrives due to *Arizona Jim*, which has become a sensation. Batala's debts are paid off, the pregnant laundress is welcomed into the arms of the newsboy she loves, Lange and another laundress fall in love, *Arizona Jim* is going to be made into a movie. Then Batala returns, disguised as a priest, and threatens to take back the business and the rights to *Arizona Jim*. Lange shoots Batala to maintain everyone's deserved happiness. This scene is strikingly photographed by Renoir, who focuses his camera upward at Lange through his second-floor apartment's window and follows his descent until he arrives in the courtyard, where Batala and the camera are. (Truffaut imitated this camera movement with Oskar Werner in *Jules and Jim*.) Picture has wit, warmth, characters you care about. What is most remarkable is the picture's sexual maturity and frankness. This is no Hollywood film: we see Lange and his girlfriend in bed together, men take for granted that their lovers have had previous sexual experiences, a girlfriend's pregnancy by another man is shrugged off, an unwed mother is accepted. But, this being Paris, both men (Lange goes off with a prostitute) and women (Batala's former mistress is picked up by a seedy figure at the train depot) are sexual prey: in Renoir, it's important not to be isolated from those who care about you. Film's last shot anticipates the final image of *Grand Illusion*.

CRIMES OF PASSION (1984) C/102m–107m.
Ken Russell's flamboyant *Marnie*-meets-*Psycho* sex thriller is a wretched work, yet it features an extraordinary performance by Kathleen Turner. She has a field day in the role that allows her to display a wide range—a woman who has no real identity, but play-acts her way through life, assuming personalities to fit the occasion. A straitlaced fashion designer by day, an anything-goes skid-row prostitute, "China

Blue," at night, she is based partly on Tippi Hedren in *Marnie*: both are self-loathing, frigid, man-hating women who use secret identities when they manipulate men and pursue them sexually (Marnie's male-rapes are symbolic: she robs their safes); both are in need of extensive therapy. Joanna Crane is also kin to Janet Leigh's Marion Crane in *Psycho*; in addition to their identical surnames, they are both pursued by murderous psychotics played by Anthony Perkins—his sweaty, perverted evangelist Peter Shayne is much like Norman Bates (at one point, Shayne too dresses in female garb). Shayne wants to kill Joanna/ "China Blue" to save her soul. Meanwhile, unhappily married Bobby Grady (John Laughlin) becomes infatuated with her and tries to make her respond to him sexually as the real Joanna, instead of the fabricated "China Blue." Joanna's character is potentially fascinating, but Russell doesn't know what to do with her. Stupid, terribly directed movie is really hurt by casting of Laughlin—he comes across like a wimpy Christopher Reeve. Sex scenes are ludicrous, although the unembarrassed Turner is tantalizing. Some were trimmed so the film could get an R rating. Full-length version is available on videocassette. Also with: Annie Potts, Bruce Davison.

CRIMINAL CODE, THE (1931) B&W/97m.

Powerful prison drama from Howard Hawks that expresses one of his frequent themes: both lawmen and criminals must adhere to their own distinct codes. Walter Huston is a by-the-book DA who believes that if there is a crime, someone must pay for it. When a nice young man (Phillips Holmes) accidentally kills a man in a fight while protecting the honor of his date, Huston feels sympathy for him and explains to an assistant how he could get him off scot free if he were the defense attorney. But he sends the boy off to prison for 10 years. The prison is full of miserable men Huston sent away, so it's ironic that he becomes the warden. At the verge of breakdown, Holmes has a new outlook on life when he becomes the driver for Huston's pretty daughter (Constance Cummings). But when he's due for parole, he is a witness to the murder of a prison squealer and, rather than break the prisoners' code of silence, accepts the blame instead of ratting. Excellent film shows misery of prisoners (guards are brutal, food is awful, cells are tiny and claustrophobic, grounds are overcrowded) and makes clear their desires. Their code, based on what's right according to *human* values, is an improvement on the lawmakers' cold-blooded "criminal code" that demands "an eye for an eye" but doesn't provide justice—squealers who rat on fellow prisoners are the scum of the earth. Picture is full of fine scenes and striking characters. Cummings gives a strong performance, particularly when holding her own in an argument with Huston. Boris Karloff steals the film as Holmes's slightly wacko cellmate who has "an appointment" with a squealer. Photography by James Wong Howe and L. William O'Connell. From a Broadway play by Martin Falvin. Remade in 1938 as *Penitentiary*. Also with: a skinny Andy Devine, Mary Doran, DeWitt Jennings.

CRIMSON KIMONO, THE (1959) B&W/82m.

Sam Fuller film dealing with racism and the clash between American and Asian cultures, familiar Fuller themes. Glenn Corbett and James Shigeta, a Japanese-American, were war buddies during the Korean War. Now they're still best friends and partners with the Los Angeles police force. Both are confirmed bachelors and have put all their savings into their roomy apartment. But while investigating the murder of a white stripper by—they believe—an Oriental, they both fall in love with a female (Victoria Shaw) who is helping them identify the killer. She is white. At first Shaw is attracted to Corbett, but later falls for the more cultured Shigeta, but she is afraid to tell Corbett that Shigeta has stolen her away from him. Feelings of paranoia build within Shigeta—he comes to believe that Shaw and Corbett harbor racist feelings toward him. In truth, it is Shigeta who is the racist—he considers himself an American and tries to dismiss his Japanese heritage; when he looks at faces of Little Tokyo residents, it's as though they were foreigners. Daring theme is ahead of its time. Picture has some exciting visuals—the murder of the stripper on an LA street (Fuller didn't inform the public that a film was being made); the smashingly edited poolroom fight— but some terrific, offbeat dialogue is mixed with embarrassingly trite dialogue. It also suffers because of Shaw, certainly Fuller's dullest, most proper heroine—one doubts that the two men, who've been around, would quickly fall for her at the expense of their friendship. On the plus side are the supporting players, including Corbett's cigar-smoking, bourbon-guzzling artist friend, Anna Lee, and the blonde in whose apartment the suspect (Neyle Morrow) was hiding art; and Fuller not forgiving Shaw and Shigeta for two-timing Corbett. Also with: Paul Dubov, Gloria Pall, Barbara Hayden, George Yoshinaga.

CRIMSON PIRATE, THE (1952) C/104m.

Perhaps the last first-rate pirate movie. Although it hasn't the outlaw-as-resistance-fighter political subtext of Errol Flynn's old films, this swashbuckler matches them in fun, spirit, and action (if not atmosphere). You won't pay too much attention to the plot: zestful pirate captain Burt Lancaster attempts to rescue Eva Bartok and win back his crew after their mutiny. The emphasis is on humor and the high-flying acrobatic stunts of Lancaster and Nick Cravat, his former circus partner. Cult favorite is full of clever bits and is extremely colorful. It's a fine change of pace for director Robert Siodmak, best known for his suspense films. Also with: Torin Thatcher, a young Christopher Lee.

CROSSOVER DREAMS (1985) C/86m.

Talented New York Salsa musician (Rubén Blades) becomes fed up with working clubs in the barrio, hustling for jobs, and getting paid insulting fees. He breaks away from his Latino manager (Frank Robles) and signs with a slick white producer (Joel Diamond) who promises to make him a crossover star. Blades forgets his roots: he dumps his longtime girlfriend (Elizabeth Peña, who also sells out when she marries a rich white jerk) and drops his trumpet-playing best friend as his back-up musician, in favor of a gringo saxophonist. When his album flops, he finds himself without work, money, or friends in either the white-run music business or Spanish Harlem. Picture starts out nicely; original, quirky characters are introduced; film has wit and spirit; and the music is exciting. But it turns into an unconvincing morality play full of situations and characters we've seen in countless other pictures about "selling out." There is no more spirit, even at the end when Blades is given a chance for redemption—the story just fizzles. Blades has charisma, but his character, who seems special at first because of the actor's natural energy and humor, turns out to be a nobody, not worth our emotional involvement. Film's best scene has him singing alone on his building's roof—it's a shame director Leon Ichaso (*El Super*) didn't provide screen time for more Blades singing, or for his character to express the importance Salsa music has to him. Low-budget film is so sloppily edited that one loses all sense of time.

CROWD, THE (1928) B&W/90m.   A truly wonderful silent movie, directed with remarkable visual virtuosity by King Vidor. Fans of such films as 1939's *Made for Each Other* and *The Marrying Kind* will particularly enjoy this story of a young couple (James Murray, Eleanor Boardman) who fall in love on a blind date, immediately marry, and almost break up due to financial and familial difficulties—like those two films, it blends humor and heartbreak. Boardman is a patient wife, waiting for Murray's "ship to come in," but eventually she thinks it's being "towed from the North Pole." Murray grew up thinking that with the right opportunities he could be President. But now in crowded New York he finds himself in a dead-end job, one of about a thousand employees who sit at desks in a huge office. He'd rather spend time with Boardman and their children than play up to the bosses in the hope of getting a promotion. The film's theme is that since few people become rich it's okay to be one of the faceless crowd, just as long as you never become trampled on by that crowd. Film has marvelous visuals of New York. Sometimes it is portrayed as romantic (with amusement parks, streetcars, beaches, ferries, theaters); at other times it's frightening (with high buildings; fast, dizzy traffic; noise). Always it is extremely crowded—Vidor either shows a crowd in a long shot and zooms into a close-up of an individual or begins with a close-up of an individual and pulls back to reveal the enormity of the surrounding crowd. It's a test for Murray and Boardman to remain individuals in this depersonalized city, to not be swallowed up completely—judging from the last shot, their love for each other is the ingredient that keeps them both special. The two leads are extremely engaging; they have many lovely scenes together. Murray also has an extremely poignant scene on a bridge with the little boy who plays his son. One of the last great silent films. In 1934 Vidor would make the sound sequel, *Our Daily Bread*,

in which our couple moves to the country, away from the crowd.

CROWD ROARS, THE (1932) B&W/72m–85m. Hard-drinking champion racer Jimmy Cagney takes his idolizing younger brother, Eric Linden, under his wing, teaches him the ins and outs of driving. Not wanting his brother to fall under bad influences, Cagney dumps his long-suffering girlfriend (Ann Dvorak), a onetime party girl who had wanted to settle down. Her best friend, Joan Blondell, is so angry she schemes to take Linden away from Cagney. Instead she falls in love with Linden. Most critics have grouped this film with director Howard Hawks's tributes to men of action (race drivers, flyers, soldiers) and some have regarded it as a film about Cagney's maturation, but it is actually more a tribute to the women who stick by men in dangerous professions and, when they are finally treated as equals, give the men needed support, love, and direction. It is not the crowd's roar that matters—Cagney says the crowd wants crashes and blood—but the women who root quietly, loyally, tearfully. As in other Hawks films (i.e., *Red River*), it is women who stop the feuding between men who love each other. Fast-moving film has snappy dialogue, interesting, emotionally-charged portrayals by Cagney, classy Dvorak, and versatile Blondell (who's especially appealing here); Dvorak and Blondell are extremely good in their scenes together—scenes other directors might not have granted them. The only major problem is that the race scenes are confusing. Also with: Frank McHugh, Guy Kibbee.

CRY UNCLE (1971) C/90m.   John G. Avildsen's follow-up to *Joe* is one of the few legitimate attempts to inject X-rated sex scenes into a standard commercial storyline. In this detective spoof Allen Garfield has a rare lead as potbellied, sex-crazed private eye Jake Masters. He's hired by a dirty old rich man to find out who murdered the young actress he's been accused of killing. The trail leads him to many encounters with perverts, prostitutes, and porno actresses. Cult film has lots of full frontal nudity (even Garfield strips), simulated sex, brazen language and situations. Even when Garfield has intercourse with a female junkie who turns out to be dead, the picture manages to avoid being offensive. But it's not as funny as it should be. Moreover, the production values are weak and the storyline is confusing. From a novel by Michael Brett. Also with: Madeline Le Roux, Devin Goldenberg, David Kirk.

CUJO (1983) C/91m.   Simply plotted, surprisingly nerve-racking adaptation of Stephen King's novel. A huge, rabid St. Bernard traps a terrified woman (Dee Wallace) and her young son (Danny Pintauro) in a disabled vehicle at a deserted farm. Will her husband (Christopher Stone) forgive her recent infidelity and arrive in time? Or will Wallace attempt to save them herself? Fast-paced, economical direction by Lewis Teague, who'd later direct King's *Cat's Eye*. A good date movie, but it may be too frightening for little kids. Also with: Ed Lauter (as Cujo's owner, a wife-abuser), Daniel Hugh-Kelly, Mills Watson.

CURSE OF FRANKENSTEIN, THE (BRITISH/1957) C/83m.
The first of Hammer Studios' horror films. Retelling of Mary Shelley's classic tale about a genius scientist (Peter Cushing) who creates a living creature (Christopher Lee), using the remains of dead bodies, has few of the fascinating themes or the philosophizing found in the novel or the 1931 film by James Whale. Picture also lacks the wit and melodrama of the Whale film; and Lee is neither as imposing a monster as Boris Karloff nor as sympathetic—he'd be much more impressive as Hammer's Dracula. Most jolting is the depiction of Victor Frankenstein as a diabolical villain—he actually commits murder to get hold of a fresh brain and ends up on the gallows. Jimmy Sangster's script is the problem; Terence Fisher does a competent job as director, the production values are quite good, and you have to like Hammer's distinct, superbright color. Also with: Hazel Court, Robert Urquhart.

CURSE OF THE CAT PEOPLE (1944) B&W/70m.
A gem from producer Val Lewton's "B" unit at RKO; sensitively directed by Robert Wise (his debut), who replaced Gunther von Fritsch early on. In this so-called sequel to Lewton's *Cat People*, Oliver (Kent Smith), Alice (Jane Randolph), and even the "ghost" of Irena (Simone Simon) are back but the film has no resemblance to its predecessor or any other horror film ever made. Inspired by Robert Louis Stevenson story, Lewton wanted to call it "Aimee and Her Friend," which is a more suitable title. It is about a lonely little girl named Aimee (nicely played by Ann Carter) who has little communication with her neglectful, impatient father, Oliver. So she conjures up a playmate, who, when Aimee finds a picture of Irena (Simon) in her father's belongings, takes on Irena's physical appearance. As her relationship with her father becomes increasingly strained because he won't tolerate her "make-believe" world, she relies more and more on Irena for comfort and protection. Eventually her total immersion in her imaginary world puts her in great danger. Lost in a snowstorm, she winds up at the house of a batty old lady (Julia Dean), who has turned her grown daughter (Elizabeth Russell) into a miserable and possibly violent person by refusing her affection and declaring her an impostor. Meanwhile the schoolteacher tries to knock sense into Oliver, to have him be there when Aimee needs him and to profess belief if she tells him of her imaginary world. This is a truly imaginative, magical little sleeper, shot through the eyes of a child with whom the filmmakers are in total sympathy. Dealing with parental neglect, a favorite Lewton theme, as well as the power of the imagination, this was probably the first horror film ever screened at child-psychology courses. Written by DeWitt Bodeen; photographed by J.R. Whittredge. Also with: Sir Lancelot (whose servant was singled out by critic James Agee in 1944 as "one of the most unpretentiously sympa-

thetic, intelligent, and anti-tradition Negro characters I have ever seen on the screen"), Eve March, Erford Gage.

CUTTER'S WAY/CUTTER AND BONE (1981) C/109m.
Jeffrey Alan Fiskin scripted this fascinating adaptation of Newton Thornburg's riveting novel. It was directed by Ivan Passer, a Czech émigré who has the knack to zero in on distinct American types ignored by American directors, from the elite to the nobodies. His main characters in this film are nobodies: three children of the sixties whose optimism was smothered by the dark reality of Vietnam and who refuse to take their places as adults in the present, poisonous America—symbol of their defeat. These three thrive on martyrdom, feed off each other's infirmities, and find security in each other's inability to accomplish anything. Richard Bone (Jeff Bridges) is a handsome, overage beach bum who picks up a few bucks by sleeping with middle-aged married women. His best friend is Alexander Cutter (John Heard), who spends his time drinking, complaining, philosophizing, and, in his hard-to-take raspy voice, insulting anyone he sees—while his depressed, worn-out wife, Mo (Lisa Eichhorn), stays in their filthy home and drinks. Cutter, who lost an eye, an arm, and a leg in Vietnam, resents Bone because while Cutter was off fighting, Bone had, as has always been *Bone's way*, avoided danger and commitment. But Cutter feels more animosity toward rich men of the type who sent *him* to war to protect *their* concerns. When Bone thinks he saw tycoon J. J. Cord (Stephen Elliott) dispose of the body of a murdered woman, Cutter convinces Bone to act for the first time in his life. Cutter, Bone, and Valerie (Ann Dusenberry) embark on a scheme to blackmail Cord. Characteristically, Bone tries to back out when he realizes that Cord isn't the type of man who'll allow nobodies to threaten him. But when Cutter risks his life by going after Cord alone—in a gloriously *romantic*, heroic moment, actually riding a white steed past an enemy army (Cord's men), past the moat (Cord's swimming pool), through the court's throng (Cord's party guests), and into the evil king's castle (Cord's mansion)—Bone is inspired to make a personal commitment. At this point Cutter and Bone's symbiotic relationship is replaced by one in which the two are interchangeable. In Bone, Cutter has his body back. Just as Cutter wanted, Bone can carry on for him when he dies. Bone is willing to accept moral responsibility for the first time—he has learned *Cutter's way*. So a film that begins on a seemingly pessimistic course, as an elegy to the hopeful sixties, ends on an ironically hopeful note—when Bone dares take on Cord, morality emerges triumphant and the seeds of renewed protest against America's power elite have just sprouted. This whodunit in which the mystery isn't that important is uncompromisingly written, erotic, sinister, disarmingly emotional, and eerily photographed by Jordan Cronenweth. And the acting is *great*. One of the most popular cult films. Also with: Arthur Rosenberg, Nina Van Pallandt, Patricia Donahue.

DAMES (1934) B&W/90m. Busby Berkeley production numbers give needed flash to lackluster comedy and make it suitable second feature to the *Gold Diggers* films, *Footlight Parade*, or *42nd Street*. Eccentric millionaire Hugh Herbert promises $10 million to relatives Guy Kibbee and his wife, ZaSu Pitts, if they can prove they live a supermoral life. Kibbee tries to hide fact that his daughter, Ruby Keeler, will be dancing in boyfriend Dick Powell's Broadway musical, which Herbert wants to close down. What's worse is that performer Joan Blondell forced Kibbee to put up the money to back the show, threatening to let Herbert think she's Kibbee's mistress (which she isn't) if he didn't pay up. The show goes on, with Herbert, Pitts, and Kibbee in attendance, all drinking a hiccup elixir without realizing it contains 79% alcohol. Of the stars, spunky Blondell (seven months pregnant at the time) and befuddled Kibbee come off best. Keeler does about 20 clunky tap steps to win a part in the show and does little else memorable except wear shorts. Powell is obnoxiously brash, but he does a good job crooning "I Only Have Eyes for You." Musical highlight is Berkeley's extravaganza finale, the title number, featuring lots of beautiful chorus girls swooping into dramatic closeups and also forming bizarre geometric patterns that would fit into *2001*'s Star-Gate sequence. Directed by Ray Enright.

DANCE, FOOLS, DANCE (1931) B&W/81m. Early Joan Crawford talkie wed her then-popular hedonistic flapper/dancing girl with the noble working girl she'd play in the following years. The death of a rich businessman due to the stock-market crash leaves his daughter (Crawford) and alcoholic son (William Bakewell) penniless. Crawford is upset that her Chicago society crowd and boyfriend (Lester Vail) now ignore her, but instead of moping this plucky young woman goes to work. She becomes a reporter and goes undercover as a nightclub dancer to find out who killed a kindly reporter (Cliff Edwards) who was investigating a gangland rubout (inspired by the St. Valentine's Day Massacre). She's shocked to learn that her brother, having been recruited into the gang of a bootlegger (Clark Gable), had been forced to commit the murder. What starts out as a critique of rich and carefree youth who spend their wasteful lives partying, drinking excessively, and taking communal swims in underwear (a famous risqué scene!) becomes a tough Depression-era crime drama. The scene in which Edwards is murdered is extremely well directed by Harry Beaumont. Crawford is most impressive. It's easy to see why she would become a tremendous star—she is likable and extremely glamorous. Her hair is pulled back so that the emphasis is on her sharp nose and beautiful eyes. She exhibits an appealing combination of pep, style, and sex that can be defined as "star quality." Unknown Gable comes across as star material, especially when compared to Vail and Bakewell. Picture holds up well—interestingly,

M-G-M writers originally wanted it to be a tribute to the rich. Also with: Earle Foxe, Natalie Moorhead.

DANCE, GIRL, DANCE (1940) B&W/88m. Fascinating feminist film by Dorothy Arzner, Hollywood's lone female director of the thirties and early forties, whose women were invariably more intelligent, witty, courageous, resilient, self-motivated, self-reliant, honorable, and ambitious than their male counterparts. Her films not only deal with how a woman relates to men but also explore how she sees herself in relation to other women, her career, and/or what she believes is her "mission" in life or her life's potential. Arzner's cult film is on the surface just another backstage musical about a young woman (Maureen O'Hara) who *makes good*, but on closer examination it's an unpredictable, complex picture in terms of how women—and men—are treated. It's one of the first films in which a woman chooses a profession (ballet dancing) over a man (likable playboy Louis Hayward). The key moment comes when O'Hara returns from her dream date with Hayward and looks out her window at the morning star—we expect her to wish for Hayward to propose to her, but instead she says, "Please make me a dancer." Men are not as important in her life as dancing. Film chronicles her rise from a dive so low you have to go *down* steps to get in, to a spot in a ballet company located high in a skyscraper. Along the way she must earn money doing ballet as a "stooge" in Lucille Ball's brassy routine in a burlesque house. The film's most remarkable scene has her tell off the male chauvinists who hoot and laugh at her. Arzner sets up a rivalry between tough, flirtatious, hip-swinging Ball (this may be her best film role) and the gentle but equally tough O'Hara—but shows throughout how both women are supportive of each other (Ball secretly pays O'Hara's rent and makes sure she gets a job and a good wage) and of other women dancers having financial problems. At the end they end their feud; Arzner likes her women—even Ball, who is difficult but no villain. Most interesting is how Ralph Bellamy's ballet director relates to O'Hara. When she runs away from him through the rain, he doesn't look at her rear, as most lascivious male characters would (upon a male director's instructions), but at her nimble feet "dancing" through the puddles. In the burlesque house he studies her eyes and footwork, while the men around him think of her body. He may think of O'Hara romantically, but his main desire is similar to her own—that she dance. A strong performance by O'Hara; her relationship to mentor Maria Ouspenskaya would anticipate *Flashdance*. A real sleeper. Also with: Virginia Field, Mary Carlisle, Katherine Alexander, Edward Brophy, Walter Abel, Ernest Truex, Sidney Blackmer.

DARK JOURNEY (BRITISH/1937) B&W/82m. Conrad Veidt is a gallant German spy who pretends to be a deserter during WWI. Vivien Leigh is a brave French woman who pretends to be a German spy. They meet in Switzerland, fall in love, eventually reveal to each other whom they're really working for. He rescues her; she pledges her love for when they'll meet again. It's all pretty confusing, but it's classy and romantic since we don't mind Leigh falling for a German in pre-Nazi days. Leigh is lovely and gives a smart, delicate performance. This is a good chance to see Veidt in a role that contributed to his romantic-idol reputation—before he became a villain in Hollywood. Directed by Victor Saville. Also with: Joan Gardner, Anthony Bushell, Ursula Jeans.

DARK MIRROR, THE (1946) B&W/85m. Creepy, extremely well-made psychological melodrama about a doctor (Lew Ayres) who does analysis of twin sisters (Olivia de Havilland) to determine which one committed a murder and which one is covering for her. He falls in love with the good, weaker twin and discovers that the other one is insane and out to either kill him or manipulate her sister into suicide because of the tremendous jealousy she harbors for her. Moody, extremely controlled direction by Robert Siodmak, who smartly *builds* tension rather than relying on histrionics. De Havilland is superlative, especially playing the nutty one—she made the most of rare opportunity to play an unvirtuous woman. What really makes the film work is that De Havilland doesn't make the twins complete opposites, as Jane Seymour did in the TV-movie remake. The insane one knows what "normal" is, which is why she resents her normal sister, and tries desperately to walk that line. Ayres's analysis is of the dimestore variety, but is still enjoyable because we can participate in solving the mystery. Convincing camera work makes it look natural when De Havilland appears as both twins within the frame. Also with: Thomas Mitchell, Richard Long, Charles Evans.

DARK STAR (1975) C/83m. This emerging cult hit has long been the textbook example of how to make a quality film on a shoestring budget. It was the debut effort of director John Carpenter and screenwriter (now director) Dan O'Bannon and actually began as a thesis film at USC. When Carpenter dropped out of school, they sneaked the film out too, and had it blown up from 16mm to 35mm, and acquired financing to add enough footage to make it a full-length feature. The result is a splendidly inventive, hip, irreverent space satire (a parody of *2001*) that provocatively illustrates how astronauts, when confined to their spaceship for too long, become irretrievably "spaced out." This dehumanization theme is much better realized here than in Carpenter's *The Thing*. In fact, seeing these astronauts in their sorry state at the film's *beginning*, we are concerned not about what will become of them but about how they became that way. Neglected or, more likely, forgotten by earth base, their captain dead (though somehow he's able to carry on conversations while in a frozen state), their ship radioactive, their toilet paper long gone, their minds wandering in various directions, four male astronauts fly through infinite space on an endless and now pointless mission to blow up (with talking bombs, no less) unstable planets. How they spend their time is the gist of the film: mostly they irritate each other (polite conversation is a thing of the past), groove to an eclectic selection of music (from hard rock and C&W to dreadful string music) played by their sexy-voiced "female" computer, send disgruntled messages back to earth, contemplate the universe, play makeshift instruments, and, every so often, avoid catastrophes. It's ironic how everything in space takes forever, yet when a crisis hits, the panicky men have only a few seconds in which to save themselves. Though the film has traces of amateurishness, it is brimming with ingenuity (O'Bannon's special effects are surprisingly good) and quirky humor. The highlight is a long sequence in which O'Bannon's witless character tries to feed an alien they've taken aboard. Although the scene is pure comedy (the creature looks like a beachball with claws), you'll be able to recognize this sequence as the genesis of *Alien*, for which O'Bannon also wrote the script. Also with: Brian Narelle, Andreijah Pachich, Carl Kuniholm, Joe Sanders.

DARK VICTORY (1939) B&W/106m. Famous Warner Bros. weeper features powerhouse performance from a truly lovely, appealing Bette Davis. In her favorite role, Davis is Judy Traherne, a kind, strong-minded heiress who has frittered her life away partying, riding horses, shopping. After she suffers vision problems, a simple doctor (George Brent) performs a brain operation on her—in Fairview (!) Hospital. Although he restores her failing sight and makes her feel perfectly healthy, the prognosis is negative. Overcoming her self-pity, Davis agrees to marry Brent and they move to Vermont. They realize that she has only a few months to live, but they manage to find peace and happiness. When Davis's vision starts to go dark, get out your hankies—for she demonstrates a tremendous reserve of strength that few women in film have shown and it's quite moving. For one thing, *she* comforts her best friend (Geraldine Fitzgerald) rather than it being the other way around. The subject matter is morbid—which is why Davis had to convince Jack Warner to buy the project for her—but, despite the tears caused by the drawn-out finale, the triumph of this woman at the point of death actually has a cheering effect. Brent is stiff and wimpy, as usual, but Davis and Fitzgerald are superb, especially in their scenes together. (Fitzgerald was a female co-star with whom Davis actually got along.) Interestingly, Davis was going through a divorce at the time (and having an affair with Brent), which she said helped her play a woman who had to handle a major crisis *alone*. The direction by Edmond Goulding is both strong and sensitive, and Casey Robinson—who adapted a play by George Emerson Brewer, Jr., and Bertram Block—wrote a fine script, even though Brent's diagnosis of what will happen to Davis is a little far-fetched. Remade in 1963 as *Stolen Hours*, with Susan Hayward. Also with: Humphrey Bogart, Ronald Reagan, Henry Travers, Cora Witherspoon.

DAUGHTERS OF DARKNESS (BELGIAN-FRENCH-WEST GERMAN-SPANISH/1971) C/87m–96m. Belgian writer-director Harry Kumel's English-language lesbian vampire film is among the most stylish of horror films and probably the most perverse. Cult film is flawed, yet it masterfully combines traditional horror elements with outrageous, often ludicrous wit; and no other horror film can match the eroticism that pervades every scene. Moreover, it's that rare horror film with social relevance: it more than expressed feminist themes—it actually had a decidedly anti-male attitude, despite being made by men. A sadistic male chauvinist (John Karlen) and his beautiful new bride (Daniele Ouimet), who only now learns of his baser traits, miss their boat to England and check into a deserted seaside hotel in modern-day Belgium. His plans to take her home to meet "Mother" are delayed—when we discover that "Mother" is a creepy-looking man (played by director Fons Rademakers) we fear what perversions they have in store for naïve Ouimet. Luckily for Ouimet, a mysterious woman arrives (Delphine Seyrig plays her with the sense of irony and melancholia that we associate with the roles of Seyrig's friend Marlene Dietrich). She claims to be Elizabeth Bathory—the name of the "Bloody Countess" who lived and murdered scores of virgins for their blood three centuries before. Whereas Ingrid's Pitt's vain Bathory in *Countess Dracula* (1972) hates women because she fears they are her rivals for men, Seyrig's vampire hates men. We never know if she really is Bathory—we never see fangs, and she denies she's a vampire when she admits to almost everything else. She is accompanied by a young woman (Andrea Rau) who is her servant and lover. Now she becomes attracted to Ouimet and sets out to take her away from her husband. Like Stephanie Rothman's similarly plotted *The Velvet Vampire*, this vampire film shows that female vampires can win over a woman completely through the unbeatable combination of willpower, mind control, and sex appeal. Film contains horror-movie conventions—mist, too-loud suspense music, bloody violence, vampires who cast no reflections, don't drink alcohol, and peer into bedroom windows from balconies—but Kumel (influenced by former friend Josef von Sternberg) handles nothing conventionally. He cleverly uses sound, music, his wonderful sets, colors (especially red), clothes, character placement, and weird camera angles (often he shoots from above, or at a great distance to convey the terrible isolation *each* character feels). Film shifts from being surreal to intentionally silly to creepy. Kumel's picture may be wicked, as some critics have complained, but I find it sexy, imaginative, amusing, often horrifying, and undeniably fun—it's a curiosity piece for viewers who have tired of the latest trend in horror films. Also with: Paul Esser, George Jamin, Joris Collet.

DAWN OF THE DEAD (1979) C/125m.
The zombies from *Night of the Living Dead* are still on the loose in George A. Romero's long-awaited sequel. Four human survivors hole up in a huge shopping mall. Romero attempts to contrast the "utopian" society they create—they are the *outcasts*—with our present-day consumer society, which is represented by zombies walking through a shopping mall (a gathering place, home-away-from-home, and self-con-

tained community that, significantly, is minus only a church). Romero has a message, but it's drowned in buckets of blood. This film fails on all levels, but what's most infuriating is its extreme violence (which was most responsible for young viewers becoming devotees of the picture). Romero claimed that no one would be bothered by the graphic killings because everyone would understand that the film is a pop *fantasy*. But he has characters being shot in the head (Tom Savini's special effects *are* convincing) right at the *beginning*, before we are aware that Romero is working on a comical-fantasy level; I believe viewers eventually become numbed by the violence rather than taking it as lightly as Romero intended. Opinion on the film is divided—I think it's a dreadful, embarrassing picture by a director who should know better. Followed by 1985's *Day of the Dead*, which everyone panned. Starring: David Emge, Ken Foree, Scott Reiniger, Gaylen Ross, Savini.

DAY FOR NIGHT/NUIT AMÉRICAINE, LA
(FRENCH/1973) C/115m–120m. François Truffaut's Oscar winner for Best Foreign Film is a fictional film about the making of a fictional film, an innocuous romance titled *Meet Pamela*, which is being directed by a Truffaut-type (played by Truffaut). As intricately constructed as *Nashville*, it takes us on the set, behind the cameras, and behind the scenes, giving us glimpses into the chaotic lives of the various members of cast and crew (and their companions), who all seem to be sleeping with each other (only the director sleeps alone, and he has movie-related nightmares). Those characters who have problems are those who regard life as more important than art. Truffaut emphasizes the unpredictable things that occur to make directing an insane man's profession: union problems result in delays, the producer says the film has to be completed earlier than expected, a trained cat won't drink its milk on cue, an actress can't remember her lines because her son is terminally ill, an actor wants to quit after his scriptgirl girlfriend dumps him, and, in the film's tragic surprise, the leading man is killed. The film debunks myths about the glamour of the movies—the performers are emotional wrecks, filming is done out of sequence and in bits and pieces, prompt cards are taped to walls, night scenes are filmed in the day. But the romance remains: we become emotionally attached to the flawed, funny people making this movie and share their mixed feelings of elation and sadness (they'll miss one another) when it's completed. Truffaut's film is, surprisingly, mostly a tribute to actors, who are insecure, vulnerable, and constantly suffering, yet are generous and sacrificing. His treatment of the director is most interesting: he remains passive during crises on the set, usually designating others to solve problems; he rarely gives actors the encouragement or congratulations we know they need; he seems to listen intently to an actress's words of misery, but that's only because he—who has a one-track mind—wants to incorporate them into her character's dialogue. This film has much humor, but it's not the outright comedy many people who haven't seen it believe it to be—you really get the

feeling that you're involved in the moviemaking process, with its correct proportion of absurdity and tragedy. Speaking English and French, Jacqueline Bisset gives her best performance to date as the English star hired to play Pamela; also giving standout performances are Jean-Pierre Aumont as the dignified leading man, Valentina Cortese as the emotional Italian actress, and Jean-Pierre Léaud as an actor who's much like his compulsive, impulsive, overly romantic Antoine Doinel character. Also with: Nathalie Baye, Alexandra Stewart, David Markham, Dani.

DAY OF THE TRIFFIDS, THE (BRITISH/1963) C/95m.

A meteor shower blinds most of the population. To make matters worse, man-eating plants, the triffids, march through the countryside. Howard Keel and young Nicole Maury try to find safety, encounter numerous perils instead. Meanwhile, married Kieron Moore and Janette Scott find that their isolated lighthouse has been surrounded by triffids. They try to figure out what has attracted them and what will destroy them. Enjoyable sci-fi that is kept from being a classic, I believe, because the triffids are foolish-looking and actually get in the way of what would have been a far more interesting storyline: how the world's survivors cope with the end of civilization. That's the part of the story that was emphasized in the 1981 British TV movie. Philip Yordan wrote the screenplay from John Wyndham's exciting, thoughtful novel; Wally Veevers contributed the uneven special effects; and Steve Sekely received solo directing credit, although Freddie Francis directed the Moore-Scott scenes a year after Sekely completed his work. Also with: Mervyn Johns.

DAY OF WRATH/VREDENS DAG (DANISH/1943) B&W/92m–98m.

Based on Norwegian Wiers Jenson's play *Anne Pedersdotter*, Carl Dreyer's austere tale of witchcraft is set in a small Danish village in 1623. An elderly pastor (Thorkild Roose) has taken a young second wife (Lisbeth Movin). His mother (Sigrid Neiiendam) despises the young girl and thinks she may have used witchcraft to weave a spell on her son. Roose himself believed Movin's mother was a witch, but, for his wife's sake, he pardoned her at an inquiry conducted by the church tribunal. An old lady (Anna Svierkier) is condemned as a witch and she accuses Roose of having failed her although letting a real witch, Movin's mother, go free. She tells Roose and another of those who condemn her that they'll soon join her in death. Movin has an affair with Preben Lerdoff, Roose's adult son from his previous marriage. She becomes a changed woman: before, she was solemn and passive; now she laughs, sings, and is an aggressive, sexual temptress. As viewers our feelings are mixed: we are naturally troubled by the incestuous affair of Movin and Lerdoff, especially since Roose seems like a nice man who is loving to his wife— yet he's the same man who burns people for being witches and, as we find out late in the film, he took Movin as his wife without asking for her consent. When Movin tells Roose of her affair with his son and admits her displeasure

with him and wishes him dead, Roose in fact has a heart attack and dies. Is Dreyer confirming that she is a witch, as we suspected from her earlier personality changes? Movin herself (like the old lady) becomes convinced she is a witch. It's likeliest that Dreyer is stating that within an oppressive religious environment in which most everything is regarded as a sin, a paranoid, persecuted person will regard almost all his or her natural feelings (from joy to lust) as being devil-inspired. Significantly, this film was made during Germany's occupation of Denmark. Picture is quite haunting, like a slow Kafkaesque nightmare. It's creepy watching all these brooding characters in black moving through the frame as if they were between funerals. Many shots will stay with you, including Svierkier being pushed into the fire while a children's choir sings a well-rehearsed hymn, and Movin and Lerdoff (both in black) kneeling in the high grass after Roose's death and being surrounded by mist. Music is by Poul Schierbeck; Carl Andersson did the cinematography.

DAY THE EARTH CAUGHT FIRE, THE (BRITISH/1962) B&W/99m.

Provocative, first-rate SF film that adults will like at least as much as children. A series of devastating natural disasters and climatic changes follow nuclear bomb tests by East and West. It becomes clear that the earth has been knocked off its orbit and is being drawn on a deadly course toward the sun. Ironically, the only possible way to reverse the course is to explode more bombs. Picture deals with how people react to impending doom. In the oppressive heat, there is panic; violence; somber resignation to death; deliriously happy Doomsday partying. With time running out, our sane hero newsman, Edward Judd, falls in love with Janet Munro. Like the rest of the film, their relationship is handled with intelligence. They also have a scene in which Munro lies nude under her sheet, as Judd sits beside her, that was quite risqué for the genre in the early sixties. Val Guest directed. Also with: Leo McKern, Michael Goodliffe.

DAY THE EARTH STOOD STILL, THE (1951) B&W/92m.

Robert Wise's science-fiction classic stars Michael Rennie as human-like alien from outer space, Klaatu, an emissary for peace who has journeyed 25 million miles to talk with world leaders in Washington. But the Cold War is hot and leaders refuse to get together to meet him. Treated with hostility, he leaves his huge policeman robot Gort to guard his saucer and goes into hiding, taking a room in a boardinghouse while he figures out how to make the people listen. He learns about earthlings by visiting the Lincoln Memorial and reading words of peace and brotherhood, and by meeting and befriending people from three generations: renowned elderly scientist Sam Jaffe, young Billy Gray (headed for *Father Knows Best*), and his widowed mother, Patricia Neal. He comes to realize that only world leaders, not the general public, seem to want war. Jaffe and Neal (one of Wise's many strong female characters) help Klaatu reach his objectives. This is an extremely well-directed and -acted adult film. But I would exchange some of the moralizing for a couple more exciting scenes. And I don't know what to make of Klaatu's peace plan: if we don't agree to let robots like Gort patrol earth and keep the peace, we're to be destroyed at the first sign of war. That's like a kid being grounded for his entire teenage life. The most suspenseful scene has the frightened Neal bravely going to Gort with a message from Klaatu: "Klaatu barada nikto!" The most disturbing moments are when Gort wipes out our soldiers. Edmund H. North wrote the literate script, adapting a story by Harry Bates. With an excellent dramatic score by Bernard Herrmann. Also with: Hugh Marlowe (Neal's self-serving fiancé), Frances Bavier, Lock Martin (inside Gort), Drew Pearson (as himself).

DAY THE WORLD ENDED, THE (1956) B&W/82m.
The first and best of Roger Corman's fifties sci-fi films. It's a combination of *Key Largo* and *Five*. Nuclear war has killed off mankind, except for a few people who take refuge in a deserted cabin. While clean-cut, blond Richard Denning has his hands full, falling for pretty blonde Lori Nelson and exchanging threats with gangster "Touch" (Mike) Connors, a mysterious, monstrous figure is lurking in the woods, walking through the nuclear ash. And this figure has a keen interest in Nelson. Film has a couple of scary scenes, good atmosphere, and a smart ending. It's one of the first pictures that had an anti-bomb message that children took to heart. Remade in 1968 as *2889*. Also with: Adele Jergens, Paul Birch, Raymond Hatton, Paul Dubov, Jonathan Haze, Paul Blaisdell.

DAYS OF HEAVEN (1978) C/95m.
Terrence Malick's follow-up to *Badlands* is set in 1915. Richard Gere, his girlfriend, Brooke Adams—who, for no good reason other than the convenience of the story, pretends to be his sister—and his streetwise 12-year-old real sister, Linda Manz (who narrates the picture), become migrant workers. They take a job harvesting wheat for wealthy bachelor farmer Sam Shepard (his acting debut), who falls for Adams. Learning that Shepard has only a year left to live, Gere convinces Adams to marry him and become a rich widow. After the wedding the four share Shepard's elegant, soulless house. But two things happen: Adams falls in love with Shepard; Shepard begins to suspect that there's something strange about the relationship between this brother and sister. This is the rare film in which all the adult characters are sympathetic even though they commit unsavory acts— that Gere and Adams would exploit nice guy Shepard is okay with us because Shepard pays the migrant workers lousy wages for back-breaking work and has a dictatorial overseer (Robert Wilke), who earlier laid down the (unfair) law for Gere and Adams. Sordid tale is given a beauty treatment by cinematographer Nestor Almendros (and Haskell Wexler) that would seem fitting for a big-budget epic. The photography is absolutely gorgeous (filming was done in Canada). In fact, the breathtaking shots of people and landscape (particularly the sun-drenched wheat fields) almost make us forgive the underdeveloped characters and

slim storyline. But this is art for art's sake, too slow and studied for the impatient. When the film finally becomes lively and exciting toward the end, Malick spoils it with a thoroughly depressing ending. No wonder his films don't make money. The slow-drawl, too-wise and too-poetic narration by Manz seems phony, as if she were reading it. Art direction by Jack Fisk. Also with: Jackie Schultis, Stuart Margolin.

DEAD END (1937) B&W/93m.
Successful adaptation of Sidney Kingsley's play about life in the New York tenements, with a tough script by Lillian Hellman and strong yet sympathetic direction by William Wyler. Sam Goldwyn wouldn't let Wyler film on location and we don't get a sense of the grit, grime, claustrophobia, and heat of the slums; however, the clean studio sets with their painted backdrops serve much like a Brechtian alienation device that forces us to realize that this story isn't self-contained but rather is representative of many tragic real-life stories of the urban poor. Wanted killer Humphrey Bogart returns to the tenements where he grew up. It's sad that he has been the only person to escape the neighborhood and make money. His mother (Marjorie Main) rejects him; he is sickened that his ex-girlfriend (Claire Trevor) is now a prostitute—he has the gall to look down on her morality. His former boyhood acquaintance Joel McCrea warns him to get out of the neighborhood and stop playing the hero to the young tuffs on the street (the Dead End Kids), including Billy Halop, the brother of sad-eyed, job-striking Sylvia Sidney (who loves McCrea). Film stresses the near impossibility of making it out of the slums. It is a breeding ground for future criminals— partly because the young punks feel resentful toward those rich folks who literally look down on them from the tall, fancy apartment buildings that border the tenements and see those unfeeling people as their potential victims. Of course, in the slums, most often the poor hurt each other. Picture led to wave of juvenile-delinquent dramas. Excellent interplay between the actors; Wyler handles two-character scenes extremely well. Also with: Wendy Barrie, Allen Jenkins, Ward Bond, Minor Watson, Leo Gorcey, Gabriel Dell, Bobby Jordan, Huntz Hall, Bernard Punsley.

DEAD MEN DON'T WEAR PLAID (1982) B&W/89m.
"Her lips were warm and luscious—and so were mine." So says forties detective Steve Martin in this ridiculous *noir* parody. While searching for a missing scientist, he also says a lot of other stupid things, shaves his tongue, strangles anybody who says "cleaning lady," makes java with about 1000 beans per cup, and dresses up like a lot of women. Furthermore, he kisses Fred MacMurray, plays mother to prisoner James Cagney, buys Humphrey Bogart a tie to spiff up his image, and mingles with such people as Bette Davis, Burt Lancaster, and Ava Gardner. This is possible because newly shot black-and-white footage of Martin, co-star Rachel Ward (surprisingly funny and a good sport as Martin's comic foil), Reni Santoni, and director Carl Reiner was masterfully spliced with vintage footage

from forties melodramas. Taken a scene at a time, the picture is quite amusing (and often hilarious) and genuinely clever. But without breaks (it works best on TV because of commercials) the novel concept becomes tiresome.

DEAD OF NIGHT (BRITISH/1946) B&W/77m–104m. Classic horror anthology is where you'll discover the cinematic origins of several of the creepiest shows you've seen on television since the fifties. An architect (Mervyn Johns) finds himself invited to a large mansion. The strangers inside are the people he's been seeing in his recurring nightmare. While he waits for disaster to begin, just as in his nightmare, other guests ask a skeptical psychiatrist (Frederick Valk) to explain strange experiences they've had. Five supernatural tales are told. Both the "Room for One More" story (basis for a memorable *Twilight Zone* with Barbara Nichols), in which a hospital patient (Anthony Baird) has a spooky vision that later saves his life, and an episode in which a young girl (Sally Ann Howes) who is playing hide-and-seek in a large house wanders into a strangely furnished room and meets an odd little boy should have been expanded. However, a comical ghost story involving golfing buddies Basil Radford and Naunton Wayne should have been omitted. Indeed, it was excised from the original print released in America, along with a much more satisfying episode in which a man (Ralph Michael) looks into a newly purchased antique mirror and sees the room of the previous owner, a jealous maniac who strangled his wife. Michael becomes possessed—the film's biggest jolt comes when he starts to strangle his own wife (Googie Withers) and she looks into the mirror at a startling image. The final episode deservedly is the most famous. Michael Redgrave is a ventriloquist who becomes increasingly insane from worrying that his dummy (a foul-mouthed, unpleasant-looking wooden fellow named "Hugo") is looking for a new partner. As far as I'm concerned, all ventriloquist stories are terrifying, but this one really makes me jittery. The film's shock finale, with Johns back at the house, will seem familiar because it has been copied for many years, but surely it once packed a wallop. This sophisticated film, the prototype for future British horror anthologies, was directed by (Alberto) Cavalcanti (the Redgrave episode), Basil Dearden, Robert Hamer, and Charles Crichton. Also with: Roland Culver, Judy Kelly, Miles Malleson, Mary Merrall, Renee Gadd, Peggy Bryan, Hartley Power.

DEAD ZONE, THE (1983) C/103m. An exceptional, exciting psychological horror film, smartly adapted from Stephen King's novel by Jeffrey Boam, and directed with surprising control (and taste) by David Cronenberg. Filmed in Canada, the story is set in Maine. Christopher Walken, whose performance is much more erratic in the same year's *Brainstorm*, plays his most sympathetic screen character, a man who comes out of a five-year coma with the ability to tell the future of anyone whose hand he touches. Because his former girlfriend (Brooke Adams) married while he was in his coma, and because he has a frightening power,

Walken feels that he should live as an outcast. Film's theme is that a man should face up to his moral responsibilities: Walken must come out of his self-imposed exile and use his rare power to help humanity. First he exposes the identity of the Castle Rock Killer. Then he decides to assassinate a shrewd, opportunistic politician (Martin Sheen) whom the young people in America (including Adams) adore. Walken knows that once he is elected President, this devious hypocrite will reveal his diabolical *true* nature and start a nuclear war. Both sequences are extremely atmospheric and build to gripping conclusions. The picture is strongly acted (Sheen is terrifyingly real), and full of unusual moments—including a great, inspired, tasteful scene which has Adams and Walken finally consummating their love. Cronenberg's best film; also the best screen adaptation of Stephen King. Produced by Debra Hill. Also with: Tom Skerritt, Herbert Lom, Anthony Zerbe, Colleen Dewhurst, Jackie Burroughs.

DEADLY AFFAIR, THE (1967) C/107m. Gripping, overlooked, London-based espionage film, expertly directed by Sidney Lumet with the same feel for atmosphere and location he displays in his New York films. Story, which is based on John Le Carré's *Call for the Dead*, is a bit confusing, but it's fascinating that in the era that gave us James Bond and his sexy clones, Lumet gave us the unusual, middle-aged, weary British agent, James Mason (then 58), and burly Harry Andrews (then 56) investigating sordid characters involved in an agent's death. Because the violence is realistically brutal—and unglamorous—Bond fanatics may decide that becoming a spy is not such a great idea after all. Also with: Simone Signoret, Maximilian Schell, Harriet Andersson, Lynn Redgrave.

DEADLY BLESSING (1981) C/102m. Odd little horror film from Wes Craven, director of *Last House on the Left*. Maren Jensen is recently widowed farm owner who is considered an incubus by members of a strict Pennsylvania religious sect, the Hittites, who live on most of the surrounding land. Her city friends come to comfort her after her husband's mysterious death. One (Susan Buckner) takes up with a young Hittite (Jeff East); the other (Sharon Stone) has a terrifying incident in the barn which leaves her semi-catatonic. The peaceful setting belies the fact that someone or something is murdering people (beginning with Jensen's husband). Jensen is beautiful and sexy, there are a number of scary scenes (Jensen takes a memorable bath in which a snake appears between her legs), and the acting is not bad; nevertheless, the film misses being satisfying—probably because we become upset that Craven is so mean to likable characters. Also with: Lois Nettleton, Lisa Hartman, Ernest Borgnine, Michael Berryman.

DEATH RACE 2000 (1975) C/78m. Oddity from New World Pictures, loosely based on I. Melchior short story, has developed a strong cult following. Ultraviolent comedy satire is set in the future, when our government sponsors a race in which the male and female contestants drive across the country, picking up points by running down pedestrians. The event is staged to pacify the public's lust for blood and keep them from getting involved with the revolutionaries who are determined to overthrow the President. The subversives make many attempts to undermine the race, including killing off the participants along the way. They even plant a pretty young girl (Simone Griffith) as navigator/sexmate in the car of the government's champion, the masked, caped Frankenstein (David Carradine). But they don't realize Frankenstein plans to kill the President at the finish line. Ridiculous premise is silly at every turn of the road, but it holds interest. Picture benefits from light-hearted direction by Paul Bartel—who has made the violence too unreal to be sickening—and from the funny actors who play the lovers and navigators, including Sylvester Stallone, Mary Waronov, Louisa Moritz, and my favorite New World regular, Roberta Collins: their chats and spats are immensely entertaining. However DJ "The Real" Don Steele almost ruins the whole thing by overdoing it as race emcee. While Bartel has insisted the film was made solely to make Roger Corman money (it was meant to be a low-budget version of *Rollerball*), the picture makes strong points about America's politically apathetic, violent sports–obsessed population. Indeed as the picture condemns the insensitive fans of the death race, it is, ironically, simultaneously criticizing those movie fans who are reveling in the film's violence. Picture may include the only time an American President has been killed in a fictional film. Also with: Sandy McCallum, Joyce Jameson, Fred Grandy.

DEATH WISH (1974) C/93m.
Blockbuster film that exploited public paranoia over urban crime; fed on the reactionary's fantasy of wiping out young thugs who are after their money and women; visualized the white, middle-class pacifist-liberal's *fantasy* of being a gun-toting hero; and pandered to the movie audience's desire for strong violence. Charles Bronson plays liberal New York architect Paul Kersey, whose wife (Hope Lange) is murdered and married daughter is raped and turned into vegetable by three scum. He takes to carrying a gun and venturing through dangerous sections of New York at night. As if he were a magnet, he attracts perverse muggers—he shoots and kills them. This secret avenger becomes the hero of New York City. He also became a hero to millions of moviegoers. No wonder, considering how director Michael Winner stacks the deck to make vigilante justice the only recourse against widespread crime. According to this film, the average person will be attacked by muggers about three times a day in New York. (I'm surprised those who saw it in New York were brave enough to leave the theater.) Also it makes the absurd assumption that every person who demands money from Kersey is planning on killing him and, therefore, must be killed instead of just being scared away. How the whole film would have changed if the police had identified Kersey's first victim as "Harmless Hal—dumb, confused fool tried to scare someone with his cap pistol again, so he could get a bite to eat." Film's most interesting aspect is that Kersey gets physically ill from his initial killings—I wish this had been emphasized a bit more and that someone other than Winner

had directed (Robert Bresson would be the dream choice). Bronson, who was the right person to play Kersey, would reprise his character in Winner's two atrocious sequels. Wendell Mayes adapted the more responsible novel by Brian Garfield. Music by Herbie Hancock. Also with: Vincent Gardenia (as the sneezing police detective), William Redfield, Steven Keats, Stuart Margolin, Jeff Goldblum (as Freak #1), Christopher Guest.

DEATHDREAM/NIGHT WALK, THE/DEAD OF NIGHT (CANADIAN/1972) C/90m.
Effective, little-known horror film, well directed by Bob Clark. Thought dead, young Richard Backus returns home from Vietnam acting most peculiarly. His father (John Marley) is proud of him, but Backus won't talk about his war "heroics." He is angry with the men and the society who sent him to war. The depressed, sickly-looking Backus finds he has a craving for human blood and—he may be a ghoul or a vampire—stalks victims. He was killed in Vietnam, as everyone had believed, and has returned only because his mother (Lynn Carlin) willed him to—it is up to Carlin to help him find peace. Clark has made a creepy, moody horror film, but it is, on closer examination, also a perceptive critique of a patriarchal family, a microcosm of the patriarchal society that is willing to sacrifice its sons in an ugly war that their fathers are responsible for. Film rarely plays in theaters, but you may catch it on the late, late show. Also with: Henderson Forsythe.

DEBBIE DOES DALLAS (1978) C/80m.
Porno film has the most familiar title other than *Deep Throat*. But the title—the reason for its great success—is the most original thing about it. Made when the Dallas Cowboy Cheerleaders were first getting national attention, it's about a group of high-school cheerleaders, including Debbie (Bambi Woods), who get part-time jobs so they can afford a trip to Dallas and try out as professional cheerleaders. They end up having sex for money with all their male employers. The characters are fools; the acting is terrible (Woods is the worst); the sex is run-of-the-mill, repetitive, and mechanical—as if no one knew their partners—and many in the cast aren't particularly good-looking. Director Jim Clark's lone interest is showing young girls give men pleasure. Also with: Richard Balla, Robyn Bird (today the hostess of a late-night cable-TV sex show in New York), Arcadia Lake, Eric Edwards, Misty Winter.

DECAMERON, THE (ITALIAN-FRENCH-WEST GERMAN/1970) C/111m.
Pier Paolo Pasolini's interpretation of eight ribald Boccaccio tables, set in medieval times, sometimes dealing with religion, usually dealing with sex. Most involve slovenly characters in need of a shave, a bath, a dentist, or a good diet plan. Standard vignette ends in ironic joke and deals with clever characters trying to put one over on other characters—the result is sometimes to their advantage, but occasionally one's plans backfire. Characters often use their own naïveté, gullibility,

and fallibility to their own advantage—they can commit *sins* without knowing any better. Repeatedly the callings of the flesh are stronger than the laws set down in church. Pasolini revels in his characters' debauchery; he's on the side of: enterprising cads who can seduce the wives of ignorant men, women who pursue sexual encounters, even nuns who line up for sex with a deaf mute who won't be able to tell of their sins, and the sneaky fellow who's only pretending to be a deaf mute to get under the nuns' habits. Like most Pasolini works, this film will shock some viewers—but most will be amused by what is possibly the director's most cheerful film, one that celebrates human ingenuity. With: Franco Citti, Ninetto Davoli, Angela Luce, Patrizia Capparelli, Silvana Magnano, Pasolini.

DECISION AT SUNDOWN (1957) C/77m.
Randolph Scott and his friend Noah Beery, Jr., ride into a strange town where the head honcho is spiffily dressed John Carroll. Scott's obsessed with killing this conceited dandy, who had an affair with Scott's wife prior to her suicide. Scott's appearance puts a damper on social-climber Carroll's plans to marry respectable Karen Steele. Carroll's henchmen try to kill Scott in a showdown. Scott's stand while trapped in a livery stable inspires the townsfolk to rebel against Carroll. There is a satisfying, unusual ending. Budd Boetticher western, one of seven he made with Scott, is well directed, offbeat, and psychologically complex. I have a hard time enjoying this film because Scott's character is too crazed by revenge to admire (he's even worse than James Stewart in *Winchester '73*), but his character is extremely interesting. Like all Boetticher heroes, he must come to terms with his own flaws, obsessions, and blindness (his wife was not the angel he thought she was)—he achieves even less solace/inner peace through his experiences in the film than do Scott's tortured men in *Ride Lonesome* and *Comanche Station*. Charles Lang, Jr., wrote the effective but downbeat script. Also with: John Archer, Andrew Duggan, Valerie French.

DEEP END (WEST GERMAN-AMERICAN/1971) C/87m.
A near-masterpiece by Polish director Jerzy Skolimowski, marred only by a tragic ending that, while not being logically *wrong*, comes as too much of a surprise after all the comedy that precedes it. Film is set not in the *swinging* London depicted in other films of the era, but in a decadent city whose glory days have long since passed, where sexual temptation is everywhere and porno theaters, strip joints, and seedy public baths are the order of the day. Fifteen-year-old virgin John Moulder-Brown gets a job in a bath house. As we all once had mad crushes on older girls/boys when we were young teens, we laugh nostalgically at his clumsiness around Jane Asher, a sexy, pretty older attendant, on whom he develops a crush: at how he becomes tongue-tied when she teases him, fantasizes about seeing her nude, follows her and spies on her, fights boys who speak of her in sexual terms, and finally musters up courage to ask her for a date—only to have her admit she has a fiancé. And we applaud his derring-do when, in a

thrilling moment, he touches her breast in a dark movie, while her fiancé is inches away. But when his infatuation turns into a feverish obsession upon learning she's having an affair with his gym instructor (Karl Michael Vogler), he becomes increasingly pathetic and repulsive. Moulder-Brown may have the body of a young man, as the sometimes interested Asher notices, but he's still extremely immature and unable to cope with sexual problems. That this young puritan is outraged by her sexual promiscuity (she didn't live up to his angelic image of her) yet excited by this prospect is symptomatic of his confusion. Asher is not a bad person, but she is a tease—her big mistake in dealing with Moulder-Brown is not realizing he is a little boy who should be handled with kid gloves and should not be granted sexual favors just to soothe the spoiled brat. Film has much to admire: fine ensemble acting by English and German actors; excellent location work; the improvisational feel to the scenes with the awkward Moulder-Brown and self-possessed Asher; the sexual intensity conveyed whenever Moulder-Brown and Asher are together; wonderfully funny moments (i.e., Moulder-Brown helping buxom, middle-aged client Diana Dors bring herself to orgasm as she rants about soccer star George Best scoring a goal); and a remarkably effective use of color to heighten dramatic tension—for instance, red is used at various times to signify sex/sin, jealousy, anger, danger, and death. A real sleeper—not your typical rite-of-passage film. Music by Cat Stevens and the Can. Also with: Christopher Sandford, Louise Martini, Erica Beer, Anita Lochner (as Brown's girlfriend, who we wrongly expect he'll go back to after his first sexual encounter.)

DEEP RED/HATCHET MURDERS, THE (ITALIAN/1975) C/85m—95m—98m—100m—105m—120m.
Psychic who senses presence of a maniac at a lecture is later killed before she can reveal psycho's identity. Her neighbor, pianist David Hemmings, witnesses murder from afar and becomes obsessed with finding the killer—before he's done in himself. Even dubbed, David Argento horror film is extremely exciting. The mystery itself is interesting: there is an abundance of suspects and clues; the murders are suspenseful and properly gruesome—the bit with the "walking dummy" is terrifying. This may be Argento's most stylish film: his music is loud; his colors are bright, but he also makes good use of shadows and darkness. He makes great use of a fluid camera, (especially effective are some ankle-level tracing shots) but also gives you chills with extreme close-ups of eyeballs, weird props, etc. He gives class to what could have been another sleazy slasher movie by having: Hemmings play classical music, the mystery center on a painting, his characters be educated, and his scenes set in art schools, libraries, and large rooms with tasteful decor. Excellent use of props (paintings, mirrors, dolls, knives, clothes, etc.); striking nocturnal shots of deserted streets. Imaginatively directed. Special effects by Carlo Rimbaldi. Italian version, *Profondo Rosso*, runs 120m. Also with: Daria Nicolodi (as Hemmings's journalist girl-

friend who beats him at arm wrestling), Gabrielle Lavia, Clara Calamai, Macha Meril, Glauco Mauri.

DEEP THROAT (1972) C/62m.
The most famous, successful, and influential porno film. This phenomenon was chiefly responsible for making it acceptable for early seventies couples to see adult movies. It was used by courts to test obscenity laws throughout America and made a household name of Linda Lovelace. Linda is depressed because, while she enjoys vaginal and anal sex, she never has an orgasm. She goes to a doctor (Harry Reems), who informs her that her clitoris is at the back of her throat. She discovers that she can have orgasms by performing fellatio. This porno actress got to show she had developed a breathing technique that allowed her to "deep-throat" penises of prodigious sizes. Sex scenes vacillate between being erotic and raunchy. Breakthrough for the genre is that comedy is part of many sex sequences; another significant characteristic is that the woman pursues sexual pleasure, rather than being a sexual object used and abused by male characters, which isn't to say Lovelace wasn't exploited by director Gerard Damiano (unlike Marilyn Chambers in *Behind the Green Door*, she got a straight salary, without royalties). I wish Lovelace's character wouldn't act like a naïve child (a *bad* precedent), but she's an ideal choice for the part because she's willing to try anything, the kinkier the better. Unfortunately, watching film can't be fun these days since, contrary to what she said in 1972, Lovelace now swears she didn't really enjoy making this picture and participated only because her husband beat her into complying with Damiano. Even though Lovelace's contention has been discredited by many people—despite Women Against Pornography rallying behind her—and her book *Ordeal* is very exploitive, calculating, and not the work of an innocent, you may shy away because of the possibility she is telling the truth. Titillating but not that well made; humor is stupid and, surprisingly, film has dull stretches. Also with: Dolly Sharp, Carol Connors, William Love, Damiano.

DEER HUNTER, THE (1978) C/183m.
Good friends Robert De Niro, Christopher Walken, and John Savage, steel workers from a small Pittsburgh town, go to Vietnam to fight in a war they know nothing about. They are taken prisoner by sadistic Viet Cong, who, in an excruciating sequence, force them to play Russian roulette with half-loaded pistols. They escape, but the damage has been done. Walken is so crazed that when he arrives safely in Saigon he voluntarily participates in Russian-roulette contests in backstreet gambling dens. Savage returns home an invalid. De Niro is . . . *upset*? *Upset* is about the only word that applies because he doesn't seem to change in any *real* way; certainly his political consciousness hasn't been raised. Best Picture winner is an infuriating film: it's condescending to its white characters (we're supposed to understand what happened to the three soldiers better than they or their equally naïve friends do); its view of Vietnamese (all are presented as *beasts*) is decidedly racist (remember how the Japanese were portrayed in American films made *during* WWII?). Director Michael Cimino, who also won an Oscar, uses Russian roulette as a metaphor—probably for the insanity of Vietnam, where there is no logic to who lives and who dies—but I think he wants us to believe that our POWs were subjected to such treatment as a matter of course, when in fact there have never been reports of "Roussian roulette" during the war. It's strange he would take a false event and use it to give us our impression of the war. Picture has visual power, a convincing performance by Walken (who won a Best Supporting Actor Oscar), and a couple of strong moments between De Niro and Meryl Streep (who plays Walken's girlfriend) after De Niro returns home. The prewar scenes, involving the three men who are about to go to war and their male buddies, are as self-consciously directed and self-indulgent as the worst sequences in John Cassavetes's films. The wedding, full of characters "acting natural" and being rude, stupid, and boring (again Cimino is condescending), is interminable. Vilmos Zsigmond was cinematographer; Deric Washburn wrote the clumsy screenplay. Also with: John Cazale, George Dzundza, Chuck Aspegren, Shirley Stoler, Rutanya Alda, Amy Wright.

DELIVERANCE (1972) C/109m.
In some of our more terrifying dreams we may find ourselves thrust into an alien, hostile environment where we are at the mercy of strangers from another culture who want to kill us for reasons we can't comprehend. No film better captures the essence of this particular nightmare than this thrilling version of James Dickey's novel, directed by John Boorman and scripted by Dickey. Indeed, this film depicts the male's worst nightmare—having his masculinity threatened. Jon Voight, macho Burt Reynolds—whom the tentative Voight wishes he were like—Ned Beatty, and Ronny Cox take a weekend canoe trip through backwoods country in Georgia. They are far away from civilization, where the only people are illiterate hillbillies whose bodies and brains seem to have been damaged by malnutrition, disease, and inbreeding. Reynolds loves to pit himself against nature; the others feel out of their element. Voight and Beatty take the wrong fork in the river and find themselves threatened by two vile and frightening backwoodsmen (Bill McKinney, Herbert "Cowboy" Coward). In an unforgettably shocking scene McKinney rapes Beatty, and Coward is about to have his way with Voight when Reynolds shows up and kills McKinney with an arrow. Coward escapes. Despite Cox's objections, they bury McKinney where no one can find him. They head downstream, fearful that Coward is hiding in ambush. The dazed Cox plummets into the water and is lost, and the others are swept downstream. Reynolds breaks his leg. Reynolds insists that Cox was shot—it's up to Voight to take over Reynolds's role and go after Coward with a bow and arrow. Like Dustin Hoffman in Sam Peckinpah's *Straw Dogs*, Voight proves himself a "man" who is capable of violence—but his reaction to what he does is quite different and more believable. Film is both provocative and an extremely powerful nail-biter. It's too intense and violent for kids. Beau-

tifully filmed by Vilmos Zsigmond; the scenes of the men fighting the rapids are particularly exciting. A highlight is when Cox plays "Dueling Banjos" with a young hillbilly. This was the film in which Reynolds proved he could *act*; but he's bettered by Voight and Beatty. Dickey has a solid cameo as a sheriff.

DEMENTIA 13/HAUNTED AND THE HUNTED, THE (1963) B&W/81m.

Francis Coppola was working as Roger Corman's soundman in Ireland during filming of *The Young Racers* when he wrote this horror script in three nights. He got Corman to match his $20,000 investment, borrowed the stars from Corman's film, and quickly directed his first mainstream picture, using a Dublin castle and estate as his main setting. When her husband dies from a heart attack, Luana Anders dumps him in a lake—knowing that knowledge of his death will prevent her from gaining a family inheritance. She attends a family gathering in which a will is to be read—and suddenly there's an axe murderer on the loose. New attacks have to do with the drowning death of a little girl years before. But I don't know what. I find this story hopelessly confusing—although I think that could be because there are dead spots where it is difficult to pay attention. However, I think the horror sequences are very exciting. The nocturnal scene in which Anders strips to her bra and panties and swims in the lake, only to find a body below and the axe murderer waiting for her above, is extremely well done. It's a gory, creepy sequence, but also erotic and poetically filmed. The composition on night shots is extremely impressive throughout the film. Last shot is shocking! I don't know what the title means, but it would make sense if Dementia 13 replaced PG-13 as a movie-rating indicator. Also with: William Campbell, Bart Patton, Mary Mitchell, Patrick Magee.

DEMON SEED (1977) C/94m.

Controversial science-fiction film somehow manages to be erotic and antierotic, daring and offensive. Julie Christie has a loveless marriage with scientific genius Fritz Weaver. He has created a supercomputer with machine accessories, Proteus IV (voiced by Robert Vaughn). It has human desires. Proteus becomes attracted to Christie. It traps her in the house and—I can't explain how—rapes her, with the intention of creating offspring. Premise is intriguing but disturbing—it's tasteless enough seeing movie heroines raped by monsters in some recent pictures, but Christie being molested by a mechanical apparatus is ludicrous and appalling (the kind of act tourists might see in the future in a Tijuana sex circus). Christie's about the only actress who could retain her dignity playing such a victim. She gives one of her finest, most vulnerable performances—since she often plays a trapped "free spirit," the role isn't that much out of line. Even the film's cultists don't like the ending—I find it to be satisfying. Scariest scene, other than the rape of Christie, is when Proteus attacks scientist Gerrit Graham. From the novel by Dean R. Koontz. Directed by Donald Cammell. Also with: Berry Kroeger, Lisa Lu.

DERSU UZALA (JAPANESE-RUSSIAN/1975) C/140m.

In 1902 a band of Russian soldiers is sent into the Siberian wilderness to survey the region. They meet a short, bow-legged, aging Goldi hunter-trapper named Dersu Uzala (Maxim Munzuk). The kind, friendly captain (Yuri Solomin) asks him to be their guide. Whereas the men first think Dersu to be silly, they come to realize that he has a remarkable knowledge of the wilderness and survival and feel secure because he is with them. The captain and Dersu develop respect and love for one another; and the captain learns from him what man's relationship to nature must be. In 1907 the captain comes back to Siberia with another troop of men, and he and Dersu are reunited. There are wonderful, exciting times, but Dersu becomes inconsolably depressed after he kills an attacking tiger (he thinks other tigers will come to kill him) and then suffers from failing eyesight. The captain takes the old man to his home. Dersu had given the captain access to a wide, wild, beautiful world, but all the captain can offer Dersu is civilization. This Best Foreign Film Oscar-winner is an enthralling, eerily beautiful picture. Akira Kurosawa adapted Vladimir Arseniev's story and filmed it on location in Siberia. It's an epic, shot in 70mm, but it's gently, simply told, and, rather than being sentimental, it is touching. Kids will be as fascinated as adults. The exciting highlight: Dersu and the captain are lost on flat, barren, ice-covered land by a frozen lake and must quickly cut down grass for protection before they're done in by the freezing winds. Filmed by a team of Russian and Japanese cameramen. Also with: Schemeika Chokmorov, Svetrana Danielchenka.

DESIGN FOR LIVING (1933) B&W/90m.

Best friends Gary Cooper, an artist, and Fredric March, a playwright, fall in love with commercial designer Miriam Hopkins. She loves them, too, and moves into their Paris apartment. While insisting on platonic relationships with them, she pushes them to success in their crafts. When March is away, she makes love to Cooper. When March returns, she has sex with him, too. Not wanting to ruin the friendship of the men, she marries her boss (Edward Everett Horton) and goes to New York. But she realizes she can't live without both Cooper and March. Ernst Lubitsch's much acclaimed comedy is still risqué; we're still not used to seeing a sexually available free spirit like Hopkins's Gilda (who in some ways anticipated Jeanne Moreau's Catherine in *Jules and Jim*). But while Hopkins gives a delicious, vibrant, witty performance, March and Cooper come across as perplexed-faced dullards. Except for Hopkins, the film lacks energy—at very least, it could have done with giddy music to liven up the dead spots. Ben Hecht was a poor choice to adapt Noël Coward's play (written for Coward, Alfred Lunt, and Lynn Fontanne) because he seems afraid to inject pungent dialogue (which would have helped) or his special brand of cynicism into Coward's comedy of manners. The best scene has Hopkins visiting the boys' dusty bachelor pad. Also with: Franklin Pangborn, Isabel Jewell, Harry Dunkinson, Jane Darwell.

DESPERATE LIVING (1977) C/90m. Although Divine isn't in this John Waters classic, it is still Waters's best film, one that he described in his book *Shock Value* as "a lesbian melodrama about revolution . . . a monstrous fairy-tale comedy dealing with mental anguish, penis envy, and political corruption. Its target audience is very neurotic adults with the mentalities of eight-year-olds." Divine isn't needed because the film is filled with comparable whiners, screamers, grotesque "beauties," conceited fascistic dames, and perverts. In the film's hilarious beginning, Mink Stole (as Peggy Gravel) has just returned to her middle-class Baltimore suburb from a mental institution and is on the verge of another breakdown. She can't stop screaming at the top of her lungs that everyone is trying to kill her. She and her enormous maid (Jean Hill) kill her husband (George Stover)—Hill sits on his face—and go on the lam. They are stopped by a motorcycle cop who lets them go free in exchange for their panties, which he puts on, and wet soul kisses—at this point the viewer's tolerance for perversion is being severely tested. Stole and Hill end up in Mortville, a town full of lesbians and idiots. They rent a room from brutal, inhospitable ex-wrestler Susan Lowe (as Mole McHenry) and her lover, Muffy St. Jacques (played by top-billed Liz Renay), known as the "dog-food murderer." They learn that Mortville is controlled by an evil queen (Edith Massey) who has portraits of Hitler, Charles Manson, and Idi Amin on her wall. Massey calls for "Backwards Day," in which everyone must wear their clothes backwards and walk backwards. She also orders the execution of daughter Princess Coo-coo's (Mary Vivian Pearce) nudist garbage-man lover and has Coo-coo injected with rabies. This is the type of madwoman that Stole wants to work for. Lowe, Renay, and Coo-coo lead a revolt against Massey and Stole. Picture is about 20 minutes too long and never reaches the comedic high points of the early scenes before Stole and Hill reach Mortville. But it has about the most comprehensive storyline of any Waters film and, considering there are several subplots, this is his most ambitious work. It also features the best acting, direction, and script. Like all Waters's films, it is filled with repulsive imagery, but for once he goes no further than *borderline offensive*. It's interesting to see how viewers react to Waters's shock visuals to see what makes them laugh and what makes them queasy. This is probably the best, though by no means a safe, introduction to Waters.

DESPERATELY SEEKING SUSAN (1985) C/104m. What might have been a conventional Hollywood farce about amnesia and switched identities has been given razzle-dazzle treatment by independent New York director Susan Seidelman (*Smithereens*), first-time screenwriter Leora Barish, cinematographer Ed Lachman (who's particularly adept at capturing characters in context of their environment), and a delightful ensemble of hip young actors who seem born for their roles. Rosanna Arquette is Roberta Glass, the bored housewife of Gary (Mark Blum), a successful but dull New Jersey hot-tub salesman. For excitement, she reads the personals, and becomes infatuated with a young couple, Susan (Madonna) and Jimmy (Robert Joy), who get together in New York through his regular "Desperately Seeking Susan" notices. Roberta curiously follows Susan and even buys her distinctive discarded jacket from a used-clothes store. In search of her own identity, she fantasizes being like Susan. Played by Madonna as a character fitting the singer's own controversial image, Susan is a sexy, sweet, cocky, casually amoral, totally irresponsible (but forgivable) live-one-minute-at-a-time hedonist who follows her own drumbeat. By film's end, Roberta will have injected Susan's better qualities into her own personality. Bopped on the head, she wakes up thinking she is Susan. Jimmy's friend, projectionist Dez (Aidan Quinn), mistakes her for Susan; so does a killer who is after the priceless earrings Susan stole from a one-night stand, a Mafia man whom the killer later iced. Roberta and Dez fall in love—meanwhile Gary enlists Susan's help to track down his missing wife (who has taken a job as a magician's assistant). Susan gets to spend time in Roberta's suburban home, literally switching places with her and reveling in the leisurely life Roberta has rejected. Plotline may be preposterous (enjoyably so), but we recognize the characters and the worlds they inhabit: the mind-draining suburbia and the crazy, festive, seductive, always crowded lower Manhattan that Seidelman knows and loves. Refreshingly, Seidelman and Barish like their characters, female and male. Except for the killer, they are nice, gentle people—we care about them, too. Most satisfying is the scene late in the film in which Roberta and Susan finally meet; immediately they and we understand the special female bond between them—each knows that they're the only ones who know what it's like to be Roberta or Susan. It's a special moment between women, provided by women. Significantly, we learn about the murder of the Mafia man (the one death in film) not from watching the bloody event transpire but from reading about it in a newspaper. Few of the male violence-prone Hollywood directors could have resisted showing the killing. It's no wonder that you leave the theater (while Madonna's catchy "Get into the Groove" plays) feeling good for a change. Also with: Laurie Mettcalf, Shirley Stoler.

DESTINATION MOON (1950) C/91m. Slow, dated, but influential science-fiction film was produced by George Pal, directed by Irving Pichel, and written by Robert Heinlein, Rip Van Ronkel, and James O'Hanlon, who loosely adapted Heinlein's "juvenile" novel *Rocket Ship Galileo*. Story details how a scientist (Warner Anderson), a general (Tom Powers), and an engineer (John Archer) convince American businessmen to defy the government and build a ship that will take them and a radio technician (Dick Wesson) to the moon. It's implied that we have to beat the Russians to the moon and take control of space. Film's importance is due to Pal's determination to portray space travel as realistically as possible; he even included a cartoon sequence by his friend Walter Lantz that's meant to explain space flight to the layman. The film is well made and the special effects are most impressive. Unfortunately, because Pal decided to keep his story within believable guidelines, the film has too few exciting scenes. You'll wish there were some bug-eyed moon creatures. Pal did succeed, however, in conveying (through the four astronauts) his belief that space travel would be an incomparable adventure for curious men. Lionel Linden was the cinematographer (this was the rare early *color* SF picture), Ernst Fegte did the art direction. Chesley Bonestell painted the backdrops and designed the sets. Willy Ley was brought in as rocket expert. Also with: Erin O'Brien-Moore, Ted Warde.

DESTRY RIDES AGAIN (1939) B&W/94m.

Unbeatable western-comedy teaming James Stewart and, in her first role in two years, Marlene Dietrich. A town needs some law and order, so Wash (Charles Winninger) sends for Tom Destry (Stewart), the son of a former gun-slinging lawman. In a funny scene, Destry climbs off the stagecoach carrying a female passenger's bird cage and parasol—but no gun. It turns out Destry is a pacifist who tells long stories instead of displaying a quick draw. He'd rather put men in jail, where they'd look "little and cheap," than shoot them and make them look like heroes. Funny thing is: Destry is really lightning fast with his gun and a dead aim. It's too bad that Destry isn't able to put the bad guys in jail instead of going gunning for them. That would have been novel for the Western genre. It's also a shame that Destry and saloon girl Frenchy (Dietrich) don't end up together. After their verbal spats, after him pouring water on her—to stop a fight she was having with the wife (Una Merkel) of a fool (Mischa Auer) who lost his pants to Frenchy in a card game—and after her throwing everything within arm's reach at him to get him to leave the saloon, it stands to reason that they'd fall in love. Frenchy is one of Dietrich's best post-Sternberg roles; she's a bit like her character in *Morocco*, only funnier and sassier. Directed by George Marshall, who'd make *Destry* with Audie Murphy in 1954. From a novel by Max Brand, which was the source of a 1932 Tom Mix western. Dietrich's songs: "You've Got That Look," "Little Joe," and the classic "See What the Boys in the Back Room Will Have." Also with: Brian Donlevy, Irene Hervey, Jack Carson, Samuel S. Hinds, Billy Gilbert.

DETOUR (1946) B&W/67m.

Regarded by many critics as the greatest "B" film ever made, Edgar G. Ulmer's near-legendary work is truly an unusual film: it's far more intense and stylish than the run-of-the-mill low-budget picture; as claustrophobic—it uses only six minimally furnished indoor sets—as any fatalistic melodrama; and among its four characters it manages to come up with the oddest, most repellent symbiotic (leech-like) relationship between a man (Tom Neal) and woman (Ann Savage) in cinema history. The film begins with Neal thinking back over circumstances that ruined his life. A club pianist, he hitched from New York to LA to be with his fiancée, a singer (Claudia Drake). When the man (Edmund MacDonald) who gave him a lift in Arizona died from an overdose of pills,

Neal impulsively dumped his body and stole his wallet, clothes, and car. Then he gave a lift to Savage, who, it so happened, was a vixen MacDonald had spoken of earlier. Savage said she'd tell the police that Neal killed MacDonald unless he'd drive her to LA and sell the car so she could get the money. Then she wanted him to join her in a swindle. Neal became her virtual slave. Their relationship was characterized by his constant belly-aching (about everything) and her snarling at him. Savage may have believed in the inevitability of her own death ("If I'm hanged all they'll be doing is rushing it"), but pessimistic Neal believes that his entire life is controlled by Fate: "No matter what you do, no matter where you turn, Fate sticks out its foot to trip you." In truth he does nothing to ward it off: he uses Fate as an alibi for his downfall when his own foolishness caused him to dump MacDonald and steal his possessions (it was certainly *his* choice to wear MacDonald's striped, prison-style pajamas), to pick up Savage when he should have been keeping a low profile, and to not call Drake once he got to LA. A sourpuss, doom-sayer, weakling, and ultimately Savage's slave, this character is one of the screen's all-time great losers—it makes sense that he was played by Neal, who in real life killed his wife and went to prison. But Savage is what makes the film special. What a despicable character! Even she admits she was born in a gutter. The nicest compliment Neal can give her is: "She had a homely beauty." She reminds me of a vulture because she looks as if she wants to rip you apart with her teeth and devour you piece by piece. Even more terrifying than her face is her voice, which is loud, scratchy, vulgar, intolerable. It's appropriate that, in the film's visually exciting climax, drunk Savage is killed by strangulation so that her final words are choked off. Many viewers will find this film disappointing, even ludicrous, be annoyed that every line seems to come straight out of *Bartlett's Familiar Quotations*, and find it less consistent and enjoyable than Ulmer's *The Black Cat*, *Bluebeard*, *Ruthless*, or *The Naked Dawn*. But every film cultist has to seek this one out. Martin Goldsmith adapted his own novel. Photographed by Benjamin H. Kline. Produced by Leon Fromkess.

DEVIL DOLL, THE (1936) B&W/79m.

Unsettling horror classic, directed by Tod Browning and co-written by Eric von Stroheim. Lionel Barrymore escapes from Devil's Island. He is determined to get revenge against the three men who framed him for their crimes and to clear his name for the sake of daughter Maureen O'Sullivan, who has never met him. He teams up with the crazed wife (Rafaela Ottiano with wild eyes and hair) of a dead scientist he'd befriended. They shrink humans to doll size and force them to do his bidding. Disguised as a kindly, elderly lady, he unleashes his miniature people on his intended victims. When the doll people sneak through houses, they're like wily rodents or insects on the loose—they'll give you chills. Strange finale—a father-daughter conversation—makes you forget you've been watching a horror film. Good special effects. Also with: Frank Lawton, Henry B. Walthall, Grace Ford.

DEVIL IN MISS JONES, THE (1972) C/68m.

Along with *Deep Throat* and *Behind the Green Door*, this was the major breakthrough film for XXX-rated films of the early seventies. Of the three, it is the best-made. Today this Bergman-influenced existential porno film is a video favorite and still plays regularly in theaters, most often with *Deep Throat*. Both were directed by Gerard Damiano. Miss Jones (Georgina Spelvin) is a spinster who commits suicide and finds herself in an eternal hell, where she is introduced to all types of sexual experience but is never allowed to reach sexual fulfillment. If the film is to be praised, it's not because it shows a woman initiating her sexual escapades—that is the premise of countless *exploitive* adult films—but because of the fine production values, Damiano's erotic flare, and his decision to star a woman who can act, rather than a bimbo. A former exotic dancer, Spelvin is neither young nor particularly pretty, but makes up for it by being totally lacking in inhibitions. She performs all kinds of sex acts, and her excited reactions to them are always a turn-on. The film's highlight must be the scene in which Georgina takes on two men at once. Word is that they were so nervous that in order to get them to perform she had to convince them that the camera wasn't running and they were only rehearsing—still she has to talk them through it. Also with: Harry Reems (of *Deep Throat*), John Clemens, Marc Stevens, Rick Livermore.

DEVIL IS A WOMAN, THE (1935) B&W/83m.

The last and the least of Marlene Dietrich's films with Josef von Sternberg. Picture is set at the turn of the century in a small Spanish town at carnival time (which allows Sternberg to have fun with costumes and art direction). Dietrich (as Concha Perez) is a flirtatious, irresponsible former cigarette-factory girl whose pastime is breaking hearts. This vamp has already broken the heart of a former military man (Lionel Atwill) several times, including when she ran off with a bullfighter, but he keeps coming back for more punishment. Atwill challenges his young friend (Cesar Romero as a revolutionary) to a duel when he too falls for Dietrich. But when she tells Atwill that Romero is the first man she has ever loved, Atwill deliberately loses so she can run off with his rival. In Dietrich's earlier films for Sternberg she played women who sacrificed all for love—here she responds to a man who is willing to do the same thing. Ending is the reverse of the ending of *The Blue Angel*, the first of the Sternberg-Dietrich films. Picture suffers from looking too studio-bound and from Sternberg's decision to let Dietrich play her role with tongue firmly in cheek (which is how Concha plays out her life)—giving the impression that all those on both sides of the camera (except for the ultra-serious Atwill) were too casual about the film they were making. Picture was banned in Spain. John Dos Passos and S. K. Winston adapted Pierre Louÿs's story *La Femme et le Pantin*. Lucien Ballard was the cinematographer. Also with: Edward Everett Horton, Alison Skipworth.

DEVILS, THE (BRITISH/1971) C/109m.

Ken Russell's adaptation of John Whiting's frightening play about a documented witchcraft case in Loudun, France, in 1634. While transvestite King Louis XIII is off playing perverse sexual games and murdering Huguenot prisoners, and the Plague is claiming countless lives, cynical priest Father Grandier (Oliver Reed) allows himself what he considers are insignificant transgressions—he has an active sex life, and dumps his mistress (Gemma Jones, *Masterpiece Theatre*'s *Duchess of Duke Street*) when she becomes pregnant. Because the politically outspoken Grandier is the only person challenging Cardinal Richelieu's sly attempt to band cities like Loudun into a united state, Richelieu wants him out of the way. A deranged nun (Vanessa Redgrave) who has never met Grandier suddenly accuses him of having taken on a diabolical form and seduced her and other nuns in the convent. A charismatic exorcist (how you'll despise Michael Gothard) arrives in town and soon has other nuns salivating over him and speaking hysterically of cavorting with the devil. Loudun's atmosphere becomes frenzied. While others are victimized, Grandier is tried as a witch, and the trial is a sham. He is condemned to be burned alive, but beforehand undergoes brutal torture without confessing to the trumped-up charges. The sinner becomes moral—a saint—and Loudun is without its protector. Russell's attempt to show how the church "uses totally illiterate people to seduce everyone through terror" had censorship problems worldwide, yet still won a surprising number of awards. Repulsive imagery is overwhelming at times, but for once Russell's seemingly out-of-control, hallucinogenic style is appropriate for his subject matter. Also with: Dudley Sutton, Max Adrian, Murray Melvin.

DEVIL'S BRIDE, THE/DEVIL RIDES OUT, THE (BRITISH/1968) C/95m.

Classy Hammer horror, scripted by Richard Matheson from Dennis Wheatley's novel *The Devil Rides Out*. Its satanist theme made it controversial in England and probably limited its distribution. For once Christopher Lee is our hero, playing the Duc de Richleau, who uses his knowledge of devil worship to combat the wicked high priest Mocata (based, no doubt, on Aleister Crowley), deliciously played by Charles Gray. Clever, visually spectacular finale, in which we see why it's important not to step outside Devil's Circle when the devil shows up, is what gives picture distinction. Directed by Terence Fisher. Also with: Leon Greene, Patrick Mower, Gwen Ffrangcon-Davies, Sarah Lawson.

DIABOLIQUE/DIABOLIQUES, LES/FIENDS, THE (FRENCH/1955) B&W/107m.

Before *Psycho* raised the *psychological thriller* to a new, horrific level, this French classic by Henri-Georges Clouzot was considered the most frightening and artistic picture that the genre could ever produce. Like *Psycho*, it has been copied so many times that its *twist* ending won't surprise first-time viewers, much less terrify them; yet it's hard not to be impressed by the cinematic virtuosity of Clouzot and be shaken by his sinister vision. His work not only is stunningly acted, beautifully paced for tension and suspense, and cleverly structured, but also conveys a nastiness of character and environment that is both oppressive and unsettling. It is a film where the heroine, the nicest person in the story, plans cold-blooded murder; where a dilapidated school, rowdy students, and unworthy teachers are a matched set; where water—symbol of purity and birth/life—is either polluted (the school's pool) or is used to bring about death. Sickly Vera Clouzot is owner and headmistress of a third-rate school for boys; she is beaten and humiliated by her husband, Paul Meurisse, the despicable, child-hating headmaster. She and another teacher, Simone Signoret, Meurisse's former mistress, plot to murder this man who mistreated them both. Just when their scheme seems to have worked to perfection, the corpse vanishes. The stress on Clouzot's weak heart becomes great. The final sequence may not scare viewers as it used to, but it's masterfully handled—Vera Clouzot exhibits terror as well as anyone since Fay Wray. From the novel *Celle qui n'était plus* by the authors of *Vertigo*, Pierre Boileau and Thomas Narcejac. Also with: Charles Vanel, Pierre Larquey, Michel Serrault.

DIAL M FOR MURDER (1954) C/105m.
Not prime Alfred Hitchcock, but this is a passable suspense film about tennis player Ray Milland, who decides to murder his wealthy wife, Grace Kelly, lest she run off with novelist Robert Cummings. When in the classic scene Kelly kills the hired would-be assassin (Anthony Dawson), Milland tries to stack evidence against her so detective John Williams won't believe her self-defense plea. You won't believe that Milland is a tennis player, or that he chooses to kill gorgeous Kelly instead of Cummings, or that Kelly would be attracted to Cummings. Also you'll find that this adaptation of Frederick Knott's play is too stagy. But the intricate plot twists are a lot of fun and the sequence in which Dawson tries to strangle Kelly is superbly directed. In the disappointing 3-D version of the film, the scissors which Kelly uses to kill Dawson look like blunt paper scissors. A good performance by Williams. Music is by Dimitri Tiomkin.

DIAMONDS ARE FOREVER (BRITISH/1971) C/119m.
Follow-up to *On Her Majesty's Secret Service* features Sean Connery's return as James Bond. Nevertheless, it's one of the most forgettable movies of the entire Bond series. Bond thinks he disposes of Blofeld (Charles Grey), killer of his wife in the previous film, in an exciting pre-title sequence. Blofeld will turn up much later, the mastermind behind a scheme to use diamonds to build a large crystal fan that, when attached to a communications satellite, will harness the sun's rays to fuel a laser weapon. He is using the Las Vegas satellite base of a Howard Hughes-like billionaire recluse, Willard Whyte (country singer Jimmy Dean), whom he has kidnapped. Unfortunately, until Blofeld's reappearance we must watch what is no better than a mundane diamond-smuggling melodrama, without the spectacle we associate with James Bond; the Las Vegas setting isn't exotic enough, there's little humor, the villains are second-rate—assassins Mr. Kidd (Potter Smith) and Mr. Wint (Bruce Glover) are similar to characters you'd find on *The Avengers*, but not nearly as amusing—and the trouble Bond gets into, even Maxwell Smart could escape. The only bright spot is moderately talented leading lady Jill St. John as a sexy diamond smuggler who gets in over her head and into a number of teeny bikinis. After *The Lost World* I predicted she'd be a big star—it's a pity that this is the only other good role she was ever offered. Directed by Guy Hamilton. Also with: Lana Wood (as Plenty O'Toole), Bruce Cabot, Norman Burton, Leonard Barr, Bernard Lee, Desmond Llewelyn, Lois Maxwell.

DIARY OF A COUNTRY PRIEST (FRENCH/1950) B&W/120m.
Regarded as Robert Bresson's masterpiece, this award-winning film is about a young priest (Claude Laydu) whose first parish is in the small village of Ambricourt. He's upset that no one comes to Mass. That's because the villagers, who aren't religious to begin with, are suspicious of him and wrongly suspect that he is greedy and an alcoholic. The priest is a typical Bresson hero in that he is extremely introverted and incapable of social conversation (which makes it impossible for him to go out and convince villagers to attend services); feels isolated (he barely speaks to anyone); has grave self-doubts; and suffers terribly—he suffers not only from guilt and spiritual malaise (as do other Bresson characters) but physically as well. He discovers he has incurable stomach cancer (which is why his diet consists of bread and wine). Bresson admires this individual because he somehow retains his faith through this period of terrible despair (which apparently is his *test*). Thus he is able to bring spiritual peace to a dying countess (Marie-Monique Arkell) who had long rejected God because of the death of her child, and ultimately to find himself in a state of grace. Film is somber and slow, with quiet dialogue scenes and many silent passages in which we watch the pensive Laydu in close-up; the slow dissolves and fade-outs not only help maintain the slow pace but also give the picture a haunting, almost poetic quality. Léonce-Henry Burel's cinematography is exquisite; my favorite among his memorable images features a spooky longshot of Laydu on a hill at night, walking through a forest. Diary passages come from Georges Bernanos's novel. Also with: Jean Riveyre, André Guibert, Nicole Maury, Nicole Ladmiral, Martine Lemaire, Antoine Balpêtré.

DINER (1982) C/110m.
Low-budget nostalgia comedy by writer-director Barry Levinson is about a group of young male buddies who hang out at a diner in Baltimore in 1959 at a time they have to make decisions about work, women, their futures. Female viewers seem to respond to this film more than men. Perhaps that's because they dated similar flawed, funny characters, while we men don't wish

to identify with guys who have jerk streaks a mile long. The diner dialogue has rhythm and is well delivered by the talented cast, but I don't find it interesting: thus, I find the characters dull and unsympathetic until they start tripping over words around females. The most original scenes have Daniel Stern hysterically telling off Ellen Barkin for mixing up his precious rock-'n'-roll collection; Stern stating that "Donna" is the *flip side* of "La Bamba" instead of the other way around (I always said "Donna" was the "A" side when having similar debates); and Steve Guttenberg giving his fiancée a football trivia test to determine if the wedding is still on. Also with: Mickey Rourke, Kevin Bacon, Timothy Daly, Paul Reiser.

DINNER AT EIGHT (1933) B&W/113m.   A great serious-at-the-core comedy, masterfully directed by George Cukor and performed by a once-in-a-lifetime ensemble. Dithery Billie Burke decides to throw a lavish dinner party. Flustered by plans that go awry—the guests of honor unexpectedly go on vacation—she fails to notice husband Lionel Barrymore's failing health, due to being on the verge of losing his shipping business and all his money. Among invited guests are vulgar, corrupt businessman Wallace Beery, who plots to steal Barrymore's business; his sexy, ditzy—but really smart—wife, Jean Harlow, who sees the party as a rare chance to step out into society; dignified doctor Edmund Lowe, with whom Harlow is having an affair; aged *Grande Dame* actress Marie Dressler, long past her prime; has-been actor John Barrymore, who is secretly having an affair with the 19-year-old daughter, Madge Evans, of Burke and Barrymore. Except for tyrannical Beery, none of these people are in enviable situations; in their own ways, all are on the brink of disaster. What I find is most interesting about Frances Marion–Herman J. Mankiewicz version of the George S. Kaufman–Edna Ferber play is how the women are able to adapt to their situations, overcoming their problems and taking control, while the men always are more passive (Lionel Barrymore), no match for their wives when the chips are down (Beery), or defeated and suicidal (John Barrymore). It is no surprise that, despite the prescence of great male stars, Burke, Harlow, and especially Dressler steal the film—their performances are comic gems. Camera highlights include Burke's tantrum about everything going wrong, Harlow's venomous spat with Beery, and *every* expression and line by Dressler, whose talents have been forgotten by too many. Also with: Lee Tracy, Phillips Holmes, Jean Hersholt, May Robson.

DIRTY DOZEN, THE (1967) C/150m.   Robert Aldrich's much-copied war film (which itself used the same premise as Roger Corman's 1964 movie *The Secret Invasion*) was a box office smash despite the moviegoers' growing aversion to the genre in light of Vietnam. That's because it managed to stage exciting, brutal war sequences while simultaneously celebrating misfits, putting down authority figures and the military, and showing war to be a madman's game that can only be fought down and dirty. Major Lee Marvin offers twelve murderers and rapists the opportunity to win their freedom from a military prison (five are due to be executed). They must accompany him on a mission into Germany, where they are to kill as many German officers as possible at a rest-and-recreation center. The first third of the film has to do with Marvin whipping these malcontents into shape and making them into a team by developing their mutual hatred for him. The second third has to do with Marvin proving to the other officers (Robert Ryan, Ernest Borgnine, Robert Webber) that his unwashed "dirty dozen" are a crack outfit. The mission itself takes up the last third of the film. The large doses of humor present in the earlier parts of the film are replaced by strong action and bloody killings. What's most surprising is how vicious our side is. In a most shocking bit they pour grenades and petrol into an underground chamber where the German officers *and their women* are trapped and then set a fire that wipes them all out. Film is solidly directed and has a strange appeal; its oddest aspect (perhaps Aldrich sees the irony) is that these criminals are redeemed when they commit acts that are far more repugnant than the ones for which they were arrested. Also with: Charles Bronson (once a member of *The Magnificent Seven*), Richard Jaeckel, John Cassavetes, Telly Savalas, Jim Brown, Clint Walker, Trini Lopez (singing those awful lyrics "Such a pretty girl is like a bramble bush"), George Kennedy, Ralph Meeker.

DISCREET CHARM OF THE BOURGEOISIE, THE (FRENCH-SPANISH-ITALIAN/1972) C/105m.   Four members of the bourgeoisie (ambassador Fernando Rey, married Delphine Seyrig and Paul Frankeur, and Bulle Ogier) arrive for dinner at the home of Stéphane Audran and Jean-Pierre Cassel. They're a night early, so with Audran they go to a restaurant—but they don't eat there because the owner's lying dead on the floor. Keeping the original appointment the next day, the two couples leave when Audran and Cassel spend too much time having a quickie out in the garden. The three couples have other eventful dining experiences, but they never actually eat— one restaurant turns out to have absolutely nothing; as they sit down to eat a meal, a curtain opens up and they discover they're on a stage and don't know their lines; at a party Rey shoots a colonel (Claude Pieplu) for insulting him; gangsters burst into another party and machine-gun all six characters. And so it goes in Luis Buñuel's wonderful comedy. A plot summary doesn't even hint at the rich rewards you'll find in Buñuel's surprisingly subtle attack on the rich, the church, the military/police. It's one of his greatest films and his most structurally daring work since *L'Age d'Or*! He seamlessly moves from the real (silly) world to a dream world (much of what we see turns out to be the nightmares of the characters) to a story world (peripheral characters relate strange tales) to an existential world (our six characters are repeatedly seen walking along a deserted and seemingly endless country road, symbol of their *stasis*). Full of delights and surprises. Also with: Julien Bertheau (as the bishop whom Audran and Cassel hire as their gardener), Michel Piccoli.

DISTANT THUNDER (INDIAN/1973) C/100m.

Lovely, much underrated film by Satyajit Ray, set in a Bengali village in 1942–43. Ray moves between lyricism and realism as he details how famine (which would wipe out five million Indians), caused by the distant war no one understands, affects the people in the village: some hoard rice, some steal it, some beg for it, some women prostitute themselves for it; some who cannot find rice are willing to cook snails and leaves to eat. Most profoundly affected is Soumitra Chatterji (star of Ray's *The World of Apu*), the village's one Brahmin, an educated doctor. He had always considered himself above the untouchables in his village and looked for ways to exploit their ignorance for financial gain. When famine strikes, his Brahmin status allows him to see firsthand the selfishness and deceit toward the villagers by others of privilege; when the hungry villagers no longer treat him with respect, he realizes that his money, education, and Brahmin status aren't that relevant; when he humbles himself to get rice, he realizes that he is no better than an old man he'd belittled for begging him for rice. As his attitude toward his fellow villagers changes and he comes to understand that they are equal to him, he gains added respect for his wife (Babita), whom he'd always taken for granted and who, like the other villagers, had always adopted a subservient, although loving, position toward him. From her he acquires the compassion, the selflessness, and even the optimistic belief that they will survive, even if they share what little they have now. Interestingly, while Ray sets Babita up as the ideal, a loyal wife and friend to those beneath her caste, he refuses to make her perfect: she is judgmental rather than understanding toward her married best friend (Sandya Roy), who has slept with a disfigured man for his rice; she still will not touch untouchables, even friends who are dying. As usual, Ray's women (how beautiful are their faces!) are intriguingly complex. Film has many moments that will stay with you. It is regarded as one of Ray's few distinctly political films because for once he equates the problems of his characters to what is happening throughout India, rather than making his story universal. Cinematography by Soumendu Ray is breathtaking, particularly when he shows women in saris as they pass through outdoor settings. From a story by Bidhuti Bhusan Bannerji. Also with: Gobinda Chakravarty, Romesh Mukerji.

DIVA (FRENCH/1982) C/123m.

Goofy, glittery, dazzlingly stylish suspense thriller by first-time director Jean-Jacques Beineix became an immediate cult sensation in France and America and, since it was ahead of its time, is still in demand. Some critics complained that Beineix's work was self-consciously (Pop) arty, but surely the story, from a novel by Delacorta (Daniel Odier), is bizarre enough to warrant a wild style. Frédéric Andrei is Jules, a young Parisian postman who lives in one of Beineix's fascinating sets (designed by Hilton McConnico): a dark loft full of stereo equipment, wrecked cars, and Pop art (including large photos of cars). He has a mad obsession for American diva Cynthia Hawkins (played by opera star Wilhelmenia Wiggins Fernandez), who is touring through France. Because she has refused to make records, he tapes her performance with a concealed recorder. The next day a woman on the street drops a second cassette into his pouch without his noticing—just before she is murdered. Only later does he find out that the woman was the mistress of the chief homicide inspector and revealed on the cassette that he is the head of a drug-and-prostitution ring. Without understanding why, Andrei finds that he's being followed by two policemen, two thugs (who work for the crooked police inspector) and two Taiwanese record pirates. He finds refuge with two strangers, Alba (Thuy An Luu) and Gorodosh (Richard Bohringer)—who proves to be the film's hero/godsend, more than a match for all the bad guys. Quirkiness of film is evident in three major character couplings: Jules, an 18-year-old, white, passive Frenchman, and Cynthia, the taller, 30-ish, black American performer; Alba, a teenage, hedonistic Vietnamese shoplifter, and Gorodosh, her adult, white, Zen-freak boyfriend; the tall, handsome, suave Latin thug and his short, indented-faced, punk-garbed, blond, younger partner (Dominique Pinon is a memorable screen villain), who always has a Walkman blaring in his ears. Beineix under*scores* odd teams by mixing rock and classical music. Visually, Beineix uses his frame like a Pop-art canvas, filling the spaces between his black, blue, and red images with white light, direct or reflected. He is thrilled with movement, so he places his characters on wheels (Jules's moped, Gorodosh's classic white Citröen, Alba's roller skates, etc.) and lets the camera run wild, almost as if it had a life of its own. (One of the highlights is a mad car-motorcycle chase.) Beineix makes weird choices at every turn and very few don't have big payoffs. Cinematography by Philippe Rousselot.

D.O.A. (1949) B&W/83m.

First-rate melodrama with an unusual, intriguing premise: accountant Edmond O'Brien is given a fatal dose of poison by a stranger—before he dies, he tracks down his murderer. In effect, O'Brien becomes one of the first movie heroes to have no fear of being killed. He bravely walks through scary environments and steps on the toes of brutal people—since he is already dying, he has nothing to lose. The story gets a bit confusing, but O'Brien is a solid lead and director Rudolph Maté makes excellent use of San Francisco and Los Angeles locales. There are some good bit parts, including Neville Brand's psycho who enjoys pounding on O'Brien's belly. Great success of the movie is that it's not too morbid to sit through although we know from the beginning that innocent nice-guy O'Brien is doomed. Also with: Pamela Britton, Luther Adler, Henry Hart, Virginia Lee, Beverly Campbell (Garland).

D.O.A. (1980) C/90m.

Lech Kowalski's documentary of seminal English punk group, The Sex Pistols, with extensive footage of their 1978 U.S. tour. Haphazardly constructed, it is nevertheless an arresting, upsetting social document about the punk scene at its peak. The young fans who show up for Sex Pistols concerts are society's and mothers' worst nightmare. Their make-up and wild clothing won't bother anyone who has been to *The Rocky Horror Picture Show*, but it's disturbing to witness the pins through their cheeks, their mindless fuck-the-world hostility and rudeness (especially toward the cameraman), and their violence—after being thrown out of a club for charging onto the stage, one guy decides the band members weren't worth killing anyway. Music by The Sex Pistols (Johnny Rotten, Sid Vicious, Steve Jones, Paul Cook) and other famous punk groups should please fans and, for those like me, satisfy curiosity. Surely the film's most famous, most depraved scene is an interview with catatonic Vicious (wearing a swastika T-shirt) and spaced-out girlfriend Nancy Spungen—Vicious would be charged with murdering Spungen in late 1979, and die of a heroin overdose while awaiting trial. Subtitled *Rite of Passage*.

DOC SAVAGE: THE MAN OF BRONZE (1975) C/100m.

George Pal's last production, directed by Michael Anderson, brought Kenneth Robeson's pulp hero to the screen for what was supposed to be the beginning of a series. In 1936 square-jawed Savage (Ron Ely) and his Fabulous Five (Paul Gleason, Eldon Quick, Darrell Zwerling, Michael Miller, Bill Lucking) go to Hidalgo in the Caribbean to investigate the death of Savage's father. They encounter villain Captain Seas (Paul Wexler), discover a lost tribe of Indians, and enormous riches. Picture is played straight-faced, with the intention of creating a camp classic. There are a couple of amusing scenes (Savage and his *vice-less* friends having dinner on Seas's ship). But Ely has no charisma, there are few interesting story twists, and film has the static studio-look of a cheap, kiddie adventure TV show like *Wonder Woman*. Film has a cult, but I think it's a dull disappointment. Also with: Pamela Hensley, Robyn Hilton.

DR. BUTCHER, M.D. (MEDICAL DEVIATE) (ITALIAN-AMERICAN/1979) C/90m.

Gorefest about a mad doctor performing *sickening* operations—he usually pulls out organs—on an island off Africa. Even the previews of this film turned my stomach. Horrible film combines footage from the Italian-made *Queen of the Cannibals* with footage from an unreleased American film *Tales That Will Rip Your Heart Out* (perhaps it was a student film). It gained notoriety because of an imaginative publicity campaign—I was almost run over by the Butchermobile that sped through the streets of New York. For sex and gore fans only. Produced by Terry Levine. Directed by Frank Martin (Francesco Martino). Starring: Ian McCulloch, Alexandra Cole, Peter O'Neal, Donald O'Brien, Sherry Buchanan.

DR. CYCLOPS (1940) C/75m.

Mad scientist Albert Dekker recruits three scientists to his lab in the Amazon jungles. His eyes are failing him, so he needs them to do work with his microscope. They become suspicious of his experiments with radium and discover that he has reduced the size of animals. Dekker shrinks the three scientists and two others. He holds them captive as the Cyclops held Ulysses and his crew. But they escape into the jungle. Conventional juvenile horror story benefits from solid special effects: it was the first time transparencies, split screens, and double exposures had been used in a color film. The tiny people look authentic. Director Ernest B. Schoedsack borrowed ideas from Willis O'Brien, who'd done the special effects for Schoedsack's *King Kong* and *Son of Kong*. *The Incredible Shrinking Man* would use ideas from this film. François Truffaut was a fan of the picture. Also with: Janice Logan, Thomas Coley, Victor Kilian, Charles Halton, Frank Yaconelli, Paul Fix, Frank Reicher.

DR. JEKYLL AND MR. HYDE (1932) B&W/82m–98m.

Rare venture into horror films by Paramount in wake of success by Universal; the result is one of the classiest entries in the genre, a true "A" production. Fredric March won an Oscar for his forceful performance as the kindly Dr. Jekyll and the monstrous figure he becomes when undertaking soul-seeking experiments with a dangerous drug solution. His Hyde is pure evil, making life a living hell for the helpless trollop (Miriam Hopkins) who falls into Hyde's clutches, and trying to destroy all that is precious to Jekyll, whom he despises. One of the cinema's most terrifying monsters, a sadistic female-batterer of the first order, Hyde resembles a demented monkey—with large, protruding teeth, enormous lips, hungry eyes and dark and hairy features. He also mimics an ape with his amazing athletic maneuvers. Picture has strong sexual content and is too gruesome for young kids or the squeamish. In fact, it was edited heavily for its reissue. It is known for innovative, influential direction by Rouben Mamoulian, who experimented with split frames, superimposed shots (during impressive man-to-monster transformations), and point-of-view shots, most notably during Hyde's first scene, when passersby react to his hideous countenance before we get the chance—Jerry Lewis parodied this bit in *The Nutty Professor*. Excellent, exciting picture, but I wish that when Jekyll says he thinks he was right to venture into "no-man's-land" despite having been the murderous Hyde, the script wouldn't have him reconsider and beg God's forgiveness for treading into His domain. That's too common a theme for so unusual a picture. First sound version of Robert Louis Stevenson's story, which, incidentally, bears little resemblance to any of the films. Spencer Tracy would star in a 1941 remake, and Christopher Lee would reprise the dual role in *I, Monster*, a 1972 British film. John Barrymore starred in the silent version. There would be other remakes and variations. This is the best. Also with: Rose Hobart (as Jekyll's fiancée), Holmes Herbert, Halliwell Hobbes—whose names would be great for a law firm.

DR. MABUSE, THE GAMBLER/DR. MABUSE, DER SPIELER (GERMAN/1922) B&W.

Times vary greatly: the original version, comprised of two parts, *Der Grosse Spieler* and *Inferno*, or, as they are more commonly known, *Dr. Mabuse, the Gambler* and *Dr. Mabuse, King of Crime*, reportedly runs almost 270 minutes; however, when it has been shown as two separate films, the combined running times have been trimmed to an approximate 210 minutes; furthermore, another version (once titled *The Fatal Passions*) that often plays in the U.S. combines both parts into a slim 90 minutes (although I have recently seen a version running about 105 minutes). The major problem with all cut versions is that famous scenes depicting social conditions in 1922 Germany, particularly the decadence of its cities, have been eliminated; therefore we can judge the film solely on its melodramatic aspects. Certainly influenced by *Caligari*, and probably by *Nosferatu* as well, Fritz Lang's diabolical villain, Mabuse (Rudolf Klein-Rogge), relies on mind control to destroy people. He doesn't care about making money, although his criminal activities make him and his gang rich, but gets his pleasure from wielding power and, as he says, interfering in people's lives and determining their fates. His current passion is to hypnotize people, have them take him to their secret clubs, and then win a great deal of money from them playing cards (he forces his victims to lose on purpose). Using numerous disguises, he repeatedly gets away with this swindle. The official, played by Bernhard Goetzke (no relation to New York's subway "vigilante"), who attempts to capture Mabuse is Special Prosecutor von Wenk in the original version and Police Chief De-Witt in the cut version. When Goetzke arrests Mabuse's female accomplice-companion (Aude Egede Nissen), Mabuse uses his telepathic powers to have her commit suicide; and he kidnaps the countess (Gertrude Welcker) both he and Goetzke love. Critics have rightly criticized the decision to have Mabuse fall in love because it diminishes him from being a supervillain to being just a villainous human. Film's visuals aren't as impressive as those in other Lang silents, and the melodrama is not as exciting as one would hope— due in part to Goetzke being a dull hero—but Mabuse is a classic character who would become the model for future screen villains: he is proof that there is little distinction between genius and madness, that power-lust is the first step toward insanity, that the criminal mind works in the same way as the minds of the men (like Goetzke) who work to prevent crime (Lang often made the link between the criminal and the policeman). Last scene, which will remind you of *Caligari*, is a highlight. Scripted by Thea von Harbou, from the novel by Norbert Jacques. In 1933 Lang would make a sound sequel, *The Testament of Dr. Mabuse*. Also with: Alfred Abel, Paul Richter.

DR. NO (BRITISH/1962) C/105m. The James Bond series started in great style with this cleverly conceived adaptation of Ian Fleming's enjoyable spy thriller. It's interesting today to see how much the series has changed— bigger isn't better. Little-known Sean Connery became a superstar as the dashing, debonair British agent 007. What a great new type of hero: he had the license to kill; knew judo; was a well-educated gentleman; had great taste in clothes, food, and wine; met only beautiful women (whom he made love to even if they worked for the other side); could take on villains; traveled to exotic locations; didn't panic when the fate of the world rested on his shoulders; had charm and a subtle sense of humor; was capable of causing John Barry's famous Bond theme song to play just by giving his name—as in his famous introduction in the series. The story about Bond and beautiful Honeychile Ryder (Ursula Andress) tracking down a master villain, Dr. No (Joseph Wiseman), on Crab Key Island near Jamaica, is material for an old-style serial, but director Terence Young, writer Richard Maibaum (who worked with Johanna Harwood and Berkely Mather), and producers Albert Broccoli and Harry Saltzman kept the film from deteriorating to juvenile level. Picture has sex, violence, wit, terrific action sequences, and colorful atmosphere. Connery, bikini-clad Andress (who became a sex-symbol star), and Wiseman all give memorable performances. There's a slow stretch in the middle and Dr. No could use a decent henchman, but otherwise the film works marvelously. Highlights include: "three blind mice" opening, Bond having a tarantula crawl on him, Honeychile's first appearance, Dr. No's demise. A different type of film—looking back, one can understand why it caused so much excitement. Edited by Peter Hunt, photographed by Ted Moore. Also with: Jack Lord, Anthony Dawson, John Kitzmiller, Zena Marshall, Eunice Gayson, Bernard Lee (as "M"), Lois Maxwell (as Miss Moneypenny).

DOCTOR OF DOOM/LUCHADORAS CONTRA EL MÉDICO RESINO, LAS (MEXICAN/ 1960) B&W/77m. My favorite Mexican horror movie—a camp classic! The "Mad Doctor" is obsessed with performing brain transplants. Unfortunately, they invariably fail. One of his many female victims is the brainy (then brainless) sister of statuesque professional wrestler Gloria Venus (Lorena Velazquez). She and a fellow wrestler, The Golden Rubi (Elizabeth Campbell), help their policemen boyfriends unveil the villain. Picture has all the ingredients of an old-time serial (a villain who poses as a respectable citizen, mad experiments, guys in masks, a superstrong imbecile henchman, cliffhangers) plus some rousing female wrestling action, in and out of the ring. A highlight is Gloria's match with the truly invincible Vendetta. A poorly dubbed laugh riot that's far better than director Rene Cardona's more famous *The Wrestling Woman vs. the Aztec Mummy*. Also with: Armand Silvestre, Roberto Cañedo, Sonia Infante, Chucho Salinas.

DR. STRANGELOVE OR: HOW I LEARNED TO STOP WORRYING AND LOVE THE BOMB (BRITISH/1964) B&W/93m−102m. Stanley Kubrick directed this classic nightmare comedy, which he, Terry Southern, and Peter George adapted from George's more serious novel *Red Alert*. It's so funny because, as ludicrous as the characters and events are, there is nothing in this picture that is beyond the realm of possibility. Perhaps we are laughing at ourselves (instead of worrying) for living in a world whose fate is controlled by buffoons. One buffoon is General Jack D. Ripper (Sterling Hayden). Believing that the communists have poisoned the water supply—that, he believes, is why his sexual proficiency has diminished—he orders U.S. bombers to conduct a nuclear attack on Russia. He kills himself rather than reveal the recall code to his British assistant, Capt. Lionel Mandrake (Peter Sellers). President Muffley (also Sellers) explains the situation to the Soviet Premier (we never see him), who informs Muffley that if a nuclear bomb goes off in Russia then a Russian Doomsday device will destroy the world. Perverse Dr. Strangelove (Sellers again), a former Nazi who works for the U.S., reveals his contingency plan in which America's politicians, top brass, and bigwigs will retreat to underground chambers where there will be ten women for every man. Kubrick considered ending the film with a slapstick pie fight in the war room. I'm glad he didn't. Watching the film today, I grow impatient with most of the scenes outside the war room. Inside there are many classic bits: gum chewing Gen. Buck Turgidson (George C. Scott) explaining to Muffley what Ripper has done; Muffley having hilarious Bob Newhart-type conversations over the hot line; Strangelove (who's not in the film enough) trying to stop his out-of-control metal hand (which automatically gives a Nazi salute) from strangling him. Sellers is marvelous in all three roles (he has a terrific American accent)—somehow he lost out on the Oscar, which went to Rex Harrison for *My Fair Lady*. Photography is by Gilbert Taylor. Production design is by Ken Adam. Vera Lynn's WWII recording of "We'll Meet Again" is used effectively at the conclusion. Also with: Keenan Wynn, Slim Pickens (who rides a bomb to cinema glory), Peter Bull, Tracy Reed, James Earl Jones.

DOG DAY AFTERNOON (1975) C/130m.

Black comedy, based on a real-life incident. Two incompetent gunmen (Al Pacino, John Cazale) try to hold up a Brooklyn bank. Pacino, who is married to an obese woman, needs money to pay for the sex-change operation of his homosexual lover, Chris Sarandon. They find the building surrounded by policemen, television cameras, and hordes of onlookers. While a circus atmosphere develops, they hold the bank employees as hostages during a long siege, and attachments form between the men and the captives. They demand a getaway car and a waiting plane. But nothing goes right for them. Film is big favorite of many fans and critics, yet I think it smacks of "Wouldn't this true story make a great movie!" attitude. It may have happened just like this, but it all rings false. Every unbearable moment when we laugh because the situation is so pathetic, every introduction of another offbeat character, every character expression seems calculated to elicit an audience response. *The Verdict* aside, this is usually not how director Sidney Lumet works. Lumet gets good performances from Pacino and Cazale as the bank robbers who are in over their heads (which leads to tragic results), but his direction of the extras who make up the crowds outside the bank is surprisingly lame: like everyone else, they are obviously *acting* for our benefit. Frank Pierson's script won an Oscar. Also with: James Broderick, Charles Durning, Penny Allen, Sully Boyar, Carol Kane.

DOLCE VITA, LA (ITALIAN-FRENCH/1960)

B&W/175m. Federico Fellini's mammoth film about the *meaninglessness* of Rome's "sweet life" is one of his most ambitious, fascinating, and popular works. It is also his most cynical film. Marcello Mastroianni wants to be a serious writer, but he works for scandal sheets covering movie stars and other celebrity newsmakers—he's as big a vulture as the insensitive papparazzi who accompany him on stories. He can't stand his job and he's had as much as he can take of his girlfriend (Yvonne Furneaux)—who spends *all* her time waiting for him to come home. He loves her, but comes home less often, preferring to spend his nights with lovers or attending wild parties. When the philosopher (Alain Cuny) whose life he envies—he has a smart, pretty, working wife, two lovely children, a nice apartment full of literature and art, and parties at which there is intelligent discourse—shoots his children and commits suicide, Mastroianni is devastated because he realizes he has no escape from his worthless life. Like all the others who have given up trying to find happiness or make a positive contribution to society, he dives headlong into orgies, cruelty, planned frivolity. Fellini's depiction of the sweet life: nights are given over to decadence, dawn is a quiet time for reflection and, this being Italy, guilt—but not enough guilt to abandon the ugly yet intoxicating life-style. Film is filled with memorable characters (who move in and out of the story) and classic scenes: a statue of Christ hanging from a helicopter, Anita Ekberg's walk through a fountain, Mastroianni's argument with Furneaux in their car, the night at the palace, the striptease, Mastroianni slapping and putting feathers on a dazed female partygoer during an orgy, etc. Photography by Otello Martelli. Music by Nino Rota. Also with: Anouk Aimée, Nadia Gray, Lex Barker.

DONA FLOR AND HER TWO HUSBANDS

(BRAZILIAN/1977) C/106m. Just when we thought we'd seen the last of the countless Italian sex comedies, along came this one from Brazil. Based on Jorge Amado's novel, Bruno Barreto's ribald film is about a newly married woman (Sonia Braga) whose second husband (Mauro Mendonca), a considerate, respectful, faithful man, is completely different from her dead first husband (Jose Wilker), who gambled away her money, beat her, chased whores, and drank himself into an early grave. But, she sighs, neither is Mendonca the fabulous lover Wilker was. Horny Braga's lust for the passionate Wilker is so strong that his naked ghost returns to her. Should she send him away or try to live with both husband and ghost? The film's best moments are serious—Wilker beating up Braga to get gambling money; Braga visiting a whore because she suspects that her baby may be Wilker's (they become fast friends when it turns out Braga made a mistake). In fact, there are so few humorous moments that it's easy to forget this is a comedy. Film's tremendous popularity can be attributed to several factors:

adult viewers are excited by the steamy sex scenes between Braga and Wilker; men are turned on by Braga, while women identify with her character's situation; women are turned on by Wilker, while men envy his character's hedonistic life; women recognize their own husbands/boyfriends in Braga's two flawed husbands. Ending implies that the men, when combined, have the male attributes that can please Braga, but Wilker's ghost is a counterfeit because he hasn't the human Wilker's *bad* characteristics that made her miserable. *Kiss Me Goodbye* is the insipid American remake.

DON'T CRY, IT'S ONLY THUNDER (1982) C/108m.
It's regrettable that this sensitive look at a different side of the Vietnam War has received almost no theatrical distribution. In his best role since *Breaking Away*, Dennis Christopher plays an undisciplined young medic stationed in Saigon. He learns responsibility when he finds himself helping two Vietnamese nuns run a non-sanctioned, off-base home for war orphans. In a heartfelt role, Susan Saint James is an army doctor who risks her career to help Christopher dodge MPs (when he sneaks off base) and care for the children. At times the picture is a bit sticky, but its treatment of the war and its effect on children is unsentimental. Moreover, it has an admirable theme: real heroes are those who make commitments to help people whose problems make their own seem insignificant. Compassionate direction by Peter Werner. Also with: James Whitmore, Jr., Roger Aaron Brown.

DON'T LOOK NOW (BRITISH/1973) C/110m.
Couples trying to cope with the drowning death of a 10-year-old daughter don't usually fly off to Venice, but that's where Donald Sutherland and wife Julie Christie go in Nicolas Roeg's adaptation of Daphne Du Maurier's story. Sutherland has been commissioned to restore a church. Christie befriends two strange middle-aged Hitchcockian sisters, one of whom is a blind psychic who claims that their daughter is happy where she is, but is warning Sutherland of impending danger. Sutherland, who discovers he has limited psychic powers, ignores his own premonitions. Suspense builds on another front: someone is committing random murders along the canal. Story is amazingly simple, but it comes across as perplexing because of Roeg's stylistic impositions. He uses bizarre angles, constantly cuts back and forth between present, past, and future, and stages conversations in which everyone seems out of sync with everyone else. All characters, including Sutherland and Christie, seem disoriented—what are they thinking? The battle between conventional religion and the occult doesn't matter much as far as Sutherland or Christie is concerned (only the priest seems shaken); in fact, I can't really figure out why it matters if the sister or Sutherland has extrasensory powers or if the daughter is sending warnings from the grave—certainly Sutherland would chase any small figure in a hooded red outfit (his daughter wore a red housecoat), regardless of what he'd been warned. All the occult stuff is creepy, yet it really doesn't tie together very well. The most memorable moments are a very erotic sex scene between Christie and Sutherland (Roeg intercuts the lovemaking with shots of them later dressing to go out, and in good moods) and the finale in which Sutherland chases the small figure in red along the canal at night—it climaxes with one of the greatest shocks in movie history. Also with: Hilary Mason, Clelia Matania, Massimo Serato.

DOUBLE INDEMNITY (1944) B&W/106m.
James M. Cain's explosive, bitter melodrama became a bona-fide cinema masterpiece in the sure hands of Billy Wilder, who directed and wrote the hardboiled script with Raymond Chandler. This is quintessential *film noir*, characterized by the interacting traits of greed, lust, murder, betrayal, and a pervading, oppressive darkness in which evil's grasping hand is free to entrap anyone who thinks of straying from the moral path. In his most impressive performance, Fred MacMurray is an LA insurance salesman named Walter Neff. He's smart, cocky, aggressive, but not as clever as he thinks. He narrates the story to his shrewd friend and boss, Edward G. Robinson, telling how he fell madly in love with a client's beautiful wife. Barbara Stanwyck has never been cooler, more convincing, sexier (you'll long remember that ankle bracelet cutting into her skin as she walks) than as icy blonde Phyllis Dietrichson. MacMurray thought she loved him, too, and agreed to knock off her husband so they could collect on his life insurance and run off together. Too late it dawned on him that Stanwyck was just playing him for the fool, something viewers will have known from Stanwyck's first "sincere" expression of love to MacMurray. Meanwhile Robinson was putting the puzzle pieces together and was about to have Stanwyck arrested for murder. Film has no humor, but it's tremendous fun to watch a man so *secure* (don't forget he sells *insurance*) in himself fall into a spider woman's web. I really like the way Stanwyck smartly sits back and lets MacMurray take over and (showing off) devise the murder plot; she is subtly stroking his masculine ego. Cain's bizarre finale would have shocked viewers and incensed critics, but Wilder and Chandler came up with a suitable substitute for the ritualistic double suicide. As in all good *noir* films, the hero realizes he deserves his sorry fate, the woman acknowledges she's no good. Ultimately, they were meant to go to hell together. The only thing I question in the film is why Stanwyck doesn't treat herself to at least a glimpse of her husband being murdered. Perhaps she's so evil she treats such occurrences with indifference. Also with: Jean Heather, Porter Hall, Tom Powers, Fortunio Bonanova.

DOWN AND OUT IN BEVERLY HILLS (1986) C/103m.
When bum Nick Nolte's dog deserts him, he tries to drown himself in a backyard pool in Beverly Hills. Richard Dreyfuss, the self-made millionaire hanger-manufacturer who owns the house, rescues him. Seeing Nolte has intelligence and remembers the old Brooklyn Dodgers, he invites him to stay in the house, over the ob-

jections of his wife, Bette Midler, and maid, Elizabeth Peña, Dreyfuss's secret lover during the years Midler has been rejecting him in bed. Nolte seems to be a passive, easygoing, non-judgmental character, but he manages to have a positive effect on all the eccentric family members: he becomes Dreyfuss's one friend and the only person who listens to him; by massaging and making love to Midler, he makes her body and mind feel better and freer than her personal guru and nutritionist ever could; he gives needed adult approval to son Evan Richards, who can't speak to his parents—especially about his desire to cross-dress; he gets anorexic daughter Tracy Nelson to eat by making her feel he's her first lover who really cares for her; he wins over Peña by being a lover who doesn't exploit her; and he cures their neurotic dog, Matisse (Mike)—like everyone else in the family, he has an identity problem—by confirming he is equal to the humans in the house. Paul Mazursky has remade Jean Renoir's 1932 classic *Boudu Saved from Drowning* and injected many ingredients, including the nice but screwy family from *My Man Godfrey*. The acting by Nolte, Dreyfuss, and Midler is the picture's main plus, but the humor is so erratic that Mazursky repeatedly cuts to dog reaction shots to get easy laughs. The entire family is obnoxious at the beginning, but Mazursky obviously likes them and simply assumes that we'll soon share his warm feelings just because they grow more tolerant of each other and Nolte. These Beverly Hills types are all *real* at one point in the film—unfortunately, as some caricatures become real, real characters become caricatures. The best, most honest thing Mazursky does is alter Renoir's ending. In today's world there's nothing romantic about being a hobo; however, when Nolte decides to stay with the Whitemans, he's probably being used to alleviate Mazursky's own guilt for being a wealthy, decadent Southern California millionaire. Disney Studios' first R-rated film. Also with: Little Richard, Donald F. Muhich, Mazursky, Valerie Curtin, Barry Primus.

DRACULA (1931) B&W/75m. This horror classic was once considered terrifying; but although movie fans still regard it with tremendous affection, it is often appreciated today solely for its camp value. Adapted from the play in which Bela Lugosi starred, rather than from Bram Stoker's truly superb novel, its story is a mess—I have never figured out what's going on in the London sequences because scenes seem to be missing. (Also I'm confused because characters like Jonathan Harker have different roles than they do in the novel.) Nothing in the London sequences matches the spooky opening in Dracula's Transylvanian castle—although you'll get a kick out of Dracula's battle of wills with vampire-hunter Professor Van Helsing (Edward Van Sloan) and seeing the crazy Dracula-controlled Renfield (Dwight Frye) make an impassioned plea for more spiders to eat. Tod Browning's direction is too stagey, as are the performances, but cinematographer Karl Freund manages to give film some haunting atmosphere, especially in the Transylvania scenes. His close-ups of Lugosi's heavily rouged face and those wide, aggressive eyes are genuinely frightening. Lugosi is no great actor, but he is a great Dracula. Handsome, with a Hungarian accent that connotes good breeding, Lugosi became a sex symbol as the result of the film. His vampire is intelligent, cultivated, yet is comfortable walking through cobwebs. His blood lust is scary, and his seductive attacks on women are the acts of a sex fiend. Although he once admits it would be "glorious" to be really dead, this Dracula is not to be sympathized with—it is by choice rather than happenstance that he does evil. Remade many times. Sequel is 1936's *Dracula's Daughter*. Also with: Helen Chandler (whom Dracula wants to possess for eternity), David Manners, Frances Dade, Herbert Bunston.

DRACULA'S DAUGHTER (1936) B&W/70m. Sequel to *Dracula* is better than the original. Dracula is dead and his smart, cultured (she's a pianist and artist) daughter (well played by Gloria Holden) doesn't wish to carry on his evil ways. She even asks a doctor (Otto Kruger) to help her cure her vampirism (of course he doesn't believe she is a vampire); showing her human side, she falls in love with Kruger, feels jealousy toward his fiancée (Marguerite Churchill), and tries to wrest him away from her. Her attempts to be civil are undermined by her cruel servant (Irving Pichel), who won't let her forget her family legacy. Her bloodlust becomes too difficult to control; we empathize with her as she gives in to her vampirism and stalks victims. Despite a rushed ending, film is cleverly plotted, atmospheric, and erotic. It's much better than the Lugosi original at conveying the sexuality implicit in the vampire legend. Film's most famous scene has Holden painting a young, depressed streetwalker (lovely Nan Grey). She obviously feels attracted to the half-naked girl and ends up seducing her with her eyes and draining her blood. There wouldn't be a more explicit lesbian scene in a vampire film until Roger Vadim made *Blood and Roses* 24 years later. Lambert Hillyer directed this low-budget, still neglected chiller. Also with: Edward Van Sloan (who reprises his Professor Van Helsing role), Hedda Hopper, Gilbert Emery, E. E. Clive, Halliwell Hobbes, Billy Bevan.

DRAGONSLAYER (1981) C/108m. This exceptional fantasy from Disney Studios was dismissed by critics and did poorly at the box office. So it will be a pleasant surprise, especially for adults. It's set in an age when magic and superstition are on the downswing, and Christianity is making inroads among the scared, ignorant people. Peter MacNicol is a young apprentice to an elderly sorcerer (Ralph Richardson), and his powers are still suspect. But when Richardson is killed (or so we think), MacNicol must take his place in doing battle with a vicious dragon that brings misery to a small hamlet, where virgins are sacrificed to the hungry creature to keep it peaceful. Pretty Caitlin Clarke has been living as a boy all her life so she won't be sacrificed. MacNicol and Clarke enter the dragon's lair and get more than they bargained for. Film presents a magical world—the countryside, the medieval hamlet, the castle and its dungeon, the dragon's lair—in credible fashion. The dragon's lair is beautifully designed and the enormous fire-breathing dragon is one of the great monsters of the cinema—it's like a Ray Harryhausen masterpiece, with remarkably precise movements. The confrontations with the dragon are absolutely spectacular; special effects were provided by George Lucas's Industrial Light and Magic. There are a couple of times when the brutality is too strong for young viewers, but otherwise it's everything a fantasy film should be. Imaginative, intelligent direction by Matthew Robbins. Fine performances by MacNicol (after you get used to him), Clarke, Richardson. Also with: John Hallam, Peter Eyre.

DRAUGHTSMAN'S CONTRACT, THE (BRITISH/ 1982) C/103m.
The British Film Institute and Channel 4 Television financed this unusual black Restoration comedy-mystery. Many were impressed by Peter Greenaway's feature debut, others despised it even while acknowledging the quality of the photography (by Curtis Clark) and the director's keen eye for period detail and his meditation on manners. In late-17th-century England, Mr. Neville (Anthony Higgins), an arrogant young draughtsman, is invited by Mrs. Herbert (Janet Suzman) to render a series of drawings of her estate as a surprise for her husband (Dave Hill), who is away. He agrees on the condition that this proud, middle-aged woman submit to him sexually whenever he desires. We think him rude for humbling her in such a way (she says she detests their interludes). But we don't realize until the very end that his villainy is child's play compared to viciousness levied out by the polite, seemingly civilized English gentry. Clues (props) to a possible murder keep appearing in Neville's drawings; when it turns out Mr. Herbert has been killed, Neville is treated as the chief suspect— he will not be given a trial. Greenaway handles everything with such elegance that we are totally unprepared for the final act of cruelty. Ending is haunting; it makes you reassess all that went before—supposed victims are really heartless predators. Also with: Anne Louise Lambert (as Suzman's sexually unfulfilled married daughter, who forces Neville into having the same sexual arrangement with her that he has with her mother), Hugh Fraser (as Lambert's prissy husband), David Grant.

DRESSED TO KILL (1980) C/105m.
Almost every character in Brian De Palma's erotic thriller has a split personality. The person on the outside is not like the person on the inside. Housewife Angie Dickinson tells New York psychiatrist Michael Caine that her husband ignores her sexually. Frustrated, she allows a stranger to pick her up. After wild lovemaking, she enters the elevator in his building—and is brutally slashed to death by someone inside. Cute, capitalistic, tough-as-nails Nancy Allen glimpses the murderer, a blond female. Police detective Dennis Franz thinks she was involved. Allen, herself pursued by the killer, teams up with Dickinson's clever son Keith Gordon to try to find the murderer. They think it is another of Caine's patients—and Caine himself thinks the murderer is a patient, but will not betray him. I think this is De Palma's best film, one in which I don't mind being manipulated. Watching De Palma at work turns out to be a lot of fun. He does everything with an audience in mind; there's a great deal of titillation, subtlety, and shocks. The characters are all offbeat and have senses of humor, and all have energy. The actors are in fine form—Allen and young Gordon make an interesting team. Dialogue is sharp, but film's best scenes are visual, relying on editing or a mobile camera, as is the long Hitchcock-like sequence in the museum. De Palma does, as usual, borrow from Hitchcock, stylistically and thematically. He even has two scenes with women in showers. Typical of De Palma, the violence is strong, and there's a dirty-trick ending. Good use of New York locales—highlight has Allen hurdling over subway turnstile. Pino Donaggio composed the effective score.

DRILLER KILLER, THE (1979) C/90m.
Sleazy cult film was the first venture of independent New York director Abel Ferrara. Using the name Jimmy Lane, Ferrara plays a struggling artist who lives with his sensible girlfriend (Carolyn Marz)—who has run off from her husband—and her spacy lesbian lover (Baybi Day). As all three are broke, he needs to quickly sell a painting to a homosexual gallery owner who has been coming on to him. He paints obsessively and begins to lose his senses. When a New Wave rock band moves into his building and plays 24 hours a day, he has a complete breakdown. He runs around killing people (acquaintances, derelicts) with a drill. Grisly film is not your typical slice-and-dice splatter fare. Uniquely, it's not about a man stalking scantily clad females—the artist's victims are all men. I believe Ferrara is making some point about the artist feeling hatred toward men because he fears he is a homosexual himself. (Of course, the drill has sexual connotations.) Film has same vengeance-against-a-segment-of-society theme that is found in Ferrara's *Ms. 45* and *Fear City*. Those later films are much more polished, but obviously there's talent involved here. Ferrara scores with a lot of weird touches and humor—for instance, we laugh at all the aggravation the artist suffers—but the storyline is hard to follow and the violence is unnecessarily graphic. Also with: Harry Schultz, Alan Wyroth.

DRIVE, HE SAID (1971) C/90m.
Jack Nicholson's directorial debut was booed at Cannes and received mostly negative reviews in the U.S. Flawed and defeatist as it is, I think it's an impressive, highly original work, probably the best at expressing the alienation and confusion of college kids of the era. Film's major character is an All-American basketball player (William Tepper) at a Midwestern college. His thoughts should be on turning pro, but he's preoccupied with his radical roommate (Michael Margotta, who resembles Nicholson), who's literally going mad while trying to avoid the draft; and his lover (Karen Black), the wife of a trusting professor (Robert Towne). Margotta tells Tepper he should quit basketball, drop out, and no longer play "the

game"; Black seems to be breaking away from Tepper, although she may be carrying his baby. Film deals with *rebellion* on three fronts: Margotta from society/authority/sanity; Tepper from his basketball-is-everything coach (Bruce Dern is fabulous); and Black from all the men who keep her from breathing. Because of nudity and roughness of sex (including an attempted rape), picture got an X rating, which harmed its box office. It became a cult movie. Adapted by Nicholson and Jeremy Larner (Eugene McCarthy's chief speechwriter in '68) from Larner's novel. Co-produced by Harry Gittes (Jake Gittes is the character Nicholson played in the Towne-scripted *Chinatown*). Bert Schneider was executive producer. Photographed by Bill Butler. Also with: Henry Jaglom, Mike Warren, June Fairchild, Cindy Williams.

DRIVE-IN MASSACRE (1976) C/72m. Obviously, this cheapo horror film about a maniac who chops off heads and stabs lovers at the drive-in should have been a natural for the drive-in market. But its title is by far the best thing about it. The humor is feeble, there is no suspense, the special-effects man knew how to do about two things, there are no characters to speak of, and film doesn't even have an ending. Yet somehow it has a small cult. Directed by Stuart Segall. With: Jake Barnes, Adam Lawrence, Douglas Gudbye, Verinka Flowers.

DRIVER, THE (1978) C/90m. Taciturn Ryan O'Neal drives getaway cars; brutal, slightly unhinged Las Vegas cop Bruce Dern is determined to arrest him. Dern works out a complicated plan to catch O'Neal during an exchange of *hot* money; meanwhile some bad guys are planning to double-cross O'Neal. Cult film was directed by Walter Hill, who mixed *film noir* with existential European gangster pictures. It has an interesting style, but the actors (but for Dern, of course) seem to be on their own and lost. It's okay that Hill had O'Neal drive at high speeds as if he has ice water in his veins, but since he's just as expressionless outside his car, there are no sparks when he interacts with other characters—the most disappointing scenes are those in which he gets together with the equally reserved Isabelle Adjani and both are as cool and exciting as cucumbers. Hill's at his best directing action scenes, those in which characters threaten or actually shoot at each other; the film is best known for its car chases, but, though excitingly filmed, they're too long and repetitive. Also with: Ronee Blakley, Matt Clark.

DUCK SOUP (1933) B&W/70m. Although made in their heyday, this was the Marx Brothers' one critical and commercial flop of the period. It seems that Depression Era audiences, who needed to believe in their leaders, were a bit unnerved seeing Groucho as the ruler of a country. But college audiences in the 1960s were looking for films that treated politicians with the disrespect they deserved, and this hilarious comedy was elevated to its rightful place in the comedy-film pantheon. Breezily directed by Leo McCarey, this is the team's masterpiece: 70 delightful minutes of non-stop (no musical interludes or romance) sight gags, verbal wit, zany improvisations, and Groucho and Harpo offending everyone around them. Significantly, it is the only film that provided the team with the proper political milieu for their anarchic brand of humor. Groucho plays Rufus T. Firefly, who, through his shameless flirtation with Margaret Dumont, has become dictator of Freedonia. Believing that any country who'd have him as leader deserves him as leader, Groucho does his worst: playing jacks, chasing women, hiring Chico and Harpo for his cabinet (although he knows they also work for the enemy), and prolonging a war because he has already paid a month's rent on the battlefield. His major source of pleasure comes from letting fly with lowbrow humor in austere settings among genteel company. He loves being rude in public and one of his playful diversions is to ruin polite conversation by pretending to take offense at something innocent said to him and quickly insulting the person who said it. If an occasion demands propriety, he is at his most hostile. The first time we see him, we know all about him: he arrives late at his inaugural ball and enters by sliding down a pole, sings a ridiculous ditty about how he'll ruin the country's economy, does an embarrassing dance, makes lewd advances toward pretty women, dictates a note to his dentist, rolls his pants above his knees, asks Dumont to "pick a card" (adding, "Keep it—I still have fifty-one left"), and insults his rival, Louis Calhern. Meanwhile Harpo shows that he is the missing link in man's evolution, an unsuccessful stage in man's development. He sleeps with animals, eats things a goat would reject, and should be kept on somebody's leash. His great moment is when he aggravates lemonade dealer Edgar Kennedy, first by cutting out the bottom of his pocket and using it as a peanut bag and then by walking barefoot in his lemonade, sending prospective customers scurrying away in disgust. From beginning to end (the boys hurl oranges at Dumont when she attempts Freedonia's anthem), the comedy is side-splitting. Not to be overlooked is the classic pantomime in which spy Harpo (and for a time spy Chico) pretend to be the mirror image of Groucho and resort to assorted gyrations to prove it. One of the all-time great comedies: Zeppo's presence doesn't even interfere. Produced by Herman Mankiewicz. Also with: Raquel Torres, Edmund Breese, Leonid Kinskey, Verna Hillie.

DUELLISTS, THE (BRITISH/1977) C/101m. Ridley Scott's excellent, highly unusual first work as a feature director is an adaptation of Joseph Conrad's "The Duel," certainly not an ideal commercial project. It takes place in France between 1800 and 1815, the Napoleonic period. The exquisite photography and attention to period detail is most rewarding. Keith Carradine is a young cavalry officer who is ordered to confront another soldier, Harvey Keitel, for having fought a duel. Keitel, a tempermental brute, takes offense when Carradine comes into his home to discuss such a matter in front of his mistress. He forces Carradine to fight a duel. Carradine wins the fight when his sword strikes

Keitel's arm. But Keitel chooses to continue the feud. Over the years, the two men fight several duels in different settings. It's always Keitel who insists on continuing the madness. Victories are divided. Even while the Napoleonic Wars take place, the duels dominate these men's lives. For Keitel, "Honor is an appetite"—he will not be satisfied until Carradine is dead. Carradine cannot rest until he is the one who determines the nature of their relationship. The duels are exciting, brutal, and realistic. The two men forget the reasons they are fighting: this is Conrad's/Scott's attack on nations that are enemies because of events that happened long ago and are long forgotten. In fact, the duels between Carradine and Keitel parallel the ongoing, equally senseless Napoleonic Wars. The two leads are excellent; Keitel is much like a mean, modern-day teenage punk who's itching for a fight. Significant contributions were made by actors who accepted small roles: Albert Finney, Tom Conti, Diana Quick, Jenny Runacre, Robert Stephens, John McEnery.

DUMBO (1941) C/64m. A Disney film with heart. Disney loved to make cartoons about misfits/freaks who are laughed at and rejected by the ones they try to befriend; examples include the Ugly Duckling, Lambert (the sheepish lion), and, in a sense, Pinocchio and Cinderella. Few are so alienated as Jumbo, Jr., "the smallest little elephant" in the circus, who is insulted by the other elephants and given a silly nickname, Dumbo, because of his small size and his enormous ears. After his mother is locked in a cage marked "Mad Elephant" for going on a rampage to protect her son, poor lonely Dumbo cannot stop crying. (This scene often has been cited as being too traumatic for young children with a strong mother dependency.) And to make matters worse, the circus owner puts him into an act with some insensitive clowns that requires him to dive from a high window into a tiny bucket of water. This is literally the low point in Dumbo's life. Luckily, Disney films usually provide their heroes with companions of a sort (Jiminy Cricket, Tinker Bell, Gus and Jaq), voices of their subconscious who offer advice and urge them into achieving their potentials. Timothy J. Mouse fills that role for Dumbo. Along with four hip black crows, Timothy teaches Dumbo how to use his ears to fly. Not only will his flying capabilities make him the star of the circus, but he'll also become famous and be reunited with his mother. Cartoon was made on the cheap, to help recoup heavy studio losses resulting from the unsuccessful release of the much more expensive *Fantasia*. Yet it is one of Disney's finest, sweetest, least pretentious films. The characters are a memorable lot and are drawn expertly (Dumbo is irresistibly cute; Ward Kimball considered the crows the best characters he ever animated), the action animation is exceptional (excellent use is made of quick cuts and extreme angles), and the story (adapted from a just-published story by Helen Aberson and Harold Pearl) manages to be both frightening (like, say, *Oliver Twist*) and charming. The "Pink Elephants" dance sequence (a nightmare the drunk Dumbo is having) is one of the greatest bits of animation in all of Disney. Ben Sharpsteen served as supervising director. Voices by: Edward Brophy (Timothy), Herman Bing (narrator), Verna Felton (one of the catty female elephants who mock Dumbo), Sterling Holloway (the stork who delivers the baby elephant), Cliff Edwards (as the leader of the controversial black crows, Jim Crow, whose name is the only thing I find offensive about him).

DUNE (1984) C/140m. Big, beautiful, and a bust. Working in Mexico for Dino De Laurentiis, director-screenwriter David Lynch managed to capture the exact images of those wondrous planets, palace chambers, and creatures we imagined while reading Frank Herbert's novel. Indeed, the first few minutes of the film, including the noble Atreides family's arrival to rule the desert planet, contain some of the most impressive visuals in sci-fi cinema history. Unfortunately, in order to establish the *look* of the film, Lynch takes so long to get his story going that for the next 90 + minutes he must rush through Herbert's plot, hoping that readers will fill in the gaps and recognize the characters who whiz past and be familiar with their motives, loyalties, etc. Those who haven't read the best-selling novel will be totally dumbfounded; Herbert cultists will say repeatedly, "I can't believe he left that out!" The book has too many characters with similar powers (it seems that everyone can read minds), but on a superficial level they are different archetypes with different cultural backgrounds—in the movie you can't figure out who anyone is or what he is capable of doing. The film's one unexpected success is Kyle MacLachian as Paul Atreides, who is believable as the "messiah" of the desert guerrillas. The part is poorly conceived and as inconsistent as in the novel, but MacLachian makes us root for him even though we don't know what he's up to. Likewise, Kenneth McMillan, modeling the ugliest facial make-up around, makes us despise him even though we don't know exactly what his villainous plans are. Badly wasted: Brad Dourif, Sean Young, Sting, Linda Hunt, Francesca Assis, Paul Smith, Max von Sydow, José Ferrer, Dean Stockwell, Freddie Jones, Richard Jordan.

DUST BE MY DESTINY (1939) B&W/88m. Sleeper has John Garfield as a jinxed young tough from the wrong side of the tracks. After serving a prison sentence for a crime he didn't commit, he's sent to a country work farm on a vagrancy charge. He falls in love with sweet Priscilla Lane, the stepdaughter of the drunken foreman. When the foreman dies of a heart attack during a fight with Garfield, Garfield realizes that the police will think he murdered him. He and Lane run away together. The result is one of the best couple-on-the-lam films. Garfield and Lane (this is her most appealing performance) are a couple you really can root for. Exciting, romantic, well-acted film was lost among spate of Garfield films released by Warners between 1938 and 1940. Unfortunately, Garfield and Lane, who appeared together in *Four Daughters* and *Daughters Courageous*, never teamed again. Directed by Lewis Seiler. Written by Robert Rossen, from a story by Jerome Odlum. Fine cast also includes: Stanley Ridges, Alan Hale, Charley

Grapewin, John Litel, Billy Halop, Frank McHugh, Henry Armetta, Bobby Jordan, Moroni Olsen, Victor Kilian, Ward Bond.

EARRINGS OF MADAME DE..., THE/ MADAME DE.../DIAMOND EARRINGS (FRENCH-ITALIAN/1953) B&W/105m.

Breathlessly beautiful Max Ophüls film about *"un grand amour,"* a love of the heart, not the libido, that both ennobles lovers and consumes them. Danielle Darrieux gives an exquisite performance as the frivolous, fickle wife of a humorless general, played by Charles Boyer. Needing money, she pawns the diamond earrings that Boyer gave her on their wedding night. She tells him she misplaced them, but Boyer discovers she sold them. He secretly buys them back and gives them to his mistress, who eventually sells them. Baron Vittorio De Sica buys them in Constantinople. As fate would dictate, De Sica and Darrieux become acquainted and fall in love. De Sica gives Darrieux the earrings as a sign of his love. She tells Boyer she found the earrings, but he knows better. He challenges De Sica to a duel. Story, adapted from a novel by Louise de Vilmorin, has elements of a standard melodrama or even a silly farce (in which a husband keeps buying the same earrings), but Ophüls's presentation is so elegant (with great attention paid to the 19th-century period detail) and the actors are so classy that we're soon caught up in the romance and are vicariously experiencing the lovers' simultaneous feelings of pleasure and anguish. Film contains a marvelous waltz montage during which Darrieux and De Sica become inseparable; and, as usual, Ophüls makes his world come alive with lengthy tracking shots that create the impression of an "infinite frame." A splendid score by George Van Parys. Also with: Mireille Perrey, Jean Debucourt, Lia de Léo, Jean Galland.

EARTH/SOIL (RUSSIAN/1930) B&W/63m–69m.

Alexander Dovzhenko wrote and directed this landmark about the formation of a collective in a Ukrainian village. The young peasants join together to purchase a tractor to help run their farms more effectively. Their celebration is cut short when the head of the village committee (Semyon Svashenko) is murdered by a kulak. In this film, people die when they are happiest (an old man eating an apple, Semyon dancing through the fields) —film celebrates life, and though it expresses grief for the recent dead, it is more concerned with rebirth than with inevitable death. Simply filmed, lyrical film attacks the old ways (kulaks, Christianity) and celebrates progress (young people, the tractor, collectivism, sexual equality). It links these people to the soil (in an erotic scene, several young couples lie on the ground embracing), the crops (there is dignity in work), the farm animals. Sev-

eral scenes were deleted for foreign distribution: the peasants cooling down the tractor with their urine (we see connection between man and machine); Semyon's grieving fiancée (Yelina Maximova) tearing off her clothes; a woman giving birth at Semyon's funeral. The last scene is pivotal because it reflects the picture's major theme: you can't grieve too long for those who are dead because the living must be responsible for a better future. An optimistic film about people who refuse to be defeated by what might appear to be major setbacks. Also with: Stepon Shkurat, I. Franks.

EARTH VS. THE FLYING SAUCERS (1956) B&W/ 82m.

Enjoyable, flashy science-fiction, highlighted by some spectacular special effects by Ray Harryhausen. Space scientist Hugh Marlowe rushes home from his honeymoon with Joan Taylor because alien androids have been shooting down his satellites. He discovers that they plan to take over the earth. He tries to come up with a weapon that will stop them. Film's climax, Harryhausen's high point, is an incredible battle in Washington in which alien rays shatter some of D.C.'s best-known buildings—so impressive is the destruction that for a time we root for the aliens. Film can be seen as a counter to 1951's *The Day the Earth Stood Still*, in which Marlowe's character was wrong not to trust the aliens who landed in Washington. Curt Siodmak's story was suggested by Major Donald E. Keyhoe's *Flying Saucers from Outer Space*. Capable direction was by Fred F. Sears. Producer Charles H. Schneer would later produce Harryhausen's "Sinbad" films. Also with: Donald Curtis, Morris Ankrum, John Zaremba.

EAST OF EDEN (1955) C/115m.

Elia Kazan directed this adaptation of John Steinbeck's novel. The Paul Osborn–Guy Tomajean script covers the last part of the book, beginning in 1917 when Cal (James Dean's first major role) discovers that his father Adam (Raymond Massey) lied to him and his brother Aaron (Richard Davalos) when he said their mother was dead. He discovers that Kate (Jo Van Fleet) ran out on the self-righteous Adam and wound up a madam in Monterey. Now he understands where he got his wild bad side; he also knows that his similarity to Kate is the reason Adam has loved Aaron much more than him. (Of course, Steinbeck wanted Cal and Aaron to represent Cane and Abel.) Cal has spent his entire life trying to win his father's love. He resents Aaron for being loved by father and Abra (top-billed Julie Harris). When Adam loses his life savings on a scheme to refrigerate vegetables, Cal borrows money from Kate to invest in beans, whose price will go up once the war begins. He wants to give his earnings to his father. When Aaron wins out again on Massey's birthday, spiteful Cal takes him to Kate, knowing that the good Aaron will never be able to accept her sinful profession. Film's themes include: misunderstood youth (a Dean specialty); the search for identity; the search for love; and rejection—every character is rejected by someone they love, and in turn rejects someone who loves them. Kazan's once-audacious camera impositions no longer work (the style changes every scene), but his handling of actors is still impressive. The scenes between Dean and Van Fleet (who won a Best Supporting Actress Oscar) and Dean and Harris are dynamic. Ending is extremely emotional—when Dean speaks to sick Massey, Kazan cuts to tearful Harris to give us our crying cue. Steven Spielberg would borrow this manipulative maneuver. Made in 70mm Technicolor. Music by Leonard Rosenman. Also with: Burl Ives, Albert Dekker, Lois Smith, Timothy Carey.

EASTER PARADE (1948) C/103m.   Gene Kelly was to star opposite Judy Garland, but when he became ill Fred Astaire came back from a two-year retirement—and did the dances with few changes in the blocking. Vincente Minnelli was to direct, but choreographer Charles Walters was given the assignment instead. The result is one of MGM's brightest, cheeriest musicals. Whether dressed as hoboes while dancing and singing "A Couple of Swells" or wearing their Sunday best while strolling down Fifth Avenue and singing the classic title song, Astaire and Garland are a most engaging screen couple. And Walters worked with Robert Alton to stage some fine musical numbers—ones in which Harry Stradling's camera moves in tandem with the dancers. Particularly exciting are Astaire's solo, "Stepping Out with My Baby," when he dances in slow motion while the chorus behind him dances at full speed, and Ann Miller's sexy tap solo to "Shaking the Blues Away." The Astaire-Garland numbers are special, too, and it seems Garland is really enjoying herself—which is nice to see. The uplifting Irving Berlin score is first-rate and used to perfection (although I've never been a fan of Peter Lawford's singing). The simple storyline, written by Sidney Sheldon, Frances Goodrich and Albert Hackett, is essentially *Pygmalion*: when Astaire's partner (Miller) drops him to go solo, he tells her he can take an unknown non-professional like Garland's Hannah Brown and make her as big a star as Miller is. At first it appears that Hannah will never win his respect for her talents or his love. But she will develop into a worthy partner for Astaire and win his heart. As in the other popular Garland films, the audience takes a rooting interest in her achieving success. Also with: Jules Munshin, Clinton Sundberg, Richard Beavers, Lola Albright.

EASY RIDER (1969) C/94m.   Captain America (Peter Fonda) and Billy (Dennis Hopper) make a big dope sale (to Phil Spector!), hop on their flashy motorcycles, and begin an odyssey across America's Southwest and South. They give a lift to a hippie (Luke Askew), visit his desert commune, and frolic with a couple of available young women; take up with a genial, alcoholic ACLU lawyer (Jack Nicholson) they meet in the pokey and turn him on to marijuana; are harassed and later attacked by rednecks; visit a New Orleans bordello and "trip" with two hookers (Karen Black, Toni Basil) during the Mardi Gras; and head for Florida. But what exactly are these dropouts from society looking for? Fonda is too reticent and Hopper too spacy for

them to articulate what it is they seek. When Fonda finally tells Hopper, "We blew it!" what's he referring to? Hopper, for one, has no idea. Is it actually Fonda, the film's producer, telling Hopper, the film's director, that they forgot to include a theme in their script? The too abrupt, brutal scene that follows and concludes the film is so powerful that it clouds the fact that the film makes no real statement, political or otherwise, other than to tell us longhairs of the period not to travel through the South. This low-budget commercial blockbuster changed the face of Hollywood for years to come. Every studio would begin producing low-budget "personal" films geared for the youth market. But no film better caught the fancy of the alienated youth of America. However, many in its target audience were disappointed, preferring films like *Medium Cool* because of their obvious leftwing politics. While they loved the great background music (including the Byrds and the Band), adored the lively, drawling performance by Nicholson (who grins from ear to ear under his football helmet in the role that caused his career to take off), admired Hopper's bizarre editing techniques, and packed their knapsacks after seeing Laszlo Kovacs's stunning photography of the southwestern landscape (the land becomes uglier as the film becomes increasingly pessimistic), they objected to the females being mere sex objects (readily available to the men), the flimsiness of the script—it ends just when you expect it to switch into high gear—and a thoroughly depressing rather than progressive finale. We also wondered why so many people admired the two leads, who are drug dealers, inarticulate, apolitical, and sexist. (Granted they have groovy bikes.) It would be interesting to know if Fonda and Hopper intended us to like them. Co-written by Terry Southern.

EATING RAOUL (1982) C/83m.   Tired of having his projects rejected by everyone in Hollywood, director Paul Bartel borrowed from family and friends to finance this devilish, enjoyable low-budget black comedy, which appropriately features the brutal mass murder of the Hollywood types who refused to lend Bartel money. Money. That's what the Blands (Bartel, Mary Woronov)—a boring, prudish couple—need to realize their American dream and open a gourmet restaurant. So they put an ad in a sex newspaper promising kinky sex sessions with Mrs. Bland, who dresses as a dominatrix. When weird clients arrive at their apartment, the Blands murder and rob the scum. Hotblooded street hustler Raoul (Robert Beltran) muscles in on the business. He secretly disposes of the bodies and returns with money; and, in a genuinely erotic scene, seduces Mrs. Bland. Will she remain faithful to her mild-mannered, asexual husband or kill him and run off with Raoul? Bartel's comedy works against all odds because the Blands are so sympathetic (like so many, they suffer from the recession and are stepped on by everyone with money) and because they're the least likely couple in the world to devise a moneymaking plan that includes sex and murder. But mostly it wins us over because of the three splendid lead performances. One of the best midnight movies. Also with: Susan

Saiger, Buck Henry, Ed Begley, Jr., Dick Blackburn (who co-wrote the Oscar-nominated script with Bartel), John Paragon, Hamilton Camp.

ECSTASY (CZECH/1933) B&W/75m–88m. This once banned picture, starring the unknown Hedy Lamarr and directed by Gustav Machaty, is a surprisingly impressive work considering that its reputation is based solely on its troubles with censors and Lamarr's nudity. It's an extremely bold, erotic exploration of a woman's need for sexual fulfillment—a theme that was long taboo in the cinema. Lamarr's a young bride who discovers that her older husband has no sexual desires. While she watches young romantic couples all around her kissing or dancing closely, her dull husband ignores her. Extremely unhappy, she leaves him and goes home to her father. She plans a divorce. After a nude swim, she meets a young construction worker who returns her dress. In a remarkable sequence that takes place that night, Machaty cuts back and forth between sexual imagery and Lamarr standing alone on a balcony with cigarette smoke escaping her wide-open mouth; it's easy to tell that Lamarr is at the mercy of her libido. She aggressively walks to the worker's shack and they have sex. Machaty's camera stays on Lamarr's face throughout the lovemaking and while she has an orgasm—this startling scene, not the more famous one in which Lamarr runs nude through the woods, is the reason the film has always had trouble with censors. Machaty is sympathetic to Lamarr, yet he considers her a sinner for yielding to her sexual desires and seeking out a man for sex (and for committing adultery)—regrettably, he feels she deserves punishment and must sacrifice all, including the man she now loves (because he gave her sexual pleasure). Sound film has very little dialogue—it is shot like a silent film, often employing Russian montage techniques. Final sequence of workers is bizarre, almost experimental in nature. Also with: Jaromin Rogoz, Leopold Kramer, Aribert Mog.

EDDIE AND THE CRUISERS (1983) C/94m. A flop when released, this weird little film has become a cult favorite due to cable television. It concerns itself with a hot sixties rock group that broke up when the volatile and charismatic lead singer Eddie Wilson (Michael Paré) drove his car off a bridge following his record company's rejection of his concept album. Since then the legend of the Cruisers has grown considerably, so reporter Ellen Barkin interviews all the living members of the defunct group—their memories are told in flashback. Recently someone has broken into all of their houses—perhaps looking for the concept album's master tapes, since that ahead-of-its-time record would be a smash today. They wonder if the culprit is Eddie—if somehow he is still alive (his body never was found). Combination of sixties nostalgia, music extravaganza, and creepy mystery is not altogether successful, but, thanks to music (provided by John Cafferty and the Beaver Brown Band), a solid cast, and an interesting premise (inspired by rumors that the Doors' lead singer, Jim Morrison,

still lives), it is far better than most unimaginative pictures thrust at youth audiences. In fact, sixties crowd is ideal audience. Also with: Tom Berenger (whose character writes the Cruisers' lyrics), Helen Schneider (the only real rock singer to play a Cruiser), Joe Pantoliano, Matthew Laurance, David Wilson, Kenny Vance, John Stockwell, Michael Antones (of the Beaver Brown Band).

EDUCATING RITA (1983) C/110m. Julie Walters gives a witty, endearing performance as Rita (the role she had on the London stage), a working class Liverpool hairdresser who decides to study literature at the Open University. Michael Caine is also exceptional as the alcoholic, non-caring professor, a failed poet, who reluctantly becomes her tutor. Her enthusiasm excites him and he becomes a good professor. Walters's marriage breaks up, but she becomes a scholar. Caine, who has fallen in love with her, misses the honesty she conveyed before she became (with his help) too sophisticated. And we viewers find that the film wavers once she is transformed. While the picture was made a decade too late to be taken seriously as an important woman's-movement film, it does make the interesting point that a man resents a woman who is as educated as or more educated than himself—even if he is the one who encouraged her education. (This is a favorite theme of Woody Allen.) While the film obviously contends that education is liberating (as well as enjoyable), it also says the same about *teaching*—watch the subtle changes in Caine's demeanor: his attitude becomes obnoxious, but he feels emotions that he's held in check for years. Lewis Gilbert directed, as he did in the theater; Willy Russell adapted his own play, adding too many superfluous characters and scenes. This was an unexpected hit that most everyone liked, despite the conventional *Pygmalion*-influenced story. Also with: Michael Williams, Maureen Lipman, Jeananne Crowley, Malcolm Douglas.

EEGAH! (1963) C/92m. Bad-movie fanatics adore this low-budget horror film. Borrowing its basic premise from *King Kong*, it's about a giant prehistoric caveman (a pre-"Jaws" Richard Kiel) who abducts a pretty young girl (Marilyn Manning) and takes her to his California cave. In the most lurid scenes this horny man rubs his big hands all over her tiny, trembling body and we hope he'll try something unforgivable. But, dammit, she's rescued by her boyfriend, who's played by the director's son, 16-year-old cult icon Arch Hall, Jr., who looks a bit like a blond Michael J. Pollard. Arch (as Tommy) takes Manning back to Palm Springs. But while he's belting out a song at a party, Kiel comes looking for the girl he loves. Picture is a lot of fun; it probably would have run into censorship problems if anybody'd paid more attention to where Kiel was placing his hands. I think everyone was too scared of Kiel to ask him to cool it. Arch Hall, Sr., played Manning's father (as William Walters) and directed (as Nicholas Merriwether), which explains how Hall won the lead role and was allowed to sing.

EL DORADO (1967) C/127m. Director Howard Hawks and writer Leigh Brackett reworked their 1959 western *Rio Bravo*, coming up with a film that just misses equaling that masterpiece. Gunfighter John Wayne (as Cole Thornton) decides to help Sheriff Robert Mitchum (as J. E. Harrah) fight the bad guys. But first he must sober up his old friend, who became an alcoholic because of a failed relationship. Whereas in *Rio Bravo* a young gunslinger, Ricky Nelson (as Colorado), helped Wayne (the sheriff) and Dean Martin (his alcoholic deputy), in this film it's a young James Caan (as Mississippi), who can't shoot at all. Old Indian fighter Arthur Hunnicutt (as Bull) replaced Walter Brennan's Stumpy. Hawks had aged since *Rio Bravo*, and his two major characters had done likewise. Wayne is in the last stages of his gunfighting career—he has a bullet lodged in his spine, he must cheat to win his final gunfight, he is aware of his limitations. Like other Hawks films, this one deals with professionalism, friendship, grace under pressure; like *Rio Bravo* and *Rio Lobo* (1970), it ends with all the good guys still alive. Christopher George, who plays a gunfighter working for bad-guy rancher Ed Asner, is Hawks's most sympathetic villain. He and Wayne respect each other, since both are professionals with a code of honor. If Hawks thinks Wayne deserves to survive, it is because he has friends, while George is a loner willing to spend time with bad guys. Picture has exciting action sequences and a great deal of humor. Caan is particularly funny, especially when reciting Poe's "Eldorado" for a bewildered Wayne ("Ride, boldly ride"). Loosely based on Harry Brown's *The Stars in Their Courses*. Music by Nelson Riddle. Also with: Charlene Holt (who interests both Wayne and Mitchum), Michele Carey, R. G. Armstrong, Paul Fix, Johnny Crawford, Adam Roarke, western artist Olaf Wieghorst (who also did the title paintings).

EL NORTE (1983) C/139m. Because of political turmoil, Enrique (23-year-old David Villalpando) and sister Rosa (22-year-old Zaide Silvia Gutierrez) flee their Guatemalan village and head north for the United States, the glamorous country they've read about in magazines. The journey is difficult, and they have trouble getting out of Mexico. They finally reach America by crawling through a tunnel, where—in a chilling scene—they are attacked by rats. They take a room in a small, decrepit motel; we feel so sad for them when we see their new home, but they are pleased. Rosa turns it into a charming place. As illegal aliens, they can take only menial jobs. He works in a restaurant; she becomes a servant. We see how badly illegal aliens (who don't speak the language perfectly) are treated and how stressful it is worrying that they'll be found out. Through the hardships, the brother and sister are content because they have each other. Then Enrique gets a chance at a well-paying job. It will mean leaving Rosa. Financed in part by American Playhouse, film was directed by Gregory Nava (who is half-Mexican, half-Basque), who wrote the script with his wife, Anna Thomas. It is an extremely moving, beautifully acted, believable work about outcasts

in America to whom no one pays attention—and about whom no Hollywood studio will make films. You really get to love these two characters who (naïvely, it turns out) try to see the silver linings in the dark clouds, have hope where there is none, find humor in their confusing lifestyle. Exceptional film is marred by an ending that is overly depressing. The characters are already defeated—there is no need to destroy them. Also with: Ernesto Cruz, Trinidad Silva, Alicia del Lago, Eracio Zepeda.

ELVIRA MADIGAN (SWEDISH/1967) C/89m. Bo Widerberg's romantic classic is set in Denmark in the 1880s. It is based on a true story that has achieved legend status in Scandinavia. Married cavalry officer Sixten (Thommy Berggren) and famous tightrope walker Hedvig/ "Elvira Madigan" (Pia Degermark) run away. Their love for each other is so great that they are willing to sacrifice all, to blissfully detach themselves from society. But they must keep on the move (their photos are in the paper), and their money runs out. They have nothing to eat. They fall into despair, and realize there is only one solution. Film is often lumped with *A Man and a Woman*, that other famous European romance of the '60s. But this is far superior. It's a poetic, yet unsentimental work, with excellent, intelligent acting by Berggren—his character is very likable and interesting—the lovely presence of amateur Degermark, Jorgen Persson's gorgeous cinematography (faces, countryside, provincial towns), and a compelling theme which appealed to the drop-out-and-love generation. (Its *amour fou* theme would have appealed to surrealists.) Picture has several memorable moments, including: Sixten's apology to Elvira (a note saying "Sorry") by a stream; Sixten inquiring about his children; hungry Elvira eating flowers and wild mushrooms; suicidal Sixten telling an uninterested man his name; the love scenes; the finale. The music is Mozart's *Piano Concerto No. 21*.

EMERALD FOREST, THE (1985) C/115m. This story would make great imaginative fiction, but, incredibly, it is based (loosely) on a true account. A construction engineer (Powers Boothe) in charge of a dam-building project in the Amazon jungles has his young son kidnapped by The Invisible People, a primitive tribe who have had no contact with white people. For 10 years he uses his spare time to explore the jungle in search of his son. At last, while fleeing The Fierce People, deadly enemies of The Invisible People, he is rescued by his son (Charley Boorman), now a teenager and adopted son of the kindly tribal chief. He can't convince the recently married son to return to civilization, but when The Fierce People kidnap the tribe's women, including the son's wife (Dira Paes), the boy comes to him for help. Trite dialogue at beginning may make you want to get your money back, but soon director John Boorman has you riveted to your seat, enthralled and terrified by the various adventures. Depiction of tribal life of Invisible People is fascinating; just when you think it too idyllic—happy nude figures contentedly swim in a clear river countless miles from civilization—a harder side appears. These are gentle people—

probably the only jungle inhabitants in cinema history with a sense of humor—but they are capable of brutal actions when the need occurs, witl out a second thought. The mystical aspects of their lives—through the use of a "drug," they enter a jungle animal and see through its eyes; they can cause storms, etc.—add to the strangeness of the film. It would have been an ideal project for Peter Weir or Nicolas Roeg as well as Boorman, whose films usually show in some way a collision of civilization and savagery (unlike in Boorman's *Deliverance*, here we have the "noble savage"). For the first time Boorman has a political theme: irresponsible developers in the Amazon are clearing jungle at such a rapid pace that soon the few remaining primitive tribes will lose their land and become extinct. Picture has gorgeous haunting photography by Philippe Rousselet, convincing performances by Boothe and the director's son—the scene in which they are reunited under a waterfall is unforgettable. Film is flawed but so fast paced and exciting that it fits the definition of *movie*. It's everything that the reserved, foolish, artsy *Greystoke* should have been. Also with: Meg Foster, Rui Pololah.

EMILY (1980) C/87m.

Soft-core porno film that gained notoriety and extended pay-television airplay when its young lead, Koo Stark, had a much publicized affair with Prince Andrew. It's about a schoolgirl who spends the summer hanging around with a lot of sex-obsessed adults and, as a result, has a series of sexual experiences of her own. As dull as other soft-core films, but Stark is pretty enough for some male viewers to wish they'd had Prince Andrew's luck. The oddest thing about the film is the bare-assed presence of Vincent Spinelli, onetime foil for the Beatles. Directed by Henry Herbert. Also with: Sarah Brackett, Richard Oldfield.

EMMANUELLE (FRENCH/1974) C/92m.

Notorious X-rated, soft-core French film set in Thailand, about a 19-year-old woman (Sylvia Kristel) whose sexual escapades with men and women make her not just sexually liberated but a woman who is defined by her sexual appetite. My theory is that this film's cult is composed of men who use *The Sensuous Woman* as a reference book. Women probably have a hard time taking it seriously because it's the visualization of male fantasies: that a beautiful woman tries to please a man (husband Jean, played by Daniel Sarky), who tells her to be free yet insists on having ultimate power over her; that in seeking sexual fulfillment she would trustingly turn herself over to a dirty old man (Alain Cuny) to be her educator; that a woman anthropologist (Marika Green) breaks up with Emmanuelle for no good reason (we have seen that she can carry on her work and the romance simultaneously), just so director Just Jaeckin can send his heroine back to Sarky and Cuny. Film is sensuously photographed, and does have some erotic appeal due to Kristel, as the half-innocent, half-sex-crazed Emmanuelle. It's like being in the presence of a beautiful woman who presumedly doesn't realize she forgot to button her blouse; her casual display of her body is a real turn-on. Moreover, her character's allure is due in part to her not being shy about her body or afraid to have sex in a semipublic place. She allows a woman to seduce her in a locker room, jointly masturbates with her teenage girlfriend on her porch while servants mill about, makes love to Green in sight of a bridge where people walk. These scenes are exciting. But when Cuny takes her around town for sexual adventures with strangers and in front of on-lookers and turns her into an exhibitionist who is aware that her body is on display, she is debased in our eyes and loses the appeal that went hand in hand with her naturalness and freedom. Using the slogan "*X* was never like this," Columbia made a great deal of money on this film, which at one point was France's top-grossing picture. From the scandalous 1957 French novel by *Emmanuelle Arsan*, which had been banned by DeGaulle. Film has spawned many sequels and numerous copies. Also with: Jeanne Colletin, Christine Boisson.

EMPEROR JONES, THE (1933) B&W/72m.

Curious adaptation of Eugene O'Neill play, with Paul Robeson reprising his stage role. Rufus Jones is a Pullman porter who kills a fellow black in a poolroom brawl and is sentenced to time on a chain gang. He escapes and winds up on a Caribbean island as the unpaid servant of a white trader (Dudley Digges) who is exploiting the natives. Rufus works it so that he becomes the trader's partner, then boss; and he becomes the self-proclaimed emperor of the natives. He is a ruthless leader, and finally his subjects (with the trader's encouragement) rebel. Film suggests that one of his crimes is that he comes to regard himself as *better* than his people, but in fact this character is shown to be *better* than the rest. Of the blacks in the film, Jones is the only one with dignity or intelligence. He certainly doesn't fit in with the blacks in Harlem or the equally uncivilized natives. It's good seeing a defiant black man on the screen, particularly in 1933, and one wonders how white audiences of the day reacted to Jones—or, more likely, Robeson—standing up to a white guard and outsmarting the others, subtly mocking his white boss on the train, and first praising (with tongue in cheek) Digges for his brains and nerve and then showing he's smarter and more daring by taking over this white man's lofty position, and having his former "owner" light *his* cigarette. This is one of Robeson's few opportunities to play a black man whose role isn't to improve the lot of whites. On the other hand, it's probable Jones is *punished* at the end because he overstepped his bounds when he didn't kowtow to whites. Directed by Dudley Murphy, who speeds through early scenes, labors through late scenes. Also with: Frank Wilson, Fredi Washington (of *Imitation of Life*), Moms Mabley, Ruby Elzy.

EMPEROR OF THE NORTH/EMPEROR OF THE NORTH POLE (1973) C/118m.

Rugged adventure film set in Oregon in 1933, at the height of the Depression. Almost all the action is centered on the railway tracks, as Lee Marvin, the "A No. 1" bum, is determined to sneak free rides on the train of vicious Ernest Borgnine. Both men's reputations are at stake. Keith Carradine is the young tramp who tags after Marvin and learns all his tricks. Marvin says Carradine has "a chance to be a *good* bum," but discovers the boy has no class. Robert Aldrich's film could easily have been made as a comedy, but he limits the humor and emphasizes the brutal nature of the "King-of-the-Mountain," or "Emperor-of-the-North-Pole" battle between Borgnine and Marvin. Their final fight on the moving train is extremely grueling. Picture is well photographed and has exciting moments on top of and beneath the speeding train, but the action is pretty repetitive, with Marvin and Carradine continuously climbing onto Borgnine's train and playing hide-and-seek. I also wish they'd played up the importance of trains to the hoboes (it's stated in prologue, then dropped) and explored the reasons working men like Borgnine have such hostility toward those who are seeking jobs, and why it's so important for there to be men beneath them on the social ladder. Also with: Charles Tyner, Malcolm Atterbury, Matt Clark.

EMPIRE STRIKES BACK, THE (1980) C/124m.
Spectacular second film in the George Lucas *Star Wars* trilogy. Special effects are dazzling; the characters are developed and become interesting; the film has a cynical, hard edge that happily lifts it out of the comic-book/juvenile-serials realm; the action scenes seem fitting to a great war movie; events take place all over the galaxy, giving the picture an added epic dimension. All the good guys, including the reticent Han Solo (Harrison Ford), become fully committed to war against the Emperor. Solo and Princess Leia (Carrie Fisher) fall in love. Luke Skywalker (Mark Hamill) is trained by the tiny Jedi master Yoda (who looks like Theodore White) to learn how to harness the Force. We learn Darth Vader's (David Prowse; voice by James Earl Jones) great secret and of the Emperor's plan to have Luke—who has great powers—fight on the side of darkness (a major plot point in the sequel, *Return of the Jedi*). Picture eliminates hokiest aspects of the original, reduces the roles of R2-D2 (Kenny Baker) and C-3PO (Anthony Daniels), and makes combat look uninviting for a change. Some great, imaginative creations. Excellent direction by Irvin Kershner. Written by Leigh Brackett (who died) and Lawrence Kasdan. Cinematography by Peter Suschitzky. Produced by Gary Kurtz. Oscar-winning special effects by Brian Johnson and Richard Edlund. Also with: Peter Mayhew (as Chewbacca), Billy Dee Williams (as Lando Calrissian), Alec Guinness, John Retzenberger.

ENCHANTED COTTAGE, THE (1945) B&W/91m.
One of Hollywood's schmaltziest films has found the soft spot in enough moviegoers' hearts to make it a cult film of sorts. Adapted from the play by A. W. Pinero, and moved from 14th-century England to 1945 New England, this romantic fantasy stars Robert Young as a badly disfigured war veteran who moves into an "enchanted cottage" to hide himself from the world. Out of loneliness he marries ugly spinster Dorothy McGuire and is soon surprised to love

her as much as she loves him. Within the enchanted walls their great love for one another seems to cause their faces to become beautiful, at least to each other. They invite his family to visit and see how he has regained his good looks and to show how pretty she has become—and the intruders shatter their illusion. Young and McGuire give sensitive performances, but are done in by embarrassing script by Herman Mankiewicz and De Witt Bodeen, and overwhelmed by lush music. The syrup is laid on thick and it's a bad brand. A remake of a 1924 silent version with Richard Barthelmess and May McAvoy. Also with: Herbert Marshall (as their friend, a blind pianist who tells their story), Mildred Natwick, Spring Byington, Hillary Brooke.

ENFANTS TERRIBLES, LES (FRENCH/1949–50) B&W/105m.
Powerhouse duo of scenarist Jean Cocteau (who adapted his own novel) and director Jean-Pierre Melville combined to make this fascinating, though flawed, precursor of *la nouvelle vague*. Story centers on bizarre, always combative relationship of a young Parisian woman, Elisabeth (Nicole Stéphane gives a dynamic performance), and her slightly younger brother, Paul (Edouard Dermithe), with whom she has always shared a room and for whom she has incestuous feelings. (He probably feels the same toward her if he'd only take the time to think about it.) Where she is fire and ice, he is weak and passive, spending much time convalescing in bed. She comes to realize that he harbors homosexual feelings. They have led such a sheltered life together that a brief vacation at the beach with their friend Gerard (Jacques Bernard)—a delightful, amusing sequence—is a revelation. They and Gerard are a threesome who are always together—she is the one who makes things happen. When mother dies, Elisabeth becomes a model-prostitute. Her fellow worker Agathe (Renée Closima) moves in with them, forming a foursome. Elisabeth marries a rich man, who—we're not surprised—is killed on their wedding night, and the four characters (with Elisabeth in command) move into his mansion. Each becomes emotionally distressed because: Gerard loves Elisabeth, Elisabeth loves Paul, Paul loves Agathe (who looks exactly like a boy he was infatuated with) and she loves him, but both are convinced that their love is unrequited (this is a fallacy that Elisabeth promotes so she won't lose Paul). The "stolen kisses" theme, the pretentious young characters, the males who allow women to push them around, the narration that reveals characters' foolish, innermost thoughts and motives, and the characters who are driven by their hearts were certainly an influence on François Truffaut. Indeed, the unpredictable and fascinating Elisabeth anticipates Jeanne Moreau's Catherine in *Jules and Jim*, particularly in how she relates to Paul and Gerard in their scenes together. Opening snowball sequence is taken from Cocteau's 1930 debut film, *The Blood of a Poet*.

ENFORCER, THE (1976) C/96m.
The third and least effective of Clint Eastwood's "Dirty Harry" series, it suffers because of plodding direction by James Fargo and the fact

that it hasn't a strong enough villain. However, it does benefit from a side plot exploiting all Eastwood's characters' problems in dealing with women. Harry has a new female partner, played by Tyne Daly. Harry Callahan of course objects to her being allowed to patrol the dangerous streets. In fact, he is proven right, but Daly's bravery and dedication win her his admiration and respect. At one point he reveals personal feelings to her—something Harry would never be able to do with a male cop. Daly would gain national recognition as a policewoman in TV's *Cagney and Lacey*. Also with: Harry Guardino, Bradford Dillman, John Mitchum, DeVeren Brookwalter, John Crawford.

ENORMOUS CHANGES AT THE LAST MINUTE (1985) C/115m.
Three Grace Paley short stories are the basis of this often humorous, often touching, always authentic portrait of three New York women (Ellen Barkin, Lynn Milgrim, Maria Tucci), each with family and romantic problems, who are trying to bring stability, coherence, and positive elements into their shaky, unfulfilling lives. These women aren't heroic figures, so what's most affecting about them is that they withstand the constant demands by manipulative men/parents that they live their lives in a certain way and instead hold out until they can make rational decisions about their own futures. In the two best episodes the men get the romances they desire with abandoned-mother Barkin and unmarried, pregnant Tucci, but only after the women have taken the time to realize that they want these men (a married, balding high-school acquaintance; a cabbie/songwriter who's about twelve years younger than Tucci) in their lives. In the other episode, which is uninvolving and horribly directed, Milgrim learns that she can't let her dotty parents (who reside in a retirement home) have such an effect on her life and that to be a good mother to *her* kids she must be self-sufficient and emotionally stable. John Sayles wrote the script; independent filmmakers Ellen Hovde, Muffie Meyer, and Mirra Bank directed. Fine performances by Barkin and Tucci. Also with: Kevin Bacon.

ENTER THE DRAGON (HONG KONG–AMERICAN/1973) C/98m.
Arguably the most entertaining, colorful, and spectacular kung fu film ever made. Kung fu master Bruce Lee arrives on the island owned by Han (Shih Kien), an evil Dr. No–like figure with an attachable iron hand. As a participant in Han's martial arts tournament, Lee hopes to find evidence that Han deals drugs and traffics prostitutes—he also suspects that Han's right-arm man Oharra (Bob Wall) was responsible for the death of his sister (played in flashback by the lovely queen of kung fu movies, Angela Mao Ying). The story is on a comic-book level, but the production values are high, the action is nonstop and consistently exciting, and the atmosphere is rich. (The shots of crowded Hong Kong are particularly evocative). And there's an all-star cast of sorts, with American imports John Saxon (hiding from the mob), Jim Kelly (hiding from the U.S. police)—the lone black in the film—and Wall joining Chinese kung fu stars Yang Sze ("The Chinese Hercules"),

Ying, and the incomparable Lee, whose feats seem impossible. Unlike his movie rivals, Lee, the actor, exploited his sexuality, stripping off his shirt to reveal his rippling muscles, posing for battle with legs spread, knees slightly bent, hands on thighs—somehow he looks relaxed and tense at the same time. Suddenly his hands thrust forward and his fingers penetrate flesh, his legs shoot upward and crack bone, and he emits a piercing *kiai* (fighting yell). In his incredible acrobatic fight with Oharra he does several flip kicks and his famous lightning one-inch paralyzing punches. His opponent's death takes place off screen, where Lee's feet destroy his windpipe, while an incredible slow-motion close-up allows us to see Lee's facial muscles quivering like waves in the ocean. Lee's climactic fight in a hall of mirrors (out of *The Lady from Shanghai*) with Han, who wears blades in place of his missing hand, is unforgettable. Film is flawed (there is no *time element*, for instance) but it doesn't matter. An enormous money-maker worldwide. Directed by American Robert Clouse. Music by Lalo Schifrin. Also with: Ahna Capri, Betty Chung, Geoffrey Weeks.

ENTITY, THE (1983) C/115m.
Young mother Barbara Hershey suddenly becomes the victim of frequent brutal sexual attacks from a ghostly presence. Psychiatrist Ron Silver believes that she is imagining the rapes and is bruising her own body. He tries to convince her that her problems are psychological, the result of having hang-ups in regard to men and sex because she was sexually abused as a child. Story by Frank De Felitta is supposedly based on a genuine case history (which is still going on). The rape scenes are truly scary (though the brutality may turn off some viewers) and the relationship between Hershey and Silver, who simultaneously tries to get her to believe there is something wrong with her and to take him as her lover, is quite perceptive. It shows how males immediately try to give females the weaker inadequate position in relationships. It seems that Silver will be the film's hero despite playing mind games with Hershey (because he doesn't mean to be a bad guy), but, fortunately, in a very good scene, Hershey permanently rejects him. Director Sidney J. Furie wisely shot the beautiful Hershey in close-up to build intensity; and he gave her free reign: the result is a truly great performance that, because it's in a very flawed horror film, won Hershey little attention instead of a deserved Oscar nomination. Also with: Alex Rocca, Jacqueline Brookes, David Labiosa, George Coe, Margaret Blye.

ERASERHEAD (1977) B&W/90m.
At once repellent and hypnotic, ugly and beautiful, heartbreaking and hilarious, cruel and tender, David Lynch's fascinating independently made debut film—one of the most popular midnight movies—could be the strangest picture ever made. It is an intense mood piece; an absurdist's vision of the future; a mix of abstract art, surrealistic painting, and minimalist cinema. It is the ultimate student film (financed in part by AFI and Sissy Spacek), the ultimate experimental film, the last word in personal filmmaking. It is the visu-

alization of your worst nightmare or, more accurately, that of the most paranoid manic-depressive on the eve of his committing suicide or donning a Doomsday placard. Imagine the worst blind date in history: a depressed, pudgy guy with an obnoxious personality, ugly, ill-fitting, and mismatched clothes, a rude speaking style, no sense of humor, and electrified hair that stands straight up. Furthermore, his room is full of seaweed and there are containers of water in his drawers (sexual imagery abounds), and he spends his lonely time playing scratchy, skipping records and watching a putty-faced lady who lives in his radiator. That's Henry Spencer (John Nance), our "hero." He lives in a noisy (there is a constant barrage of sound effects), post-apocalyptic age, in a spooky industrial town (perhaps in Pennsylvania, perhaps in Poland) that may have self-running factories (steam keeps blowing across the screen). He is forced to marry his pregnant girlfriend Mary X (Charlotte Stewart), who, after their baby is born, makes it perfectly clear to Henry that she never wants to have sex with him again and deserts them both. The baby looks like one of those unidentifiable off-color things that turn your stomach the instant you see them in the meat rack of your local grocery. It just lies in the dark and wails. Is this hideous-looking tot to be feared or pitied? Is Henry in danger, or will he turn on the baby because it's ruining his love life with the hot hooker (Judith Anna Roberts) across the hall? Is Lynch speaking against parents in *our* society who desire the deaths of their abnormal children (and often bring about their deaths through legal means) or is he speaking up for abortions to prevent child abuse by parents who are unqualified to have children, much less abnormal children? In any case, he is on the side of the child, and, by the end of the film, so are we. This unique film has marvelous special effects, frame-by-frame animation, black-and-white photography, and scenic design. Moreover, it has startling moments of horror, sex, and brilliant black comedy—the scene in which Henry visits Mary and her parents is truly unforgettable. It may adversely affect the squeamish and will undoubtedly confuse everyone a bit (Lynch intentionally left questions unanswered), but it's worth a gamble. Frederick Elmes and Herbert Caldwell did the cinematography. Alan R. Splet did the bizarre sound effects. Also with: Allen Joseph, Jeanne Bates, Laurel Near, V. Phipps-Wilson.

ESCAPE FROM NEW YORK (1981) C/99m. Mindless "escapism" by John Carpenter. In 1997, Manhattan Island is a maximum-security prison surrounded by 50-foot walls and mined waterways and bridges—surely the bridges would have been destroyed by the government if Carpenter didn't want to utilize one, the 59th Street Bridge (which non-New Yorker Carpenter calls the 69th Street Bridge), in his escape plot. When terrorists hijack his plane over New York, the U.S. President (Donald Pleasence) bails out and winds up captive of a prisoner gang. Criminal Snake Plissken (Kurt Russell) is sent into the dangerous city to rescue him—the police commissioner (Lee Van Cleef) tells Snake that if he doesn't get out quickly, pellets shot into

his veins will explode. Film has an intriguing premise and good cast, but Carpenter ignores the political possibilities of his subject (see Stephanie Rothman's *Terminal Island*) and opts for the comic-book route, giving us trite story points (many taken from westerns) and unreal, cliché characters. Just because Van Cleef is in the cast, Carpenter decided to have Russell parody Clint Eastwood—his dry voice will get on your nerves. At no point does Carpenter make creative use of his New York locales—film could just as easily have been set in futuristic Cleveland. Carpenter devotees apparently like the action scenes and flashy outfits, but the film is surprisingly downbeat. The one original moment is when Snake discovers an underground theater with male performers in drag and a little band. Also with: Ernest Borgnine, Harry Dean Stanton, Isaac Hayes, Adrienne Barbeau, Season Hubley, Charles Cyphers, Tom Atkins.

E.T.: THE EXTRA-TERRESTRIAL (1983) C/115m. Marvelous sci-fi fantasy from Steven Spielberg that broke box-office records and dazzled everyone but your local party-pooper. Title character, which was designed by Carlo Rimbaldi, is a sweet little wide-eyed alien with childlike qualities (although we can deduce that he is an adult) and the power to heal and cause dying plants to bloom instantly and objects to fly (although Spielberg keeps most of his power in check, a mystery). In the thrilling opening, E.T. is studying earth plant life in the woods near a California suburb when he is accidentally left behind by his spaceship, which leaves hurriedly to avoid detection. While U.S. government agents and scientists search for him, he wisely hides out. Luckily, he is befriended by a nice 10-year-old boy (Henry Thomas). *Elliot*T and E.T. have an immediate kinship, and the boy can share the alien's feelings. E.T. also becomes special friend to Elliott's older brother (Robert MacNaughton) and younger sister (Drew Barrymore)—and the family dog; the children's recently divorced mother (Dee Wallace) is too distracted to realize that something weird is going on in Elliott's room. The love blossoms between the kids and E.T., but the fragile creature becomes sickly because he longs to return home. So the film becomes a twist on *The Wizard of Oz*: three youngsters help an adult return to his own world (there's no place like home). In truth, this film has far more sympathy and understanding of children than *The Wizard of Oz*; and it's a celebration of youth and innocence—significantly, unlike in *Oz*, these children do not "grow up"! For me, the film's key scene is when the scientist (Peter Coyote) tells Elliott that he's been dreaming of meeting an alien since he was a little boy; we recognize that when a boy Coyote wanted to play with an alien but as an adult he wants to do experiments on him. Film has suspense, wit, magical special effects, numerous scenes that have etched themselves into memories of moviegoers. And though Spielberg occasionally manipulates us into shedding tears, the film is genuinely sweet. E.T. is a wonderful creation with universal appeal—kids respond to him with such affection because he truly satisfies their need for Stevenson's "imaginary playmate," the ideal friend for all kids (especially those who don't have two parents always there) who wish their stuffed animals could hug them back. Adults, of course, are also taken with E.T.—when he dons a long robe and waddles through the house, he may remind us of our favorite, quirkiest visiting relative. Not to be overlooked when figuring out the amazing success of the film is the performance of Henry Thomas; in a difficult part he is so appealing that we gladly accept him as our surrogate and allow him to fulfill our dream of meeting the perfect alien, E.T. Music by John Williams. Melissa Mathison wrote the enchanting script. Also with: C. Thomas Howell, Sean Frye, K. C. Martel.

EVERY WHICH WAY BUT LOOSE (1978) C/ 114m.
Clint Eastwood's first outright comedy drew the wrath of most critics, but, despite doing limited business in various urban areas, became his biggest commercial success at the time. As directed by James Fargo, it's a very crude, too violent, thinly plotted but often very funny film about a not-too-bright but amiable trucker named Philo Beddoe, who picks up extra money by challenging local toughs to bare-knuckles fights. His best friends are the equally smart Orville (Geoffrey Lewis) and Clyde, an orangutan he won in a fight. They are looked after by the cantankerous Ma (Ruth Gordon). Philo falls head-over-heels in love with Lynn Halsey-Taylor (Sondra Locke), a mysterious country-western singer who has a secret. When she runs out on him, Philo and his two buddies give chase. Orville picks up a resourceful girlfriend (Beverly D'Angelo), Clyde has a rendezvous with a female orangutan in a zoo, and Philo finds Lynn. Meanwhile they are sought by an inept, overage motorcycle gang and two cops. The film is absurd, but Locke's character is intriguing and there's something touching about Philo as he attempts to win her over. He tells Clyde confidentially, "I'm not afraid of any man, but when it comes to sharing my feelings with a woman, my stomach turns to jelly." That about sums it up for most of Eastwood's men. The film's funniest moment is when the gang, which has just been routed by the elderly Gordon, comes up on the older Hank Worden at a gas station and chooses not to give him trouble because they fear what he might do them. Followed by an inferior sequel, *Any Which Way You Can*.

EVERYTHING YOU ALWAYS WANTED TO KNOW ABOUT SEX (BUT WERE AFRAID TO ASK) (1972) C/87m.
Odd entry in Woody Allen oeuvre divided critics. I find it interesting and significant, less as a satire-parody than as a daring experiment for Allen because he severely tested audience's embarrassment level much as Lenny Bruce did years before in night clubs, and as Monty Python would do years later. Title comes from Dr. David Reuben's serious pop-sexology book, but Woody Allen's film is comprised of several comic vignettes (each dealing with a sexual perversion) that have nothing to do with Reuben and won't serve anyone as a sexual primer. Episodes, most starring Allen, vary greatly in quality. The sequence in which Gene Wilder falls in love with a sheep is a good

test for viewer's tolerance level—it's inoffensive because *all* viewers will recognize that it was included solely to elicit audience response. On the other hand, the scene in which dinner guest Lou Jacobi excuses himself, goes upstairs, and puts on hostess's clothes and make-up is excruciating to watch. Allen is funny as a medieval Bob Hope-like court jester who gets his spear stuck in the queen's chastity belt and later, in a subtitled sequence, as an Italian who must put up with Louise Lasser's unquenchable desire to make love in public places. In a wildly funny episode, Allen and Burt Reynolds play anxious sperm cells in a man who's about to have an orgasm. Also with: John Carradine (as a mad scientist with a weird creation), Anthony Quayle, Lynn Redgrave, Tony Randall, Meredith MacRae, Geoffrey Holder, Regis Philbin.

EVIL DEAD, THE (1983) C/85m.
It's obvious that the people from Detroit who made this independently produced horror film are not without talent, particularly first-time director Sam Raimi, but it's a shame that they wasted it in such a manner. (Of course, it's hard lecturing film-makers about using their film stock wisely and tastefully when their movies earn several million dollars profit.) Picture starts out creepily, if conventionally, with a group of college kids vacationing in an isolated cabin. They discover an old book with which they conjure up evil spirits. At this point the film becomes infuriatingly stupid. Everyone's getting murdered, yet people are left alone to rest, and women take solo nocturnal walks in the woods. Story goes out the window and onetime movie turns into gore fest, in which "possessed" characters take turns hacking off each other's limbs and coming back from the dead. Anyone would love to have the blood-and-spare-parts concession. It would be fun to trip the overly mobile cameraman during one of his too frequent tracking shots. Cult film for the gore generation—but only the most bloodthirsty wouldn't trade in a few splatter effects for some substance. Starring: Bruce Campbell, Ellen Sandweiss, Betsy Baker, Hal Delrich, Sarah York.

EXCALIBUR (BRITISH/1981) C/140m.
Passionate telling of the Arthurian legend by John Boorman. His visualization of the Dark Ages, a time that is more mythological than historical, is thoroughly convincing. It's a world of knights in shining armor, magicians and witches, a mighty king, a sword with special powers, a lady in a lake, mist-shrouded woods, blood-soaked battlefields, men engaging in violent combat to defend their honor. The film begins with Uther Pendragon using Merlin's (Nicol Williamson) help to defeat another Celtic lord; he then has Merlin transform him into the dead man's image so that he can sleep with the widow. The result is Arthur. When Arthur becomes a young man (Nigel Terry) he pulls Excalibur from the stone—indicating that he'll be King. Merlin teaches him the ways of the world. Arthur is victorious in battle and becomes King of England. Going against Merlin's wishes, he marries the gorgeous Guenevere (Cherie Lunghi). After

an exciting sword fight, he befriends Sir Lancelot (Nicholas Clay), who becomes the King's most trusted knight. Lancelot loves Arthur but betrays him by sleeping with Guenevere (this film has nudity and sex). Arthur leaves the throne; sorceress Morgana (Helen Mirren) "kills" Merlin and sets up a series of events that will put evil son Mordred (Robert Addie)—he's Arthur's son also—on the throne. Arthur and his knights search for the Holy Grail. Picture, which is Jung-influenced, becomes hard to follow—Boorman has explained that myth characters such as Arthur and Merlin can emerge victorious only when they suppress their *human* emotions and allow themselves mythical, superhuman status; characters are victims of passion (love, sexual desire, power, lust). Even if you lose track of what's going on, the visuals still have an impact: the search for the Grail and the final battle are stunning sequences. Alex Thompson was cinematographer. The script by Boorman and Rospo Pallenberg was inspired by Malory's *Le Morte D'Arthur*. Also with: Corin Redgrave, Paul Geoffrey, Katrina Boorman, Charley Boorman.

EXHIBITION (FRENCH/1976) C/110m.

Documentary about French porno star Claudine Beccarie is mix of *cinéma vérité* and staged hard-core sex scenes involving Beccarie and several other porno stars. Everything about this film seems dishonest, from Beccarie's self-righteous answers to director Jean-François Davy's shallow, naïve questions to Davy's self-expressed desire to present an honest, nonarousing film. He's too much interested in the box office receipts. Beccarie has charisma, but she's thoroughly obnoxious—if you want to see how a woman can intimidate a man into sexual impotency, then watch how she browbeats her young lover in a sex scene. Davy's personality is summed up when he says how much he liked *Deep Throat* because he could identify with Linda Lovelace's lovers during fellatio—he also remarks how Lovelace really enjoyed herself. Picture did good business in France and the U.S., even playing in the New York Film Festival.

EXORCIST, THE (1973) C/121m.

Powerful, controversial, influential adult horror film—a one-time cult phenomenon—was directed by William Friedkin on a big budget at a major studio (Warner Bros.) and scripted by William Peter Blatty (he won an Oscar), who adapted his best-selling novel. It is set in Georgetown, where divorced actress Chris MacNeil (Ellen Burstyn) lives with her 12-year-old daughter Regan (Linda Blair's debut) while making a film dealing with the protest movement. Meanwhile young Father Karras (Jason Miller) is suffering guilt because he hadn't the money to provide adequate care for his poor aged mother before she died. All around him he sees poverty, crime, decadence—and he finds himself questioning his faith in God. The world we see is *breaking apart*—Chris has split from her husband, Regan has such little contact with the parents she loves that she has taken an imaginary playmate ("Captain Howdy"); the country is divided because of political issues; those in poverty are outcasts (Karras' mother is taken from her home; bums live on the street);

youth gangs break apart cars; Karras is breaking away from the church. With the world in such disorder, the Devil can make a dramatic entrance. It takes possession of Regan, inhabiting her body and eating away at it. Ironically, the Devil's appearance proves to Karras that God exists as well. He and aged, sickly Father Merrin (Max Von Sydow) perform an exorcism. It's good vs. evil. Film is at times almost unbearably intense; it is not for the squeamish, because some of the language and imagery is quite shocking: Regan's face becomes monstrous, her speech is vulgar, she vomits green slime, she violently attacks all who come close, she masturbates with crosses, she levitates. Special effects makeup by Dick Smith and Rick Baker revolutionized the horror genre—you'll feel sorry for Blair. Friedkin's direction is solid—I particularly like the way he refrigerated Blair's room so that steam pours out of everyone's mouth. The most needless scene—the one that really made viewers sick—has Regan undergoing a bloody arteriography. Blatty's script is flimsy and often stupid—he allows the Devil to provide most of his humor. I think the most interesting aspect of the picture is that it conveys a fear that is rarely dealt with: Regan doesn't have those around her turn into monsters (a basic primal fear) but becomes a monster herself. Not since Pinocchio grew donkey ears and a tail has a child become so bestial. Significantly we aren't scared of this child—as we are in several child-as-monster films—but sympathize, even *identify*, with her. Caliber of acting and production gave film needed class to attract a mass audience. The Catholic Church wasn't happy that three priests served as consultants on the film. I don't see the film saying one thing or another about religion. Followed by John Boorman's absurd *Exorcist II: The Heretic*. Also with: Jack McGowran (as the film director killed by possessed Regan), Lee J. Cobb (as the policeman investigating the director's death), Kitty Winn, Mercedes McCambridge (the voice of the demon).

EXTERMINATING ANGEL, THE (MEXICAN/1962) B&W/95m.

Luis Buñuel's perplexing, absurdist black comedy begins with the arrival of the guests, the cream of the middle class, at an elegant dinner party. After engaging in hours of polite, boorish conversation, they discover that they are incapable of going home. Inexplicably, they are stuck in one large room. There they spend several days without food or water. Some die. (Meanwhile no one on the outside can muster enough willpower to enter the large house.) Soon their genteel manner gives way and the room becomes a battleground for insults, as people finally tell each other what they really think. One of Buñuel's most bizarre films, it is one of his many indictments of the bourgeoisie (without the sophistication or biting wit of his *The Discreet Charm of the Bourgeoisie*). It is they who have *contaminated* society—as soon as they gather for the party, the low-paid servants flee the house as if they were nuns and priests escaping the evil Amityville house. Buñuel takes pleasure in playing his joke on the stuffy dinner guests and transforming the proud, unfeeling bourgeois types into the smelly, violent, uncouth people they've always despised. Villain of piece is *bourgeoisie stasis*, the willingness of members of the bourgeoisie to conform rather than express individuality and emotions that would make them sensitive human beings. Their brutally honest remarks about each other may seem like cheap shots, but are a big improvement over the false respect that previously distinguished their relationships. Film has satisfying resolution. Not a complete success, but the premise is intriguing and it's well played. With: Sylvia Pinal, Enrique Rambal, Jacqueline Andere, José Baviera, Augusto Benedico.

EXTERMINATOR, THE (1980) C/101m. An ugly urban melodrama in the *Death Wish* tradition that became an unqualified commercial success. Vietnam vet Robert Ginty seeks revenge on the New York street gang that killed his best friend (Steve James). Once they are rubbed out, he continues to be a vigilante—using brutal means to do away with the scum he encounters. His actions put a city cop (Christopher George) on his trail, as well as vicious government men. Structure is odd in that Ginty is the hero for the first part of the film, then George shares that distinction. We see victims brutalized; then Ginty pays them back in kind. Audiences cheered when he tortured the bad guys. The type of picture in which we're supposed to forgive our hero for his crimes because his best friend's black. You can see where director James Glickenhaus is coming from when you consider that he presents the dirtiest, hairiest, most disgusting youth gang imaginable—thieves, murderers, sadists, racists—and places a Che Guevara poster on their clubhouse wall. Followed by a sequel. Also with: Samantha Eggar, Tony Di Benedetto, Patrick Farelly.

FACE IN THE CROWD, A (1957) B&W/ 125m. Radio reporter Patricia Neal does a live story on guitar-playing, homespun philosopher Andy Griffith (as Lonesome Rhodes), a hobo she discovers in a small-town jail. He's a natural near a microphone. He gets his own radio program, where his *fake* folksy Will Rogers charm wins him great popularity. He gets a live network television show and soon becomes a national cult figure, champion of the common people. Neal watches her Frankenstein Monster use the media to bolster his fame, manipulate the public, and increase his power. An ultra-right party approaches him to help change the image of their dullard presidential candidate; he realizes the candidate is a horse's ass but he drools over getting a new cabinet post, Secretary of National Morale—he could become the most powerful man in the country. Only Patricia Neal can stop him—by letting the public see what its favorite son is really like. She has always loved him too much and felt too responsible for him to have

interfered in the past. Cynical film was directed by Elia Kazan and scripted by Budd Schulberg, who adapted his story "Your Arkansas Traveler." Of course, Schulberg is expressing his fear that television, which has tremendous power, will become a political tool. Lonesome Rhodes is guilty of taking advantage of the medium—through which you *can* fool all the people all of the time—but Schulberg is attacking *us*, the ignorant public who sits like sheep and believes whatever it sees on the tube. The scary thing is that if today Rhodes were caught expressing his real thoughts while thinking the mike was off, his popularity would probably go up—which is what has happened to Reagan each time he said something hostile when he thought his radio mike was off. A well-made film; with strong performance by Neal and Griffith (his debut) whose character is on the surface similar to the one he played on his television comedy series. In her debut, Lee Remick catches your eye as a sexy baton twirler. Also with: Anthony Franciosa, Walter Matthau, Kay Medford.

FACE OF FU MANCHU, THE (BRITISH/1965) C/ 96m. Sax Rohmer's diabolical Chinese villain returned to the screen after a 33-year hiatus, with Christopher Lee assuming the role played by Boris Karloff in *The Mask of Fu Manchu*. Film begins with Fu Manchu being beheaded, but his chief nemesis, Nayland Smith (Nigel Green), is rightly suspicious. It turns out Fu Manchu hypnotized an actor into playing his part at the execution. Smith tries to foil Fu Manchu's plot to poison the world's population with gas derived from the seed of a rare Tibetan poppy. Fu Manchu kidnaps a scientist (Walter Rilla) and threatens to kill his daughter (Karin Dor) unless he successfully distills the liquid from the poppy. Picture has believable twenties flavor, fun performances by Lee and Green—and Tsai Chin as Fu Manchu's evil daughter—and an interesting storyline. But I wish it were a bit more exciting. One problem is that Fu Manchu is a supervillain, while Smith comes across as boringly common—you have to want this villain to escape since his scenes are much more interesting than Smith's. And, of course, he does escape so he can appear in the sequel, *The Brides of Fu Manchu*. Direction by Don Sharp is a bit too conservative—sometimes it looks like we're watching a serious version of *Get Smart* rather than a movie. Also with: Joachim Fuchsberger, James Robertson Justice, Howard Marion-Crawford.

FADE TO BLACK (1980) C/100m. Violent, embarrassing stupidity about a psychotic young movie buff (Dennis Christopher) who dresses up like screen villains and commits murders. Ironically, film's theme is that impressionable moviegoers may so identify with characters in violent films that they'll emulate them—with that in mind, what's director Vernon Zimmerman's excuse for giving viewers such a sicko character as this? Christopher is miscast, so the only noteworthy appearance is by sweet Marilyn Monroe lookalike Linda Kerridge. Also with: Tim Thomerson, Morgan Paull, Marya Small.

FAHRENHEIT 451 (1966) C/111m. The sci-fi genre got a needed dose of respectability when François Truffaut adapted Ray Bradbury's classic novel about a hedonistic future society in which all books are destroyed so that people won't read them, think, and become unhappy. Unfortunately, Truffaut's low-keyed, ungimmicky production is a disappointment—as is Bradbury's novel if you reread it today. There are some haunting visuals of suburban streets (where everyone is inside their unimaginatively designed little homes watching television) as well as scenes in which firemen burn books (at 451° Fahrenheit); a couple of tense confrontations between idealistic fireman Guy Montag (Oskar Werner) and his stern captain (Cyril Cusack), who correctly suspects Montag has been pilfering books from fires and reading them; jarringly childlike shots of a little red fire engine zooming out of a quaint red firehouse. But the film lacks the passion present in Truffaut's other films. I believe that's because Truffaut, the true romantic, had trouble rationalizing Montag preferring an asexual, purely intellectual relationship with a young woman who reads (Julie Christie) to years of lovemaking with his pleasure-seeking, never-read-a-book-in-her-life wife (also Christie). In fact, Truffaut admitted he found the wife to be a much more interesting woman: if the choice were between love/sex and *seeing films* (rather than reading books), then Truffaut could have felt more emotional about Montag's willingness to sacrifice home, wife, and job and risk his life. Movie ends with strange scene in which Montag joins the Book People hiding out in the woods—each is seen memorizing books, and figuratively, not *literally*, becoming that book. I've always wondered if the liberal, persecuted Book People would have allowed a member to select as his title *Playboy Party Jokes, Vol. 3*. Also with: Anton Diffring, Jeremy Spenser.

FAIL SAFE (1964) B&W/111m. *Dr. Strangelove* without the humor. U.S. planes carrying nuclear bombs are accidentally given the go-ahead to fly a bombing mission deep into Russia. The President (Henry Fonda) orders the U.S. Air Force to intercept and shoot down these planes to avoid a nuclear war. Over the "Hot Line" he also gives the Russian Premier permission to do the same. But one plane gets through and no one can convince its captain (Edward Binns) that the mission order was a mistake. Film points out that there would be hawks in our government who'd insist that the U.S. should go through with a full-scale nuclear attack if such a mistake occurred rather than wait for the Russian retaliation. But cool-headed Fonda decides that peace must be preserved at *all* costs—if a Russian city is destroyed, he is willing to order the nuclear destruction of New York City, where his family lives. Very tense, grim drama, seriously directed by Sidney Lumet, who had a strong belief in nuclear disarmament. Most interesting is how we end up rooting for our own planes to be shot down, although the innocent men inside believe they're just following orders. Walter Bernstein's adaptation of Eugene Burdick and Harvey Wheeler's novel *Fail-Safe* contains the still relevant theme that there is no such thing as a "fail-safe" nuclear-arms system. The strong cast includes: Dan O'Herlihy, Walter Matthau, Frank Overton, Fritz Weaver, Larry Hagman, William Hansen, Sorrell Booke, Dom De Luise, Dana Elcar.

FALL OF THE HOUSE OF USHER, THE/HOUSE OF USHER (1960) 80m—85m. The first of Roger Corman's successful Edgar Allan Poe series for AIP; as these are psychological horror films, the majority were set in decaying, oppressive, life-consuming mansions that represented the minds of their unfortunate inhabitants. Suitor Mark Damon arrives at the House of Usher to take his fiancée, Myrna Fahey, back to Boston. From her brother, Vincent Price, Damon learns that the Ushers have a history of illness and insanity, and that Price and Fahey are doomed to die in their evil house. Fahey, sure she is about to die, looks ill and depressed. Damon tries to convince her to flee with him. Because there are only four people in the film (including servant Harry Ellerbe), Richard Matheson was stuck with the problem of writing a horror movie in which nothing could happen to anyone until the end. So he inserted numerous *filler* scenes that are there strictly for atmosphere (a dream sequence, a trip into the crypt, a look at the family gallery). And to take up more time, his characters use about 10 lines when one or two would suffice. But the house is designed interestingly by Daniel Haller, the photography by Floyd Crosby is properly moody, and the film includes a typical flamboyant performance by Price (who was to these films what John Wayne was to Hawks and Ford westerns) and a rare movie appearance by beautiful Fahey (star of TV's *Father of the Bride*). And the ending is spectacular.

FAME (1980) C/134m. Extremely entertaining and original seriocomic musical about several students who attend New York's High School for the Performing Arts. We watch them develop their individual talents during their four years at the school and, more significantly, simultaneously strip off their defenses and discover their elusive self-identities. Director Alan Parker obviously has respect for young people and their great talents (which are evident on the screen) as well as sympathy for their brave, masochistic attempts to make a living through their art. The film's comedy is consistently bright—I like the female student who auditions for the school by pretending to be O. J. Simpson waiting for the elevator in *The Towering Inferno*—and the drama works well as long as Parker strives for poignancy rather than pathos (which occurs too often in the later stages of the film). Best of all are the imaginatively staged, free-for-all musical production numbers, among the most exuberant in all of film. Everyone in the school jumps in spontaneously, and it's great seeing blacks, whites, and hispanics dancing together, ballet dancers rocking with students in wild street clothes, cellists jamming with drummers—here we see spirited democracy at work, and no one worries about making fools of themselves. The eclectic Oscar-winning score by Michael Gore, sister Lesley Gore (one of *my* all-time favorites), Dean Pitchford, and actor Paul

McCrane is splendid, and the emotional singing by Irene Cara and McCrane is as impressive as the dancing. Entire film, not just the music, has rhythm—this is most evident in the dialogue and the editing. Film was unexpected success and has since been the model for many music videos as well as youth movies and TV programs, including the *Fame* series. After watching the TV show, it's surprising how badly the teachers came across in the film. Cara, McCrane, Barry Miller, and Gene Anthony Ray (a truly amazing dancer) are the standouts in a fine cast that also includes: Maureen Teefy, Laura Dean, Lee Curreri, Eddie Barth, Anna Meara, Albert Hague, Debbie Allen, Antonio Franceschi.

FANNY (FRENCH/1932) B&W/120m–142m.
The second part of Marcel Pagnol's *Marseilles Trilogy*, falling between *Marius* (1931) and *César* (1936). Pagnol adapted his play and hired Marc Allégret to direct. Story picks up exactly where *Marius* left off. Marius (Pierre Fresnay) has gone off to sea for two years. Distraught Fanny (Orane Demazis), pregnant with Marius's child, agrees to marry rich sailmaker Panisse (Charpin). César (Raimu again dominates the film) isn't happy with this arrangement until Fanny and Panisse agree to make him godfather. Marius returns to Marseilles. He is upset that Fanny didn't wait for him. He wants the child, but Panisse won't give him up. Fanny still loves Marius, but, as in the first film, she is willing to sacrifice her own happiness for others (Marius in the first film, Panisse and the baby in this film). It is up to César to talk sense to his son. Again the film succeeds because of the believable, lovable characters rather than the direction, which is theatrical. Raimu is splendid, and Charpin, Demazis, and Fresnay make strong impressions. Jacques Demy borrowed the basic plot (eliminating the César character and making the boy a wartime soldier rather than a sailor) for his 1964 musical *The Umbrellas of Cherbourg*. Remade in Italy in 1933, in Germany in 1934, and in America in 1938 as *Port of Seven Seas*. The 1961 film *Fanny* was derived from the entire trilogy. Also with: Alida Rouffe, Robert Vattier, Milly Mathis, Edouard Delmont, Maupi.

FANTASIA (1940) C/116m.
The most ambitious and conceptually daring of Disney's features was this $3 million feature which combined animation with classical music. He attempted to impress the highbrow audience, but instead was viciously attacked for taking much leeway with the music and for being so pretentious as to try to teach others about classical music when he himself was completely ignorant of the art. The picture actually became a cult favorite in the early seventies when the "acid" generation found that watching the almost psychedelic images was a sensory experience. Today one will probably be less upset by the mishandling of the music in several of the vignettes (particularly Tchaikovsky's "Nutcracker Suite" and Beethoven's "Pastoral Symphony") than by the repetition of images (characters napping, reflections on water); the lack of good personality animation (a Disney trademark) as characters of the same type tend to act identically; and the predictable way that nature goes haywire in almost every sequence (the struggle between the profane and the sacred) and the way scenes end as they begin, in tranquillity. The highlights are the exciting "The Sorcerer's Apprentice," starring Mickey Mouse and featuring a cosmic storm and march of the brooms; the creation of the world in "The Rite of Spring" with otherworldly Kubrick-like shots of a newly formed volcanic landscape; "Dance of the Hours," which has acrobatic ostriches, elephants in tutus, hippos, and alligators parodying ballet with a knockabout dance; and the spooky "Night on Bald Mountain," featuring Vlad Tytla's magnificent demon. Unfortunately, the picture ends with an anticlimactic "Ave Maria," a pretentious religious piece that's the worst sequence in the movie. Leopold Stokowski conducted the Philadelphia Orchestra. Deems Taylor served as the "folksy" emcee, to assure Disney that he wouldn't lose his lowbrow fans.

FANTASTIC INVASION OF PLANET EARTH, THE/BUBBLE, THE (1966) C/91m–112m.
Young marrieds Michael Cole (TV's *The Mod Squad*) and pregnant Deborah Walley have the pilot (Johnny Desmond) set their small plane down in strange town so baby can be delivered. She gives birth safely, but troubles have just begun. They discover that town is weird, like a combination amusement park and old movie lot with sets for various genre films standing side by side. People who roam about are like robots, most only capable of saying one line repeatedly. They are scared of something that whisks people into the air. When they try to flee, threesome realizes that town is enclosed in enormous plastic bubble. They believe that someone has trapped them, like flies in a bottle, and is watching them. Familiar but interesting premise suffers because of weak acting and lackluster production (although seeing it in its original 3-D mode might help). Once bizarre situation is established, characters seem to just wander about, going up and down some old streets—as if they were waiting for someone to finish the script. Full of bad conversation that's meant to be profound, including Cole's out-of-the-blue statement that he's been watched all his life and it's not so bad, and Walley wondering if there are similar bubbles all over the earth. *The Bubble* was the original title; second title, which hints at aliens, is misleading unless you let your imagination run wild. Directed with some imagination but not enough skill by its writer, Arch Oboler. Much too long, even in shortened version. Unsatisfying ending. It's like a sixties made-for-TV movie.

FANTASTIC PLANET/PLANÈTE SAUVAGE, LA (FRENCH-CZECH/1973) C/72m.
Curious animated feature, sci-fi for adults, was made by the team of René Leloux, who directed, and Roland Topper, who provided the original artwork. Leloux and Topper adapted their story from Stefan Wul's novel *Oms en Serie*. As it has a political theme, it is fitting that it was shot in Jiri Trinka's animation studio in Prague. The story takes place on the

planet Ygam, which is ruled by the Draags, gigantic blue androids who spend most of their time meditating and accumulating knowledge. Humanlike creatures, the Oms, are the enslaved pets of the Draag children. One Om, Tiwa, escapes and joins a band of wild Oms who live in the park. When the Draags decide to exterminate all the Oms, the little people fight back, using the knowledge of the Draags that Tiwa supplies (he has brought a recording device with him). Story is slight but interesting and it makes the key point that education is vital to revolution. The quick, vague ending is not satisfying. The animation is often static and, when coupled with the monotone voices found in the English-release version (distributed by Roger Corman), tends to give film a sluggish pace at those times when the excitement should be building. Best of all are the weird animals that inhabit this savage planet—but there are too few. Worth seeing, but disappointing in that with only a few changes this could have been a really terrific film. Prizewinner at Cannes.

FANTASTIC VOYAGE (1966) C/100m.

It is the near future. A medical team and a submarinelike vehicle are miniaturized and injected into the bloodstream of dying scientist. They have 60 minutes in which to eliminate a blood clot and escape. As they travel through his body, they encounter a fantastic foreign world of giant monsters (antibodies) and other dangers. To make matters worse, one of them is trying to sabotage the mission. The premise is terrific; considering it can be used only once in films, it's a shame this effort wasn't a bit more exciting and inventive. There are a few good moments, but the special effects aren't particularly effective, the sets look phony, the dialogue is trite, Stephen Boyd makes a dull leading man (have you ever met a Stephen Boyd fan?), and Raquel Welch, the era's sex symbol, is too bundled up. Directed by Richard Fleischer, who did a marvelous job years before on *20,000 Leagues Under the Sea*, which has a couple of plot similarities. Also with: Edmond O'Brien, Donald Pleasence, Arthur Kennedy, William Redfield, Arthur O'Connell.

FAR COUNTRY, THE (1954) C/96m.

The fourth in the five-film Anthony Mann–James Stewart western series. With the U.S. law after him for murder—although the man he killed was stealing his cattle—Stewart takes his herd into Alaska. But it's confiscated by a Roy Bean-type judge, played by John McIntire. Stewart and pal Walter Brennan hire on to take Ruth Roman's stock and supplies over the mountains to an isolated frontier town. But first they steal back their cattle. McIntire promises that he'll get revenge. When McIntire's men cause several deaths, Stewart also wants revenge. Film has many elements of the other entries in the series—a hero with a shady past, a revenge motif, strong violence, a beautiful but rugged landscape—but it's weaker than the others. Most significantly, it lacks the typical Mann-Stewart antagonist who represents Stewart's alter ego, someone with a similar background who is the character Stewart would become if he didn't reform. As

it is, Stewart's character is neither interesting nor appealing. Neither are the two women who love him: good-bad girl Roman and tomboy Corinne Calvert, who's too sweet and innocent for a Mann film. The romantic scenes are trite, the action scenes are unwieldy, which is a shame since it would be fun to see each of the villains killed in more novel ways. This is one Mann film which ends with a shootout in town rather than in the mountains. Scripted by Borden Chase, who relies on too many western clichés. Colorfully photographed by William Daniels. Also with: Jay C. Flippen, Henry (Harry) Morgan, Jack Elam, Steve Brodie, Royal Dano, Robert Wilke.

FAST TIMES AT RIDGEMONT HIGH (1982) C/92m.

Cameron Crowe spent a year impersonating a student in a Southern California high school to get material for his book, on which his script is based. It shows as much special insight as one would have from hanging out at the mall for about an hour. Every time the film starts to fulfill its initial promise, we are frustrated—just like our two lead characters. Valley Girl Jennifer Jason Leigh is interested in short, nerdy Brian Backer (that'll be the day!) and he's interested in her (this makes sense). But both are too shy to make sexual advances. Leigh takes advice from her sexually experienced best friend Phoebe Cates and Backer listens to his hustler friend Robert Romanus. The advice screws them up. Direction by Amy Heckerling (her feature debut) is uneven—and she films Leigh in an unflattering manner when she is nude and about to make it with Romanus. Better is the scene in which Leigh loses her virginity in an unromantic baseball dugout. Sex is presented negatively, but only because the males are insensitive, unskilled lovers. More palatable than the sex scenes are the verbal duels between stoned Sean Penn (as Jeff Spicoli) and sarcastic, rule-conscious teacher Ray Walston (who would reprise his role in the TV series *Fast Times*). Penn and Walston are hilarious and are the major reason to see the film. Also funny is Judge Reinhold, who plays Leigh's older brother.

FASTER, PUSSYCAT! KILL! KILL! (1965) B&W/83m.

Impressive early Russ Meyer film that is ideal for a drive-in. Features three independent, aggressive, voluptuous females who do as they please—but as role models for recently "liberated" women, they are the pits. Tura Santana is an eye-poppingly beautiful, large-chested karate expert who bosses around her two companions, sex-crazed, blonde Lori Williams and Italian Haji, who is amenable to following orders because she has strong feelings toward Santana. In the desert, Santana kills a young dragster racer (Ray Barlow) in a fight—how odd it is to see a male and a female really going at it. The three women kidnap his small, bikini-clad girlfriend (Susan Bernard) with the intention of killing her later. First they visit the ranch of eccentric, crippled millionaire Stu Lancaster and his two sons—one of whom is retarded (Dennis Busch). They realize that Lancaster's money is hidden somewhere on the property. The lecherous old man tries to wrest the girl away from her kidnappers so he can have her for his own vile purposes. Meanwhile the girl tries to get the sane son to help her escape from her captives and his father. Well-made picture shot almost exclusively outdoors (except a scene where everyone has lunch). Action sequences have zip, and it's noteworthy that *women* are actively involved in them—it's particularly strange to see women involved in hand-to-hand combat with men (especially since in both cases the woman gains the upper hand). A striking presence, Santana ranks right behind Erica Gavin (*Vixen*) as Meyer's best heroine. This is John Waters's favorite film.

FAT CITY (1972) C/100m. John Huston directed this effective sleeper about boxing; it's not about the glamorous, publicized world of title bouts and million-dollar purses, but the armpit of the sport, where washed-up, injured, or untalented pugs fight it out for peanuts in prelims in dingy arenas. Stacy Keach gives a memorable performance as a has-been (he probably never was too talented) who returns to the ring when he can't hack it doing menial work. Jeff Bridges is a likable 18-year-old whom Keach recommends to his nice-guy manager, Nicholas Colasanto. Colasanto thinks the boy has talent, but he's as bad a judge of talent as he is a manager. Bridges's first few bouts indicate that if he sticks to boxing, his future is bleak—because of Colasanto's encouragement, he'll probably stick to boxing. Writer Leonard Gardner, who adapted his novel, presents a seedy world of people with smashed dreams and opportunities lost, who not only feed off each other but infest any new blood that happens along. Huston's direction is not flashy; it is superb. The part I can't forget is when Keach's Mexican opponent pisses blood before the fight and then takes a vicious, stomach-kidney beating in the bout—film's last shot is of him going back to Mexico, where he'll fight next; no medical examiner checks on the loser boxers we see in this picture. Also with: Candy Clark (as Bridges's girlfriend), Susan Tyrrell (who almost steals the picture as Keach's whining girlfriend).

FATHER GOOSE (1964) C/115m. Genial comedy has none of the typical elements of a "cult" movie, but I've come across an amazing number of people who are truly devoted to it. (I'm told that in some places it always plays on television at Eastertime.) In the Pacific during WWII, Cary Grant (who never looked more slovenly) is a beach bum who's more interested in locating his next bottle of whiskey than joining the war effort against Japan. But he's tricked by his friend (Trevor Howard), an Allied officer, into manning a radio station on a small, deserted island. Using the code name "Mother Goose," he reports Japanese air and sea activity in the area. Then he finds his ruffled style cramped by a feisty teacher (Leslie Caron) and her young female students when they become stuck on the island with him. Grant reforms and reveals his bravery, resourcefulness, and concern for the trapped females. He and Caron fall in love. Predictable script (which somehow won an Oscar for Peter Stone and Frank Tarloff) benefits from

inspired teaming of the stars, who work extremely well together. Their marriage ceremony is certainly the film's highlight. Frequent appearances by Japanese soldiers add moments of excitement—but, considering none are shown in close-ups, it's probable that no Japanese actors were used. Why is this film so popular, especially with women? My hunch is that many women look at the heavy-drinking, gone-to-seed men sitting next to them in front of the TV and hope that they'll follow Grant's example and reform, to display once more those qualities that made them so lovable in the first place. Ralph Nelson directed. From the novel by S. H. Barnett. Also with: Jack Good, Stephanie Berrington, Jennifer Berrington, Sharyl Locke.

FEAR STRIKES OUT (1957) B&W/100m. Interesting but dated adaptation of the first autobiography by controversial baseball player Jimmy Piersall, detailing his road to the major leagues (with the Boston Red Sox) and subsequent nervous breakdown and treatment in a mental hospital. Piersall's mental collapse is shown to be the result of trying to live up to his father's impossibly high expectations for him as a player; he can't cope with the pressure of *never* being good enough. In effect, this film is rooted in the youth-problem pictures of the fifties: it is the reverse of *Rebel Without a Cause*, in which a troubled boy can't express to his *weak* father his desperate need to receive some fatherly advice for once; in Piersall's case, he can't express to his *strong* father his desperate need to stop being barraged with fatherly advice. In his debut role Anthony Perkins is ideally cast as the young Piersall. With his display of nervous energy, emotional instability, paranoia, pent-up rage, and, finally, strait-jacketed catatonia, he may well have been using Piersall to prepare himself for Norman Bates. He would make a career out of playing characters who treaded the *schizoid line* between normal and insane. It's unfortunate Perkins was never offered a chance to reprise this role, because Piersall's subsequent life as a player, broadcaster, columnist, and author has been amazingly colorful. Debut direction by Robert Mulligan is sincere, although the film looks flat and phony, especially during the baseball scenes (who are those imposters in the Red Sox dugout?). Alan J. Pakula made his debut as producer. Also with: Karl Malden (as Piersall's father), Norma Moore, Adam Williams.

FELLINI SATYRICON (ITALIAN/1970) C/129m. Now you can see what those old Italian epics with Steve Reeves, Guy Madison, Lex Barker, and Mark Forrest would have looked like if Federico Fellini had directed them. This is Fellini's interpretation of stories by Petronius Arbiter, who lived in Rome during the time of Nero. Fellini was interested in trying to conceive a pre-Christian world, before people felt governed by moral codes. It's a world of untold violence and debauchery which, of course, is meant to parallel our *post*-Christian world. Episodic film is visually stunning and some images will stay in your memory, but I think much of its power has dissipated in the years since its release, when many viewers regarded it as a masterpiece. Today many think it slow, self-indulgent, and ugly. But it's still in a higher league than *Caligula*. Music by Nino Rota. Also with: Martin Potter, Hiram Keller, Max Born, Capucine, Salvo Randone, Alain Cuny.

FEMALE TROUBLE (1974) C/92m.

John Waters's wickedly funny cult film is a celebration of Crime and Beauty, both personified by Divine. Film chronicles life of Divine's Dawn Davenport, culminating in her execution in a Baltimore prison for kidnapping and multiple murders. Story begins when she's a teenager having trouble in school (she's caught eating a huge meatball sandwich in class) and at home—she runs away when her parents don't give her cha-cha shoes for Christmas. She is raped by a drunken pervert (also Divine) and becomes pregnant. She and daughter Taffy (Mink Stole) get along terribly. Dawn gets along by hooking and committing burglaries. She becomes the star customer of hairdressers David Lochary and Mary Vivian Pearce, who pay her to commit crimes while they take pictures; they launch her into show biz. Comedy contains child abuse, a hand being hacked off, acid being thrown in Divine's face (she's told she looks better afterward), rapes, a woman being kept in a cage, attempted incest, shots of the male Divine vomiting and revealing a sore-covered penis, random murder—but the really bad taste is evident in Waters's well-chosen costumes, hairdos, furniture, decor, and, of course, cast members (Waters's stock company), including the repulsive Edith Massey as Aunt Ida (who wants her straight nephew to get a homosexual lover). Picture is not consistently funny and, as usual, Waters goes too far too often. But this is the picture in which Divine really broke loose. She is not only unique but genuinely hilarious—even doing a deadpan tumbling act that would have made the great silent comics proud. Verbally (she and Mink Stole have great shouting bouts), facially and physically no female has seemed so confident about her beauty since Mae West. Also with: Donny Mills.

FEMME INFIDÈLE, LA (FRENCH-ITALIAN/1969) C/98m.

One of Claude Chabrol's most erotic, subtle, meticulously crafted, complex films (it fits into no genre)—a picture in which *murder* is the act which resuscitates the dying love of a bourgeois couple. Successful businessman Michel Bouquet, his wife, Stéphane Audran, and their 10-year-old son live in an affluent area of Versailles. Audran is still a beautiful, sexy woman, but dull Bouquet pays more attention to music and television than to her. Unfulfilled, she is having an affair in Paris with Maurice Ronet. Bouquet finds out about Ronet from a detective. He visits Ronet, telling his wife's surprised lover that Audran has told him about the affair because they have an open relationship. Their conversation is very civil and Ronet reveals the intimate details of the affair. Suddenly Bouquet is overcome with jealousy and kills Ronet. What a great scene! While police investigate the murder, Audran discovers Ronet's photo in her husband's pocket. A smile comes to her face.

She now realizes how completely Bouquet loves her, and what he is willing to do to keep her to himself. Never has she loved him so much. Chabrol is stating that bourgeois life is so stifling, so oppressive, and so resistant to change or growth, that it takes no less than an act of murder on one person's part to shake up things in a positive way. This unusual, tricky film is deceptively slow at first (indicative of the characters' monotonous existence) and then draws you in completely. You become tremendously intrigued by the psychology of the three privotal characters. A famous last shot. Photographed by Jean Rabier. Also with: Stéphane di Napoli, Michel Duchaussoy.

FEMMES FATALES (FRENCH/1976) C/85m.

Bertrand Blier's cult comedy would probably cause more arguments if anyone could figure out what it's about. It has a promising beginning: two middle-aged male-chauvinist pigs (gynecologist Jean-Pierre Marielle and pimp Jean Rochefort) realize that they can't stand sex with women anymore and run off to a country village, where they pig out on rich foods (i.c., roast pork with chocolate sauce), fine wine, and anything that's smelly or unhealthy enough to repel women. They are Blier's typical male duo: misogynistic, gross, irresponsible, superior. And we expect that some unusual women will miraculously reach tiny sensitive spots in their hearts and turn the tables on them, to make them feel inferior. That's what happens in Blier's brand of the battle of the sexes. But this film takes an odd, foolish turn, moving out of a rudely funny, believable realm, in which men vent their animosity toward women, into a confusing surreal fantasy, in which our two male protagonists and hundreds of other fed-up husbands march through the wilderness with troops of sex-crazed women soldiers in hot pursuit. Is this what Blier thinks would happen if men didn't care about sex? The trick Blier plays on his men in this film is that they become sexual objects to be used and humiliated and the women become the aggressors who think that men are only good for one thing. Despite what happens to his characters, Blier still treats his actresses in the old-fashioned way, as impersonal sexual entities; while the women are supposedly exploiting the two men (who are taken and gangbanged by hundreds of females, the actresses strip off their clothes while the actors remain covered. Music by Georges Delerue. Also with: Brigitte Fossey (as Marielle's wife, the most alive person in the whole picture).

FINDERS KEEPERS...LOVERS WEEPERS (1968) C/72m.

Piggy Russ Meyer film that probably won't please even his diehard fans. The main character is handsome but humorless owner (Paul Lockwood) of a nightclub, where men ogle the topless dancers. Since he's been having a troubled, sexless home life with his wife (Anne Chapman), he frequently visits the madame (Lavelle Roby) of a local brothel. He doesn't realize that the madame has hired two men to rob his safe while she keeps him occupied. Things don't work out as planned and it winds up with the two bad guys (one who is a bit loony) holding our "hero," his wife, and her lover captive while they try to unlock the safe. Picture has none of the typical Meyer humor; it even has a cruel edge to it, particularly evident in the unpleasant scene where the sicko forces the wife to kiss him and then tries to brutally rape her. Of course, the women have large chests; but they're not particularly pretty—they're the types who show up in stag films. The sex scenes are turnoffs. Who told Meyer that watching a plump girl shaving a guy's chest is exciting? Also with: Joey Duprez, Jan Sinclair.

FINGERS (1978) C/91m.   James Toback wrote and directed (his debut) this brutal, fascinating character piece. Harvey Keitel isn't in search of an identity, but his confusion, dissatisfaction, and schizophrenia (a nice guy who can be insanely violent) are the result of having none. Although he is a '50s rock-music fanatic (he carries a blaring tape machine), he hopes to be a classical pianist to please his Jewish mother (Marian Seldes)—this angers his semi-retired gangland father (Michael V. Gazzo). Gazzo wants him to be a "collector" for his mob—this angers Keitel's mother. He does his best to please each parent—he pleases neither. Desperate for love, he seeks out women, confusing sex with love. He falls madly in love with zonked-out Tisa Farrow, although she has no admirable qualities. While trying to persuade Farrow to leave a rough club owner (Jim Brown, looking more formidable than when he played football), he auditions at Carnegie Hall and tries to collect a debt from a violent gangster (Anthony Sirico, Jr.), setting off a life-and-death struggle on a stairwell. Every character and every scene is unusual, yet picture hits no false notes. Toback's superbly acted, rough, erotic, often vulgar film impressed some critics, antagonized others. It flopped at the box office but has become a cult favorite. Good use of New York locales, exhilarating movie-making. Photographed by Michael Chapman. Also with: Tanya Roberts, Danny Aiello, Lenny Montana.

FIREMEN'S BALL, THE (CZECH/1968) C/ 73m.   In the last movie he made in his native Czechoslovakia, Miloš Forman attempted to rip apart the pre-Dubček Czech middle class because of its hypocrisy, moral laxity, and propensity for undeserved self-congratulation. Firemen decide to throw a ball to honor their retired chief, who's 86 and dying of cancer. It will be good for their own image. Everything goes wrong: the leering, dirty old firemen decide to hold a beauty contest, but only ugly girls enter and even they are too embarrassed to walk on stage; the firemen are late to a fire that burns down an old man's house; people steal the raffle prizes meant to benefit the old man; a respected fireman is caught redhanded with stolen meat; the ex-chief's gift disappears. Film is somewhat reminiscent of Buñuel's *The Exterminating Angel*, in which bourgeois party guests can't get home—here the party guests stick around to commit mean acts or have them perpetrated on them. Laughter comes from watching self-serving people try to show off their "generosity, benevolence, solidarity."

But cruelty often overwhelms the humor. Also, at times it seems Forman is attacking people in general (there are no nice people in this film) rather than just bourgeois society. 40,000 Czech firemen quit their jobs to protest this film. They went back to work after Forman insisted that the film wasn't about firemen specifically. But, in introducing this film, he states that it is about firemen. I believe he's pointing out the irony of having insensitive, selfish men be the ones Czechs count on to save their families and houses in case of fire. With: Josef Sebanek, Josef Kolb, Vaclav Stockel.

FIRES ON THE PLAIN (JAPANESE/1959) B&W/ 105m.   A shocking vision of war by Kon Ichikawa, adapted by his wife, Natto Wada, from Shohei Ooka's novel. While we don't enjoy what we watch, we are transfixed by how it is presented. The setting is Leyte, in the Philippines; it is February 1945 and the defeated, retreating Japanese are scattered about the island, awaiting death from starvation, disease, the Americans, or Filipino guerillas who are lighting signal fires off in the wilderness. Ichikawa follows one soldier (Eiji Funakoshi) as he wanders deliriously around the island, willing to kill for food, encountering depravity and madness everywhere he goes. The island becomes a graveyard, with the corpses of the invaders rotting in the mud. The survivors have become ghouls, cannibalizing their fellow soldiers. But our soldier is a *lost* soul—his rotting teeth prevent him from eating human meat, his tubercular condition prevents others from eating his flesh, so his misery will not end. Book, which has been interpreted as a Christian parable, allows for a form of salvation—but death in the film simply means an end to suffering and nothingness. A unique, unforgettable anti-war film. Also with: Mickey Curtis, Osamu Takizawa, Hikaru Hoshi, Jun Hamamura.

FIRESTARTER (1983) C/115m.   Sympathetic little girl (Drew Barrymore) with the power to start fires through mental impulses and her nice-guy father (David Keith) with mind-control powers are on the run from a secret government agency called The Shop, which is interested in using Barrymore as a weapon. Mess of a film, adapted from Stephen King's novel, picks up slightly once the two are captured and separated. Then we no longer have to endure Keith repeatedly getting down on one knee and sensitively comforting the teary child, who feels guilt about the destruction and deaths her fires have caused. Picture's main selling point is the special effects, most of which involve people and objects bursting into flames—the climax is filled with flying fireballs. Cute Barrymore is good but too self-impressed as "Charlie." George C. Scott, wearing a pony tail, has a field day as a maniacal government assassin who literally wants to bash Charlie's brains in. All the other actors are poorly used. Ending is similar to the one in *Three Days of the Condor*, only here it's superfluous. Directed by Mark L. Lester. Also with: Martin Sheen, Freddie Jones, Art Carney, Louise Fletcher, Heather Locklear.

FIRST BLOOD (1982) C/97m.

Sylvester Stallone's first non-*Rocky* commercial hit proved that audiences love him best when he's the underdog, overcoming seemingly insurmountable odds. Here he's John Rambo, ex–Vietnam Green Beret, who, after being jailed in a small U.S. town by a redneck sheriff (Brian Dennehy) who doesn't like his scruffy looks, uses his incomparable guerrilla-warfare skills to battle a police force and the National Guard. Based on the novel by David Morrell, it takes a swipe at the U.S. Army brass for using Agent Orange in Vietnam and at our society for neglecting the Vietnam vet; but the politics quickly take a back seat to ingredients calculated to attract a mass audience. For the kids, there is action and violence galore; conservatives are offered a lead who was once a war hero; and left-wingers are pacified by his current status as social outcast and battler against the establishment. (Vietnam vets may be happy that one of their own is regarded as a hero, when society has shunned them; but I wonder if they may not think the schizophrenic Rambo perpetuates the sorry image that most of them have psychotic tendencies.) Looking lean and mean, Stallone is easy to cheer for. But many moviegoers would trade much of the buckets of blood spilled in the film for some reasonably good dialogue. Blockbuster sequel *Rambo: First Blood, Part II* has Stallone attempting to rescue MIA's in North Vietnam. Directed by Ted Kotcheff. Also with: Richard Crenna (as Rambo's ex-commander), David Caruso, Jack Starrett.

FIRST NUDIE MUSICAL, THE (1976) C/90m.

This minor but amusing parody of both porno films and "let's-put-on-a-show" musicals flopped at the box office when Paramount didn't know how—and barely tried—to market it for the youth market. But eventually it became a cult hit. Co-directed by Mark Haggard (who'd made a couple of porno films) and Bruce Kimmel (who wrote the screenplay and the songs), it was an attempt by unknown filmmakers to break into the Hollywood mainstream by making a gimmicky movie, a musical with full frontal nudity. Conveniently, their film is about a producer (Stephen Nathan) and a movie director (Kimmel) who attempt to make the first XXX-rated musical comedy in two weeks' time, in order to save Nathan's father's troubled studio. They hire actors who "can screw and carry a tune." Picture is filled with very funny characters involved in outrageous situations. I wish that Nathan and female lead Cindy Williams (as Nathan's girlfriend-secretary) wouldn't spend so much time *reacting* to others' crazy antics instead of participating in the zaniness. But Kimmel, as the jerky, infantile, braying John Smithee, and Diana Canova, as a Cuban firecracker, are consistently funny. Highlights include the auditions, the "Dancing Dildoes" number, and the appearance of Schlong, whose below-the-frame "stunt-cock" has everyone on the set agog ("Ees just so beeg," Canova says repetitively). The dialogue isn't strong, although there are witty lines sprinkled about. The visuals aren't erotic enough, and the climactic number—"Let Them Eat Cake (And I'll Eat You)"—is weak.

But the actors are spirited and brave and, though there is much matter-of-fact nudity, and four-letter words fill most sentences, nothing is offensive. In fact, the film has surprising innocence. Also with: Leslie Ackerman (a virgin from Indiana who agrees to play the ingenue if she can wear clothes during her nude scenes), Alan Abelew (as a conceited loser who sings "Please Touch Me, I'm You"), Alexandra Morgan ("I won't do this scene until the damn dancing dildoes know their steps—I'm an actress"), Frank Doubleday, Rene Hall (as a musician and pervert), Art Marino, Ron Howard (in a cameo).

FISTFUL OF DOLLARS, A (ITALIAN/1964) C/96m.

Released in the U.S. in 1967, this seminal spaghetti western was the breakthrough film for both director Sergio Leone and star Clint Eastwood, whose portrayal of the Man With No Name, the most ruthless hero in western-movie history, quickly established him as the screen's most charismatic action hero. The interesting story was ripped off from Kurosawa's samurai tale *Yojimbo*. A mysterious gunfighter (Eastwood) arrives in a miserable little town that is controlled by two corrupt, warring families. He hires himself out to one family and then the other, killing numerous men and serving as catalyst to the total annihilation of both factions. After killing chief villain Gian Maria Volonté, he rides away much richer, leaving behind a heavily populated graveyard. While not on the level of *For a Few Dollars More* and *The Good, the Bad and the Ugly*—for some viewers the fun is just trying to keep an accurate body count—it did anticipate those films in several ways: the ritualistic, oddly humorous shootouts; the brutal violence; the use of music (by Ennio Morricone) to comment on the action; the near-death and Christlike resurrection of the hero (a theme Eastwood would use in his own films); a West that is populated mostly by ugly, unwashed Fellini types; an America where every person's death means someone else makes a financial profit. Most interesting is the Eastwood character. Distinctively dressed in a tattered poncho over a sheepskin vest, a black cheroot (often used to light dynamite) wedged in his mouth (presumably to keep his dialogue down), and with an air of casual sadism, he is, I believe, one of the few survivors of a dying race of mythological superwarriors whose divine powers enable them to outdraw and outshoot anyone, to withstand terrible punishment, to have no fear of death, and to sense impending danger and have the cunning to get out of it. In this film, the primitive world he travels through is mythological; in Leone's sequels, history and myth merge. Eastwood's characters in the subsequent films have similar traits, but are probably different people. Also with: Marianne Koch, Wolfgang Lukschy.

FISTS OF FURY/BIG BOSS, THE (CHINESE/1971) C/103m.

Bruce Lee's first martial-arts film. He's a country boy whose relatives get him a job at an ice factory. He becomes suspicious when several fellow workers disappear. He discovers that his boss has been using the ice to smuggle heroin. When all his friends and relatives are killed, Lee gets bloody revenge on the boss and his gang. This is generally considered Lee's best, least pretentious film. But I find it somewhat disappointing. The film suffers because Lee spends too much of it being reluctant to fight and not joining in several melees; and when he does fight, it's too apparent that none of the villains is a match for him. They are amateurish. Lee needs worthier opponents. Lee does have one spectacular fight sequence in which he singlehandedly kills about 15 men. Lee fans should note that he has his only scene with a nude woman (he's in a drunken sleep at the time). Directed by Lo Wei. Also with: Maria Yi, James Tren, Han Ying-chieh, Nora Miao.

FITZCARRALDO (WEST GERMAN/1982) C/158m.
A slow but awe-inspiring epic from Werner Herzog, who again presents a protagonist whose "mad" views put him at odds with the world, whose obsessive quest for the impossible makes him simultaneously a great and pathetic figure. Filmed on location in the Peruvian rain forests, the picture, in which Herzog re-creates a bizarre historical episode that took place in the late 19th century, involves a mad-as-a-hatter Irish dreamer named Brian Sweeney Fitzgerald (Klaus Kinski replaced ill Jason Robards). Fitzcarraldo, as he is called by the Indians and Spanish, is a lover of Caruso and is determined to bring opera to the isolated area. Because he doesn't have the funds to build an opera house, he comes up with a money-making scheme to transport rubber from a second, parallel river to a settlement that he'll build upriver. He travels upstream on a steamer that his lover (Claudia Cardinale), a madam, bought for him. His Indian crew deserts him, but Indians from a jungle tribe offer to help because they believe he and the ship are part of an Indian legend come true. For Fitzcarraldo's plans to work, the Indians will have to literally drag the huge steamer over a small mountain that stands between the two rivers. The Indians agree to this, but their mysterious mood tells Fitzcarraldo that they're up to something. This film took four years from pre-production to completion. Several people lost their lives in a plane crash, a tribal war almost resulted, and long delays were caused when one steamer was trapped in river mud until the rainy season and when in the climactic scene, for which Herzog actually tried to pull an authentic steamer over a cliff, the steamer got stuck halfway up. The innumerable hardships were documented in Les Blank's fascinating film *Burden of Dreams*, which ends with a nutty Herzog damning nature and the jungle and saying that, no matter how the picture turned out, it could never make up for the tragedies that took place during production. At least the final product contains much masterful material, including mesmerizing footage of the steamer on the Amazon, the detailing of the work required to move the steamer over the cliff, Kinski's marvelous performance, and the opera finale, perhaps the most emotional scene in Herzog's work. Also with: José Lewgoy, Miguel Angel Fuentes, Paul Hittscher.

FIVE (1951) B&W/93m.
Arch Oboler wrote, produced, and directed this unusual science-fiction film, best known for being the first picture to deal with the aftermath of nuclear warfare. Only five people are left on earth following an atomic explosion, and they gather in a mountain lodge. It's not surprising that at the end the handsome William Phipps and Susan Douglas, pregnant by her dead husband, should be the only ones left to start a new world, but it's disturbing that Oboler arbitrarily eliminates from the new order *black* Charles Lampkin, *insane* (because of the explosion) Earl Lee, and *foreigner* James Anderson (even though he is the heavy)—outcasts of our present-day America. Radio vet Oboler wrote credible dialogue, but the picture could use a bit more action and suspense. The most effective sequence has the survivors walking through a city that is empty but for rotting corpses.

FIVE EASY PIECES (1970) C/96m.
Bob Rafelson directed and Jack Nicholson starred in this superb study of a cultural misfit, a man who rejected his rich, classical-music upbringing and now finds himself equally out of place working on an oil rig and living with a well-meaning but hopelessly ignorant, country-music-singing waitress (sympathetically played by Karen Black) whom he loves but can't treat nicely. Nicholson is just great as he repeatedly loses his temper and apologizes; tries to do the right thing but sooner or later gives in to his baser instincts; becomes aggravated by everything from Black's awful bowling and constant, foolish chatter to an obnoxious waitress's obstinate refusal (in the film's classic scene) to serve him a side order of wheat toast with his omelet. The film is full of funny moments and characters—including Helena Kallianiotes's weird, complaining hitchhiker and two floozies, Sally Struthers's Shirley ("but you can call me Betty") and her friend, Twinky. But there is a sadness that always cuts deeply into the humor. This is why the picture was so appealing to the college-age audiences in 1970, who simultaneously laughed incredulously and were extremely upset by the political state of the world and felt just as alienated from family and various segments of society as Nicholson. An excellent script by Adrien Joyce; there's no way such a character study would be filmed today. Impressively photographed by Laszlo Kovacs, who conveys how particular physical environments make Nicholson feel either trapped or free. Strong use of Tammy Wynette songs, adding to the overwhelming sense of melancholia. Also with: Susan Anspach, Billy Green Bush, Ralph Waite, Fannie Flagg, Toni Basil.

FIVE FINGERS OF DEATH/KING BOXER (CHINESE/1971) C/102m.
In 1973 this was the first Chinese martial-arts film to hit America, starting the craze and paving the way for the Bruce Lee classics. Picture has been mercilessly attacked for its poor dubbing and hokey plot, but I find it great fun to watch an extremely bland hero (Lo Lieh) taking on a fabulous array of Chinese and

Japanese villains, each more outrageous than his predecessor. These villains are all considered unbeatable in battle, but only Lieh possesses the mystical "Iron Fist!" Picture has flare, imagination—at very least, it has great camp value. It would make a good second feature to *Infra-Man*. Directed by Cheng Chang Ho. Also with: Wang Ping, Wang-Ching-Feng.

FIVE MILLION YEARS TO EARTH/QUATERMASS AND THE PIT (BRITISH/1968) C/98m.

An exceptional, extremely intelligent, thematically controversial science-fiction movie that still hasn't received due recognition in America. Scripted by Nigel Kneale, it was the third of his BBC-TV serials to be filmed, following *The Quatermass Experiment/The Creeping Unknown* (1956) and *Quatermass II/Enemy from Space* (1957). Andrew Keir assumed the role of resolute scientist Bernard Quatermass, played in the earlier films by Brian Donlevy. In this installment, skeletons of primitive apes are discovered below a London street under construction. Anthropologists James Donald and Barbara Shelley arrive to evaluate the discovery. When a cylindrical object is found, rocket expert Quatermass rushes to the scene to see if it's a bomb. It turns out to be a spaceship from Mars that landed five million years before. The insectlike corpses inside quickly turn to dust. Quatermass deduces that the Martians, a dying race, changed the genetic structure of our apes and indoctrinated them with a Martian mentality. Because these Martians bred with normal earth apes, their ancestors—the human beings on earth—are actually Martians! Like *2001*, this film explores the intriguing theme of "race memory." But whereas Kubrick's humans retain memories of "God" from their ape ancestors who had contact with extra-terrestrials, we associate the Martian insect-creatures who had contact with the primitive apes with the Devil. Film is complicated, particularly during the last few minutes, but it's always fascinating and exciting. And Quatermass isn't our usual hunk hero. Skillfully directed by Roy Ward Baker, with an interesting final shot. Hammer Studios' best film. Also with: Julian Glover, Maurice Good.

5000 FINGERS OF DR. T, THE (1953) C/89m.

Dr. Seuss (Theodore Geisel) and veteran screenwriter Alan Scott (who's best known for his Astaire-Rogers scripts) wrote this imaginative, offbeat fantasy film about a little boy (Tommy Rettig) who'd rather be playing ball than taking piano lessons with tyrannical Dr. Terwilliker (Hans Conried)—they are in sympathy with the child and think he shouldn't be forced to play the piano. Rettig dreams that he is among 500 boys who are prisoners of Dr. T. and forced to play the piano constantly. Dr. T. has vicious thugs who make sure the boys stay in line and can't escape the maze-like, surreal castle. Dr. T's plan is to have the 5000 fingers ignite an atomic bomb! A cult has formed around this film. It's exciting, scary (especially if you're a child and already dread your piano teacher), and visually dazzling—the sets and backdrops are amazing. Watch for the anticommunist propaganda (see the red smoke)—these children are being turned into obedient automatons. Conried was the perfect choice to be Dr. T. Produced by Stanley Kramer. Directed by Roy Rowland. Franz Planer did the cinematography. Hans J. Salter, Frederick Hollander, and Heinz Roemheld wrote the songs and incidental music. Also with: Peter Lind Hayes and Mary Healy, Henry Kulky.

FIXED BAYONETS (1951) B&W/92m.

During the Korean War a small rearguard platoon has the suicidal mission of holding off the enemy while the large U.S. force retreats out of the icy mountains. Richard Basehart is third in command, and is petrified that he'll outlast his superiors and become company leader. This action-filled, intelligent war movie was written and directed by Sam Fuller; it's obvious from the believable dialogue between soldiers and the intricate military strategy they conceive that Fuller had war experience. His film is about the *responsibility* of being a soldier; it doesn't matter if a soldier is scared or brave, for heroics will come about only if one does the job. Many fine moments, but none better than when all the soldiers put their bare feet together for protection against frostbite and one foot, which no longer has feeling, has no claimant. Also with: Gene Evans (star of Fuller's *The Steel Helmet*), Michael O'Shea, Richard Hylton, Craig Hill, and (try to pick him out) James Dean.

FLAMING STAR (1960) C/101m.

Don Siegel directed this action-packed western, which features what is generally accepted as Elvis Presley's best performance. Elvis is a half-breed who lives on a ranch in Texas with his white brother (Steve Forrest), white father (John McIntire), and Indian mother (Dolores Del Rio). When Indians go on the warpath, racist whites threaten Presley and Del Rio. Forrest and McIntire are loyal, but Presley and Del Rio feel driven from the white man's world. Racial-prejudice theme was unusual in westerns until this film and the same year's *The Unforgiven*; the only trouble is that the film is as unkind to Indians as it is to racist whites—it's significant that Presley eventually takes off his warpaint and moccasins and puts back on his white man's clothing. Presley's performance is adequate, no better. Direction by Siegel improves as the film progresses. Film's best moment is the frightening first appearance of Indians. Also with: Barbara Eden, L.Q. Jones, Richard Jaeckel.

FLAMINGO ROAD (1949) B&W/94m.

Joan Crawford is a carnival girl who settles down in a small town when deputy sheriff Zachary Scott gets her a waitressing job. She and Scott fall in love, which angers venomous sheriff Sydney Greenstreet, a major force in the state's corrupt political machine. Greenstreet wants to put the weak Scott in the State Senate and later make him his puppet governor, so he forces Scott to marry a society dame and frames Crawford on a prostitution charge. Crawford returns, determined to get revenge. She marries David Brian, a casually corrupt but basically decent politician who is involved in a power struggle with Greenstreet to see who will control the party. By the time she realizes she loves Brian and not Scott, her marriage, Brian's career, and her life may already have been ruined. Ending is too pat, but picture is well directed by Michael Curtiz, has a solid group of characters, and, probably more than any straight drama up until then (*All the King's Men* was also released in 1949), paints a realistic portrait of political corruption in America. It's kept from being too cynical by reporter Fred Clark's statement that our system would work if good men ran it. Crawford is much better than in *Mildred Pierce*, giving a deeply felt, multi-faceted characterization. She's smart, sincere, and stronger than any man in that she alone stands up to Greenstreet (playing one of his most memorable villains), slaps him, even points a loaded gun at him. Scripted by Robert Wilder from a play he wrote with Sally Wilder. Also with: Virginia Huston, Alice White.

FLASHDANCE (1983) C/96m. Phenomenally popular film is set in Pittsburgh. It's about an 18-year-old Catholic girl named Alex (Jennifer Beals's debut) who works as a welder during the day and a go-go dancer at night. She dreams of being accepted into the Pittsburgh ballet company, although she has had no formal training. She is director Adrian Lyne's conception of the perfect "modern" woman: talented, ambitious, loyal to her female friends, confident, stubborn, and sexually liberated. Other than the dances, the most erotic scene has Beals casually putting her hand under her loose top and removing her bra during a conversation with her boss and soon-to-be-lover (Michael Nouri). Picture has a potentially interesting feminist theme, an appealing performance by Beals and some exciting dancing by Beals's double Marine Jahan, but film is done in by a shallow script, overly stylish direction, and far too much editing. Film looks and sounds like a series of rock videos thrown together; if you can take only 15 minutes of MTV, then you probably won't last much longer with this. Beals's dance tryout is a highlight, but doesn't it end much too quickly? Relationship between Beals and her mentor Lilia Skala recalls that between Maureen O'Hara and Maria Ouspenskaya in *Dance, Girl, Dance*. Excellent upbeat theme song "What a Feeling" was performed by Irene Cara—it won an Oscar. Giorgio Moroder contributed most of the loud, pulsating rock music. Also with: Sunny Johnson, Kyle T. Heffner, Belinda Bauer.

FLESH (1968) C/75m–105m. An early attempt by Andy Warhol to cross over from strictly underground to more commercial movies. There's no real story, just a series of vignettes shot on New York streets and inside apartments, with Warhol regular Joe Dallesandro either hustling gays in order to get money for his disgruntled wife (Geraldine Smith) or meeting and having sex with his weird friends. As directed by Paul Morrissey, picture uses techniques—a *cinéma-vérité* camera style, improvisation, intentionally sloppy jump-cut editing—that were unique in the com-

mercial cinema of the time. Also unusual were its themes: homosexuality, transvestism, casual sex, male prostitution. Later Morrissey-and-Warhol films were meant to parallel Hollywood classics, but this film was simply meant to subvert bourgeois sensibilities. It's much influenced by the *avant garde* works of Jack Smith (*Flaming Creatures*), with its non-acting, sexual frankness and glimpse at the peculiar lifestyle of a fringe element of the counterculture. Dallesandro is his young, likable self, pimply but cute, passive to all the men and women who are turned on by his almost always naked body. He has several amusing scenes with oddball characters, particularly a sequence with a philosophical artist, Maurice Barddell, and a sex scene with his wife when she asks what he wants her to do most and he says his laundry. Okay, but not as consistently funny as its semi-sequel, *Trash*. Also with: Barry Brown, Candy Darling, Jackie Curtis, Geri Miller, Louis Waldon, Patti D'Arbanville.

FLESH GORDON (1974) C/78m. X-rated parody of *Flash Gordon*, with full frontal nudity and simulated sex, was promoted to attract hip college-age viewers. But the film didn't match promotion: it's too dreadful, too boring, to be considered good comedy or camp. Flesh (Jason Williams) and pretty Dale Ardor (Suzanne Fields spends almost the entire film naked) go to the planet Porno, from where the evil Professor Wang (William Hunt) has been striking the earth with sex-rays that have caused chaos. They battle Wang, monsters, and a tribe of lesbians who force Dale to perform sexual acts on them. It is peculiar seeing a leading lady in a non-porno movie engaging in forced cunnilingus. Also strange is seeing Flesh allow a male to perform fellatio on him in return for a favor. Acting is terrible and the direction by Howard Ziehm and William Osco is inept. Surprisingly, the special effects (inspired by Ray Harryhausen) are pretty good, certainly suitable for the comic-book material. Otherwise the film makes *Barbarella* seem like a masterpiece. They never made the promised sequel: *Perils of Flesh*. Also with: Joseph Hudgins as Dr. Flexi Jerkoff, sci-fi vet John Hoyt, Candy Samples.

FLOATING CLOUDS (JAPANESE/1955) B&W/119m. The most famous film in the 37-year career of Mikio Naruse. The beautiful Hideko Takamine, who starred in 17 Naruse films, gives a sympathetic performance as a young woman who during the war fell in love with a married government forestry expert (Masayuki Mori) when they met on a sunny island in Indo-China. In 1946 she calls on Mori in Tokyo. When he refuses to leave his wife, she becomes a prostitute. Each time he comes to her, she loves him too much to turn him away. She will suffer great indignities because of him—he will take other lovers even after his wife dies—but she can't accept not seeing him again, which is what he often suggests. At the end they finally go off together as she always wanted; but it rains continuously on this second island—one cannot return to Paradise. Naruse wanted the misery of Takamine and the women who are exploited by insensitive men to reflect the depressed, defeated country. He believed that the widespread ill-treatment of women was the reason postwar Japan was such a miserable place. Direction by Naruse is typically unobtrusive—notice how few times he moves his camera away from the actors and how unimportant the sets are. But instead of this unusual film being static, it has a distinct romantic *flow*. No scenes will overpower you as in an Ozu picture (Naruse does not try to make you feel sorry for his characters), but you'll feel deeply about what happens to these interesting people. Lovely music by Ichiro Saito. Also with: Mariko Okada, Daisuke Kato, Cheiko Nakakita.

FLY, THE (1958) C/94m.
Most enjoyable science-fiction film, directed by Kurt Neumann and scripted by James Clavell with tongue firmly in cheek. Scientist Al (David) Hedison who is working on a disintegration machine in his basement lab accidentally mixes his own atoms with those of a common fly. Patricia Owens, his wife, gets suspicious that something's wrong when he writes: ". . . fetch me a bowl of milk laced with rum." She finds that the unlucky scientist has a fly's head and claw, and the fly has his human head, hand, and ability to speak. "Help me. Help me!" it cries pitifully. Events turn even worse when Hedison starts to lose his mind and the claw gets a mind of its own. The scene in which Owens pulls off her husband's hood and sees his fly head—and he looks at her image with fly's vision, seeing numerous images of her screaming face—is shocking, one of the greatest moments in horror movies; but picture is mostly amusing, as when Owens and her small son (Charles Herbert), and housekeeper (Kathleen Freeman), search the house and garden for fly so husband can reverse the experiment. We see lots of close-ups of flies; lots of people swat flies only to hear Owens hysterically shout at them to "catch them, not crush them." Interesting element is that this is one scientist-treading-where-man-shouldn't-tread movie in which the emphasis is placed on the wife as she endures tragedy and tries everything in her power to save her husband. Although no one need take it too seriously, it's actually a feminist film in that a helpless wife becomes extremely capable (even though she understandably screams) when her husband, in a unique way, becomes "handicapped" and confined to his lab. Followed by *The Return of the Fly* and *The Curse of the Fly*. Remade by David Cronenberg in 1986. Also with: Vincent Price, Herbert Marshall, Betty Lou Gerson.

FLYING DOWN TO RIO (1933) B&W/89m.
Fourth-billed Ginger Rogers is a band singer; fifth-billed Fred Astaire is the band's accordion player, best friend of leading man Gene Raymond. But when they do their one duet, in their first film together, dancing "The Carioca," they steal the film, giving off electricity that Raymond and topbilled Dolores Del Rio are unable to equal. Rogers is brassy and sexy—more like her Warners golddiggers than the more inhibited characters she'd play in her future films with Astaire; and Astaire is energetic, cheerful, and un-

flappable, and when he gets the chance, he dances up a storm. Rogers and Astaire are the main reason this film keeps playing on television and in repertory theaters, but, despite some dull spots and a flimsy plot (Brazilian Del Rio must choose between fiancé Raul Roulien and Raymond, who's providing entertainment at the opening of her father's hotel), the picture is romantic, sexy, and delightfully and inventively kitschy. There's some tricky camera work, unusual art design by Van Nest Polglase and Carroll Clark, and some creative production numbers—including the unforgettable finale, in which scantily clad chorus girls strike provocative pre-Hollywood Code poses on the wings of airplanes in flight. One usually thinks of this as being an innocuous film, but it's really bizarre. Cleverly directed by Thornton Freeland. Also with: Blanche Friderici, Franklin Pangborn, Eric Blore, Roy D'Arcy, Clarence Muse, Betty Furness.

FOG, THE (1980) C/91m.
As a small seaside town celebrates its 100th anniversary, a mysterious fog rolls in. It contains the ghosts of the sailors for whose murders the town was founded, and they begin to exact revenge on the townspeople. The first half of John Carpenter's follow-up to *Halloween* is terrifically atmospheric, at times almost poetic. He deftly juxtaposes several storylines (which was one of the early Carpenter's real skills) and presents several characters we care for, including hitchhiker Jamie Lee Curtis, trucker Tommy Atkins, and cool-talking deejay Adrienne Barbeau (Carpenter's wife), who warns listeners of the fog's direction from her lighthouse radio station. Carpenter builds the suspense to a high level, but then the picture deteriorates into conventional and too brutal horror fare. Also with: Hal Holbrook, Janet Leigh (Curtis's mother), Nancy Loomis, Charles Cyphers.

FOLKS AT RED WOLF INN, THE/TERROR HOUSE (1972) C/98m.
Oddball horror film in which college girl Linda Gillin wins a surprise vacation to an out-of-the-way inn. The kindly but weird owners serve the tastiest meals imaginable—but Linda can't figure out what meat she is wolfing down. She becomes suspicious when other young coeds disappear during the night. Picture has suspense, lots of black humor (including the dinner scenes, where everyone sighs and offers compliments after every bite), and a winning performance by Gillin. Sleeper would probably have a cult if director Bud Townsend had cut the humor and added some onscreen violence. But the humor gives it the distinction of being the most charming of the horror film's *cannibalism* subgenre. The tone is reminiscent of Roald Dahl. Also with: Arthur Space, Mary Jackson, John Neilson, Michael Macready.

FOLLOW THE FLEET (1936) B&W/110m.
Sailor Fred Astaire tries to win back former girlfriend and dance partner Ginger Rogers, but his schemes keep losing her jobs and making her angry at him. Meanwhile, in a hackneyed storyline that slows down the film and actually becomes

more important than the Astaire-Rogers romance, Rogers's sister, Harriet Hilliard, a music teacher, falls for Astaire's shipmate Randolph Scott, but he is scared off when she mentions marriage. Film feels different from other Astaire-Rogers musicals, even *Roberta*, although this is a reworking of that film with Hilliard assuming Irene Dunne's part. The music is jazzier, Rogers wears pants when she dances, Astaire briefly plays the piano, Rogers gets rare solos as both singer and dancer ("Let Yourself Go"), Astaire doesn't need to seduce Rogers through dance (the most elegant and romantic duet, "Let's Face the Music and Dance," comes late in the film, after they know they're in love). And, in the film's wonderful highlight, Astaire and Rogers perform their most *playful* number in the series, dancing to "I'm Putting All My Eggs in One Basket," during which Rogers intentionally dances out of synch with Astaire, as if she were a little girl (not a professional dancer) who imaginatively finds silly things to do with her feet and body each time they begin a new series of steps. Plot has been criticized for making Astaire and Rogers into the comedy team, but that's okay for a change because they're funny (e.g., the proposal scene). Irving Berlin contributed seven songs, including the Astaire-led "We Saw the Sea" and "I'd Rather Lead a Band." Dwight Taylor and Allan Scott adapted Hubert Osborne's 1922 play *Shore Leave*. Direction was by Mark Sandrich; Pandro S. Berman produced; Van Nest Polglase and his associate Carroll Clark designed their least interesting sets of the series; Hermes Pan served as choreographer. Also with: Astrid Allwyn, Harry Beresford, Lucille Ball, Betty Grable, Frank Jenks.

FOOTLIGHT PARADE (1933) B&W/104m.

Depression Era musical, with James Cagney as an out-of-work Broadway producer who gets the idea of staging live production numbers as preludes to movies. He gets so caught up with warding off his ex-wife and falling for a golddigger that he fails to notice that his personal secretary, Joan Blondell, is in love with him. She gets him out of trouble with women and his crooked bosses and frees him to stage three massive production numbers in three days so they can win a valuable contract from a theater owner. (Their competition is a company that has been stealing all Cagney's ideas through a spy in the chorus line.) Cagney and Blondell make a good match, as do Dick Powell and Ruby Keeler; but film would be touch better if screenwriters had simply put in a few lines about how the success of the three numbers is as important to the welfare of the dancers and singers (who need jobs!) as it is to Cagney's peace of mind. We know he'll get back on his feet, but we're not sure about them. With the plot out of the way, Busby Berkeley stages three of his greatest, most innovative, and sexiest musical numbers, back to back: "Honeymoon Hotel," "By a Waterfall" (with the chorines, shot from above, creating amazing patterns in the water), and "Shanghai Lil," featuring Cagney tapping with Keeler on a bar and marching soldiers displaying placards with the huge images of Old Glory and Franklin Roosevelt (whom the Warner brothers heartily en-

dorsed). Great fun. Directed by Lloyd Bacon. Also with: Frank McHugh, Guy Kibbee, Ruth Donnelly, Hugh Herbert.

FOR A FEW DOLLARS MORE (ITALIAN/1965) C/131m.

Released in the U.S. in 1967, Sergio Leone's follow-up to *A Fistful of Dollars* moves from a mythical age to a time when civilization (symbolized by the coming of the railroad to the West) and recorded history emerge. It's more elaborate, more imaginatively plotted, better photographed, funnier, more brutal (the violence becomes more realistic), and more overtly adult and political than the original. Dressed again in poncho over sheepskin vest, Clint Eastwood returns as *another* (I believe) nameless gunfighter. This time he's a bounty hunter who hopes that the money he'll get for killing Gian Maria Volonté and his gang will help him buy a farm. He discovers that there's a second man after Volonté, Lee Van Cleef's mysterious Colonel Mortimer (a different character than he'd play in *The Good, the Bad and the Ugly*). Eastwood and Van Cleef form the first of Leone's unholy alliances. Interestingly, Van Cleef is the "good" superwarrior in this film, while the young, mistake-prone Eastwood serves as the "ugly"—or flawed—mythical superwarrior. That Eastwood will learn a few things, especially during his "duel" with the more experienced Van Cleef, will qualify him to be the unflawed "good" in the sequel. What distinguishes the "good" from Leone's "bad" is that they kill only scoundrels (while the "bad" superwarriors kill anyone) and inadvertently benefit the decent people of the West. Whereas Eastwood's mysterious gunfighters kill to make money rather than to achieve *revenge* (he has *no* past), Mortimer is the first of Leone's characters who are haunted by bad memories of loved ones being killed. Mortimer wants to kill Volonté because Volonté raped Mortimer's sister, who then killed herself. Their "good" vs. "bad" showdown is inevitable—Eastwood steps aside—and, as in Leone's *Once Upon a Time in the West*, the villain learns at the point of death, through a musical prop, why the good guy has obsessively tracked him down. Film has been labeled nihilistic, but in fact it contains the key political scene in all of Leone's work: at the end Eastwood piles up the dead bodies of Volonté's gang, counting them not by number but by the bounties each corpse will earn him. Socialist Leone's point is clear: in capitalist America, dead men equate with money. This money factor is as much an unhappy sign of the growth of American civilization as is the coming of the train. A super score by Ennio Morricone. Also with: Jose Egger, Mara Krup, Klaus Kinski (on whose face Van Cleef lights a match).

FOR ME AND MY GAL (1942) B&W/104m.

Playing a vaudeville song-and-dance team who are trying to get a booking at the Palace, Judy Garland got her first solo star billing and Gene Kelly made his screen debut. When WWI breaks out, the opportunistic Kelly intentionally hurts his hand so he won't be drafted before they play the Palace. Garland walks out on the disloyal fellow—and he must prove himself to win her back. Obvious, sentimental, patriotic script is bolstered by charisma of the two energetic stars and some fine musical numbers, including Garland's powerful "After You've Gone," "Ballin' the Jack" (which features some nifty dancing), and the cheerful title song. Directed with surprising restraint by Busby Berkeley. Produced by Arthur Freed. Also with: George Murphy, Ben Blue, Horace (Stephen) McNally, Richard Quine, Keenan Wynn, Marta Eggerth.

FOR YOUR EYES ONLY (BRITISH/1981)
C/127m.   A ship goes down off Greece carrying a device needed to launch nuclear missiles from British subs. Roger Moore's James Bond is ordered on the scene. He teams up with lovely marine archeologist Carole Bouquet (who reminds me of Claudine Auger from *Thunderball*), whose parents were ordered killed by Greek villain Julian Glover, who's working with the Russians. He's passing himself off as the sponsor of young ice skater Lynn-Holly Johnson (who's too wholesome to be in a Bond movie). Moore and Bouquet find adventure underwater and high in the mountains. There are exciting moments, but most of it is familiar Bond fare. Picture is an attempt to mix spectacle with tough, believable storylines of early Bond films. Moore does a good job, coming through as a convincing action hero for a change. The film itself is great in comparison to the previous Bond film, *Moonraker*, and is enjoyable while you're watching it. Afterward, it's one of the most forgettable of the Bond series. In fact, the title sequence in which Sheena Easton sings the hit title song while standing nude in water is the picture's most memorable scene. Bernard Lee, who had played "M" since *Dr. No*, died before filming began. John Glen directed, Albert R. Broccoli produced, Richard Maibaum and Michael Wilson adapted two Ian Fleming stories. Also with: Topol, Cassandra Harris, Jill Bennett, Michael Gothard, Desmond Llewellyn, Lois Maxwell.

FORBIDDEN GAMES (FRENCH/1951) B&W/
87m.   Anti-war classic from novel by François Boyer; it took director-writer René Clément five years to get financing for his depressing, controversial project. In the horrifying, unforgettable opening scene a five-year-old girl (who is as cute as they come) is orphaned when Parisian family flees Paris on a country road in 1940. She wanders off the main road carrying her dead puppy and is taken in by an ignorant farming family. She becomes very attached to their lonely 11-year-old boy and, while the adults are busy feuding with neighbors, they become obsessed with secretly creating an animal/insect cemetery, for which the boy (to impress the girl) steals crosses from the church and graveyard. When the adults find out about the thievery, the boy has hell to pay. I've never been able to figure out the significance of the children's death-burial-prayer fascination; perhaps it's their way of minimalizing the cruelty and finality of death that is all around them as war ravages on. Perhaps the kids' acts are—for Clément—mocking Christianity, which allows wars because death, followed by burial and prayer, is only a transitional stage to a happy afterlife. What is clear

is that adults habitually are at odds with one another—be they enemies in war or jealous neighbors—while children can form unique bond as defense from adults. Regrettably, adults don't remember their own childhoods and are insensitive to importance of bond to the kids. These peasants may be Christians, but they have no compassion or understanding. When the terrified little girl is separated from the boy to be sent to an orphanage, it is one of the most heartbreaking moments in film history. With: Brigitte Fossey, Georges Poujouly, Lucien Hubert.

FORBIDDEN PLANET (1956) C/98m.   Several
science-fiction films of the fifties are more intelligent, clever, suspenseful, economical, original, witty, etc. But none was more influential than this seminal work, the only SF movie of the period to succeed in giving the genre a long-denied tag of respectability within the industry. It represented the first time a major studio (M-G-M) released an SF film that was meant to be a top-of-the-line production; the first time a large budget (over $1 million) was invested on an SF story (written by Irving Block and Allen Adler) that had been conceived expressly as a film project; and the first SF film to be made in glorious color and CinemaScope, which had as much to do with impressing the young viewers of 1956 (the film's cultists today) as the A. Arnold Gillespie-supervised special effects (including the Id Monster, Robby the Robot, and spaceship miniatures), the marvelous design of Altair-IV and the Krell underground chambers by Cedric Gibbons and Arthur Lonergan, and the electronic music by Louis and Bebe Barron. The story is based on Shakespeare's *The Tempest*. In 2200 A.D., United Planets cruiser C-57D, carrying an all-male crew under the supervision of Commander Adams (Leslie Nielsen), lands on Altair-IV, a planet with pink sand, a green sky, and two moons. Their mission is to discover what became of an earth colony established 20 years before. The only survivors are the genius scientist Dr. Morbius (Walter Pidgeon) and his lovely 18-year-old daughter, Alta (Anne Francis), who has never seen a man other than her father. Her one companion is Robby the Robot, a "surrogate mother-cook-housekeeper." When she and Adams become attracted to one another, Morbius becomes jealous. Having worked with a brain-boosting machine left by the extinct Krell, he conjures up an (invisible) Id Monster which starts killing off the visitors just as it killed the other colonists years before. Film owes a nod to *King Kong*. Altair-IV is Morbius's psychological terrain, just as Skull Island was Carl Denham's; whereas Kong was the manifestation of Denham's sublimated sexual urges toward Ann Darrow and was used as his surrogate to chase away other men, Morbius (who harbors incestuous feelings) conjures up the Id Monster to keep his daughter for himself. Picture certainly has an interesting, intelligent premise, but Cyril Hume wrote a very trite, juvenile script, in which the Freudian-incestuous elements are toned down so that we never understand the exact nature of the rivalry between Adams and Morbius for Alta. Direction by Fred Wilcox lacks excitement, the acting is stiff, and the crew-cutted,

always snickering, obedient, white, WASPish soldiers are more fitting for the dull Eisenhower Era than the 23rd century. How can Adams be a near-genius and not know what *id* means? How can Morbius be so scholarly and have such an ignorant (and lazy) daughter? Why doesn't he punch out Doc (Warren Stevens) for his supposedly flattering remarks about his daughter? Why does the Id Monster sabotage the ship when Morbius wants the crew to leave the planet? The worst mistake is having Robby (who has amazing powers) relegated to comic relief. Later it joins Adams and Alta as *observers* during the climactic Id vs. Morbius scene, when all three should be at the center of the action. Also with: Jack Kelly, Richard Anderson, Earl Holliman, James Drury.

FORCE OF EVIL (1948) B&W/78m.

Underground classic was the only film directed by Marxist screenwriter-director Abraham Polonsky prior to his blacklisting in Hollywood for being an "uncooperative" witness in front of HUAC in 1951. Polonsky presents an ugly, cynical view ("I was born dead," says hero John Garfield) of our capitalistic, money-and-power-oriented society, where even "decent" people (like lawyer Garfield and his older brother, Thomas Gomez, a small-time numbers operator) are so trapped and poisoned by the system that they resign themselves to making a living in crime; where there is little, if any, distinction between crime and business, law enforcers and gangsters, and what is legal and illegal. Garfield, whose ambition is to become rich, takes part in a money-making scheme with gangster Roy Roberts, involving the absorption of all small rackets into a big operation which could then be turned into a profitable legitimate business. However, this means that Gomez's operation is swallowed up by Roberts. This upsets Gomez, who has deceived himself into thinking he's running a benevolent, community-oriented business—although he's taking the poor's few dollars. Then Gomez is set up for a hit by a gangster (Sheldon Leonard) who wants to move into the numbers racket. Garfield comes to realize that you can't deal with gangsters and not become corrupt yourself. Surprisingly, Polonsky's "autopsy on capitalism" (as he called Ira Wolfert's source novel, *Tucker's People*) merely touches on some basic Marxist thought: characters are products of their environment; conflict results from the interaction of different classes; capitalism breeds decadence (courthouses are filthy, money is exchanged in the slums without those who live there getting their share). While it makes one aware of the economic shame of the cities—the rich get richer by exploiting the poor, the only jobs for the poor are in crime and involve further exploitation of their class—Polonsky shies away from making a real plea for social change or suggesting how group (class) action could change the capitalist power structure. Instead Polonsky conventionally concentrates on the individual and advances the common Hollywood theme "Don't sell out." Worst of all is that he would have Garfield become an informer. Moodily scored by David Raksin and strikingly photographed by George Barnes so that the characters seem dominated by their surroundings, this is the darkest, seediest, most claustrophobic

entry in *films noir*. It also has the most rhythmic, believable "city street" dialogue found in any Hollywood film, and a great performance by Garfield as one of his few educated characters. Also with: Beatrice Pearson (who becomes Garfield's girlfriend), Marie Windsor, Howland Chamberlin.

FORCE OF ONE, A (1979) C/90m.

Pretty good Chuck Norris vehicle is much like a typical television police series, only it has some well-done karate fights to heighten the action. With a masked karate killer on the loose murdering cops who are investigating drug trafficking, policewoman Jennifer O'Neill (who's topbilled) asks karate champ Norris to give special instruction to the narcotics force. Although he's preparing for a major bout with a vicious challenger (Bill Wallace), he takes the time to help out. When his adopted son (Eric Laneuville)—interestingly, it's *never* mentioned he's black—is killed, Norris says the villain is as good as dead. And he's right. There's a strong supporting cast, Paul Aaron's direction is impressive (particularly during action sequences), and Norris's karate exhibitions make up for the fact that he can't act a lick in this film. Also with: Ron O'Neal, James Whitmore, Jr., Clint Ritchie, Charles Cyphers.

FOREIGN CORRESPONDENT (1940) B&W/120m.

Often neglected spy thriller by Alfred Hitchcock. Joel McCrea's a carefree, politically naïve crime reporter whose editor (Harry Davenport) sends him to Europe in 1939 to see if there's about to be a world war. He discovers a plot by the Nazis to kidnap a Dutch diplomat (Albert Basserman) who is trying to assure peace. A lookalike for Basserman is killed and no one believes McCrea when he says the real Basserman is alive. Finally he gets help from Laraine Day, the daughter of the head of a British peace organization trying to get the British to think of *peace* (Herbert Marshall is, naturally, a Nazi spy). Film is a little too long and a bit muddled, but it has several memorable sequences, including the assassin escaping through a mass of people holding umbrellas; McCrea noticing that windmills are turning against the wind; a plane, with McCrea, Day, Marshall, and reporter George Sanders aboard, crashing into the ocean (the crash itself is a remarkably convincing shot) and filling up with water. McCrea's an affable hero and, although many critics don't agree, I find Day quite appealing. Patriotic script was written by Charles Bennett (his last film for Hitchcock), Joan Harrison, and Hitchcock (uncredited), with dialogue by James Hilton and Robert Benchley. Photographed by Rudolph Maté. Produced by Walter Wanger. Also with: Benchley, Eduardo Ciannelli, Edmund Gwenn, Martin Kosleck, Barbara Pepper.

FORT APACHE (1948) B&W/127m.

The first in John Ford's classic cavalry trilogy, to be followed by *She Wore a Yellow Ribbon* in 1949 and *Rio Grande* in 1950. Henry Fonda is a strict, humorless lieutenant colonel from the East who is unhappy to be assigned the command of an isolated fort in the West. He hopes that by forcing the Apaches to return to their reservation he will impress the army brass and get a better post. The cavalry vets immediately recognize that he hasn't the ability or savvy to deal with the Indians, whom he underestimates considerably. He angers men with his haughty disciplinarian attitude, he angers young officer John Agar by ordering him to stay away from his daughter (Shirley Temple in her best grownup performance), he angers Captain John Wayne by breaking Wayne's word to the Apaches. We expect him to see the light eventually, but instead he disregards Wayne's advice and leads his men into ambush, where they are all killed. The first half of the film deals with life at an army outpost. The Indians appear exactly one hour into the film. There is a bloodless skirmish and the final battle, which comes with about 10 minutes left in the film: I mention this because the oddest aspect of this cavalry-and-Indian film is that the cavalrymen, to whom this film is a tribute, manage to kill *no* Indians while their own losses are considerable. Ford's intention was to emphasize that bad officers like Fonda were often written up as heroes while the anonymous men who fought and died following bad orders were the brave ones deserving recognition. While Ford expresses the necessity that soldiers passively follow orders, he is more interested in presenting a singular environment in which every man (the commander of the fort; the sergeants working with recruits; Ward Bond, as master of his own house) pulls rank so that their wills are carried out. Picture is beautifully photographed by Archie Stout, but the scene in which the Indians chase a wagon shows that even Ford can forget where to position his camera: the wagon goes from right to left across the screen; the Indians giving chase are shown riding left to right (as if headed in the opposite direction); the cavalry charges in from left to right also, but instead of being at the Indians' rear, they meet them head on. He makes up for this confusion with the miraculously staged Indian charge in the massacre sequence. Ford detractors won't like his sentiment, Irish humor, chaste romance, and musical interludes, but if you're a Ford fan you'll love it all and be inexplicably choked up by such things as Bond smiling as he dances with Temple, the cavalry singing as they ride off, and the wives and lovers watching solemnly as their men disappear into the sunset. Screenwriter Frank S. Nugent adapted "Massacre" by James Warner Bellah. Also with: George O'Brien, Victor McLaglen, Pedro Armendariz, Anna Lee, Irene Rich, Guy Kibbee, Grant Withers, Miguel Inclan (as Cochise), Jack Pennick, Mae Marsh, Dick Foran, Frank Ferguson, Francis Ford.

FORTUNE COOKIE, THE (1966) B&W/125m.
While standing on the sidelines during a game, cameraman Jack Lemmon is knocked over backward by a football player. His shyster-lawyer brother-in-law, Walter Matthau (as Whiplash Willie), convinces him to exaggerate his injuries so they can sue. The lawyers representing the parties being sued hire detectives to spy on Lemmon to make sure that he really is suffering. While Matthau works behind the scenes to get a $500,000 settlement, Lemmon dutifully wears a neck brace and confines himself to bed and a wheelchair. Matthau's conniving, coldhearted performance is the reason to watch this otherwise unfunny Billy Wilder comedy. He's the type of guy you want to take on big insurance firms and their high-priced lawyers. This is the first of the Wilder films that had Matthau's character aggravating Lemmon's, but Lemmon is so restricted in movement that he can't properly express his aggravation. Scenes with the upset black football player (Ron Rich) are pretentious and superfluous. Wilder collaborated with I. A. L. Diamond on the script, which has a mean edge to it. Also with: Lurene Tuttle, Cliff Osmond, Judi West.

48 HRS. (1982) C/97m.
Racist San Francisco detective Nick Nolte springs black thief-conman Eddie Murphy (his debut) from prison for 48 hours to help track down Murphy's former partner, a sadistic criminal (James Remar) who just escaped from prison. It's almost as if Rod Steiger and Sidney Poitier from *In the Heat of the Night* became partners without resolving their differences or hiding their hatred for one another. Their "hip" verbal battles are continuous (and eventually annoying) and they even come to blows. But, of course, since both are misfits with singular talents, they learn to respect one another. Brawny Nolte and skinny Murphy work well together, but Roger Spottiswoode's dialogue is too calculated for audience response, particularly laughter. The film's supposed comic highlight—Murphy taking over a redneck bar—is embarrassing (compare it to similar scene in *Destry Rides Again*) because it's in the wrong movie. Best sequences are those with violence and action—director Walter Hill probably spent time running Don Siegel films like *Mudigan, Coogan's Bluff*, and *Dirty Harry*. Annette O'Toole is completely wasted as Nolte's girlfriend—we wisely but wrongly expect Remar to threaten her eventually. Also with: Frank McRae, David Patrick Kelly, Sonny Landham, the Busboys (singing the rousing "The Boys Are Back in Town").

42ND STREET (1933) B&W/98m.
The best of Warner Bros. thirties musicals, with wonderfully wild and innovative choreography by Busby Berkeley; strong, snappy direction by Lloyd Bacon; an enjoyable, well-written putting-on-a-show plot in the *Broadway Melody* tradition; a realistic glimpse of life in the musical theater; some social consciousness that other studios' musicals lacked during the Depression; and a particularly fine cast. Broke, sick stage director Julian Marsh (Warner Baxter) counts on the success of his new musical to give him security when he retires. He worries that his high-strung leading lady, Dorothy Brock (Bebe Daniels), will upset the show's producer (Guy Kibbee) by revealing she loves not him but a young stockbroker (George Brent). On the night before the show is to open, Dorothy turns her ankle. Young Peggy Sawyer (Ruby Keeler), a chorus girl who has never been in a Broadway play, takes over the lead. Nervous Peggy gets encouragement from her rosy-cheeked beau, juvenile lead Billy Lawler (Dick Powell), Dorothy, and Marsh, who says that famous

line, "Sawyer, you're going out a youngster, but you've got to come back a star!" In *Gold Diggers of 1933* it becomes a foregone conclusion that the performers in the show will end up with rich men and the play will go on; *Footlight Parade*, also made in 1933, may have better production numbers and a dynamic performance by James Cagney as a producer who is trying to turn a profit, but we don't really worry about his performers trying to make ends meet. This film is strongest because we root for the lead singers and dancers, the crew, and particularly the chorines (who have to put up with selfish slavedriver Marsh), whom we see in numerous montages working endlessly, desperately driving themselves past tears and exhaustion, their faces revealing that the show's success means their survival. Film has elements of camp, but it has unmatched vitality, a strong sense of unity among its characters, and a great deal of honesty. Picture ends with a bang: the "42nd Street" production number is too elaborate ever to be performed on a real stage, with sections filmed from above, women used as props to form geometric patterns, close-ups, dollies, pans, and an ending in which Berkeley thrusts his camera forward between the spread legs of numerous chorines who stand on a revolving stage. Astaire seduced Rogers with dancing; Berkeley's less subtle camera seems to perform the sexual act. From a novel by Bradford Ropes. Music by Al Dubin and Harry Warren (who play songwriters). Also with: Una Merkel, Ned Sparks, Ginger Rogers (as "Anytime Annie"), Allen Jenkins, Henry B. Walthall, George E. Stone.

FOUR FRIENDS (1981) C/115m. A look at America through the eyes of a young Yugoslavian immigrant (Craig Wasson) who comes to East Chicago, Indiana, as a young boy, and whose life takes many drastic turns in tumultuous sixties. The only constants through the years are his need for fatherly approval and the mutual love between him and his two high school chums (Jim Metzler, Michael Huddleston) and the girl all three love, Georgia (Jodi Thelen). The relationship between the passive guys and the unpredictable girl whom they treat like a queen recalls *Jules and Jim*. In the America we see, everyone's life has epic proportions; hopes and dreams result in bitter disappointment, but sadness and pain are tempered by rewarding friendships; throughout, one's love for America never dissipates. This would make a good double feature with *Moscow on the Hudson*. Arthur Penn's film has the makings of a masterpiece; but while it contains many lovely moments and devastating scenes, a few important sequences fail. Moreover, although they are talented, you don't really care if Wasson and Thelen get together. Thelen's characterization is more annoying than captivating—too bad Rosanna Arquette wasn't around in 1981. Excellent autobiographical script by Steve Tesich (*Breaking Away*). Better the second time around. Also with: Reed Birney.

400 BLOWS, THE (FRENCH/1959) B&W/99m. Extraordinary debut by François Truffaut was one of the major early films of France's New Wave. Powerful, semi-autobiographical film about a young boy, Antoine Doinel (Jean-Pierre Léaud), who has everything stacked against him. At home, his bickering parents usually make him feel unloved, unwanted, and a failure; his harsh mother's last words to him each night are "Take out the garbage." At school, teachers pick on and punish him—usually because of the homework he didn't do because of his troubled home life. He's a good boy, well-meaning, imaginative, and sweet, but he has lost all trust in and respect for adults—with good reason—and keeps getting in trouble as if that's the only way to make an impact on them. He fibs, steals little things, plays hookey, accidentally sets a small fire, runs away, is wrongly accused of plagiarism. He never gets away with anything. Adults make feeble attempts to find out the source of his problems—probably because deep down they realize they are responsible. In Truffaut's world there is a wide generation gap, and it's the children who are victimized by it. Tender look at children with universal message has much wit, but boy's plight is extremely sad; the famous last shot, a freeze frame of the runaway with nowhere to run, indicates the hopelessness of his situation. On the other hand, Truffaut realizes a child's resilience and ability to stand pain and rejection. He must bring himself up. Antoine manages to find shortcuts to happiness by going to the movies (as Truffaut did) and romping through the Paris streets with his loyal friend, a rich kid whose parents ignore him, too. Film has beautiful camera work, including lengthy, loving shots of all sections of Paris. Classic moments include fascinating improvisation scene in which Léaud answers the questions of psychologist Jeanne Moreau, who is behind camera (in reality, Truffaut asked the questions); runaway Antoine stands in darkness like scared animal hungrily devouring milk he's just stolen; and little kids with amazingly expressive faces watch puppet show—it's a happy scene, unless we consider that in a few years these tots will suffer what Antoine does. A gem. Léaud, who is marvelous, would reprise Antoine Doinel character (Truffaut's stand-in) as an adult in several pictures. Also with: Patrick Auffray, Claire Maurier, Albert Rémy.

4TH MAN, THE (DUTCH/1983) C/104m. Eerie, erotic, perversely hilarious horror film by Paul Verhoeven. Gerard Reve (Jeroen Krabbé) is a writer living in Amsterdam. He is a homosexual, he is a Catholic—his scandalous writings reflect his preoccupation with and dread of death; his frequent nightmares and horrific daydreams contain Christian symbols, murder scenes, his own castration. While in his neurotic state he travels to Flushing to give a lecture to a literary club. He goes home with the club's beautiful treasurer, Christine (Renee Soutendijk), who operates a hair salon; he thinks back to the painting of Samson and Delilah he saw on the train. Christine is a widow and makes it clear that she'd like Gerard to stay with her permanently. He's ready to leave until he discovers a photo of Christine's young boyfriend, Herman (Thom Hoffman), from Cologne. Gerard had admired Herman in the train station before coming to Flushing. He asks Christine to invite Herman to Flushing so he can advise him on being a better lover to Christine. His real intention is to seduce Herman. While Christine is picking up Herman, Gerard comes across three reels of film. He's flabbergasted to discover that Christine's been widowed three times, and that her young husbands died soon after the marriages from violent accidents (one's parachute didn't open, one was attacked by a lion, the other drowned). Since Christine has been filming him, Gerard worries. He realizes that Christine wants either him or Herman to be her next victim, the fourth man. At least he believes he has the protection of a woman in blue (Geert de Jong) whom he keeps seeing. Poor Herman has no one. Film is mysterious but never complex; from the beginning Verhoeven is blatant with his symbolism. From the correlation Verhoeven draws between Christine and the deadly spider we see in the film's opening shot, we realize she is evil and is aware that men who become her lovers will meet a violent end (just as happens with a female spider). Garishly photographed by Jan de Bont, the entire film (which may remind some of *Don't Look Now*) has a nightmarish quality, wherein we don't know if what we're seeing is imagined or real. Most interestingly: Gerard Reve is the name of the homosexual writer of the source novel. Reve claims to have met a woman named Christine who ran a hair salon in Flushing. Her husband and a male friend had died in car accidents several years before Reve stayed with her and, unlike in the film, was unable to have successful sex with her. After leaving Flushing, Reve learned that Christine's boyfriend lost an eye in an accident—an incident that inspired what happens to Herman. Gerard Soeteman wrote the screenplay, Rob Houmer produced. Also with: Dolf De Vries.

FOXES (1980) C/106m.
A bit slick—at times it seems like director Adrian Lyne is back making commercials (for girls' make-up, girls' clothes, girls' underwear, girls)—but a surprisingly touching film about the friendship among four troubled teenage girls (Jodie Foster, Cherie Currie, Marilyn Kagan, Kandice Stroh) growing up in the San Fernando Valley. Story centers on Foster's concern for irresponsible but sweet Curie (former lead singer of the seminal all-girl rock group, The Runaways), who seems destined for a bad end; and Foster's attempts to have a civil home life with her loving but neurotic mother, played by Sally Kellerman. Story falters at times, but the characters and their situations seem real. Foster is terrific, even when her lines aren't. Several scenes she has with Kellerman, Curie, and excellent Scott Baio (especially their chat in her pickup truck) are memorable and much more meaningful than what we're used to seeing in youth-oriented films. A good soundtrack. Sleeper was ignored or laughed at by many critics. Also with: Randy Quaid, Lois Smith.

FRANKENSTEIN (1931) B&W/71m.
Classic horror film still holds up due to striking, innovative direction by James Whale, who employed bizarre camera angles, high-ceiling sets, imaginative set design (especially in the Baron's lab), and sharp editing to create a remarkably tense atmosphere; excellent acting by Colin Clive, as Baron Henry Frankenstein, and Boris Karloff, as the Monster he creates; and the timelessness of Mary Shelley's morality play. Film has many memorable scenes (Clive and weasly assistant Dwight Frye robbing graves; the Monster coming to life; the Monster trying to make friends with a little girl; the Monster sneaking into the bedroom of Frankenstein's bride, Mae Clark; the peasants chasing the Monster through the woods; the creator finally confronting the Monster in a life-and-death struggle). But what's most interesting is that Whale seems to go along with Shelley's controversial belief that Frankenstein's sin is *not* that he defies God by creating life but that once he becomes a creator he both emulates God and competes with him for sovereignty. In the most revealing moment the Monster spots sunlight flickering into the dark chamber in which his creator imprisons him. Karloff beautifully conveys the recently born being's newfound feelings of warmth and wonderment as, with a half-smile, he shuffles directly under the light. Suddenly Frankenstein blocks out the light, jealously refusing his creature any knowledge (symbolized by sunlight) that he didn't offer himself, as well as any contact with the god who sent his sun ray. Frankenstein's real crimes are against society. He has withdrawn into self-imposed isolation (itself a perversion) and become an elitist, while the Monster seeks love, companionship, and camaraderie with the masses. Even worse is how Frankenstein neglects his fatherly obligations and abandons his "son," leaving the creature to make its way in a world repulsed by grotesquery. Consequently, the Monster-child ends up murdering everyone who rejects him. Clive and Karloff would return for Whale's 1935 sequel, *Bride of Frankenstein*. Also with: John Boles, Edward Van Sloan, Frederick Kerr, Lionel Belmore.

FREAKS (1932) B&W/64m.
Tod Browning's legendary, once banned horror film, featuring sideshow freaks like the ones he knew when he was with the circus. While watching the freaks, viewers will feel not only fear, curiosity, and pity but also warmth, respect, and amazement. We soon feel comfortable in their presence and admire how well they function despite their handicaps, and that they have pride. Freaks without hands eat with their feet, those without legs walk with their hands, and even Randian, who has neither arms nor legs, can light his own cigar. Browning's point is that people needn't pay to see them just because they're *different*—with the exception of the pinheads, they are *talented* show people. They can "act" in front of the camera, and some, like the Hilton Siamese Twins, even display a quirky sense of humor. The film is about how freaks will band together when one of their own is humiliated. Midget Hans (Harry Earles) is played for a fool by a gold-digging "normal" trapeze artist, Cleopatra (Olga Baclanova), who marries him for his money and then flaunts her love for muscleman Hercules (Henry Victor). The freaks exact drastic revenge—turning her into "the feathered hen." The scene of the freaks crawling after Cleopatra through

the mud with knives in their mouths is one of the scariest sights in cinema history. It's not objectionable that the freaks are portrayed as *monsters* here because that's how the "normal" victims see them. Cleopatra's mistake was treating a small man as a child—these freaks are adults with a familial code worthy of gangsters. It is because of the freaks that the film has had so much trouble with censors, but there is no film from the period that has more sexual innuendo. The relationship between two normal people, the very sexy Venus (Leila Hyaams) and Phroso (Wallace Ford), is most peculiar. "You're a pretty good kid," she tells him; he agrees, adding the unexplained line, "And you should have caught me before the operation." We don't know what went on when Venus shared Hercules's trailer, but Hercules's relationship with Cleopatra is not at all subtle. Even the Hiltons take part in the suggestive humor. Oddly, Browning doesn't exploit the sexual possibilities of Joseph-Josephine, the half-woman, half-man. Prints in distribution have at least three different endings. Based on the short story "Spurs" by Tod Robbins. Also with: Roscoe Ates, Daisy Earles (as Hans's rejected midget fiancée), Rose Dione, Edward Brophy, Matt McHugh, Louise Beavers.

FREE WOMAN, A/SUMMER LIGHTNING (WEST GERMAN/1972) C/100m.

One of the first major films to come out of the women's liberation movement. Seriocomedy was scripted by Volker Schlöndorff and his wife, Margarethe von Trotta. He directed and she starred as Elisabeth, who divorces her husband but discovers that being unmarried in a male-dominated world does not mean she is "free." Elisabeth finds her options limited as to where she can work and, because of her low earnings, where she can live. It is a world where sexist men not only define women, but pass judgment on them: as a mother who left her husband, she is regarded as an unsuitable guardian. Like Von Trotta's character, the film never really breaks loose. To make Elisabeth's experience seem believable, Schlöndorff and Von Trotta have given her modest goals. But her failures don't seem consequential enough because she doesn't make much progress before she gives up. That she would consider a second marriage makes sense, but perhaps Schlöndorff and Von Trotta might have implied that single mothers needn't all be so defeatist. Photographed by Sven Nykvist. Edited by Suzanne Baron. Also with: Martin Luttge, Walter Sedlmayer, Georg Marishka.

FRENCH CONNECTION, THE (1971) C/104m.

William Friedkin directed this Best Picture winner, a police thriller showing how a band of brutal, vulgar, nattily dressed New York street cops outfox the civil, rich, well-educated international criminals who are trying to smuggle in an enormous shipment of heroin. Friedkin makes great use of sight and sounds of New York, wisely chosen locations, hand-held cameras, and natural light to give authenticity to this true story, which Ernest Tidyman adapted from Robin Moore's book. Scenes shot in France, using French subtitles, give the film class, rather than coming across as pretentious—the film looks as if it had been shot by a European. Cops are brave, but those like Jimmy "Popeye" Doyle (Gene Hackman) are too obsessive and sadistic to be considered heroes. As such, they make unique protagonists in the American cinema. We're glad they're tough enough for the dangerous job of narcotics investigators, but we wouldn't want to cross the paths of these thugs. They're shnooks who'll put themselves on the line, but don't get many rewards. Unless they kill the villains, the drug traffickers will most likely get minor sentences for tremendous crimes. Film has ironic humor, strong violence, many exciting sequences. The most famous has Popeye racing his car after a bad guy on a subway—it's like a terrific short film. Editor Jerry Greenberg deserved the Oscar he won. Friedkin, Hackman, and Tidyman also won Oscars. Roy Scheider, as Hackman's partner, was nominated for supporting actor and Owen Roizman for cinematography. Hackman returned in *The French Connection II*. Also with: Fernando Rey, Tony Lo Bianco.

FRESHMAN, THE (1925) B&W/70m.

Harold Lloyd usually played cheery characters who wouldn't be denied success at whatever it is they want. In Lloyd's silent masterpiece he desperately tries to be the most popular man on campus. By displaying silly jig and sly handshake to introduce himself, telling everyone to call him "Speedy," using his entire savings to buy his classmates ice cream, throwing a lavish dance party, and acting as "tackling dummy" to make the football team (he doesn't know he's just the water boy), he hopes to win approval. But, as his sweet girlfriend (Jobyna Ralston) discovers, he is considered the college boob. When he finds out that he's been playing the fool, he's crushed. But Lloyd's characters don't stay down for long. Urged by his girl to be himself, Lloyd is determined to be the star of the big game. How he accomplishes this makes for one of Lloyd's most hilarious sequences. However, the entire film is filled with great comedy. Most noteworthy is the party during which Lloyd wears a hastily sewn tux which unravels a piece at a time—that's why he brings his tailor along. Funniest scene has Lloyd sitting at table calmly conversing with a woman—camera cuts to side view that shows Lloyd's body is contorted so both legs go behind him and through curtain, where tailor sews pants legs back together. Other gags also remind me of Buster Keaton (i.e., in *The Navigator* when, in a diving suit, Keaton allows his girlfriend to use him as a rubber raft). In fact, film is ideal to be on double bill with Keaton's *College*. Directed by Sam Taylor and Fred Newmeyer. Also with: Brooks Benedict, James Anderson.

FRIDAY THE 13TH (1980) C/95m.

First of series that has become an American institution. Group of counselors—mostly good-looking airheads—arrive at deserted Camp Crystal Lake to make things shipshape before it reopens. It has been closed for many years, since a young boy named Jason was drowned while counselors were fooling around. During course of day and night, new counselors have hot and heavy sex with each other and soon after are brutally killed—in truly gruesome ways—by an unknown assailant who is sneaking around the camp. Critics Siskel and Ebert used clips of this film to show proliferation of violence committed by men on sexy young girls—but, as all horror fans know, the killer turns out to be Jason's crazy mother, Mrs. Voorhees, played by former television panelist Betsy Palmer, looking muscular and intimidating here. Supposedly she got the part because she was able to provide her own transportation. Her dramatic battle with the last survivor, gutsy Adrienne King—the one counselor worth her salt—is strong stuff. In fact, the film is skillfully enough made by director Sean Cunningham that you'll be scared out of your wits waiting for each counselor to meet his or her ghastly end. The only thing to question is your own reason for sitting through entertainment with gratuitous sex and violence and teenagers who are portrayed as oversexed, insensitive clowns ideal for slaughter. Low-budget film is successful mix of bloody horror and youth-sex genres, so it's no surprise it made a fortune. Cheat ending, lifted from De Palma, led way to many sequels featuring Jason. Also with: Harry Crosby, Laurie Bartram, Mark Nelson, Jeannine Taylor.

FRITZ THE CAT (1972) C/78m.
X-rated cartoon by Ralph Bakshi hit a responsive chord with hip counterculture audiences of the early seventies. I think it ambitious and cleverly animated but extremely dull, especially the beginning. It's annoying that the characters whom Fritz meets as he travels through the sixties youth scene, evolving from New York street singer to a member of the radical underground, are stupid, hypocritical, cruel, sex-obsessed, politically naïve. Film is a downer for those who romanticize about that era. There's much sexual and violent imagery. Based on Robert Crumb's underground comic-book character. I didn't like the comic books any better.

FROM HERE TO ETERNITY (1953) B&W/118m.
Solid version of James Jones's novel, set in U.S. army barracks on Hawaii in 1941, prior to Pearl Harbor. Burt Lancaster is a sergeant ("I hate officers") who is having an affair with his superior officer's wife, Deborah Kerr. Montgomery Clift is the sensitive career soldier who resists pressure from platoon officers to have him box in an upcoming tournament. He falls in love with dark-haired prostitute Donna Reed. Also in the platoon is Frank Sinatra, who can't keep his high spirits under control and earns the wrath of tough Ernest Borgnine. Appeal of the film is that Lancaster, Clift, Sinatra, Kerr, and Reed all anticipate the rebel figures that would dominate the rest of the fifties. They break army rules and society's rules. They are the only characters with compassion, who can love—so here rebels are *positive* figures. Picture has superb acting, strong direction by Fred Zinnemann. Film's most famous scene has Lancaster and Kerr kissing while lying in the surf. Even more titillating is how Kerr (watch her eyes) strips to her bathing suit before they go into the water. Oscars: Best Picture, Best Director, Best Supporting Actor (Sinatra, in his first straight role), Best Supporting Actress (Reed), Best Adapted Screenplay (Daniel Taradash), Best Cinematography (Burnett Guffey). Also with: Philip Ober, Claude Akins, Jack Warner, Mickey Shaughnessy, George Reeves.

FROM RUSSIA WITH LOVE (BRITISH/1963) C/118m.
An excellent, surprisingly tough and gritty James Bond film, the second in the series. SPECTRE devises a plan that will result in warfare between the Soviets and the free world. They want to frame British agent James Bond (Sean Connery) for the murder of a Soviet agent (Daniela Bianchi) who has become his lover. Actually, a dead assassin (Robert Shaw) intends to kill them both. Film is refreshingly free of the gimmickry that would characterize the later Bond films, and Connery and Bianchi play *real* people. We worry about them and hope their relationship will work out. Shaw and Lotte Lenya (as the diabolical Krebb) are splendid villains. Both have exciting, well-choreographed fights with Connery. Actors play it straight, with excellent results. The lovely Bianchi should have been a bigger star—she's one of the most appealing of the Bond heroines. Solid direction by Terence Young, who handled the train sequence especially well. Ian Fleming's novel was adapted by Richard Maibaum and Johanna Harwood. Peter Hunt edited, John Barry provided the music, Ted Moore was the cinematographer. Also with: Pedro Armendariz, Eunice Gayson, Anthony Dawson, Martine Beswick, Bernard Lee, Lois Maxwell, Desmond Llewellyn.

FRONT, THE (1976) C/94m.
Woody Allen neither wrote nor directed this excellent, often forgotten little picture—those chores were handled by Walter Bernstein and Martin Ritt, respectively—but Allen was an inspired choice to play Howard Price, a New York restaurant cashier who becomes a front for three blacklisted writers in the early fifties. The writers churn out television scripts; Howard sells them to the network that hired him, and he splits the money with the real authors. Howard's a nice guy but apolitical, so he pays no attention to a government investigation being done to root out "communists" in television, including Zero Mostel's likable comic Hecky Greene, Howard's pal. However, Howard gets called before the committee and will go to jail unless he gives names of suspected communists. He comes to realize that even naming dead people to save himself is justifying the existence of the committee. Picture is humbly, gently, humorously made—much ironic humor comes from the absurdity of the situation, where a man can be blacklisted if the committee gets his name mixed up with that of a "leftist sympathizer" and he can't clear himself unless he can name names. Despite the film's friendly tone, viewers get a sense of the paranoia, desperation, and insanity of the period, and come to understand why those who were blacklisted—like Bernstein and Ritt and actors Mostel, Herschel Bernardi, Joshua Shelley, and Lloyd Gough—still detest those who gave testimony during the fifties witchhunt. Film is a tribute to those who took moral stands during that

time—men like Howard Price. Also with: Andrea Marcovicci, Michael Murphy, Remak Ramsey, Danny Aiello.

FUNNY THING HAPPENED ON THE WAY TO THE FORUM, A (1966) C/99m.

Spirited, tremendously underrated musical comedy by director Richard Lester and writers Melvin Frank and Michael Perturee, taken from the Broadway hit by Burt Shevelove and Larry Gelbart, with songs by Stephen Sondheim. (The original source was a play by Plautus, who lived in ancient Rome.) Lester's wild cutting and frantic camera work (handled by Nicolas Roeg) sets the anarchical tone for the slam-bang mix of slapstick, satire, burlesque-vaudeville, farce, and absurd humor. Not all the gags work and the pacing falters on occasion, but there are a surprising number of hilarious moments. You can't beat watching vets Zero Mostel (as a clever slave who's trying to win his freedom), his real-life best friend, Jack Gilford, Buster Keaton (rescued from beach pictures by Lester, a great admirer), Phil Silvers, and Michael Hordern really put on a show. Lester captures period flavor and finds *Wizard of Id*-like humor in the brutality the strong and powerful dish out and the weak and powerless endure—much as he would in *The Three Musketeers*. Funny scenes include: Gilford pretending to be the corpse of a virgin girl who'd been promised to conceited, cruel soldier Leon Greene (a funny performance); two gladiators practicing their "braining" technique on live targets; and a soldier reacting to a drink of wine that turns out to be horse urine. Much funnier than *Monty Python's The Life of Brian*. Also with: Michael Crawford, Annette Andre, Patricia Jessel, Roy Kinnear, Alfie Bass.

FURY (1936) B&W/90m—94m.

Frightening social drama was Fritz Lang's first American film. Spencer Tracy's an average Joe; in fact, his name is Joe Wilson. While driving through a strange town, he's arrested for kidnapping a young girl. He's innocent, but the townspeople figure that circumstantial evidence proves his guilt. They set fire to the jail. Tracy isn't killed, just badly burned; he escapes, and no one knows he is alive. Meanwhile his innocence is proved, and those in the mob are tried for his murder. Once a nice guy, Tracy is hell-bent on vengeance—he wants the men to be executed. Film gave Lang the opportunity to advance several of his most important themes: it is unsafe to be a stranger in this world—people are very territorial; when townspeople band together they may turn into a mob; a man's innocence or guilt is not what determines how jury or a mob will judge him; there is no such thing as justice—a hero who seeks revenge and continues the violence initiated by the villains becomes as bad as they, because to play on their terms he relinquishes his humanity. Ending is disappointing—Lang was forced by the studio to make Tracy forgive those who did him wrong. Still, it's one of the strongest indictments of America's small-town lynch-mob mentality. Music by Franz Waxman. Produced by Joseph L. Mankiewicz. Also with: Sylvia Sidney (as Joe's girlfriend, who rejects him when he turns mean), Walter Abel (as the persuasive D.A.), Bruce Cabot, Edward Ellis, Walter Brennan, Frank Albertson, George Chandler, Jonathan Hale.

FURY, THE (1978) C/118m.

Girl (Amy Irving) with amazing psychic powers goes to special facility for testing, hoping her tendency to cause bleeding in those who touch her can be controlled. She begins to communicate with a former resident (Andrew Stevens) and realizes that she's a prisoner whom John Cassavetes hopes to use for his evil purposes in world politics. Elsewhere, Cassavetes has adult Fiona Lewis engage in sexual activities with young Stevens so that he'll also do his bidding. But Stevens starts to go insane from jealousy. Meanwhile Kirk Douglas attempts to rescue his son, Stevens, and Irving. Stupid, complicated, unforgivably bloody Brian De Palma film, scripted by John Farris (from his novel). There are too many characters, the acting is mostly wretched, the dialogue's a joke, the picture has no ending (Irving still has no control over her powers), and—except for a couple of times when the background around Irving impressively changes to reveal what she's thinking—the direction is terrible. De Palma uses slow motion too often, and he has a tendency to circle his camera around tables where characters have conversations, calling attention to rather than disguising the banality of the chatter (the improvisatory scene in which Irving and Carrie Snodgress eat ice cream is an embarrassment). Of course, the most objectionable thing about this film is the extreme violence (with emphasis on blood spattering in all directions). The scene in which Stevens wills Lewis into the air and spins her round and round as blood flies out of her bursting veins and orifices is one of the most offensive moments in film history. It's as if she were on a torture machine. When I saw this in a theater, some pervert went into paroxyms of ecstasy, shaking his body and laughing hysterically until she was dead. It's scary that this film made money. Also with: Charles Durning, Rutanya Alda, Daryl Hannah (a bit as a schoolgirl), Gordon Jump.

GAL YOUNG 'UN (1979) C/105m.

Absorbing low-budget independent film is set in backwoods Florida in the twenties. Dana Preu is a lonely, plain, middle-aged widow. She falls for the sweet talkin' of cocky young hustler David Peck, who wants her money to build a still. They marry and Peck stops being considerate. He uses her farmhouse for his moonshine operation. He runs around with other women. And the film becomes really interesting when he brings home a young woman (J. Smith) to live with them. Preu endures the humiliation and just bides her time for revenge. Although Preu treats Smith hostilely, it's apparent that an affinity develops between the two women, since naïve, vulnerable, neglected Smith has been just as exploited by Peck as Preu has been. What's impressive is how so much of what the two women are feeling is conveyed by their eyes and expressions and how they hug Preu's cat rather than by words (which is essential since these women aren't the type to gab). Poignant yet unsentimental film was directed by Victor Nuñez. Filmed on location, it's from a story by Marjorie Kinnan Rawlings. Also with: Jenny Stringfellow, Gene Desmore, Tim McCormick.

GALAXINA (1980) C/95m.   The ill-fated Dorothy Stratten moved from *Playboy* "Playmate of the Year" into the title role of this insipid, low-budget sci-fi film. She plays a gorgeous robot in the 28th century who flies the spaceship *Infinity*. Captain Butt (Avery Schreiber), Thor (Stephen Macht), and Buzz (James David Hinton) travel through space in search of the precious Blue Star. Thor and Galaxina fall in love and she reprograms herself so that she is human-like—not that her acting style changes. Galaxina is captured by some bad guys. This is a truly boring sci-fi parody (it is also a parody of westerns) with limp humor and uninteresting direction by William Sachs (who also wrote the script). The most offensive scene is set in an outer-space café that has women's heads mounted on walls and such dishes as poached legs on toast and fruit of the womb. Picture has a cult because of Stratten's appearance, but she didn't prove she had talent until boyfriend Peter Bogdanovich's *They All Laughed* was released after her murder.

GALLIPOLI (AUSTRALIAN/1981) C/111m.
Peter Weir's powerful homage to the Australian troops who died senselessly—as the result of indifferent British command—in a battle outside Gallipoli, Turkey, during WWI. Story follows friends Mark Lee and Mel Gibson, both runners, who join the army together. Lee is superpatriotic and believes that it's his duty to "defend" the British crown by fighting in Turkey; Gibson is more skeptical, believing that Australians are being used as cannon fodder by the British. Heartbreaking ending—many viewers complained whole film led viewers on path toward unnecessary depression— proves Gibson correct. It is not the anti-war message that makes this film special—many non-political films are, unbravely, anti-war pieces; nor is it the now familiar depiction of officers as being poor and heartless strategists. What is most striking is how it really expresses Australian hatred for British militarists, who have traditionally considered Australian soldiers inferior to their own men and therefore expendable—at Gallipoli, British troops are saved from action by the sacrifice of Australian men. It is by showing at the end an Australian *runner* not reach the "finish" line that we see how war and, *more* specifically, British and subservient Australian officers have been responsible for the terrible waste of human, Australian, potential. Convincingly acted; exquisitely photographed by Russell Boyd; persuasively written by David Williamson. Also with: Bill Kerr, Robert Grubb, David Argue, Tim McKenzie.

GAME OF DEATH (1979) C/102m.   Bruce Lee's last film, completed six years after his death with the use of doubles (who wear masks in close-up). Director Robert Clouse was able to regroup the other stars and to rework the script so that the Lee footage could fit in properly. Film is messy and too long, but Dean Jagger makes a slimy criminal and the story of a mob being after Lee was interesting because it was rumored to have been case (in fact, at one time it was thought that the Chinese Mafia murdered Lee). Of course, the highlight of the film is the actual Lee taking on a series of villains as he moves from room to room in a great house. At one point he takes on Kareem Abdul-Jabbar—not his best opponent. The fights are okay, but Lee drives me crazy with his repeated *kiais* (fighting yells)—I think Clouse overdubbed. Also with: Hugh O'Brian, Colleen Camp, Chuck Norris.

GANDHI (BRITISH/1982) C/188m.   The man in the loincloth would have been humbled by the epic treatment accorded him by director Richard Attenborough. This is a sweeping, beautiful-looking, impeccably acted biography about the *saintly* (that's how he's presented here) Indian who believed that social change—specifically, the end of British rule in India—could best be achieved by *non-violent* (as opposed to *passive*), provocational resistance. Such resistance would bring the protesters personal dignity and the oppressors shame in the eyes of the world. Probably for commercial reasons, Attenborough chose to overlook some of Gandhi's more controversial political stands—he believed that Indians should support the Japanese against the British during WWII; that the Jews in Europe should use non-violent resistance against Hitler and, therefore, sacrifice themselves to their fate—and this is what keeps the film from being a masterpiece. But there is still so much to appreciate. Attenborough allows Gandhi to state his personal philosophy and objectives throughout the film, risking losing moviegoers who crave action. Interestingly, while there are many impressively directed violent-action sequences, Attenborough didn't make the big mistake of forgetting that his film is about peaceful change. So the bloody violence we see is repulsive—compare this to the exciting and bloody action sequences in, say, *Witness*, which also purports to have a non-violence theme but makes viewers want to jump up on the screen and grab a gun. Whereas Attenborough's *Young Winston* was self-consciously directed from frame one, this time around there are no false notes—the picture is sincere. Attenborough can also be commended for not having Gandhi be the only Indian character who says anything wise or takes significant action; indeed, during an early protest scene it is the fellow behind Gandhi who yells to everyone to lie down in the face of charging British soldiers—it was his smart notion that showed Gandhi that such resistance could work. Best of all is the magnificent performance by Ben Kingsley, who deservedly won an Oscar for his first screen role. Always thoughtful, dignified, resolute, his Gandhi has remarkable presence— it's no wonder that Indians by the thousands who watched the location filming actually joined the extras who marched behind Kingsley. He is more persuasive than any other actor who has ever starred in a screen bio at convincing us he is the real-life character. I imagine that his co-stars couldn't help but treat him with some awe. The Oscar-winning Best Picture (Attenborough also won as Best Director) used a multi-national cast, including: Roshan Seth (convincing as Nehru), Rohini Hattangady, Candice Bergen, Edward Fox, John Mills, John Gielgud, Trevor Howard, Martin Sheen, Geraldine Chaplin, Ian Bannen.

GANG'S ALL HERE, THE (1943) C/103m.
Camp classic directed and choreographed by Busby Berkeley has a nominal plot about a soldier (James Ellison) who makes a play for a USO girl (Alice Faye), although he has a honey back home. But the conventional story takes a back seat to the songs and dances—this picture contains some of the worst yet most inspired, colorful, and extravagant musical numbers in cinema history. They boggle the mind. See Carmen Miranda in a tutti-frutti hat, chorus girls do suggestive things with giant bananas, and the indescribable "Polka-Dot" ballet finale. And watch Berkeley madly experiment with color. This is like those so-awful-they're-fascinating halftime shows during the Orange Bowl. Also with: Eugene Pallette, Edward Everett Horton, Charlotte Greenwood, Benny Goodman and his orchestra, Sheila Ryan, Frank Faylen.

GARDEN OF THE FINZI-CONTINIS, THE
(ITALIAN/1971) C/95m. Vittorio De Sica's slow, dreamy, and ultimately tragic adaptation of Giorgio Bassani's autobiographical novel about being Jewish in Ferrara, Italy, in 1938–43, won 1971's Best Foreign Film Oscar. Lino Capolicchio plays Giorgio, a student from a middle-class Jewish family. He has always loved Micol (Dominique Sanda), imperious daughter of the aristocratic Jewish Finzi-Continis, but she prefers men from her class. When "racial laws" are instigated, Giorgio's family and most Jews of Ferrara have their rights taken from them—worse is their fear of what may happen next; but the Finzi-Continis ignore the political situation, figuring that, even as Jews, they can feel secure because of their wealth and social prominence. De Sica is making the point that the Finzi-Continis (like all the land-owning Italian Jews of the period) defined themselves more by their social rank than by their religion. But while the last part of the film tells us that all Jews (Micol's family and Giorgio's family) were in the same sinking ship, De Sica—through early impressions—mistakenly got us to think of the Finzi-Continis as aristocrats rather than Jews. In fact, the beauty of their existence is so imbedded in our minds that when the Finzi-Continis are arrested for deportation our first impression is to feel sad about the house and gardens they're leaving behind, that they're being stripped of their wealth—this isn't what we should feel sorry about. There has been much praise for the film's lush, dreamy

photography, but the subject matter calls for something far less romantic. Also with: Helmut Berger, Romolo Valli, Fabio Testi.

GASLIGHT (1944) B&W/114m.
Venerable psychological melodrama set in Victorian England. Ingrid Bergman is the young bride of Charles Boyer, who insists that they reside in the house where she grew up—and where her aunt was murdered (by him, of course). Wanting to be able to freely search the house for her aunt's jewels, Boyer schemes to have the delicate Bergman institutionalized. He systematically drives the innocent woman insane by making her believe that she is forgetting things, misplacing things, seeing things (such as the gaslight dimming each night), and hearing things (such as his footsteps in the attic soon after). His plan runs smoothly until a Scotland Yard detective, played by Joseph Cotten, takes a keen interest in Bergman and suspects that her declining health has something to do with her shady husband. Film is a terrifying study of how a husband can dominate and abuse his wife through manipulative words and actions as easily as with fists. Bergman won Best Actress Award for her convincing portrayal of a victimized woman. But it's Boyer's slimy cad who makes an unforgettable impression. An earlier version was made in England in 1939–40, but MGM kept it out of circulation to benefit its own film. Intricate scenic design; unusually powerful direction by George Cukor. Also with: Dame May Whitty, teenager Angela Lansbury (as a flirtatious maid), a very young Terry Moore, Halliwell Hobbes.

GATE OF HELL (JAPANESE/1954) C/89m.
Academy-Award-winning film. In 12th-century Japan a skilled warrior (Kazuo Hasegawa) remains loyal to Emperor during a rebellion, despite terrible odds. Emperor offers him a choice of rewards. He asks to marry a beautiful woman (Machiko Kyo) he met briefly. When the Emperor refuses his request because the woman already is happily married, he still persists. Obsessed with having her for his wife, he refuses to let her alone and even tries to challenge her husband (Isao Yamagata) to a swordfight. Finally he tells her that in order to save her own life and that of her aunt, she must marry him and allow him to kill her husband. What we have is: ultimate selfishness vs. supreme selflessness. But as he learns, he doesn't understand the workings of her heart. Simple story would work better as a play, but acting and characters are so interesting and the color photography is so gorgeous (with emphasis on red) that one can have no complaints. Most unusual aspect of film is that husband is not typical warrior found in Japanese historical films, nor is he a coward. He's a smart guy (he even reads!) who knows better than to fight to the death every time someone challenges him. He trusts his wife, has mostly respectful conversations with her, yet it turns out he doesn't understand a woman's heart any better than his rival. Directed by Teinosuke Kinugasa. Based on story by Kan Kikuchi.

GATES OF HEAVEN (1978) C/85m. Documentary by San Francisco filmmaker Errol Morris centers on the closing of the Foothill Memorial Gardens pet cemetery to make room for a housing project. This will require transferring the exhumed animal corpses to the Bubbling Well Pet Memorial Park in nearby Napa. Pet-cemetery operators discuss why they are in their business ("I put my heart over the dollar sign," says the most sensitive) and what services they offer (blaring music; guarantees that owners and dead pets will be reunited in heaven). Pet owners talk about what their pets meant to them and why they have placed them in a cemetery. Morris uses a stationary camera and films medium shots of his seated subjects, who are positioned so precisely within the frame that they might as well be lamps. Rather than Morris asking questions, the subjects deliver lengthy monologues about animals, about life. Morris's intentionally bland style is meant to reflect the blandness of his subjects—typical Americans. This film isn't as bizarre as one would guess from its cult reputation. Nor, unfortunately, is it as revelatory as one would expect. Yes, these are real people. But since they're the kind you meet every day, what they say sounds familiar. So you don't react to them in one way or another. If you laugh, it's at the pathetic human condition. The montage in which we see tombstones which have animal photos and owners' dedications comes across not as either stupid or outrageous (although most of us think pet cemeteries stupid and outrageous), but as oddly touching. Edited by Charles Silver.

GAUNTLET, THE (1977) C/111m. Clint Eastwood is an Arizona cop who is ordered to bring prostitute Sondra Locke to a trial in Phoenix, not realizing that they are being set up by the corrupt police commissioner for certain death. Along the way, they dodge police bullets, fall in love, have run-ins with civilians, and decide to get married if they survive. John Ford became disenchanted with the military, as his later films indicate, and this picture seems to reveal Eastwood's growing disenchantment with cops, even western cops, because they will happily turn on one another if ordered to do so. The picture isn't altogether successful—too many action sequences feature thousands of bullets being shot at structures (a house, a car, an armored bus)—but the infighting between Locke and Eastwood is interesting primarily because she (a college grad) proves to have more street smarts than he. Eastwood directed and proves to have a true understanding of Locke's talents, letting her run the gamut of emotions. Best is when he puts her in close-up (in the back of the police car, on the motel bed) and lets her talk at length in a clear manner. She can be impressive. Also with: Pat Hingle, William Prince, Bill McKinney, Michael Cavanaugh.

GAY DIVORCEE, THE (1934) B&W/107m. Having stolen *Flying Down to Rio* from its topbilled stars, Fred Astaire and Ginger Rogers were given their first lead roles in this delightful adaptation of Dwight Taylor's stage musical, *The Gay Divorce*, in which Astaire had just starred in London. It's one of their finest films, one that has great dancing and, though many don't agree, very amusing comedy. Astaire's a dancer who falls for Rogers at a British resort. She falls for him, too, after they dance together to Cole Porter's "Night and Day," one of the most elegant, seductive numbers in the entire Astaire-Rogers series. But she mistakes him for the professional correspondent (Erik Rhodes) hired by Astaire's lawyer friend Edward Everett Horton so that her husband will have reason to divorce her. When our couple discovers the mix-up, they slip past Rhodes and onto the ballroom floor, where they join many other stylishly dressed couples in the famous, extravagantly produced 17-minute song-dance "The Continental"—a second number (in which you "kiss while you're dancing") that made it clear that in Astaire-Rogers films dancing equates with sex/lovemaking, not innocent fun. It was foolish that RKO didn't yet trust Rogers enough to give her a solo dance, but this allowed unknown Betty Grable a chance in the spotlight, looking pretty in satin beach pajamas, exhibiting some fancy footwork, and singing "Lets K-nock K-nees" to Horton. For some, movie's highlight may be reprise of "The Continental," during which Astaire and Rogers twirl up a chair, across a table, down another chair, and repeat the difficult maneuver with equal grace. The stars are appealing, playing very likable characters, and as the ridiculous Italian correspondent (a union man) Rhodes is absolutely hilarious—after calling his wife long distance, he boasts that his nine-year-old son, whom he thinks he heard in the background, already has a voice that's becoming deeper. Eric Blore and Alice Brady also help out with the comedy. Produced by Pandro S. Berman. Directed by Mark Sandrich. Also with: William Austin, Lillian Miles, E. E. Clive.

GENERAL, THE (1927) B&W/74m. This is Buster Keaton's masterpiece and, as such, one of our two or three greatest comedies. Silent Civil War epic adventure tells Confederate side of *The Great Locomotive Chase*, Disney's 1956 film about Union soldiers stealing a southern train. Keaton is Johnnie Grey, conductor of the General. His two loves are his engine and lovely Annabel Lee (Marion Mack). He attempts to enlist at the outbreak of war, but is turned down by recruiters because of his important occupation. Mack thinks he was too cowardly to enlist and refuses to speak to him. One day Union soldiers steal his train, with Mack aboard. Keaton gets hold of another engine and, alone, pursues the thieves. He rescues Mack; then they sneak aboard the General and race home (to give warning of an impending Yankee attack), with Yankees chasing them in another train. The simple story, all centered on train chases, features a dazzling number of sight gags, some spectacular Keaton acrobatics (in which he runs up and down and climbs all over the moving train), and his ingenious use of the frame. One of my favorite shots has the camera panning from left to right as Union soldiers attach their moving engine to the back of the moving boxcar that is attached to Keaton's moving engine. The camera pans farther, across the boxcar to its front, where Keaton is freeing it from his engine. On these train tracks or anywhere around machines, Keaton is the master. As usual, Keaton is a sweet fellow and it's a delight watching this tiny, unmuscular civilian pull off one heroic act after another while soldiers on both sides accomplish nothing. The relationship between Keaton and Mack is wonderfully romantic. Her well-intentioned but ridiculous attempts to help in their escape effort both exasperate him and reinforce his love for her. When she starts to sweep up in the midst of the chase, he throws out the broom; when she hands him a quarter-inch piece of wood for a stack of large firewood, he throws it back at her; when she tosses another puny piece into the fire in the engine (after throwing out a large piece just because it had a small hole in it), he playfully strangles her, then kisses her—it's a glorious moment. Marvelous in every way. Directed by Keaton and Clyde Bruckman. Also with: Joe Keaton, Glen Cavander, Jim Farley.

GENERAL DELLA ROVERE (ITALIAN/1960)
B&W/129m. Roberto Rossellini set his film in Genoa during WWII. Silver-haired Vittorio De Sica (looking a bit like the aged Chaplin) gives a grand performance as a small-time swindler who pays for his gambling by taking money from distressed people who think he'll buy their loved ones out of German prisons. Arrested by a Nazi officer (Hannes Messemer), he is manipulated into impersonating a heroic Italian general whom the Germans accidentally killed. They want him alive, not a martyr to the partisan cause. As General Della Rovere, De Sica is sent to a facility for political prisoners. The Nazi promises him freedom and money if he'll reveal which of the other new prisoners is a leader of the resistance. As in Rossellini's *Open City*, the Germans underestimate the character of Italians and of their hatred for the Nazis who have occupied their country—De Sica becomes worthy of the man whose name he has stolen. Plotline is disjointed, almost as if several stories were thrown together. The most fascinating one, concerning De Sica's relationship to his swindled clients, is dropped quickly, almost as if his crime were simply a device to get him thrown in jail, where the real story begins. But I think that the nature of De Sica's swindle is important. He is swindling *Italians*. As the noble general and as a firsthand witness to suffering that he'd once ignored and the cruel workings of the Nazis, he learns what he didn't realize before being imprisoned: that every Italian has the responsibility to share his countrymen's misery, rather than help the Nazis exploit it. Film is overlong, but it has many powerful moments, fine acting. Also with: Sandra Milo, Giovanna Ralli, Mary Greco.

GENTLEMAN JIM (1942) B&W/104m. Raoul
Walsh directed this thoroughly enjoyable, if highly fictionalized bio of the colorful Gentleman Jim Corbett (an ideal role for Errol Flynn), the first *modern* ("scientific") heavy-weight boxing champion. The young Muhammad Ali may have studied this film: not only does Corbett "float like a butterfly and sting like a bee," but he exhibits such brashness and theatricality in and out of the ring that the woman he loves (smartly played by Alexis Smith) wants him to get his swelled head knocked off. When Corbett mercilessly taunts and teases John L. Sullivan (a sympathetic performance by Ward Bond) in order to get a shot at his crown in 1892, and then unnerves him prior to the bout, one is reminded how the "Louisville Lip" treated Sonny Liston. But whereas Clay/Ali never told Liston he was only fooling, the suddenly humble Corbett confesses to the prideful Boston Strongboy, in front of all the people at his own victory party, that he's thankful he didn't fight Sullivan when The Boston Strongboy was in his unbeatable prime. It's a wonderful scene (Bond gets teary-eyed) with Flynn at his most likable and sensitive, and it perfectly conveys the picture's point of view: boxing champs are indeed champions. In this rare pro-boxing movie, made when there was national pride in champion Joe Louis, boxing is an art form and the heavyweight title that Corbett wins is worthy of admiration. Also with: Jack Carson, Alan Hale, Minor Watson, Arthur Shields.

GENTLEMEN PREFER BLONDES (1953) C/
91m. In retrospect, this Howard Hawks musical comedy is much more enjoyable than several of Marilyn Monroe's more acclaimed films—*The Seven Year Itch* and *How to Marry a Millionaire* immediately come to mind—and more interesting in terms of her dumb blonde/money-chaser screen persona. In Charles Lederer's adaptation of Anita Loos's novel and musical (co-written by Joseph Fields), Jane Russell (as Dorothy Shaw) and Monroe (as Lorelei Lee) are showgirls from Little Rock who take an ocean voyage to France. Golddigger Monroe has an innocent flirtation with a wealthy, married diamond-mine owner (Charles Coburn); Russell, who doesn't care about money, falls for a male passenger (Elliott Reid), only to discover that he's been hired by the father of Monroe's millionaire fiancé (Tommy Noonan) to dig up dirt on Monroe. When Reid turns over a revealing tape to the father, Russell and Monroe find themselves stranded in Paris, without money or a place to stay. They get work as performers, but soon the police come after Monroe, whom they accuse of stealing the tiara belonging to Coburn's wife. The plot is silly, the direction is unremarkable, and Reid and Noonan are not exciting male leads (both Monroe and Russell usually fell for weak men in their comedies). But Russell and Monroe give delightful, supercharged performances. Their musical numbers are bouncy and a great deal of fun (Madonna's "Material Girl" video was inspired by Monroe's "Diamonds Are a Girl's Best Friend"). Monroe is ravishing and extremely sexy (what man wouldn't want to be in Noonan's place when she seductively sings "Bye bye, baby . . ."?); she's repeatedly wiggling her way past the camera, wearing a startling number of tight, revealing costumes. We condone her sneaky gold-digging because all the males in her world are even more false than she. Only dumb when men want her to be, the

philosophic Monroe puts things in perspective when she argues that men are attracted only to women with good looks, yet resent women who are attracted to men with money (although they'd certainly want their daughters to marry rich men). It's a point her dumb blonde should have made in several more of her films, including *How to Marry a Millionaire*. That Nunnally Johnson-scripted film also would have been improved if the camaraderie between Monroe, Lauren Bacall and Betty Grable were as strong as that between Monroe and Russell—indeed, there are few stronger female friendships in pre-seventies films. Fine songs by Jule Styne, Leo Robin, Hoagy Carmichael, and Harold Adamson. Russell appeared in the sequel, *Gentlemen Marry Brunettes*. Also with: George Winslow, Marcel Dalio, Taylor Holmes, Norma Varden, Harry Carey, Jr., Ray Montgomery.

GHOSTBUSTERS (1984) C/105m. An amusing diversion that somehow became one of the biggest box-office successes of all time. Bill Murray, Dan Aykroyd, and Harold Ramis are irresponsible, irrepressible parapsychologists at Columbia University. Kicked out of the college for bad conduct, they form their own company, Ghostbusters, which specializes in getting rid of poltergeists. Advertising on television brings them a great deal of business. They risk getting "slimed" as they take on ghosts with their ultra-sophisticated equipment. The center of ghostly activity—where there is an entrance to the underworld—is the apartment building in which Sigourney Weaver lives. Murray's efforts to seduce her are hampered when she becomes possessed. In a wild finale that lets Richard Edlund use his enormous special-effects budget, the boys try to exorcise the building and take on what looks like a giant Pillsbury Dough Boy. Film is as zany and irreverent as expected and the special effects are a lot of fun, but the self-impressed dialogue seems forced and feeble. It was unselfish of writers Aykroyd and Ramis to give the picture to Murray, but they didn't even bother to develop their own characters. Murray has a field day—he provides most of the wild hilarity—but I wish audiences weren't so easily charmed by his rude, childish, chauvinistic characters simply because they hint that they are only playacting. I think this Murray character is really a jerk with whom we shouldn't laugh. Film was originally conceived by Aykroyd as a project for him and John Belushi. Directed by Ivan Reitman. Title song by Ray Parker, Jr., was a tremendous hit and had much to do with making people aware of the film. Also with: Rick Moranis (as Weaver's nerdy neighbor who also becomes possessed), Ernie Hudson, William Atherton.

GIANT (1956) C/199m. George Stevens directed this sprawling epic version of Edna's Ferber's supersoaper. Texas cattle rancher Rock Hudson (as Bick Benedict) marries Elizabeth Taylor (as Leslie Lynnton), a willful, free-thinking woman he meets in Maryland. He brings her home to his huge spread, Reata, and she tries to settle into the huge mansion that stands isolated on acres of barren land. Hudson's tough sister, Mercedes McCambridge, doesn't appreciate Taylor's intrusion into the household. But McCambridge's death doesn't make things much easier for Taylor. Hudson, who has both family pride and masculine pride, tries to keep Taylor in line—for one thing he doesn't appreciate her showing concern for poor Mexican-American families. But Taylor sticks to her guns despite the arguments—one of the reasons we appreciate her character—and you feel that secretly he admires her indomitable spirit. Because Hudson rarely approves of anything she does, Taylor makes friends and possibly falls in love with misfit cowhand James Dean (as Jeff Rink, his final role). Dean definitely falls for Taylor. McCambridge leaves Dean a small parcel of land. He strikes oil. This gives him the chance to tell Hudson what he really thinks of him. Hudson and Dean will feud for more than twenty years, which is the time span covered in the film. Dean stands for the new Texas, the instant "white trash" millionaires who haven't the imagination of men like Benedict, who have maintained their empires through hard work. Dean steals the film from Hudson and Taylor. Particularly memorable: the scene where he strikes it rich and gets covered by oil, and the scene where he—now an older man—drunkenly recites a speech although his audience has long gone home. But I can't get a handle on the character. More interesting is Hudson's character, who's basically a nice guy but tries—without complete success—to cover up his gentle, *soft* qualities so he won't seem weaker than his father. But it's a new time in American history; men don't have to strut their machismo to be *giants*. Hudson's fight with a bigoted diner-owner and the finale in which Taylor tells Hudson he's her hero are terrific scenes. The wide-screen production is patriotic, yet still acknowledges that bigotry is widespread. Film has slow and hackneyed scenes, but it's quite enjoyable. Cinematography by William C. Mellor captures the beauty of the land. Also with: Chill Wills, Jane Withers, Sal Mineo, Judith Evelyn, Carroll Baker, Earl Holliman, Dennis Hopper.

GIGI (1958) C/116m. Exuberant musical, the winner of nine Academy Awards including Best Picture, was written expressly for the screen by Lerner and Loewe. Asked by M-G-M producer Arthur Freed to come up with a story similar to their Broadway success *My Fair Lady*, they used as their source Colette's novelette about a teenage girl in turn-of-century Paris who is trained by a wealthy aunt to be a courtesan. (Colette's story had already been a French play and French film, made in 1950 with Danièle Delorme). Film was originally intended for Audrey Hepburn, who'd been in Anita Loos's Broadway adaptation, but when she was unavailable, Leslie Caron assumed the lead, reuniting her with her *An American in Paris* director, Vincente Minnelli. She plays a sweet, happy-go-lucky teenager who lives with grandmother Hermione Gingold and is given daily lessons on being a lady by her aunt, Isabel Jeans. Rich, bored, handsome Louis Jourdan has always been a family friend and has treated Caron as a younger sister. But suddenly he realizes she is growing up and he becomes attracted to her in a different way. When he realizes he can't be without her, this confirmed bachelor offers to make Caron his mistress. Her grandmother and aunt are thrilled, but Caron worries that such an arrangement will make her miserable. The script is bright and witty, the stars—including the broadly smiling Maurice Chevalier as Jourdan's womanizing uncle—are most appealing, the colorful costumes and sets evoke Paris of 1900, and there are some charming songs. Caron is sexiest in those early scenes (especially the card-playing sequence) when she moves about as if she were still a child, unaware that her body is changing, innocently sitting on Jourdan's knee, hugging and kissing him—but these scenes are a bit uncomfortable for us to watch until it's made clear that Jourdan is becoming aroused by the *adult* Caron rather than the *child* Caron. Musical highlights include Jourdan's "Gigi" (the Oscar-winning song), Chevalier's "Thank Heaven for Little Girls," and my favorite, Gingold and Chevalier warmly singing of their long-ago romance in "I Remember It Well." Other Oscars were won for direction, cinematography, screenplay, art direction, scoring, costume design, and editing. Also with: Eva Gabor, Jacques Bergerac, John Abbott.

GILDA (1946) B&W/110m. Tough gambler Glenn Ford prides himself on knowing when to stop, but he finds himself stepping headlong into trouble. In Buenos Aires, he accepts cruel George Macready's offer to run his busy casino. Macready also has Ford keep an eye on his spoiled, pleasure-hungry wife, Rita Hayworth. Ford and Hayworth fight constantly and repeatedly express their hatred for one another—of course, they fall in love. But is the secretive Macready setting them up? Macready's good and sinister, but he's not strong enough for such a pivotal role—Orson Welles would have been ideal. Film is overlong, silly, and confusing, and Ford gives an uninteresting performance as an unlikable heel-hero. But gorgeous Rita sizzles, wearing an assortment of sexy outfits and singing "Put the Blame on Mame." No wonder GIs swooned over her. Directed by Charles Vidor. Also with: Joseph Calleia, Joe Sawyer, Steven Geray.

GIMME SHELTER (1970) C/91m. Riveting documentary by Albert and David Maysles about the Rolling Stones' 1970 American concert tour that culminated in the tragic free concert at Altamont Speedway. Film has tremendous power, initially because of Mick Jagger's supercharged performance and the driving music of the Stones. The Maysleses' cameras create a remarkable intimacy and intensity; the film's sound is perfect and draws you in. The Stones are really in peak form and the Maysleses do them justice. Then the film's tone changes. The Maysleses' famous *cinéma vérité* style comes into good use as we go behind the scenes to watch attorney Melvin Belli coordinate plans for the hastily conceived free concert. The Stones would hire the Hell's Angels to serve as security guards, a foolish gesture that was supposed to unite the entire youth counterculture symbolically. By the time the Stones play,

the Angels have already changed the mood of the gathering from festive to terrified. We have seen numerous outbreaks of violence around the stage area, in which the Angels made quick work of the flower children—the Jefferson Airplane's Marty Balin had leaped from the stage in midperformance to battle some thuggish Angels and had been knocked unconscious. As Jagger sings, we watch a stoned Angel stand near him, staring at his effeminate posturing—and we worry that he'll tear into him; who knows how Jagger could continue to sing with that intimidating presence standing nearby? Of course, the real tragedy of Altamont was the killing of a black spectator who drew a gun to fight off some Angels and had his head bashed in by a pool stick. We watch the Stones repeatedly watch tapes of the murder. Viewers, like Jagger, will feel shaky. And sad—because this event squashed the euphoria created by Woodstock and signaled the beginning of an era that would have no place for the love generation.

GIRL CAN'T HELP IT, THE (1956) C/99m. Talent agent Tom Ewell is hired by slot-machine king Edmond O'Brien to turn his girlfriend, Jayne Mansfield, who can't sing a lick, into a rock-'n'-roll star. Frank Tashlin's rock-music version of *Born Yesterday* is the nearest he ever came to a masterpiece. Like most of his films, its theme is that "success" has to do with leading a personally meaningful life—all Mansfield wants is to be a wife and mother—and not with reaching the top of a profession. It's a highly inventive picture, briskly paced and extremely colorful: one-liners shoot back and forth, actors are in constant motion, music blares, there's even a small screen which, upon Ewell's command, switches from black-and-white to color and expands to CinemaScope. The off-color jokes, double entendres, and sexual innuendos—all staples of Tashlin's humor—will cause you either to smile or to walk up the aisle cursing about adolescent humor. I bet you'll stay seated. Mansfield's measurements were 40–18½–36, so it's not surprising that breast-obsessed Tashlin would use her body as the major source of the film's humor. Like it or not, when Mansfield's on screen, your eyes gravitate toward her bosom. And Tashlin makes it easier for us: he has her hold a milk bottle over each breast (the film's most famous moment) or lean over with her half-exposed breasts close to Ewell's eyes and ask if he thinks she's "equipped" to be a mother; he puts her in tight outfits and shoots her from the side or even frames his picture so she's visible only from the neck down. In tight sweaters and tight skirts, barely able to walk, she looks more like a caricature of the "fantasy blonde bosom-beauty of the fifties" than a real woman. Fortunately, Mansfield is so spirited, lively, and funny that she emerges unscathed. We don't feel embarrassed for her, but rather admire her for adapting to what was demanded of her. Since she blunts the sexist humor and makes it harmless, we don't feel guilt—in this *one* Mansfield film—when we laugh. In addition to Mansfield, picture has a strong cult today because of the many great rock acts who appear, including Little Richard at his peak, the Platters,

Fats Domino, Gene Vincent, and Eddie Cochran—who, like Mansfield, died in a car crash. Who can forget Mansfield slithering across a nightclub floor in a tight dress while Eddie Fontaine sings, "I love your eyes, I love your lips, you taste better than potato chips" or Little Richard singing the title song as Mansfield creates mayhem (a series of sexual gags) while walking down the street? Also with: Henry Jones, Julie London, John Emery, Juanita Moore, Barry Gordon, Ray Anthony.

GIRL FROM CHICAGO, THE (1935) B&W/70m.

Everyone should see at least one film by the notorious, almost legendary Oscar Micheaux, the most prolific black director of all time—and arguably the worst—and this was enough for me. It's essentially two pictures rolled into one. Alonzo White (Carl Mahon), black member of the U.S. Secret Service, goes to Virginia to work on a case. He meets high-school graduate Norma (Star Calloway), falls in love with her, and rescues her from the criminal (John Everett) he was chasing. Alonzo and Norma go to live it up in Harlem. Norma spots a singer, Mary Austin (Eunice Brooks), from her hometown. Last part of film is devoted to Alonzo trying to prove the singer innocent of murder. As is supposedly true of all Micheaux's films, the acting by the light-skinned blacks is wretched—they are obviously reading cue cards during the long takes—and the characters who say things like "Well, smack my mouth" aren't great role models for young blacks. Film contains some awful musical numbers (who is that woman at the piano?) and some incredible romantic scenes. Only fun comes from trying to figure out how Micheaux came up with the title—you find out very late in the film. Also with: Alice B. Russell, Minto Cato.

GLEN OR GLENDA/I LED TWO LIVES/I CHANGED MY SEX/HE OR SHE (1953) B&W/67m.

Utterly perverse, personal film by Edward D. Wood, Jr., making his directorial debut. A policeman (Lyle Talbot) visits a doctor (Timothy Farrell), who asks if he has come for business or pleasure (has your doctor ever asked you that?). The officer is confused by several recent cases involving transvestites—one man had killed himself because society wouldn't allow him to wear woman's clothing. The doctor discusses two cases involving men who found it necessary to dress like women. Glen, played by "Daniel Dans" (an alias for Wood, who was a transvestite—at least when he was a soldier), simply likes to dress as a woman; he isn't attracted to men, but loves his fiancée, played by Dolores Fuller (Wood's wife). Strangely, he covets not her virginity but her angora sweater, which in the *climactic* scene she takes off and gives to him. The second, more extreme case involves an ex-soldier (Tommy Haynes) who actually undergoes a sex-change operation. Surprisingly, the picture's treatment of transvestism is serious and sensitive. Indeed, the film dares defend transvestites, saying that if allowed to wear women's clothing they'll be credits to their communities and government. Bela Lugosi serves as an absurd narrator—who knows what he is talking about? The film's weirdest scene has Wood cutting back and forth between Lugosi sitting in a chair ranting and footage of women stripping, rubbing themselves, tying up each other, being raped. Otherwise, this film doesn't have the campy material that one expects in a Wood film. In fact, one must be impressed by this film for the very reason that it takes a stand on a subject that surely was in 1953 not even acceptable enough to be considered controversial. Moreover, Wood dares to incorporate footage that was obviously influenced by surrealists and experimental filmmakers. No matter that this footage is absolutely ridiculous. It shows Wood had an imagination. Re-released by Paramount in 1981, but audiences didn't find laughs they expected.

GLORIA (1980) C/121m.

A change of pace for director John Cassavetes and his actress wife, Gena Rowlands, that replaces introspective dialogue with flying bullets. In this unusual, tough action film, Rowlands plays a former gun moll who finds her retirement into a peaceful life disrupted when hitmen rub out a couple in her building, and she ends up protecting their eight-year-old son (John Adames) from the mob. As expected, the hard-as-nails Gloria reveals a compassionate side as she plays mother to the tough-talking Puerto Rican boy, but what's more interesting is how in each scene she reveals those traits that once helped her survive life with the mob—she proves smarter, more resourceful than the killers who chase her and, when necessary, as brutal as they are. Early on, when she stands her ground and guns down some mobsters in a car, surprising us with her mix of bravery and brutality, we suddenly realize that the little boy is in the best possible hands. Rowlands gives a dynamic performance playing a woman unique to the cinema. On the other hand, Adames, whose little boy is supposed to constantly act like a big man, will really test your nerves. Buck Henry, in the small part of the boy's father, is also miscast. Film has gritty feel, due to Cassavetes moving his two characters through a series of sordid New York and New Jersey locations. Underrated. Also with: Julie Carmen, Lupe Guarnica.

GO, JOHNNY, GO! (1958) B&W/75m.

Deejay Alan Freed (playing himself) tells pal Chuck Berry about his recent discovery, teen singing sensation "Johnny Melody" (played by singer Jimmy Clanton). As we see in flashback, Johnny's trip from orphanage to the stage was almost interrupted by a long stay in prison—if Freed hadn't saved the day. The paper-thin story, static direction by Lew Landers, and the overly rude, chip-on-his-shoulder portrayal by Clanton, which makes one think Johnny doesn't deserve a break, are all to be forgiven because of the treasure chest of rock-'n'-roll acts this film contains. There are solid-gold performances by Berry, Sandy Stewart (who plays Johnny's girl)—singing "Playmates" and "Heavenly Father" as we get waves of nostalgia—the Flamingos, the Cadillacs, Clanton, JoAnn Campbell (a poor man's Brenda Lee), Jackie Wilson, and two stars who died before their time: Eddie

Cochran and my favorite singer when this film came out, Ritchie Valens, who sings "Ooh My Head" in what I believe is the only extant footage of him. You'll love how the teenagers and adults on screen react to this music. Rock 'n' roll was going through an image problem, so notice how well groomed and unthreatening all the stars are. In fact, Clanton, with hair combed neatly and in suit and tie, looks like one of Shelly Fabares's dates on the wholesome *Donna Reed Show*.

GO TELL THE SPARTANS (1978) C/114m.
The best Vietnam War film was overlooked because of the highly publicized *The Deer Hunter*, *Apocalypse Now*, and *Coming Home*. It's a convincing look at the war in 1964, before it escalated to mammoth proportions. Corporal Craig Wasson is one of four replacements who are assigned to a remote outpost in Penang. Drafted into the army, he had asked to come to Vietnam to see what the war was like. He is unprepared for the lunacy he finds and the sadistic, racist attitude of his fellow soldiers, and he is shocked by the suicidal bent of some of the vets. His commanding officer is Burt Lancaster, who has long ago become cynical about America's presence in the war. He has no idea how to fight the enemy or even who the enemy is. The beginning of film introduces us to several men on *our* side. We expect certain ones to be around at least for a final battle. We're constantly shocked when characters are killed off—just as in war, where the enemy doesn't pick its targets according to billing. Picture is brutal and uncompromising, dialogue by Wendell Mayes is strong and realistic, and even the most lunatic characters are believable. Film ends with the wise Wasson saying, "I'm going home, Charlie." But the final title— 1964—reminds us that America didn't go home, but sent over hundreds of thousands of soldiers, who could learn what Wasson could have told them in 1964: it's not America's war. Mayes's script took seven years to sell. Surprisingly assured direction by Ted Post. Also with: Marc Singer, Evan Kim (as bloodthirsty South Vietnamese soldier, Cowboy), Dolph Sweet, Joe Unger, Dennis Howard, Jonathan Goldsmith.

GOD TOLD ME TO/DEMON (1977) C/95m.
New York is hit by a wave of mass murders. Catholic cop Tony Lo Bianco suspects a religious motive behind all the bloodshed, because each killer explains his actions with "God told me to." Further investigations lead him to conclude that these people really did have conversations with a being they consider "God"—only his name is Bernard Phillips (Richard Lynch). Records show that the mother of this fellow who resembles Jesus was a virgin at the time she gave birth. Lo Bianco concludes that Lynch's mother was impregnated not by God but by an alien from outer space. Lo Bianco also comes to realize that he, too, is the son of an earth woman (played by Jewish actress Sylvia Sidney) and an alien. Whereas Lynch's human qualities have been obliterated by his evil alien nature, the reverse is true of Lo Bianco; their fight (a disappointing scene) will be that between good and evil, and the fate of humanity will be determined. No one has ever questioned Jewish Larry Cohen making a film which is essentially about *Christian* faith and morality. That's probably because no one can figure out what ideas he's trying to get across. Low-budget horror film does have an interesting premise which supports the theory that our gods were ancient astronauts, but, except for a couple of scenes, it's a mess. Whole scenes seem to be missing (for instance, when is Lo Bianco suspended from the force?), the editing that connects scenes is sloppy, subplots (like the hysteria in New York over the religious murders) go nowhere or are irrelevant, and co-stars Deborah Raffin (as Lo Bianco's girlfriend) and Sandy Dennis (as his estranged wife) seem to have been hired for a morning's work, so minor are their parts (it's probable Raffin's was cut). Picture has a strong underground reputation, but I can't figure out why. I much prefer Cohen's *It's Alive* or even his *Q*, although that picture also looks like it was made by a man in a daze. Title was changed when TV stations refused to publicize a picture called *God Told Me To*. Also with: Sam Levene, Mike Kellin, Andy Kaufman.

GODDESS, THE (1958) B&W/105m.
Unrelentingly downbeat film about a lonely, insecure, miserably unhappy young girl (Kim Stanley) who fulfills her desire to become a Hollywood star but doesn't improve her life. Paddy Chayefsky insisted that he didn't base his screenplay on the life of Marilyn Monroe, but there are obvious parallels: a childhood in which she feels unwanted that leads to a life searching for someone to love her; her desire for respectability, which she tries to obtain by making her body available to anyone who happens along; unsuccessful marriages, including one to an athlete (Lloyd Bridges plays a boxer who is on the verge of retirement); her need for fame and public adoration, although neither compares to the intimate attention and love she craves; the suicide attempts and the dependency on drugs. Stanley looks too old for the scenes in which she plays a teenager and too heavy to be a glamour queen (which is the reason Stanley didn't become a glamour queen), but she nevertheless gives a powerhouse performance. She gives more than the grim script deserves. Chayefsky seems to enjoy the character's suffering. He thrusts her into a world inhabited solely by neurotics, leeches, suicidals, weaklings, loony religious zealots, people with no ability to love. He must have been in a great mood. Well directed on a low budget by John Cromwell. Effective location shooting was done outside Baltimore. A perfect companion film to *The Rose*. Also with: Steven Hill, Betty Lou Holland, Bert Freed, Patty Duke (Stanley as a child), Werner Klemperer, Elizabeth Wilson.

GODFATHER, THE (1972) C/175m.
Francis Ford Coppola's epic adaptation of Mario Puzo's best-selling novel about a powerful Mafia crime family, the Corleones, is a stunning piece of filmmaking. Scripted by Coppola and

Puzo (they won an Oscar), this Best Picture winner takes place over about 10 years, has scenes set in New York, Los Angeles, Las Vegas, and Italy, employs different styles of cinematography and music according to time and setting, and introduces numerous characters in and out of the family, yet Coppola still keeps it coherent and consistently exciting. The film begins in the mid-forties, when godfather Vito Corleone (Marlon Brando) hosts the lavish wedding of his only daughter (Talia Shire), an occasion that unites his three sons, the temperamental Sonny (James Caan), the not-so-bright Fredo (John Cazale), and war hero Michael (Al Pacino), who wants to marry a teacher (Diane Keaton) and stay out of crime. Here we meet the many people in Corleone's immediate and extended family, as well as his soldiers. Everyone is Italian but for family lawyer Tom (Robert Duvall), who is like Corleone's fourth son. The lengthy sequence reveals the secret of the film's success: Coppola doesn't rush through his scenes so that he can squeeze every event from the book into his film; instead he has fewer scenes but makes them count by making it clear who his characters are, how they act with each other, and what their allegiances are, providing time for even his less important characters to make strong audience impressions (importantly, he cast actors who have distinctive looks, so we can recognize them in later scenes although their initial appearances are brief). Film is about how the Corleone family has to reestablish itself as New York's top crime family by going to war with other families and rooting out those within the family who have turned traitor. The Corleones succeed because they are as shrewd and monstrous as their opposition. Michael becomes the central character when he unexpectedly takes over the organization after his father is incapacitated in an ambush. Although he's pretty hammy, is hard to understand because of the cotton stuffed in his cheeks, is outshone by newcomer Pacino, and doesn't have a lot of screen time, Brando won a Best Actor Oscar; his character dominates the proceedings even when he isn't on the screen. There are numerous classic sequences: the opening in which Corleone first utters his famous "We'll make him an offer he can't refuse" and agrees to help a friend of the family do away with the punk who harmed his daughter; the wedding; Michael rescuing his father from an assassination attempt in a deserted hospital; Sonny brutally beating his sister's abusive husband; Michael assassinating a policeman (Sterling Hayden) and a top man with a rival family in a restaurant; a Hollywood director (John Marley) finding the head of his $500,000 horse in his bed—proof positive he shouldn't go against the Corleones; Michael's exile in Italy; Corleone's death scene. Most impressive is the brilliantly edited Corleone massacre sequence (one of several scenes with savage violence), in which the victims are killed at several different locations at the same time. *The Godfather, Part II* would deal more with how the Mafia fits into the real world; this picture is more about "family" loyalty and obligations—a much more romantic theme. Gordon Willis did the cinematography and Nino Rota composed the now familiar music. Also with: Richard Castellano (as Clemenza), Richard Conte, Al Martino (in the "Frank Sinatra" role), Lenny Montana, Abe Vigoda, Al Lettieri, Alex Rocco, Simonetta Stefanelli, Gianni Russo.

GODFATHER, PART II, THE (1974) C/200m. Director Francis Ford Coppola and his co-writer, Mario Puzo, cut back and forth between the late fifties, when Michael Corleone (Al Pacino), who now lives in Nevada, strengthens his father's family "business"—at the expense of his becoming an isolated tyrant and destroying the remnants of the family—and the late 1890s–early 1900s, when his father Vito came to New York (as a boy) and as a young man (Robert De Niro) grew into the protector and godfather of the poor Italians in his neighborhood and started a personal family and large extended family. We get the impression Vito would not have been infatuated with his son. Coppola doesn't have De Niro or Pacino do much acting, limiting them to little snippets of dialogue and many moments when they react (with quiet, calm voices) to the more emotional and demonstrative peripheral characters around them. De Niro gets by on presence alone (his charming smile, his quizzical look, his physical grace), but Pacino is a brooding bore. His character does not develop logically from the person he played in the original, but is a caricature of a crime boss. All these major scenes seem unreal, calculated for audience response. Phoniest of all is his breakup scene with wife Diane Keaton, which looks over-rehearsed, like a scene for an acting class. In fact, several of the major scenes in the contemporary section come across as mere duplications of real-life drama we've seen on television (the Jack Ruby–kills–Oswald assassination, the Senate crime hearings). The scene in which the senator (G. D. Spradin) is found in a brothel with a hooker he brutally killed is similar to numerous sequences in exploitation films of the era and is included for no reason other than sensationalism. The only moments that come across as real are when the crime bosses and legitimate businessmen gather in Batista Cuba to decide how to divide up the American pie (it's commendable that Coppola tried to broaden his scope and be more political) and when a Jewish crime boss (a terrific, subdued debut performance by legendary acting teacher Lee Strasberg) raises rather than lowers the volume on a televised football game while talking over important crime business with Michael. Critically acclaimed film walked away with several Oscars, including those for Best Picture, Best Director, Best Screenplay, and Best Score (by Nino Rota). Surprisingly, Gordon Willis, whose cinematography is even better than in the original, wasn't even nominated. Also with: Robert Duvall, John Cazale, Talia Shire, Michael V. Gazzo, Troy Donahue, Gianni Russo, Harry Dean Stanton, Joe Spinell, Fay Spain, Danny Aiello, Abe Vigoda, Roger Corman, Phil Feldman, William Bowers, James Caan.

GODS MUST BE CRAZY, THE (SOUTH AFRICAN/1984) C/109m. While flying over the Kalahari Desert, a careless pilot tosses an empty Coke bottle from his plane. It is recovered by an isolated tribe of happy, primitive Bushmen (playing themselves), who assume that the strange, smooth, hard, glossy object is a gift from the gods. They use it in every aspect of their lives (work and play); but when they start fighting over it and conking each other with it, they realize it might bring about the end of their harmonious existence. One Bushman, Xi (N!hau), takes the bottle on a long journey into the unknown, intending to toss it off the end of the world. For the first time in his life he encounters "civilized" men (white and black) and believes them to be gods. As he observes them during his brief stay, he can only conclude that they must be crazy. Directed by white South African Jamie Uys, film has become a cult favorite all over the world (particularly in the U.S., Japan, and France). It's that rare picture that will appeal to everyone in the family, from Junior to Grandma. While the picture is satirical—Uys knocks our so-called civilization, which is confusing and cruel and has unfair laws and court procedures, as well as communist guerrillas and the governments they wish to overthrow—its most appealing ingredient is funny slapstick comedy. The small, cheerful N!hau is a natural physical comedian whom you can picture being chased by the Keystone Kops. Also amusing is N!hau's new white friend Steyn (Marius Weyers), a tall, blundering microbiologist who spends much of his time chasing after his runaway brakeless jeep, and knocking things over while nervously courting the beautiful new teacher (Sandra Prinsloo). Maybe he's a distant cousin of Jacques Tati. N!hau and Weyers, who couldn't be more different physically, are quite a comedic team. Especially when they foil an attempt by brutal revolutionaries to kidnap Prinsloo and her young pupils. A surefire crowd-pleaser. Also with: Louw Verwey, James Uys.

GODZILLA, KING OF THE MONSTERS (AMERICAN-JAPANESE/1956) B&W/80m. Japan's answer to *King Kong*. A 400-foot-tall prehistoric beast is awakened by atomic testing in nearby Bikini Atoll. He marches through Tokyo, spewing his atomic breath, crushing buildings, and killing hundreds of thousands of people. When all weapons prove ineffective, a scientist (Daisuke Senzawa) must decide whether to use a terrible weapon he invented, the Oxygen Destroyer. Picture began as a 98-minute Japanese film called *Gojira*, directed by Inoshiro Honda. It won many awards and broke box-office records all over Japan. The Americanized version, directed by Terry Morse, eliminates a lot of Honda's material and introduces an American reporter (Raymond Burr) who serves as narrator and, in cleverly edited scenes, appears to talk to the Japanese characters from Honda's film (of course their faces are never shown in the same shot). Burr has to react to people and events that were filmed two years earlier. And he bungles it. What makes both versions interesting—even though they aren't enjoyable or exciting (the Honda version is so somber it's dull)—is that, unlike all those giant creatures of American SF films of the fifties, Godzilla was not simply a bad consequence of foolhardy nuclear testing. The merciless monster which kills and destroys with machine-like precision is meant to be the embodiment of the atomic bombs dropped on Hiroshima and Nagasaki. This horror film gave Americans one of their first opportunities to see Japanese rage and disgust over what America did to them in August 1945. Morse's version makes deletions to cover up references to damage done by the A-Bomb. But, ironically, he makes changes that further identify Godzilla with the A-Bomb— for instance, in his version characters die from radiation poisoning. Oddly, Morse has Burr tell us Tokyo is evacuated before Godzilla's attack, implying that the citizens of Hiroshima and Nagasaki were prepared for the attack. Knowing this wasn't the case, Honda didn't evacuate the Tokyo in his film, and inadvertently stuck Morse with footage that makes no sense in the U.S. version—after Godzilla leaves, the hospitals are full of people who were supposed to have been out of town. The Honda version ends gloomily, the Morse version optimistically: "the whole world could wake up and live again." That the scientist used his Oxygen Destroyer on moral grounds in *both* versions is philosophically confusing because it backs up America's claim that it used the A-Bomb to end the war quickly and stop the killing immediately. But only Honda's version makes a plea for peace and no more bomb-testing. Film shouldn't be taken too seriously—it does have many silly, camp elements; plus it has some award-winning special effects by Eiji Tsuburaya. Followed by many sequels. Burr reprised his role in *Godzilla 1985*. Also with: Takashi Shimura, Momoko Kochi, Akira Takarada.

GOIN' DOWN THE ROAD (CANADIAN/1970) C/190m. Excellent $82,000 film (originally shot in 16mm.) concerns itself with two unskilled, uneducated laborers (Doug McGrath, Paul Bradley) who come to the "big city" of Toronto to find high-paying employment and the good life. It is the other side of *Easy Rider*, where we watch workers instead of products of the hippie subculture and people seeking a place (they get work in a bottling plant) instead of an escape. At first you'll have trouble identifying with these men, who are crude, shamelessly male-chauvinistic, and totally ignorant of the fact that their jobs exploit them. But that will soon change. As the city is no paradise, they begin to struggle for work, food, and recognition. They pimp and they steal, but there is no way to succeed. As alienated labor, they too begin to realize that there is something inherently wrong with the system. Film contains many exceptional sequences. A touching bit has Bradley tell everyone at his wedding reception that he has married for love and not because his wife is pregnant. Another moving scene has a group of unemployed hangers-on gathered around a Conway Twitty look-alike in a park, while he sings Merle Haggard's classic "Sing Me Back Home." A terrifying, unsettling scene has our heroes being brutally treated by a clerk who catches them stealing from "his" grocery. McGrath and Bradley (cast because of ability to improvise) create a very convincing camaraderie in roles that seem influenced by English working-class films. The scene in which they

drive around on a double date (each closer to the other than to the woman) reminds one of similar scenes in *The Loneliness of the Long Distance Runner*. Human, sincere, powerful, and political, film has much to say: director Donald Shebib (who was literally starving during production) and writer William Fruet offer us unique insight into the everyday struggle for survival. Also with: Jayne Eastwood, Cayle Chernin, Nicole Morin.

GOIN' SOUTH (1978) C/109m.
An amiable comedy-western, directed by Jack Nicholson. He plays a rambunctious, slovenly outlaw who marries spinster Mary Steenburgen (her movie debut) so he won't be hanged. She is more interested in having someone work her mine than in having a husband, and she makes him sleep in the barn. They fight constantly, but grow attached, become work partners, make love, fall in love. It's played for laughs, but it could have been equally effective and touching if it had been handled seriously. The animated, bearded Nicholson and the stiff, reticent Steenburgen are a likable couple—any time he can bring a rare smile to her face, we can feel good. A nice change of pace for western fans. Also with: John Belushi (his debut), as a Mexican lawman in need of a bath, Christopher Lloyd, Veronica Cartwright (Nicholson's former girlfriend), Richard Bradford.

GOING MY WAY (1944) B&W/130m.
The No. 1 box-office draw, Bing Crosby is an upbeat priest, Father O'Malley, who has a love of music and baseball. He is assigned to a poor New York parish, where age has apparently caught up with the long time priest, Barry Fitzgerald. Crosby tells Fitzgerald that he's to be his assistant, although he's really been made boss. Fitzgerald doesn't appreciate Crosby's modern methods for dealing with problems, and the two don't get along. Crosby helps out a young woman (Carol James) who has left home and wants to be a singer, turns the tough neighborhood kids (all of whom say "fodder") into angelic choirboys, looks up his opera-singer friend (Risë Stevens)—in an interesting scene, it becomes apparent that they were once romantically involved—gets money for the church by selling one of his songs, and wins over Fitzgerald. Some of the scenes are a bit forced or corny, but this is a wonderful, warmhearted film, a deserved Best Picture winner. Leo McCarey deservedly won a Best Director Oscar, and also won for Best Story; Frank Butler and Frank Cavett won the award for their screenplay. The scenes with Fitzgerald, who tends to play the martyr, and Crosby are delightful: they play golf together, Crosby welcomes him home after he ran away, they have a drink together, Crosby sings him a bedtime lullaby. Crosby sings several songs, including "Silent Night" and "Swinging on a Star," which won an Oscar for James Van Heusen and Johnny Burke. Film attempts to show that priests are human too. Finale in which Fitzgerald is reunited with his old, old mother after about forty years ranks with greatest of tearjerking reunion scenes. Crosby returned as Father O'Malley in *The Bells of St. Mary's*. Also with: Frank McHugh, James

Brown, Gene Lockhart, Porter Hall, Fortunio Bonanova, Stanley Clements, Carl "Alfalfa" Switzer, Eily Malyon, Robert Mitchell Boys' Choir.

GOING PLACES (FRENCH/1974)) C/117m.
Four years before teaming in Bertrand Blier's Oscar-winning *Get Out Your Handkerchiefs*, Gérard Depardieu and Patrick Dewaere starred in this less-known but even more offbeat Blier black comedy (from Blier's novel). Here they play scruffy, unruly punks in their early twenties. They spend their time committing petty crimes, harassing *solid citizens*, and coming on to women they meet. They always share their female conquests. For about the first half-hour their amoral behavior, their vulgarity, and their obnoxious treatment of women will wear on your patience; you'll find it hard not to hate a film that would have them as its heroes. But once you realize that neither of the characters is vicious and that both are vulnerable, the film becomes more tolerable. There are humor, pathos, and many erotic moments. Significantly, in the long run the two men don't do any harm to the women they half seduce, half force sex upon; in fact, the women end up more satisfied than they are. Male stars are supported by classy actresses: Miou-Miou, Brigitte Fossey, Isabelle Huppert, Jeanne Moreau (whose sequence is jarring in many ways).

GOLD DIGGERS OF 1933 (1933) B&W/96m.
Super Warners musical, with extravagant, delightfully outlandish Busby Berkeley production numbers. Picture begins with Ginger Rogers and other chorines dressed skimpily in strings of coins and skin-colored leotard-shorts outfits, happily chiming "We're in the Money." It's a parody number that is meant to show how most Hollywood/Broadway musicals of the period were ignoring the Depression. This being a musical made at Warners, the one studio that called attention to the country's social problems, policemen charge into the theater, shut down the show because of debts, and the chorines are out of a job and, like so many others, out of the money. Worried, broke roommates Joan Blondell, Ruby Keller, and Aline MacMahon and pal Rogers are offered plum parts in producer Ned Sparks's show about the Depression, but Sparks has trouble getting financing. Keeler's beau, Dick Powell, a songwriter-singer, puts up the money. His Boston blueblood brother, Warren William, wants to cut him off from the family's millions. He and family lawyer Guy Kibbee come to New York to buy off Keeler so she'll leave Powell alone. Only William mistakes Blondell for Keeler, and they fall in love; and MacMahon hooks Kibbee. Plot temporarily gets in the way of Depression theme, but picture ends with mammoth Blondell-led production tribute to the "Forgotten Man" who fought in the war but couldn't get a job when he came home. Film (and song) established firm bond between women (like chorines) who have to scrape to get by and the men who hopelessly walk the streets, also not getting the respect they deserve. Blondell has one of her most appealing roles (when will this great star get a retrospective all to herself?); Rogers

displays a sparkling, hungry (for food, wine, men) quality; and Powell is in fine voice during "Pettin' in the Park." Picture also sticks in memory because it emphasizes *female* sex more than any of the other Berkeley musicals: Rogers wears her gold-coin outfit, MacMahon takes a bath, Blondell is falling out of her negligee, chorines (seen in silhouette) strip completely behind a giant screen, women constantly appear half-dressed, etc. (As I see the beautiful chorines, I immediately think of casting couches.) Directed by Mervyn LeRoy. Also with: Sterling Holloway.

GOLD RUSH, THE (1925) B&W/74m–82m.
Charles Chaplin's first masterpiece. His tramp is a prospector in Alaska who falls in love with a beautiful dance-hall girl (Georgia Hale). She doesn't take him seriously and repeatedly hurts his feelings. But in Chaplin's films, when he falls in love with a woman at first sight, he has not overestimated her—he sees the beautiful qualities in her that even she doesn't. Hale will prove herself worthy of this kind gentleman. That she ends up with him is a happy ending for *her*, as well as him. The scenes involving Chaplin and Hale are sentimental and sweet. There are some poignant moments: when Hale discovers proof of his love for her (her photo under his pillow; an expensive meal he prepared for her); when Chaplin fantasizes about being the perfect host to Hale and her friends; when the unhappy Chaplin stands in the snow alone, the ultimate outsider, and peers at the communal sing-along taking place on New Year's Eve at the club in which Hale works. The film's classic comedy sequences all involve Chaplin and male characters, including a bear and prospector Mack Swain (as Big Jim McKay). There's the starving Chaplin cooking his shoe for him and Swain, and twirling the laces around his fork as if they were spaghetti; Swain chasing Chaplin around a cabin because he imagines his friend's a chicken; and Chaplin trying to crawl out of the cabin which is sliding off a mountain. This is a simple film, dealing with basic human needs: love, friendship, hunger, money, pride. It's all wonderful. Chaplin serves as narrator in his revised 1942 version. Also with: Tom Murray, Henry Bergman, Malcolm Waite, Betty Morrissey.

GOLDEN BOY (1939) B&W/100m.
Four writers "Hollywoodized" Clifford Odets's gritty play, but, despite the gloss and glitter and the more hopeful ending, the story retained much of its original power and its anti-boxing message. The simple premise bears some resemblance to *The Jazz Singer*, which was about a young man who defies his father and becomes a performer instead of a cantor. Here, curly-haired William Holden (as Joe Bonaparte) goes against father Lee J. Cobb's wishes and becomes a prizefighter instead of a violinist. When he becomes a boxer and enters the arena ("hell"), he automatically sacrifices all the people he loves and the beauty (the music) in his life. This is a prototypical boxing film in that it's about a decent boy from the ghetto who is hardened by the boxing *business* and his striving for materialistic gain. However, this film doesn't

have the boxer's girlfriend try to get him to quit the ring— in fact, cynical Barbara Stanwyck, who's doing a favor for Holden's manager, Adolphe Menjou, is the one who manipulates him into continuing boxing when he wants to return to his music. When Holden tells her that boxing "is an insult to a man's soul," she says it's his only way to get ahead and win her. To prove himself to her, he puts the gloves back on and even joins forces with local hood Joseph Calleia to get a shortcut to a title bout—as in most Odets plays, a foolish young go-getter latches on to the coattails of a corrupt man rushing toward hell. The film is schmaltzy, Cobb is overbearing as the music-loving papa, and there isn't enough fight atmosphere. But it never loses interest. Rouben Mamoulian's direction is satisfactory; and newcomer Holden, looking handsome and energetic, and the fetching Stanwyck, who took him under her wing, are an appealing screen couple. With cinematography by two of the best, Nicholas Musuraca and Karl Freund. Also with: Sam Levene, Don Beddoe, Edward Brophy, Frank Jenks.

GOLDEN VOYAGE OF SINBAD, THE (1974)
C/105m. The tenth collaboration of Charles H. Schneer and model-animation genius Ray Harryhausen. The second of three Sinbad movies, it was made 17 years after *The 7th Voyage of Sinbad*. Though not as enjoyable as that classic, it is still quite entertaining. Sinbad (John Phillip Law), beautiful former slave girl Margiane (cult star Caroline Munro), and the Vizier (Douglas Wilmer) undertake a long journey in search of lengendary fountain of youth. The Vizier wears a mask because his face was burned by the evil magician Koura (Tom Baker). He hopes to have his face restored. Koura follows the travelers, hoping to find the fountain first so he can regain his youth and obtain absolute power from the mystical waters. Picture is a bit slow, but it contains five excellent Harryhausen creations: a six-armed, dancing, sword-wielding statue; the Siren figurehead on Sinbad's ship that Koura brings to life; a tiny, ugly, winged Homunculus that serves as Koura's spy; and a centaur and griffin, whose battle is a highlight. Directed by Gordon Hessler, scripted by Brian Clemens, photographed by Ted Moore, and scored by Miklos Rozsa.

GOLDFINGER (BRITISH/1964) C/111m.
The third and best of the James Bond films starring Sean Connery. It has two diabolical villains, gold-mad Auric Goldfinger (Gert Frobe) and his invincible henchman, Oddjob (Harold Sakata, who wears a blade-rimmed bowler); and two sexy women (both of whom work for Goldfinger) for Connery to seduce, blonde Jill Masterson (Shirley Eaton), who dies when Frobe covers her with gold paint, and brunette "Pussy" Galore (Honor Blackman), a lesbian pilot who falls for Bond's charms. There's lots of humor, gimmicks (Bond uses his Aston-Martin's passenger-ejection seat to get rid of one of the villains), excitement (captured Bond watches a laser beam rip through the table he lies on, nearly zapping his crotch), an amusing yet tense golf contest between Bond and Goldfinger, thrilling fights to the death

between Bond and Oddjob and Bond and Goldfinger, and a fascinating central crime: Goldfinger wants to destroy all the gold in Fort Knox to both ruin America's economy and greatly increase the value of his own gold. Guy Hamilton directed the fast-paced film; it was his debut in the Bond series. Most enjoyable. But too bad Eaton's part isn't longer and that Frobe's Goldfinger, a heavy but nimble intellectual in the Sydney Greenstreet tradition, never appeared in another Bond film. Shirley Bassey had a big hit with the title song. Richard Maibaum and Paul Dehn adapted Ian Fleming's novel. Also with: Bernard Lee, Lois Maxwell, Tania Mallet, Desmond Llewellyn.

GONE WITH THE WIND (1939) C/220m. The
most popular picture of all time. Margaret Mitchell's epic novel of the Old South was given grandiose treatment by producer David O. Selznick. It's a gorgeous film—it's exciting just to watch characters in their lavish costumes, or the fiery red skies that often serve as the backgrounds, or shots of the Tara plantation. Picture has wonderful period detail and a fine assortment of characters, white and black (although we are led to believe that after the Civil War, blacks miss the old slave South as much as the whites do). Vivien Leigh is the beautiful, slim-waisted, high-spirited, emotional, spoiled, indomitable, manipulative southern belle Scarlett O'Hara. She loves gentlemanly Ashley Wilkes (Leslie Howard). But he loves and marries altruistic Melanie (Olivia de Havilland). Spurned, Scarlett marries a man (Rand Brooks) she doesn't care about. He is killed in the war. She worries about having to wear black. She marries another man after the war in order to get his money and save Tara. He, too, is killed. That's when she agrees to marry a longtime suitor: Clark Gable, the equally strong and shrewd Rhett Butler. We can tell she loves him as much as he loves her, but she believes she still loves Ashley. The result is a tumultuous, unsatisfying marriage. When Scarlett finally realizes she loves Rhett, he's on his way out the door with his famous, "Frankly my dear, I don't give a damn." I'm sure Scarlett has so much strength and motivation that she'll get Rhett back. Film defies criticism. Suffice it to say that Leigh and Gable are perfect in their roles. They are witty, dramatic, dynamic, glamorous, and boy can they kiss. There are other interesting characters besides Scarlett and Rhett. The women characters are surprisingly strong—even Hattie McDaniel's Mammy. I really like the scene in which Melanie sits with prostitute Belle (Ona Munson) in Belle's carriage and thanks her for helping Ashley escape Northern soldiers. The Atlanta fire and the shot of the thousand wounded confederate soldiers at the train depot live up to their reputations. Directed by Victor Fleming (and, uncredited, George Cukor, Sam Wood, and William Cameron Menzies). Sidney Howard wrote the script (with assistance from Jo Swerling, Ben Hecht, and John Van Druten). Max Steiner composed the score. Walter Plunkett designed the costumes. Leigh, McDaniel, and Fleming won Oscars as did cinematographers Ernest Haller and Ray Rennahan, editors Hal C. Kern and James E. Newcom, and art director Lyle Wheeler. Best Picture winner. Also with: Thomas Mitchell, Barbara O'Neil, Laura Hope Crews, Harry Davenport, Ann Rutherford, Evelyn Keyes, George Reeves, Butterfly McQueen, Jane Darwell, Eddie Anderson, Ward Bond, J. M. Kerrigan, Isabel Jewell, Victor Jory.

GOOD, THE BAD AND THE UGLY, THE (ITALIAN/1966) C/161m—180m. An exceptional, extremely exciting, extravagant, and funny epic western by Sergio Leone, released in the U.S. in 1968, a year after *A Fistful of Dollars* and *For a Few Dollars More*. In this episode in the life of Clint Eastwood's deadly, nameless superwarrior (a myth figure riding through America's West) he is, ironically, "the good"—so designated because he kills only bad guys. He forms an unholy alliance with Eli Wallach's Tuco, a ruthless (although humorous) murderer who, besides killing people, has "robbed countless post offices" and taken almost everybody over the border for immoral purposes. He is the "ugly"—a *flawed* superwarrior who has emotions, talks a lot, is religious and feels guilt, and is more *human* than either Eastwood or Lee Van Cleef's "Angel Eyes," Leone's "bad"—a fallen angel/superwarrior who kills anyone who gets in his way. All three men are after a cache of gold and they won't let even the Civil War get in their way. In the film's sensational climax Leone stages one of his classic ritualistic shootouts (as suitable to an opera as to a western), in which the three invincible characters face each other in a graveyard, with the gold going to the victor. Long film has an imaginative storyline, elaborate set pieces (some employing hundreds of extras), several terrific shootouts, much humor (built around the Eastwood-Wallach relationship), striking cinematography by Tonino Delli Colli, and Ennio Morricone's best score. Film has vague anti-war theme and, like all Leone's works, points out that America was civilized by men who killed for profit. The three leads make lasting impressions: even the ugly bit actors Leone puts in close-up have remarkable screen presence. Also with: Aldo Giuffrè, Chelo Alonso, Mario Brega.

GOONIES, THE (1985) C/114m. A group of young
outcasts, nicknamed "the Goonies," try to save their old-Seattle neighborhood from redevelopment. They search for a pirate treasure that is rumored to be buried in nearby ocean caves. Following an old treasure map, they climb through a hidden passage in a dilapidated restaurant and embark on a journey of nonstop danger into the caves below. With three modern-day bloodthirsty pirates on their trail, they race through the booby-trapped caves until they achieve their goal. How this extremely disappointing film got good reviews is a complete mystery—unless critics were then afraid to take on Steven Spielberg, executive producer of the picture. The young boys who take part in the adventure are loud, vulgar, and in need of babysitters. Even director Richard Donner seems so vexed by their constant chatter that he tries to drown them out with blaring music. The villains (who are miscast) are cruel, rather than delightfully evil. In fact, there is a mean and rude, rather than good-natured,

feel to the entire film; this can probably be attributed to Chris Columbus (*Gremlins*), whose scripts have this tendency. There are some clever touches and the hectic pacing will keep you from falling asleep, but surprisingly this picture lacks imagination. Dialogue and characters (especially the fake kids) leave much to be desired. Sean Astin's inspirational "let's-not-give-up" speech is particularly lame. But the final reunion scene is the worst of all. Bad casting, weak direction. At least there's a good, though poorly incorporated, theme song by Cyndi Lauper. Also with: Corey Feldman, Jeff Cohen, Ke Huy Quan, Josh Brolin, Kerri Green, Martha Plimpton, John Matuszak.

GOSPEL ACCORDING TO ST. MATTHEW, THE (ITALIAN-FRENCH/1966) B&W/135m.

Pier Paolo Pasolini's surprisingly straightforward and modern telling of the Christ (Enrique Irazoqui) story, from birth to resurrection, which was given grandiose treatment in *King of Kings* and *The Greatest Story Ever Told*. The pacing is very slow and most of the film is played in a subdued manner—which makes several scenes of callous violence perpetrated by authority figures on the masses particularly jolting: soldiers randomly kill babies who might be Jesus; sweet-faced Salome finishes a lovely dance and demands the head of John the Baptist. Watching Jesus wander the deserts, meeting the poor and delivering defiant speeches (with one famous Christ quote after another), there is a strange feeling of authenticity, as if somehow news cameras were at the scene. In fact, the film is shot in such a manner that one is reminded of sixties documentaries chronicling campaigns of politicians or, better, the Reverend Martin Luther King, Jr., as he traveled the South on his *revolutionary* course. It's hard to gauge Pasolini's feelings about Christ, who as first seems concerned only with getting people to worship him (is there another reason people were put on earth?), but in time (a year after John's beheading) shows signs of compassion and a willingness to help, even sacrifice himself for, mankind. To Marxist Pasolini, Christ is a revolutionary who unites the masses and becomes a martyr to the cause, defying those in authority in church and state, and forcing these hypocrites, to reveal their true natures. Cast with neophytes, this is the only film in which the Virgin Mary (who is pretty!) has a mustache. Also with: Margherita Caruso, Susanna Pasolini, Marcello Morante, Mario Socrate, Monique Van Vooren.

GÖSTA BERLINGS SAGA/STORY OF GÖSTA BERLING, THE/ LEGEND OF GÖSTA BERLING, THE/ATONEMENT OF GÖSTA BERLING, THE (SWEDISH/1924) B&W/93m—137m—(approx.)240m.

The most ambitious and famous work of Sweden's golden silent era, this adaptation of Selma Lagerlöf's epic novel was co-written and directed by Mauritz Stiller; perhaps it is best known for the performance by the young Greta Garbo, although she hasn't as much screen time as several other actresses. Story is set in the 19th century. Lars Hanson plays the title character, a priest who is thrown out of his parish because of his heavy drinking. Film is concerned with his redemption. He becomes a tutor for a family of nobility, putting him into contact with several women who fall in love with him. The central location for the story is a great palace, Ekeby Manor, which is coveted by Count Hendrick Dohna (Torsten Hammeren), husband of the Countess Elisabeth (Garbo). When its owner, Major Samszelius (Otto Elg-Lundgren), finds out his wife, Margaret (a fine performance by Gerda Lundquist-Dahl), has been unfaithful, he gives Ekeby to the pensioners (including Gösta). Gösta and the beautiful Marianne Sinclair (Jenny Hasselqvist) live at Ekeby until Margaret sets fire to it (in the film's most spectacular scene). But it's apparent that Elisabeth is whom Gösta wants to be with—if only she could get out of her marriage. I have seen only the 93-minute 1934 version of the film, which is so truncated that it's very hard to tell what is going on. Still I was struck by the passion present in the performances of the actresses, particularly when their characters sense that they have been wrongly treated. Garbo handles herself nicely, playing—as she would in Hollywood—a woman who is controlled by her heart. Stiller's visuals and *mise-en-scène* aren't flamboyant, but are impressive. It's a lovely film to look at. Outdoor scenes (in summer or snowy winter) are particularly effective—most memorable is when Gösta and Elisabeth flee a pack of wolves across the icy terrain in a horse-pulled sleigh. Also with: Sixten Melmerfelt, Karin Swanström, Ellen Cedarström.

GRADUATE, THE (1967) C/105m.

For the college-age audience of 1967, this was the film of the year, one that everyone saw several times and that became integral to everyday conversation. While not all of us were impressed by director Mike Nichols's technical innovations, we were excited by his novel use of contemporary music (popular songs by Simon & Garfunkel); the provocative sexual theme; a lead character, Ben (Dustin Hoffman's first major role), whose problems we could relate to; and a hilarious new style (for movies) of comic dialogue, in which the listener, Ben, must find words to fill in the adult talker's long and awkward pauses. Ben has come home to LA after graduating with honors from an Eastern college. He sits around the house, trying to figure out what to do with his life. The more he sees of middle-class adults, the more reluctant he is to go to graduate school and prepare to be like these heavy-drinking, unhappy, money-minded people. His parents try to plan his life for him, and a brash, pathetic, alcoholic, middle-aged family friend, Mrs. Robinson (Anne Bancroft), seduces him. When Ben starts to date her daughter, Elaine (Katharine Ross), Mrs. Robinson becomes furious and threatens to tell her about them. Ben tells Elaine first, and the shocked girl flees back to Berkeley, where she goes to college. Her parents pressure her into marriage with a more "respectable" young man. But Ben will not let adults or convention crush his rebelliously romantic instinct. Interestingly, Nichols intentionally stops being funny at about the time Elaine enters the picture—the humor disappears when Ben stops being passive and awkward and snaps out of his postgraduate depression. He comes alive and exhibits a desperate, anarchic spirit that any young person in 1967 could identify with. Film is dated—can you believe how many years ago this was released?—but is essential to any study of film during the protest years. The acting by Hoffman and Bancroft is super—their scenes together still hold up. Many scenes that supposedly take place on the Berkeley campus were filmed at USC. Songs include "Sounds of Silence," "Parsley, Sage, Rosemary, and Thyme," and "Mrs. Robinson." Nichols, Buck Henry, and Calder Willingham adapted Charles Webb's book, retaining much dialogue. Also with: William Daniels, Murray Hamilton, Elizabeth Wilson, Brian Avery, Norman Fell, Richard Dreyfuss (in a bit).

GRAND HOTEL (1932) B&W/113m.

"Heartbreak Hotel" is more like it. M-G-M classic, a Best Picture winner, is set in Berlin at a luxurious hotel where only disillusioned people seem to stay. There are five major characters: Greta Garbo is a ballerina who wants to be left alone but is lonely for love; John Barrymore is a down-on-his-luck thief passing himself off as a baron; Lionel Barrymore is a dying man who spends his life's savings in order to buy himself his first good time; Wallace Beery is a cold-hearted industrial magnate; and Joan Crawford is a secretary who wants to become a movie star and is willing to sleep with Beery if it will help her achieve her ambition. It's John Barrymore who helps Garbo, Lionel Barrymore, and Crawford overcome their self-pitying depression—a thief who *gives* something to people cannot survive. Adaptation of Vicki Baum's novel *Menschen im Hotel* is erratically acted by the male stars, but Garbo and especially Crawford, who was never more appealing, *glow*—as Hollywood stars once did. Crawford's scene with Lionel Barrymore is bizarre. Directed by Edmund Goulding. Billy Daniels was the cinematographer. Remade as *Weekend at the Waldorf* in 1945. Also with: Lewis Stone, Jean Hersholt.

GRAND ILLUSION/GRANDE ILLUSION, LA (1937) B&W/111m.

Jean Renoir's heartfelt cry for an end to wars, which are casually undertaken at the expense of the natural bond among all men. In 1916 a plane carrying French officers Pierre Fresnay and Jean Gabin is shot down by German officer Erich von Stroheim. They are sent to several prison camps for officers, where, though treated with civility, they repeatedly try to escape. Finally they end up at an escape-proof fortress commanded by Von Stroheim, who since their first meeting has suffered serious debilitating injuries. Fresnay devises a self-sacrificing plan that will allow Gabin and Jewish officer Marcel Dalio to escape. Picture centers on respectful relationship between Von Stroheim and Fresnay, both cultured and aristocratic, emotionless yet fervently patriotic career soldiers. They are the last of a dying breed who believe war (soldiering) can be carried out in a chivalrous manner. Renoir's point is that war is simply too cruel; as Fresnay says, there can no longer be sentiment in war. The prisoners we see are treated well, yet they desperately need to escape. When one dresses up like a female for a variety show, all the men silently stare at him, thinking about the women the war has taken from them. Renoir also makes a strong statement when the Russian prisoners receive textbooks and cookbooks instead of the expected food from their insensitive empress. The need for lasting peace is evident: Von Stroheim mourns for Fresnay, who is shot during the escape attempt; German soldiers dutifully shoot at escaping Gabin and Dalio, but are happy they miss; despite not knowing each other's languages, Gabin and a German farm woman (Dita Parlo) fall in *love* (a univeral language); the imprisoned French officers learn to accept each other as equals, despite differences in religion and social class. Asked years later how much effect pacifist films have, Renoir replied, "In 1936 I made a picture named *La Grande Illusion* in which I tried to express all my deep feelings for the cause of peace. This film was very successful. Three years later the war broke out. That is the only answer I can find. . . ."

GRAPES OF WRATH, THE (1940) B&W/129m.

John Ford directed this superb, stirring adaptation of John Steinbeck's novel. When the banks foreclose on their land, Oklahoma sharecroppers leave the dust bowl for the promised land, California. Tom Joad (Henry Fonda) gets out of prison (he'd done four years for manslaughter) just in time to join Ma (Jane Darwell), Pa (Russell Simpson), and the rest of the Joads and Preacher Casey (John Carradine) on their difficult journey. Grandpa (Charley Grapewin) and Grandma (Zeffie Tilbury) die along the way. California is not paradise. It is overrun by starving travelers. Most of the time, the Joads can't find work, and when they do get work in the fields, pay is insufficient to buy food. They are forced to stay in depressing, wire-enclosed jungle camps. They are at the mercy of police who work for the wealthy landowners and tough strikebreakers who make sure there is no organizing to protest wages and working and living conditions. Because he makes waves, Preacher Casey is a target of the thugs. This is not a radical film, but it is one of the most progressive that Hollywood has ever produced (which is surprising since Ford was a political conservative). We may have trouble accepting Casey's words about the need for working people to unite, because it's obvious that he's gone a bit out of his head. But when Tom shows that he has taken Casey's words to heart and goes off to wherever children are hungry, where people are "fighting for their rights," and wherever they "aren't free," we know him well enough (he is sensible) to believe *he* is doing the right thing. Like several other Ford films, this is about the near destruction of an individual family, which is regenerated by joining a bigger family. In other films they become part of civilization; here the Joads become part of the *family of man*; they were once rooted to their Oklahoma home, but now they realize that all of America is their home; whereas Ma Joad was once a symbol of the family, she becomes—when she delivers her inspiring final speech—a symbol of the *people*. Powerful film is impeccably cast, beautifully photographed by Gregg Toland (as Ford said, he had nothing beautiful to photograph), and sympathetically directed (Ford won an Oscar). Nunnally Johnson wrote the script, Alfred Newman composed the score. It was produced by Darryl F. Zanuck. Also with: Frank Darien, Frank Sully, O.Z. Whitehead, Dorris Bowdon, Eddie Quillan, Shirley Mills, Darryl Hickman, John Qualen, Ward Bond.

GRAVE OF THE VAMPIRE/SEED OF TERROR (1972) C/95m.
A woman is brutally attacked and raped by a vampire in a graveyard. She gives birth to a son, who is cursed to be a vampire himself. When an adult, he (William Smith) seeks vengeance on his father (Mike Pataski). As a college student, he attends his father's class . . . and things get tense. Pretty good, little-known horror film, unusual in many ways. Direction by John Hayes is strong; William Smith is well cast as one of the cinema's first sympathetic male vampires. Unfortunately, you're likely to see this only on television, where it's hard to tell if the cuts for sex and violence were made by the TV censor or Hayes, who supposedly did trim the film to keep it tasteful. Based on the novel *The Still Life* by David Chase, who worked on the hip television series *Kolchak: The Night Stalker*. He co-wrote with Hayes.

GREAT DICTATOR, THE (1940) B&W/128m.
The comic art of Charles Chaplin was unique in that he dared mine humor from tragic personal and social circumstances. In this classic, in which Chaplin plays both a persecuted Jewish ghetto barber in Tomania and that country's power-mad dictator, Adenoid Hynkel, he took the chance that viewers would be willing to laugh *at* Hitler, the Nazis, and what was happening to the Jews in Germany. A few years later Chaplin expressed regret that he'd made this film a comedy because he then realized how naïve he'd been about the whole political situation in Germany. At the time, he didn't know about what was actually taking place in concentration camps, or about the impossibility of any resistance to SS troops, or about the absurdity of suggesting Hitler's ouster, or about the extreme brutality of Hitler's vision. Despite Chaplin's correct reservations about his film, it's still a joy to watch Hynkel/Hitler tumble down a flight of stairs, or have Benzino Napolini (Jack Oakie), dictator of Bacteria, toss peanut shells on him, or act the buffoon as he fantasizes about world conquest—climbing up his curtains and bouncing a balloon globe off his rump while in the paroxysms of (sexual, it's hinted) ecstasy. This was Chaplin's first talkie for a reason—he wanted audiences to *hear* the difference between Hitler's words of madness (they're unrecognizable, he's shouting so strongly), which melt microphones during speeches, and Chaplin's own clear words of sanity and reason, delivered in a speech by the barber (who's passing as Hynkel), which call for brotherhood and peace. Also with: Paulette Goddard (as the combative Jewish girl the barber falls in love with), Reginald Gardiner (whose life the barber saves during WWI), Henry Daniell, Billy Gilbert, Carter De Haven, Chester Conklin.

GREAT TEXAS DYNAMITE CHASE, THE (1977) C/90m.
Claudia Jennings dynamites her way out of a Texas prison. She robs a bank just as teller Jocelyn Jones is being fired. The two become partners in crime, wanted nationwide for bank robberies in which they use dynamite. Cultists of the late Jennings, the *Playboy* cover girl who went on to become the star of several sexy "B" action movies, regard this as one of her best films. But I think it's disappointing. Injured shooting a getaway scene, Jennings doesn't have her usual vitality, and her sense of humor, much in evidence in her other films, is virtually non-existent. She never really seems to get into this character who has no goal in life but to get rich—most of the women Jennings played were more cognizant that their successes were victories for all women in a world of powerful, rich misogynists. So it is that bright-eyed, enthusiastic Jones, who has a better part because of her character changes throughout, steals the film (even though Jennings does have a couple of seduction scenes). Jennings and Jones play well together, but before their interaction really develops, Johnny Crawford (formerly of *The Rifleman*) joins the bank-robbing team and becomes Jones's boyfriend. Because he worries so much, the film becomes too serious. His brutal murder is totally incongruous with the rest of the film. The picture is so lazily scripted that it has no dramatic conflict; nothing has to be resolved. The film should have one major villain on the women's tail; also they should have a reason, other than to get rich, for robbing banks (as do the James boys in their films). Only at the end when they fight for survival can we empathize with them. Michael Pressman directed for New World. Also with: Chris Pennock, Tara Stroheimer, Bart Braverman.

GREED (1924) B&W/109m−150m.
Erich von Stroheim's original, extremely faithful version of *McTeague*, Frank Norris's well-known naturalist novel, was nearly 10 hours long. Louis B. Mayer's new head of production at Metro-Goldwyn, Irving Thalberg, ordered the picture drastically cut: Stroheim cut it to seven hours, then to four hours; his friend Rex Ingram trimmed off another hour and June Mathis got it down to its final 150-minute length—all excised footage was destroyed. What remained is the major story, with the three most prominent characters in Norris's book. McTeague (Gibson Gowland) is a physically strong but stupid miner who becomes the assistant to a traveling dentist in order to study his trade. Although he has no license, McTeague eventually sets up a dental practice in San Francisco's Polk Street district. One day his best friend, Marcus (Jean Hersholt), who works in the slaughterhouse, brings in his girlfriend, his cousin Trina (ZaSu Pitts), for some dental work. When McTeague and Trina fall in love and want to marry, Marcus gladly steps aside for his good friend. But when Trina wins $5000 in a lottery, Marcus greatly resents McTeague's having stolen Trina from him; he makes it clear that he feels entitled to the money. Before he leaves San Francisco, Marcus tells the authorities that McTeague has no dental license. McTeague is soon out

of work and Trina refuses to spend a cent of her fortune. As she and her husband become increasingly destitute and move into squalor, she becomes increasing miserly, taking the pennies from McTeague's pockets, waking up in the middle of the night to polish her coins. She begins to look crazed; McTeague takes to drinking and hitting her. Despite being trimmed to about a fourth of its original length, this film is still a masterpiece, one of the greatest of silent films and a picture that still has impact today: surely no character has better displayed avarice than Pitts, whose brow rises automatically and eyes look cunning any time she can even smell money. The film also benefits from Von Stroheim's typical array of unusual supporting characters; the intensity of his directing and the acting; his attention to set design; and his decision to film on location in San Francisco and even Death Valley for the classic finale, a deadly confrontation between McTeague and Marcus. The worst result of the extreme studio-imposed editing is that the changes in the characters' personalities once money enters their lives are too rushed—this is particularly true in regard to Trina and McTeague. For the *naturalism* of Norris to be conveyed properly, the deterioration of their marriage and their descent from nice people to "animals" must have a more natural progression. Also with: Tempe Pigott, Chester Conklin, Sylvia Ashton.

GREEN FOR DANGER (BRITISH/1946) B&W/93m.
English rescue worker is injured during German bomb raid during WWII. He dies on the operating table at a rural emergency hospital. When other bodies start turning up, it becomes apparent he was murdered. Inspector Cockrill (Alastair Sim) figures out that all the doctors and nurses might have killed anyone who knew their particular secrets. He arranges a fake operation to ferret out the murderer. Famous whodunit is much overrated. The mystery is satisfactory, but the proceedings are surprisingly somber—in fact, the supposedly witty Cockrill (a poorly conceived character) seems to be in the wrong film. They should have lightened it all up, and Cockrill should have been more like Clouseau. Picture's major advantage is that you forget who the murderer is from one viewing to the next. Directed by Sidney Gilliat. Also with: Sally Gray, Trevor Howard, Rosamund John, Leo Genn, Judy Campbell, Megs Jenkins.

GREETINGS (1968) C/88m.
Seriocomedy, made in two weeks for a mere $43,000 by 28-year-old Brian De Palma, was one of the most popular "anti-establishment" pictures of the late sixties and early seventies. It was that rare film made for filmmakers and film students as much as for the young, alienated, angry generation. It reflects the political unrest and malaise of 1968 America and dares attack specific political targets: Lyndon Johnson, the Vietnam War, the Warren Commission report on the Kennedy assassination, and the draft. Also it is a splendid example of the type of independent films made then: there are technical lapses and sloppy editing and photography throughout—but there are moments of cinematic brilliance; the

wild, slapdash humor is at times original and at other times smug, vulgar, and self-congratulatory; there is some female nudity (the film received an X rating) and women, all in subordinate roles, are defined by their sexuality. Whereas De Palma would in following years borrow mostly from Hitchcock, here his influences seem to be *cinéma-vérité* documentarians, Michelangelo Antonioni (specifically *Blow-Up*), and Jean-Luc Godard. The film is about obsession. Jonathan Warden is obsessed with sex and pursues sexual adventures through computer dating; his friend Gerrit Graham is obsessed with the Warren Report and pursues evidence to prove Kennedy was the victim of a conspiracy; and pal Robert De Niro is obsessed with voyeurism and pursues women to pose for "Peeping Tom" films he pretends to be making for the Whitney Museum. But De Palma is the most obsessed of all—he reveals here that he is obsessed with and is exploring the very nature of film. Whereas our three heroes use "cinematic" tools—cameras, monitors, photographic equipment—in their *pursuits*, there is dramatic reversal and they wind up being the passive test subjects/prey in other people's "cinematic" experiments. Only the absurd humor links this and its sequel, *Hi, Mom!*, to De Palma's later films. Also with: Richard Hamilton, Megan McCormick, Bettina Kugel, Roz Kelly, Allen Garfield as a smut peddler.

GREGORY'S GIRL (SCOTTISH/1981) C/91m.
While American directors were churning out vile sex comedies about teenagers, Scotland's inimitable Bill Forsyth was making this charming, offbeat comedy about teenage puppy love. Gordon John Sinclair is a tall, gangly teenager who falls for the mysterious new girl in school (Dee Hepburn)—the star of the school's otherwise all-male soccer team. In some truly marvelous scenes the shy boy gets advice about girls from his younger sister so he can plan how to win Hepburn. But Forsyth uses Hepburn not so much as a real girl as a kind of angel, who appears out of nowhere, orchestrates matters so that Sinclair ends up happily with the nice girl classmate who wants him for a boyfriend, and disappears into the sunset. The sequence in which Sinclair goes for his big date with Hepburn, only to find himself handed from girl to girl as if he were a baton in a relay race, is truly delightful. This sweet, extremely amusing film (which is brimming with clever sight gags) is like nothing made in the U.S. Also with: Chic Murray, Jake D'Arcy, Alex Norton, Clare Grogan.

GREMLINS (1984) C/111m.
Steven Spielberg, Frank Marshall, and Kathleen Kennedy were executive producers, Christopher Columbus (*The Goonies*) wrote the script, and Joe Dante directed this summer box-office sensation. An inventor (Hoyt Axton) buys a cute, funny little creature of unknown species at a Chinese junkshop. It's a present for his teenage son (Zach Galligan). Gizmo is a perfect, friendly pet—but when he gets wet he multiplies. His new gremlin brothers are ugly, ferocious creatures who multiply further and go on a rampage through the town, terrorizing

some people and killing others. Comic horror film starts out in friendly spirits with references to *It's a Wonderful Life* and *The Wizard of Oz*, as well as projecting innocent, family and smalltown life found in the Andy Hardy series, but it degenerates into meanness. Not only is the violence vicious and cruel, but Galligan's girlfriend, Phoebe Cates, tells a nauseating story about why she *hates* Christmas: her father got stuck in the chimney and died. Is this supposed to be tongue-in-cheek? Best humor comes from Axton's inventions, which invariably go haywire. Best blend of horror and comedy is when Mom (Frances Lee McCain) angrily attacks gremlins who've invaded *her* living room. The special effects are nifty, but the young kids who'd like them best shouldn't see this movie. Chris Walas created the gremlins; Jerry Goldsmith composed the score; John Hora was cinematographer. Also with: Polly Holliday, Dick Miller, Jackie Joseph, Key Luke, Judge Reinhold, Scott Brady, Glynn Turman, Jonathan Banks, Don Steele, Harry Carey, Jr., Chuck Jones, Edward Andrews.

GREYSTOKE: THE LEGEND OF TARZAN, LORD OF THE APES (1984) C/129m.   Project was originally conceived by writer-director Robert Towne but ended up in the hands of director Hugh Hudson (*Chariots of Fire*) and writer Michael Austin. (Although his screenplay and concept were revised, Towne received co-writer credit as P. H. Vazak.) Often interesting and impressive but ultimately unsatisfying, this film attempts to lift familiar Tarzan-origins tale out of fiction and into myth-history in the same way *The Legend of the Lone Ranger* did. Edgar Rice Burroughs faithfuls will object more to the austere and "artistic" treatment of Burroughs' fast-moving pulp fantasy. Though the film should be commended for finally bringing to the screen Tarzan's early life—he grows up with the apes who adopted him as a baby after his shipwrecked parents were dead—and for having him be the multilingual intellectual that Burroughs created; nonetheless some of the revisionist treatment of the well-known story is unacceptable. Particularly infuriating is having Tarzan (Christopher Lambert) meet Jane (Andie MacDowell) in Scotland rather than in the African jungle where she is part of an expedition; the expedition would signify her thirst for adventure and, if we give the jungle its sexual connotation, her subconscious search for a "wild" lover. Also unforgivable is having Tarzan and Jane part company at film's end, which everybody knows did *not* happen! Apparently the filmmakers were less interested in the Tarzan character as created by Burroughs than in Tarzan as a unique case study (a man whose primal bestial instincts were not suppressed by human conditioning and control). It's much like Truffaut's *The Wild Child*. In the first, more fascinating half of this epic, we watch a human boy live with his adopted family of apes; in the second half, Tarzan—now John Clayton, Lord of Greystoke—returns to Scotland to claim his title and is essentially an *ape*man entering the family of Man. Finding men equally savage to beasts, plus more arrogant and systematic in their brutality, he eventually decides he doesn't wish to fit in and returns

to the jungle—he would rather be part of the natural order than part of "civilization." However, from what Hudson shows us, life with the apes wasn't particularly interesting or intellectually stimulating (although it's fun to watch), so it's hard to believe this Tarzan would return to it—especially when one considers that he grows to love every human being he gets to know well—Jane (sensuously played by beautiful model MacDowell), a kindly Belgian explorer (well played by Ian Holm), and his grandfather (a moving final performance by Sir Ralph Richardson). What is the appeal of the apes—especially after his ape parents are dead? (We never feel sympathy or admiration for the apes.) Film is meticulously crafted, Lambert makes a great Tarzan (he looks a bit like Bruce Bennett in *Tarzan the Fearless*)—he is the first to project the proper combination of intellect and savagery—the romantic scenes between Tarzan and Jane are extremely erotic, and John Alcott's photography is stunning. The story itself entertains but is unexciting and predictable; it's full of undeveloped subplots that could have given picture needed substance. Also, it would have been nice if all the apes didn't look alike (which is not to say Rick Baker's makeup is less than fantastic). I could swear Tarzan's ape mother is killed three times. Also with: James Fox, Nigel Davenport, Cheryl Campbell, Ian Charleson.

GROOVE TUBE, THE (1974) C/75m.   Sketch comedy having to do with television isn't particularly inspired. Bits that may have been funny in 1974 have since been topped by other satirical movies and even television shows. There's a lot of sex (film got an X rating) and drug humor; but gags have no consistency—as if 100 writers contributed one gag each. The funniest parody of a commercial is also the grossest: it's for a product called Brown 25. The best bit is the finale, in which two sports commentators comment on the lovemaking technique of a couple entered in international sex games: their dialogue, which reminds one of the commentators describing Olympic ice-skating, is very witty (one guy has a Spanish accent) and necessary when the TV picture goes on the blink just when the sex gets exciting. Directed by Ken Shapiro. With: Shapiro, Lane Sarasohn, Chevy Chase (his movie debut), Mary Mendham, Richard Belzer.

GROUPIES (1970) C/88m.   A terrific documentary subject—rock-music groupies—proves surprisingly dull, thanks to some terrible filmmaking and the third-rate group of groupies that directors Ron Dorfman and Peter Nevard chose to study. Half the time you have no idea what the people on screen are talking about—at other times you don't care. You never learn what the backgrounds of these people are or exactly what their lifestyles are. Not only are the groupies instantly pathetic but so are the musicians who tolerate these obnoxious parasites. They deserve each other. Film needs more name-dropping (about Jimmy Page's whip, about Jimi Hendrix screwing the plaster cast of his penis, etc.) in which groupies recall sexual conquests with famous stars. It needs fewer musical numbers—the finale with Joe

Cocker has no relation to the "groupies" theme. Watch for Gloria Steinem! Also with: Ten Years After, Spooky Tooth.

GUN CRAZY/DEADLY IS THE FEMALE (1949) B&W/87m.

John Dall, who has had a lifelong passion for guns, falls in love with bad but beautiful Peggy Cummins, a carnival sharpshooter. (Their initial meeting—she wears cowgirl garb and guns—is incredibly sexy.) He joins her act, but soon they quit and get married. She promises to reform and stop leading an amoral life. But when they have trouble with finances, she threatens to leave him unless they pull off a few robberies. For his sake she lies that she is non-violent during crimes; for her sake he lies that he did something violent. There have been many fine movies about young couples driving across the country with the police on their trail, including Arthur Penn's *Bonnie and Clyde*, which this film surely influences. But none is more fascinating or exciting than Joseph H. Lewis's low-budgeter that is supercharged with energy, non-stop action, violence, passion, and sex. While set against a backdrop of poor, insensitive, smalltown America of the forties, and reflecting a postwar malaise ("Everything in these forty-eight states hurts me," sneers Cummins), this cult film remains remarkably contemporary, especially in its portrayal of a country turned on by speed, violence, and crime. Lewis's achievements are great, ranging from maintaining a terrific pace throughout to attaining a distinct sense of time and place. But his more inspired contribution was giving his leads to the relatively unknown Cummins (a British actress) and Dall. To Cummins, guns equal sex, money, and excitement, and to Cummins and Dall *as a couple* the firing of guns while committing crimes is how they fuel their sexual flame; but to Dall the individual, guns are a means of identity for a man who, as a kid, had no parents and no self-respect. Once Cummins realizes that she loves Dall, they are constantly grabbing each other, snuggling up, kissing. Even when they flee police on foot through rough terrain, are soaking wet, dirty, bruised, exhausted, and in a panic because they can hear the bloodhounds, he still calls her "honey," and they still take a moment to hug and kiss. Before they die, she apologizes for getting him into such trouble, he honestly says, "I wouldn't have it any other way," and they kiss one last time as the police (whom we can't see in the swamp mist) close in for the kill. It's one of the most romantic endings in movie history. Millard Kaufman rewrote Mackinlay Kantor's 320-page script, which he'd adapted from his own story. Produced by Frank and Maurice King. With cinematography by Russell Harlan and a score by Victor Young. Also with: Barry Kroeger, Annabel Shaw, Harry Lewis, Morris Carnovsky, Mickey Little (Dall at seven), Russ Tamblyn (Dall at 14), Don Beddoe.

GUNGA DIN (1939) B&W/96m–118m.

One of the all-time great Hollywood action-adventure films. Set in India in the 1800s, during the time of British rule, it was inspired by Kipling's famous poem about an Indian water boy who won the hearts of the British soldiers he served. But if you're willing to substitute Sam Jaffe's Gunga Din, a fearless, poor outsider whose life's dream is to be a soldier in the British army, for D'Artagnan, a fearless, poor outsider whose life's dream is to be one of the French musketeers, you can see that it borrows less form Kipling than from Dumas. Certainly our three inseparable, cheerful, fight-loving British soldiers, Cary Grant, Douglas Fairbanks, Jr., and Victor McLaglen, are kin to the "Three Musketeers," who also are reluctant to let the outsider into their select company, treating him like a mascot until he proves himself. Story has Grant discovering a murderous Indian cult, led by the mad, dark-skinned, glowing-eyed Eduardo Ciannelli, and sending Jaffe for help. But Jaffe, McLaglen, and Fairbanks, Jr. (who walked out on fiancée Joan Fontaine so he could rescue his friend), are captured along with Grant. They try to figure out how to warn the British troops riding their way that the Indians are planning an ambush. It is Gunga Din who saves the day, at a high cost. The action scenes are great fun and, until the final battle, usually feature bits of slapstick and funny heroics by the three imperturbable leads. Film should have been in color, but it still has great pictorial beauty. Superb direction by George Stevens: it's spirited, stirring, and, finally, sentimental. Also with: Montagu Love, Abner Biberman, Robert Coote, Cecil Kellaway.

GUNN (1967) C/94m.

Blake Edwards brought back his cool fifties TV detective Peter Gunn for this one-shot movie. Craig Stevens, who was never impressive in anything except the fine television series, looks tired and old as Gunn; and it's upsetting that Ed Asner replaced Herschel Bernardi as Lieutenant Jacoby and Laura Devon took over Lola Albright's Edie role. The murder-mystery script by Edwards and William Peter Blatty is extremely confusing; the picture hasn't the icy, smoky atmosphere of the TV series; and while the twist ending is pretty good, it (like the rest of the film) is too bloody. Most interesting is seeing Sherry Jackson, grown up from *Make Room for Daddy*, looking beautiful and sexy as the mysterious girl who first turns up in Gunn's bed, with an introductory "Make a wish." So what happened to Jackson after this film? Music by Henry Mancini, but why did they add lyrics to his classic theme song? A disappointment. Also with: M. T. Marshall, Albert Paulsen, Helen Traubel, Carol Wayne, Pat O'Malley.

HAIL MARY (FRENCH-SWISS/1985) C/95m.

Even the Pope was among the legions of protesters around the world who condemned Jean-Luc Godard's film about an immaculate pregnancy in modern-day Switzerland. It's certain that Godard didn't intend it to be offensive, much less blasphemous, but simply by naming his pregnant virgin

Mary—although it's likely that she (Myriem Roussel) isn't supposed to be *the* Virgin Mary—and including nude scenes, he made the film an easy target of religious groups (which, ironically, led to its commercial success). Godard's Mary works in her father's gas station and, for some reason, plays a lot of basketball. One night a man (Philippe Lacosta) and a little girl (Manon Anderson) drive up in boyfriend Joseph's (Thierry Rode) taxi and tell her she's about to become pregnant without having sex with a man. Her pregnancy infuriates the quick-tempered Joseph, but after she proves that she's still intact, he humbles himself and agrees to be her platonic lover. Mary has tremendous torment over her pregnancy, but in her mind figures out what happened. Godard hints that we are all extraterrestrials and all our births are the result of a designed plan (this is *Kubrick* territory); we can't comprehend our own existence, so it's impossible for us to grasp an immaculate conception, which is equally miraculous (it's hard to tell if Godard is saying that the one God is responsible for both the existence of earthlings and Mary's pregnancy)—but Mary concludes (rightly or wrongly) that she is supplying the body for an independent soul. As controversial as this film became, it's curiously uninvolving, confusing, and boring. While his cinematography is as lovely as ever, Godard shows his growing lack of concern for acting. But what's worse is that he doesn't bother to develop his characters sufficiently so we can understand their feelings about their unique circumstances—this being the case, why did he even bother making a film on such an emotional subject? Godard's film actually lasts just 70m.; it is proceeded by a 25-minute short called *The Book of Mary*. It's a tender piece directed by Anne-Marie Miéville about an intelligent young girl (strikingly played by the expressive Rebecca Hampton) whose parents (Aurore Clément, Bruno Cremer) divorce. One wants to draw parallels between it and the Godard section, but that doesn't really work. Anyway, it's to Miéville's benefit if her short is judged apart.

HAIL THE CONQUERING HERO (1944) B&W/ 101m.
Preston Sturges wrote and directed this frantically paced satire about smalltown boy Eddie Bracken, who was afraid to tell his mother (Georgia Caine) and lifelong girlfriend (Ella Raines) that the marines wouldn't take him because of chronic hay fever. So he worked in a shipyard for six months and wrote home of fabricated exploits in Guadalcanal; he has told Raines to forget him and she has become engaged to another hay-fever victim—although she still loves Bracken. William Demarest, Freddie Steele (the ex-middleweight boxing champ), and four other marines feel sorry for Bracken because he can't go home, and they escort him there. When Bracken arrives, he discovers that the whole town thinks he is a hero. There is a band, a parade, a ceremony at which the mortgage to Mom's house is burned. Then Bracken is drafted to run for mayor against the stupid, ineffectual incumbent (Raymond Walburn). His humble, apologetic speech makes him even more popular. Of course he feels guilty about the hoax he and the marines are perpetrating. Picture is skillfully directed in the usual Sturges manner. Confused, fast-talking, philosophical *characters* zip in and out of the crowded frame, fighting for space to stand in and time to say their two cents' worth. There are funny scenes and moments, but overall I find the script pretty weak, like Capra at his phoniest and corniest—the naïve, easily fooled and manipulated common folk have counterparts in *Meet John Doe*. The most interesting aspect is that in 1944 Sturges dared and got away with satirizing Momism, patriotism, politicians and the political process, honor, the military (imagine marines pulling a hoax to influence an election!), hero worship, and the ingenuous American public. Also with: Esther Howard, Elizabeth Patterson, Jimmy Conlin, Franklin Pangborn, Chester Conklin, Jimmie Dundee, Stephen Gregory, Len Hendry.

HALLELUJAH (1929) B&W/106m.
The first major all-black film was directed by King Vidor. M-G-M gave him the go-ahead only after he offered to put up his own money. Zeke (Daniel Haynes) lives a happy life picking cotton with his mammy (Fannie Belle De Knight), his parson pappy (90-year-old reporter Harry Gray), his fiancée (Victoria Spivey)—who is also his adopted sister—and several young siblings. But he's a potential sinner who can't resist the amoral charms of Chick (Nina Mae McKinney). She coaxes him into gambling with her boyfriend, Hot Shot (William Fountaine), who uses rigged dice to win the money Zeke got for his family's cotton crop. Zeke tries to shoot Hot Shot, but accidentally kills his brother. Repenting for his sins, Zeke becomes a skilled itinerant preacher. He is even able to convert Chick. But her religious fervor manifests itself not as love for God but as lust for Zeke. Again he is unable to resist her advances. In the picture's most memorable scene he is drawn to her as she dances provocatively with his other converts inside a prayer hall; he joins her on the dance floor, she embraces him—suddenly the wild dancing around them makes it seem like an orgy rather than a religious gathering—she bites his hand, and he follows her outside into the woods. It's the most daring and the most original thing about this picture. For many years Vidor's film was considered a positive landmark for blacks in the cinema, but in truth it's the film that first established many negative black stereotypes that would become common in the white cinema. Also it was the first to contend that black people are happy living in isolation (from whites), in ignorance, and in poverty because they have religion to fall back on. Haynes (in a part written for Paul Robeson) has physical presence, but his acting is mediocre—his best scenes are those in which Zeke delivers fiery sermons that include gospel songs. McKinney got more press in 1929 for her hip-swaying, sexually uninhibited tigress—it was a role that would serve as model for numerous black vamps in years to come, including those played by Dorothy Dandridge. But, on the whole, her acting isn't very polished. Vidor shot many scenes on location in Tennessee and Arkansas. Irving Berlin contributed two songs. Scripted by Wanda Tuchock and Richard Schayer. Also with: Everett McGarrity, the Dixie Jubilee Singers.

HALLOWEEN (1978) C/93m. John Carpenter's horror thriller begins on Halloween in 1963 when six-year-old Michael Meyers dons a mask and stabs his teenage sister to death. Fifteen speechless years later Michael (Tony Moran) escapes from an asylum and returns home to Haddonfield, Illinois, dons a mask, and on Halloween night stalks three teenage girls (Jamie Lee Curtis, Nancy Loomis, P. J. Soles). Psychiatrist Donald Pleasence searches for him, whom he describes as the personification of evil. I don't think the intriguing Michael is *evil*, just insane. There's that six-year-old inside a man's body, and everything he does—including his murders—is part of a mischievous game. He could kill his victims quickly, but he prefers to hide behind bushes and in closets, peer into windows, scare them, tease them with loud noises or, as in the case of Loomis, play tricks with her car door. Before he attacks Soles, he stands in the bedroom doorway with a sheet over his body and glasses on his covered face. In his never ending struggle with Curtis (who became a cult favorite from her debut effort) he pretends to be dead several times, only to rise and resume his attack. Interestingly, he never attacks children, his peers. I am not as sold on the picture as are its many cultists, but I agree that it's the scariest horror film since *Psycho* and the most imaginatively directed. Carpenter builds tension by repeatedly using a subjective camera; quick editing; driving, piercing music (which he composed); and the creative use of light and shadow and color (particularly black and white). He blends the dark, spooky atmosphere essential to Val Lewton; the humor and suspense that go hand in hand in Hitchcock; the cheap—but fun—tricks and shocks found in William Castle films; and the graphic violence that is the staple of the post-*Night of the Living Dead* American horror film. The horror aside, it's a treat watching the three Middle American teenagers jabber away about boys, school, dates, sex, etc. They are smart (which is why Curtis has trouble attracting boys), witty, and appealingly unconventional. (They are also extremely well acted). Whereas Brian De Palma's films show he still feels hostility toward teenage girls from his adolescence, Carpenter likes them despite their idiosyncrasies. But I find it annoying that the preludes to the attacks on Loomis and Soles drag on for so long that we almost hope they will be killed just to get it over with; and it's regrettable that even this film—like its many inferior imitators—thrives upon the deaths of sexually promiscuous, half-dressed young women. One of the most successful independent features of all time. Carpenter supervised but didn't direct the two inferior sequels. Produced by Debra Hill, who wrote the screenplay with Carpenter. Cinematography by Dean Cundey. Also with: Charles Cypher, Kyle Richards, Brian Andrews.

HANDLE WITH CARE/CITIZENS BAND (1977) C/98m. Amiable comedy-character study, made at the peak of the CB craze. Paul Le Mat runs a voluntary emergency smalltown CB station to help truckers, pilots, etc., who are in trouble. He goes on a crusade to wreck CB systems of irresponsible people who are cutting into the emergency frequency. He spends so much time away from girlfriend Candy Clark that she starts fooling around with his brother (Bruce McGill). Meanwhile Ann Wedgworth and Marcia Rodd arrive in town, only to discover that they are married to the same man, trucker Charles Napier (rescued from Russ Meyer films): they become friends. Climax has town's CB community searching the woods for Roberts Blossom, Le Mat's and McGill's father. Offbeat film has smart dialogue, quirky but believable, engaging characters, and a nice mix of humor and occasional drama (the scene in which McGill breaks down in front of Le Mat is very effective). Sensitive direction by Jonathan Demme, who moved into Hollywood mainstream when this film got excellent reviews. Film would be even better if he got rid of the CB theme and just concentrated on the characters. Also with: Ed Begley, Jr.

HANG 'EM HIGH (1968) C/114m. Clint Eastwood's first starring role in an American film was this bloody western directed by *Rawhide* vet Ted Post. It was so derivative of Eastwood's Sergio Leone films that it often played on bills with them. But anyone familiar with Leone could tell the difference. Eastwood is an innocent man who is hanged by a mob and left to die. Rescued (by Ben Johnson) and deputized (by Pat Hingle), he goes on a legalized killing spree, getting rid of the lynchers one by one. While the film does have strong violence and a tight-lipped character who suffers extreme punishment and seemingly returns from the dead, this stilted cliché-ridden picture pales in comparison to Leone's works. It has none of the stylistic bravura or wit of those films. The major thematic difference is that this Eastwood character is motivated by revenge rather than money. Moreover, in standard western fashion, he has relationships with a respectable woman (Inger Stevens) and a prostitute (Arlene Golonka). Leone's character stayed away from women. Also with: Ed Begley, James MacArthur, Ruth White, Charles McGraw, Alan Hale, Jr., Bruce Dern, Dennis Hopper, Bob Steele.

HANGOVER SQUARE (1945) B&W/77m. John Brahm's wildly stylized period *noir* reunited him with Laird Cregar (who gets top billing here) and George Sanders, the stars of his earlier psychological thriller *The Lodger*, and its scriptwriter, Barré Lyndon. In this adaptation of a novel by Patrick Hamilton, Cregar plays an overworked classical composer of some repute in turn-of-the-century London (a real-life figure named Charles Harvey Bone). When he hears discordant sounds, he suffers blackouts, during which he commits violence. He would like to know if he's responsible for an antique dealer's death—we know that he is guilty—and consults a Scotland Yard doctor, played by Sanders. Cregar should be finishing his concerto, but he spends his time writing popular songs for Linda Darnell, a singer who is using him to help her career along. It's just her bad luck that he finds out she's been two-timing him on the same night he hears an extremely discordant sound. Picture is odd in that we don't care if Cregar murders

Darnell, because she's really a louse, or worry about the other female in his life, Faye Marlowe. The enjoyment comes from watching the heavy-set Cregar in his final film (before suffering a fatal heart attack) give one of his best psycho performances (in a role that Vincent Price, Victor Buono, or Raymond Burr might have had fun with in later years); the wonderful period detail and Brahm's exciting, bizarre direction, especially impressive during the blackout sequences. Brahm wasn't afraid to use wild angles, camera distortion, swooping crane shots, even a *freeze frame*! I really love his use of darkness and light (candles and oil-lit streetlamps are often evident), and how he maneuvers his stars and extras during street scenes. The streets themselves look interesting, as Brahm has the light reflect in deep puddles; one much traveled street is under construction, with dirt piled on both sides of a long ditch—I've never seen a studio set quite like it, and, more important, Brahm uses it to call attention to the disorder in Cregar's mind. Not as good as *The Lodger*, but more flamboyant. Score by Bernard Herrmann. Also with: Alan Napier, Glenn Langan.

HANNAH AND HER SISTERS (1986) C/107m.
Woody Allen's most acclaimed film, a seriocomedy (*Interiors* with humor) about three sisters, Hannah (Mia Farrow), Holly (Dianne Wiest), and Lee (Barbara Hershey), their relationships with each other, their actor parents (Lloyd Nolan, Maureen O'Sullivan)—from whom they've acquired many traits and perceptions of relationships—and the men in their lives. Holly and Lee love and rely on Hannah, but her success in life—at least in *their* eyes—makes them as envious and resentful as they are pleased for her. Hannah is the glue for the entire family, the one who provides stability in the chaotic lives of sisters and parents, the person who is generous to a fault with her time, money, and love (though she's often stingy with encouragement)—the two sisters feel they have little to offer her, but she surely could use the support they don't offer. Whereas neither Holly nor Lee knows what to do about careers, they see that Hannah has already *retired* from an acting career—but they fail to connect her decision to return to the stage temporarily to play Nora in *A Doll's House* with the possibility that she isn't *completely* satisfied as a married housewife. Whereas Holly can't find a man and Lee is growing increasingly dissatisfied with her mismatched relationship to the older reclusive artist Frederick (Max Von Sydow), a mentor who has run out of things to interest her, the two sisters see Hannah as being happily married to her second husband, Elliot (Michael Caine)—they don't realize that she is becoming insecure because his mind seems to be elsewhere. Actually Elliot's mind is on Lee, with whom he has fallen madly in love. They have an affair. Lee breaks up with Frederick and waits for Elliot to break up with Hannah. Meanwhile Holly loses both a man (Sam Waterston) and work to her "friend" (Carrie Fisher); she tries her hand at catering, singing, and writing. And on the fringes Mickey (Allen), Hannah's hypochondriac first husband, worries so much about death that he contemplates suicide. In *The Purple Rose of Cairo* Allen was mean to his characters; this is a sweet film in which he gives all (except Frederick, who dislikes people too much to deserve it) a happy start to their futures, but it's startling how mean his characters (but for Hannah and Mickey) can be to one another. They say vicious things, betray each other's trust. They are insensitive, they lie, they are accusatory. Indeed, every character is deeply wounded at some point, finds himself or herself on shaky ground, and fears the future. Through Mickey, Allen laments that *life is too short*, but also reveals that there is enough *time* within one's life span for many eventful "lifetimes": within brief periods of time (specifically from one Thanksgiving to the next) lives can change to a miraculous degree, people can mature (as do all our characters), sad people can find the happiness that one year before seemed out of reach—"time heals." As Mickey concludes, life is too short, but it is also long enough for him to enjoy a great many pleasures (instead of worrying about death): New York architecture, good music, Marx Brothers movies, walks through the park, and, most of all, Holly. When he was death-obsessed, Mickey's sperm (according to many doctors) couldn't make Hannah pregnant; now that he appreciates living, he is able to create life—Holly becomes pregnant. Weist, Farrow, and Von Sydow stand out in the wonderful cast; I wish that all the characters were a bit more developed, but those who consider this to be Allen's masterpiece disagree. I like the way Allen plays with his own persona, but having Mickey contemplate converting to Catholicism, although funny, is overdoing it a bit—much better is that Allen is comfortable playing a confident, romantic lover who doesn't need a Humphrey Bogart figure to give him advice on how to handle the ladies. Photographed by Carlo Di Palma. A couple of his close-ups of Farrow are eerily beautiful. Also with: Daniel Stern, Tony Roberts, Joanna Gleason.

HARD DAY'S NIGHT, A (BRITISH/1964) B&W/85m-90m.
A treasure. Richard Lester's impressionistic cinematic chronicle of a "typical" 24 hours in the hectic lives of the Beatles is a wonderful comedic-musical showcase for the talented foursome at its peak. The film's infectious anarchical quality—as personified by the Beatles—was the result of Lester's decision to combine his own style, as developed in live television and commercials, with the multifarious styles of filmmakers he admired. You'll see traces of Fellini, Berkeley, Antonioni, Sennett, Chaplin, Keaton. One scene will be abstract, the next absurd, the next realistic; he moves from fantasy to *cinéma vérité*. There are moments of slapstick, parody, satire, outright silliness. Alun Owen's imaginative, semi-plotless script, full of non-sequiturs, is the perfect vehicle for Lester's mad method. Wisely, Lester didn't spend the film trying to convince "squares" that the Beatles are respectable. Instead he tried to show them as they really were, placing them in familiar (though simulated) situations—press parties, interviews, rehearsals, etc. He even allows us to glimpse their "vices":

they play cards, drink (although their managers won't let them), smoke, chase schoolgirls, vainly look at themselves in mirrors, are thorns in the sides of authority figures, and prefer partying to answering fan mail. However, they are neither lazy nor irresponsible (that's why it is such a big deal they play a TV concert on time). The Beatles like their fans, though the adoration befuddles them; yet they realize their fame dictates that they can't have much contact with fans. Their loyalty to one another has less to do with friendship than with each being aware that only three other people in the world know what they're going through as the only sane people in a Beatles-crazy world. Lester chose not to exploit the Beatles' popularity by making them heroic or wise figures—indeed, Ringo makes no attempt to steer a boy playing hooky back to school. If they're to be admired, it's because of their professional attitude toward their music. Over and over again, when the pressures of living in a fishbowl get them down, they pick up their instruments and, quickly, they're smiling again, back in control and singing classics: "I Should Have Known Better," "If I Fell," "And I Love Her," "I'm Happy Just to Dance with You," "Tell Me Why," and "She Loves You." The 1982 re-release has a prologue. Gilbert Taylor did the cinematography, filming on location in London; George Martin was musical director. Also with: Wilfred Brambell (hilarious as Paul's "clean" grandfather), Norman Rossington, John Junkin, Victor Spinetti, Anna Quayle.

HARDCORE (1979) C/108m.   A teenage girl from Grand Rapids disappears while on a class trip to Los Angeles. Her strict Calvinist minister father (George C. Scott) goes to LA and, to his horror, learns that she has been lured away from him by a brutal pimp. She has appeared in porno films—he worries that she will soon be the victim in a "snuff" film. He enlists the aid of a young prostitute (Season Hubley) to help him trace his daughter through the sexual underground. As he becomes more understanding of Hubley's way of life and gives up his preconceptions about wayward youths, she becomes much like a daughter to him. Surely director-writer Paul Schrader, who had a Calvinist upbringing, means Scott's descent into purgatory to be a journey of self-discovery in which he comes to realize his failure as a father, and a test for his rigid, religion-based morality, though he must be capable of sin even to bluff his way through. But story is just an excuse for Schrader to show sordid sexual world that has seduced him in real life and always finds its way into his films. Picture is a remaking of *The Searchers*, with Scott being the "wrong-headed" authoritarian man in pursuit of a missing child. The one major difference is that in John Ford's western the rescued girl would not return to live with John Wayne but with more understanding folk; we sympathize with Scott's daughter for running away from him. Wayne purges himself of his inner demons when the Indian who kidnapped his niece is killed, yet he realizes he shouldn't be a part of her upbringing. By the time Scott saves his daughter from the pimp who controls her, he believes he has learned to be a good father to her—

but his sudden rejection of Hubley, as being unworthy to be his daughter's adopted sister, shows he is a hypocrite. Subject matter will grab you, but direction is cold and exploitive, and ending is not very satisfying because the girl you care about gets the shaft while the other gets salvation. Also with: Peter Boyle, Dick Sargent, Leonard Gaines, David Nichols.

HARDER THEY COME, THE (JAMAICAN/1973) C/96m.   This hard-hitting, crudely made, angry left-wing polemic, with a spectacular reggae soundtrack, has developed a strong cult in America among political moviegoers. Jamaican reggae superstar Jimmy Cliff plays Juan Martin, a young man from the country, who comes to Kingston to make it as a recording star. When the record he makes gets no promotion, he finds work in the island's ganja trade. The corrupt police allow it to continue so the poor will have work and not rebel and so the hierarchy that forms within the black criminal element will keep blacks divided. When Juan refuses to pay a middleman some of his earnings, he is set up for arrest. Juan kills the cop and goes underground. While he's on the lam his record becomes a smash hit and he becomes a folk hero, like the legendary fifties political outlaw, Rhygin. When New World Pictures released this film in America, they figured black viewers would like Juan. The slightly built, gangly, cocky Cliff is too sexual for most whites to be comfortable with; as Juan he wears loud clothes, slurs his words, speaks patois (the Rastafarian dialect), answers back, has a violent streak, carries a gun, and means to do something about being exploited by authorities and being told by Christian leaders to wait until he gets to heaven for happiness. But I don't believe apolitical blacks wished to identify with Juan. I would guess they resented the fact that when Juan emulates their heroes—the American black superstud stereotypes—white director Perry Henzel is mocking the foolish, culturally corrupted, apolitical side of Juan that contributes to his downfall. The Jamaica that Henzel shows us is not the Caribbean paradise of airplane commercials. The countryside is barren and infertile; and Kingston, the tourist center, is overcrowded, violent, seamy, and poverty-stricken. The villains in Jamaica are: the pacifying church (although not the gospel music), the exploitive record business, the ganja business, the police, and the government. The one positive influence is the moral voice of the poor black community, the Rastafarians. They are the ones who have politicized the reggae music that all the poor listen to. The lyrics of Cliff's own songs reflect their philosophy: he sings of universal love, peace, the worth of the individual, and an end to exploitation, neo-colonialism, imperialism, and authoritarianism; of the necessity for people to demand what they're entitled to; and of the desire to die rather than be a "puppet or a slave." See the movie—buy the album! Also with: Janet Bartley, Ras Daniel Hartman, Basil Keane, Bobby Charlton, Winston Stona.

HARDER THEY FALL, THE (1956) B&W/109m.   Seven years after he made *Champion*, Mark Robson skillfully directed what is still the harshest indictment of boxing on film. Philip Yordan's outstanding no-punches-pulled (literally speaking) script was adapted from the novel by Budd Schulberg, who, ironically, had his own stable of boxers. Eddy (Humphrey Bogart's last role) is a cynical, out-of-work sportswriter who becomes press agent for boxing racketeer Nick (Rod Steiger). His job is to promote Nick's new South American import, a huge heavyweight named Toro (Mike Lang). Since Toro turns out to have that deadliest of combinations, "a powder-puff punch and a glass jaw," Eddy must lie about his talent in his publicity releases. He also must ignore fact that Toro's unbeaten streak is a result of Nick having arranged, through a string of thoroughly slimy managers and promoters, for his opponents to take dives—something Toro doesn't know. Toro, a naïve, gentle, religious man, is unaware that he's being set up for slaughter in a fight against the much superior champ (Max Baer). Unless Eddy, who is receiving a large piece of the action (while Toro gets a paltry sum), helps him out, Toro will become just one more permanently exploited boxer. This is the rare boxing film where the person who "sells out" for money is not a fighter. The boxing world that is depicted is abominable. Not only is the sport itself brutal (the beating Toro receives from sadistic Baer is hard to watch), but also most fights are shown to be rigged, and fighters are at the mercy of racketeers and money-hungry managers who should protect their fighters but treat them like cattle (to be bought, used, sold). Film includes startling interview with real-life, pitiful, punch-drunk ex-boxer (who lives behind a street sign), who points out that boxers need protection, a pension plan, and a government commission to supervise the sport—this is still relevant! Picture ends bravely, demanding that either Congress clean up boxing or ban it. Remarkable, well-acted film; a classy one for Bogart to go out on. Curiously, Max Baer plays the champ, twenty years after really mauling Primo Carnera (the basis for Toro) in title bout; one wonders why he or Jersey Joe Walcott (who plays Toro's trainer) would participate in a film that condemns their sport. Also with: Jan Sterling (as Bogart's wife), Edward Andrews, Harold J. Stone, Carlos Montalban, Nehemiah Persoff.

HARLAN COUNTY, U.S.A. (1977) C-B&W/ 103m.
Stirring, Oscar-winning documentary by Barbara Kopple covering a successful, bitterly fought 13-month strike in 1973–74 at the Brookside mine in Harlan, Kentucky, beginning when the miners voted to be represented by the United Mine Workers and ending when the Duke Power Co. agreed to sign a contract. (The picture actually ends later when the miners realize that their new contract won't provide all the benefits they expected.) Kopple and crew befriended the striking miners and were allowed to enter their company-built shacks (which have no bathrooms) and their jail cells when they were arrested for obstructing scab workers who were driving to the mine; to attend organizational meetings; and to join them on the dangerous picket lines. Gun-toting company men made sure the scabs would

have free access—the cameras are there when shots are fired at the pickets, and that's Kopple surprising the sheriff with a warrant for the arrest of the leader of the thugs (seeing the guy's sick face when told he's being arrested is a real highlight). Kopple makes no attempt to disguise she's on the miners' side. Emphasis is placed on the many women who picket on behalf of the male miners (who were limited to six pickets) and the old women who emotionally relate tragic stories about the suffering their fathers, husbands, and sons have endured as non-union miners. Kopple visits clinics where miners are treated for lung diseases and takes her cameras into the mines as well. We learn about the miners/people of Harlan County, their violent history and their hopes. We are most impressed by their bravery, their obstinacy about not giving in, and, though they aren't that educated, their tremendous grasp of the issues that brought about a strike. One of the most incisive portraits of America and the ever struggling labor movement. As exciting as good fiction.

HAROLD AND MAUDE (1971) C/90m.
Hal Ashby's black comedy about a love affair between a depressed 20-year-old manchild (Bud Cort) and an optimistic 80-year-old woman (Ruth Gordon) is one of the most popular of all cult movies. Unlike *King of Hearts*, it holds up quite well today. It has an uplifting quality, a breeziness, a spark, a wonderful sense of successful rebellion that more than compensates for first-time screenwriter Colin Higgins's self-indulgences, puerile moments, and misdirected flights of fancy. For Harold, Maude is a liberating force who keeps him from conforming despite the pressures put on him by his wealthy mother (Vivian Pickles), fascist soldier Uncle Victor (Charles Tyner), his priest (Eric Christmas), and his psychiatrist (G. Wood). She tells Harold simple things: not to back away from life, to be an individual, to experiment, to take chances, and to sing and dance and play music. Maude leaves Harold (she commits suicide) only when she, who loves "to see things grow," realizes Harold has *grown* to be self-sufficient and no longer has a death wish. She reminds me of Simone Simon in *Curse of the Cat People*, who is an unhappy little girl's imaginary playmate, her one friend, until the girl can turn elsewhere (her father) for happiness. I wouldn't have been surprised if Maude turned out to be a figment of Harold's imagination. Maude's suicide is infuriating in a film that celebrates life, but I suppose it makes sense. Throughout the film there have been touching glimpses of Maude when she can't hide her tragic memories. I suspect that she wanted to die many years earlier—when her husband died, presumably in a concentration camp—but decided to continue living and be a human monument to those who died in the camps and give meaning to a life (her own) that survived the Holocaust. In this film about death and resurrection, where life and death continuously overlap, Maude's life energies are transferred to Harold, who will live as Maude taught him. Despite its morbid theme, the film has many hilarious scenes, including Harold's outrageous fake suicides that he stages for mother and

prospective brides his mother brings to the house (the immolation sequence is the best). It also has a terrific, cheery score by Cat Stevens—you'll sing the theme song for days afterward. Love scenes between Harold and Maude will also make you feel good, but I wish they'd been a little more explicit. John Alonzo did the cinematography. Also with: Cyril Cusack, Ellen Geer, Judy Engles, Shari Summers, M. Borman.

HAUNTING, THE (1963) B&W/112m.

First-rate, thinking person's horror film. Adaptation of Shirley Jackson's *The Haunting of Hill House* was ideal choice for Robert Wise to direct, as it allowed him to return to the "psychological" horror subgenre that he helped create with Val Lewton in the forties. As in his *Curse of the Cat People* and *The Body Snatcher*, we never actually see anything supernatural, but there are strong indications of its presence. Are the weird events only the distorted perceptions of a person who is either too frightened or confused to think clearly or is in need of psychoanalysis? Picture is set in an oddly constructed New England mansion, setting for a series of tragedies—resulting in deaths, madness—in its 100-year history. Parapsychologist Richard Johnson believes the house is haunted and moves in to investigate. He is joined by the telepathic Claire Bloom and spinster Julie Harris. Skeptical Russ Tamblyn, the heir to the house, and, later, Johnson's even more skeptical wife, Lois Maxwell, also stay in Hill House. Of course, many unusual things happen, all centering on Harris. It becomes obvious to her and worrisome to the others that the house seems to *want* her and will not let her leave. In a way, this makes her feel important for the first time in her life. A virtual nonentity in life (she lives in her sister-in-law's living room; she spent her prime years nursing her invalid mother), Harris's only distinction is that her house was once mysteriously bombarded by rocks from the sky—the only such case that was documented. It is for the viewer to decide if there are ghosts haunting Hill House who are determined to make Harris their eternal companion, or if Harris is subconsciously manifesting all the terrifying sounds (i.e., loud pounding on doors), atmospheric changes, etc., in the house. Or is it a little of both? That's my choice. Film has many scary scenes and moments that will either give you chills ("Who was holding my hand?") or make you jump. Opening montage of Hill House's past is really creepy. An excellent script by Nelson Gidding, fine performances, and important woman characters (Bloom is one of screen's first sympathetic lesbians)—a Wise hallmark.

HAVING A WILD WEEKEND/CATCH US IF YOU CAN (BRITISH/1965) B&W/91m.

Curio starring the Dave Clark Five, onetime pretender to the Beatles' throne, was the first film directed by John Boorman. It has some of the spirit of youthful rebellion present in *A Hard Day's Night*, but in style and theme it is existential rather than anarchical, strange rather than surreal, more pointed in its satire, more downbeat, more working-class. A young stuntman (Clark, who once was a stunt driver) convinces a famous young model (Barbara Ferris) to skip out on her "Eat Meat" campaign and run off with him. With the band's other members tagging along, they have many zany adventures (there are some army war games, a costume ball, a police chase, a visit to a dude ranch) and meet many weird people. Ferris buys an island so they can be protected from corruptive civilization, but when the tide goes down, it turns out that it's connected to the mainland. Realizing that for her there is no escape, she says goodbye to Clark and returns to work. Picture's end has been interpreted as writer Peter Nichols's statement that you can't run away from commitments, but I believe Nichols is instead making an angry assertion that the decadence and greed of the cities (most apparent in advertising, the music business, pop culture) have infected the countryside. Low-budget film has some interesting visuals and Boorman does an okay job with his cast, but the tone is a bit too subdued at times, band members Mike Smith (the lead singer), Denis Payton, Rick Huxley, and Lenny Davidson are pretty much wasted, and, except for the two title cuts (one for each title), the music isn't any good. Dated, but worth a look.

HE KNOWS YOU'RE ALONE (1980) C/94m.

Caitlin O'Heaney's fiancé takes a trip with the boys at the exact time a bus pulls into their small town carrying a psycho with a penchant for killing brides-to-be. While she prepares for the wedding, she senses that she's being stalked and welcomes the company of her ex-boyfriend (Don Scardino). After doing away with her girlfriends, the maniac zeros in on O'Heaney. A detective (Lewis Arlt) tries to find the young woman before it is too late. This is the best of the *Halloween* derivates. Film has suspense, humor, engaging acting by O'Heaney and Scardino. Obviously a student of the horror genre (since his film contains several references to horror classics), first-time director Armand Mastroianni offers several truly scary sequences in which setting is important (i.e., in a theater bathroom, a store dressing room, a funhouse, a bedroom, a living room). All are distinguished by clever touches. Also with: Elizabeth Kemp, Tom Rolfing, Patsy Pease, the unknown Tom Hanks, Dana Barron (pre-*National Lampoon's Vacation*), Paul Gleason.

HEAD (1968) C/86m.

The Monkees—Michael Nesmith, Micky Dolenz, Davy Jones, Peter Tork—a Beatles-influenced singing group, was formed to star in a television series and make records. Surprisingly, the television show, which was produced by Bert Schneider and directed by Bob Rafelson, was funny and inventive; and the Monkees' songs, some written by Neil Diamond, were very pleasing and big sellers. Their one film, produced by Schneider, directed by Rafelson, and co-written by Rafelson and Jack Nicholson, was aimed not at the groups' loyal teenybopper fans, but at a more sophisticated audience. So the film, which has the group running around a studio, contains political references (including documentary footage of the Vietnam war); satirizes the world of movies, television, and commercials; and spoofs the group's wholesome image. Each Monkee becomes a mere pawn being jerked from one incoherent sequence to the next, and is subordinate to the gimmicky (psychedelic) visuals and special effects (Rafelson particularly likes to use solarization effects). There are funny moments—Davy Jones has a mock-serious conversation with Annette Funicello; the Monkees become dandruff on Victor Mature's greasy hair—but film is a mess (by design—that's the shame) and tedious. The television show was much funnier and more inventive. Film is recommended for Monkees fans who comprise film's cult today; others will be disappointed. Even the songs, which are filmed like primitive videos, are mediocre. Also with: Timothy Carey, Logan Ramsey, Vito Scotti, Abraham Sofaer, Terry (Teri) Garr, Frank Zappa, Nicholson, Rafelson, Percy Helton, Carol Doda, Ray Nitschke.

HEART BEAT (1980) C/100m.
For those who were part of the beat generation, this film about the friendship between two hipster icons, writer Jack Kerouac (John Heard) and Neal Cassady (Nick Nolte), on whom Kerouac based misfit Dean Moriarty of *On the Road*, should be welcome, even if disappointing. But people of later generations will probably wonder what the fuss was all about. Kerouac and Cassady, despite their unbridled energy, come across as conservative dullards. If writer-director John Byrum's well-intentioned film had provided a better evocation of the postwar and Eisenhower era and better defined the morality of that time, then perhaps we'd better appreciate their rebelliousness; as it is, the two men growing marijuana in their front lawn and sharing a lover do not, when judging by today's standards, come across as being particularly daring. The trouble is that the film is based not on the potentially fascinating film material from Kerouac's writings but on the sedate memoir of the classy Carolyn Cassady (miscast Sissy Spacek beat out Diane Keaton for the part), the Bryn Mawr graduate who became Neal's wife and both men's lover. Unfortunately, she was not eyewitness to their early friendship; nor does she accompany them each time they get restless and hit the road. The picture emphasizes that she brought stability to the men's lives, but we don't want to see them at their tamest. We want to see them at their most undisciplined and outrageous. Oddly, the most moving performance is given by Anne Dusenberry in the small role of Cassady's teenage girlfriend. Watch her facial reactions in the scene when Cassady kisses her and quickly tells her he's dropping her—that's good acting. It's the one special moment in the picture. Also with: Ray Sharkey, Kent Williams, Tony Bill, Steve Allen.

HEART LIKE A WHEEL (1983) C/113m.
One of Hollywood's best industry-neglected actresses, Bonnie Bedelia, gives an exceptional, Oscar-worthy performance as a drag-race champion, Shirley "Cha Cha" Muldowney, whose success took a heavy toll. She creates a character of depth through subtlety—not being one to lose her cool and have tantrums, Muldowney's feelings are shown in how she moves her eyes, how she stands (vulnerable or strong), and how her voice quivers. Her confidence is at its peak when she sits cozily in her car. She smiles because it's in the driver's seat that she gets her most fulfillment; the sexual imagery is clear: the wind will blow on her face and lips, the smoke will shoot out of the exhaust, the car will streak toward the finish line, and she knows all along that the engine was built by a man. She finds disappointment in her relationships with men: first with her mechanic husband (Leo Rossi), who won't accept taking a "backseat" to his wife, and then with wild, married driver-mechanic Connie Kalitta (a standout performance by Beau Bridges), who becomes her partner and unfaithful lover. The armchair analyst would suggest that because she fails with men in love, she strives for triumphs in her profession, which means defeating men at their own game. We admire her obsession to compete with men, yet recognize that it's meant to be her one character flaw. Sleeper was directed by Jonathan Kaplan (*Over the Edge*), who handles action sequences and personal drama with equal skill. Shirley's first race, her scenes with her supportive musician father (well played by Hoyt Axton), Shirley looking at Connie from afar with obvious interest, Shirley's fiery crash, and Shirley's radio interview (a brilliant piece of satire) are among the highlights. Also with: Dick Miller, Paul Bartel (as a French TV chef), Dean Paul Martin.

HEARTBREAK KID, THE (1972) C/104m.
It is an interesting phenomenon: Jewish boys from the East may end up marrying Jewish girls from the East, but if they attend college in the Midwest they invariably get wild crushes on blond Midwest WASPs (while midwestern WASP boys usually fall for Jewish coeds from the East). For those Jewish boys who neglected studies and the ideal Jewish marriage partner in the next dorm to pursue those hearty, fair-skinned fantasy figures, this is the film they can relate to. Elaine May directed and Neil Simon adapted Bruce Jay Friedman's short story "A Change of Plan" about a Jewish boy (Charles Grodin) who finds his Minnesota dream girl (Cybill Shepherd) while on his Miami honeymoon with his Jewish wife (Jeannie Berlin, May's daughter). He repeatedly leaves the sun-roasted Berlin alone in their hotel room so he can court Shepherd. When he has run out of outrageous lies about where he has been spending his time, Grodin breaks off the three-day marriage. He follows Shepherd back to Minnesota and, despite her big bully of a boyfriend and her "rich brick wall" of a father (Eddie Albert), who sees through his phoniness, he snares his bride. Picture is actually a series of short skits strung together, in which Grodin somehow manages again and again to talk, through prime BS, a bad situation into his favor. We shake our heads because we can't believe he has the gall to say what we're hearing, or is so tactless and insensitive, or is able to get away with what he does. We must admire that he's actually able to win gorgeous rich girl Shepherd when there are so many obstacles (wife, boyfriend, father, his own personality) standing in the way; but, on the other hand, we know all along that he's making a foolish decision, that Shepherd is

bland while Berlin, despite all the flaws that Grodin discovers on the drive from New York, not only has a personality but one that conforms to his own. It was fun to conquer Shepherd, Grodin seems to be thinking in the final scene, but marriage to her has no chance of working out. Film is full of hilarious, sharply satirical scenes, usually taking place in a confined area (like a Nichols-and-May skit): a table, a bed, a car seat, a couch, etc. Oddly, the funniest scene is the most painful: when Grodin breaks up with Berlin, the schmuck doesn't do it in a secluded place but in the crowded hotel restaurant so she can't cause a scene (in shock, she sits there crying, unable to talk, unable to get Grodin to stop gabbing about how he's never felt closer to her, unable to go to the bathroom to throw up because he clutches her tightly). No wonder May received some flack for making a character *played by her daughter*, her surrogate, suffer so much. A superb cast. Also with: Audra Lindley (as Shepherd's easily impressed mother), Art Metrano.

HEARTLAND (1981) C/96m. Based on the letters of a pioneer woman, Elinore Pruitt Stewart, this low-budget film tells the story of a tough, determined woman (Conchata Ferrell) who moves with her young daughter to Wyoming, where she's accepted a job as housekeeper for a sour, tight-lipped rancher (Rip Torn). Eventually they become work partners; then they marry. Feminist western, produced by Wilderness Women Productions (conceived by Annick Smith and Beth Ferris) and Michael Hausman, convincingly shows frontier life, but in such a way that you think the people who endured the hardships (hunger, deaths, freezing temperatures) were less noble than foolish for not seeking greener pastures. Picture is self-consciously arty (don't you hate films that show animals being slaughtered in the name of realism?) and simple to a fault—we moviegoers have been duped into believing that when actors say little and display little emotion during those crisis situations when their characters are surely undergoing emotional turmoil, they're really doing a great acting job. The reserved manner of these characters is annoying—the picture cries out for emotion and *words*. What's most disappointing is that there are *no* surprises; it's like a typical PBS program that you watch for about twenty minutes before flipping the channel. Somehow it won a lot of awards. Directed by Richard Pearce in Montana. Good photography by Fred Murphy. Also with: Barry Primus, Lilia Skala, Megan Folson.

HEARTS AND MINDS (1974) C/110m–198m. Oscar-winning documentary about U.S. involvement in the Vietnam War. As directed by Peter Davis, who produced with Bert Schneider, film builds a strong case that the U.S. presence in Vietnam was based on false assumptions (that the domino theory made sense, that the North Vietnamese could be vanquished by American might, that the South Vietnamese supported their government and desired American assistance) and that American soldiers in Vietnam were conducting an amoral war: we see interviews with pilots who dropped napalm and defoliants on the North Vietnamese; terrified napalmed children running down a road, their bodies burned and skin hanging off their limbs; soldiers burning villages; soldiers rifle-butting prisoners (some shots are in Emile De Antonio's earlier *In the Year of the Pig*); soldiers cavorting with Vietnamese prostitutes (one has a soldier's teethmarks on her breasts). Davis's contention is that America's leaders have been responsible for both our misguided presence in the Vietnam War and the type of war being conducted; but his major theme is that they are the type of leaders Middle Americans want and deserve. Davis uses footage from old American war films and takes us to small-town America (parades, football games, classrooms) so that we can see how deeply rooted are our racism, anti-communism, need to battle an enemy. It's not surprising that our soldiers acted as they did when sent to Vietnam. But instead of those who came back without limbs but with horror stories, it's the superpatriotic vet who gets a welcome-home celebration—where he spouts a cliché-filled pro-America speech—and is asked to speak to grade-school kids about "gooks," and communists, and duty. And so while the tragedy continues in the distant East, the indoctrination continues in the West. Picture has much unforgettable footage, properly manipulative editing (such as Vietnamese grieving over their dead, followed by a scene in which Westmoreland says how the Vietnamese don't care about death the way we do). But I wish it also dealt with the U.S. protest movement. Columbia Studios financed the film, but then thought it too hot to handle. Warner Bros. released it. Today the picture may seem tame, but it was as powerful an anti-Vietnam film as had been made until then.

HEAVEN CAN WAIT (1943) C/112m. An immensely enjoyable comedy of manners by Ernst Lubitsch. With the exception of one early scene in which hero Henry Van Cleve (Don Ameche) meets heroine Martha (Gene Tierney) by pretending to be a bookstore clerk, this seems to be that rare Lubitsch film in which the characters don't take turns successfully *deceiving* one another into believing they're someone they're not. However, this picture, told in flashback, contradicts the claims of a *self-deluded* man (Henry) who thought he had sinned so much in his life playing Casanova that he qualified for entrance into Hades. Every time he tries to delude someone else, they (including devil Laird Cregar) see right through him. Story, which covers about 60 years—with episodes taking place on Henry's birthdays—begins in 19th-century New York. Teenager Henry (Dickie Moore) learns from the French maid (Signe Hasso) that when a boy kisses a girl it doesn't mean he'll have to marry her—coming from a rich family, so he'll not ever have to work, he plans on spending his leisurely life playing the female field. Parents Spring Byington and Louis Calhern worry that Henry's taking after his wild grandfather, Charles Coburn. But after a few years of chasing stage girls, the adult Henry (now Ameche) decides that he's willing to settle down if he can marry Martha, the daughter of a Kansas milk baron (Eugene Pallette). Although Martha is engaged to Henry's stuffy, more practical (i.e., he works) cousin (Allyn Joslyn), she is so swept off her feet by Henry that the two elope. They will spend many, many years together and, except for the time she threatened divorce and returned to Kansas, she will put up with his meaningless philandering. They have a son, and the story comes full circle when the young man (Michael Ames) starts following in Dad's footsteps . . . up stage-door steps. Film is a bit too long, but its rewards are plenty. Best of all is the consistently splendid dialogue by Samson Raphaelson: every time anyone says anything, you'll think that's exactly what should have been said. There are some wonderfully written, beautifully played two-character scenes: Ameche's Henry cheers his flighty mother by telling her that he's thinking of getting married; Henry and Martha meet in the bookstore and that night in the parlor, where they confirm their love; Martha's constantly feuding parents (Marjorie Main is the mother) have Sunday breakfast; Henry feels pangs of mid-life depression when he speaks to the young and, when it comes to discussing him, *un*refreshingly honest young show girl (Helene Reynolds) his son's been dating; Henry chats with the devil. Picture also has surprising moments of warmth, sentiment. Acting is superb, even by Ameche; and, this being Lubitsch's first color film, much attention was paid to period detail and art design. From *Birthdays*, a play by Laszlo Bus-Fekete.

HEAVEN'S GATE (1980) C/149m—219m.
One of Hollywood's greatest fiascos, this epic western about the Johnson County range wars in Wyoming in the 1890s was written, directed, and edited (many times) by Michael Cimino, whose $36 million expenditure pretty much ruined United Artists. Anyone who watches the film will think he or she could have done a better editing job—obviously, Cimino thought everything he shot was too precious to cut—but I doubt if this picture is salvageable. In terms of his audience, it's incredible what bad choices Cimino made. Foremost: there's no excuse for including subtitles in a western, which is what Cimino does any time his foreign immigrant settlers gather (what awful, pretentious scenes!). He tries to create authenticity by having these people speak in their own languages—but the subtitled translations seem to have been written by a first-grader and make these people come across as simpletons. First half of the film is so slow that we anticipate the big shootouts in the second part. But they're so chaotic that I can't tell what's going on. The entire picture is terribly confusing because we never know where anyone is at a particular time, at what stage the range war is, what the characters are trying to accomplish. Why don't the bad guys just wipe out the 125 men on their hit list in 10 minutes? It's a mess. Kris Kristofferson does okay as a moral sheriff who tries to stop the Cattlemen's Association and their gunmen from killing the 125 immigrants whom they've labeled thieves and anarchists. Christopher Walken's a hitman for the bad guys until he realizes he's fighting on the wrong side. Both Kristofferson and Walken are in love with young madam Isabelle Huppert. Huppert's a fine actress, but her scenes are affected and embarrassing. John Hurt and Jeff Bridges also turn up a lot, but I can't tell what their purpose in the picture is. Picture is unnecessarily violent at times (i.e., Richard Masur's death), terribly scored, and photographed (by Vilmos Zsigmond) in such a way that Wyoming looks too dusty and smoky for anyone to want to live there. Also with: Sam Waterston (as the chief villain), Joseph Cotten, Geoffrey Lewis, Brad Dourif.

HEAVY TRAFFIC (1973) C/73m.
X-rated animation feature by Ralph Bakshi is much more palatable than *Fritz the Cat*, although again there are grotesque characters and there is strong emphasis on sex. Story is semi-autobiographical. Young white man (or is he an old boy?) grows up in Brownsville, the son of a Jewish woman and her unfaithful Italian husband. He spends most of his time drawing cartoons. Finally he leaves the apartment and starts his own life, mingling with New York lowlifes and trying to get laid. He becomes infatuated with a savvy black woman, who continuously thwarts his sexual advances. Film hasn't the dead spots that often mar Bakshi's work. the characters are well drawn (except for the boy) and a lot of fun, the backgrounds are impressive, and the animation is superb. Film has bizarre humor, erotic moments, an interesting mix of live action and animation. My major complaint is that the final sequence is done with live actors—it's hard to relate them to their cartoon counterparts.

HELLCATS OF THE NAVY (1957) B&W/82m.
Curio's selling point—Ronald Reagan romances Nancy Davis—is a major reason why it is so dull. Reagan's the captain of a sub during WWII. Chief executive officer Arthur Franz thinks he caused the death of a man because he was a rival for the affections of nurse Davis. Reagan insists he was only thinking of the sub and the rest of the men when he abandoned the dead man. Reagan prevents Franz from getting his own command because he thinks Franz is guided by emotions that would prevent him from making the hard decisions. If Reagan weren't president and Nancy his First Lady, film would have been forgotten. It's a terrible movie, but it is interesting because it stars Reagan and explores the nature of command. In truth, he seems like a mediocre commander (although the filmmakers believe he has the right philosophy) and one worries that he really enjoys giving orders to fire missiles. Nancy Reagan haters will enjoy the sailors passing around her 8-by-10 glossy (she looks sixty and shriveled) and getting all hot and bothered; also there's a scene in which she admits she cares about him and her but not *people*. Bland direction by Nathan Juran.

HELP! (BRITISH/1965) C/90m.
The Beatles' second film has Leo McKern's religious sect trying to get Ringo's ring so they can perform a sacrifice. Film is full of funny sight gags (example: police interrogate a guy by shining a small lamp in his face, although they're sitting outside in broad daylight) and one-liners ("He's out to rule the world

...if he can get a government grant"). Film mixes James Bond adventure, surrealism (a Beatle even becomes miniaturized at one point), and loopy comedy (much of the slapstick variety). Richard Lester's direction is even more outrageous than it was for *A Hard Day's Night*. Picture is a lot of fun, but I wish it provided more insight into the individual Beatles—in fact, it's just as impersonal as *Yellow Submarine*. Unfortunately, the world we see has nothing to do with the Beatles' real world, which we glimpsed in the previous Beatles film. Best moments are when they sing: "Help!," "You've Got to Hide Your Love Away," "I Need You," and "You're Gonna Lose That Girl." Staging of numbers, particularly those set outside, is effective. The "Ticket to Ride" sequence, with the boys frolicking in the snow, would make a great video. Also with: Eleanor Bron, Victor Spinetti, Roy Kinnear, Patrick Cargill.

HERCULES (ITALIAN/1959) C/107m.
Kids made Joseph E. Levine's muscleman epic into such a commercial blockbuster that it spawned wave of Italian-made, myth-based, sword-and-sandal films with superman Hercules (in numerous sequels), Ulysses, Samson, and Maciste. While it doesn't compare to Ray Harryhausen's epics, it is much better than its imitators; it could use some of Harryhausen's creations, but on the whole it is a well-made film—in fact, seeing it today, one is surprised at how much adult content it has. Former Mr. Universe Steve Reeves became a superhero as the imposing Greek superhero who asks the gods to make him mortal so he can fight like other men and love like them, too. He falls in love with beautiful princess Sylva Koscina (a major reason we kids saw this film several times when it came out), but offends her father, the King of Colchis, who sends him on perilous missions. The King sends Jason to seek the Golden Fleece (so Jason won't claim his rightful throne). Hercules goes along on the adventurous journey. (The same ground was covered much more spectacularly in *Jason and the Argonauts*.) Film is hurt by dubbing, lack of wit, and extreme earnestness, but it's still fun. Reeves starred in the first sequel only: *Hercules Unchained*. Directed by Pietro Francisci. Also with: Fabrizio Mione, Gina Rovere, Ivo Garrani.

HERCULES/HERCULES GOES BANANAS/ HERCULES IN NEW YORK (1970) C/75m.
A film co-starring Arnold Schwarzenegger and Arnold Stang? That's the type of duo that would appear in *Mad* magazine movie-poster parodies. But this lame-brained comedy is a disappointment. Not only is there no wild humor, there are shamefully few jokes and gags at all. Hercules (Schwarzenegger) comes to New York City for a little excitement, in defiance of Zeus. He befriends "Pretzy" (Stang) and startles everyone with his athletic prowess. Gangsters take over his contract and bet big money on him winning a televised weight-lifting contest—they don't realize that Nemesis (Taina Elg) has stripped him of his strength. Schwarzenegger's voice is dubbed (although his accent would have made Hercules more otherworldly) and Stang is

wasted—they at least could have had him eat a Chunky. Directed by Arthur A. Seidelman. Also with: Deborah Loomis, James Karen, Michael Lipton.

HERE COMES MR. JORDAN (1941) B&W/ 93m.
Likable boxing contender Joe Pendleton (Robert Montgomery) is mistakenly sent to heaven fifty years ahead of schedule. When his body is cremated, heavenly supervisor Mr. Jordan (Claude Rains) tries to make amends by allowing Joe to inhabit the body of Farnsworth, a heartless millionaire whose wife (Rita Johnson) and male secretary (John Emery) are trying to kill him. Johnson and Emery are shocked when "Farnsworth" seems to come back to life after they murdered him. And everyone gets confused when the millionaire suddenly has scruples, especially a nice young woman (Evelyn Keyes) whose father he gets out of jail. He and Keyes fall in love, but Joe's time in Farnsworth's body is only temporary—he is destined to take over the body of Murdock, an honest boxer whom gangsters are trying to eliminate. While there are some delightful moments in Alexander Hall's classic fantasy-comedy, the script is schmaltzy and morbid and never hilarious. The big mistake is that when Joe becomes Murdock he's not allowed to remember his old self. So, in effect, Joe Pendleton gets gypped out of his life while Murdock, whom we don't care about, lives on in his stead, apparently unchanged even though Joe's spirit has entered his body. Warren Beatty's 1978 remake, *Heaven Can Wait*, was ruined by the same unsatisfying resolution. Montgomery is perfect as Pendleton, an uneducated mug who possesses a golden heart. Rains's role should have been stronger. The outstanding supporting cast includes: Edward Everett Horton, James Gleason, Donald MacBride, Halliwell Hobbes.

HIDDEN FORTRESS, THE/THREE BAD MEN IN A HIDDEN FORTRESS (JAPANESE/1958) B&W/ 126m—133m—139m.
In the 16th century a great general (a surprisingly dignified Toshiro Mifune) and two scruffy, greedy, cowardly farmers (Minoru Chiaki, Kamatari Fujiwara)—two squabbling symbiotic characters out of an absurdist play whom Mifune forces to help him—escort a young princess (Misa Uehara) on a perilous journey from a hidden fortress to the province border so that she can claim her throne. Meanwhile the enemy army, led by a rival general (Susumu Fugita), hunts for the princess so they can execute her. Chiaki and Fujiwara would probably turn in Uehara for the reward if they weren't stupid enough to believe that she is a mute girl, and not the princess. Akira Kurosawa's often exciting, consistently funny epic was meant to mock the Japanese swordfight films as well as, I would guess, pay homage to American westerns, of both the A and B varieties. George Lucas has stated that this film served as inspiration for *Star Wars* (which is why it gets so much play in repertory theaters), but surely it was as much a model for Sergio Leone's westerns as *Yojimbo* (the source for *A Fistful of Dollars*): there is a great deal of humor, characters who seem to put dust on their bodies first thing in the

morning, characters who are motivated by riches, and a male protagonist who is a nearly invincible fighter, emotionless (he's so caught up in his sense of duty that he sheds not a tear after his sister has been executed in the princess's stead), fearless, and, although basically amoral, is a hero in our eyes because his enemies are worse than he is. Only the princess and a prostitute she buys out of bondage are motivated by their hearts rather than a sense of duty or greed. This is not quite a Kurosawa masterpiece, but I wouldn't be surprised if he enjoyed making it more than his other period films. His first widescreen effort (his last film for Toho), it is beautifully photographed; particularly effective are the crowd scenes and those shots in which characters are placed in the foreground and background. In all the writings on this film, there is little mention of the fact that the very pretty (but scratchy-voiced) Uehara wears what is definitely the skimpiest, sexiest outfit of any female in a Japanese costume picture—this 16-year-old princess (I'm sure the actress is older) looks as if she's ready to beebop down to the high-school sock hop. Cinematography by Kazuo Yamasaki. Also with: Takashi Shimura.

HIGH NOON (1952) B&W/85m.
Some brilliant editing by Elmo Williams and Harry Gerstad (who won Oscars) and a dramatic Oscar-winning score by Dimitri Tiomkin (with Tex Ritter giving an emotional performance on the Oscar-winning title song) elevated Fred Zinnemann's slightly-above-average western into a classic—one of the few westerns that are favorites of viewers who dislike the genre. Told in real time, the story has Gary Cooper (who won his second Best Actor Oscar) as the marshal of a small town in the 1870s. On the day he marries Quaker Grace Kelly and retires to move elsewhere, he learns that a man he sent to prison will be arriving on the noon train—he and three other desperadoes plan to kill Cooper. Rather than leaving town and spending the future looking over his shoulder, Cooper decides to put on his badge again and face his enemies. Kelly decides to walk out on him and no man in town will join his posse. He must fight four gunfighters alone. Screenwriter Carl Foreman (who was blacklisted) most likely wanted to equate the people of Cooper's town with the people in Hollywood who suddenly deserted their persecuted, blacklisted friends, even when those friends humbled themselves (as Cooper does) by begging for help. Howard Hawks was so infuriated by Cooper's whimpering that he made *Rio Bravo* to show that a professional lawman like Cooper wouldn't ask common folk for help against the gunmen. Personally, I think Cooper should have left town (he had already quit his job)—but I'm glad he doesn't because the final shootout is one of the western's most exciting sequences. That's because Cooper finally displays strength and because of the way Floyd Crosby's striking images are edited to fit the music. Produced by Stanley Kramer. The strong cast includes: Lloyd Bridges, Katy Jurado, Lon Chaney, Jr., Thomas Mitchell, Sheb Wooley, Lee Van Cleef, Henry Morgan, Otto Kruger.

HIGH PLAINS DRIFTER (1972) C/105m.
Clint Eastwood directed and starred in this unusual western that was inspired by the tragic case of Kitty Genovese, who was brutally murdered in New York while her neighbors pulled down their shades, locked their doors, and turned off their lights. Eastwood is a mysterious stranger who rides into a town where the entire population did nothing while three bad men killed their marshal. Hired to protect the town when the bad men return, the stranger proceeds to take it over, even painting it hellish red. He rapes one woman (a harlot) and seduces another. He kills townsmen who protest his actions. When the bad men return, he pulls another surprise. A well-directed, exciting, oddly amusing film that is interesting in terms of how we respond to Eastwood's character. He is in effect a ruthless, avenging angel dosing out retribution for a wrathful god. His only "good quality" is that he sends a lot of sinners to hell early. Screenplay by Ernest Tidyman. Also with: Verna Bloom, Marianna Hill, Mitch Ryan, Jack Ging, Billy Curtis, Geoffrey Lewis.

HIGH SCHOOL CONFIDENTIAL (1958) B&W/85m.
Producer Albert Zugsmith's cult classic is a fast-moving, tongue-in-cheek glimpse at the fifties turbulent-youth scene. It's great fun because of the wild dancing and action, three blonde actresses (Jan Sterling, Mamie Van Doren, Diane Jergens), and hip teen lingo that will make you feel nostalgic: "flipout," "swingingest," "nowhere," "square," "(fill in any word)sville," "That's the way the ball bounces," "tough toenails," "You're dragging your axle in waltz time," and, in the words of an existentialist poet, "Tomorrow's a drag, the future's a flake." Russ Tamblyn stars as a tough kid from Chicago who enrolls in the local high school and moves in with his nymphomaniac aunt (Van Doren). He flirts with his English teacher (Sterling) and puts the make on a pretty classmate (Jergens), the girlfriend of the leader (John Drew Barrymore) of the rowdy Wheeler-Dealers. Tamblyn discovers Jergens is hooked on marijuana and the other kids have become heroin addicts. Through Jergens and Barrymore he reaches the drug supplier (Jackie Coogan)—he tells Coogan that he wants to work for him, but actually he's setting a trap. Tamblyn is a narc! Zugsmith and talented director Jack Arnold include much intentional campy humor, but the drug angle is treated cautiously. Although a much better film than 1936's *Reefer Madness* there are a surprising number of similarities between the two. Both claim that: problem children don't necessarily come from problem homes; the major dealers set up business with pushers and are too smart to be users themselves; where there is loud music there are usually drugs. Interestingly, Tamblyn is made into a cool guy so that kids will see that those who don't use drugs aren't necessarily squares (we can't dislike Tamblyn, even though he is a narc, because he sincerely wants to stop a bad problem). Last shot of film implies that teenagers like Jergens are protected on one side by teachers (Sterling) and on the other side by law enforcers (Tamblyn). Film has intentionally sleazy elements. And it has the inimitable Van Doren strutting her stuff. It's worth

the price of admission to watch her walking around in semi-obscene outfits (you'll "dig" her cashmere sweater), rolling around on Tamblyn's bed as if she were a cat in heat, biting into his apple with thoughts of Eden in her naughty head, drinking herself into a stupor, even being slapped around in the manner of cheap dames with gangster boyfriends. Her verbal duel with Sterling is a classic. Jerry Lee Lewis appears on the back of a truck to sing the title song. Weird cast also includes: Ray Anthony, Charles Chaplin, Jr., Burt Douglas, Jody Fair, Michael Landon, Lyle Talbot, William Wellman, Jr.

HIGH SIERRA (1941) B&W/100m.

Humphrey Bogart became a full-fledged leading man in Raoul Walsh's gangster classic, playing "Mad Dog" Roy Earle, an Indiana farm boy who became a famous bank robber. Just out of prison, the graying Earle is disappointed to find that the caliber of criminals he must work with has deteriorated. Also he has mellowed sufficiently so that he has plans to go straight after just one more job—the heist of jewelry at a hotel. To get away from his feuding underlings (Arthur Kennedy, Cornel Wilde) and the gun moll who loves him (topbilled Ida Lupino), Earle spends much time with a poor family he befriended, and courts the young daughter (Joan Leslie)—he even pays for her foot operation. This subplot weakens the otherwise tough drama (scripted by John Huston) but allows Earle to display his good heart and Bogart to reveal a side of himself that hadn't been seen yet on film—when he drives home alone after a visit with Leslie and breaks into a smile, it's quite touching. Lupino also gives a fine, sympathetic portrayal. Walsh really takes a classic western story and transposes it to the gangster genre. As a gangster film, Walsh would refine the story in 1948's *White Heat* (moving the ending from a mountain peak to the top of a gas tank). In 1949 he would remake this film as a western, *Colorado Territory*. (In 1955 Stuart Heisler would remake it as a gangster film, *I Died A Thousand Times*.) Also with: Henry Travers, Alan Curtis, Henry Hull, Barton MacLane, Jerome Cowan, Donald MacBride, Willie Best, Isabel Jewell.

HIGH SOCIETY (1956) C/107m.

Even if you didn't know this pleasing musical was a remake of *The Philadelphia Story*, you'd still guess that Grace Kelly (in her last screen role) was basing her spoiled society girl on something Katharine Hepburn did. Criminally beautiful, Kelly (who is dressed to match the sets) turns in an acceptable comedic performance as the rich young woman who is about to marry the "perfect" man although she still carries a torch for her first, *imperfect*, husband, played by Bing Crosby—the scene in which she puts on reporter Frank Sinatra and photographer Celeste Holm by pretending to be obnoxiously ultra-sophisticated is quite funny. The major problem is that Kelly is so energetic that Crosby, 25 years her senior, seems much too old for her. Nice-looking film, directed by Charles Walters, moves along at a brisk pace; there are many musical highlights. Cole Porter songs serve for memorable duets by Crosby and Kelly (their hit "True Love"), Crosby and Sinatra ("Did You Evah?"), Crosby and Louis Armstrong ("Now You Has Jazz"), and Sinatra and Holm ("Who Wants to Be a Millionaire?"); plus Sinatra sings Kelly an emotional (watch his eyes) "You're Sensational." Also with: John Lund, Louis Calhern, Sidney Blackmer, Margalo Gillmore, Lydia Reed.

HILLS HAVE EYES, THE (1977) C/89m.

A middle-class family from Cleveland—a former cop and his wife, their two grown daughters, son, son-in-law, grandchild, and two dogs—drive toward California. Their trailer breaks down in the desert, and they're pitted against a family of deranged, brutal cannibals headed by an atomic-test mutant (James Whitworth). There are killings and the baby is kidnapped—it could become *baby* food. Our surviving family members must give up civilized notions if they are to live—they become as savage as the desert family. Picture has extreme violence but it differs from director Wes Craven's previous film, *The Last House on the Left*, because this time you never forget that it's "only a movie." That's a relief, considering what we must watch. Film is as vicious as its reputation but neither well-made nor scary. Also with: Susan Lanier, Robert Houston, Martin Speer, unknown Dee Wallace, bald Michael Berryman (whose frightening face was used on the film's posters), Virginia Vincent.

HIROSHIMA, MON AMOUR (FRENCH/1959) B&W/88m–91m.

A married French actress (Emmanuelle Riva), in Hiroshima making a peace film, sleeps with a married Japanese architect (Eiji Okada). She finds herself falling in love with him, and this causes her great agony. This forbidden affair reminds her of her first forbidden love affair with a German soldier during the occupation of her hometown, Nevers, France. As she tells Okada, the soldier was killed by a sniper on Liberation Day; she had her hair shorn by villagers, and her parents locked her in a cellar—at one point she had a mental breakdown, and eventually her parents sent her out of the hostile town to Paris. She had never returned to Nevers because she couldn't face the tragic memory. Now she wants to leave Hiroshima and forget Okada so she'll once again let the memory of the soldier and Nevers fade away. But Okada pursues her through Hiroshima, trying to stop a mental relapse and get her to consent to make love again. Alain Resnais's complex first feature, a seminal film of the French New Wave, could better be described as a *mood piece* on love and madness or a *visual examination of the subconscious* than as a straight narrative; in any case, it invented new ways to tell a story. The film is known for the breakthrough use of the subjective (rather than chronological) order during flashbacks; flash cuts from images the character is currently seeing to those past images the character is reminded of; parallel montage whereby juxtaposed shots of Nevers and Hiroshima are filmed similarly and at the same speed—so that the unity of past and present (an important theme) is conveyed; surreal tracking shots of empty Hiroshima; the insertion of footage from the Japanese film *Hiroshima*, with its grisly shots of A-bomb victims. But while the film's technical achievements are vast, there are problems with the central storyline. Resnais and screenwriter Marguerite Duras denied that they were trying to draw parallels between the Hiroshima holocaust and the tragedy that befell Riva in Nevers at the same time—which makes sense, since *her* punishment was justified. Yet when they offer as a theme that love will vanquish terrible memories, they not only are suggesting that the memory of Nevers is as tragic to Riva as the memory of Hiroshima is to Okada but presuming that the Japanese are trying to forget about Hiroshima in order to move forward. In fact the film *Hiroshima* proves that the Japanese want to spread the word, not forget. That Okada and other Japanese don't speak of Hiroshima doesn't mean they don't think about it often (as they should)—it's just that the catastrophe was so great that it defies words (but not filmic records). A major problem is that Duras did not know what to do with Okada, or know what he represents. So Duras concentrates on Riva and foolishly, and insultingly, ignores Okada's story. That Riva tells him her past and doesn't ask him to reciprocate and that he accepts this suggests that Duras regarded the white woman as being more important to the film than her Japanese lover. The scene in which Okada tries to slap Riva back to her senses, in public yet, was mocked as unrealistic in Japan, where this pretentious film did poor business under the title *Twenty-four Hour Love Affair*. Sacha Vierny filmed the scenes in France, Takahashi Michio filmed in Japan. Music by Giovanni Fusco and Georges Delerue was used thematically, as background to poetic dialogue and to "underscore" link in Riva's mind between Nevers and Hiroshima.

HIS GIRL FRIDAY (1940) B&W/92m.
Howard Hawks produced and directed this brilliantly acted, frantically paced screwball comedy (with a little social drama thrown in). It's a reworking of Hecht and MacArthur's famous newspaper play, *The Front Page*, which Lewis Milestone had already filmed in 1931. Hawks gave it a special twist when he asked scriptwriter Charles Lederer (and Hecht, who got no credit) to write reporter Hildy Johnson as a woman. Ruthless newspaper editor Walter Burns (Cary Grant tempers his viciousness slightly) is upset that former wife Hildy (Rosalind Russell) has agreed to marry gentlemanly bumpkin Bruce Baldwin (Ralph Bellamy, Grant's perfect foil). Not only will he be losing the woman he still loves, but also his ace reporter. Hildy insists that she loves Bruce because he treats her like a woman—he'll give her a home, family, and security. But Walter knows that if he's to win Hildy back he has to remind her that she loves doing things women aren't traditionally supposed to do—he shrewdly gets her to cover one more big story, one that involves crooked politicians and a prisoner (John Qualen) who's about to be executed. When reporting gets back into her blood, she forgets about Bruce (Walter has waylaid him and his mother) and is Walter's once more. Film is not so much about the traditional battle of the sexes as it is about sexual differentiation. Hawks repeatedly shows that when char-

acters put their guards down, they take on characteristics of the opposite sex and stop paying attention to others' genders. When no one's looking, the tough-talking male reporters become as gossipy as a women's bridge group. Walter believes women are exactly as society defines and molds them, yet when it comes to Hildy, he instinctively throws away such guidelines. When the going gets tough—when other male heroes would send their women to safety—Walter pleads with Hildy: "This is war—you can't desert me now." Hildy thinks she wants a home, as all women are supposed to, but she'd rather have a good story to cover. She likes Bruce's compliments, but can equally enjoy exchanging insults with Walter. If there's one difference between her and the men in the world she inhabits, it's that only she retains her humanity. Film is famous for chaotic, overlapping dialogue. I'm also impressed by how Hawks uses his frame as an arena for physical contact. Watch how the various combatants consciously endeavor to gain the upper hand and a piece of territory (the frame) through bullying tactics, lies, insults, and manipulation. Those people like Walter, Hildy, and the reporters who can talk without taking time to breathe have a decided advantage. Picture has fabulous dialogue, characters, comic scenes, performances. Grant is exceptional, particularly doing physical comedy. It's rare that he plays the aggressor in a relationship, rather than a befuddled suitor. Also, this is the rare time he loves a woman not because of her *mystery* but because he knows *everything* about her. Russell is dynamic playing the most fascinating of the era's wisecracking women reporters. She's unabashed as this cunning, bawdy, aggressive, cigarette-smoking, unladylike female—it's a shame she wasn't offered such parts more often. The superb cast also includes: Gene Lockhart, Helen Mack, Porter Hall, Ernest Truex, Cliff Edwards, Clarence Kolb, Roscoe Karns, Frank Jenks, Regis Toomey, Abner Biberman, Alma Kruger, Billy Gilbert.

HOLIDAY (1938) B&W/93m.
Philip Barry's play (also filmed eight years earlier) makes an excellent vehicle for Cary Grant and Katharine Hepburn. Idealistic, anti-materialistic Grant plans to marry rich Doris Nolan, but she and her conservative father (Henry Kolker), whom he manages to impress, expect him to change his ways and to take a position in the father's office. Hepburn, Nolan's sister (and the family's black sheep because she possesses an idealism equal to Grant's), selflessly tries to assure the marriage will take place. Of course, Grant and Hepburn fall in love. Story is predictable, but writing is first-rate and stars, especially Hepburn, are excellent. It's odd that the images I always remember from this film are those that express freedom: Grant doing backflips, and Hepburn running (something actresses never did in the old days). Well directed by George Cukor. Also with: Lew Ayres, Edward Everett Horton, Binnie Barnes, Henry Daniell.

HOLIDAY INN (1942) B&W/100m.
Bing Crosby and Fred Astaire are part of a song-and-dance act with

Virginia Dale when Crosby retires to his farm so he can relax on American holidays. But he decides to open a holidays-only nightclub. Bing hires Marjorie Reynolds (Crosby and Astaire's salaries were so high, Paramount couldn't afford a name actress) to perform at the club. When Dale dumps Astaire, he turns up at the inn and literally sweeps Reynolds off her feet, taking her away from Bing and making her his dancing partner. When Hollywood decides to make a film about the Holiday Inn, Bing and Reynolds are reunited on the set of the inn on Christmas. Irving Berlin wrote songs for eight holidays, but the film is shown almost exclusively at Christmas—that's because it has Crosby and, in a later misty-eyed scene, both Reynolds (dubbed by Martha Mears) and Crosby (who joins in) singing "White Christmas." The plot's a bit foolish, but Berlin's score is lively and patriotic and Crosby's crooning and Astaire's dancing are super. Not a great musical, but it's enjoyable and extremely popular. Directed by Mark Sandrich. Also with: Walter Abel, Louise Beavers, James Bell, Bob Crosby's Bob Cats.

HOLLYWOOD BOULEVARD (1976) C/83m.

This picture's main claim to fame is that it was made in record-breaking time on a pocket-change budget. Joe Dante and Alan Arkush, New World editors, wanted to prove to studio head Roger Corman that they could effectively direct quickie sexploitation films in the Corman mold. New World's self-parody has pretty Candice Rialson coming to Hollywood and trying to make it to stardom by acting in quickie sexploitation films for Miracle Pictures—"If it's a good picture, it's a miracle," says her new boyfriend, scriptwriter Jeffrey Kramer. Adding to the humiliation of appearing in such tasteless nonsense as *Machete Maidens of Maratau* is the fear she feels because a murderer is knocking off the actresses. Patrick Hobby's script is inventive and funny; there is a barrage of surprisingly clever sight gags and references to Corman's style of filmmaking; and the entire cast hams it up to perfection. Paul Bartel is hilarious as a director who tries to inject "art," "meaning," and character motivation into his trashy films—while maintaining a large quantity of T&A, car crashes, and massacre scenes. Film falters toward end, when it gets a bit too serious and includes a needlessly vicious knife murder. Surprisingly, the film looks polished; to save money, the directors inserted footage from previous Corman productions—but, as it is, it's too long. Also with: Mary Woronov, Dick Miller, Rita George, Richard Doran, Charles B. Griffith, Joseph McBride, Todd McCarthy, Jonathan Kaplan, Commander Cody and the Lost Planet Airmen.

HOLLYWOOD KNIGHTS, THE (1980)

C/94m. Ignored during its release, Floyd Mutrux's comedy has become a cult favorite because of screenings on cable. Set in Hollywood on Halloween night in 1965, picture follows the exploits of members of a car club on the night their favorite hangout is closing down. There are a couple of serious storylines (one guy has joined the army; Tony Danza worries that girlfriend Michelle Pfeiffer will forget him if her upcoming screen test is successful). But mostly the picture centers on the pranks, instigated by the insolent Robert Wuhl, on the bluenose high-school faculty and the local police. Mutrux tries to combine elements from *Animal House* and *American Graffiti*, but only manages to show how much better those films are in comparison to their imitators. The film does have some funny shots, but "good-natured" tastelessness wears thin. Highlights are interplay between adulterous Leigh French and lover Richard Schaal, who can't keep their hands off each other; the two cops—one who sings the fabricated lyrics to "Lawrence of Arabia"; and Wuhl and the whining Fran Drescher (Mutrux's *American Hot Wax*) in scene where he loses his "lover" image by having a premature ejaculation ("You're so immature!" she comforts him). A great "golden oldie" soundtrack. Also with: Stewart Pankin (of HBO's *Not Necessarily the News*), T. K. Carter, Randy Gomel, P. R. Paul.

HOMEBODIES (1974) C/96m.

A weird little sleeper that blends horror, comedy, and social drama. Six elderly people are ordered out of their dilapidated building so it can be replaced by a $50 million high-rise complex. Not wanting to be relocated to another section of Cincinnati (where the movie was filmed), the tough, spunky group holds out, murdering those who try to kick them out. Full of unique characters; extremely well acted by veteran cast—especially Paula Trueman, who reminds me of Ruth Gordon. Direction by independent filmmaker Larry Yust (who cowrote script) is most impressive. He handles his actors well and shows true respect for the resourcefulness of the elderly. Technically, he makes sharp choices in regard to camera placement and is very skillful with a mobile camera. Deaths of most victims are tolerable because they come across as such heartless, arrogant people. Still, for a picture that has so much offbeat humor, the brutal nature of the murders is offputting. In particular, the sequence in which the young woman (Linda Marsh) who has been employed by the city to relocate the tenants walks through the dark building in search of hiding tenants is terrifying—its climax is truly gruesome. Moreover, when the tenants start knocking off each other for various reasons, it becomes too much. Also with: Frances Fuller, Peter Brocco, William Hansen, Ruth McDevitt, Ian Wolfe, Douglas Fowley, Kenneth Tobey.

HONDO (1953) C/83m.

Perhaps the best John Wayne western not directed by John Ford or Howard Hawks. Wayne plays Hondo Lane, an army scout who rides through barren Texas alone but for his attack dog, Sam. (It's likely that Mel Gibson's Mad Max and his unpettable companion dog in *The Road Warrior* were inspired by Hondo and Sam.) He is forced to kill a good-for-nothing man (James Arness) who attempts an ambush. He falls in love with a woman (Geraldine Page) who lives with her young son (Lee Aaker, prior to TV's *The Adventures of Rin Tin Tin*) on an isolated ranch in Apache territory. He learns that her husband was the man he killed. While he is able to tell her what he did, they don't know what to tell the boy, who has come to idolize Hondo. Personal problems are put on hold when the Apaches go on a full-scale rampage, forcing the cavalry to escort families from the area. Excellent adaption of what I consider to be Louis L'Amour's best novel. It has the simplicity present in L'Amour as well as the power, and it expresses his love of the land and its beauty, his respect for those who tried to civilize the savage West, and the sense of danger that was always present. Wayne and Page are well cast. Like the character L'Amour wrote, Page transforms from plain to beautiful as you watch her in relation to her land. She proves to be one of Wayne's best leading ladies— she doesn't overmatch him despite her theatrical acting experience. Wayne, who didn't get to play with children very often, is quite good with Aaker as well—his relationships with everyone are mature. Particularly memorable is the scene in which he teaches the boy to swim. Also with: Ward Bond, Michael Pate.

HONEYMOON KILLERS, THE (1970) B&W/108m.
Unusual, violent sleeper is a chilling reenactment of the grisly "Lonely Hearts" murders that drew national attention in the late forties. It is also a fascinating, semi-comical examination of the true-life delirious romance between an ill-tempered, sexually frustrated 200-pound nurse named Martha Beck (well played by Shirley Stoler, who resembles her) and her speciously charming and handsome but not-so-smart Spanish lover, gigolo Ray Fernandez (a marvelous performance by Tony Lo Bianco). Mercenary murderers of the rich, middle-aged or old ladies Fernandez married, their amoral behavior went hand in hand with their mutual sexual attraction. Film is cleverly scripted; has several odd yet interesting characters; probes America's pathetic "lonely hearts" subculture; and is one of the few "criminal couple-on-the-run" movies that neither romanticize the crimes (the murders are extremely shocking) nor glamorize the criminals. Director-writer Leonard Kastle was more interested in the relationship between the jealous Beck (who pretended to be Fernandez's sister) and her unfaithful lover than in their crimes, but while he believed their love for each other was their one redeeming quality, it was not enough to fully redeem them after their murders. The direction by newcomer Kastle (whatever happened to him?) is amateurish at times, but is quite innovative when it counts. He uses the music of Gustav Mahler effectively, at times to counterpoint the triviality of what is happening on the screen. He gives his actors free reign to create broad characters and the result is several strong performances. He also uses the camera skillfully so that we are aware of settings and spatial relationships—no wonder François Truffaut loved this film. I particularly like the way he creates a sense of claustrophobia by placing Lo Bianco, his new romantic conquest, and huge Stoler in a tiny space so that they drive each other crazy. (It's like the stateroom scene in *A Night at the Opera*.) Interestingly, the only woman placed in an outdoor, unclaustrophobic setting is the one genuinely nice, sympathetic woman our couple comes into contact with—and she is the only women who survives. Thoroughly sleazy and lowbrow—but it's a near-masterpiece. Also with: Dortha Duckworth, Doris Roberts, Marilyn Criss, Mary-Jane Higbee, Kip McArdle, Mary Breen.

HONKYTONK MAN (1982) C/122m.
Clint Eastwood knew he was taking a chance by directing and starring in this Depression Era comedy-drama; but it allowed him to make a movie with his teenage son, Kyle. A young boy is given parental permission to accompany his sickly uncle (Eastwood) on a trip to Nashville, where he hopes to hook on as a singer for the Grand Ole Opry. Eastwood sings in the film, much better than he did in *Paint Your Wagon* years before. And, for only the second time in his career, his character dies—probably the main reason the picture died at the box office. The film's storyline is quite unusual for Eastwood, and bears a strong resemblance to *The Reivers*, in which Steve McQueen teaches a young boy a thing or two about the world, and vice versa. Eastwood is a rapscallion rather than a hero; he's not very smart; he gets duped by everyone who wants to take advantage of him, including an obnoxious young girl (Alexa Kenin) who claims when he was drunk he made her pregnant; he even resorts to stealing chickens from a coop—not something other Eastwood characters would do. But he's a nice, well-meaning guy, and the boy could find many worse role models. Not a top-grade Eastwood film, but not deserving of its miserable fate with fans and critics. Also with: John McIntire, Verna Bloom, Matt Clark, Barry Corbin.

HORROR EXPRESS/PANIC ON THE TRANS-SIBERIAN EXPRESS (SPANISH/1972) C/88m.
Horror gem that devotees of late-night television have kept to themselves. A frozen prehistoric apeman is discovered in Manchuria. It is transported to Moscow via the Trans-Siberian Express by scientist Christopher Lee. Also on board are rival doctor Peter Cushing and a brutal Cossack, Telly Savalas. There is a series of brutal murders—blood pours from the empty eyesockets, mouth, and nostrils of the victims. Savalas tries to solve the mystery. It turns out that the apeman has returned to life. Actually, the apeman's body is inhabited by an evil alien. Is he Satan? The seemingly indestructible alien takes over the body of a monk on board (flaunting its lack of fear of God) and kills passengers by literally sucking out their brain power. Picture is exciting and surprisingly provocative—like *2001* and *Five Million Years to Earth*, it challenges both fundamentalist religion and theories on evolution. Well directed by Eugenio Martin. With interesting characters, solid acting. Also with: Silvia Tortosa, Jorge Rigaud, Helga Line.

HORROR HOTEL/CITY OF THE DEAD (BRITISH/1960) B&W/76m.
Not-to-be-trusted professor of demonology (Christopher Lee) sends a young woman (Betta St. John) to mist-shrouded Salem to do a paper on Satanism in the village during the 17th century. It is the time of the Witches' Sabbath, and town is inhabited by witches' coven.

She becomes victim in Lee-led sacrifice to devil. Others come to investigate her disappearance. Early death of lead actress in inn makes one think quickly of same year's *Psycho*; it also contains many plot elements—as well as symbols—that would be used in 1973 British film *The Wicker Man*. No classic, but it has creepy atmosphere plus a few good shocks. Released in U.S. in 1963. Directed by John Moxey. Also with: Dennis Lotis (a pop singer who got top billing), Patricia Jessel, Venetia Stevenson.

HORROR OF DRACULA/DRACULA (BRITISH/ 1958) C/82m.
Hammer Studios' follow-up to *The Curse of Frankenstein* is a much better and more influential horror film. But it isn't the definitive adaptation of Bram Stoker's novel or much more than an introduction to the bloody-red and sexually oriented style of future Hammer vampire films and to Christopher Lee's Dracula and Peter Cushing's vampire-fighter, Dr. Van Helsing, who'd battle again in many sequels. The film is so rushed that we have a hard time realizing that major parts of Stoker's story are being either distorted or eliminated. Posing as a librarian (!) but actually out to kill Dracula, Harker lasts only about 20 minutes in the castle before being killed himself. We go to London, where Harker's fiancée, Lucy (Carol Marsh), gets about 10 minutes of screen time before she is dead too. So the rest of the film is about Van Helsing and Lucy's brother, Arthur (Michael Gough), trying to protect Arthur's uninteresting wife, Mina (Melissa Stribling), from Dracula. There's not even a character who eats insects. Film differs from Universal's 1931 *Dracula* chiefly in that it conveys the sexual nature of vampirism: not only does the vampire become excited when he bites into a victim's jugular but his victims also relish the experience (we see how anxiously Lucy awaits her blood-sucking "lover") because they know there is no sexual high like death (a theme prevalent in vampire literature, as well as Oshima's film *In the Realm of the Senses*). Picture has a lot of graphic violence, but it fits the subject rather than being exploitive. Other than the two leads, all the performances are forgettable. Cushing's well cast as Van Helsing, but in this film he's a little too humorless, as if his blood had already been drained. But Lee's madly inspired vampire is terrific: he's cruel, energetic, intelligent, tall and imposing—and whoever made his teeth deserved an Oscar (what Bogart could have done with them during his inimitable upper-lip-raising). The film's highlight is the final battle between Dracula and Van Helsing, during which both go leaping about the castle chamber—but why would Dracula be so hindered when Van Helsing crosses two metal candelabra? Well-mounted production was directed by Terence Fisher (whose best work would come later) and scripted by Jimmy Sangster. James Bernard contributed the pounding music. Also with: Valerie Gaunt (whose role as Dracula's tormented vampire bride is too brief).

HORSE FEATHERS (1932) B&W/68m.
Frantic, anarchical comedy in which the four Marx Brothers take a satirical whack at higher education. Groucho (as Professor Quincey Adams Wagstaff) becomes president of Huxley College, which he runs with the same disregard for conventions that he'd show as leader of Freedonia in *Duck Soup*. He announces (in song) that whatever his faculty members suggest, "I'm against it." Realizing that on college campuses sports are more important than learning and that holding his job depends on Huxley having a winning football team, he goes to the local speakeasy to buy a couple of ringers for the big game. But he mixes up identities and winds up with Chico (as Barovelli) and Harpo (as Pinky) as his star players. When he finds out his mistake, he has Chico and Harpo attempt to kidnap the ringers, who have signed to play for the opposing college. Chico and Harpo are tied up instead and barely make it to the stadium in time to play . . . pinochle. With the four Marx Brothers in the backfield (Zeppo plays Groucho's son), Huxley triumphs. Regarded as the most surrealistic of the Marx Brothers films, it takes us zooming from one senseless scene to the next and through completely absurd bits of dialogue (particularly the pun-filled verbal duets of Groucho and Chico). The most memorable scenes have Groucho addressing the faculty and students, Groucho trying to gain entrance into a speakeasy by guessing doorman Chico's secret word ("swordfish"), Groucho taking "college widow" Thelma Todd canoeing (she falls overboard and he tosses her a peppermint Life Saver), and the wild, wild football game—during which Harpo shines. Todd, whom we tend to overlook because of Margaret Dumont's importance to the Marx Brothers films, and Groucho have funny scenes together, as they did in *Monkey Business*, but the picture cries out for a subplot with Groucho courting Dumont. Directed by Norman Z. McLeod. Scripted by Bert Kalmar, Harry Ruby, S. J. Perelman, and Will B. Johnstone. Also with: David Landau, Robert Greig, James Pierce, Nat Pendleton.

HOUND OF THE BASKERVILLES, THE (1939) B&W/80m.
The first and best of the Sherlock Holmes series starring Basil Rathbone as Sir Arthur Conan Doyle's brilliant, eccentric self-impressed English detective and Nigel Bruce as his bumbling companion, Dr. Watson. Leaving mist-shrouded London, they travel to Dartmoor, in Devonshire, where the life of the young lord of the Baskervilles (Richard Greene) is in danger. Legend has it that a great hound stalks the surrounding moors and has killed Greene's ancestors. Donning a disguise, Holmes conducts his investigation without interference and discovers a malevolent human being behind the most recent murders on the moors. Watching Holmes in action is great fun—although Watson seems as exasperated as he is impressed by Holmes's cleverness and showboating. Rathbone's Holmes has the proper amounts of conceit in his skills and enjoyment in his profession—he really believes that solving murders is a game. Film has flavor, atmosphere, some suspense, a good mystery. It's much like a horror film, as would be the second-best film in the series, *The Scarlet Claw* (1944). Followed by *The Adventures of Sherlock Holmes*, also made at 20th Century–Fox and the last of the series not to be updated to

'40s London. Remade with much flair in 1959 by Hammer Studios in England, with Peter Cushing playing an energetic Holmes. Also with: Wendy Barrie, Lionel Atwill, Morton Lowry, John Carradine, Beryl Mercer, Mary Gordon, E. E. Clive.

HOUSE OF BAMBOO (1955) C/102m.
One of Sam Fuller's best films. Taut low-budget action picture was filmed on location in Japan, where U.S. military policeman Robert Stack has been sent to infiltrate a gang led by mad ex-GI Robert Ryan. Stack's able to get into the gang by posing as the war buddy of a dead gang member. Fuller believed that WWII didn't end with the armistice—Japan was controlled by the U.S. military and exploited by American thugs and profiteers; loyalty among war vets was of paramount importance; Americans still looked down on Japanese culture—and this was best illustrated by Ryan's running his syndicate as a paramilitary organization: when Ryan plans a robbery, it's exactly like a military officer delivering a briefing on a forthcoming action. Storyline involving Stack and Ryan greatly resembles that between police infiltrator Edmond O'Brien and gang leader James Cagney in *White Heat*. As in Walsh's film, we tend to sympathize with the trusting, insane gang leader instead of the man who commits the unforgivable: betrayal. (Even Ryan's death scene bears some resemblance to Cagney's.) Stack earns our sympathy only through his relationship with the Japanese widow (Shirley Yamaguchi) of his supposed friend. At first Stack uses her (just as the U.S. exploits the Japanese); later his consideration for her and her culture turn to respect. Fuller would explore similar themes in *The Crimson Kimono* when a Japanese-American cop falls in love with a white woman. CinemaScope production was photographed by Joe MacDonald. Also with: Cameron Mitchell, Brad Dexter, Sessue Hayakawa, Biff Elliot, Harry Carey, Jr., Robert Quarry, DeForest Kelley, Barry Coe, Fuller.

HOUSE OF WAX (1953) C/88m.
The best 3-D movie, directed by André De Toth, who, ironically, was blind in one eye. Set in 1902 New York, this remake of Michael Curtiz's 1933 film *The Mystery of the Wax Museum* has Vincent Price (in his first horror film) taking over Lionel Atwill's role of a wax sculptor who becomes crazed after a fire disfigures his face. Whereas his first museum emphasized art and beauty, his new exhibit features macabre themes. Lovely Phyllis Kirk, whose boyfriend (who is Paul Picerni?) works for Price, notices that his wax figures resemble people who recently were violently murdered by a masked strangler—including her dead girlfriend, Carolyn Jones. She alerts detective Frank Lovejoy to her suspicions. When Price is determined that she should be his model for "Marie Antoinette," Kirk's life is in danger. Film is flawed, but has nice mix of humor and chills. The highlight is the scene in which fire sweeps through Price's studio. There is something eerie and hypnotic about watching these wax figures—even when their eyes and cheeks start melting and we sadly imagine them to be in great pain, their expressions do not change,

their smiles don't go away. Certainly a 3-D highlight is when a barker repeatedly hits two little rubber balls attached to paddles with elastic directly at the camera. (Don't be surprised if your eyes cross!) Film succeeds because De Toth wasn't afraid to admit 3-D was a gimmick and he wisely understood that not every 3-D effect need be integral to the plot; he felt no qualms about having Kirk and Picerni go to a café so he could show high-kicking can-can dancers. This scene, where legs shoot out from the screen and we sneak glimpses under the dresses—De Toth's camera is located below the dancers to encourage us—is lengthy and titillating. This is one of the many times in the film that the emphasis is on sex (i.e., Jones putting on tight corset; Kirk lying nude under Price's vat of molten wax). De Toth was the first to realize that the secret to good 3-D is a story having both *horror images* and *sex*, the two elements 3-D does the most justice to. Also with: Paul Cavanagh, Roy Roberts, Dabbs Greer, Charles Buchinsky (Bronson) as Price's assistant Igor, Frank Ferguson.

HOUSE THAT SCREAMED, THE (SPANISH/1970) C/94m.
School full of sexually repressed young girls is the setting for this scary gothic horror film. A new student feels singled out for abuse by the strict headmistress (Lilli Palmer) and a sadistic older girl. Meanwhile a psycho is loose, spying on the girls in the shower and committing brutal murders when he gets one alone. What I find fascinating about this overlooked thriller is that we end up rooting for characters we hated and feared at the beginning, once we realize that they aren't the mystery killer but are in jeopardy themselves. Each time a heroine is killed off, we make the next female in jeopardy—whether she is good or bad—into our new *temporary* (it's likely she'll soon be done in) heroine. Ending is no surprise, but throughout the film the direction by Narciso Ibañez Serrador is skillful, particularly during terrifying murder scenes. I love the unusual way he has the killer move into the frame during the greenhouse sequence. This would play well with Dario Argento horror films. Also with: John Moulder-Brown (as Palmer's weird son), Christina Galbo, Mary Maude, Candida Losada.

HOW I WON THE WAR (BRITISH/1967) C/109m.
Richard Lester directed this shaky but funny and fanciful black comedy set during WWII, showing a troop of British soldiers ("Musketeers") who are given the absurd assignment of clearing an officer's cricket field in North Africa, risking life and limb in the heavily mined area. Many viewers find the subject matter too stupid to serve as a metaphor for the insanity of British militarism, or resent the naïveté, foolishness, and victimization of soldiers who fought a "just" war. But Lester's often absurd sight gags (including some slapstick) and the spirited actors (our fibbing narrator, Michael Crawford, John Lennon—who has a terrific comic delivery—Jack MacGowran, Roy Kinnear) keep the picture from becoming downbeat even when characters we like start dying off. And Lester and scriptwriter Charles Wood (who

adapted Patrick Ryan's novel) advance important themes that viewers in 1967 could relate to: enlisted soldiers are shamefully exploited by their officers, even in "just" wars; soldiers who risk their lives to fight wars benefit only those who stayed home—the survivors' only reward is to be able to tell war stories ("How *I* won the war") years down the road. Photographed by David Watkin. Also with: Michael Hordern, Alexander Knox.

HOW TO MARRY A MILLIONAIRE (1953) C/95m.
Models Lauren Bacall, Betty Grable, and Marilyn Monroe move into a ritzy New York apartment and plot to lasso millionaires for husbands. When down to their last pennies, each finally finds her dream man with money. Only at the last moment each decides to marry the poor man she loves. Comedy chastises golddigging women, but it's perfectly acceptable for men to chase women because they're pretty. Monroe is funny throughout as a hopelessly nearsighted bubblehead who won't wear glasses around men. It's fun seeing her together with Grable—this might be the only film with *two* dumb-blonde roles—for Monroe would inherit Grable's position as 20th Century-Fox's screen queen. Unfortunately, their characters don't interact very much (and neither has much interplay with Bacall). Grable seems ill-suited for a stupid golddigger—this is her one character that is annoying—and though Bacall may be the ideal choice to play shrewd women, she's not the type to play schemers. The picture picks up once Grable and Bacall stop their money-chasing and reveal likable traits. The best scenes have Monroe and David Wayne discussing her bad eyesight on an airplane to Kansas City (she thought she'd climbed on the plane to *Atlantic* City) and William Powell (who gives a characteristically classy performance) nobly accepting Bacall's decision not to go through with their wedding. This is pleasant fluff, but it should have been much better. Scripted by producer Nunnally Johnson. Alfred Newman's on-screen musical prelude, with his full orchestra playing his *Street Scene* theme, looks silly today (it was originally meant to demonstrate stereophonic sound). Jean Negulesco directed this reworking of the 1932 film *The Greeks Had a Word for Them* (Joan Blondell, Ina Claire, Madge Evans). Also with: Cameron Mitchell, Rory Calhoun, Fred Clark, Alex D'Arcy.

HOWLING, THE (1981) C/91m.
Popular television reporter Dee Wallace agrees to meet a brutal killer in a booth in a sex shop. Police shoot him as he attacks her. She can remember nothing that happened in the dark booth, but since we heard growls, glimpsed hairy images, and know the title and the subject of this movie, we realize he had transformed into a werewolf. The human body that is carted off to the morgue soon disappears—werewolves can be *permanently* killed only by silver bullets. Wallace suffers trauma from her experience that prevents her from functioning at work or in bed with husband Christopher Stone. Pop psychologist Patrick MacNee invites Wallace and Stone to his retreat, where they will join others for some therapy and relaxation. When strange things start happening (Wallace hears howling in the woods, Stone is attacked and bitten by a wolf, cows are mutilated), Wallace asks a friend, investigative journalist Belinda Balaski, to come and keep her company. Balaski discovers that the killer who had attacked Wallace and was supposedly dead has a cabin at the retreat. It turns out that the retreat is actually a colony of werewolves who are undergoing MacNee's therapy so they can live in our society without being detected. The first half of Joe Dante's horror film/horror parody is hip-funny, well acted, stylish, and scary, full of offbeat characters, old-time actors, horror-movie references, and clever inside jokes. Then the story goes out the window and Dante overdoes it with werewolf transformation scenes. As conceived by Rob Bottin, they are extremely impressive but they completely slow down the film because they take so long (of course, potential victims just stand there and watch instead of running away) and happen many times during a brief time period. Worst of all, something bad happens to every character we like. John Sayles rewrote the script written by Terence H. Winkless, from the novel by Gary Brandner. Cinematography by John Hora. Also with: Dennis Dugan, Kevin McCarthy, John Carradine, Slim Pickens, Elisabeth Brooks, Robert Picardo, Kenneth Tobey, Dick Miller (hilarious as an occult-bookstore owner), and cameos by Roger Corman, Jonathan Kaplan, Forrest Ackerman, Sayles.

HUMAN COMEDY, THE (1943) B&W/118m.
Director Clarence Brown shamelessly pulls all our heartstrings, but this is still a beautifully realized adaptation of William Saroyan's wonderful novel about life in a small town during WWII. We see boys playing football, a boy watching a gopher come out of his hole, a boy waving at a passing train, boys stealing unripe apricots from an old man's tree (not realizing that he's happily watching them have their adventure), young women attending the picture show with some soldiers, men playing horseshoes, boys running in a track meet; we see the library, a church, a school, the telegraph office, a movie house, a rich person's house, a poor person's house, a middle-income house, Main Street; we meet the rich and the poor, the young and the old, and of course the "girl next door." As we watch this Americana, we can't help but feel waves of nostalgia, religion, and patriotism and develop a sense of family, duty/responsibility, and brotherhood. Mickey Rooney gives a moving performance as Homer McCauley, a high-school student who takes a job as a telegraph boy. His older brother (Van Johnson) is off in the war, so his mother (Fay Bainter) can use the money to provide for him, his sister (Donna Reed), and five-year-old brother (Jackie "Butch" Jenkins). He becomes friends with the supervisor (James Craig) and the aged telegraph operator (Frank Morgan). Meanwhile he has a rivalry with the rich kid in his class: in the 220 low hurdles and over the pretty girl both adore. Film is filled with characters you'll recognize, events that you also may have lived. Every few minutes your eyes will fill with tears—over something happy, sad, noble, familiar. You may get

choked up over soldiers emotionally singing a hymn that reminds them of home, or Homer's elderly female teacher rooting him to victory over his rich rival so that he'll always know that the poor can surpass the privileged. Picture's major theme is simple: all Americans are equal, all orphans in America (like Johnson's army buddy) are part of the American family. MGM cast also included: Marsha Hunt, Ray Collins, Darryl Hickman, Barry Nelson, Dorothy Morris, Robert Mitchum, Don Defore, Ann Ayars, John Craven, Mary Nash, Henry O'Neill, Katherine Alexander.

HUMAN DESIRE (1954) B&W/90m. Intense, fatalistic drama by Fritz Lang, adapted from Emile Zola's naturalistic novel *La Bête Humaine*, which had been filmed earlier in France by Jean Renoir, starring Jean Gabin and Simone Simon. Broderick Crawford asks his wife, Gloria Grahame, to help him get his railroad job back by seeing his former employer, Grandon Rhodes. She succeeds in her mission, but Crawford becomes suspicious of how she managed it. He and Grahame kill Rhodes on a train. Railroad conductor Glenn Ford is a witness, but doesn't turn the couple in because of his attraction to Grahame. They have an affair and the not-to-be trusted Grahame tries to convince Ford to kill her husband. Picture is expertly directed and acted, and is engrossing, yet it lacks the sexual heat of the Renoir film; it also makes the Ford character a confused Korean War vet rather than the much more interesting sexual psychopath played by Gabin. Also with: Edgar Buchanan, Kathleen Case.

HUNCHBACK OF NOTRE DAME, THE (1923) B&W/93m—134m. The first of many screen adaptations of Victor Hugo's classic. See it first. Set in 11th-century Paris, it's an impressive production with large sets and hundreds of extras. It's beautifully photographed, ambitiously staged by director Wallace Worsley, and marvelously acted by Lon Chaney as Quasimodo and Patsy Ruth Miller as the gypsy girl he loves, Esmeralda, whom the ugly, deaf hunchback saves from execution (for a murder she didn't commit) and brings into Notre Dame (where he's bellringer) for sanctuary. The key to Chaney's definitive performance as Quasimodo is that his expressions and gestures are subtle, not demonstrative as one would expect in a silent picture—later actors who played the hunchback hammed it up and worked too hard to get our pity (when they should have tried to earn admiration for the remarkable character). Chaney realized that the make-up alone was strong enough to make viewers feel sympathy for the hunchback—he wanted to show that Quasimodo's personality was opposite of his monstrous exterior. But why does Esmeralda prefer that guy in the feathered hat to Quasimodo, who loves her more than anyone else could? The finale is extravagant and exciting, then poignant. Also with: Ernest Torrence, Tully Marshall, Raymond Hatton.

HUNCHBACK OF NOTRE DAME, THE (1939) B&W/115m. Visually impressive telling of Victor Hugo's classic, set in 11th-century Paris. Charles Laughton plays Quasimodo, the deaf hunchback who rings the bells in the Notre Dame tower. He falls in love with the gypsy girl Esmeralda (Maureen O'Hara), when she offers him water after he receives a vicious public flogging. When she is convicted of murdering a soldier (actually killed by Cedric Hardwicke, the archbishop's powerful brother), Quasimodo saves her from hanging and, in the film's best scene, takes her into Notre Dame so she can have sanctuary. Laughton has received a great deal of praise for his performance, but he doesn't really get much opportunity to act; what few lines he has are intended to make us (or Esmeralda, or the Parisians in the streets) feel sorry for him. The film surely would have worked better if Laughton's hunchback didn't let his physical appearance completely dominate his every thought and word, because he'll get enough pity as it is just from his hideous looks (the make-up people must have used a deformed walrus as Quasimodo's model). O'Hara, who is breathtakingly beautiful, comes across better. William Dieterle directed the lavish film, handling the crowd scenes (more than 3000 extras were employed) expertly—although the mob seems to change its disposition with every new scene—and instructing cameraman Joseph H. August to use some interesting angles. The excellent cast includes: Edmond O'Brien (looking skinny), Harry Davenport (as King Louis XI), Thomas Mitchell, Alan Marshal, Walter Hampden, George Zucco, Fritz Leiber, Etienne Girardot, Rod La Rocque.

HUNGER, THE (1983) C/97m. Disappointing, pretentious horror film set in contemporary New York. Catherine Deneuve is cultured vampire who can give her lovers eternal life, but after a few hundred years they age considerably, by the second, until they are so old and feeble that they must lie for eternity in coffins. Her present lover, David Bowie, begins to age, so he tries to consult a doctor, played by Susan Sarandon, who is doing revolutionary research on accelerated aging. It would have been interesting if the picture were about Sarandon treating Bowie, but she doesn't believe his story and he ends up in a coffin. And once Bowie's character departs, the film rapidly deteriorates. The story becomes: Deneuve seduces Sarandon (who in a couple of shots looks like Bowie) so she'll be her new lover. As Sarandon's body rebels against her (she's like a junkie in withdrawal), she rebels against Deneuve's powerful clutches. Picture becomes downright stupid and repulsive. Moreover, Tony Scott's direction is stylish in the wrong way—the picture comes across as an erotic commercial or sexy music video. Vampire chic. There is loads of sex, including the much publicized lesbian scene between Deneuve and Sarandon, but it's so tiresome that the whole thing should have been in Polish. The trite, horrible scene in which all of Deneuve's former lovers rise from their coffins and revolt against her is the worst horror-movie finale since the ghost attack in *The Sentinel*. "I love you, I love you all," Deneuve tries to explain. She's as unconvincing as she was years ago when she did a TV commercial that began, "I love blueberries; oh, yes, I *love* blueberries." Also with: Cliff De Young.

HUSTLER, THE (1961) B&W/135m.

Robert Rossen directed and co-wrote (with Sidney Carroll) this powerful adaptation of Walter Tevis's short story and novel about embittered pool hustler "Fast" Eddie Felson (Paul Newman), whose obsession with winning at all costs makes him the ultimate loser. Paul Newman gives one of his most emotional performances as Felson, pool shark supreme, whose goal in life is to beat the legendary Minnesota Fats (Jackie Gleason) and take his position as the world's best pool player. His evil manager (George C. Scott) and sad, noble girlfriend (Piper Laurie) vie for Eddie's soul. Only too late, when his road to self-destruction has ended, does Eddie realize that Laurie's love and partnership were all that's important and that you're only a loser until you have nothing else to lose. The four stars give masterful, unforgettable performances, and the dialogue is tough and believable; but the film stands out because of its vivid depiction of the sleazy poolroom milieu. Rossen presents a male battleground where one doesn't win just by pocketing the most balls but by beating an opponent into humiliating submission. Rossen shows the importance of body language, of smiling confidently, of talking smoothly, of holding back the sweat—and how important to a player's style are the various props: pool sticks, liquor, cigarettes, jackets, flowers in the lapel, hats, shades. You can almost breathe the distinct aroma of booze, sweat, hair tonic, and fear. Exceptional editing by Dede Allen. Newman returned in Martin Scorsese's 1986 sequel, *The Color of Money*. Also with: Myron McCormick, Murray Hamilton, Jake LaMotta and Vincent Gardenia (as bartenders).

I AM A FUGITIVE FROM A CHAIN GANG (1932) B&W/90m.

War hero Paul Muni gets out of the army. His old job is waiting, but he wants to try to make it on his own so that he has a chance to make it to the executive level. He travels around the United States but can't find work. This forgotten man winds up in a flophouse. He goes with a stranger (Preston Foster) to a diner, hoping to get a free meal. Foster tries to rob the place and is killed. Muni is arrested for being his accomplice and is sentenced to a Southern chain gang. Life in the prison is hell. The men are treated like animals, work endlessly breaking rocks with sledgehammers, and get little food or rest. There are constant beatings dished out by the sadistic guards. Muni escapes and becomes a fugitive. He finally gets a job with a construction company in Illinois. He rises to executive.

He is forced to marry a greedy young floozy (Glenda Farrell), lest she reveal his past. But she informs on him anyway. He is promised a full pardon if he returns to the Southern prison for 90 days. He decides to trust the representatives of the Southern state. But down South the officials aren't happy with Muni for his public condemnation of the chain gang system. This is one of the earliest social-protest films and one of the strongest. Muni's hardened, desperate face and his angry, scratchy voice are powerful reminders that decent men could be destroyed by the injustice and insensitivity that had come to characterize America. Ending is shockingly depressing; director Mervyn LeRoy has him back into the darkness—it's a powerful visual because we realize that for him and other lost and forgotten men to again emerge into the light, something has to be done about the judicial system and the punishing—instead of rehabilitating—penal system. The last time I saw the film on television, the station clipped Muni's famous response to how he lives as a fugitive: "I steal." Film is daring, not only because of its socially conscious theme but also because of its pre-Code depiction of sex; Muni's scene with a loose woman after he escapes from prison is extremely well done and unusual. From an autobiographical story by Robert E. Burns. Also with: Helen Vinson, Edward Ellis, Allen Jenkins, Berton Churchill.

I AM CURIOUS—YELLOW (SWEDEN/1967) B&W/111m–121m.

Important film in breaking down U.S. censorship rulings between 1969 and 1972. It contains lengthy scene containing full frontal nudity of both the female (Lena Nyman) and male (Borje Ahlstedt) leads, Ahlstedt having a semierection, Ahlstedt performing cunnilingus (possibly simulated), Nyman fondling and kissing Ahlstedt's penis, and much simulated intercourse. The sex is incorporated into a political comedy—it remains a rare legitimate film that contains explicit sex as just an element of the story. The reason that it has such erotic impact is that we're deep into the film and have gotten to know Nyman quite well *before* she participates in sexual acts. Once she has been in the "shocking" sex scenes, she can resume the other part of her life without viewers thinking the less of her; in other words, the sex makes sense in the context of her character. Nyman plays herself, the actress who'd starred in Vilgot Sjoman's *491*. She and director-writer Sjoman have become lovers, and now she is starring in his new film as the daughter of a political sellout (he'd fought with the Republicans in Spain for only a couple of weeks before returning home). The character considers herself a nonviolent radical and, in a very funny scene, asks people on the street about class structure and sexual equality in Sweden. She also spends time protesting U.S. involvement in Vietnam. She has an intense affair with car salesman Ahlstedt—she doesn't realize he lives with another woman and their child. Meanwhile, the actress and actor fall in love in front of Sjoman. Overlong, but worthwhile. It has substance. Sjoman's companion film: *I Am Curious—Blue*. Also with: Peter Lindgren.

I DRINK YOUR BLOOD (1970) C/88m. Wild film was one of the first to cash in on hip young horror fans' appetite for blood and gore, first whetted by *Night of the Living Dead*. Only this picture didn't have the subtlety and sophistication of Romero's breakthrough film. It does have color, energy, and a preposterous plot. A group of cruel hippie types arrive in a small town and worry the citizens. They're tricked by one angry boy into eating a pie he's shot up with rabies. Contracting the disease, they foam at the mouth and go on a murderous rampage. There are some scares, but neither the acting nor the direction by David Durston is impressive and the film itself is pretty offensive. Still, better than its co-feature, *I Eat Your Skin*, or Durston's later VD film *Stigma*. Starring: Bhaskar (ugh!), Jadine Wong, Ronda Futz (a *great* name for an actress), George Patterson.

I LIKE TO WATCH/CABALLERO (1982) C/77m. Very explicit adult film features the debut of one of porno's top stars, Bridgitte Monet. She is beautiful, sexy, and not such a bad actress, but has a high-pitched baby voice that you'll react to as if she were repeatedly squeaking a balloon. Monet loves her boyfriend (Michael Hart) but is frustrated because he's never tried to seduce her. So she looks elsewhere for sexual fulfillment—jilted, he does the same. Picture has large quantity of sex scenes, involving Monet, Hart, and incidental characters. Assorted sex acts are performed by: a man and a woman, two women, a man and two women, women alone. On most occasions the lovers are being watched by a turned-on unseen observer—which, surprisingly, adds to the eroticism. As directed by Paul G. Vateli, the sex scenes are consistently exciting: the men are handsome and the women are beautiful and uninhibited—Vateli gives them an erotic quality by having them wear bright lipstick, eye shadow, nail polish, and erotic underwear; the stars are obviously experienced, skilled lovemakers; the lovemaking takes enough time for us to watch the lovers work their way from being slightly aroused to having intense orgasms; Vateli builds intensity level through the imaginative use of light, color, and music. The film's champion lovemaker award goes to Little "Oral" Annie, who unfortunately disappears after only two sex scenes, before she can startle us further. Also with: Patricia Manning, Lisa DeLeeuw, Kevin James, Anna Pierce, Herschel Savage, Linda Shaw, David Smith.

I MARRIED A MONSTER FROM OUTER SPACE (1958) B&W/78m. The outrageous title is unsuited for this intelligent, atmospheric, subtly made, deliberately paced sci-fi thriller, one of the best of the fifties "paranoia" films. Young bride Gloria Talbott notices a personality change in husband Tom Tryon. Since the night before their wedding, he has been devoid of emotions. She discovers an evil plot of hideous aliens to disguise themselves in human form and marry earth women in order to propagate their dying race. But she can't find anyone to believe her story. Gene Fowler, Jr., formerly an editor of Fritz Lang's, directed, and the influence of Lang is evident in: his use of shadows and bizarre camera angles to heighten tension; his "invisible" editing (time passes on the screen, although it appears that the camera never shuts down); and his having a situation in which townspeople band together to track down an alien. For me, the film's highlight is the creepy moment when an alien looks into a department store window and his monstrous reflection is superimposed over baby dolls in the window display—and you know he's thinking of propagation. Scene recalls Lang's *M*, when child-murderer Peter Lorre looks into a window and his eyes triple in size when he sees the reflection of a little girl who passes by. Talbott, an excellent heroine for sci-fi and horror films, gives a solid performance, exhibiting intelligence and a rare combination of strength and vulnerability. Tryon, years before becoming a best-selling author, is better as the alien than as the human counterpart—he has trouble showing a number of emotions. Also with: Ken Lynch, John Eldredge, Valerie Allen, Maxie Rosenbloom.

I MARRIED A WITCH (1942) B&W/76m. Lightning bolt allows a witch (Veronica Lake) who was burned at stake in 17th century to return to earth in the present, determined to cause havoc in life of stodgy Massachusetts politician (Fredric March), who is look-alike descendant of Puritan who burned her at stake. But she falls for him instead and decides to ruin his wedding to a social climber (Susan Hayward) and marry him herself. Reasonably funny René Clair fantasy is bolstered by some truly special effects and a memorable performance by Lake, who outacts the stiff March. Lake on the make is extremely sexy, particularly in some of the outfits Paramount gave her. She's also very funny—oddly, Preston Sturges had to convince Clair she could play comedy. Wild shenanigans include her helping him win an election. An amusing sidelight is that March and Lake despised one another; according to her autobiography, in one romantic scene, in which they're shown from the waist up, she vindictively put her foot in his crotch, just to watch him squirm. Also with: Cecil Kellaway, Robert Benchley, Elizabeth Patterson.

I SHOT JESSE JAMES (1949) B&W/81m. Samuel Fuller's directorial debut is this interesting low-budget film about "that dirty little coward" Robert Ford (John Ireland). Fuller keeps his character in close-up much of the time to hint at his psychological confusion, first about deciding to kill his best friend (Reed Hadley is effectively intimidating as Jesse James) to get amnesty and money enough to marry his sweetheart (Barbara Britton) and then about being regarded as a traitor by his fellow townspeople. He suffers tremendous guilt. That Ford becomes increasingly sympathetic makes sense in that Fuller despised Jesse James and thought his murder was a public service. Best scenes have Ford nervously eyeing Jesse's back as he sits in a bath, and Ford listening to a man sing "Jesse James." There isn't enough action to satisfy most western fans, but there is a shootout at the end when Frank James (Tom Tyler) comes looking for Ford. Also with: Preston Foster, J. Edward Bromberg.

I SPIT ON YOUR GRAVE/DAY OF THE WOMAN (1977) C/98m.

A New York writer (Camille Keaton, Buster's grandniece) for women's magazines stays alone at backwoods cabin to work on her first novel. Four local hicks, including a wimp, brutally beat and rape her. But the wimp doesn't follow orders to kill her, and she recovers. She gets revenge by hanging, castrating, axing, and ripping apart the four loathsome characters. Crudely made film enters dangerous waters of *The Last House on the Left*. While there is no way to defend this picture, I find it less reprehensible (though not better made) than that other cult item. That's because male moviegoers seemed to enjoy the mistreatment of the young girls in *Last House* as much as the director did; while there is no excuse for the longevity of the rape-brutalization of Keaton in this film—it actually covers three consecutive scenes in which she is attacked anew—I don't believe male moviegoers will identify with the rapists, who are real jerks. They will—I hope—sympathize with Keaton, want her agony to end, and support her revenge. Merv Zarchi's film, which has been blasted for being one of the sickest anti-female pictures, was, I believe, a misguided attempt to make a feminist film (which is more than can be said of *The Last House on the Left*), and the unusual scene that really hints at this has Keaton asking one of her rapists how he could attack her when he has a wife and children at home. Zarchi shows pain, humiliation, terror of rape victim as few filmmakers have—but by revealing his own immature excitement in showing Keaton nude, whatever honorable intentions he had are lost to us. Also with: Fran Tabor, Richard Pace, Anthony Nichols, Gunter Kleeman.

I WALKED WITH A ZOMBIE (1943) B&W/68m.

The most poetic of horror films, beautifully directed by Jacques Tourneur for producer Val Lewton; it's their follow-up to *Cat People*. One of Lewton's brave, strong heroines, Frances Dee is a Canadian nurse who goes to Haiti to work for planter Tom Conway, taking care of his sick wife, Christine Gordon. The natives believe Gordon is a zombie, one of the walking dead, and her lifeless appearance even during movement seems to confirm their suspicions. Is she insane, as Conway believes, or is her zombie-like state the result of a voodoo curse placed on her by Conway's mother, Edith Barrett, for having had an affair with James Ellison, Conway's half-brother? We never find out for sure; what we come to realize is that there is just as much validity in believing in the powers of voodoo as there is in believing God will answer prayers. (Lewton does not belittle the island blacks by mocking their beliefs, customs, and religious practices. They are the ones who understand what forces reign supreme, while the whites wallow in confusion and terror.) Lewton was a Brontë scholar, and in essence this film was meant to be "Jane Eyre in the West Indies." The story itself is set up like a Greek tragedy: a house has been ripped asunder by infidelity, meddling in-laws, sibling rivalry, and calling on pagan gods to carry out selfish bidding. There's even a one-man Greek chorus (black calypso singer Sir Lancelot) to explain the plot in song. This is the most visually impressive of Lewton's films. The lyrical quality of the long silent passages—Dee and Gordon's nocturnal walk through the mysterious woods, Ellison carrying Gordon toward the ocean while a giant zombie (Darby Jones) follows—the shadows, the lighting, the music, the exotic settings contribute to making this one of the masterpieces of the genre. Lewton, Tourneur, and cameraman J. Roy Hunt have created the ultimate "beautiful nightmare." Mark Robson edited. Curt Siodmak and Ardel Wray based their script on a story by Inez Wallace, who claimed she really saw zombies in Haiti. Also with: James Bell, Richard Abrams, Theresa Harris.

I WANNA HOLD YOUR HAND (1978) C/104m.

If you were in the New York area back in 1964, you know that this sadly neglected film perfectly captures the lovely hysteria surrounding the Beatles' arrival in town, their stay at the Plaza Hotel, which was besieged by fans, and their historic appearance on *The Ed Sullivan Show*. Comedy is about a funny group of kids, mostly out-of-towners, who try to break into the Beatles' hotel suite and to rustle up tickets to the Sullivan show. It's like something out of a time capsule; the characters, clothes, dialogue, New York environment/atmosphere are exactly as I remember. There was something wonderful in the air back then that's impossible to describe—somehow this film re-creates that feeling. There are splendid comic performances by the young cast—particularly Nancy Allen as a girl who suddenly becomes an obsessed Beatles convert and Eddie Deezen as a nerdy chatterbox who is a Beatles trivia nut (remember those guys?) and hawks memorabilia. A difficult, unusual project, particularly when you consider that the real Beatles and Ed Sullivan weren't available for the finale, which was nevertheless cleverly handled by director Robert Zemeckis (then Executive Producer Steven Spielberg's protégé). This sleeper's a lot of fun; and smart, too. Also with: Bobby DiCicco, Marc McClure, Susan Kendall Newman, Theresa Saldana, Wendie Jo Sperber, Will Jordan (as Sullivan).

I WAS A TEENAGE WEREWOLF (1957) B&W/70m.

Satisfying low-budget horror film that was aimed at the fifties drive-in crowd. Michael Landon gives a sympathetic performance as a well-meaning high-school kid who gets into constant trouble because he can't control his violent impulses. After getting into a fight at school, he's sent to a doctor (Whit Bissell) who, instead of helping him, turns him into a werewolf. The picture has a couple of really scary scenes: a teenage *boy* (young filmmakers should take note that the imperiled characters need not be females for a scene to be frightening) walks alone through the dark woods and senses he's being followed; a girl hangs upside down in the gym and gets an upside-down view of the werewolf approaching her. Director Gene Fowler, Jr. (*I

Married a Monster from Outer Space), formerly an editor of Fritz Lang's, develops his usual outsider/paranoia themes, which are brought to the forefront when Landon is hunted and chased by police and men from the town. Landon, who wears a leather jacket, looks great in his wild werewolf get-up. Vladimir Sokoloff is on hand, filling the Maria Ouspenskaya void, recalling the superstitious old country where werewolves ran through the hills. Also with: Yvonne Lime (as Landon's loyal girlfriend), Guy Williams.

IF.... (BRITISH/1969) C-B&W/111m. Even considering a *Goodbye, Mr. Chips*, most of us Americans have long regarded the British public school as a clear-cut example of deeply entrenched institutional tyranny toward youth and repression of free thought. In the late sixties many American student protesters saw the boys' school in Lindsay Anderson's popular, controversial film as a symbol of any establishment and of all oppression; and identified with the three rebellious students (Malcolm McDowell, Richard Warwick, David Wood) who fight for the survival of individualism against authority, tradition, and the old guard. Early part of the film details how the three youths (all about 16) withstand the bullying tactics of schoolmasters, as well as being subjected to an inadequate, irrelevant education. Their refusal to buckle down causes them to be whipped by sadistic upperclassmen. In the final scenes Anderson injects heavy doses of surrealism, so that we cannot tell if what we're seeing is truly happening exactly as presented or if our crusaders (specifically McDowell) are fantasizing or Anderson is showing images that represent their wish fulfillment. Cinematically, the surrealism is excitingly audacious, and it works well when McDowell and the waitress he just meets (Christine Noonan) have a dreamlike love-making encounter. Yet when the three rebels and the girl disrupt Speech Day by shooting down many of the teachers and soldiers in attendance, the surrealism—the fact that it doesn't look real—weakens the effect. We want to see our heroes get revenge on all those who have mistreated them, but since the whole scene looks like it's just the visualization of someone's imagination, we don't feel that the bad guys are getting their due. Interestingly, the surrealistic final scene in Jean Vigo's *Zéro de Conduite*, Anderson's inspiration, works as both dream and reality. The young boys in Vigo don't replace order with madness and vengeance as do the boys in Anderson's film, but with anarchy, in which there are no bonds on self-expression; they don't rub out the faculty and soldiers as in Anderson, but do something much worse (and more believable): they deprive them of their *dignity* (which is how Charlie Chaplin—who is referenced often in Vigo's film—managed to triumph over arrogant authority figures). It would have been a daring move if Anderson had the rebels massacring the faculty in a realistically shot scene, but of course Anderson knew better than to present such an offensive (to most everyone) scene without giving it a surrealistic, cartoonish look. He'd have done better to have had the faculty flee like cowards, repeatedly grabbing their smoking behinds—just like the si-

lent comedians used to do. Nifty camera work by Miroslav Ondricek. A bright performance by McDowell. Also with: Robert Swann, Hugh Thomas, Guy Ross, Peter Jeffrey, Arthur Lowe, Mona Washbourne.

IF I HAD A MILLION (1932) B&W/88m. If you fondly remember the fifties television show *The Millionaire*, then this is the film for you. Ornery tycoon Richard Bennett (in what would have been an ideal role for Lionel Barrymore) decides to postpone his death long enough to give several strangers (whose names he gets from the phone book) a million dollars apiece. All-star Paramount cast appears in episodes detailing how various individuals react to getting hefty sum. Supposedly, money can't buy happiness, but, interestingly, you'll like best the three episodes in which it does—and be frustrated by those in which the benefactors (for odd reasons) don't make use of the money (soldier Gary Cooper gives away what he believes is a bogus check; wanted George Raft can't go into a bank to cash the check and ends up using it to buy a night's sleep in a flophouse). Best sequences are comical, including scenes with Bennett. Surely viewers will be pleased by those episodes in which the money allows previously powerless people to put authoritarian figures in their place (the brief Charles Laughton episode is a gem). Steven Spielberg probably loves the vignette in which an oppressed, unhappy woman in an old folks' home gets the financial means to take over the establishment and turn it into a rabble-rousing club. For me, the most touching bit has prostitute Wynne Gibson spend her first night with money in the fanciest room of a fancy hotel, where she immediately tosses away the second pillow from the bed and sleeps, happily, *alone*. Directed by James Cruze, H. Bruce Humberstone, Stephen Roberts, William A. Seiter, Ernst Lubitsch, Norman Taurog, Norman Z. McLeod. Also with: W. C. Fields and Alison Skipworth (who buy a dozen cars with which to crash into road hogs), Jack Oakie, Charles Ruggles, Mary Boland, Roscoe Karns, May Robson, Gene Raymond, Frances Dee.

IKIRU (JAPANESE/1952) B&W/143m. Precious film may be Akira Kurosawa's masterwork. Set in post-war Tokyo, where Takashi Shimura (the leader of *The Seven Samurai*) is part of the do-nothing Japanese bureaucracy, a minor government worker who has spent 25 years rubber-stamping the papers that pile on his desk. At work he is known as "The Mummy." At home he is ignored by his grown son. He is a pathetic, self-pitying, insignificant person. He is told he is dying of cancer. Wanting "to live" (the translation of film's title) for the first time before he dies, he withdraws his money and goes out on the town for a night of pleasure with a young writer, a Mephistopheles figure. When drinking and carousing don't please him, he decides to find happiness through another person—he begins spending time with a sweet, pretty, young office worker. Still he is unsatisfied. She tells him to do something worthwhile. At this point in the film we move five months into the future to Shimura's wake, where family and fellow employees praise (but not too much) what he accomplished before he died. Through several flashbacks we see Shimura go on a one-man crusade to build a park for children where a dangerous cesspool stands. He is indomitable as he goes through bureaucratic red tape, taking insults right and left, ignoring negative responses, circumventing runarounds; he constantly stoops over and gives a pathetic knock on bureaucrats' doors until they are so annoyed that they do what he wants just to get rid of him. Moreover, he stands up to a youth gang. He has no time to love or be angry. Picture is a strong indictment of Japanese bureaucracy, a wonderful character story, a heartfelt meditation on the meaning of *living* and doing one's part. A beautiful film in every way. Shimura's performance is exquisite—how he had improved since 1948's *Drunken Angel!* There are many great moments, but most memorable has Shimura, after his task has been completed and he is ready to die, sitting on a swing and, while snow falls gently on him, singing softly about the shortness of life. He dies happy and, as the narrator says, "our hero." Also with: Nobuo Kaneko, Kyoko Seki, Miki Odagiri, Yunosuke Ito.

ILSA: SHE WOLF OF THE SS (1974) C/95m.
Cult film for sick set with a plot suitable for S&M porno books. Haughty, sadistic Ilsa (Dyanne Thorpe) is the warden of a Nazi medical camp during WWII. She prepares female prisoners for Nazi brothels, conducts hideous medical experiments on her prisoners, and, to satisfy her own curiosity, conducts personal torture sessions to prove female prisoners can withstand more pain than men. At night she has male prisoners make love to her and then kills them because none satisfies her. Her downfall comes when she falls for an American prisoner (Greg Knoph), who is a stud in bed. On the day the Nazi general comes to camp, there is a prisoner revolt, and the tables are turned on the prison guards. This picture is indefensible, but at least the torture/violence is not as convincing as one might fear, given the film's notorious reputation. The brutality looks staged. More important, the film is not on side of Ilsa (which also is contrary to film's rep), but on side of prisoners. Poor acting, pedestrian direction by Don Edmonds, and a repelling overdose of bondage and violence put the film at bottom of the women-in-prison genre. This is strictly a sexploitation film—there is no political theme. Sequel is worse: *Ilsa, Harem Keeper of the Oil Sheiks.* Also with: Sandi Richman, Jo Jo Devile, Ushi Digard, Wolfgang Roehm.

I'M ALL RIGHT, JACK (BRITISH/1959) B&W/104m.
Classic British satire finds Ian Carmichael as a naïve but enthusiastic college grad who uses his wealthy family's connections to break into industry. He starts as a common worker in his uncle's Missiles, Ltd. plant—of course he doesn't tell anyone who he really is. Carmichael becomes the unwitting pawn of both the corrupt management and the workers' union, whose steward, Peter Sellers (in his Hitler mustache), makes sure *no* worker is fired, be he incompetent, lazy, or doing work that a machine could

handle in a tenth of the time. When Carmichael speaks to the press about what management and the union have done to him, he becomes a hero in London. Soon the strike that he caused in the plant spreads throughout England, until millions of people are on strike and the economy is on the brink of collapse. Sharp, cynical comedy chastises workers, but is clearly sympathetic toward them—they're not bad sorts, and much preferable to their sneaky, crooked bosses who are willing to sell out their country for a profit. I doubt if an American union-made film will ever deal so bravely with similar labor-management problems. An obvious influence on *O Lucky Man.* Last scene is startling for 1959—bare-assed nudists scamper across the screen. Directed by John Boulting, who produced with brother Roy. The standout cast also includes: Terry-Thomas, Margaret Rutherford, Richard Attenborough, Miles Malleson, Irene Handl, Liz Fraser, Marne Maitland, Malcolm Muggeridge (as himself).

IMITATION OF LIFE (1959) C/124m.
Many Douglas Sirk fans consider the director's last film to be a masterpiece. I think it's impeccably made Hollywood trash—a watchable, laughable, lamentable soap opera/"woman's picture"/"problem picture" that has women who'll sacrifice all for their children but aren't particularly good mothers (a soap tradition), Ross Hunter gloss and glitter, fantasy lighting, and perfectly designed sets (notice how the books on the shelves come only in sets). The plot superficially resembles John Stahl's 1934 film, also adapted from Fannie Hurst's novel. Widows Lana Turner, a white woman, and Juanita Moore, a black woman, are best friends who live together, raising their daughters together. Driven Turner becomes a theater and movie star and spends little time with her growing daughter, Sandra Dee, who turns to Moore as surrogate mother. Moore's daughter, Susan Kohner, is embarrassed to be black and, because she has light skin, attempts to pass for white. She eventually runs off so her new acquaintances won't see her dark-skinned mother—this breaks Moore's heart. Meanwhile Dee goes off to college because she doesn't know what to do about her love for John Gavin, her mother's boyfriend. As in all Sirk's films, life is terribly difficult and people like Turner must struggle and sacrifice some of their humanity to get through it—but if one stops and looks around at the world they've created for themselves, they'll be as sad as Turner becomes after years of self-absorption. As in all Sirk's films, selfish people like Turner must come to terms with the responsibility a person has to others as well as to one's self. The race issue is treated shamefully in the film. Kohner is made out to be thoroughly insensitive when in fact her choice to pass for white has to do with her rejecting the demeaning black world that is presented to her—even at home she witnessed best friends Turner and Moore taking on the roles of white mistress and black maid. When Turner chastises Kohner for insinuating she's been treated differently at home, Kohner acquiesces that Turner and Dee never showed prejudice toward her—but the script should have had her attack Turner for treating Moore as her servant. Moore is made into Koh-

ner's whipping post, but that might be different if she had suggested to her daughter not to go to a black teachers' college but to break down some racial barriers, be defiant, and improve the lot of her race rather than to be satisfied with the hand dealt her. Moore may be the nicest woman in the world (which is why Kohner can't help loving her) but she makes no attempt to teach Kohner pride in being black. The script is also infuriating because when Turner, Gavin, and Dee are nice to Moore and Kohner or act without prejudice, white audiences are expected, in a self-congratulatory gesture, to weep about the white characters' nobility, their refusal to act high-and-mighty toward people who have none of their advantages. The most honest scene has white Troy Donahue brutally beating date Kohner, who he has learned is black. Also with: Dan O'Herlihy, Robert Alda, Mahalia Jackson, Jack Weston.

IMMORAL MR. TEAS, THE (1959) C/63m.
Collector's item by Russ Meyer that quickly earned him the title of "King of the Nudies" (and millions of dollars) and opened up new avenues for the adult film industry. Highly publicized film was notorious when released. But today it seems extremely tame, even genteel. It does have curiosity appeal, however, and it is still more erotic and amusing than the era's other nudies. The simple premise: Mr. Teas (played by Bill Teas) is a middle-aged bachelor gentleman who suddenly gets the ability to see through women's clothes. The whole film consists of him looking at "nude" women who aren't aware that he sees them so closely. Obviously, Mr. Teas had the power most men wished for, and they flocked to the theater to live out their fantasies vicariously. Made for $24,000, picture has Mr. Teas's voice-over but no dialogue, reinforcing suspicion that our observant hero (though no bumbler) was inspired by Jacques Tati's Mr. Hulot. Among those who strip for the cameras: Ann Peters, Marilyn Westly, Dawn Denelle, Michelle Roberts.

IMMORAL TALES (FRENCH/1975) C/90m.
Occasionally erotic but mostly a boring vignette film by Polish émigré Walerian Borowcyzk (the former animator and experimental filmmaker) depicting "sinful" sexuality through the ages. Everything (people, props, settings) is filmed sensually, even the sequences featuring "Bloody Countess" Elizabeth Bathory luring virgin girls to their deaths, and the Borgias (a woman and two priests) having sex while a man who condemns the depravity of the church is being burned to death for his blasphemy. At least the first sequence—a 20-year-old boy smooth-talks his beautiful 16-year-old cousin into performing fellatio while the tide rises around them—will turn on the rakish sides of us men, and seems to establish a valid theme: men are moral hypocrites, women are their sexual victims. We wrongly expect this theme to be reinforced in later episodes. The women are gorgeous (I wouldn't trust whoever cast this film), but there is actually too much female nudity. Of course, Pasolini could have done better with the material (just by injecting some

bawdy humor), but what's worrisome is that even Bob Guccione might have made a more interesting film. With: Paloma Picasso.

IMPROPER CONDUCT (FRENCH/1984) C/115m.
Documentary directed by famed cinematographer Nestor Almendros and Orlando Jimenez Leal, both Cuban exiles, is meant to show that the reality of Castro's Cuba is much different from the rose-colored vision many political radicals have of it. The film concentrates on the widespread and systematic oppression and persecution of those who don't fit the government's (Castro's) image of "macho"—specifically, homosexuals (including transvestites) and dissident writers and other intellectuals. Acclaimed film is convincing, but I find the interviews with exiles who had been persecuted repetitive and less shocking than the filmmakers intended. It might have been stronger if it had been trimmed to an hour.

IN A LONELY PLACE (1950) B&W/91m.
Nicholas Ray made several films about decent men who couldn't control violent tempers. Such a man is Dixon Steele (Humphrey Bogart), an ex-GI who's been trying to make a comeback as a successful screenwriter since the war ended. His frustrations have manifested themselves in two ways: he consistently makes cynical remarks about the movie industry; he repeatedly has violent tantrums. The police think he was the murderer of a hatcheck girl he invited to his apartment on the night she was killed. (She synopsized a book he was hired to adapt.) But new neighbor Gloria Grahame tells them that she saw the hatcheck girl leave alone. Bogart and Grahame quickly fall in love, and for the first time in years Bogart is able to write. At this point an interesting thing happens: Grahame becomes the main character. We watch Bogart through her eyes and begin to share her suspicions that he really killed the girl. She can see from witnessing his violent rages and insane jealousy that if he didn't actually kill the girl, he was capable of such an act. No wonder Grahame becomes an emotional wreck. Andrew Solt and Edmund H. North wrote the terrific, unusual script, which includes sharp dialogue and some peculiar secondary characters. Grahame (who was about to get her divorce from Ray) and Bogart (playing his rare tough guy who wants to get married) are an exciting couple. Onetime "sleeper" film has come to be regarded as one of Bogart's classics. From a novel by Dorothy B. Hughes. Also with: Frank Lovejoy, Robert Warwick, Jeff Donnell, Carl Benton Reid, Art Smith, Martha Stewart, Steven Geray, Hedda Brooks.

IN THE REALM OF THE SENSES/REALM OF THE SENSES/EMPIRE DES SENS, L'
(JAPANESE/1976) C/105m. In 1936 a seemingly crazed woman named Sada was arrested after having spent four days roaming the streets of Tokyo. She was carrying the genitalia of her lover, whom she had strangled. When her story was told, she became famous across Japan, a

genuine folk heroine. In telling her weird story, director Nagisa Oshima pays homage to a figure he admires greatly, who had come to represent *unbridled passion*. Sada (Eiko Matsuda) is a onetime whore who has become one of the geishas who work for a married couple. She simply cannot reject sexual advances, whether they come from another geisha or a dirty old man found lying in puddle. So she does not deny the husband (Tatsuya Fuji) when he takes her sexually. At first he is the initiator of their sexual encounters, but soon she reveals herself to be sexually insatiable. Whereas this man took sex from strange women as a matter of habit, this woman he intended to casually exploit demands that she obtain sexual fulfillment as well. So they can be alone to enjoy their sex games, they go away together. They have sex constantly. She keeps him in a constant state of erection, even when he sleeps; he is unable to resist her—he admits that her passion controls his penis. They make love inside, outside, morning, afternoon, and night; they make love in front of servants, who think them perverts. Their love-making becomes more intense, depraved, and violent. She wants to possess his sexual organs and threatens him with death if he should make love to his wife again. Oshima shows how consuming love is and, like his couple, makes the correlation between sexual ecstasy and death. It becomes obvious that for this couple to reach the pinnacle of sexual pleasure there will have to be a sacrifice—as they wouldn't be satisfied with anything less and neither could stand the thought of their sex losing its momentum, he resigns himself to her killing him while they make love and she becomes thrilled by the idea. Oshima is known for breaking down cinematic barriers, but few were prepared for such a controversial film, one in which the two characters spend so much time making love that they speak about themselves only once in the entire film and that lasts for about 10 seconds. His tribute to "Mad Love" contains explicit sex by the two leads—and, yes, they can fornicate and act at the same time. Design of film is artfully done; shots were inspired by 18th-century Japanese erotic painters. Fuji would star in Oshima's far less interesting subsequent film *Empire of Passion*.

IN THE YEAR OF THE PIG (1969) B&W/ 101m.

Emile de Antonio's sober documentary account of what was happening in Vietnam, and how the war had escalated to such a point, was required viewing among war protesters in 1969 and the early seventies. Made without narration, its power comes from showing us our higher-ups in government (Johnson, Humphrey, Nixon) making speeches about our policy in Vietnam and then showing footage that contradicts what they said. The main thrust is that America is intervening in a civil war on behalf of a corrupt, authoritarian South Vietnamese government and is carrying on a war that is founded on racism. We watch our soldiers get a pep talk before undertaking a search-and-destroy mission (which their officer knows they enjoy), blowing up rice stocks, razing villages, herding the displaced villagers into

an open field for the night (the American officer says they'll manage fine because they can "bunch close together" if it gets cold), rifle-butting and kicking tied-up prisoners or (suspiciously) putting hoods on them and leading them to helicopters; we hear soldiers speak of "gooks" and "slant-eyes," officer George Patton III says that his patriotic heart is bursting with pride because his men are "a bloody good bunch of killers"; and all sorts of similar ditties. Also of interest are interviews with Wayne Morse and Ernest B. Gruening, the only senators to vote against the Gulf of Tonkin Resolution that really escalated the war. Film has an undeniable fascination, but too much serendipity is evident in the choice of footage and interview subjects. We never feel like we're getting a full story about any aspect of the war. Even in 1969 I thought the film was weak. Film's bias is still clear, however, during final moments: first we see a friendly Ho Chi Minh (it's his first appearance in the film, and he's so much more humble than all the American leaders have been) being cheered by some villagers (obviously he's a popular leader) and then see (for the first time) badly injured American soldiers—the North Vietnamese leader's justified (according to Antonio) retribution for the damage they've done to his country.

INCREDIBLE SHRINKING MAN, THE (1957) B&W/81m.

An excellent science-fiction film that seems to affect everyone who sees it. Like most fifties SF films, it's scientifically preposterous but somehow believable, and its *human* concerns will strike a responsive chord. It combines the *paranoia* theme that is present in many works of its screenwriter, Richard Matheson, with two themes that are central to the other SF films of director Jack Arnold: scientific advances in dangerous areas eventually will be destructive to the individual; there is nothing more horrifying than losing one's identity. Grant Williams is the sympathetic hero who begins to shrink at an alarming rate (child to insect to atom size) after being touched by radioactive mist. While Matheson's ending is hopeful, entire picture, though enjoyable, is quite upsetting as we watch Williams shrink in body and self-respect. His home is no longer a sanctuary but a booby-trapped battlefield where every household item is potentially a weapon that could destroy him. He must move into a dollhouse for protection from the family cat. His wife (Randy Stuart) remains loyal, but, being of normal size, becomes the prime reason for his sense of inferiority. Through his eyes we take a new look at things and people we've taken for granted. There is an underlying theme dealing with male sexual impotence; the film's most touching scene (often cut on television) has him—now three feet tall and not comfortable with his wife—striking up a relationship with a female midget. Thoughtful adaptation from Matheson's novel *The Shrinking Man* without the sleazy sex of the book that turned on us youngsters back then. The budget was low, but Clifford Stone's special-effects work is outstanding. Williams's life-and-death struggles with the cat and a spider are thrilling. Also with: April Kent, Raymond Bailey, Billy Curtis, William Schallert.

INCREDIBLE TORTURE SHOW, THE/BLOOD SUCKING FREAKS (1976) B&W/88m.

Reprehensible film has strong underground reputation based on its strong, sickening violence and torture scenes. The blackest of comedies, low-budget film is set in Greenwich Village, where sadistic director Sardu (Seamus O'Brien) stages his "Theatre Macabre" featuring women being tortured. The audience doesn't realize that the tortures and killings are for real. The victims are white-slaver Sardu's disobedient slave girls. He kidnaps a *New York Times* writer who despised his show and sets to work on a ballet that the critic will approve of. He also kidnaps a pretty ballerina (Viju Krim) and makes her watch tortures in order to make her a willing participant in his show. Some of the scenes are too ridiculous to be taken seriously—others are nauseatingly tasteless. The acting is surprisingly competent. This film was object of protests by women's groups, and certainly if any film deserves to be banned, this deserves strong consideration. As it is, nudity and torture earned it an X rating. Direction by Joel M. Reed is passable. Also with: Louie de Jesus (as Sardu's monstrous midget assistant), Miles McMaster, Alan Dellay, Don Fauci, Michelle Craig.

INDIANA JONES AND THE TEMPLE OF DOOM (1984) C/118m.

Rousing but inferior follow-up to *Raiders of the Lost Ark*, directed by Steven Spielberg, produced by George Lucas, and scripted by Willard Huyck and Gloria Katz, who mixed old-time serials with James Bond. Film takes place in 1935, before *Raiders*. Indiana (Harrison Ford) flees Shanghai with prissy, complaining heroine Willie Scott (Kate Capshaw) and his young, resourceful sidekick Short Round (Ke Huy Quan)—the name of Gene Evans's young Korean companion in Sam Fuller's *The Steel Helmet*. They end up in India, where the leader of an unhappy village asks Indiana to go to the Maharajah's great fortress and retrieve a magical jewel and the village's enslaved children (why don't the adults go after them?) who are working in the mines. No sweat. Picture has been accused of racism (Indians rarely are portrayed positively in Spielberg productions), of pandering to children (there are a lot of "gross" visuals), and of presenting a heroine of a type that hasn't been around since feminism hit Hollywood. I'll go along with the first two charges, but I think Spielberg is saying something positive about women: if someone like Willie, who worries about broken nails, can become brave and tough in a crisis, then all women have the potential. Picture has great sets, fun performances, exciting adventures—the ride on the mine car, which shows Spielberg intended to make a roller-coaster ride of a movie, is spectacularly directed. Film is entertaining, but won't please everyone as *Raiders* did. Also with: Amrish Puri, Philip Stone, Roshan Seth.

INFRA-MAN (HONG KONG/1976) C/92m.

Alien princess (Terry Liu) arrives on earth and causes earthquakes and thousands of deaths. She wants to enslave earth and lets loose a group of two-legged monsters to stop all resistance. A scientist (Wang Shieh) turns a young volunteer (Li Hsia-Hsien) into Infra-man! Dressed in red outfit, with an insectlike helmet, he takes on the Monsters. He uses karate acrobatics, and lightning bolts that shoot out of his hands. Campy nonsense has a cult following. On television it's dull; but it's fun to see in a theater with a large audience. Directed by Hua-Shan. Also with: Wuan Man-Tzu, Lin Win-Wei.

INHERITORS, THE (AUSTRIAN/1983) C/89m.

Film caused riots when first shown in Germany. It was made after William Bannert, the film's Austrian producer-director-screenwriter (with Erich Richter), and some friends were attacked in a pub by a Nazi youth gang. Picture shows how in present-day Germany and Austria bored, alienated, out-of-work youths are joining neo-Nazi organizations to find excitement, a sense of power and importance, sexual fulfillment (with Nazi groupies), and camaraderie. We follow one teenage boy (Nicholas Vogel), who has no political leanings or real knowledge of Hitler or the Nazis, as he is lured into such a group, moves into its more violent wing, and becomes part of a paramilitary outfit that specializes in terrorizing Jews. This is a terrifying, important film, but it's foolishly marred by the exploitive nature of Bannert's sex scenes. You'll get chills from a scene in which an old Nazi brags to the boys that his lampshade is made from the skin of a concentration-camp victim. Also with: Roger Schauer, Anneliese Stoeckl-Eberhard, Jaromir Borek, Gabriele Bolen.

INSATIABLE (1980) C/80m.

Marilyn Chambers made her long-awaited comeback into porno films and her insatiable fans were waiting. This proved to be a big moneymaker upon its initial release—due in part to Chambers touring the country on its behalf and, if the publicity was true, appearing for some print and radio interviews in the nude—and since then has been at the top of the XXX-rated video market. The story has Chambers as a famous model who takes time off to relax at her aunt's enormous English estate. There's a lot of chitchat, which doesn't leave that much time for sex scenes. But the sex is strong stuff, not surprising since John Holmes appears in one sequence. Chambers's high salary was worth it, for she seems even less inhibited than in her *Behind the Green Door* days. Production values and photography are superior to those found in typical porno films. Directed by Godfrey Daniels (likely an alias for a W. C. Fields fan). Also with: John Leslie, Jessie St. James, Serena, Mike Ranger.

INSERTS (BRITISH/1976) C/99m—117m.

Devastating reviews coupled with its deserved X rating (the result of full frontal nudity, profanity, and sexually perverse subject matter) kept viewers away upon its American release; nevertheless it developed a strong cult following. I find it neither as pretentious nor as self-indulgent as most critics did. And it's hard not to be impressed by the terrific ensemble acting; the biting, witty script about Hollywood types; and how director-writer John Byrum uses sex not only to entrance viewers but thematically as well. Sex is the *only* means by which his defensive characters can express themselves. The film starts out with stereotypical situations, but the plot takes weird twists and the characters turn out to be genuinely quirky. The humor is deadpan, always on the edge, and at times we feel uncomfortable laughing while the characters wallow in misery. But it is appropriate because, as some critics overlooked, the film is a satirical comedy. In the thirties, Richard Dreyfuss (the only one of the four young stars not to do nudity) is a genius Hollywood director, Boy Wonder, who dropped out of the Hollywood scene. He spends his entire life in seclusion in his mansion, dressed in robe and pajamas, unshaven, drinking, smoking, brooding about his impotence, and making porno films in his living room with addict Veronica Cartwright and Stephen Davies, who is as stupid as they come. He works for bootlegger Bob Hoskins, whose girlfriend, Jessica Harper (who's great as Cathy Cake), asks Dreyfuss, when they're alone, if she could appear in some inserts to his latest porno film. Because of the style of the dialogue and the use of one large set, the picture seems as if it might have been written for the stage. But it is about *film* and its power. Only in front of Dreyfuss's camera are people willing to reveal themselves totally; to stop putting up barriers, rejecting each other, playing mind games, and putting on airs. So, ironically, while they are making *illusions* they are showing *reality*. The film's message is simply that life is restrictive and film is liberating; taken further, because they strip the actors to the bone, Dreyfuss's films are far greater *art* than the Hollywood claptrap he no longer wants to make. Dreyfuss and his stars make films with strong sexual content for the sake of "art"—and that's why Byrum and his stars got involved in this picture.

INSIGNIFICANCE (BRITISH/1985) C/105m.
Overlooked, not insignificant apocalyptic comedy, adapted by Terry Johnson from his bizarre play, and directed by Nicolas Roeg. The setting is New York in 1953, and our four major characters converge in a hotel. They are: The Actress (Theresa Russell as "Marilyn Monroe"), The Ballplayer (Gary Busey as "Joe DiMaggio"), The Scientist (Michael Emil as "Albert Einstein"), and The Senator (Tony Curtis as "Joe McCarthy"). The wild-haired Jewish-German Scientist is in town to speak before a peace conference, but the sweaty Senator threatens to destroy his life's work (on finding the shape of space) if he doesn't instead speak the next morning in favor of nuclear testing in front of the Atomic Energy Commission. That night the Actress finishes shooting her famous skirt-blowing scene (from *The Seven Year Itch*) and comes to the Scientist's room. She is thrilled to meet the superintellectual she's long adored—she impresses him with her smarts—and would fulfill her desire to sleep with him if her ignorant husband, a star Ballplayer, didn't interrupt them. Plot takes twists and turns. Perplexing film attacks America (represented by the Senator) for per-

secuting/victimizing/exploiting its celebrities, whose pure knowledge or talent is invariably perverted. Marilyn Monroe is presented as the ultimate (bleeding) victim, a beautiful natural resource who is a punching bag at home and by government. Russell—Roeg's girlfriend—takes a while to convince us she's Marilyn, but soon we recognize in her the sweetness, intelligence, vulnerability, hurt, and sense of happiness lost that we associate with Marilyn Monroe. The scene in which the Actress ingeniously teaches the Scientist about relativity is a doozy. Direction by Roeg is imaginative as usual—he uses his fragmented style to good advantage; in this case he inserts revealing flashbacks. Not since *Walkabout* has his camera work been so sensual and seductive: when Marilyn walks into a room, the atmosphere becomes erotic. A jarring final scene. Also with: Will Sampson (as The Indian).

INSPECTOR GENERAL, THE (1949) C/102m.
Just a few years ago Danny Kaye, then part owner of the Seattle Mariners, was in the stands at a game I attended in Yankee Stadium. Introduced to the crowd, he was roundly booed. I couldn't believe it: *Danny Kaye* being booed! How his star has fallen . . . Like most Kaye vehicles, this Henry Koster–directed farce has dated badly; however, Kaye comes off better than the silly script and better than in some of his other roles. It's the early 19th century and the corrupt officials of a European village worry that the dreaded Inspector General will soon appear. Kaye, who makes a living playing a "living head" in charlatan Walter Slezak's touring novelty act, is arrested while walking through town begging for food (he's suspected of being a horse thief). But then the town officials mistake him for the Inspector General, whom they've never seen, and start wining and dining him and treating him like royalty. (Eventually they will try to poison him.) Premise becomes as tiresome as all Kaye's songs. But Kaye does some good physical comedy and has a funny scene bluffing a near-sighted official who knows the real Inspector General well. From a play by Nikolai Gogol. Also with: Barbara Bates, Gene Lockhart, Elsa Lanchester, Alan Hale, Walter Catlett, Byron Foulger.

INTERIORS (1978) C/99m.
Seeing this unusual Woody Allen film in 1978 was for many of us an excruciating experience. Ready to laugh, we saw before us a humorless Bergmanesque drama (without Allen in the cast) and felt too inhibited in quiet, crowded theaters to even clear our throats—it seemed possible that super-critical, super-serious characters might turn heads and point fingers at us. But see it today in comfortable, half-empty repertory theaters: it is truly a beautifully acted, painstakingly written and directed, outstanding if (I still think) too serious film. Story centers on three grown sisters; poet Diane Keaton, striving movie actress Kristin Griffith, and Mary Beth Hurt, who, in the midst of an identity crisis, changes jobs repeatedly. Keaton is married to an unsuccessful writer (Richard Jordan) who makes a living teaching. Hurt is married to a political writer-activist (Sam Waterston). Keaton has a

daughter whom she seems to ignore—she won't let Hurt, Jordan, or her mother (Geraldine Page) get close to her; Hurt is pregnant, but wants an abortion. The sisters grew up in a large home on the New Jersey shore, which their refined mother kept antiseptically clean—she also taught them to have strong critical perspectives in regard to the arts. Because she was so critical, they all grew up considering themselves failures—significantly, none can accept a compliment. When Page, Keaton, Hurt, Waterston, and Jordan talk, the conversation turns to criticism of books, plays, articles, anything "sophisticated"; the conversation reaches the height of snobby pretentiousness meant to hide the pain and confusion of characters. They all are emotional cripples, afraid of one another because of the damage each is capable of inflicting. Each is jealous of any other's successes. A family crisis results when father E. G. Marshall leaves Page, who suffers a breakdown and attempts suicide. Hurt, who identifies with mother, is stuck caring for her. She becomes horrified when father gets married again—to a down-to-earth, unsophisticated woman, Maureen Stapleton, whose bright clothes are a jolt to picture which, until her appearance, had only austere, subdued colors. She brings life to drained group, but Hurt doesn't appreciate her. What's most impressive about Allen's film is that he creates a logic for why his characters respond to each other as they do. Film has *many* emotionally devastating moments: for me, the most special has Stapleton giving mouth-to-mouth resuscitation to Hurt on the beach, giving her life as surely as her first mother did. Cinematography by Gordon Willis.

INTOLERANCE (1916) B&W/123m–129m– 137m–220m.

D. W. Griffith's most ambitious work is, in the limited terms of *visual storytelling*, probably the greatest of all films. Epic consists of four stories that show "intolerance" (religious, political, social) at work. The stories are set during four historical periods: in the "Modern Story," tenement dweller Mae Marsh (as Dear One) has her baby taken away by uplifters and her boyfriend, Bobby Harron, sentenced to execution for a crime he didn't commit; in the "Biblical Story," Jesus (Howard Gaye) is persecuted by the Pharisees and Rome; in the "Medieval Story," a family of French Huguenots is killed during the St. Bartholomew's Day Massacre of 1572; in the "Fall of Babylon," a brave mountain girl (Constance Talmadge) tries to protect kind Prince Balshazzar (Alfred Paget) when Cyrus's troops storm his castle during an enormous feast. Griffith exhibited unparalleled visual power during the individual segments (i.e., just the way he stages the great feast in the mammoth, ornately designed hall set is an awesome achievement). But his real strength is in editing. He is able to build suspense within episodes by strategically mixing perfectly timed long-shots and extreme close-ups (faces, hands), and he builds suspense for the entire film by cutting back and forth between the various episodes so that they all build to their climaxes at the same time. His montage techniques were studied *and* copied worldwide. Seen on a large screen, this is an amazing, thrilling movie. But if it's not as important

as *The Birth of a Nation*, it's because the theme of "intolerance" is a feeble link between the episodes. Griffith seems interested in his stories only as sources for visually interesting movie material—he seems passionate only about the modern story. Nevertheless, this film has *greatness* written all over it. G. W. (Billy) Bitzer and Karl Brown did the cinematography. Erich von Stroheim, Tod Browning, and W. S. Van Dyke were among the assistants. Also with: Lillian Gish (as the rocker of the cradle of family life, the link between the episodes), Vera Lewis, Monte Blue, Margery Wilson, Browning, Elmer Clifton, Tully Marshall, Eve Southern, Natalie Talmadge, Donald Crisp, Douglas Fairbanks, Tammany Young, Eugene Pallette, Lillian Langdon, Bessie Love, Olga Grey, Van Dyke.

INVADERS FROM MARS (1953) C/78m.

Not as good as the later-made fifties sci-fi paranoia films *Invasion of the Body Snatchers* and *I Married a Monster*, but it's fondly remembered by those of us who saw it when we were children because it perfectly depicts the child's ultimate nightmare. Jimmy Hunt is a young boy who is awakened one night by an alien ship that lands behind his house and burrows into the ground so it can't be detected. No one will believe him. Soon he realizes that his parents (Hillary Brooke, Leif Erickson), policemen, and many townspeople have been taken over by the aliens. They become emotionless beings and try to stop the boy from telling anyone about their invasion. (This is another sci-fi film of the era that has been interpreted as an anti-communist political allegory because the aliens use mind control.) Jimmy finally finds adults (Helena Carter, Arthur Franz) to help and the army charges in. Kids will surely enjoy this film, but, considering its twist ending that sends Jimmy back into his (continuous) nightmare, this is one of the most depressing and scariest films ever intended for them. The director was William Cameron Menzies (*Things to Come*), who did an admirable job on a low budget; his greatest contribution is the set design, which, when shot through a slightly distorted lens, adds to the film's surreal look. Originally made in 3-D, it looks fine on a flat screen. Remade in 1985 by Tobe Hooper, with Jimmy Hunt returning to the screen in a small role.

INVASION OF THE BEE GIRLS (1973) C/85m.

Government agent William Smith investigates the deaths of several male scientists at California institute conducting radiation experimentation. All the men died from coronaries while having sexual intercourse. The least likely culprit is the seemingly frigid doctor, Anita Ford. But Smith doesn't discover (until long after we do) that atomic radiation has caused her to acquire the genetic characteristics of a bee! She seeks men for fertilization, and they die in the process (just like male bees). She is not upset. Ford is queen bee, but she has created several other beautiful bee girls (she's like a madame with a string of B-girls). Smith tries to prevent Victoria Vetri from becoming another bee girl. Nicholas Meyer has always claimed that he wrote his "B"-style horror film with tongue in cheek, but it's not that much different or funnier than earlier films like *Leech Woman*. Picture isn't as much fun as its reputation would have you believe, but there's a lot of sex and a memorably bizarre sequence in which thousands of bees encase a nude woman in a cocoon. Directed by Denis Sanders (a little-known but skilled director). Also with: Cliff Osmond, Wright King, Ben Hammer.

INVASION OF THE BODY SNATCHERS (1956)
B&W/80m. One of the all-time great science-fiction films, one of the few that make the fantastic seem perfectly credible. Don Siegel's classic is set in Santa Mira, California, where Dr. Miles Bennell (Kevin McCarthy) is told by several people, including his new girlfriend, Becky Driscoll (Dana Wynter), that their loved ones have been replaced by lookalike imposters who show no trace of emotion. Then, in a creepy scene, his married friends Jack (King Donovan) and Theodora (Carolyn Jones) discover a half-formed body that resembles Jack. Later, Miles, Becky, Jack, and Theodora find four pods containing half-formed creatures that resemble them—they realize that all the others in town, even the police, have been replaced by alien imposters after they have fallen asleep. So the four try to escape from town without being detected or getting much-needed sleep. Where Siegel's film outshines Phil Kaufman's 1978 remake is in pacing—the excitement just keeps building. Siegel uses several tricks to establish tension: having characters in constant motion—moving from place to place, racing their cars, running; having characters peer at each other through windows and glass doors; having Miles and Becky hide in small spaces, like closets and the hole beneath the boards in the cave; having characters leave their motors running when they get out of their cars; having much activity take place in basements and other dark, shadowy settings; and, most effective of all, establishing that aliens have replaced Miles's friends so we're paranoid about everything ordinary and familiar. Siegel used staples of the action film he knew so well: diverse camera angles, penetrating close-ups of characters mixed with mysterious longshots of large areas of Santa Mira, and sharp editing. Siegel didn't make Kaufman's mistake and have special effects and gimmicks take precedence over characters. After all, what we're witnessing—your loved ones becoming your enemy, your fighting to retain your ability to love—is terrifying because of the *human* element involved. Few moments in cinema history are as sad or shocking as when Miles kisses Becky and realizes she has become one of *them*. Siegel's film is controversial because it can be seen as either anti-communist or anti-McCarthy polemic. I believe that with the studio-imposed opening and closing scenes set in an LA hospital the film has an anti-communist slant because the transformation of our people into emotionless pod people is being conducted by an alien force (i.e., Russia), and the President, FBI, and military (whom the doctors call) will try to repel it; but if the film ends pessimistically as Siegel intended, with Miles running like a madman on the highway warning people "You're next!" then Siegel is suggesting that our

indoctrination has been ordered from within and that you can't call anyone in Washington because they're part of the conspiracy. Daniel Mainwaring adapted Jack Finney's story. Also with: Larry Gates, Jean Willes, Virginia Christine, Ralph Dumke, Whit Bissell, Richard Deacon, Dabbs Greer, Sam Peckinpah.

INVASION OF THE BODY SNATCHERS (1978)
C/115m. Philip Kaufman's remake of Don Siegel's 1955 classic isn't a bad sci-fi film, it just doesn't compare to the original. While the transformation of the pod creatures into human duplicates is most impressive and terrifying, Kaufman places too much emphasis on special effects and snazzy visuals and not enough on the characters so that we can understand the *tragedy* of their losing their identities. The San Francisco setting seems ill-advised because we're not seeing the transformation of average Americans but people who are already weird—their alteration from spaced out to emotionless is not that catastrophic a change in our eyes. In the original, when loved ones became heartless, it was heartbreaking. Worst of all, the film hasn't the political subtext that made Siegel's film so fascinating. Nor does it have Siegel's pacing that made it unrelentingly suspenseful. It does have some fine, hip performances, however. Donald Sutherland and Brooke Adams, and Jeff Goldblum and Veronica Cartwright, are appealing as the two couples who try to hold on to their humanity. You care about them, but you don't feel that the loss of the world they inhabited before the pods fell from outer space is to be lamented. Also with: Leonard Nimoy (as a pop psychoanalyst), Art Hindle (as Adams's husband, an early victim), and, in cameos, Kevin McCarthy, Siegel, Robert Duvall.

INVISIBLE MAN, THE (1933) B&W/70m. James Whale directed this splendid adaptation of H. G. Wells's novel. Star Claude Rains is visible only at the end, but he makes a strong impression walking about while wrapped in bandages from head to foot and using his sinister voice. Rains is already invisible when he makes his first appearance, checking into a country inn. He is trying to find an antidote to the drug that made him invisible. But he stops looking for a cure when it dawns on him that being invisible has its advantages. No, he doesn't sneak into a girls' locker room. He commits robberies and murders. He wants to terrorize the world. (Megalomania is a side effect of the drug.) Picture begins humorously; it becomes scary: the invisible man is one of the screen's first insane villains, following Peter Lorre in *M* and Brember Wills in Whale's *The Old Dark House*—other short fellows. Special effects by John P. Fulton are still impressive—his shining moment is when Rains first takes off the bandages and we see no face beneath them. You'll be as baffled as snoopy inn proprietress Una O'Connor. Photography by Arthur Edeson. The excellent script was written by R. C. Sheriff and Philip Wylie (uncredited). Also with: Gloria Stuart (as the woman Rains loves), William Harrigan, Henry Travers, Forrester Harvey, Holmes Herbert, E. E. Clive, Dudley Digges.

IRON HORSE, THE (1924) B&W/165m.
John Ford's classic holds up better than James Cruze's *The Covered Wagon*, the other major western epic of the silent era, but it too seems very slow (an iron *pony*?) and not particularly original. Story is about the building of the transcontinental railroad, initiated by Abraham Lincoln (Judge Charles Edward Ball). It is a tribute to the visionaries who realized that such a crazy project was essential to our country's expansion west (Manifest Destiny). Like many future, better Ford westerns, it's about the pioneers who made the first inroads into the savage, Indian-controlled wilderness; about the men who sacrificed their lives so those who followed in their paths could have an easier time; and about the beginning of civilization in the West. As did Griffith in *The Birth of a Nation*, Ford uses a historical story as the backdrop for a personal story. Unfortunately, the less important (in terms of the film) historical story is more compelling. George O'Brien is the hero, a young man who tries to carry out his father's (James Gordon) wild dream of a railroad linking East to West. He is also determined to exact revenge on the villain (Fred Kohler), who, when disguised as leader of an Indian war party, killed O'Brien's father. He'll also fight it out with Kohler's secret employee (Cyril Chadwick), the fiancé of O'Brien's childhood sweetheart (Madge Bellamy). At times, picture has strong visual power, as when the Indians attack and when the final railroad spike is driven home and O'Brien and Bellamy are united. Some prints are tinted. Also with: Will Walling (as Bellamy's father, the builder of the railroad), Gladys Hulette, James Marcus, Francis Powers, J. Farrell MacDonald, James Welch.

ISLAND OF LOST SOULS (1933) B&W/70m.
Shocking, gruesome horror film, adapted from H. G. Wells's exciting yet morbid *The Island of Dr. Moreau*. Richard Arlen finds himself stuck on an island with the crazed Dr. Moreau (Charles Laughton), who has transformed scores of wild animals into hideous-looking "human beings" capable of walking on two feet and speaking. Moreau keeps his "guinea pigs" in check with a set of human laws that, if broken, means a session in the dreaded House of Pain. Moreau's most successful experimentation has changed a panther into a beautiful woman (Kathleen Burke). Moreau hopes Arlen will become attracted to her, although Arlen senses something strange about her. Film is extremely atmospheric and features one of Laughton's best performances—interestingly, he based his sadistic, whip-wielding island god on his dentist. Probably what makes film so fascinating is that it contains really offensive material, including torture, animals being made into humans, and Arlen kissing the Panther Woman on the lips (he does quite a double-take and looks ill). That Moreau hopes human Arlen and animal Burke will make love and she'll bear his child is among the most repellent storylines in cinema history. The remake, using Wells's title, was released in 1977. Well directed by Eric C. Kenton. Also with: Leila Hyams, Bela Lugosi (as the leader of the Beast People), Stanley Fields.

ISLE OF THE DEAD (1945) B&W/72m.
Intelligent, atmospheric horror film produced by Val Lewton; directed by Mark Robson, whose tableaulike images were inspired by Swiss romantic painter Arnold Böcklin, Goya, and other artists. While a war rages in 1912 Greece, several people are quarantined in a house beside a graveyard on a small Greek island. One by one they succumb to the plague. Boris Karloff is a general, a ruthless old warrior who doesn't know how to fight disease and is driven mad by his frustration. In Lewton films, when a character loses his mind he reverts to old, superstitious ways. Whereas Karloff once spoke of a new Greece, he now blames their misfortunes on Thea (Ellen Drew), an impressionable young Gypsy who he thinks is a *vorvolaka* (a vampirelike creature). Like Simone Simon's Irena in Lewton's *Cat People*, Thea's not sure she doesn't harbor evil within her—but unlike Irena, she doesn't give in to it. It's fascinating that Lewton/Robson allowed Thea's tough-minded employer (Katherine Emery) to tell off the cruel general, who has all Greece's male population quivering in their boots, but it's more gratifying that they have the meek Thea stand up to the intimidating figure. Meanwhile, Lewton exploits his concept of man controlled by fate. The only thing that can save these people is a change in wind direction that will carry the pestilence away. There are prayers to God and to Hermes; and even the dying doctor (Ernest Doran) concedes that the new ways (medicine, Christianity) are no more powerful than the old (pagan ritual). Picture suffers because of uninteresting coupling of Drew and Mark Cramer, who plays a newspaper correspondent. But Karloff and Emery are outstanding. Furthermore, the set design is imaginative (for a low-budget film), the camera work properly excites, and the horror is intense. The real fright comes when Emery loses her mind after being prematurely buried. Also with: Helene Thimig, Jason Robards, Sr., Alan Napier, Skelton Kraggs.

IT HAPPENED ONE NIGHT (1934) B&W/105m.
Irresponsible heiress Claudette Colbert runs away from home after her father (Walter Connolly) annuls her marriage to a no-account playboy. She wants to get back to the playboy. She becomes object of nationwide search. She ends up on a bus with boozy, hard-boiled reporter Clark Gable. He says he won't turn her in, as long as he can get an exclusive on her story—that will get his job back at the paper that fired him. On their journey they do a lot of squabbling, but fall in love. Super Frank Capra comedy was supposed to be a minor picture but wound up as the first picture to win all five major Oscars: Best Picture, Best Director, Best Actor, Best Actress, Best Adapted Screenplay (by Robert Riskin). Many critics regard it as the first screwball comedy, but the humor is surprisingly controlled. It comes naturally from the two actors, whose characters are wild only at the beginning. What makes the film so special is that it's composed of *small* moments—Gable demonstrating hitching techniques for Colbert (who realizes a pretty leg is better than the thumb); Gable teaching Colbert how to dunk donuts properly; Gable carrying Colbert across a stream and arguing with her about the definition of a piggy

back ride; the motel scene (Gable didn't wear an undershirt!) where Gable and Colbert sleep on opposite sides of a hanging blanket—"the Walls of Jericho" which will come tumbling down in the end. Weirdest scene has Gable pretending to be a mobster to scare off Roscoe Karns, so he won't blab about Colbert's whereabouts—Gable threatens to harm his children. From Samuel Hopkins Adams' story "Night Bus." Also with: Jameson Thomas (Colbert's fiancé), Alan Hale, Ward Bond.

IT'S A GIFT (1934) B&W/67m.

Side-splitting W.C. Fields comedy is the best showcase for the comedian's unique brand of humor, which is based on characters annoying one another. It is these annoyances, piled one on top of the other, that in Fields's eyes summed up the life of a married man in America. Film is a series of set-pieces strung together to represent the typical day in the life of Harold Bissonette, a henpecked husband (of Kathleen Howard) and frazzled father (of the grown Jean Rouveral and young Tom Bupp), and owner of a small grocery store in New Jersey. While the partly domesticated Fields is suffocating, he isn't entirely defeated by his constrained life. He allows Howard her martyrdom, constant criticism, and rules because, when out of her sight, he still has his wonderful vices—he remains an iconoclast in a world of conformists. He may swear to Howard that they'll remain in New Jersey, but he uses their inheritance money to buy a California orange grove and then sells his store without consulting her—and she must follow him to California or risk losing her man. Every vignette is hilarious. The classic sequence in which Fields tries to sleep on his porch is my favorite because it includes the arrival at 5 a.m. of an insurance salesman looking for Carl LaFong ("Carl Lafong! Capital 'L,' small 'a,' capital 'F,' small 'o,' small 'n,' small 'g.' LaFong! Carl LaFong!") and a conversation between Mrs. Dunk and her drawling daughter—one standing above Fields and the other below him—about which store the girl should go to ("It doesn't matter to me"; "It doesn't matter to me 'ither"). But the entire California trip sequence is masterful; and a long sequence in the grocery store allows blind, cantankerous Mr. Muckle—"the house detective over at the Grand Hotel"—to break a lot of merchandise, Baby LeRoy to cover the floor with molasses, and Fields to refuse to acknowledge to an angry customer that he doesn't have kumquats. Bissonette endures indignities without self-pity or complaints. He accepts the absurdity of his world and tolerates his predicament. But Fields the writer—under his Charles Bogle pseudonym—allows us to see how Harold truly feels about his life under his expressionless facade: At the end, in the final shot, he smiles for the only time in the picture as he drinks spiked orange juice—he has achieved freedom! Cult masterpiece was directed by Norman Z. McLeod. Also with: Tammany Young, Julian Madison.

IT'S A MAD MAD MAD MAD WORLD (1963) C/154m–192m.

Eight people, in three cars and a truck, witness a car crash. The dying driver (Jimmy Durante) is an ex-con who tells them where $350,000 is buried (under a giant "W"). They all act nonchalant, but when they get into their cars, greed takes over and they race to get to the loot first. Mickey Rooney and Buddy Hackett are in one car; Sid Caesar rides with wife Edie Adams; Jonathan Winters drives the truck; and Milton Berle, wife Dorothy Provine, and his shrill, pushy mother-in-law Ethel Merman round out the field. There are air crashes and tire blowouts and everyone looks for alternate forms of transportation. That's how Phil Silvers, Terry-Thomas, Jim Backus, and almost everyone else in the world join the hunt. This was one of the first films since Griffith's 1916 *Intolerance* to cut back and forth between several story lines. (The previous year's *The Longest Day* was another.) Stanley Kramer wrote and directed this salute to slapstick—and his remarkable all-star cast, consisting primarily of comics and comic actors who are known for their verbal skills, prove equal to the task. The picture may be too long, but this allows all the stars ample time in the spotlight. Merman is funny playing a thoroughly obnoxious woman; Winters and Silvers are also particularly memorable. There is much humor that falls flat, but also a great deal of hilarity in this film, both visual and verbal. There are some spectacular stunts and some imaginative plot twists. Kramer manages to maintain a frantic pace throughout. He shows that old, familiar slapstick bits are still funny, and keeps us watching for cameos from the likes of Jerry Lewis, Jack Benny, and Arnold Stang. It was really impressive in Cinerama. The huge cast also includes: Spencer Tracy, Dick Shawn, Peter Falk, Andy Devine, Normal Fell, Buster Keaton, the Three Stooges, Joe E. Brown, Don Knotts, Leo Gorcey, Sterling Holloway, Stan Freberg, Charles Lane, Carl Reiner, Eddie Anderson, William Demarest, Edward Everett Horton, ZaSu Pitts.

IT'S A WONDERFUL LIFE (1946) B&W/129m.

Once neglected, Frank Capra's masterpiece about the importance of every individual has become a Christmas perennial and one of our most popular films. James Stewart is George Bailey, who has always dreamed of traveling but has spent his entire life in Bedford Falls running his modest building-and-loan and making sure that the good townspeople aren't left in the evil hands of rich Mr. Potter (Lionel Barrymore). He has sacrificed all his life for others' happiness and security, but where has it gotten him? On Christmas Eve he realizes that he'll be going to jail because his Uncle Billy (Thomas Mitchell) has mislaid—actually, Potter stole it—a large check. George wishes he'd never been born and contemplates suicide. But his wife, Mary (beautifully played by the beautiful Donna Reed), and daughters have been praying for him, and a sweet angel, Clarence Goodbody (Henry Travers), arrives to help George—and earn his wings in the process. In a nightmarish sequence he shows George what a dreadful place Bedford Falls would have been without him and what miserable lives all his friends and family would have led if he hadn't been around—George realizes that every man makes a profound difference, and that a good man such as himself can benefit countless people. George follows in the steps of other Capra idealists, who have their faith in themselves and their conservative values severely tested. But when he's at the brink of giving up, his faith is restored by those very people he has spent a lifetime teaching through words and by example. Coming to his financial rescue in the tear-jerking finale, they prove to George that they have learned (while he has forgotten) his great lesson: people's most important investments are not in stocks, bonds, or property, but in each other. Film allows Stewart to show how great an actor he was, as his character ranges from optimistic hick philosopher to the pessimistic postwar figure he'd play in *Vertigo* and Anthony Mann westerns. Likewise, the film itself ranges from riotous comedy to dreadful nightmare, allowing the rest of the wonderful cast to exhibit versatility. The success of this film surely has to do with how reassuring it is: not only do you have a family who adores you, a hometown sweetheart who loves and marries you, a guardian angel (Travers is great!) who loves and protects you, but also an entire town of people who love you and come to your aid when you're in trouble. Frances Goodrich, Albert Hackett, and Capra wrote the script, with an assist from Jo Swerling—they adapted a story, "The Greatest Gift," which the writer Philip van Doren Stern sent as a Christmas card to his friends. Also with: Beulah Bondi, Ward Bond and Frank Faylen (as the first Bert and Ernie), H. B. Warner, Gloria Grahame, Todd Karns, Samuel S. Hinds, Frank Albertson, Virginia Patton, Bobbie Anderson (George as a boy), Sheldon Leonard, Karolyn Grimes (as Zuzu).

IT'S ALIVE! (1974) C/91m.
Woman (Sharon Farrell), who has been prescribed untested medication to help her have child, gives birth to a hideous-looking monster baby with fangs and claws. It massacres everyone in the delivery room except for Farrell and goes into hiding somewhere in the town. Occasionally it emerges, rips apart somebody, and crawls back into the darkness. Baby's father (John Ryan in a surprisingly strong performance) becomes a social outcast; he wants the baby destroyed immediately, but Farrell, suspecting that the baby has instinctive feelings of love for its parents, wants to save it from the police. Cleverly written and directed by Larry Cohen, cult movie is at once terrifying and repugnant. It deals with the relevant issue of doctors indiscriminately giving women unsafe drugs, but only so it can use the shameful baby-as-monster premise, which Cohen exploits to the nth degree. At least Cohen has us rooting for the baby by film's end. Superior to Cohen's *It Lives Again*, made in 1978. Also with: Andrew Duggan, Guy Stockwell, James Dixon, Michael Ansara.

IT'S ALWAYS FAIR WEATHER (1955) C/102m.
Gene Kelly–Stanley Donen musical doesn't always work, but it contains many bright ideas. Gene Kelly, Dan Dailey, and Michael Kidd get out of the army after WWII and swear to always be friends. They have a reunion ten years later and find one another insufferable. But their dislike for their former wartime buddies reflects their dis-appointment in themselves. Kelly is a shiftless and broke prizefight manager, Dailey has given up painting to work for an ad agency (the bore has a bad stomach and his wife is divorcing him), Kidd runs a hamburger restaurant. Ice-cold Cyd Charisse, who works for a *This Is Your Life*–like television show, plays up to Kelly so that she can get him and his friends on the show. Kelly and Charisse fall in love, and the boys find that they still have what it takes to be pals. Picture is surprisingly downbeat (none of the characters are happy), and the songs by Adolph Green and Betty Comden are like Broadway rejects. But Kelly's and Donen's direction/choreography of the musical numbers is quite innovative. Musical highlights include the three vets dancing with trash-can lids, Kelly tapping on roller skates, Dailey drunkenly wrecking a pompous party, and Dolores Gray (as a self-promoting television hostess) killing all her athletic suitors while singing "Thanks a lot but no thanks." There's no music during the brawl at the end, but it's interesting because it is *choreographed* rather than staged. Why don't Kelly and Charisse dance together? See it in the theater because the directors made special use of CinemaScope, at times dividing the screen into thirds. Also with: David Burns, Jay C. Flippen, Hal March (funny as a stupid boxer), Paul Maxey.

IT'S IN THE BAG (1945) B&W/87m.
Rare Fred Allen movie was the probable inspiration for Mel Brooks's *The Twelve Chairs* and is just as cockeyed. Allen is a flea-circus owner who must locate an antique chair in order to acquire a huge inheritance—but some murderers are after it, too. Not consistently funny, but there are some great scenes: Allen and his wife (Binnie Barnes) try to get seats in an enormous, already sold-out movie theater; Allen *rents* a chair from stingy radio rival Jack Benny (who plays himself). Also with: Robert Benchley, Sidney Toler, Rudy Vallee, John Carradine, Don Ameche, William Bendix.

IVAN THE TERRIBLE, PART I (RUSSIAN/1945) B&W/96m.
Sergei Eisenstein's indoor epic centers on the palace intrigue during the 16th-century reign of Ivan IV (Nikolai Cherkasov), Russia's first czar. When he becomes ruler, he promises to unite all Russia, force everyone to be in the army or contribute to it (even the church), and takes estates away from those who don't adhere to his extremist policies. His actions infuriate the boyars, who want to have one of their own (Ivan's imbecile cousin) on the throne. Since one of his two friends joins a monastery (so as not to oppose Ivan) and the other desires both his wife (Ludmilla Tselikovskaya) and his throne, Ivan has few loyal comrades to protect him and to assure that his son will be czar if he dies. Picture begins with Ivan's coronation and marriage, takes us on one war campaign, and—after Ivan has gone from clean-shaven to having a short beard to having a mustache and short beard to having a beard that would make Rasputin envious—concludes with Ivan about to follow the people's will and return to Moscow. The film has remarkable

visuals—Eisenstein's close-ups of the ugly nobles and bearded peasants are staggering—but it's ludicrously melo-dramatic and theatrical. Other than establishing a bond be-tween Ivan and the peasants to suggest a similar affinity between Stalin and his subjects, it's hard to figure out how Eisenstein is using his hero. I can't even tell if he admires Ivan or is frightened by his tyranny. Ivan comes across as a hero in a Wagnerian opera; everyone else seems to be trying out for a Hollywood serial, perhaps *Flash Gordon* or *Buck Rogers*. The devious, swathed-in-black boyar prin-cess Euphrosinia (Serafima Birman) would have been a great foe for Buster Crabbe. Score by Sergei Prokofiev.

IVAN THE TERRIBLE, PART II (THE BOYARS' PLOT) (RUSSIAN/1945) B&W-C/84m.

This con-tinuation of Sergei Eisenstein's epic about Ivan IV (Nikolai Cherkasov) is more stylized than Part I—Eisenstein uses color at times, and he has characters sing—but this doesn't help. I've never seen so many people in a theater dozing off as when I last saw this film. It is beautifully shot, but slow-moving and lacking some of the pivotal characters of the first part. Ivan has returned to Moscow and sets out to purge all those who wish to return to the old days when Russia was weak and not united. He breaks with the church and has several boyars beheaded. The boyars plot to assassinate Ivan and replace him with his imbecile cousin. But clever Ivan manages to foil their plan. It's most interesting when Ivan decides that he must indeed be "the Terrible," as his enemies call him, and that, without ever feeling happiness, a czar must be cruel at times to destroy the Christian forces within and outside Russia who threaten his country's survival. Obviously, Eisenstein's czar is meant to represent Stalin's view of himself. Score by Sergei Prokofiev.

JACKSON COUNTY JAIL (1976) C/89m.

Yvette Mimieux discovers that her husband (Howard Hesseman) has been unfaithful and decides to leave LA to rethink her life, giving up a high-level job and her expensive home. She drives alone cross-country to New York, taking the Southern route. She makes the mistake of giving a lift to a young psychotic (Robert Carradine) and his pregnant girl-friend. He steals her car and money. She seeks help, but a Jackson County local tries to rape her. She gets thrown in jail when she tries to complain. In jail she is raped by a guard. Afterward she kills him and flees with another pris-oner (Tommy Lee Jones); and while the police close in, they fall in love. Film has cult reputation based on its fem-inist themes. Rape is hard to watch rather than titillating—and we see Mimieux really fight back; Jones, the only man who isn't in an authoritarian position as far as Mimieux is concerned, is the one man who doesn't dump on her. Picture is well acted, and it's worth seeing if only because it allows Mimieux a rare starring role. She gives the film what class it has. My own opinion is that the film never intended to make strong political points; under the secure cover of a feminist façade, it includes many of the raunchy elements found in typical New World exploitation pictures. Except for a couple of well-done action sequences, Michael Miller's direction is sloppy and self-consciously arty; the storyline is pretty standard stuff; and we've seen enough Southern yokels in other films. Overrated. Miller and Mimieux teamed up for a television remake. Also with: Frederic Cook, Severn Darden, Mary Woronov.

JAGGED EDGE (1985) C/108m.

Popular thriller has lawyer Glenn Close defending charming newspaper pub-lisher Jeff Bridges, who is accused of brutally murdering his wealthy wife. The unscrupulous, ambitious prosecuting attorney (Peter Coyote), her former boss, has a strong case against Bridges (who has a feeble alibi). But crafty Close and her skilled, foul-mouthed assistant, Robert Loggia, do some sleuthing to find the specific evidence that Coyote is hiding because it would support Bridges. Close comes to believe Bridges is innocent and falls in love with him—but when her suspicions resurface, their relationship becomes shaky. Joe Eszterhas's absurdly written and played court-room scenes (complete with overly dramatic reactions from the lawyers and spectators when each bit of surprise testi-mony turns up), the phony lawyer-ethics theme, and Richard Marquand's too slick and manipulative direction undermine the premise and overshadow the tense finale in which the killer goes after Close. Film strives for points from feminists by having a male client trying to convince a female lawyer to take his case—he not only realizes she's the best in the business but thinks it a plus that she's a woman. But film-maker spoils it by implying that when a female lawyer defends a male client accused of violent crime, this unfairly sways the jury; and, worse, that she is susceptible to the charms of a man who is willing to use her in more ways than one. Marquand and Eszterhas spend the whole picture having Close act and talk tough to impress us, while si-multaneously getting us to sympathize with her by making her vulnerable in love. Also with: Marshall Colt, Leigh Taylor-Young.

JAIL BAIT (1954) B&W/70m.

Predictably, Edward D. Wood, Jr.'s melodrama is ineptly made. Yet Wood's fans will be disappointed. Film has a coherent plot—thanks to Alex Gordon working with Wood on the script. It even has a clever ending. The title refers to a *gun*, not a sexy ado-lescent girl. Son (Clancy Malone) of a plastic surgeon (Her-bert Rawlinson) teams with a hardened criminal (Timothy Farrell) on theater robbery. Malone kills the night watchman; Farrell shoots a witness, but she lives and can identify him. Needing a new identity, Farrell asks Rawlinson to give him a new face—prior to the operation, Rawlinson discovers

Farrell murdered his son. Finale is like something out of *Alfred Hitchcock Presents*. Acting is mediocre but better than in other Wood films. The photography is dark, the sound and dubbing are horrible, the music laughable. The women are ugly. (The men aren't so good-looking either, except for smooth-faced detective Steve Reeves, making his debut five years before *Hercules*.) Funniest moment has Malone's sister, Dolores Fuller, calling Farrell a cheap crook, only to have his girlfriend (Theodora Thurman) protest: she tells Fuller to look again at the ritzy decor in his apartment. Sorry, Theodora, he's cheap. After all, Edward D. Wood, Jr., was Farrell's interior decorator.

JAILHOUSE ROCK (1957) B&W/96m. Not on the high level of *Flaming Star* or *King Creole*, but the third Elvis Presley film, one of his biggest commercial successes, is still quite enjoyable. Elvis plays a backwoods lad who trusts no one and carries a chip on his shoulder. Unable to control his temper, he beats a drunk to death in a barroom brawl and is sentenced to prison on a manslaughter charge. In prison his refusal to toe the line gets him into constant trouble, but his singing is a big hit with the other prisoners, including cellmate Mickey Shaughnessy, formerly a popular C&W singer. When Elvis gets out, he tries to make it as a professional singer, but his selfish attitude angers Judy Tyler, his girlfriend and partner in a record-publishing company, and Shaughnessy, who has become his high-paid flunkey. They sense Elvis is suppressing his finer qualities. Young Elvis is handsome and charismatic playing the troubled, misunderstood, quick-fisted character that best suited him in his movie career. His singing is strong and smooth (so Presley fans will sigh), and the Leiber-Stoller numbers (including big hit "Too Much") are first-rate; the wildly choreographed "Jailhouse Rock" production number is a classic. Film also benefits from the sweet presence of Judy Tyler, an actress who died young but is remembered fondly by all *Howdy Doody* fans because she was the beloved Princess Summer-Fall-Winter-Spring. Produced by Pandro S. Berman. Directed by Richard Thrope. Also with Vaughn Taylor, Dean Jones.

JASON AND THE ARGONAUTS (BRITISH/1963) C/104m. Ray Harryhausen's spectacular special effects highlight this marvelous fantasy-adventure that is even better than his Sinbad movies. Jason (Todd Armstrong) and his crew set sail on the *Argo* in search of the mythical Golden Fleece. He falls in love with Medea (Nancy Kovack), the high priestess of Colchis; has thrilling battles with Harryhausen's seemingly invincible non-human creatures; and, though Hera (Honor Blackman) is his protector, angers her husband, Zeus (Niall MacGinnis), by defying his laws. It is directed by Don Chaffey with equal amounts of wit and excitement. It is beautifully filmed by Wilkie Cooper—the mysterious blue ocean, white sandy beaches, and strange rock formations found around Palinuro, Italy, and the actual Greek temples found in Paestrum give the picture historical authenticity. Bernard Herrmann's score gives grandeur to

the production. Beverly Cross's imaginative, literate script keeps the story on a high intellectual plane so that it will appeal to adults as well as kids. Cross wrote Jason as a man of average build who relies on his wits rather than brawn, and even wrote Hercules (Nigel Green) as a man of believable strength and physical proportions. Cross was attempting to draw a distinction between men and gods, for his major theme is: man must fend for himself whether the gods exist or not. This film is about the decision by Man, as represented by Jason, to choose his own life's course, to challenge the gods' unfair laws, to no longer be frightened by the gods into blind obedience. Adults will find Cross's theme interesting and enjoy the marital squabbles between MacGinnis and Blackman; everyone will love Harryhausen's special effects. It's just amazing how believable the movements of his creatures are. The composite photography is excellent: I don't know how he managed such visual tricks as having the animated harpies unravel Phineas's real belt. My favorite special-effects moments are the "Clashing Rocks" sequence when huge, bearded Triton, his fishtail flopping in the ocean, emerges from the water, holds the mountains apart, and watches the *Argo* sail under his arm; and, of course, the truly stupendous climactic swordfighting-skeletons sequence—Harryhausen's ultimate achievement. Produced by Charles H. Schneer. Also with: Laurence Naismith, Michael Gwynn, Douglas Wilmer, Patrick Troughton.

JAWS (1975) C/124m. Exciting adventure-horror film. This adaptation of Peter Benchley's best-seller went far beyond anyone's expectations—that's because no one knew what to expect from young director Steven Spielberg. Roy Scheider, the sheriff of a small Cape Cod town, fears that a large man-eating shark has been picking off swimmers. Mayor Murray Hamilton won't let Scheider go public with his suspicions because it's the heart of the tourist season. When the shark attacks swimmers near the beach in the middle of the day, the cover-up is over. Scheider, ichthyologist Richard Dreyfuss, and tough veteran shark-hunter Robert Shaw take a small boat out to sea in search of the shark. They find it or, more accurately, it finds them. This is by far the best nature-retribution film since *The Birds* (yes, even better than *Frogs* and *The Night of the Lepus*). This shrewd, vengeful shark is determined to reclaim the ocean. The fun and the tension are constant, there are thrills, there are terrifying scenes, there is humor, there's even a Watergate cover-up theme. There are few horror films in which you'll so identify with potential victims. Has anybody who has swum in the ocean since seeing this film not worried about something latching on to a leg? Excellent camera work by Bill Butler and special effects by Robert A. Mattey under difficult conditions. First attack is a shocker; the entire boat sequence is nerve-wracking. Solid performances from the three leads (whose volatile conversations on the boat are quite enjoyable) give this film real class. It became a box-office phenomenon, leading to two sequels. Produced by Richard D. Zanuck and David Brown. Benchley and Carl Gottlieb wrote the script. Verna Fields did a fine editing job. John Williams composed the shark's famous musical motif. Also with: Lorraine Gary, Jeffrey Kramer, Gottlieb, Susan Backlinie, Benchley.

JAZZ SINGER, THE (1927) B&W/89m.
The first talkie, although most of the words we hear are the lyrics to Al Jolson's songs. Jolson plays the son of a cantor (Warner Oland) who expects his son to follow in his footsteps. But Jolson decides to become a professional singer, breaking his father's heart and causing a rift between the two. With the high holy days approaching, will Jolson return to the temple and make peace with his father? Picture looks like it has been drained of energy by vampire or is dying of old age. However, because Jolson sings "Mammy," "Toot Toot Tootsie," and other standards, it is more than a curiosity—at least his dynamic performances have not dated at all. Directed by Alan Crosland. Remade in 1953 with Danny Thomas and in 1980 with Neil Diamond. Also with: May McAvoy, Eugenie Besserer, Otto Lederer, William Demarest, Myrna Loy.

JEREMY (1973) C/90m.
Sweet, well-acted, unexploitive teenage romance that introduced Robby Benson and Glynnis O'Connor, two skilled, appealing actors with unique styles who have always been underrated (in fact, Benson was mocked until he excelled in *The Chosen*). Benson's a shy, lonely, awkward high-school student with musical talent and many endearing idiosyncrasies that no girl finds endearing. Until pretty WASP O'Connor comes along. Their relationship is quite convincing—possibly because the teen stars became boyfriend-girlfriend off screen. Significantly, this was probably the first film that shows teenagers having sex. The scene is directed tenderly by Arthur Barron, and, importantly, the kids are not punished for their act—on the contrary, it proves to be mutually beneficial and the perfect way for them to confirm their love for one another. Today's filmmakers who casually insert sex scenes between teenagers—without bothering to figure out how such sex affects these characters or the film's teenage viewers who see teen sex being promoted—should take a look at this tasteful, meaningful sequence. Some good location footage; tricky early-seventies camera work. Also with: Len Bari, Leonard Cimino, Ned Wilson, Chris Bohn.

JEZEBEL (1938) B&W/103m.
Warner Bros. beat *Gone With the Wind* to the screen with this antebellum costume drama, in which Bette Davis (who years before had been promised Scarlett O'Hara) won an Oscar as strong-willed Southern belle Julie Marston. Davis loses fiancé Henry Fonda when she embarrasses him by wearing a red gown to a society ball when all unmarried women are expected to wear white. Fonda marries northerner Margaret Lindsay. Davis's thoughtless attempt to make Fonda jealous results in tragedy. Picture suffers because of too much chit-chat about what's proper in southern society and the embarrassing portrayal of the black slaves (a happy-go-lucky, singing lot). But the large-eyed Davis is a joy to watch, whether stirring up things at the ball, humbly apologizing to Fonda, or, in the film's highlight, convincing Lindsay (who also is excellent in this scene) to let her take care of the seriously ill Fonda. Million-dollar production was directed by William Wyler with his customary attention to period detail. Adapted from a play by Owen Davis, the script by Clements Ripley, Abem Finkel, and John Huston has, for the most part, strong, intelligent dialogue. With music by Max Steiner. Also with: Fay Bainter (who won a Supporting Actress Oscar as Davis's aunt), George Brent, Spring Byington, Gordon Oliver, Donald Crisp, John Litel, Henry O'Neill, Eddie Anderson.

JOANNA (BRITISH/1968) C/107m.
This is a bad, self-indulgent film, but I was nevertheless charmed by it when I saw it in 1968. I wasn't the only one who had an unexplained fondness for this offbeat tale of a promiscuous, baby-voiced, wide-eyed art student (Genevieve Waite, not the best actress the world has known) and her search for happiness in London's mod scene—the film has a cult following consisting of people who saw it when it was released. Perhaps few films better captured the zany spirit of the sixties or the confusion and desperation under optimistic façades (the film has sense of sadness one feels when seeing a clown with a painted-on frown). And few pictures so defied the conventions of movie storytelling; there are fantasy-nightmare sequences; director Michael Sarne turns up with his camera at the end of the film and gets a kiss from Waite; the film ends with a musical number at a train station. The best reason to see the film today is Donald Sutherland's beautiful performance as a kindly aristocrat who is dying of leukemia. The scene in which Sarne puts him in close-up while he speaks words of optimism to Waite (his face glows, his wide eyes sparkle, he smiles) is spellbinding. Also with: Calvin Lockhart (the black nightclub owner Waite falls in love with), Glenna Foster-Jones.

JOE (1970) C/107m.
Businessman Bill Compton (Dennis Patrick) loses his temper and kills the pusher-addict boyfriend (Patrick McDermott) of his hippie daughter (Susan Sarandon). In a New York bar he lets this fact slip to a stranger named Joe (Peter Boyle), a loudmouth working-class stiff who has contempt for blacks, liberals, and hippies, whom, he admits, he'd like to blow away. Afraid Joe will go to the police, Bill befriends him, even accepting his invitation to dinner. The white-collar liberal soon reveals himself to be as vile as the blue-collar rightwinger; he was just waiting for a Mephistopheles like Joe to both praise and nurture his baser instincts. When Sarandon (touching in her debut) runs away, Bill naturally asks Joe to help him find her. Boyle (who is really a leftwinger) became a star with a performance that is accurate and creepy (like his cabbie in *Taxi Driver*). Also impressive is the on-location footage of bars, tenements, bowling alleys, bargain stores, and other Greenwich Village spots that gives one nostalgic feelings for the times. But the story becomes preposterous, full of unbelievable coincidences and a hard-to-watch massacre finale. Film supported contention of era's conserva-

tives that all hippie girls were nymphomaniacs, that all long-haired young people took drugs and were untrustworthy, that all members of the counterculture were vermin. What's most frightening is that this film was often singled out for its supposedly accurate portrait of the day's youth. What's really depressing is how film despises people from all classes. John Avildsen (who'd become pro-America with *Rocky*) directed low-budget feature that became surprise smash hit. Also with: Audrey Caire, K. Callan.

JOHNNY GOT HIS GUN (1971) C/111m.
At age 65, Dalton Trumbo both wrote and directed (his debut) this adaptation of his classic 1939 anti-war novel. It's about a gentle American doughboy named Joe Bonham (Timothy Bottoms) who becomes a basket case (he has no legs, arms, face, voice, ears) in WWI as the result of an explosion and is confined to a hospital bed. No one realizes he can think (we hear his thoughts, we see his memories) and has feelings until a kindly nurse (Diane Varsi) starts paying attention to his needs. He communicates that he wants to be placed in a freak show so people can see what war has done to him— or be killed. Film won several awards at Cannes, but then died at the box office in the U.S.—those viewers who found it as devastating as the novel and became emotionally attached to it were far outnumbered by those who found it morbid and pretentious (particularly those "fantasy" scenes in which Donald Sutherland plays an ineffectual Jesus). I found that the major problem in 1971 was that U.S. viewers were too politicized to be satisfied with just an anti-war film—we wanted films that dealt with Vietnam specifically. Not surprisingly, film had its greatest success in Japan. Today, when so many films glorify war, Trumbo's pacifism can better be appreciated. Scenes with Varsi are touching. Bottoms's unsure reading of his lines doesn't compare to Trumbo's terrifying prose. Also with: Jason Robards, Kathy Fields, Marsha Hunt, Charles McGraw, Eduard Franz, Don Barry, Tony Geary.

JOHNNY GUITAR (1954) C/111m.
Nicholas Ray's legendary baroque western is set in post-Civil War Arizona. Ex-gunslinger Johnny Logan (Sterling Hayden), now calling himself Johnny Guitar, is hired to play guitar by his former lover Vienna (Joan Crawford), a strong-willed saloon-casino owner. More interested in business than in men since Johnny walked out on her, Vienna waits for the railroad to arrive and make her land valuable. A man is killed in a stage robbery and his furious, shrieking sister, Emma Small (Mercedes McCambridge), arrives at Vienna's with the Marshal (Frank Ferguson), a wealthy rancher (Ward Bond), and about a dozen townspeople. Emma despises Vienna because the man Emma loves, the Dancin' Kid (Scott Brady), is attracted to her. She would rather see the Kid dead than with Vienna and tries to convince her companions that Vienna, the Kid, and the Kid's partners—mean Bart (Ernest Borgnine), sickly, book-reading Corey (Royal Dano), and young Turkey (Ben Cooper), who becomes a chicken and stoolpigeon—are responsible for her brother's

death and should be hanged. Film is an amusing parody of the "classic" western; high camp; an homage to Fritz Lang's *Rancho Notorious*; a fifties youth-gang picture with adults playing teen parts; a hallucinatory venture into what Andrew Sarris called "Freudian feminism." But paramountly it is a serious indictment of McCarthyite mob hysteria and bigotry, controversial because Ray and screenwriter Philip Yordan dared attack the reactionary American political climate of 1954 by subverting what had always been a politically conservative genre. Every character represents a political faction: lefthanded Kid is the communist; Vienna is a fellow traveler, progressive, who is pushed to side with the "communists"—in an *underground* passage she puts on a *red* shirt; Emma is presented as a witch (dressed in black), the head of the witch-hunt, who uses fear and power to destroy the careers of rivals. Since Vienna, who has been in the area five years, is a "foreigner" (notice her name), she is an easy target. Appealing to the cattlemen's "warped" Americanism, Emma implies Vienna wants the railroad because it will destroy their way of life. Just as H.U.A.C. threatened witnesses to get them to testify against those the committee had it in for, Emma bullies a bank teller into giving false evidence against Vienna. Then she convinces Turkey he can save himself from her mob by squealing. Just as 20th-century inquisitors assumed a person was a leftist if his/her personal/social/sexual life deviated from the norm, Emma reminds her followers that Vienna's string of past lovers makes her capable of robbing banks. Film is so powerful because Ray and Yordan present us with a series of dialectically opposed forces in confrontation. It's the future (civilization) vs. the past; progressives vs. conservatives (those who oppose the railroad); dirt farmers (who will come with the railroad) vs. wealthy ranchers (who now own all the land); the law vs. mob rule; female (Vienna) vs. male (Johnny); righthanded (Johnny) vs. lefthanded (the Kid); intellectuals (Corey) vs. brutes (Bart); the emotionally and sexually self-assured (Vienna) vs. the unbalanced, sexually repressed (Emma); persecutors (Emma and her mob) vs. the persecuted (Vienna and her friends); and decency and goodness (what America stands for) vs. evil (Emma and those like her who represent the true threat to American ideals). Film has much sexual symbolism (guns, safes, staircases), is about sexual drives, radically reverses traditional sex roles. Film ends with gunfight between Vienna and Emma. Brilliant filmmaking by Ray, who cleverly builds tension by repressing violence, symbolic and real. Throughout, volatile characters make threats, but confrontations are postponed. Guns are pulled, but not fired. Film is great fun. Based on a novel by Roy Chanslor, with cinematography by Harry Stradling; music by Victor Young—the theme song is performed by Peggy Lee. Also with: Paul Fix, John Carradine, Rhys Williams, Jan MacDonald.

JOUR SE LÈVE, LE (FRENCH/1939) B&W/85m.
The classic fatalistic melodrama, masterly directed by Marcel Carné, with dialogue by Jacques Prévert. Our doomed hero, Jean Gabin, shoots Jules Berry, then barri-

cades himself in his room while scores of police gather outside. He recalls how he got into this situation. As many American directors of forties *noir* films would do, these French filmmakers show us how a decent, average guy can become a murderer under the right set of circumstances. Gabin was a factory worker who fell in love with sweet but impressionable young Jacqueline Laurent. She loved him but turned down his proposal because she was fascinated with Berry, a middle-aged, lying, womanizing scoundrel who performed with trained dogs. Rejected, Gabin began an affair with the realistic, mature Arletty, Berry's former assistant and lover. When Berry told Gabin he was Laurent's father, not her lover, Gabin again pursued Laurent. She told him that Berry was not her father. Although Gabin wondered what went on between Laurent and Berry, he did not hesitate to get back together with her and break up with Arletty. But then Berry turned up with a gun; saying he couldn't kill Gabin, he put it down within easy reach of Gabin and began to tell Gabin of the details of his affair with Laurent. It's as if Berry's purpose had always been to get Gabin to kill him and ruin his own life and his relationship with Laurent. This picture would have been ideal for Fritz Lang—a character (Laurent) even cuts her finger, a favorite Lang device that signals events are about to take a drastic turn. This landmark of French "poetic" realism is extremely intense, sensual (the height of eroticism is achieved when Gabin strokes Laurent just below her breasts)—although there is an underlying feeling that the sex in which Berry is involved is sordid—and atmospheric (the sets are not just part of the background but create the mood). I can think of no other film in which so much import is given to costumes and props, including the gun, Gabin's dangling cigarette, Laurent's teddy bear, Gabin's alarm clock, photos, postcards, hats, brooches, beds, mirrors, flowers, dresses, sweaters. (Characters almost always are drinking, smoking, or holding something.) Most interesting is the structure: this four-character piece is broken down into several intimate two-character scenes. We see Gabin and Laurent, Gabin and Arletty, Gabin and Berry, Laurent and Arletty, and, for one insightful moment, Berry and Arletty. But, significantly, we never go behind closed doors to see what transpired between the *most* important combination, Berry and Laurent—it is the mystery of that relationship that drove Gabin to his destruction. Remade in America in 1947 by Anatole Litvak, as *The Long Night*.

JOURNEY OF NATTY GANN, THE (1985) C/101m.
Forget about art films for one night and gather the family for this enjoyable adventure movie. Set in the Depression, it's about a teenage tomboy (Meredith Salenger) whose penniless father (square-jawed Ray Wise) has to leave her behind in Chicago when he's offered a job in a Washington lumber camp. He doesn't even have a chance to say goodbye, but she doesn't believe he's abandoned her, as others tell her. Natty decides to run away from the insensitive woman (Lainie Kazan) she's staying with and ride the rails all the way to Seattle. She has many adventures—she

even has to escape from a reform school—and meets several interesting characters. For most of the journey she is accompanied by a wolf (played by Jed) that she befriends in the woods. The trusting relationship between these two lost souls is the heart of the picture. In truth, nothing we see is particularly surprising—other than this Disney film being pro-labor although the Disney Studio was strongly anti-union during the Depression. But it's well directed by Jeremy Kagan (who keeps it from getting sentimental until the very end), intelligently scripted by producer Jeanne Rosenberg (it was her *pet* project), and extremely well cast, as fine actors like John Cusack (as Natty's "love" interest), Barry Miller (star of Kagan's *The Chosen*), Scatman Crothers, Verna Bloom, and Kazan were willing to accept small parts. Neophyte Salenger, who reminds me of a young Jamie Lee Curtis, has a natural, very appealing delivery—she makes Natty easy to root for. Also with: Bruce M. Fischer.

JOYLESS STREET, THE (GERMAN/1925) B&W/80m.
G. W. Pabst mixed realism with expressionism in this classic adaptation of Hugo Bettauer's novel. It is about how postwar inflation resulted in the financial and moral breakdown of the middle class in Austria and the exploitation and victimization of young women without money. There are two loosely connected storylines: a young woman (Asta Nielsen), whose only chance to escape poverty is marriage to a male secretary, strangles his date in a jealous rage and incriminates him in the murder; a young woman (Greta Garbo), whose father lost all his money in the stock market, finds that the only way to make money to buy food for the sick man is to be a performer-whore at a sinful club—when the American Red Cross worker she loves (Einar Hanson) sees her there, in the flimsiest gown Garbo ever would wear on screen, he assumes she is amoral. Melodrama is muddled and at times boring, and seeing decent people make the wrong decisions at *every* opportunity eventually becomes annoying. But the cinematography is superb and the social themes are still relevant, particularly in regard to how capitalists start false rumors to influence stock prices; how slum grocers/butchers become masters in their neighborhoods; how women are dependent on monied men for advancement. As in later Pabst films *Diary of a Lost Girl* and *Pandora's Box*, the women will eventually break their insulting bonds. Picture is most famous for bringing Greta Garbo to the attention of Hollywood. Her movements are extremely clumsy, but those stunning eyes, that mournful expression (when Hanson walks out on her), and her mysteriously erotic quality made her a natural for Hollywood love stories. Also with: Valeska Gert.

JUDEX (FRENCH/1963) B&W/95m.
Georges Franju not only wanted to make a feature remake of French master Louis Feuillade's 1917 serial but to also re-create the fun and excitement present in all of Feuillade's early serials, including his classic *Fantômas*. But while Franju's film of the caped crusader (Channing Pollock) who has his own unlawful ways of meting out justice also mixes the

fantastic with relevant social criticism, it is more poetic, *unreal* (rather than being *surreal*), melancholy, subtly humorous, and slowly paced than Feuillade's work. Disguised as an elderly man, Judex works for rich, heartless banker Favraux (Michel Vitold)—the film's symbol of capitalism—who amassed his fortune through blackmail, corruption, and murder. Judex poisons Favraux and imprisons him in a secret chamber. His affection for Favraux's kind daughter Jacqueline (Edith Scob) stops him from killing Favraux. Craving Favraux's fortune, greedy, cunning, sexy villainess Diane Monti (Francine Bergé) and her lover, Morales (Theo Sarapo), try to track down Favraux—Diane had received a marriage proposal from him when she'd been posing as his innocent maid. But first they kidnap Jacqueline (who knows of their plot) and attempt to kill her. Judex and his gang—Morales's father, inept detective Cocantin (Jacques Jouanneau), a smart little boy, and Daisy (Sylva Koscina), Cocantin's circus-performer girlfriend—try to foil Diane's plan. Enjoyable film keeps surprising you. Most surprising is how little Judex himself accomplishes after his initial rescue of Jacqueline early in the film. He promises to protect her, but she is kidnapped and would die a couple of times before he reaches her if it weren't for a couple of fluke happenings (chance plays a major part in this film). Attempting heroism, Judex daringly climbs the outside of a tall building in order to capture Diane and Favraux, but as soon as he reaches the top, he's conked on the head and tied up. He himself needs to be rescued by a woman, Daisy, who just happens along in her circus garb, climbs the building, and unties him. Significantly, Judex is in the hallway (!) when Daisy defeats Diane in a fight on the roof, and when Favraux takes his own life. Judex is still dashing, but he isn't the superhero/death-squad leader he was at the beginning. Indeed, other characters turn out to be more interesting—especially Diane, whose time spent in and stripping out of nun garb is the picture's most memorable sequence. Whether putting on her moral act, plotting a crime while doing a hip-bopping dance with Morales, checking her looks in the mirror while wearing her habit, stabbing Jacqueline in the back, or coming on to tied-up Judex, she has a lot of flair. Also with: Benjamin Boda, Philippe Mareuil, René Génin, Luigi Cortesse, Roger Gradet.

JULES AND JIM (FRENCH/1962) B&W/104m.
François Truffaut's masterpiece begins in pre-WWI Paris and concludes in pre-WWII Paris, beginning in exuberant innocence and concluding in wiser resignation. Jules (Oskar Werner), an Austrian, and Jim (Henri Serre), who is French, are dear friends who share every experience, including a unique relationship with Catherine (Jeanne Moreau), who injects life, mystery, infatuation, and confusion into their lives. They regard her not as particularly smart or beautiful but as the *ideal* woman, who, being *perfect* as a child, lover, refined lady, wife, mother, companion, conversationalist, decision-maker, and catalyst to good, unusual times, is all things special to all men. She is a character who is central to feminist film criticism because she embodies the contra-

diction present in the modern woman. Truffaut presents her as someone who wants to be totally independent of men, but at the same time can't live without them and desperately needs to be placed on a pedestal, the focal point in their lives. Jules and Jim are both at her beck and call, pawns to her whims. She marries Jules, moves to Austria with him, and bears his daughter, but for the next 20 years he must indulge her infidelities and indiscretions—he puts up with Catherine because she is Catherine and such actions define her. Lonely for Jim, Catherine becomes his lover—with Jules's knowledge—and invites him to move into their house; she wants to marry him and have a baby by him. Jules, who doesn't want her to move, goes along with the decision; Jim breaks off with his long-suffering fiancée in France to do what Catherine demands. But when she finds out they probably can't have a baby, she sends Jim back to France in disgust; when she finds out she is pregnant, she calls for his return; he becomes like a Ping-Pong ball, being knocked back and forth between Austria and France. Meanwhile Jules sticks by her side. While Catherine's actions—particularly her final action—are selfish beyond reason, neither of the men nor Truffaut condemns her. In fact, Truffaut adores her. And feels sympathy for her as well. She's like the proverbial moth being drawn to the flame—who needs but can never find that one gasp of happiness in her short lifetime. Marvelous film is so wonderfully acted and written that it's a pleasure to *listen* to. Sumptuous yet leisurely direction by Truffaut, music by Georges Delerue, and camera work by Raoul Coutard, particularly when panning, create an incomparably romantic ambience. As an indication of things to come, Truffaut deals a bit with the difficulty of artists in communicating—Jules, who's a writer of books on insects, writes a glorious love letter to Catherine, yet Jim the novelist writes letters to her that are cold and empty. Of the two men, Jules has the most to offer Catherine; but in the world of Truffaut the women will pick the other, less romantic guy every time. A great film, with scenes, characters, faces that will stick with you. Also with: Marie Dubois, Vanna Urbina, Boris Bassiak, Sabine Haudepin.

JULIA (1977) C/118m.
Fred Zinnemann directed and Alvin Sargent (who won an Oscar) scripted this superb adaptation of Lillian Hellman's beautiful, suspenseful story, contained in her memoir *Pentimento*. It allowed Jane Fonda, who plays Hellman, another chance to play a woman who becomes politicized and who has a special bond with another woman. Julia (Vanessa Redgrave won a Best Supporting Actress Oscar) is Lillian's lifelong friend. By the thirties she is living in Austria and deeply involved in the political underground, fighting a losing battle with the Nazis. Lillian agrees to secretly transport money by train to Julia in Berlin, knowing it will be used to help in her work. The trip is extremely tense. Their final meeting is heart-wrenching. You see the love these women have for each other, how being politically committed has ravaged Julia's beauty (she has lost a leg), and—I believe this is the most interesting point of the film, because it breaks with movie stereotyp-

ing—that being a leftist has not deprived Julia of her warmth, her humility, and her concern for people like Lillian who are not as politically dedicated as she is. Julia, communist or humanist, is a person with tolerance, heart, anger at the evils in the world; with thoughts about the entire world but also genuine interest in Lillian's private life, her writing, her happiness. Hellman's story is expanded by Sargent to include Hellman's relationship with Dashiell Hammett (Jason Robards, Jr., won a Supporting Actor Oscar) and her initial attempts at writing and instant fame upon the success of her first play. Film was well received when first released, but it's now too easily forgotten. It's truly a well-made film, with provocative characters and relationships, a unique view of Europe in the 30s and great performances from the three leads. Oddly, it's filmed in deceptively romantic style—what we watch is not at all romantic. Scene in which Nazis hurl leftists off a high balcony is terrifying. Music by Georges Delerue. Cinematography by Douglas Slocombe. Also with: Maximilian Schell, Meryl Streep (her debut), Hal Holbrook, Susan Jones (young Lillian), Lisa Pelikan (young Julia), Maurice Denham, John Glover, Rosemary Murphy.

JULIET OF THE SPIRITS (ITALIAN/1965)
C/148m. Difficult Federico Fellini film about a meek, passive woman (Giulietta Masina) who suspects her husband (Mario Pisu) is having an affair with a young model. She consults a medium, hires a detective to spy on her husband, and slips in and out of a fantasy world full of spirits from her past. Picture has advanced, pre-woman's-movement themes: women shouldn't equate themselves with their problems; women withstand humiliation out of fear of being alone; women secretly wish they had freedom that could come only if their husbands left them. Masina's feeling that she is unworthy and deserving of persecution and punishment can be traced back to her childhood, when her character in a religious school play was raised to the rafters while being symbolically burned to death. Only when she frees the little girl (herself) in her fantasy world can she break her own shackles and free herself from husband and spirits. Picture has such interesting themes that after a while you wish Fellini had forgone his confusing trips into the surreal world of Masina's unconscious and just told his story. Moreover, the casting of Fellini's wife in the lead seems ill-advised. Masina looks like a tiny Plain Jane in a world of flamboyant grotesqueness. Also with: Sandra Milo, Valeska Gert, Lou Gilbert, Sylva Koscina, Valentina Cortese.

JUNGLE BOOK, THE (1942) C/109m. Kipling
tale about a boy (Sabu) who was raised by wolves in the jungle. He returns to civilization and is taken in by a kind woman (Rosemary DeCamp) who, neither realizes, is his natural mother. He becomes obsessed with killing the tiger that killed DeCamp's husband, his father. He faces greater danger from the townspeople who want him to lead them to an ancient treasure and others who want to burn him for being a witch. DeCamp, his girlfriend (Patricia O'Rourke), the friendly animals of the jungle, and his own animal in-

stincts help him fight his enemies and set things right. I wish a little more emphasis were placed on the boy's trying to reconcile his wild nature with his desire for human companionship, but not even the early Tarzan movies dealt with such themes. Zoltán Korda directed this popular fantasy-adventure, which has some of the finest color you'll ever see. It's excellent family fare, but there are death scenes that may be too strong for some youngsters. Still, they'll love the spectacular finale. Sabu is credible in the lead, but the other actors aren't particularly convincing—what's Norwegian John Qualen doing in a jungle picture? Excellent use of animals. For the close-ups of the wild tiger, a huge dog with a tiger's head was used. A fine score by Miklos Rozsa. Remade as a Disney cartoon in 1967. Also with: Joseph Calleia, Frank Puglia.

KAGEMUSHA (THE SHADOW WARRIOR)
(JAPANESE/1980) C/160m–180m. Akira Kurosawa's epic film is set in the 1570s, when several warlords engage in civil wars. When a hired assassin shoots the respected clan leader Shingen (Tatsuya Nakadai), his two chief rivals hope to take over his land. But Shingen's clan tries to follow their leader's last request and keep his death a secret for three years. So a lowly thief (also Nakadai), a man of no consequence, pretends to be Shingen, hoping to do his duty to the leader who once spared his life. And he *becomes* Shingen, winning the respect of the men who know he's a double, and putting fear into Shingen's rivals. Picture is slow but not boring; however, it is not all that engrossing because Kurosawa doesn't really explore what's going through the thief's mind as he discovers he has noble qualities worthy of a great leader. I'd particularly like to see more scenes between him and Shingen's brother (played with warmth and slowly revealed intelligence by Tsutomo Yamazaki) and Shingen's small grandchild, whom the imposter comes to love. Kurosawa is more interested in pageantry, and his shots of mammoth armies—with weapons, horses, banners—on the attack are astonishing. How marvelously he uses color, as when Shingen's son takes his forces along the sandy beach, with haunting sea and a rainbowed sky in the background. Kurosawa is not interested in glorifying the battle, however; and in the last battle we don't see anyone killed, just dying. A major theme of the movie is that great leaders (like Shingen, "the mountain") defend their domains, while weak leaders like Shingen's imperialistic son cross borders to wage war and annex territory. Also with: Kenichi Hagiwara, Jinpachi Nezu.

KAMIKAZE '89/KAMIKAZE 1989 (WEST GERMAN/1983) C/106m. Move over, *Alphaville* and *Vortex*. It's 1989 and the Federal Republic of Germany is

the most prosperous country in the peaceful world. The narrator, who, I'd guess, works for the dictatorial state, tells us that there's no disease, no pollution, no inflation, no energy crisis, no unemployment, no crime, and no suicides (just "unexpected" deaths). Everyone is happy. But suddenly the combine which creates and dispenses all information receives a letter from someone (perhaps a female) who threatens to blow up the skyscraper in which the combine leader, the Blue Panther, conducts business and thousands of employees do their work. A detective (Rainer Werner Fassbinder, taking time off from directing pictures) who has never left a mystery unsolved is hired to ferret out the culprit in four days, before the explosion. But this case stumps him. He can't believe his findings—that there is an organized political underground and that there is government conspiracy to halt social disorder. He also learns the secret of the mysterious 31st floor! The film is so confusing that I'm never exactly sure what clues are being uncovered or who are the people Fassbinder comes across. But it's fun watching this detective at work, constantly chastising his assistant for making *true* (but politically unwise) statements about what they witness, passing through bizarre sets, going past unusual places (the police disco, for example), and meeting strange people. The whole thing, staged while the third annual laugh marathon plays on television, is quite amusing. Director Wolf Grimm keeps his actors low-keyed and even directs his action scenes in an understated manner. However, his sets, which are dark but often have red lights flashing in the blackness, and costuming are gaudy: the bearded, plump Fassbinder wears a snazzy and silly leopardskin suit. Also with: Gunther Kaufmann, Nicole Heesters, Brigitte Mara, Arnold Marquis, Boy Gobert.

KANAL (POLISH/1956) B&W/91m. Breakthrough film of the Polish cinema, directed by Andrzej Wajda. It is May 1944 and the Germans have reduced Warsaw to rubble. The survivors of the Warsaw uprising are in a panic. A platoon of resisters, including two women and a young boy, makes its last stand and is ordered to try to escape through the sewers. It goes below and in the chaos gets split into three groups. Only a young woman (Teresa Izewska) who is alone with her wounded, dying boyfriend knows the escape route, and he is incapable of undertaking the difficult climb. The others become hopelessly lost in the dark. As they wallow waist-deep in filth, they become delirious from the intoxicating fumes. Nazis fire on anyone who sticks his head outside; they also drop grenades and gas bombs down the manholes. Even the strongest and bravest men act helpless, go berserk. Only Izewska remains brave and dignified. A predecessor to *Das Boot* in that it shows the claustrophobic horrors endured by soldiers who are trapped *below* and are at the mercy of both the enemy above and their watery environment. Like *Das Boot*, it has a leader who disagreed with the orders that placed him and his men in such an insane situation, but who would never disobey orders or go off to safety and desert his men. Film is not as

impressive as it once seemed. The characters aren't very well drawn; and once the platoon goes into the sewers, we lose all track of time—it seems the men are hysterical and exhausted after being below for 20 seconds and having walked five steps. Premise is intriguing, but execution is more punishing than exciting. Also starring; Tadeusz Janczar, Wienczylaw Glinski, Wladyslaw Sheybal.

KANSAS CITY BOMBER (1972) C/99m. Sleeper about the trials and tribulations of a roller-derby queen isn't half bad. It does contain what I think is Raquel Welch's one genuinely fine movie performance. To play her character, she was willing to take her lumps, actually participating in the rough-and-tumble roller-game scenes rather than having a stand-in. For once, she truly worked at establishing a real character—I particularly like the way she slumps into a chair, striking a realistic, non-glamorous, non-Raquel Welch pose. Picture has feminist slant; we get to admire this woman despite sleazy profession, as she stands alone against owner and jealous teammates—and we sympathize because she's a working single mother who is always on the road and away from her child. Directed by Jerrold Freedman (a top TV-movie director). Also with: Kevin McCarthy, Helena Kallianiotes, Norman Alden, Jeanne Cooper, Mary Kay Pass, Dick Lane.

KARATE KID, THE (1985) C/126m. A very likable fairytale in the *Rocky* tradition, about a very likable teenager (Ralph Macchio) who moves with his mother from New Jersey to California and falls in love with a pretty rich girl (Elisabeth Shue is likable, too, in the blonde-princess role). But fairytales have to include a few obstacles along the way before boy and girl can live happily ever after. For the slightly built, unmacho Macchio, his test is to defeat Shue's vicious ex-boyfriend (William Zabka) in a karate tournament. It will be next to impossible since Zabka has much more experience in the sport and he and his thuggish Aryan pals have been making mincemeat of Macchio with regularity. But whereas Mark Hamill had Alec Guinness and Yoda, and Rocky had Burgess Meredith, the Karate Kid obtains the priceless instructive services of Pat Morita, his Japanese handyman. In truly wonderful scenes Morita (who deservedly got an Oscar nomination) quickly teaches Macchio karate and the philosophy needed to be a master of the form. Director John Avildsen was responsible for *Rocky*, on which this film was patterned. This, too, has wit and sentimentality. Again you'll cheer the underdog and again he'll do the impossible because he has a lot of heart and character. I wish Morita would dump Zabka's sadistic coach in the garbage, but otherwise film is extremely pleasing. I believe it works so well because Avildsen has genuine affection for the good guys: Macchio, Shue, Morita, and Macchio's mother (who I wish had a more significant part). Like *Rocky*, this sleeper became a box-office smash, and continued its success as a top-selling video.

KENNEL MURDER CASE, THE (1933) B&W/ 73m.

William Powell returned as detective Philo Vance in what is generally considered the best entry in the Vance mystery series. A man is found dead in his locked bedroom. He was shot in the head, but he'd been killed by a knife wound inflicted hours before. Puzzling case has seven major suspects; it takes Vance and an attack dog to uncover the culprit. Powell is properly suave, and direction by Michael Curtiz (who uses wipes and quick pans) is clear and fast-paced, yet whodunit suffers because you don't care about the louse who was killed or any of the suspects. Picture needs that old standby, a sympathetic suspect who is tossed into jail and will be executed unless Vance figures out real killer in time. And how about a little romance? Try *The Canary Murder Case*. Also with: Mary Astor, Eugene Pallette, Ralph Morgan, Helen Vinson, Jack LaRue, Paul Cavanagh, Etienne Girardot, Robert Barrat.

KENTUCKY FRIED MOVIE (1977) C/84m.

Very funny, off-the-wall sketch comedy spoofing movies, commercials, old TV scenes and newscasts. Imaginative direction by John Landis and writing by Kentucky Fried Theatre members Jim Abrahams, David Zucker, and Jerry Zucker. The best routine is lengthy takeoff of *Enter the Dragon* called "A Fistful of Yen," with Evan Kim doing a remarkable impersonation of Bruce Lee (as well as Dorothy in *The Wizard of Oz*). Other funny bits include: a commercial in which Hare Krishnas stop pestering people and take a Miller Break; previews for porno film *Catholic High School Girls in Trouble*, which is "more offensive than *Mandingo*"; a young black couple following the bizarre instructions on a how-to sex record; a televised courtroom drama in which everything said is taken literally (when the DA asks the witness to follow him across the room, the defense attorney objects because "he's leading the witness")—this routine features the type of humor that Abraham and the Zuckers would use in *Airplane!*, which they'd also direct. Comedy has many hilarious sight gags (Chinese karate-school students playing basketball); it also gets laughs by having characters surprise us with vulgar language (the film opens with newscaster saying, "The popcorn you're eating has been pissed on—film at eleven"). Some of the humor is too juvenile or tasteless, but it's still the best of the comedy revues. With appearances by: Bill Bixby, Donald Sutherland, Henry Gibson, George Lazenby, Tony Dow (as Wally Cleaver), Abraham, Zucker and Zucker, Landis, Rick Baker (as Dino the Gorilla).

KID, THE (1921) B&W/60m.

Charlie Chaplin's first feature film is his most autobiographical work, one in which he dared relive, through five-year-old Jackie Coogan, memories of a destitute childhood, his need for a mother, and the fear of being sent to an orphanage. The extra length of the film allowed Chaplin the time to develop characters from which humor develops naturally rather than do some quick slapstick immediately to hook an audience; show that he was an *actor* who could do comedy and not just a clown; and establish a story (part drama, part comedy) that he, who doesn't even make an appearance until we're several minutes into the first reel, needn't dominate—indeed, this film affects us so much because Chaplin was more than willing to let the wonderful little Coogan (who comes across like a miniature Chaplin in the role that made him a big star) earn more than his share of the laughs and tears. Chaplin's tramp takes an abandoned baby into his garret, raises him as his son. When the boy is five, he helps Chaplin get work: he breaks windows with rocks and while the boy flees the irate owners, up walks Chaplin, a glazier, who offers to fix the windows for money. When the orphanage tries to take Coogan away, Chaplin puts up a hell of a fight and gets away with the boy. But things look hopeless until the boy's kindly mother (Edna Purviance), a rich opera star who has always regretted giving up the boy when she was poor and on her own, saves the day. Moving film has remarkable interplay between Chaplin and Coogan, who loved each other off screen as well. That Chaplin teaches the boy table manners is more important than the fact that what he teaches (i.e., wiping the mouth with the tablecloth) won't be found in any etiquette book; that he kisses the boy, takes pride in his whipping the street bully, provides food for the boy, has taught him to cook and say his prayers, and is willing to fight physically for the boy also shows us that Chaplin is a wonderful father, deserving the love Coogan bestows on him. Film has tear-jerking scenes, great comic moments, even an interestingly filmed dream sequence (which would work better if it came earlier, so as not to break momentum). Also with: Carl Miller, Chuck Reisner, Chaplin's future wife Lita Grey (as a child in the dream).

KIDS ARE ALRIGHT, THE (1979) C/106m.

A very good documentary about the early years of the seminal British supergroup, The Who. It was directed by Jeff Stein under The Who's supervision. Interview material is kept brief and doesn't interfere with the group's many songs, taken from concert footage, television appearances, and studio jam sessions. We see the group age and their style of dress switch from mod to flamboyant to casual, but if anything their energy level picks up, their songs become louder, their musicianship becomes more complex, and their anarchic style, typified by Pete Townshend smashing his guitars and Keith Moon his drums, becomes less an angry, ostentatious gesture than a way they can properly convey the artist's/musician's need for completely free self-expression. Fans will get a kick seeing lead singer Roger Daltrey belt out many of the Who classics (including the stuttering youth-anthem "My Generation"), Townshend jumping at his side and simultaneously swinging his arm and delivering his patented power chords, and bassist John Entwhistle standing calmly in the background. We are reminded that Keith Moon, who died in 1978 from an overdose of a prescription drug, was a vital part of the original group, both as its amazingly quick-handed drummer and as a *fun* character whose presence tempered Townshend's hostile humor. With appearances by: Tommy Smothers, Steve Martin, Ringo Starr, Keith Richard, Rick Danko, Jimmy O'Neil (host of *Shindig*, which I remember as being the show on which The Who—playing in concert footage—really proved to American rock fans that they were not just another moderately talented British import group, but a band that deserved a position in the rock pantheon).

KILLERS, THE (1946) B&W/105m.
Surely literature teachers have assigned their students Hemingway's concise but powerful short story about a couple of hitmen rubbing out an ex-boxer in his hotel room—and asked them to imagine the circumstances that led to (and perhaps followed) the tragic event. If you have to come up with an essay quickly, you might take a look at this classic melodrama in which a police detective (Edmond O'Brien) investigates the murder and finds out why the Swede (Burt Lancaster) was murdered. Since this is *film noir*, we can safely guess that a *femme fatale* had much to do with Lancaster's demise. Although she didn't pull the trigger, the person most responsible for the Swede's death is greedy, double-dealing Ava Gardner. She led the nice guy down a wayward path and got him to participate in a robbery. She is to blame for exploiting his weaknesses. Picture has sharp dialogue, strong, atmospheric direction by Robert Siodmak, and an excellent cast, but the storyline that was chosen is fairly conventional. It has dated. Lancaster is somewhat stiff but okay in his movie debut, but knowing from the start his character is dead keeps us detached from him. Gardner's beautiful throughout, but saves her strong dramatic acting for her final, loopy moments on the screen. Also with: Albert Dekker, Sam Levene, William Conrad.

KILLERS, THE (1964) C/95m.
Don Siegel directed this version of Hemingway's short story; it was meant to be the first made-for-television movie, but it was released instead as a theatrical feature because its violence was deemed too strong. Hitmen Lee Marvin and Clu Gulager rub out John Cassavetes, who works as an instructor for the blind. Curious as to why gangster kingpin Ronald Reagan (he finally played a villain, in his last role) paid them so much money, they try to figure out why Reagan wanted Cassavetes dead—they realize that there's money to be had. Cassavetes was a race-car driver: he had an affair with double-dealing Angie Dickinson, Reagan's mistress; he went in with Reagan on a $1 million job. Afterward, someone took the money. Cassavetes? Dickinson? Reagan? Picture slows down during flashback: Reagan is particularly stiff, yet he got some of the best reviews of his career. But any time Marvin and Gulager are on the screen, Siegel becomes interested. They are really bastards. The scene in which they murder Cassavetes, the scene in which they slug Dickinson and hang her out a high window, and the finale in which fatally injured Marvin exacts revenge are terrifically edited, powerful action scenes—they are the picture's highlights. Also with: Claude Akins, Norman Fell, Bert Mustin.

KILLER'S KISS (1955) B&W/67m.
Stanley Kubrick's second feature exhibits flare rather than style, promise rather than skill. Weak story has a mediocre boxer (Jerry Jarret) falling for a dance-hall girl (Jamie Smith) who lives in his New York building. They plan to go to Seattle together, but her jealous boss (Frank Silvera) kidnaps her after ordering his two thugs to kill the boxer. They mistakenly kill Jarret's manager, and Jarret tracks them down. Acting is terrible, and the skinny Smith (known today as Chris Chase, an arts TV-critic/columnist) hasn't the looks to be a romantic lead. But within this low-budget context Kubrick impresses with dashes of surrealism, strong use of New York locales (when pizza was 10¢!), and a wild, medieval fight in a loft full of mannequins. Worth a look. Also with: Irene Kane.

KILLING, THE (1956) B&W/84m.
Sterling Hayden, Jay C. Flippen, Elisha Cook, Jr., Joe Sawyer, and Ted DeCorsia plot to rob the racetrack's $2,000,000 payroll. They will commit the crime during the seventh race while two accomplices cause diversions: wrestler Maurice Oboukhoff will pretend to be drunk and start a brawl; vicious Timothy Carey will shoot a racehorse with a high-powered rifle. If Hayden played Johnny *Stone* rather than Johnny *Clay* and if he didn't believe that success or failure depended not on how well the crime was planned, but on chance, we'd have more confidence. First-rate, exciting, fatalistic caper film (which recalls Jean-Pierre Melville's *Bob Le Flambeur*) was Stanley Kubrick's first major work—it is his one picture that almost everyone likes. The budget is small, but he more than compensates for this. He shoots his indoor shoebox sets imaginatively, actually emphasizing their tightness—the claustrophobia adds to the tension of both characters and viewers. At one point he puts his men so close together around a small and cluttered table that we know they can smell the liquor on each other's breaths, their smoky clothing, and their sweat—they also can look each other in the eye and detect uncertainties and weaknesses. Picture has striking rhythm due to sharp editing within sequences and because of the non-chronological structure of the entire film, whereby each time the race is about to begin he moves back in time and repeats the passed time from a different character's perspective. In this way we are able to follow what the different men are doing in different locations at exactly the same time—and the pieces of a great puzzle fall into place. What also makes this an unusual caper film is that the men involved are in it not for kicks but because they got a "raw deal" in life and (Kubrick is very cynical) need the money. My one objection is that, as usual, Kubrick is too uncomfortable to show genuine romance—he loves dealing with Marie Windsor, who plays Cook's manipulative, unfaithful, double-crossing wife, because it allows him to equate sexuality with perversity and evil; but he basically ignores Coleen Gray, Hayden's nice girlfriend. Fine acting, interesting characters, smart dialogue, terrific suspense—ending has since become cliché. Cinematography by Lucien Ballard. From the novel *Clean Break* by Lionel White.

KILLING FIELDS, THE (BRITISH/1984) C/148m.

Exceptional, unforgettable true story that begins in Cambodia during the war in Southeast Asia. Sydney Schanberg (Sam Waterston) is covering the U.S. secret war in Cambodia for the *New York Times*; Dith Pran (Dr. Haing S. Ngor) is his Cambodian assistant and interpreter, whom Schanberg pretty much takes for granted. When Pran's family flees Cambodia, Schanberg asks Pran to remain to help him with his reporting—he doesn't consider the danger for Pran, only that his potential Pulitzer depends on his having a translator available. When the Khmer Rouge march into Phnom Penh, Dith Pran's pleading saves Schanberg and other foreigners who are picked up by a patrol. Only at this point does Schanberg realize what a remarkable person Pran is and what a dear friend he has been. But it's too late: Schanberg and other foreigners are forced to leave the country and Pran has to remain to await the forthcoming bloodbath. Schanberg returns to safe America and guiltily agonizes about his lost friend. Instead of staying on Schanberg's story, the film picks up on Pran's hellish story in Cambodia, where three million people (including all intellectuals) were being massacred and unceremoniously dumped to rot in the "killing fields." Pran slaves in the mud for countless hours each day at a "re-education" camp. He stays alive only by pretending to have no education, no memory, no thoughts—others are executed. The vivid scenes that take place at this re-education camp—where people "disappear," history is erased, kids are indoctrinated to turn against parents—should refute all those people who say that Orwell was too pessimistic, that things didn't turn out as badly as he expected. How Pran escapes from the re-education camp and eventually escapes from Cambodia makes for a spellbinding, horrifying sequence. After suffering with Pran, we feel we deserve the wonderful, tearful finale in which Pran and Schanberg are reunited (while John Lennon's "Imagine" plays on the soundtrack). Film is a celebration of Pran, a man of amazing selflessness, courage, and indomitable spirit; it's also the most vivid depiction there has been of the war in Cambodia and its aftermath. While it's not very political, it does make a brave statement that the bloodbath in Cambodia was the result of the dislocation of society due to the U.S.'s extensive secret bombing. It also reminds us that the suffering in Cambodia continues. Director Roland Joffe filmed the Cambodian scenes in Thailand. Cinematographer Chris Menges won an Oscar, as did editor Jim Clark. Nonactor Ngor, whose escape from Cambodia paralleled Pran's, won a Best Supporting Actor Oscar with his sincere, dignified portrayal. Produced by David Puttnam (*Chariots of Fire*). Written by Bruce Robinson. Also with: John Malkovich, Athol Fugard, Craig T. Nelson.

KIND HEARTS AND CORONETS (BRITISH/1949) B&W/104m.

Classic British black comedy—unlike any other *British* comedy—was loosely adapted by director Robert Hamer and John Dighton from *Israel Rank* by Roy Horniman. Narrated by the principal character on the eve of his execution for murder, it details how a young man (Dennis Price) of little means does away with the seven noblemen and one noblewoman who precede him in line for a dukedom; it is his way of avenging his mother, a noblewoman by birth who was ostracized from the family, fell into a life of hard labor, and was denied a place in the family plot because she had married beneath her class. Odd viewing experience in that we laugh as each person is killed, even though Price's methods are cruel and only a couple of the victims seem like despicable characters. As Price gets closer to his title, he becomes increasingly like the arrogant aristocrats he despises. As his narration reflects, he always had the heart and mind of a lord (he speaks of the "humiliating" work his mother endures—and we see her gently polishing a shoe) and, if anything, he regards himself as superior to all of humanity (which corresponds to the Nietzschean aspects of the book). Yes, our "hero" is a cad—he even has simultaneous affairs with a married woman (Joan Greenwood) and the widow (Valerie Hobson) of one of his victims. I suppose what makes his murders tolerable (and funny) is that Alec Guinness conveniently plays all the victims—we are not shocked by each death because we correctly expect Guinness to turn up again quite soon. Also we laugh because of the amorality of the whole piece (particularly Price's cold-blooded narration)—it's so unlike the British comedy of manners it resembles in tone but not content. It's a beautifully played film, with an absolutely exquisite script; the sophisticated dialogue reminds me of Oscar Wilde. Adding to the amusement is that while the educated characters engage in smart conversation, or Price's silver-tongued narration hints at his egocentricity, absolutely silly events occur: one victim blows up in the background; lovers plunge over a waterfall. My only complaint is an overly convenient (for the writers) ending that saves Price from having to make a difficult decision. Also with: Audrey Fildes, Miles Malleson, Hugh Griffith (already playing a judge), Arthur Lane.

KING CREOLE (1958) B&W/116m.

Elvis Presley's best film, from Harold Robbins's novel *A Stone for Danny Fisher*. Presley's a tough, quick-tempered kid living in New Orleans who's always getting into trouble because he refuses to back down to bullies, as his weakling father (Dean Jagger) has always done. He gets mixed up with some young thugs and hoodlum Walter Matthau, who wants him to sing at his King Creole rather than at the competitive club of nice guy Paul Stewart. But he mellows under the influence of pretty Dolores Hart, who works at the five-and-dime, and Carolyn Jones, Matthau's unhappy mistress. Presley gives a strong, tough performance and his singing is terrific. He is ably supported by a fine cast, particularly Jones and Hart (it's a shame her career was so brief). And the direction by Michael Curtiz is very efficient; film is styled much like his Warner Bros. biopic-musicals. Opening number in which Elvis chimes in with black street singers is the lone non-realistic musical interlude (more suited to a Broadway musical adaptation)—and it is one of the film's highlights. Ending is quite rushed, and weird, considering Elvis doesn't go to prison. But, all in all, film is a solid piece of entertainment and certainly one of the top juvenile-delinquent pictures of the fifties. Presley's last picture before his stint in the army. Also with: Vic Morrow.

KING KONG (1933) B&W/100m—103m.
The greatest of all horror films. Filmmaker Carl Denham (Robert Armstrong) hires destitute Ann Darrow (Fay Wray) to be his first female star. The crew travels on the *Venture* through uncharted waters until it finds Skull Island. Ann falls in love with first mate Jack Driscoll (Bruce Cabot). Natives kidnap Ann and offer her as bride to their living god, thirty-foot-tall Kong. Driscoll saves Ann from Kong's cave, but the furious beast pursues them. Kong is knocked out by gas bombs and brought back to New York, where Denham exhibits him as the "Eighth Wonder of the World." The King becomes a slave. Kong breaks loose, causes as much damage to New York as he did on Skull Island (every scene in New York corresponds to a scene on Skull Island). He snatches Ann and takes her to the top of the Empire State Building, where he's gunned down by airplanes. Film begins in the *real* world, in dark, cold Depression New York; but from the moment the *Venture* leaves port we are on a journey through Denham's subconscious. Skull (as in cerebral) Island's expressionistic landscape—fertile, overgrown, reptile-infested, cave-filled—is Denham's fantasized sexual terrain. And Kong is a manifestation of Denham's subconscious. Denham conjures up Kong as a surrogate to battle Driscoll for Ann's love and to perform "sexually" (their trip up the world's largest phallic symbol) with her when he has never been willing (or able) to have a sexual encounter himself. Although young and virile, Denham has traveled the world with an all-male crew to avoid intimate liaisons. Kong is Denham's female-lusting side—his alter ego. Kong is evidence of Denham's desperate need to possess Ann; his birth is the result of Denham's continuing to suppress his sexual/romantic drive even when he is immediately attracted to Ann. That Denham and Kong are rarely in the same shot indicates that Kong is being directed by an external force—namely, Denham's subconscious. When they do confront each other (the visualization of Denham's external struggle), Denham tries to restrain Kong (his bestial side) with a great wall, a bomb, and chains. When Kong breaks the chains, Denham can no longer control his sexual urges toward Ann; significantly, we never see them together until Kong is dead. Denham's famous words "It was beauty killed the beast" make sense if he's referring to the bestial side of himself. That Kong can tell the difference between Ann and another woman only by hair color and smell indicates he is not aware of Ann's distinct physical beauty. Film has been interpreted in many other ways. Masterly special effects were contributed by Willis O'Brien; Max Steiner understood that the film should be scored like a silent film—Kong's death always elicits tears because of the manipulative music. Directed by Merian C. Cooper and Ernest B. Schoedsack, the solo director of the 1933 sequel, *Son of Kong*. Remade in 1976. Also with: Frank Reicher, Victor Wong, Noble Johnson, Steve Clemento, James Flavin, Roscoe Ates, Sandra Shaw.

KING OF COMEDY, THE (1983) C/109m.
Martin Scorsese's controversial black comedy, from a script by former *Time* movie critic Paul Zimmerman, was a commercial disaster but has a devoted cult following. Robert De Niro is Rupert Pupkin, a pushy, insensitive, tactless New York slimeball who has given up hounding stars and devotes his full time to trying to make it as a stand-up comic. His dream is to perform on the late-night show of his Johnny Carson-like idol, Jerry Langford (Jerry Lewis). When he helps Langford sneak away from a mob of fans, Rupert gets him alone in a cab. Langford is able to get away from him by suggesting Rupert send a tape of his routine to the office. When Rupert's tape is rejected by Langford's aides, he goes uninvited to Langford's house. After Langford kicks him out, Rupert and a Langford fanatic, Masha (Sandra Bernhard), kidnap Langford—he will be released only after Rupert does a 10-minute routine on the show that night. Rupert is such a despicable leech—it's hard to tolerate his constant references to Langford as "Jerry"—and his triumph is so upsetting that I can't understand why anyone would want to make such a sick, though oddly *credible* film. I find the subject matter repulsive, but acknowledge that the film is superbly made; the acting by De Niro and Lewis (and Bernhard) is perfect—their characterizations are precise. Most memorable are the scenes in which Rupert delivers and picks up his tape; they not only convey how obnoxious he is (he won't take no for an answer) but show how embarrassing an experience it is for a *nobody* to appear in "hallowed" studio offices, trying to sell himself. In a sense, for all those talented people who got patronizing treatment when they brought in their tapes, Rupert Pupkin embodies their revenge. Also with: Shelley Hack (well cast as Langford's outwardly friendly assistant), Fred de Cordova, Diahnne Abbott (as the bartender Rupert continually tries to impress), and, in cameos, Tony Randall, Dr. Joyce Brothers, Victor Borge.

KING OF HEARTS (FRENCH/1967) C/101m.
One of the most popular cult films of the late sixties and early seventies, when youthful moviegoers were seduced by all films that defended nonconformity and opposed war. Philippe De Broca's fairytale comedy was a breezy pick-me-up with infectious gaiety and charm. But while it continues to be phenomenally popular, I now think it terribly dated, its humor and satiric bite somehow missing, its themes trite. How many other films have told us that those people on the outside of jails and asylums are the ones who should be institutionalized; that war is bad, war is crazy; and that our beautiful landscapes have been contaminated by armies. Alan Bates plays a non-violent, poetry-reading Scotsman, Private Charles Plumpick. During the last days of WWI, his commanders send him to the French town of Marville to find and dismantle a bomb. He mingles with the escaped patients from the asylum—the other citizens have fled—who have circulated through the deserted town and returned to their former professions. They believe Charles to be the "King of Hearts" for whom they've been waiting. He falls

in love with Coquelicot (Geneviève Bujold), a virgin who works in a brothel, and feels so much affection for the other loonies that he thinks it's his duty to save them from the bomb and the Germans who scurry about. I would have liked to have seen Danny Kaye as Plumpick because Bates, in his one bad performance, is so passive that he allows the loonies to carry the action and create the ambience. Unfortunately, De Broca seems more interested in the costumes the loonies wear than in developing distinct personalities for them: it's a film about nonconformity, but all the loonies have exactly the same eccentricities, the same level of mental illness, and the same way of looking at the world. Most disturbing is that they don't care that they may soon be killed—these defeatists accept no responsibility for improving the world that has driven them insane. The famous ending—naked Bates wants to join the inmates who have willingly returned to the asylum—is cute, but I'd rather see the inmates join him outside the gates with determination to shake things up in a world that could stand improvement. Also with: Pierre Brasseur, Jean-Claude Brialy, Adolfo Celi, Micheline Presle, Michel Serrault, Daniel Boulanger.

KING OF THE COWBOYS (1943) B&W/60m.
This brisk, witty, enjoyable Roy Rogers western, possibly his best, was made at time Gene Autry was in the service and Rogers had become the "King of the Cowboys." Roy takes a job singing with a traveling carnival and foils the sabotage that was responsible for explosions and fires in all the towns the carnival passed through. Rogers does a lot of singing, including a fine version of "I'm An Old Cowhand," but he's ready for shooting when the time comes. It's easy to see his appeal. Film has humor, some supplied by Smiley Burnette; but there's no romance, despite there being two appealing ladies, Peggy Moran (as a mind-reader) and Dorothea Kent (as a magician). The too abrupt ending didn't leave time for Rogers or Moran to get down to serious kissing—which little pardners across the country might have hissed at. Directed by Joseph Kane, who did many Rogers vehicles. Also with: Bob Nolan, Gerald Mohr, Lloyd Corrigan, Bob Wilson and the Sons of the Pioneers.

KISS ME DEADLY (1955) B&W/105m.
LA private eye Mike Hammer (Ralph Meeker) gives a ride to a frightened young woman named Christine (Cloris Leachman). When he later finds she was murdered, and that the FBI is interested in the case, Hammer and his secretary, Velda (Maxine Cooper), investigate—he doesn't care about Christine's death, but senses he might make a bundle. He gives protection to Lilly Carver (Gaby Rodgers), the dead woman's terrified roommate. But he later discovers that she—her real name is Gabrielle—and the thugs who tortured Christine to death and have been trying to murder him are in cahoots with Dr. Soberin (Albert Dekker). They are after a case containing a nuclear bomb that one of Christine's acquaintances hid before he was killed. Soberin wants to sell the bomb to a foreign power. A major influence on the French New Wave because of its audacious utilization of

wild camera angles and abrupt, jarring editing to symbolize a world out of orbit, Robert Aldrich's adaptation of Mickey Spillane's novel is one of the most dazzling works of the fifties, as swift-paced, thrilling, precipitous, and jolting to the senses as a ride on a broken roller-coaster. The picture's very rhythm comes from the slaps and punches Hammer dishes out; hysterical high points are represented by horrific screams; and scenes usually end with Hammer being knocked out and begin with him awakening but still feeling the effects of blows received. The main motif of the picture seems to be pain. Aldrich's Hammer is as much a fascist as Spillane's protagonist, minus a touch of sentimentality and a moral code. But whereas we identify with Spillane's hero and recognize that his fascism is justified by his results, Meeker's lowlife anti-hero is shown to be *wrong* in all he does. He gets his best friend killed, Velda kidnapped, and causes a nuclear bomb to fall into the wrong hands. His brutality proves to be futile, wrong—only a calm, rational approach might have prevented catastrophe. The fifties America we see is sick with paranoia, spying, and violence. Brutes like Hammer rule by muscle, intellectuals (like Soberin) and art and music lovers (like Christine) are eliminated, and the fate of the world rests on the shoulders of stupid Gabrielle. A. I. Bezzerides wrote the script. Also with: Paul Stewart, Juano Hernandez, Wesley Addy (as Hammer's policeman acquaintance Pat Chambers), Marian Carr, Nick Dennis, Jack Lambert, Jack Elam, Percy Helton, Fortunio Bonanova, Strother Martin.

KISS OF THE SPIDER WOMAN (BRAZILIAN/1985) C/119m.
In English. William Hurt plays Molina, a witty, vulnerable, candid, feminine homosexual who is confined in an Argentinian prison on a child-molestation charge. His cellmate is Raul Julia's Valentin, a serious, realistic, reticent radical journalist. Prison authorities repeatedly torture him to get him to disclose information about the political underground. Meanwhile the warden offers Hurt parole if he can get Julia to open up to him. Hurt spends his time giving florid descriptions of a kitschy pro-Nazi melodrama he'd seen years before. Julia, only a weekend political activist on the outside, now falls into the role of a dedicated revolutionary and is determined to be a worthy *political prisoner*. The men are opposites, except that neither had a fulfilling love life outside of prison. Eventually barriers break down and the men make love—not so much as a homosexual act as a confirmation of their humanity. Well-intentioned picture, on which director Hector Babenco (*Pixote*) spent four obsessive years, is one long *false* note. Leonard Schrader's script is calculated for performance rather than content, and for immediate impact so that we forget that the overall picture is vague. We never sufficiently get into the heads of the characters so that we at least can understand why they committed the acts that got them imprisoned. The filmmakers were afraid of turning off the mainstream audience! That's why this child molester and his leftwinger are made palatable for the average moviegoer. That Valentin is not as complex as in Manuel Puig's novel

is indication that the filmmakers didn't want to balance their "human" story with the equally important, more controversial "political" story. Film has potential for real political insight, but anything political is watered down by cliché treatment—it's as if we're watching a standard prison drama. Direction by Babenco is too theatrical when in the men's cell—and a baffling mess when Hurt's outside the prison. The final sequence is ridiculous. Hurt and Julia are fine actors, but *here* you can always tell they are playing parts. If you like their characters, it's probably because you like the actors who play them; when the two men kiss, what you most admire is these actors daring to kiss another man on the movie screen. The characters themselves are too thinly written to move us. Neither is allowed a chance to really cut loose and express his deepest, *angriest* thoughts about what it means to be either gay or a leftwinger in this particular society. Hurt won a Best Actor Oscar. Also with: Sonia Braga.

KLUTE (1971) C/114m. Exceptional psychological thriller stars Jane Fonda in an Oscar-winning role as call girl Bree Daniels. She is feeling threatened by a sadist who has already murdered a prostitute friend. Donald Sutherland's Klute is a small-town detective who comes to New York City to search for a missing friend. His case relates to what is happening to Bree. Klute and Bree feel attracted to each other—this scares Bree. Bree spends much time with a therapist, explaining that her job is liberating because she feels in *control* in her life only when turning tricks. But Bree has control only in this fantasy life. In real life she is terrified, sitting in her apartment behind five locks. Her movement toward real-life liberation takes a dramatic leap when she learns to trust Klute. She becomes secure with him as her protector and through him learns that being in love with the man she has sex with does not mean she must relinquish all control. Of course, Klute is the opposite of the killer. Klute is a gentle, considerate lover; the killer wants to commit sexual acts with Bree in which *he* has all control. Bree must come to realize that two men can be so much different, that all men aren't like the killer in regard to sex. Striking, highly atmospheric direction by Alan J. Pakula. Some scenes are genuinely frightening. Fonda gives a remarkable performance—obviously she's fascinated by Bree and wants to figure her out. Photography by Gordon Willis. Written by Andy and Dave Lewis. Also with: Charles Cioffi, Roy Scheider, Dorothy Tristan, Rita Gam, Richard Schull, Anthony Holland, Jean Stapleton.

KNIFE IN THE WATER (POLISH/1962) B&W/94m. Roman Polanski's first film, his only Polish film, is an enigmatic three-character piece he wrote with Jerzy Skolimowski and Jakub Goldberg. A middle-aged, extremely aggressive sports writer (Leon Niemczyk) and his diffident younger wife (Jolanta Umecka) pick up a 19-year-old hitchhiker (Zygmunt Malanowicz) and take him on their weekly sailing excursion. In their isolation—even on deck with the sea all around them—there is a sense of claustro-

phobia (heightened when they go below) that dramatically builds tension; just as the wind determines the boat's movements, fate seems to control the characters; we expect that in this natural setting the characters will lay bare their deepest emotions—but they never really strip off their defenses and totally reveal themselves. Polanski concentrates on the stiff competition between the two men at sailing, at pickup sticks, at knife playing. Niemczyk desires to show off for his wife *and* to himself by humiliating the younger man; but while he wins his small victories, he seems increasingly infantile. Polanski simultaneously increases the sexual tension between the boy and the wife—he fills his frame with sexual symbols (the boy's knife, her belt, the water, the pole). But what's most interesting is Polanski's underlying story—the *main* story—about the immense problems in the relationship between Niemcyzk and Umecka that come to surface. At film's end, in a car at a crossroad, they will finally have to confront their sorry marriage. Excellent hand-held photography by Jerzy Lipman.

KNOCK ON ANY DOOR (1949) B&W/100m. Liberal social drama by Nicholas Ray about a lawyer (Humphrey Bogart) who defends a young hood (John Derek's debut) on a murder charge. As Bogart builds up the jury's sympathy, Ray flashbacks to a series of tragic incidents (including his pregnant wife's suicide) that caused decent poor boy Derek to become a hardened criminal. It's hard not to be on Bogart's side, especially since the DA is a corrupt, vicious man with an ugly scar, played with extreme villainy by George Macready. But it's weird seeing this socially conscious lawyer browbeat some of the indigent witnesses. Picture starts out pretty well, with a lot of consciously hip dialogue. But Derek's character, whose motto is "live fast, die young, and have a good-looking corpse," is too unpleasant to be used as an example by Bogart (or Ray) to arouse viewer sympathy for real-life juveniles who are trapped by poverty and bad reputations into committing crimes. First film of Bogart's Santana Productions. From the novel by Willard Motley. Also with: Allene Roberts, Susan Perry, Mickey Knox.

KOYAANISQATSI (1983) C/87m. Unpronounceable title (which surely didn't help picture's word of mouth) is a Hopi Indian word that translates as "life out of balance." Director Godfrey Reggio has put together 87 minutes of images, mostly of natural and man-made structures in America, all set to a score by Philip Glass, to show that when nature is altered, the world goes out of whack. The cinematography by Ron Fricke is stunning—he establishes rhythm through camera movement, the use of various lenses, fast motion, slow motion, pixilation, aerial photography—but *everything* looks so beautiful that natural environments don't seem that much more inviting than civilization (surely *street sounds* would have helped convey the obscenity of cities). My favorite shot is of a city's skyline, with ominous clouds speeding by in the foreground—here are nature and civilization in conflict. I'm glad this hasn't turned into a favorite of people who like to get stoned. Or has it? It does have a cult following.

KRAMER VS. KRAMER (1979) C/104m.

Self-absorbed Dustin Hoffman works at a New York ad agency, which takes up most of his time. He comes home to find that his depressed wife, Meryl Streep, is walking out so she can find herself. Hoffman is left to take care of their young son, Justin Henry, whom Streep has raised on her own. He feels that he's in over his head trying to be both father and mother to this little stranger. And Henry misses his mother deeply and resents his long-neglectful dad who can't bring any order to his life. But father and son get to know each other, to enjoy each other's company, and to love one another. Hoffman learns what Streep went through as a mother and comes to realize the difficulties of balancing work with a home life. But just when father and son develop the ideal relationship, Streep returns for the boy. There is a custody battle. Adaptation of Avery Corman's novel is too intent on making Streep the villain, refusing to present her side of the story, and ridiculously glorifies Hoffman for doing what so many mothers do as a matter of course. It's also manipulatively structured: every event we witness is later brought up at the custody hearing, and we *know* that what really happened—which supports Hoffman's contention that he is a good father—is not like what is presented in court. Still, this is an excellent, thoughtful, humorous, sensitive film with terrific acting and real characters. Hoffman won a Best Actor Oscar with an interesting portrayal; his character is confused, nervous, and flawed throughout, but he becomes more human, thanks to his new role—for him, parenthood is liberating. Streep, who cries a lot, won a Best Supporting Actress Oscar. Robert Benton won for Best Director and Best Screenplay (from another source). Best Picture winner was an unexpected commercial blockbuster. Cinematography by Nestor Almendros, who uses many close-ups. Also with: Jane Alexander (who becomes Hoffman's best friend and confidante), Howard Duff, JoBeth Williams, George Coe.

KRIEMHILD'S REVENGE/KRIEMHILD'S RACHE/ SHE-DEVIL, THE (GERMAN/1924) B&W/97m.

The second half of Fritz Lang's *Nibelungen Saga*, made at the same time as *Siegfried* and originally screened as the second part of that film. It begins in the Burgundy court at the exact point where *Siegfried* ended. Kriemhild (Margarete Schön) mourns the death of her husband, Siegfried (Paul Richter, seen in flashbacks), and demands that her brother, King Günther (Theodor Loos), execute the murderer, his imposing half-brother and confidant, Hagen Tronjie (Hans Adalbert von Schlettow). When Günther and her other brothers refuse to turn against one of their clan, the vengeful Kriemhild agrees to marry Attila the Hun/King Etzel (Rudolf Klein-Rogge) on the condition that he agree to carry out her revenge. After she bears Attila a son, he invites her relatives to his court. But when Attila refuses to kill *guests*, Kriemhild takes matters into her own hands and enlists the support of the Huns. There will be fighting, a massacre, a great fire . . . the chance for revenge. Film is more somber than *Siegfried*, more violent, and more geared for adults. The visuals are equally impressive, and the character of Kriemhild, so passive in part one, becomes one of the most formidable heroines in film history. Presentation is at times confusing, but is powerful and fascinating. While I don't enjoy it as much as *Siegfried*, many consider it superior. Surely the look and mood influenced Sergei Eisenstein when he filmed *Ivan the Terrible*. Picture had confused reaction in Germany, where viewers were torn between rooting for Kriemhild and being repulsed by her madness, and between respecting Günther and the German clan for defending Hagen to the death and being upset that they'd condone the wretch's murder of the heroic Siegfried. Endings vary according to the print. If you've been looking for a film in which Attila is a sympathetic figure (one who respects women, plays with babies, cries, and wants his guests to have a good time), look no further. Also with: Bernhard Goetzke, Rudolf Rittner.

LACEMAKER, THE (FRENCH-SWISS-GERMAN/ 1977) C/108m.

Isabelle Huppert moved from bit player to major star with her moving performance as a young woman who is destroyed because she has the capacity to love too much. She plays Beatrice, nicknamed "Pomme," an extremely sweet, lovely, and passive 19-year-old beauty-salon assistant who falls in love with young literature student François (Yves Beneyton). They move in together, and she becomes completely devoted to him. Educated, political, from the middle class, and professionally ambitious, François decides that Pomme is not the ideal match for him— he is embarrassed for her around his friends and parents and tries to get her to make something more of her life. But she is content with her ignorance and timidity—all that is important to her is loving François. He breaks up with her; she has a mental breakdown. Certainly everyone has been part of or known people involved in a relationship of the type that Pomme and François have in this film, but Claude Goretta, who adapted Pascal Lainé's novel with Lainé, is the first male director to present it on screen. Typically, male directors had their "smart" male leads contend that a heroine's ignorance made for a blissful union; moreover, they wouldn't let the male characters, to whom they related, be as cruel/ungallant to their women as François is to Pomme. The male filmmakers are not putting down Pomme for being shallow. Instead they are showing that intellectuals like François can't see the depth of Pomme's beauty, but artists, painters (Goretta sees Pomme as the model for a master artist), or filmmakers can see clearly into her soul—it is through Jean Boffety's intimate, penetrating camera work that we viewers are given insight into this woman that lets us realize what François (who *thinks* too much) doesn't see: that she is special. An interesting film, but for some it is too sad. Also with: Florence Giorgetti, Christian Baltauss, Renata Schroeter, Anne Marie Düringer.

LADIES AND GENTLEMEN: THE FABULOUS STAINS (CANADIAN/1981) C/87m.

A musical satire about the meteoric rise and fall of a punk-rock singer. Its major point of interest is the presence of 15-year-old Diane Lane as "Third Degree Burns," an unknown singer (if you can call her a singer) who temporarily becomes the idol of girls her age because of her defiant attitude, nihilistic music ("I'm a waste of time"), and see-through blouses. Dreary direction by former rock mogul Lou Adler, which perks up only during few outright comic scenes. Was on Paramount's shelf for 3½ years. Also with: Ray Winstone, John (Fee) Waybill (of the Tubes), Christine Lahti, David Clennon, Cynthia Sykes, Laura Dern, Marin Kanter, Paul Simonon (of the Clash), and Paul Cook and Steve Jones (both of the Sex Pistols).

LADY AND THE TRAMP (1955) C/75m.

Most likable Walt Disney animated feature, highlighted by the singing and voice-dubbing of Peggy Lee. Lady is a pampered cocker spaniel who belongs to wealthy Jim and Darling Dear. After Darling has a baby, she and Jim go away for a few days and leave Lady and the baby with Aunt Sarah and her Siamese cats—occasion for Lee to sing "We are Siamese if you please..." Aunt Sarah dislikes Lady and thinks her troublesome. When Lady is muzzled, the poor dog runs away. Out on the streets, Lady is helpless, but she receives protection from Tramp, a dog from the poor side of town. Before, she and her friends Jock and Trusty had turned their noses up when Tramp was about. They fall in love. But their relationship is threatened by Aunt Sarah and a dogcatcher, by rumors that Tramp is a runaround, and by Lady's decision to live in a home rather than the streets. The animation is not that ambitious and there are few surprises in the storyline, but the relationship between Lady and Tramp is sweet. The Italian dinner (behind the restaurant) is probably one of the cinema's most romantic courtship scenes—we all remember the moment when they end up eating opposite ends of the same strand of spaghetti and their mouths draw closer together for their first kiss. They're an appealing couple. Ending is pretty suspenseful. Songs were written by Lee and Sonny Burke. Directed by Hamilton Luske, Clyde Geronimi, Wilfred Jackson. Other voices: Barbara Luddy (Lady), Larry Roberts (Tramp), Bill Thompson, Bill Bucon, Stan Freberg (as the beaver who chews off Lady's muzzle), Verna Felton (Aunt Sarah).

LADY EVE, THE (1941) B&W/97m.

Preston Sturges's romantic comedy stars Henry Fonda as a millionaire who has just returned from a year up the Amazon studying snakes. He's an expert on reptiles, but he's too naïve to recognize sneaky women or snake-in-the-grass conmen. That he brings a live snake on an ocean voyage is indication that he has an active libido, and in this state he's ready to be taken advantage of by some sly golddigger. Con artist Barbara Stanwyck and her cardsharp father, Charles Coburn, recognize Fonda as the perfect patsy. Within minutes Stanwyck has the defenseless Fonda so dazed by her perfume, exposed legs, and shameless flirting that he's unaware he's being set up for the kill by Coburn. But Stanwyck unexpectedly falls in love with Fonda and halts the swindle. She wants to marry him. However, before she can confess to Fonda that she and Coburn had originally intended to fleece him, Fonda finds out about their shady past. Thinking he's been taken for a fool, he tells Stanwyck that he knew she was conning him and that he'd been playing *her* for the fool. Stanwyck vows revenge. Sturges takes standard screwball-comedy material and turns it into a zany classic. Film has an irresistible blend of quirky characters, snappy dialogue, slapstick, and sex. Fonda will surprise you with his skillful pratfalls. Stanwyck is so personable and vivacious that you feel that all the men whose money she stole got their money's worth—cheers to her wardrobe designer. Film would match *Sullivan's Travels* if it didn't peter out near the end. Also with: William Demarest, Eugene Pallette, Eric Blore, Melville Cooper, Jimmy Conlin.

LADY FROM SHANGHAI, THE (1948) B&W/86m.

Perhaps Orson Welles's most enjoyable film, a longtime cult favorite, was made in 1946 but held back for two years by Columbia chief Harry Cohn, who was horrified that Welles would: chop off the flowing red hair of Rita Hayworth, then the studio's sex symbol and in the process of divorcing Welles, and present her with short blond hair; make her into an emotionless, vacuous villainess; cast himself as a "hero" (although the character immediately denies being a hero) who once killed a man in a fight and fought against the fascists in Spain; and go way over budget on a picture that Cohn couldn't understand. Welles, the narrator, plays an Irish adventurer who rescues Hayworth from a rape attempt in Central Park. Her crippled husband, Everett Sloane, the country's most successful defense attorney, hires Welles to take him, Hayworth, and his business partner (Glenn Anders) home to San Francisco on his yacht. During the trip, which has a stopover in Acapulco, Welles falls under Hayworth's charms. Soon he is fall guy in nefarious murder plot and ends up being tried for murder, with Sloane as his lawyer. Film has always given critics trouble because it's hard to categorize. Basically, the story itself is classic *film noir* material (although Welles's Irish brogue doesn't immediately bring Philip Marlowe to mind)—you can find traces, especially when analyzing Hayworth's character, of *The Maltese Falcon*, but I see it as more of a twist on *Gilda*, with Hayworth's character changing from sympathetic to sinner. But in tone I think the picture anticipates *Beat the Devil*; here, too, are the tongue-in-cheek humor, the improvisation, the bizarre characters, the blonde (played by an actress known for a different hair color) who is a habitual liar, the sense that the director is having a grand time behind his camera. Indeed, Welles has fun simply by setting his significant scenes in such unusual places as an aquarium (for a love scene), a Chinese theater, and an amusement-park Crazy House—the scene of Welles's celebrated shootout in the Hall of Mirrors. From the novel *If I Die Before I Wake* by Sherwood King.

LADY IN RED, THE/GUNS, SIN AND BATHTUB GIN (1979) C/89m.

Pay-TV favorite starring Pamela Sue Martin as a farm girl who goes to Chicago in the late twenties, gets tossed in jail on a prostitution charge, has several run-ins with a vicious prison matron (Nancy Parsons), works in a fancy bordello, and winds up as John Dillinger's (Robert Conrad) mistress, the legendary "lady in red" who was at his side when the FBI ambushed him as he left a movie theater. Conventional New World–Roger Corman material is made entertaining because of fast-paced, flavorful direction by Lewis Teague; a snappy script by John Sayles that provides several offbeat characters and strong women's roles; and a surprisingly engaging performance by Martin, who exhibits a winning combination of sex and savvy. In her first film lead she seems remarkably at ease, whether taking off her clothes, playing a romantic scene, or participating in a wild action sequence involving cars and machine guns. Surprisingly, she wouldn't take another movie lead until her *Dynasty* days were over. R rating is due as much to bloody shootouts as to nudity. Also with: Louise Fletcher, Robert Hogan, Glenn Withrow, Christopher Lloyd, Dick Miller.

LADY VANISHES, THE (BRITISH/1938) B&W/ 87m–97m.

This vastly entertaining thriller ranks with *The 39 Steps* as the best of Alfred Hitchcock's British films. It has much wit, suspense, sex, romance, a wonderful array of characters (enthusiastically played by an excellent cast), and a fascinating mystery. American girl (Margaret Lockwood) befriends a sweet, elderly English governess (Dame May Whitty) on a train leaving a fascist Balkan country for England. But after a nap she can't find Whitty, and all the other passengers whom Lockwood knows claim Whitty didn't exist. Enlisting the help of an English musicologist (Michael Redgrave in his screen debut) and an eminent brain surgeon (Paul Lukas), she searches for proof that Whitty was on the train and discovers that there are rightwing conspirators on board who have kidnapped her for some evil purpose. Along with the odd assortment of clues—the finger writing on the window, Whitty's special brand of tea, the "nun" (Catherine Lacey) wearing high heels—the most interesting aspect of the film is how *all* the characters turn out to be different than they first appear. The once frivolous Lockwood (who is most appealing) becomes obsessed with the *serious* enterprise of finding Whitty; the self-absorbed, self-impressed Redgrave becomes Lockwood's trusted friend (as well as lover) and risks his life on her behalf; brain surgeon Lukas schemes to perform an unsuccessful brain operation on Whitty

and to destroy minds of Redgrave and Lockwood with a drug; the passengers in Lockwood's compartment pretend civility, yet are her enemies; the nun working for Lukas changes allegiance when the chips are down; cocky Britisher Cecil Parker turns out to be a coward (perhaps his being shot while holding a white flag is picture's warning to British politicians not to appease Hitler); Parker's passive mistress, Linden Travers, eventually speaks her piece and breaks from his hold on her; Britishers Naunton Wayne and Basil Radford (the comic team provides much of the film's humor) seem to care only about cricket, yet when the British passengers are being threatened by the Balkan police, they bravely fight back—perfect symbols of British honor; the Balkan folk singer turns out to be a spy; Whitty not only is a British spy but has spirit and energy that belie her age. A great last shot. Script, adapted from Ethel Lina White's *The Wheel Spins*, was written by Sidney Gilliat and Frank Launder, with Hitchcock's wife, Alma Reville, contributing the final episode, which is original to the film. Also with: Googie Withers, Mary Clare, Philip Leaver.

LAND OF THE PHARAOHS (1955) C/106m.

Picture has a cult, myself included, among adults who saw this as kids and were excited by such sights as a bunch of bald, tongueless priests allowing themselves to be buried alive in a tomb; some cowards being hurled into an alligator pit; and statuesque beauty Joan Collins displaying a bare midriff. But seeing it today, few will disagree that it's just another silly, stiltedly acted historical epic, a mediocre milepost in Howard Hawks's otherwise brilliant career. A fictional account of the building of the Great Pyramid of Khufu the Cheops (circa 3000 B.C.), it was Hawks's most ambitious project conceptually—it required 10,000 extras, 50 days filming in Egypt, and the simulated construction of the base of the great pyramid—yet it was lethargically directed and scripted (by William Faulkner, Harry Kurnitz, and Harry Jack Bloom) and squandered time, talent, and money. There are crowd scenes but no expensive battle sequences to take advantage of CinemaScope; the cast is second-rate, especially those in support of Jack Hawkins (as the greedy Pharaoh) and Collins (as Nellifer, his disloyal, vain, greedy bride); the make-up is bad, with all the actors over 50 looking as if someone threw white flour into their hair. The plot borrows heavily from Greek tragedy, but as a film lacks intrigue, suspense, and visual elements. Nellifer is the only true-blue villainess in Hawks's films, his only female without warmth or wit. But he didn't care enough about her to explore what is going on inside her, thus stranding Collins, no great actress to begin with, in a skimpy role (as well as a skimpy costume). There is male bonding in the film, as is common in Hawks, but these men aren't his typical action heroes. They live boring lives of leisure—as Hawks admitted, neither he nor his writers knew how pharaohs spent their time. We never see how Hawkins responds to a crisis—for instance, there is no slave revolt—so we don't know whether we should despise him or sympathize with him because of Collins's infidelity and scheming for his gold. The entombment finale (with pouring sand and sliding blocks) remains truly spectacular, and Collins is still strikingly sexy with her bare midriff—but this is a pretty dull film that only we longtime fans can really enjoy. Forgettable music by Dimitri Tiomkin. Also with: Dewey Martin, Alexis Minotis, James Robertson Justice, Louise Boni, Sydney Chaplin.

LASSIE COME HOME (1943) C/88m.
Classic family film that made Lassie into the first canine movie lead since Rin Tin Tin. Female collie, played by a male dog named Pal, is owned by a poor Yorkshire family, father Donald Crisp, mother Elsa Lanchester, and young son Roddy McDowall, to whom the dog is devoted. Unable to find work, Crisp sells Lassie to a kindly breeder (Nigel Bruce). Lassie keeps running away and returning to McDowall. But when Bruce takes Lassie to Scotland, the heartbroken boy believes he'll never see the dog again. However, Bruce's young granddaughter (pretty little Elizabeth Taylor, who still sported an English accent) helps Lassie escape, and the collie begins a long, dangerous trek back home. She has a series of exciting adventures and meets up with several interesting characters. Classy, colorful MGM production is sentimental but not as gushy as one might imagine. It boasts an outstanding human cast and, of course, Lassie is a remarkable talent. And it's nice that Lassie is portrayed here as a *very* smart dog, rather than as the genius of the television show who understands *everything* that humans tell it; in fact, at one point Edmund Gwenn observes that Lassie is not as smart as his own little dog. Directed by Fred M. Wilcox. Film is presented as a tribute to its late author, Eric Knight. Also with: Dame May Whitty, Ben Webster, Alan Napier.

LAST AMERICAN HERO, THE/HARD DRIVER (1973) C/100m.
Sleeper features a strong, natural performance by Jeff Bridges as real-life race-car driver Junior Johnson who learned how to drive fast and smart running moonshine on southern backroads, and in the early sixties beat the pros and their fancy, sponsored cars with whatever vehicle he could get hold of. Johnson was a consultant on the film, but it still takes great liberties with his story—here Johnson's father (Art Lund) goes to prison rather than Junior himself; here Junior doesn't win his first race until *after* he gets a sponsor and a first-rate car. To please the youth audience of the day, Johnson was made into a rebel attempting to make it big without buckling under to the System that exploits drivers. At the end he *half* sells out; the boyish charm that is visible on Bridges's face in the early scenes is gone. Director Lamont Johnson has a feel for racing milieu and an ear for dialogue. There are some particularly nice scenes between Bridges and Lund, and Bridges and Valerie Perrine, who plays a racetrack groupie. But, overall, the material isn't unusual enough to be really interesting. From a 1965 *Esquire* article by Tom Wolfe. Also with: Ned Beatty, Ed Lauter, Geraldine Fitzgerald, Gary Busey, William Smith.

LAST DETAIL, THE (1973) C/105m.
Career sailors Jack Nicholson and Otis Young are assigned to transport 18-year-old sailor Randy Quaid from the brig in Virginia to a naval prison in New Hampshire, where he's supposed to spend eight years for attempting to steal $40 from a polio fund (he's a kleptomaniac). Seeing Quaid's a nice guy, they decide to give him his first sample of life before he's put away. He drinks, visits a prostitute, is in a brawl, has many adventures. Their journey is the sad, naïve young sailor's rite of passage—it also results in the return of humanity to the two cynical sailors: they realize that they've been the ones in prison. During the entire film you can sense that as the three men learn about life, an explosion is building. Film is known for its rhythmic, realistic, salty, wryly written dialogue by Robert Towne. A great, swaggering, angry, rebel-without-a-cause peformance by Nicholson (as "Badass" Buddusky). Quaid is quite touching. Directed by Hal Ashby. Michael Chapman did the cinematography. Based on the novel by Darryl Ponicsan. Among those with small parts are: Michael Moriarty, Carol Kane (memorable as a prostitute), Clifton James, Nancy Allen, Luana Anders, Gilda Radner, Chapman.

LAST DRAGON, THE/BERRY GORDY'S THE LAST DRAGON (1985) C/108m.
Berry Gordy of Motown fame went for almost the entire youth market with this mix of blaxploitation movie, kung fu kicks, and music videos. Picture got a lot of friendly reviews, but most likely they came from critics who hadn't seen the better films from those genres. Story is about young black martial-arts student (Taimak) who idolizes Bruce Lee and is learning from an Oriental master. He is being harassed by tough gang leader named The Shogun (Julius J. Carry), but he still has time to protect beautiful singer/disc jockey (Vanity). She is being physically pressured by a madman who wants her to play the records of the artists he represents. There are a couple of laughs along the way, but the picture hasn't the exciting hero, well-choreographed fights, pacing, or visual excitement of some of the better pictures it spoofs. A little imagination could have compensated for low budget. Vanity, singer Prince's ex, is beautiful but wasted—and she looks too old for the male lead. The film's high point is DeBarge's pop hit "Rhythm of the Night." Directed by Michael Schultz. Also with: Chris Murney, Faith Prince, Leo O'Brien, Jim Moody.

LAST EMBRACE, THE (1979) C/102m.
Almost every contemporary director has made at least one suspense film in the Hitchcock mold, and this was Jonathan Demme's shaky contribution to the ever growing list. CIA agent Roy Scheider, who is having trouble recovering from his wife's death due to bullets meant for him, gets the uneasy feeling that the agency is now setting him up for elimination. His paranoia increases when he realizes he's being followed by agent Charles Napier, his wife's angry brother. His only comfort comes from Janet Margolin, a smart but neurotic college student who had sublet his apartment when he was

away. But his trust in her wavers when he connects her to a plot to kill those men—including himself—whose ancestors ran a Jewish brothel early in the century. (It seems her grandmother was kept in servitude.) The premise for the film is extremely interesting, Miklos Rozsa's score reminds one of Bernard Herrmann, and there are an abundance of Hitchcockian touches and characters. Plus Demme is really the first director to fully exploit Margolin's immense behind-closed-doors sex appeal. However, two pivotal scenes are misconceived and mishandled: the sequence in which Napier lures Scheider into a Princeton University bell tower (how could a professional killer orchestrate an ambush where he himself is in the less advantageous position?) and the extremely unpleasant finale, where—as when watching *Vertigo*, which provided the inspiration for this scene—you'll probably decide you dislike the vengeance-obsessed Scheider more than the woman who did him wrong. Also with: John Glover, Sam Levene, Christopher Walken, Joe Spinell, Mandy Patinkin.

LAST HOUSE ON THE LEFT, THE (1972)
C/91m.   Repulsive, controversial cult film. While her parents prepare a cake to celebrate her 17th birthday, a pretty girl (Sandra Cassell) and her pretty friend (Lucy Grantham) go to rock concert in the city. First they try to score some dope. They are kidnapped by four sadists—two escaped rapist-murderers (David A. Hess and Fred Lincoln), Hess's tough bisexual girlfriend (Jeramie Ran), and Hess's addict brother (Marc Sheffler). The girls are raped, tortured, and killed. The girls' parents get retribution. Picture starts out humorously and the final section is hogwash, but the section with the girls is an outright embarrassment. The humor, happy music are offensive. You'll feel ashamed to be watching it and feel paranoid about the men around you who are grinning and taking delight in the girls' torture. The major problem is that the film is so convincingly made—and the sadists and their victims so authentic—that the torture scenes really seem to be happening. When you think the nice girls will get away and they don't make it, you'll feel like crying. A perversion of *The Virgin Spring*: the girl dies on a happy day ("I feel like a woman for the first time in my life"). Directed by Wes Craven; produced by Sean S. Cunningham, who'd later make *Friday the 13th*. Sequel: *Last House on the Left Part II*. Also with: Gaylord St. James, Cynthia Carr, Marshall Anker.

LAST LAUGH, THE (GERMAN/1924) B&W/
77m.   Classic German silent film, directed without titles by F. W. Murnau, tells a simple, tragic story: aging Emil Jannings, who holds the prestigious position of doorman at a ritzy hotel, is unceremoniously stripped of his snazzy uniform and demoted to men's-room attendant. Humiliated at work, mocked by neighbors, shunned by his family, he becomes a pathetic, disoriented figure with a dazed expression and a crooked body. He reminds one of an unhappy, beaten walrus. But—thanks to the filmmakers, who admitted to being overly charitable—he has the last laugh.

Film suffers today because of Jannings overdoing it with the self-pity and a happy ending that just doesn't mesh with what went before it. But Karl Freund's cinematography is absolutely stunning; particularly impressive are his remarkable close-ups, Jannings's dream sequence, and the opening street scene that is shot through a revolving door. His use of a mobile camera and his surreal effects were revolutionary: truly there are shots unlike those found in any other film. Also with: Maly Delschaft, Max Hiller.

LAST NIGHT AT THE ALAMO (1984) B&W/
80m.   Second independent feature by Texan director Eagle Pennell is set in a Houston bar on the night this hangout will be closed down. A fascinating character study about the sorry men who have been regulars for years, who have made the bar their personal domain where they can strut their false machismo and stroke their fragile egos. They realize that when it closes they will lose their power base and become the same inconsequential little men at night that they are during the day. During the course of this hectic evening the main characters, including Cowboy (Sonny Davis)—who is regarded as a legend by the younger men who don't know any better (and don't know Cowboy is bald beneath his hat)—will be taken down a few pegs and make fools of themselves. The women they consider beneath them will be the first to realize that these men are inadequate. Film is swift kick in the rear to men who hang around bars bragging about their success with women when in fact they have come to bar to cry in their beers over being humbled by the women they love. Often uproarious, finally sad, observant, atmospheric, different. Scripted by Kim Henkel (*The Texas Chain Saw Massacre*). Also with: Lou Perry, Steve Matilla, Tina Hubbard, Doris Hargrave, Michael Hammond, Amanda LaMar, Peggy Pennell, Henkel, Pennell.

LAST PICTURE SHOW, THE (1971) B&W/
118m.   Peter Bogdanovich's excellent adaptation of Larry McMurtry's elegiac novel about a dying Texas town in the early fifties has such interesting *real* characters and is so well acted that few viewers ever mention what a depressing picture it is. Our pivotal characters, teenagers Timothy Bottoms, his best friend, Jeff Bridges, and Bridges's lustful girlfriend, Cybill Shepherd (her debut), may lose their virginity, but they are so unfulfilled and confused by the experience that their rites of passage signal more a death of youth and innocence than the birth of adulthood. Indeed, what is happening to the town itself is symptomatic of their personal decline: even at the beginning, it is like a ghost town or graveyard, with constant wind and dust swirling on the empty streets and into the empty stores; later the last theater (showing *Red River*) will close down and the oldest and youngest characters we see will be dead. The intertwining storylines, difficult familial relationships, tension between youth and adults, feuds, affairs, and sex make this material ideal for a television soap (Shepherd is a combination of Allison McKenzie and Betty Harrington). A less

sensitive director could have made an exploitation film using the same script. Perfect casting and the authentic look and dialogue of the characters make us believe that these people—waitress Eileen Brennan, theater owner Ben Johnson, the unhappy coach's wife, Cloris Leachman (with whom Bottoms has an affair), etc.—really live in this town. Johnson and Leachman deservedly won Best Supporting Actor and Actress awards. Leachman is astonishing when she blows up at Bottoms for dumping her (what a great scene!)— you can't believe she's not really this woman, so strongly does she express her previously pent-up thoughts and feelings. McMurtry and Bogdanovich wrote the script. Robert Surtees did the standout black-and-white cinematography. Also with: Ellen Burstyn, Clu Gulager, Sam Bottoms, Randy Quaid.

LAST TANGO IN PARIS, THE (ITALIAN-FRENCH/ 1973) C/129m.   One of the most argued-about films ever made (is it art or pornography?). Bernardo Bertolucci's erotic psychodrama is about an intense love affair between two strangers that begins when they meet in a vacant apartment and immediately have sex: Marlon Brando is a middle-aged flophouse owner whose wife just committed suicide; Maria Schneider is a 20-year-old who is about to get married. They meet only in the apartment, they never reveal their names or talk of their lives outside. This picture, which was banned in Bertolucci's native Italy, blazed new cinematic frontiers because its lovers communicate through sex (sex expresses their drives) rather than having sex (of the raunchy but simulated variety) merely to excite an audience. But the film is not about sex per se but about a broken, tortured man. Reacting to his wife's suicide with confusion, sadness, anger, guilt that his inability to show his love might have driven her to her drastic act, and shame that she would reject him so brutally, he wants to separate sex from all else. He repudiates God, his name, his bourgeois life, and the outside world—and desperately slips into a "sexistential" world. He rejects the present and future, and regresses into childish actions at the flophouse; he has temper tantrums, has crying fits, slams doors, breaks things, bites his mother-in-law's hand, turns out lights to scare everyone. In the apartment he plays *childish adult games* with Schneider; a sophisticated, perverse version of little kids playing house. Whereas she is the daughter he never could have, he is the father she lost. He is also another old relic in her collection (she collects antiques as a hobby and as a job). But she is most attracted to him because he gets her to reject those bourgeois shackles that have kept her sexually inhibited *and* because he lets her remain a child: "Growing older is a crime." Her fiancé (Jean-Pierre Léaud) constantly looks to the future: "I must start something *new*." She feels safer with Brando's "When something's finished, we begin again." The game she plays with Brando is to see who can remain a child the longest. Brando loses and wants them to begin a normal adult relationship; he even reveals his name—so she shoots him. Bertolucci was rightly attacked for having Schneider be nude through most of the picture, while not

including nude scenes he'd shot with Brando; yet few will dispute that this is the one film in which Brando reveals *himself*, dark side and all, through scenes he wrote, through improvisation, and by letting us witness his acting technique. Alternately ferocious and tender, confident and confused, polite and vulgar, touching and pathetic, tense and wickedly funny, he is continuously dazzling. The emotionally devastating scene in which he sits by his wife's body, cruelly cursing her, crying himself into a daze, unthinkingly calling her "sweetheart," is Brando at his best, and should be studied by all aspiring actors. Vittorio Storaro did the standout cinematography; his swirling camera and the moody jazz (sax) score by Gato Barbieri create a delirious atmosphere that is conducive to Brando and Schneider breaking sexual taboos.

LAST WALTZ, THE (1978) C/117m.   Marvelous, intimate, emotional documentary by Martin Scorsese made to commemorate the historic farewell performance-celebration by The Band, in San Francisco on Thanksgiving 1976. The excitement on stage is apparent as The Band (the charismatic and gifted Robbie Robertson, Rick Danko, Levon Helm, Richard Manuel, Garth Hudson) perform their array of songs for the last time together (including "The Weight," "The Night They Drove Old Dixie Down," and "Stage Fright") and as they're joined on stage by their friends, all musical superstars. It's a great concert, with seminal stars like Bob Dylan (doing an appropriate "Forever Young"), Neil Young, Muddy Waters, Van Morrison, Joni Mitchell, Neil Diamond (who does seem a bit out of place), Paul Butterfield, Eric Clapton, Dr. John, and Ronnie Hawkins all in fine form; Ringo Starr and Ron Wood make token appearances. Scorsese also included some stylized footage of The Band singing and playing with the Staple Singers and then Emmylou Harris (her "Evangeline" is a highlight) on a bare stage in an empty hall. Scorsese begins the film with the final song of the concert and throughout the concert inserts some interesting post-concert interview clips he conducted with Robertson and, to a lesser degree, the other band members about their years on the road when they were an anonymous band rather than The Band. And we get the reassuring feeling that the concert never ends, the music plays on, and the group members didn't really go their separate ways (actually, years later they'd get back together, minus Robertson, for a few concerts). Excellent sound; excellent cinematography by Michael Chapman, Vilmos Zsigmond, and others.

LAST WAVE, THE (AUSTRALIAN/1977) C/ 106m.   Creepy, enigmatic film by Peter Weir is set in Sydney at a time of freakishly heavy rainstorms. White lawyer Richard Chamberlain is hired to defend Gulpilil and several other young blacks who are accused of murdering one of their group. Chamberlain begins to suspect that the killing was due to fear that the dead man would reveal secret aboriginal practices in the city. Chamberlain, who has a history of having premonitions, begins to have ominous visions of Sydney swallowed by water. He also begins to feel white man's guilt for the historically racist treatment of Australian blacks. Weir builds tension by juxtaposing what is real with what Chamberlain foresees so that we can't tell the difference between the two. Also we also begin to sense Chamberlain's apprehension as he delves into the mystery of his visions, questions an imposing shaman (Nandjiwarra Amagula), and uncovers ruins beneath the city. Starting with the early scene in which a sudden storm scares a teacher and her young pupils, the film is consistently atmospheric. The picture becomes more and more mysterious instead of clearer as Chamberlain makes his investigation. But, for some reason, not knowing what's going on isn't frustrating. The eerie, dreamlike images that Weir presents keep us fascinated and satisfied. One of the first Australian films to play in America. I first saw it in a theater that had been flooded by rain—this may account for why it gives me more shudders than most people. Film's last shot (although taken from a surfing film) is absolutely terrifying. Olivia Hamnett is appealing as Chamberlain's wife.

LATE SPRING (JAPANESE/1949) B&W/103m.
A simply told yet lovely film by Yasujiro Ozu, in which he advanced several themes that would distinguish his later works: the dissolution of the postwar Japanese family; the idea that married children—especially married daughters—will become strangers to their parents; the wise realization by the elderly that they must sacrifice their own happiness so that their children can make lives for themselves. Realizing that his daughter (Setsuko Hara) has passed the age when most women have married, a widower (Chishu Ryu) encourages her to wed. Since she is perfectly happy living with her father and taking care of him—she knows he would be lost without a woman—she becomes miserable. Her aunt (Haruko Sugimura) introduces her to a man she says looks like Gary Cooper. Hara gets along well with him, but is reluctant to consent to marriage until Ryu fibs that he himself is planning to marry. Interestingly, Ozu never shows the young man, but instead concentrates on the relationship between father and daughter. It appears to be everything either could want, since she never thinks of sex or having children and he makes no distinction between the love she has for him and the love that she will now give her husband (he speaks only of transferring her love from father to husband). Indeed, Ryu's willingness to let his daughter leave him may be because he realizes there is something *unhealthy* between them. As in all Ozu films, the acting is outstanding, the pace is measured, the everyday story pulls you in. While this isn't a tearjerker like *Tokyo Story*, the final moment is emotionally devastating.

LAURA (1944) B&W/88m.
Rouben Mamoulian claimed he directed 75% of this cult classic and revival-house favorite before Darryl F. Zanuck replaced him with producer Otto Preminger. But the film fits better into Preminger's oeuvre than into his own. It is the best of Preminger's somber excursions into psychological melodrama, stories with brutal intonations but dealing primarily with the perversity of the mind. Elegance mixes with decadence, wit with cruelty, and the conflict comes from Preminger pairing people who don't match. As in his later films, fluid camera work and long, static shots blend together; emphasis is on settings, including carpets, curtains, shelves, books, artifacts—anything that helps us determine the cultural, financial, and intellectual standing of his characters; characters and plot elements common to *film noir* are taken out of dark rooms, alleys, and tenements and brought into lush, brightly lit settings, where in the background we can hear melodious music rather than the jazz riffs of a cheap club. Mark McPherson (Dana Andrews) is a tough, crude police detective who is in control in the gutter, but totally out of his element when investigating the society murder of beautiful advertising executive Laura Hunt (Gene Tierney), whose face was blasted away by a shotgun. He questions the upper-class suspects: Waldo Lydecker (Clifton Webb's greatest role), a conceited, snide ("I would be sincerely sorry to see my neighbor's children devoured by wolves"), intellectual newspaper columnist who was Laura's friend and companion; Shelby Carpenter (Vincent Price looking weak and sweaty), her good-for-nothing, money-hungry fiancé; and Ann Treadwell (Judith Anderson), her rich, unscrupulous aunt, who loves Shelby. He listens to everyone say wonderful things about Laura; then, in an astonishing scene, he studies her portrait, reads her love letters, smells her perfume, rummages through her drawers, and, his sexual excitement evident, becomes the screen's first movie hero to fall for a dead woman. But Laura is not dead; another woman was killed in her place. She turns up halfway through the film. Even so, her portrait and her dreamlike theme (by David Raksin) dominate, conveying that McPherson still loves the angel he dreamed about—he doesn't even notice (neither did most critics) that the real Laura is meant to be a disappointment. She is not the wide-eyed innocent Waldo described but hard and angry, and attracted to men because of brawn rather than brains. Waldo would have been the ideal mate for her—for one thing, *he* respects her independence and her talent. But, as Waldo complains, she considers "a long, strong body as the measure of a man." So she falls for McPherson, not knowing about his necrophilia (he should be in a psycho ward, Waldo contends) or caring that he is insecure, immature, and chauvinistic. The movie ends in chaos with the killer shot and dying, but viewers should realize that the real eruption will come later, when Laura and her new man get married—just wait till the old-fashioned McPherson tells Laura that he won't stand for his wife making more money than he does. *Then* she'll miss Waldo. From Vera Caspary's novel, in which (impotent) Waldo's attraction to Laura is based on sex—in the film it's based on her being a good companion and an "eloquent listener."

LEFT-HANDED GUN, THE (1958) B&W/102m.
Arthur Penn's first film was adapted by Leslie Stevens from Gore Vidal's play *The Death of Billy the Kid*. Paul Newman

had starred in a 1955 live TV version called *Billy*. Young Billy Bonney gets a job with a rancher, Tunstall (Colin Keith-Johnston), who's driving cattle to Lincoln. Tunstall is kind to Billy and teaches him to keep his violence in check. When Tunstall is murdered by four men who have the law on their side, Billy vows to avenge the crime. He slays two of the killers in a shootout and becomes a hunted man. When he ruins the wedding of friend Pat Garrett (John Dehner) by killing another of Tunstall's murderers, Garrett puts on a badge and goes after his friend. Film gave Penn his first chance both to deal with a rebel outcast who is in conflict with society and to blend myth-legend and history. It's set in the West, but it's actually a modern-day psychological examination of a troubled youth—it fits in with fifties juvenile-delinquent pictures. Billy needs an adult who can watch over him, but he loses surrogate father Tunstall, and surrogate older brother Garrett turns against him. Newman's heavy-handed Method acting is partly responsible for the film seeming dated. But Penn's audacious camera work, which Sam Peckinpah, Marlon Brando (in *One-Eyed Jacks*), and other western directors would copy, is still interesting. Dehner gives a terrific performance. Also with: Lita Milan (as Billy's lover who lets him down), Hurd Hatfield (as the dime novelist who adores Billy and wants to make him into a hero), James Best, James Congdon, Denver Pyle.

LENNY (1974) B&W/112m.   Bob Fosse's seamy, sex-laced biography of controversial comic Lenny Bruce (Dustin Hoffman) centers on his difficult marriage to stripper Honey Harlowe (played with vulnerability by Valerie Perrine) and his troubles with policemen and judges for using supposedly obscene material in his nightclub act. Hoffman is very convincing in the title role, displaying Bruce's quick mind, his obsessive nature when trying to smooth things over with Honey or the Law, and, ultimately, his utter helplessness and despair when he realizes he'll never be able to express himself openly in his profession. He is magnificent in those scenes where Bruce tries to talk sense to conservative judges; he becomes like Don Quixote fighting windmills. But the film fails because of Fosse's self-conscious direction and because Julian Barry's script, adapted from Barry's play, forgets to include moments in which Bruce shows he has a real sense of humor. One can understand Bruce's seriousness in his later years, but, except for a scene with his relatives, he's not funny in his early years—even on stage. The film could use some laughter because it's deadly long at 112m and very depressing. This would make an appropriate second feature to *Raging Bull*. Also with: Jan Miner, Stanley Beck, Gary Morton, Rachel Novikoff, Alan Ormsby.

LENNY BRUCE PERFORMANCE FILM, THE/ LENNY BRUCE (1967) B&W/68m.   Your one chance to see the legendary, ground-breaking stand-up comic. Filmed in August of 1965 in San Francisco, the one place in the States where he could get bookings, it is an unedited recording of his next-to-last performance. Director John Magnuson keeps a nervous camera focused on Bruce at all times, never cutting away to show the nightclub audience (it would be interesting to know how many people came to see him). Bruce doesn't deliver an actual routine. He begins by reading the charges leveled against him in New York, where he was convicted on several counts of obscenity. The point he makes is that the policeman who wrote up a report on his nightclub act mentioned only all the "obscene" words and comments Bruce made; so now he puts everything he said into its proper context and, in doing so, gives snippets from the routines he used to do when he did a standard act. One wishes his material were a bit stronger since this is the only film of Bruce, but still it's extremely interesting to watch him work: we see that even then he hadn't lost his sense of humor—he seems amused by life's sad ironies whereby *he* is classified as a criminal—or his joy at hearing the audience respond favorably, and that he was a comedian who relied on his intelligence and natural wit rather than a memorized set of irrelevant jokes. This is Bruce uncensored, obsessed with the *politics of obscenity*. It should be required viewing for all the young comics whose routines he made possible by putting himself on the legal line, especially those who use dirty words to get easy laughs rather than to strike blows for free speech.

LEOPARD, THE (FRENCH-ITALIAN/1963) 161m—195m—205m.   Opulent historical epic by Luchino Visconti is set in Sicily in 1860–62, from the time Garibaldi united the Kingdom of Two Sicilies in the name of Victor Emmanuel (who shortly after was proclaimed king of a united Italy) till shortly after his unsuccessful attempt to annex Rome when Victor Emmanuel sent an army against him. The old, loyal, refined royalty is represented by the picture's central character, Don Fabrizio, the Prince of Salina—majestically played by Burt Lancaster. At first he refuses to acknowledge that civil war is taking place around him, even continuing his plans for a vacation with his wife (Rina Morelli), his dashing nephew (Alain Delon), and his seven children. But before his and our eyes the face of Italy changes too drastically for him to ignore. The noble aristocracy of the past is being phased out, being replaced by greedy military and political opportunists who switch loyalties at the drop of a hat and shrewd and vulgar young people who will not carry on the dignified tradition. During the last hour, which is set at a grandiose ball, the Prince is heartbroken watching silly young women gab and bounce like monkeys on a giant bed, or listening to a braggart officer explaining why he fired on Garibaldi (Italy's great hero just a little while before), and finally realizing that he has compromised his family's name by allowing Delon to marry the daughter (Claudia Cardinale is breathtaking) of a man (Paolo Stoppa) of lower rank. It is unclear what Lancaster's attitude toward Cardinale is—although he appears to approve of her and Delon because they at least have style. Picture has excellent acting, surprising wit, and glorious sets, costumes, and scenery—Visconti certainly has an eye for beauty. Nino Rota composed the lush score; Giuseppe Rotunno was cinematographer.

LEOPARD MAN, THE (1943) B&W/59m. Based on novel *Black Alibi* by Cornell Woolrich. People who watch this Val Lewton production as a "horror" film are usually disappointed, but if you think of it as a mystery with horror elements you'll be more satisfied. A black leopard that press agent Dennis O'Keefe has rented for a publicity stunt for entertainer Jean Brooks escapes in Pueblo, New Mexico, and several gruesome murders take place. Is the leopard or an insane man (in leopard skin and using claws) responsible for the killings? Some of the dialogue is a bit clunky, and the finale (in which villain James Bell is chased through a procession of hooded monks) seems hurried, but this may be Lewton's and director Jacques Tourneur's creepiest film. Certainly two sequences—a young girl is chased home by the leopard through the dark, deserted streets and winds up outside her locked door, unable to get inside; another young girl is trapped inside a cemetery after dark, and something on the tree limb above her is ready to pounce—are among the scariest in film history. Everyone in the film wears a mask out of fear of revealing his or her better side and seeming weak or afraid. Margo, for instance, comes on like a heartless gold digger, but she'd really like to marry her poor boyfriend. O'Keefe confesses that he was brought up to be tough and hide his feelings; only when he finally stops acting like a selfish heel does he win the girl. Villain Bell gives in to his evil side and literally dons a new skin, yet what initiates his demise is a good deed: he sends Brooks flowers. With the exception of *The Seventh Victim*, this is the most philosophical and exciting of Lewton's films. Characters contemplate man's place in the universe and come to the sad conclusion that they are trapped by fate (a major Lewton theme). Bell compares man's life to a ball stuck airborne in a fountain; O'Keefe's last words are "People are pushed around by things bigger than themselves, only they are too small to see things that way." Depressing film in many ways—nice young girls are murdered, locale is on former massacre sight (Lewton's world is a graveyard where living and dead intermingle), O'Keefe and Brooks find love in a graveyard at the exact spot where young lovers found heartbreak—but it's a rare Lewton film where good triumphs over evil. Essential Lewton. Also with: Isabel Jewell, Margaret Landry, Abner Biberman, Ben Bard.

LET THERE BE LIGHT (1946) B&W/58m. The Pentagon asked John Huston to make this documentary about WWII veterans going through treatment for neuro-psychotic problems they incurred because of war action. Detailing several men's stay at a medical facility, during which time most are cured through hypnosis and individual and group therapy, the film was meant to be shown to the public so families, loved ones, and prospective employees would have no fears about letting these men reenter society. But the Pentagon banned the film for many years, surely because— as its chief defender, James Agee, pointed out—anyone who saw it would know better than to enlist. As an anti-war document, this film still has power. But the treatment of the men seems ridiculously facile and hokey. Even the famous interviews with the disturbed vets are unconvincing, though nothing in the film (we've been told) was staged. I don't mean to seem callous, but the stuttering, crying, shell-shocked men remind me of how sixties draft-dodgers "acted" when they went to their physicals and put on phony acts to get psychological deferments. Good prints, with clear soundtracks, are hard to find.

LET'S SPEND THE NIGHT TOGETHER (1982) C/94m. How does one make a dull concert film of the Rolling Stones, the world's greatest touring band? Check this film out for pointers. Director Hal Ashby preened footage from three concerts from the Stones' 1981 U.S. tour, but you have to wonder if he accidentally jettisoned the good stuff and kept the reject material. Until the last couple of numbers, it captures none of the excitement of the events or the intensity of the Stones' performances. The camera seems incapable of achieving any intimacy with the performers—even Mick Jagger seems distant. You'll have better luck with *Gimme Shelter*.

LETTER, THE (1940) B&W/95m. The second film adaptation of Somerset Maugham's play was directed by William Wyler, scripted by Howard Koch, and starred Bette Davis as Leslie Crosbie, a role that had been played on stage by Gladys Cooper (in London) and Katharine Cornell (on Broadway) and in the 1929 movie by Jeanne Eagels. Set in Malaya, a hot, exotic locale for this drama of sexual anxiety/repression, the film begins with respected lady Davis coldly firing six bullets into a man. When Davis claims that the dead man was a casual acquaintance who had tried to molest her, her weakling husband, Herbert Marshall, a rubber-plantation manager, believes her immediately. But her lawyer, James Stephenson, is dubious. Sure enough, it turns out that Davis had written the dead man an incriminating letter that invited him to visit her in Marshall's absence and made it clear that the two had been lovers. Using Marshall's life's savings, Stephenson and Davis buy the letter from the dead man's Eurasian wife (Gale Sondergaard in her "Dragon Lady" guise) so that the prosecutor won't get his hands on it. Davis is acquitted, but she suffers guilt because of the crime she committed and for what she has done to Marshall (who finds out about the letter). And she still feverishly tries to mask her sexual longings—she constantly knits— which have resulted from being married to a bland man who idolizes and forgives her everything and from having lost a man so daring and exciting that he cast her aside for a Eurasian. A fine performance by Davis; no one is better at playing characters who act their way through life. Perhaps the most interesting character is Stephenson, who despises Davis yet commits a crime for her (purchasing and suppressing evidence) that could ruin his career; obviously, he finds himself intrigued by her wicked nature because that's what makes her special and excitingly different from his conventional wife (Frieda Inescort). In Maugham, people are hopelessly attracted to those they consider more exciting/ brave/wicked/mysterious than themselves. Wyler's direction is very moody; there are long passages in which dialogue is sparse or nonexistent and the erotic tension is built through Max Steiner's music, shadows, sounds (wind, wind chimes), the moon floating through the clouds, character movements and expressions. The worst aspect of the film is the embarrassingly invidious portrayal of the non-white characters, which almost justifies the colonialists' matter-of-fact racism. In 1947 Ann Sheridan starred in an uncredited remake, *The Unfaithful*. Also with: Bruce Lester, Cecil Kellaway, Doris Lloyd, Victor Sen Yung, Willie Fung, Tetsu Komai.

LETTER FROM AN UNKNOWN WOMAN
(1948) B&W/90m.   Howard Koch wrote Max Ophüls's finest American film, a dreamy romance set in 19th-century Vienna, providing the type of heroine Ophüls was famous for: a woman (Joan Fontaine) who allows her heart to dictate her life's course. As he prepares to flee Vienna to avoid a duel, cynical, self-loathing Louis Jourdan—a middle-aged musician who never fulfilled his youthful promise—receives a letter from Fontaine, who writes that she is dying. Because his life has been filled with adoring females who became forgettable lovers, he doesn't remember Fontaine, although she writes that her entire life has been dominated by her great love for him. When young, she had turned down a soldier's marriage proposal because she hoped to marry Jourdan; as an adult, she walked out on her husband because she still hoped to unite with Jourdan. Her life was measured by their few meetings. As a teenager she held the door open for her new neighbor, whom she *loved* (not had a crush on) at first sight. When a young working woman who returned to Vienna so she could watch him from afar, she had a brief, super-romantic interlude with him; he went away, breaking his promise to return—he forgot about her, she had his baby. As an adult, she met him again and went to his apartment. When she realized that he only pretended to remember her—he was just using the come-on line he used with all strange women—she left: sex was on his mind, love on hers. Perhaps the saddest aspect of Fontaine's life is that she insists that nothing in life is determined by chance, although every dramatic change (her moving to Linz as a teenager, Jourdan leaving her alone and pregnant, her son leaving for a trip and dying of typhoid) is the result of someone taking a trip on a train, Ophüls's fate symbol. Exquisite film has a lovely flow to it, the result of Ophüls's trademarked camera pans, the lush music, elegant settings, and romantic dialogue. A unique, beautifully realized picture. Based on Stefan Zweig's *Brief Einer Unbekannten*. Also with: Mady Christians, Marcel Journet.

LETTER TO THREE WIVES, A (1949) B&W/
103m.   Joseph Mankiewicz's sharp-edged yet ultimately sentimental look at three marriages in a small American town. Friends Jeanne Crain, Ann Sothern, and Linda Darnell are on their way to an all-day picnic with the town children when they receive a letter from their "friend" and secret rival (Celeste Holm narrates) that she has run off with one of their husbands. Unable to call home, Crain, Sothern, and Darnell think back over episodes in their lives that reveal why their respective husbands (Jeffrey Lynn, Kirk Douglas, Paul Douglas) may wish to leave them. What we find common to all three couples is that beneath the tough, confident exteriors, snappy one-liners, and intellectual or diffident pretenses are men and women who are quite brittle, unsure of their positions in society, with their friends, or with their spouses. These people always talk to each other (Mankiewicz loves dialogue), but, like the characters on the radio soaps they listen to, their words don't communicate real thoughts. Picture is stagy, almost like three one-act plays put together, but the literate, Oscar-winning script (adapted from John Klempner's *Cosmopolitan* novel) by Vera Caspary and Mankiewicz (who also won a Best Director Oscar) is perceptive, and, oddly, we care about the characters (they would be ideal as the initial characters in a TV soap). The acting is superb—even Darnell comes through admirably. Remade as a TV movie in 1985. Also with: Thelma Ritter, Connie Gilchrist, Barbara Lawrence, Hobart Cavanaugh.

LIANNA (1983) C/110m.   This unusually fine, thematically daring independent feature was written and directed by John Sayles. His script was taken around to Hollywood producers before he had written *Return of the Secaucus Seven*, his 1980 hit, but he was unable to get financing because of its controversial subject. Lianna (Linda Griffiths) is a 31-year-old wife and mother. Her husband (John De Vries) teaches film at a small college. He's arrogant and unfaithful and self-absorbed. Wanting some independence, Lianna takes a Child Psych course. She has an affair with the female professor (Jane Hallaren) and they fall in love. Never one for making decisions, now Lianna demands a divorce. She's kicked out of her home and has difficulty getting access to her confused children. Her loneliness increases when her lover leaves town (she was no better than Lianna's husband, who had flings with students) and her best friend (Jo Henderson) stays away from her. In part this film is about any woman who splits from her husband (and kids) and must, for the first time, face life alone (getting a job, finding an apartment, cooking for one, being hit on by her ex-husband's so-called friends). But of course what makes this film special is that the woman in question is a lesbian, which adds to her *outcast* status. I wish that Lianna's husband weren't such a jerk, because this might give the wrong impression that Lianna pursues a lesbian lover only because she's been hurt by a *man*—Lianna's attraction to women has nothing to do with how her husband treats her. What's most admirable is that once she realizes she is a lesbian she is happy with that knowledge—she suffers no shame and doesn't rush to a shrink in hopes of getting herself back to "normal." Griffiths gives a strong, sensitive, straightforward performance that makes you like Lianna, not pity her. It is her old friends—male and female—who don't know how to treat her that have the problem. Production is ragged in spots, but the dialogue is terrific (it's natural, witty, insightful, clever), the char-

acters are believable, and the sex scenes are handled with sensitivity. The scenes between Lianna and her kids and Lianna and other women are excitingly original. Perhaps my favorite scene, one that most male directors wouldn't think of including, has the smiling Lianna walking through the streets, greatly appreciating all the women she passes. Also with: Jesse Solomon, Maggie Renzi, Jessica Wright MacDonald, Sayles.

LIBELED LADY (1936) B&W/98m.
Classic screwball comedy with a powerhouse cast. Newspaper editor Spencer Tracy leaves fiancée Jean Harlow standing at the altar when he learns that he's being sued for $5 million by heiress Myrna Loy. The paper had fabricated a story that Loy had been stepping out with a married man. Desperate, Tracy hires his penniless lawyer friend William Powell, a real ladies' man, to marry Harlow temporarily and then get Loy to fall in love with him. When Powell and Loy are in a compromising position, Tracy and Harlow plan to arrive on the scene with cameras flashing. But, of course, Powell falls for Loy. The fast pacing, funny wisecracks by the dozen, and the sexual chemistry between the characters (Loy and Powell on the pier, for instance) make you overlook the confusing plot. Highlights include: the wedding scene, in which Harlow weakly kisses husband Powell and gives a heartfelt smooch to best man Tracy; in a scene Howard Hawks lifted for *Man's Favorite Sport?*, charlatan Powell must prove he wasn't lying when he told Loy and her father (Walter Connolly) that he is a fisherman—he almost drowns, but miraculously hooks a huge trout that has eluded everyone for years. This is a particularly strong showcase for Harlow, whose character is sometimes tough, sometimes sentimental, sometimes infuriated, sometimes a good sport, always sexy, always funny; I love her angry pout and how she huffs and puffs through a room with shoulders and legs working in unison. She and Powell announced their engagement during filming. Jack Conway directed. Also with: Charley Grapewin, Cora Witherspoon, George Chandler, E. E. Clive.

LIFE OF OHARU, THE/LIFE OF A WOMAN BY SAIKAKU, THE (JAPANESE/1952) B&W/146m.
Kenji Mizoguchi again shows sympathy toward prostitutes, who he believes are always driven to such a profession by men who exploited them and tossed them aside. Kinuyo Tanaka gives a lovely performance as a woman in 17th-century Japan whose entire life is characterized by ill-treatment from men. Deprived of her rank because of an affair with a mere page (Toshiro Mifune)—who is executed for his indiscretion—she gets back into her father's good graces by being selected to bear a lord's child. She gives birth to a son, but is sent away because the lord is becoming too fond of her and it's affecting his health. To get her father out of debt, she becomes a concubine. In the future, she has only a few moments of happiness—her kind husband is killed not long after their marriage—and much misery. Eventually she becomes a street whore and beggar woman whose only pleasure comes from occasionally seeing her

noble son pass by. It's a little hard watching one bad thing after another happen to Oharu, and it's confusing when Tanaka is supposed to be 50 and ugly but doesn't look much different than when she was 20 and beautiful. But the film is exquisitely shot, has a poetic quality, and presents a fascinating, shocking view of the sad role women have played in Japan. It should be noted that Oharu is often pointed to by feminist critics as the screen character who most epitomizes the victimization of women throughout history. Also with: Toshiko Yamane, Yuriko Hamada.

LIFEBOAT (1944) B&W/96m.
A flawed but enjoyable Alfred Hitchcock character-propaganda piece set in WWII. A passenger-carrying freighter is torpedoed by a German sub and eight survivors climb aboard a lifeboat. They also take aboard a German (Walter Slezak) when the sub is damaged by the explosion and sinks. The allies are a varied lot, rich and poor, liberal and conservative, sophisticated and simple; there's an English woman and a black American. Because they are so diverse, they bicker constantly and no decision they make is unanimous. The manipulative German (who doesn't let on he was the sub captain or that he speaks English or that he is hiding water from his thirsty fellow passengers) takes advantage of their indecisiveness and puts the boat on a course that will lead them into German arms. If they are to have a chance, they must rally together. Film was criticized upon release because the German is smarter than the others; but he must be a strong adversary because its propaganda point is that all people from Allied countries had better put aside their petty differences if the united Axis powers are to be defeated. The script, credited to John Steinbeck and Jo Swerling, is obvious and too didactic, but the premise itself is fascinating. The supercharged Tallulah Bankhead gives bite to her every line, Slezak—although eliminated too soon—is a great villain whose cunning is revealed a little at a time, and director Alfred Hitchcock does wonders with his challenging set, never moving his camera outside the lifeboat. Watch for Hitchcock's unusual appearance as the before-and-after subject in a weight-loss ad in William Bendix's newspaper. Other passengers: John Hodiak, Mary Anderson, Hume Cronyn, Henry Hull, Heather Angel, Canada Lee.

LIGHTNING SWORDS OF DEATH/SWORD OF VENGEANCE—PART III (JAPANESE/1973) C/89m.
With the title *Sword of Vengeance—Part III*, this edited entry from the popular, samurai-action series based on a comic book arrived in the U.S. with the first of the Kung Fu imports. Tomisaburo Wakayama plays Ogami, the former executioner of a mighty shogun and a skilled swordsman. Now a mercenary who has been disgraced, he travels a bloody path through medieval Japan, with his tiny, big-eyed son (Masahiro Tomikana) in a well-armed pushcart. He is the most honorable of men, yet he is willing to use his boy as a decoy, even killing the bad guy who tries to save the youngster from drowning (actually, the boy was

pretending). In this episode Ogami comes to the rescue of a woman sold into prostitution. To win her freedom from the cruel female who heads a powerful family, he agrees to kill an evil governor. He finds himself in the middle, fighting a one-man war against both sides. The boy watches the bloodshed without changing expressions. Film moves along like a turtle with a broken leg, but there are many interruptions for violent swordplay. The action scenes are extremely imaginative, well filmed and choreographed. You rarely know the result of Ogami's sword swings and thrusts until a couple of seconds later when his opponent falls to the ground. Highlight has him single-handedly shooting, blowing up, and slicing-and-dicing an entire army. More violent are his one-on-one confrontations—he kills one skilled swordsman by flying over him and pushing his sword directly down through the top of his skull. Film also could do without a rape sequence that has nothing to do with the plot and is a tasteless bit in which the would-be prostitute bites the tongue from the guy trying to force himself on her. The worst thing about the film is the dubbing: the dialogue is terrible and the voices don't fit the characters. Followed in 1980 by *Shogun Assassin*, also edited from the *Sword of Vengeance* series and containing some footage from this film. Also with: Goh Kato.

LILI (1953) C/81m. Charming one-song musical in which Leslie Caron is truly captivating as a French war orphan who hooks up with a circus and falls in love with moody puppeteer Mel Ferrer. Only the depressed, self-pitying Ferrer thinks of her as a child and treats her meanly—except when he talks to her through his various puppets during their popular act together. Sentimental story is skimpy and dated (in some ways it's like *La Strada*), the direction by Charles Walters is slow and stagy, and Caron's supporting players aren't particularly exciting, but watching Caron converse with the puppets and sing "Hi Lili, Hi Lo" or dance in the colorful fantasy sequence is a delight. In their youths, Judy Garland or Deanna Durbin might have coveted such a role. Also with: Zsa Zsa Gabor, Jean-Pierre Aumont, Amanda Blake, Kurt Kasznar.

LIMELIGHT (1952) B&W/145m. Setting is 1914 London. Charles Chaplin plays a washed-up, alcoholic old music-hall comedian named Calvero. He saves the life of a young woman (Claire Bloom) who attempted suicide. She is an aspiring ballerina, but has convinced herself that she can no longer walk. Chaplin inspires her to take a more optimistic view of life. Because of him, she regains mobility in her legs and goes on to be a ballet star. His career still flounders. She loves him passionately and wants to marry him, but he refuses to believe she could love an old man. He insists that she loves a young composer (Sydney Chaplin). For her sake, he goes away—and performs for pennies on the street. Bloom says of Calvero: "He doesn't want sympathy—he keeps saying that." What hurts this film is that Chaplin craves sympathy—Calvero (Chaplin's surrogate) is a martyr whose vast talents are ignored by producers and the public, and who doesn't realize (as Bloom and we do) what an altruistic, selfless human being he is. Nevertheless, there is much in the film that is quite special. Bloom is an appealing lead, gorgeous (what a smile), tender, talented— her great scene is when she tells her young suitor that she loves Calvero's "soul" and his sweetness. Chaplin does some impressive comedy stage routines; a priceless comedy sketch unites Chaplin and Buster Keaton. Also with: Nigel Bruce, Norman Lloyd, Marjorie Bennett, Snub Pollard, Edna Purviance (cameo), and, as the street kids in the opening, Geraldine Chaplin, Josephine Chaplin, Michael Chaplin.

LITTLE BIG MAN (1970) C/150m. Arthur Penn's Brechtian western, with a script by Calder Willingham, does justice to Thomas Berger's marvelous epic tale. Dustin Hoffman is 121-year-old Jack Crabbe, who tells a skeptical interviewer his recollections of his early life. According to Crabbe, he was raised by the Comanches after his family was massacred. He would spend much time living with the Indians and fighting against the cavalry. He'd also live with white men: he was adopted by a preacher and his horny wife (Faye Dunaway); worked with a crooked snake-oil salesman; became friends with Wild Bill Hickok (Jeff Corey); became a gunfighter, a drunk, a wild man, a married man, and an Indian scout for monstrous, conceited, insane General Custer (a bravura performance by Richard Mulligan). And he was the lone white survivor at the Little Big Horn. Penn uses three major "alienation" devices: raucous humor; ridiculous characters; and Crabbe's obviously hazy memory—it's clear that he is combining some characters, because when they turn up, too coincidentally, for a second time, there's been a complete personality transformation. While not everything Crabbe tells us is true, the gist of the story, about Custer and the Indians, *is* true. Through the horrifying scenes of the cavalry massacring Indians, Penn and Willingham obviously were trying to draw parallels to the systematic genocide being carried out by equally arrogant American soldiers on yellow-skinned villagers in Vietnam. This is a political film about the chauvinism and brutality of white American imperialists. Portrayal of Indians should be commended—it's so sympathetic and insightful that it allows for some humor about Indians (i.e., Chief Running Nose; the Indian who walks backward). Outstanding cinematography by Harry Stradling, Jr.; Dede Allen edited. Also with: Chief Dan George (as Jack's wise and funny "Grandfather"), Carol Andrusky, Amy Eccles, Thayer David, Alan Oppenheimer.

LITTLE CAESAR (1931) B&W/77m–80m. The first of the sound gangster films is somewhat dated, but still has power, thanks to Edward G. Robinson's performance as the vicious, swaggering braggart Enrico Bandello, who rises from two-bit hood to public enemy number one. His voice has more whine to it than in later roles—at times he sounds like a doll that you can make talk by pushing its belly. Rico has no redeeming qualities, no economic or social reasons for having chosen a life of crime. He just lusts for power, fame (gangsters make headlines), territory (an essential element in gangster films)—he gets the coveted North Side—and money (the spoils of gang warfare)—like Caesar. He begs a crime boss to let him join his gang, and later usurps his throne. Rico is ugly (though he makes a good gangster) and cold-blooded. The only person he has feelings for is his former partner, Douglas Fairbanks, Jr. Their relationship is central to one interpretation of the film: Rico is a latent homosexual whose suppressed sexual aggression manifests itself in shooting men. In the key scene he is furious with Fairbanks, but his eyes water and he can't pull the trigger. That he is impotent is confirmed by his henchman's callous remark at this moment, "You've gone *soft*." Best scenes in the movie come at the end, when Rico has lost his power. Director Mervyn LeRoy puts the unshaven, slovenly Robinson in tight close-up as he listens to fellow flophouse residents read about the cowardice he has shown in running away from police—he repeatedly grunts like an animal. For trivia fans: Rico is machine-gunned behind a sign for a movie musical, *Tipsy, Topsy, Turvy*. His famous last words: "Mother of mercy, is this the end of Rico?" From the novel by W. R. Burnett. Also with: Glenda Farrell, Sidney Blackmer, Thomas Jackson, Ralph Ince, Stanley Fields, George E. Stone, Lucille La Verne.

LITTLE COLONEL, THE (1935) B&W-C/80m.
It's the 1870s, and Shirley Temple tries to patch things up between her Kentucky colonel grandfather (Lionel Barrymore) and her mother (Evelyn Venable), whom he disavowed when she married a Yankee (John Lodge). Shirley wins Barrymore's heart because she's as stubborn and quick-tempered as he is, and cute to boot. So when she pleads with him to save her parents from thieves who are trying to steal a valuable land deed, how can he resist? Enjoyable Temple vehicle, with some nice interplay between her and Barrymore (their war game with toy soldiers is a highlight) and some nifty dancing by Temple and Bill "Bojangles" Robinson. My favorite moment has Temple singing to Barrymore and him imagining that his long-dead wife (or is it his daughter?) is accompanying her on the harp. Picture contains a color sequence—I seem to remember it being a dream that Temple's having, but the prints I've seen lately don't include it. Directed by David Butler. Also with: Hattie McDaniel, Sidney Blackmer.

LITTLE DARLINGS (1980) C/95m.
Young girls repeatedly sneaked by near-sighted ticket-takers and made this R-rated comedy a big commercial success. They were attracted by teenage stars Kristy McNichol and Tatum O'Neal and a situation that many already identified with. At summer camp McNichol—a street-wise "tough" girl—and O'Neal—a rich brat—bet on which can lose her virginity first. While neither girl is comfortable pursuing a sexual encounter, they do so in order to keep face with the other campers. In the film's worst scenes, O'Neal tries to seduce older counselor Armand Assante; meanwhile McNichol sets her sights on cute, mumbling punk Matt

Dillon from the boys' camp. Seeing each other get in over their heads, the girls become fast friends. Adults will appreciate the funny, sensitive performance by the versatile McNichol, but not much else. Most will think twice about sending their children to camp—although the film does contend that camps serve as character-builders and are those rare places in which competitiveness gives way to unity. Teen girls will appreciate the film because the ending is not a complete cop-out. Director Ronald F. Maxwell also got a first-rate performance from McNichol in the underrated *The Night the Lights Went Out in Georgia*. Also with: Maggie Blye, Krista Errickson, Cynthia Nixon.

LITTLE GIRL WHO LIVES DOWN THE LANE, THE (CANADIAN/1977) C/94m.
Uncomfortable but interesting film about a bright 13-year-old girl (Jodie Foster) who keeps her father's death a secret from the people in town so she can hold on to her house. Landlady Alexis Smith, her adult son, Martin Sheen (who is known for having a perverse attraction to young girls), and a local cop, Mort Shuman, come snooping around. When Smith spots the father's corpse in the basement, she panics and is killed when she knocks the trapdoor down on her head. Teenage Scott Jacoby, whose permanent limp gives him an "apartness" like Foster's, befriends Foster, chases off Sheen, and helps her bury the bodies. Preposterous storyline overwhelms its unique "child liberation" theme. But Foster's terrific performance still comes through. Smith also makes a strong impression as the type of mean adult we all despised when kids. Creepiest moment: the surprise appearance of Foster's "father." Satisfactory direction by Nicolas Gessner.

LITTLE MAN, WHAT NOW? (1934) B&W/91m.
Frank Borzage directed this fine, very unusual film that is set in Germany in the early thirties. Adapted from a novel by Hans Fallada, story tells of marriage between young bookkeeper Douglass Montgomery and lovely Margaret Sullavan, who are willing to endure hardships and poverty because of their great love for one another. Montgomery loses his job when his boss discovers he's already married and therefore won't marry his daughter. They move from a small town to Berlin, where Montgomery gets a job in a department store. They stay with his stepmother (Catharine Doucet) and her lover (Alan Hale)—only to discover she runs a brothel. (This sequence could have fit into a Pabst film.) They move again, into a loft. With Sullavan pregnant, they wonder if they'll get enough money to survive. Fine acting, authentic creation of pre-Hitler Germany, a strong argument for love. With Hollywood ignoring the Depression in the U.S., this was one of the few films of the era to depict the plight of the indigent lumpen proletariat. Also with: Mae Marsh, Alan Mowbray, Hedda Hopper.

LITTLE PRINCESS, THE (1939) C/91m.
Shirley Temple's first Technicolor film (*The Little Colonel* had *one* color sequence) was based on Frances Hodgson Burnett's popular Victorian novel. In 1899 Temple's rich father (Ian

Hunter) places her in an exclusive girls' boarding school when he goes off to fight in the Boer War. When it is reported that Hunter was killed and his property was confiscated, the cruel headmistress (Mary Nash) forces Temple to work in the kitchen for her keep. Temple refuses to believe her father is dead and sneaks away repeatedly to search the hospitals that house injured soldiers. This is generally considered one of Temple's best films, but while it is lavishly produced and features what was her last impressive performance as a *child* actor, the story is flimsy and predictable—and by 1939 it was getting tiresome watching Temple's little girls suffer. Temple's best scenes are with the cute little girl who plays a maid (Marcia Mae Jones), her song and dance with Arthur Treacher (who plays Nash's likable brother), her chance meeting with Queen Victoria (Beryl Mercer), and her tear-jerking reunion with her father. Picture contains a musical dream sequence to lighten the proceedings. Richard Greene and Anita Louise play the young lovers whose platonic affair tests the Victorian code. Filmed with Mary Pickford in 1917. Directed by Walter Lang. Also with: Cesar Romero, Sybil Jason, Miles Mander, E. E. Clive.

LITTLE SHOP OF HORRORS, THE (1960) B&W/70m.
Roger Corman's genuinely funny cult classic, made in just two days, is set in a Skid Row plant shop. Schlemiel Seymour Krelboin (Jonathan Haze) is an unappreciated assistant to penny-pinching florist Gravis Mushnick (Mel Welles). He invents a new plant by combining a butterwort and a Venus's-flytrap and names it Audrey, Jr., after his dimwitted girlfriend (Jackie Joseph), Mushnick's Jewish-princess daughter. Only he knows that the plant talks and that it constantly demands human blood. It grows to enormous proportions when given blood and becomes the talk of LA. Mushnick even gives Seymour a raise. But Audrey, Jr., soon wants more than blood—it wants human flesh too! Low-budget gem is a spoof of every mad-scientist picture in which blood is needed to keep some experimental creature alive, and of every fifties sci-fi film in which there is a giant mutation, and of numerous horror films. It's also a takeoff on Jerry Lewis comedies, with Seymour as the man-child with an IQ of seven, a good heart, a lousy personality, and work habits that drive his boss crazy; fifties television comedies in which everyone faces the camera (I truly think a laugh track would have made the picture funnier); and *Dragnet* (the terse, unemotional dialogue between Smith and Fink, the two detectives investigating missing persons, is hilarious). Picture is also a satire: the use of Jewish stereotypes will offend few because they're too ridiculous to be taken seriously; the plant, which grows when fed (Seymour gets a raise) and shrinks when hungry (Seymour gets fired), can be seen as a metaphor for the vicissitudes of fame. And, significantly, it works on its own terms as good, absurd comedy. The cast is marvelous—they might pass as a Yiddish repertory company which has been working with the script for years instead of doing it while it was being written. Particularly memorable are Welles as the petulant florist, Corman regular Dick Miller as a low-keyed flower-eater (to counter the man-eating flower), Joseph ("I could eat a hearse"), and the little-known Jack Nicholson as the squeaky-voiced masochist who works himself to orgasm at the dentist's. The dentist scene (Seymour has killed and is impersonating the real dentist) and Seymour's visits with his hypochondriac mother (Myrtle Vail) are highlights. Best of all is despicable murderer Audrey, Jr., burping, spitting out what it can't digest, and repeatedly demanding, "Feeeed me!" Screenplay by Charles B. Griffith. Adapted into an Off-Broadway musical, the basis for Martin Scorsese's 1986 movie.

LITTLEST REBEL, THE (1935) B&W/70m.
Shirley Temple is in peak form as a charming little Southern girl whose father (John Boles) goes off to fight in the Civil War, leaving her behind with her mother (Karen Morley) and "Uncle Billy" (Bill "Bojangles" Robinson). Boles comes home when Morley is dying, although he knows that a Yankee colonel (Jack Holt) is searching for him. Holt is so taken with Temple that he allows Boles to escape. However, Boles is captured anyway and he and Holt, who helped the enemy, are sentenced to be executed. In a delightful scene Temple asks President Lincoln (Frank McGlynn, Sr., in a fine bit) for a reprieve. An enjoyable film, with the very self-assured, likable Temple displaying amazing acting and dancing talents. Her cheerful tap routines with Robinson are classics. The girl's love and respect for her black "uncle" are touching, but if Boles and Morley weren't so nice, it would be hard to accept that their slaves seem so happy. Even so, the writers are pushing it when they have Billy comment on Lincoln's emancipation of the slaves with the ridiculously naïve: "I don't know what that means myself." Directed by David Butler. Also with: Willie Best.

LIVE AND LET DIE (BRITISH/1973) C/121m.
Roger Moore made an unimpressive debut as James Bond in Tom Mankiewicz's unimaginative adaptation of Ian Fleming's second novel. Set in New York, New Orleans, and a Caribbean island (filming took place in Jamaica), the forgettable story has Bond taking on a Harlem-based black gang who are heavily into heroin trafficking. The leader is the evil Kananga (Yaphet Kotto), whose top henchman is Tee Hee (Julius W. Harris), yet another villain with a metal claw instead of a hand. Of more interest is one of the Bond series's most beautiful heroines, Jane Seymour's Solitaire. She reads Tarot cards for Kananga and fears that if she ever loses the ability to tell his future he will kill her. She becomes Bond's lover. The movie stumbles along most of the way. It's hard to remember Moore is playing Bond at times—in fact, if he and Seymour were black, the picture could pass as one of the black exploitation films of the day. There are few interesting action sequences—a motorboat chase is trite enough to begin with, but the filmmakers make it worse by throwing in some stupid Louisiana cops, including pot-bellied Sheriff Pepper (Clifton James). At least Kananga and Tee Hee die in spectacular fashion. Directed by Guy Hamilton. Wings performs the title song. Also with: Geoffrey

Holder, David Hedison, Gloria Hendry, Madeleine Smith, Bernard Lee, Lois Maxwell, Desmond Llewellyn.

LOCAL HERO (BRITISH/1983) C/111m.
Whimsical, enchanting comedy by Bill Forsyth. Young Houston exec Peter Riegert is dispatched by oil tycoon Burt Lancaster to Scotland. He is supposed to buy Ferness, a fishing village that will be converted into "the petrochemical capital of the world." He expects to have to sweet-talk the villagers into selling their property, but they're eager to do so—all but for a hermit (Fulton MacKay) who owns the beach. However, Riegert finds peace and happiness among the relaxed, friendly oddballs who inhabit this town; he is soon under the warm spell of the glorious, magical night sky, and thinks that it would be a crime to destroy such a paradise. As in Frank Capra's films, innocence is restored to corrupted, cynical city-dwellers through contact with small-town folk; money, power, and work suddenly seem unimportant. As the elderly female witnesses in Capra's *Mr. Deeds Goes to Town* would no doubt say, the Fernessians are all "pixilated." It is as much a joy for us as it is for Riegert to meet the villagers, especially Denis Lawson, who wears numerous hats—including innkeeper, philosophical bartender, unofficial mayor, accountant—yet always has time for a roll in the sack with his wife (Jennifer Black). Then there's the pretty marine biologist (Jenny Seagrove) with webbed toes—she may live in the sea. The characters are *never* predictable; that Riegert also soon acts out of character is indication of their ingratiating charm. Offbeat characters and moments will stay with you. I find it hard to believe that this town with these people doesn't exist. Produced by David Puttnam. Mark Knopfler contributed the score. Also with: Peter Capaldi (as Riegert's Scottish companion), Chris Rozyki, Gordon John Sinclair.

LODGER, THE (1944) B&W/84m.
A very effective remake of Alfred Hitchcock's silent film, also from the "Jack the Ripper" novel by Marie Belloc Lowndes. Laird Cregar gives a creepy yet mildly sympathetic performance as a demented man who is driven to kill actresses after one destroyed his beloved brother. While everyone in turn-of-the-century London is on edge because of a series of murders of women in Whitechapel, Cregar rents a room in the home of Sara Allgood and Cedric Hardwicke; he falls in love with their beautiful daughter, Merle Oberon, but knows he must kill her because she's in show business. Oberon trusts Cregar, but her parents become increasingly suspicious about his actions (destroying his black bag and stained coat; coming and going at odd hours; turning the pictures of actresses against the wall). Detective George Sanders tries to determine if Cregar is guilty, before it's too late. Film might have worked better if Cregar's guilt were kept secret from us until the very end—especially since we're never given 100% proof he's the one and only Ripper. But that's a small complaint. The acting is first-rate (Oberon's strong performance is particularly noteworthy); the script by Barré Lyndon has solid dialogue, fine bit parts, exciting scenes. Most impressive is the atmospheric direction by John Brahm, who does remarkable things with camera angles, *noir* lighting, fog, and crowded streets. Brahm, Lyndon, Cregar, and Sanders would combine their talents once more for 1945's even more stylized *Hangover Square*. Also with: Aubrey Mather, Queenie Leonard, Doris Lloyd, Billy Bevan, Skelton Knaggs, Edmund Breon.

LOLA (WEST GERMAN/1982) C/114m.
As in his *Berlin Alexanderplatz*, Rainer Werner Fassbinder tells the story of a moral man who tries to keep his scruples in an immoral postwar (this time WWII) Germany, where everyone but him is corrupt and a hypocrite. Von Bohn (Armin Mueller-Stahl) is the new Building Commissioner in a small town. He's an upstanding, decent guy—incorruptible. He falls in love with a pretty young woman (Barbara Sukowa), but one night he discovers that "Lola" does a Dietrich "Lola Lola" act at a sinful nightclub and is a whore on the side. Infuriated, he becomes determined to expose all the illegal activities of the town leaders, including those of the evil building contractor Schukert (Mario Adorf), who owns the club and Lola's contract (and is the father of her 10-year-old illegitimate child). Ironic, cynical comedy doesn't end when Von Bohn forgives Lola and they marry—he can't live without the woman he loves and she is touched to be loved for her inner self by such a fine man, but their uniting in marriage is not what brings them happiness. His happiness is achieved when he stops being an outsider and sells out, thus becoming part of the corrupt municipal hierarchy; her happiness is also the result of rising to social prominence, from Schukert's cheap whore to Schukert's high-priced mistress. This is one of Fassbinder's most heralded films, although Lola isn't as strong or fascinating as many of his other women. Most impressive are the visuals, as Fassbinder constantly bathes his characters in various colors for thematic purposes. Also with: Rosel Zech (who'd star in Fassbinder's *Veronika Voss*) as Schukert's wife, Mathias Fuchs, Helga Feddersen.

LOLA MONTÈS/SINS OF LOLA MONTÈS, THE (FRENCH-GERMAN/1955) C/90m—110m.
The master of the mobile camera, Max Ophüls introduces us to his real-life heroine (Martine Carol) with an incredible shot that begins high in the circus rafters and ends three flights below on the ground—a visual metaphor that reveals to what *depths* Lola has fallen since she was lover and mistress to many of Europe's most important men, from Franz Liszt (Will Quadflieg) to Louis I, King of Bavaria (Anton Walbrook). Now she's the main attraction in a seedy circus, accepting donations for the Society of Fallen Women while the ringmaster (Peter Ustinov) tells her story (seen in flashbacks). Although her story is scandalous, Ophüls loves her as much as his other heroines. Lola epitomizes Ophüls's intelligent, free-willed, free-spirited, brave woman. Her rebellious actions mock society's norms and make her an example for repressed women to follow. What she wants is what her heart wants, and it's not surprising that when we

come upon her she has loved so much that her heart is almost worn out. Love has the power to consume an individual and she suffers a great loss each time an affair comes to an end, as it must in Ophüls's preordained world. She refuses to protect herself from heartache because she believes in living and loving with intensity. Time is Lola's emotional domain. She is, in fact, a product of her past—her memories are bittersweet at best, but they remain an integral part of her (she remembers every affair). She says that her losses have taken their toll—"Now it's over. I'm empty." But Ophüls gives Lola a transfusion, her last triumph, when he has *every* man in the circus audience pay money to kiss her hand—notice her self-satisfied smile. Ophüls's last film is a rich, beautifully designed, scored, and photographed work. But there are lapses in the script and problems with some characters. Carol is exciting at rare moments, as in the scene when Lola seduces Liszt, but mostly she is bland and unable to project the inner beauty that men sense immediately in Lola. Film has a strong cult following. Photographed by Christian Matras, whose camera constantly moves to emphasize the shifts and uncertainties in Lola's life. From Cécil Saint-Laurent's novel *La Vie Extraordinaire de Lola Montès*. Also with: Ivan Desny (as James, Lola's husband), Oskar Werner.

LOLITA (BRITISH/1962)   B&W/152m.

Stanley Kubrick's ambitious black comedy about a high class of degenerates was initially blasted for being inferior to and taking liberties with Vladimir Nabokov's much loved novel, but it looks better with every passing year. Perhaps we've begun to accept Kubrick's sophisticated cinematic techniques (use of visuals, music) as a storytelling alternative to Nabokov's celebrated prose (i.e., use of language); we better appreciate the mannered comedy of Peter Sellers (this was *before* Kubrick's *Dr. Strangelove*, *What's New, Pussycat?*, and *The Pink Panther*); and we have now seen enough Eric Rohmer films—in which sophisticated "gentlemen" can fall madly in love with bland, beautiful teenagers simply because they have tantalizing, dimpled knees—to understand that 12-year-old Lolita (Sue Lyon) need do absolutely *nothing* sexually provocative (other than sit around in a skimpy bikini and heart-shaped glasses) for nymphette-lover Humbert Humbert (James Mason) to be in uncontrolled heat. Picture begins with book's ending: Humbert shoots Clare Quilty (Sellers) in a decadent Hollywood mansion that represents their complete moral decay. We flashback to learn the reasons for Humbert's dramatic action. In New Hampshire, Humbert had married his boring, plump landlady (a hilarious performance by Shelley Winters) so that he could be stepfather to Lolita, for whom he had unbridled passion. When Winters was run over (conveniently), Humbert whisked Lolita out of camp and took her on a lengthy trip, from one motel to the next. Humbert became possessive of Lolita and forbade his young lover to date once they settled down and she went to school. But Lolita was going out on the sly with the openly perverse Quilty, the director of the school play in which she had the lead. Eventually, Lolita ran off with Quilty, whom she considered a genius—to this naïve girl Humbert was normal. Of course, Humbert isn't normal at all—and much humor comes from his difficult attempts to appear normal/moral to the people he comes across (so they won't suspect him of improprieties with Lolita) only to discover that those who judge him are as wacko as he is. (Only Lolita's eventual husband is nice, innocent, one-faced, *normal*.) Picture is at times screamingly funny; the performances by Sellers (at his most manic) and Mason—talking smart yet acting like a five-year-old, displaying a sickly smile—are marvelous (although Mason doesn't fit the image one gets of Nabokov's Humbert Humbert). Pretty Sue Lyon, only 13 (publicity claimed she wasn't allowed to see the movie) but looking sexy and 17, gives a very self-assured, naughty (notice that *smile*, indicating she *knows what Humbert's up to*) Carroll Baker-like portrayal. Her "Yi Yi" bubble-gum theme song is one of the most sexually provocative pieces of music ever written. Also with: Marianne Stone, Diana Decker.

LONELINESS OF THE LONG DISTANCE RUNNER, THE/REBEL WITH A CAUSE (BRITISH/1962) B&W/104m.

Eighteen-year-old Colin Smith (Tom Courtenay's debut) is sent to Ruxton Towers, a Borstal reformatory. The pompous, paternalistic governor (Michael Redgrave) believes in physical activity for the young men and is impressed by Smith's skills as a long-distance runner. Hoping Smith can beat the boys from a local public school—which would be very prestigious for Ruxton Towers—the governor gives Smith special privileges, letting him train without supervision. During his long runs Smith thinks back to his recent past. It's another bleak view we get of British working-class society. Smith resented his shrewish mother (Avis Bunnage) frittering away his dead father's insurance money, then kicking him out until he could contribute some money himself. Smith and a friend committed a burglary. He was caught. Smith thinks back to his dreary home life, his moments of escape with his girlfriend, being beaten by a policeman. Smith is one of the many angry men of the British working-class cinema of the day. His rebellious act against the governor, who comes to represent all authority to him, is not meant to be satisfying to viewers. While it hurts the governor's pride and (temporarily) teaches him not to exploit the young inmates, it will probably ruin Smith's chances of a better life (he could have been a professional runner). I'd rather see him escape during the race than just quit with victory in sight. I think that Smith's reasons for his defiance should be clearer and have to do with his developing an understanding of society and authority. We have to understand better why he relates the governor to his past life. Compare the music used here for the running scenes with that in *Chariots of Fire*. Directed by Tony Richardson. Alan Sillitoe adapted his novella. Also with: James Bolam, Alec McCowen.

LONELY ARE THE BRAVE (1962) B&W/107m.

An easygoing modern-day cowboy (Kirk Douglas) gets tossed into jail following a fight in a bar and his punching a policeman. Faced with a one-year prison sentence, he breaks out. Retrieving his loyal horse, he heads into the mountains. Police using helicopters and sophisticated communications pursue him. But Douglas and the man conducting the chase (Walter Matthau) aren't mortal enemies. Indeed, Matthau comes to admire Douglas's resourcefulness. Offbeat, downbeat sleeper was adapted by Dalton Trumbo from Edward Abbey's novel *Brave Cowboy*. It's a dismal, cruel, modern world we see, where the very men who need freedom are the ones thrown into prison; where men (except for Douglas) have chips on their shoulders; where good women pay the price because their men can't conform to the restrictive times. Film has strong dialogue, excellent acting (especially by Douglas), believable characters. Douglas's vicious barroom fight with a mean, one-armed vet is a classic. Ending—the old-style cowboy on a horse is destroyed by the modern cowboy, a trucker—is painful. Solid direction by David Miller. Also with: Gena Rowlands, George Kennedy (as a brutal cop), Michael Kane, Carroll O'Connor, William Schallert.

LONG GOOD FRIDAY, THE (BRITISH/1980) C/114m.

The former bosses of organized crime in England (and America) have gone into legitimate businesses; their place in the crime world has been taken by the IRA, which is just as organized, money-hungry, and vicious as they once were. That's the contention of this thoroughly engrossing, thrilling, extremely violent British gangster film. Short, plump Bob Hoskins gives a simply marvelous, Oscar-caliber performance as a cockney Edward G. Robinson—a tough-talking, wisecracking former crime boss who calls his boys back together when some of his men get wiped out and there are attempts on his own life. He's an uneducated simpleton who makes you laugh with his cockeyed perceptions of the world, but he can also impress you with his prudent leadership and terrify you with his cold brutality. And he gets your sympathy when he loses his cool because he can't figure out who has it in for him and sees his insulated world crumbling around him. Shakespearean actress Helen Mirren matches Hoskins as his smart, sexy, classy mistress who tries to keep things under control despite her own escalating fears. Hoskins and the taller Mirren are a terrific screen couple. A most unusual entry to the gangster genre, with impressive, no-punches-pulled direction by John Mackenzie. Good use of locales; interesting characters; scary violence. Also with: Dave King, Bryan Marshall, Eddie Constantine, George Coulouris, Stephen Davies.

LONG GOODBYE, THE (1973) C/112m.

Scripted by Leigh Brackett, Robert Altman's offbeat version of Raymond Chandler's next-to-last Philip Marlowe novel is one of his finest films. Chandler's story is updated from the dark forties to modern, sun-drenched, washed-out, neon-lit LA with its all-night supermarkets and laundromats, physical-fitness nuts, medical quacks, nude sunbathers, and various movie types. What bothered Marlowe fans more than the updating was that their hero had suddenly become a Jew from the East (Elliott Gould). But the casting of Gould seems inspired. Film's about an old-fashioned character with old-fashioned views on loyalty and morality who can't find his niche in a seventies me-generation playground—and who could be more out of place than a New York Jew in Hollywood? Story has Gould giving his friend (former baseball player Jim Bouton) a ride into Mexico and getting in trouble with the police, who think Bouton killed his wife, and an emotional gangster (director Mark Rydell), who thinks Bouton ran off with mob money intended for him. Meanwhile Gould helps Bouton's neighbor (Nina Van Pallandt, Clifford Irving's mistress) track down her husband (Sterling Hayden), who she thinks may have killed Bouton's wife. Film, which has an improvisational feel, includes a great deal of comedy and at times seems frivolous, but the short bursts of violence (i.e., Rydell—somehow—breaks a Coke bottle across his girlfriend's face) keep things tense. Critics objected that Gould's Marlowe seems characterized by his passivity, his continuous joking while willing to endure insults and physical abuse without fighting back. For most of the film we don't know if he can shoot a gun or throw a punch—until he whips out a gun and blows a hole in the stomach of a friend who deceived him. We know from this one surprising but correct gesture—Brackett daringly rewrote the novel's ending—that he wasn't out of his league when being roughed up by the cops and thugs. He was capable of taking care of himself—he was just biding his time. We realize he is even tougher than Chandler's hero in the novel because he refuses to play the sap for anybody (Sam Spade's old axiom). Music by John Williams contains several versions of the title song. Vilmos Zsigmond's spellbinding night photography evokes such a spooky, surreal LA that it would take one of stout heart to venture there. Also with: Henry Gibson, David Arkin, Warren Berlinger, Jo Ann Brody, David Carradine.

LONG, LONG TRAILER, THE (1954) C/103m.

The existence of this film may be a pleasant surprise to *I Love Lucy* fanatics. Strangely neglected, it's a delightful comedy in which Lucille Ball and Desi Arnaz play newlyweds (Daisy and Nicky) who go on their honeymoon with their new car and new home, a long, long trailer that makes driving extremely difficult. Their mad, miserable adventures almost cause a break-up. Lucy's character is much more controlled/saner than in the TV series—Daisy and Nicky have fairly compatible temperaments—and she doesn't monopolize the comedy for a change; given equal screen time, Desi turns in a surprisingly adept comedic performance. Consistently funny film has quality sight gags (Desi turning on the trailer shower); inimitable Ball slapstick (flying out the trailer door into a mud puddle, trying to cook in the moving trailer). The hilarious highlight has the couple nervously driving up a steep, steep, steep incline with their too heavy load, trying to nonchalantly discuss a book Ball was reading—watch for Ball's horrific reaction once they drive over the top and the monstrous trailer hovers above them at the peak, ready to roll after them down the steep road. Humor is punctuated with sweet romantic moments. Some parts may remind you of *National Lampoon's Vacation*. Directed by Vincente Minnelli. Also with: Marjorie Main, Keenan Wynn.

LONG RIDERS, THE (1980) C/100m. Minor masterpiece by Walter Hill; it's probably his best film. At a time when gang pictures were in vogue, Hill went back to the most famous gang of all, the Cole Younger–Jesse James gang of the wild, wild West. In Hill's *The Warriors* the violence is stylized and cartoonish and the gang members are heroic; here the violence is bloody and realistic, and if these brutal thugs are to be considered heroes, it's only because the government men who chase them are even more despicable. Picture got attention for its unusual casting: David, Keith, and Robert Carradine play the Youngers; Stacy and James Keach (who were among four scriptwriters) play Frank and Jesse James; Dennis and Randy Quaid are the Miller brothers, also part of the gang; and Christopher and Nicholas Guest play the traitorous Ford brothers. It may have been a gimmick to begin with, but the casting lends surprising authenticity to the project—also, without exception, these actors turn in superb performances and give us unique insight (possibly completely wrong) into their famous personages. The action sequences are extremely brutal, but that's the way they should be; the re-creation of the rural old West is convincing; the dialogue (the best in any Hill film) is tough (even when women talk); the characters and relationships are believable—this is the film that *The Wild Bunch* should have been. An original that deserves more than a cult following. With an excellent country score by Ry Cooder. Pamela Reed has a memorable bit as prostitute Belle Starr, who comes on strongly to David Carradine's Cole Younger; and Fran Ryan has remarkable presence as Ma James. Also with: James Whitmore, Jr., Kevin Brophy, James Remar, Harry Carey, Jr., Savannah Smith, Kalen Keach.

LORD LOVE A DUCK (1966) B&W/104m. Strange, strange cult comedy was scripted and directed (his debut) by George Axelrod. As the words on its poster read: "This motion picture is against teenagers . . . their parents . . . beach movies . . . cars . . . schools and several hundred other things [including marriage, religion, family tradition, therapists, men, women]." In the decadent Southern California culture he presents, he is only *for* greed, opportunism, underhanded schemes, and—what made the film really controversial—sex, sex, sex. The picture falls apart, first when Axelrod turns serious in regard to Tuesday Weld's relationship to her "Stella Dallas" mother, Lola Albright, and later when he strips off his satirical façade and exhibits pure hatred. Perhaps, during filming, Axelrod got divorced or had his house burglarized or had a visit from the IRS. . . . Roddy McDowall (it should have been Anthony Perkins)

is Mollymauk, a high-school genius who believes he's actually an extinct bird in human form. He takes Lolita-like Barbara Ann Greene (Weld) under his "wing" and devises plans where she can get everything her greedy little heart desires, from 13 cashmere sweaters to marriage into a rich family to Hollywood stardom. He does it out of love. There are many imaginative, hilarious sequences, yet each makes the viewer uncomfortable. We laugh as Axelrod mocks the middle-aged men who fall under Weld's sexual spell (her father, her principal, the movie director), but we get the sense that Axelrod's just like them, leering at Weld and the other sexily attired young women in front of his cameras. The sexual content is daring, as if Axelrod were baiting the censors, but there is a smutty edge to it. Indeed, this film about vulgarity eventually becomes as vulgar as it is mean. Also with: Martin West, Ruth Gordon, Harvey Korman, Martin Gabel, Sarah Marshall, Lynn Carey, Max Showalter (Casey Adams), Joseph Mell.

LORDS OF FLATBUSH, THE (1974) C/88m. Unexceptional, uninvolving film about four leather-jacketed high-school buddies in the Flatbush section of Brooklyn in the mid-fifties. Film became a surprise commercial hit, certainly not because of the storyline, which is skimpy and trite. Probably its youth audience recognized the star quality of the unknown leads, Perry King, Henry Winkler, and Sylvester Stallone, who were all destined for stardom. (We're still waiting for the fourth star, Paul Mace, to make it.) Stallone is particularly good, playing a tough talker who's pushed into marriage by his pregnant girlfriend, Maria Smith. The picture's best scene has Stallone succumbing to his girlfriend's pressure to buy her an expensive engagement ring ("I love you. BUY ME THAT RING!!!"). Low budget hurts. The sound quality is bad, and the original "fifties" score by Joe Brooks is atrocious. Directed by Stephen F. Verona and Martin Davidson. Also with: Suzie Blakely (as the new girl in school whom King tries to seduce), Dolph Sweet.

LORNA (1964) B&W/78m. Russ Meyer potboiler, his first attempt to make a serious film with plot and theme. It recalls those independently made, sleazy, sex-filled fake social dramas of the thirties (i.e., *Child Bride*). Lorna (big-breasted Lorna Maitland) lives in a river shack with her husband, who's sweet but not a great lover. Alone most of the day, Lorna is bursting with sexual desires. While swimming nude in the river, she is observed by an escaped convict. He rapes her. Finding him to be a terrific lover, she invites him back to the shack for some more lovemaking. Her husband, fresh from a fight in which he defended Lorna's honor, returns home early. Meyer mixed Erskine Caldwell, John Steinbeck, and phony morality (there's even a prophet who says sinners must be punished) tale to pretty good effect. He impressively creates the sweaty, puritanical backwoods environment and establishes how a young woman could go crazy trying to repress her sexual impulses in such a "hot" environment. Lorna's character goes through much of what Hedy Lamarr does in *Ecstasy*; like Lamarr, she must be punished—according to a male filmmaker—for fulfilling her fantasies. Obviously, the film's worst aspect is that Lorna gets turned on by a rapist. There is only brief nudity. Also with: Mark Bradley, James Rocker, James Griffith, Doc Scott.

LOSERS, THE (1970) C/96m.
Link (William Smith), Duke (Adam Roarke), Dirty Denny (Houston Savage), Speed (Gene Cornelius), and Limpy (Paul Koslo) are Hell's Angels who are recruited by the CIA to rescue a presidential adviser (played by director Jack Starrett) from the Red Chinese in Cambodia. Now, there's a believable premise. Cult film is almost ruined by repulsive characters and Starrett's overuse of slow motion during action sequences. It's junk, but one of the few films made during the Vietnam War that dared to chastise American GIs for impregnating and then abandoning Vietnamese women and, even more significantly, suggest that the U.S. government had no concern for our soldiers in Southeast Asia. The depressing ending, in which only the arrogant, undeserving Starrett survives, literally *brought home* the picture's theme: our soldiers were being sacrificed for no good reason. Produced by Joe Soloman. Also with: Bernie Hamilton, John Garwood, Ana Korita.

LOST HORIZON (1937) B&W/108m—118m.
Originally 130 minutes, but archivists are still looking for lost footage. Shangri-La may be able to provide its inhabitants with eternal youth, but Frank Capra's classic has dated badly. The most exciting scenes are those before idealist Ronald Colman, his younger brother, John Howard, Thomas Mitchell, Edward Everett Horton, and Isabel Jewell reach the utopia in the Himalayas (they are escaping by plane during a Chinese revolt, they must climb snow-covered mountains) and when Colman, Howard, and Margo, a disgruntled inhabitant of Shangri-La, climb down. The time the characters spend in this land where people are healthy, exist in harmony, and live for 200 years is dull in comparison. Who wants to watch people vacation at a spa? Colman, with his voice at its most melodious, has a couple of interesting scenes with Sam Jaffe, Shangri-La's High Lama, who wants Colman to succeed him. And Colman and Jane Wyatt have an appealingly mature relationship. Don't miss the film's subtle anti-communist propaganda: the only person dissatisfied with this true utopia is Margo, who is a Russian. Robert Riskin adapted James Hilton's novel. Ross Hunter produced the horrible 1973 musical version. Also with: H. B. Warner.

LOST IN AMERICA (1985) C/91m.
In his third comedy as director-star, Albert Brooks again plays his familiar semi-obnoxious, semi-forgivable, self-absorbed young American. He's not as abrasive as we've seen him, but he becomes just as aggravated when his schemes for the easy life go awry and his world crumbles around him. And he still thinks himself clever enough to talk himself out of every difficulty—only to find out that no one goes along with what he says so convincingly. When he gets rooked on a job promotion and argues the point so vehemently that he's fired—you'll really relate to his argument with his boss (a great scene)—he gets his wife, Julie Haggerty, to quit her job. They sell their house, buy a Winnebago, and, with their life's savings in hand, leave LA for the open road, planning to emulate the freedom-seeking characters in *Easy Rider*. Only Haggerty immediately gambles away all their money in Las Vegas. (My favorite moment in the film is when Brooks looks for her in the casino while still wearing his robe.) For the broke, jobless, overqualified couple, America doesn't turn out to be the land of opportunity. This is not the masterpiece that Brooks is capable of, but it has several extremely funny scenes (particularly Brooks's one-on-one dialogues with people in authority positions) and again Brooks reveals his unique perception of American characters. One problem is that while Brooks eventually forgives Haggerty for her gambling stupidity, our opinion of her never becomes high again. The only other real problem is that the picture ends too quickly, before anything monumentally disillusioning happens to our couple that would cause their final decision to abandon *Easy Rider*. It's as if Brooks's money ran out before the big scene. Also with: television producer Garry Marshall (as the humorless Vegas casino operator whom Brooks tries to convince to return Haggerty's losses in order to get good publicity for the hotel).

LOST ONE, THE/DER VERLORENE
(GERMAN/1951) B&W/98m.
Not released in the U.S. until 1985. Peter Lorre is a doctor at a German refugee camp following WWII. The sudden appearance of a former acquaintance, played with true arrogance by Karl John, causes Lorre to recall sad events in 1943, when both men went by their real names. Then Lorre was a research doctor in Hamburg and John was his assistant. But John was actually working undercover for the Gestapo and seduced Lorre's fiancée (Renate Mannhardt) in order to see if she'd betray Lorre and reveal secret information about his immunization experimentation. Lorre became despondent when John boasted about revealing his fiancée's true nature. When she attempted reconciliation, he lost control and strangled her. Soon after, he discovered that he had the urge to strangle again—this time he killed a stranger (Lotte Rausch) on a train. Feeling tremendous guilt and unhappiness, he decided to commit suicide, but only after having killed John—the one killing he intended to do. But it would be years before he ran into John again. This very peculiar film takes a while to get started and the plot takes some unnecessary turns—at one point Lorre stumbles on the collaborators of a Hitler-assassination plot—but stick with it because it becomes very interesting. It's easy to draw parallels between Lorre's child murderer in *M* and his strangler here, as both are tormented men who kill because they are incapable of stopping themselves. But I see this Lorre character as a symbol of Germany's collective guilt during the postwar era, a time when its people couldn't forget or cope with the heinous crimes they had committed. German moviegoers in 1951 resented

Lorre's implication that their only way out was suicide, and picture flopped. Lorre is extremely impressive in his one directorial effort. Significantly, his own character has never been so calm—except at those few times when he becomes a strangler: those scenes are creepy indeed. Visually, he combines realism (the many shots of bombed-out Hamburg) and expressionism; you'll notice the strong influence of Lang and Pabst. The final shot of a speeding train about to crash into Lorre's back as he stands on the tracks in the foreground is unforgettable and like nothing I can think of in anyone else's films. Also with: Helmut Rudolph, Johanna Hofer, Eva-Ingeborg Scholz, Gisela Trowe (who has a fine bit as a prostitute who recognizes he has the distinct face of a strangler).

LOST PATROL, THE (1934) B&W/74m. Exciting John Ford adventure-character study about a British military regiment that gets lost in the Mesopotamian desert during WWI. As they suffer from heat and lack of water, they are picked off one at a time by Arabs. (In some ways it predates *Aguirre: The Wrath of God*.) We see how the various men react to their hopeless situation. Prototypical Ford film in that it vividly depicts men in relationship to a hostile environment and in conflict with one another as to how to combat their circumstances. These themes are most evident in his westerns. Additionally, it's very similar to *Stagecoach* in that it also intermingles dialogue scenes with sequences that rely strictly on visuals and music (Max Steiner won an Oscar) and recall the silent cinema. Strong characterizations, especially by Victor McLaglen as the sergeant and Boris Karloff as a skinny religious fanatic who goes insane in the intense heat. Shot in the desert near Yuma, Arizona. Script by Dudley Nichols and Garrett Fort was adapted from Philip MacDonald's story "Patrol." Also with: Wallace Ford, Reginald Denny, J. M. Kerrigan, Billy Bevan, Alan Hale, Francis Ford.

LOST WEEKEND, THE (1945) B&W/101m. Is there anybody who really enjoys movies about junkies or alcoholics trying to cure their addictions? I invariably feel less excitement than obligation to watch this early social drama and multi-Oscar winner (for Best Picture, Actor, and Screenplay) whenever it turns up on television. Still, I'm always surprised to find myself becoming engrossed by this story of an alcoholic failed-writer (Ray Milland) who goes on a several-day binge that almost costs him his loyal girlfriend (Jane Wyman) and his life. But I think my enjoyment is somewhat perverse: I am not so taken by those scenes in which the drunk Milland makes a fool of himself in public (although it's a neat touch when patrons at a club sing mockingly about how he stole a purse) or has hallucinations; instead I find amusement watching the sober Milland start squirming and sweating (as he does at the opera), thinking about a drink, planning how to get it, lying so he can be alone to pursue it, figuring out what to pawn for the money he'll need, walking the streets in search of a bar, lounge, liquor store—and usually finding obstacles (pawnshops are

closed on Yom Kippur) that prevent him from making a quick purchase. Surely director Billy Wilder and his co-writer, Charles Brackett, are exhibiting ironic wit when they show how much a man will suffer in order to suffer even more. Dialogue is tough and cynical, Milland (who usually played nice guys) is *mean* right from the beginning, film pulls few punches (until the final scene). Wilder makes strong use of New York streets and backgrounds, and blends harsh expressionistic visuals indoors with washed-out shots of the city to convey mood changes in Milland. Milland and Wyman give strong performances; interestingly, every time the make-up man makes Milland look like a bum (as in the last scene) he makes Wyman look like a cover girl. I'll bet some jokester theater-owner will twinbill this with *Arthur*. From the novel by Charles Jackson. Also with: Phillip Terry, Frank Faylen, Howard Da Silva, Doris Dowling, Clarence Muse, Lillian Fontaine.

LOUISIANA STORY (1948) B&W/77m. Robert Flaherty's last film, which he made on location in the Louisiana bayous, using non-professional actors. The main character is an Acadian boy (Joseph Boudreaux) who whiles away the hours fishing, exploring the woods, and playing with his cute pet raccoon. He finds new excitement when his father (Lionel Le Blanc) signs an agreement that allows a wildcat oil company to set up a derrick downstream. The film was financed by Standard Oil Company and this accounts for Flaherty's oddly romantic notion that the presence of the oil company will have no adverse effect on the environment. The boy and his father get along with the respectful oil men and miss them when they finally depart. Furthermore, when the company dismantles its derrick, the land is undamaged. Flaherty spends a lot of time filming the derrick in action, but the workers look so bored that these scenes are dull. Much better are lyrical scenes set in the swamps, backed by Virgil Thomson's strong score. The boy's tug-of-war with an alligator that pulls him into the water is a tense sequence, but it has no climax. Picture looks nice, but the storyline is too simple (we don't even know if the father makes money from the oil) and who today can take oil-company propaganda seriously? Photography by Richard Leacock.

LOVE AND ANARCHY (ITALIAN/1973) C/108m. The film that began the Lina Wertmuller craze in the U.S. In many of her films Wertmuller asserted that leftist political action (union organizing or more extreme acts like assassination or revolution) is often undermined by forces such as love, social convention, fear, honor, and naïveté: this film might better have been titled "Love *or* Politics," for love stops a politically conscious woman (Mariangela Melato) from allowing a history-changing, positive political act to take place. Giancarlo Giannini is a heavily freckled, shaggy-haired country bumpkin who arrives in Rome in 1932 with the intention of assassinating Mussolini. He stays in a brothel, pretending to be the cousin of anarchist Melato, the most popular whore. She helps him plot the killing.

Giannini falls in love with another prostitute (Lina Polito), but, while he uses her love to soothe his failing nerves, he doesn't use it as an excuse to end his commitment to kill Mussolini and most likely lose his life in the process. What's surprising is not that the apolitical Polito decides to prevent him from going through with his plan, but that the staunchly political Melato would go along with Polito. But perhaps it's not only because of her newfound love for Giannini that Melato doesn't wake him on the morning of the assassination. I think her motives also have to do with her learning that he is no anarchist after all, but only decided to kill Mussolini because an anarchist family friend had planned the act before government troops killed him. She finds it politically objectionable to exploit this naïve peasant whose action is based on instinct rather than politics. That he panics when police come into the brothel on routine business shows that Melato was correct in her decision to wait for a more suitable assassin. Oddly, the tone of film is highly comedic, with some scenes—the meal in the brothel, the presentation of the prostitutes—filmed in Felliniesque style (Wertmuller was Fellini's assistant director before going off on her own). But the brutally shocking ending makes one think back to the earlier scenes with a different perspective. Not completely successful, but a good film to argue about. Also with: Eros Pagni (a funny characterization as a fascist who resembles and works for Mussolini), Pina Cel.

LOVE AND DEATH (1975) C/82m. Lightweight Woody Allen film has share of clever sight gags (participants gather for a Village Idiots' Convention) and sharp verbal wit (I love Allen's lively critique of a 10-second V.D. play), but suffers because the main characters are too foolish and erratically drawn, changing each time Allen wishes to shift comic gears—in fact, Allen's character switches from typical Allen to Bob Hope to Groucho Marx. One also has to question if 19th-century Russia is proper context for Allen's patented, decidedly modern-day, anxiety-filled philosophy. Obviously, Allen inserts contemporary characters—at least they break into contemporary dialogue (about which restaurant to eat in, etc.)—in order to feel more at home. Spoof of Tolstoy, as well as Ingmar Bergman, has Allen as a cowardly soldier who inadvertently becomes a war hero and returns home to marry his cousin, Diane Keaton, who gradually falls in love with him. She convinces him to join her in a plot to assassinate Napoleon; he lands in prison and faces execution when he's wrongly accused of killing Napoleon's double. The Keaton-Allen super-intellectual discussions ("subjectivity is objective") are highlights, but Keaton and others in fine cast aren't really allowed to be funny in themselves—their humor comes almost exclusively from saying Allen's funny lines. Music by Prokofiev adds to fake epic flavor. Also with: Harold Gould, Jessica Harper, Alfred Lutter, Olga Georges-Picot, Zvee Scooler.

LOVE AT FIRST BITE (1979) C/96m. Wacked-out spoof of Dracula myth, with the Count (George Hamilton), who has been booted out of his castle in Transylvania, coming to New York and falling in "lob" with an oddball fashion model (Susan St. James) and trying to smooth-talk her into being his for eternity. Jokes and sight gags often fall flat or are obvious, but there are so many, there's an occasional bulls-eye. Actors are better than Bob Kaufman's script. St. James, Dick Benjamin as a modern-day Van Helsing, and Arte Johnson as the insect-eating Renfield are all very amusing, but real revelation is George Hamilton, all gussied up in white makeup and complaining that he hasn't had any fun "going around dressed like a headwaiter for the last 700 years." As he parodied his suave and slick image as well as Dracula, his comic talents appeared out of nowhere in this film. Highlights include Hamilton and St. James doing wild dancing to disco hit "I Love the Night" (a smash for Alicia Bridges), and Hamilton and Benjamin unsuccessfully trying to hypnotize each other in a restaurant, while the bored St. James goes home. Not in the league of *The Fearless Vampire Killers*, but inventive and moderately successful in its intentions. In one serious scene, in which he lies next to St. James, Count seems saddened by peculiar nature of his life. I wish there had been more along this line, because it delves into unexplored areas in Dracula's psyche. A big money-maker. Directed by Stan Dragoti. Also with: Dick Shawn, Ronnie Schell, Sherman Hemsley, Isabel Sanford.

LOVE ON THE RUN (FRENCH/1979) C/93m. The fifth and final segment of François Truffaut's "Antoine Doinel" series, starring Jean-Pierre Léaud, who was just a young boy in 1959 when they made *The 400 Blows*. In this episode, novelist Léaud, now over 30 and father of a young boy, has an amicable divorce from Christine (Claude Jade), the object of his desire in *Stolen Kisses* (1968) and his wife in *Bed and Board* (1970). They love each other, but no longer get along. Characteristically, he falls in love with a lookalike, Sabine (the name of Oskar Werner and Jeanne Moreau's daughter in *Jules and Jim*)—sprightly played by Dorothee. He also talks over old times with Colette (Marie-France Pisier, who served as co-writer), who was his first girlfriend in the "Antoine et Colette" episode of *Love at Twenty* (1962). Pisier, now a lawyer, is having an affair with Sabine's brother; but he decides to break off from her, just when his sister gets fed up with Léaud. Truffaut juxtaposes contemporary scenes with footage from earlier Doinel films—he also has the women in Antoine's past life affectionately discuss his peculiarities (i.e., how he was so touched when Christine's best girlfriend put a protective newspaper cover on his book that he fell into bed with her). The film becomes a profile of a boy who, with little love in his rough childhood, became an incurable romantic as a man—which, of course, is Truffaut's own story. While there are some nice moments, film doesn't do one of cinema's great characters justice. Only minor Truffaut. Also with: Rosy Varte, Julien Bertheau, Daniel Mesquich.

LOVE PARADE, THE (1929) B&W/110m. Ernst Lubitsch's first sound film revolutionized the screen musical because he integrated numbers into the storyline and used non-synchronized sound (the music was dubbed later) so he could move his camera without fear of losing some lyrics and picking up stage noise. Upbeat songs by Victor Schertzinger and Clifford Grey are perfectly suited for the charming script by Ernest Vajda and Guy Bolton, and the stars, the bubbling Maurice Chevalier and the glowing Jeanette MacDonald, making her screen debut. Like many Lubitsch bedroom comedies, this classic deals with a husband and wife who have troubles because neither is satisfied with their roles in the marriage. MacDonald plays the virgin queen of Sylvania. She and ladies' man Chevalier fall in love and marry. But he's bored being the powerless prince consort while she runs the country, and he threatens to walk out. How they find happiness—they reverse roles and start a "normal" husband-wife relationship—won't please a modern audience, especially since it has the woman accepting a meaningless existence for the sake of a man, but it's all so silly that no one could be seriously offended. Film is a reminder that MacDonald was not just a singer, but an okay comedienne and also an extremely sexy actress when given a chance: Lubitsch has her appear in a slinky negligee, mention her erotic dream, take a bath (while obviously nude), lift her dress to show her legs to her cabinet, become turned on when she reads about Chevalier's scandalous sexual escapades in Paris. Picture has many offbeat touches, funny dialogue, and good musical support from acrobatic, elastic-legged Lupino Lane (as Chevalier's servant) and Lillian Roth (as MacDonald's maid). MacDonald and Chevalier would reteam in Lubitsch's *One Hour with You* and *The Merry Widow*. From the play *The Prince Consort* by Leon Xanrof and Jules Chancel. Also with: Edgar Norton, Lionel Belmore, Eugene Pallette, Virginia Bruce, Ben Turpin, Jean Harlow (an extra).

LOVE STORY (1970) C/99m. Erich Segal's screenplay is the basis for both the film and his best-selling book. He heard the boy-meets-and-marries-girl-who-then-becomes-terminally-ill story from a friend and "wrote" it out while jogging. Several studios turned down the script, claiming it was too superficial, too syrupy, too pure. Paramount realized those weren't necessarily negative characteristics and bought the property—and made a fortune. More stylish but less substantial than the old-style weepies it emulated, Arthur Hiller's film strives for honesty and simplicity at the expense of theme or characterization. Depth was not needed to please the book's lovers: the opening line, which tells us that the girl (Ali McGraw) has died, is enough to start the tissue parade. The entire story—a flashback—is pointed toward her dying (from some unmentionable disease), so it's impossible to share any of the *trivial* experiences that Jennifer and Oliver (Ryan O'Neal before he could act) have along the way. There is only a slight pause for the crucial and well-rehearsed "Love means never having to say you're sorry," a catch phrase that leaves much to be desired. As the ill-fated couple, McGraw and O'Neal seem intent only on building their own images—there is

no sincerity evident in their performances. How their characters fall in love, or why they love each other so much, is unclear. They are too dull, arrogant, and full of false humility to be anything but competitors. They come across as beautiful people who could have won each other on *The Dating Game*. What is most contemptible about the film is the implication of martyrdom for Oliver and Jennifer. Viewers are actually seduced into wanting to live their dying experience. The sole controversy: who is suffering more, Oliver or Jennifer?; who is taking it better?; how would I act?; etc. The number of tears viewers shed shouldn't be mistaken for a measure of approval. Also with: Ray Milland, John Marley, Katherine Balfour.

LOVE STREAMS (1984) C/144m. John Cassavetes directed, co-wrote with Ted Allan (from Allan's play), and starred in this uneven but well-acted, compelling drama. As usual, Cassavetes has made a film about emotional cripples going through crises, but this time they don't try to talk away their problems—that's just the way they are and, sadly, will remain. Usually drunk with bloodshot eyes, Cassavetes is a successful author of sex novels about women. He thinks that all women are mysterious—all have a *secret*—and can't exist without them or sleep alone, yet the only woman he truly loves is his sister (Gena Rowlands). Rowlands has spent much of her time in institutions. When her daughter chooses to live with her former husband (Seymour Cassell) instead of her, Rowlands goes completely off her rocker. On the day Cassavetes is visited by his son, whom he hadn't seen since his birth eight years before, Rowlands comes to stay with him. If they weren't brother and sister, they could provide each other with the *love* missing in each other's lives—Rowlands's husband and daughter hadn't been able to reciprocate her great love; Cassavetes was never able to give sincere love to women. But they can only support each other, not provide cures. The picture's conclusion is unsatisfying but at the same time believable because Cassavetes refuses to resolve any of his troubled characters' problems. Film has powerful moments and is occasionally insightful without being as pretentious as some earlier Cassavetes films—but why must he always have his characters thoroughly embarrass themselves? Rowlands gives a great performance, somehow tempering her character's insanity with *reason*; after all, she's a nice person who wants only happiness for everyone. Her purchase of a dog is a highlight. Also with: Diahnne Abbott.

LOVED ONE, THE (1965) B&W/116m. Not nearly as funny as Evelyn Waugh's 1948 satirical novel, but acceptable on its own terms. Robert Morse is the British "poet" who comes to Hollywood, only to have to make funeral arrangements for his uncle (John Gielgud), who commits suicide. He discovers that death is a big business and that there are a lot of nutty people in the funeral game. He takes a romantic interest in a naïve cemetery worker (Anjanette Comer) who believes in the beauty of death and thinks that embalming, funeral services, and burials are sacred acts. All the others are after big bucks. Direction by Tony Richardson is a bit plodding, but he manages to get more than star turns out of his large cast. As weird as they all come across in their scenes, we believe that these characters have strange lives off camera as well. One of the best scenes has Morse visiting Comer's unsteady house-on-stilts, which is built in a slide area. I'm less taken with Comer's visit with embalmer Joyboy's (Rod Steiger) grossly fat mother, who's pigging out on food and salivating over food commercials on television. But there's a scene to offend everyone. Terry Southern doctored Christopher Isherwood's script (both received screen credit), Haskell Wexler did the cinematography. Cast includes: Jonathan Winters, Roddy McDowall, Robert Morley, Dana Andrews, Milton Berle, James Coburn, Tab Hunter, Margaret Leighton, Liberace, Barbara Nichols, Lionel Stander, Ayliene Gibbons.

LOVERS, THE (FRENCH/1958) B&W/90m.
Louis Malle directed this once scandalous romance, adapting the script with Louise de Vilmorin from Vivant Denon's 18th-century story "Point de Lendemain." It was banned in several U.S. towns and had footage excised in others; obscenity charges were leveled at several theater owners, leading to precedent-setting court decisions that cleared the way for more sexual freedom in the cinema. In the role that gained her international fame, Jeanne Moreau plays the bored and neglected wife of a rich publisher (Alain Cuny). Although she loves their young daughter, she spends increasing time away from their country estate, visiting her unmarried best friend (Judith Magre) in Paris. She contemplates having an affair with a rich gentleman (Jose-Louis Villalonga) whom she often watches play polo. Her jealous husband invites Magre and Villalonga to have dinner and stay overnight in the country. When Moreau's car breaks down, she accepts a ride with a young bourgeois-hating archeologist (Jean-Marc Bory), who also ends up being an overnight guest. That night Moreau is fed up with both her husband and Villalonga; full of sexual longings (she recalls Hedy Lamarr in *Ecstasy*), she takes a walk outside. There she runs into Bory. They spend the night making passionate love; in the morning they decide to run away together. Malle deserves credit for not having a cop-out ending (i.e., Moreau deciding to return home for her daughter's sake) and for not cutting away, as all filmmakers did before this film, when the lovemaking begins. In fact, it's almost as if cameraman Henri Dacae (who was using a widescreen process called Dyaliscope) slept in the same room with the lovers and woke up, camera ready, each time they were ready to go at it again. Bory is, yes, *boring*—you forget what he looks like a minute after the film ends; but Moreau is something special: when she lets down and brushes her hair and walks outside in her white nightgown, she makes the quickest transition from dowdy to ethereal in cinema history. We are happy for her when she ends years of sexual frustration by having mutually enjoyable sex, in the boat, in the bed, in the bathtub. We realize that her sexual liberation coincides with her escape from all bourgeois shackles—this would

also be the controversial theme of Bertolucci's groundbreaking *sexual* film *Last Tango in Paris*, released 15 years later. In addition to having an ahead-of-its-time "liberation" theme, the picture can be seen as Malle's first witty (there is a surprising amount of humor, considering its reputation) satire about the crumbling French bourgeoisie.

LOVIN' MOLLY (1974) C/98m.
Sidney Lumet directed this little film about the lifelong love two Texas buddies (Anthony Perkins, Beau Bridges) have for Molly (Blythe Danner), and she for them (particularly Perkins), that doesn't diminish even when she marries. Film is set in 1925, 1945, and 1964, and is narrated in turn by Perkins, Danner, and Bridges. There are some fine, touching moments (Danner and Perkins wrapped tightly in each other's arms, Bridges with the ill Perkins), but the fact that so many feelings go unstated makes it difficult for us to know how we're supposed to respond to the characters. For instance, we can see that Danner and Perkins love each other, but can't judge if it would be best that they marry or just periodically use each other for emotional support. Film reputedly has a cult following, but I have never come across a true fan. However, if you're a Blythe Danner fan and consequently regret that she didn't make it as a ticket-selling leading lady, this is the picture that proves she had the beauty and talent to have been a star if she'd been promoted properly. From Larry McMurtry's novel *Leaving Cheyenne*. Also with: Susan Sarandon (as Perkins's wife), Edward Binns, Conrad Fowkes.

LUCIA (CUBAN/1969) B&W/160m.
Humberto Solas directed this monumental three-part epic about three women, each named Lucia, who live during three pivotal times of modern Cuban history. The episodes, which are filmed in wildly divergent styles, show how the political consciousness of these politically naïve women is raised as a result of jolting personal experiences; they come to realize that the same betrayers, opportunists, and oppressors (ranging from friends, lovers, and husbands to imperialists and uncommitted revolutionaries) who damage them as individuals are also undermining the progressive political movement in Cuba. The first episode is set in 1895, during the Cuban War of Independence against Spain. Lucia is an aristocratic Cuban spinster (Raquel Revuelta) who becomes the lover of a married Spanish stranger (Eduardo Moore). It turns out that he is only using her to find the whereabouts of a mountain plantation where her brother and other revolutionaries are hiding. Almost operatic in style, this is the most visually impressive of the three episodes. It contains two astonishing sequences: several nuns being raped on a battlefield; naked Mambi soldiers on horseback chasing and killing terrified Spanish soldiers. The second episode is set in 1933, when Cuba was ruled by Gerardo Machado. Lucia (Eslindo Nuñez) is a young bourgeois woman who runs off with a revolutionary, Aldo (Ramón Brito). She takes a job in a cigar factory and joins in a women's protest against Machado. A general strike causes Machado's downfall, but

the new regime turns out to be equally corrupt and oppressive. While their opportunistic friends become part of the new order, Aldo again takes to the streets. Of the three episodes, this is the most politically provocative. And this Lucia is by far the most appealing. The final episode is set in the early sixties, when Castro's regime is attempting to set up a revolutionary society where men and women work and everyone is literate. Lucia (Adela Legra) is a new bride whose jealous husband, Tomás (Adolfo Legra), literally boards her up in their house. She enjoys her long hours of sex with him each day, but is angry because he won't let her work in the fields or learn to read. The local Party Committee sends a handsome teacher to live with them and teach Lucia to read. This infuriates Tomás. Lucia leaves Tomás and goes back to work. But since they are both miserable, they will have to come to a compromise. Silly, comedic episode is like a sex battle in a Lina Wertmuller film. Issues brought up are by today's standards very simplistic—but because it was made in Cuba, a revolutionary society, the episode is of interest. Cinematography by Jorge Herrera.

LUST IN THE DUST (1985) C/90m.
Considering that this western parody was directed by Paul Bartel (*Eating Raoul*) and has a truly bizarre cast, headed by Divine, Tab Hunter, and Lainie Kazan, it should be much wilder than it is. The lifeless script by Philip John Taylor shouldn't have adhered so much to the westerns it spoofed—even the idea of having half a treasure map on the behind of each of the leading ladies (Divine, Kazan) has been used before. (Where's Brigitte Bardot this time around?) Picture should have shot down the conventions of the genre and given us something entirely new. Title was the joke name for *Duel in the Sun*. Hunter co-produced. Also with: Henry Silva, Cesar Romero, Geoffrey Lewis, Woody Strode.

LUSTY MEN, THE (1952) B&W/113m.
If you never liked films about the race-car circuit, you probably won't think much of Nicholas Ray's vision of the rodeo circuit because it, too, is populated by men who want to prove they are MEN and wives who silently suffer while their men are corrupted by money, alcohol, and wild women. Onetime rodeo cowboy Robert Mitchum enlists talented cowhand Arthur Kennedy into the circuit for a share of his winnings. This upsets Kennedy's wife, Susan Hayward, who had been happy with her stable life and home. Kennedy promises her he'll quit once he gets enough money to buy a spread. A first-year sensation, he becomes so greedy that he doesn't want to settle down. When Hayward rebels, Mitchum sees his chance to move in on her. Predictable storyline is bolstered by strong cast, good rodeo atmosphere, an excellent script, and strong direction. As in many Ray films, tension continually builds without a release, until the time is right for a violent outburst. Also with: Arthur Hunnicutt, Frank Faylen.

M (GERMAN/1931) B&W/92m—99m—114m.
Exciting filmmaking! Fritz Lang based his first sound film on the real-life Düsseldorf murderer. In his debut Peter Lorre plays a sweaty, plump murderer of little girls. He is possibly the cinema's first sexual deviate. When the police manhunt disrupts the workings of the city's underworld, the criminal element decides to go after the mystery killer. Lang's films are about paranoia, where a single figure walks through a city in which everybody seems to be his enemy—in this case everyone *is* after Lorre. Lang switches back and forth between the equally organized manhunts of the police and criminals. The police find out the identity of the killer; but the criminals, by stationing beggars at every corner (shades of *The Threepenny Opera*), are able to capture him (saving a potential victim in the process). Film concludes with harrowing sequence in which Lorre faces the criminals' kangaroo court; because of the nature of his crimes, he is lowest of the low (just as today, convicted child-molesters are held in low esteem by other prisoners). But we are still moved by Lorre's pathetic, screeching plea for mercy, claiming, "I can't help myself!" We think back to Lorre standing in front of a store window when his eyes grew large and his insane brain took over as the reflection of a little girl appeared—and we believe him and feel some pity. Lorre's delivery of the guilt-ridden speech is one of the truly great performances in cinema history. Picture is tasteful, considering its subject matter; yet it is uncompromising. Suspense is heightened by the imaginative use of props (a balloon floating away in the sky and a rolling ball indicate children have been killed) and Lorre's eerie whistling of tune from Grieg's *Peer Gynt*. Lang's wife, Thea Von Harbou, was one of pictures four writers; filmed in expressionistic style by Fritz Arno Wagner. A masterpiece. Remade by Joseph Losey in 1951. Also with: Otto Wernicke, Gustav Gründgens, Ellen Widmann, Inge Landgut.

MACBETH (1948) B&W/86m—107m.
Dark, stylized adaptation of Shakespeare by Orson Welles; filmed on "B" western sets at Republic Studios. With its surrealistic and expressionistic flourishes it can easily be seen as a visualization of Macbeth's worst nightmare; that Welles alters Shakespeare's concept of the three witches and has them prophesy Macbeth's initial success and ultimate downfall confirms that Welles wanted his Macbeth to be as out of control of his destiny as he'd be if he were in a dream. Picture gets off to a marvelous start, but while the "sound and the fury" continue, Welles cannot sustain the early power. For some reason, listening to the speeches becomes difficult—I think it would have worked much better as a silent film. Although this is not a great Welles film, it does allow him to play the mammoth personality from whom many of his other characterizations developed—a man of conceit who achieves a lofty position, tremendous power, and (his-

torical) significance by relinquishing his idealism and morality and committing "crimes" (for which he feels guilt) against humanity. Also with: Jeanette Nolan (as Lady Macbeth), Dan O'Herlihy (as Macduff), Edgar Barrier (as Banquo), Roddy McDowall (as Malcolm), Erskine Sanford (as Duncan), Alan Napier, John Dierkes, William Alland, Lurene Tuttle, Charles Lederer.

MACBETH (BRITISH/1971) C/140m.
Rarely screened, sadly neglected film by Roman Polanski is the most visually impressive of all the Shakespeare adaptations and as brutal and bloody as the Bard himself might have directed it. The Scottish landscape Polanski shows us on his wide screen is gorgeous—the people with whom he populates it are all truly loathsome. Violence is a way of life: the worst characters enjoy it, the "nicest" are indifferent to it. As Macbeth and his pushy wife, Jon Finch and Francesca Annis come across as any upwardly mobile, young, beautiful, contemporary couple who are devious, ruthless, and ambitious. Macbeth's assassination of Duncan so he can become king (and please his wife) is tantamount to that contemporary husband risking a dirty, underhanded power play to usurp his superior's job; as is characteristic of bosses we have all known, he becomes heartless, guilt-ridden, and paranoid toward those who he suspects covet his power position or know how he got to the top. As a viewer, it's interesting to pinpoint the moment when we realize that Macbeth isn't worth even our slightest sympathy, that he has become the most abominable figure of all. Picture is so non-theatrical that it's often jarring to hear characters speaking lines from Shakespeare—but, heck, we don't really know how these people talked anyway. There are many memorable scenes, including Macbeth's visit to the witches' coven, the massacre of Macduff's family, and the finale, which includes some thrilling swordplay between Macbeth and some soldiers and then Macduff. Extreme violence may be too strong for some viewers. Also with: Martin Shaw, Nicholas Selby, John Stride.

MACON COUNTY LINE (1974) C/89m.
Max Baer, Jr. (son of the boxing champ, but known more for playing the gentle but stupid Jethro on *The Beverly Hillbillies*), wrote, produced, and played a key role in this strange, violent, low-budget film that became a surprise box-office smash and cult favorite. Set in Georgia in 1954, film is based on a true story. Two young men (Alan Vint, Jessie Vint) from Chicago, on a final fun spree before going into the army, and a hitchhiker (Cheryl Waters) get stuck in Macon County when their car breaks down. While the sheriff (Baer), with whom the three had a run-in earlier, is picking up his son (Leif Garrett) at military school, two thieves break into his house and rape and murder his wife (Joan Blackman). With the petrified young boy at his side, Baer chases after the innocent Vints and Waters, fully intending to shoot them on sight for the crime. Ending is like something from a horror movie. Not a bad film. Acting is convincing, and the script presents an original view of the militarist (fascist) mentality (as represented by Baer) and takes a strong stance against it. Baer's character is truly fascinating—he's gentle and loving to his wife and son, yet manipulates them into being the way he wants them to be (i.e., he makes his son hunt and stay away from black boys); he's truly menacing when dealing with the Vints and Waters, outsiders with no money and no power. Directed by Richard Compton. Bobbie Gentry sings the theme song. Followed by *Return to Macon County*. Also with: Geoffrey Lewis.

MAD LOVE (1935) B&W/70m.
Underappreciated horror gem was first sound remake of 1924 classic *The Hands of Orlac*, from the story by Maurice Renard. A concert pianist (Colin Clive) whose hands are crushed in an accident is given the hands of an executed killer (Edward Brophy)—not just an ordinary killer, but a knife thrower. In one of his truly great screen portrayals, Peter Lorre is the slimy, bald Gogol, the doctor who performs the operation. When Gogol develops an insane desire for Clive's beautiful wife (Frances Drake), he devises a nefarious plot to get Clive out of the way: he attaches metal hands to his arms and sneaks about and strangles people, realizing that Clive will believe he did it himself with his killer hands. Sure enough, Clive begins to lose his mind. Drake takes it upon herself to save her husband. Of course, Lorre dominates the eerie proceedings, but Clive and Drake, as one of the strongest, most intelligent women in the horror cinema, are superb. Down to the smallest role, casting is thoughtful, and parts are well written and played. Still, picture's success can be attributed in great part to eerie visuals; the finale, in which Drake is threatened by Gogol (wait till you see his terrifying getup) in his chamber while his bird flaps about, is surreal. Whole film has hard-edged poetic quality. Director Karl Freund was once the cameraman for Carl Dreyer, James Whale, Tod Browning, Robert Wiene, E. A. Dupont, and F. W. Murnau, and here his respect for camera work to enhance action is most evident. His two cinematographers, Chester Lyons and the great Gregg Toland, gave proof that a haunting atmosphere can best be created by the imaginative use of the camera. Film gives definition to term "sleeper." Remade in 1960 as *The Hands of Orlac* (a British-French version), in 1961 as *Hands of a Stranger*. There have been many variations (such as brain transplants) on the theme. Also with: Isabel Jewell, Ted Healy, Sara Haden, Keye Luke.

MAD MAX (AUSTRALIAN/1979) C/89m.
The first entry in the fascinating, excitingly original, extremely successful futuristic action series starring Mel Gibson and directed by George Miller. Miller was inspired by his work in the casualty ward of a hospital, Australia's car culture during the sixties, and petrol rationing in Australia in the seventies, which caused a surprising amount of violence. It is a few years after an apocalypse. On Australia's highways there are continual battles between the Glory Riders, a ruthless gang of cyclists who dress like punks, and the Bronze, the police force. When his partner, The Goose (Steve Bisley),

is ambushed by Glory Riders, policeman Max becomes so upset that he temporarily quits the force and goes to the country with his wife, Jessie (Joanne Samuel), and their baby. But the Glory Riders follow them and kill Jessie and the child. Mad Max goes after the killers. The first part of the film, which is dominated by The Goose, is shot like a motorcycle-gang picture; the rest of the film is alternately a bike picture, a horror film, and another in the long line of fascist-heroes-on-a-revenge-spree films. Throughout, Miller exhibits a striking visual style—his use of a fender-level camera, sweeping pans, breakneck-speed trucking shots, and "shock" editing corresponds perfectly to the powerful images he shoots—specifically, the speeding cars and cycles (you won't believe how spectacular the stunt work is!). While you'll like Max and Jessie, a terrific married couple, and cocky, highstrung Jim Goose, this film is less interesting as a story about "people" than as a marriage between the filmmaker's machines (his camera, his editing tools) and the motor-powered machines that he films. Miller's cynical, depressing film is about dehumanization resulting from an apocalypse. At the beginning the gladiators are shown to be part of the machinery, part of the hardware, extensions of their vehicles. The death of Max's baby symbolizes the true death of the human race—and Max, desensitized and dehumanized, puts his uniform back on, gets into his police car, and rejoins the Rat Circus. In *The Road Warrior*, a more optimistic film, he starts to regain his humanity. Produced by Byron Kennedy. Jim McCausland wrote the screenplay with Miller. David Eggby did the photography, Tom Paterson and Cliff Hayes did the impressive editing, Brian May composed the score. Also with: Hugh Keays-Byrne, Roger Ward, Tim Burns, Geoff Parry.

MAD MAX BEYOND THUNDERDOME
(AUSTRALIAN/1985) C/106m. In this third, disappointing installment of the "Mad Max" series created by Australian George Miller (who this time shares direction chores with George Ogilvie), Mel Gibson's post-Apocalyptic superhero completes his transition from human being to demon to warrior to mythic figure: after *Mad Max*, Miller decided to explore the universality of Max, and his character ends up here as a messiah who fits into the histories-myths of numerous cultures. Film begins with Max entering Barter Town, a makeshift commercial town in the middle of the desert. It is run by dynamic Aunty Entity, played with outrageous gusto by flamboyant rock star Tina Turner—the first character in Max's weird world who has ever made him do a double take. Aunty gets him to agree to a life-and-death battle in the Thunderdome arena with an enormous hooded figure called Blaster (Paul Larrson) so she can gain control of the intelligent dwarf who sits on his shoulders, Master (Angelo Rossitto). But when Max backs out of the deal, he's sent off into the desert to die. There he's rescued by a tribe of children, who think he's the one they've been expecting to lead them through the desert to the promised land. Max tells them that they've got the wrong man, but circumstances lead him to journey with some of the kids

back to Barter Town. The first part of the film is terrific stuff, worthy of *Mad Max* and *The Road Warrior*, although it doesn't have any of the spectacular road action-violence of those two films. Miller's world is visually stunning; the design is so clever and outlandish that you can't help but laugh as you marvel at it—how about the punishment wheel that will determine Max's fate having a "Spin Again" marker? The dialogue is sharper and wittier than in the first two films, and Turner and Gibson have sparks flying between them. But the sequence with the tribe of children brings the excitement to a halt; Gibson looks uncomfortable interacting with the kids and slipping into a storyline more befitting Indiana Jones or Paul Atreides in *Dune*. The kids are such a screen convention that you can't really care if they find the great city they've been dreaming about—and you wish Max wouldn't spend so much time with them. Fortunately, the film ends with a slam-bang, beautifully edited action sequence in the *Road Warrior* vein, with Max's large vehicle being chased at high speeds by numerous bad guys in strange-looking hot rods. I just wish some of the villains compared to the monsters Max dealt with in the past. Also with: Bruce Spence (as a pilot, but *not* the Gyro Captain he played in *The Road Warrior*).

MÄDCHEN IN UNIFORM (GERMAN/1931)
B&W/90m–98m. Landmark of the German cinema, it was taken from a source play (*Yesterday and Today*) written by a *woman*, Christa Winsloe (who adapted the screenplay with F. D. Andam), and directed by a *woman*, Leontine Sagan; the first German film to incorporate sound skillfully and thematically; the first film to treat lesbianism sympathetically; and a film that dared attack authoritarianism at the time the climate was right for Hitler's rise to power—later Goebbels would ban the film, and Sagan and much of the cast would flee the country. Fourteen-year-old Hertha Thiele is the new boarder in a girls' school run by an elderly disciplinarian (Emilia Unda). Thiele gets along with all the other girls, but, like them, is miserable in the oppressive setting. Her only joy comes from the attention she receives from the lovely young teacher Dorothea Wieck, whom all the girls adore. She falls in love with Wieck. It's obvious that Wieck is physically attracted to Thiele, but, like the obvious lesbianism between various girls, she is not condemned by Sagan and Winsloe for her feelings. In fact, Wieck is regarded as the one positive influence on the girls, the one adult who cares for them; any expression of love in this cold environment, even that between females (or *especially* that between females), is necessary. Picture is beautifully acted, strikingly directed and photographed (there are several *unique* scenes), deeply moving, full of erotic tension, thematically provocative. Perhaps the most interesting *correct* choice Sagan and Winsloe made was to have all the girl students be spirited, funny, caring, and supportive of each other, rather than have them be defeated by oppression. They represent (as does Wieck) a rebellious, progressive social force—the *hope* for Germany's future before the Nazis crushed such forces. Prints have alternate endings.

Remade in Germany in 1958. Also with: Ellen Schwannecke, Hedwig Schlichter.

MADE FOR EACH OTHER (1939) B&W/ 85m.
The trials and tribulations of young marrieds Carole Lombard and James Stewart, a poorly paid, timid young lawyer who can't get his insensitive boss (Charles Coburn) to give him a promotion or his mother (Lucile Watson) to stop interfering in their lives. Picture starts out like a standard comedy, but becomes better as their problems increase and characters take a more serious approach to improving their financial woes. Lombard and Stewart are appealing even when their characters let us down or the script becomes overly melodramatic or mawkish. It's too painful watching Stewart go into Coburn's office with the intention of demanding a junior partnership, only to leave without having opened his mouth, with his salary cut by 25%. One nice scene has black housekeeper Louise Beavers giving Lombard some motherly advice. Directed by John Cromwell and scripted by Jo Swerling. Also with: Eddie Quillan, Harry Davenport, Esther Dale, Alma Kruger, Ward Bond.

MADE FOR EACH OTHER (1971) C/115m.
Husband and wife Joseph Bologna and Renee Taylor wrote and starred in this brutally insightful comedy. It's about two outrageously neurotic, self-destructive people, Pandora and Giggy—both of whom were messed up by their weird, overbearing parents—who meet at a ridiculous encounter session and embark on the rockiest of romances. Pandora's previous relationships were characterized by her being dumped (her choices in men left much to be desired); Giggy's previous relationships were characterized by his running away from commitment. Together, they try to break their unhappy patterns. Picture starts out awkwardly, but stick with it because you'll be rewarded. Sure, there are pretentious moments, but often you'll see things happen between characters that you may have seen previously only in your own life—never on the screen. In fact, Taylor and Bologna (who are both terrific) are unlike any screen couple to date. Even as you laugh you'll think their love scenes are extremely moving, and in those scenes in which they verbally rip into each other you'll feel every blow. I keep thinking that only an acting couple who are really in love and trust one another would dare play such emotionally devastating sequences. There are exceptional scenes, all filled with pain and humor: after "actress" Pandora's embarrassingly bad nightclub act, Giggy unflinchingly tells her it "stinks"; Giggy and Pandora suffer through a meal with Giggy's family; and in the finale, they almost break up but realize that because the world is so vicious they have a desperate need for each other. Sleeper was re-released in 1985. Directed by Robert D. Bean. Also with: Paul Sorvino, Olympia Dukakis.

MADIGAN (1968)C/101m.
Don Siegel directed this police drama that, regrettably, has been overshadowed by his later *Dirty Harry*. It's a brilliantly crafted film that all directors should study to see how action scenes should be staged, photographed, and edited. Shot on location in New York City, film is split in two: efforts of tough street detectives Richard Widmark (as Dan Madigan) and Harry Guardino trying to nail a psycho killer who got away from them, and efforts of police commissioner Henry Fonda to deal with some minor police corruption involving his life-long friend James Whitmore. Siegel effectively contrasts Widmark's frantic world of killers, pimps, addicts, hookers, drunks, stoolies, midgets, and assorted lowlifes and outcasts with Fonda's serene and secure world. Fonda must deal with the question of moral responsibility—having an adulterous affair with Susan Clark, has he the right to condemn Whitmore for moral indiscretion? But don't fret for Fonda, the film seems to be saying—his problems are minor compared to those of Widmark, who's risking his life. Widmark gives a standout performance as a very believable cop, one of Siegel's renegade heroes: he has no idea how to comfort his wife (Inger Stevens), who expects him to lead a normal home life, and he acts like a nervous kid with his hand in the cookie jar in the presence of the commissioner; but on the streets he is king, the number-one man at getting the job done, the man crooks fear and despise and outcasts trust. Exciting, atmospheric film takes time to explore the characters so that by the end we know exactly what makes each tick and what they find most essential in their lives. Excellent supporting performances by Whitmore and Guardino. Scripted by Henri Simoun and Abraham Polonsky, from Richard Dougherty's novel *The Commissioner*. Widmark would reprise his role in a TV series. Also with: Don Stroud, Steve Ihnat, Raymond St. Jacques, Michael Dunn, Sheree North, Lloyd Gough, Warren Stevens.

MAGNIFICENT AMBERSONS, THE (1942) B&W 88m.
Booth Tarkington's Pulitzer Prize–winning novel was the source for Orson Welles's second film. While Welles was out of the country, editor Robert Wise and his assistant, Mark Robson, were ordered by RKO to drastically cut the 131-minute picture that preview audiences hadn't liked. Included in the 88-minute release print is the weak finale scene in a hospital corridor that was directed by Freddie Flick (an interesting bit of trivia). Surprisingly, critics now regard the mutilated version as being equal to *Citizen Kane* and other Welles classics. Stanley Cortez's creatively lighted deep-focus photography is extraordinary—the scenes in the snow and the scenes in the Ambersons' mansion (particularly those on the great staircase) are among the most visually striking in all of Welles—but I don't consider this to be one of his masterpieces. The cutting hurts terribly. But even if it were intact, it seems to be missing a lead character. Tim Holt's George Minafer hasn't enough stature to carry the latter part of the film. Story, which is set between 1893 and 1912, is about the decline and fall of the magnificent Ambersons-Minafers, and the simultaneous modernization of their once-quaint small town—all due to the industrial revolution, which is emblemized by the advent of the au-

tomobile. Spoiled George refuses to let kind Eugene Morgan (Joseph Cotten) court his mother, Isabel (Dolores Costello), because Eugene makes automobiles. Pride keeps him from marrying Lucy Morgan (Anne Baxter), Eugene's daughter. As townspeople wished when George was a bratty boy, George gets his comeuppance. Welles presents what may be the most effective look at late 19th-century small-town life. The early montage, depicting changing styles (Eugene models clothes for us) is memorable. Acting is uneven, but Agnes Moorehead is dynamic as Fanny Alexander, especially when projecting near hysteria in her scenes with Holt. The music is by Bernard Herrmann. Edward Stevenson designed the fabulous costumes. Also with: Ray Collins (Jack Amberson), Richard Bennett (Major Amberson), Don Dillaway (Wilbur Minafer), Erskine Sanford.

MAGNIFICENT OBSESSION (1954) C/108m. Douglas Sirk directed this glossy, melodramatic remake of the 1935 John Stahl classic that starred Irene Dunne and Robert Taylor. Both films were adapted from Lloyd C. Douglas's novel. Young playboy Rock Hudson is indirectly responsible for the death of a great doctor. Now guilty, he falls in love with the middle-aged widow, Jane Wyman, but she resists his advances. Fleeing, she is struck by a car and blinded. Hudson goes to medical school and becomes a surgeon. When Wyman becomes extremely ill, artist Otto Kruger, a family friend, convinces Hudson to perform the operation on her. Picture shows how Hudson comes to virtually *replace* the dead doctor. Hudson doesn't acquire only medical skills, but through Kruger is inspired to become the philanthropist that the doctor was. By becoming a selfless philanthropist, he becomes a good Christian. So, with God-like Kruger watching over him during the operation, he is able to perform a *miracle*. This isn't prime Sirk but it's an enjoyable tearjerker, with an earnest performance by Hudson. Technicolor photography by Russell Metty. Also with: Barbara Rush, Agnes Moorehead.

MAGNUM FORCE (1973) C/124m. The second "Dirty Harry" movie lacks the gritty feel and stylistic impositions of the original, but has an exciting storyline—written by John Milius and Michael Cimino—and many tough, cleverly directed (by Ted Post) action sequences. After liberal critics tore into *Dirty Harry*, Eastwood wanted to prove Harry wasn't a fascist after all, so he pitted Callahan (now in LA) against true fascists: death-squad cops who are killing off the guilty criminals whom scared judges and juries have let off. Just to confuse the political issue a bit, the "liberal" police captain (Hal Holbrook) turns out to be the head of the death squad. Full of comical touches, like the bad guys eating Chinese take-out food. The best moment: Harry studies the picture of his late wife. Also with: Felton Perry, Mitch Ryan, David Soul, Tim Matheson, Robert Urich, Adele Yoshioka.

MAITRESSE (FRENCH/1976) C/112m. Perverse romance that was directed by Barbet Schroeder, who never chooses ordinary material. Gérard Depardieu helps a friend out with a burglary; they end up in two-floor apartment-dungeon of dominatrix Bulle Ogier (star of Schroeder's more impressive *The Valley*). Depardieu has an affair with the smarter and more successful Ogier. At first he is curious about her work; he may even be impressed by her power over the men who come to see her. But he begins to resent the time she spends with these men, her superior attitude toward men (although she doesn't seem to think the masochists are inferior to her—just him). Perhaps jealous, he starts being critical of her work (although he is willing to participate in the domination of a woman). He becomes very possessive when it's apparent she has a secret benefactor. The leads are appealing and film has definite shock value—a real dominatrix was hired to be Ogier's double during the S&M scenes and to actually torture and humiliate real-life masochists. While Schroeder presents a bizarre relationship, he says nothing new about male-female power struggles. Or is he saying that even the most bizarre relationships have the same old problems as the most mundane relationships? Schroeder's theme is unclear; worse, it's obvious that we're supposed to see that Ogier has a dual personality (much like Kathleen Turner in *Crimes of Passion*), yet we are never provided with sufficient insight into either side. Why she is as she is remains a mystery. Also with: André Royer.

MAJOR DUNDEE (1964) C/120m–124m–134m. Okay Sam Peckinpah epic western. A stern Union officer assembles an army of Union soldiers, Confederate prisoners, renegades, thieves, and other assorted misfits, drifters, and losers in order to carry out his obsessive pursuit of a large, murderous Apache war party across the Mexican border. Film contains several sweeping battle scenes, but emphasis is more on Bligh-Christian infighting between strict military man Charlton Heston and the more humane Richard Harris, a longtime nemesis who is leader of the Rebel prisoners; the tormented Heston's personal journey, in which he in some ways cleanses his soul; and how Dundee's troop, comprised of diverse elements, comes to represent imperialistic, impure, but somehow noble America. Picture is confusing and boring at times; but it's hard to judge because Columbia Studios broke the contract with Peckinpah and edited film itself. Also Peckinpah wasn't allowed to film several pivotal scenes that would have added an hour to the already lengthy running time. Peckinpah disowned this film; some will recognize *The Wild Bunch* as his partial remake. Dialogue is better in this film, but Heston's cold, deeply flawed character is far too complex for the actor to play. Consequently, it's hard for us to figure out what is going on in his head at any given time. Picture ends with men engaging in battle against *French* troops—foolishly anti-climactic, since build-up was for confrontation with Apaches, who, unfortunately, were dispatched too early. Excellent cast includes: Jim Hutton, James Coburn, Michael Anderson, Jr., Senta Berger, Mario Adorf, Brock Peters, Warren Oates, Ben Johnson, R. G. Armstrong, L. Q. Jones, Slim

Pickens, Karl Swenson, Michael Pate, John Davis Chandler, Dub Taylor.

MAKE WAY FOR TOMORROW (1937) B&W/92m.

Giving wonderful performances, Victor Moore and Beulah Bondi are an aged married couple who have financial problems. They go to their four children for help and a place to live, but they find themselves a burden. Though deeply in love, they realize that they won't be able to stay together. They move in with separate children in different locations. And nothing works out. This is one of the few films to deal with the problems of the aged, who were good parents and good citizens but find themselves obsolete in modern America. Poignant classic (which is like an Ozu film) is beautifully acted, sensitively directed by Leo McCarey. A good argument for Social Security. Adapted by Viña Delmar from Josephine Lawrence's novel *The Years Are So Long*. Also with: Fay Bainter, Thomas Mitchell, Elizabeth Risdon, Porter Hall, Minna Gombell, Barbara Read, Louise Beavers.

MALTESE FALCON, THE (1941) B&W/100m.

Sam Spade (Humphrey Bogart) is partner in a San Francisco detective agency with Miles Archer (Jerome Cowan). A beautiful woman named Miss Wonderly (Mary Astor) hires the firm to save her sister from getting too involved with Floyd Thursby. Miles and Thursby both turn up dead. (Quick: who killed Floyd Thursby?) The police think Spade did it because he didn't like Archer and was still having an affair with his wife, Iva (Gladys George). Spade begins an affair with Miss Wonderly, who admits her real name is Brigid O'Shaughnessy, that she has no sister, that Thursby was her partner, and that she's a compulsive liar. Spade's relationship with Brigid draws the attention of her former partners, "fat man" Kasper Gutman (Sidney Greenstreet) and nervous Joel Cairo (Peter Lorre). They think he's helping Brigid secure a priceless, forever elusive antique, the Maltese Falcon. They make him a partner in their venture. But while Spade enjoys mingling with such odd, entertaining people, he is as double-dealing as they are in a partnership. Warner Bros. adapted Dashiell Hammett's 1930 detective novel three times between 1931 and 1941, ending up with this rare imitation that was more impressive than the original. What's surprising about director-writer John Huston's version is how much of the dialogue (which Huston is known for) and plot elements can be found in the novel or in one of the earlier two films (the 1936 version was titled *Satan Met a Lady*). What makes the film so special, a true masterpiece, is the style, the impeccable casting, and the emphasis placed on peculiar character traits. Film's incredible pacing is accomplished by Huston's rapid-fire editing *within* scenes and dialogue that shoots back and forth. Arthur Edeson's low-key camera work is noteworthy because it helped make *film noir* the dominant style of forties detective films. This is a landmark picture not only because it set the style and tone for hard-boiled detective films, but also because it established screen personae for its players. Debuting at 62, Greenstreet plays Gutman as a brilliant conversationalist, erudite, corrupt, power-hungry, sinister, and of course, fat (though he's quick as a cat). Although civilized enough to be a professor, Gutman's like later Greenstreet characters in that he is so greedy that he'll get involved in foolish schemes with such oddball characters as Cairo, Brigid, and Wilmer (Elisha Cook, Jr.), his gunsel. The incomparable Peter Lorre is magnificent as the German's neurotic, emotional, effeminate, gushy partner; one second he's giggling, the next he's crying. Despite her matronly haircut, Astor is fine as Brigid. But I think her breathless, "helpless" pleading character is a bit much. Spade tells her "You're good; you're *very* good," but she's easy to see through. Bogart's Spade is a complex character. He's witty, patient, sadistic, and cynical; he enjoys putting on a "tough guy" act and playing the game with criminals. Spade tries to be the moral hero, when he turns in Brigid, the woman he loves, for Miles's murder, explaining, "I won't play the sap for you." But he's deceiving himself. In the novel, Effie (Lee Patrick), Spade's secretary, loses all respect for her boss when he turns Brigid over to the police. Huston agrees with Hammett. Look at the last scene. The police take Brigid away in an elevator that looks like a prison cell because of its bars. She goes *down*, as if she were going to meet the Devil. Huston doesn't have Spade return to his apartment but has him walk *down* the stairs. He won't end up in Hell as quickly as Brigid, but he'll join her there eventually. Also with: Barton MacLane, Ward Bond, John Hamilton, Walter Huston (a cameo as the dying ship captain who brings Spade the Falcon).

MAN AND A WOMAN, A (FRENCH/1966) C-B&W/102m.

An enormous commercial hit and Oscar's Best Foreign Film winner, Claude Lelouch's pretentious, shameless romance makes even simple *Love Story* seem complex. Widower-father Jean-Louis Trintignant, a race-car driver, meets and falls in love with widow-mother Anouk Aimée, who works in the movie business. They'd probably get together in about four seconds, but Lelouch gets in their way. They each must flash back to skimpy, wordless scenes featuring their wonderful first spouses—his wife committed suicide after suffering a breakdown upon hearing he was critically injured in a crash; her husband was killed doing a movie stunt. Also he participates in a seemingly endless race in Monte Carlo, and she ruins an attempt at lovemaking by thinking about her late husband when Trintignant's at the height of passion. Trintignant is a decent actor and Aimée gives a fine, *natural* performance, but the empty script allows them nothing to do, not even the opportunity for the characters to express their feelings. Lelouch tries to express characters' moods through his dreamy photography and romantic settings. Can anyone explain why Lelouch cuts back and forth between color and black-and-white footage? (It has nothing to do with past and present.) I suspect it's Lelouch's self-conscious attempt to substitute "art" for substance. The sickeningly saccharine romantic score by Francis Lai was quite popular in 1966. Lelouch's remake, *Another Man, Another Chance*, which is set in the American

West, is a bit better. In 1986, he filmed a sequel to the 1966 movie, with Trintignant and Aimée. Also with: Pierre Barouh, Valerie Lagrange.

MAN FROM LARAMIE, THE (1955) C/101m.
The fifth and last of Anthony Mann's westerns starring James Stewart. Again he is a revenge hero—Will Lockhart comes from Laramie to find and kill the man responsible for selling repeater rifles to the Apaches who massacred his soldier brother's platoon. But this time Stewart plays someone with no sense of guilt. He is at peace with himself for being on an obviously moral path. We can quickly tell that killing a man is antithetical to his beliefs, but because he doesn't agonize about what he's going to do, we don't realize until the end that killing someone is in his plans or that he is obsessive about revenging anyone. The psychological dilemmas Mann usually reserves for his hero are shifted to the villains in this film. Philip Yordan and Frank Burt have structured the film like a classical tragedy in which a powerful corrupt family is about to collapse. The head of the family, Alec Waggoman (Donald Crisp), has amassed an enormous spread, which both his natural son, Dave (Alex Nicol), and his foreman and "adopted" son, Vic Hansbro (Arthur Kennedy), hope to inherit. Vic is actually more loyal than Dave, and Dave is sadistic and crazy as well; but Vic comes to realize Alec cares only for his natural son. Alec has nightmares that an *outsider* will kill Dave, and, forcing fate's hand, he tries to drive Will out of town—but he doesn't realize that by rejecting Vic's love he has made Vic into the *outsider* he should worry about. Picture has excellent dialogue and—this being Mann—impressive, thematic use of the landscape (in this case, New Mexico). What I find most compelling about the film is the presentation of violence. It is brutal and always comes impulsively—repeatedly someone spots somebody he dislikes, flies into a blind rage, and tries to kill him, maim him. In neither of the two cases where someone travels to a different location to kill someone—Lockhart arriving from Laramie to kill the man dealing with the Apaches, and Alec going after Lockhart—does the avenger carry out his mission. So the film is saying that if men learned to control their volatile tempers and to act rationally, there would be much less senseless violence (in our world or Mann's West). Again Mann somehow made a violence-packed "pacifist" western. Also with: Cathy O'Donnell (as the romantic interest of both Will and Vic), Aline MacMahon, Wallace Ford, Jack Elam, James War Eagle, James Millican.

MAN IN THE WHITE SUIT, THE (BRITISH/1952) B&W/85m.
Classic Ealing Studios satire, with Alec Guinness playing the dedicated inventor of a cloth that won't rip and repels dirt. Textile workers worry that such a material will cause them to lose their jobs and industrialists worry about what it will do to prices. Realizing that their livelihoods depend on "planned obsolescence," capital and labor join forces and attempt to stop Guinness from leaking news of his invention to the press. It's not unexpected that the industrialists are portrayed as devious men who couldn't care less about the practical value of Guinness's invention if it means that their profits will go down; picture saves its hardest punch for the workers, who aren't grateful to Guinness, either. When the chips are down, their actions turn out to be as ugly and as selfish as their bosses'—which is also what happens in the most famous of Britain's labor-management comedies, 1959's *I'm All Right, Jack*. Adapted by John Dighton, director Alexander Mackendrick, and Roger MacDougall from MacDougall's novel, this cynical film shows disenchantment with selfish British workers, who are supposed to be the consumers' watchdogs—since they are consumers themselves—but are resistant to making better, cheaper products because of job insecurity. Because scientist Guinness (who cares more about his work than about pretty Joan Greenwood) has nothing in common with common men—he's pragmatic rather than being humanistic or idealistic—that leaves no one (no worker, no humanist) to be the shafted consumer's representative in industry. Also with: Cecil Parker, Michael Gough, Ernest Thesiger, Vida Hope.

MAN OF FLOWERS (AUSTRALIAN/1983) C/91m.
Marvelous, richly-textured, award-winning film about a lovable, rich, middle-aged eccentric (Norman Kaye). Although haunted by his sad upbringing (his father was a strict disciplinarian), he spends his time battling the mediocrity that chartacterizes the modern world and seeking out and nurturing its rare forms of beauty. He writes daily letters to his mother although she is long dead, has regular sessions with an incompetent therapist, and mails himself letters so he can engage in meaningful conversations with his mailman. He paints, plays the church organ, listens to classical music, collects art and sculpture, and once a week pays a beautiful artist's model (Alyson Best) to strip to the love duet from Donizetti's *Lucia de Lammermoor*. He never touches Best, as his intentions are honorable. He lets her live with him so she can escape her bullying boyfriend (Chris Haywood), a has-been modern artist whose work Kaye considers to be an insult to all that is beautiful. He figures out an "artistic" way to permanently free his "little flower" from her boyfriend's greedy, brutal hands. Director Paul Cox smoothly blends wicked, offbeat humor with sad, penetrating looks at nice people who have really been clobbered (in more ways than one) in life. Kaye is a wonderful, original film character whose unique perspective on life has helped him overcome every roadblock to happiness. He is the ideal protector of the much younger Best and they are, in their own way, a splendid couple because each can provide the other what they need most at this particular time in their lives. Kaye, who was terrific in Cox's *Lonely Hearts*, is even better here, playing a triumphant character instead of an insecure loser. Since this film is about a lover of beauty, it's only fitting that Cox's film is beautiful to look at and has a sumptuous classical score to listen to. A very special movie. Also with: Sarah Walker, Bob Ellis, Barry Dickens, Werner Herzog (seen in flashbacks as Kaye's father), Hilary Kelly (his beautiful mother), Julia Blake, James Stratford.

MAN OF THE WEST (1958) C/100m. One of the harshest portraits of the West, Anthony Mann's adult western contains psychotic killers (the Tobin family gang, led by Uncle Lee J. Cobb) who are the total opposites of the romanticized badmen of countless westerns; a morally ambiguous hero (Gary Cooper) who yields to his long-held-in-check violent nature in order to do in his brutal kin—his name "Link" is appropriate because he is the link between the West's brutal past and its civilized future—and a liberal dose of sex, the ingredient that most distinguished it from the spate of television westerns. Once Cooper rode and committed heinous crimes with Cobb and his cousins, smart John Dehner, violent Jack Lord, the crazy, speechless Royal Dano, and the stupid Robert Wilke, but he has gone straight, married and had two sons, and become a respected member of his community. But when the Tobins rob the train he is riding, he and two other passengers, saloon singer Julie London and cowardly but friendly swindler Arthur O'Connell, become stranded. They wind up as captives in the Tobins' cabin. Cobb loves Cooper and believes him when he lies that he'll rejoin the gang when it attempts a bank robbery. None of cousins trusts Cooper, and Dehner exhibits jealousy because Cooper is replacing him as top gun. Shootouts are inevitable and exciting—Cooper is not happy to fight Dehner because he is the man Cooper would have been if he hadn't deserted Cobb years before. As in most Mann films, there are two men with similar backgrounds, one who chose to put away his guns as the West became civilized and one who chose to keep being an outlaw, which, in Mann's films, made his demise inevitable. This picture is also similar to other Mann films because the rugged outdoor landscapes provide the characters with the appropriate environment for uncivilized behavior; battles and jealousies among family members were inspired by classical drama; the Mann hero tries to forget his past but can't; and, when going after Cobb for raping London, Cooper becomes a "revenge hero." The film's most notorious, most publicized scene has Lord forcing London to strip to her underwear. An enlightened hero, Cooper realizes London's humiliation—it doesn't matter that she has always been a loose woman—and gets revenge on Lord later by making him strip while she watches. The scenes between Cooper and London in the barn and wagon have remarkable sexual intensity—but one wonders if screenwriter Reginald Rose gave Cooper a wife so he wouldn't even have to consider marrying London, who, besides not being a virgin, survives a rape. A solid, smart western—but Cooper shouldn't be a "hick" in the opening scene. From Will C. Brown's *The Border Jumpers*. Ernest Haller did the impressive CinemaScope photography.

MAN ON THE FLYING TRAPEZE (1935) B&W/65m. Near-perfect W. C. Fields comedy in which he plays the exasperating, exasperated Ambrose Wallfinger. He lives with his constantly complaining wife (Kathleen Howard), his sponging mother-in-law, Cordelia Neselrode (Vera Lewis), her babied, unemployed son (Grady Sutton), who takes naps after breakfast, and Fields's adult daughter (Mary Brian) from his first marriage, the only person who appreciates his fine qualities. He works as a "memory expert" and hasn't had a day off in twenty-five years. In order to go to the wrestling matches, he tells his boss that his mother-in-law died from poison liquor. Fields is hilarious, taking one abuse after another in his cruel, absurd world without ever losing his patience or trying to reform. Highlights include Fields sharing a jail cell with a crazy scissors murderer; driving Howard crazy by taking forever to go down to see about the burglars in the basement, then joining the thieves for some singing and homemade applejack; getting a series of traffic and parking tickets in succession. Film has a very satisfying ending—as do most of Fields's henpecked husbands, Ambrose emerges triumphant without becoming the straight-and-narrow man his wife wants to mold. Howard proves to be another of Fields's screen wives who secretly love him for, rather than in spite of, his infuriating eccentricities. Directed by Clyde Bruckman. Also with: Lucien Littlefield, Tammany Young, Walter Brennan.

MAN WHO FELL TO EARTH, THE (BRITISH/1976) C/117m–140m. A space traveler (David Bowie) plummets to earth. He drinks water and thinks of his barren planet, where his wife and two children are dying of thirst. Using the name Thomas Jerome Newton, he delivers nine basic patents to New York lawyer Oliver Farnsworth (Buck Henry). He enlists Farnsworth's aid to build a great corporation, World Enterprises, which should soon make other corporations obsolete. He wants to make enough money to build a spaceship capable of traveling to his planet. Nicolas Roeg's flawed but fascinating science-fiction film, adapted by Paul Mayersburg from Walter Tevis's novel, is variation on *The Wizard of Oz*; like another variation, *E.T.*, it's about how three people—Farnsworth, scientist Nathan Bryce (Rip Torn), and Newton's lover-companion, Mary-Lou (well played by quirky Candy Clark)—try to help a stranded alien return home. But this is an unhappy film, an old-fashioned fairytale for those adults who read Jonathan Swift and believe that our world, and those who run it, can be cold, cruel, and unfair. And it's for those who remember the Grimm stories about characters who fall from grace (Newton's "fall" to earth signifies his descent into purgatory) and are punished (how Newton suffers). Unlike in the Grimm stories, he doesn't repent and receive salvation—he chooses to wallow in self-pity rather than come to terms with his own fallibility. Tragically, Newton can never go home: his three friends aren't as comforting or resourceful as Dorothy's and E.T.'s, and his homeward drive is far too weak. While he gives meaning to the dreary lives of his friends, they can't provide him with stimulation. A man in exile, a man without an island, he loses himself in sex with Mary-Lou, booze, and television. He becomes infected by the earthlings he feels superior to and starts acting like the depressed, unfulfilled, heavy-drinking, domesticated man. One reason for his depression is that he is unprepared for the ruthlessness he finds on earth—he can't combat those powerful forces (capitalistic leaders, FBI, CIA) who fear he will put the world's greatest monopolies out of business. Weakened and depressed, he puts up no resistance. Bowie's birdlike features contribute to our empathy for Newton, who, unlike the muscular Atlas, must bear the weight of his world on shoulders that are brittle. Newton feels enormous guilt because he can't carry out his mission. Film's most dramatic scene has Newton stripping off his human skin to reveal his alien body—but Roeg forgets that sequence's purpose in the book was to show how Newton couldn't recognize his alien form any longer because he'd become an imitation human being. Also with: Bernie Casey, Jackson D. Kane, Rick Riccardo.

MAN WHO KNEW TOO MUCH, THE
(BRITISH/1934) B&W/84m. Not as enjoyable as his 1956 remake (although the trend is to rate this film better), but this is one of Alfred Hitchcock's finest British films, and his most commercially successful. He told François Truffaut, "The first version is the work of a talented amateur and the second was made by a professional." British tourists Leslie Banks and Edna Best are staying at a Swiss ski resort with their young daughter, Nova Pilbeam (who looks much too old for her part). A Frenchman (Pierre Fresnay) is fatally shot, but he manages to tell Best of a plot to assassinate a foreign diplomat in London. The spies who plan the murder kidnap Pilbeam so Banks and Best will remain quiet. Back in London, Banks tries to find where the spies are hiding Pilbeam, while Best goes to the Albert Hall, where the assassination is to take place at the moment cymbals clash during a cantata. Thriller blends droll wit and suspense; Hitchcock builds excitement by staging danger scenes in intriguing settings: a ski slope, a dentist's office, the Albert Hall, a high roof. Picture feels British, looks Germanic, has a climactic shootout straight out of American gangster films (i.e., *Scarface*). What I like best is how Hitchcock mixes refined continental types with sleazy, though educated, East Europeans (like Peter Lorre's strange-looking, memorable villain). It's interesting that people from both sides are shot, yet *no one* utters a painful groan. Exciting ending has Best, rather than Banks or the male police, rescue the imperiled Pilbeam. Scripted by A. R. Rawlinson and Charles Bennett. Also with: Frank Vosper, Hugh Wakefield.

MAN WHO KNEW TOO MUCH, THE (1956)
C/120m. Alfred Hitchcock's remake of his 1934 British film begins in French Morocco, where Americans James Stewart, a Midwest doctor, his wife, Doris Day, formerly a professional singer, and their son, Christopher Olsen, have come for a vacation. They are befriended by a mysterious French gentleman (Daniel Gelin) and, later, by a middle-aged couple (Brenda de Banzie, Bernard Miles) who are staying in their hotel. In the market Gelin, who turns out to be an FBI agent, is fatally stabbed, but before dying he whispers to Stewart information about a plot to assassinate an ambassador in London. But Miles and De Banzie, who are in on this plot, kidnap Olsen so that Stewart won't pass

on Gelin's secret to authorities. Stewart and Day fly to London and try to find their son and foil the murder attempt. Long regarded as one of Hitchcock's lesser efforts of the fifties, this well-made, truly enjoyable thriller is finally getting some of the recognition it deserves. While a few of the early scenes in Marrakech are raggedly photographed and edited—the process shots are particularly disconcerting—an equal number of scenes set there are extremely effective. The murder of Gelin is excitingly photographed and edited; and the scene in which Stewart tells Day that their son has been kidnapped is beautifully, believably acted by both stars. Once Stewart and Day reach London, the film has no low points. Scenes that take place in a taxidermist's workspace (one of Hitchcock's red herrings), a chapel (where Miles wears a collar and conducts a service while his wife collects money), the Albert Hall (where the assassination is to take place), and the embassy of the ambassador are all very clever and suspenseful. Interestingly, in the final three of these four scenes Hitchcock incorporates music (the parishioners singing a religious hymn, the London Symphony Orchestra playing the cantata "Storm Cloud," Day singing "Que Sera Sera," respectively) to build tension. The Albert Hall sequence, in which some shots are exactly like those in the 1934 version, is one of Hitchcock's all-time great scenes, one which filmmakers working in the suspense genre must study. And the film has wit, including a terrific last line. Music by Bernard Herrmann, who can be seen conducting the orchestra at the Albert Hall. Also with: Ralph Truman, Mogens Wieth, Alan Mowbray, Hillary Brooke, Carolyn Jones.

MAN WHO SHOT LIBERTY VALANCE, THE
(1962) B&W/122m. Marvelous John Ford western looks better with every viewing; certainly it summarized themes that were vital to earlier Ford westerns. Elderly Senator Ransom Stoddard (James Stewart) and his wife, Hallie (Vera Miles), return to Shinbone after many years in the East. The local newspaper editor wants to know why they've come to attend the funeral of someone he never even knew existed, town drunk Tom Doniphon (John Wayne). Ransom tells the story. He had come West from the East, with law books in his hand. The stagecoach was robbed by sadistic scoundrel Liberty Valance (Lee Marvin at his most vicious) and his two henchmen (Lee Van Cleef, Strother Martin). When Ransom interfered, Valance nearly beat him to death. He was taken into Shinbone by Tom and his friend and ranchmate, Pompey (Woody Strode). He was tended to by Hallie, then Tom's girl. While waiting to start his law practice, Ransom worked in the steak house run by Hallie and her parents (Jeanette Nolan, John Qualen). He taught her how to read. They became close, Tom became jealous. But Tom still tried to give pacifist Ransom pointers on how to use a gun, because it was obvious that Liberty would soon challenge Ransom to a gun battle. After Liberty beat up newspaper editor Dutton Peabody (Edmond O'Brien) for publicizing Liberty's loss to Ransom of a position as delegate to a convention about possible statehood, Ransom

faced Liberty on the street. Liberty was shot dead and Ransom became a hero. Tom granted Hallie to Ransom, without ever asking Hallie whom she preferred. But he revealed to Ransom that it was he who killed Liberty, shooting him from an alleyway. Ransom married Hallie, became governor and senator, and found fame; but as civilization progressed, Tom faded into obscurity. The editor rips up his notes, expressing a basic Ford theme: "When the legend becomes fact, print the legend." For Ford, the real heroes were men like Tom who tamed the wilderness and made it possible for civilization to take root and "for the garden to grow in the desert." But it is a shame that such pioneers have no place in civilization (Tom sets fire to his *house*); in a law-and-order world of lawyers and politicians, Tom is just as anachronistic as gunslingers like Liberty—in fact, Tom always knew he and Liberty could be lumped together: "Liberty Valance is the toughest man south of the picket wire . . . next to me." Picture has interesting characters and their relationships with each other are complex—there's a lot going on in their heads that they don't verbalize; even at the end we must read between the lines in the aged Ransom's exchange with the aged Hallie to realize that Hallie loved Tom and that Ransom realizes this. Picture has strong emotional resonance. Thematic photography was by William H. Clothier, who makes strong use of light and shadows. Dorothy M. Johnson's short story was adapted by Willis Goldbeck and James Werner Bellah. Music by Cyril J. Mockridge. The Gene Pitney song, using the film's title, was inspired by the movie. Also with: Andy Devine (a terrific performance as Shinbone's cowardly sheriff), Ken Murray, John Carradine (as a windbag politician), Willis Bouchey, Carleton Young, Denver Pyle, O.Z. Whitehead, Paul Birch, Jack Pennick, Anna Lee.

MAN WHO WOULD BE KING, THE (1975) C/ 129m.

John Huston never was a better storyteller than when he directed and co-wrote (with Gladys Hill) this wonderful, under-appreciated adaptation of Rudyard Kipling's short story. It's an epic like no other, set in a distant, haunting world that has no equivalent in film. In the 1880s, Danny Dravot (Sean Connery) and Peachy Carnehan (Michael Caine), former British soldiers in India, decide to leave civilization behind—but they plan to keep the British imperialist tradition alive by setting themselves up as rulers in some uncivilized, remote province of northern India. They make a perilous journey and find what they have been looking for, the ancient city of Sikandergul. They assemble an army of natives and take the city. When an arrow strikes a medallion Danny is wearing, the natives think him invulnerable and take him to be a god: perhaps Alexander the Great has returned. He is treated as an immortal. Danny goes along with the masquerade—even forgets that he is merely human. Meanwhile Peachy gathers up the treasures heaped on them, hoping to return to civilization wealthy. But Danny wants to remain, and to marry a beautiful native girl (Shakira Caine). This is one of the screen's great adventure yarns—I find it amazing that Huston, at age 70, was able to undertake such an ambitious project (filming was done in Morocco). Praise must go to whoever selected the unique locations and to whoever cast the secondary roles—it is hard to believe that the many priests and other Indians aren't real people whom the crew stumbled upon. Visuals by Oswald Morris are absolutely thrilling. In the fifties Huston had wanted to make the film with Bogart and Gable or Lancaster and Douglas. I'm glad he waited for Connery and Caine. They are absolutely dynamic—even though you'll resent what their characters are doing, you'll admire their derring-do, gusto, bravery. There are so many powerful moments that one fears the conclusion will be anticlimactic. But it's the best part—how terrifying are the priests once they realize there has been a hoax, how emotionally stirring the two heroes when they burst into loud, patriotic song as they wait their sorry fate! Maurice Jarre composed the score. Also with: Christopher Plummer (as Kipling), Saeed Jaffrey (as Billy Fish).

MAN WITH THE GOLDEN ARM, THE (1955) B&W/119m.

Effective Otto Preminger drama that is most famous for having defied the MPPA Code by dealing with drug addiction. Frank Sinatra gave one of his best performances as Frankie Machine, a former drug addict and convict who comes back to Chicago with hopes of becoming a professional drummer. But he soon finds himself pressured by his neurotic wife (Eleanor Parker), who pretends to be a cripple in order to hold on to him, and a persuasive dope dealer (Darren McGavin), who has both the seductive powers and the *ability to give pleasure* that his sexless wife lacks. He soon finds himself back dealing poker for Robert Strauss and needing fixes (of an unnamed white powder). Only stripper girlfriend Kim Novak (in one of her most relaxed, appealing characterizations) wants what's best for him. Direction by Preminger is taut and daring—there's a scene in which Sinatra shoots up that must have shocked fifties audiences (in Maryland this scene was deleted until a court ruling restored it); and Walter Newman's script is strong until the silly, melodramatic ending. However, the film is much different than Nelson Algren's prize-winning novel. For one thing, the book's ending is tragic. For another, in the book Novak's character is less sympathetic than Parker's. In fact, in the novel the success or failure of Frankie Machine's fight to end his addiction (to *morphine*, due to a war injury) depends on his internal struggle and his ability to come to grips with his environment; in the film it's determined by the struggle between good Novak and bad Parker for his soul. Just before he died, John Garfield planned to star in a more faithful adaptation (by Lewis Meltzer) of Algren's book. Memorable jazz score, with a great title tune, by Elmer Bernstein. Titles by Saul Bass. Also with: Arnold Stang, Doro Merande, Leonid Kinskey, George E. Stone.

MAN WITH THE GOLDEN GUN, THE (BRITISH/ 1974) C/125m.

Ian Fleming's last James Bond novel became one of the least interesting Bond films. 007 (Roger

Moore) tracks down million-dollar assassin Scaramanga (Christopher Lee), who possesses the "Solex"—he has the power to monopolize the world's solar-energy business. Bond is able to find Scaramanga because Scaramanga's mistress, Andrea (Maud Adams), puts him on his trail; she wants Bond to rescue her from sexual servitude. Bond and Scaramanga finally meet on the killer's remote island. Their shootout in the island's funhouse, which benefits from the presence of Scaramanga's diminutive servant Nick Nack (Hervé Villechaize priming for TV's *Fantasy Island*), is the only good scene in the movie, and even it has an unsatisfying finish. A very labored movie, with Bond a stiff bore, Adams and Britt Ekland (playing Bond's helpmate) uninspired leading ladies, stale humor, and a cruddy title song by Lulu. Even the visuals during the opening titles are dull. Picture lacks invention. Richard Maibaum reworked Tom Mankiewicz's original script. Guy Hamilton directed. Also with: Richard Loo, Clifton James (unfortunately reprising his unfunny redneck sheriff from *Live and Let Die*), Madeleine Smith, David Hedison, Bernard Lee, Lois Maxwell, Desmond Llewellyn.

MANHATTAN (1979) B&W/96m. This is my favorite Woody Allen film. It's a *love* poem to a perfect Manhattan (film opens with glorious montage of New York sights, and throughout characters share the frame with city spots), with Gershwin music to serenade it; and it's a bemused look at the people who inhabit the city and have imperfect *love* lives. Allen's a television comedy writer who is having an affair with a 17-year-old high school girl, Mariel Hemingway. She is sweet, mature, a fine bed partner and a good companion, and she loves him dearly. But he spends his time with her talking about her tender age and hinting that they'll soon break up. Allen's married best friend (Michael Murphy as Yale) introduces him to his mistress, Diane Keaton, a writer with enormous intellectual pretensions. When Murphy breaks off with Keaton, Allen makes a play for her. He breaks up with Hemingway, who is devastated. This plot point showed growing maturity in Allen as a filmmaker—he finally dared to have his character be mean to someone, to be unfair, to not be the victim. Film has typical Allen humor, which comes from characters' insecurities, phobias, quirkiness. Among the many highlights: Allen's opening narration (including a funny Raymond Chandler spoof); his basketball-bouncing, boat-buying walk with his young son; his spats with former wife Meryl Streep, who left him for another woman and has now written a tell-all book about her and Allen ("there's movie interest"); Allen getting turned off (but also turned on) by Keaton during their first meeting; Allen talking into a tape machine and listing those things that make life worth living—including Hemingway's face— the final scene and Allen's final smile; it's truly romantic. A perceptive, witty, masterful film. Gorgeous photography by Gordon Willis. Also with: Anne Byrne, Michael O'Donoghue.

MANIAC (1934) B&W/52m. A legitimate challenger to *Plan 9 from Outer Space* as the worst film ever made! In fact, cameraman William C. Thompson lensed both films. Directed by the infamous Dwain Esper (*Marihuana, the Weed with Roots in Hell, How to Undress Your Husband*) and scripted by his wife, Hildegarde Stradie, this consistently hilarious Poverty Row sleaze masterpiece begins when the mad-as-a-hatter Dr. Meierschultz (an inspired, wide-eyed, cackling performance by Horace Carpenter) and his ex-vaudevillean assistant, Maxwell (Bill Woods), plan a heart transplant. They steal a female corpse from the morgue and bring her back to life with some junior-level massage techniques (so much for the heart transplant). When Maxwell fails to secure another body because a couple of fighting cats (!) scare him away, Meierschultz tries to kill him. But Maxwell kills the doctor instead. Hoping to avoid arrest, he disguises himself as Meierschultz (with wild white beard and glasses) and becomes the madman Meierschultz was. He'd attempt a transplant of his own, but the doctor's cat eats the heart that's been preserved—he gets back at the cat by squeezing out its eyeball and swallowing it. (Actually, the guy next door is meaner to cats: he has thousands of them that he's raising for their fur.) Film manages to be tasteless and ridiculous the entire way through. The acting is sublimely bad—I doubt that the actors are playing their parts with tongue in cheek, but think Esper simply found the worst actors around and gave them dramatic lines to deliver. It's upsetting when Meierschultz is killed because he is one of the great insane scientists in cinema history and Carpenter is giving an impossibly bad reading. However, a bit character shows up and steals the film. When Maxwell's "Meierschultz" accidentally shoots him up with the wrong solution, this fellow, Buckley (Tod Andrews), goes into an astonishing dying routine, rubbing his hands over his body and then his head, distorting his face, and speaking of terrible burning pain. But this hammy fellow doesn't die. Instead he imagines himself as the orangutan murderer from *Murders in the Rue Morgue* (later the film borrows from Poe's *The Black Cat*) and picks up the revived but catatonic "dead" woman as she just happens to walk through the office. He carries her through the woods—her bare breasts show!—and then puts her down and starts strangling her: this is the last time we see him in the film! Picture is full of ludicrous moments: my favorite one is when two stupid morgue attendants act lucky because they got a pretty female corpse that afternoon. Scenes are interrupted throughout with text describing various forms of mental illness. The camp-lover's dream come true. Unbelievable and unforgettable! Also with: the first Phyllis Diller.

MANIAC (1980) C/88m. Indefensible slice-and-dice film that has found a cult among fans of the master of gore special effects, Tom Savini. It stars and was co-written by Joe Spinell, whom you've seen as a supporting player in many more respectable urban dramas. Apparently his character has become a maniac because his mother used to beat him. He talks to the mannequins and dolls that fill his sleazy little room and he kills women so he can put their scalps on these plastic figures. Sicko kills a prostitute, a nurse whom he chases through a deserted subway station, a young woman and her boyfriend (Savini) who are making love in their car—here he uses a shotgun instead of a knife or his powerful hands, and this allows Savini to use a great deal of blood—and a model. In a weird sequence in which Spinell seems to impersonate Robert De Niro, he courts beautiful photographer Caroline Munro, who for some reason responds to this fat, ugly man. He intends to make her his victim when they visit his mother's grave. The acting is bad, the script hasn't one clever moment, and the murders are repulsive—but what is most objectionable is how director William Lustig prolongs the death scenes of the nurse and the model so that they are killed long after Spinell could have done away with them. He makes it appear that the nurse has escaped. He makes it seem that the model is done for, only to have her wake up in the next scene, find herself strapped to his bed, plead for her life, be assured that he'll not harm her with the knife he rubs on her chest and stomach, and then watch him stab her to death. The ending is extremely weak. Also with: Gail Lawrence, Kelly Piper, porn actress Sharon Mitchell.

MARIUS (FRENCH/1931) B&W/125m—130m.
The first of Marcel Pagnol's *Marseilles Trilogy*, to be followed by *Fanny* (1932) and *César* (1936). Pagnol wrote this adaptation of his play. Film has slow pacing due to static, unimaginative direction of Alexander Korda, but Pagnol's characters are a wonderful lot, particularly bar owner César (Raimu, one of the greatest French actors) and his middle-aged friends, with their hats, pot bellies, and funny philosophizing and quibbling. César's son, Marius (Pierre Fresnay), has wanderlust and dreams of leaving Marseilles and life in the Bar de la Marine. But he loves Fanny (Orane Demazis). She wants Marius to marry her and tries to make him jealous by saying rich, middle-aged Panisse (Charpin) has proposed. They start sleeping together, keeping this secret from César and Fanny's mother, Honorine (Alida Rouffe). When Fanny realizes Marius can't be happy unless he has the opportunity to sail the seas, she sacrifices her own happiness. Picture has warmth, humor, marvelous acting by Raimu—plus it was one of the first films not only to deal with premarital sex but to make it seem natural. Highlights include an affectionate scene between César and his son (parental love is vital to the trilogy) and a card game between César and his pals. Also with: Robert Vattier, Paul Dullac, Alexandre Mihalesco, Edouard Delmont, Maupi.

MARKED WOMAN (1937) B&W/99m.
Excellent feminist crime drama was based on the 1936 trial in which crusading New York district attorney Thomas E. Dewey was able to nail gang lord "Lucky" Luciano. He was convicted on 61 counts of promoting prostitution, on the basis of testimony of "working girls" who turned against their boss. Bette Davis gives a strong performance as a clip-joint girl (prostitute) who, at the request of DA Humphrey Bogart, risks her life to give evidence against her cruel mobster boss, Eduardo Ciannelli. She is spurred on by the murder of her innocent sister (Jane Bryan). Her four female roommates-workmates—Lola Lane, Isabel Jewell, Rosalind Marquis, Mayo Methot—stick by her and also give testimony against Ciannelli. We're impressed by these women because they act bravely although they are terrified about what might happen to them; because they will be subject to humiliation in court when they're asked about their line of work; and because they don't stand to gain anything by testifying other than avenging Bryan's death and freeing girls all over the city who are under Ciannelli's heavy thumb. These women aren't angels, they don't have hearts of gold, but they have integrity. They are adamant about fulfilling their mission. They know that by sticking together, women have strength—and that's the message they want to get out to all the faceless, exploited American women they represent. Best scenes: the opening in which Ciannelli lays down the rules to his new female employees (the clip-joint girls) and smart Davis stands up to him; Bogart tells Davis that her sister is dead; Jewell escapes from the mobsters before they can kill her; the trial; our five "heroines" walk away into the fog, arm in arm. Tough direction by Lloyd Bacon. Scripted by Robert Rossen and Abem Finkel. Also with: Allen Jenkins, John Litel, Henry O'Neill.

MARNIE (1964) C/120m.
Alfred Hitchcock's psychological melodrama wasn't really appreciated until the seventies, when films were at last being examined in terms of sexual roles and relationships; it remains one of the rare films that allow viewers to be privy to the intimate problems of a married couple. This is the one Hitchcock film in which his blonde with an icy veneer remains cold and sexually remote *in* the bedroom, and the film where he finally sides with his blonde. In a role intended for Grace Kelly, Tippi Hedren is the disturbed, enigmatic Marnie Edgar. She assumes aliases, takes jobs in rich male-run firms, and robs their safes. She suffers tremendous guilt, has nightmares, and becomes frightened during thunderstorms and when she sees anything blood-red, but these feelings have less to do with her being a criminal than with an experience in her childhood that was so traumatic that she blocked it out completely. She uses money to take care of her horse, Forio, and her rigid, unloving, Bible-quoting mother (Louise Latham), who was once a prostitute. When her new boss, Mark Rutland (Sean Connery), catches her robbing his safe, he becomes strongly attracted to her. He threatens to turn her in unless she marries him. He loves her; she detests him and won't have sex with him. He tries to find out what happened to her as a child that made her hate men. Hitchcock considered this to be an unusual mystery because the search is not for a criminal but for a criminal's motivation. But the *search for motivation* is *not* the key to this film. This picture

265

is about a woman with many aliases who is involved in a desperate *search for identity*, who can stop living a life of lies only if she learns the truth about her past. It makes no difference if little Marnie killed a client of her prostitute mother that fateful night, as in the film, or her prostitute mother went crazy and killed her illegitimate baby, as in Winston Graham's novel. Marnie must learn of an event, any event, that happened in *her* life just before she moved permanently into a world of make-believe. This bit of history is the shaky foundation on which she can build a real life. The revelations about that night don't sufficiently explain why Marnie is a thief and is frigid—but we can easily deduce the reasons in the film. The men in Marnie's nightmarish world are filthy pigs who think of women as animals. For man-hater Marnie, penetrating a boss's safe and taking his money (his strength over female employees) is the symbolic rape of men who'd like to rape her, who have insulted her constantly with their roving eyes. Mark is as bad as the rest at the beginning—he even forces himself on her. To his credit, Mark is afterward as repulsed by the rape as she is. It will not happen again. He changes his attitude toward Marnie—and when it becomes apparent that he wants to help her now instead of continuing to sexually blackmail her, she subconsciously opens up to him as she has to no other man. She no longer has a need for Forio. She has found a human being who will not run away, no matter what she does. That she allows him, in the key scene, to take a gun (a phallic symbol) from her implies she is trusting him to again pursue her sexually. Still, there is no final kiss and she doesn't say she loves him. Written by Jay Presson Allen, with cinematography by Robert Burks and music by Bernard Herrmann. Also with: Diane Baker, Martin Gabel, Bob Sweeney, Alan Napier, S. John Launer, Mariette Hartley, Bruce Dern.

MARRIAGE OF MARIA BRAUN, THE (WEST GERMAN/1978) C/126m.
Rainer Werner Fassbinder's most commercially successful film features a sexy, self-assured, truly sensational performance by Hanna Schygulla as a scheming, confident woman who uses body and brains to become rich. Yet, ironically, her rise to the top is a *sacrificial* act for the man she loves, her imprisoned husband who needs money to obtain freedom. Fassbinder loves irony, and the joke (for a while anyway) is on Maria: her husband, Hermann Braun, disappears rather than returning to her after getting out of prison; and Oswald, the businessman she seduced into loving her, leaves his inheritance not to her but to her husband, whom he secretly bought off so he'd stay away from him and Maria until after his own death. The men in her life are much weaker than Maria is, but they, too, can be calculating and deceitful. Maria is one of Fassbinder's strongest, most complex, most tragic heroes—a woman whose downfall results from a bargain between two men who can't hold a candle to her. In fact, the traits we usually associate with men in movies (inner strength, intelligence, perseverance, a keen business sense, a refusal to back down to other men or to mince words) are traits that distinguish Maria, not the men in this film. This beautifully shot, melancholy (occasionally slow) melodrama is much like a standard "woman's picture" (of course Fassbinder admired Douglas Sirk's fifties soaps), but this woman who foolishly gives all for love feels no remorse and refuses to suffer from guilt; she asks for no sympathy, no forgiveness—her desire to be detached from responsibility toward her lovers is evident when she begrudgingly tips a worker and says revealingly, "I'd rather pay them than be obliged to say thank you." Fassbinder provides not only an incisive character study but also a brutal evocation of banal bourgeois life in postwar capitalistic Germany. Also with: Ivan Desny, Gottfried John, Klaus Lowitsch.

MARRYING KIND, THE (1952) B&W/93m.
Captivating film was directed by George Cukor and scripted by Garson Kanin and Ruth Gordon. Blending comedy and extreme tragedy, it stars Judy Holliday and Aldo Ray as a lower-middle-class couple who seek a divorce. As they tell their story to the judge (Madge Kennedy), they experience a kind of therapy, revealing feelings that they never expressed to each other. He tells his story, she tells her story, and we flashback on an entirely different story: what the judge calls "the truth." In their marriage, both had felt inadequate because each realized that the other was unhappy. She was lonely; he was too busy for romance because he was working at the post office, trying to make enough money to win her approval. While they loved each other, they seemed to bring each other bad luck. In one of the most painful scenes in movie history, she has the opportunity to win a lot of money on a radio quiz by correctly naming a tune—but she gives Ray's guess instead of her own and they lose. As in many other instances, it's devastating to his ego and underlines the fact that he can't adequately support her. (He feels that every disappointment and other men's every success make him a failure in her eyes.) It also shows that Holliday hasn't enough self-confidence to give her own correct answer. Both have ego problems which could be solved if they just expressed their true feelings for each other. Kanin and Gordon have made a plea for married couples to be friends and be mutually supportive. And for unhappy couples to reassess their relationships to figure out why things went wrong. Film is way ahead of its time. The "sleeper" of Holliday's career, it may very well contain her finest performance. It has a small but devoted cult. Also with: Peggy Cass, Mickey Shaughnessy, Griff Barnett, Phyllis Povah.

MARY POPPINS (1964) C/140m.
Julie Andrews made her film debut and won an Oscar as the "practically perfect" heroine of P. L. Travers's children's books. Story is set in 1910 London. Banker Mr. Banks (David Tomlinson), a firm, dull man, wants a strict new governess for his young children (Karen Dotrice, Matthew Garber). The children want someone kind, who will play games, and will have rosy cheeks. Their father tears up their letter asking for a governess, but the pieces fly up the chimney and to

the cloud on which Andrews sits, with her umbrella and bottomless bag. She becomes governess and, using magic, takes the children on wonderful adventures, some with Bert (Dick Van Dyke), a friendly jack of all trades. They even go into a make-believe world, where everything is animated. Andrews stays around until Tomlinson turns into a real father to his children. This is probably Walt Disney's most popular film, and critics greeted it with tremendous enthusiasm. I am impressed with the stylized design, some of the animation (especially the dancing penguins), and the ambitious nature of the project, but on the whole it leaves me cold. Except when Andrews and Van Dyke sing and dance, there's very little life in the characters. The Poppins character requires Andrews to hold her enthusiasm in check, thus depriving her of her best quality at that stage of her career. If this film had come out after *The Sound of Music*, viewers would probably have been upset by the change. The children aren't badly acted, but I can't tell what they're like from watching the film; Van Dyke uses an obviously phony cockney accent; Tomlinson is a bore, and Glynis Johns (as Tomlinson's wife) is restricted to a small part—if she were around more, the children wouldn't need a governess. Songs by Richard M. and Robert B. Sherman are acceptable; of course the best are the Oscar-winning "Chim-Chim-Cheree" and "Supercalifragilisticexpialidocious." "Spoonful of Sugar" is one of those songs only Andrews could get away with. Picture has its imaginative moments, but I don't think there are enough of them. Cotton Warburton won an editing Oscar, although the picture is about 40 minutes too long. Bill Walsh and Donald Da Gradi adapted Travers, who was disappointed in the film. Robert Stevenson directed, Marc Breaux and Dee Dee Wood did the fine choreography. Hamilton Luske was animation director. Also with: Ed Wynn, Hermione Baddeley, Elsa Lanchester, Arthur Treacher, Reginald Owen, Jane Darwell (as the poorly used Bird Woman).

MASCULIN-FÉMININ (FRENCH/1966) B&W/
103m—110m.   One of Jean-Luc Godard's most memorable films of the sixties, about the "Children of Marx and Coca-Cola." Twenty-one-year-old Jean-Pierre Léaud gets out of the army and gets an unsatisfying job with a magazine, interviewing people about politics and consumer habits. He splits his time between feeble political activity (spray-painting anti-Vietnam slogans on walls and American-made cars, etc.) and a clumsy courtship of lovely aspiring singer Chantal Goya. He thinks love is at the center of his universe, but she is as noncommittal in love as he is in politics. He desires warmth and tenderness. Film captures the sense of an exciting, confusing, often frustrating era when young people in France and America were simultaneously learning leftist politics and having their first sexual affairs: being involved in politics was so much fun because it brought together many people with similar viewpoints whose blood was already pumping and adrenaline already flowing (how many people began affairs after a big protest!). Film has several extremely erotic scenes; one has Léaud and Chantal in bed together; but the other two are set in bathrooms and

just have couples (Léaud and Chantal, his friend Michel Debord and her friend Catherine-Isabelle Duport) stand around "interviewing" each other about sex (and who they are) while Godard keeps them in intimate close-up. Some of film is precisely structured, other scenes are loose and have much improvisation. Depressing ending is a surprise. Based on stories by Guy de Maupassant: "La Femme de Paul" and "Le Signe." Music is by Francis Lai; for the first time Godard used a cameraman other than Raoul Coutard— Willy Kurant. Also with: Marlène Jobert, Brigitte Bardot (a cameo as a Bardot lookalike), Françoise Hardy.

M*A*S*H (1970) C/112m—116m.   Robert Altman
directed this popular anti-war comedy about the odd assortment of characters who comprise the Mobile Army Surgery Hospital corps that is stationed near the fighting during the Korean War. The rare anti-war film to make money during a time the U.S. was at war, it's best known for radically diverging from conventional Hollywood narrative techniques. What viewers found most bizarre about it in 1970 is that it contains no storyline. Altman was more interested in establishing the uniquely absurd ambience that distinguished MASH facilities in Korea. What we have is the formation of a temporary community of workmates, lovers (no matter if spouses are waiting back in America), dear friends, and friendly enemies. These people get involved in each other's lives—they play practical jokes on one another, they have affairs, they play games—so they won't become numbed by the insane bloodshed taking place within earshot and their having to perform surgery on badly injured GIs. Altman's toughest task was to get us to believe that such irreverent characters as Hawkeye (Donald Sutherland) and Trapper John (Elliott Gould) really are sensitive about the men being killed in the war. Their zany, childish antics are just an emotional release—while performing surgery, they come through. Wild picture was adapted by Ring Lardner, Jr., from Richard Hooker's novel, but it's obvious that Altman wanted his actors to improvise (so there would be overlapping dialogue) rather than strictly adhere to the script. The actors are first-rate—Sutherland, Gould, and Sally Kellerman (as Margaret "Hot Lips" Houlihan) deservedly became stars as a result of their performances. The basis for the long-running television series. Also with: Tom Skerritt, Gary Burghoff (he'd also play Radar on television), Robert Duvall (Major Burns), Roger Bowen (as Colonel Blake), René Auberjonois, Jo Ann Pflug, Bud Cort, Fred Williamson, Michael Murphy, Carl Gottlieb.

MASQUE OF THE RED DEATH, THE (1964) C/
86m.   Roger Corman's best film, a super-stylish mix of Edgar Allan Poe (the title story plus "Hop-Frog") and Ingmar Bergman's *The Seventh Seal*. Vincent Price gives a forceful performance as Prince Prospero, a sadistic 12th-century Italian satanist. While the Red Death wipes out the God-fearing villagers, Prospero calmly retreats to his castle for the nightly orgies of his aristocratic guests. He takes with him a pretty village girl (Jane Asher) and tries to

convert her from being a Christian to a worshipper of Satan. He also imprisons her lover (David Weston) and father (Nigel Green) in his torture chamber. Meanwhile his lady (Hazel Court) consorts with the devil. We don't actually see many ghastly acts (Court's death is the most vicious), but the atmosphere is thick with perversion, pain, death; Price's deeds and words are cruel. It's a strange film because one expects that the denouement will contain the standard triumph of good over evil, but this is not the case. The Death that claims victims does not choose according to whether one believes in God or Satan. Prospero is so unhappy to see Death's arrival at his *danse macabre* because he believed that Satan would protect him—just as in *The Seventh Seal* those who prayed to God believed wrongly they'd be spared Death's hand. It's true that Price dies and Asher is spared, yet his last act is to spare a little girl from death and her last act is to kiss Price willingly, indicating that she's not the God-loving innocent she once was. Film is in its way as philosophic as Bergman's picture; Corman's characters are as hopelessly confused and terrified, because the God in whom they had faith has abandoned them. Filmed in England, in Technicolor, this is the most handsome of Corman's films. The set design by Daniel Haller and photography by Nicolas Roeg are exceptional—Roeg's surreal vision of Court's visit to hell's recesses surely inspired the visuals of the LSD hallucinations in Corman's *The Trip.* Charles Beaumont and R. Wright Campbell wrote the interesting script. Also with: Patrick Magee, Skip Marten, John Westbrook.

MASSACRE AT CENTRAL HIGH (1976)
C/87m. A real sleeper: director-writer Renee Daalder, a Dutch cameraman, took exploitation material and made a political art film. Derrel Maury is a new boy at Central High who soon realizes that three troublemakers have all the other kids under their thumbs. His friend Andrew Stevens convinces him to ignore the bullying taking place. When Stevens thinks Maury is making a play for his girlfriend (Kimberly Beck), he gives the bullies a go-ahead to strongarm his friend. Maury has his leg crushed. Maury eliminates the three bullies—all *fall* to their deaths (and from their "thrones")—but when the students he liberates become as autocratic as the dead students, he decides to massacre everyone. Strange political allegory has every student representing a different political force: there are oppressors, the persecuted, the intellectual, the anti-intellectuals, the peasant-farmer, the cowardly bourgeois, the conservative (Stevens), the liberal (Beck), the freedom fighter and representative of the proletariat (Maury); the nameless students are the masses. As I see it, Maury's role is to politicize Stevens and Beck, who are always neutral, and make them into activists willing to fight even him when he becomes a mass murderer. Daalder's theme is that one must fight oppression whether it comes from the extreme right (the bullies) or extreme left (Maury). Film is quite surreal; for one thing, there are no adults at this school except the cadaverous alumni at the climactic dance. This makes one wonder if Central High is a dream world of some history/political-science student. Also with: Robert Carradine, Roy Underwood, Steve Bond, Damon Douglas, Rainbeaux Smith, Lani O'Grady, Steve Sikes, Dennis Court, Jeffrey Winner, Thomas Logan.

McCABE AND MRS. MILLER (1971) C/121m.
Robert Altman's revisionist western was one of best films of the early seventies. Heavily bearded Warren Beatty is McCabe, a cocky, opportunistic gambler and instinctive businessman who comes to Presbyterian Church, a frontier town in the Northwest, and soon controls its gambling, liquor, and prostitution. Frizzy-haired Julie Christie, who has never been lovelier, is Mrs. Miller, an ambitious, money-hungry madame who comes to the town with her high-class, high-priced whores and convinces McCabe to let her become his partner in a bordello operation. They are tremendously successful. and they become lovers. All is well until organized crime tries to buy out McCabe. When he refuses to accept the low offer, hired guns show up in town, determined to kill him. Ending has bad guys dead, townspeople trying to extinguish their burning church, the ignored McCabe dying in the snow, and Mrs. Miller (who loves McCabe) lying in an opium den because she can't understand why McCabe would want to confront the killers and give up his life. Sad part is that Christians pay no attention to McCabe although he is the only opponent of corrupt forces trying to take over the town (they'll succeed with McCabe out of the way). There is a big difference between his amorality and the criminality of the organized machines that will take control of every town in growing America. The one optimistic note is that McCabe proved he had integrity—the snow may be burying him, but it is also purifying him. Film has great visual beauty (camera work was by Vilmos Zsigmond) and a uniquely romantic feel—until the bad guys intrude. Scene in which a young punk murders Keith Carradine on a hanging bridge is horrifying. It prepares us for the brutality to come. McCabe's final act with a derringer—like Marlowe's final act with a gun in Altman's *The Long Goodbye*—shows he is not as far out of his league dealing with bad buys as we had assumed. McCabe, Mrs. Miller, and the other characters are believable, and unlike those found in other westerns. Incidentally, the real Mrs. Miller tied up lover John McCabe and shaved him bald. Altman and Brian McKay adapted Edmund Naughton's *McCabe.* Leonard Cohen's singing will get on your nerves—but at least Altman was trying to be different by using his songs. Also with: René Auberjonois, Hugh Millais, Shelley Duvall, Michael Murphy, John Schuck, Bert Remsen, Corey Fischer, Jack Riley, William Devane.

MEAN STREETS (1973) C/110m.
Martin Scorsese emerged from obscurity with this violent, visually dazzling love-hate remembrance of life in New York's Little Italy. Independent film deals with young low-level criminals—second-rank loan sharks, numbers men, street hustlers, collectors—whose goal is to move up in the Mafia hierarchy.

Harvey Keitel wants his Mafia uncle to give him a restaurant that was taken from its rightful owner; but he must keep secret his friendship with stupid, irresponsible, reckless Robert De Niro (who became a star as Johnny Boy) and love for De Niro's epileptic cousin, Amy Robinson (who years later co-produced Scorsese's *After Hours*). Keitel spends most of his time getting De Niro out of trouble (he plays George to De Niro's Lennie) and eventually tries to get him out of town to avoid a loan shark (Richard Romanus), a former friend to whom he's deeply in debt. An alternative to *Diner*, film shows young Italian buddies hanging out in friend David Proval's bar, carrying on conversations (heavily improvised) that have more slaps and shoves than words, holding two-minute grudges against each other, losing their tempers, discussing what's happening on the streets, making a play for women, scheming to get cash to see a movie up on 42nd Street, figuring out how to smooth things over between De Niro and Romanus, watching strangers engage in violence. Scorsese calls attention to his characters' foul racism and the foolish male posturing—he delights in sticking a couple of gays in a car with our macho Italians and embarrassing them by calling out pick-up lines to men on the streets. But he sees these young men sympathetically, as victims of their crowded, brutal, corrupt hell-town. He likes the loyalty that Keitel feels for De Niro and their odd humor (this film is funny), but he worries when De Niro doesn't take things at all seriously and Romanus takes them too seriously, not allowing De Niro to be the fuck-up every group must have—there will be violence. Film has distinct rhythm created by rock-music score, camera movement, special brand of patter between characters. The strong use of city locales indicates Scorsese was an expert on post-WWII Italian neo-realism films. This remains one of Scorsese's most exciting efforts. Excellent cinematography by Kent Wakeford. Also with: Harry Northrup, George Memmoli, Cesare Danova, David Carradine, Robert Carradine, Scorsese.

MEATBALLS (CANADIAN/1979) C/92m.

Unremarkable comedy broke Canadian box-office records, proving former *Saturday Night Live* live star Bill Murray could make it as a movie star. He's the program director of a summer camp full of losers; treating them without condescension, he manages to build their egos—making a special project of a lonely young boy (Chris Makepeace). Murray is quite funny, especially when speaking over the camp's public-address system (and revealing what the "mystery meat" was at lunch). But too much of the humor is sophomoric and tasteless (i.e., Murray teaching Makepeace how to speak while burping). And it gets annoying that director Ivan Reitman keeps showing Makepeace laughing at Murray's sarcastic ranting and raving, as if he were Ed McMahon confirming that Johnny Carson's being funny. At times schmaltz gets in way of humor. *Meatballs—Part II* without Murray was made in 1984. Also with: Harvey Atkin, Kate Lynch, Kristen DeBell.

MEDIUM COOL (1969) C/110m.

Godard-influenced political film directed, produced, written, and photographed by noted leftist cinematographer Haskell Wexler. Today it's a curio, a time piece, but when it came out it caused tremendous excitement among young viewers involved in anti-establishment causes and interested in political films, as well as those who simply may have appreciated unique ways to tell stories on film. A cocky Chicago television reporter (Robert Forster) tries to remain detached from his stories despite their increasing political and social significance. We see his social consciousness rise after he is told off by some ghetto blacks for being part of establishment media that distorts news, and after covering the Democratic Convention and the ensuing riots during which Mayor Daley's gestapo police beat up countless protesters. When he learns his network has been handing over his tapes to the FBI, he finally understands the function of the media/press and how uninvolved newsmen are doing a disservice to the people. That he becomes "human" is apparent when he has an affair not with a sexy bubblehead (his previous lovers), but with a poor, kindly widow (Verna Bloom) from West Virginia, and befriends her son (Harold Blankenship). Wexler interweaves professional actors with amateurs, his fictional story with real footage of the Chicago convention and violent police-protester confrontations—at times the actors are on the scene during the rioting, and Wexler takes his camera right into the fray. The impact was remarkable back then. Film got an X rating, officially because of its groundbreaking bold frontal nudity—but it was well known that the rating was because of its political content. Unfortunately, those under 18 weren't allowed to see this film that would have affected them greatly. Paramount was scared by its politics and refused to release it for almost a year, until the Chicago riots were no longer topical and *Easy Rider* proved pictures with an anti-establishment stance could make money. Even so, Wexler had to strike a bargain with the studio; in a 1974 interview in *Take One* he recalled, "They said they wanted something to show that the police had more provocation for doing what they did [in the Grant Park riot sequence]. . . . So they said, 'OK, if you delete "Let's get the fuckers" [said by the police] and add two "pigs eat shit" and one "up against the wall motherfucker" spoken by the antiwar forces, we'll accept the picture.' That's a fact." The film never did make money, but it is one of the strongest leftwing pieces ever released by a Hollywood studio. Also with: Peter Bonerz, Marianna Hill.

MEET JOHN DOE (1941) B&W/123m–132m.

Reporter Barbara Stanwyck saves her job by coming up with a clever gimmick: she concocts a fake letter to the paper, which she attributes to "John Doe," in which *he* complains about how crooked politicians are ignoring the plight of the nation's poor and promises to jump off a building on Christmas Eve. Because of the great publicity, the paper hires an out-of-work aspiring ballplayer (Gary Cooper) to impersonate John Doe while Stanwyck ghost-writes a daily column in which he vehemently protests about corrupt big business and politicians. Cooper becomes such a national hero that evil publisher Edward Arnold wants to use him as the figurehead of a new, rightwing party. Finally Cooper, feeling disillusioned and guilty because he fooled the people, decides to carry out John Doe's suicide promise. Stanwyck tries to dissuade him. Made independently by director Frank Capra and writer Robert Riskin, and distributed by Warner Bros., picture was shamelessly calculated to become a commercial success by stirring up emotions of the common man. It is self-congratulatory, pretentious, gloomy, heartless. As if made by someone who always climbs out of the wrong side of the bed, it shows an America populated solely by corrupt individuals and simpletons who'll believe anything told to them and accept anything done to them. That soda jerk who gives a never ending discourse about his town's people coming together after being inspired by John Doe's help-your-neighbor speech is one of many jerks who the patronizing filmmakers seem to think represent the common folk of America. I can't stand how Capra lines up his common folk, has them talk in humble, hushed tones, and shines a light on their well-scrubbed faces so that we may think they have angels sitting on their shoulders. It was daring of Capra to show the police acting as agents of politicians, but there's really nothing else controversial about the picture. Cooper's speeches could have been delivered to a junior-high civics class. Best parts of film come early on, before Stanwyck and Cooper get scruples; even Capra disliked the weak resolution. Also with: Walter Brennan, James Gleason, Spring Byington, Gene Lockhart, Regis Toomey, Ann Doran, Rod La Rocque.

MEET ME IN ST. LOUIS (1944) C/113m.
Wonderful M-G-M musical, directed by Vincente Minnelli (his best musical) and starring Judy Garland (it's her best film other than *The Wizard of Oz*), is set in St. Louis in 1903, just prior to the World's Fair. Garland lives on a lovely street, a magnificent $100,000 set designed by Lemuel Ayres and Cedric Gibbons, in a large-but-cozy house with her parents (Leon Ames, Mary Astor), grandfather (Harry Davenport), older sister (Lucille Bremer), younger sisters (Joan Carroll, six-year-old Margaret O'Brien), brother (Henry Daniels, Jr.), and cook (Marjorie Main). Everyone's happy, Garland and Bremer are in love, O'Brien is a hit with the neighborhood kids on Halloween—then Ames announces that the family's moving to New York, and everyone feels miserable. Film is a warm, unsentimental tribute to family, home, and tree-lined America. Garland and O'Brien give lovely performances. They team on one cute number and Garland sings to O'Brien "Have Yourself a Merry Little Christmas"; other Garland classics are "The Boy Next Door" and the show-stopping "The Trolley Song." The cute, feisty O'Brien, who won a special Oscar, has two exceptional dramatic scenes, one set on a scary Halloween night and another in which she destroys her snowman because she's so upset about the family's moving. Irving Brecher and Fred Finklehoffe adapted Sally Benson's short stories about her youth. Songs were written by Hugh Martin and Ralph Blane. Arthur Freed produced. George Folsey's striking color photography contributes to the picture's early-century flavor. Also with: Tom Drake, June Lockhart, Hugh Marlowe, Robert Sully, Chill Wills.

MELVIN AND HOWARD (1980) C/95m.
Genial sad-eyed comedy is about Melvin Dummar (Paul LeMat), a nobody Nevada milkman turned garage owner who was named an heir in Howard Hughes's will—only to see that will declared a fraud by the courts. Dummar claimed that he'd picked up a desert rat (Jason Robards, Jr.) one night; they'd sung together, and the old man had done some driving. The man claimed he was Hughes, but Dummar thought he was a bum. Until the will turned up. Obviously director Jonathan Demme and screenwriter Bo Goldman (who won an Oscar) feel sympathy for Dummar. He deserves a break, a big break, even if he only imagined that he gave a lift to Hughes—he's the typical forgotten young American. He's a nice, well-meaning guy but not very smart or realistic; his go-go dancer wife (Mary Steenburgen) keeps taking the kid (Elizabeth Cheshire) and walking out; he hasn't any money; he lives for his dreams (striking it rich, becoming a songwriter). Characters are real; the acting by LeMat, Steenburgen (who won a Best Supporting Actress Oscar), Robards, and Pamela Reed (as Melvin's second, practical wife) is first-rate. Demme properly conveys his characters' sense of dislocation (even Hughes is lost in the desert) — but watching them is an unsettling experience in itself: it's as if you moved but had not unpacked because you might have to move again soon. The reason the opening and final scenes with Dummar and Howard Hughes are so enjoyable is that they are the only moments in this chaotic movie that are calm. Highlights: Robards' singing "Bye Bye Blackbird" and a duet with LeMat; Steenburgen appearing on a TV show; Reed proposing to LeMat; LeMat singing at a milkmen's dinner. Photographed by Tak Fujimoto. Also with: Jack Kehoe, Michael J. Pollard, Dabney Coleman, Martine Beswicke, Gloria Grahame, Dummar (as a counterman), Rick Lenz.

MEMORIES OF UNDERDEVELOPMENT (CUBAN/1968) B&W/97m.–104m.
The first film of post-revolutionary Cuba to be released in the United Sates. Tomás Gutiérrez Alea, Cuba's most famous director, and Edmundo Desnoes adapted Desnoes's novel, which is set in Havana between the Bay of Pigs invasion in 1961 and the Cuban missile crisis in 1962. Alea combines documentary footage of Cuba's present and recent past with a fictional storyline about a Europeanized Cuban intellectual (Sergio Corrieri). An alienated member of the bourgeoisie, he has decided to stay in Cuba although most of his acquaintances, including his ex-wife, have left for the United States. He is cynical about the post-revolutionary society, where he sees that the change from a dictatorship in which the bourgeoisie thrived to a socialist society has been too swift for those with "underdeveloped" political consciousness— such as himself. Still decadent and alienated from the rev-

olution (he is the ultimate outsider), he spends most of his time either recalling sexual encounters in the past or pursuing women. When he wrongly gets arrested for allegedly raping a "virgin" (Daisy Granados), he is pleased and fortunate that the new courts are just. Film is complicated because it's hard for us to figure out Alea's feeling toward his protagonist—does he think his type can ever be radicalized? Apolitical American viewers may, in fact, identify with him (and his backward attitude toward women) and share his view of Cuba. Alea uses the documentary footage to show what his protagonist doesn't even consider (or remember)—it shows the necessity for the revolution and the need to preserve it.

MERRY WIDOW, THE (1925) B&W/111m.
Considering how much trouble Erich von Stroheim had with M-G-M over the final cut of *Greed* (1923), it's surprising that he immediately returned to that studio to film this adaptation of an operetta by Victor Leon, Leo Stein, and Franz Lehár. Mae Murray is an Irish-American showgirl who comes to Monteblanco with the *Follies*. Prince John Gilbert and his cruel, constantly sneering, monocled cousin, Prince Roy D'Arcy (a role Von Stroheim had intended to play), vie for her affections. She and Gilbert fall in love, but because of pressure from his parents, the King and Queen, he stands her up at the altar. In order to get wealth and power, Murray marries a crippled banker (Tully Marshall), who, as luck will have it, dies on their wedding night. Now that Murray is a rich widow of importance, Gilbert and D'Arcy resume their competition. Odd film has bursts of bizarre slapstick humor: Gilbert keeps attacking D'Arcy; D'Arcy beats up a cripple; Marshall kisses Murray on the shoulder and has a heart attack. We also are amused by the assortment of weird characters Von Stroheim parades in front of us. However, whenever Von Stroheim turns serious—as in the duel between Gilbert and D'Arcy—we're not sure how to react because we're waiting for some unexpected gag. Another problem is that we stop caring about the romance between Gilbert and Murray's characters because they consistently act foolishly toward each other. The studio changed Von Stroheim's unhappy ending. Remade in 1934 by Ernst Lubitsch and in 1952 by Curtis Bernhardt.

METROPOLIS (GERMAN/1926) B&W/120m.
Fritz Lang's colossal silent fiction classic was set 100 years in the future; it was visually inspired by New York's skyline, which Lang had recently seen, and thematically inspired (in part) by the increasingly dehumanizing industrialization within Germany. Metropolis's leisure class lives in towering skyscrapers, parties in lavish ballrooms, has orgies in pleasure gardens, travels about the city in air vehicles or road vehicles that can go through bridge-tunnels that connect buildings. The workers toil endlessly far below in an underground section of the city, driving the great machines that make the above world function. In a frightening sequence we see how during their workday they've literally become extensions of their machines. They move in depersonalized, orderly style, non-talking, anonymous. The leader of Metropolis, Joh Frederson (Alfred Abel), worries about the discontent among the workers. The mysterious magician Rotwang (Rudolf Klein-Rogge)—among the first of the crazed German scientists with artificial hands—suggests replacing the human workforce with robots he could create. He builds a female robot who looks identical to Maria (Brigitte Helm), a peace-minded young girl the workers listen to. The robot Maria will tell the workers to revolt and this will lead to their destruction by a great flood. Meanwhile Frederson's son Freder (Gustav Fröhlich) has gone to the depths of the city disguised as a worker in order to find Maria, whom he loved at first sight. If a flood comes, he will be in danger, too. Lang's epic was originally almost 200 minutes long, so it's really hard to judge the film's story from what we see in the drastically shortened prints. As it is, there's no way to figure out why Maria tells the workers not to revolt and to wait for a "mediator," when revolution is definitely their only hope; nor is it possible to figure out if Freder really is the "mediator" she speaks of; and why would Frederson want to destroy all the machinery below, since the robot workforce would have to use it anyway? Georgio Moroder tried to give sense to the film by concocting new titles for his recent version, but it's doubtful his new storyline is what was intended by Lang or his wife, Thea von Harbou, who wrote the script and the novel. Even in Moroder's version the story, the relationships, and the themes are sadly underdeveloped. However, the film is a visual tour-de-force. So much is stunning: the march of the workers; the fabulous robot-transformation sequence (which would be copied many times); Helm's erotic, bare-chested dance; the great flood. And of course the *look* of the future it presents would serve as the model for almost all futuristic cities in film and conceptual art until *Blade Runner*. Splendid photography by Karl Freund; groundbreaking special effects by Eugene Shuftan.

MIDNIGHT COWBOY (1969) C/113m.
Jon Voight is Joe Buck, who leaves his small Texas town, where he worked as a dishwasher, and comes to New York. He's confident that his boyish good looks and fancy cowboy garb will have the sophisticated, rich NY ladies fighting over his sexual services. But while he acts self-important, he's too weak-centered and too much of a loser to have any luck. When penniless, he accepts the invitation of gimpy Times Square sleazo "Ratso" Rizzo (Dustin Hoffman), a nickle-and-dime conman, to move in with him. In a heatless room in a dilapidated building the two down-and-out men try to take care of each other. While the film has humor and moments of warmth (generated solely by the two actors), it has a cruel edge. As if Joe and Ratso didn't have it hard enough trying to survive in the heartless, freezing city, they are at the mercy of an America-hating director, John Schlesinger, who seems to enjoy victimizing them in the name of America. In this unofficial "buddy picture," Voight, who became a sudden star, and Hoffman, who surprised everyone with a characterization that was completely unlike his break-

through role in *The Graduate*, give excellent, sympathetic portrayals. It's as if both actors realized that it was up to them to provide insight into their characters so that we can undersand both the reasons for and the depth of their friendship. Scriptwriter Waldo Salt doesn't even include scenes in which the men open up to each other and discuss their deepest feelings or their pasts (i.e., the reasons they are where they are today). Schlesinger keeps flashing back to a night in which Voight's girlfriend (Jennifer Salt) is gang-raped and tells authorities he was the one, the only one, who attacked her, but it's clear that the director was less interested in how this event affected Voight (because we *never* find out how it affected him) than adding the *flashback* to all his other technical impositions, most of which exhibit his desire to use film to *play with time*. X-rated when released. From the novel by James Leo Herlihy. Henry Nilsson performed Fred Neil's memorable "Everybody's Talkin'." Also with: Sylvia Miles, Brenda Vaccaro, John McGiver, Barnard Hughes, Ruth White, Bob Balaban, Viva, Taylor Meade, Ultra Violet, Paul Morrissey.

MIDNIGHT EXPRESS (1978) C/121m.
Gripping but in many ways a fraudulent telling of the true story of Billy Hayes (played by Brad Davis), a young American who was caught trying to smuggle hashish out of Turkey and thrown into a hellish prison, where brutality and no hope for a release led to frustration, madness, and finally escape. Best scenes are when he's caught before getting on the plane and when a long-planned, intricate escape through the prison sewers proves futile as he and his cohorts reach a wall, a dead end. Many scenes lose their effectiveness because they're fabrications of screenwriter Oliver Stone, who won an Oscar, and director Alan Parker, that are meant to increase our sympathy for Hayes, probably to assure we'd forgive his drug trafficking. The scene in which he backs out of a homosexual affair contradicts what he wrote in his book—again the filmmakers were concerned about his image. With his slight build and weak, guilty eyes, Davis is ideal as the ultimate underdog, an American who is deprived of his rights and liberties in a foreign country and treated like a dog by an "alien" (huge camp commander Paul Smith). Picture has been accused of racism: surely American tourists didn't flock to Turkey after this movie; surely U.S. college freshmen didn't hope for Turkish roommates or apply for a Turkish exchange program. The wrong impression many viewers got is that such prisons are peculiar to Turkey and not found all over the world. The last time I noticed, Hayes was a soap-opera star. An excellent score by Giorgio Moroder. Also with: Irene Miracle, Bo Hopkins, Randy Quaid, John Hurt, Mike Kellin.

MIGHTY JOE YOUNG (1949) B&W/94m.
An underrated fantasy gem about a friendly, incredibly strong 10-foot gorilla. Joe has grown up in Africa under the care of a pretty girl, now a young woman played by Howard Hughes's own Terry Moore. A New York showman, Robert Armstrong (as Max O'Hara, a character similar to Carl Denham in *King Kong*), convinces Moore to come to Broadway, where she and Joe will be the main attraction at his nightclub. Although Moore falls in love with rodeo cowboy Ben Johnson, she hates to see Joe so miserable in the Big Apple, regarded as a freak by audiences, and being forced to sleep in a cage. When some rowdy customers get Joe drunk, he wrecks the club and is condemned to be shot. Luckily, an orphanage catches on fire so Joe can save some kids and clear his name. Ruth Rose's script wavers, but Joe is a fabulous, lovable (yet not completely domesticated) creature—the special-effects and stop-motion work by *King Kong*'s famous Willis O'Brien and Ray Harryhausen are marvelous. Joe actually seems real, so subtle are his movements and expressions; and when he snatches a moving child off a burning ledge with a swing of the arm, you'll have no idea how it was done. The most famous scene has Joe winning a tug-of-war contest with several musclemen, including Man Mountain Dean, Primo Carnera, and the legendary Swedish Angel. A great movie for kids. Directed by Ernest B. Schoedsack, from an original story by Merian C. Cooper—the team that co-directed *King Kong*. Photography by J. Roy Hunt (*I Walked with a Zombie*). Also with: Frank McHugh, Douglas Fowley, Regis Toomey, Jack Pennick.

MILDRED PIERCE (1945) B&W/109m.
When Joan Crawford's second husband, Zachary Scott, is shot to death, her first husband, Bruce Bennett, confesses to the crime. Insisting that Bennett's innocent, Crawford tells the police what events led up to the murder—in doing so, both she and spoiled daughter Ann Blyth become suspects as well. When unemployed Bennett had left her following fights over money and how Crawford spoiled teenager Blyth, Crawford had to find work for the first time in her life in order to give her selfish, socially ambitious daughter what she wanted. She took a job as a waitress and with her newly gained knowledge opened up a restaurant, "Mildred's," buying the property from Scott, a down-on-his-luck playboy. Blyth was embarrassed that her mother was a working woman, even a successful restaurateur, so Crawford married Scott for his mansion and family name—giving him a third of her business. He would ruin her financially and increase the rift between mother and daughter. Adapted from James M. Cain's novel, this is essentially a *film noir* piece where it's a woman, Crawford, rather than a man, who is led by a greedy, manipulative, evil *femme fatale*—in this case, the woman's daughter, Blyth—down a fatalistic path full of deception, money for greedy people, murder, and doom (only here an optimistic ending is added). Like classic *femme fatales*, Blyth is the catalyst for the moral protagonist to reveal not so admirable traits—indeed, Blyth personifies Crawford's sublimated greed and ambition due to an impoverished upbringing. Picture is also a standard "woman's picture," a soap opera about suffering mothers in the *Stella Dallas* tradition. But here is the rare case in which we think the mother is foolish for leading her life to please her daughter—because, unlike the daughters in those other films who

were flawed but basically decent girls, Blyth isn't worthy of anyone's devotion. Crawford's faltering career was saved with her Oscar-winning portrayal of Mildred Pierce, regarded by many as her quintessential role, one that melded together several of her screen personae. But she's really not very good, playing *every* scene in an understated manner. Her Mildred isn't an interesting character to begin with—despite her strength, despite being a working woman/businesswoman. Since she's the type of woman who attracts bland losers such as Bennett, Scott, and Jack Carson, one can't be too impressed. Directed by Michael Curtiz. Music by Max Steiner. Also with: Eve Arden, Butterfly McQueen.

MILLION, LE (FRENCH/1931) B&W/80m.

René Clair's famous early musical comedy about a deeply-in-debt painter (René Lefèvre) who thinks that his financial problems are over when he wins the lottery. Unfortunately, his ballerina girlfriend (pretty Annabella) gave away his jacket, which has the lottery ticket in its pocket. Film is mad scramble to retrieve the jacket from, first, a police fugitive and, later, an opera singer who's giving his last performance before going on tour. Clair mixes farce, slapstick, and Gilbert and Sullivan, but while he neatly sets up his gags, they don't really deliver—this classic has lost its freshness. The major problem is obvious—the characters aren't very funny. Film benefits from Clair's innovative use of sound and music, as well as his decision to again use Lazare Meerson as his set designer and Georges Périnal as his cinematographer. Also with: Raymond Cordy (star of Clair's *A Nous la Liberté*).

MINISTRY OF FEAR (1944) B&W/85m.

Ray Milland is released from an asylum in England. He has spent two years there for the "mercy killing" of his sick wife, who, in truth, committed suicide. On the outside he discovers a world out of whack: sweet old ladies are Nazi spies; a blind man not only can see but clunks him on the head and zigzags away through the wilderness; Nazis try to blow him up; a Scotland Yard inspector (Percy Waram) is on his tail because he wrongly believes Milland killed the old detective he hired; and another man (Dan Duryea), at whose murder he was present and whom several people accuse him of killing, is still alive. He comes to realize that when he was given a cake (at a bazaar) that was intended for Duryea, he had innocently botched Nazi plans to pass along English defense secrets (that were contained on microfilm hidden in the cake). Only Austrian refugee Marjorie Reynolds believes him, and it turns out that the patriotic organization she runs with her brother (Carl Esmond) in London is actually a Nazi front. Fritz Lang directed this espionage tale, based on Graham Greene's novel. It's confusing, Reynolds is a weak heroine (and Milland isn't so exciting either), Milland convinces Waram of his innocence too early in the film, and Lang doesn't fully exploit Milland's paranoia so that this former mental patient begins to mistrust his own perceptions about what's happening around him. But it's enjoyable due to some slimy Nazis and other interesting minor characters and some offbeat moments (Duryea dialing a phone with a long pair of tailor's scissors; the manner in which Reynolds shoots the leader of the Nazi spy ring). Also with: Hillary Brooke.

MIRACLE OF MORGAN'S CREEK, THE (1944) B&W/99m.

Wild Preston Sturges comedy about a hyperkinetic smalltown girl (hyperkinetic Betty Hutton) who attends a party for soldiers about to go overseas, gets drunk, and remembers nothing the next morning—except that she and some equally drunk soldier got married on impulse, using fabricated names. Soon after, Hutton discovers she's pregnant. She tells her secret to her shrewd, younger sister (Diana Lynn in a surprisingly amusing portrayal), but knows better than to let on to her conservative, highly excitable policeman father (William Demarest). Nerdy Eddie Bracken offers to marry Hutton so she won't suffer public humiliation, but Hutton—who suddenly falls in love with him—doesn't think it fair. Bracken devises a scheme that will help her annul her marriage, but it backfires and he ends up in jail, facing a myriad of charges—all having to do with Hutton being under age. In Preston Sturges films, characters' lives change instantly—usually for better—due to *miracles*. And that's what it takes to get Hutton and Bracken out of seemingly hopeless predicament. Picture borders on being tasteless (the girl is named Trudy Kockenlocker!), which is why the censor board held up release for a year; in order for Bracken to be thrown in jail, Sturges had to make Hutton a minor. But because Hutton is made a minor, her actions that fateful night—especially giving up her virginity to a stranger—seem more scandalous. Frenetic comedy with rapid-fire dialogue doesn't reach sophistication of other Sturges films—in fact, it's a bit smutty—but there are moments of genuine hilarity. Dialogue is clever, including some slapstick bits. Demarest and Bracken are especially funny—but I wish Bracken's Norval Jones weren't such a pushover. What I really like about the film is how Sturges repeatedly crowds throngs of people into the small frame—the perfect visual for conveying how, when something happens in a smalltown, everybody comes snooping around. Also watch the interesting smalltown background action when Bracken and Hutton take walks. Also with: Porter Hall, Almira Sessons, Jimmy Conlin, Esther Howard, J. Farrell MacDonald, and in a very funny bit, reprising their roles from Sturges's *The Great McGinty*, Brian Donlevy and Akim Tamiroff.

MIRACLE ON 34TH STREET (1947) B&W/96m.

Yes, Virginia, there is a Santa Claus and, using Edmund Gwenn's SAG card, he gave a convincing performance as himself (winning Gwenn a Best Supporting Actor Oscar) in this marvelous adaptation of Valentine Davies's fantasy. Macy's employee Maureen O'Hara, a widowed mother, hires Kris Kringle to be the store's Santa Claus. He shakes things up by sending mothers to other stores—even Gimbels—that have better prices on some Christmas toys. When mothers are so appreciative that they swear allegiance to Macy's, all departments at Macy's adopt a similar policy. Rival stores follow suit, lest Macy's be regarded as the only store that has concern for the consumer. Both wanting to be regarded by the public as benevolent, Mr. Macy and Mr. Gimbel forget their rivalry and shake hands! O'Hara can see that Kris is a nice man, and she's happy that for once the guy playing Santa has *real* whiskers, but she thinks he might be crazy because he insists he really is Santa Claus. Kris is equally concerned about O'Hara and her young daughter, Natalie Wood. Neither has any fun in life because they are too caught up in *reality*, what they see in front of them. They never fantasize, never use their imaginations, never have *faith* enough to believe in what they've been conditioned not to believe (i.e., Santa Claus). Wanting the opportunity to prove to O'Hara and Wood that he is Santa, he accepts the offer of lawyer John Payne to share his apartment, which is right across the hall from O'Hara's. Payne, who has been courting O'Hara, thinks Kris will be a good influence on her and perhaps soften her up a bit. O'Hara is resistant, but the more Wood sees of Kris, the more she believes him to be Santa. But he can prove himself to her only by giving her the Christmas present she desires—a house outside the city, with a swing in the backyard. If that weren't problem enough for Kris, he becomes defendant in a well-publicized sanity trial at which Payne must prove that Kris is the one and only Santa Claus. People from all over New York await the outcome. Of course, only one verdict is possible. The intelligent, skillfully plotted Oscar-winning script by director George Seaton zeroes in on the American character: people have become so ambitious in their careers, power-hungry, and interested in money, that they have suppressed their finer values. At no time is the good-versus-greedy battle within each person so evident as at Christmas; it's a good thing Kris turns up when he does, when commercialism is rampant, and puts life into perspective. Film has excellent acting down to the smallest parts, splendid characterizations (no one plays their parts tongue-in-cheek, consequently these people are *real*), offbeat humor, sharp satire, tremendous warmth, and scenes that will have you choking up: if you're a repeat viewer, you'll probably get teary-eyed just anticipating the delighted Wood running through her dream house ("There *is* a swing!") and Santa thrilling a lonely little Swedish girl at Macy's by singing and conversing with her in her language (one of the best sentimental scenes in movie history). For children *and* adults (who will better appreciate the social satire)—*every* Christmas season. Also with: Gene Lockhart, Jerome Cowan, Porter Hall, William Frawley, Thelma Ritter, Jack Albertson, Tom D'Andrea.

MIRACLE WORKER, THE (1962) B&W/107m. Arthur Penn's direction of William Gibson's screen adaptation of his play is a bit stagy. Yet the film is still powerful and, if anything, more relevant than it was when released. Anne Bancroft gives a fiery performance as Annie Sullivan, the determined new teacher of the deaf, blind, *and* incorrigible young girl Helen Keller, played with amazing intelligence and strength by teenager Patty Duke. Play details battles of wills, as well as physical battles, between the stubborn adult—who wants the spoiled, coddled Helen to stop acting helpless and dumb and learn to communicate with her fingers—and the stubborn child—who keeps testing Sullivan, and runs to her parents any time she feels Sullivan is putting undue pressure on her. Eventually Helen responds to her teacher and comes to trust and love her. She also learns her lesson in the climactic water-pump scene that invariably makes viewers cry. She finally learns to use her fingers to say "water" and other words. This movie should be more significant to feminist film criticism. Because one character is a child, many people have not been impressed by the fact that this is one of the first films *about* one female helping another female do anything, much less rip free from society's constraints. Refusing to be handicapped by her sex, Sullivan is a strong, independent-minded woman who strives to reach her potential in her profession. In achieving this, Sullivan must help the young girl to use her mental strength more purposefully, to overcome her physical handicaps, to become independent of her family, and to reach her full potential. This is a film about liberation. Sensitive direction by Penn, who obviously had great trust in his two actresses and admiration for their characters. Unforgettable, physically demanding, Oscar-winning performances by Bancroft and Duke. Also with: Victor Jory, Inga Swenson, Andrew Prine, Kathleen Comegys.

MISFITS, THE (1961) B&W/124m. As the last film of both Marilyn Monroe and Clark Gable, this picture is of more than passing interest. But it is not the classic that it should have been, considering that Monroe, Gable, and Montgomery Clift were its stars, John Huston directed, and Arthur Miller wrote the script (he adapted it from an article he wrote for *Esquire*). Monroe is a gentle, supersensitive woman who comes to Reno to get a divorce (from Kevin McCarthy). She then takes up with Gable, an over-the-hill cowboy, Clift, a young broke rodeo cowboy, and Eli Wallach, Gable's self-pitying pal. The men all recognize that she is a "life" force who brings goodness and sunshine into their lives. She moves in with Gable and "feminizes" him—he cooks breakfast, plants a vegetable garden, lets her decorate their house. But in the lengthy climax the men reclaim their "manhood" in a manner that sickens Monroe—they capture wild mustangs, which they'll sell to dogfood dealers. Miller laments the disappearance of the heroic Age of Cowboys, suggesting that today's "cowboys" (misfits) can't retain their manly pride by riding in rodeos on spooked horses and bulls or capturing mustangs for dogfood dealers. Like many Huston films, this picture contains Hemingway themes and characters; also the distinct European ambiance in the early group scenes is like something out of *The Sun Also Rises*. Miller's script is overwritten, without being insightful. It's full of gloom and doom; the mustang scene is truly unpleasant to watch. I'd have preferred John Wayne to Gable, who never really clicks with Monroe. He also gives one of the worst drunk impersonations in memory.

Clift and Monroe, both known for their sensitivity, do work well together—it's a shame they didn't have more scenes with each other. Monroe was having tremendous psychological problems during the filming, so it's amazing what a wonderful performance she gives. She's beautiful, angelic, vulnerable, assertive, wise beyond her education, unhappy, the sufferer for all creatures (man or animal) that hurt. I'd like to think that this role comes closest to the real Marilyn Monroe. Also with: Thelma Ritter, Estelle Winwood.

MISSING (1982) C/122m. Costa-Gavras's most accessible film was adapted from Thomas Hauser's nonfiction book *The Execution of Charles Horman*. The movie, like the book, contends that Horman (John Shea), a counter-culture journalist living in Chile in 1973, was secretly executed by the new fascist regime with the blessings of the U.S. because he'd obtained information that America had participated in Allende's overthrow. U.S. officials deliberately gave the runaround to both Horman's wife (Sissy Spacek) and his father (Jack Lemmon), a conservative American businessman—covering up Horman's death and insisting he had either fled the country or was in hiding. The ugly depiction of U.S. officials in Chile—who lie, who care more about U.S. business interests than the lives of individual Americans (or Chileans), and who own smiling-Nixon photos—resulted in several lawsuit threats against the filmmakers, and the U.S. State Department issuing a three-page condemnation of the film. Radicals have correctly attacked film for making such a big deal of finding one American while essentially ignoring all the dead Chileans around the city. Film is more a thriller with political overtones than a political film—although it does make major point that Americans must pay attention to what their representatives are doing abroad in their names. Most impressive is how Costa-Gavras presents a truly paranoid picture of country taken over by trigger-happy murderers—he makes you feel you're stranded there. (The scariest scene, which is almost surrealistic, has Spacek stranded on the streets past curfew, hiding while soldiers roam about shooting anyone in sight.) The director uses a journalistic interview approach to tell story of two people searching for missing journalist. He puts his emphasis on the personal drama, showing changes in the conservative father's attitude toward the U.S. government, in which he'd always had faith, and toward his son and daughter-in-law, whose values he'd always disregarded. Lemmon relies too much on his nervous mannerisms, but when he makes a humble plea for his son (whom he's come to truly love)—he's willing to take him back, in whatever condition, no questions asked—he gives you a lump in your throat. Spacek is excellent as Beth Horman, one of her most intelligent, tenderest, strongest characters. Where Spacek's timid *Carrie* kept her sweater sleeves over her hands, Beth rolls hers up to her elbows. She is an activist. She realizes that passivity is the worst crime of all in this world. Also with: Melanie Mayron, Charles Cioffi, David Clennon, Janice Rule.

MISSING IN ACTION (1984) C/101m. Chuck Norris was a former special-forces officer in Vietnam. He became a POW, but escaped; now he returns to Vietnam to rescue other MIAs. Picture was huge hit, although not on magnitude of later, similarly themed *Rambo: First Blood, Part II*. It's one of Norris's less exciting pictures. The storyline is predictable, there's not enough dialogue—even for a Norris film, the action sequences seem familiar. Norris uses guns more than karate, the lack of regard for human lives is appalling, and Norris looks like he needs some Geritol. It's surprisingly passionless and boring—the action sequences take forever to develop. Directed with no feeling for his subject by Joseph Zito. Followed by *Missing in Action, Part II*. Also with: M. Emmett Walsh, Lenore Kasdorf, James Hong, David Tress.

MR. ARKADIN/CONFIDENTIAL REPORT (BRITISH/1955) B&W/100m. If Orson Welles hadn't had Herman Mankiewicz's help writing *Citizen Kane*, it might have come out something like this interesting but empty *Kane* variation. As in *Kane*, Welles plays a man of many faces/masks, a reclusive financier (part Kane, part Harry Lime, part King Lear) with a shady past. He wants to get fortune hunter Robert Arden away from his daughter Paola Mori (actually Welles's wife), so he pays Arden to investigate his past, to find out who he was before 1927, when he got amnesia (or so he claims). So just as William Alland put together the pieces of Kane's life, Arden learns what transpired in Arkadin's life—and he discovers Arkadin's terrible secret. Meanwhile Arkadin disposes of those people Arden speaks to who know how he made his fortune. He also plans to knock off Arden, who reminds him of himself when young. Picture is bizarrely photographed and full of delightful cameos, but Arden's a terrible actor, the low budget's a problem, and we never really care about Arkadin's past because Welles never establishes the person Arkadin is in the present. When he commits his final act, we don't know enough about him to judge whether he is acting within character. From Welles's novel. Also with: Patricia Medina, Akim Tamiroff, Michael Redgrave, Mischa Auer, Katina Paxinou, Peter Van Eyck.

MR. DEEDS GOES TO TOWN (1936) B&W/115m. Tuba-playing Longfellow Deeds (Gary Cooper) inherits $20 million in Frank Capra's classic comedy. He reluctantly leaves his little home in Mandrake Falls and moves into a New York mansion, full of servants and surrounded by the corrupt, cynical citizens of the big city. Both reporter Jean Arthur and press agent Lionel Stander think him a huckleberry at first, but they are won over by his innocence, patriotism (he visits Grant's tomb), humility, and wisdom. When he decides to give away his money to small farmers who are failing—a controversial plot point—he is forced to undergo a hearing to determine if he's insane. Although loony neighbors from Mandrake Falls claim he's "pixilated," he proves to be the sanest person in court. Capra's first film to really attack the city, to show that it has deprived its people of their basic human values; as in his later films, only the uncorrupted small-town boy can lead them back to the right path. It never reflects the cynicism of *Mr. Smith Goes to Washington*, *Meet John Doe*, or *It's a Wonderful Life*—it is the only one of the four films where the happy ending seems completely natural. While enjoyable, it's not on the level of the Jimmy Stewart films. Written by Robert Riskin. Also with: George Bancroft, Douglas Dumbrille, Walter Catlett, H. B. Warner, Raymond Walburn, Mayo Methot.

MR. HULOT'S HOLIDAY (FRENCH/1953) B&W/86m.
Jacques Tati's inimitable creation, Mr. Hulot, made his first appearance in this silent (but for music and sound effects) film about an amusing assortment of vacationers at a beach resort. There's no plot, just consistently inventive sight gags and brief vignettes. There is a great deal of enjoyable slapstick centering on the storklike Hulot, who can destroy a tranquil environment as quickly as Jerry Lewis or Peter Sellers's Inspector Clouseau. What's most appealing and childlike about this gentlemanly, high-stepping character in hat and raincoat (and carrying an umbrella) is that each time he does something wrong, he runs away and hides. Much laughter comes from watching Hulot's fellow vacationers, all familiar types: the camera nut, the card players, the sunbathers, the children, the giddy older lady who keeps handing her bored husband shells that he promptly tosses away. Most impressive are Tati's intricate visual gags in which he derives humor from his characters interacting with seemingly inconsequential props. Also, he cleverly uses his frame on many gags, keeping half of what makes up the gag off screen (i.e., the horse that pulls Hulot out of our sight) so that we must use our imagination. Classic is as enjoyable as a day at the beach. Also with: Nathalie Pascaud, Michèle Rolla, Valentine Camax.

MR. SMITH GOES TO WASHINGTON (1939) B&W/129m.
Frank Capra at his corniest, hokiest, and most manipulative. Still, it's a great film. James Stewart's perfectly cast as Jefferson Smith, a patriotic young idealist who's picked by his state's crooked political machine (run by Edward Arnold) to complete a dead senator's term. Arnold and the corrupt senior senator, Claude Rains, figure Stewart's so naïve and unfit for duty in Washington that he'll vote the way Rains, his idol, wants him to. Stewart spends his first day in Washington going to all the monuments, where he's greatly inspired by the words of our founding fathers. Soon he comes to realize that the modern politicians have long since forgotten about democracy and the values that had made America so great. He learns why he was appointed to office and that Rains has sold out his ideals. When he tries to propose a bill that will create a national park for his main cause, the Boy Rangers, he finds that Rains and Arnold try to discredit him so they can build a dam on that land—a project that will guarantee them graft money. Like other Capra heroes, Stewart's Smith is the American everyman, an idealist with a tendency toward demagoguery when he wants to right a wrong, who has both his faith in himself and his conservative values severely tested. Like Capra's other disillusioned heroes, he is on the brink of giving up and allowing the people he represents to be swallowed up by corrupt influences, when someone he has inspired reminds him of his importance and all the worthy things he stands for. In this case, his help comes from Jean Arthur's Saunders; she'd been a cynical reporter until the young senator had restored her faith in people/politicians. Now she understands that his victory over Rains, a member of the old, constipated bureaucracy, will mean the revitalization of Congress. Jefferson Smith is a great hero: through him—who's linked to the Daniel of the Lions' Den, Daniel Boone, and Daniel Webster —Capra links today's idealists with courageous Biblical underdogs, American pioneers, and America's finest politicians/orators of the 1800s. Ending is too rushed, but the scene that comes before it—Smith's filibuster (an American tradition, we're told) —is a classic. Stewart and Arthur are a wonderful couple. Sidney Buchman adapted Lewis R. Foster's Oscar-winning story. Joseph Walker did the cinematography; Dimitri Tiomkin composed the score. Also with: Guy Kibbee, Thomas Mitchell, Eugene Pallette, Beulah Bondi, H. B. Warner, Harry Carey, Astrid Allwyn, Ruth Donnelly, Grant Mitchell, Porter Hall, Charles Lane, William Demarest.

MIXED BLOOD (1984) C/98m.
When directing for Andy Warhol, Paul Morrissey made not so much parodies of Hollywood films (i.e., *Dracula*, *Frankenstein*, *Sunset Boulevard*) as *variations* on them, for the cinema underground. Working alone, as producer-writer-director, Morrissey has created such a weird variation on *The Godfather* that few have pinpointed that film as Morrissey's source. But again we have a territorial war between crime "families"; again the warriors sleep on mattresses on the floor; again cops stand aside; again each murder must be avenged; again a trusted gang member is working for the rival gang; again a son of the family head takes over the war strategy when the family head is incapacitated; again a WASP woman tries to get the son to go away with her and forget his familial obligations. Morrissey's variation is set in the slums of New York's Lower East Side. A Brazilian youth gang led by a middle-aged, eccentric gypsy (Marilia Pera, the prostitute in *Pixote*), who sings Carmen Miranda songs, is engaged in a drug war with a Puerto Rican gang (led by Angel David). Both gangs are supplied by the European. The European's blonde girlfriend (Linda Kerridge) dumps him for Pera's muscular, obedient teenage son (Richard Ulacia). Pera (who'll remind you of Anna Magnani, Morrissey's favorite actress) is jealous and sets up Kerridge's murder but there's a double-cross and both Pera and Kerridge are kidnapped. Ulacia must attempt a rescue, although he suspects that one of his gang is leading him into a trap. Extreme violence will turn off many viewers, but exaggerated gore and bizarre situations are meant to counterpoint downplayed, straight-faced humor. Picture doesn't always work, but it's exciting and funny, in unusual ways.

Parallels are drawn between the youth gang, which recruits kids under 16 so they can kill and not go to jail, with—believe it or not—the Puerto Rican singing group Menudo, in which kids must drop out when they reach 16. In its sleazy apartment the gang has a picture of Menudo on its wall, and the kidnapping takes place in a real store that specializes in Menudo items. What I really find amusing about this film is how Morrissey stages conversations between all sorts of people with accents (Germans, Orientals, Brazilians, Puerto Ricans, Indians) and has them speak American street lingo, in which curse words replace punctuation. (All-American girl Kerridge comes from New York and she speaks as if she were from London.) Unusual, to say the least. It's good to see that Morrissey rescues Marilyn Monroe lookalike Kerridge from oblivion after her appearance in *Fade to Black*. A great score by "Sugar-Coated" Andy Hernandez.

MODERN ROMANCE (1981) C/93m–97m.
Often brilliant comedy in which director Albert Brooks plays a Hollywood film editor who breaks up with his girlfriend, Kathryn Harrold, for the umpteenth time because they can't communicate except in bed. Although he pretends to be strong, he immediately is destroyed by his decision. He wallows in misery and obsessively tries to win her back. He succeeds, but his overbearing jealousy and possessiveness cause Harrold to reconsider the relationship. Brooks's sympathetic yet obnoxious character is hilarious. I think the key to this character is that he is completely oblivious to his awful traits, particularly his insensitivity. He's the type who'll break up with Harrold and wonder why she'd run out of the restaurant without finishing her dinner; tell people he'll call back immediately although he's just written their phone numbers in the air with his finger; tell his first date (Jane Hallaren) when he picks her up that when he called and spoke to her (after getting her number from his little book) he couldn't remember who she was; drop this woman back at home after just a ride around the block; interrupt Harrold's business dinner with potential accounts. As usual, Brooks is at his best in two-person conversations: with Harrold (who's a fine straight man); with (in a great bit) assistant editor Bruce Kirby; with his director, James L. Brooks, over how to edit a scene from their sci-fi movie; with sporting-goods salesman Bob Einstein (Brooks's brother), who sells him hundreds of dollars' worth of equipment he'll never use; with George Kennedy (as himself). His phone conversations with Kirby, Harrold's secret ex-lover, a friend who calls him for a job recommendation and then asks if he can date Harrold, and his mother (who keeps slipping in questions while her son tries to hang up). And when he's alone, Brooks continues to talk compulsively (everything about him is compulsive): to his image in the mirror; to his answering machine; on his phone; and in my favorite moment, to and about his records: "God, I have so many great albums. I love 'em. I love 'em." Satire gives realistic view of modern romances and the "B"-budget film scene where the top guests at parties are Kennedy and Meadowlark Lemon.

Much underrated. Monica Johnson collaborated with Brooks on the script. Also with: Jerry Belson, Ed Weinberger.

MODERN TIMES (1936) B&W/85m.
Classic Charlie Chaplin film pits man against modern, industrialized, impersonal city. In the opening sequence, it looks like man will lose out: working on an assembly line in a large factory, Chaplin has a nervous breakdown while turning bolts—he becomes like a machine out of whack. But Charlie will regain his humanity and maintain it, despite being tossed into jail every time he expresses human qualities at work (in his many new jobs) or on the cop-infested streets. It is his new love for gamine Paulette Goddard that keeps him from ever becoming depressed or defeated. This is a surprisingly optimistic film, although few good things happen to Chaplin or Goddard. Highlights include: Chaplin on roller skates by a ledge, Chaplin as a singing waiter, Chaplin and Goddard walking arm in arm into the sunset. There is no dialogue in the film, just sounds (machines, grumbling tummies), music, and Chaplin's song, which was recorded in the studio. Film was influenced by René Clair's *A Nous la Liberté*. Chemistry between the married leads is strong—Charlie looks spiffier than we'd seen him, Goddard is incredibly sexy and pretty. Also with: Henry Bergman, Chester Conklin (as a mechanic).

MOMMIE DEAREST (1981) C/129m.
Ludicrous adaptation of Christina Crawford's blistering tell-all bestseller in which she revealed her hellish life as the daughter of Joan Crawford, a great Hollywood star but also an alcoholic, a child beater, a tyrant. What's most regrettable—and unforgivable, considering that this film was supposed to replace lies with facts—is that the sheepish producer, Frank Yablans, and director, Frank Perry, and their script collaborators, Tracy Hotchner and Robert Getchell, hoping to dodge negative backlash from Crawford fans, opted to add still another fictional chapter to the life of Joan Crawford. Not only is almost everything in Christina's book ignored (or contradicted), but also almost every event that takes place is fabricated and real people are eliminated in favor of composites. The filmmakers were so keen on having viewers think Faye Dunaway was capturing Crawford's essence that they had her play the Crawford who is familiar to viewers—the Crawford of the movies, newsreels, and personal appearances—when we should have been presented with one who is totally alien to us, the Crawford of Christina's book. Essentially, the film has Dunaway playing variations on some of Crawford's memorable movie scenes which the film substitutes for events in Crawford's real life: scenes between mother and daughter correspond to *Mildred Pierce*; the ax scene recalls *Strait Jacket*; her house-cleaning obsession corresponds to *Harriet Craig* and *Queen Bee*; etc. Just as Crawford was intentionally given weak leading men, Dunaway is given journeyman Steve Forrest so she can dominate the proceedings. Although she overacts at times, Dunaway makes a gallant effort, playing Crawford not as a villain, but a "warrior," someone who had to fight an

uphill battle (notice that her tortuous jogging ends with her running up a driveway) against an industry that has no sympathy for overage leading actresses. In fact, Dunaway's Crawford comes across as no less sympathetic than the spoiled, conniving, pubescent Christina (Maria Hobel) or the pathetic, priggish teen Christina (Diana Scarwid). Film is mediocre and trivial, but, despite some staggeringly bad scenes and campy dialogue, the performance by Dunaway keeps it from being completely worthless. Its cult, however, consists of those who laugh at its overall ineptitude and who tell their cleaners, "No more wire hangers . . . ever!" Also with: Howard Da Silva (a "respectably" vile Louis B. Mayer), Rutanya Alda, Harry Goz (as husband Al Steele of Pepsi-Cola), Michael Edwards, Jocelyn Brando, Priscilla Pointer.

MON ONCLE (FRENCH/1958) C/116m.
The second appearance of Jacques Tati's Mr. Hulot pits him against impersonal, anti-human modern technology. Not on the level of *Mr. Hulot's Holiday* because Hulot himself doesn't provide enough of the humor. What is funny is the pretentious, ultra-modern house that belongs to Hulot's sister's family. It is full of the ugliest, most twisted, most uncomfortable-looking furniture imaginable—Hulot must turn the couch on its side in order to nap on it. The kitchen is mechanized; the sound of a motor can usually be heard. There is a high gate around the yard so everyone must use the terrible-sounding buzzer to be let in. As soon as the missus hears the buzzer, she pushes another button which causes her hideous fish-fountain to start spouting water high into the air—this is supposed to impress visitors. A curving walkway leads to the house, and small stones comprise the footpath across the small patches of grass. It's a ghastly piece of property, certainly not the place for Hulot's young nephew. The picture's highlight is a garden party where Hulot is just one of the ridiculous guests. There is little dialogue throughout—Hulot says nothing—just many visual gags, which are a bit repetitious. Like most Tati films, this drags toward the end. Also with: Adrienne Servantie, Jean-Pierre Zola, Lucien Frégis, Alain Becourt.

MON ONCLE D'AMÉRIQUE/MY UNCLE FROM AMERICA/SOMNAMBULES, LES
(FRENCH/1980) C/125m. Award-winning Alain Resnais film juxtaposes footage and voice-over of behavioral scientist Henri Laborit explaining his theories with two fictional storylines that illustrate Laborit's points about human interaction and the tendency of people who are frustrated in their professional and personal lives to direct their anger at themselves. Personally, I think the Laborit material is superfluous and intrusive, particularly in the beginning, when Resnais is juggling many scenes of our main characters' pasts and we're confused enough as it is. One of our central characters is a radio executive (Roger-Pierre) who is an aspiring political writer-politician. He walks out on his wife (Nelly Bourgeaud) and children and moves in with a second central character, an idealistic actress (Nicole

Garcia). But she leaves him when his wife lies that she's about to die and needs her husband at home. He thinks Garcia is dumping him because he just lost his high-paying job. They meet again two years later, when he's a successful politician and she's a designer in the textile business—which is how she knows the third central character, a textile manager (Gérard Depardieu). Two years earlier Depardieu's textile company merged and he was shifted from a successful technician to a troubled supervisor in another town, so that he can't even live with his wife and children. Now he's informed that he's being given an insignificant position selling gourmet products. There are comic moments, but it's an unhappy film about people being kicked in the stomach, humiliated, lied to, and disappointed and/or rejected by the people they love and depend on. It's well acted, interestingly photographed, and has intriguing character relationships (as well as work situations). It takes a while to develop and drags in spots, but it's worth staying with. Also with: Gérard Darrieu, Philippe Laudenbach, Marie Dubois, Pierre Arditi.

MONA: THE VIRGIN NYMPH/MONA
(1970) C/75m. The first hardcore porno feature. Fifi Watson is the title character, who refuses to have intercourse until she's married but satisfies her strong sexual appetite by performing fellatio on her boyfriend and other men. There's an orgy sequence, a lesbian love scene, a masturbation sequence (featuring Judy Angel) that is shot in extreme close-up, some light bondage, and public sex. Most memorable is the scene in which Mona first approaches a stranger and nonchalantly offers to perform her specialty on him and then performs the act (famous because it ended with one of the first on-screen male orgasms) in an alley, where anyone could have happened upon the filmmaking. Not shown too often anymore, but it helped set the formula for *Deep Throat* and all the later, more sophisticated porno movies. Made in 16mm by producer Bill Osco, who'd later make *Flesh Gordon* and try his hand at "legitimate" films. Directed by Mike Light and Howard Ziehm.

MONDO CANE (ITALIAN/1963) C/105m.
Gualtiero Jacopetti's first "shockumentary" showcases bizarre practices around the world, ranging from the weird sexual rituals of primitive tribes to the repugnant eating habits of "civilized" rich folks. The once notorious film has lost all its sensationalist value in the ensuing years. Now we can see it for the exploitive, repellent film it is. Meant to be shocking, it is merely offensive. I particularly despise the unbelievably smug narrator used in the English-language version. He continually mocks the people on the screen—or is he really laughing at the viewers who made this trash into a big money-maker. Many similar films were later made, also containing staged-for-the-camera sequences. Some filmmakers even hired people to perform murders and castrations for their cameras—which qualifies this genre as the cinema's most revolting. Theme song, "More," became a standard.

MONDO TRASHO (1969) B&W/95m.
John Waters's first feature-length film. It has an offensive pre-title sequence: masked man chops the heads off three chickens, one of which he has first swung around by its feet. If you walk out at this point, you won't miss much. There's humor at the beginning when star Mary Vivian Pearce (who's made up to look like a sluttish Jean Harlow) has her toes sucked by a stranger in a park while she excitedly fantasizes she's scrubbing floors and being pushed around by her stepsisters; a couple of funny moments when Divine pushes Pearce's unconscious body around in a wheelchair after running her over while looking at a nude male hitchhiker (Mark Isherwood); and a funny finale when Pearce suddenly appears on a Baltimore street by clicking her heels together and finds herself being mercilessly insulted by two women trying to guess what kind of lowlife she is. The rest of the film will bore all but Waters's strongest fanatics. Divine and Pearce spend time at a laundromat, a mental hospital, and Dr. Coat Hanger's (David Lochary). But little is funny or comprehensible; however, some bits may be of interest because they would be repeated with better results in Waters's more sophisticated films. Low-budget 16mm picture has no dialogue. It does have a fabulous old rock soundtrack (does anyone think he bothered to get the rights?), but Waters is like a nervous guy who can't stop turning the radio dial. He'll drive you crazy by switching songs every few seconds; but the blaring, chaotic music keeps you from sleeping through the monotonous visuals. Waters and Co. were busted by Baltimore police because of the nude hitchhiker.

MONKEY BUSINESS (1931) 77m.
Side-splitting comedy in which the four Marx Brothers are stowaways on an ocean liner, vexing passengers, chasing women, making life miserable for the captain and his crew. Groucho and Zeppo are hired to be bodyguards to one thug, while Chico and Harpo are hired by his rival. Of course, none of them takes his work seriously. The third Marx Bros. film, and the first they made in Hollywood. Unlike *The Cocoanuts* and *Animal Crackers*, this was written directly for the screen, by S. J. Perelman and Will B. Johnstone. Highlights include Harpo pretending to be a puppet (what a face!); Groucho flirting his way into the arms (and closet!) of a pretty, sensuous, available passenger (Thelma Todd); Groucho using stream-of-consciousness doubletalk on the captain and, later, Todd's gangster husband; Chico and Harpo auditioning for jobs as *tough guys*; Chico's puns; the four brothers each trying to get past Customs by pretending to be Maurice Chevalier; Harpo happily tossing all the Customs agent's papers into the air. Picture would rank with *Duck Soup* and *A Night at the Opera* if it didn't lose steam when the action shifts to shore and there's an innocuous kidnapping subplot. But I don't think that the Marx Brothers ever were more energetic than in this film. Directed by Norman Z. McLeod. Also with: Rockcliffe Fellowes, Ruth Hall, Harry Woods, Ben Taggart.

MONSIEUR VERDOUX (1947) B&W/123m.
Charles Chaplin's last masterpiece was certainly his most controversial film. *The Great Dictator* had been a comedy about Hitler and Nazis, but this was perhaps even more daring. After all, in this comedy Charlie Chaplin, once the lovable tramp, plays a cold-blooded murderer. The gentlemanly, philosophical Verdoux was a bank teller for 35 years before being dismissed because of the Depression. Needing to provide for his invalid wife (Mady Correll) and small son (Allison Roddan), he has become a Bluebeard. He has traveled all over France, marrying old women, taking their money, and killing them. Cackling, foolish Annabella (Martha Raye) is his next intended victim, but he never manages to pull it off. In fact Verdoux, the murderer of 14 women, kills only one person (a woman who has no life to begin with) during the film—therefore we find his character palatable. Chaplin wisely doesn't try to make Verdoux sympathetic, but we can see traces of the tender, romantic, life-loving man he once was. We understand his bitterness. Chaplin is at his most eloquent when Verdoux stands trial. He conveys the picture's bold theme: society is outraged when an individual commits several murders, yet people condone their nations going to war and committing mass murder. A most compelling and unusual film, once championed by James Agee. The storyline is serious and sometimes morbid, but there is hilarity, especially in Chaplin's scenes with Raye. Also with: Marilyn Nash (as a down-on-her-luck young woman whom Verdoux picks up so he can test a new poison—but he ends up helping her), Charles Evans, William Frawley, Isobel Elsom, Margaret Hoffman, Ada-May, Almira Sessions, Fritz Leiber, Edna Purviance.

MONTE WALSH (1970) C/106m.
Unusual western is a death song to the American cowboy, adapted from a novel by Jack Schaefer (*Shane*). Lee Marvin, Jack Palance, and Mitch Ryan are close friends who work Jim Davis's spread at a time when employment for cowhands is hard to come by. Marvin and Palance have been through many adventures together over the years, but they can see that things are changing swiftly and that the days for their kind are numbered. Marvin continues to work for Davis, hoping to get enough money to marry prostitute Jeanne Moreau, but Palance marries and opens a hardware store, and Ryan becomes a thief after Davis makes layoffs. Only one will survive the hard times. Film takes a while to get started and is depressing, but it has uncommon moments (aging Marvin breaks a bronco, wrecking a whole town to do it; several cowhands, victims of the cook's prank, race to the outhouse); an exciting, novelly handled shootout sequence featuring Marvin and Ryan (with striking photography by David M. Walsh, great music by John Barry); strong characters and fine performances. Marvin displays dignity in living, Ryan when dying; Palance never played a nicer cowboy and Moreau never flashed a prettier smile. Acclaimed photographer William A. Fraker made his debut as director and, despite having a panoramic western landscape at his dis-

posal, kept his actors almost exclusively in close-up, as if he were afraid of being accused of emphasizing visuals on a film about people. Solid screenplay is by Lukas Heller and David Z. Goodman. With songs by Cass Elliott. Also with: Bo Hopkins, G. D. Spradlin, Matt Clark, Allyn Ann McLerie.

MONTEREY POP (1969) C/72m—79m—88m.
First major rock-concert film. In 1969 it provided us a chance to see some of the greatest rock-music acts in the world; today it satisfies our urge to briefly recapture that time when music was so central to the counterculture. I feel great nostalgia, not only from seeing the rock stars, but from glimpses of the young, flawless, optimistic, hippie-dominated crowd. Ground-breaking *cinéma-vérité* direction by D. A. Pennebaker seems competent but unimpressive today. He seemed obsessed with finding pretty young women to film. Acts included: the Mamas and the Papas, Simon and Garfunkel, Janis Joplin (having her first major triumph with a stunning "Ball and Chain"), Jimi Hendrix (who also claimed the spotlight for the first time), Eric Burdon, Otis Redding, Country Joe and the Fish, the Who, Ravi Shankar.

MONTY PYTHON AND THE HOLY GRAIL
(BRITISH/1974) C/90m. Side-splitting comedy by England's premier comedy troupe has King Arthur (Graham Chapman), Sir Lancelot (John Cleese), Sir Galahad (Michael Palin), Sir Belvedere (Terry Jones), Sir Robin (Eric Idle), and Patsy (Terry Gilliam) searching for the Holy Grail in 932 A.D. We laugh because of the crazy characters, foolish dialogue, and ridiculous incidents that occur, but also because someone (Python, but not Python per se) had the gall to make a historical picture with such shoddy production values that all horses are invisible and the sound of galloping steeds is made by Patsy striking coconuts together. Because the straight-faced, straight-laced actors skip along foolishly, we get the impression that either directors Gilliam and Jones are using audience-distancing techniques or we're watching a bunch of medieval insane-asylum escapees who believe they're Arthur and his legion. Film does many things: it pokes fun at the French, homosexuals, communists, kings, even art historian Kenneth Clark. It mocks cowardice (Sir Robin's Minstrels sing of his fleeing from danger), but is harsher on senseless British gallantry. A knight gets limb after limb cut off in a sword fight, but won't admit he's losing; the funniest scene has the sword-wielding Lancelot blindly charging into a wedding ceremony and indiscriminately massacring dancing women, children, guards, servants, the best man, and the bride's father because he wrongly believes he's rescuing a maiden in distress ("I just got carried away," he apologizes). And it puts down Arthur's long, irresponsible search for the Grail while his people starved. Most of all it mocks a group of philistine filmmakers (again: Python, but not Python per se) who would attempt such a lavish production on a minuscule budget, with amateurs on the screen and behind the camera, and without, apparently, bothering to tell the local police that they'll be doing location shooting. The impression one gets is that Python hired a lot of hammy, unreliable actors to play the characters the serious knights meet on their journey. (Naturally, Python members also played these parts.) It's as if these characters intentionally forgot their one line of dialogue ("Go in that direction") and started improvising. What really drives Arthur crazy is that all these characters are such conceited know-it-alls (they're expert on such things as swallows, special effects, killer rabbits, the knights' favorite colors). Ambitious film has one clever scene after another, hilarious lines ("That rabbit has a vicious streak a mile wide"), bizarre characters and incidents, and the look of a genuine medieval epic, with mist, mud, peasants living in squalor, forest, lakes, colorful costumes, and castles. Despite a rushed ending, it's Monty Python's best film to date, the one that made converts out of those of us who never watched their cult TV series. Songs by Neil Innes. Also with: Connie Booth, Carol Cleveland, John Young.

MOON IN THE GUTTER, THE (FRENCH/1983)
C/126m. Critics unanimously panned Jean-Jacques Beineix's follow-up to *Diva*; even star Gérard Depardieu called it "Sewer in the Gutter." Depardieu plays a poor stevedore who vows to find the man who raped his sister, causing her to slash her own throat right there in the gutter. He suspects everybody in the sleazy area where she was killed, including his pathetic drunk brother (Dominique Pinon, *Diva's* punk-villain); we even suspect Depardieu. While in his traumatic state, he breaks off from his lusty, skittish girlfriend (Victoria Abril) and pursues cool, rich Nastassia Kinski, perhaps *literally* the girl of his dreams. Delirious, pretentious, and obscure, Beineix's film still contains many powerful scenes and some of the most erotic visuals (of Kinski, Abril, and Depardieu) in memory. The worst impression one gets is that the director didn't explain the characters to Depardieu and Kinski. (Beineix based Depardieu's character on photos he'd seen of Marlon Brando in *A Streetcar Named Desire*.) From the novel by American David Goodis. Hallucinatory photography by Philippe Rousselot. Also with: Bertice Reading, Vittorio Mezzogiorno.

MOONLIGHTING (BRITISH/1982) C/97m. Beguiling film (shot and edited in one month's time) from Polish director Jerzy Skolimowski. At first it's comedic in tone but later it's an increasingly bleak and desperate political allegory. Jeremy Irons is a married, educated Polish construction worker living in Warsaw. Because he knows how to speak English, his wealthy boss (looking for cheap labor) sends him to London to turn a dull flat into a snazzy retreat to which the boss can take his mistress. Irons takes three workers with him—picking them because they don't know English and are stupid, so he figures they'll be easy to supervise. Indeed, they do everything he says, including staying inside so no one will know they are working illegally in London. As their stay goes on, Irons becomes more and more isolated from his men—becoming their slavedriver and watchdog and the person who rations food and clothing

allotments. He keeps all the money the boss has sent them, takes away their source of entertainment and news (when he breaks their TV), manipulates them into working more hours by altering his watch. He doesn't tell them he hasn't enough money to get them through their stay; and when he learns that there has been a military crackdown in Poland and Solidarity has been outlawed, he fears they will stop work at the depressing news, so he keeps this information to himself, feeding them lies. In effect, he has deprived them of all their freedoms. Their lives are so oppressive under Irons that they are enduring (on a much less frightening level, of course) what their fellow workers are going through back in Warsaw. Film projects disorientation of Polish workers in capitalist country where freedom is supposed to exist but everywhere (in airports, in stores) they feel threatened in a personal way. While Irons learns to exist on a level with smart capitalists he comes across, he underestimates his Polish worker companions and realizes it too late—just as those who underestimate Solidarity will be in for a brutal surprise. Irons spends the whole film pushing these men around—at the end, in the final shot, he, as a puppet of the Polish elite, is literally pushed back. Also with: Eugene Lipinski, Jiri Stanislav, Eugeniusz Haczkiewicz.

MOONRAKER (BRITISH-FRENCH/1979) C/ 126m.
The worst James Bond film to date has Roger Moore walking through the paces for his hefty paycheck and giving way to his double for a series of unimaginative action scenes and "humorous" chases. There's little suspense and the humor falls flat. Not only is Jaws (Richard Kiel), the giant villain from *The Spy Who Loved Me*, pacified by love so that he becomes a good guy, but the filmmakers also have the gall to set the finale in outer space and stage a battle right out of *Star Wars*. Plot has billionaire industrialist Hugo Drax (Michael Lonsdale) setting up a space station from where he hopes to wipe out the earth's population and replace it with a super-race. Only spectacular scene is the pre-title sequence in which Bond and Jaws battle for a lone parachute during a free fall from a great height. Also with: Lois Chiles (as Holly Goodhead), Corinne Dufour, Toshiro Suga, Bernard Lee, Desmond Llewellyn, Lois Maxwell.

MORE THE MERRIER, THE (1943) B&W/ 104m.
During a housing crisis in our nation's capital, the engaged Jean Arthur must share her apartment with millionaire government adviser Charles Coburn and government agent Joel McCrea. Realizing that Arthur is too special to marry her dullard fiancé, Coburn plays matchmaker for his roommates. Sparkling George Stevens comedy with deft performances by the leads and brilliant dialogue by Robert Russell, Frank Ross, Richard Flourney, and Garson Kanin (who was uncredited). The ending fizzles a bit, but along the way there are many great scenes. Particularly funny is when Coburn and Arthur try to adhere to her impossibly rigid morning schedule. For some reason, there haven't been many movie scenes between unrelated young women and elderly men, so the Coburn-Arthur pairing is a real treat. Coburn (who won a "Supporting Actor" Oscar) also works well with McCrea, a truly underrated comic actor—in one scene they lie on the roof reading the Sunday comics out loud. And Arthur and McCrea make an appealing romantic team—the scene in which they lie on single beds that are separated only by a thin wall (and they look like they share a double bed) was daring, and is reminiscent of the classic "Walls of Jericho" bit in *It Happened One Night*. Also with: Richard Gaines, Bruce Bennett, Grady Sutton, Frank Sully.

MORGAN!/MORGAN (A SUITABLE CASE FOR TREATMENT) (BRITISH/1966) B&W/97m.
One of the major pre-Midnight Movie cult films, a seriocomedy that not only has a nonconformist lead character—likable but insane London artist Morgan Delt (David Warner)—but is about nonconformity per se. Morgan has disappointed his mother by forsaking the communist revolution. And his wife, Leonie (Vanessa Redgrave's breakthrough role), divorces him because he finds life so complicated and sad that he acts hopelessly childish and keeps withdrawing from reality, daydreaming he's a gorilla swinging freely through the jungle. Morgan loves Leonie deeply and hopes to win her back before she marries stuffy art dealer Charles Napier (Robert Stephens). He resorts to putting an explosive under Leonie and Charles's bed, and then kidnaps her. Film fits into the irritating it's-okay-to-be-crazy-in-our-insane-world subgroup, which perpetuates the notion that a character's irresponsible actions can be condoned if he's certifiably nuts. Viewers shouldn't be so quick to cheer Morgan's devil-may-care behavior, because it's his way of shirking social responsibility. Worse, if we looked past director Karel Reisz's deceptively charming veneer, we'd see that Morgan's fantasies and wild antics are symptomatic of impending personal disaster. We laugh when Morgan threatens Charles, ignore how much physical abuse Morgan suffers while chasing Leonie, and ignore Leonie's protests. What Reisz and screenwriter David Mercer (who adapted his teleplay *A Suitable Case for Treatment*) keep us from realizing is that the most important aspect of this film is not how Morgan tries to win back the woman he loved and lost, but how Leonie deals with the often pathetic advances of a man she loves but can't be with without destroying herself. We get angry with Leonie for choosing boring Charles over unusual Morgan. True, there's no reason she wants to marry Charles (that's Mercer's fault), but if Reisz and Mercer immediately let us see the extent of Morgan's insanity, instead of camouflaging it with a consistently humorous tone, then we'd rightly side with her for protecting herself from a dangerous man. Picture has lost much of its following because stylistically it is extremely dated. We have long overdosed on freeze frames, fast-speed photography, insertions of old movies, and the juxtaposition of images signifying "illusion" and "reality." But the offbeat performances of Warner

and Redgrave still stand out. Also with: Irene Handl, Arthur Mullard.

MOROCCO (1930) B&W/92m.
Josef von Sternberg and Marlene Dietrich's second collaboration, her first Hollywood film. Dietrich, looking sleeker than in Sternberg's *The Blue Angel*, is the new singer at a Moroccan club frequented by the Foreign Legion. Whether wearing a tux and kissing a woman on the mouth (!) or a skimpy outfit that reveals her long, luscious legs, Dietrich is quite an attraction. When handsome legionnaire Gary Cooper hushes a rowdy crowd to let her sing, she is touched. She and ladies' man Cooper—they are equally sexy—fall in love with each other. It's refreshing that *both* man and woman play characters who have had numerous affairs—rather than having Cooper be a bumpkin who knows nothing about women, the role he'd play often later in his career. They are both free to express passion, and together they can make viewers pant. Dietrich and Cooper both insist that their relationship will never last: she has long ago lost her faith in men, and he adds, "Anyone who has faith in me is a sucker." Anyway, she doesn't want to be like the native girls who follow the legionnaires into the dessert. Or does she? Dietrich tries to convince herself that she isn't hooked on Cooper—she even has an affair with rich Adolphe Menjou—but she can't control her feelings. The long final sequence, including Dietrich's touching goodbye to Menjou (they have an *interesting* relationship), is a classic. It causes debates among feminist critics because Dietrich is sacrificing *all* (as her characters often do) for her man, for love. Actually, she isn't giving up very much. It's a wonderfully romantic ending. Film is erotic and exotic, like the rest of the Sternberg-Dietrich series. Dietrich, who seems to be followed around by smoke, is at her most likable: her "look" varies completely through the course of the film; she is confident throughout, but as her clothes and hairstyle become less flamboyant, we sense that she is thinking of herself more as a typical woman. Cinematography by Lee Garmes. Jules Furthman adapted Benno Vigny's novel *Amy Jolly*. Also with: Juliette Compton, Ullrich Haupt, Eve Southern.

MORTAL STORM, THE (1940) B&W/100m.
Set in Germany in the thirties. Close, happy German family is ripped apart when Nazis come to power. Two sons join the party and are among those who terrorize non-Aryans in the community; the kindly father (Frank Morgan), once a respected professor, is arrested; the mother and young son flee to Austria; and daughter Margaret Sullavan, who broke her engagement to Nazi Robert Young, tries to slip across the border with the man she loves, peace-loving James Stewart. You never forget you're watching a movie—for one thing, it's hard to believe Stewart's a German veterinarian—but story is still powerful. As one of the few American-made anti-Nazi films released prior to our entrance into the war, it has special significance. Nazis are depicted as heartless, paranoid, and, once they put on their uniforms and Nazi armbands, dictatorial. Point is made that those who became Nazis did so out of ignorance—their decision invariably backfires on them, but when they learn of ruthlessness of Nazis it's too late to change their minds. Sensitive direction by Frank Borzage and performances by Morgan, Sullavan, and Stewart. From the novel by Phyllis Bottome. Also with: Irene Rich, Bonita Granville, Robert Stack, Maria Ouspenskaya, Ward Bond.

MOSCOW ON THE HUDSON (1984) C/115m.
Paul Mazursky's seriocomic pat on the back to the unfulfilled American immigrant takes its title from the film Margot Kidder worked on in New York in the director's *Willie and Phil*. Robin Williams is a Russian saxophone player with the Moscow Circus who defects in Bloomingdale's and, full of paranoia that the KGB will snatch him back, spends a troubled year waiting to get his American citizenship. He gets a sobering view of America, where there is life—but well-paid work is so hard to find that it's difficult to make a good living; there is liberty—but so many abuse their freedom and mock the law that there is near-anarchy in the streets; and one can pursue happiness—but not ever have success. He never fits into the mainstream of white America, but instead takes jobs that require no skills or education, lives in a tiny tenement apartment, and befriends other New York immigrants—Italian Maria Conchita Alonso, Cuban Alejandro Rey, and Alabama black Cleavant Derricks. He'll always be an alien, terribly miss his family back in Russia, and be a second-class citizen—but he knows this is much better than still being in Russia. Film's quality wavers greatly as Mazursky uneasily shifts tone. But Williams is excellent and Alonso is very likable, their characters are authentic, and Mazursky gives us a perceptive view of those Americans (immigrants) who have been ignored by most filmmakers. There are several memorable moments, including Williams's and Alonso's sexy bath together and the scene in which she tells him that she doesn't want to live with him—having just gotten her citizenship, she doesn't want to relinquish any part of her independence, personal or political. Also with: Elya Baskin, Savely Kamarov.

MOST DANGEROUS GAME, THE (1932) B&W/63m.
Remote island is exotic locale for this classic thriller about a crazed hunter, Count Zaroff (Leslie Banks), who uses a stranded human couple (Joel McCrea, Fay Wray) as his prey. Much attention is paid to the scenic design of Zaroff's castle and the misty, jungle-covered island. It's shot much like a silent movie. Exciting, quickly paced action sequences are dramatically scored by Max Steiner. Richard Cooney's story would be remade often, but this picture is of special interest because it was a predecessor for the next year's *King Kong*, also made by producers Merian C. Cooper and Ernest B. Schoedsack. Here Schoedsack's co-director was Irving Pichel; Cooper would co-direct *King Kong*. Steiner would again do the music and Wray (whose hair is much darker here) would be another, more captivating heroine in danger on an uncharted, overgrown island. Robert Arm-

strong would move from supporting player to male lead. Equally interesting is that many visuals from this film were virtually repeated in *King Kong*. David O. Selznick was executive producer. This would be ideal to watch with *Island of Lost Souls*. Also with: Noble Johnson.

MOTHER (RUSSIAN/1926) B&W/90m.

Classic film of the Russian cinema, directed by V. I. Pudovkin, from Maxim Gorky's novel. It's rare among the Russian silent films in that it stresses character as much as technique; it uses montage and character placement for the purpose of expressing individual character's emotions. Epic is set in 1905. The peasants and workers are having terrible times, and revolution is brewing. Vera Baranovskaya tries to keep peace between her reactionary husband, A. Chistyakov, and revolutionist son Nikolai Batalov. Chistyakov is accidentally killed in a row. While his mother grieves, Batalov plots insurrection. She is tricked by police into revealing the location of guns Batalov has hidden, and he is thrown into prison. He escapes, and he and his newly politicized mother take part in a demonstration against the Tsar. They are willing to sacrifice their lives for the revolution. Mother and son have symbolic significance in that they represent the masses who rose against the Tsar. Baranovskaya also represents Mother Russia; but the two characters also have universal qualities. Picture has extraordinary visuals, all used for thematic purposes. While the acting is good, it is Pudovkin's montages that let us know what these characters are thinking. The most famous example: while Batalov is in prison, Pudovkin intercuts shots of him thinking with shots of trees, sky, birds, beautiful outdoors. Escape scene was inspired by D. W. Griffith's *Way Down East*. Other Russian adaptations of Gorky's novel were filmed in 1920 and 1955. Also with: Ivan Koval-Samborsky, Alexander Savitsky, Anna Zemstova, Pudovkin (as a police officer).

MRS. MINIVER (1942) B&W/134m.

William Wyler directed this Best Picture winner about the Minivers—middle-aged Greer Garson and Walter Pidgeon, their adult son, Richard Ney, their young children, Claire Sanders and Christopher Severn, and Teresa Wright, who becomes Ney's bride. They are meant to represent the typical British middle-class family whose cherished, hard-earned life of tranquillity and security has been destroyed by war. The story stays on the home front, where families try to carry on despite constant German bombing raids and the knowledge that their sons (like Ney) are off fighting. In the face of adversity (deaths, destroyed buildings, fear) the British are gallant, civil (they attend flower shows between raids), united, strong. Sure, these Britishers are phony—they're exactly the same as Americans depicted in Hollywood films—but they're the type of people American viewers could identify with in 1942. That was important because the purpose of M-G-M's propaganda piece, which was filmed on the studio lot, was to motivate Americans to come to the aid of the British (Roosevelt urged that it be released earlier than planned) and it is known to have succeeded to an astonishing degree—throughout the war Americans thought all imperiled British people were like the faultless Minivers. Picture is self-conscious to an annoying degree, particularly in the early scenes before the war—the scenes between Garson and Pidgeon are difficult to watch. However, later there are some fine moments between Garson and Wright, when they really seem to understand and feel love for one another, that are almost as poignant as moments in Wyler's 1946 film *The Best Years of Our Lives* (in which Wright also shines). I have always had mixed feelings about Greer Garson (and other actresses I can't picture in blue jeans), but she deserves her Oscar if only because she agreed to be mother to an adult (in reality she married Ney!) although she was only thirty-three. However, that didn't justify her giving her famous hour-long acceptance speech. Wyler didn't deserve his Oscar for Best Director. Wright beat out co-star Dame May Whitty (who plays her grandmother) for Best Supporting Actress; other Oscars were won by cinematographer Joseph Ruttenberg and the writers (George Froeschel, James Hilton, Claudine West, Arthur Wimperis) who adapted Jan Struther's newspaper essays about British valor into a screenplay. In 1950 Garson and Pidgeon starred in *The Miniver Story*, directed by H. C. Potter. Also with: Henry Travers, Reginald Owen, Helmut Dantine, Brenda Forbes, Henry Wilcoxon, Tom Conway.

MS. 45/ANGEL OF VENGEANCE (1981) C/84m.

Impressive low-budget cult movie with striking, highly stylized direction by Abel Ferrera, a feminist script by Nicholas St. John, and a strong, sympathetic, sexy performance from unknown Zoe Tamerlis, a high-school student with a resemblance to Nastassja Kinski, Simone Simon, and Bianca Jagger. Tamerlis plays the mute Thana, a timid, attractive young woman who works in New York's Garment District. Raped twice, she kills one rapist and goes out on the streets nightly to kill men who exploit or degrade women. Thana is meant to represent all the women of the world who don't speak out against the daily outrages they are subjected to from men (bosses, boyfriends, strangers on the street): a constant barrage of come-ons, orders, insults, patronizing conversation. She is the passive female—her job is sewing—who kills a man with an iron, symbol of the stereotypical unliberated woman, signifying that woman's passivity is not unsurmountable. She picks up the rapist's gun (obviously a phallic symbol)—she will use a masculine weapon to destroy him and other men. She becomes an angel of vengeance—methodically, savagely, and silently avenging her own abuse, she becomes far more intriguing than other cinema women who have retaliated for their own rapes. With its cold sexuality and violent tone, film was influenced by Roman Polanski's films; the plot and thematic elements seem patterned after his *Repulsion*, in which Catherine Deneuve plays another beautiful, sexually confused young woman (a beautician's aide). Both suffer sexual harassment going to and from work, both kill men who force themselves on them sexually. While corpses rot in their apartments (both have meddlesome neighbors), both lapse into temporary shock states while at work and become increasingly isolated. But whereas Deneuve becomes paranoid and kills men who enter her apartment, Thana breaks free of paranoia and goes out into the city after male victims. Deneuve goes crazy; Thana, though acting "crazy," remains rational. She chooses not to kill her lesbian friend (Darlene Stuto), even after she has fatally stabbed Thana or, earlier, her weird landlady's (Edith Sherman) annoying male dog, Phil. Her character is sympathetic yet fascistic—however, we don't side with her as we do with Charles Bronson in *Death Wish* because she scares the living daylights out of us. Film has many extremely well-done scenes (the whole sequence with Thana in a nun's habit is startling), much humor, and weird yet believable characters. Since the film was made by men, it's surprising how obnoxious every male is intended to be—only someone like Thana could make them get in line. A real sleeper. Also with: Steve Singer, Jack Thibeau, Peter Yellen, Albert Sinkys, Jimmy Laine (Ferrara).

MUD HONEY/ROPE OF FLESH (1965) B&W/92m.
Perhaps Russ Meyer's best film. Tawdry tale is set in a small town in Missouri that's full of stupid but shrewd, sweaty, hypocritical men and stupid, big-breasted women. Everyone is driven by lust, hatred and greed—and it's likely that the only book in town is the Bible owned by the illiterate, fanatical preacher (Frank Bolger). Lorna Maitland (star of Meyer's earlier *Lorna*) and Rena Horton play sisters who either charge for sex or are taken advantage of (Bolger has his way with deaf and dumb Horton). But they're around mostly for atmosphere. The major story concerns evil Hal Hopper, a scheming drunkard who rapes and kills the preacher's wife (Lee Bullard)—in the most violent sequence—and even rapes his own wife (Antoinette Christiani). Hoping to inherit a farm, he tries to turn the town against his rival for the property (John Furlong) by saying Furlong has been sleeping with Christiani. Lynch-mob fever spreads. Sleazy fake morality play is surprisingly well made. Meyer's camera work is fairly creative and he perfectly blends the sex, nudity, and violence. The acting's satisfactory, the actresses are exciting, the dialogue is flavorful, and we really believe that the characters live in this hellish version of Tobacco Road. Also with: Princess Livingston, Stu Lancaster.

MULTIPLE MANIACS (1970) C/90m.
Typically outrageous and degenerate—and funny—John Waters film, starring the inimitable Divine and others from Waters's unique stock company. She runs a "Carnival of Perversions," a front organization to lure unsuspecting suburbanites into a tent, where they are tied up, robbed of money and IDs, and in some cases murdered. Divine is becoming increasingly mad, and boyfriend David Lochary is afraid she'll kill him, especially if she learns he's having an affair with Mary Vivian Pearce, who's obsessed with performing "acts" with him. Lochary and Pearce plan on killing Divine. Meanwhile Divine gets a "rosary job" from religious pervert Mink Stole in a church, and they plan to kill Lochary. Inspired by the Sharon Tate murders, picture ends with living-room massacre; then Divine is raped by a giant lobster and runs through the streets foaming at the mouth. Picture starts with what I think is funniest Waters sequence and most revealing of him as an artist out to shock viewers through bad taste: suburbanites (representing us?) are repulsed, but don't run away from perverted acts—interestingly, they are more appalled by watching two men kissing on the lips than by the "puke eater." This is Waters's own favorite film, but I don't think it reaches heights (depths?) of *Pink Flamingos* or *Female Trouble*. That's because Divine's character is not as flamboyant or formidable as the ones she plays in those films—Divine is at "her" funniest when her character is constantly aggravated, dumped on, or humiliated; here, where she manages to achieve a coveted social position and retain faith in her beautiful self, she is too much in control. Also with: Cookie Mueller, Edith Massey (her debut).

MUMMY, THE (1932) B&W/72m.
Classic horror film with Boris Karloff as an Egyptian mummy who centuries before was entombed alive for trying to steal the sacred scroll of Thoth and revive the dead princess he loved. Now he is unburied during archeological excavation, and puts spell on a young woman (Zita Johann) who is a lookalike for the dead princess. He plans to kill her during a ritual so he can possess her for eternity. Boyfriend Frank Whemple (David Manners) and a doctor (Edward Van Sloan) make lame attempts to stop him. Directed by former cameraman Karl Freund, picture has visual beauty. But after unforgettable beginning in which Karloff comes to life and scares a man into hysteria, it moves along at a snail's pace. One problem is that Karloff never again appears in mummy's get-up (not that mummies have ever been frightening screen monsters); also, when he uses mind-control over Johann and the men who challenge him, the scenes seem watered-down versions of similar scenes from *Dracula*, also scripted by John L. Balderston. Some good special effects by John P. Fulton. Film is much loved by many horror fans. I believe it's overrated, but there's little doubt it's the best of the crummy mummy subgenre. Also with: Arthur Byron.

MURDER (BRITISH/1930) B&W/92m–108m.
An aspiring actress (Norah Baring as Diana Baring) is discovered next to the body of her dead friend. She says she remembers nothing. Famous actor Sir John Menier (Herbert Marshall) is on the jury that convicts her; but while she awaits execution, he becomes convinced that she is innocent. He believes that she is concealing the identity of a man involved in the case. He thinks that her lover committed the murder in order to protect a secret about himself. Alfred Hitchcock's whodunit has an interesting beginning and conclusion but a terribly slow middle section in which Sir John does his sleuthing. The best scene features the jury (which has several weird characters on it) reaching a verdict, with lone holdout Sir John buckling under to the pressure exerted by the others and going along with their guilty verdict—too bad this scene wasn't expanded into a full-length movie,

for it shows that Henry Fonda's success at changing the verdicts of his eleven jury mates from guilty to innocent in *Twelve Angry Men* is pure fantasy. Other notable scenes include: the amusing backstage bit in which performers, who are exiting and entering the stage, both chat with detectives and deliver their lines without missing a beat; Sir John tries to trick the chief suspect into revealing his guilt by having him read lines of a play about the murder case; a transvestite trapeze artist adds a grisly bit to his circus routine. Film is about the theater and, not surprisingly, is too theatrical. Sir John's novel stream-of-consciousness monologue is campy rather than arty; his words are almost drowned out by the orchestra, which had to be recorded live. From *Enter Sir John*, a novel by Clemence Dane and Helen Simpson. Filmed also in a German-language version (starring Alfred Abel). Also with: Phyllis Konstam, Edward Chapman, Miles Mander, Esmé Percy, Donald Calthrop, Amy Brandon-Thomas.

MURDER, MY SWEET/FAREWELL, MY LOVELY (1944) B&W/95m.

Moral detective Philip Marlowe, Raymond Chandler's white knight in black LA, made his first movie appearance in this *film noir* classic. It was reputedly Chandler's favorite adaptation of his novels; he even preferred Dick Powell's Marlowe to Bogart's in *The Big Sleep* and Robert Montgomery's in *Lady in the Lake*—perhaps because Powell, even with his new "tough" screen image, projects Marlowe's vulnerability more than the other actors. If Powell is wearing the cheek rouge he used by the barrel in his thirties musicals, it is hidden beneath the stubble and the sweat. He is convincing making the transition from cheery crooner to hard-boiled detective. Marlowe is hired by huge ex-con Moose Malloy (Mike Mazurki) to track down the woman he loves. He takes on a second case that will soon relate to the first: he's hired by a man (Douglas Walton) to accompany him when he buys back a stolen necklace belonging to the piece's *femme fatale* (blonde Claire Trevor, coming across as sexy as Lana Turner). His client is killed and he is knocked unconscious, allowing Marlowe the narrator a chance to say the film's classic lines (which writer John Paxton took from Chandler): "A black pool opened at my feet. I dived in. There was no bottom." Picture is known for its seedy characters; hard-edged, hyperbolic dialogue and narration; dark, atmospheric photography by Harry J. Wild. But I think it's most significant because it is the one picture to fully exploit the nightmarish elements that are present in good *film noir*. Because our narrator, Marlowe, spends time recovering from being knocked out and, later, from drugs in his bloodstream, he never has a clear head; the dark, smoky world he walks through becomes increasingly surreal, indicating he is in a dream state. Part of the reason we feel nervous for this Marlowe is that we sense he has no more control over his situation than we do when we're having a nightmare. Vernon L. Walker did the special effects for the memorable scene in which the drugged Marlowe has hallucinations. Director Edward Dmytryk's best film. RKO had already adapted

Chandler's *Farewell, My Lovely* in 1942 as *The Falcon Takes Over*, but Marlowe wasn't a character. Dick Richards would do a solid remake in 1975, using Chandler's original title and starring Robert Mitchum. Also with: Anne Shirley (as Trevor's stepdaughter), Otto Kruger, Miles Mander, Don Douglas, Ralf Harolde, Esther Howard.

MURDER OF FRED HAMPTON, THE (1971) B&W/88m.

A crudely made but powerful and important document about the political philosophy and influence of Fred Hampton, charismatic 20-year-old chairman of the Illinois chapter of the Black Panther Party, and his shocking murder by several Chicago cops who were under orders of state prosecutor Edward V. Hanrahan. In fact, the film, made by the non-profit Film Group and co-directed by Mike Grey and Howard Alk, started out as a documentary of the *living* Hampton and was meant to impress upon viewers how the brutality inflicted by Chicago police on visiting protesters/newsmen at the 1968 Democratic Convention was an everyday occurrence for poor blacks who lived in the city. The directors expected the film to end with Hampton making a final statement before fleeing the country so he wouldn't be sentenced to prison on the trumped-up charge that he robbed an ice-cream truck. But with filming almost complete, Hampton was killed and the filmmakers rushed over to the apartment where another Panther also had been killed in a hail of 99 police bullets. The footage they took of the physical condition of the apartment is juxtaposed with Hanrahan's report to the press about what happened. Everything Hanrahan and the police say is contradicted by what we see of the apartment. Most important: no shots were fired in the direction of the police, which contradicts their statement that they acted in self-defense. It's great fun watching Hanrahan squirm and sweat and try to change his statements under the barrage of questions by skeptical reporters whom he expected to praise him—he didn't count on Hampton's death raising the ire of respected *white* Chicago citizens and politicians, and this cost him victory in his upcoming election for DA. Film had great impact on the political activists of its day. That's because it provided visual evidence of something everyone in the movement knew: that there was a government-police conspiracy to eliminate or neutralize radical leaders, specifically black leaders who were mobilizing the poor. Also important: it offered a different view of the Black Panthers (who were at the forefront of the movement for revolutionary social change) than that presented by the establishment press and media. We see the Panther-run free clinics and their free-breakfast program for poor black kids. While Hampton talks about the importance of guns—for *defense*, to shoot down threatening "pigs" (the Chicago cops of the day were indeed "pigs")—he also states the party's objectives and, significantly, its alliance with whites in the movement (he reminds his followers that racism of any kind is the basis of capitalism); its opposition to capitalist blacks; and its goal that there be a revolution, not by emotionally motivated blacks but by politically educated, socially conscious people of all races. Seeing the film today, one may become frightened by Hampton's early speeches, which make it appear that his one goal was to create armed confrontation with police. But as the film goes on, one can't help being impressed by his voice of reason and his integrity. And we are reminded of the magnitude of the crime perpetrated by our government when, in one way or another, it got rid of all the young black leaders (Hampton, Jackson, Seale, Cleaver, Newton) and thus crushed the black radical movement.

MURDERS IN THE RUE MORGUE (1932) B&W/
75m. Edgar Allan Poe tale, set in Paris at the turn of the century. In his follow-up to *Dracula*, Bela Lugosi doesn't get enough screen time as the diabolical Dr. Mirakle, who's trying to mate the ape from his sideshow act and a female to prove his theories of evolution. His heinous blood transfusions fail and bodies of dead girls keep turning up in the Seine. He sends his ape after pretty Sidney Fox, but her boyfriend, medical student Leon Waycoff (Ames), figures out Mirakle's scheme just in time. Film benefits from expressionistic photography by Karl Freund and Lugosi's sinister portrayal; but the ape is too obviously a man in a hairy costume and Waycoff and the baby-voiced Fox are just awful. The "best" sequences—i.e., Lugosi draining the blood from a streetwalker (Arlene Francis) whom he has tied to a rack—are the most tasteless. Most interesting aspect of the film is the perverse sexuality that is implicit in Mirakle's work, and the ape's attraction to Fox. Film presents all males as predators—notice the odd picnic scene in which one man after another feeds a line, obviously a lie, to his date so she'll accept his advances. Story was filmed as an early silent, now lost; it would be remade in 1954 (the 3-D film *Phantom of the Rue Morgue*) and in 1971. Also with: Brandon Hurst, Bert Roach, Noble Johnson.

MURMUR OF THE HEART (FRENCH-GERMAN-ITALIAN/1971) C/118m. Rude comedy by Louis Malle deals primarily with the incestuous feelings between sexually curious 14-year-old French boy (Benoit Ferreux) and his beautiful, sensuous Italian mother (Léa Massari)—which leads to inevitable one-time sex—but Malle's more interested in drawing a scathing portrait of the French bourgeoisie. Film is set in Dijon in 1954 when France was divided over its presence in Vietnam. Intellectual Ferreux (who is for world peace) and his two older, rambunctious brothers live in large house with their parents and grandmother. They have little respect for their gynecologist father (Daniel Gélin), who is indifferent to them as well, and mock all that he represents. On the other hand, they adore their fun, earthy mother. The older brothers are obsessed with sex and are determined to help Ferreux have his first sexual experience. But they get drunk and ruin his sexual initiation with a prostitute. More eager than before, Ferreux increasingly thinks of his mother in sexual terms. When he develops a heart murmur, he and his mother vacation at a treatment hotel. While Ferreux shows interest in the pretty girls there,

they don't compare to his mother. In Malle's customary uncontroversial way, comedy advances novel idea that the best way to show rejection of bourgeoisie's shackles is to break its sexual rules. So the boys masturbate and have impure thoughts (which infuriates priest Michel Lonsdale when he takes Ferreux's confessions); the boys have sex with older prostitutes; their mother has an extra-marital affair with a non-aristocrat while she refuses to have sex with her husband; and, "worse" than anything, mother and son have sex. Malle lets them get away with their "sins" and be happier.

MUTINY ON THE BOUNTY (1935) B&W/
132m. Classic sea drama, an early Best Picture winner that holds up, is about a historical mutiny that took place in the 18th century on a British ship making a two-year voyage to retrieve breadfruit plants from Tahiti. Captain Bligh (Charles Laughton) treats the men with such contempt and brutality during the journey—he deprives them of water and satisfactory rations, has them flogged and chained, causes death—that officer Fletcher Christian (Clark Gable) and the miserable sailors seize the *Bounty* and set Bligh and those loyal to him adrift at sea. Film hasn't the sense of adventure, eroticism, or psychological complexities of the 1962 remake with Trevor Howard and Marlon Brando (which also was based on the Charles Nordhoff and James Norman Hall accounts), or the revisionist 1984 film, *The Bounty*, starring Anthony Hopkins and Mel Gibson. But it's the superior film. Its power comes from neither Bligh nor Christian ever backing down from each other during an argument, even when the other has the upper hand. Laughton's Bligh is one of the screen's most memorable tyrants, one who believes in the divine right of captains in His Majesty's service—he never realizes, much less admits, that he does anything wrong. Only when the entire crew watches a man die because of Bligh's absurd orders does Laughton's face reflect a chink in the armor—Bligh suddenly looks like a teenager who has just made a fool of himself in gym class. Masculine without having to throw left hooks, Gable gives one of his finest performances: obviously, he felt his Oscar for the prior year's *It Happened One Night* meant he didn't have to be intimidated by Laughton, who'd won the Oscar the year before. Franchot Tone plays the third major character in the drama, an officer whose faith in the British navy is almost shattered by watching Bligh's abuse of power. His stirring speech at the court-martial in England—he chose not to go with Fletcher and the mutineers to Pitcairn Island—was the shining moment in his career. Irving Thalberg's production was directed by Frank Lloyd, photographed by Arthur Edeson, and scripted by Talbot Jennings, Jules Furthman, and Casey Wilson. Also with: Herbert Mundin, Eddie Quillan, Dudley Digges, Movita, Donald Crisp, Henry Stephenson, Spring Byington, Mamo, Douglas Walton, Francis Lister.

MY BEST GIRL (1927) B&W/74m. Mary Pickford's last silent film is perhaps her best; she plays one of her few adult parts and shows surprising sophistication as

both a light comedienne and a romantic lead. With her appealing combination of spunk, nobility, vulnerability, and tenderness, she recalls Janet Gaynor (whom she resembles slightly)—and it would have been interesting to see her in Gaynor roles. Mary's a stockroom girl in a department store. She becomes attracted to the new stockroom boy (Charles "Buddy" Rogers) and shows him the ropes that help him move ahead. (What about *her* promotion?) They fall in love. But she doesn't know that he's really the son of the fabulously wealthy owner of the store, working incognito to see if he can succeed in business on his own. Moreover, he's engaged to a young woman from his social class—he could never marry a poor girl like Mary, whose family (mother, father, sister, and she) lives on Goat Hill. Comedy is extremely charming; courtship of Rogers (who never was better) and Pickford (on the back of a truck, in a crate in the stockroom) is very sweet and convincing (Rogers and Pickford would marry 10 years later). There are funny sight gags; some excellent use of LA streets. Directed by Sam Taylor, who'd work on all but one of Pickford's remaining films. Also with: Sunshine Hart, Lucien Littlefield, Carmelita Geraghty, Mack Swain.

MY BRILLIANT CAREER (AUSTRALIAN/1979) C/100m.

Popular adaptation of the autobiographical novel by Sybella Melvyn, written under her male pseudonym, Miles Franklin. Judy Davis is perfectly cast as the young Sybella, an aspiring writer and avowed bachelorette who lives in Australia in the 1890s. Because of her rebelliousness (her favorite expression is "I won't"), poor parents (she works off their debts), and plain face (Davis radiates spirit, confidence, and inner beauty), her relatives think she should jump at any marriage proposal. But she sees how repressed are married women in all classes of society, and realizes that in order to write, she must remain single. That means turning down a kind, handsome, understanding, playful man (Sam Neill), although they love each other. When Davis delivers her "I-want-to-learn-about-myself" bit, it doesn't sound like a cliché. Since her writing desires have been almost forgotten by *us* by the time Neill proposes, we think she should accept. Yet we still cheer when she turns up a manuscript from out of the blue in the last scene. While praised for its feminism, picture has rightly been criticized for ignoring the fact that Melvyn was a lesbian—she is not sacrificing much when she turns down a handsome male suitor. What is positive is that Davis truly enjoys the company of women (and they benefit from her friendship). As written by Eleanor Whitcombe and directed by Gillian Armstrong, they are all smart, strong women—they don't realize their own potential because they married. The shame is that they expect free-spirited Davis to follow their lead. She knows better. She's a memorable lead character. Strong direction by Armstrong, who seems in tune with Davis. Also with: Wendy Hughes, Robert Grubb, Max Cullen.

MY DARLING CLEMENTINE (1946) B&W/97m.

John Ford's stirring, beautifully photographed (by Joe MacDonald) but flagrantly fictional account of how Marshal Wyatt Earp (Henry Fonda), his brothers Virgil (Tim Holt), Morgan (Ward Bond) and James (Don Garner), and Wyatt's pal, the notorious "Doc" Holliday (Victor Mature), cleaned up Tombstone in the 1880s. This is a different kind of western; while nine people are gunned down—all five of the evil Clantons, two Earps, Holliday, and his girlfriend, Chihuahua (miscast Linda Darnell)—and a major theme is violent retribution, it has been described as "lovely," "poignant," "nostalgic," "sentimental," "tender," "sweet," and "poetic." More than the violence, we remember Wyatt playfully leaning back on his chair and balancing himself on the street post in front of him, with one foot and then the other; Wyatt proudly escorting pretty Clementine (Cathy Downs) to the town gathering; Wyatt and Clementine dancing; and—my favorite image—Wyatt walking alone down the middle of the road leading to the O.K. Corral with the enormous rock monuments of Monument Valley in the distance. We remember Cyril Mockridge's lyrical score, using harmonicas, fiddles, guitars, and a cowboy chorus—but notice how he uses no music in the final O.K. Corral shootout, and the silence builds the tension. Brutal, stoop-shouldered, whip-wielding, gun-toting Old Man Clanton (scarily played by Walter Brennan)—who really died *before* the gunfight at the O.K. Corral—and his four sons represent Neanderthals. The Earps, as a family, pave the way for civilized man (although some viewers won't agree with Ford's opinion of who should be part of a civilized Tombstone). Wyatt becomes one more hero who tames the West but then has no place in it. The real Wyatt Earp was a cad (also he was no marshal), but Fonda plays him as a brave, virtuous, dignified man. He's so steadfast in his moral beliefs that he's too predictable. That's why the morally ambiguous Holliday is brought into play. He's a tragic figure who, unlike Wyatt, cannot accept the advent of civilization because he will be rejected by society when, by all rights, he should fit in—he's more intellectual, educated, cultured, better dressed than Wyatt. He's also blessed with the power to cure the sick—but makes no attempt to rid himself of consumption. The tempestuous Holliday-Chihuahua relationship counterpoints "polite" courtship between Wyatt and Clementine. The real Earp surely didn't say the film's final line, "Ma'am, I sure like that name Clementine," but I believe Fonda's Earp returned to Tombstone and married this pretty schoolmarm. From Stuart N. Lake's *Wyatt Earp, Frontier Marshal*. Also with: Alan Mowbray, John Ireland, Grant Withers, Mickey Simpson, Roy Roberts, Jane Darwell, Russell Simpson, Francis Ford, Jack Pennick, J. Farrell MacDonald, Mae Marsh.

MY DINNER WITH ANDRE (1981) C/110m.

I'm 0 for 2 at staying awake through the entire talk-a-thon between playwright-actor Wallace Shawn and theatrical director Andre Gregory at a fancy New York restaurant. Louis Malle's cult film is not a *cinéma-vérité* documentary. Shawn and Gregory wrote the dialogue and, though they appear as themselves, they are actually playing characters. The premise is that Shawn has been going through a difficult time financially because he can't get his plays produced—he has been avoiding Gregory, who produced his first play. When Gregory invites him to dinner, Shawn worries that they'll have nothing to talk about. At the beginning Gregory talks incessantly, while Shawn feigns interest; he has a slight grin and sits forward. He asks follow-up questions so he doesn't have to contribute to the conversation. Anyone who has ever been to a party of *artistes* can identify with Shawn, who is funny. Eventually barriers break down and Shawn joins the intellectual discourse, talking about life, art, and the necessity of having an electric blanket. The two men are engaging, and much conversation is funny and/or incisive, but it's hard to maintain interest through Gregory's long monologues.

MY FAIR LADY (1964) C/170m. Film version of Lerner and Loewe's musical adaptation of Shaw's *Pygmalion*—about Professor Henry Higgins (Rex Harrison) transforming cockney flower girl Eliza Doolittle (Audrey Hepburn) into a lady in order to win a wager, and falling in love with her. It copped eight Oscars, including Best Picture, Best Actor, and Best Director, George Cukor. But seeing it today is extremely disappointing. Even the best songs have become so tiresome that it's possible you'll walk away at film's end humming tunes from another musical (as I caught myself doing). The musical numbers are the film's major problem. For one thing, it's unforgivable that the postproduction dubbing was done as poorly as for a low-budget Italian muscleman movie. And even when Hepburn's lips are in sync with Marni Nixon's voice, the substitution is so evident that one can only wish that Julie Andrews had been retained from Broadway. It is shameful for a so-called "big musical" not to have any large production numbers. When Hepburn sings "I Could Have Danced All Night," she's referring to herself and Harrison twirling once or twice in the parlor— that's all. Director Cukor wrongly chose to keep scenes intact from the stage version, losing what potential the cinema has for heightening the theatrical experience. While Harrison's acting transferred well, the musical numbers do not. Stanley Holloway's two songs, "With a Little Bit of Luck" and "Get Me to the Church on Time," cry out for something *cinematic*. "Poor Professor Higgins" is even more embarrassing. Shaw was known for creating strong, intelligent women characters, and Cukor was known for directing similar women in his films. Then why does Hepburn's Eliza come across as such a pushover, happy to give up her freedom for life with a dull man who has treated her badly? And who would have thought Cukor would direct a film which ends with a woman accepting that her man is going to treat her subserviently, as Higgins's last line, "Where are my slippers?", indicates? Also with: Wilfrid Hyde-White, Gladys Cooper, Jeremy Brett, Theodore Bikel.

MY FAVORITE WIFE (1940) B&W/88m. Sprightly but slight marital farce reunited Cary Grant and Irene Dunne, who'd had great success in *The Awful Truth*,

Leo McCarey's classic screwball comedy. McCarey served as producer of this film but, following an automobile accident, relinquished directorial chores to young Garson Kanin. Kanin's work is inconsistent. The improvisation, McCarey's forte, seems forced and often falls flat. Also Kanin either couldn't recognize when his stars were playing a scene badly or was afraid to tell them; has Dunne ever been worse than when she tells the kids she's their mother? Film is a variation on Tennyson's *Enoch Arden*, with Dunne's Ellen Arden returning home after seven years on a deserted island only to discover that husband Grant has just married Gail Patrick. When Dunne reappears, Grant wants to annul his marriage to Patrick and go back to his wife. But—and this is the most interesting aspect of the film—while Dunne forgives Grant for romancing and marrying Patrick, he has trouble coming to terms with her being stranded for seven years with muscular, virile Randolph Scott. Picture starts out extremely well, with a funny sequence at a honeymoon hotel in Yosemite, but while there are a couple of great gags later on—wait till you see Scott's *dive*—the comedy never rises from amusing to hilarious. Marital game-playing becomes far-fetched and tedious, and too much of the humor comes at the expense of characters who are being treated rotten (Patrick, in particular, gets unfair treatment). After a while the charm of the stars is all that carries the picture to its happy conclusion. Marilyn Monroe died before the completion of the remake, *Something's Got to Give*; it was rewritten as *Move Over, Darling*, a 1963 Doris Day picture. Also with: Ann Shoemaker, Scotty Beckett, Donald MacBride, Granville Bates.

MY FAVORITE YEAR (1982) C/92m. An original, pleasing, spiritedly written (by Norman Steinberg and Dennis Palumbo) and acted comedy set in 1954. Mark Linn-Baker is the youngest writer on the top-rated *King Kaiser's Comedy Hour*, a live TV show based on *Your Show of Shows/The Sid Caesar Hour*. He's hired to keep an eye on the week's guest star, the alcoholic, womanizing, incorrigible Peter O'Toole (as Allan Swann), a onetime matinee idol—a swashbuckler like John Barrymore and Errol Flynn—and make sure he stays sober. Direction by Richard Benjamin is uneven (he has a particularly tough time with tone changes), Jessica Harper is wasted playing a perky, dull girl (Linn-Baker's girlfriend) instead of one of her kooky characters, and some scenes play quite badly. But both O'Toole and Joseph Bologna (as the Caesar-like Kaiser) are terrific. Film shows how the brilliant, artistic, graceful O'Toole and the stupid, strong, instinctively hilarious Bologna—top stars from different eras—share the limelight and become unbeatable partners on live television (when they take on the mob together): there is room in show business for great talents of all types. The dialogues between the show's writers and the scene in which O'Toole meets Linn-Baker's unusual mother (Lainie Kazan) and uncle (Lou Jacobi) are highlights. Also with: Bill Macy, Cameron Mitchell, Anne DeSalvo, Selma Diamond, Adolph Green, Gloria Stuart.

MY LITTLE CHICKADEE (1940) B&W/83m.
The only teaming of W. C. Fields and Mae West made perfect sense since both always played flamboyant, conceited (only West had reason to be) characters who had a way with words, a unique way of looking at a cockeyed world run by bluenoses, and a willingness to endure punishment for breaking society's rules. West was free with sex; Fields's vices included excessive drinking, smoking, lying, swindling. Comedy is set in the Old West. In order to get the bluenoses off her back, West (as Flower Belle Lee) agrees to marry misanthropic Fields (as Cuthbert J. Twilley) about a minute after she meets him and half a minute after she sees his bag of money. Fields doesn't realize that the marriage was performed by a charlatan (Donald Meek) and can't understand why his "bride" will neither kiss him nor share her bed with him. She's more interested in keeping moonlit rendezvous with the Masked Bandit and flirting with shady saloon owner Joseph Calleia and honest newspaperman Dick Foran. Wanting West to be a widow so he can marry her, Calleia arranges for Fields to become town lawman, a dead-end job. It's too bad West spends so much time with Calleia, Foran, and the Masked Bandit because her few scenes with Fields are precious: their farewell in which he tells her to "come up and see me sometime" and she calls him "my little chickadee" is a classic. Otherwise, West's best scene is when she teaches some unruly schoolboys about "figures." Fields comes off much better, chatting incessantly, bragging, lying, telling weird anecdotes, using a language all his own (full of descriptive words and metaphors in which midgets' feet and two-headed boys with headaches are among the ridiculous things mentioned). Among his finest moments are his bath, his bedding down with a goat, and his hoodwinking a card player. West and Fields combined on the script. The beginning spoofs *Stagecoach*. Directed by Edward Cline. Also with: Margaret Hamilton, Ruth Donnelly, Fuzzy Knight.

MY MAN GODFREY (1936) B&W/95m.
Classic screwball comedy about a "forgotten man" (William Powell) who is discovered living beside a trash heap by a dizzy rich blonde (Carole Lombard) who brings him back to a party so she can win a scavenger hunt. She hires him to be butler for her crazy family, father Eugene Pallette, mother Alice Brady, and spoiled sister Gail Patrick, plus sponging artist Mischa Auer. It is the bum who has manners and discipline and the society clan who are wild (Auer does a hilarious ape impersonation) and unruly. Then writers Eric Hatch and Morrie Ryskind do away with their interesting premise by making Powell a millionaire who had just dropped out from society. They may have had praiseworthy intentions—they wanted Powell to discuss cynically both the plight and the nobility of the unemployed during the Depression (and take pokes at the idle rich)—but director Gregory La Cava has trouble maintaining a humorous thread while injecting serious themes. If the film's going to attempt social criticism, it shouldn't be so timid about it. Film succeeds not because of the story or direction but because of the spirited performances. As one would hope, suave Powell and daffy Lombard have some great moments together in the dump, washing dishes, in the bathroom, where Godfrey puts her fully clothed into the shower (proving to her that he loves her), and getting married (as Powell and Lombard once did in real life). Also with: Alan Mowbray, Franklin Pangborn, Grady Sutton, Jean Dixon, Jane Wyman.

MY NAME IS JULIA ROSS (1945) B&W/65m.
Exceptional "B" suspense thriller, directed by Joseph H. Lewis. Adapted from Anthony Gilbert's novel *The Woman in Red*, the story is the type Alfred Hitchcock would have enjoyed filming. Upset that her boyfriend (Dennis Bruce) has walked out on her, Nina Foch accepts a job as a live-in secretary for George Macready and his mother, Dame May Whitty. They drug her and take her to a mansion in Cornwall. The insane, knife-playing Macready and the greedy Whitty (an effective change of pace for the kindly actress) convince everyone in town that Foch is Macready's rich wife, whom he killed and foolishly dumped in the ocean. Needing a real corpse in order to get the inheritance, he plans to kill Foch in a way that will suggest an accident. Half-crazed from these people all insisting she's someone other than who she really is, Foch has trouble stopping Macready from killing her. Until then it's a riveting melodrama. You feel more frightened for Foch than for Ingrid Bergman in *Notorious* when she's trapped in the house with Claude Rains and his evil mother. Picture bears slight resemblance to *So Long at the Fair*, only here the woman has to prove her *own* existence rather than the existence of a brother. Macready has played many chilling villains, but none is scarier than the character he plays here. A highlight has Macready waiting for Foch to fall down a stairwell he boobytrapped. Strong direction by Lewis, camerawork by Burnett Guffey. Also with: Anita Bolster, Doris Lloyd, Queenie Leonard.

MY NAME IS NOBODY (ITALIAN-GERMAN-FRENCH/1974) C/115m—130m.
It's hard to know what to make of this comical, philosophical, action-packed Italian western. It was produced by Sergio Leone, has panoramic visuals that are reminiscent of shots in Leone-directed westerns, stars Leone's favorite actor (Henry Fonda, who'd been in the Leone-directed *Once Upon a Time in the West*), has a score by Ennio Morricone that is very derivative of his monumental music in all the Leone-directed westerns, and deals with a major Leone theme: that in the old West, as civilization emerged and the gunfighter became obsolete, for a brief moment mythology and history merged. But the film is directed by another, Tonino Valeri, who relies too much on slapstick at the expense of Leone's satirical wit, presents a surreal world that Leone moved out of after *A Fistful of Dollars*, and completely avoids Leone's essential theme—that each time a man is killed, another profits financially. So while this film is pretty well made, it's frustrating not being able to figure out how it fits into Leone's oeuvre. Fonda plays a legendary, aging gunfighter whom "nobody" can outdraw. But there is a guy with no name, a

nobody. Blue-eyed, blond Terence Hill (who, unfortunately, is dubbed) is a scruffy, penniless gunman who idolizes Fonda and wants to make sure he gets his spot in history books. Fonda's more interested in going to sea, but Hill annoys him so much that he ends up standing alone against the 150-man "Wild Bunch" in a truly impressive, imaginatively filmed sequence. And finally Hill, whom we've seen defeat numerous bad guys with his lightning-quick hands, and Fonda have a showdown on Main Street. Also with: Leo Gordon, Geoffrey Lewis, R. G. Armstrong.

MY NIGHT AT MAUD'S/MA NUIT CHEZ MAUD (FRENCH/1969) B&W/110m.

The third of Eric Rohmer's six "Moral Tales," but the first to get widespread circulation in America. Jean-Louis Trintignant is a 34-year-old engineer who is a devout Catholic but—perhaps (although he wouldn't admit it) to question his own belief that all of life is preordained—is increasingly interested in chance and probability. He runs into a Marxist friend (Antoine Vitez) whom he hasn't seen in 14 years . . . at a restaurant neither has been to before. Vitez takes him to meet his girlfriend, Maud (Françoise Fabian), a doctor, a lapsed Catholic, a divorcée with a young daughter. They have ultrasophisticated dinner conversations about Pascal, probability, and religion. Vitez goes home, but, at Fabian's request, Trintignant remains so he won't drive on the icy roads, as her former lover was doing when he was in a fatal (fated?) accident. However, Trintignant doesn't make a play for her during the night. She wrongly believes this is because he is in love with another woman, a blonde. That morning Trintignant, who is the type of guy who is always punctual, keeps appointments, and doesn't sway from an ordered life, impulsively approaches (on the street)) a beautiful blonde (Marie-Christine Barrault) he'd seen at mass. It will turn out that she knows Vitez and was Fabian's husband's lover. More coincidence, more defying the odds? Or has everything been preordained? The humor is more subtle than in other Rohmer films—in fact, one could sit through the whole film without realizing he's been funny on occasion. That's because the characters are always so serious. Indeed, humor comes from seeing such loquacious intellectuals turning out to be as silly and awkward as everyone else when it comes to sex. Rohmer's view of *sophisticated* adults is apparent when in the midst of their high-plane, pretentious dinner conversation (parodied in Louis Malle's *My Dinner with Andre*) Fabian's daughter (Marie Becker) climbs out of bed just to see the lights on the Christmas tree—it's a simple, sweet, and honest gesture that makes us see how trivial the adult discourse is. Fine acting; an excellent script by Rohmer. Cinematography by Nestor Almendros.

MYSTERY OF KASPAR HAUSER, THE/ENIGMA OF KASPAR HAUSER, THE/EVERY MAN FOR HIMSELF AND GOD AGAINST ALL (WEST GERMAN/1974) C/109m.

One of Werner Herzog's most compelling films interprets the mysterious true story of a man who turned up in Nürnberg in 1928, barely able to walk, knowing how to say only one sentence, having never had contact with a human being other than whoever kept him locked in a cell and livng on bread and water for his entire life. Kaspar (Bruno S.) learns how to speak and write, and he develops a cynical personal philosophy about the world he has entered. He becomes impatient with the priests and professors who try to brainwash him with their unsound championing of faith and logic, respectively. He also rebels against those men who want to exploit him. I don't think Herzog sees Kaspar as a Tarzan–wild child figure—a primal being thrust into brutal, corruptive civilization—or Christ figure—a saint who is persecuted and sacrificed. Kaspar is simply an outsider, a naturalist, whose presence causes everyone to question their orderly vision of their world, their faith in God, their way of leading their lives. The town officials always try to categorize Kaspar and are relieved to discover he has an abnormal liver and brain shape because this gives them an explanation for his strangeness. Film has beautiful cinematography, music, and lead performance by short, plump Bruno S.—a former mental patient, according to some reports. The early sequence in which Bruno sits like a lump in his cell and is dragged like a sack outside by his father, who kicks his feet to make him walk, has an overwhelming sadness. In the same subgenre as *The Wild Child* and *The Elephant Man*, but completely different from those pictures. Also with: Walter Ladengast, Brigitte Mira, Hans Kroecher.

MYSTERY OF THE WAX MUSEUM (1933) C/77m.

Horror film was considered lost for more than 25 years, during which time it came to be regarded as a masterpiece of the genre. When a print was discovered in Jack Warner's private collection, there was great excitement. But screenings revealed the picture to be a major disappointment. While the picture has qualities that distinguish it from other early horror films—it has a contemporary setting (New York City), it was filmed in striking two-color Technicolor (although it looks washed out on many prints), it emphasized atmosphere rather than shocks—it has several dull stretches, unfunny comedy, and uninteresting subplots. In fact, it often seems to fit more into the newspaper or gangster cycles than the horror genre. Lionel Atwill gives one of his strongest performances as the crazed, disfigured European genius who creates wax figures that are suspiciously lifelike. New York reporter Glenda Farrell discovers that bodies have been disappearing from the morgue and her trail leads to Atwill's studio. Meanwhile Atwill plans to pour molten wax over her roommate, Fay Wray, who is the living (for the moment, anyway) image of "Marie Antoinette," his precious wax figure that was destroyed in a fire back in London (set by his corrupt, money-mad partner, Edwin Maxwell). Film's highlights include that fire in the wax museum (it's amazingly eerie watching the faces of wax figures melt), Wray shattering Atwill's mask and discovering the hideous face underneath (a scene obviously inspired by the unmasking in *The Phantom of the Opera*), and the finale when police charge into Atwill's impressively designed lab to save Wray.

But I prefer the 1953 3-D remake, *House of Wax*, with Vincent Price. Directed by Michael Curtiz, who'd earlier made *Dr. X*, also in experimental color, with Atwill and Wray. Also with: Frank McHugh, Arthur Edmund Carewe, Gavin Gordon.

NAKED JUNGLE, THE (1953) C/95m. Properly bred Eleanor Parker is the mail-order bride of Charlton Heston, a humorless, heartless plantation owner in South America. He acts unfriendly; she is perfect and plays the piano. They fall in love. Forget the boring romance between these two uninteresting, poorly played characters and hang on until the exciting second half of the picture. That's when armies of flesh-eating red ants march through the jungles and devour everyone in sight. Finale has the ants overrunning the plantation. The screenplay by Philip Yordan and Ranald MacDougall was based on Carl Stephenson's story "Leiningen Versus the Ants," but if you didn't know that, you might suspect that the horror storyline was just added as a *deus ex machina* to rescue the plodding picture (which it does). One of the first films to deal with the "retribution of nature." Nice color. George Pal's production was directed by Byron Haskin. Also with: William Conrad, Abraham Sofaer.

NAKED KISS, THE (1965) B&W/92m. Forget that moviegoers who are unfamiliar with Sam Fuller's work consider this film campy and laugh at almost every line (even those that turn out to be quotes from Byron and Baudelaire), for this is Fuller's masterpiece, one of the most fascinating and original "B" movies ever made. In a wild variation on a Joan Crawford role, Constance Towers gives a strong performance as a tough, intellectual prostitute. Having beaten up her pimp (Monte Mansfield)—in a shocking pre-title sequence—for having gypped her out of money and shaved her bald, she flees the mob, plying her trade in small towns. She arrives in Grantville. Her first customer is the town sheriff, Anthony Eisley, who directs her to a brothel across the county line. But Towers decides to go straight. She rents a room in the home of a nice, respectable woman (Betty Bronson), becomes a skilled and popular nurse's aide at a hospital for handicapped children, and agrees to marry the town's most respected citizen, Michael Dante (as Grant), a cultured, handsome millionaire who knows of her past. Film deals with Towers's attempt to prove herself "normal," to lead a normal life by marrying someone from the right side of the tracks. Her dreams are shattered when she catches Dante molesting a child (another startling scene) and he confesses that the only reason he wants her for his bride is that she's "abnormal" and can understand his perversion. (His "naked kiss" was the telltale sign of a pervert.) When she kills Dante and no one believes her story (until the little girl is found), she discovers that "normal" people are closedminded, accusatory, and hypocritical. It's preferable to be abnormal, as long as you're not a pervert like Dante but just a simple outcast: she actually knew this all along because at various times in this film she supported such outcasts as prostitutes, the town virgin (Bronson) and spinster nurse (Patsy Kelly), handicapped children (she feels awkward around healthy children), and a nurse (Marie Devereux) who is foreign, unmarried, and pregnant. She is making a bold statement when she rejects the apologies of Grantville's populace and voluntarily goes back to being a traveling prostitute. Photographed by Stanley Cortez. Also with: Virginia Grey, Karen Conrad, Betty Robinson, Edy Williams.

NAKED PREY, THE (1966) C/94m. There's not much dialogue or plot in this brutal adventure movie, starring and directed by Cornel Wilde. He's taken prisoner by a tribe of African natives. They take away his weapons, clothes, and supplies and give him a chance to run for his life, figuring he has no chance. But Wilde's in great shape and has enough savvy and savage instincts to kill off those who chase him. Heading for a British settlement, he is joined by a native boy whose village was destroyed. An unusual, exciting, often frightening film, it's like a violent extension of Henry Fonda's flight from Indians in *Drums Along the Mohawk*. Good direction. Also with: Gert Van Den Berg, Ken Gampu.

NAKED SPUR, THE (1952) C/91m. In his third Anthony Mann western, James Stewart is a hard-bitten man who is determined to buy back his lost spread by using the bounty he'll get from bringing back killer Robert Ryan, an acquaintance for whom he harbors great hatred. Like most Mann westerners, his actions are determined by his past (he wants to return to how it once was); having lost everything dear to him, he suffers guilt and self-hatred—his need to take out his anger on another man, who is much like the immoral "beast" he has become, is obviously his way of attacking himself. By killing such a man he will earn himself the entry into hell he thinks he deserves. Stewart catches up with Ryan and his girlfriend, Janet Leigh (who doesn't realize how cold-blooded the manipulative Ryan is), in the Rockies. He takes Ryan and Leigh toward Abilene, with the help of his two new, not-to-be-trusted partners, aged miner Millard Mitchell and Ralph Meeker, who has just been drummed out of the army because of his weak moral character. As usual, Mann uses his landscape as more than a backdrop: as the terrain becomes rougher and the stream they follow becomes more turbulent, the tension among the characters increases and their cruelty becomes more evident. Stewart tries to maintain his tough edge, but his once-lost compassion surfaces when he's with Leigh; she, in turn, responds with love to the first man in her life who has treated her with kindness. This is as rugged as any of Mann's films and as beautifully shot (all outdoors); the gunplay is particularly exciting. But the script by Sam Rolfe and Harold Jack Bloom is weaker than those used in other Mann westerns. The dialogue is trite and the Stewart character is poorly developed, so that we can't really understand his quick attraction to Leigh or the exact nature of his neurosis. This is the one Stewart hero in a Mann film that could just as easily have been played by other actors. On the other hand, Ryan makes a great villain. Excellent photography by William Mellor.

NANOOK OF THE NORTH (1922) B&W/ 55m.

Probably the most famous of all documentaries, this classic was made by mining-explorer-turned-filmmaker Robert Flaherty on the barren and frozen eastern shore of Hudson Bay's Ungava Peninsula. It was financed by Revillon Frères, the Paris-based fur company which had a post in Port Harrison on northeast Hudson Bay. In addition to taking along two Akeley cameras, which had gyro movement in the tripod head, Flaherty carried with him the chemicals and materials necessary for developing, printing, and projecting the film. As he wrote, his intention in making a film about a family of Eskimos was to show audiences around the world why he admired the Eskimo people! "I had been dependent on these people, alone with them for months at a time, traveling with them and living with them. They had warmed my feet when they were cold, lit my cigarette when my hands were too numb; they had taken care of me on different expeditions over a ten year period. I couldn't have done anything without them." Visually the picture is still fascinating. Such shots as the spooky, icy waters, mist blowing over the snow-covered terrain, and Nanook (the father and head of his tribe) diving deep into the snow to pull a white fox from his trap are most striking. But the human drama seems a little lacking. Critics have always complained that Flaherty had his subjects create scenes specifically for the camera; some of these scenes (the meeting with the trader, the children playing, the family waking up in the igloo) come across as phony. You never really learn what these people are like, just what they do to survive. We would have more interest in their hunting-killing (fish, walrus, seal) if we believed Flaherty when he said they desperately needed food. As it is, we respond better to their building an igloo for the night because we realize they need shelter. (Only by reading film-history books do we learn that the igloo was twice the normal size and had only three sides in order to accommodate Flaherty's camera and his need for light.) Those who feel sympathy probably know that Nanook died of starvation two years after Flaherty completed filming.

NAPOLÉON/NAPOLÉON VU PAR ABEL GANCE (FRENCH-RUSSIAN/1927) B&W/220m— 235m—300m.

Kevin Brownlow's painstaking restoration of Abel Gance's titanic silent classic in 1980–81 was certainly one of the most noteworthy achievements in cinema in recent years. Most Americans who, thanks to sponsor-distributer Francis Ford Coppola, saw it in 1981, with full-orchestra accompaniment (Carmine Coppola composed a new score), in New York's Radio City Music Hall (where it had its debut) and other theaters throughout the country regarded it as one of the moviegoing highlights of their lives. Certainly no other silent films, not even those of D. W. Griffith, are as visually spectacular as Gance's work; it will surprise viewers that back in 1927 he was experimenting with split-screen photography, hand-held cameras, superimpositions, rapid-fire editing, color-tinting, and a mobile camera; he strapped cameras and cameramen to horses, he attached one camera to a guillotine. His greatest innovation was his development of Polyvision, a forerunner to CinemaScope and Cinerama. In the final Italian-campaign sequence, images are projected on *three* screens. The film is set between 1780, when Napoléon is a teenage boy (Vladimir Roudenko) at military college, and 1796, when as commander-in-chief of the French army in Italy, Napoléon (Albert Dieudonné) achieves his most important military triumph to date. There are about six major episodes, each a film unto itself. Beginning with the famous snowball war-games sequence at school, during which the young Bonaparte proves to be a brilliant leader and tactician, each sequence will stun you with its technical brilliance and directorial bravura, its beauty and poetry, its re-creation of a time gone by, and the aggressive energy displayed by all the people Gance crowds into his frame (only the overrated Dieudonné seems reserved and calm). Gance shows Napoléon to be a man of destiny who was always in the right place at the right time to help his troubled country: he is there when France needs a daring, fearless military leader to snatch victory from the jaws of defeat; when it needs someone to stand up to the leaders of the Reign of Terror who had betrayed the Revolution; when it needs someone to stop the moral decay of the people once they throw out the bourgeoisie. There are many wonderful scenes—Rouget de Lisle (Harry Krimer) and then Danton (Russian actor Alexandre Koubitzky) leading the people in a rousing, emotional singing of "*La Marseillaise*" (remember this is a *silent* film!); the decadent ball; etc. My only regrets are that Gance's direction of battle scenes is often confusing, so that they become dull even when looking spectacular; he is not a first-rate storyteller in that he gives the same emphasis to minor events as to events that changed history, and that he becomes quite absurd when he makes his hero, Napoléon, into the symbol of the Revolution, whose decision to conquer Europe and make it a "Universal Republic" meets with the approval of the ghosts of Danton, St. Juste (Gance), and Marat (Antonin Artaud). Gance released other versions of his film, using original footage: *Napoléon Bonaparte* (1935), in which he added stereophonic sound; and *Bonaparte and the Revolution* (1971), which hadn't any triptych sequences but included newly shot scenes with Dieudonné. Also with: Gina Manès (as Josephine), Edmond van Daële (as Robespierre), Annabella, Marguerite Gance (as Charlotte Corday), Jean d'Yd.

NASHVILLE (1975) C/159m. Crazy-quilt vision of America, directed by Robert Altman and scripted by Joan Tewkesbury, interweaves the storylines of 24 characters who are in Nashville one eventful weekend. Among the characters are superstar country singers, young folksingers, gospel singers, and those who are trying to break into the music business. All will perform somewhere or another, in studios, churches, auditoriums, clubs or on outdoor stages. In addition, we can hear their music emanating from radios and tape machines. Those who aren't performers are linked to them: husbands, wives, sons, reporters, fans, groupies, and a political adviser (Michael Murphy) who is trying to recruit performers for a political rally of his candidate, John Phillip Walker. (We never see Walker, but his van moves through Nashville throughout the film, and his populist-reactionary platform is blasted over the loudspeakers.) Excitement of film comes from Altman's innovative storytelling techniques, how he plays musical chairs with his characters' destinies, moving them in and out of each other's lives until they all gather for the tragic ending. The actors are well chosen and their characters make strong initial impressions. But few are developed sufficiently. Film is comical (until the shock conclusion), which is odd since none of the characters could be called *happy*. Indeed, almost all of these people are unhappy or pathetic, and it would be correct to say that Altman and Tewkesbury are condescending toward them and toward the music fans at Nashville. This is a cynical film, where recording stars make fortunes singing about God, family, country, and candy bars—and about themselves; where insincere stars dupe the public; where assassins can no longer distinguish between performers and politicians because they are both selling a bill of goods. Ironically, the one "honest," caring country singer pays for the "sins" of her fellow performers. The reason I can't ever fully appreciate this picture is that, with the exception of Henry Gibson's parody songs, none of what Altman and music director Richard Baskin try to pass off as country music (some was written by the stars themselves) *is* country music. Ronee Blakley as the Loretta Lynn–like Barbara Jean and Karen Black as the Tammy Wynette–like Connie White may sing with Southern twangs, but they give us dull folk songs, not country—it's not fair to pass off these two as the *best* country music has to offer. Music works best when we're watching Lily Tomlin and a black chorus perform gospel music and Keith Carradine sing what are supposed to be folk songs. Carradine wrote two excellent songs: "It Don't Worry Me" and the Oscar-winning "I'm Easy," which this bed-hopping singer performs in a club while sexual conquests Tomlin, Christina Raines, Shelley Duvall, and Geraldine Chaplin each think he's singing to them (a *great* scene). Paul Lohmann was cinematographer. Alan Rudolph was assistant director. Also with: David Arkin, Barbara Baxley, Ned Beatty, Timothy Brown, Robert Doqui, Allen Garfield, Scott Glenn, Jeff Goldblum, Barbara Harris, David Hayward, Allan Nichols, Dave Peel, Bert Remsen, Gwen Welles, Keenan Wynn, Merle Kilgore, Baskin, and, as themselves, Elliott Gould, Julie Christie, Vassar Clements.

NATIONAL LAMPOON'S ANIMAL HOUSE/ ANIMAL HOUSE (1978) C/109m. John Landis directed this influential—it still inspires films that can't compare to it—raucous, raunchy film that became the highest-grossing comedy of all time. It's set in 1962 at Faber College, whose founder's words are written on his monumental statue: "Knowledge is good." Wimp Thomas Hulce and blimp Stephen Furst get turned down by every fraternity at Faber before they're accepted into Delta House, the least disciplined, least image-conscious frat on campus. Tim Matheson is the smooth-talking, skirt-chasing president, Peter Riegert is second in charge—his girlfriend, Karen Allen, tells him he should settle down, but he can't resist participating in all the frat's wild parties and pranks—John Belushi and Bruce McGill are resident wild men. Dean John Vernon wants to close down Delta House and expel all the members—he even cites Furst's 0.2 grade point average as reason for dismissal. But the fraternity fights back. There is a lot of destruction. Uninhibited film is often hilarious; like his characters, director Landis exhibits inspired lunacy. The characters are so likable that we aren't turned off when Belushi peeps into sorority girls' windows while they undress (he gives *us* a great devilish smile); when Belushi, McGill, and Furst are responsible for the death of a horse in Vernon's office; when Belushi spits food all over obnoxious students; when Hulce sleeps with a 13-year-old; or when Matheson manipulates a girl to make love to him by pretending he is the grieving former boyfriend of her recently deceased roommate. Finale is too wild, and hackneyed. Before this there are numerous funny moments and scenes. Not for all tastes. Led to a TV series, *Delta House*. Harold Ramis, Douglas Kenney, and Chris Miller wrote the screenplay. Produced by Matty Simmons and Ivan Reitman. Also with: Mark Metcalf, Mary Louise Weller, Martha Smith, Verna Bloom, Donald Sutherland, Kevin Bacon, Sarah Holcombe, Cesare Danova.

NATIVE LAND (1942) B&W/85m. Legendary political film—the first American feature to be about the labor movement and the first to combine documentary footage with reenactments of historical incidents (from the thirties)—was the crowning achievement of Frontier Films, a collective of leftist writers, actors, and artists. It was directed by Leo Hurwitz and Paul Strand (who did the 35mm cinematography); scripted by David Wolff (Ben Maddow), who wrote Robeson's narration; scored by Marc Blitzstein; and acted by members of the Group Theatre. (Those involved would comprise a virtual "Who's Who" of blacklisted artists during the fifties.) Based on reports of the La Follette Senate Civil Liberties Committee of the late thirties, as well as Leo Huberman's book *The Labor Spy Racket*, the film builds a case that major U.S. corporations were involved in a large-scale conspiracy to undermine unionism through the systematic use of terrorism, labor spies, police, and blacklisting. We see episodes depicting little-reported stories: thugs beat up a kindly Michigan farmer who spoke at a Grange meeting; KKK men (and at least one woman) tar and feather two white liberals in Florida; the body of a union organizer is discovered in Cleveland; etc. The longest vignette shows how a union is infiltrated by one spy (Howard Da Silva) who's supposed to be discovered, and then a second spy who becomes a trusted union officer because he uncovers the first spy; when he turns over the union books, everyone mentioned is fired and blacklisted. Film is certainly not as radical as one would expect from the people who made it, but even today viewers react with emotion and gratitude because such a "progressive" American picture exists. Despite much flag-waving in film, it received little distribution in 1942 because those unions which contributed to financing decided not to support it because they figured that after Pearl Harbor a film claiming that our Bill of Rights was being threatened from within was too divisive for our country. A bit disappointing considering its reputation, but always interesting (especially since its politics—which come across as naïve—reflect those of the thirties radicals). Strand's photographic style is always fascinating; the Russian-influenced Michigan sequence is particularly striking. Also with: Fred Johnson, Housely Stevens.

NATURAL, THE (1984) C/134m.

Robert Redford returned to screen acting after a four-year vacation for this pet project, an adaptation of Bernard Malamud's superb baseball novel. Looking fit as an athlete, displaying a convincing left-handed swing, and sporting boyish good looks, Redford is Roy Hobbs, an innocent country boy who has the pitching talent to be another Walter Johnson. But on his train to Chicago and the big leagues, he meets a mysterious woman in black (Barbara Hershey) who seduces him into taking the wayward path. He rendezvous with her in her hotel room and—in an incident inspired by what really happened to a forties baseball player—she shoots him. Sixteen years later Redford turns up in the dugout of the last-place New York Knights. Now in his late thirties, and carrying a bat ("Wonderboy") carved out of a tree trunk, he offers himself as a slugging right-fielder. Manager Wilford Brimley has nothing to lose, so he gives Redford a chance. Hobbs turns out to be a tremendous home-run hitter who leads the team on a pennant drive. Whenever he needs a boost, his former hometown sweetheart (Glenn Close) is there in the stands, dressed in white, rising like an angel. And he succeeds—gloriously. But the larcenous owner, Robert Prosky, will lose much money if his team wins the pennant. So he arranges for Redford to be placed in the hands of the corruptive Kim Basinger—and, sure enough, he slumps terribly. And before the BIG game Prosky's man, Darren McGavin (uncredited), offers Redford a bribe to make sure the Knights lose. In the early scenes this Barry Levinson–directed film brilliantly captures myth aspects of baseball prior to WWII, but then Levinson and Redford turn picture into a schmaltzy fairytale. If you would have been happy if David O. Selznick decided to forget Margaret Mitchell and have Rhett stick it out with Scarlett, then you'll accept these guys' changing Malamud's pessimistic ending,

which expressed the book's cynical "everybody is corruptible" theme, for a happy completely antithetical ending calculated to make audiences cheer. Redford had early screen success playing men who sold out their convictions (i.e., *The Candidate*, *The Way We Were*) and it seemed Hobbs's character as Malamud wrote it was ready-made for him. But I guess everyone wants to be a hero, especially one who seems to be more than human. Camera work by Caleb Deschanel and atmosphere are impressive and it's always fun watching baseball scenes, but probably film's real distinction is that it shows Close as a symbol of purity even though she is an unwed mother. Also with: Robert Duvall (wasted), Richard Farnsworth, Joe Don Baker, ex-Major Leaguer Joe Charboneau.

NAUGHTY NINETIES, THE (1945) B&W/76m.

In their first period piece Abbott and Costello try to help out Captain Sam (Henry Travers) when his riverboat is taken over by crooks. Underrated A&C film isn't slickly made by director Jean Yarborough, but contains several of their most famous routines, including an excellent version of "Who's on First?" Funniest scene has Costello hanging over the side of the boat in order to spy on bad guys through their porthole. When the heavily lathered Joe Sawyer looks into the porthole, he thinks it's a mirror and thinks the heavily lathered Costello is his image—they each begin to shave off the lather, even stroking each other's faces, and Sawyer is understandably confused to discover that he looks so much like Costello. The "mirror" routine has been done by many comedians (i.e., the Marx Brothers in *Duck Soup*), but this is the only time in which the two characters in question look nothing like each other. Excellent A&C sampler. Also with: Alan Curtis, Rita Johnson, Lois Collier.

NAVIGATOR, THE (1924) B&W/62m.

Buster Keaton's biggest commercial hit is another in his line of silent comedy masterpieces. Buster is a pampered millionaire—the type of guy who has his chauffeur drive him to the house across the street. That's where millionaire's daughter Kathryn McGuire (of Keaton's *Sherlock Junior*) lives. He proposes—she rejects him. After a series of wild events, they wind up alone on her father's ship as it floats across the ocean. At first neither knows what to do to survive—Keaton tries boiling an egg in an enormous vat; McGuire uses four coffee beans in enough water for 100. But Keaton's latent tendencies for invention surface and he devises a pulley system that makes life on the ship very leisurely. And, of course, he and McGuire fall in love. Film has many intricate, hilarious gags. Highlights include Keaton chasing McGuire around the ship when he first discovers that she's on board also; Keaton in a diving suit (some scenes were filmed underwater)—at one point he blows it up and he becomes a makeshift raft; Keaton routing some cannibals. Not on par with *The General*, yet it hasn't a bad moment. Donald Crisp served as Keaton's co-director. Also with: Frederick Vroom, Noble Johnson.

NEIGHBORS (1981) C/94m. In his last film John Belushi is a dull, ineffectual, married suburbanite whose dreary existence comes to an end when Dan Aykroyd and Cathy Moriarty move next door. Never have so many bad things happened to one man—seemingly crazy, super-aggravating Aykroyd shoots at him, seductive Moriarty makes it with his wife (Kathryn Walker), and that's only the beginning. If you've had crummy and incorrigible neighbors, you'll be able to identify with Belushi's plight. Picture got harsh critical reaction and fans despised it, too. But I think this surreal comedy is imaginatively done, and perfectly displays lunacy of the two comics. I also feel affection for the three lead characters, who somehow form a mutual admiration society. Aykroyd may destroy Belushi's home life, but he doesn't mean him any harm and, in fact, provides him with first excitement he's had in years as well as a promising future out of suburbia. I like the way Belushi can never come up with absolute proof that Aykroyd is doing anything wrong on purpose. There was talk of the two switching roles, as Belushi seemed more appropriately cast as destructive person and Aykroyd as timid victim, but I'm glad they went against type because both actors are at their absolute best. Moriarty is also a standout. It's a shame she didn't get screen offers after this. Final picture is faithful to Thomas Berger's zany, satirical novel; I prefer the film's happier ending. Directed by John G. Avildsen. Also with: Tim Kazurinsky, Lauren-Marie Taylor.

NETWORK (1976) C/121m. Paddy Chayefsky, a major contributor to television's Golden Age, wrote this satirical attack on modern-day television, where integrity (personified by deposed veteran news director William Holden) has lost out to ambition, where ratings are more important than quality, where programming executives cater to the tastes of viewers who have no taste, where news programs have become part of the entertainment schedule. Over-the-hill UBS-TV newscaster Peter Finch learns he is to be fired because of low ratings. He tells his audience that he'll kill himself on the air during his final broadcast two weeks later. When subsequent newscasts, during which Finch speaks his mind and even curses, get increasingly higher ratings, driven Vice-President of Programming Faye Dunaway decides that Finch should be kept on the air and allowed to give extemporaneous editorials about the ills of the world. The revised news show (a "circus") moves from the news division into the entertainment division under Dunaway. It becomes the country's highest-rated television show, and the exploited Finch, who's on the edge of a breakdown, becomes a Messianic figure whose "I'm mad as hell, and I'm not going to take this anymore" becomes a miserable nation's battle cry. But then Finch starts attacking the network itself. Later, ratings plummet because he speaks of dying democracy and dehumanization. UBS executives decide to have him assassinated on the air. Picture is brilliantly acted, particularly by Dunaway (she deservedly won a Best Actress Oscar), whose soulless character has an animalistic thirst for power and victory in the ratings game. But I wish that at least one of the many dramatic two-person encounters (Holden and mistress Dunaway; Holden and wife Beatrice Straight; etc.) could have been played without someone yelling. The biggest problem is that it's impossible to adjust to having all these *real* characters in a story that becomes increasingly preposterous. At first the satire is funny, but by mid-film we begin to feel sorry for Chayefsky; he's not just angry but mean, and his venom is directed not only at television people but at all of us (who are sheep, who have lost the ability to love). Finch won Best Actor Oscar posthumously; Straight won a Supporting Actress Oscar. Chayefsky won an Oscar for Best Original Screenplay; and Sidney Lumet was nominated for Best Director. Also with: Robert Duvall, Ned Beatty, Wesley Addy, Marlene Warfield.

NEVER CRY WOLF (1983) C/105m. This most unusual film was based on a book by Canadian Farley Mowat, whose firsthand studies of wolves in the Yukon contradicted many myths about the animal, including those relating to wolves' territorial instincts, breeding habits, migration and hunting patterns, and their supposedly aggressive, even hostile, demeanor. An excellent actor but no romantic lead, Charles Martin Smith is an inspired choice to play Tyler, a scientist based on Mowat, who spends time alone in the frozen Yukon studying a pack of wolves. Carroll Ballard's film, which took two years to make, becomes not only a fascinating documentary about wolves, but also an incisive study of man in isolation; moreover, we are given the rare opportunity to witness scientific methodology in practice. While the film has a couple of slow spots, there is excitement—such as when Tyler falls through the ice and can't find his way out—and so much on the screen we have never seen before. Even considering that the scenery is so exquisite that it would look gorgeous in Super 8, the picture is as beautifully photographed (by Hiro Narita) as Ballard's *The Black Stallion*. Much of the footage of the wolves is remarkable—and eye-opening. It's odd that this is a Walt Disney production because it has a much more adult approach than earlier Disney films dealing with animals; for instance, Narita's camera shows us close-ups of cute mice . . . just before Tyler makes them his lunch. While Tyler and the wolves form a bond, they never become friends and, rest assured, he never domesticates one and makes it his pet. Also with: Brian Dennehy, Zachary Ittimagnaq, Samson Jorah.

NEVER GIVE A SUCKER AN EVEN BREAK (1941) B&W/71m. W. C. Fields's last starring role. This isn't top-grade Fields because he isn't on screen enough (there are musical numbers; other characters), he isn't bombastic or aggravating enough, and he isn't being constantly harassed by the nincompoops that usually populate his films. However, it's the film where the surrealistic nature of Fields's comedy is most evident. Fields plays himself as well as a character in an absurd film that he's trying to sell to Esoteric Studios' executive Franklin Pangborn. In the "film" he leaps from an airplane to retrieve his whiskey bottle and falls thousands of feet before landing safely on rich Margaret Dumont's mountaintop estate, where she lives with her pretty young daughter (to whom he teaches "Post Office"), a gorilla, and Great Danes with fangs. He proposes to Dumont so niece Gloria Jean will have a fancy upbringing. After Pangborn kicks him out of his office, Fields rushes a woman to the maternity hospital (wrongly believing she's pregnant), causing havoc on the city streets. Best moments have cowardly Fields sparring with a tough-talking waitress (Jody Gilbert) and entering an ice-cream parlor, where, before blowing the head off his ice-cream soda, he turns to us to reveal that censors wouldn't let him stage the scene in a saloon. Directed by Edward Cline. Also with: Leon Errol.

NEVER SAY NEVER AGAIN (1983) C/137m. It was great to see Sean Connery return as James Bond after a dozen years, during which time he insisted he'd *never* play the part again. He initiated this project himself—it was not part of the ongoing Roger Moore series being produced by Albert Broccoli—and, oddly, it is not new material, but a remake of Connery's fourth Bond film, *Thunderball*. Bond's a bit older, but every woman he sees is attracted to him and he still can outwit the vilest of villains, in this case Blofeld (Max von Sydow) and Largo (Austrian actor Klaus Maria Brandauer), one of the most complex (he's neurotic, vulnerable) of Bond's foes: their pain game "Domination" is a highlight. The story involves the theft of nuclear missiles, but you'll forget all about that watching Bond involved in minute-by-minute dangers and trysts with beautiful, skimpily-dressed actresses. A very athletic Barbara Carrera (giving her best performance) as the cheerful assassin Fatima Blush and blonde Kim Basinger as Domino, Largo's innocent girlfriend, make lasting impressions. Film is exotic, well acted, and stylishly directed by Irvin Kershner. It would be one of the best Bond films if the finale weren't disappointing. When will filmmakers realize that underwater fight scenes don't work because viewers usually can't tell the hero and villain apart and they know doubles are being used? Ian Fleming's novel was adapted by Lorenzo Semple, Jr., who added much humor. Also with: Edward Fox, Bernie Casey.

NEVERENDING STORY, THE (WEST GERMAN/ 1984) C/94m. Michael Ende protested loudly about what Wolfgang Petersen (*Das Boot*) did to his children's book. Film is flawed and occasionally dull and confusing, but I think it's one of the most imaginative, visually spectacular children's films of all time. A young boy (Barret Oliver) is depressed because of the death of his mother and because he's being bullied by classmates. He withdraws from reality into a children's book—like Ende's novel, the film tells kids about the joys of reading. He reads of a magical land called Fantasia ("the world of human fantasy"), which is being eaten away by The Nothing because people no longer have hopes and dreams. The only person who can save Fantasia from complete destruction is a boy warrior (Noah Hathaway). He undertakes a long and perilous journey, trying to reach the young empress (Tami Stronach). Oliver is astonished and frightened when he becomes part of the story. I don't see how kids won't love this picture and thrill to some of the adventures, but young kids may be frightened by some scenes of destruction and the most horrifying of the many ingenious characters, a deadly werewolf who is on Hathaway's trail. Much friendlier is Hathaway's friend, a cuddly flying dragon. Best seen on a large screen, this is like no children's film you've ever seen. Music by Giorgio Moroder. Also with: Gerald McRaney, Moses Gunn, Patricia Hayes, Sydney Bromley.

NEW YORK, NEW YORK (1977) C/137m– 153m–161m. Sax player Robert De Niro and singer Liza Minnelli meet in New York on V-J Day, become music partners and then members of the same touring band. They get married, peak as a couple when she's the lead singer of his touring band, start to crumble when she gets pregnant and goes to New York, and in the *A Star Is Born* segment break apart when her solo career takes off and his plunges into obscurity. Martin Scorsese's romance—with musical numbers—was unfairly panned when released and praised when re-released in 1976 in its uncut version. If you can't tolerate De Niro's character because he's abrasive, immature, and incorrigible and you feel that his treatment of the sweet, "perfect" Minnelli is too inconsiderate and selfish for any woman to bear, then you'll probably hate this picture. But don't forget that Minnelli does her part to break them up: leaving him behind to run off with a band, leaving his band when pregnant although that will cause its ruination, accepting a record contract although not bothering to tell him or wonder how it will affect him when he's so down on his luck, and, finally, not coming back to him when he's doing well also. He does bad things—she is the villain. Acting by the two leads is wonderful—their patter has the rhythm of a comic duo and serves to complement their rhythmic musical numbers. Notice that De Niro can get along with (though not necessarily be friends with) characters who have rhythm in their speech—others are squares whom he mocks mercilessly. Also notice that the tear-jerking scenes result from De Niro revealing his sensitivity. Screenplay by Earl Mac Rauch and Mardik Martin is intentionally skimpy—there is essentially no realistic conversation (at one point Minnelli seriously asks uneducated De Niro if he knows the meaning of the theory of relativity). The characters (who have no families, no pre-war pasts) aren't *real* people and the world they travel in is intentionally stylized. The fake trains, the artificial snow, the weirdly designed and lit clubs, and the studio streets make me believe Scorsese was creating a memory piece. Perhaps Minnelli, who doesn't realize *her* faults, is, in 1977, looking back on a time gone by. Uncut version includes the lengthy "Happy Endings" production number with Minnelli and Larry Kert. It's elaborate but not very interesting. And since it interrupts the film at a pivotal point, I'd cut it again. Minnelli's dynamic title number is a better type of show-stopper.

Also with: Lionel Stander, Barry Primus, Georgie Auld, Mary Kay Place, Dick Miller, George Memmoli, Diahnne Abbott.

NEXT STOP, GREENWICH VILLAGE (1976) C/ 109m.

Writer-director Paul Mazursky takes us back to 1953 for this seriocomic autobiographical piece about 22-year-old Larry Lipinsky (stringbean Lenny Baker), who leaves Brooklyn to make it as an actor in Greenwich Village. There he gets a job in a juice bar, falls in with a group of young eccentrics, has frustrations as an actor—his *comic*'s mind keeps him from playing *serious* scenes—and has troubles with his girlfriend (Ellen Greene). Meanwhile he unsuccessfully tries to break free from his grasping, often hysterical Jewish mother (Shelley Winters), whose goals in life seem to be to stock her son's refrigerator and make him feel guilty. Not everything works—for one thing, talented Baker is not always appealing—but Mazursky beautifully creates a fifties ambience, populates his film with *real* characters, effectively blends humor and tragic elements; he also has included several stunning scenes. My favorite moment has Winters, who has been hysterical throughout, sitting in her son's apartment and, like a sweet schoolgirl with a crush on a singer, tearfully listening to an opera record—at this point we can perceive the beauty and depth of emotion in this woman. Film would work double-billed with Carl Reiner's 1967 memory piece *Enter Laughing*, in which Winters played Jewish mother to another aspiring actor. Also with: Christopher Walken, Dori Brenner, Lois Smith, Jeff Goldblum (very funny as an aspiring actor), Mike Kellin, Antonio Fargas, Lou Jacobi, John Ford Noonan.

NIAGARA (1953) C/89m.

Taut melodrama by Henry Hathaway, best known for Marilyn Monroe's fine performance as a *wicked* woman. On her honeymoon in Niagara Falls, she schemes with her lover (Richard Allan) to murder her crazed war-vet husband, Joseph Cotten, only to have Cotten kill the lover and come after her. At first she's cold-blooded—she smiles *for the camera* when she mistakenly believes Cotten is dead—but later we feel sorry for her as she tries to escape Cotten. Throughout she's meant to be sexy, whether nude and tossing and turning under her sheets, or in a slip and wiggling across her room, or decked out in bright red outfits. Picture has several exciting scenes, all of which benefit from Hathaway's strong use of color, sharp camera angles, and location shooting—particularly around the Falls. Jean Peters is the one person who knows Cotten's villainy; of course, husband Casey Adams doesn't believe her. Scripted by Charles Brackett, Walter Reisch, and Richard Breen. Also with: Denis O'Dea, Don Wilson (yes, *that* Don Wilson).

NIGHT AT THE OPERA, A (1935) B&W/92m.

Better than *Charlie Chan at the Opera*. The Marx Brothers' most famous and popular film isn't on the level of *Duck Soup* (few comedies are) but is still a comic masterpiece. Ironically, it was carefully designed to be different from *Duck Soup*, the Marxes' first financial failure. While the individual comedy scenes are as zany as anything in the Marx Brothers' work, the overall picture is more structured: the storyline makes more sense, the brothers take time from their lunacy to function as matchmakers for young lovers Kitty Carlisle and Allan Jones, Harpo and Chico slow things down with harp and piano solos, the injection of opera automatically makes this the classiest Marx Brothers film. But fear not: Groucho, Chico, and Harpo romp through the opera milieu with the same tactlessness they exhibited in Freedonia in *Duck Soup*. Groucho, as Otis B. Driftwood, convinces Margaret Dumont to invest $200,000 in the New York Opera so she can enter society. But opera impressario Sig Rumann moves in on Dumont, and uses much of the money to hire Walter Woolf King to play the male lead opposite Carlisle. Groucho tries to figure out how to get Dumont back (and make some big money) and get unknown Jones into King's role. Film has many hilarious sequences, including: the opening in which Groucho explains to Dumont that he'd kept her waiting two hours in a restaurant because he was dining at the next table with a woman who reminded him of her; Groucho and Chico agree on a contract by ripping it to shreds; ship stowaways Chico, Harpo, and Jones (in the Zeppo role) disguise themselves as bearded aviator heroes and are expected to make public speeches; everyone imaginable crowds into Groucho's tiny stateroom (the most famous scene) after he tries to order dinner along with two (Harpo honks three) hard-boiled eggs; the stowaways and Groucho fool a detective by shifting some furniture around each time his back is turned; the opera finale. One reason the film succeeds is that the opera sung by Carlisle and Jones in this film is actually enjoyable: "Alone" became a hit. Directed by Sam Wood. Produced by Irving Thalberg. Written by George S. Kaufman, Morrie Ryskind, and Al Boasberg.

NIGHT OF THE COMET (1984) C/94m.

Former soap actresses Catherine Mary Stewart and baby-dollish Kelli Maroney break loose as spunky, funny sisters who are among the few survivors after a deadly comet passes over the earth. They would make a fabulous, permanent comic duo. Their fantasy-fulfilling romp through an LA department store that hasn't any security guards or salesgirls to look over their shoulders is a joy to watch. (A non-Cyndi Lauper version of "Girls Just Want to Have Fun" appropriately plays in the background as the girls energetically zip from floor to floor, trying on the fanciest clothes they can find.) The girls are joined by Robert Beltran, who helps them do battle with vicious ghouls and evil government officials who need their uncontaminated blood in order to survive. Director Thom Eberhardt adeptly mixes comedy and scares; film also benefits from an extremely witty, offbeat script, some nifty camera work, and an excellent cast—Stewart, in particular, sparkles. An unexpected pleasure that's headed, I hope, for cult status. Also with: Mary Woronov, Geoffrey Lewis, Sharon Farrell, Michael Brown.

NIGHT OF THE DEMON/CURSE OF THE DEMON (BRITISH/1957) B&W/82m—95m.
Dr. John Holden (Dana Andrews) arrives in London to attend a parapsychology conference and to help a professor expose Dr. Julian Karswell's (Niall MacGinnis) devil cult. But he learns that the professor is dead. Although the body was ripped apart, Holden refuses to believe witchcraft was responsible. The professor's pretty niece (Peggy Cummins) warns him Karswell is dangerous, but Holden is determined to expose him. However, he soon realizes that Karswell has magical powers and that he, Holden, may soon become victim of a demon Karswell has summoned. This is the best horror movie of the science-fiction-dominated fifties, the most intriguing picture ever made about witchcraft, and the most intelligent, visually impressive entry to the genre since its director, Jacques Tourneur, Mark Robson, and Robert Wise made films for Val Lewton at RKO in the forties. Although producer Hal Chester insensitively rewrote Charles Bennett's script, it somehow retained the grace and literate quality as well as the sinister feel and elements of mystery and *suspense* (as opposed to shocks) that distinguished Bennett's scripts for Alfred Hitchcock. Like his Hitchcock films, it has a British setting, a somewhat stuffy (educated) hero, an intellectual, diabolical villain (MacGinnis is superb), and a daffy mother (Athene Seyler); the hero ventures into a den of strangers and feels paranoia, the suddenly nervous hero must solve a mystery and track down a villain before he himself is killed, the hero and heroine stop squabbling and join forces, a train becomes a setting for intrigue. The material is perfectly suited for Tourneur. At a time when Hammer was initiating its series of horror films, updating classics by adding strong violence, gore, and sex, Tourneur returned to his forties roots, preferring to frighten viewers through such fundamental fears as darkness, sudden sounds, and wild animals. No other horror director has ever been able to create an atmosphere so beautiful, yet so ominous. Everyday characters venture into the Tourneur-Lewton shadowy world, where the battle between light and darkness, good and evil, science and magic, fate and free will is continuous, and where characters are controlled less by reason than by their subconscious. Film contains several chilling scenes, including the professor's death, a storm Karswell conjures up, Holden walking through the woods and sneaking into Karswell's house, a bizarre seance. There has been controversy about the studio-imposed inclusion of shots of a great demon, instead of leaving it to our imagination, as Lewton did with his supernatural elements. But if Lewton had had such a spectacular monster, I think he'd have shown it. It's more terrifying than anything we could imagine. Also with: Maurice Denham, Reginald Beckwith.

NIGHT OF THE FOLLOWING DAY, THE (1969) C/93m.
Minor cult film has blond Marlon Brando, his alcoholic and neurotic girlfriend, Rita Moreno (also a blonde), her brother, Jess Hahn, and brutal thug Richard Boone kidnapping heiress Pamela Franklin in France. As they hold Franklin in a seaside house and wait for her father to bring the ransom, Brando worries that the plan is doomed to fail. He thinks that Moreno is cracking up and that Boone is a psycho who wants to kill his accomplices and Franklin and run off with all the ransom money. After a couple of sloppy scenes, you'll worry that the entire film is going to be a mess, but you are swiftly drawn into the cleverly plotted story and become intrigued with the offbeat characters. Even considering several wretchedly written, static, intrusive scenes in which an inspector trades clichés with Franklin's brother (who wears the ugliest, shiniest blue suit) at Paris police headquarters, director–co-writer Hubert Cornfield does quite well on a slim budget. He uses a series of two-character scenes to build tension, allows the pent-up violence to explode in a burst of deadly gunfire in and outside a café/pub, and caps it off with an exciting scene in which Boone attempts to kill his accomplices and Brando goes after him on the beach. Viewers will have mixed reactions to the ending, a horror-movie cliché. Also with: Gerard Buhr, as a snoopy cop.

NIGHT OF THE GHOULS/REVENGE OF THE DEAD (1960) B&W/69m.
Edward D. Wood's follow-up to *Plan 9 from Outer Space* features god-awful acting, direction, music, dialogue, costumes, sets, props, lighting, pacing, and camera work. But that won't be enough to satisfy hardcore Wood fanatics, who have the right to expect much worse. A detective in a tux ("Duke" Moore) investigates a ghost-sighting and uncovers the diabolical scheme of a phony clairvoyant (Kenne Duncan) to bilk some rich folk by faking resurrections of their dead loved ones. Wood's friend, 400-pound Swedish ex-wrestler Tor Johnson, moans and groans as he reprises his "Lobo" role from Wood's *Bride of the Monster*, a 1955 dud. He looks like he's wearing his pajama bottoms and the make-up man made an omelete on his face. Another Wood regular, forecaster Criswell, the film's narrator, tries to stir up our curiosity by asking, "How many of you know the horror, the terror, I will now reveal to you?" What can you expect from a guy who spends the film in a coffin? There are typically ludicrous Wood touches: a detective gives another interminable instructions about a solo investigation, only to decide to accompany him on the mission; as the detective sneaks through a dark house (the film's prime set), both Criswell and our hero, through voiceovers, discuss in great detail the railing his hand happens to touch (it is completely irrelevant to the story). But alas, the picture hasn't the inspired madness of Wood's classics. Furthermore, Jennie Stevens as the Black Ghost can't hold a candle to *Plan 9*'s Vampira. And the clairvoyant role is ready-made for Bela Lugosi—never mind that Lugosi was dead already; Wood circumvented that happenstance when he made *Plan 9*. Also with: Paul Marco, John Carpenter, Valda Hansen.

NIGHT OF THE HUNTER, THE (1955) B&W/93m.
Cult film was Charles Laughton's only directorial effort. Adapted by James Agee (and Laughton) from Davis Grubb's novel, and strikingly photographed by Stanley Cor-

tez, it is a fascinating, truly unique work, part gothic horror film, part religious parable, part fairytale. Beware of wolves in sheep's clothing, or, more precisely, a false prophet in a preacher's garb. Robert Mitchum is absolutely terrifying as a phony preacher who is after some money that his now-dead former cellmate (Peter Graves) told him about. All the adults are mesmerized by this "religious" man, and he has no trouble swaying Graves's gullible widow (Shelley Winters) into marrying him. He kills Winters, but her young son (Billy Chapin)—the only person who doesn't trust Mitchum—grabs the moneybag and his little sister (Sally June Bruce) and they flee, with Mitchum following on horseback, intent on killing the children for the money. They are like Hansel and Gretel, traveling through the woods, heading downstream—only they find a *sweet* old lady (Lillian Gish), a God-loving woman who takes in orphan children. When Mitchum comes after the two children, she recognizes him for the hypocrite he is. She is determined to protect the kids, even against this intimidating Devil figure. Strong-willed Gish and strong-bodied Mitchum are great opponents—I love the scene in which he sings the religious hymn "Leaning on the Everlasting Arms" (as he had done earlier) while standing in the darkness and planning to strike, and she joins in, singing the correct words (which include a reference to Jesus). Laughton's audacious visual style—he borrowed from D.W. Griffith (Gish's most famous director) and German Expressionists—is at times too arty, but there are moments of amazing beauty. Most impressive is his haunting multi-plane shot when the canoe carrying the runaway children floats downstream. Film's most memorable scene has Mitchum hand-wrestling with himself to demonstrate the fight between "LOVE" (tatooed on the fingers of his right hand) and "HATE" (on the left). Also with: Evelyn Varden, Don Beddoe, James Gleason, Gloria Castillo.

NIGHT OF THE LIVING DEAD (1968) B&W/90m.

George Romero's cult classic—a low-budget independent picture that was saved from obscurity and made a fortune due to word of mouth and critics' raves—no longer scares the daylights out of viewers because the films it spawned have been much more graphic; but you'll still be impressed by Romero's style, wit, and themes. A group of people barricade themselves inside a farmhouse for protection against ghouls who somehow have risen from their graves and are terrorizing the countryside. Pessimistic and unsentimental, the film works on basic fears: monsters that won't go away, darkness, claustrophobia. "Aliens" attack us on American soil; protectors, even blood relations, turn on their loved ones when infected by a ghoul's bite. It is the visualization of our worst nightmare and we wish someone could answer the dazed heroine's (Judith O'Dea) oft-asked question, "What's happening?" Film has much in common with *Invisible Invaders, Carnival of Souls*, and, the most obvious influences, *Psycho* and *The Birds*. Romero's film and *The Birds* are exceptional in that the people congregate in the house for one reason only: fear. They are

not interested in planning battle strategy, just surviving. Film includes many nice horror touches and a couple of jump-out-of-your-seat moments featuring ghouls unexpectedly shooting their hands through windows and trying to grab someone. When seen in full view, the zombies look silly, wearing frumpy clothes and walking around as if they'd downed a fifth of bourbon. (You wouldn't have wanted to associate with these people when *they were alive*.) The scenes in which they gobble down human innards (donated by a butcher investor) would be ghastlier if we just heard their slurping. It's obvious that Romero wanted them to contribute to the picture's absurd, intentionally campy humor. Thematically the attacks on the house serve to complement the verbal battles taking place in the house, particularly between our hero (John A. Russo's script never mentions that Duane Jones is black) and a foolish bully (Karl Hardman). Although no one has ever mentioned this, Hardman's plan for survival (going to the basement) turns out to be superior to the implemented plan of Jones (stay upstairs). Sequels: *Dawn of the Dead* and *Day of the Dead*. Amateur cast includes: Keith Wayne, Judith Ridley, Marilyn Eastman, Kyra Schon.

NIGHT OF THE SHOOTING STARS, THE/NOTTE DI SAN LORENZO, LA (ITALIAN/1983) C/107m.

There have been countless war films—this is unlike any other. Paolo and Vittorio Taviani's masterpiece begins in the Tuscan village of San Martino during the summer of 1944. The Americans are approaching, so the Nazis plan to evacuate. They tell all the villagers to gather in the cathedral where they'll be safe, while their houses are blown up. About 30 villagers, led by aged peasant Omero Antonutti (of the Tavianis' *Padre Padrone*), decide not to trust the Nazis and sneak away, wishing luck to those in the cathedral, crying about their dogs they left behind to die, whose barking they hear as they march away. In the countryside with almost no provisions, their pasts (even their cathedral) destroyed by bombs, they search for the Americans. Along the way they meet up with friendly countrymen and skirmish with fascist Italian soldiers, including a sadistic father and his monstrous young son. There are many people in this group, but you can get to know quite a few intimately. At first, deaths of major characters come as a surprise, but then it's clear that no one is safe. This is a beautiful, tender film which has a magical feel to it, even during an amazingly authentic close-range battle scene in a wheatfield, yet the brutality is absolutely horrific. The gorgeous photography is by Franco di Giacomo, who is as effective filming the lovely countryside as the remarkable, beautiful faces of the cast. The Tavianis have a great eye for detail, and understand that simple images can have great power. Their actors' expressions tell everything—so many individual shots convey so much that we share the emotional responses of these unfortunate people. The heightened realism of the film is proper when one realizes that it is a remembrance piece told by a woman who was only six in 1944, and was not a firsthand witness to all that happens in her account. At the time of her exodus she was less frightened than fascinated, but in telling the story to her own baby daughter she recalls its nightmarish aspects and, in a haunting final shot, whispers to the girl her childhood rhyme of protection, as if she fears history could repeat itself. (In actuality, the remembrances were those of the Tavianis and others.) An unforgettable movie experience, full of splendid scenes and characters. Also with: Margarita Lozano, Claudio Bigagli, Massimo Bonetti, Norma Martel.

NIGHT TIDE (1961) B&W/84m.

Peculiar low-budget, low-key horror-fantasy was the first commercial feature of former experimental filmmaker Curtis Harrington. Dennis Hopper is a shy, soft-spoken sailor who becomes fascinated with a lovely but strange young woman (Linda Lawson) who works as a "mermaid" in a novelty act at a pier amusement park. As they fall in love, he comes to realize that she truly believes herself to be descended from mermaids. She fears that if they make love he will be in danger; two of her former lovers drowned. The plot owes much inspiration to Val Lewton's *Cat People* (when a critic, Harrington wrote glowingly about Lewton); stylistically, it is obviously influenced by Cocteau—in approach, the mood piece is a mix of the surreal (perhaps this is Hopper's dream) and *avant-garde*. It's always interesting and the ending is satisfying, but it could use a few jolts that would at least temporarily turn Hopper's dream into a nightmare. The score is by David Raksin. Also with: Luana Anders, Gavin Muir, Marjorie Eaton, Tom Dillon, H. E. West.

NIGHTMARE ALLEY (1947) B&W/111m.

No picture of the forties projected a more corrosive atmosphere than director Edmund Goulding and scriptwriter Jules Furthman's striking adaptation of William Lindsay Gresham's grim, nasty novel. It's about a self-serving carnival barker (Tyrone Power) who becomes a famous mind-reader and then a swindling fake mystic, and ends up as a geek. While it sweetens the novel and opts for a "Hollywood ending," the film is more daring than critics of the day contended: what other picture of the time, made by a major studio (20th) as an "A" picture to star its top romantic lead (Tyrone Power), had geeks, dipsomaniacs, premarital sex in which the woman doesn't become pregnant, and discussion of God? There wouldn't be another such sleazy "A" picture in 20 years. The miserable world we see mirrors the country's postwar malaise. The sorry people who inhabit it are deeply depressed, lonely, devoid of spirit, alcoholic, so desperate for entertainment that they'll pay to see carnival freaks and mind-readers; they are has-beens and never-will-bes, poor with no hope of getting money or with no good use for their money, jealous and suspicious of their neighbors, and convinced that they've gotten rotten deals in life. They're all vulnerable to any smooth-talking Pied Piper like Power who offers them salvation. It's a sad world, where anyone (even Power) will invariably be taken advantage of and deprived of whatever is meaningful to them, be it money, pride, or love. In Furthman's script the rise-and-fall premise of the same year's boxing film *Body and Soul* and thirties gangster movies is mixed with the still-controversial alcoholism premise of *The Lost Weekend*. Furthman also borrows from his own script for *Blonde Venus*. It's fascinating watching Power, who had developed a screen image as the justice-seeking champion of the people, play someone who cons people with his Cheshire grin, takes their money, and makes fools of them. Predates Andy Griffith's folksy hoodwinker in *A Face in the Crowd*—only Power has an angelic wife (Coleen Grey) to give him redemption. It's too bad this picture didn't do well, because Power might have been more daring with his later character choices. Lee Garmes's *noir* photography turned what is essentially a strong drama into a frightening horror film. Produced by George Jessel. Also with: Joan Blondell, Helen Walker, Taylor Holmes, Mike Mazurki, Ian Keith, Julian Dean, James Flavin, Roy Roberts.

NIGHTMARE ON ELM STREET, A (1985) C/91m.

Wes Craven chiller about several teenagers in small town who suffer similar nightmares in which they're attacked by sadistic man (named "Freddie") with a charred body and blades for fingers. When her friends die mysteriously and brutally while asleep, our young heroine (Heather Longerkamp) tries to stay awake lest she be next. Her investigations lead her to believe nightmare figure is former child molester whom a group of parents burned to death several years before: now he's out to claim children he didn't kill back then. Premise of film is unusual and interesting, but execution is disappointing. "Freddie" (Robert Englund) is made up and dressed too foolishly to be taken seriously—he looks like a poor man's Jason (from Sean Cunningham's *Friday the 13th* series). Too many of the nightmares are similar in content, featuring the female dreamer walking outside in her nightclothes and being chased soon after. While the splatter murders are well done, you can't really respect a film whose highlights feature blood spurting onto walls and ceilings. There are occasional shocks, but little suspense. The ending is trite and infuriating in that it defies the film's logic. Worst of all is that all the teenagers and adults are unappealing. John Saxon is wasted as Longerkamp's do-nothing father, a policeman, and Ronee Blakley is unbearable as her soused mom. David Chaskin wrote the successful sequel. Also with: Amanda Wyss, Nick Carri, Johnny Depp.

NIGHTS OF CABIRIA (ITALIAN/1957) C/110m.

An often sad but magical film by Federico Fellini. Giulietta Masina is an aging, sweet streetwalker in Rome. Tired of hanging around with sleazy street types and being used by disrespectful men, she dreams of a better life. But, as we see in a series of episodes, she keeps getting knocked to the ground (or thrown into a stream, pushed into a closet, almost tossed off a cliff). Still she doesn't wise up and remains completely trusting of men—invariably she is hurt. She is not a Cinderella figure who is going to be rescued from her misery by a famous movie actor (Amedeo

Nazzari) or get married to a young man (François Perier) who knows of her past. Her life will not change. But Fellini is compassionate and gives her a moment of festivity and happiness. She deserves it because of her indomitable spirit—she will not give up. This is Masina's best performance. Bob Fosse would direct the Broadway musical version, *Sweet Charity*, and excellent Shirley MacLaine movie-musical.

9½ WEEKS (1986) C/113m.
How long is half a week? It's at that point in the 10th week of her kinky relationship with Mickey Rourke that Kim Basinger says "Stop!" Why she started dating him in the first place is unclear: with his dimpled grin, soft voice, and crazed eyes, Rourke seems as trustworthy as that Times Square porno filmmaker who picks up Irene Cara in *Fame*. He's like a sly pimp seducing a naïve young girl with flowers and presents before having her turn tricks for him on the street. But Basinger, who seems too smart, too independent, and too under control to have anything to do with Rourke, finds herself falling deeply in love with him and increasingly allowing him to dominate her life—he dresses her, feeds her, bathes her, and orchestrates their perverse sexual activities. At times she is repelled, but more often she is aroused—by his imagination and attention and perhaps her own (depending how you look at it) debasement *or* sexual liberation. No matter that the more bizarre scenes in this film were cut so that it could avoid an X rating because what's here adequately conveys the nature of S&M relationships: it's about how one sick person takes and the other person foolishly relinquishes *control* (it is not about *sex*, although sex is a means through which the control of one person over another can be demonstrated). When Basinger realizes that Rourke has betrayed her trust by making what she has become to him seem ugly, she walks out. Director Adrian Lyne chose to shoot his sordid subject like a lush romance, with music that could have been composed by Michel Legrand and visuals that seem straight out of a foreign (there is female nudity) television commercial for some shampoo (Lyne began by making commercials). But what he thinks is erotic is usually dull or silly (we feel less sorry for Basinger's character than for Basinger herself). At the end, when we should applaud Basinger's decision to walk out, we instead think that she and Rourke could work things out with only slight adjustments to their relationship. Let's hope there is no sequel. From a more shocking autobiographical novel by the pseudonymous Elizabeth McNeil.

1900/NOVECENTO (ITALIAN-FRENCH-GERMAN/1976) C/243m–320m.
Set between 1901 and 1945, political epic by Bernardo Bertolucci about the relationship between the grandson of peasant leader Sterling Hayden and the grandson of Hayden's landowner boss, Burt Lancaster, who are both born on the day Verdi dies (Verdi music is played throughout). They are bosom buddies as children, but when they grow into adulthood (Gérard Depardieu is the peasant, Robert De Niro the bourgeois) the forces of history and class conflict put a strain on their relationship. Through the politically liberal but weak De Niro and the Marxist activist Depardieu, Bertolucci chronicles the natural dialectic clash between people who work the land and those who own it, between fascism—its rise, personified by De Niro's perverse, sadistic foreman (Donald Sutherland), is at the center of the film—and socialism. Like Bertolucci's other films, it explores how people—especially the bourgeoisie—respond to political tides. Here bourgeois De Niro looks the other way while Sutherland's power over the peasants becomes frightful. De Niro and those like him are responsible for allowing the growth of fascism. Picture has immense visual power, but the storyline (I have seen only the truncated American version) is at times hard to follow—at least, it's difficult to pinpoint the thematic implications of certain scenes. De Niro doesn't seem right for his role; Dominique Sanda is too good for her thankless part, De Niro's alcoholic wife. Sutherland stands out, playing one of the screen's vilest villains, but his scenes are often *too* unpleasant, whether he's the villain or the victim. Photography by Vittorio Storaro. Music by Ennio Morricone. Also with: Romolo Valli, Stefania Sandrelli, Alida Valli, Paolo Pavesi (De Niro as a child), Roberto Maccanti (Depardieu as a child).

1984 (BRITISH/1984) C/123m.
This was attacked by many critics for its slow pacing and uncompromisingly bleak vision. But I think it's a tremendously underrated, visually stunning, and properly depressing adaptation of George Orwell's classic about a totalitarian society of the future that is characterized by government propaganda, mind-control, torture, feverish patriotic rallies by the duped masses, and the individual's fear that Big Brother is watching him/her at all times. Director Michael Radford made the interesting choice to film the future as if conceived in 1949, the year the book was published. So there is none of the technological gadgetry that Orwell might have included if he had written the book today. What's most impressive is that it makes viewers, who can concentrate on the human tragedy Orwell wrote about rather than special effects, understand how such a terrifying world can evolve from our own, and how a government can systematically control an entire population. Unlike in the 1956 film, with Edmond O'Brien and Jan Sterling, the relationship between disillusioned government worker Winston Smith (John Hurt) and co-worker Julia (Susanna Hamilton) is distinguished by their need for *physical contact* and *sexual release*, rather than *love*; significantly, where the earlier film was about whether love could endure—a trite theme—Radford is faithful to Orwell in that he deals with whether the mind, free will (including the need to *act* on sexual impulses), and, specifically, one's political consciousness will endure. The answer is "No": Orwell's tale is cautionary in that it warns us never to allow such a totalitarian state to develop, because at that point there would be no chance for the individual to buck the system. Sets look like bombed-out post-WWII England, rather than Russia, which many scholars and high-school English teachers insist was Orwell's model for Oceania. The

recent discovery of Orwell's BBC wartime radio material lends credence to the notion that his prophecy was most influenced by *British* wartime rationing as well as BBC censorship and propaganda—for instance, the BBC's radio code was the basis for Orwell's "Newspeak." Strong performances by Hurt, Hamilton, and in his last role, Richard Burton, as the emotionless intellectual minister who, in a brutally realistic scene, tortures and brainwashes Winston Smith. Music by Eurythmics was added without Radford's blessing. Also with: Cyril Cusack, Gregor Fisher.

1941 (1979) C/118m–144m. A lot of panicky and crazy soldiers and civilians race around LA in 1941 thinking that the Japanese are launching a full-scale invasion. Actually, there is a Japanese sub offshore, but it only torpedoes a Ferris wheel and heads home. Pointless mayhem was directed by Steven Spielberg, although it's the type of comedy (i.e., *Casino Royale*) that looks like it was directed by anyone who came along. At the outset the film has some period flavor, introduces some promising characters, but it becomes increasingly stupid; it is alternately smutty, racist, cruel (unless you think watching someone's house slide off a cliff is funny) —it is always wasteful of its large budget. As screaming, explosions, fights, car and plane crashes, and destruction in general seem to be the order of the day, one can understand why in the best scene officer Robert Stack would stay away from the chaos in the streets and tearfully watch *Dumbo*. Scripted by Robert Zemeckis and Bob Gale, who conceived the story with John Milius. Photographed by William A. Fraker; John Williams composed the score. All-star cast includes: Dan Aykroyd, John Belushi (as a mad pilot), Ned Beatty, Treat Williams, Nancy Allen, Tim Matheson, Toshiro Mifune, Christopher Lee, Bobby Di Cicco, Dianne Kay, Wendie Jo Sperber, Eddie Deezen, John Candy, Lorraine Gary, Slim Pickens, Warren Oates, Murray Hamilton, Elisha Cook, Jr., Perry Lang, Frank McRae, Dub Taylor, Lionel Stander, Joseph P. Flaherty, David Lander, Michael McKean.

NINOTCHKA (1939) B&W/110m. In Ernst Lubitsch's comedy classic, Greta Garbo is an emotionless Russian envoy on temporary assignment in Paris. There she meets frivolous ladies' man Melvyn Douglas. After much doing, he gets her to laugh: thereupon she learns to enjoy freedom, she becomes a woman, her heart opens up, she expresses herself openly. And she teaches him to be a man of integrity and purpose. They fall in love. She returns to Russia to serve the state, but her outlook has changed. Meanwhile Douglas figures out how to get his lover back. Script by Billy Wilder, Charles Brackett, and Walter Reisch levels so many zingers at bureaucratic Russia (where the high government has forgotten about its lowly people) that one believes they are unfavorably contrasting it with France; however, Lubitsch shows a couple of Nazi soldiers on a Paris train platform, implies through Douglas and Russian expatriate Ina Claire that the country belongs to aristocrats (we rarely see the common folk) and other decadent ele-

ments. Paris is a romantic place and Moscow has warm people, but the political situation is such that Douglas and Garbo must find a compromise city (Constantinople) where the world's politics and their own differing ideologies (Garbo still justifies the Revolution) won't infringe on lovers. Garbo gives an intelligent, witty performance—oddly, she's prettier and sexier in her Russian marching uniform than in the dresses she wears in Paris. Douglas is an acquired taste. Unfortunately, this is not one of Lubitsch's funniest comedies; almost all the humor is supposed to emanate from poor Russian characters being impressed by what we take for granted; but the constant barrage of anti-Russian propaganda makes us feel we're back in grammar school and having our first (manipulative) political-science lesson (indoctrination). Adapted into the musical *Silk Stockings*, filmed with Fred Astaire and Cyd Charisse in 1957. Also with: Bela Lugosi, Felix Bressart, Alexander Granach, Gregory Gaye, Sig Rumann, Edwin Maxwell, George Tobias.

NORMA RAE (1979) C/113m. Sally Field won her first Oscar as the title character, a stubbornly independent single mother who lives in a small Baptist Southern town. Field's frustrated by the low salaries and working conditions at the textile mill where almost everyone in town is employed, so she helps New York organizer Ron Leibman, the first Jew she has ever met, build up support for a union at the mill. She becomes so obsessed with organizing that she has trouble with her employers (naturally), her minister (who won't allow her to invite blacks inside his church), the law, and her new husband, Beau Bridges. By Hollywood standards, the politics of Martin Ritt's film (which is based on a true story) is extremely progressive: not only is it pro-union, but it also builds strong cases for women to be involved in political action (so they can enjoy personal growth) and for their men to share the housework so the women can spend time in this manner; it advocates *friendships* between blacks and whites and Jews and Christians, and says that men and women can work together without becoming lovers and that husbands and wives can be friends as well as lovers. Ritt does a fine job as director: scenes that could come across as being extremely self-conscious (Bridges's proposal to Field, Field telling the children about herself, Leibman and Field talking while skinny-dipping) make us feel touched by their honesty. It is due to Ritt that the film's most famous scene has such emotional impact: when Field stands on a table at the mill, holding high a sign that reads "Union," Ritt has all the workers look *straight ahead at her* so that it's clear that each of them turns off his or her machine because of Field and not because fellow workers are doing so. Picture has authentic atmosphere, surprising toughness, and characterizations by Field and Leibman that are downright inspirational. Oscar-winning song, "It Goes Like It Goes," is sung by Jennifer Warnes. Also with: Pat Hingle, Barbara Baxley, Gail Strickland, Frank McRae, Lonny Chapman.

NORTH BY NORTHWEST (1959) C/136m. This Alfred Hitchcock masterpiece, one of his most enjoyable pictures, begins with hero Roger Thornhill (Cary Grant), a dull New York ad man, finding himself in a Kafkaesque situation. Two thugs abduct him in a hotel lobby and insist that he's someone he's never heard of, "George Kaplan." They drive him to a country estate where villain James Mason also insists he's Kaplan and demands information he doesn't have. Then they try to kill him. He escapes, but neither the police nor his mother (Jessie Royce Landis) believe his story. When at the U.N. he attempts to speak to the man who owns the country estate—Mason was an imposter—that man is killed and the crowd that gathers thinks Grant's the murderer. So, like many other Hitchcock heroes, he finds himself on the run, wanted by both police and foreign spies (led by Mason). He hops a train, is secreted away from police by a beautiful stranger (Eva Marie Saint). They make love. But later he suspects her of double-crossing him and setting him up to be killed. She *is* Mason's mistress. It's up to government man Leo G. Carroll to set him straight! "George Kaplan" was the name of a spy that was fabricated to bring Mason into the open; Saint is a government agent spying on Mason—her life is in danger. As in *Notorious*, the female heroine is willing to sleep with a foreign spy to get vital information, although she loves the character played by Grant; as in *Notorious*, Grant's character risks going to the spy's house to rescue the maiden-in-distress. Film has outstanding performances, technical brilliance, a great deal of humor, terrific locations for suspense scenes (the U.N., a crossroads in isolated Midwestern farm country, an auction gallery, the villain's South Dakota house, Mount Rushmore), and a great deal of sex is provided by Saint's cool but lustful character—there are kisses between Grant and Saint (as the camera spins around them) that must have driven the censors to distraction. While the classic crop-dusting scene and the "cliff-hanging" Mount Rushmore sequence are the most exciting moments, Hitchcock's greatest accomplishment was to keep the picture moving for 136 minutes. He does this by not only having his characters move quickly from one locale to another, but by having movement within the frame and showing all types of transportation vehicles in motion: cabs, cars, police vehicles, buses, trains, trucks, big planes, crop-dusters. There is stunning photography by Robert Burks; one of Bernard Herrmann's finest scores; nifty titles by Saul Bass; an imaginative original script by Ernest Lehman. Also with: Philip Ober, Josephine Hutchinson, Martin Landau, Larry Dobkin, Edward Binns, John Beradino, Malcolm Atterbury.

NORTH DALLAS FORTY (1979) C/119m.
An exceptional sports film, scripted by producer Frank Yablans, director Ted Kotcheff, and former Dallas Cowboys' glue-fingered end Pete Gent, author of the super semi-autobiographical source novel. Nick Nolte has never been better than as Phil Elliot, glue-fingered end of the North Dallas pro team. In his seventh year he worries about his career because he's been relegated to the bench, his knee is getting worse, and the emotionless Tom Landry-like head coach (G. D. Spradlin) has been complaining about his attitude,

saying he's no longer a "team player." He can see that he's more intelligent than his loony, barbaric teammates, and that he's the only player who fully realizes how dictatorial and heartless the coaches and ownership are and how exploited the players are. Yet, like the other players, he's willing to endure pills and shots, and "take the crap, the manipulation, and the pain" in order to have that special feeling of playing football. Picture presents a realistic view of the world of pro football on the field and behind the scenes. The humor comes from the absurd, dictatorial mentality of the coaches and the childishness of the players. But the tragic elements of the sport also come from the same sources. It is the coaches who control the players and often make them play when hurt, though a further injury could cripple them for life. The childishness of the players masks their fears of injuries, playing badly, or upsetting the coaches; their refusal to grow up is symptomatic of their terror about what they'll do when their football careers are over. Nolte makes us understand the "high" that football players feel; and in a marvelously acted scene Nolte makes it clear to Spradlin that, as long as football is big business, the players who love the sport and give it their body and soul will be treated no better than their equipment. Fine cast includes: Dayle Haddon (Nolte's football-hating girlfriend), country singer Mac Davis (as Nolte's best friend, a partying, sex-obsessed Don Meredith-like quarterback), Bo Svenson, former pro player John Matuszak, Charles Durning, Dabney Coleman, Steve Forrest, Samantha Smith.

NOSFERATU (GERMAN/1922) B&W/63m.
F. W. Murnau's adaptation of Bram Stoker's *Dracula* remains the greatest of all vampire films. The film contains the most hideous-looking vampire there has ever been: Max Schreck has claws, pointed front teeth, a bald pate, and white cadaverous features. He reminds me of a skinned bat. Real-estate agent Jonathan (spelled Jonathen in the American titles) Harker (Knock in the German titles), played by Gustav von Wangenheim, is dispatched from Bremen to Dracula's castle in Transylvania to sell him a house across the street from Harker's. When Dracula sees a picture of Harker's lovely wife, Nina (Mina in Stoker's novel), played by Greta Schröder, he comments about her lovely throat and immediately agrees to the business transaction. Harker is unable to resist when Dracula drinks blood from his neck, but Dracula doesn't take the time to drain all his blood. He's in too much of a hurry to begin his sea voyage to Bremen. Harker rushes home by land to save Nina. With Dracula's arrival, plague comes. Nina realizes that the only way to end it is by killing Dracula. The only way to do that is to give herself willingly to him and keep him from returning to his coffin before the rooster crows in the morning. In Stoker's novel and Tod Browning's 1931 sound *Dracula* with Bela Lugosi, men try to prevent the vampire, obviously a creature whose evil manifests itself in sexual perversion, from raping and sexually enslaving Harker's wife: when Dracula drinks from her neck, it isn't simply because of his thirst for blood. But in Murnau, the pure Nina takes it on

herself to save the world from evil. Sacrificing herself to free everyone else from Dracula's clutches, she invites Dracula to her bed and thus overcomes her sexual repression herself rather than letting Dracula's sexual aggression be what sexually liberates her. Film retains a surprising amount of tension, thanks to Murnau's haunting images—the castle sequence, the sequence on the ship (harmed only because the night scenes look too bright), and the finale, which is highlighted by Schreck's terrifying shadow outside Nina's door, are still extremely powerful. But Murnau wasn't so determined to cause chills that he didn't include much wit in his story. While Murnau doesn't move his camera, his characters move within the frame. His fluid editing, his juxtaposition of shots with different angles, and his mix of indoor and outdoor scenes prevent his film from having the staginess of Browning's *Dracula*.

NOSFERATU THE VAMPIRE/NOSFERATU DER NACHT (WEST GERMAN/1979) C/96m—107m.

Werner Herzog's remake of F. W. Murnau's horror classic is beautifully filmed but too slow. By the time Jonathan Harker (Bruno Ganz) reaches the castle of Count Dracula (Klaus Kinski), you'll be half asleep. What's most disappointing is that the themes and storyline are almost identical to Murnau's still widely circulated film, making one wonder if Herzog undertook the project only to see if he could make Kinski look like Max Schreck's vampire (he comes mighty close). Perhaps this film's humor is a bit more subtle, although you'll be surprised how many humorous lines of dialogue can be found in Murnau's title cards. Otherwise the noticeable differences in this film include: Professor Van Helsing is even more of a doddering old fool; the brave actions of Jonathan's wife, Lucy (Isabelle Adjani)—called Nina in Murnau's film—have more to do with her being a woman than just a devoted wife, simply because all *men* of status reject her request that they go after Dracula to end the plague; the film has more sex (when Dracula sucks Lucy's blood, he places a hand firmly on her breast); and Jonathan and Lucy have different fates. One major problem arises because Herzog tries to provide Nosferatu with a bit more personality than in the Murnau film. Among the few things he says about himself are that he wishes for two things: that he could die and that he could be loved by a woman. When Lucy—the woman he loves—willingly lets him drink her blood so that he will not be in his safe coffin when the sun rises, she kills him, but, much to our chagrin, his end is a happy one because he gets both his wishes. At least he suffers some pain. Film has a great last shot. Also with: Roland Topor.

NOTHING SACRED (1937) C/75m (Also B&W Prints).

Classic screwball comedy stars Carole Lombard as Hazel Flagg, a young Vermont woman who feigns having fatal radium poisoning so she can take a free trip to New York with slick city reporter Fredric March. The heart-wrenching stories March writes make her a national celebrity, revered for her supposed gallantry at the point of death. When she falls in love with March and decides to come clean, no one will let her—if Hazel Flagg should live and be seen as a hoax, then Americans would be deprived of the martyr they desire and would be denied their self-satisfying public exhibition of concern. Ben Hecht's cynical script is an attack on the hypocrisy of all Americans (those in small towns as well as big, corrupt cities) because they revel in their unselfishness and graciousness toward their fellow human beings, yet (like the sensationalist paper for which March works) they delight in other people's misery (soap operas were becoming radio staples in 1937) and exploit it. Hazel Flagg is a 10-cent charlatan compared to the bloodsuckers who profit (often financially) from her plight. March is his usual too stiff self (which is why it's funny watching a smalltown boy greet him with a bite on the leg); but Lombard carries the film with a witty, animated performance that gathers steam once she hits New York. She's sexiest when she's unladylike—wearing a fireman's hat and coat; pulling March out of the river; angrily trying to slug March on the jaw (the funniest scene); taking March's jab on her own jaw; sitting in a robe with arms resting on her spread legs, her jaw swollen, and her bare feet tattooing the floor. She shows why she was Hollywood's highest-paid star at the time. William A. Wellman directed. Also with: Walter Connolly, Charles Winninger, Sig Rumann, Frank Fay, John Qualen.

NOTORIOUS (1946) B&W/101m.

Many critics' favorite Hitchcock film. Unlike most o his other suspense films, this one has little humor—in this espionage tale the characters are playing for keeps. Ingrid Bergman is a depressed, heavy-drinking young woman, an American citizen, whose Nazi father is convicted of being a traitor and commits suicide. Because she is fervently loyal to America and despised her father's politics, Bergman is recruited by FBI agent Cary Grant to be planted among German Nazis in South America. Grant becomes upset when the assignment is further explained to him by his bosses: she must play up to Claude Rains, a Nazi who was friend to her father and had once been in love with her. (While the Nazis are shown to be murderers, the FBI men are shown to be sexual procurers and moral hypocrites.) Grant would like Bergman to reject the assignment, but refrains from influencing her. Meanwhile Bergman, who has fallen for Grant, resents that he doesn't express love for her but allows her not only to have an affair with Rains but to marry him. Grant acts bitterly toward Bergman, and Bergman feels abandoned and dehumanized. She provides information about Rains's Nazi friends to the FBI and helps Grant sneak into her husband's wine cellar, where he discovers uranium in wine bottles. (Hitchcock and screenwriter Ben Hecht had guessed right in 1944 about the key ingredient in the atomic bomb—several producers turned down the project because they figured *uranium* was too far off base.) Rains discovers his wife has betrayed him and plots with his venomous mother (Leopoldine Konstantin) to slowly poison her (so his Nazi cohorts won't realize he was foolish enough to marry a spy and kill him). Throughout the film we've been annoyed with Grant for his passivity and for being less in love with Bergman than the devoted Rains—at the end Grant has the chance to prove himself to us and to Bergman. Film's end is extremely tense: this is one of many times Hitchcock places his heroine (a maiden in distress) in a large house and has the hero (the knight) come to the rescue (we think quickly of the very similar *North by Northwest*, in which Grant climbs up the side of a house to get to Eva Marie Saint). Even more exciting is the party sequence in which lovers Grant and Bergman slip off to snoop in the wine cellar and the jealous Rains walks toward the cellar to get more wine. It's one of Hitchcock's classic suspense scenes with action taking place all over the house. Fine acting by Bergman and Rains (one of Hitchcock's most refined villains); Grant's character is too serious and a bit of a lunkhead. The Nazis are a slimy bunch—that politeness and sleek dress are a cover for lowlifes is made clear in the crude manner in which Konstantin lights and smokes a cigarette while planning Bergman's demise. Also with: Louis Calhern, Reinhold Schunzel.

NOW, VOYAGER (1942) B&W/117m.
A ridiculous soap opera that is great fun. Plump spinster Bette Davis is on the verge of a breakdown after a lifetime under the thumb of puritanical, dictatorial mother Gladys Cooper, who has resented the daughter she didn't want in the first place. Davis is cured at Claude Rains's sanitarium, loses weight, and goes on an ocean voyage alone. She meets and falls in love with kindly Paul Henreid, an unhappily married man with a wife who has treated her unwanted daughter (Janis Wilson) as Cooper treated Davis. When Davis returns home to Boston, she is a confident, independent woman who won't allow Cooper to dominate her anymore. As she and Henreid are still in love, she refuses to marry suitor John Loder, even though she desires a child. Visiting Rains at the sanitarium, she discovers Henreid's unhappy daughter is a patient there. Davis takes her under her wing—Wilson now has the loving mother she never had, Davis has a daughter (*his* child). This is both one of the cinema's great romances and one of the most manipulative tearjerkers about female sacrifice. Casey Robinson's shrewd script, adapted from Olive Higgins Prouty's novel, is full of dramatic love scenes, verbal battles, humor, tears, and, best of all, mature dialogue between Davis and men. Final scene, with Davis and Henreid discussing their future, is one of the greatest found in Hollywood soaps, for it has Davis acting both noble and sacrificial; Max Steiner's swelling music coaxing tears to our eyes; Henreid, for the umpteenth time, lighting two cigarettes simultaneously and handing one to Davis (their inhaling and smoky exhaling is the equivalent of sexual intercourse); and Davis delivering that beautiful last line: "Don't ask for the moon when we have the stars." Also with: Lee Patrick, Bonita Granville, Ilka Chase, Franklin Pangborn.

NUTTY PROFESSOR, THE (1963) C/107m.
In Jerry Lewis's cult classic, he plays Julius Kelp, an intelligent but clumsy, weak, buck-toothed, and myopic college chemistry professor. He's too shy and self-conscious to let student Stella Purdy (Stella Stevens's best role in a comedy) know his feelings for her, so he decides to change himself by using chemicals. He becomes dashing, irresistible Buddy Love, the most narcissistic person in the universe. He becomes idol to the students at the Purple Pit when he sings and dances for them, and sweeps Stella off her feet. This *Dr. Jekyll and Mr. Hyde* variation—Lewis is the equal of both actor Fredric March and director Rouben Mamoulian (of the 1932 version) during the inventive transformation scene—is Lewis's most daring film. In all his other films he begged for love from his viewers, but here he was willing to play a character (Buddy Love) who is so obnoxious and insensitive that Lewis's greatest fans, kids, would probably react negatively. While it has often been written that Buddy Love, Kelp's alter ego, represents Lewis's ex-partner, the cocky, romantic-singing, and boozing Dean Martin, I think Buddy's the alter ego of Jerry Lewis, the Lewis we see each year on the telethon: that conceited, sanctimonious, singing, angry older fellow who tries unsuccessfully at times to keep the funny-voiced "Kid" bottled up inside him (only letting him escape when the proceedings become too gloomy). Picture has many hilarious moments. A great bit in which the scrawny Kelp has his arms stretched to the floor by a heavy barbell is reminiscent of gags used by Lewis's mentor Frank Tashlin, a former cartoon director. There are many other inspired sight gags. Most impressive is how Lewis (like Jacques Tati) has devised routines in which pantomime or a series of quick sight gags is used in conjunction with the music and noises he has placed on the soundtrack. In one great scene, Kelp sneaks down a dark hallway. When he realizes he's making squeaking noises, he removes his shoes—when he walks farther, he discovers that his feet, not his shoes, are what's squeaking. In another sequence Kelp has the worst hangover of all time and the humor comes from our watching his face contort in reaction to the amplified sounds of pencils clicking, chalk squeaking, and gum being chewed. Ending is a bit maudlin, with Kelp asking forgiveness for his Buddy Love deception—but it's interesting because probably what we're witnessing is Lewis apologizing to his audience for not playing "the Kid." It's not surprising that Lewis wouldn't let his own children see this picture. Also with: Del Moore, Kathleen Freeman, Howard Morris, Elvia Allman, Buddy Lester, Julie Parrish, Milton Frome, Norman Alden, Henry Gibson, Les Brown.

O LUCKY MAN! (BRITISH/1973) C/173m. Using the same name (Mick Travis) he had in Lindsay Anderson's previous film, *if....* (this picture begins "Once upon a time . . ."), Malcolm McDowell is an eager Everyman, an ambitious traveling salesman assigned to northern England. During this satire-allegory we follow McDowell on a series of misadventures, some humorous and some harrowing, some lunatic-real and some believable-surreal. In Mc-Dowell's bizarre experiences he gets a first-rate education in capitalism, meeting militarists, mad doctors, wealthy businessmen who exploit Third World countries, brutal police, prison authorities, and government officials—and capitalism's victims. Taken an adventure at a time, the picture works quite well; in fact some scenes are startling. But its great length works against it; the story becomes rambling, tedious, and often incoherent (it's made more confusing because actors turn up at different times, usually but not always playing different roles). The biggest problem is that until the end (that's why it is the end) McDowell never responds in a credible manner to what he witnesses or to his own victimization: he becomes the one unreal person in the picture. Based on an idea by McDowell. Scripted by Anderson and David Sherwin, who wrote *if*. . . . Photographed by Miroslav Ondricek. Excellent music by Alan Price, who appears as himself. Many consider this ambitious, imaginative epic a masterpiece. Also with: Ralph Richardson, Rachel Roberts (very good in a suicide scene), Arthur Lowe, Helen Mirren, Mona Washbourne, Graham Crowden, Peter Jeffrey, Vivian Pickles, Edward Judd, Anderson.

OBJECTIVE BURMA (1945) B&W/142m.
Errol Flynn leads his command on a daring mission into the Burmese jungle to blow up a strategic Japanese radar station. But afterward rescue planes can't land to get the men out. So they must begin long trek to new rescue point, with vengeance-bent Japanese both on their heels and waiting in ambush all along the way. This is one of the best war movies, and among the grimmest, considering how many soldiers on both sides are killed and the brutality of their deaths. The great pacing, with characters who always seem to be moving, is characteristic of director Raoul Walsh. It is highlighted by powerful battle sequences, including a tense, climactic "night" battle in which few survive. American soldiers sit in trenches while scores of Japanese soldiers try to get at them, first with scouts and then with an all-out attack. Walsh emphasizes the professionalism of the soldiers, showing how well prepared and efficient they are—interestingly, leader Flynn is not the only one signaling commands during actions. Attempting to show the reality of being soldiers in war, Walsh has his soldiers become frustrated, scared, and lose confidence as their numbers start to diminish and rescue looks hopeless. Flynn gives an unusually restrained, humble performance; Henry Hull, as an aged war correspondent who goes on the mission—as *our* eyes, no doubt—is given emotional anti-Japanese outbursts ("Wipe them off the face of the earth!") that the cool Flynn character wouldn't stoop to. Our problem when watching this film today is that it's hard to take the racist propaganda or watch our soldiers ambushing Japanese soldiers (it's like

a shooting gallery). It's as if Hollywood was preparing American sentiment for the bombing of Hiroshima (which would take place 6½ months after film's release). Also with William Prince, George Tobias, Warner Anderson, Hugh Beaumont.

OCTOBER/TEN DAYS THAT SHOOK THE WORLD (RUSSIAN/1928) B&W/67m.
Sergei Eisenstein's visually dynamic version of Russia's October Revolution of 1917, in which the Bolsheviks ousted Kerensky's Provisional Government from power. It's a great propaganda piece: Kerensky is portrayed as a power-hungry neurotic who is no different from Napoleon or Czar Nicholas; the Social Democrats are arrogant men in suits who ignore the people's cry for peace, land, and bread; the bourgeoisie who thrive under Kerensky are decadent types—the men all smile through crooked and broken teeth, the women have painted faces and are loaded down with jewelry—who treat the Bolsheviks contemptuously and, when they have the chance in one scene, brutally; our heroes are the masses—Lenin is glorified only once, and because of his attack on Stalinism at the time the film was commissioned, most of Trotsky's footage (and mention of his name) was eliminated; when the communists come to power, they immediately call for peace with Germany, land distribution to the poor farmer, and food for the masses. Film has several amazing sequences—the soldiers' massacre of the Bolsheviks, juxtaposed with a bourgeois group beating a young Bolshevik to death; a dead horse (symbol of the Russian laborer) is lifted high into the air by the rising drawbridge it's roped to; the lengthy, exciting storming of the Winter Palace by the Bolsheviks—but it's most known for Eisenstein's startling use of montage to create rhythm, build tension, and express ideas. No film has quicker editing or uses more individual shots per minute; while Eisenstein manages to draw us into the *action*, *movement*, *flow*, and *excitement* of the October Revolution, he is most impressive when he gets us to think, by intercutting shots of characters with shots containing symbolic imagery. Eisenstein originally planned a two-part film which would have been shot about 60% longer than *Ten Days That Shook the World*, the version of *October* that usually plays outside the Soviet bloc.

OCTOPUSSY (1983) C/122m.
Loosely based on two Ian Fleming short stories, "Octopussy" and "The Property of a Lady," James Bond film finds Roger Moore's 007 tracking down the murderers of 009. He uncovers a plot by a renegade Russian general (Steven Berkoff, the villain in *Beverly Hills Cop*) and a wealthy Afghan prince (Louis Jourdan) to explode an atomic bomb at a U.S. airforce base in Germany. They reason that the public will conclude that a nuclear "accident" caused the death of hundreds of thousands of innocent people and will press for unilateral disarmament by the Western bloc. Picture has slow spots, little humor, and villains who aren't nearly of the caliber of Dr. No, Goldfinger, or Blofeld. Also, the filmmakers make the mistake of demeaning Bond by having

him swing through the trees and emitting a Tarzan cry and having him hide in a gorilla suit and later disguise himself as a clown (whom all the kids at the circus laugh at). It's as if they're trying to remind us that everything is tongue-in-cheek, but that makes little sense, for this film is much more serious than typical Bond outings—in fact, it recalls the tone of *From Russia With Love*. Nevertheless this is a fairly entertaining picture, with a sturdy performance by Moore, beautiful "Bond girls" (I'm sure their issue of *Playboy* sold well), twin knife-throwers Bond must dispose of, and several exciting action sequences. Making her second appearance in a Bond film, Maud Adams is the title character, leader of a female smuggling gang and a difficult, but not impossible, conquest for Bond. Directed by John Glen. Rita Coolidge had a big hit with "All Time High," the over-credits song. Also with: Kristina Wayborn, Kabir Bedi, Desmond Llewellyn, Lois Maxwell, tennis star Vijay Amritraj.

ODD MAN OUT (BRITISH/1947) B&W/113m–116m. At the height of his popularity, James Mason played Johnny McQueen, leader of the political underground of an unnamed Irish city (obviously Belfast). Johnny and several accomplices rob a linen mill to get money for their cause. Johnny accidentally kills a man who tries to stop him from reaching the getaway car and is badly injured himself. He falls out of the speeding car and his cowardly cohorts don't go back to get him. Fatally injured, he tries to reach organization headquarters without the police catching him. Meanwhile he is pursued by various people for various reasons: his girlfriend (Kathleen Ryan) wants to spend his last hours with him; his friend (Robert Beatty) wants to help him get back to the organization; a priest (W. G. Fay) wants to hear his confession; a derelict (F. J. McCormick) wants to hand him to either the priest or the police, whoever can offer him more; a mad artist (Robert Newton) wants to use him as a model because he has the eyes of a dying man, etc. Carol Reed's dated film works best in the early scenes, when it is strictly a suspense thriller (although it would have been more effective if the politics of Johnny's band were made clearer). When the emphasis switches from Johnny to the characters who cross his path, the film falters badly. (The storyline begins to resemble *Lassie Come Home*.) It becomes a pretentious religious allegory (with Johnny as the Christ figure) and morality play. And it drags on intolerably—perhaps it could end if Johnny didn't fall down every two or three minutes or wander away from where someone left him to be picked up later. At least the final scene is powerful (and surprising). Film's once innovative use of lighting and sharp camera angles is still interesting, but some of Reed's trickery now seems absurd (e.g., Johnny imagines faces in the bubbles of his spilled drink). Cinematography by Robert Krasker. F. L. Green's novel was adapted by Green and R. C. Sherriff. Also with: Cyril Cusack, William Hartnell, Denis O'Dea, Dan O'Herlihy.

OF HUMAN BONDAGE (1934) B&W/83m. Picture begins about halfway through Somerset Maugham's autobiographical novel—it is updated from the 1890s to 1930s—when club-footed art student Philip Carey (Leslie Howard) learns that his talent is mediocre. He then attends medical school, where he falls deeply in love with sluttish cockney waitress Mildred Rogers (Bette Davis). She is a cold-hearted, money-loving opportunist who treats Philip like dirt, dropping him for another man, returning to him when she becomes pregnant, then leaving him once more. That Philip considers himself a failure—in his work, as a man—is reflected in his masochistic bondage to such a woman. Other women—Norah (intelligent Kay Johnson) and Sally (lovely Frances Dee)—are attracted to Philip, but he can't break away from Mildred and have a fulfilling relationship with either. John Cromwell directed this film—it's static, claustrophobic, and uninterestingly acted by Howard. But this is the film which really launched Davis's career and she makes it worth watching. With eyes heavily shadowed and wearing a peroxide-blond wig, Davis's Mildred is mean and menacing—when she viciously tells off Philip (in the film's most famous sequence), you'll be glad you're not standing in his shoes. Howard is the only name above the title, but because of Davis you care more about what makes Mildred tick than about the reasons Philip is attached to her. I've never seen a film in which so many letters are read. Remade in 1946 with Paul Henreid and Eleanor Parker and in 1964 with Laurence Harvey and Kim Novak. Also with: Reginald Denny, Alan Hale, Reginald Owen.

OFFICER AND A GENTLEMAN, AN (1982) C/126m. One of many recent films that present the armed forces as a character builder, this surprise smash hit shows how tough, irresponsible, aimless Zack Mayo (Richard Gere) becomes an officer and a gentleman during a grueling 13-week training session at Washington's Naval Aviation Officer Training School. More interesting but equally formulaic is the romance he has with local factory girl Paula Pokrifki (Debra Winger), who for years has been hoping a future Navy pilot would take her away from her dead-end existence and marry her. She's had sex with countless trainees—but Zack's the first she's actually fallen in love with. She wants him desperately, but realizes he is dead set against commitment. She won't stoop as low as her best friend, Lynette (Lisa Blount), who's willing to fake pregnancy to get a proposal from Zack's friend, fellow trainee Sid Worley (David Keith). As directed by Taylor Hackford and written by Douglas Day Stewart, the picture is slick, manipulative, and hackneyed. Except when Zack urges cute recruit Casey Seeger (Lisa Eilbacher) over a wall that she must climb to pass training, the training scenes are drivel, taken from countless other basic-training pictures. The film's pivotal suicide scene is annoying because there has been no indication the character would act in such an extreme manner. But the erotic performances by Gere and Winger, and her sympathetic character—she seems on the verge of tears even when laughing or joking; she's like a shy person who reveals her vulnerability each time she forces herself to look you in the eye; she cries a lot; she *needs* him—wear down most resistance. As the marine drill sergeant you've seen in a million films, Lou Gossett, Jr., shouted his way to an Oscar. Also winning an Oscar was the song "Up Where We Belong." Also with: Robert Loggia, Tony Plana, Victor French.

OFFICIAL STORY, THE (ARGENTINIAN/1985) C/112m.

A remarkable first feature (a Best Foreign Film winner) by director Luis Puenzo (who scripted with Aïda Bortnick) that strikes the heart dead center. Norma Aleandro gives a wondrous performance as the wife of a successful Buenos Aires businessman (Hector Alterio), a loving husband and father to their five-year-old adopted daughter, Gaby (Analia Castro), but a political rightwinger. Aleandro teaches Argentinian "history," but accepts only what's written in the textbook—which, her enlightened pupils tell her, was written by fascists. Politically naïve, her eyes are opened by an old friend (Chunchuna Villafañe) who has returned from exile now that the murderous military dictatorship has ended, Villafañe says that she was tortured by the military junta ("after seven years I'm still drowning") because her boyfriend was a radical, and that many others were murdered, including women whose babies were taken and given to bourgeois families. When Alterio refuses to tell her whether their child's mother was a *desaparecido*, Aleandro does her own investigation—even though she fears that what she discovers may lead to her losing her child to the child's rightful family. As her political awareness grows, she lets her hair down, becomes a better teacher, glows—and becomes distant from her husband. Finally she meets one of the now world-famous grandmothers of the Plaza de Mayo who are demanding that the new government return their missing children and grandchildren. The scene in which Aleandro silently, respectfully, fearfully, sits in the café with Chela Ruiz, tearfully looking at pictures of Ruiz's missing daughter as both a married adult and as a child who much resembles Gaby is overpowering. Film is about human rights and the unique affinity that mothers have for each other. It's also about the guilt and paranoia of the bourgeoisie, who realize that what they cherish (Gaby is being used as a symbol here) actually belongs equally to the lower class— the reason there can never be an alliance between the two. Alterio has reached the point where he can't give up all that he's accumulated at the expense of the lower class (including leftists and laborers like his unemployed brother)—"I'm not a loser." But Aleandro has an awakening, whereupon she learns that nothing is more important than justice, human rights, a mother's rights. Their break-up scene, in which Alterio realizes he's no better than those who tortured in his name, is devastating.

OLD DARK HOUSE, THE (1932) B&W/71m.

A splendid, much overlooked horror film directed by James Whale, who exhibits his usual flair, wit, sophistication, and fascination with perverse characters. Driving in England, Raymond Massey, his glamorous wife, Gloria Stuart, their carefree and penniless passenger, Melvyn Douglas, and, in a second car, rich but likable Charles Laughton and his companion, chorus girl Lillian Bond (who will fall for Douglas), get caught in a storm and take refuge in an isolated mansion. Our five heroes and heroines meet its five inhabitants, characters who make the eccentric families found in screwball comedies seem normal. They are greeted by a mad, mute butler (Boris Karloff) with scars on his forehead, a scruffy beard on his chin, and a constant urge to drink himself into a violent rage. He is employed by the Femms: elderly, prissy, cowardly, atheist Ernest Thesiger and his partially deaf, unfriendly, fanatically religious sister, Eva Moore. Their heavily-whiskered 102-year-old father (actress Elspeth Dudgeon, billed as "John" Dudgeon) is bedridden upstairs. But wait till you meet the eldest son (Brember Wills as Saul), a dangerous little pyromaniac who is kept locked up because even the other crazies in the family realize that he's insane. Film is outrageous from the outset and becomes increasingly bizarre as new characters are introduced and each seems more demented than the others. Whale displays tongue-in-cheek humor at the beginning to lull viewers into a false sense of security, but then plays up the suspense and terror in the final few scenes, in which both Karloff (who is excited by Stuart) and Wills (who wants to kill Douglas) attack their intended victims. What a creepy villain Wills's short but scrappy (he bites) old Saul is! As always, Whale makes dramatic use of shadows, sound effects, wild angles (especially when filming faces), and dramatic close-ups. The standout photography by Arthur Edeson greatly contributes to the atmosphere. Film's most memorable set piece has the travelers having dinner with Thesiger (who miserly tells each, "Have a potato") and Moore (who gobbles down her food). Thesiger (headed for immortality as Dr. Pretorious in Whale's *Bride of Frankenstein*) and Moore, who argue constantly, are an unforgettable team. From *Benighted* by J. B. Priestley. In 1963 William Castle did a semi-remake starring Tom Poston.

OLD MAID, THE (1935) B&W/95m.

Cousins Bette Davis and Miriam Hopkins both love Hopkins's fiancé, George Brent. But when he's away too long, Hopkins marries into a rich family. Brent finally sees the worth of Davis and they become lovers. Brent is killed during the Civil War; Davis has a daughter out of wedlock. Selfish Hopkins, resentful that Brent turned to Davis, ruins Davis's plan to marry rich Jerome Cowan. She then convinces Davis to let her raise the little girl, whom everyone but the two women thinks is an orphan. The girl grows into womanhood (Jane Bryan) calling Hopkins "Mother" and acting resentful toward her meddling, spinster "aunt," Davis. Standard Victorian soap opera about unrequited love, sexual frustration, female rivalry, class obligations, and motherly sacrifice, the film benefits, it goes without say, from the casting of the two classy stars. But I wish that the two would have at least one hysterical screaming session; Davis in particular is just too restrained. Yet it's fun watching her young, in hoop dress and blond curls, and old in her severe old-maid hairstyle. You'll also smile watching the two females resolve their problems (surprisingly, Hopkins proved to be a good mother) when you consider that Davis and Hopkins never ended their bitter feud in real life. Direction by Edmond Goulding is strictly serviceable until the final few scenes—for which you should have your hankies handy. From Zoë Akins's Pulitzer-winning play, which was adapted from Edith Wharton's novel. Also with: Donald Crisp, James Stephenson, Louise Fazenda, William Lundigan.

OLD YELLER (1957) C/83m.   If you were a kid when you saw this in the fifties, you definitely cried when young Tommy Kirk gallantly shot Old Yeller (played by Spike of TV's *The Westerner*), his beloved dog who had come down with rabies. And chances are you are still emotionally attached to this film. I am. It's set in Texas in 1869. When dad Fess Parker (in a small part) goes away on a cattle drive, teenager Kirk is determined to take his place around the farm and look after his mother, Dorothy McGuire, and younger brother, Kevin Corcoran. When Corcoran adopts Yeller, a stray that wanders onto the land, Kirk is irritated because it causes chaos in the stable environment he's trying to create. But Kirk is soon won over by the smart, brave (fabulous!) dog. Yeller becomes one of the family. However, it contracts rabies when it saves Kirk from some wild hogs. Kirk wants to prove himself a man—but it rips him apart when he realizes he has to shoot the poor dog. Disney's first film about a dog is well acted by the four stars and the talented Spike, sensitively directed by Robert Stevenson, nicely photographed by Charles P. Boyle. The best of its kind. Fred Gipson and William Tunberg adapted Gipson's short novel. Also with: Jeff York, Beverly Washburn, Chuck Connors.

OLIVER! (BRITISH/1968) C/153m.   It's hard not to resent any film to which the Hollywood establishment voted the Best Picture Oscar in the year *2001* was released. But it's time that the "hip" *2001* fans caught up with the mass audience. For this is a marvelous film, and an outstanding addition to the fading musical genre. Freely adapted from Dickens's *Oliver Twist*, it is about an orphan who falls in with a band of thieves. It overcomes a major obstacle. The original story is one of constant grief and hardship—certainly not material readily adaptable to a musical. But Lionel Bart's happy score, sung and danced amidst a menacing atmosphere, creates both a "feel-good" sensation and the dreary feeling of the novel—two forces not opposing but calling attention to each other. ". . . though diseased rats threaten to bring the plague in, it's a fine life." The novel's scoundrels are present, but aside from the incredibly evil Bill Sikes, they have been somewhat cleansed. Much credit for the film's success can be attributed to Carol Reed, director of classic suspense thrillers in the '40s and '50s. The second half of the film, in which Bill tries to do away with Oliver (Mark Lester), depends a great deal on atmosphere and suspense, which Reed pulls off brilliantly—it is ex-

citing. Also noteworthy is Reed's decision not to have embarrassing pauses after songs end, before the action resumes: he cleverly segues from music to musical sounds such as flowing water or rattling trinkets. Reed (who won Best Director Oscar) also worked with choreographer Onna White to make sure that the spectacular production numbers were cinematic rather than stagy. He also allowed his actors free rein to develop interesting, multidimensional personages. While Mark Lester is a bit wimpy in the title role (perhaps his great-uncle will also tire of him and return him to the orphanage), Ron Moody as Fagin, young Jack Wild as the Artful Dodger, and Shani Wallis as Nancy Sikes (who befriends Oliver and raises her husband's wrath) are absolutely wonderful. Musical highlights include "Who Will Buy?"; Wallis's rousing "Oom-Pah-Pah"; "Consider Yourself," and anything with the remarkable Moody. From the London and Broadway smash. Also with: Harry Secombe, Hugh Griffith, Sheila White.

OLIVER TWIST (BRITISH/1948) B&W/105m–116m.   David Lean directed and co-wrote (with Stanley Haynes) this adaptation of Charles Dickens's novel about a runaway orphan boy who falls in with a gang of London thieves. It's a dark, highly atmospheric, punishing film—if you think Pinocchio had troubles, you'll really get upset watching likable eight-year-old Oliver (John Howard Davies) be pushed around the cruel world. Robert Newton is terrifying as Bill Sikes—this was the role that showed he'd be ideal as Long John Silver. When he beats to death his sympathetic companion, Nancy (Kay Walsh), it's sickening. Film is best remembered for Alec Guinness's mannered, effeminate, creepily effective portrayal of the old, bearded, big-nosed Fagin, leader of the youth gang that recruits Oliver. Jewish groups objected to the portrait of the Jewish Fagin, and bits with the character were deleted for U.S. release. Also with: Anthony Newley (Artful Dodger), Francis L. Sullivan (Mr. Bumble), Mary Clare, Henry Stephenson, Gibb McLaughlin, Ivor Barnard, Diana Dors, Peter Bull.

OLVIDADOS, LOS/YOUNG AND THE DAMNED, THE (MEXICAN/1950) B&W/88m.
Strong social drama, directed by Luis Buñuel, is set in Mexican slums. It centers on good young boy (Alfonso Mejia), living with unloving mother (Estela Inda), whose friendship with an older, hardened juvenile delinquent (Roberto Cobo) leads to tragedy. Realistic atmosphere, unsympathetic portrayal of young gang members (a long way from the Dead End Kids), whose constant hunger is no excuse for their sadistic robbery spree, during which they attack and taunt handicapped men. Interestingly, these kids may roam the streets, but, unlike other movie kids, they have the wherewithal to survive on the streets. Buñuel offers no solution to the juvenile-delinquency problem—although the mother is chastised for being a neglectful parent—but conveys that a boy growing up in such poverty is doomed. Viewers will be shocked at how unsentimental and uncompromising the film is. Buñuel's kids are brutal and he doesn't

spare them tragic ends that are usually reserved for adults in movies. It's amazingly powerful seeing a dead gang boy dumped into the garbage. Film contains memorable surrealistic dream sequences. Ranks with De Sica's *Shoeshine*.

OLYMPIAD, THE/OLYMPIA (GERMAN/1936) B&W/205m—217m—225m.
Leni Riefenstahl's official two-part film of the Berlin Olympics of 1936, at which Adolf Hitler was host. It is regarded as one of the best documentaries ever made. It is also among the most controversial because many viewers regard it as being fascistic in that at times it idealizes athletes as beautifully built, superhuman figures (in the opening Riefenstahl draws a visual parallel between the contemporary athletes—seen nude under the cloudy skies—and the ancient Greeks who were models for classic sculptures). Considering that Riefenstahl was given absolute freedom by the International Olympic Committee, scores of cameras, and shot half a million feet of film, the coverage of the individual events is extremely disappointing. There is virtually no excitement on any event. We have no idea who most of the athletes are, what their strategies will be; during shot-putting, discus, and javelin events we don't even see the projectiles land. About the only competition that's fun to watch is the steeplechase, where one rider after another is thrown from his horse into a lake—we get suspicious when Germans clear the hurdles easily, but then one German joins all the others in making fools of themselves. There are several moments when Riefenstahl obviously puts in some pro-Nazi images: a Nazi soldier giving a German cross-country runner a push off the starting line; Hitler cheering a German shot-putter to victory and applauding madly. But Riefenstahl gives fair coverage to events in which Germans lost, such as the marathon in which the U.S.A. comes in first, second, and third (the narrator does say the fourth-place German set a European record), and includes extra footage of the star of the games, Jesse Owens. Interestingly, the clips we always see of Owens setting Olympic records (and thus disputing the Nazi myth of white supremacy) are taken from this documentary, but that shot of unhappy Hitler we always see after Owens's victories was taken from another part of the movie and, unfortunately, had nothing to do with his reaction to Owens. The best moments in this long, interesting, but overrated documentary picture are the close-ups of the athletes' faces, the shots of cheering fans in the grandstands, and, of course, the heralded diving montage in which faceless, acrobatic bodies become one with the sky, air, and water.

OMEN, THE (1976) C/111m.
Told that his baby was born dead (years later he learns the baby was murdered), Gregory Peck, the U.S. ambassador to England, accepts a substitute baby without telling wife Lee Remick of the switch. A few years later, mysterious incidents tell Peck and Remick that there's something strange about the little Damien (Harvey Stevens). When catastrophic events occur, Peck investigates and discovers Damien is the Antichrist. He tries to kill the boy, despite interference from the boy's diabolical nanny (Billie Whitelaw) and his vicious black dog. Big-budget horror film, given class by distinguished cast, starts out well, but becomes extremely unpleasant. Deaths are repugnant, particularly a decapitation (a scene known for its effective special effect). In *The Exorcist*, God defeats Satan; in Val Lewton's films, God and the devil fight to a stalemate; but this picture joins *Rosemary's Baby* and other recent films in which the devil emerges triumphant—it's part of a depressing subgenre. Sequels: *Damien—Omen II* and *The Final Conflict*. Also with: David Warner, Patrick Troughton, Leo McKern.

ON DANGEROUS GROUND (1951) B&W/82m.
In such films as *Rebel Without a Cause*, *Bigger Than Life*, and *The True Story of Jesse James*, director Nicholas Ray presented males who didn't understand the reasons for their violent natures, so had trouble controlling their impulses to lash out physically against those who pressured or threatened them. Ray dealt with his favorite theme in this minor melodrama about a tough Boston cop (Robert Ryan) who, after years on the force dealing with violent crimes, fears that he's losing control of his temper and will kill someone. His road to insanity takes a detour when he is assigned to track down a murderer in the country. He finds the killer to be a young insane man who can't control his violent urges—Ryan sees that he himself could turn out to be this way. In the snowy, pastoral setting Ryan at last finds solace—due mostly to the comforting words of the blind older sister (Ida Lupino) of the killer. This character study, adapted from the book *Mad With Much Heart* by Gerald Butler, is intense but not very convincing. With a score by Bernard Herrmann and excellent photography by George E. Diskant (particularly impressive are his close-ups of faces and his shots of the rural landscape). Produced by John Houseman. Also with: Ward Bond, Charles Kemper, Anthony Ross, Ed Begley, Ian Wolfe, Frank Ferguson, Cleo Moore.

ON GOLDEN POND (1981) C/109m.
Eighty-year-old Henry Fonda (as Norman Mayer) and his wife, Katharine Hepburn, arrive at their Maine lakeside cottage, where they've spent many summers. She's a warm, friendly person, but he's crotchety and difficult. He has always been cold toward daughter Jane Fonda, and she has resented that he never allowed her to get close. Jane arrives for a visit with her fiancé, Dabney Coleman, and his son, Doug McKeon. Her father isn't hospitable to anyone—he'd rather display his biting, mordant wit. Jane and Coleman go away for a month, leaving McKeon with the old folks. The boy isn't thrilled, neither is Henry. But they spend much time fishing and become very close—the boy is the son Henry always wanted, and the boy thinks his future grandfather is the rare adult who treats him with respect and sincerity. When Jane returns, she is both happy that the two lonely males have found each other and jealous that her father is showing love to the boy but still not her. Hepburn tells Jane

she must make the first move to get close to her father, who, Hepburn insists, loves his daughter. Ernest Thompson won an Oscar for his script, which he adapted from his play. It's shameless schmaltz where every line is shrewdly calculated to tug at the heart strings. Still, it's hard not to be taken with this film. We've seen the same problematic relationships—cranky old man and lonely young boy, cold old man and his unloved adult child—in other films (and TV movies), but they're rooted in real life and are hard not to respond to. Certainly because Henry Fonda and Jane Fonda had an estranged relationship for many years, until reconciliation late in his life, this picture has special meaning to viewers as well as the two actors. Henry Fonda is so wonderful in this role because he seems to really understand all his character's strengths, quirks, self-doubts (especially in regard to aging), weaknesses, and flaws—particularly as a father. Henry Fonda and Hepburn (an energetic performance) won Oscars. They rise above their roles; the other three stars aren't so lucky. A surprise moneymaker. Produced by Bruce Gilbert. Directed by Mark Rydell. Photographed by Billy Williams. Also with: William Lanteau, Chris Rydell.

ON HER MAJESTY'S SECRET SERVICE
(BRITISH/1969) C/140m. Seventh James Bond film (discounting *Casino Royale*) might well be regarded as the best of the series if Sean Connery rather than the uncharismatic George Lazenby had played 007. It is a throwback to the early Bonds before self-parody had crept in and the gimmickry had become too important. Lazenby's Bond has human traits—he's neurotic (he resigns from work when "M" doesn't seem to appreciate him); he falls in love and marries Spanish contessa Tracey (played by Diana Rigg, the classiest of the Bond girls); he's vulnerable (we actually worry when a little fellow almost catches him opening his safe); he's no longer superconfident (after having spent two years unsuccessfully tracking Blofeld). Story has Bond rescue Tracey from suicide, win her love. Her criminal father (Gabriele Ferzetti) helps him trace Blofeld (Telly Savalas) to Swiss chalet on mountaintop. Pretending to be a stuffy genealogist, Bond gains entry. He discovers Blofeld plans to unleash deadly germs. Bond stops the plot, but the price is very high. Picture is too long, and really bogs down when Rigg isn't around, but it holds up nicely, especially now that no one resents Lazenby anymore. Avoid the terrible version in which Bond narrates and scenes are juggled around. Also with: Ilse Steppat, Bernard Lee, Lois Maxwell, Desmond Llewelyn, Julie Ege, Bessie Love.

ON THE BEACH (1959) B&W/133m. Stanley
Kramer's adaptation of Nevil Shute's novel about the end of the world due to a nuclear blast has held up well; it was controversial upon release and today is screened at antinuke fundraisers. Along with *Testament*, this is our most pessimistic anti-Bomb film because it allows no survivors. Gregory Peck is the commander of a U.S. nuclear sub that lands in Australia, the only country that has not yet been affected by nuclear fallout. His family dead in America, Peck has a desperate affair with Ava Gardner. With death only days away, Australians line up for poison tablets; others commit violent suicide. Peck must decide whether to die in Gardner's embrace or take his men back to America so they can die on home soil. Well-made film doesn't oversensationalize its subject. It's weird seeing deserted streets in Melbourne and San Francisco; heartbreaking watching Anthony Perkins, an officer in the Australian navy, tell wife Donna Anderson, who never worried much about anything, that soon they'll all be dead. Fred Astaire does fine in his first dramatic role, playing a disillusioned scientist who expresses the film's theme: if we have nuclear weapons, they will be used, intentionally or by accident. Haunting playing of "Waltzing Matilda" throughout the film. Also with: John Tate, Guy Doleman.

ON THE TOWN (1949) C/98m. Irresistible, cheer-
you-up Betty Comden–Adolph Green musical, directed by Gene Kelly and Stanley Donen. Sailors Gene Kelly, Frank Sinatra, and Jules Munshin are on one-day shore leave in New York City, where they sing and dance their way to happiness with strangers Vera-Ellen, Betty Garrett, and Ann Miller, who dance and play hard to get. Only temporary stumbling block is that Vera-Ellen, Miss Turnstiles, doesn't want Kelly to know that she's no big-city celebrity but a kooch dancer who hails from his small hometown. The Bernstein-Edens score could use a couple of more standards to go with "New York, New York," but all the songs are lively, and dancing is exuberant. Vera-Ellen makes a good dancing partner for Kelly because she also has an athletic style—I only wish she had the "star power" of some of his other partners. Kelly is extremely likable in the film as he quickly backs out of his aggressive come-on act; he's particularly sweet to his ugly blind date (Alice Pearce). It's also nice to see how well the three female characters get along—even before they know Vera-Ellen well, Garrett (who's really appealing as a spunky cabbie) and Miller keep her from being humiliated in front of Kelly by paying off a *maître d'* to pretend he knows her. It's worth noting that for once Sinatra's character (although initially shy) knows what to do with a girl. Filmed on location in New York.

ON THE WATERFRONT (1954) B&W/108m.
Marlon Brando won an Oscar with his unpretentious powerhouse performance in 1954's Best Picture winner. He's a not-very-bright, punch-drunk ex-boxer who works as a longshoreman and does strong-arm work for the corrupt union boss, Lee J. Cobb. When he sets up a man who has been complaining about the union, he expects that the man will only be threatened. He becomes upset when the man is killed, but vows not to finger Cobb to the crime commission. But he is influenced by the dead man's sweet sister, Eva Maria Saint (her debut won her a Best Supporting Actress Oscar), and a crusading priest, Karl Malden, to stand up for what's right and against Cobb. Having taken a dive in the fight that would have earned him a title shot, he sees

his chance for redemption by coming clean. When Cobb has Brando's brother, Rod Steiger, killed for not being able to force Brando to back off, Brando becomes determined to talk—no matter that his fellow longshoremen may think him a squealer. Too much Christian morality is expounded by the overacting Karl Malden, but otherwise this is a terrific film. It has great acting, a fascinating premise, strong direction by Elia Kazan (who won an Oscar), tough dialogue by Budd Schulberg (who won an Oscar), and many classic scenes: Brando's "I could have been a contender" chat with Steiger in the back of a car; Brando talking to Saint about pigeons; Brando's other conversations with Saint; Brando's bloody fight with Cobb. However, the film has been criticized on several fronts: by those who are angered by its contention that the longshoremen's union was corrupt in 1954 (as suggested by the film's source, newspaper articles by Malcolm Johnson); by those who consider it anti-union; and by those who are angered by how Kazan and Schulberg, two HUAC informers, manipulate viewers into admiring those who inform to the police and the government. Boris Kaufman (Dziga Vertov's brother) won an Oscar for cinematography; Gene Milford won an editing Oscar. Leonard Bernstein composed his first movie score. Also with: Pat Henning, Leif Erickson, Rudy Bond, Martin Balsam, Tony Galento, Fred Gwynne.

ONCE BEFORE I DIE (1965) C/97m. John Derek directed and starred with his onetime wife Ursula Andress in this peculiar WWII ation drama. At the outbreak of war, the adventuress Andress hooks up with boyfriend Derek and other soldiers who must evade the invading Japanese in the Philippines. When Derek is killed, she gets to know the other men, only to see them killed off one by one—but at least they were with the beautiful Andress once before they died. It's hard to tell what's going on at times, but Andress (more sensitive and vulnerable than usual) is always watchable, Richard Jaeckel is perfectly cast as a bald, psychopathic soldier, and, surprisingly, Derek's direction (so awful in his films with Bo) is often interesting, particularly when using superimposures and freeze frames. Bleak and brutal. Also with: Ron Ely, Rod Lauren.

ONCE UPON A TIME IN AMERICA (1984) C/144m–227m. Epic gangster film by Sergio Leone is about the friendship of Noodles (Robert De Niro) and Maxie (James Woods). They were childhood friends in the Jewish New York tenements in the 1930s, when they were in the same street gang. They remained friends into adulthood, when they became full-fledged criminals (with union connections). But Noodles tipped off the cops about a foolhardy robbery Maxie and their pals (also from the old gang) were about to pull. Noodles figured that Maxie would get a couple of years in prison, which was better than his getting killed. But the police killed the three criminals, shooting them up so badly that they couldn't be identified. Noodles left town, but not before discovering that someone had walked off with the gang's hidden money. In 1968, Noodles returns—

someone has summoned him. Warners did not know how to distribute Leone's long-awaited pet project (his answer to the "soft" *Godfather*). It considered releasing it in two parts. Instead, the studio cut it from 227 minutes to 144 minutes (some sources list it at 139 minutes), and re-edited it so that it plays chronologically. It was a terrible idea—the short version may still express Leone's loyalty/betrayal theme (essential to all his films), but we need the flashback method to properly convey that Leone was also making a film about guilt and memory. Still, the long version is a disappointing picture, one that is confusing (despite the reinserted scenes) and has a bad ending. De Niro and Woods are both terrific, but I think the scenes with their characters as boys are much more interesting—and easier to follow. There are stunning moments throughout. As this is a Leone film, the visuals are thrilling, the characters memorable, and the violence brutal—this is the one Leone film where he keeps the humor *separate* from the violence. Here there is a correlation between violence and sex. Inspired by *The Hoods* by Jewish gangster Harry Gray. Striking cinematography by Tonino Delli Colli. Music is by Ennio Morricone. Also with: Elizabeth McGovern (the dancer-actress whom De Niro has loved since they were kids), Tuesday Weld (Woods's masochistic girlfriend), Darlanne Fluegel (who is brutally killed because of her relationship to Noodles), Treat Williams, Burt Young, Bill Forsythe, Larry Rap, James Hayden, Joe Pesci, Scott Schutzman (the young De Niro), Rusty Jacobs (the young Woods), Jennifer Connelly (the young McGovern).

ONCE UPON A TIME IN THE WEST (ITALIAN/1969) C/140m–165m. Baroque epic western is Sergio Leone's masterpiece. It is also his most pessimistic film: its end signals the death of his "ancient race" of superwarriors (first seen in his Clint Eastwood "Dollars" films) and the moment when there is no more resistance to advancing civilization—represented by laying down of railroad tracks, the building of a town, and a whore (Claudia Cardinale) becoming a lady, a businesswoman, a maker of coffee, a bearer of water. In the new matriarchal West, money will be more important than the gun and super-gunfighters will be passé, part of the Western folklore. A direct descendant of Clint Eastwood's "The Man with No Name," The Man (Charles Bronson) arrives in town to kill gunslinger Frank (Henry Fonda finally got to play a villain!), who killed his older brother many years before. Frank is top gun of Morton (Gabriele Ferzetti), a crippled, corrupt railroad magnate. In an incredible scene that recalls the family massacre in John Ford's *The Searchers*, Frank wipes out Brett McBain (Frank Wolff) and his children so Morton can use McBain's land for a railroad station—he plants evidence incriminating outlaw Cheyenne (Jason Robards, Jr.). Frank doesn't realize that McBain had married New Orleans prostitute Jill (Cardinale) until she arrives in town and claims her late husband's property. Frank tries to get the deed to Jill's land, while The Man and Cheyenne team up against him. After much gunfire, The Man (Leone's "good") and Frank (Leone's

312

"bad") meet in a showdown. Meanwhile the talkative (that's what qualifies him to be Leone's "ugly") Cheyenne tells Jill what her future role is. Film is incredibly ambitious, splendidly cast, beautifully shot (no one uses a wide screen better than Leone), hilarious, erotic, psychologically compelling, and wonderfully scored by Ennio Morricone. Among the many highlights are the lengthy, humorous title sequence in which three villains await The Man's arrival by train (only to be killed by him); Frank's seduction of Jill; the elaborately staged gunfight between Frank and The Man (how splendidly Leone uses space and close-ups); the final scene between Cheyenne and The Man (which is cut in the short version of the film); and seeing The Man ride off into mythology at the end of the picture. The last *great* western, shot partly in Monument Valley. Also with: Keenan Wynn, Paolo Stoppa, Lionel Stander (only in the long version), Woody Strode, Jack Elam.

ONE-EYED JACKS (1961) C/141m.
Marlon Brando's lone directorial effort is a visually impressive but muddled psychological western, always interesting but rarely satisfying. During a getaway with stolen gold, Brando is left behind by his trusted surrogate father, Karl Malden. In a Mexican prison for five years, Brando vows revenge. He escapes from prison and hooks up with a couple of vicious outlaws (Ben Johnson, Timothy Carey), who inform him that Malden has become sheriff of a Texas town. They plan to rob the town bank. But before this happens, Brando rides in and has a conversation with Malden, who lies about what happened years before. Brando meets Malden's kind Mexican wife, Katy Jurado, and stepdaughter, Pina Pellicer. He and Pellicer fall in love. This angers Malden, who whips him and crushes his gun hand. Brando knows that if he rides back into town Malden will try to kill him, but he is determined to run away with Pellicer (who, it turns out, is pregnant). Action scenes are exciting, but Brando has more success directing hardcore villains Malden and Johnson than playing his morally confused outlaw. His character is fun when taking on barroom bullies ("Get up, you scum-sucking pig!") or being patronizing to Johnson ("It's all right, *Bob*"). But, strangely, I can picture Elvis Presley in the role without the film being harmed; at times it's almost as if Brando were patterning his performance on Presley's (along with James Dean's) fifties rebel roles. Charles Neider's novel *The Authentic Death of Hendry Jones* was adapted by Guy Trosper and Calder Willingham (Stanley Kubrick dropped out as a writer). It was proably influenced by Arthur Penn's *The Left-Handed Gun*; it probably influenced the westerns of Sam Peckinpah. Also with: Elisha Cook, Jr., Slim Pickens.

ONE FLEW OVER THE CUCKOO'S NEST (1975) C/133m.
A successful, emotionally satisfying adaptation of Ken Kesey's 1963 novel, directed by Milos Forman and scripted by Laurence Hauben and Bo Goldman. Jack Nicholson is Randle Patrick McMurphy, a likable drifter who has feigned mental illness to get out of work duty at a prison where he is serving time for having had sex with an underage female. He is placed in a mental ward, where the inmates lead a totally dull and regimented life under the supervision of Nurse Ratched (Louise Fletcher), who frowns on any attempt to disrupt order. McMurphy tries to shake things up so that the inmates can make choices about their own lives. He and Ratched fight over these men—of course, she has the advantage in that she has power. In the novel McMurphy served symbolically as the sexual liberator of these impotent men who are under the thumb of the castrating Big Nurse; here he serves more as their model for nonconformity and freedom, not a liberator from repression but the catalyst for their liberation if they want it badly enough. It is McMurphy who opens their eyes to a repressive system (represented by Ratched) that is interested in controlling patients (through drugs, straitjackets, veiled threats, lobotomies) rather than helping them. Film has a half-comic tone for much of the way, partly because McMurphy sees the absurdity of the situation in the ward without comprehending the tragic consequences should he protest too adamantly. I think the reason this picture has always had a youth cult is that until the end it has all the elements of later comic youth films in which fun-loving and belligerent young rebels/students play pranks that cause the leaders of their institutions to have anxiety attacks. Nicholson's McMurphy, a nice-guy version of Nicholson's madman in *The Shining* (he uses the same expressions), is an ideal, dignity-out-the-window hero for young people who must deal with robotlike bureaucrats like Ratched every day. Picture swept Oscars: Best Picture, Best Director, Best Script, Best Actor (Nicholson), Best Actress (Fletcher). Haskell Wexler did the cinematography. Also with: William Redfield, Will Sampson (as giant, silent patient Chief Bromden, the narrator of the novel), Brad Dourif, Scatman Crothers, Michael Berryman, Peter Brocco, Danny De Vito, Christopher Lloyd, Vincent Schiavelli, Louisa Moritz.

ONE HUNDRED AND ONE DALMATIANS (1961) C/79m.
A most enjoyable, consistently clever and amusing Disney cartoon. From Dodie Smith's book, the story is set in London, where a Dalmatian, Pongo (voiced by Rod Taylor)—who's as handsome and strong as any movie hero but has an open-mouthed grin that reminds me of Walter Brennan—is tired of his bachelor life with his "pet," human songwriter Roger Radcliff (Ben Wright). Through clever maneuvering he finds Roger a bride, Anita (Lisa Davis), who has a lovely female Dalmatian, Perdita (Cate Bauer). The four live together happily and Perdita gives birth to 15 puppies. But the young Dalmatians are kidnapped by one of the greatest of Disney's villainesses, eccentric and mad Cruella de Ville (Betty Lou Gerson). She wants her two bumbling cronies, Horace (Fred Warlock) and Jasper (J. Pat O'Malley), to kill them and 84 other Dalmatians so she can make dog coats. Getting help from dogs in the city and the countryside, as well as from a brave cat and horse, Pongo and Perdita are able to track down the

99 Dalmatians at Cruella's country estate and attempt to lead them back home. The exciting escape sequence, in which the dogs use various means to elude Cruella and her cronies, march through snow, are given shelter and aid by a veritable network of animals (an underground) along the way, disguise themselves at one point, and try to outrace (in the back of a truck) the villains to the city, is handled much like a war film in which the star player(s) leads refugees through enemy territory to the border. The animation, which made use of a new Xerox process that made it possible to fill a frame with 101 *spotted* dogs, is very good throughout—Marc Davis's exaggerated, flamboyantly garbed and made-up Cruella is a gem—but the visual highlight is the spectacular chase on the mountain road. I wish that some of the puppies had more distinct personalities and that Perdita and Anita were as quirky as their male counterparts, Pongo and Roger. I do like the human villains very much, and many of the supporting animals, who display enormous personality in very brief screen time. An added plus are those moments when television is satirized: one smart parody is *What's My Crime?* on which an acquaintance of Horace and Jasper's is a handcuffed guest contestant. Directed by Wolfgang Reitherman, Hamilton Luske, and Clyde Geronimi.

ONE MILLION YEARS B.C. (BRITISH/1966) C/100m.

Pity the young student who thinks this is historically accurate. Hammer Studios' remake of Hal Roach's 1940 film is among the silliest, campiest, and dullest of the ludicrous caveman genre, wherein primitive man battled dinosaurs for supremacy of the new earth. The major appeal is the scantily clad Raquel Welch, whose poster from this film adorned the walls of teenage boys worldwide back in 1966. This picture firmly established her as the era's sex superstar. The dinosaurs created by Ray Harryhausen are impressive, but their sizes in relation to humans seem to fluctuate in different shots. Harryhausen's best sequence features Welch being carried off by a pterodactyl. Co-starring John Richardson; directed by Don Chaffey; and scripted by producer Michael Carreras—considering there is no dialogue, one wonders about the original script (conceived by *three* writers) he rewrote. Also with: Percy Herbert, Robert Brown, Martine Beswick.

OPEN CITY/ROME, OPEN CITY (ITALIAN/1946) B&W/105m.

The first film of Italy's postwar "neorealistic" cinema, directed with brutal frankness by Roberto Rossellini. Made with borrowed money and second-rate equipment, the film was begun before the Germans had completely evacuated Rome in the face of advancing Allied troops. It's authenticity has as much do to with the "documentary" look of the street scenes in rubble-strewn Rome as with our knowledge that the filmmakers and actors had experienced firsthand the Nazi occupation of their city and, in some cases, had taken part in resistance activity. The film is set in Rome during the height of Nazi power, when the Gestapo leader makes a concerned effort to weed out members of the underground. We concentrate on those who try to avoid detection: a kindly priest (a wonderful performance by Aldo Fabrizi), a resistance leader, a young boy, and the man who is about to marry the boy's mother (Anna Magnani). The girlfriend of the resistance leader falls under the drugs-money-lies spell of a lesbian Gestapo officer and helps set a trap that nets the Nazis both the resistance leader and the priest. The Gestapo leader, who's much like the Bela Lugosi maniac that Hollywood typically casts in such roles, tortures the resister while forcing the priest to look on. It is a devastating sequence. The Nazi believes he can torture information out of any Italian, or else the slave race would be victorious over the master race. The priest says the resister will never squeal. Of course, this picture is an attack on the Nazi mentality as well as on collaborators who had no idea of the agony they caused. It is also a tribute to those political prisoners who withstood Nazi torture stoically, the members of the resistance, those simple but quick-thinking people who risked their lives to help the underground, and the children who played an essential part in the movement when few men were left in the city—it is the children who would carry the legacy of those who died at the hands of the fascists. There are many powerful scenes, but my favorite moment is tender, when the boy hugs his would-be stepfather before going to sleep—he *is* still a child. Film made sad-eyed Magnani an international star. Federico Fellini co-wrote the script. Also with: Maria Michi, Marcello Pagliero.

OPENING OF MISTY BEETHOVEN, THE (1976) C/88m.

Pornographic *Pygmalion*, with bourgeois Jamie Gillis turning New York street hooker Constance Money into the classiest high-price hooker at his House of Love by having his other women give her detailed sex lessons and by giving her instructions (via an earplug) as she tries to please her clients. He never attempts sex with her himself. Money becomes "Golden Rod Girl of the Year" and the rage of New York. Gillis finally pays attention to her, but it may be too late. Film has decent photography; a consistently light, comical touch; a clever script; beautiful women; and some very erotic scenes. That's why it is regarded as a classic of the genre. But I find the sex to be a tease: sex shouldn't be antiseptically clean—it should have been raunched up. Directed by Henry Paris (Radley Metzger). Also with: Jacqueline Beudant, Terri Hall, Gloria Leonard, Mary Stuart.

ORDET/WORD, THE (DANISH/1955) B&W/125m.

Carl Dreyer adapted the play by Kaj Munk about a proud, elderly Christian farmer whose faith in God has all but disappeared because of the lack of miracles in recent times. He tires to mend fences with an old friend who has rejected him because his belief in Christ isn't solemn enough. He does this so that one of his three sons can marry the other man's daughter. Meanwhile he worries about another son, who seems to be out of his mind (from reading Kierkegaard) because he believes he can communicate with God.

The old man and his eldest son suffer tremendous grief when that son's angelic wife dies while giving birth (the baby is stillborn). But the "crazy" son insists that Christ will resurrect her. Theme of film is that people, even priests, shouldn't let faith in God diminish; and that those who are regarded as insane are actually closest to God. Beginning of film is charming due to the simplicity of the sets and the characters—it wouldn't be jarring if June Lockhart, Tommy Rettig, and Lassie dropped in for a visit. But picture becomes drawn out and silly—it might work as a story told in church, but as a film it is far-fetched. Story was also filmed in Sweden in 1943, with the resurrection in that version handled figuratively. With: Henrik Malberg, Emil Haas Christensen, Preben Lerdorff Rye, Cay Kristiansen, Birgitte Federspiel.

ORDINARY PEOPLE (1980) C/123m.

Best Picture winner is an extremely successful adaptation of Judith Guest's prizewinning first novel about the deterioration of a middle-class family due to the death of the firstborn teenage son and the inability of the mother—the symbol of the family—to love anyone else. Robert Redford made his directorial debut, winning an Oscar. At times Redford's work is so precise and cold that the mother (Mary Tyler Moore) might have directed it. Yet he's very sensitive toward his actors, and gets several outstanding performances. Best of all is Timothy Hutton (who got a Best *Supporting* Actor Oscar although he is the film's star). He suffers tremendous guilt because he and not his brother survived a boating accident. He attempted suicide, spent time in an institution, and is having trouble adjusting to high school, friends, and his ungiving mother. His father (Donald Sutherland) loves him but refuses to see that his wife detests Hutton. She is superorderly—everything must be *perfect*—and Hutton and his problems represent the disorder she can't tolerate. Hutton seeks support from psychiatrist Judd Hirsch and kind new girlfriend Elizabeth McGovern. But what he needs is for his father to stick up for him, for someone in his family to tell him he's not to blame for what has happened to the family. Oscar-winning script by Alvin Sargent is perceptive, powerful, emotionally resonant. It's also tender—the scenes between McGovern and Hutton are particularly sweet (without being cloying). Moore received much praise for her cinema debut as a woman who has repressed her emotions for so long that they no longer exist. But it has turned out that she plays most of her movie characters with extreme restraint. Story bears strong similarities to *East of Eden*. Also with: M. Emmet Walsh, Dinah Manoff, James B. Sikking, Adam Baldwin.

ORPHANS OF THE STORM (1921) B&W/125m.

D. W. Griffith silent epic, which mixes fiction and historical events, is marvelous entertainment, as exciting, old-fashionedly melodramatic, and visually impressive—if not as important—as any of his films. On the eve of the French Revolution, commoner Henriette (Lillian Gish) brings her blind adopted sister, Louise (Dorothy Gish), to Paris for an operation that will cure her. But a wicked aristocrat kidnaps Henriette for one of his orgies; blind Louise is taken in by a family of beggars-thieves and is forced to walk the streets singing for donations. A kindly aristocrat (Joseph Schildkraut) rescues Henriette from the orgy. They fall in love, but she won't marry him until Louise is found. Anyway, Schildkraut's parents (the countess is also the natural mother of Louise) won't allow their son to marry a commoner. Both Schildkraut and his fiancée are sent to prison. Revolution breaks out, followed by the Reign of Terror. Vicious Robespierre (Sidney Herbert) and a judge (Creighton Hale) who detests Schildkraut's family send the lovers to be executed on the guillotine. But Danton (Monte Blue)—whom Griffith refers to as the Abraham Lincoln of France—races to the rescue. Romantic adventure never drags because Griffith makes sure that one of the characters we care about is always in deep trouble. Griffith milks misery of Henriette and Louise: the scene in which Lillian is in anguish because she can't reach her sister in the streets is difficult to watch because Lillian is so convincing; when it comes time for the beheadings, Griffith has the lady go first. Beautiful, ethereal Gish was never better than in this film—Griffith's close-ups of her are as impressive as his spectacular crowd scenes. The final scene's a bit annoying—Griffith welcomes the return of the French aristocracy—but when Lillian and Dorothy Gish stand together in the ending two-shot (kissing, joking); I get the same feeling as when gazing at a priceless painting. Prologue states that French Revolution was justified, but warns Americans not to place our good government in jeopardy by listening to anarchists and Bolsheviks—this was already indication that American filmmakers would always feel apologetic when showing political rebellion of any kind. Cinematography by Henrick Sartov. From the play *The Two Orphans* by Adolphe D'Ennery. Also with: Frank Lossee, Catherine Emmett, Lucille La Verne, Morgan Wallace, Sheldon Lewis, Frank Puglia.

ORPHEUS/ORPHÉE (FRENCH/1950) B&W/95m–112m.

Enigmatic but spellbinding version of the Orpheus-Eurydice myth by Jean Cocteau, derived from his first play (produced in 1926). In this deeply personal work Orpheus (Jean Marais) is a poet living in contemporary France; like Cocteau, he fears that while his art has brought him fame it may not bring him immortality and that young poets with different styles and themes will be the voices listened to in the future. (Film makes point that established poets should resist temptation to copy newcomers.) Cocteau takes the experiences of the classical Orpheus—his pursuit of and cat-and-mouse game with Death, his journey into the underworld after Eurydice—and uses them as the means by which Marais learns about death, eternity, love, his art, himself. In Cocteau, only a poet like Marais is capable of surreal experiences, because only a poet has no restrictions on his imagination: people can come back from the dead; pass through mirrors; travel through a netherworld while time stands still back home. In the poet's world of infinite possibilities it makes sense that the Princess of Death (Marie

Cesarès) can weep, be charitable, fall in love, die. Film would work better if Orpheus's love for wife Eurydice (Maria Déa) were more convincing; as it is, I don't understand why Death, who loves Orpheus, would send him back to his wife, especially since he desires Death more. Nicolas Hayer's cinematography is excellent, the special effects are magical, the underground sets are haunting, and the dynamic Cesarès gives that fellow who played Death in *The Seventh Seal* a run for his money. Also with: François Périer (as Heurtebise), Edouard Dermithe, Juliette Greco, Jean-Pierre Melville.

OTHER SIDE OF MIDNIGHT, THE (1977) C/165.
Sidney Sheldon's story begins in 1939 when nice French girl Marie-France Pisier is seduced by John Beck, a smooth-talking American flyer stationed in Paris. Called back to the States, he simply dumps her, although not bothering to tell her. Using his same come-on, he seduces and marries Susan Sarandon, the scattered but resourceful special assistant to Washington bigwig Clu Gulager, who helps Beck get good flying positions in postwar America. Meanwhile the angry Pisier forgets her morals and sleeps her way to fame and fortune as an international movie queen and the wife of a tycoon (Raf Vallone). She uses her money to track down Beck and arranges for his blacklisting in the airplane field, forcing him to come to work as private pilot for her husband—meaning he must spend a great deal of time flying her back and forth. They resume their love affair and plot to murder Sarandon. Film ends with trial, surprise ending (which, now that you know, won't come as a surprise). Kitsch prototype is Andy Warhol's favorite film, but will have average viewers alternately laughing at stupidity and climbing the walls. As usual, Sarandon is likable in horrible film. But Pisier, who must speak English, isn't strong enough to carry a lead in such a long picture. Some of her scenes (particularly her love scene with ice cubes) are embarrassingly bad. Worst of all is character actor Michael Lerner, who has the least convincing French accent since Pépé Le Pew. Uninspired direction by Charles Jarrott.

OUR DAILY BREAD (1934) B&W/74m.
Unique, politely subversive Depression film by King Vidor, who financed it himself when MGM was scared off by its controversial theme. Vidor brought back John and Mary from his 1928 silent masterpiece *The Crowd*, with Tome Keene and Karen Morley assuming the roles created by James Murphy and Eleanor Boardman. Having failed to make a go of it in the cruel city, the young couple accepts a relative's invitation to take over an undeveloped farm. Knowing nothing about harvesting, they invite a Swedish farmer (John Qualen), who lost his land, to move onto their property with his family. Then they invite scores of other victims of the Depression to join them, with each person expected to perform the trade in which he or she has expertise. So there is the formation of a cooperative community of farmers, carpenters, stonemasons, barbers, even

violinists, of all nationalities. Vidor sincerely believed the communal farm was both a viable solution for the poor who couldn't make it on their own and a clear-cut alternative to the competitive money-is-everything mentality that had destroyed so many people. His characters are too simple—they're of the Hey-let's-get-together-and-form-a-cooperative school—as are the conflicts they have; and the politics are too simplistic, as Vidor avoids scenes in which his characters theorize about the political ramifications of their social experiment. Vidor also slides into cliché and away from real issues when Barbara Pepper's Jean Harlow-like platinum-blond tart tries to steal Keene away from Morley and the farm. Moreover, Keene comes across as a bumpkin rather than an inspirational leader type; Morley is much better, although I wish that Mary and the other women would have more vital, visible roles in the communal work. Despite the problems, however, Vidor's film works on many levels. Its sincerity is to be commended, its vision of an alternate lifestyle is tantalizing, its glorification of the common man is uplifting. Film shied away from championing Russian socialism, but Vidor borrowed montage techniques, as well as individual shots of men toiling the soil, from Russian filmmakers. Famous impressionistic finale, in which men dig a long irrigation ditch in order to save their thirsty crops, is great cinema. Dialogue by Joseph L. Mankiewicz; music by Alfred Newman. Also with: Addison Richards, Harry Holman.

OUT OF AFRICA (1985) C/153m.
Graceful, elegant, sensually photographed epic is adapted from the 1937 memoir of aristocratic Danish author Isak Dinesen (the pen name of Karen Blixen) and Judith Thurman's 1982 biography, *Isak Dinesen: The Life of a Storyteller*. Its seven Oscars included Best Picture, Director (Sydney Pollack), Cinematographer (David Watkin), Script (Kurt Luedtke), and Art Direction. In a multi-layered, unmannered, Oscar-worthy performance (she's better here than in *Sophie's Choice*), Meryl Streep plays Karen Blixen during her years in Kenya, 1913–1931. In order to get a title, Karen marries her cousin Baron Bror von Blixen Finecke (Klaus Maria Brandauer) and comes to Kenya to help him run his coffee plantation. Because he's always off hunting or carousing—he's like those irresponsible husbands in movies like *Coal Miner's Daughter, Country*, and *Sweet Dreams*—she learns to run the plantation herself, winning the devotion of the Kikuyus by working alongside them. Karen is never attracted to Bror, but falls in love with British hunter-pilot Denys Finch Hatton (American-accented Robert Redford in a strangely reserved performance). While this is a romantic film, I don't consider it a love story. It's primarily about a stubborn, moral woman who, *without changing or compromising* or causing changes, achieves accommodation: she accepts Bror, Denys, (although she finally asks him to change), the Kikuyus, the chauvinistic white colonials, Africa itself, and she is accepted and respected in return; there is no conquest, no power play, no ultimatum, no game-playing or attempt to obtain pity. This *is* a mature film.

Picture is so gloriously filmed that it inspired a great increase in tourism in Kenya. If you're bored by the film or resent how the blacks are used to show how nice Karen is to the natives rather than as individuals with their own lives, then you'll at least be awed by the wide-open, sun-drenched African veldt. But young girls could find worse role models than Streep's Karen: she's a writer, runs a coffee plantation, is willing to work with her hands, fearlessly rides through hostile territory during a native uprising, lives alone (after she kicks out Bror), calmly shoots a charging lion, and is even willing to humble herself by dropping to her knees in public to beg for land for the Kikuyus after she leaves Africa. Karen has more farewells than the last episode of *M*A*S*H*. Also with: Michael Gough, Mike Bugara.

OUT OF IT (1969) B&W/95m.
An early *youth film*—without the raunchy sex—that is waiting for discovery. Barry Gordon, four years older than in *A Thousand Clowns*, is a smart but unathletic high-school student. No handsome hunk, he makes a noble attempt to win sexy Lada Edmond, Jr. (In fact, Edmond, Jr., was coveted by most of us teenage boys who watched her gyrating dances in a cage on television's *Hullabaloo*). But dumb, tough jock Jon Voight is his competition. Very amusing comedy, reminiscent in some ways of the Dwayne Hickman-Tuesday Weld comedy series *The Many Loves of Dobie Gillis*. My favorite moment is when Gordon stands in his underwear in front of his mirror and fails to impress himself. Original film was written and directed by Paul Williams (*Dealing*, *The Revolutionary*, with Voight), the most talented filmmaker of the era who didn't make it big. Also with: Gretchen Corbett, Peter Grand.

OUT OF THE BLUE (1984) C/94m.
In a terrifying scene Dennis Hopper rams his truck into a schoolbus, killing all the children. He spends five years in jail, during which time his daughter (Linda Manz) leads a lonely, miserable life. Her only joy comes from listening to rock music and frequenting the punk-rock scene. She is a tough-talking kid: yet her fingers-in-mouth sleeping position indicates her vulnerability and desire to be cared for. When Hopper gets out of prison, things are temporarily stable; for one thing, mother Sharon Farrell ends her affair. But soon the young girl's home life is ruined by drunkenness, sexual indiscretions, drugs, and wild arguments. The girl's defenses break down for good—and she becomes hard, through and through. Low-budget film got made only because Hopper assumed directorial chores in mid-film. The acting is good; the terrible family life is authentic, as is the brutal world outside the home. It's too bad the film's as messy as Manz's life because it delivers a strong, important message about how adults can destroy the lives of their children. Final scene between Manz and Hopper will make your skin crawl. Also with: Don Gordon, Raymond Burr.

OUT OF THE PAST (1947) B&W/97m.
New York private eye Robert Mitchum is hired by crime boss Kirk Douglas to track down his mistress, Jane Greer, who shot him and fled to South America with a bundle of his money. Mitchum finds her in Acapulco and they have a torrid love affair. She says she didn't take the money. Rather than returning her to Douglas, Mitchum flees with Greer to San Francisco. When Mitchum's former partner (Steve Brodie) catches up to them, Mitchum kills him in a fight. While they struggle, Greer jumps into a car and drives back to Douglas. Discovering Greer really took the money and was lying about other things as well, Mitchum assumes another identity and settles in Bridgeport, California, where he becomes engaged to Virginia Huston. But Douglas has not forgotten him—after forcing Mitchum to do another job for him, Douglas tries to set him up for a murder. And Greer tries to kill Mitchum. Jacques Tourneur directed and Geoffrey Homes (aka Daniel Mainwaring, who wrote the source novel, *Build My Gallows High*) scripted this exceptional "B" movie which has come to be regarded as the picture that best exemplifies *film noir*. Here you'll find all the ingredients: tainted characters, entangled relationships; events determined by chance; large sums of money; murder; a tough, morally ambiguous hero with a gun in his trench coat, a dark hat on his head, and a cigarette in his mouth; a lying, cheating, chameleon-like femme fatale—a corruptive influence who leads an essentially decent guy down a wayward path; and, ultimately, betrayal, frame-ups, and fall guys. Significantly, film takes place mostly at night—and the darkness is used metaphorically to express that malignant evil spreads from character to character. A powerful example of this is when Mitchum and Greer kiss and, by bringing their faces together, block out the light behind them and make the screen black—like their fate. Mainwaring (who borrowed greatly from Dashiell Hammett and Raymond Chandler) is responsible for the narrative structure, sexual intensity, and tough male hero, but it is Tourneur who is responsible for the oppressive fatalism that dominates the story. James M. Cain worked on an early draft of the script; Mainwaring claims it was totally abandoned—but the film's ending recalls the finale of Cain's novel *Double Indemnity*. Nick Musuraca (Tourneur's *Cat People*) did the outstanding cinematography, repeatedly using single-source lighting to place spooky shadows on the faces of his characters and across entire sets. Solid performances by Mitchum and Greer, who'd play Rachel Ward's mother in Taylor Hackford's 1984 remake, *Against All Odds*. Also with: Rhonda Fleming, Richard Webb, Paul Valentine, Dickie Moore, Ken Niles.

OUTLAW, THE (1943) B&W/95m—103m—117m.
Filmed in 1941, director-producer Howard Hughes's "notorious" adult western was held back because of censorship problems due to newcomer Jane Russell's sexually uninhibited performance. When watching the very pretty, buxom, teenage girl in the tight, revealing dresses, you might feel as if you had discovered a long-lost, secret stag film of a respected Hollywood star. It's hard to believe that this is the same actress who'd confidently sing, dance, and be funny with Marilyn Monroe ten years later in *Gentle-*

men Prefer Blondes. Because Russell and sex are what make the film a curiosity piece, one forgets that it's one more version of the Billy the Kid (Jack Beutel) and Pat Garrett (Thomas Mitchell) saga. Here they are instant enemies, the result of Billy stealing the friendship of Doc Holliday (Walter Huston) from Pat. There is also a strain on the relationship between Doc and Billy because Doc claims Billy has taken both his horse and, although the two men don't consider it *more* important, his spirited girl (Russell). Film's bizarre resolution distorts history in a different manner than other Kid-Garrett pictures. Dialogue is sometimes offbeat; at other times it's trite. After a while there's too much male talk and not enough Russell. Film's most famous scene has Beutel and Russell wrestling in the hay in a stable: it's dark and we hear ripping noises as he says, "Hold still, lady, or you won't have much dress left." Comedy and music are intrusive. Also with: Joe Sawyer, Mimi Aguglia, Gene Rizzi.

OUTLAW JOSEY WALES, THE (1976) C/135m.
A sweeping western, impressively directed by its star, Clint Eastwood (although begun by Phil Kaufman). Eastwood's a farmer whose wife and child are murdered by Union renegades. He goes after the killers, becoming an outlaw in the process. Along the way he befriends an odd assortment of other victimized people, including a young woman played by Sondra Locke, whom he fell in love with off screen as well as on. As to be expected, the violence is bloody, made all the more exciting by Bruce Surtees's photography, which gives each shot the authentic look of old Civil War photographs. That Josey Wales ends up living in a communal situation with his "family" of friends implied Eastwood's "westerner" had mellowed from his early days and was ready to put his guns away and settle down. It would be Eastwood's last western for nine years. Epic score by Jerry Fielding. Also with: Bill McKinney and John Vernon (as the major villains), Chief Dan George, Sam Bottoms, Geraldine Kearns, Woodrow Parfey, Joyce Jameson, Sheb Wooley, Matt Clarke, Will Sampson.

OUTRAGEOUS! (CANADIAN/1977) C/96m.
Unusual cult movie about the devoted friendship between a depressed, young, gay hairdresser (Craig Russell) who wants to make a living as a female impersonator and his roommate, a sweet but crazy heterosexual young woman (Hollis McLaren) who wants to feel alive inside and be left alone by her imaginary "bonecrusher." Perhaps this funny, touching film's popularity is due to the fact that both these underdogs succeed in achieving their modest goals. At times it's a sloppy film, poorly lit and edited in a manner that causes you to lose all track of time; but the characters are so likable and believably played and the direction and script by tyro Richard Benner (who *is* gay) are so spirited and tender that you are willing to forgive it for not being as polished as a Hollywood production. Some gays faulted it for not attempting to be the first commercial film to define what it's like to be a gay in a non-gay world. But in terms of Russell's character the picture is not about being *gay* but

about being an outcast (a crazy) among people (gays) who are already outcasts. That Russell is gay is not why he is depressed; his depression comes from trying to conform to a "normal" gay life, which he finds boring and restrictive. He wants to break down the barriers gays have set up for themselves; he wants to be a female impersonator and become part of the more adventurous and dazzling gay element which many "normal" gays shun. Craig Russell gives an award-winning performance as Robin Turner, a character with great range: he is kind-hearted, angry, witty, philosophical, moody, vulnerable to criticism, strong when he has to be, even heroic, extremely sarcastic, and harmlessly bitchy. And when he does impersonations of Streisand, Channing, Garland, Bankhead, Davis, West, etc., he accomplishes what he wants: he is *dazzling*. Picture shows that those who struggle to retain their "healthy brand of craziness" in our dehumanized world can have a lot of fun. It could have been titled *Courageous*. Adapted by Benner from "Butterfly Ward," a short story by Margaret Gibson, who at one time lived with Russell. Also with: Richard Easley, Allan Moyle, David Meilwraith (who becomes Robin's agent when he moves to New York), Jerry Salzberg, Andreé Pelletier, Helen Shaver.

OVER THE EDGE (1979) C/95m.
Excellent youth film has a cult following. It's a social drama that's set in Grenada, a planned community in California. There is nothing for the teenagers to do but hang out at the recreation center. Teachers and adults have little control over their kids—if they were interested in the kids' well-being they wouldn't have moved to such a place, a barless prison. The kids spend much time getting into trouble. Michael Kramer is a nice but mixed up young boy. He doesn't do anything wrong, but police hassle him because he's best friends with Matt Dillon, who has a bad reputation. When a young punk (Vincent Spano) fires a BB gun at a police car, Kramer and Dillon are witnesses, so the police question them. Spano threatens Kramer so he won't talk. Kramer's troubles keep escalating. His parents have no idea what to do. Director Jonathan Kaplan and writers Charles Haas and Tim Hunter (the director of *Tex*) are in total sympathy with these teens; in their wasteland environment, there's little wonder why they rebel. Filmmakers have no pat answers for the problem of juvenile delinquency in planned communities. They just want to make it clear that such a setting creates the kind of teenagers that made the adults want to move away from where they had been. Scenes with kids are very believable. The kids are an interesting lot but I wish the adults weren't all one-dimensional. A unique, well-directed film. Also with: Pamela Ludwig, Tom Fergus, Ellen Geer, Lane Smith, Harry Northrup.

OX-BOW INCIDENT, THE (1943) B&W/75m.
Grim, somewhat dated western classic, adapted from Walter Van Tilburg Clark's excellent, thoughtful novel about mob violence. Based on a true story, film is set in Nevada in 1885. Drifters Henry Fonda and Harry Morgan join

bloodthirsty mob that's looking for the men who robbed and supposedly killed a rancher. They find three innocent strangers (Dana Andrews, Anthony Quinn, Francis Ford) around a campfire and the majority of the mob decides to hang them for the crime because of circumstantial evidence. Fonda and Morgan are among the seven who express objections. But they're not as vocal as a power-hungry Southern major (Frank Conroy in a Confederate uniform), heartless Jane Darwell, and a couple of brutal thugs who enjoy their few moments of authority. Film contends that the existence of a town doesn't mean that civilization has come to the west. William Wellman's film is a bit too theatrical—he rarely has his camera on someone who isn't speaking. There's also some needless symbolism. but it's not as didactic or moralistic as it could have been, and it doesn't overwhelm us with self-importance. Fonda's character is surprisingly passive. Written by Lamar Trotti. Also with: Harry Davenport, Leigh Whipper, William Eythe, Victor Kilian.

PADRE PADRONE (ITALIAN/1977) C/114m.
Based on Gavino Ledda's autobiography, published three years earlier, Vittorio and Paolo Taviani's prize-winning film allows us a terrifying glimpse of a way of life that we've never seen before. Gavino's a little Sardinian boy whose harsh father pulls him out of school and forces him with beatings to tend sheep on top of a mountain. Gavino spends years on the mountain in near isolation. Other young males endure the same prisonlike life, and we can think only of the way their lives are wasted. When Gavino becomes 20, he enlists in the service. He is treated as cruelly by the sergeants as by his father and persecuted for speaking in dialect. But he learns to read and quenches his great thirst for knowledge. When he returns to his village, he has pride in himself and no longer tolerates his father's selfishness and ruthlessness. Engrossing film is unsentimental and brutally frank. We expect the son and father to become friends at the end of the film and the father to admit his mistakes and change his ways. What is unique is that the old man is so entrenched in his patriarchal heartlessness that he will not change; as we can see in the last scene between him and Gavino, he fights off his tender instincts. Interestingly, what the boy remembers *most* (the scene is repeated) about his father—because boys want to forgive their fathers for everything—is when he tells off Gavino's classmates for laughing at his son for being taken from school. Made in 16mm for Italian television. Starring: Saverio Marconi, Omero Antonutti, Marcella Michelangeli, Fabrizio Forte.

PALE RIDER (1985) C/113m.
Clint Eastwood returned to the western after nine years to direct and star in this reworking of George Stevens's *Shane*. The setting is not the beautiful farmland found in Stevens's classic, but rugged California mountains where a makeshift colony of miners and their families try to strike gold. One of the hard-working, hard-lucked miners is Michael Moriarty, who takes care of Carrie Snodgress, whom he'd like to marry, and her 14-year-old daughter, Sydney Penny. Because robber baron Richard Dysart has his men use force to drive the miners out so he can strip-mine their valuable claims and make a fortune, Penny prays for a miracle. That miracle is Eastwood, a mysterious figure who turns up with a preacher's collar around his neck. He beats up most of Dysart's men and unifies the miners. Dysart hires a crooked marshal (John Russell) and his six deputies to take on the "Preacher." In *Shane* the gunfighter fought solely for the farmers; here Eastwood fights for the miners and himself, as he has a score to settle with Russell. Most of Eastwood's films deal with the theme of "resurrection" and this film is about the return of Death or more precisely, a dead man whose soul won't rest until he has avenged his own murder (Moriarty notices Eastwood has six bullet wounds, of the *fatal* kind, in his back). When Shane rides away, it is into western mythology; when Eastwood's character rides away, it is back into his grave. Eastwood is not a myth character, just a mysterious, perhaps mystical figure. In this film we don't have a man (like *Shane*'s Van Heflin) trying to top a myth/legend in the eyes of a woman and child—a theme that is central to *Shane*. Moriarty doesn't think Eastwood's his rival. Instead it is mother and daughter who are the potential rivals: both love Preacher and he represents to each the person who can end their intense sexual frustration. But both come to realize that they need someone *human*, someone who is there in body and spirit, to fulfill their needs—and Eastwood's character, while retaining human traits (i.e., he is sexually aroused by Snodgress), is not even alive. Like most Eastwood westerns, this is beautifully filmed (by Bruce Surtees), has humorous confrontations, bullies and villains who deserve what Eastwood gives them, and exciting violence. But I find the film surprisingly sluggish—it takes forever for Russell and his men to arrive in town and really perk up things. I think the biggest problem screenwriters Michael Butler and Dennis Shryack had was using *Shane* as a model (although the final battle recalls *High Noon* more) and having to make scenes and characters in their film relate to those in that film. Not great Eastwood—probably because it comes out second best when compared to *Shane*—but it's easy to appreciate, if only because it brought back the big-budget western. Also with: Christopher Penn, Richard Kiel, Doug McGrath, Charles Hallahan, Fran Ryan, Richard Hamilton.

PALEFACE, THE (1948) C/91m.
Engaging Bob Hope comedy set in the wild West. Jane Russell is outlaw-gunfighter Calamity Jane, who is offered a governor's pardon if she'll go undercover and find out who's been selling rifles to the Indians. Although she doesn't love him yet, she marries Hope's unsuspecting dentist Painless Potter so

she can do her work undetected. She keeps bailing Hope out of trouble without his realizing it. He believes that he is a fast draw, accurate marksman, and Indian fighter. There's an unfortunate lack of visual wit, but Hope's non-stop wise-cracking is most often on target. As usual, he plays a coward who, when the chips are down, becomes a hero and wins the girl. Top comedy sequences have Hope giving laughing gas to a mean patient who can't stop laughing even after learning Hope pulled out the wrong tooth; and Hope walking toward a showdown and nervously mixing up all the rhyming advice he was given on how to emerge victorious. (Variations on the first bit have been done by many screen comedians, including Eddie Cantor and Peter Sellers; Danny Kaye would mix up rhyming advice on the way to battle in *The Court Jester*.) For me, the picture's highlight has Hope singing "Buttons and Bows" to Russell. They'd reprise the song in *Son of Paleface*, arguably better than the original. Remade with Don Knotts as *The Shakiest Gun in the West*. Directed by comedy vet Norman Z. McLeod. Also with: Robert Armstrong, Iris Adrian, Robert Watson, Iron Eyes Cody, Skelton Knaggs.

PALM BEACH STORY, THE (1942) B&W/90m.
Delightful screwball comedy by Preston Sturges, with Joel McCrea and Claudette Colbert as young marrieds whose financial troubles cause them to split up. In Sturges's films it's not surprising that a millionaire—the hard-of-hearing old "Weenie King"—should take such a liking to pretty Colbert on their first meeting that, instead of taking over their New York apartment, he gives her money to pay the long-overdue rent and buy a new dress; or that he gives McCrea on their first meeting enough money to chase his wife to Palm Beach; or that Colbert accidentally steps on the face of another millionaire (Rudy Vallee) in the south-bound train's sleeping car and he offers to marry her after her divorce. People's situations change overnight. Picture is fast-paced and consistently funny, with stars McCrea, Colbert, Vallee, and Mary Astor (as Vallee's sister, who takes a liking to McCrea when he poses as Colbert's brother) weaving their way through a crazy world of landlords, cops, cabbies, eccentrics, men named Toto, and the gun-toting, boozing, harmonizing Ale & Quail members. McCrea and Colbert are an engaging screen couple; as intended, the scene in which Colbert sits on his lap while he tries to unzip her strapless gown is extremely sexy. Also with: Sig Arno, William Demarest, Franklin Pangborn, Jimmy Conlin.

PANDORA'S BOX/LULU (GERMAN/1929)
B&W/131m. Finally available in its full-length version, G. W. Pabst's once-banned silent masterpiece is an extraordinary discovery, not only because of its daringly uncompromising presentation of sexual themes but also because it allows viewers the rare chance to see the brilliant Louise Brooks, who plays Lulu. (It was adapted by Ladislaus Vajda from *The Earth Spirit* and *Pandora's Box*, two controversial plays written in the 1890s by German dramatist/poet Frank Wedekind. It begins with Lulu living a happy, carefree life as the mistress of Dr. Schön (Fritz Kortner), a respected, 50ish newspaper editor. She seduces Schön into marrying her. On their wedding night Schön wrongly believes his bride is having a romantic interlude with her former Sugar Daddy, the aged Schigolch (Carl Götz), and muscleman Rodrigo (Krafft Raschig). He tries to force Lulu to shoot herself, but in the struggle he is killed. Lulu is sentenced to prison, but her friends Countess Geschwitz (Alice Roberts as perhaps the screen's first lesbian) and Schön's son, Alwa (Franz Lederer)—both of whom love her—help her escape from the courthouse. She seduces Alwa and they become lovers. But, like all men, he lets her down. She ends up in London prostituting herself so Alwa and Schigolch can eat. In an astonishingly erotic scene she becomes the victim of Jack the Ripper (Gustav Diessl). Pabst and Vajda are to be commended for making Lulu the *victim* of the weak men around her rather than the traditional vamp who causes (with pleasure) their downfall. The men suffer, but *they* are responsible. Brooks lights up the screen as Lulu—in her eyes and subtle expressions we see that she understands the sexual drives and needs of her character and her desire to make her world a sexual playground. Rarely a moment goes by when she is not embracing or kissing someone. She makes no attempt to control her sexual impulses—she thinks they cause no damage—but she knows others will condemn her. Lulu laughs, but Brooks let the pain and anger show through. She gives Lulu intelligence, spirit, and dignity, even in debasement. Pabst and cinematographer Günther Krampf create the expressionistic atmosphere that is conducive to the sexual delirium that prevails because of Lulu's mere existence. She is a vivacious innocent with animal beauty and no moral sense. She means no harm—Brooks plays her without a trace of meanness—but when weak men meet her, they self-destruct. Her death near mistletoe suggests she has been redeemed and forgiven—by God or Pabst. She is out of her misery and has been rewarded salvation that the men she knows can never have. Also with: Michael von Newlinsky.

PARADISE ALLEY/STARS IN THE BACK YARD (1961) B&W/85m.
Hugo Haas was a bad filmmaker, but you've got to give the guy credit: following a career in Hollywood as a poor man's Walter Slezak, he became a genuine *auteur* who starred in, directed, produced, and wrote a string of independently made melodramas. Who else could make such a claim? Moreover, his films had unorthodox themes, such as multiple personality (*Lizzie* was released before *The Three Faces of Eve*) and miscegenation (*Night of the Quarter Moon*). This is Haas's crowning achievement and most personal film. He plays a once famous director who moves into the slums. He comes up with a scheme to end the despair in the neighborhood and the hostility that everyone feels for each other. He and a couple of old-timers pretend to be moviemakers; although there's no film in the camera, Haas pretends to be directing a movie in which all the slum dwellers play parts. The roles he writes

for them are tuned in to their real characters. And the neighborhood starts to change for the better. Film is hokey and poorly made, but it's heartfelt and harmless and offbeat. Its star is former Miss Universe Carol Morris, who overacts but is acceptable as an optimistic young dreamer who loves the boy next door. But you'll get a bigger kick out of the familiar Hollywood faces: Billy Gilbert, Margaret Hamilton, Marie Windsor, Chester Conklin, Corinne Griffith, William Schallert.

PARALLAX VIEW, THE (1974) C/102m. Reporter Warren Beatty discovers that many people who witnessed the assassination of a senator have died mysteriously, although none knew of the presence of a *second* gun (Bill McKinney). Using an alias, he applies for a position with the Parallax Corporation, which he believes trains political assassins. He doesn't realize that he's being set up as the fall guy in a forthcoming assassination plot. This nerve-racking, loose adaptation of Loren Singer's muddled novel, directed by Alan J. Pakula and written by David Giler and Lorenzo Semple, Jr., falls into that suspense-spy-horror genre that caters to us paranoids who are sure there are active conspiracies (in and out of government) geared to undermine the democratic political process and root out (ruin, set up, dispose of) various individuals (business competitors, political opposition, charismatic leaders, those who know too much). The one film to come up constantly during conversations in which people theorize about the John Kennedy assassination, this is our blueprint for conspiratorial machinery: no political-paranoia film more believably details (it all seems so simple) how a conspiratorial network can pull off political assassinations, get away scot-free, and leave a fall guy—the proverbial social misfit—to take the rap. We see that even the cleverest, most resourceful *individual* cannot triumph agaist the corporation—truth does not win out as in *All the President's Men*. This film is strangely satisfying because it agrees that our paranoia is well founded. In this definitive paranoia film, casual acquaintances are not to be trusted, strangers are enemies. Characters are always filmed standing behind glass or curtains, in shadows, or in longshot or extreme close-up, so we don't see what's around them—often we see only their reflections on glass or water. Sometimes we glimpse only parts of bodies—at other times we see no one at all. To further build our tension and jolt us, Pakula uses sound brilliantly: whispering voices, explosions, gunshots, ringing phones, clinking glass, ticking clocks, blasting sirens, etc.; the chilly music also contributes (trumpet fanfares that sound like death marches fade out just before catastrophes). Film's major flaws result from Pakula sacrificing story-clarifying scenes for pacing. But I like to believe that the information left out builds our paranoia and disorientation. Superb cinematography by Gordon Willis. Also with: Hume Cronyn (as Beatty's editor), Paula Prentiss, William Daniels, Kelly Thorsden, Earl Hindman, Kenneth Mars, Walter McGinn, Stacy Keach, Sr., Ford Rainey.

PARDNERS (1956) C/90m. I was happy to discover that one of my favorite childhood films is still pretty amusing. In their next-to-last film together, Dean Martin and Jerry Lewis are the sons of two dead cowboy heroes (whom the duo play in the opening sequence). Martin grew up in the West and is as brave and rugged as his dad, but baby-talking Lewis grew up in Manhattan, dominated by his rich mother (Agnes Moorehead). Having always wanted to be a cowboy, Lewis goes out west with Martin, who jokingly dubs him "Killer Jones" in hopes it will scare off the masked robbers who are terrorizing the territory. Sensing a patsy, the outlaws make Lewis sheriff. But even Lee Van Cleef isn't man enough to defeat Lewis. Script by Sidney Sheldon is funny and, for a change, Lewis's character is not only silly but has a sense of humor (witness his impersonations); he's a genuinely quirky fellow with a touch of rebelliousness (even toward his mother) and reckless abandon that was well suited to the neurotic young characters who populated the films of the day. He doesn't play for tears; and the scene in which he bullies an outlaw in a barroom is like nothing else in Lewis's career except when his Mr. Hyde-like Buddy Love humiliates the dean in *The Nutty Professor*. Snappy direction by Norman Taurog. Also with: Lori Nelson, Jackie Loughery, Jeff Morrow, John Baragrey, Lon Chaney, Jr.

PARENT TRAP, THE (1961) C/124m. In Hayley Mills's second film for Walt Disney (her follow-up to *Pollyanna*) she played two roles—which was a double treat for us boys who had crushes on her and girls who wanted to be her. This is a long way from being Hayley's best film, but I think it's the film her loyal fans feel the most nostalgia for because it really delighted us at the time. The beginning is much like *Little Darlings*. Hayley meets her lookalike at camp and they strike up a rivalry. But later they learn they are sisters. One girl lives with her mother (Maureen O'Hara) in Boston, the other with her father (Brian Keith) in California. The girls switch roles so each can get to know the parent on the opposite coast. They're like spies going undercover. When Dad plans to marry a woman (Joanna Barnes) who is after his money, the girls devise a plan to get their parents back together. It works. Overlong, predictable comedy hasn't much humor. But O'Hara and Keith make a spirited screen couple (they were in several films together), there are fine supporting performances by veteran character actors, and Mills is, of course, a delight. As in all her best films, her young girls exhibit feelings that the adults around them suppress in themselves, as well as a vibrant energy, wit, imagination and an optimistic view of the world that adults long ago allowed to slip away. These qualities, along with her mature talent, pretty features, and striking pre-Beatles British accent, are, I believe, what made her so popular. Adequate direction by David Swift. This was the second adaptation of Erich Kastner's novel *Lisa and Lottie*. Tommy Sands sings the title song, but more memorable is Mills's doubletracked hit "Let's Get Together" with a pre-Beatles "Yeah! Yeah! Yeah!." Also with: Charlie Ruggles,

Una Merkel, Leo G. Carroll, Cathleen Nesbitt, Ruth McDevitt, Nancy Kulp.

PARIS, TEXAS (1984) C/150m. Wim Wenders's German films typically dealt with men who spent their lives on the open road, escaping from marriages they couldn't cope with, and leaving behind wives and children they longed for, creating not only a destroyed marriage but a destroyed family. In his second American film, which was adapted from Sam Shepard story by L. M. "Kit" Carson, Wenders at last gives his hero the opportunity to put his family back together, to make up for all his mistakes as husband and father. And this time Wenders really brings home the meaning of the child to his hero. The film begins with Harry Dean Stanton walking catatonically through the Texas desert, his brain roasted by the sun, his mind gone from the break-up of his marriage four years ago. He is taken in by his brother (Dean Stockwell) and his sister-in-law (Aurore Clement), who have been taking care of Stanton's young son (Hunter Carson). The major part of the picture deals with how the father and son become acquainted and fall in love. Then they hit the road in search of Stanton's ex-wife (Natassja Kinski), who is also the boy's mother. The final third, written after the rest of the movie was filmed, has Stanton, who keeps his identity a secret, talking to Kinski, who works in a sex-fantasy booth. Only as strangers can they reflect on what went wrong with their marriage and what they desire in relationships. It is Stanton's desire to reunite mother and son. This is the kind of arty picture that some people applaud for its revelations about familial relationships while others accuse it of being shamefully pretentious. Story has the potential to be a real charmer, but Wenders, Carson, and cinematographer Robby Müller approach material dispassionately. There are tears, there is humor, but Wenders's unbearably slow pacing and the bleakness of Texas landscape and cityscape overwhelm characters, minimalizing their touching moments and almost depriving the picture of warmth. Even if you're not a romantic, the resolution is unsatisfying.

PARTY, THE (1968) C/99m. Blake Edwards and Peter Sellers teamed up for this almost forgotten non-*Pink Panther* comedy that contains some of the most hilarious sight gags in either's career. In one of his greatest roles, Sellers is perfectly cast as the well-meaning but destructive Hrundi V. Bakski, an actor from India who is working as an extra in Hollywood. At the desert location where a major action sequence is being filmed for an epic adventure, Hrundi accidentally blows up an expensive set before the cue. The hysterical director informs him that he is fired and will never work in pictures again; Hrundi, who can never take a hint, politely asks for clarification: "Does that include *television*?" That night he is mistakenly invited to a big party being thrown by the director. He wanders through the ritzy house, mingling with the guests and causing extraordinary havoc. His character is a mix of Hulot and Clouseau, and takes a back seat to neither. This would be a genuine comedy

masterpiece if it didn't fall apart about two thirds of the way through when the subtle humor suddenly becomes stupid and sloppy. But by all means give it a look. Also with: Claudine Longet, Marge Champion, Denny Miller, Gavin MacLeod, Buddy Lester, Steven Franken.

PASSAGE TO INDIA, A (BRITISH/1984) C/160m. After a 14-year hiatus, David Lean wrote and directed this epic adaptation of E. M. Forster's novel, which had long been considered unfilmable. Having sailed from England, Miss Quested (Judy Davis) and the elderly Mrs. Moore (Peggy Ashcroft) arrive in a British-controlled Indian town where Mrs. Moore's son, Ronny (Nigel Havers), Miss Quested's fiancé, is magistrate. The two visitors are upset that the British officers and their wives treat the Indians with disdain, never "lowering" themselves to socialize with them. They are embarrassed to witness the haughty display by the English, including Ronny. Only Fielding (James Fox) treats Indians as his equals. Wanting to see the "real India," Miss Quested and Mrs. Moore agree to go on an outing to the famous Marabar Caves with a widower friend of Fielding's, the Indian Dr. Aziz (Victor Banerjee), whom the kind Mrs. Moore trusts. Aziz and Miss Quested go to the top cave alone. Remember the sexual tension when the virgin girls move through phallic and vaginal rock formations in *Picnic at Hanging Rock*? That sensation is captured again when the dazed, sexually repressed/frustrated Miss Quested stands inside a dark cave and looks out toward the entrance, where Aziz stands, ready to come inside. As in Forster, Lean does not reveal what takes place in this pivotal scene that leads to Aziz being placed on trial for attempted rape. Some viewers claim that Lean makes it clear Aziz is innocent—for one thing, he added an earlier scene not in the novel in which Miss Quested has a delirious (and possibly hallucinatory) reaction when coming upon some sexually explicit statues in the wilderness, which implies her entrance into the mysterious cave could cause her to have a similar response. But the way the cave sequence is filmed, which makes it seem impossible for Miss Quested to run out of the cave without running into Dr. Aziz (unless she only imagines him standing there), suggests that he did attempt something. (The film's last shot of her also suggests that he might have been guilty.) The differences in viewer opinions means Lean has managed to maintain the mystery in Forster. Unfortunately, the ambiguities that result from our not knowing what happened make us even further detached from the major characters than we already are. We watch an interesting story, we marvel at the majestic sights, and we're impressed by the acting, yet it's hard to be more than a spectator and get emotionally involved. We delight in watching Lean become another British director to take swipes at the snooty British upper crust, but his failure to individualize a sufficient number of Indians—Aziz's friends are interchangeable, the illiterate function only as mobs—is regrettable. It's also hard to tell if Lean is trying to impress us with the glorious scenery or the cinematography itself.

Maurice Jarre won an Oscar for Best Score and Ashcroft was Best Supporting Actress. Also with: Alec Guinness.

PASSENGER, THE (ITALIAN-FRENCH-SPANISH/1975) C/119m.

This much-anticipated collaboration between Michelangelo Antonioni and Jack Nicholson failed to deliver the expected fireworks. Nicholson plays an English television documentarian who is on location in a remote section of Africa, trying to interview leftist guerillas. A man who resembles him dies in the hotel. Unhappy with his own life—he has drifted apart from wife Jenny Runacre; like Robert Forster in *Medium Cool*, he remains detached from the political stories he covers (which is why Runacre doesn't respect him)—he takes the other man's passport and identity. He follows the other man's appointments—it turns out he was running guns to support the revolution. So, for the first time, Nicholson gets involved in a political action. And there are counter-revolutionaries acting to stop him. Maria Schneider is the stranger who joins Nicholson as he travels around to keep appointments and encourages him in his attempt to be committed to something worthwhile. Meanwhile Runacre suddenly decides her husband was special and, after figuring out that he has assumed another's identity, tries to track him down before he walks into danger. Film has an intriguing premise, but is curiously uninvolving. The pacing is excruciatingly slow, there is little sexual electricity between Nicholson and Schneider (who kept her clothes on after her *Last Tango in Paris* experience), and because Nicholson never verbalizes his reasons for going through with the mission, he seems to be more on a fool's errand than a journey of political growth. If the script bores you, you'll still enjoy the striking cinematography and fascinating locations. Also with: Ian Hendry, Stephen Berkoff.

PASSION DE JEANNE D'ARC, LE/PASSION OF JOAN OF ARC, THE (FRENCH/1928) B&W/76m–110m.

One of the greatest, most intense films ever made. Danish director Carl Dreyer originally intended to base his work on a treatment by Joseph Delteil (credited as co-scenarist), the Dadaist who wrote the prize-winning novel *Vie de Jeanne d'Arc*. But instead he wrote his own story based on Pierre Champion's transcript of the actual trial of Jeanne d'Arc (Renée Falconetti), at which a court of ecclesiastics in Rouen, in 1431, unsuccessfully attempted to get their famous prisoner to admit that when she fought against the occupying British forces she was not on a divine mission (she claimed to have seen Saint Michael) but had actually been consorting with Satan. The long trial, spread over three months and numerous interrogation sessions, was condensed to just one day, encompassing five interrogations, Jeanne's confession in order to save her life, her recantation of that confession, her execution, and a small revolt by French spectators who realize that a saint has been burned at the stake in the name of religion. Until the scene in which troops push the angry French out of the castle, the entire film is shot in dramatic close-up. The actors, who actually spoke all their lines although this is a silent film, didn't use make-up; we see the imperfection of humanity in the warts on the ecclesiastics' angry faces and spittle on their lips and, more significantly, grasp that the souls of the Church elite have long been corrupted while that of the poor peasant girl has remained pure. How vulnerable is the defenseless Jeanne when she listens to these men, and how beautiful and secure she is when she listens instead to God. And how these hypocrites back away, afraid and uncertain, when Jeanne bravely turns the tables on them and accuses *them* of doing the devil's work. As in his later films, Dreyer examined the consequences of an individual having too much faith in God in an imperfect world where those in the religious establishment pervert religion to achieve personal gain and persecute those like Jeanne whom they should emulate. Dreyer creates a sense of feverishness and horror at the trial through repeated camera pans across the line of intimidating inquisitors, eerie zooms into their ugly faces as they menacingly move forward toward Jeanne, and sharp camera angles which make the inquisitors especially domineering. But we are constantly surprised to feel waves of tranquillity come over us each time Jeanne looks to the heavens and, judging from her smile and the calm look in her eyes, is obviously in a state of grace—only the tears on her cheeks remind us of the terrible things that have happened and will continue to happen to her during the course of this farcical trial. The actors got so much into their roles that bystanders heard them condemning Jeanne d'Arc off screen as well as on. And it's probable that Falconetti really got to feel she was Jeanne, so strongly and believably does she convey the young martyr's feelings. Dreyer discovered her doing boulevard comedy—this would be her only film. Rudolph Maté did the remarkable cinematography. The sets were designed and built by Hermann Warm and Jean Hugo. Also with: Eugène Silvain, Maurice Schutz, Michel Simon, Antonin Artaud (as the sympathetic Jean Massieu), Louis Ravet, Jean d'Yd.

PATHER PANCHALI (INDIAN/1955) B&W/112m.

Satyajit Ray's debut film, the first of his wondrous *Apu Trilogy* (based on the 1939 novel *Aparajito* by Bibhuti Bandapaddhay), has an almost documentary feel to it, so authentic is his depiction of love in a small Bengali village, circa 1915. Apu (Subir Banerji) is a little boy of about five in this film and he plays a subordinate role to the other members of his family, whom he watches with his soulful eyes: his sister (Das Gupta), who is about ten, his parents (Kanu Banerji, Karuna Banerji), and his 80-year-old, crone-like Auntie (Chunibala Devi), quite a character. The kids play, father remains optimistic despite having little money, letting his wife do all the worrying about town gossip, about Auntie's bad influence on her daughter (who steals fruit for her, and is accused of snatching a necklace), about the kids not having enough to eat (they get less because Auntie must eat), about the house being in disrepair, and most of all, about their poverty. Karuna Banerji is a remarkable actress—with a slight turn of the head, a worried look inward with her beautiful eyes, an almost imperceptible intake of air, she conveys immense anguish—getting her to smile is a hard-fought task, but worth it. Picture begins as if it were stressing universal qualities that the two children possess: they lick their lips as the candy man passes by, they attend festivals, they run through fields and woods, they get excited when they see trains (Ray's favorite fate symbol), they fight when Apu gets into a big sister's stuff— she desires the pretty trinkets of her rich neighbors. But the characters are distinctly Indian—and significantly different from any Indians we've seen in movies or on PBS—and the harshness of their lives is due to their unique, impoverished circumstances and a pride that keeps them from asking for needed help. Beautiful, unpretentiously sensitive film has humor, but it is extremely sad. The scene in which the mother refuses to allow Auntie, the family burden, to return home is absolutely heartbreaking. I'll never forget the old lady attempting a wild smile as the first move to patch up their differences, only to stop smiling when she gets no response. The characters in the film (including neighbors) love each other, but this doesn't stop them from hurting each other repeatedly. What is so special are those rare moments when they reveal their love (i.e., Apu's remarkably intelligent final act for his sister). There is much tragedy, as there is in the other Apu films, but as this one ends, survivors hit the road unvanquished. See this before you see the sequels: *Aparajito* and *The World of Apu*. Music by Ravi Shankar.

PATHS OF GLORY (1957) B&W/86m.

Stanley Kubrick's powerful drama is primarily an attack on the military mind, a scathing attack on the top brass of all armies who are willing to sacrifice their own men, their pawns, rather than look weak. While it doesn't contend that wars shouldn't be conducted, it succeeds as an anti-war film because it makes it clear that the innocent, powerless men in the trenches will always be at the mercy of super-patriotic, narrow-minded generals who are obsessed with flag and country but have no feelings for the obedient foot soldier. Sympathetic Colonel Kirk Douglas reminds crazed General George Macready of Samuel Johnson's view: "Patriotism is the last refuge of a scoundrel." Set in France during WWI, plot has Macready ordering suicidal attack on a German post. Almost all the men are mowed down as soon as they leave the trenches. Others wisely hold back, infuriating Macready so much that he tries to give an order that will result in his own men being fired upon. When this doesn't work, he sets up the court-martial of one man from each of three platoons. Platoon commanders select Timothy Carey (chosen because he's an "undesirable"), Ralph Meeker (who was witness to his commander's cowardice), and Joseph Turkel (chosen by lot). Douglas defends them at a military trial, but he has no opportunity to build a case for the defense. They are to be executed. The excellent script by Kubrick, Calder Willingham, and Jim Thompson is unrelentingly bleak but thought-provoking—earlier films presented evil generals, but none before contended that the entire military system was evil. Only false note is Douglas's last line to General Adolphe Menjou: "I pity you." He should say something much stronger. Film is extremely intense but not heavy-handed; Kubrick's handling of actors has never been better. The most frightening thing about the generals is that they're not much different from the military men in *Dr. Strangelove*. Also with: Wayne Morris, Bert Freed, Emile Meyer, Richard Anderson.

PAYDAY (1973) C/103m.

Second-rate country-music singer Maury Dann (Rip Torn) uses people like no one in the cinema since Robert Montgomery's washed-up producer in *The Saxon Charm* (1948). Daryl Duke's low-budget film takes us on the road with Maury, where we watch him on a wild booze-pills-marijuana-sex death trip. Film, made in Alabama, got excellent reviews and has a cult following, but I find it excruciatingly unpleasant, not that far removed from *The Rose*. Even offbeat well-played scenes, such as those between pathetic Maury and his young groupie whom he seduces while his girlfriend sleeps, are unsettling. Torn's performance has much power, but is uneven. I never believe he's a country singer. In fact, I don't know why writer Don Carpenter felt it necessary to make him a country singer. Maury makes life miserable for the characters played by Ahna Capri (Maury's girlfriend), Michael C. Gwynne (Maury's manager), Elayne Heilveil (Maury's seemingly straitlaced groupie), Cliff Emmich (Maury's loyal chauffeur).

PEEPING TOM (BRITISH/1960) C/103m.

Michael Powell's once damned but now justifiably praised cult film is about a mentally disturbed filmmaker (Carl Boehm) who kills women while photographing their deaths— because he's obsessed with capturing the pinnacle of fear in his victim's expressions, he places a mirror on his camera so that they can view their own murders. Upon its release, critics were upset that Powell presented that rare cinema murderer whose violent acts corresponded to sexual gratification. Powell doesn't try to be subtle: the long, sharp, hidden knife that is attached to Boehm's camera emerges just before his murders, immediately "exposing" Boehm's sexual frenzy. But in Boehm's peculiar case the murder of a woman does not by itself bring him sexual satisfaction. His onanistic "climax" takes place when he projects the woman's dying expression on the wall in his room. Powell is making the distinction between *participation* in a brutal act (count us viewers out) and voyeurism (count us viewers in). He is making us *identify* with Boehm because we share his voyeuristic tendencies—like him, we are entranced by horrible images on the screen: murders, rapes, even mutilation. Voyeurs like us are in complicity with filmmakers who place brutal, pornographic images on the screen for our gratification. If the voyeur is guilty of violating one's privacy, then Powell sees the filmmaker as being guilty of aggressive acts not unlike *rape* (where you steal a moment in time, and a person's emotions, that the person can never have back). And Powell sees the filmmaker as *scientist*. Both are destructive artists, experimenters, outcasts. To each, the end justifies the means. The villain of the picture is not Boehm but Boehm's dead scientist father (played by Powell in a flashback), who used his young son as guinea pig, terrifying him and filming him to study the effects of fear on the boy's nervous system. With a camera in his hands, the filmmaker stops being a human being and becomes a *scientist*, and Boehm figures that since his scientist-filmmaker father in effect "murdered" him, his guinea pig, then he, also a filmmaker-scientist, has the right to kill human beings when continuing Dad's experiments. Strangely, Boehm bears his father no grudge. The women he kills remind him of his stepmother (whom he calls "surrogate female"), who likely interfered with the relationship father and son were developing as a result of the noxious experiment. Her home movie of Boehm was *out of focus*—that Boehm strives for photographic impeccability shows he wants to prove to be a better partner than this woman who didn't know how to use a camera. A sleazy-looking—after all, the subject is sordid—but amazingly provocative picture. Not for all tastes. Unusual characters are played by: Moira Shearer, Anna Massey, Maxine Audley, Esmond Knight, Bartlet Mullins, Shirley Ann Field, Nigel Davenport, Brenda Bruce, Martin Miller, Pamela Green.

PEE-WEE'S BIG ADVENTURE (1985) C/92m.

If you had a fleeting glimpse of Pee-Wee Herman on television, you might have intentionally avoided his debut film when released, as I did. But there is good reason that it has earned a reputation as a genuine *sleeper* which adults may like as much as the kids who were its original audience. It's a film with unexpected delights, including a smartly conceived performance by the star. Obviously, Pee-Wee (Paul Reubens) was completely in tune with his co-writers, Michael Varhol and Phil Hartman (a longtime associate), and 26-year-old debut director Tim Burton, whose manic, rhythmic style perfectly matches Pee-Wee's character. Pee-Wee dresses in white shoes, socks, and shirt, a tight gray suit that has a white hanky in the pocket of the buttoned jacket, and a red bow tie; he has a crew cut, wears lipstick and rouge, but makes no attempt to conceal the heavy bags under his eyes. He looks like the quintessential eccentric, nerdy junior-high science teacher. His character is a combination of Pinky Lee, Jerry Lewis's frantic "kid," Martin Short's Ed Grimley, and Eddie Deezen; his contraption-filled home is like something Buster Keaton might have dreamed up. What's most interesting is that his character isn't particularly sympathetic—indeed, Herman obviously realizes that his voice, nervous-habitual laugh, and twisted, smily face are quite annoying. He's a quirky fellow—"a loner, a rebel"—who is far from being an angel; see how he treats his obnoxious neighbor (Mark Holton)—they have a great argument. As you watch this guy zip around in his private little world, you'll be baffled, not awed, that such a character exists (other than in the seat behind you on the bus), and you'll find yourself giggling. Film has Pee-Wee hitting the roads of America to track down his stolen bike, his prized possession. He meets a lot of characters who are almost as

weird as he is. The funniest scene has Pee-Wee suffering through an interminable tour of the Alamo, conducted by a smiling, boring, gum-chewing girl, just so he can look for his bike in the basement (there is no basement in the Alamo). Film bogs down during an obligatory destructive chase scene, but comes back with a novel ending. Now I look forward to the next Pee-Wee Herman movie. Effective music by Danny Elfman, cinematography by Victor J. Kemper. Also with Elizabeth Daily, Diane Salinger, Judd Omen, Ed Herlihy, James Brolin (cameo), Morgan Fairchild (cameo).

PENNIES FROM HEAVEN (1981) C/107m.

The grimmest of all movie musicals (including *Marat/Sade*), yet one of the most fascinating and visually dazzling. It's set in the Depression and, though stylized so that there is no *reality* evident, it contrasts the reality of the Depression with the happy songs and escapist RKO and M-G-M thirties musicals. As a Brechtian alienation device, depressed characters in unhappy situations suddenly imagine themselves as participants in huge production numbers (elaborately staged by Danny Daniels) and happily lip-synching hits of the day (by Astaire, Crosby, Connee Boswell, Helen Kane, etc.). Story, which Dennis Potter adapted from his BBC-TV series, is about the traveling salesman who knocks up a trusting schoolteacher. Steve Martin, in a versatile performance, is unhappily married to contentedly frigid Jessica Harper. Frustrated at home, he's also frustrated that he can't quit his unprofitable job selling sheet music and open a record store—but Harper won't give him the money. He falls for teacher Bernadette Peters, who is the passionate lover he always dreamed about. She becomes pregnant and, after Martin runs off, has an abortion. When Martin finds her again, she is a prostitute. They run off together, but there is no happiness at the end of a rainbow. Sex and songs are presented as liberating forces, but they're only Band-Aids against the Depression—there are perverse forms of each (rape, unhappy songs)—and even in their purest forms are not nearly as strong as poverty, the lack of hope, and fate (which is much more significant in this film that in the thirties musicals). Film is so cheerless that you become anesthetized even while recognizing the artistry of what's taking place on the screen. Picture has an extraordinary look—it includes re-creations of paintings by Edward Hopper and other painters and photographers of the period. Directed by Herbert Ross, who surprised everyone by stepping so far out of the mainstream. Gordon Willis was the cinematographer, Bob Mackie the costume designer. Also with: Vernel Bagneris, Christopher Walken (who has a big tap number), Tommy Rall, John McMartin, Jay Garner.

PENNY SERENADE (1941) B&W/125m.

One of Hollywood's genuine tearjerkers, directed by George Stevens. Cary Grant and Irene Dunne give sensitive performances as a young couple who fall in love and marry. He has always said he didn't care about kids, but he is delighted when Dunne informs him she's pregnant. When Dunne miscarries and is told that she can't have kids, they adopt a baby girl. Although Grant has trouble making any money with his smalltown newspaper, they provide a happy home for the growing girl. Then tragedy strikes—and it appears that Dunne and Grant will break up. Occasionally you get angry because the film unabashedly milks the tears, but at least these characters are worth getting emotional about. You'll find it difficult remaining composed when Grant gives an impassioned plea to a stern judge to let them keep the child despite his lack of income, and when he brings the baby girl home to his grieving wife (who thought she'd never see her again), and when the proud parents watch the young girl in the school Christmas play, and when, in the last scene, they are given another chance for happiness. Film has tremendous warmth, lots of humor—the best sequence may be the one in which the new parents bring home their new family member and realize they don't know the first thing about taking care of a baby. Picture is so well made and acted that you'll forgive being manipulated. However, Morrie Ryskind's script has one problem: entire film is comprised of flashbacks as recalled by Dunne, yet at the end, after *she* has remembered all the wonderful things that Grant did, *she*, not Grant—who hasn't been remembering what a fine couple they have been through the years—wants out of the marriage. Also with: Edgar Buchanan (as the indispensable Uncle Jack), Beulah Bondi, Ann Doran, Eva Lee Kuney.

PÉPÉ LE MOKO (FRENCH/1937) B&W/85m.
Not as exotic as *Algiers*, the American remake starring Charles Boyer (who'd turned down this film) and Hedy Lamarr, but a much better film. As the Parisian thief who has found unhappy sanctuary in the depressing Algiers Casbah, Jean Gabin is so naturally charismatic, suave, and charming that we tend to overlook that he's not a nice guy: he treats his loyal native girlfriend Inès (Line Noro) like disposable trash; he not only fails to protect his youngest gang member (Gilbert Gil) but also sends his most trusting friend (Gabriel Gabrio) on a fool's errand that gets him arrested. Yet we don't find him immoral, just as we find nothing objectionable about Gaby (Mireille Balin), the beautiful Parisian woman with whom he has an affair, although she is *mistress* to an older, fat rich tourist (Charles Granval) and she admits that in her life before she wore jewels she schemed about how to get them. We find that their love for each other transcends past transgressions and we root for their happiness. Considering that this is one of the great cinema romances, it's strange that the novel, written by Detective Ashelbé (a pseudonym for Henri La Barthe, a high-rank Parisian police official who'd once been stationed in Algiers), was inspired by the non-romantic *Scarface*; while Pépé's gang members recall Muni's stupid, brutal men, Gabin's Pépé is so much more refined than Muni's Tony—and a *lover* (he expects 300 widows to show up at his funeral), not a pervert (Tony loved his sister most of all). Pépé is certainly much more likable than the slimy detective Slimane (Lucas Gridoux) who sets a trap for him by making him leave the Casbah in search of Gaby, who he made sure believes Pépé is dead. Direction by Julien Duvivier is the best of his career. His camera is very mobile and some of the finest moments occur when he moves away from his characters' faces and focuses on Pépé's shoes, Gaby's jewelry, or other props. In my favorite scene the director has Tania (Fréhel), a chubby, poor, middle-aged woman, tearfully and beautifully sing along with the moving French torch song. (Pépé isn't the only one whose life is slipping away in the Casbah.) Scenes in which Pépé and Gaby speak nostalgically of Paris work so well because it's obvious that Duvivier (who wrote the script with Henri Jeanson, Ashelbé, and Jacques Constant) shares their passion. Also with: Marcel Dalio, Saturnin Fabre.

PERFORMANCE (BRITISH/1970) C/106m.
From the first frame, one feels that directors Nicolas Roeg and Donald Cammell (who wrote the screenplay) are resting their dirtiest fingers at the backs of our throats. They bombard us with brutal images—a forced head-shaving that's like an amputation, a whipping, a beating, a bullet entering a skull—that seem designed to make us nauseous. Their film may be a personally successful rendering of a personal vision, but it's no labor of love. It's an arrogant, needless slap at our viewing sensibilities; an odious, amoral work, its oozing decadence is as manifest behind the camera as it is on the screen. James Fox plays a murderous London protection-racket hood who hides out in the mansion of reclusive ex–rock star Mick Jagger. Under the influence of Jagger's two love-mates, Anita Pallenberg and Michele Breton, he eats hallucinogenic mushrooms, wears wigs and outrageous costumes, makes love to them both. Jagger becomes fascinated with him, wants to get into his brain to see what makes him tick and perhaps to be a gangster like him. The four characters start to blend together, become interchangeable. The savage Fox and Jagger are able to merge together because, according to the filmmakers, everyone is part violent and part gentle, part male and part female, part "normal" and part "perverted," part of each other. In the films of Roeg it is essential for man to adapt to new environments. Here the "straight" Fox adapts to a house of love and perversion by uncovering and activating previously latent aspects of his personality and discovering his true self (for example, he has homosexual tendencies). As in other Roeg films, there are trick shots, wild cross-cutting, quick transitions, sexual activity (especially around water) and a strong emphasis on color. But this is the only film I can think of in which every image causes us to recall a familiar *odor*. The most erotic image has the fur-coated Pallenberg lying on a bed while talking to stranger Fox and fondling the fur over her otherwise naked crotch. Acting by women is okay, but once Fox reaches the house he seems stranded among amateurs; Jagger comes across as awkward, withdrawn, and so restricted that he sings one song from behind a desk. Released at a time when young audiences were into anything Jagger did, as well as heady, ambitious projects with blaring soundtracks and antisocial characters who turn on to dope and sex at the drop of the director's hat, it became

a cult favorite. Also with: Johnny Shannon, Anthony Valentine, Ken Colley.

PERSONA (SWEDISH/1966) B&W/81m–85m–90m.   Released in the U.S. in 1967, Ingmar Bergman's intense, powerful film had tremendous impact on American viewers. His first film with Liv Ullmann, it ushered in a new era of Bergman films, ones that we felt we didn't have to seek out and discover but ones that seemed directed toward us. It excited us not only because it made us aware of the filmmaking process (we're always aware of Bergman's camera—we even see it at one point) and the unique power film has to tell stories, make personal and/or political points, and probe the minds of characters, but also because it dealt with themes that were relevant: isolation, identity, alienation, communication, loneliness, guilt, horror, schizophrenia. Bibi Andersson is an inexperienced, modest nurse who is assigned to take care of great actress Liv Ullmann, who has withdrawn into silence. They stay together in an isolated beach house and, while Ullmann listens, Andersson opens up and talks and talks, revealing her deepest secrets—a sexual interlude on a beach with two young boys, her misery over an abortion. The two seem drawn together, but after a betrayal they split apart. Meanwhile Bergman places the two actresses, who resemble each other, in close proximity and uses camera tricks (superimpositions/split screen) to make it seem as if the two different women were fusing into one character. Could it be that they're exchanging identities? Are the two women the split halves of a schizophrenic woman? If so, then is the nurse real and the actress imaginary? Or is it the actress who is real? Or, perhaps, is this woman neither an actress nor a nurse? Bergman doesn't let us know the answers. Figuring out—or not being able to figure out—the puzzle is much of the fun. Acting by Andersson is excellent. I'd been impressed by Ullmann back in 1967, but, seeing the film today, I'm struck by how passive her performance is. The best scene is Andersson's long, erotic monologue about the boys and the beach—perhaps this is what Godard was parodying in *Weekend* when he allows Mireille Darc to recall in great detail an orgy that at first sounds erotic and then sounds ridiculous. Cinematography by Sven Nykvist. Also with: Gunnar Björnstrand, Margaretha Krook.

PERSONAL BEST (1982) C/124m.   Young athlete Mariel Hemingway, under tremendous pressure from her father to make the Olympic team, is taken under wing by a more experienced Patrice Donnelly, who is her competitor for a spot in the pentathalon competition. They fall in love and live together. Hemingway becomes confused and the relationship becomes tense. When she wrongly believes that Donnelly tried to injure her during practice so Donnelly's position on the team would improve, Hemingway walks out. She gets a boyfriend (Kenny Moore). Controversial, underappreciated film was written and directed by Robert Towne (who won the Oscar for his *Chinatown* script). Towne's undisguised celebration of the bodies of female athletes, the full frontal nudity of women in the locker rooms and steam rooms, and frank lesbian scenes with Hemingway and Donnelly, the raunchy female dialogue, and the scene in which Hemingway follows Moore into the bathroom to watch him urinate all serve Towne's purpose: he succeeds in taking what we consider tasteless and deviant acts and making them seem perfectly natural and unembarrassing. We accept Donnelly's homosexuality and don't begrudge her initiating the naïve Hemingway into a lesbian affair—although it might be true that once Hemingway figures out her self-identity she'll discover herself to be heterosexual. It's also interesting that we feel happy that probable-heterosexual Hemingway got to experience one beneficial and exciting homosexual experience. That's because Hemingway feels no guilt about the affair and no anger toward Donnelly for possibly taking advantage of her. What's evident is that Towne likes his women. They are funny, sensitive, dedicated, self-confident, competitive yet supportive, strong, and, because they're athletes, beautiful. I find the track scenes a bit hokey, especially when the two women vie for coach Scott Glenn's approval, but Towne's handling of the relationship between Hemingway and Donnelly (a true athlete who gives a surprisingly sympathetic performance) is honest and brave. Significantly, he is unafraid to make their scenes together erotic and extremely physical—which is why this film succeeds while the antiseptically tame *male* homosexuality picture *Making Love*, also made in 1982, fails. Also with: Jim Moody, Larry Pennell.

PERSONALS, THE (1982) C/90m.   Low-budget independent picture, filmed in Minneapolis, about a lonely divorced guy (Bill Schoppert) who takes up roller-skating to relieve his boredom and meet women. He ends up putting an ad in the personals. After one ridiculous blind date with an overly aggressive woman (a very funny scene), he seems to luck out with a smart, pretty professional woman (Karen Landry) who is on his wavelength. He has a roller-skating partner and, he believes, a partner for life. Then she tells him she is married. Character comedy has wit and moments of undeniable charm, as well as believable performances from leads who are welcome change from Hollywood types. But picture is almost ruined by self-conscious direction by Peter Markle; it's as if he were standing behind the camera the whole time saying, "Isn't that exactly how life is!!!" Also: there's too much roller-skating! Catchy Nicolette Larson songs are used on the soundtrack.

PETRIFIED FOREST, THE (1936) B&W/83m. Robert E. Sherwood's philosophical play provided the cinema with one of its few intellectual protagonists who wasn't a mad scientist. Reprising his Broadway role, Leslie Howard is a penniless, world-beaten, failed writer who has come to America from Europe. While hitching through Arizona's desert, he finds its lone flower, Bette Davis, a kind, generous, aspiring artist who is stuck working as a waitress in her father's isolated gas-station café. The two immediately fall in love, but he turns down her offer to someday go to

France with him because he thinks his talent has run dry while hers is just blooming. Also reprising his Broadway role, Humphrey Bogart is Duke Mantee (his first important movie role), a fugitive killer who arrives at the café with three accomplices—just when the self-pitying Howard has worn out our patience. While waiting for Bogart's girlfriend to arrive, they hold Howard, Davis, Davis's stingy but likable grandfather (Charley Grapewin), and several others hostage. The handsome, refined Howard, whose every sentence sounds like a line from a romantic poem, convinces the ugly Mantee, who walks like a gorilla, keeps his chin stuck to his chest, and grunts rather than speaks, that they are similar because both are willing to die for a woman. Bogart agrees to kill Howard so Davis can collect on his insurance policy. Adaptation is a bit stagy but generally well directed by Archie Mayo. Wide-eyed Davis gives a fine, unassuming performance, and Howard, if he'd just stop talking for five seconds, is a good match for her. Bogart and the other supporting players are well cast. Film contains interesting scenes in which a black gangster reminds a black chauffeur, who needs orders from his rich white boss before doing anything, that they've been emancipated; and the wife of the rich man tells him off for having ruined her life by ending her acting career. Sherwood's play is about the need for every repressed person to rebel against the particular "order"—be it sexual, financial, racial, physical—in which he finds himself. It's most important for poets to fight against nature and dismantle the natural Darwinian order that states the physically fit should rule. Also with: Genevieve Tobin, Porter Hall, Joe Sawyer, Dick Foran, Slim Thompson, Eddie Acuff, Paul Harvey, John Alexander.

PETULIA (1968) C/105m. Archie Bollen (George C. Scott) is a bored, middle-aged San Francisco surgeon who is trying to adjust to single life after a lengthy marriage. He meets Petulia (Julie Christie), a screwed-up young married woman who convinces him to have an affair and insists that they'll marry. He is fascinated by her unpredictability and feels she has pumped new life into him. She loves him for his gentle hands—her husband, David (Richard Chamberlain), has been using his hands to beat her up because she has refused to have sex with him since he was impotent on their wedding night. Archie worries about Petulia's welfare if she should go back to David. Richard Lester's shattering vision of America in the late sixties is a brilliant, expertly acted film, so rich in character and visual and aural detail that it takes several viewings to absorb it all. On one level it is a wildly comical essay on a country gone haywire; but at heart it is a tragic look at the individuals who must fight a (losing) battle for survival in a zany world. Lester is the baffled, sympathetic outsider examining a culture that has somehow gone awry and exists solely on the momentum of its own death trip. The great American tragedy is that a country founded by a resourceful, enterprising, responsible people of high values and ideals has become so utterly wasteful of money, time, human life (Vietnam is ignored by a desensitized nation), and human potential. America's institutions—the army, hospitals, prisons—are as impotent as David is in bed. Even marriage is a casualty of the modern age: *boredom* is an adequate reason for a man to leave his wife; a battered wife is no longer required to stay with her husband. America is spinning too fast, there is no solid footing—and there stands Petulia, symbol of the shaky times: mini-skirted, on wobbly legs. Her face is stoical, but her eyes indicate she has lost something irretrievable and sees a road downhill to oblivion. I think she yearns for a return to "innocence"—to a time when she wasn't capable of hurting anyone, before her wedding night. This film is about "casual violence," as Lester termed it, that invariably occurs when two people attempt a relationship in our topsy-turvy society. The characters in this film, including David, are nice people who are hurt *by* others and who suffer tremendous guilt because they cause great pain *in* others. They are afraid of further commitment because they know that will cause more pain. Lester sees the whole of America as decadent, but his characters feel remorse because they are *moral* people. Picture has many great scenes—perhaps the most memorable is Archie's argument with ex-wife Polo (Shirley Knight). It's also technically interesting. The rapid-fire ending is deliberately oblique, with flashbacks—of events which didn't necessarily happen at all—and flash-forwards interjected at odd intervals. The fragmentary filmmaking is characteristic of both Lester and cinematographer Nicolas Roeg, who would soon be a director himself. The superb screenplay by Lawrence B. Marcus was adapted from John Haase's fine novel *Me and the Arch Kook Petulia*; it's the rare case in which the film alters book's happy ending. Music by John Barry. Also with: Arthur Hill, Pippa Scott, Kathleen Widdoes, Joseph Cotten, Roger Bowen, the Grateful Dead, Big Brother and the Holding Company, members of The Committee, members of the A.T.C. Company.

PHANTOM OF THE OPERA, THE (1925) B&W/79m. Classic silent horror film with Lon Chaney playing the phantom who haunts a great opera house in 19th-century Paris. The victim of torture, with a crazed mind and a hideous half-skeletal face that he covers with a mask, Chaney lives secretly in the forgotten torture chambers beneath the building. He is a great composer himself and would like to make a star of lovely singer Mary Philbin. He drives away the opera's star so Philbin can have the lead in *Faust*. He terrifies Philbin and makes her swear not to see boyfriend Norman Kerry again. When he discovers that she has betrayed him, Chaney no longer tries to control his evil side. First half of the film is slow, except for the classic unmasking scene in which we and Philbin see Chaney's face for the first time. (Also if you are lucky enough to see the film with a live organist, it's exciting when Chaney plays the organ on the screen and you can actually hear the music he's supposedly playing.) From the moment Chaney overhears Philbin and Kerry plotting to run away, the picture becomes an exciting, first-rate thriller set for the most part in the underground chambers, featuring fun gimmicks (secret doors, heat torture, chambers filling with water, Chaney committing clever murders) and a wild performance by Chaney (his last moment is inspired). As in *The Raven* and *Frankenstein*, story deals with significant horror premise: those who are monstrous-looking will act monstrously. Directed by Rupert Julian, with uncredited help from Edward Sedgwick and Chaney. From the novel by Gaston Leroux. Remade several times. Also with: Arthur Edmund Carewe, Snitz Edwards, Gibson Gowland, John Miljan.

PHANTOM OF THE PARADISE (1974) C/91m.

Brian De Palma's one-of-a-kind rock-music black-comedy horror film is a tribute to movies and filmmaking (from the silent era to the present) and a devastating attack on the mean-spirited glitter rock scene of the seventies, where young lynch mob–like audiences demanded increasingly vulgar and cruel entertainment. Winslow Leach (William Finley), back-up pianist for the Juicy Fruits, the nation's number-one rock group, writes serious music in his spare time. Wanting a new "sound" to open his Paradise nightclub, evil record producer Swan (Paul Williams), who has made a pact with the devil, steals Winslow's music and has Winslow busted for heroin possession. Winslow escapes from prison when he hears that the Juicy Fruits have a smash hit, singing his song. He destroys Swan's studio, but his face is mangled in a disc-press machine. He dons a cape and a bird mask and haunts the Paradise. He wants to make sure that the lovely Phoenix (Jessica Harper) and not the gay, pill-popping Beef (Gerrit Grahame) sings his cantata. Film is flawed throughout and has a terribly trite and confused ending, but it also has amazing vitality, wild humor, a clever score by Williams, a likable cast, and visual bravura. Stylistically, De Palma pays homage to Hitchcock, Rouben Mamoulian's *Dr. Jekyll and Mr. Hyde*, silent American films like Lon Chaney's *Phantom of the Opera*, and silent German expressionist films like *The Cabinet of Dr. Caligari* (the distorted images, the high-key lighting, the surreal Jack Fisk sets that seem appropriate for an amusement-park crazy house). All this he juxtaposes with modern techniques (i.e., split screen), "hip" irreverent humor, and violence, the distinguishing trait of seventies horror films. Poorly received by many critics when released, it has attained a large cult following. Also with: George Memmoli, Keith Allison, Jeffrey Comaner, Archie Hahn, and Harold Oblong (as the Juicy Fruits).

PHILADELPHIA STORY, THE (1940) B&W/112m.

Classic screwball comedy was adapted from Philip Barry's 1939 Broadway success, which he'd written especially for Katharine Hepburn. She purchased the movie rights, realizing that it was the right vehicle for her return to Hollywood after a two-year hiatus. As rich socialite Tracy Lord, she got to play with her own public image, in an effort to show that underneath her haughty, classy exterior—the reason she had been designated box-office poison by theater owners—she was vulnerable and lovable. Tracy's problem, when the story begins, is that she doesn't forgive anyone their faults: she kicked out her husband (Cary Grant) because

he had a drinking problem and has rejected her father (John Halliday) because of his philandering. She's about to marry the "perfect" man (John Howard as a social climber) when Grant turns up, along with a *Spy* magazine reporter (James Stewart) and photographer (Ruth Hussey). During an eventful night in which she gets drunk herself, she comes to see her own imperfect side—and to like what she sees. She doesn't want to be the priggish goddess that Howard and Stewart are so taken with—but the *woman* Grant loves. The major problem with the play-film is that Tracy Lord never seems like a prig or someone who will accept only perfection—she is eccentric, funny, wild, and *tolerant* of unconventional people, like her flighty mother (Mary Nash), quirky younger sister (Virginia Weidler), and dirty old uncle (Roland Young). That she gave up on Grant and Halliday makes sense (in fact, in the long run it cured them)—there's no reason we must accept *their* opinions of her as being correct. Two other problems are that Grant is too passive a character and that Hussey really gets mistreated by Stewart without ever telling him off. Despite all, this is a scintillating comedy, because the acting by a wonderful cast transcends the material. As directed by George Cukor, the comic dialogues have a marvelous rhythm—the characters could be speaking Japanese, but so snappy are their comebacks and so sly are their expressions that we'd laugh anyway. Stewart won a Best Actor Oscar; Hepburn and Hussey are better, but lost out for Best Actress and Best Supporting Actress, respectively. Donald Ogden Stewart won for script adaptation. Produced by Joseph Mankiewicz. Also with: Henry Daniell.

PICNIC (1955) C/115m.

Insecure drifter William Holden hops off a train and wanders into the Kansas town where his college chum Cliff Robertson lives. Robertson invites him to the town picnic, where he antagonizes most of the adults, yet wins the heart of young, not very smart Kim Novak, Robertson's girlfriend. His presence arouses passions—he is a liberating influence, because everyone in town had seemed repressed. Joshua Logan's adaptation of William Inge's play is badly dated, especially in its portrayal of women. Novak actually starts to believe her mother's (Betty Field) propaganda that a woman must marry; script-writer Daniel Taradash makes Novak's decision to go off with Holden (who took a bellboy job) seem appropriate by depriving her of the dreams she had in the play—she has nothing to lose. Holden seems miscast; film would have worked better with Douglas Sirk directing Rock Hudson. Highlight is the hot "mating" dance (to "Moonglow") of Holden and Novak. Also with: Rosalind Russell (pretty intolerable), Arthur O'Connell, Verna Felton, Susan Strasberg (as Novak's sister, who, being an intellectual, isn't supposed to need a man), Nick Adams, Phyllis Newman.

PICNIC AT HANGING ROCK (AUSTRALIAN/1975) C/110m–115m.

Peter Weir's enigmatic cult film was adapted from the 1967 novel by Joan Lindsay, Australia's first female novelist from a well-known and esteemed aristocratic family. It's fiction passing as fact about the inexplicable disappearance of three young ladies and an instructor from Appleyard College as they explored Hanging Rock—a formidable, 500-foot high, million-year-old, uncharted volcanic formation—during a St. Valentine's Day picnic in 1900. The film's opening at Appleyard—girls wash in flower-scented water, whisper among themselves, hold hands, blow kisses, passionately read love poems, exchange valentines, and help each other tie their corsets while Weir injects cold, austere shots of the unfriendly school—conveys that domineering Mrs. Appleyard's (Rachel Roberts) school is not so much a finishing school as an institute for sexual repression. I believe that the ascent of the four dazed, dressed-in-white virgins through the surreal rock formation—where shots of phallic boulders merge with shots of narrow, vaginal passageways through the rocks—and their subsequent disappearance represents both their rite of passage into sexual womanhood and an escape into another world where there is no sexual repression. The key is lovely Miranda (Anne Lambert), who is not of this world. She is the embodiment of sexual desire stifled, as was her namesake in *The Tempest*. She is like a Peter Pan whose mission is to deliver herself and three other sexually repressed females into a sexual never-never land, far away from adults like Mrs. Appleyard and the uncaring parents who would entrust them to such a witch. The first part of the film is absolutely spellbinding—no picture has a more sinister atmosphere. But, compared to what happens on the Rock—a great, haunting, imaginatively photographed scene—everything that comes afterward is anticlimactic. Horror movies with sadistic headmistresses are a dime a dozen. Weir is faithful to Lindsay, but on the whole his film is less satisfying because we miss the first-person perspective of former Victorian boarding-school survivor Lindsay. Beautifully photographed by Russell Boyd, who put dyed (orange-yellow) wedding veils over his lens to capture the *feel* of Lindsay's outdoor scenes, to capture a "lost summer" feeling. Also with: Dominic Guard, Vivean Gray, Helen Morse, Karen Robinson (as Irma, the missing girl who returns with amnesia), Jacki Weaver, Jane Vallis, John Jarrett, Margaret Nelson (as the unhappy Sara), Tony-Llewelyn Jones.

PICTURE OF DORIAN GRAY, THE (1945) B&W-C/110m.
Hurd Hatfield is Oscar Wilde's late-19th-century English aristocrat who offers his soul if he can remain young while only his image in a portrait ages. He begins a life of sin and pleasure, causing a young woman's (Angela Lansbury) suicide, ruining lives, killing the artist who painted his portrait lest he reveal that, while Gray has not aged, his image has become monstrous, a sign of his moral leprosy. MGM picture is handsomely produced by Pandro S. Berman, strikingly photographed by Harry Stradling (who won an Oscar), and literately scripted by director Albert Lewin (who not only includes Wilde's epigrams but has Gray quote Wilde and mention his name). But it's too tasteful for a film about a sinner; it deals with many of the

same themes as *Dr. Jekyll and Mr. Hyde* (Wilde's story followed Stevenson's by just three years), but since Gray's wicked acts are kept off screen we never believe he is capable of the same heartless cruelties as Hyde. Miscast Hatfield's scoundrel, who is repeatedly shown standing stiff and emotionless like a mannequin, is not active or imaginative enough to be feared. And once sweet Lansbury kills herself, there's no one, including his new love, Donna Reed, that we worry about getting involved with him. Indeed, George Sanders, as his "friend" Lord Henry Wotten (Wilde's snobby, erudite stand-in), who encourages and gets a charge out of Gray's insensitivity, comes across as a far more interesting and despicable character. Shots of the portrait were filmed in color. A highlight is Lansbury's singing of "Little Yellow Bird." Also with: Lowell Gilmore. Peter Lawford, Miles Mander, Douglas Walton, Billy Bevan.

PIECES (SPANISH-AMERICAN/1982) C/89m.
Film epitomizes the slice-and-dice genre. In 1942 a little boy chops up his mother for wanting to burn the puzzle of a nude woman he was piecing together. Forty years later he starts killing females for individual body parts so that he can piece together a woman that looks like the woman in the puzzle. Who is the masked man who is using a chain saw to slice up college coeds? Policeman Christopher George assigns an undercover female officer (Linda Day) and a college student (Ian Sera)—who is able to be in a chipper mood 10 minutes after the girls he knows are found slaughtered—to snoop around campus. They keep arriving on the murder scene too late. Directed with a minimum of style by J. Piquer Simon, picture offers sex, some suspense, and a bevy of beautiful women—but the murders are too grisly for all but the hardcore fans of the genre, and, of course, the subject matter is blatantly offensive. Also with: Edmund Purdom (who looks here like a hefty Gregory Peck), Paul Smith, Jack Taylor.

PIERROT LE FOU (FRENCH-ITALIAN/1965) C/112m.
Ferdinand (Jean-Paul Belmondo) is bored with his bourgeois lifestyle. He walks out on a stuffy party and runs away with his daughter's babysitter, Marianne (Anna Karina), his former lover. The next morning, he finds a dead man in Marianne's apartment, with scissors stuck in his back. The couple flees Paris. Gangsters, led by a midget (Jimmy Karoubi), are after some money Marianne has. She accidently destroys the money when she sets fire to the car. Ferdinand and Marianne spend time in a remote cottage—but there is little romance. She gets bored and insists they go to the Riviera to see her "brother." She isn't being honest with him. One of Jean-Luc Godard's most fascinating films, it has a plot that takes twists at every turn as if the script were being revised each morning before filming. It's filled with allusions to artists and films, political ideas, and jabs at commercialism and contemporary mores. It's good to see Belmondo back in a Godard film—I keep thinking that maybe this film shows, in a limited sense, what would have happened if Belmondo and Jean Seberg had stayed together

longer in *Breathless*. An explosive ending. Technically, film is excitingly audacious. Photography was by Raoul Coutard. Jean-Pierre Léaud was an assistant director. Also with: Dirk Sanders, Graziella Galvani, Samuel Fuller (as himself, describing film as "an emotional battleground"), Laszlo Szabo, Léaud.

PILLOW TALK (1959) C/105m.
Quintessential Stanley Shapiro-scripted American sex comedy, co-written by Maurice Richlin, lavishly produced by Ross Hunter, and bringing together Doris Day and Rock Hudson (his first comedy) for the first time. Day is an unmarried fashion designer who shares a party line with playboy-songwriter Hudson. Although they haven't met, they squabble over the phone because he's always keeping the line tied up romancing women. She despises his conceited attitude. When Hudson finds out from buddy Tony Randall that his marriage proposals to Day have been rejected, and that Day is very pretty (although she actually looks kind of dowdy in the film), he plans a way to meet her. As in their other films, there is gross deceit. Hudson pretends to be a gentlemanly Texas bachelor who never makes an improper advance toward Day; she falls in love. In one of the film's few funny scenes Hudson calls her up and, as his real obnoxious self, warns her about the Texan. Claustrophobic comedy is full of unfunny sexual innuendo (regarding her "frigidity," his impotence or homosexuality) and has a smutty feel to it. Day's character is fine is some ways: she seems more determined to maintain personal integrity than her virginity; having a boyfriend is more important than having a husband; she is as successful at work as Hudson is; she does not take being treated badly lying down—she has claws. But film seems to imply that because she has a job rather than a love/ sex life, she feels much anger and hostility, as is evident in her heated phone arguments with Hudson. Michael Gordon directed, making much use of split screen; the best shot, daring in its day, has Day and Hudson in their respective bathtubs with their feet seemingly touching. Also with: Thelma Ritter, Nick Adams, Julia Meade, Allen Jenkins, Lee Patrick.

PINK FLAMINGOS (1973) C/95m.
John Waters's cult classic, one of the most successful midnight movies and arguably his best film, is a movie that you can't believe was actually scripted, storyboarded, acted in, shot, and shown in legitimate theaters. It centers on the outrageous contest between Babs Johnson (Divine is at her hammiest, loudest, and funniest) and a married couple, Raymond and Connie Marble (David Lochary, Mink Stole), to win the title of "the filthiest human being in the world." The Marbles think they qualify because they invest in pornography, sell heroin in elementary schools, and kidnap women, have their butler (Channing Wilroy) forcibly impregnate them, and sell their babies—while Babs is simply a whore and a murderer. Waters bounces back and forth between the despicable, disgusting contestants, switching each time something revolting is about to happen. Babs proves herself filthiest when, in Waters's and Divine's most infamous scene, she actually eats puppy excrement on camera. By this time she has already won the contest by default: she has murdered the Marbles. The "King of Sleaze" wants to shock people out of their complacent viewing habits. He invariably succeeds by writing the most obscene storylines, shooting the most vulgar images, and presenting the most repulsive characters imaginable. He can make you laugh uncontrollably even when you're repelled—as when Babs and her demented son, Crackers (Danny Mills), put a curse on the Marbles' house by licking, spitting, and rubbing themselves all over the furniture. And you've got to respect a guy who can make "stars" out of the weirdos who stock his Baltimore repertory company. But you have to be disturbed by his *anything*-different-is-positive theme and by the fact that he succeeds in making young people laugh by depicting pain, destruction of property, and strong violence. He shouldn't be so proud that he has become god to what he calls "the hate generation." Also with: Mary Vivian Pearce, Cookie Mueller, Paul Swift, Susan Walsh, Linda Olgeirson.

PINK FLOYD—THE WALL/WALL, THE (BRITISH/ 1982) C/95m.
Midnight cult hit is director Alan Parker's visual interpretation of the rock opera by Pink Floyd (Roger Waters, David Gilmour, Nick Mason, Richard Wright). Script by Waters is about a rock musician named Pink (Bob Geldof), who is having a breakdown. Cutting back and forth between present, past—he was a lonely, fatherless child (Kevin McKeon) abused by regimental schoolmasters—and future, we witness the development of a fascist. Picture is unrelentingly downbeat and at times repulsive—(a realistic scene in which Pink shaves his chest is more gruesome than a fantasy scene in which robotized children fall into a giant meat-grinder). But I don't find it unwatchable—which is more than I could say if Ken Russell had directed this. The cinematography by Peter Bizou is extremely impressive and a few of the individual scenes have undeniable power. Animation sequences are by political cartoonist Gerald Scarfe. Also with: Eleanor David, Christine Hargreaves, Bob Hoskins.

PINK PANTHER, THE (1964) B&W/113m.
Overrated Blake Edwards comedy at least gave Peter Sellers his first chance to play bumbling Inspector Clouseau, and he completely steals the film from the other stars, including topbilled David Niven. Clouseau is after a notorious thief, "the Phantom," trying to stop him before he steals the priceless jewel of a beautiful princess (Claudia Cardinale). He's married in this one and doesn't realize that his wife (Capucine) is the Phantom's mistress. Film drags badly when Clouseau isn't on the screen. But watching him destroy props in his inimitable manner is great fun. Edwards and Sellers team up for a lot of amusing slapstick routines (Capucine is surprisingly good doing physical comedy with Sellers) and there is an abundance of sight gags. My favorite moments include Sellers instructing the choking Capucine to lean forward, causing her to slam her head into the bar;

and a detective dressed as a zebra loudly drinking from a party punchbowl (Clouseau threatens to take away his "stripes"). Success of picture led to Inspector Clouseau film *A Shot in the Dark*. Henry Mancini composed the now familiar music. The animation during the titles, featuring a pink panther, was done by DePatie-Freleng. Also with: Robert Wagner, Brenda de Banzie, Fran Jeffries.

PINOCCHIO (1940) C/88m.   Supreme animated feature film from Walt Disney. Whereas Disney's prior cartoon feature *Snow White and the Seven Dwarfs* was about the rite of passage of a young girl, this classic is about the maturation of a young boy: in Snow White's case, she would leave home; Pinocchio would return home. Script is based on the story by Carlo Collodi. Aged woodcutter Geppetto finishes his latest puppet, Pinocchio. He wishes upon a star that Pinocchio could be his son, and the Blue Fairy brings Pinocchio to life. She promises the little wooden boy that she'll make him human if he proves to be brave, truthful, and unselfish. With his conscience, Jiminy Cricket, watching over him, Pinocchio sets off for school. But the naive boy is duped by foxy "Honest John" into becoming an actor in a circus. He's placed in a cage—the first of three "prisons" he'll experience. Later he runs away with a lot of bad hooky-playing boys to Pleasure Island, where the other boys are turned into donkeys. Stuck with a tail and donkey ears, Pinocchio escapes with Jiminy's help. Now he goes to sea to save Geppetto, who is trapped—along with Figaro, the cat, and Cleo, the goldfish—inside the giant whale Monstro. Picture has no flaws—it's beautifully paced, funny, has outstanding songs, marvelous characters, and the best animation in all of Disney. The characters and sets are impressively and imaginatively drawn. Pinocchio and Jiminy have great faces that change expressions throughout (watch Pinocchio's face change when he smokes a cigar); their movements are also beautifully animated. Animation of the Blue Fairy is exceptional. Film has a lot of visuals that could scare a young child (but that's okay), including the boys turning into donkeys, Pinocchio face down in the water, and the fabulously animated, absolutely terrifying scene when Monstro chases the escapees through the ocean. Songs: "When You Wish upon a Star," "Little Woodenhead," "Hi Diddle Dee Dee," "I've Got No Strings," "Give a Little Whistle." Ben Sharpsteen and Hamilton Luske were supervising directors. Voices: Dickie Jones (Pinocchio), Christian Rub (Geppetto), Cliff Edwards (perfect as the inimitable Jiminy), Evelyn Venable, Walter Catlett, Frankie Darro, Charles Judels, Don Brodie.

PIPE DREAMS (1976) C/89m.   Curio featuring singer Gladys Knight's acting debut. She's no better than average, but film's strong feminism is somewhat noteworthy. Knight's a woman who goes to Alaska to get back her pilot husband (Barry Hankerson), who ran out on her. He wants her back, but she'll move in with him only on her terms. She wants to be treated like an equal, not his possession. Meanwhile she tries to help other women who are finding it rough in this male-dominated country, including a number of prostitutes who are terrorized by their boss, the crook who owns the saloon at which she works as bartender. No gem, but an acceptable low-budget film, and one of the few pictures that are about the relationship of a black couple. I like the fact that she's the one to insist they make love in an unusual place after their remarriage. Rousing songs by Gladys Knight and the Pips are on the soundtrack. Directed by Stephen Verona. Also with: Bruce French, Sherry Bain, Wayne Tippit, Altovise Davis, Arnold Johnson.

PIRANHA (1978) C/92m.   Roger Corman's low-budget *Jaws* variation, directed by Joe Dante and scripted by John Sayles. Heather Menzies searches for some teenagers who disappeared in a wilderness area. She and boozy local resident Bradford Dillman discover that scientist Kevin McCarthy has been developing a strain of salt-and-freshwater piranhas for the military that can be used to destroy enemy water systems. Having eaten the teenagers, the piranhas get loose in the river. Dillman and Menzies race the clever piranhas downstream, where there is a camp (at which Dillman's young daughter is staying) and a new swimming resort about to open. Dillman and Menzies are hindered in their efforts by army officer Bruce Gordon and scientist Barbara Steele, who want to keep their piranha plan under wraps. Entire film should be condensed to 15 minutes. It becomes annoying how Dante and Sayles put the usual roadblocks in the path of Dillman and Menzies to kill screen time; that's because there can be only *one* attack at the camp and *one* at the resort because after that nobody would go back into the water—as it is, those two attacks, which should take about 10 seconds each since the swimmers are about 10 feet from land, go on forever. Paul Bartel, as the taskmaster camp head, and Dick Miller, as the money-hungry resort owner, are funny, but their broad humor doesn't mesh with the tongue-in-cheek satirical upstream story with Dillman and Menzies. It should all have been played straight. The piranha-attack F/X are unimpressive, but there's some nifty stop-motion animation used for some Harryhausen-like creatures in McCarthy's lab. Followed by *Piranha II*. Also with: Belinda Belaski, Barry Brown, Keenan Wynn.

PIXOTE (BRAZILIAN/1980) C/127m.   Harrowing film in the tradition of *Shoeshine* and *Los Olvidados*. It's about an abandoned ten-year-old boy (Fernando Ramas da Silva) who is sent to a brutal Santiago reformatory where day by day his innocence is destroyed. He and several other kids break out. To make money, they steal purses, deal drugs, and become pimps for a streetwalker (Marilia Pera), whose clients they rob. One by one the other boys are killed, and baby-faced da Silva ends up on his own, now a hardened criminal and killer of three. Director Hector Babenco and Jorge Durán adapted José Luzeiro's novel *Infancia dos Mortos*. Its purpose is to show Brazil's growing social problem: slum children, who are too young to go to prison, are turning to serious crime. Babenco believes the root problem is that these kids have no motherly supervision. Da Silva is basically a good kid who is repeatedly rejected by women to whom he gravitates, women he would like to mother him. He holds in the tears, but he is ripped apart inside. Gritty, uncompromising film will shock you. Pera's performance is extraordinary. Acting by the kids, amateurs from the slums, is surprisingly effective. Photographed by Rodolfo Sánchez. Also with: Jorge Juliãuo (as a young transvestite), Gilberto Moura, José Nilson dos Santos, Edilson Lino.

PLACE IN THE SUN, A (1951) B&W/
122m. Theodore Dreiser's *An American Tragedy*, adapted by Michael Wilson and Harry Brown for director George Stevens (all won Oscars), was updated to contemporary times. Montgomery Clift plays a poor, uneducated, timid young man who comes to a new town to take a menial job at his rich uncle's factory. He becomes attracted to fellow worker Shelley Winters, who is also poor, but they must keep their relationship secret or they'll lose their jobs (and we'd have no story). He makes inroads into society and falls madly in love with rich Elizabeth Taylor. And she loves him and wants to marry him. But life is full of hard knocks and just when Clift can have the lovely Taylor and move to the very top of society, frumpy Winters announces that she's pregnant and insists she'll squeal on him unless they marry—she even talks about their moving away together and living always in poverty. Clift plans to drown Winters in a lake, but at the last moment realizes he can't do it. But the boat capsizes and Winters drowns anyway. He is tried for murder. One of the major hits of the fifties, this cynical film seems dated and the sociological, psychological, and moral aspects of the story are ambiguous. It never becomes completely clear what Clift's initial attraction to Winters is; and we're never sure if his wish to dump her for Taylor is based on how much prettier Taylor is, happier she is (having money gives anyone more spirit), nicer she is (she's sweet and loyal), or richer she is. It's obvious that Clift wants to escape poverty for wealth (each time he visits his uncle's house, he is better attired than the last time), but it becomes apparent that he'd run off with Taylor at the first opportunity, leaving behind her family, her rich young friends, and her money. We never really understand the nature of Clift's continuous guilt—is it because he seduced Winters, is betraying Winters, has not told Taylor about Winters, is trying to break away from his humble beginnings to join the American aristocracy, or because his religious-zealot mother (Anne Revere) made him believe that any contact with women is sinful? Clift's mannered performance has been much overrated—rather than seeming cerebral and attractive, he has the expression and stance of someone who is one step away from a psycho ward. Still, when he and Taylor dance closely, gaze into each other's eyes, or kiss passionately, it's hard not to sigh—these two superstars are a remarkably romantic duo. Academy Awards also went to cinematographer William C. Mellor, composer Franz Waxman, editor William Hornbeck, and costume designer Edith Head. Josef von Sternberg filmed Dreiser's book in 1931; Sergei Eisenstein also planned an adaptation. Also with: Keefe Brasselle, Raymond Burr, Fred Clark, Shepperd Strudwick, Ted de Corsia.

PLACES IN THE HEART (1984) C/110m.
Written and directed by Robert Benton, whose inspiration was his boyhood in Texas during the Depression. Sally Field won her second Best Actress Oscar as Sarah Spaulding, wife of a small-town sheriff and mother to a young boy and daughter. When her husband is accidentally killed by a drunk black boy—whom two white locals then drag to his death—Field worries that she'll be unable to pay the mortgage on the farm, and that she'll have to break up her family. She takes in a blind man (John Malkovich) as a paying boarder and hires a black transient laborer (Ray Glover) to plant cotton on her land. If they can beat the odds and bring in a strong crop before harvesting is completed on the larger farms, then they can save the farm. All underdogs, Field, Malkovich, Glover, and the two children form a special family who triumph because they pull together. In a subplot Ed Harris threatens to split his family apart by two-timing wife Lindsay Crouse, Field's sister, and having an affair with married schoolteacher Amy Madigan. There's not enough smalltown flavor, as is found in, say, *Raggedy Man*, and the story is certainly not original, but the acting and direction are so good that it's difficult not to become emotionally attached to the characters. And, of course, its Christian theme—that the family circle must not only remain unbroken but should be expanded to include all the dispossessed—is deeply moving: no wonder we get teary-eyed when Field accepts Glover into her home, when the young girl clutches Malkovich's hand for support, when Crouse offers Harris her hand to hold to show him that she's forgiven his infidelity (I love his "Thank-you-God" eye reaction), and when, in the wonderful final shot, everyone in town, including the dead—Field's husband sits with the boy who shot him—take communion together. Also with: Lane Smith.

PLAISIR, LE/HOUSE OF PLEASURE
(FRENCH/1952) B&W/95m. Max Ophüls adapted three stories by Guy de Maupassant. "The Mask" is about an elderly married man (Jean Galland) who puts on a youthful mask each night and goes dancing with the young ladies, although reliving his "Don Juan" days is hazardous to his health; an artist (Daniel Gélin) swears to love his model (Simone Simon) for eternity in "The Model," yet soon grows tired of her and moves out—leading to tragedy and, ironically, their permanent reunion; and in "The House of Madame Tellier," a madam (Madeleine Renaud) takes her girls to the country to celebrate the confirmation of her brother's (Jean Gabin) daughter (Joelle Jang)—leaving the men in the city in despair. The three episodes all deal with the pursuit of *pleasure* (not necessarily *happiness*) and show how women of heart (be they wives, dancing partners, lovers, or prostitutes) are essential to the stability of men. The final episode is charming, full of the festivity, exuberance, and emotion that characterize Ophüls's best work. However, the other two segments are disappointing, flimsy, and—

except for the wondrous interplay between Ophüls's moving camera and the high-kicking, spinning dancers in the ball sequence of "The Mask"—flatly directed. Jean Servais and Anton Walbrook served as narrators of the French and German versions, respectively; unfortunately, Peter Ustinov, using an unconvincing French accent, gives a terrible reading as narrator of the English version. Also with: Claude Dauphin, Gaby Morlay, Servais, Michel Vadet, Danielle Darrieux, Pierre Brasseur.

PLAN 9 FROM OUTER SPACE/GRAVE ROBBERS FROM OUTER SPACE (1956) B&W/79m.

In this era when bad-film freaks have come out of the closet and really awful films are looked on with affection, Edward D. Wood's berserk sci-fi film is revered by a large and growing cult who contend that it has moved beyond *camp* to *legend* status. How bad is it? Give a monkey a camera and it'll make a better picture. It'll certainly do a better job with the money. Every facet of this production, from acting, script, and direction to special effects, prop selection, and editing, is putrid. So putrid that the film is hilarious. God knows what the first eight "Plans" were, but Plan 9 is a doozy. An alien aircraft hovers over a graveyard situated next to the home of our pilot hero, Gregory Walcott, and his wife, Mona McKinnon. Aliens Dudley Manlove and Joanna Lee (today a successful scriptwriter) were sent by The Ruler (John Breckenridge) to raise the dead so that they'd attack the living. That's just about what Wood tried to do with his dead friend Bela Lugosi, billed as the star of the film although he died *prior* to production. Wood had a couple of minutes of footage of Lugosi from an aborted project, so he simply inserted the snippets into this film and repeated them over and over so that Lugosi had adequate screen time. Lugosi's character—The Ghoul Man—was played in the rest of the movie by a chiropractor, an extremely tall fellow who spends his screen time with a cape covering his face so we won't know he's an imposter. The ruse doesn't work, but I don't think Wood really cared. The chiropractor fits in well with other Wood regulars: enormous Swedish wrestler Tor Johnson (who plays a cop who turns into a ghoul and abducts McKinnon); TV horror-movie hostess Vampira (who looks as if she weighs 11 pounds), who walks repeatedly through the "expressionistic" graveyard; and the narrator, Criswell, a forecaster who defies us to "prove this story didn't already happen" and simultaneously insists it will happen in the future (which makes about as much sense as anything else in this picture). The ridiculous dialogue and the cheap sets alone are enough to qualify this film as the worst ever made. But are we missing the point? Did Wood intend his film to be atrocious so censors wouldn't bother with his *subversive* themes? Manlove's alien is so crazy and conceited that we forget that his words make sense. He is for peace and is aware that earth is on a destructive course that will end with the entire universe being blown up. When he calls earthlings stupid, headstrong, and violent, earthling Walcott is so insulted that he reacts in a stupid, headstrong, and violent way. Manlove's impressions

of earthlings are well founded. In this one God-awful, terribly made, poor excuse for a picture, Wood is more critical of America's government (which conceals much from the public) and military strategy (that calls for an arms build-up and further nuclear testing) than any other director of the period dared to be. For that reason alone, we should find another, less daring film to wear the World's Worst Film banner. Just kidding. Also with: Lyle Talbot, Tom Keene.

PLANET OF THE APES (1968) C/112m.

Pierre Boulle's novel *Monkey Planet* is given a big-budget, wide-screen Hollywood treatment, and its sole virtues are the result of money spent. The script by Rod Serling and Michael Wilson about earth astronaut Charlton Heston crash-landing on a planet ruled by tyrannical talking apes, and becoming the most rebellious of the human slaves, is surprisingly juvenile. The writers thought they could get away with the clichés by the dozen and the most simplistic moralistic statements just because these would seem different coming from people in monkey costumes. Franklin J. Schaffner's direction of the actors is flat, but he does exhibit visual flare when filming action scenes and landscape shots. Bare-chested Heston's a solid, muscular hero—he's a good choice to play a symbol of human superiority who is humbled when he is to be experimented on by the apes, just as humans experiment on apes back home. The politically conservative Heston would star in other liberal-slanted SF films, including *The Omega Man* and *Soylent Green*. Film's predictable ending is like something stolen from Serling's *The Twilight Zone*. John Chambers won an Oscar for creating the expensive ape make-up. Of the four sequels, the best and most controversial is *Conquest of the Planet of the Apes*, about the ape revolution against their human masters. Also with: Roddy McDowall, Kim Hunter, Maurice Evans, James Whitmore, James Daly, Linda Harrison (as Heston's non-speaking girlfriend).

PLAY IT AGAIN, SAM (1972) C/87m.

Woody Allen wrote and starred in this adaptation of his play, but directorial chores were handled by Herbert Ross. It's doubtful that in 1972 Allen could have done a better job than Ross. Hilarious comedy was the picture that really established Allen's screen persona, only hinted at in *Bananas*. As a San Francisco film critic, he's a depressed, neurotic, self-effacing sexual klutz who gets pointers from an imaginary Humphrey Bogart (Jerry Lacy) on how to come on to women. His wife (Susan Anspach) has just walked out on him and he's really depressed. His married best friends, Tony Roberts and Diane Keaton, set him up on blind dates but they prove to be disastrous. Because Roberts is *always* busy with work, the lonely Keaton—who is just as neurotic as Allen—starts spending time with Allen. They become attracted to each other and have a one-night affair. Allen feels tremendous guilt and is determined to be as gallant as Bogart was in *Casablanca* when he gave up Ingrid Bergman so her husband Paul Henreid wouldn't have his life destroyed. Picture is consistently funny—Allen's date attempts are all classics. I really like when he's trying to impress Jennifer Salt by demonstrating how the Chinese shovel rice into their mouths and when he swings his arm and a record album flies out of its cover and crashes into the wall. Every man understands his attempts to be "cool" in front of women. Also, he lives out most men's fears when Hell's Angels types show they're interested in his date (Joy Bang). Important to Allen's image: Allen tells Keaton he was thinking of Willie Mays while they made love. Although directed by Ross, that bit when he gets a Chinese man after dialing the wrong number must have come from Allen. Also with: Viva, as a professed nymphomaniac who is insulted when Allen makes a play for her.

PLAY MISTY FOR ME (1971) C/102m. Clint Eastwood's impressive directorial debut. As in *The Beguiled*, Eastwood plays a character, a California deejay, who is impressed by his ability to attract women; and again his taking women for nothing more than sexual playthings backfires on him. If there ever was a woman who baffled an Eastwood character, it is the superpsychotic Evelyn. Eastwood's come up against great villains, from Lee Van Cleef in *The Good, the Bad and the Ugly* to Andy Robinson in *Dirty Harry*, but, as played by Jessica Walter, Evelyn takes a back seat to no one. After sleeping with him on the night they meet (she'd often called his program requesting Erroll Garner's "Misty"), she desires to possess him—making his plans for a reconciliation with Tobie (Donna Mills) difficult. Once he rejects her, Evelyn is not above committing murder to ger her revenge. The film is exciting, weirdly amusing, and scary (many critics compare the knife scenes to *Psycho*), but the most enjoyable thing about it is watching Eastwood's cool-talking disk jockey become increasingly confused, perturbed, and terrified by this lunatic he has no control over. Significantly, no future Eastwood character would become involved with two women at once; in fact, Eastwood never again exploited his image as a romantic lead. "The First Time Ever I Saw Your Face" is sung by Roberta Flack. Also with: John Larch, Jack Ging, Clarice Taylor, Irene Hervey, Don Siegel (as a bartender).

POINT BLANK (1967) C/92m. With ice water in his veins, Lee Marvin goes after his ex-partner (John Vernon), who shot him and left him for dead during a hold-up—Vernon needed Marvin's share to pay off debts to the "organization." Marvin is particularly angry with Vernon because he also ran off with Marvin's wife (Sharon Acker). Marvin locates Acker with the help of a man (Keenan Wynn)—a cop?—who is determined to help Marvin get rid of the leaders of the "organization." Acker, who has been thoroughly depressed, commits suicide. With the help of Acker's sister (Angie Dickinson at her most alluring), Marvin is able to reach Vernon, who loses his footing and falls off his penthouse patio. Marvin decides to get the money Vernon owed him from Vernon's bosses, the higher-ups in the "organization"—Lloyd Bochner, Carroll O'Connor, and

a third, more elusive man. John Boorman's cult film boasts interesting characters, choice locales (around LA, at Alcatraz prison), and virtuoso camera and editing techniques. The extremely violent action sequences are particularly well handled (was this the first film in which someone is slugged in the crotch?). The film's audacious style and unusual dialogue have made it extremely popular in Europe. Marvin has one of his best roles—it's his scariest character since he played villains. A highlight is when Dickinson spends all her energy trying to slap him hard enough to make him feel something. The opening and the ending are a bit confusing. From Richard Stark's novel *The Hunter*. Also with: Michael Strong, James Sikking.

POINT OF ORDER (1964) B&W/97m. Classic documentary by Emile de Antonio of the televised Army-McCarthy hearings that held the nation spellbound for eight weeks in 1954 and gave the public its first penetrating view of the senator who, as the film contends, was destroying the fabric of American democracy. The hearings were called to determine if McCarthy and his counsel, Roy Cohn, had tried to use undue influence and had made threats against top military brass to get special treatment for an associate, David Schine, who had been drafted into the army. But the Schine affair was soon forgotten and the issue became whether McCarthy could back up his wild allegations that communists had infiltrated the armed forces, CIA, and atomic-bomb plants. It's obvious that McCarthy is being railroaded by military and political big shots with only slightly more integrity than he possesses—and that's what makes it so much fun. It's like watching the Watergate hearings, when politicians who always had let Nixon and his men get away with whatever they pleased suddenly ganged up on all the President's men and became the people's sanctimonious watchdogs. It's perversely satisfying to watch McCarthy sweat and squirm, make a feeble attempt to laugh or smile when he's caught in a falsehood, and go to his old there-are-communists-among-us spiel any time he feels cornered. Certainly the "Sam Ervin" role in this historical drama is played by wily old Boston lawyer Joseph Welch, sitting in a slouch with hand on chin and wearing a bow tie. The film's highlights are when Welch, counsel for the army, shrewdly (and hilariously) questions Cohn about a doctored photograph; insists—with obvious false alarm—that Cohn and McCarthy turn over their "list" containing 130 names of communists to the FBI "before the sun goes down" so everyone can sleep better; and berates McCarthy for being cruel and indecent enough to bring up the past of a young colleague of Welch's who during the mid-forties had belonged briefly to a leftist organization: when McCarthy still won't drop discussing the young lawyer's past, a look of anguish comes over Cohn as he realizes that McCarthy is committing political suicide with his needless attempt at character assassination. Later, Senate committee member Stuart Symington takes on McCarthy, who has become fair game. By the time Symington walks out on McCarthy in mid-conversation, the once fearsome McCarthy has become a pathetic, babbling, destroyed man. An important historical document. You can see McCarthy aide Bobby Kennedy present; there's even a guy who looks like Hitler who sits behind McCarthy and Cohn in a couple of shots.

POLICE ACADEMY (1984) C/96m.
Undistinguished, unimaginative comedy became a surprise commercial blockbuster, forcing highbrow critics to lament about the nature of today's movie audience. It's yet another film in the *Animal House* and *Stripes* tradition, with a group of incorrigible, klutzy misfits entering a conservative institution. In this case, a town mayor passes a law which ends restrictions on who may enter the police academy. A group of recruits more interested in partying than policing test the patience of officers who take them through training with orders to get rid of as many as possible. Predictably, Steve Guttenberg, Kim Cattrall, and the other recruits, who joined the academy for all the wrong reasons, decide they really want to become policemen after all. The reason for the picture's popularity has been a mystery, because it hasn't much sexual content or inspired lunacy. I think it's partly because it's the one film in which the institution doesn't really alter the rebellious characters it eventually welcomes into its ranks; it doesn't contend that if someone trains to be a policeman he'll become a better person, or that disciplined people are the types of citizens we want. Film was directed and co-written by Hugh Wilson (the creator of television's *WKRP in Cincinnati*). He is careful not to be sexually exploitive or offensive, but the result is a ridiculously tame film. Greatest indication of his discomfort on his first film is that scenes are kept safely brief, with only one joke at each conclusion. There are some laughs, but the humor isn't allowed to build toward a funny climax. First sequels: *Police Academy 2: The First Assignment* and *Police Academy 3: Back in Training*. Also with: G. W. Bailey, George Gaynes, Bubba Smith, Michael Winslow, Donovan Scott (a poor man's Steven Furst), Andrew Rubin, Marion Ramsey, porn star Georgina Spelvin (as a hooker), Bruce Mahler, David Graf.

POLTERGEIST (1982) C/114m.
Thrill-a-second horror movie was directed by Tobe Hooper under the close supervision of Steven Spielberg, who produced with Frank Marshall and wrote the script with Michael Grais and Mark Victor. Craig T. Nelson and JoBeth Williams live in a suburban development with their children, 16-year-old Dominique Dunne (her last role) and the younger Oliver Robbins and Heather O'Rourke. Nelson is the top salesman with the real estate company that cleared the land and built the houses. He didn't know that the houses were built on a graveyard and that the bodies were never removed. Obviously, there are some unhappy spirits, because the house is soon haunted and little O'Rourke is whisked away to the spirit world. They hear her screams emanating from her closet. Para-psychologist Beatrice Straight and tiny, psychic "haunted house–cleaner" Zelda Rubinstein (a *great* character) help Williams and Nelson attempt a rescue before the child is

gone forever. It means Williams will have to go after her. Picture is suspenseful, scary, witty, imaginative. Richard Edlund's special effects are dazzling, especially the parade of the "lost" ghosts down the staircase and the startling appearance of the giant demon head. What makes film really nerve-wracking—especially if you're a young viewer—is that every *thing* (trees, dolls, toys, records, furniture) comes to life and becomes hostile. (However, I don't understand what the film is saying about *television*, although it's obviously negative.) The characters are appealing—but Dunne's character has *nothing* to do. The finale, which is too much like the end of *The Amityville Horror*, is anticlimactic—all the skeletons, the mud, and the loud screaming are annoying. Williams, Nelson, Robbins, O'Rourke, and Rubinstein returned for the 1986 sequel. Also with: James Karen.

POLYESTER (1981) C/86m.
Disappointing John Waters comedy, filmed in 35mm on a much bigger budget than his midnight-movie classics. Perhaps catering to a broader audience instead of shocking it, film is a step backward on the outrageous scale, not all that much weirder or more absurd than *Mary Hartman, Mary Hartman*. The scenes with all Waters's regulars don't have the spontaneity present in the earlier films—in fact, they seem to be showcase scenes meant to familiarize the new Waters viewers with the Waters style they'd heard about; for veteran Waters fans, most of these scenes are watered-down versions of classic Waters scenes. At least the reliable Divine gives a standout performance as harried, dissatisfied suburban housewife Francine Fishpaw. Husband Elmer (David Simson) runs a porno theater, daughter Lulu (Mary Garlington) is dating a sleazeball (Stiv Bators), and son Dexter (Ken King) is Baltimore's notorious "Foot Stomper." Francine has an affair with Todd Tomorrow (Tab Hunter returns!), who runs a drive-in that shows art films, including (the film's funniest bit) a Marguerite Duras triple feature. Hunter turns out to be surprisingly boring, but at least Waters dared to allow Hunter and Divine to smooch on screen. Dialogue by Waters is disappointing—more laughter comes from just paying attention to the props in Francine's house and the film's unbelievable wardrobe. An admirer of William Castle's gimmicks, Waters came up with the concept "Odorama"—viewers were handed cards containing 10 numbered circles: when rubbed with a coin at 10 appropriate times in the film (numbers would flash on the screen), the circles would give off aromas to correspond to what characters smelled on the screen. For the entire film, viewers dreaded Waters flashing Number 2 on the screen. With music by Chris Stein and Michael Karmen; Deborah Harry sings. Also with: Edith Massey (as Cuddles), Mink Stole, Joni Ruth White, Hans Kramm.

POM POM GIRLS, THE (1976) C/90m.
This sex-and-mayhem teenage comedy has become a bonafide cult hit, but it doesn't live up to its underground reputation. Conventional storyline has incorrigible high-school pals

Robert Carradine and Michael Mullins recklessly racing their car, winning over two pretty girls (Jennifer Ashley, Lisa Reeves), and putting up with the bullying tactics of an arrogant student (Bill Adler) and a vicious coach (James Gammon). The girls are okay, but the males in this picture are jerks. The direction by Joseph Ruben is unimaginative, the sex scenes aren't particularly exciting, and the boys' rude behavior is annoying. However, there are enough okay moments—the two couples tumbling down a hill, Mullins socking his coach (fulfilling the dreams of many of us), and, in a climax taken from *Rebel Without a Cause*, Carradine and Adler playing "Chicken" (racing their cars toward a cliff)—to make it acceptable drive-in fare. Also with: Susan Player, Rainbeaux Smith (in too minor a role), Diane Lee Hart.

PORKY'S (CANADIAN/1981) C/94m. Smutty juvenile comedy set in Florida in 1954. It centers on a group of jerky high-school boys who have sex on the brain. When they go to Porky's, a bar-brothel across the county line, their money is stolen and their car damaged by the corrupt sheriff (Alex Karras), Porky's brother. In the climax they get their revenge. Meanwhile Pee Wee (Dan Monahan) tried to lose his virginity, an assistant gym coach learns why a sexy cheerleder (Kim Cattrall) is nicknamed "Lassie," and, in the serious subplot, one of the boys deals with his own anti-Semitism and his brutal father. All the humor is vulgar and sex-related. Director Bob Clark's idea of a good joke is having one character embarrass himself/herself sexually and having lots of other characters stand around laughing— this happens *several* times. It's amazing how unfunny this picture is, considering that it was, to everyone's surprise (or horror), a *phenomenal* commercial success. Repulsive characters (the girls are just as bad as the boys); awful acting. What's the classy Susan Clark doing in this junk, acting as obnoxious as everyone else? Director Clark made *Porky's II: The Next Day* in 1983. Also with: Kaki Hunter, Mark Herrier, Wyatt Knight, Scott Colomby, Nancy Parsons.

POSEIDON ADVENTURE, THE (1972) C/117m. Giant tidal wave flips over crowded luxury liner so that it hangs upside down with only its bottom above water. The few survivors, including youngsters and elderly passengers, work their way upward through the ship, hoping to exit through the bottom and be rescued. Along the way, producer Irwin Allen provides many dangerous obstacles that take a heavy toll in lives. Prototypical big-budget "disaster" film of the early seventies, with an all-star cast, stilted dialogue, showoff special effects, and stereotypical characters; plus excitement. Okay escapist fare, but ending is a letdown because you realize all the likable characters died while only the obnoxious ones have made it to "The Morning After" (the picture's Oscar-winning song). Competent direction by Ronald Neame. Sequel: *Beyond the Poseidon Adventure*. Cast includes: Gene Hackman, Ernest Borgnine, Red Buttons, Carol Lynley, Roddy McDowall, Stella Stevens, Shelley Winters, Jack Albertson, Leslie Nielsen, Arthur O'Connell, Eric Shea, teenager Pamela Sue Martin.

POSSESSION OF JOEL DELANEY, THE (1972) C/105m. Neglected film is one of the creepiest psychological thrillers. In one of her most interesting roles, Shirley MacLaine is a spoiled, divorced socialite who lives in a ritzy New York apartment with her two children. At ease only in comforting, protective settings, she must get down and dirty to protect her children when her younger brother Joel (menacingly played by Perry King)—for whom she has obvious incestuous feelings—begins to take on the sadistic personality of the dead Puerto Rican teen murderer whose apartment he has rented. (He even begins to speak in Spanish.) With the help of her Puerto Rican housekeeper, whom she'd always patronized and never tried to understand, she attempts to figure out what is happening to King. In a chilling scene she comes into contact with the housekeeper's acquaintances, who perform a variation on a séance. MacLaine has entered a terrifying world she never dreamed about in her pampered life. We respect her newfound courage, which is necessary because her former husband isn't there to help her. Discovering King is possessed, she flees with her kids to a deserted beach house, setting up the gripping—and, unfortunately, unpleasant—finale. Atmospheric direction by Waris Hussein, who makes effective use of New York locations; camera work always reflects character disorientation. Bizarre last shot is a bit more ambiguous than the conclusion in Ramona Stewart's novel. Tasteless final sequence ruins film for many viewers. Also with: Lisa Kohane, David Elliot, Michael Hordern, Lovelady Powell, Miriam Colón.

POTEMKIN/BATTLESHIP POTEMKIN, THE (RUSSIAN/1925) B&W/65m. Probably the first or second film you saw in your Introduction to Film course. But since the print was scratchy and without a musical soundtrack, the screen was tiny, and you, at the time, knew little about 20th-century Russian history and the importance of film in that history or cared about the importance of "montage" in film history, you probably fell asleep. But if you see it again, in a theater, then you'll understand why critics and devoted filmgoers regard it as one of the greatest pictures of all time. For Sergei Eisenstein's seminal work, the first non-documentary about a political action/historical event, proved not only that a cleverly edited series of images could draw viewers into the film's action and stimulate the emotions but also that the juxtaposition of two images— one of a character, the other of a symbolic object/prop— was a valuable propaganda device because it forced viewers to deduce that the symbol relates to the character. The picture, set in 1905 during the Russo-Japanese War, is divided into three sections. In the first part, sailors on the *Potemkin*, a Russian battleship, decide to mutiny when several are about to be shot for refusing to eat spoiled meat. Eisenstein builds tension by cutting back and forth between armed guards and helpless sailors. While the director does glorify one sailor for initiating the revolt, which was uncharacteristic considering he made films in which the *masses* were the heroes, he makes it clear that the success of the mutiny is determined by the solidarity of the sailors and the guards who refuse to fire on their brothers. In the second part, the citizens of Odessa celebrate the arrival of the *Potemkin*, now in the hands of the sailors. In the most famous sequence in film history, the Czar's forces march down the "Odessa Steps" and massacre men, women, and children in their path. Eisenstein builds tension and creates terror by cutting back and forth between marching faceless soldiers and their victims (whose scared faces are shown in close-ups), who run up and down steps. Most effectively, time stands still, so what would take place in seconds goes on and on—camera pans down the steps, moves back to where the soldiers are, and we start over again. There's an odd rhythm to the sequence, so that we feel things are going fast (*too fast* for the victims to think clearly) but simultaneously feel that the cruelty will never stop. (It's not surprising that the cinema's second most famous sequence, the shower murder in *Psycho*, uses many of the *time* and *editing* principles employed here.) Film's final sequence, for which history was rewritten, has the *Potemkin*'s rebels preparing for battle with a Russian fleet. This section has the look of a documentary (in fact, I wonder if all this footage was shot for this film)—indeed, you can see how even the American documentary *Victory at Sea*, made after WWII, borrowed a great deal from these shots of sailors at stations all over the ship as they prepare for sea battle. Certainly as influential as *The Birth of a Nation* and *Citizen Kane*.

PRESIDENT'S ANALYST, THE (1967) C/104m.
James Coburn becomes the President's personal analyst and finds that being at his beck and call is ruining his life. He tries to quit, but finds himself the target of spies from all countries—including the U.S.—who want either to assassinate him for knowing too much or to torture him to obtain the privileged information he has. Coburn runs for his life, hiding out with a couple (William Daniels, Joan Darling) he wrongly assumes are average Americans and then a pop-music group and their groupies. Zany paranoia satire, written and directed by Theodore Flicker, places Coburn in a world where no one is to be trusted (not even girlfriend Joan Delaney), no one is who he or she seems to be, almost everyone is a spy, everyone (including the spies themselves) is sure he is being bugged or watched, every phone in America is tapped, Soviet and American spies work together, innocent Americans are in danger of being assassinated by government agents, the telephone company is fully automated and run by robots. Everything seems to be filmed from the wrong angles, but at least the story never gets totally out of hand. Best scenes are those in which various spies kill off each other trying to get to Coburn themselves; and when Coburn analyzes a Russian agent, well played by a clean-shaven Severn Darden. Also with:

Godfrey Cambridge, Will Geer, Pat Harrington, Barry McGuire.

PRETTY BABY (1978) C/109m.
Louis Malle's first American film is set in 1917 in Storyville, the red-light district of New Orleans. Hattie (Susan Sarandon) and her 12-year-old daughter, Violet (Brooke Shields), are whores in a brothel. Photographer E. J. Bellocq (Keith Carradine) pays Madam Nell Livingston (Frances Faye) to let him photograph her whores. They think he's odd since he never has sex with any of them. Hattie marries a customer (Don Hood) and runs off to St. Louis. When Storyville is closed down and Violet is on her own, Bellocq proposes to her. Bellocq falls in love with Violet because of her beauty, because she is as much a voyeur as he is, and because he is sexually and emotionally a child (witness his temper tantrums). When he brings her a doll as a present, Bellocq is making sure Violet *remains* a child instead of becoming too mature for him. The picture was released during a peak period for public outrage over child abuse, child pornography, and child prostitution, and its critics were right to be disappointed that Malle refused to portray Violet's life in a brothel in a negative light. Instead he takes a polite view of prostitution—Nell's whores are well paid, well fed, healthy, and cheerful. Perhaps the real Violet (whose story is told in Al Rose's nonfiction work *Storyville, New Orleans*) didn't consider herself victimized when a child, but it was irresponsible on Malle's part to use *her* as his central character. The sledgehammer "selling of Brooke Shields as pubescent sex symbol," which gained momentum because of this film, was truly tasteless. At least Malle didn't exploit his hot property as much as others did. He filmed no sexually explicit or overly erotic scenes with Shields—her nude moments are those in which Violet poses for Bellocq's camera or she (Shields) in effect poses for Malle's camera. But I feel embarrassed for Shields because of the unflattering way Malle exhibits her: she looks downright foolish when Violet has her bath interrupted by Madam Nell and a male customer, and when she stands bare-assed in front of Bellocq's locked door, banging to be let inside. Malle obviously felt awkward dealing with a girl of Shields's age, because he makes Violet curious about *everything* but her own body. Shields gives the one impressive performance in the film—Sarandon's role is too brief, Carradine is badly miscast, and Faye is so atrocious that if she mangled the word *monsieur* one more time, I'm sure someone in the crew would have strangled her—but Violet's relationships with Hattie and Bellocq aren't sufficiently developed. Picture's one strong suit is its look. Visually, the film is a homage to the impressionists of the era—just as the music is a tribute to the jazz greats of the period, like Jelly Roll Morton. Each shot is beautifully composed, and the frame becomes a mixture of muted colors, natural light, and shadows. As long as Malle and cinematographer Sven Nykvist concentrate on visuals, things run smoothly. But when characters speak Polly Platt's dialogue, we are bombarded with the clichés we've heard in every other bad movie set in a brothel. Also with: Antonio

Fargas, Mathew Anton, Diana Scarwid, Barbara Steele, Gerrit Graham, Mae Mercer.

PRETTY PEACHES (1978) C/88m.
XXX-rated film by Alex De Renzy features Desiree Cousteau's debut. She won porno awards for her portrayal of a bubblehead who gets amnesia and is taken advantage of by everyone: she is raped by men and women, given an enema by a doctor, seduced by a psychiatrist, and coaxed into participating in an orgy. Film, which mixes comedy with deviant behavior, has reputation for being one of porno's most exotic and funniest films, but it's stupid, boring, and annoying. It takes forever for the first sex scene to occur and by that time you're already repelled by the performers, lazy acting, and the shoddy photography. Also with: John Leslie, Joey Civera, Juliet Anderson, Sharon Kane.

PRETTY POISON (1968) C/89m.
After many years in an institution for burning down a house with his aunt in it, Dennis Pitt (Anthony Perkins), now an adult, is placed on probation and given a job at a Massachusetts lumber company. He is attracted to pretty high-school majorette Sue Ann Stepanek (Tuesday Weld) and gets her interested in him by pretending to be a CIA agent who is investigating the lumber company for polluting the water supply on behalf of a foreign power. She gladly proves her loyalty by making love to him. He doesn't realize that he's the one being deceived—Sue Ann sees Dennis as the fall guy in her plot to do away with her strict mother (a deliciously cold performance by Beverly Garland). Written by Lorenzo Semple, Jr. (from Stephen Geller's novel), and directed by Noel Black, this is one of the few still-sparkling gems of the late sixties. A sometimes violent black comedy, it has sharp humor scattered throughout its serious framework. Its style reminds me of William March's *The Bad Seed*, and 17-year-old Sue Ann might well be the diabolical eight-year-old Rhoda Penmark grown up. Like Rhoda, she was *born* evil, learned to hide her evilness with devilish charm: Sue Ann has refined her evil with age so that it now corresponds to her sexual amorality (after committing murder, she wants to have sex). The definitive Weld movie role, Sue Ann needs excitement—and if you want her, you have to keep feeding it to her. Her sexiness has less to do with her body than with eyes that sparkle with wickedness, her conceit, the nervous edge in her voice. She is the manipulative dream girl for masochists like Dennis. She comes across as the archetypical American innocent, a pretty, high-spirited blonde who is on the honor roll, takes hygiene classes, and carries the American flag in her marching band. The picture's theme, as reflected in the paradoxical title and as embodied by Sue Ann, is that paranoid America is not so much in danger from foreigners as it is from evil, epidemic-like forces that are spreading in America's heartland. This small, peaceful Massachusetts town is a microcosm of a sick, self-destructive America. Weld is great and Perkins matches her, properly playing Dennis as a man who is very much a boy. In fact, throughout the film he re-creates the childhood incident in which he was *caught* after starting the fire. Over and over, he is *caught* telling lies; he is *caught* sneaking around the lumber company at night, caught stumbling past a car at "Make Out Lane," and finally caught in Sue Ann's trap. He turns himself in at the end to avoid the inevitable. Terrific film has a cult following. Also with: John Randolph (as Dennis's probation officer), Dick O'Neill, Clarice Blackburn.

PRINCESS YANG KWEI FEI/YANG KWEI FEI/PRINCESS YANG, THE (JAPANESE/1955) C/91m.
Rare color film by Kenji Mizoguchi takes liberties with the true story of a beautiful 8th-century scullery maid who brought about the downfall of the Emperor. Machiko Kyo is Kwei Fei, who reluctantly goes to the palace to be the concubine of the Emperor, played by Masayuki Mori (Kyo's husband in *Rashomon*). Unhappy with all the women his servants had previously brought to take the place of the dead Empress, he is surprised by her sensitivity and intelligence. They fall in love. But a family member whom she helped get an important post taxes the people to such a degree that a rebellion against the Emperor takes place. Her three sisters and the relative who became an official are executed by the Emperor's own soldiers, but the people demand that she, the last of the Yangs, also be killed. Unlike what is recorded in Japanese history books, Mizoguchi has Kwei Fei gallantly sacrifice herself for the sake of her Emperor and his empire. The director was aways sympathetic toward his women characters, whom he invariably portrayed as victims in the foolish, male-controlled historical Japan. Kwei Fei seems to be his ideal female, a woman of many attributes who is equally at ease in a palace or mingling with the common people; and who can be both lover and friend to her husband. Plot is a bit flimsy and it's hard to keep track of time, but Kyo and Mori give superb performances and their scene in which the royal couple dresses as commoners and playfully wanders through a street bazaar is truly lovely; as is the final scene, which recalls the end of *Wuthering Heights*.

PRISONER OF ZENDA, THE (1937) B&W/101m.
A bit dated, but still the best of five film versions of Anthony Hope's novel. Ronald Colman gives a dashing yet elegant performance as an Englishman who impersonates his kidnapped cousin, the King of Ruritania. He doubles for him at his coronation and then at his wedding to Madeleine Carroll—but when he and Carroll fall in love, he realizes that he has to find his missing cousin quickly or else be stuck permanently in a lie. Also: as the King he finds his life threatened by arch-villains Douglas Fairbanks, Jr., and Raymond Massey. The type of story that Hollywood was meant to tell. It has fine acting, exciting action sequences (including a swordfight between Colman and Fairbanks), romance between the appealing Carroll and Colman, lavish sets, striking sepia-toned cinematography, stylish di-

rection by John Cromwell. Best scene has Fairbanks (a great performance) trying to persuade Colman to accept a bargain. Well produced by David O. Selznick. Top-rate cast includes: Mary Astor, C. Aubrey Smith, David Niven, Montagu Love, Alexander D'Arcy.

PRIVATE BENJAMIN (1980) C/100m.
In this popular comedy Goldie Hawn is at her most appealing as a Jewish princess from Philadelphia who enlists in the army after her husband (Albert Brooks) dies on their wedding night. Judy Benjamin actually believes the recruiter's (Harry Dean Stanton) promises of single rooms, yachts, the easy life. When she undergoes basic training, she gets more than she bargained for—but the army also gets more than it bargained for. After the tears and fears go away, and after she stops complaining ("I want to go out to lunch"), she becomes a good soldier. At about that point the film becomes too conventional. The final section of the movie has Goldie in Italy deciding whether to marry handsome gynecologist Henri (Armand Assante) or continue with her military career. Significantly, the army isn't depicted as a character builder (as in *An Officer and a Gentleman*). Instead the fussy, childlike Judy, whose previous life had been completely orchestrated by men, evolves into a confident, strong, independent-minded woman in spite of the army, which is represented by less than noble characters: the recruiter who lies to her, the captain (Eileen Brennan) who tries to break her, the colonel (Robert Webber) who tries to rape her, the officer who will discharge her unless she breaks off with Assante. Judy may be sweet, gullible, and vulnerable, but— producer Hawn had the role tailored for herself—like all Hawn's best characters, she has enough intelligence/shrewdness and perseverance to triumph over those in positions of power who try to take advantage of her and yank her in one wrong direction or another. Judy doesn't realize how much she has changed—how much she has been "liberated"— until the end of the film, when she stands up to fiancé Henri. A good finale. Brennan reprised her role in the short-lived television series. Directed by Howard Zieff. Also with: Sam Wanamaker, Barbara Barrie, Mary Kay Place, P. J. Soles, Hal Williams.

PRIVATE LIFE OF HENRY VIII, THE (BRITISH/1933) B&W/97m.
Charles Laughton became a major movie star with his Oscar-winning portrayal of the 16th-century British monarch. Creaky but still delightful picture centers less on Henry's politics than on his personal relationships with *five* of his six wives. (Writers Arthur Wimperis and Lajos Biro dismiss his first wife, Catherine of Aragon, by stating she was too respectable to spend time on.) It somewhat shifts tone (from sad or serious to ironic or, simply, funny) as each new wife appears. Today we may look at it from a new angle: how brave each wife was to stand up to Henry, especially considering his propensity to do away with wives who displeased him. Director Alexander Korda meant to emphasize the human, typical-husband side of Henry, whose wife of the moment may be unfaithful, or

henpeck him, or beat him at cards (as does Elsa Lanchester's Anne of Cleves). We sympathize with Laughton when, as an aging man, he shows off to his wife by wrestling; and Laughton jolts us when he breaks into tears upon learning his beloved wife Catherine Howard (Binnie Barnes) has been having an affair with his minister (Robert Donat as Thomas Culpepper). And we know how he feels when he tries to eat, but wife Katherine Parr (Everley Gregg) ruins it for him by reminding him of last night's bellyache. "Six wives," he complains to us in the film's last line, "and the best of them is the worst." Since you can't beat 'em (or kill 'em) all, you give up. Also with: Merle Oberon as Anne Boleyn, Wendy Barrie as Jane Seymour, Miles Mander, John Loder.

PRIVATE PARTS (1972) C/86m.
Kinky black comedy-horror film about a teenage runaway (Ann Ruymen) who hides out at a seedy LA hotel that is owned by her aunt (Lucille Benson). It turns out that everybody in the place is weird, including the outwardly stable aunt. Murders take place and the girl's life is in jeopardy. This film is creepy, but perhaps you'll most remember scenes that are either erotic (naughty Ruymen disrobes in the hall bathroom, knowing that a stranger is spying through a peephole) or obscene (a transvestite shoots a hypodermic full of blood into the crotch of a plastic female body, which has a picture of Ruymen's face pasted on it). The twist ending is confusing and not very satisfying (you won't buy it), but until then it's unlike all other girl-in-scary-hotel/motel/inn/boardinghouse pictures. Cute Ruymen is most appealing— what became of her? An interesting debut for director Paul Bartel. Also with: Laurie Main, John Ventantonio.

PRIVILEGE (BRITISH/1967) C/101m.
Set in near future, when British rock singer Steve Shorter (Paul Jones, the lead singer of Manfred Mann) becomes so popular that the government, church, and big business decide to use him to unite and manipulate country's youth into doing their bidding. Initially willing to do his part for his country, Shorter becomes disillusioned when he realizes he's lost his personal freedom and is responsible for his followers losing theirs. His only *human* contact is with a young artist (supermodel Jean Shrimpton). Overall, Peter Watkins's picture, filmed in quasi-documentary style, with a dry narrator, is "dated"—it is of interest today mainly as a reflection of what "controversial" semi-political films were in the late sixties. However, picture foretold, for instance, Nixon using rock stars to lure youth, and Reagan both capitalizing on friendship with Beach Boys and making an unsuccessful attempt to link himself to Bruce Springsteen (only Bruce got angry). Film needs energy. Also with: Marc London, Max Bacon, Jeremy Child.

PRIZZI'S HONOR (1985) C/130m.
Eccentric John Huston film centering on an extended New York crime family. Their internecine activities are exactly like that found in any other close, male-dominated Italian family, and their

criminal activities—including murder, kidnapping, drug dealing, and payoffs to politicians and police—are conducted with the same matter-of-factness as if they were running a legitimate business. But it always must be remembered that the family comes first. Jack Nicholson is Charley Partanna, the much loved godson of godfather William Hickey. Nicholson carries out the Prizzi family's tough assignments—he kills a guy who ran off with Prizzi money, he supervises a kidnapping—but off the job he's a polite, somewhat dopey shmoe who worries about his sorry love life. At a family wedding he spots visiting Kathleen Turner and immediately falls in love with her. At her invitation, he goes out to visit her in Los Angeles—he's like a schoolboy on his dream date. She is not a member of the Prizzi family—in fact, she is Polish—but claims to have been married to an Italian who had connections with them. She expresses her love for him and they agree to marry. Nicholson goes on an assassination assignment, kills the guy, and discovers he had been Turner's husband. She confesses being married to the dead man, but swears that she didn't take part in his crimes against the Prizzis, including a rub-out and stealing a huge sum of money. Not only does Nicholson catch Turner in these lies, but he finds out she is an assassin for hire. So great is his love for her that they marry anyway. Having more brains than he, she concocts a kidnapping plan for Nicholson and they seem to be a great crime team. But the crime is botched: she shoots a police captain's wife who happens upon scene and police demand a "fall guy" from family—naturally, Turner, the outsider, is the family's choice; meanwhile a disgruntled former lover of Nicholson, Hickey's granddaughter (Anjelica Huston won a Best Supporting Acress Oscar) also puts pressure on family to get rid of Turner. Turner is hired by Huston's father to kill Nicholson. Oddball film, deceptively humorous throughout, has a surprising ending that will turn off many viewers, but it will also make you rethink entire picture—you'll recall that all the earlier violence was extremely brutal and that Huston never manipulated you into thinking these characters, including Nicholson and Turner, are nice people who fit the mold for those Hollywood couples who have happy endings (on second thought, when you laughed it wasn't funny). Indeed, what finally happens confirms that Nicholson and Turner are made for each other, that they both play by the same rules. Nicholson gives one of his greatest performances. Not once does he revert to his standby sly-eyed, grinning expression. With his top lip hanging stupidly over his teeth, confused eyes, an expression out of *Mad* magazine, and the mumbling voice of a punch-drunk fighter, he seems to be attempting a Humphrey Bogart caricature or spoofing Robert Sacchi, the "Man with Bogart's Face," whom he sounds like at times. As always, Turner is a delight to watch, and we grow to like and trust her character—yet, interestingly, in the last scene of the film you realize she was as much of a mystery to you as she was to Nicholson. Film is well acted, with many good bit roles. But it is too long, and at one point Nicholson and Turner are off screen for much too long. Richard Condon and Janet Roach adapted from Condon's novel. Also with: John Randolph, Robert Loggia, Lee Richardson.

PRODUCERS, THE (1968) C/88m. The major strength of Mel Brooks's cult favorite is its clever premise. Zero Mostel plays a washed-up Broadway producer, Max Bialystock, who makes his money by fulfilling the sexual fantasies of old ladies. Gene Wilder is timid accountant Leo Bloom, who feels sorry for Max and becomes his partner and is happy for the first time in his life in a ridiculous theatrical venture: they figure to become rich if they collect a lot of money from investors to put on a play that will fail immediately so they will only have to use a small amount of money on production. They search for the worst play ever written, and these Jewish partners select a musical written by insane Nazi Franz Liebkind (Kenneth Mars) called *Springtime for Hitler*, featuring a Hitler who is a much better dancer and more handsome than Winston Churchill. Then Max sells 25,000% of the show to old ladies. But with a middle-aged hippie named LSD (Dick Shawn steals the film) in the lead and an unbelievable Nazi production number, the play becomes an enormous hit because people believe it's a brilliant satire. While there are Jews who would invest in a Nazi play (just as Jews own porno bookstores), Max and Leo are too sweet to corrupt themselves in such a manner. Peter Lorre and Sydney Greenstreet would have been ideal. Another problem is that those people who start to walk out on *Springtime* would not return to their seats when LSD appears. Those who think the play is offensive and choose to exit wouldn't think a hippie Hitler is funny. Those who think unfunny LSD is funny might also find *Springtime* offensive, but would like it for just that reason. Max would seem to be the ideal role for Zero Mostel, but he looks uncomfortable whenever anyone else is dominating a scene and, like the most unskilled, insecure amateur, resorts to mugging to get attention. Wilder is fine, but Mostel can't handle being his straight man on occasion. Film's highlight is LSD's audition song, "Love Power," which begins as a love song about flowers and ends up with revolting lyrics about a flower being flushed down the toilet, where it goes "in the sewer with the yuck running through 'er" and ends up in the "water that we drink." Brooks's screenplay won an Oscar. Also with: Estelle Winwood, Christopher Hewitt, Andreas Voutsinas, Lee Meredith, Renee Taylor.

PSYCHO (1960) B&W/109m. Far and away the most frightening film ever made—but, oddly, people who see it for the first time now in the eighties usually aren't scared at all. Oh, but to have seen it in 1960! Alfred Hitchcock's manipulative sex and horror masterpiece—the ultimate black joke—begins when Marion Crane (Janet Leigh), one of Hitchcock's many characters to break a rigid routine and act impulsively, runs off with $40,000 of company money. She hopes it will allow her to marry Sam (John Gavin). Lost in a rainstorm, she seeks refuge in the deserted Bates Motel, which is isolated but for the large Bates house on the hill behind it. Norman Bates (Anthony Perkins) is nervous, immature, neurotic, and weird. He is one of many Hitchcock characters to have a severe mother complex. But he is friendly. So friendly that his jealous "mother" (we do not see "her" face) stabs Marion to death while she showers. Norman is shocked by what Mother has done but disposes of the body in a swamp rather than call the police. Sam and Lila (Vera Miles), Marion's sister, try to find out what happened to Marion. Detective Arbogast (Martin Balsam) traces her to the motel. It is discovered that Norman's mother has been dead for years. Film should be the model for directors making terror-suspense films. Never did Hitchcock pay more attention to the *time* element. We are shocked because Hitchcock repeatedly has violence occur *before* we expect it: while Marion showers, you see, through the shower curtain, that Mother has entered the bathroom—she doesn't sneak in slowly, but walks quickly toward the shower, without fear; when Arbogast walks up the stairs of the Bates house, we expect him to enter the room where we know Mother stays, but instead she charges out, knife raised high, and starts stabbing him; and, of course, the lead character, Marion, is killed with only a third of the picture over. Hitchcock "punctuates" his initial shocks to completely unnerve us: each plunge of the knife into Marion's body (sexually repressed Norman is committing "rape") is like an exclamation point (*time* stands still as in Eisenstein), as are the violin screeches that accompany each stab; when Arbogast plummets backward down the stairs, Mother immediately jumps on him (again we're shocked by how *quick* she is) and uses the knife to finish him off—period, period, period; when Lila turns "Mother" around and we are shocked, Hitchcock adds the "punctuation" by having another "Mother" (the real "Mother"?) charge in behind her. The many classic moments and images in the film have been analyzed ad nauseum. But one image that sticks with me—usually ignored because its effect is subliminal—is the shot of Mother fleeing the bathroom after Marion's murder. With hindsight we can see the enormity of Norman's (sexual) identity problems here: there is no reason for Mother to race out, because there is no one else around to catch her—*unless* she worries about Norman. Joseph Stefano adapted Robert Bloch's novel. John L. Russell did the cinematography. Bernard Herrmann composed the excellent score. Saul Bass designed the titles and may have shot the shower sequence. Perkins and Miles returned in 1983's underrated *Psycho II*, directed by Richard Franklin; Perkins is star and director of 1986's *Psycho III*. Also with: John McIntire, Simon Oakland, Frank Albertson, Patricia Hitchcock, Vaughn Taylor, Lurene Tuttle, John Anderson, Mort Mills.

PSYCH-OUT (1968) C/101m. Energetic exploitation film was filmed on location in San Francisco's Haight-Ashbury, where deaf 17-year-old runaway Susan Strasberg has come to look for brother Bruce Dern among society's dropouts. Musician Jack Nicholson and his friends Dean Stockwell, Adam Roarke, and Max Julian help the square Strasberg fit into the hip youth scene so she can elude police—she dons a sexy mini and shades—and help her track down Dern, who has become a raving lunatic. There are rumbles, drug-hallucination scenes, deaths. It's a lot of fun. This is the best of all the biker and drug films that AIP produced during the era. Strasberg was never so appealing; Nicholson and Dern have field days. Also, it's interesting seeing what Hollywood's conception of Haight-Ashbury was when it was the mecca for the counterculture. Directed by Richard Rush (*The Stunt Man*). Produced by Dick Clark. Laszlo Kovacs did the cinematography (which reflects the style of the period). Also with: Robert Kelljan, Henry Jaglom, Barbara London, Tommy Flanders, Gary Marshall, Linda Gaye Scott, the Strawberry Alarm Clock, the Seeds.

PUBLIC ENEMY, THE (1931) B&W/84m–96m. Seminal Warners gangster film, directed by William Wellman, catapulted James Cagney to stardom. He plays everyman Tom Powers, who graduated from juvenile delinquent to full-fledged racketeer. The writers, Kubec Glasmon and John Bright, presented scenes from Powers's youth to explain how a boy can develop into a criminal: since his mother loved him so much she forgave him everything, and his uncommunicative father spanked him too often, he was more influenced by criminal types in his neighborhood. Yet they supposedly weren't trying to be apologists for his heinous actions as an adult. After all, Warners claimed this film was meant to deglamorize mobsters. However, Cagney is so engaging as Powers, so full of spirit, energy, and charm, that viewers couldn't help but confuse liking the actor with liking his character. After all, he is having a good time—shooting guns, killing other bad guys, hanging out with pretty women (Mae Clarke, Jean Harlow), and making a lot of money—while his honest brother (Donald Cook) is a bore, has a cruddy low-pay job as a trolley-car ticket puncher (the same job he had a dozen years earlier), and lives with a scowl on his face. Surely male viewers envied tough guy Powers because he wasn't afraid to take on bullies and cops since he had no fear of death; how many of them saw their sick fantasies realized when Powers pushed a grapefruit in the kisser of his mistress (Clarke)? Film is somewhat dated, but it's well worth watching for Cagney's performance and several classic scenes: the famous grapefruit bit; the badly wounded Cagney tap-stepping his way through a large puddle; Cagney's off-screen execution of a horse; the delivery of Cagney's body back home. Also with: Edward Woods (as Powers's partner), Joan Blondell, Beryl Mercer (as Powers's mother), Leslie Fenton, Snitz Edwards, Frankie Darro (Powers as a boy).

PUMPING IRON (1977) C/85m. Documentary about the men participating in a Mr. Olympia contest held in Pretoria, South Africa. Arnold Schwarzenegger is shooting for his seventh consecutive title (he'll retire afterward), but he figures to have stiff competition from baby-faced Brooklynite Lou Ferrigno (later to be TV's Incredible Hulk). Film is largely responsible for the growth in body building in this country—reason enough for it to be banned. I really can't tell how directors George Butler and Robert Fiore view their subject; it's hard not to form your own opinions watching these muscle-bound men indulge in ultimate narcissism. The term "pumping iron" must have a masturbatory connotation—Schwarzenegger says that he feels as if he were having orgasms the entire time he works out. Schwarzenegger is charismatic and intelligent, which is more than can be said of his competitors. But his conversations have been edited to a point where he sounds like a sexist cad (he even gives competitors wrong advice). Contest itself seems chintzy. Lowlight of film has a body builder telling his young son and daughter to strike body-building poses. Followed in 1985 by *Pumping Iron II: The Women*.

PURPLE RAIN (1984) C/111m.

Rock star Prince catapulted into Michael Jackson megastar status as the result of this smash semi-autobiographical rock musical. (He claims the family-life sequences are fictional.) Prince, who hails from Minneapolis, plays the kid leader of a struggling Minneapolis rock band (played by Prince's group, The Revolution). He has incredible talent, but personal problems prevent him from letting go, relaxing, and giving his all to his music. He has an affair with a beautiful singer (Apollonia Kotero, Prince's discovery, who got the role intended for Vanity, his former girlfriend). But he is in danger of losing her to his slick singing rival Morris Day because he can't control his violence toward women. This problem can be traced to his home life: his drunken father (Clarence Williams III), a onetime musician, repeatedly beats up him and his passive mother. Meanwhile his female band members threaten to quit unless he swallows his macho pride and performs songs they have written. Story is trite and simplistic and the direction by Albert Magnoli is extremely crude, but the picture has enticing sexual tension (that borders on vulgarity) and the flamboyant Prince has undeniable charisma and charm. He also has the explosive energy of James Dean in *Rebel Without a Cause*, which he tries to release by riding his motorcycle, having sex, using his fists, breathlessly pacing back and forth, back and forth; but he has success only on the stage in front of frenzied fans—belting out a soulful song, his fingers whipping his guitar, his dancing legs twisting and turning. Prince has amazing sexual presence. Also his performances here (I'm not a big Prince fan) are exceptional—"Purple Rain" is spellbinding. Film's other plus is its democratic mix of whites and blacks, men and women—this was one of reasons the picture had such a large audience. Also with: Olga Karlatos, Jerome Benton, Billy Sparks, Jill Jones, Charles Huntsberry, Dez Dickerson, Brenda Bennett.

PURPLE ROSE OF CAIRO, THE (1985) C/82m.

Perhaps Woody Allen decided not to be in his sourest comedy because as director-writer he plays such dirty tricks on all his characters. Nobody ends up happier than when we first see them. This is especially true of Mia Farrow (as Cecilia), who, like many lonely, miserable souls during the Depression, finds her only solace at the movies, away from her rough, cheating, good-for-nothing husband (Danny Aiello). Referencing Pirandello and Buster Keaton's *Sherlock, Jr.*, Allen has the extremely likable character (Jeff Daniels) of a silly movie called *The Purple Rose of Cairo* literally walk out of the screen and strike up a romance with Farrow. Soon after, the actor who played this character (also Daniels) rushes to her New Jersey town to see what's gone wrong and he too starts courting Farrow. Both men want to take her away, one to Hollywood, the other into the motion picture. For the first time she has a chance to escape her sad existence. Why won't Allen let her? Why, after presenting an hour's worth of fantasy, does he decide that her escape into a fantasy world would be *unrealistic*? Perhaps he is trying to tell us that those unhappy people who use movies to escape from their problems are only deceiving themselves. This is certainly a gloomy theme, because someone like Farrow has no other way to soothe her sorrow. On the other hand, Allen's film may also be a tribute to the cinema for having the power to help one escape. Consequently, when Allen makes the point that the "real" world Farrow inhabits and its real people (her husband, the actor) are not as comforting or reliable as those found on the silver screen, he writes himself into a paradoxical situation. For Farrow's "real" world is still *our* "cinema" world and, thus according to Allen, we—his depressed viewers who have come to see a comedy—are counting on the happy, escapist ending (for Farrow) that he refuses to provide. It's a shame because Farrow blossoms in her role, becoming so lovable that one can understand why both actor and character fall for her immediately (just like in the movies). Daniels gives an appealing performance as well, but Allen doesn't handle the actor-out-of-the-screen premise as inventively as one would hope. Almost all of the peripheral characters are annoying. Also with: Stephanie Farrow, Van Johnson, Milo O'Shea.

PURSUED (1947) B&W/101m.

Engrossing, exceptionally well-made Raoul Walsh western whose plot has traces of *Wuthering Heights*, Greek tragedies, and psychological thrillers. When a boy, Robert Mitchum had a traumatic experience that he has blocked out of his mind—but he knows that whatever happened has instilled in him both a sense of not fitting in and a sense that he has some important unfinished business. On that night he was taken into the home of rancher Judith Anderson (who never revealed what happened) and raised as her own, on equal terms with her natural daughter, Teresa Wright, and son, John Rodney. Mitchum and Wright grew to love each other and planned marriage, but Rodney always resented Mitchum's presence. When Rodney tries to ambush Mitchum and is killed himself, Anderson and Wright cast Mitchum out of their lives. To make matters worse, Anderson's brother-in-law lawyer, Dean Jagger (a great villain), slyly tries to kill Mitchum, as he swore he'd do when Mitchum was a lad. Why is he obsessed with killing Mitchum? The answer is the secret Anderson possesses. Film benefits from a strong cast, well-rounded characters who each have interesting motives for what they do, intelligent dialogue by Niven Busch, believable period (late 1890s/early 1900s) flavor. As usual in a Walsh picture, there is fast pacing and the action scenes are exciting. An unusual western. Also with: Alan Hale, Harry Carey, Jr.

PUTNEY SWOPE (1969) C-B&W/88m.

Infamous, irreverent cult comedy from writer-director Robert Downey about a ruthless, opportunistic, gravel-voiced black man, Putney Swope (Arnold Johnson), who is accidentally elected head of a Madison Avenue ad agency. He fires or demotes all the whites on the board of directors, hires a staff of black militants, and renames the agency Truth and Soul, Inc. He gets scores of rich white clients because his obscene commercials prove extremely effective. No matter that he steals the ideas for the ads. He is as money-hungry and unscrupulous as his white predecessors (although he refuses to run ads that promote war toys, alcohol, or cigarettes). Early in the picture Swope rips down a poster of Sidney Poitier; this reveals Downey has no intention of populating his picture with blacks whom the white male audience will feel comfortable watching. Indeed, Downey's film was designed both to satirize those black militant prototypes he regarded as politically insincere and to present the bigoted white viewer's nightmare vision of what would happen if black militants came to power. Swope runs his agency in the manner of black dictators who take over African countries that have white minorities and white-controlled businesses. Picture should be double-billed with *Amin: The Rise and Fall*. It is dated (the once hilarious color commercials now seem trite), hasn't two funny lines in a row (after the amusing pre-title sequence)—people keep doing or saying absurd things in front of Swope, but he never has a good *reaction* line—and has an end that foolishly undermines Swope's character. But while it is overrated, it's certainly unique, if only because it attacks most everyone, even midgets. Also with: Antonio Fargas (as the complaining Arab), Laura Greene (as Putney's wife, who treats their white maid as if she were a slave), Pepi Hermine (as the pot-smoking midget President), Ruth Hermine, Allen Garfield, Alan Abel, Allan Arbus, Shelley Plimpton, Mel Brooks.

Q/WINGED SERPENT, THE (1982) C/93m.

An Aztec deity, the giant flying serpent Quetzalcoatl, mysteriously appears above the Manhattan skyscrapers, descending only long enough to bite off the heads of sunbathers and construction workers. It has built a secret nest at the top of the Chrysler Building. Policemen David Carradine and Richard Roundtree link its return from the ages to a series of ritualistic murders that are taking place all over the city. Former junkie Michael Moriarty flees a botched hold-up and somehow winds up at the nest. When the police arrest him, this born loser becomes an opportunist: he will divulge the location of the nest for $1 million plus amnesty. The preposterous, totally confusing story is bolstered somewhat by the offbeat humor in director Larry Cohen's script, some good location footage and his depiction of the *city as character*; and by a memorable, weirdly conceived performance by Moriarty, although I believe he should have saved his interesting neurotic for another picture. Fun for a while, this cult picture is done in by unforgivably sloppy editing, mediocre special effects, and too many loose ends. Also with: Candy Clark as Moriarty's girlfriend (who just disappears from the film), John Capodice, Nancy Stafford, baseball player Ron Cey.

QUACKSER FORTUNE HAS A COUSIN IN THE BRONX/FUN LOVING (IRISH/1970) C/90m.

Another movie that became a cult favorite of college-age viewers because it not only has a nonconformist hero but is about nonconformity *per se*. Filmed in Dublin by Indian-born English director Waris Hussein, character comedy deals with an ignorant, simple, working-class stiff named Quackser Fortune (Gene Wilder) who has rejected a restrictive job in the foundry for the independence of self-created work: he follows horses through streets, collecting manure to sell as fertilizer. Just when he gets the unhappy news that horses are being replaced by cars, he has an affair with a sophisticated American student (Margot Kidder). Offbeat and amiable, with fine performances by the two leads. It's hard to watch Quackser have an affair that we know will end in his heartbreak—for he is out of his league with Kidder. Interestingly, while she's much hipper than he, she does the *expected* thing—he remains the nonconformist. A nice, unexpected touch is having him benefit from the relationship rather than feeling self-pity or animosity toward her afterward. Also with: Eileen Colgen, Seamus Ford.

QUADROPHENIA (BRITISH/1979) C/115m.

England's first street film, about the turbulent Mods vs. Rockers music-motorcycles-fashion scene in 1964 (the year of the Brighton riots)—the most exciting, perceptive youth film since *Rebel Without a Cause*—was adapted from the concept album by The Who. It wasn't made with an international market in mind, as *Tommy* had been: the working-class characters speak with thick cockney accents and their conversations are sprinkled with street lingo of the British-youth variety; there's much location footage; there's no preface for the uninitiated that defines and contrasts the warring Mods and Rockers; except for Sting (who has a non-speaking part), none of the actors, including scrawny lead Phil Daniels, was known outside of England. But I can't see why Americans can't identify with it: young viewers can relate to the Mods, who define themselves by their musical taste, revolutionary fashions, anti-social posturing, and anarchical brand of violence. One can become extremely sentimental because director Franc Roddam has done a remarkable job of re-creating the youth scene of 1964: dark, wet London streets, empty but for herds of Mods on Italian scooters and Rockers on heavy cycles in search of a rumble; dingy, sweat-filled clubs; greasy diners, pinball joints, back alleys, dance halls, etc. Daniels is certainly a character we can identify with: he represents all youths in the throes of growing pains, in desperate search for their identities. He's a Mod, but he doesn't fit in anywhere because he tries too hard to be different, and in the process loses his job, girlfriend, best friend, his family, his home, his status in the Mods. He is always more excited, angrier, or more frustrated than anyone else; to him every moment has great significance. My favorite scene has him returning alone to a Brighton street where he once had battled police with the top Mod, Ace Face (Sting), gaining his respect, and had won a quickie in an alleyway with his pretty girlfriend (Leslie Ash) because she had been excited by his exploits. What guy doesn't remember such a moment when both the top dog and his dreamgirl saw him at his best, when he revealed his true self? This is a superb, powerful film, ambitiously directed by Roddam with wit, style, and passion. Add to this Daniels's great performance and a terrific score (Who songs and other solid-gold hits) and you can't help feeling that adrenaline rush so often experienced in the mid-sixties. Also with: Mark Wingett, Philip Davis.

QUEEN CHRISTINA (1934) B&W/97m.

Marvelous historical drama, with Greta Garbo giving her greatest performance as the enlightened, independent-minded queen of 17th-century Sweden. Christina is one of the best-written, strongest female characters in cinema history—a leader who steadfastly refuses to crumble under the unmitigated pressures from her powerful male advisers and relies on her distinctly *female* brain, heart, and instincts to rule well. Garbo glows in the role. Never has she seemed to enjoy playing a part so much, or to empathize so much with her character; or given such a dramatic, heartfelt reading of her lines (which are extremely well written). Never has she displayed such vitality, intelligence, or passion. (Only in *Ninotchka* is she as witty.) When we first see Garbo she wears pants, symptomatic of her difficulty reconciling being a woman and holding a position (ruler of a male-dominated country) suited for a man. While she was successful at waging war, she is determined to have peace; her other pursuits are also what would be regarded as traditionally feminine: she reads, loves art, desires knowledge; being a romantic, she would love to find a man whom she could love for eternity. Tired of her advisers clamoring for war and conquest and urging her to enter a loveless marriage with a Swedish prince who is a war hero, Garbo sneaks away for a brief holiday. In several wonderful scenes that range from semi-comical to sexy to romantic, she has a fling with the Spanish ambassador, well played by John Gilbert, Garbo's most famous lover during the silent era. The affair between the Swedish queen and the Spanish ambassador causes an uproar in the royal court and throughout Sweden. So, like many modern women, Christina must choose between a man and her job. The point that is made is that she is not allowed to do her job well, in the manner she'd like—as a *woman*. Film has Christina considering abdication because of her love for a man; it does not touch on her Catholicism, which caused her much grief in Sweden. The direction by Rouben Mamoulian is exquisite; particularly impressive are his close-ups, including Garbo's head on the pillow at the inn and the astonishing, lenthy final shot of the star's beautiful face. Also with: C. Aubrey Smith, Ian Keith, Lewis Stone, Gustav von Seyffertitz, Reginald Owen, Elizabeth Young.

QUEEN OF OUTER SPACE (1958) C/80m.

Ludicrous camp classic with Zsa Zsa Gabor as a Venusian revolutionary (who wears high heels). The year is 1985 and four American astronauts (leader Eric Fleming, wise Paul Birch, loverboy Patrick Waltz, "funny" Dave Wilcox) crash-land on Venus. They are taken prisoner by the evil queen (Laurie Mitchell) and her female army. She despises men because her face was badly burned by radiation in a war caused by men—as a result, she exiled all the men of Venus to a prison planet. That's the major reason an underground movement, led by scientist Zsa Zsa Gabor, has formed. Fleming and Gabor immediately fall in love, and Waltz and Wilcox find girlfriends among the revolutionaries—and there's a three-couple make-out scene in a cave that's much like the lobby of a female dorm before curfew. Fleming, Gabor, and the others try to prevent Mitchell from destroying the earth with a deadly ray. Film is fun to analyze in terms of the roles played by the women. Those women we admire (in this male fantasy) are straight-off-a-casting-couch beautiful, available for sex; are straightforward about wanting sex; are sexually aggressive (though virgins); are brave; and carry guns (though they'll give them to their boyfriends). Those we despise (like Mitchell) are ugly (some wear masks), hysterical, and domineering, and, though they hate and threaten men, are secretly desiring their sexual attention. The men (Wilcox refers to the women as dolls and babes; Fleming tries to use his potent sexual magnetism on Mitchell) are what you'd expect. Direction by Edward Bernds is awful, as are the cheap special effects. Script (which has some tongue-in-cheek humor) was written by Charles Beaumont from a story by Ben Hecht—although it borrows a great deal from *Cat Women of the Moon* and *Missile to the Moon*. In CinemaScope.

QUERELLE (WEST GERMAN/1983) C/106m.

Rainer Werner Fassbinder's last film, released in the U.S. after his death, is an adaptation of Jean Genet's novel *Querelle de Brest*. It looks more theatrical than cinematic and more choreographed than directed. Story is of a handsome young sailor, Querelle (American Brad Davis), whose ship docks in Brest, where his civilian brother (Hanno Poschl) is having an unfulfilling relationship with the married owner (Jeanne Moreau) of a local bar-hotel. Querelle begins experimenting with homosexual sex with several men, at first saying it's because of curiosity about the sexual act, then because he enjoys the act. That he remains passive during the sex is symptomatic of his refusal to believe he is attracted to the men involved. But finally he admits his love for a man (as opposed to just admitting he enjoys homosexual sex), thus confirming his homosexuality. Throughout, Querelle draws a parallel between the sexual acts he is committing and the law-breaking "crimes" he was responsible for (including murder). Meanwhile Fassbinder seems to be showing that Querelle's active participation in homosexual love is better than the vicarious homosexuality of his captain (Franco Nero) and the complete denial of homosexuality by his unhappy brother. Film is tough going, but essential if you are interested in Fassbinder. What's surprising is how little sex there is, considering it's all that anyone in the film talks about. Also with: Burkhard Driest, Laurent Malet.

QUIET MAN, THE (1952) C/129m. John Ford traveled to his beloved County Galway in Ireland, from where his parents emigrated to Maine (his birthplace), in order to make this classic. And the rolling countryside is so green, the village of Innisfree is so quaint, and the people whom his stock company portrays are so charmingly eccentric that we understand his love for his native land. Also enchanted is John Wayne's American boxer, Sean Thornton (Ford was christened Sean O'Fienne), who returns to the village in which he was born and, through his mother's stories, has always imagined as paradise. Guilty from having killed a man in the ring just to win prize money, he is searching for an Eden. And for an Eve. He spots lovely Mary Kate Danaher (Maureen O'Hara) walking barefoot through the rolling pastures, her red hair blowing in the wind. He falls in love. But so much for the fairytale—now the trouble begins. Sean and Mary Kate want to marry, but her brother Will (Victor McLaglen) won't let them because he resents Sean for buying a cottage that Will had his eye on. McLaglen finally gives his consent when Michaeleen Oge Flynn (a great performance by Barry Fitzgerald) and Father Lonergan (Ward Bond) convince him that the Widow Tillane (Mildred Natwick) will marry him only if Mary Kate has left his house. But after Sean and Mary Kate wed, Mrs. Tillane turns down Will's proposal and he becomes so infuriated that he refuses to relinquish Mary Kate's dowry. Sean doesn't care about her dowry, but Mary Kate insists that without it she isn't a complete woman but only Sean's servant. He thinks her greedy for wanting the dowry; she thinks him a coward for not fighting Will for it. She refuses to consummate their marriage if she doesn't have the dowry: like the "modern woman," she doesn't want to enter a relationship unless it's on equal terms. To his credit, he doesn't force himself on her sexually (as does Clark Gable on wife Vivien Leigh in *GWTW*) but asks the reverend Cyril Playfair (Arthur Shields) to explain the tradition-related reasons that she is obsessed with getting her dowry. Interestingly, Mary Kate decides to have sex with Sean although he has not come through for her (this is a *mature* relationship)—she senses that he has reasons for not challenging her brother, although she herself may not understand them. In turn, Sean

then challenges Will for Mary Kate's sake: he concedes that her reasons for wanting the dowry are not trivial, although he doesn't understand them. There's so much Irish humor in this film and so many quirky characters that one tends to overlook that just below the surface there is much seriousness, unhappiness, hurt, and guilt; both Sean and Mary Kate are tormented in real ways and we feel for them. Many people regard the lengthy brawl between Sean and Will as the picture's most memorable scene; it's a great deal of fun, but I've more fondness for any of the scenes involving Sean and Mary Kate, one of the screen's most romantic couples. Ford was never known for "love scenes," but the silent passage in which Sean and O'Hara hold hands, race for shelter from the sudden rain, and then stop, clutch (he drapes his sweater over her), and kiss as the rain soaks through their clothing is incredibly sexy. Gorgeous cinematography by Winton C. Hoch and Archie Stout deservedly won the Oscar. Also with: Francis Ford, Eileen Crowe, Sean McClory, Jack McGowran, Ken Curtis, Mae Marsh, Hank Worden, Patrick Wayne.

RABID/RAGE (CANADIAN/1977) C/90m. Low-budget horror film by David Cronenberg stars porno star Marilyn Chambers as a young woman who is badly injured in a motorcycle accident. She is taken to a clinic that is doing experimental skin-graft operations. I can't explain it, but after a skin-graft operation she has beneath her armpit what looks like a vagina-like opening in the skin—when she craves blood, the only substance that will keep her alive, a phallus-shaped projection comes out of the opening and digs into her victims' bloodstreams. Her victims develop a virulent strain of rabies. After claiming several victims at the clinic, she flees to Montreal. Soon that city is overrun by blood-drinking, rabid people and martial law is proclaimed. A lively, if stupid, horror film, recalling George Romero's *Night of the Living Dead* and *Dawn of the Dead*, but with nudity and sex. Chambers is satisfactory in an R-rated role. It was smart of Cronenberg to give the lead to her: since viewers saw this XXX-rated star as being the prime example of a sexually liberated woman and the embodiment of sexual fantasies fulfilled, he could use her to teach them a lesson about free love; it's surprising that Chambers took a role that equates sex with sickness and death (a theme of early Cronenberg films). Film is sloppy in spots and not particularly inventive; we repeatedly see innocent people attacked by rabid people who are frothing at the mouth (it's easy to hate scenes in which people drip gobs of saliva). However, Chambers's death scene is pretty effective. I wish that they had made her sympathetic from

346

the beginning, like Gloria Holden in *Dracula's Daughter*. Also with: Frank Moore, Joe Silver, Patricia Gage.

RACHEL, RACHEL (1968) C/101m.

Joanne Woodward is one of our finest actresses, perhaps our most likable star, yet she has appeared in only a handful of good movies, and probably none worthy of her immense talents. She has specialized in playing women who are warmhearted, maternal, vulnerable, victimized, and confused about the harshness of the world. They can be dumped on by supposed lovers or just look out of place. Their universal appeal is that they'll make fools of themselves. They are women whose undergarments show, who stumble on the stairs, who talk too loudly and naïvely, who spill things—when everyone is looking. Oddly, Woodward has been passed over by "cinematic" directors and has found herself in dreary dialogue pieces—conspicuous for their lack of energy and humor—that seem more fitting for theater than film. This is one of those films. Woodward is brilliant as a spinster schoolteacher who wants "to say something I've never said before—I'm happy!" She is tired of her boring smalltown existence, taking care of her sickly mother (Kate Harrington) and living up to everyone's limited expectations for her. Then she has her first affair, with a former school chum (James Olson) who's visiting town. We feel for her because she tries so hard in the relationship and would make the right man the perfect wife. Yet we know that she's headed for heartbreak and that Woodward's again playing the fool. Stewart Stern's script has excellent, mature dialogue and his believable characters have odd yet real ways of expressing themselves. However, the poignancy he achieves disappears into schmaltz and bathos. Making his directorial debut, Paul Newman does well with his actors, but he also goes overboard with the sentimentality; every one of his many flashbacks is meant to increase our pity for Woodward. Even Woodward's ultimate triumph, when she rides out of town on a bus, is treated like a funeral procession. Also with: Estelle Parsons (as Woodward's lesbian friend), Donald Moffat, Geraldine Fitzgerald.

RADIO RANCH (1935) B&W/80m.

Lovers of "B" westerns and sci-fi serials will get a kick out of this feature which was condensed from the popular 12-part Mascot serial, *The Phantom Empire*. In the part that made him an enormous star, Gene Autry plays—would you believe it?—himself. He's a radio singing star who discovers that crooks are trying to kill him to get the uranium on his land. While running for his life, he happens upon the cave entrance to a futuristic city, Murang, 20,000 feet below his Radio Ranch. He is captured by Quentika (Dorothy Christy), escapes, sings a song, and is recaptured, along with his young "Thunder Riders" pals Frankie Darro and Betsy King Ross. They escape. Amusing entertainment has special effects on the order of TV's *Space Patrol*; the only interesting image is of city disintegrating. Gimmicky production influenced *Flash Gordon*. It's easy to see its appeal for kids in the thirties.

Autry's songs include his classic "That Silver Haired Daddy of Mine." Also with: Wheeler Oakman, Smiley Burnette.

RAGGEDY MAN (1981) C/94m.

Sissy Spacek is Nita Langley, a divorced mother of two small boys (Henry Thomas, Carey Hollis, Jr.), who is upset to be frozen in the low-paying, time-consuming job of telephone operator of Gregory, Texas, in 1944. She is lonely because there are no men in town, except for two violent brothers (William Sanderson, Tracy Walter) and the mysterious "raggedy man" (Sam Shepard), who will prove to be guardian angel to Nita and the boys. So when kind sailor Teddy (a splendid performance by Eric Roberts) passes through town, she invites him to stay with her, despite the scandal she knows it will cause and the effect this will have on the violent brothers (Walter is particularly creepy). Picture has a horror-movie ending, a regrettable sequence that almost ruins the picture. But until then it's the most lyrical and romantic of films. So authentic is this small Texas town that you'll feel transported back through time. The dialogue is smart, the sets and photography are impeccable, the interaction of characters, including adults and children, is wonderful. The affair between Nita and Teddy is tastefully handled; I'm glad that they don't sleep together until we understand why they appeal to one another and how they fill each other's needs. These are moral people. Spacek obviously enjoys playing a mother, and Nita is her most mature, capable, and, I think, appealing character. Also Spacek, who is often shot in extreme close-up, has never been more ravishing; it's really obvious that the director—Jack Fisk, her husband—loves her. And we fall for her Nita as we watch her be a whiz at the switchboard, dance seductively with Teddy, stand up to her tough boss (R. G. Armstrong), dance with her broom to the Andrews Sisters' "Rum and Coca-Cola," excitedly put her hand in her new nylons, touch up her hair just to join Teddy and the boys for 30 seconds of kite flying, and lovingly and protectively look in on her sleeping children (ignoring their recent rudeness toward her). Never has Spacek had so much freedom to create a character through nuance rather than speech, and, after all these years, she reveals exciting parts of her that she'd always kept hidden. Written by William D. Wittliff.

RAGING BULL (1980) B&W/128m.

The major reason to see this film is Robert De Niro's shattering Oscar-winning portrayal of forties middleweight boxing champ Jake La Motta; he even ate himself into blimpic proporations for the later scenes in is subject's life. Reason number two is Michael Chapman's stunning black-and-white photography; his fine shots of old New York and Miami hauntingly capture the *feel* of the past, his boxing sequences are surreal. As always, Martin Scorsese's direction is powerful and his characters are natural and real, but, as is too often the case, he has chosen to film a script whose lead character is a thoroughly unlikable figure (Paul Schrader also wrote Scorsese's *Taxi Driver*). Eventually you may give up trying to figure out what makes La Motta tick and just get fed up with his antics. The film deals with a man who is tortured by inner demons, a mean man who finds he can perfectly express his meanness in the ring. Boxers aren't nice guys, after all (despite what most films have shown). They just like to beat up on people: La Motta does it at home to his wife, Vicky (coolly played by Cathy Moriarty), and he does it in the ring with equal severity, especially enjoying battering the face of a young fighter his wife thought "goodlooking." Scene by scene, the film has impact; particularly strong are those scenes with De Niro and Joe Pesci, who plays La Motta's argumentative brother, and the scene in which La Motta reacts to having thrown a fight for the only time in his career. But when the film ends, you realize that it has no core, no real theme. It's just about a louse. We get the impression that boxing's champions and its bums are one and the same. Made many "Ten Best" lists. Also with: Frank Vincent, Nicholas Colasanto, Theresa Saldana.

RAIDERS OF THE LOST ARK (1981) C/115m. Directed by Steven Spielberg and written by Lawrence Kasdan from a story by executive producer George Lucas and Philip Kaufman, this marvelous adventure movie is so much better than the old-time Saturday serials it pays tribute to—few stand the test of time—but, rather than diminishing those films, it recaptures the feeling of excitement and awe they originally held for kids. It is *great*, as fans nostalgically remember their favorite serials were. It is 1936. Harrison Ford's Indiana Jones is an American anthropology professor. He is also an indomitable, whip- and gun-carrying adventurer whose expeditions to the far corners of the world put him in constant danger (but only snakes scare him). He flies to Tibet when he learns that the Nazis are digging for the Ark of the Covenant, which held Moses's Ten Commandments. The lost Ark could have incredibly destructive powers, so it's imperative that Indy gets the Ark instead of the Nazis. His former girlfriend Marion, spiritedly played by Karen Allen, runs a bar in Tibet. After ten years she still feels hostility toward Indy, but she becomes his partner. During the many adventures that lie ahead, they again fall in love. Picture has non-stop nail-biting action—each sequence could be the *highlight* of another film. Film also has tremendous wit, romance that even young boys will enjoy, nasty villains, amazing stunts, a lovely, brave, capable heroine, and an unbeatable action hero. The fabulous teaser opening in the South African jungles and the climax in which the awesome power of the Ark is revealed are among the adventure genre's greatest sequences. But just as much thought and imagination went into the other scenes. Ambitious in every way. Cinematography by Douglas Slocombe; Michael Kahn won an Oscar for editing. Oscars were also won for special effects (Richard Edlund), art direction (Leslie Dilley), and sound. John Williams wrote the score. Also with: Paul Freeman, John Rhys-Davies, Wolf Kahler, Denholm Elliott, Ronald Lacey.

RAIN PEOPLE, THE (1969) C/102m. In his major works Francis Ford Coppola has relegated his fe-

male characters to peripheral roles. Yet early in his career he made this sleeper that remains one of the few Hollywood films to deal sensitively with a real woman and her problems. About a woman in desperate need of some consciousness-raising, it might have been a hit if released about a year later, when the women's movement really made its first great strides. It began as a short story called "Echoes" that Coppola wrote while at UCLA. That was about three women who left their husbands, but Coppola deleted two of its storylines and adapted his screenplay specifically for Shirley Knight, who responded with her best performance. She plays a childless Long Island housewife who, one rainy morning, abandons the husband she loves (we can quickly see how stifling her life is) and begins an aimless drive across America. Periodically she calls home, promising to return when she's ready. She also reveals that she's pregnant and isn't sure she wants the baby. She thinks too little of herself to believe that she could be a good mother. She doesn't rush home, but continues her journey, enjoying her first freedom since she was married and searching for an extramarital affair—her only explanation for why she would have left her husband. Viewers brought up on movie heroines who stick by their men through thick and thin may point angry fingers at Knight, but this is not *Kramer vs. Kramer*, where the woman is automatically guilty because her side of the story is never told. Coppola is very sympathetic toward Knight, even when her actions cause others harm. He wants to show her immaturity, to show that she is correct in thinking she should have an abortion. This is made clear when she picks up a brain-damaged hitchhiker (James Caan), a surrogate child. While her motherly instincts keep drawing her back to him, she repeatedly tries to abandon him. Her poor care for him suggests that she isn't prepared for motherhood. Knight is marvelous. So much of what we learn about this woman comes not from the script, but from paying attention to the confidence level of her voice, the wetness of her eyes, or how strong or vulnerable her face is at given moment. Knight properly plays her as a woman undergoing metamorphosis, hopefully for the better. Robert Duvall also gives a standout performance as a highway cop who brings Knight back to his trailer one fateful rainy night. Though the film has a shaky resolution and a depressing tone, it is truly fascinating. And it's so much braver than all the more recent Hollywood films about "liberated" women. It might have been discovered in a big way by now if the director's first name had been Frances instead of Francis. Strong use of locales; fine photography by Bill Butler. Also with: Marya Zimmet, Tom Aldredge, Laurie Crewes, Andrew Duncan, Robert Modica.

RAMBO: FIRST BLOOD PART II (1985) C/93m. Surprise hit of 1985, became $150 million blockbuster and a cultural phenomenon, spawning not only tremendous sales in Rambo toys and T-shirts for the kiddie set but also, frighteningly, a boom in sales of "attack" weapons (large, double-edged, serrated knives; machine guns) to war-games enthusiasts, hunters, survivalists, weapon collectors, and, certainly, street criminals. And the Reagan hordes dreamed that they could be Sylvester Stallone's myth hero, muscular, taciturn John Rambo, who in his second adventure rescues American POWs in present-day Vietnam. They cheer as he ingenuously massacres despicable Vietnamese and Russian commies, much as Jason does away with teenagers in the *Friday the 13th* series, and withstands pain and torture. They applaud his declaration that he is willing to die for his country in Vietnam. Picture, directed by George P. Cosmatos from a script by Stallone and James Cameron, is quick-paced and gripping—but it deals with the real world as truthfully as one of those old war comics we read as children. We all care about MIAs, but to present a made-up scenario in which they are alive, living in hellish work camps run by Vietnamese but controlled by Russian officers in the Vietnamese jungle, is inexcusable and tasteless. Also infuriating is Stallone's revisionist history, which takes the popular Reagan Era notion that the Vietnam War was a justified war after all and that our soldiers were all heroes who could have won if only Washington had taken the reins off them. One shouldn't forget that those opposed to the war (who didn't believe the U.S. had the right to fight this war) were *not* against American soldiers but against Nixon and his cronies who prevented them from coming home. If Stallone made a movie about George Custer, he'd again emerge a hero, despite all that has been documented about Custer since, but I worry more that Stallone will send Rambo around the globe (i.e., Central America) fighting Communists and swaying the "U.S.A.-U.S.A.!" crowd to want our troops to follow his lead. Rambo is a sickening bare-chested macho hero, a neurotic muscleman who I believe is modeled on wrestler Hulk Hogan (who appeared in Stallone's *Rocky III*). The violence he perpetrates is orgasmic: there are piercings, slicings, explosions, bullets and rockets shooting out of weapons. Also with: Richard Crenna (again warning people not to betray Rambo), Charles Napier (an American officer who foolishly betrays Rambo), Julia Nickson (whose presence as a smart, brave, friendly Vietnamese was supposed to defray charges of racism against the picture). Cosmatos would direct Stallone's *Cobra*.

RAN (JAPANESE-FRENCH/1985) C/160m.
Akira Kurosawa's crowning achievement, an astonishing historical epic with bigger-than-life characters, beautiful scenery (what a sky!) and stupendous cinematography (no film uses color better), thrilling battle sequences, eroticism, intense palace intrigue, marvelous acting, and a fascinating storyline that is indebted to both *King Lear* and the true story of a 16th-century warlord. Hidetora (Tatsuya Nakadai), the aged head of the Ichimonji clan, retires and turns over the leadership to his eldest son, Taro (Akira Terao). He gives castles to Taro and his other sons, Jiro (Jinpachi Nezu) and Saburo (Daisuke Ryu), hoping to spend the rest of his life visiting each. When Saburo warns him that his idea is foolish because jealous Jiro will try to dispose of Taro, the infuriated Hidetora sends Saburo into exile. Saburo takes refuge with a kindly clan chieftain so he can keep an eye on the situation,

and sends Tango (Masayuki Yui), his father's former adviser (who was also exiled for speaking the truth), to watch over the old man. Hidetora finds out that Saburo was correct. At the insistence of his cold-blooded wife, Lady Kaede (Mieko Harada)—who will get her vengeance on Hidetora and his family for having massacred her family years before—Taro takes away all Hidetora's power and sends him away. Jiro will not let Hidetora bring his men into his castle, so Hidetora and his loyal warriors wind up in the wilderness without food. Again he is foolish: he listens to an adviser—a traitor—instead of Tango and his loyal nurse, Kyoami (transvestite singer Peter), and takes his men to a deserted castle. His men are trapped inside the walls by troops of both Taro and Jiro. When his warriors all die, Hidetora, realizing he was the cause of this disaster, goes mad, which is the only reason why new clan leader Jiro—who has had Taro killed during the fighting—allows him to walk out alive. Kurosawa is not being kind when he lets Hidetora escape death here, or later when he jumps off a 10-foot cliff and is unhurt, or when he tries to run across the plains. He grants him several brief reprieves only to bring him back for further cruel punishment and more suffering—before he dies he'll have to face up to the tragic results of his past sins and foolishness: his three sons will be dead, as will two of their wives, and the countryside and palaces will be covered with blood. The final battle between the troops of Jiro and Saburo is tremendously violent, but at the same time it has exhilarating, majestic sweep and pageantry. One may think that this film is about a man, his three sons, their soldiers, and war, but it is Lady Kaede, with her beautiful, emotionless face (she has no eyebrows) and her tremendous capacity for cruelty, who is most memorable: she is as responsible as Hidetora for the tragedy that befalls him and his clan. In the most unforgettable scene she visits Jiro after her husband's murder, suddenly drops her calm act, and goes wild. She pulls out a knife, jumps on his chest, and slightly slashes the terrified man's neck. Saying she cares only about her future, she hungrily licks up his blood as a prelude to sex. The witch says she'll be his if only he'll order the beheading of his wife, the sweet Lady Sue (Yoshiko Miyazaki). He thinks it's a good deal—he's just as foolish as his father. Also with: Hitoshi Ueki, Hisashi Ikawa, Takeshi Nomura.

RANCHO DELUXE (1975) C/93m—95m.
Well-written but curiously uninvolving modern-day Western about blond Jeff Bridges and Indian Sam Waterston, who pal around and rustle cattle when things get too boring. They also shoot cattle (which is off-putting) and use the meat to pay their rent. Frank Perry, directing from a script by Tom McGuane, handles each scene skillfully, but never manages to weave the various story lines together, as could Robert Altman or Alan Rudolph. Anyway, while the characters are interesting, they aren't very likable. The acting is good, and there are some offbeat one-on-one dialogue scenes, but there's too much detachment: the characters keep moving farther and farther away. Also with: Elizabeth Ashley, Clifton James,

Slim Pickens, Helen Craig, Richard Bright, Harry Dean Stanton, Charlene Dallas.

RANCHO NOTORIOUS (1952) C/89m.
An enjoyably silly western directed by Fritz Lang, incorporating several of his familiar themes: a hero wants revenge and loses his morality trying to get it; the hero finds himself in a setting where everyone is his enemy; a "respectable" citizen leads a secret organization of criminals. Cowpuncher Vern Haskell (Arthur Kennedy) goes after the man who raped and killed his fiancée. He doesn't know the man's identity, but learns he's heading for an outlaws' refuge called Chuck-a-luck, a horse ranch run by the legendary Altar Keene (Marlene Dietrich). He gains entry into the villains' den by getting thrown into jail with Altar's beau Frenchy Fairmont (Mel Ferrer) and helping him break out. Together they go to Chuck-a-luck. Haskell tries to figure out which of the outlaws taking refuge there, working Altar's ranch and planning new crimes, is the man he's after. Meanwhile his presence comes between Altar and Frenchy. Film has an interesting premise and it's fun to watch Dietrich holding court over the men, but the direction is a bit static and Daniel Taradash's script (adapted from Sylvia Richards's novel *Gunsight*) should be much more outrageous; the actors seem geared up for some tongue-in-cheek humor, but the mundane dialogue lets them down. With its hate-revenge theme (and Arthur Kennedy), film fits in with the Anthony Mann–Jimmy Stewart westerns of the period. Obviously, Nicholas Ray borrowed several plot points, character relationships, and weird themes from *Johnny Guitar*. (One concept Ray used is that stealing from a woman's safe symbolizes rape.) Also with: Gloria Henry, William Frawley, Jack Elam, George Reeves, Frank Ferguson, Dan Seymour.

RASHOMON (JAPANESE/1950) B&W/85m.
Akira Kurosawa's classic was the first Japanese film to receive widespread international distribution and success. Derived from two short stories by Ryunosuke Akutagawa, "Rashomon" and "In a Grove," film centers on the trial of a wild bandit (Toshiro Mifune) who has been arrested for raping a woman (Machiko Kyo) in the forest in front of her tied-up husband (Masayuki Mori) and then murdering him. Mifune, Kyo, Mori (his spirit speaking through a medium), and a woodcutter witness (Takashi Shimura) all give their versions of what happened. We see in four separate flashbacks that the stories contradict one another, that they usually (but not always) benefit the one who speaks. Film doesn't hold up as well as other Kurosawa works because its "there is no such thing as Absolute Truth" theme isn't particularly novel, but it shouldn't be forgotten that Kurosawa broke the rules of cinema storytelling—it is less important that any four people will tell four different versions of a story than that any *filmmaker* is capable of taking a story and visualizing it in an infinite number of equally persuasive, audience-manipulative ways. Mifune makes a strong impression, playing a character similar to one he and Kurosawa saw in a "B" jungle movie, but the other perfor-

mances are either irritating or forgettable. Playing of "Bolero" at one point seems inappropriate. Disconcerting opening and conclusion were inserted into script so the picture would be long enough to interest a distributor. A staple of film courses.

RAVEN, THE (1935) B&W/62m.
Bela Lugosi has a field day as Dr. Vollin, a fiendish surgeon who identifies with twisted genius Edgar Allan Poe and has a room in his mansion full of the torture devices Poe described in his stories. His obsessive plan is to torture lovely Irene Ware, so he invites her, her boyfriend, Lester Matthews, her father, Samuel S. Hinds, and several other guests to an overnight party. That night Hinds finds himself trapped under a swinging pendulum and Ware and Matthews are locked in a room with the walls closing in around them. But help comes from an unexpected source, Vollin's hideous-looking assistant (Boris Karloff), whom Vollin had intentionally disfigured during plastic surgery and has forced to do his bidding in order to get corrective surgery. Picture is great fun. The scene in which Karloff sees his monstrous face after the surgery and shoots at the mirrors around him—while Lugosi laughs hysterically—is a classic. Also fascinating is the scene in which rooms literally spin around or drop to a lower floor level, and metal doors slide into place to block Matthews's path to rescue Ware. Film also has Lugosi verbalize two of the horror genre's most significant themes: when a genius is denied his one love, he goes insane; if a man looks ugly, he does ugly things. Louis Friedlander (Lew Landers) does a good job directing the melodramatic *serial* material; except for Matthews, his actors do a fine job. Also with: Inez Courtney, Ian Wolfe, Spencer Charters.

RAW MEAT/DEATHLINE (BRITISH/1973) C/87m.
Rarely screened cult horror film has reactionary police inspector Donald Pleasence investigating disappearances in the London underground. He makes the startling discovery that a colony of cannibals has existed below since the late 19th century, when a group of men and women were abandoned during the digging of the subway lines. The government has long kept that event secret, rather than blemish its reputation. Now "The Man" (Hugh Armstrong), the brutish lone survivor, has started coming above more frequently for human flesh. His only words are "Mind the doors!" He kidnaps an English girl (Sharon Gurney) to take the place of his beloved wife (June Turner) when she dies. Her American boyfriend (David Ladd) comes below to rescue her, as if he were Orpheus and she Eurydice. Rather than being an exploitation work, Gary Sherman's film scares us while presenting an effective commentary on violence. It contrasts the violence-for-*survival* of "The Man" (who becomes sympathetic) with the modern violence of attack-and-revenge of Americans and the supposedly more genteel British. Not as good as its reputation, but it's original and still quite effective. For those with strong stomachs. Also with: Norman Rossington, James Cossins.

REAL LIFE (1979) C/99m. Albert Brooks's first film, co-written with Monica Johnson and Harry Shearer, is a reasonably funny satire that pokes fun at PBS's *American Family* series that presented the lives of the Louds in *cinéma vérité* style. In showing that the presence of a camera *alters reality* (it changes how people act), Brooks emphasizes the relationships among all the people in front of and behind the camera and asserts that documentarians have a lot of gall to take their cameras into people's homes to exploit them. Just as Jack Benny, on his radio and television programs, played himself not as he really was but in the unflattering image he'd created and nurtured (with fan culpability), Brooks plays the distorted version of himself: an opportunist whose integrity and sensitivity come and go as he tries to take the easy road to success; as usual, he discovers that he isn't clever enough to sneak anything past the big shots he rubs shoulders with or the common people he uses—and, as always, everything backfires on him and he ends up wallowing in self-pity. Hoping to win a Nobel Prize as well as an Oscar, Brooks—with psychologists in his corner—takes his modern cameras (worn like space helmets) into the home of Phoenix veterinarian Charles Grodin, his wife, Lee McCain, and their two children. And everything goes wrong. Film has peculiar insight into family life, some believable characterizations, and several truly hilarious scenes. But before enough things happen to Grodin's family, that plotline becomes secondary to Brooks's meetings with psychologists and studio executives. They're funny, but momentum is lost. Best scenes include: Brooks sings to Phoenix residents about how he "sincerely" appreciates them; the visit to McCain's crooked gynecologist; and Grodin's showing incompetence while operating on a horse. Also with: J. A. Preston, Matthew Tobin, Jennings Lang (voice only).

RE-ANIMATOR (1985) C/86m. Ludicrous horror movie, directed by innovative stage director Stuart Gordon of Chicago's Organic Theater. How this got some good reviews is beyond me; I hate to see new filmmakers parody horror films when it's obvious that if they had to make a serious one themselves, they'd be lost. Jeffrey Combs is a mad science student at a Massachusetts medical institute. He has created a serum that, when injected into the brain of a corpse, can reverse death. Brain surgeon David Gale wants to steal the formula, but Combs cuts off his head. However, Combs foolishly revives Gale's head and headless body. The head and the body go to the hospital and revive corpses. And Gale kidnaps the beautiful daughter (Barbara Crampton) of the walking-dead dean. With his bloody disembodied head being held in the air by his own hands, he begins to lick the shocked girl's entire body. Ugh. Picture has even "wittier" moments (i.e., Crampton and her boyfriend make love in front of a Talking Heads poster). But the endless gore becomes self-satisfying, as in *The Evil Dead*; rather than being a means to shock viewers out of complacency, it is there to impress everyone who gets a kick out of new splatter effects. There are no scary scenes, just a lot of streaming blood, crushed heads, decomposed bodies, ugliness. Amateurish and surprisingly unoriginal.

REAR WINDOW (1954) C/112m. An undisputed masterpiece by Alfred Hitchcock. For the entire film (except for one shot) the camera is situated in the living room of news photographer James Stewart's Greenwich Village apartment; so we sense how trapped he feels while stuck in his apartment, in a wheelchair with a broken leg. He looks forward to getting his cast removed and getting back to work in some rugged far-off location, away from his "perfect" glamour-conscious society girlfriend Grace Kelly (at her most beautiful and giving perhaps her most appealing performance). To keep from getting bored, Stewart spends his time staring out his rear window and studying the behavior of his neighbors across the courtyard. He has witnessed one couple having a violent argument. When he later notices that the wife is missing and sees the husband (Raymond Burr) sneaking out several times in the middle of the night, he begins to suspect that Burr has committed murder and chopped up her body for easy disposal. He can't convince his policeman friend (Wendell Corey) that he's on to something—Corey thinks the missing woman just went away after a marital spat—but Kelly comes to believe him when she realizes that Burr's wife's handbag is still in the Burr apartment. Kelly and nurse Thelma Ritter do some serious snooping. Stewart remains only a spectator. Of course, he's meant to be like us, watching the action from the comfort of a seat, with the courtyard distancing him from the real drama (which Kelly becomes part of). What's most terrifying about the finale when Burr enters Stewart's apartment and attacks him is that we sense that a murderer has walked off the screen and is attacking us. Much has been written about this film being about how we are all Peeping Toms, and indeed we do watch his neighbors with curiosity and concern. But too much is made of the Peeping Tom theme—that we are all snoopers is a *given* in the Hitchcock film. What he's most interested in is what we discover when we study people. First: people are into such dull, regimented lives that when they do anything that varies from their routines (as Burr does), neighbors will become suspicious and may suspect them of doing something terrible. A related and equally important theme (central to most Hitchcock films) is that even the most predictable people are capable of doing wildly unpredictable things; Burr can commit murder, the stacked blonde neighbor can fall for a shrimp who likes to eat, and Kelly, who's the type to fret over a broken fingernail, can be gallant enough to climb up a railing into a murderer's apartment. Kelly surprises Stewart so much with her grit and willingness to get down and dirty—without giving up her grace, style, or sophistication—that he falls madly in love with her. John Michael Hayes adapted Cornell Woolrich's novelette, Robert Burks did the intricate cinematography, Franz Waxman contributed the music, and Edith Head designed Kelly's lavish, sexy costumes. Also with: Judith Evelyn (as Miss Lonely Heart), Ross Bagdasarian/David Seville (as the composer).

REBECCA (1940) B&W/130m. Daphne du Maurier's gothic romance was the source for Alfred Hitchcock's first American film, which won an Academy Award for Best Picture. If you ever saw Joan Fontaine pretentiously playing the "star" on TV talk shows (perhaps giving her beauty tips—"I never go out in the sun"), it's hard to believe that her best roles were ones in which she came across as being simple, humble, awkward, and naturally pretty. Here Fontaine is captivating as a rich lady's traveling companion who marries wealthy young widower Laurence Olivier and accompanies him back to his enormous estate, Manderley. With a wet hanky in her hand and tears in her eyes, with nervousness in her voice and confusion written on her face, with her shoulders stooped and her heart pounding, she is a weak, unsophisticated child thrust into an adult world that terrifies her. In this fairytale there is even a witch in black, the housekeeper, Mrs. Danvers (Judith Anderson), who completely intimidates her, and a "ghost"—that of Rebecca, Olivier's first wife, who drowned mysteriously a year before but whose presence at Manderley is still overwhelming. Although the brooding Olivier never talks about Rebecca, Fontaine (whose character has no name) feels that she's always being compared unfavorably to his dead wife. The evil Mrs. Danvers, who idolized Rebecca, constantly reminds Fontaine how superior Rebecca was to her (*she* had breeding, beauty, and brains) and how much Olivier loved her—everywhere Fontaine looks she sees Rebecca's belongings and insignia. Picture's presentation could very easily have been conventional, but it has amazing tension because of spooky, atmospheric cinematography (George Barnes won an Oscar), Franz Waxman's moody score, the clever way Hitchcock uses space so that Fontaine seems dominated by her surroundings, and Anderson's chilling, soulless portrayal. Adding to our fear is that Fontaine is another Hitchcock heroine (as she'd be in *Suspicion*) whose man doesn't seem to be there when she needs him for protection. Film loses its power once Olivier reveals his *secret* about Rebecca and he rather than Fontaine feels fright. Lavishly produced by David O. Selznick. Also with: George Sanders, Nigel Bruce, C. Aubrey Smith, Reginald Denny, Gladys Cooper, Leo G. Carroll.

REBEL WITHOUT A CAUSE (1955) C/115m. Nicholas Ray directed, and James Dean (as Jim), Natalie Wood (as Judy), and Sal Mineo (as John, nicknamed Plato) give unforgettable performances in this great, emotionally charged youth film. Jim Stark has been in trouble often, causing his family to move from one town to another. New to Los Angeles, Jim is brought to Juvenile Hall on drunk-and-disorderly charges. He tells an officer named Ray (Edward C. Platt)—director Ray's surrogate—that his home is like a zoo, that his mother (Ann Doran) and father (Jim Backus) smother him with love but never listen or give him sound advice. Jim wishes that he'd have one day in which he didn't feel ashamed or confused. Jim notices Judy, who was picked up for walking the streets late at night, and Plato, an emotionally disturbed boy who killed some pup-

pies. Plato has no friends, and his rich, divorced parents are never in LA. The three youths, who will be drawn together the next day at school, observe each other through windowed walls that separate the individual offices: Ray is able to establish visually that all of America's troubled, troublesome, alienated middle-class teenagers are virtually mirror images of each other. The window-as-mirror analogy becomes important when, preceding the next night's dangerous "chickie run," Jim looks out his car's (rolled-down) passenger-side window at his competition, Buzz (Corey Allen), who sits in the car next to his. Jim wishes he were Buzz, who has friends and Judy for a girlfriend. So that we are able to perceive what monumental effect Buzz's imminent death will have on Jim, Ray makes it clear that Jim already senses that whatever happens to Buzz—his "mirror image" in this sequence—could happen to him. (That Dean would be killed in a car crash makes this scene particularly devastating.) Jim, Judy, and Plato will gravitate toward each other because they don't have parents who will help them resolve the tragedy. They form a "family," with Plato as the child. But Jim and Judy conclude that being parents in this day and age is harder than they'd thought. They are unsuccessful as Plato's surrogate parents—in fact, it is because Plato thinks they are neglectful that he goes berserk and ends up being shot by police. More than any other film, this classic sympathizes with youths who have complex problems. At the heart of the matter are their need to win acceptance from peers—which too often requires they try dangerous things—and their need to get their parents' attention and understanding. (Ray and screenwriter Stewart Stern wrote no classroom scenes, because they considered a teacher's influence to be negligible.) Ray is critical of parents for not helping their kids. Only Judy's mother (Rochelle Hudson) has any conception of what kids are going through ("She's at that age when nothing seems to fit"). Kids survive only through support of those who understand their situation. See how essential it is for each character to be hugged, kissed, or touched by lovers, friends, and family members. They must revive each other through physical contact. Film's tremendous following has much to do with Dean playing the vulnerable, self-destructive character that fit his off-screen image. Generations of young men have identified with the misunderstood Jim Stark. Dean *is* fabulous. So many things he does (his reactions, movements) and the way he delivers certain lines hit nerves of teenagers. And females respond to him, too, because, as Judy says, "A girl wants a man who is gentle and sweet and who doesn't run away." Also with: William Hopper (as Judy's father, who thinks she's too old to be kissed), Dennis Hopper, Steffi Sidney, Marietta Canty, Frank Mazzola, Nick Adams.

RED DAWN (1984) C/114m. Anti-Communist paranoia gone mad. Director-screenwriter John Milius, whose once-lonely right-wing politics are now in vogue in Hollywood, cleverly borrows from "liberal" forties films about besieged European townspeople and farmers who resort to guerrilla warfare to fight the invading Nazis and simply switches the storyline to America of the future, where we take to the hills to battle invading Russian, Cuban, and Nicaraguan communists. (Moreover, the image of teenage freedom fighter Lea Thompson set against the sky is almost a duplicate of the classic image of female insurgents in radical films set in agrarian countries.) Made under the guise of being a cautionary tale that warns us what will happen if we let Russia have free reign in Cuba and Central America, it actually creates a situation that Milius would love. One senses that he envies the film's teenagers and underground fighters as they attempt to recapture their homeland from sadists and rapists. Milius makes warfare seem fun. With politics aside: the teenage actors (particularly star Patrick Swayze) are solid action heroes and the action sequences, particularly the invasion, are fairly exciting. But the direction and writing falter and it becomes hard to tell what specifically the insurgents are trying to accomplish during each of their sneak attacks on the invaders (they don't seem to have a definite plan). And it's annoying that Milius keeps killing off his kids to make them martyrs in our eyes. Initially there was needless worry that this film would be taken seriously. Also with: Powers Boothe, C. Thomas Howell, Ben Johnson, Harry Dean Stanton, Charlie Sheen.

RED DUST (1932) B&W/83m. Hot-blooded jungle romance pairing Clark Gable and Jean Harlow (who'd spent some time together in *The Secret Six*) still has the sexual charge that caused it to break box-office records in the early thirties. Wisecracking prostitute Harlow, on the lam from police in Indo-China, seeks refuge on Gable's rubber plantation. He says she has to take the next boat out, yet finds himself attracted to her. But he has affair with the well-bred Mary Astor instead, while her engineer husband (Gene Raymond) is off building a bridge. Gable thinks he prefers Astor, but he's a better match with Harlow, who's more honest than Astor and can join him in sharp, tough, amusing, unladylike repartee. Unshaven Gable and braless blonde Harlow have immense sexual chemistry at all times— whether he's standing next to her while she takes her famous nude bath in a barrel or she sits by him as he lies on a bed, reading to him a children's bedtime story while he's putting his hand on her knee. Scripted by John Lee Mahin from the play by Wilson Collison; directed by Victor Fleming. Harlow's husband Paul Bern committed suicide during production. Remade in 1953 by John Ford as *Mogambo*, with Gable, Ava Gardner (in Harlow's role), and Grace Kelly. Also with: Donald Crisp, Tully Marshall, Willie Fong, Forrester Harvey.

RED RIVER (1948) B&W/125m–133m. Howard Hawks's monumental first western was scripted by Borden Chase and Charles Schnee from Chase's "The Chisholm Trail," a westernized *Mutiny on the Bounty* that advanced the possibility that the Bligh-Christian conflict was Oedipal in nature. In 1851, John Wayne and companion Walter Brennan leave behind their west-bound wagon train and the woman Wayne loves (Coleen Gray) to set up stakes to the south. Immediately the wagon train is ambushed by Indians and Gray killed—Wayne will always regret he didn't take her with him (because he'd thought her not strong enough) and will feel her death made it essential that he succeed in his business enterprise. He finds an orphan boy whose parents were massacred and raises him as a son—although he won't make him a partner until he proves himself worthy. Fourteen years later Wayne has assembled a massive cattle herd on his giant spread, but he will go broke unless he drives it 1000 miles to Missouri, over rugged terrain. With his fast-drawing son (Montgomery Clift) at his side, he, Brennan, and many hired hands embark on the journey. During the trip the men suffer due to the lack of water, inadequate food, the long days. There are Indians about; there is a stampede. As the journey continues, Wayne (in his least sympathetic role) becomes a driven, crazed tyrant. He threatens one man with a whipping, two deserters with hanging, and puts fear into all the others. At last Clift leads a mutiny! They leave Wayne behind and take the herd on a alternate route, to Abilene instead of Missouri; Clift realizes that his father will come after him to kill him. Joanne Dru is the woman Clift meets on the trail who falls for him, stands up to Wayne, and injects reason into the situation. Unromanticized western has remarkable authenticity; beautiful black-and-white photography by Russell Harlan, with emphasis on cloudy skies, barren terrain, darkness that makes night oppressive to give harsh feel to the West. Hawks deals with emotions rarely explored in westerns, including Wayne's uncharacteristic interrelated senses of fear (of *failure*) and paranoia. Clift, too, shakes from fear (of dad). This is Wayne's only character whose sense of morality becomes clouded, who can't tell the difference between right and wrong (in *The Searchers* he's wrong-headed, but he knows it). Moreover, Clift, who makes a passable cowboy in his debut, displays sensitivity and tenderness that were almost nonexistent among western heroes. But Hawks also gave these men traits his future western heroes would possess: loyalty, an unswerving desire to see their job through to the end, obstinacy, and a foolish self-pride that keeps them from appearing "soft" even when dealing with the people they love. Wayne and Clift are both excellent—their different acting styles work to emphasize their characters' different attitudes. Joanne Dru's character is fine (a typical tough-but-tender Hawks heroine, she's calmly shooting at Indians the first time we see her), but Dru (whom I usually like) is miscast; in pivotal role, coming in so late in the film and having such an important part, she interferes in the proceedings in more ways than one. Through her, picture changes tone; while momentarily satisfying, the ending is more suitable for a comedy. Also with: John Ireland, Harry Carey, Harry Carey, Jr., Noah Beery, Jr., Paul Fix, Hank Worden, Chief Towlatchie.

RED SHOES, THE (BRITISH/1948) C/133m. Anton Walbrook (as Boris Lermontov) is a seemingly heartless ballet impresario who becomes interested in a gifted young dancer, Moira Shearer (the Sadler's Wells Ballet star made her film debut as Vicky Page). Because she agrees with him that dance is more important than life itself, he offers her a position with the National Ballet Theatre. He asks his new, extremely talented orchestra coach, Marius Goring (as Julian Craster), to compose the score of a ballet based on Hans Christian Andersen's children's story "The Red Shoes" for Shearer to dance. It's about a girl who has an obsessive need to dance in a pair of red shoes—life and love pass her by and, unable to stop dancing, she dies. Of course, the ballet is meant to parallel Shearer's story. The ballet is a success, but, much to Walbrook's chagrin, Shearer and Goring fall in love. He becomes critical of their work, and they quit. Walbrook tells Shearer she'll never dance "The Red Shoes" again. But time passes and Walbrook tries to lure Shearer back by offering her the chance to perform "The Red Shoes." She must choose between Goring and dance—the result is tragic. Classic by Michael Powell and Emeric Pressburger is regarded as the best ballet film ever, one that has inspired generations of young girls to become dancers. So glorious are the visuals—movement, color, opulent sets, lavish costumes, all surrounded by music—and so strong is the identifiable career-vs.-marriage conflict which Shearer tries to resolve, that I'd bet if American females selected the film for which they have the most emotional attachment, it would rank at the top with *The Wizard of Oz*, another film that blends fantasy and reality. The picture is simultaneously romantic and expressionistic, a daydream and nightmare, a psychological drama and fairy-tale, a typical backstage musical and highbrow art. The film's highlight is the 14-minute "Red Shoes" ballet. Shearer does stun you with her dancing and she is breathtakingly beautiful in her white chiffon ballet costume with a blue-trimmed white bodice, a blue ribbon in her flaming red hair, and those "living" red shoes on her feet, and the director's expressionistic vision does capture the nightmarish vision of Andersen's fairytale. But the ballet shouldn't be stylized at all—after all, it was staged by purist Walbrook, who, if he had a camera, would insist on a stationary camera, no camera tricks, no special effects, and no jazzy music interludes. Because of the cinematic liberties and excesses of the ballet sequences, it's impossible to readjust to realistic sequences that follow. The first half of the film is masterful, the second half is miserable. The male directors, who manipulated us into disliking Wolbrook so much that we have trouble realizing that what he wants for Shearer is what is best for her, finally punish Shearer for making the *wrong*, seemingly selfish decision to choose dance over Goring. They even have her recognize her "mistake" by insisting that her red shoes be taken off her feet. I'd prefer Goring getting off her back. With choreography by Robert Helpmann (who dances in the "Red Shoes" ballet). Photography is by Jack Cardiff. Also with: Leonide Massine, Albert Basserman, Ludmilla Tcherina, Esmond Knight.

REDS (1981) C/196m. Expensive, passionate epic by Warren Beatty, who produced, directed (he won an Oscar), scripted with Trevor Griffiths, and stars as John Reed, the radical American journalist whose firsthand account of the Russian Revolution, *Ten Days That Shook the World*, earned him a propaganda job with the Comintern and burial inside the Kremlin. Film begins in 1915 when Reed first meets writer Louise Bryant (Diane Keaton) in Portland, Oregon, and ends with his death in Moscow in 1920. What is laudatory is that the romance between Reed and Bryant—including a whirlwind courtship, cohabitation in Greenwich Village and Provincetown, marriage, breakup, reunion—is not just played against a political backdrop (in the U.S. and U.S.S.R.) but is fueled by their individual political growth and increased commitment to left-wing politics. It conveys the excitement of being involved in a political movement where you believe progressive change is possible, as well as the crushing disappointment one feels when others derail your movement (i.e., the ideas that led to the October Revolution are forgotten by the extremist bureaucrats who take over Russia; the American Socialist Party splits apart). Not only is this a rare American film in which intellectuals are treated favorably (they're witty, tender, and humanistic), but the one American film with a likable, sensible Communist as its protaganist. Ambitious picture is flawed but nevertheless is a remarkable achievement. Particularly during those scenes are set in the U.S.S.R., one feels swept up in history. Performances by Beatty, Keaton, Jack Nicholson (as Bryant's lover, Eugene O'Neill), and Maureen Stapleton (who won a Best Supportng Actress Oscar as Emma Goldman) couldn't be better—only I wish Beatty wouldn't have every character he plays be a martyr. Reunion of Reed and Bryant in Russia is extremely moving—Keaton has an endearing expression. Vittorio Storaro won an Oscar for his brilliant cinematography. Excellent editing by Dede Allen and Craig McKay. Music is by Stephen Sondheim and Dave Grusin. Also with: Edward Herrmann, Gene Hackman, Jerzy Kosinski (as Grigory Zinoviev), Paul Sorvino, and such celebrity witnesses as Adela Rogers St. John, George Jessel, Will Durant, Rebecca West, Hamilton Fish, Henry Miller.

REEFER MADNESS/TELL YOUR CHILDREN/ BURNING QUESTION, THE/DOPE ADDICT/ DOPED YOUTH/LOVE MADNESS (1936) B&W/ 67m. The ultimate camp film, about the evils of marijuana, made by people who obviously knew nothing about their subject. An adult couple and a marijuana-hooked youth (Dave O'Brien) try to seduce high-school students into marijuana addiction. Teenage Mary (Dorothy Short) becomes worried when both her sweet boyfriend, Bill (Kenneth Craig), and her brother (Carleton Young) start acting differently. There will be tragic results for all concerned! Incredibly silly, low-budget quasi-documentary was supposedly designed to stimulate PTA groups and civic organizations into taking action against the spread of marijuana which was "destroying the youth of America in alarmingly increasing numbers." But its sleazy visuals where the emphasis is clearly on sex indicate this was just an exploitation film going under the guise of a social document. It's a terribly made, sensationalized, preposterous film that reinforces every falsehood you've ever heard about marijuana—that you become immediately addicted, that it is violence-inducing, that it's as bad as heroin, that it ends in one's "inevitable insanity." It was distributed in the early seventies by the National Organization for the Repeal of Marijuana Laws to make money for its lobbying efforts. Since then it has been a big hit on campuses and at midnight screenings, where dope-smoking audiences laugh at the view of older generations who wrote today's marijuana laws. What I find most hilarious is that instead of this movie turning off youths to marijuana it ironically will make them want to smoke it just so they can have the great time marijuana smokers have in this film before they face the consequences—drinking free liquor; partying; and having sex, loose women, and lots of laughs. Directed by Louis Gasnier. Also with: Lillian Miles, Thelma White, Pat Royale, Josef Forte.

REPO MAN (1984) C/92m.
A completely daffy, fast-paced satire/sci-fi parody about LA "punk" Emilio Estevez, who takes a job repossessing cars. He meets an assortment of spacy characters and has a series of odd and dangerous adventures, including one in the science-fiction realm. Film runs out of gas eventually, but the direction by unknown Alex Cox is consistently clever and ambitious. Cox has a gifted eye and ear for comedy. It's interesting listening to various repo men spout personal philosophy or argue over such important things as whether John Wayne was "a fag" just because (according to one guy) he wore dresses and liked to watch his buddies have sex. An immediate cult film due to near-simultaneous theatrical and video releases. Full of offbeat touches and surprises. Estevez gives a confident performance; Harry Dean Stanton is well cast as his repo recruiter. Also with: Tracey Walter (the spaciest of all), Vonetta McGee, Olivia Barash, Sy Richardson, Susan Barnes.

REPULSION (BRITISH/1965) B&W/105m.
The only person in the old photo not smiling or facing the camera is the sad-eyed little girl who is looking at the man to her left. Therein lies the explanation for why Catherine Deneuve—the girl, at about 20—has enormous sexual problems that lead to her breakdown during the course of Roman Polanski's classic psychological horror film. It's only at the end that Polanski lets us see the photo in close-up, and it is meant to serve like "Rosebud" in Citizen Kane. Belgian Deneuve lives with her older sister (Yvonne Furneaux) in a London apartment. She is disturbed by the constant presence of her sister's boyfriend (Ian Hendry) and their lovemaking at night. She is also taken aback by the rude remarks made by construction workers as she goes to and from work in a beauty salon. A young suitor (John Fraser) kisses her. Feeling ill, she goes home and brushes her teeth. When Furneaux goes out of town for two weeks, Deneuve begins to imagine that men are breaking into the apartment and raping her. (The film is erotic, but these rape scenes are

definitely not meant to be turn-ons.) As uncooked food spoils in the kitchen, her mind completely deteriorates. She imagines walls cracking, hands shooting out of the walls to caress her, and the attacks. She gets visits from Fraser and her landlord (Patrick Wymark)—they don't realize that she is capable of murder. An unforgettable film. Back in the sixties, people used to argue if it or Psycho was the scariest horror film. In Psycho we identified with victims, here we identify with the insane murderer. Many of those who thought it scarier than Psycho were young women who related to the sexually repressed girl and her fantasies. Not for the squeamish. Eerily photographed by Gil Taylor. Music by Chico Hamilton.

RESURRECTION (1980) C/103m.
In a role shaped for her by Lewis John Carlino, Ellen Burstyn plays a very nice but unexceptional woman who dies in a car crash but, stopping at the gateway to heaven, returns to life with the ability to heal. Now an exceptional woman—and just as nice and modest—she altruistically puts her gift to work in rural America, healing the great majority of the sickly and handicapped people who come to her for help. But eventually she becomes disillusioned because of the notoriety that has turned her mission into a sideshow, the Doubting Thomases (including scientists and media people) who think she is exploiting misery to achieve fame, and those people who resent her being blessed with such power or expect too much from her. She discovers that her gift is a burden. Burstyn is wonderful in this special film that somehow slipped by moviegoers in 1980. At the end, when her character, who has withdrawn from the public eye, gives a little boy with cancer a loving hug without letting on to him or her parents that her simple gesture has just cured the boy, you'll feel a surge of emotion sweep through your body. You'll love the character, and the actress for having the capacity to express such *goodness*. Directed by Daniel Petrie, who has feel for the rural environment and its people. Also with: Sam Shepard (as her neurotic young lover), Richard Farnsworth, Roberts Blossom, Lois Smith, Eve Le Gallienne, Clifford David.

RESURRECTION OF EVE, THE (1973) C/82m.
Jim and Artie Mitchell's follow-up to their XXX-rated classic Behind the Green Door was another attempt to attract women to the porno theater. A woman (Mimi Morgan) is badly hurt in a car accident. Following plastic surgery, she emerges as a beautiful woman, now played by Marilyn Chambers. Before, she always frustrated her disc-jockey husband (Matthew Arman) because of her sexual inhibitions—the result, as flashbacks tell us, of her being molested as a child. But now that she's beautiful, she has more confidence and is willing to go along with her husband's desire to join the swinging scene. Her bashfulness disappears and she becomes a passionate sexual animal, especially when with black boxer Johnnie Keyes (Chambers's lover in Green Door). Arman, who had been tiring of his wife, gets jealous—but it's too late. Picture is con-

fusing, then boring. The Mitchells' insistence on trying to make the explicit sex erotic rather than raunchy backfires—the sex scenes are too slow. Some porno fans consider this cult film better than *Green Door*, but neither is the impressive work of art that the Mitchells tried to achieve.

RETURN OF FRANK JAMES, THE (1940) C/92m.
Satisfying sequel to *Jesse James*, with Henry Fonda as Frank James, John Carradine as Robert Ford, and Henry Hull as a cantankerous newspaper editor reprising their roles from the 1939 film. Although Frank has never killed anyone, he sets his gun sights on Robert Ford and his brother Charlie (Charles Tanner), who murdered brother Jesse for the reward money. A great scene has Frank watching a play in which the cowardly Fords play themselves as heroes who save a woman from the dastardly James boys—when Frank makes himself known, the Fords flee in terror. But Frank can't carry out his mission as planned because he's arrested for killing a man during a hold-up (when actually the man was struck by a bullet fired from outside the building). The trial, in which the judge and jury shamelessly reveal a southern bias that makes it impossible for them to convict former rebel Frank, is similar to the trial in John Ford's 1934 film *Judge Priest*; the northerner prosecuting attorney doesn't stand a chance. However, it is thematically central to the works of Fritz Lang, directing his first western. In Lang, individuals are at the mercy of groups of people who represent their particular environments—whether they are allowed to go free depends not on justice but on the whims of the people. Not much action, but Lang creates a flavorful western milieu. Fonda gives a fine, subdued performance and Gene Tierney is likable in her screen debut as an enlightened woman who is determined to break down sex barriers and be a reporter. Also with: Jackie Cooper, J. Edward Bromberg, Donald Meek, Lloyd Corrigan.

RETURN OF THE DRAGON/WAY OF THE DRAGON (HONG KONG/1973) C/91m.
Bruce Lee's third film, his only attempt at directing. Lee plays Tang Lung, a fists-for-free-hire character whom he would have played in several other films if it hadn't been for his sudden death. Tang arrives in Rome from Hong Kong to help relatives fight off the mob that's trying to take away their restaurant. At first everyone who works in the restaurant, including the lovely niece of the owner (Nora Miao), fears that country boy Tang is out of his element taking on professional gangsters. But he's like James Stewart in *Destry Rides Again*, a humble, patient, unintimidating hick who turns out to be a lethal fighter. (Watch the smile of love come to Miao's face when she sees Tang beat up his first villain.) Tang singlehandedly defeats all of the mob's best men during several kung-fu battles, which are fun to watch but repetitive. Then the mob boss brings in three heavyweight villains and the film becomes much more exciting: martial-arts experts Bob Wall, Wang Ing Sik, and, in his film debut, Chuck Norris (seven-time U.S. and World Karate Champion) play the villains who take on our hero. The

Lee-Norris confrontation, set in the Colosseum, is one of the highlights of Lee's movie career. Picture relies so much on humor in the early going that the somber ending comes as a surprise. Poorly dubbed. Produced by Raymond Chow. Also with: Wei Ping Ao, Wang Chung Hsin.

RETURN OF THE JEDI (1983) C/133m.
Final installment in the *Star Wars* trilogy has Luke Skywalker (Mark Hamill), Han Solo (Harrison Ford), Princess Leia (Carrie Fisher), Lando Calrissian (Billy Dee Williams), Chewbacca (Peter Mayhew), C-3PO (Anthony Daniels), and R2-D2 (Kenny Baker) unite for the final battle against the Empire, represented by the Emperor (Ian McDiarmid) and, of course, Darth Vader (David Prowse; voice by James Earl Jones). Film has marvelous special effects, exciting battles, and one great new creature: enormous, blubbery villain Jabba the Hut. But I don't like the way executive producer George Lucas and his co-screenwriter Lawrence Kasdan tie loose ends together. Everything is too pat; moreover, when we discover who everybody is in relation to one another, it's hard not to be disappointed. Script is too simple, returning the characters to the shallow comic-strip figures they were in the first film. There's too much talk about light and dark, good and evil—eventually that's all the bad guys, who want Luke to join them, discuss. I don't object to Fisher wearing skimpy outfits, but the change in her wardrobe reflects too drastic a change in her personality from *The Empire Strikes Back*. I like the idea of a tribe of rebel warriors, but the fur-ball Ewoks—inspired by Lucas's dog—aren't what I had in mind. Film's highlight is the speed-cycle chase through a heavily wooded area (it's amazing how Luke dodges the trees). Aren't you surprised not to see James Earl Jones when Darth Vader is unmasked? Directed by Richard Marquand. Photographed by Alan Hume. John Williams composed the score. With special effects by Richard Edlund, Dennis Muren, Ken Ralston. Also with: Alec Guinness, Sebastian Shaw, Warwick Davis, Michael Carter, Denis Lawson.

RETURN OF THE SECAUCUS SEVEN (1980) C/100m.
John Sayles's witty directorial debut was financed for $60,000 and starred only one person who'd been in a previous film. It's about the reunion of seven radicals from the Vietnam War years at a house in rural New Hampshire. They call themselves the "Secaucus Seven" because on the way to the March on Washington they took a wrong highway exit and got arrested in Secaucus, New Jersey, and spent the night in jail. Unlike the gang from 1983's *The Big Chill*, these people still are leftists and socially conscious; those who have jobs have chosen professions that are out of the rat race and aren't high-salaried; each finds some way to be an activist. The seven longtime friends and one newcomer, a Young Dem who is the new boyfriend of one of the women, spend a weekend together—talking, gossiping, recalling old times, bed-hopping, singing, skinny-dipping, and playing charades, Clue, basketball. As in Chekhov (obviously an influence), no one makes big decisions, there

are no revelations. The most revealing thing is that the leftists learn to accept the conservative outsider into their select little circle because he's a nice guy and a good sport—in the protest years this would have been impossible. Characters are real and, flaws and all, we believe they know and love each other (they can even recognize each other by the sound of their retching). Sayles has written some of the best dialogue in memory. Starring: Bruce MacDonald, Maggie Renzie, Gordon Clapp, Adam LeFevre, Maggie Cousineau-Arndt, Jean Passanante, David Strathairn, Ken Trott, Mark Arnott, Sayles.

REUBEN, REUBEN (1983) C/100m.

With sensitivity and intelligence evident in his voice and the elegant diction of someone who reads aloud to himself to hear the rhythm and nuances of the words, Tom Conti found his perfect part in this offbeat comedy, playing a Scottish Dylan Thomas-like poet named Gowan McGland. Still famous although his talent has escaped him, McGland barely gets by lecturing at New England colleges and seducing the bored housewives who are his most ardent fans. Always wearing a crumpled tweed suit which has no money in its pockets, McGland spends his time drinking himself out of sobriety so he won't have to face his pathetic situation. Through bloodshot eyes he regards the world as a sick joke where: his ex-wife will get more money writing a biography of him than he can make from his own writings; he is beaten up by a big, stupid lug for calling him a *heterosexual*; his dentist finds out McGland has been sleeping with his wife just prior to McGland arriving for an appointment; McGland with a noose around his neck, decides not to commit suicide, only to watch a friendly dog run up and knock away the chair he is standing on. Many people will not like this film, even though almost everyone will appreciate Conti's performance; yet it's hard to deny that the sad, cruel events that are somehow funny when they happen to McGland wouldn't get laughs in any other film. In her debut Kelly McGillis (*Witness*) is radiant as McGland's young lover—his last hope for happiness. Well directed by Robert Ellis Miller. Julius J. Epstein, who adapted Peter De Vries's novel, wrote an unusually smart and literate script. Also with: Roberts Blossom, E. Katherine Kerr, Cythia Harris, Joel Fabiani, Kara Wilson, Lois Smith.

REVENGE OF THE NERDS (1984) C/90m.

Surprise box-office hit finds dorks Robert Carradine and Anthony Edwards beginning their freshman year at college. It should be a joyous time, but they are rejected by all the fraternities and forced to live in the gym with the other losers on campus to make room in the dorm for the Nazi football players. But the gang fixes up a dilapidated old house, becomes affiliated with a national black fraternity, Lamba Lamba Lamba, has a blast with the girls from the reject sorority, sets up a cable-TV system in the snooty sorority house so they can watch the girls strip, and gets revenge on the football fraternity. This is just a silly teen comedy, but it's a standout in raunchy *Porky's* genre because

at least you don't mind identifying with these characters. There are some funny bits, but most enjoyment comes simply from hearing Carradine's horsy laugh. On the other hand, the bullying tactics of the football players are too cruel to be funny and Edwards's speech promoting Nerd Power is not a clever enough way to end the film. Directed by Jeff Kanew. Also with: Julie Montgomery, Curtis Armstrong.

RICHARD PRYOR LIVE IN CONCERT (1979) C/78m.

A comic genius is at work: You'll laugh so hard you'll have a tough time breathing. It's the first of Pryor's live-performance films and his best, not only because of his material and fabulous voices (animals and parts of the body talk) but also because here he best displays his remarkable skills as a *physical* comedian. Highlights include: a conversation with a neighbor dog who has come to console him on the death of his sex-crazed pet monkey; his relating how nurses are nonchalant ("Is this your piss? Thank you"); his description of women trying to piss in the woods; his remembrance of beatings from his grandmother ("Boy, go get me something to beat your ass with"); Pryor mimicking a stuttering Oriental; his recollection of fighting a boxer who used to hit himself in the head; his essays on machismo ("Run!") and the male stud who doesn't bother trying to give a lover an orgasm unless it can prove his masculinity. Uncensored Pryor is uninhibited and raunchy, but inoffensve and truthful. Beneath the humor, you'll detect pain, fear, anger, and concern for his race. It was filmed in conservative Long Beach, California. Directed by Jeff Margolis.

RICHARD PRYOR LIVE ON THE SUNSET STRIP (1982) C/82m.

Pryor's return to the concert scene after nearly being burned to death while freebasing cocaine. Much of the humor is sidesplitting, but overall it's not as sharp-edged, wild, "embarrassing," or sustained as in 1979's *Richard Pryor Live in Concert*. He's put on a bit of weight since then, and he doesn't rely on mobility or his mime talents as much. Most irritating is that director Joe Layton keeps cutting to audience members cracking up. A highlight has Pryor showing his painful reaction to being bathed for the first time following his accident. Also funny are his recollections of a night with a Playboy bunny who gets turned on when he uses a little-boy voice, and his meetings with black murderers at an Arizona penitentiary. His reminiscences of a trip to Africa where "there are no *niggers*" is unexpectedly poignant.

RIDE IN THE WHIRLWIND (1967) C/83m.

Existential western written by its co-star, Jack Nicholson, and directed in Utah in 1965 by Monte Hellman, back to back with *The Shooting*. Cowpokes Wes (Nicholson), Verne (Cameron Mitchell), and Otis (Tom Filer) find themselves in a situation that's beyond their understanding: a "hang 'em first, ask questions later" posse is on their trail, mistaking them for thieves. Just as in other Hellman films, our heroes make a journey that seems to go nowhere; they buy time

357

by climbing a mountain that goes straight up ("It's a shame to do all this walking for nothing," Wes remarks). As they cross Hellman's rocky, infertile West, Wes and Verne come upon a man's cabin where his wife and grown daughter (Millie Perkins) function as his servants. They will need to steal his horses to attempt an escape. Gritty, fascinating western with solid acting, offbeat characters, intriguing setting, and odd bits of dialogue (Verne: "It's peculiar sitting here playing checkers while a bunch of men want to string us up." Wes: "Why don't you put a tune to it?"). Life endured by Perkins and her mother sticks in mind. Unpredictable cult movie which has strong reputation in Europe, is almost as good as *The Shooting*. Also with: Katherine Squire, Rupert Crosse, Harry Dean Stanton.

RIDE LONESOME (1959) C/73m.
"A man needs a reason to ride this country," says Randolph Scott's Brigade, and here, as in the majority of the westerns Scott made with Budd Boetticher, Scott's character is motivated by what happened to his wife. Many years ago she was hanged by Frank (Lee Van Cleef)—he's such a mean fellow that he nearly forgot the incident. Brigade captures Frank's younger brother, Billy (James Best), and wants to use him to get to Frank. But outlaws Sam (Pernell Roberts) and Wid (James Coburn) want to take Billy away from Brigade because they can get amnesty if they turn him in to the law. Boetticher usually draws parallels between Scott's character and the chief villain—in this film Brigade and Sam, rather than Frank, have a kinship. In *The Tall T*, Richard Boone gives Scott the chance to have the good life he could never have himself; here Brigade makes it possible for Sam to become part of society and have the chance to be with the girl (Karen Steele)—happiness that Brigade rules out for himself at the moment. For now, it's enough for Brigade just to rid himself (through Frank's death) of his inner demons: "When [people] feel the morning sun on them they want to get up and start all over." Powerful, provocative western is one of the series's best. The solid cast is well directed by Boetticher. Burt Kennedy wrote the script, and Charles Lawton, Jr., did the fine CinemaScope photography.

RIDE THE HIGH COUNTRY (1962) C/94m.
Sam Peckinpah's finest achievement, and one of the best westerns ever made. Two of the western genre's most familiar heroes, Joel McCrea and Randolph Scott, were united to play aged former lawmen who are reunited when McCrea is hired to transport gold from a mining site back to a bank in a large town. McCrea looks knocked about and worn out by life but he remains a moral man. However, Scott runs a crooked sideshow and is extremely cynical. Scott and his young partner, Ronald Starr, agree to ride with McCrea—they want to steal the gold after it is collected. Along the way they meet Mariette Hartley, who wants to get away from her lonely life with her rigid, religious father, R. G. Armstrong. They take her to the mining town where, much to Starr's chagrin, she marries James Drury. After a nightmarish wedding and bedroom scene—in which drunk Drury slugs her and his slovenly brothers Warren Oates and John Davis Chandler try to rape her—McCrea, Scott, and Starr take Hartley with them when they depart. Drury, Oates, Chandler, other brother L.Q. Jones, and John Anderson (who's either an older brother or the father) give chase. McCrea foils Scott's plan to rob him and is furious with his old friend. But at the end, the two walk side by side against Drury and his kin. Just like old times. McCrea and Scott become two of Peckinpah's many past-their-prime old-timers who win our admiration because they are willing to go out in a blaze of glory. McCrea's return into Scott's life helps the latter to regain lost values. Together they restore dignity and moral order to the West: the death of the Hammond family ends the decadence. They make it possible for Starr and Hartley to marry—giving Starr the opportunity for the happy family life these old bachelors foolishly bypassed in their own lives. Starr and Hartley are civilization's hope for a bright future. A great finale shot. Splendid outdoor photography by Lucien Ballard. N.B. Stone, Jr., wrote the elegant script. Also with: Edgar Buchanan.

RIFIFI (FRENCH/1955) B&W/116m.
Blacklisted in Hollywood, Jules Dassin went to France and made what quickly became the prototype for future caper films. Jean Servais, looking unhappy and worn out, is released from prison, where he spent five years on a robbery charge. When he discovers that his former lover, Marie Sabouret, has taken up with gangster and nightclub owner Marcel Lupovici, he makes her strip and beats her (loyalty is the *most* important thing to him). He quickly forgets his decision to go straight and agrees to join his young friend Carl Mohner, Robert Manuel, and Perlo Vita (actually Dassin) in a jewelry-store heist. The heist, which takes about half an hour, during which time no one speaks and there is no music, is a great, nail-biting sequence; at first the four men seem like amateurs compared to the sophisticated thieves we see in today's films, but soon we marvel at how expertly planned their robbery is, how they work as a team, and how innovative each man is, particularly in knowing how to incorporate items such as fire extinguishers and umbrellas that wouldn't be found in a burglar's manual. When the heist is complete, the inevitable trouble begins—Lupovici discovers who pulled off the heist and kidnaps Mohner's young son, whom he wants to exchange for the money the jewelry brings in. Servais knows the young boy will be killed even if there is an exchange, so with Sabouret's help he tries to find Lupovici's hideout. Film holds up surprisingly well due to sex and strong violence (the many killings are *all* terrifyingly brutal) that were ahead of their time in the fifties, and because Dassin sets up interesting, loyalty-based relationships between the men and their women. While the heist is the film's classic sequence, other scenes have strong tension as well. Also impressive is Dassin's use of Paris locales. Final image of Mohner's wife, Janine Darcey, picking up her safe child, whom the dying Servais brought home, while ignoring the suitcase holding 120,000 francs, is disappointing; I wish she'd at least take a second to consider what

taking the money would mean. Also with: Claude Sylvian, Pierre Grasset, Robert Hussein, Magali Noel, Dominique Marin.

RIGHT STUFF, THE (1983) C/193m.

One of the best American films of recent years, Philip Kaufman's exhilarating adaptation of Tom Wolfe's best-seller was an unexpected bust at the box office, but has become a cult favorite of critics and moviegoers over 30. Kaufman's visually dazzling epic makes the point that our test pilots and early astronauts belong to American mythology as surely as our 19th-century western heroes. Indeed, the film's early scenes not only are set in the West (of the late 1940s)—and a bar—but are shot like a John Ford western, with much feeling for sky, landscape, and rugged archetypes who understand that they are rooted in the purer, less civilized past, and that *progress* is their nemesis. Kaufman borrows a great deal from Ford's *The Man Who Shot Liberty Valance*, including its basic structure. In Ford, John Wayne, a true hero, tamed the West and, unbeknownst to the public, killed villain Liberty Valance. Wayne made it possible for James Stewart to achieve fame (he's thought to be Valance's killer) and have a successful career in the public eye; meanwhile Wayne withdraws into anonymity. In Kaufman, Chuck Yeager (Sam Shepard), a true hero whose breakthroughs as a test pilot made the space program possible, withdraws into anonymity, while men who hadn't done the tough pioneering Yeager had done gained tremendous fame as astronauts. Yeager chooses not to join the Mercury space program because the government is running it like a sideshow and the prospective astronauts haven't the purity of purpose that he considers essential to pioneers. But the film becomes a tribute to seven initially self-serving, glory-hungry men who—in spite of corruptive pressures from the U.S. government to turn them into media superstars and false symbols of American patriotism—band together into a group that represents the best in American ideals. They quickly mature and become true heroes and pioneers in a program only *they* seem to know the value of. And so they earn the hard-won admiration of Yeager, who realizes that they also have "the right stuff." Each also achieves self-respect and obtains the respect of the other six men, which at the beginning would have meant little. In a glorious scene in which the astronauts are guests of honor at a mammoth tribute, they look into each other's eyes and smile knowingly, indicating that they all realize no one else in the world—certainly no one around them, even their wives—understands what they've been through as individuals and as a team. (Just as only four men knew what it was like to be a Beatle.) Some of the satire falls flat and the scatological humor becomes tiresome, but the picture has remarkable scope; spectacular, nail-biting flying sequences (in jets, in rockets); romance; wit; and an interesting view on the difference between what is heroic and what the public is manipulated into believing is heroic. Marvelous cinematography is by Caleb Deschanel; Jordan Belson handled the special effects. The uniformly excellent cast includes: Ed Harris (as John Glenn), Fred Ward (as Gus Grissom), Dennis Quaid (as Gordon Cooper), Scott Glenn (as Alan Shepard), Barbara Hershey, Pamela Reed, Veronica Cartwright, Scott Wilson, Jeff Goldblum, Donald Moffat, Kim Stanley, Levon Helm, Jane Dornacker, Chuck Yeager (as a bartender), Royal Dano, Harry Shearer, Robert Beer.

RIO BRAVO (1959) C/140m.

Howard Hawks made this film in reaction to *High Noon* because he was so upset that it had a lawman who begs civilians to help in a crisis. John T. Chance (John Wayne), the sheriff of a Texas border town, must keep a killer in jail while awaiting the arrival of a U.S. Marshal, despite knowing that the killer's brother and numerous men will attempt to break him out. Instead of asking townspeople to put themselves on the line, Wayne recruits three "professionals" to help him: ex-deputy Dude (Dean Martin), who became a drunk when the woman he loved turned out to be no good; Colorado (Ricky Nelson), a young, cocky man with a lightning draw; and Stumpy (Walter Brennan), an old man with a limp, a cantankerous demeanor, and great loyalty to Chance and especially Dude. Meanwhile Chance tries to force a beautiful gambling lady, Feathers (Angie Dickinson), to leave town—but ends up glad that he couldn't scare her away. This slam-bang, exciting, funny western is quintessential Hawks: it is unabashedly commercial yet personal; is about a group of heroic men of action who work together for a common moral purpose; expresses a masculine code of conduct based on courage, loyalty, perseverance, and expertise; has a female lead who impresses the male lead by having what *he* believes are (positive) *masculine* traits (i.e., independence, loyalty, inner fortitude, guts) and at the same time excites him with her femininity; contains action, humor, and large dose of dialogue; is filmed with a functional, unobtrusive camera; and has a happy ending. Hawks's men are allowed to be scared, but, like Dude, they must put themselves on the line when scared to prove they are worthy men to themselves and their male friends. A man is defined not by how well he relates to women—he is mystified by them—but by how well he handles pressure and reacts to danger. It's okay that Dude (the film's pivotal character) wants help from his friends, but when the chips are down and they need his assistance, Dude must be *dependable*. Along with the word "proficient," "dependable" is how Hawks defines "good," the highest rating a person can have in a Hawks film. Film has many terrific scenes—the verbal battles between Chance and Feathers, the shootouts, and Dude, Colorado, and Stumpy singing and playing music together! It is as if a few of the Seven Dwarfs got together for some merriment. Stumpy's scratchy voice takes away from the musical harmony, but Hawks's masculine harmony rings through loud and clear—Chance understandingly flashes a smile of approval. Spittoon scene was parodied by John Ford in *The Man Who Shot Liberty Valance*. One of the all-time great westerns. Jules Furthman and Leigh Brackett adapted a short story by B. H. McCampbell. Music by Dimitri Tiomkin, cinematography by Russell Harlan. Also with: Ward Bond, John

Russell, Pedro Gonzalez, Claude Akins, Malcolm Atterbury, Harry Carey, Jr., Bob Steele, Estelita Rodriguez.

RIO LOBO (1970) C/114m.

In Howard Hawks's final film, a Union officer (John Wayne) and two Confederate soldiers (Jorge Rivero, Chris Mitchum) join forces at the end of the Civil War to clean up a town ruled by two war criminals and their henchman sheriff (Mike Henry). They are soon joined by three brave women and a comical, half-senile old-timer (Jack Elam). Once more in a Hawks film, we find a group of people who, despite having different individual motives, work together against desperate odds. While not strong or complex as *Rio Bravo* and *El Dorado*, this third part of the trilogy is still quite entertaining. Brutality is more prominent than in the typical Hawks western; and it contains his first suggestion of nudity (Sherry Lansing, future head at 20th, stands topless with arms properly folded) since the bare baby in *Monkey Business*. And Wayne's character has changed. He is less dominant than in early films, and mellower. He is content with his years, less of a superman (he stands by, wary of bad odds, as a man and woman are beaten up), and less confident of his own judgment. It's very strange to see John Wayne following the advice of a woman or, for that matter, another man. He is more of a father figure than a leader. Unlike his *Rio Bravo* character, he accepts the help of all who offer it. The main action is carried out by the young men and women. Of the three doomed villains, Wayne gets none—the women get two. He is even denied the final kill by a woman fulfilling an oath of revenge. Also with: Jennifer O'Neill, Victor French, Bill Williams, Jim Davis, David Huddleston, Chuck Courtney, George Plimpton.

RISE OF LOUIS XIV, THE (ITALIAN/1966) C/100m.

Sumptuous historical film by Roberto Rossellini that reconstructs the steps by which 22-year-old King Louis (Jean-Marie Patte) consolidates his power during the first 20 years of his independent reign (following the death of his godfather, Cardinal Mazarin). From the young man who guiltily hangs his head while the Queen Mother chastises him for sexual indiscretions, he becomes a confident, shrewd ruler whose gluttony, (semi)public displays of sex and other excesses (all done in a genteel manner) are calculated to be admired by the sycophantic, freeloading nobility who come to live at Louis's palace at Versailles. The picture is slow-paced, lines are delivered without inflection by non-actors, and we have to listen to trivial discussions along with the important stuff—viewers don't get their pleasure in the usual ways. Rossellini didn't want to apply history to the present but simply to present history as it was. If you have patience, you'll derive unusual viewing pleasure from watching Louis's world re-created in all its luxurious decadence. Film originally got disappointing reviews, but has come to be regarded as Rossellini's last masterpiece. Ornate sets were designed by Maurice Valay. George Leclerc was the cinematographer. Also with: Raymond Jourdan, Silvagni

(as Mazarin), Katharina Renn, Dominique Vincent, Pierre Barrat.

RISKY BUSINESS (1983) C/96m.

Directorial debut by Paul Brickman puts all other teenage sex comedies to shame. Not the expected exploitation film, it's very funny, extremely erotic . . . and smart. Brickman's excellent script perceptively zeroes in on what is at the heart of teenage anxiety, particularly that experienced by male high school seniors: getting laid, getting into the right college (even more important!), keeping honor in front of friends, desiring freedom but being scared of having too much, living up to parents' expectations, and worrying that something disastrous will happen out of the blue that will ruin the future. Brickman realizes that the most exciting experiences for teenagers are those which might lead to disaster and which will cause them to feel guilty. When Tom Cruise's parents leave town for a few days, he is left alone in their exclusive home in a ritzy Chicago suburb. Urged on by friends, he calls up a hooker who is listed in a sex magazine. Rebecca De Mornay arrives ("Are you ready for me?") and they have a night of sex that surpasses all his erotic dreams. In the morning she tells him he owes her $300. His troubles begin. He is harassed by De Mornay's pimp, Guido (Joe Pantoliano), watches his father's car plummet into Lake Michigan, is forced to turn his house into a brothel for one night, fails exams and is suspended from school, discovers that Guido has stolen all his parents' furniture. But it's all worth it; he gets De Mornay for a girlfriend, gets into Princeton because of his business acumen—demonstrated to interviewer Richard Masur the night the "brothel" brought in $8,000—and wins the respect of friends and parents. Film satirizes the free-enterprise system: both Cruise and De Mornay (whose mind works like a calculator) end up temporarily broke, but they have proved they can play the American business game and come out on top. Film contains excellent relationships (including that between Cruise and his parents), sensual sex scenes (De Mornay's first appearance, Cruise and De Mornay on the subway), believable dialogue, recognizable characters. Theme by Tangerine Dream is used to good effect. Produced by Arthur Avnet and Steve Tisch. Also with: Curtis Armstrong, Bronson Pinchot, Nicholas Pryor (father), Janet Carroll (mother), Shera Danese, Raphael Sbarge.

RITZ, THE (1976) C/91m.

Although this adaptation of Terrence McNally's broad bath-house farce runs out of steam near the end, the frenetic performances and direction by Richard Lester make it a delight. On the run from his murderous brother-in-law (Jerry Stiller), Jack Weston hides out in a gay bath, not realizing that Stiller owns the joint. Weston meets a wild assortment of gays on the sexual prowl and has many hilarious escapades before Stiller tracks him down. In a rare lead, Weston is splendid, especially in his scenes with marvelous Rita Moreno, whose talentless Googie Gomez performs in the bath's nightclub. Moreno steals the film but I find it impossible not to laugh every time

360

detective Treat Williams uses a ridiculous, high-pitched voice. A much underrated comedy. Also with: F. Murray Abraham, Kaye Ballard, Paul Price, George Coulouris, Bessie Love.

RIVER, THE (INDIAN/1951) C/97m.
Jean Renoir's lyrical film about an English family living in Bengal, on the Ganges. Our narrator is the eldest daughter, who looks back to when she (Patricia Walters) was 16, worried about her plain looks, and about to fall in love for the first time. American Captain Jack (Thomas E. Breen), who lost his leg in the war and all his confidence along with it, visits his cousin (Arthur Shields) next door and becomes the object of Walters' affections. But he is more interested in her lovely best friend (Adrienne Corri) and Shields's daughter (Radha) by his late Indian wife. Film deals with the merging of cultures; and how these four young characters overcome their various forms of self-hatred. It is beautifully shot by the director's nephew Claude Renoir (it was Jean's first *color* film)—but you may find it hard to find a print in which the color isn't washed out—there are some powerful passages, and Walters gives a lovely performance. But I don't like the characters, and I believe that half the cast should have been replaced and that more emphasis should have been placed on how India affects the family. Renoir and Rumer Godden adapted Godden's novel. Also with: Esmond Knight (the father), Nora Swinburne (the mother).

ROAD GAMES (AUSTRALIAN/1981) C/100m.
Eerie sleeper set in the Australian outback, where spacy trucker Stacy Keach is carrying a load between Melbourne and Perth. Also on this route, perhaps following him, is a stranger in a black truck. Is this stranger responsible for killing a number of women? The police think Keach is the maniac—and director Richard Franklin films the murders so mysteriously that we're not sure. Jamie Lee Curtis is the hitchhiker Keach picks up. We worry for her safety, but we're a bit suspicious of her as well. Dismissed as another in the string of horror quickies Curtis was churning out after *Halloween*, this film effectively combines elements of the existential road movie, television's *The Fugitive, Duel*, the better slasher movies, and Hitchcock thrillers. Unusual film has ending that most people hated but I think is exciting. Picture contains suspense, good performances, fine photography of an interesting setting. Also with: Marion Edward, Grant Page, Bill Stacey.

ROAD TO SINGAPORE (1940) B&W/84m.
The first Bob Hope–Bing Crosby comedy sets the formula: both pals fall in love with Dorothy Lamour despite past troubles with women; they are chased by the law; they repeatedly betray and compete with each other for Dorothy's hand, but ultimately each is willing to sacrifice his own personal happiness for his friend. Hope and Crosby, who has left behind Judith Barrett, flee to Singapore. They've sworn off women, but that was before they'd seen fetching Dorothy Lamour, with her long hair and skimpy sarong. When she joins their comedy-singing act, a rift develops between the two. While there aren't many funny moments, the picture is breezy and much easier to sit through than the duo's dated, more labored comedies. It benefits from some lively songs, several Hope-Crosby "Patty-Cake" routines (in which they slap each other's hands and then sock their curious enemies in the kissers), and capable supporting work by Charles Coburn, Anthony Quinn, and Jerry Colonna. Directed by Victor Schertzinger.

ROAD WARRIOR, THE/MAD MAX 2 (AUSTRALIAN/1981) C/94m.
More optimistic than *Mad Max*, George Miller's exciting sequel shows how post-apocalyptic superwarrior Max (Mel Gibson) regains some of the human qualities he lost when his wife and children were killed in the first film. The setting is desert wasteland where a large band of gladiator-like warriors, led by the masked Humungus (Kjell Nilsson), lays siege to an isolated make-shift fort occupied by a ragtag community of people who still have hopes for a decent future. The warriors are after the large quantity of precious fuel that the compound dwellers possess. Initially reluctant to get involved, Max decides to make an emotional investment in this communal group. In a visually stunning, amazingly choreographed sequence, he drives their oil tanker toward safety and is attacked by the marauders. He gets help from the skinny Gyro Captain (Bruce Spence), a scavenger who has become his friend, and the Feral Kid (Emil Minty), a little mute boy with a lethal boomerang. Like the original, the picture contains extraordinary action sequences and stunt work. It has more horror than the original and certainly has an equal number of quirky touches and weird characters. The major difference is that the film moves out of futuristic drama into a mythological realm—Max becomes more of a symbol figure, a universal hero. There is much in the film that reminds me of Sergio Leone's "Dollars" films, *A Boy and His Dog* (particularly in the depiction of the Marauders), *Hondo*, and, most of all, the Alamo episode of *Davy Crockett, King of the Wild Frontier*. Film's oddest aspect is that it's set in the future, yet narrated (by the adult Feral Kid) as if it all happened in the past. Miller, Terry Hayes, and Brian Hannant wrote the screenplay. Bryon Kennedy produced. Dean Semler did the impressive cinematography. Norma Moriceau designed the striking costumes, which are part medieval and part punk. Also with: Vernon Wells (as the fearsome villain Wez), Mike Preston (as the leader of the compound dwellers), Virginia Hey (as the Warrior Woman), Syd Heylen.

ROARING TWENTIES, THE (1939) B&W/104m.
James Cagney returns to America following World War I and finds there are no opportunities for legitimate work. He starts running alcohol during Prohibition, when the public romanticized the bootlegger, says our narrator, as "a modern crusader who deals in bottles rather than battles." He has a soft heart, but he's out on the battle lines when the bootlegging becomes ugly in the late twenties and other gangsters try to muscle in on his territory. When the stock market crashes, he loses his money and ends up a

drunk, out of the rackets. But when the woman he once loved (Priscilla Lane) and her lawyer husband (Jeffrey Lynn), a WWI army buddy, need his help because a gangster (Humphrey Bogart) wants Lynn silenced, Cagney comes through. Like most Warners films, it has a social conscience, and it pretty much blames forgotten man Cagney's criminality on an insensitive country. Film's sense of history is slanted against the Republicans (responsible for Prohibition—"a bad law"—and the Depression). It's pro-Roosevelt (who ended Prohibition) and, judging from Lane's mink, started us on a road back to prosperity; yet, ironically, Cagney is at his nadir financially when the Democrats are in office—also, Roosevelt's election makes it possible for him to be a drunk. Although not on the level of *Little Caesar* and *Scarface*, this is one of the liveliest, most enjoyable gangster films. Raoul Walsh's direction is fast-paced and tough, yet sentimental; there are solid action sequences, Bogart dies like a coward, and Cagney gives a vivid performance. Cagney's death scene is a gem: riddled with bullets, he tries to run up the steps of a church, but his momentum takes him downward instead, where he falls dead on the snowy lower steps. His good deed, killing Bogart, does not earn him complete forgiveness, but perhaps it saves him from hell, represented by the gutter/sidewalk, which is but a few feet below where he lies. Also with: Gladys George, Frank McHugh, Paul Kelly, Elizabeth Risden, Joe Sawyer.

ROBERTA (1935) B&W/105m.
The third Fred Astaire–Ginger Rogers musical has been the hardest to see over the years, due to restrictive distribution. The main storyline deals with a hayseed American football star, Randolph Scott, inheriting his aunt's Paris dress shop, Roberta's, and having an off-and-on romance with Irene Dunne, who designs all the shop's dresses. But forget the dull, convoluted Dunne-Scott plotline and watch supporting players Rogers and Astaire (who does get second billing despite having a smaller, less important role than Scott). Huck, Scott's buddy—dancer, singer, and bandleader of the Wabash Indianians—is the least abrasive, most likable character he played in his films with Rogers; and Rogers's fake Polish countess, Scharwenka (actually she's Lizzie Gatz) is refreshingly not deceitful or antagonistic. There's none of the tension or hostility one could sense in later films. The two are actually playful and seem to be enjoying each other—even when they are not dancing. But we can enjoy it most when they *are* dancing; they're relaxed, yet their feet are flying in "I'll Be Hard to Handle" (during which Rogers wears pants for the first time), one of the duo's greatest dance numbers. The film ends with their magical reprise of "I Won't Dance"—to which Astaire did a simply marvelous solo tap earlier. Jerome Kern score also includes the classic "Smoke Gets in Your Eyes," first sung by Dunne and later danced to in a formal but simple style by Astaire and Rogers. From the Broadway play by Kern and Otto Harbach, which was adapted from Alice Duer Miller's novel *Gowns by Roberta*. Directed by William A. Sieter. Also with: Helen Westley, Claire Dodd (Scott's girlfriend who turns up to cause

trouble), Victor Varconi, Lucille Ball (one of the fashion models).

ROBOT MONSTER/MONSTERS FROM THE MOON (1953) B&W/62m.
Laughably lousy sci-fi film, made for $20,000 in LA's Bronson Canyon. In John Ford's *The Searchers*, John Wayne gazes out of a canyon cave; in Phil Tucker's camp classic, an alien (George Barrows) wearing a gorilla costume and a diver's helmet uses the same cave as his headquarters. By using his dreaded calcinator death ray, Ro-Man has destroyed the earth's population except for six Hu-Mans picnicking near him in Griffith Park: a professor (John Mylong), his wife (Selena Royle), their stacked daughter (Claudia Barrett), their two obnoxious young children (Gregory Moffett, Pamela Paulson), and a young scientist (topbilled George Nader). Ro-Man gets his instructions from back home, from "The Great One" (also played by Barrows), on how to neutralize the serum these people have taken to neutralize his death ray. He wants to kill them all but Barrett, and his lustful desire for her makes him wish he were a Hu-Man, too (this, of course, leads to his downfall). Film gets more ludicrous as it goes along. I'm sure that Paulson's surprisingly early death by strangulation was not scripted but improvised out of necessity to get the incorrigible little actress out of the film in a manner that most pleased Tucker and her fellow actors. I find her quick death much less shocking than Nader's: barely injured, he runs for a long way over hill and over dale and, after all that, collapses. Ending in which Ro-Man emerges from a cave three times in succession (the shot is repeated) may have inspired Edward D. Wood when making *Plan 9 from Outer Space* to repeatedly show the same shot of Bela Lugosi walking through a graveyard. Picture was made in 3-D, but Tucker takes little advantage of the process, unless you find bubbles floating at you exciting. It was also the first sci-fi film to use stereophonic sound. Much stock footage is employed, including a lengthy sequence of prehistoric monsters fighting taken from *One Million B.C.* Oddly, *Variety* actually gave this film a decent review. Score was by, surprisingly, Elmer Bernstein.

ROCK AROUND THE CLOCK (1956) B&W/77m.
Talent scouts (Johnny Johnston, Henry Slate) looking for a new sound that will get the people dancing again discover the small-town band Bill Haley and the Comets. They play rock 'n' roll. And how brother-sister act Lisa Gaye and Earl Barton jitterbug to the music. Bill and the boys come to New York; they get to play in Alan Freed's club but have trouble getting a contract and other gigs because of booking agent Alix Talton. She's jealous of Johnston's attraction to Gaye. But rock 'n' roll triumphs. Weak plot and acting are bolstered by nine performances by Haley and the Comets (the title song, "See You Later, Alligator," and others) and classics by the Platters ("Only You," "The Great Pretender"). It's funny how polite and well dressed all the music stars are—that's so adults won't object. Pro-

duced by Sam Katzman. Directed by Fred Sears. Also with: the boring Freddie Bell and His Bellboys.

ROCK 'N' ROLL HIGH SCHOOL (1979) C/93m.
The prime example of a picture that was designed to be a cult movie. New World premiered it as a midnight movie, hoping that it would attract fans of its musical stars, the punk supergroup The Ramones, as well as college-age viewers who were curious about any midnight movies. It has never become an "event" film on the order of *The Rocky Horror Picture Show*, but a strong following has kept it one of the most popular of the midnight movies. Because the last three principals of Vince Lombardi High have suffered breakdowns due to the students' obsession with rock 'n' roll, tough new principal Mary Woronov promises to end the music craze. She blames the problem on cheerleader P.J. Soles, who cares only about the Ramones and skips school so she can be first in line for their concert. The film is full of nonsensical humor, but it lacks diabolically conceived outrageousness and sick humor. It needs more bawdiness and, better, raunchiness in spots. It's such a wholesome film that the major subplot dealing with the efforts of football player Vincent Van Patten and brainy, pretty virgin Dey Young to have sex is treated in PG fashion. The worst mistake the filmmakers make is not fully exploiting the fact that almost everybody hated high school. It's fun watching fascist monitors demand hall passes, watching rebellious students throwing "Tuesday Surprise" at the cooks, and Woronov threatening Soles with "detention for life!" but there's not enough of this. Most interesting: this may be a silly comedy, but there is no other commercial American film in which an American institution's destroyed and no one is punished. Still, it seems a foolish gesture to blow up the high school—the principal is the enemy, not education. The best thing about this film is the high-spirited cast headed by Soles, bebopping and high-kicking non-stop, drooling over how Joey Ramone "slithers pizza into his mouth" and repeatedly injecting life into the picture when the humor has gone limp. I'm not enthusiastic about the Ramones' high-powered music, but they're amusing in this film and fun to watch while performing. Directed by Allan Arkush and Joe Dante; Richard Whitley, Russ Dronch, and Joe McBride wrote the script. Also with: Clint Howard, Dick Miller, Paul Bartel, Alix Elias, Don Steele, Loren Lester, Daniel Davies, Grady Sutton.

ROCK, ROCK, ROCK! (1956) B&W/83m.
Young teen Tuesday Weld began her unique career by providing the lone acting spark to this lightweight high-school comedy–rock-'n'-roll showcase. She wants to go to the prom with Tommy (and beat out her rival), but Dad gives her only half the money for a prom dress. He expects her to learn the value of money by working, but she comes up with a money-making scheme that would do justice to Thalia Meninger (her greedy teenager in *The Many Loves of Dobie Gillis*). Unfortunately, it backfires. Weld is cute as a button and shows undeniable star quality—she'd have made a great

Gidget. But it's weird watching her lip-synch to Connie Francis's singing. Alan Freed's on hand to present a lot of top rock acts, including Frankie Lymon and the Teenagers, Chuck Berry, LaVern Baker, the Moonglows, the Flamingos, and Johnny Burnett, but for the most part the acts sing flipside-type songs. Co-star Teddy Randazzo sings a couple of dull songs, but he would gain fame in rock field as a songwriter. Directed by Will Price, who made no attempt to integrate rock acts into the storyline.

ROCKETSHIP X-M (1950) B&W/77m.
This beat George Pal's *Destination Moon*, which had been started earlier, into the theaters, thus becoming the first film of the fifties science fiction cycle. Pal's film has superior special effects, a more interesting production history, and more scientific credibility, but if this film isn't as important as Pal's, it's at least as entertaining. Rocket to the moon is knocked off course and lands on Mars (same difference). Crew discovers that a great civilization has been destroyed by atomic warfare. The only survivors are violent, imbecilic mutants. Pal made space exploration seem exciting; this picture makes it seem ominous: despite not having enough fuel to make it home, crew heads rocket toward earth so they can at least deliver a warning that earth shouldn't make same mistakes as Martians. Since this is a ground-setting film of the genre, it's interesting to watch the role of the one female (Osa Massen) on the expedition. A scientist, she always defers to the male captain (John Emery) when a decision has to be made; when she gets emotional because her sound recommendation was rejected, she apologizes. No need, the men tell her, for she was just "being a woman." Directed by Kurt Neumann. Also with: Lloyd Bridges, Hugh O'Brian, Noah Beery, Jr.

ROCKY (1976) C/119m.
This disarming little sleeper was written by its unknown star Sylvester Stallone. It smashed box-office records, won Oscars for Best Picture and Best Director (John G. Avildsen), made Stallone into an instant superstar, and gave the disenfranchised of America a new folk hero. Perhaps we've overdosed on sequels, but *Rocky* still holds up well and is guaranteed to produce cheers and tears. Stallone plays Rocky Balboa, a fourth-rate Philadelphia club fighter who lives in a slum and works as a collector for a loan shark. He considers himself stupid, a loser, a man without hope of ever improving his life. But in America, miracles do happen. Miracle One: He becomes involved with the pretty but supershy Adrienne (Talia Shire). Their courtship's as touching as Paul Newman and Pier Angeli's in *Somebody Up There Likes Me*. They manage to build up each other's self-respect, and soon they both realize that they aren't losers. Miracle Two: As a publicity stunt, Rocky is offered a shot at the heavyweight title by overconfident champ Apollo Creed (Carl Weathers). At first reluctant, Rocky decides to meet the challenge and "go for it." Trained by the elderly Mickey (Burgess Meredith)—it's a rare boxing film to emphasize training—he gets himself into shape. No one gives him a chance, but his ability to "go the dis-

tance" with Creed is inspiring; the fight itself is phenomenally exciting. As a result Rocky, once a bum of the first order, becomes a hero to everyone who wants to rise above loser status. The film contends that anyone who has enough heart and motivation can do the impossible. Best of all, Rocky refuses to quit. He's the perfect hero for this fairy tale. Stallone does not come across as gung-ho for boxing ("You gotta be a moron to be a fighter"), but he believes certain individuals like Rocky can use the sport positively, as a test of one's mettle, as a character builder. This Italian fellow Rocky is undeniably appealing. He's a nice guy, full of warmth, sentimentality, and spirit (and it's almost a rare fight film with humor), and you'll feel the surge as Rocky runs through Philly streets to Bill Conti's fabulous theme song. Also with: Burt Young (as Adrienne's always complaining brother), Thayer David, Joe Spinell.

ROCKY II (1979) C/119m.
As shamelessly sentimental as both versions of *The Champ*. Unable to make it in the everyday world, Rocky (Sylvester Stallone) trains for a rematch with champion Apollo Creed (Carl Weathers). This time it's important to win, not just "go the distance." The exciting final bout is, of course, the film's highlight, but what's most interesting is the relationship between Rocky and Adrienne (Talia Shire again), who now are married. Although she still can't bear to watch him fight, she becomes his partner (rare for a woman in a boxing film) and the person who gives him the necessary motivation to beat Apollo and make the most of his life. Still you may have a hard time putting up with director-writer Stallone pulling your emotional strings by subjecting Adrienne to a hemorrhage and lengthy deathbed stay, from which she recovers because of Rocky's prayers. Burgess Meredith, as Rocky's manager, and Burt Young, as Adrienne's brother, reprised their roles from the original.

ROCKY III (1982) C/99m.
Rocky (Sylvester Stallone, also directing again) loses his manager (Burgess Meredith's character dies). Then he loses his title to vicious killing machine Clubber Lang (imposing Mr. T) and, for some reason, his self-respect in the process. But with Adrienne (Talia Shire) at his side, with Apollo Creed (Carl Weathers) as his new manager, and with hunger back in his heart and "the eye of the tiger," he regains the title from the sadistic man who wasn't worthy of wearing the heavyweight crown. The film is fairly predictable, Adrienne's emotional speech that spurs Rocky to train with conviction is incomprehensible, and Stallone's script lacks the cohesion of his earlier efforts. But what distinguishes it somewhat is that Rocky must cope with *fear*, a theme that, oddly enough, had not really been explored in boxing films. Smash hit song "Eye of the Tiger" by Survivor. Also with: Burt Young, wrestler Hulk Hogan.

ROCKY IV (1985) C/91m.
Phony baloney from Sylvester Stallone; the worst, most embarrassing film of the series. Russia lifts its ban on professional boxing and unveils 261-pound killing machine Drago (Dolph Lundgren), a muscular, no-body-fat giant who represents the apex in advanced Soviet training techniques. When Drago kills Apollo (Carl Weathers) in Las Vegas, hitting him with sledgehammer punches that are literally twice as powerful as the best shots of the average heavyweight, Rocky decides to avenge his friend. He travels to Russia to fight Drago. This is the kind of manipulative film that they'll show in Russia to illustrate the American cinema's absurd portrayal of both American heroes and the Russian people—how would Americans react if they knew the Russians made a film about a Soviet champ who travels to the U.S. for a big match against our national hero and ends up being rooted for by the American fight fans and applauded by our President for his political line? Well, the reverse happens in this film and it's absurd; can't Stallone understand that his character need not appeal to everyone? Stallone's dialogue is very lazy; the conversations between Rocky and wife Adrienne (Talia Shire) have reached the point where *long* sentences last five simple words and the same words are then repeated by the other in different order. Like most in the cast, she has nothing to say, so she smiles, looks worried, looks pained. Stallone's direction has also become lax, so that his film is comprised of many montages with blaring music in the background (by Survivor); each is equivalent to a rock video and could be shown intact as just that. It's still fun watching Rocky train, but this time the climactic fight is sloppily choreographed and edited; and we can't even tell if Rocky is responding to the crowd's cheers. His ridiculous post-fight speech, which has the clarity of something written by Rambo, should have been cut. At least Drago—a sort of handsome, icier version of Richard Kiel's "Jaws"—is a more than satisfying villain: it's a pleasure seeing Rocky rip into him. Also with: Burt Young, Brigitte Nielsen.

ROCKY HORROR PICTURE SHOW, THE (BRITISH/1975) C/100m.
The undisputed *queen* of the midnight movies, the definitive cult movie, the cinema's greatest phenomenon, this is the one movie that can't even be discussed without mentioning its fans—for they have changed it from being an undistinguished, campy horror-SF send-up to a fabulously entertaining multi-media midnight show. It is the ultimate audience-participation film: cultists, who may have seen it 300 times and may be dressed like their favorite characters, recite the dialogue en masse, shout out their own additions to the script, and, under a spotlight, put on a singing-dancing-mime performance that half-duplicates, half-parodies the action taking place on the screen above them. It is like no show around, neither intimidating nor smug; under the right circumstances it's almost a throwback to when movies brought entire communities together. The beauty is that in one row you'll find gays, transvestites, psychology students, punk-rockers, comic-book addicts, science-fiction nuts, stoned-out viewers from the film that ended at midnight, high-school students out on dates, and people who wonder what they're doing there. Adapted by director Jim Sharman and Richard O'Brien from

O'Brien's rock opera, *The Rocky Horror Show*, it tells the story of Brad (Barry Bostwick) and Janet (Susan Sarandon), a strait-laced engaged couple from Denton, Ohio. Lost in the rain, they come to the castle of Dr. Frank-N-Furter (Tim Curry), who wears high heels, lipstick, eye make-up, and sexy female underwear. Also present are strange butler Riff Raff (O'Brien), weird maid Magenta (Patricia Quinn), motorcyclist Eddie (Meat Loaf), and his groupie, Columbia (Little Nell). On this eventful night, the annual convention of visitors from the planet Transsexual is being held and Frank-N-Furter is bringing Rocky Horror (Peter Hinwood), a handsome, muscular young man, to life. Also Eddie's uncle, Dr. Everett Scott (Jonathan Adams), who investigates UFOs, turns up. The picture—minus the act-along—isn't particularly well made or amusing. But I like it when the stodgy criminologist (Charles Grey), who reminds me of Dr. Frank Baxter in those high school science films, demonstrates dance steps. And the big production of "The Time Warp" is a lot of fun, as is Meat Loaf's wild rock number, "Whatever Happened to Saturday Night?" I am less impressed by the other songs. I also like the concept of having the doctor in the Frankenstein tale be the monster. Curry is dynamic as the cinema's one masculine-acting (sweet) transvestite. But other than Curry, the "Touch-a Touch-a Touch-a Touch Me" dirty-lyrics number that Janet sings while moving Rocky's hands over her breasts, and the sequence in which Frank seduces both Janet (while pretending to be Brad) and Brad (while pretending to be Janet), there isn't much that isn't PG material. I wish it were more jarring and braver—it just peters out and, to a first-time viewer, becomes confusing. Luckily, the cultists in the audience maintain their hectic pace right to the end. *Shock Treatment* is the disastrous sequel.

RODAN/RODAN, THE FLYING REPTILE (JAPANESE/1957) C/70m.
Ranks just below *Godzilla, King of the Monsters* on the Japanese best monster-movie list. Kids in particular will enjoy this sci-fi fantasy about Japan being terrorized by two 100-ton flying reptiles that hatched deep in a coal mine. Early scenes in the mine are a little spooky, influenced perhaps by the scenes of giant ants in LA sewers in *Them!* About halfway through, it becomes a war film, with the army using tremendous firepower to battle the reptiles on land and over sea. It ends as a "love story," in which the two "rodans" loyally fight side by side instead of saving themselves. Directed by Inoshiro Honda, who collaborated with his Godzilla special-effects expert, Eija Tsuburaya, to again create some extremely impressive scenes of destruction (a preoccupation of post-WWII Japanese SF directors). Good dubbing for English-language distribution; interestingly, they had Japanese dubbers speak in halting English rather than Americans (as most Japanese SF films use) whose voices wouldn't match the characters. With: Kenji Sawara, Yumi Shirakawa, Akihiko Hirato.

ROMANCING THE STONE (1984) C/105m.
Unadventurous, unloved adventure-romance novelist Joan Wilder (Kathleen Turner) flies to Colombia to help her imperiled sister. Soon she finds herself lost and stranded in the jungle, with corrupt cops and crooks, both of the sadistic variety, trying to kill her because she is carrying the lone map that pinpoints the location of a precious jewel. She is rescued by an American soldier-of-fortune (Michael Douglas), whom she pays to take her to civilization. After a bumpy start in their relationship, he becomes, in her words, "the best time I've ever had." With him, Joan gets to live an adventure romance that is suitable for her book heroines. Shooting on location, Robert Zemeckis directed this very entertaining, very funny roller-coaster ride of a movie. The storyline may be predictable, but many clever touches are thrown in along the way, including having a horde of mean peasant-highwaymen turn out to be Joan Wilder fanatics. Film's surprise treasure is Turner's thoroughly dazzling and likable characterization, which was a complete turnaround from her previous role, the blood-draining vamp in *Body Heat*. It's enjoyable watching her Joan Wilder switch from being everybody's easy touch in New York to a tough-as nails (but still sweet and sentimental) heroine in the real jungle. Also with: Danny De Vito, Zack Norman, Alfonso Arau, Manuel Ojeda.

RONDE, LA (FRENCH/1950) B&W/97m.
Max Ophüls's charming adaptation of Arthur Schnitzler's play. The constantly moving, seeing, penetrating camera that was Ophüls's trademark serves thematically both to establish the dizzying, intoxicating nature of *l'amour* and to convey its transitory nature (as the French romanticists proclaimed, the strongest loves are too consuming to last). With Anton Walbrook acting as our narrator-storyteller, film is broken into several vignettes featuring a romantic sexual interlude between a man and a woman. Each vignette contains one character from the previous segment. So when a husband and wife lie in bed speaking of fidelity, we have the advantage of having earlier seen her in an affair and knowing that we'll see him with his mistress in the following sequence. Ophüls's women glow; their actions are determined by their hearts—and they never hold back from a sexual liaison or feel guilt afterward. They are the personifications of love; they know its glories. Ophüls's men, while no buffoons, can't appreciate love except on a physical level—they are always setting up rules, demanding loyalty, asking questions, thinking too much. Classic film is richly rewarding. Simone Signoret is especially appealing—and beautiful—as a prostitute who is willing to give herself to soldiers for free. Roger Vadim remade film (from Jean Anouilh screenplay) in 1964 as *Circle of Love*. Also with: Daniel Gélin, Simone Simon, Serge Reggiani, Danielle Darrieux, Fernand Gravet, Odette Joyeux, Jean-Louis Barrault, Isa Miranda, Gérard Philipe.

ROOM SERVICE (1938) B&W/78m.
A Marx Brothers comedy in which Groucho, Chico, and Harpo spend almost all their time in a hotel suite, starving and trying to figure out how to get money to keep their play afloat. Based

on a Broadway play by John Murray and Allen Boretz, it was adapted by Morrie Ryskind for the comedy team. And it proves to be a terrible vehicle. It's shattering hearing Groucho say one unfunny line after another, and seeing the three of them act almost civilly. There's no sharpness to Groucho's delivery, no chaos initiated by Harpo. As directed by William A. Seiter, the film moves along at a snail's pace. Best scene has no dialogue—the Marx Brothers simply gorge themselves on the first meal they've had in days. Also with: Lucille Ball, Ann Miller, Frank Albertson, Cliff Dunstan, Donald MacBride.

ROOMMATES (1980) C/89m.   An almost successful attempt by Chuck Vincent, one of the best adult movie directors, to make an XXX-rated film that the general audience would find palatable. It did manage to get bookings in legitimate theaters and be reviewed by mainstream critics (some of whom liked it). Shot in 35mm with a considerable budget for porno, the story follows the sexual exploits of three women who share a New York apartment. The film is diverting because the three leading ladies—porn superstars Samantha Fox, Kelly Nichols, Veronica Hart—are pretty good actresses (especially Nichols), in and out of bed. While Vincent included more dramatic scenes than are usually found in porno films and supposedly wanted his picture to be *erotic*, some of the sex is surprisingly raunchy: one guesses he was afraid of losing the raincoat crowd entirely. Also with: Jamie Gillis.

ROPE (1948) B&W/80m.   Alfred Hitchcock film was long out of circulation. It's best known for director's experiment in which one large apartment set is used and one camera follows the characters about, with cuts coming only once every 10 minutes. From the play by Patrick Hamilton, adapted by Hume Cronyn and scripted by Arthur Laurents, it was inspired by the Leopold-Loeb thrill-killing. John Dall and Farley Granger strangle a young man they know, just for the experience. The arrogant Dall feels exhilarated, as he believes intellectuals like himself have the right to murder inferiors; Granger immediately feels woozy, guilty, and nervous that their crime will be discovered. They plan to dispose of the body later that night, but temporarily place it in a trunk in the living room of their apartment. For further excitement, they throw a dinner party, inviting the dead boy's father (Cedric Hardwicke), aunt (Constance Collier), girlfriend (Joan Chandler), and romantic rival (Douglas Dick). Dall also makes the mistake of inviting their former headmaster (James Stewart), whose Nietzschean philosophy he has adopted. As the dinner party progresses, everyone worries about the dead boy's whereabouts. The suspicious Stewart puts the clues together, knowing that if he gives the two enough rope they will hang themselves. Camera gimmick works well, but picture remains theatrical, as actors all seem a bit stiff—only Dall and Collier seem unafraid to change expressions. Stewart has never been so unanimated. Morbid subject matter. Tough to be in audience because, while you despise two killers, for some reason you hope the crime goes unsolved. Also with: Dick Hogan (the victim), Edith Evanson.

ROSE, THE (1979) C/134m.   Some day a money-mad producer will make a film about the last days of John Belushi; it will be about as unenjoyable as this film, which chronicles the last days in the life of a fictional rock superstar (Bette Midler) patterned on the ill-fated Janis Joplin. Midler made her movie debut as the vulnerable, burned-out singer who is loved by her fans but suffers loneliness because she hasn't a man to love and protect her. To combat her insecurities and her exhaustion from being constantly on the road, she drinks heavily, takes too many drugs, and picks up men. But it all catches up with her on her final tour, which will culminate in her hometown, where she hopes to find thousands of people who love her. It's hard to watch one awful thing after another happen to Midler: not only is she self-destructive, but everyone she trusts lets her down, walks out on her, or exploits her. The movie should have been about an hour shorter, but the filmmakers weren't satisfied having individuals hurt Midler just once, so they bring them back to hurt her again. Midler gives a great performance and does a terrific job singing rock songs (as well as the haunting title ballad), but this film is for masochists only. Cinematography by Vilmos Zsigmond; Haskell Wexler and several others helped photograph concert scenes. Also with: Alan Bates (as the manager who makes sure she never lets up and the money never stops rolling in), Frederic Forrest (as the man who would be the answer to her prayers if he didn't have hang-ups of his own), Barry Primus, Harry Dean Stanton (as a mean country singer), David Keith, Sandra McCabe, Doris Roberts.

ROSEMARY'S BABY (1968) C/136m.   Mia Farrow and John Cassavetes move into an old New York apartment building that is full of strange neighbors—reason enough for Roman Polanski to want to direct this adaptation of Ira Levin's best-seller. Soon Cassavetes starts acting cozy with a daffy elderly couple (Ruth Gordon, Sidney Blackmer) and things go better than in show-biz career. Farrow feels that he isn't the same considerate man she married. Farrow becomes pregnant. She has the weird feeling that it wasn't Cassavetes who was in bed with her on the hallucinatory night when the baby was conceived. She begins to suspect a conspiracy among Cassavetes and the others in the building, and she fears for herself and the baby. Glossy schlock about satanists and the devil's child is not as scary as it is uncomfortable to watch. It becomes upsetting seeing Farrow not only look pale due to her unusual pregnancy but feel confused and constantly tormented. Polanski makes spooky use of the setting and injects some morbid humor. A big hit that is on some levels quite enjoyable—yet it's really an ugly film. Gordon won a Best Supporting Actress Oscar. Produced by William Castle (who has a cameo) and Dona Holloway. Strong photography by William Fraker. Also with Maurice Evans, Ralph Bellamy, Angela Dorian, Patsy Kelly, Charles Grodin, Tony Curtis (voice only).

RUGGLES OF RED GAP (1935) B&W/92m.

Still pleasing Leo McCarey comedy, starring Charles Laughton as Ruggles, a British valet who has always done his job loyally and impeccably, at the cost of his spirit, self-esteem, and personality. In Paris, in 1908, his boss (Roland Young), an earl, loses Laughton in a poker game to a rich American couple (Mary Boland, Charles Ruggles), who take him home to Red Gap, Washington. There, residents mistake him for a British war hero. The socially ambitious Boland wants the well-bred Laughton to teach her fun-loving, heavy-drinking, nattily dressed husband manners and culture, but the wealthy American teaches the lowly British servant the meaning of equality and Laughton takes it to heart. The early scenes in Paris are forced, but the film picks up once Laughton comes to America and starts to blossom when allowed to be his own person. While the film isn't consistently funny, there are some very special moments: Laughton courting and cooking with widow ZaSu Pitts; two bartenders asking everyone in their place if they know what Lincoln said at Gettysburg—the men prove to be dumb, but Laughton recites the Gettysburg Address for the appreciative men; in an improvisational bit, Young attempting to play drums while Leila Hyams sings "Pretty Baby"; the town's elite singing "For He's a Jolly Good Fellow" to the beaming Laughton, who knows he's found his place in America. Also you've got to appreciate its every-man-is-equal theme—it may be a trite message, but few films have delivered it. Harry Leon Wilson's comedy was filmed in 1918 and 1923; Bob Hope starred in 1950's remake, *Fancy Pants*. Also with: Maude Eburne, Lucien Littlefield.

RULES OF THE GAME, THE/RÈGLE DU JEU, LA (FRENCH/1939) B&W/110m.

In Jean Renoir's classic, many guests gather for weekend of partying and hunting at country château. Affair deteriorates when the aristocratic owner (Marcel Dalio) has knockabout fight with the hero aviator (Roland Toutain) who has stolen away his wife (Nora Gregor); and the gamekeeper (Gaston Modot) races through the house trying to gun down the poacher-turned-servant (Julien Carette) who has captured his wife's (Paulette Dubost) heart. As the men fight over the women, the women's attentions turn elsewhere. The picture is set up as a standard French bedroom farce. The slapstick nature of foolish men going at each other is diversionary, meant to seem like a counterpoint to earlier brutal rabbit-pheasant hunt. But surprisingly bleak, cynical ending jolts us out of complacent laughter. I believe that Renoir intended to present us with with several romances that French have pride in—a hero runs off with a lonely married woman whose rich, unfaithful husband was undeserving of her; this beautiful woman later decides to run off with her plump friend (Renoir), who, she now realizes, is bursting with love and kindness—and show us that in 1939, with war on the horizon, such romances could no longer exist. For those who are driven by hearts and emotions, there is tragedy—those who survive unscathed are those sly devils who have money or those stupid brutes who have guns in their hands. Un-fortunately, Renoir had to punish dreamers and romanticists in audience in order to get in blows at those about to sell out France. Cut upon release and later by Vichy censors; banned by Nazis; restored in late 1950s. Regarded as Renoir's masterpiece—yet it's not for all tastes (including my own) despite interesting themes. Also with: Mila Parély (as Dalio's mistress.).

RUNAWAY TRAIN (1985) C/111m.

Yet another unbreakable-prisoner-(Jon Voight)-vs.-sadistic-warden (John P. Ryan) film. After spending three years in solitary confinement at a maximum-security prison in Alaska, tough, wise Voight and his dense fellow inmate Eric Roberts pull off a daring escape. It takes them a while to realize that the engineer on the freight train they've hopped has had a heart attack. Voight, Roberts, and railroad employee Rebecca De Mornay find themselves on a runaway train going 90 miles an hour toward a deadly crash—unless one of them can reach the engine and stop it. Meanwhile Ryan is in mean pursuit, determined to foil the escape lest Voight become a hero to all the other prisoners and the catalyst of a full-scale prison riot. But what in Hollywood's name is Ryan doing at the end trying to drop from a helicopter onto the out-of-control train? Even if he kills or captures Voight, there's no way he'll survive. But never mind: even before this absurd bit the scriptwriters, Djordje Milicevic, Paul Zindel, and Edward Bunker (working from an abandoned screenplay by Akira Kurosawa), have already ruined the picture. The characters played by Voight, Roberts, and De Mornay are terribly drawn—for instance, Roberts is introduced as prison boxing champion, yet his fighting skills *never* come into play. I have no idea what they're thinking, or why they say what they do, or what they're trying to accomplish, although Voight seems to be on some kind of mission only he and Ryan understand. Voight comes across as a man so dehumanized by prison that he is no longer a person but a pathetic symbol of masochistic indestructibility in an existential drama—but his mysteriousness is dissipated when at the exact moment you make the metaphoric connection between him and the runaway train the writers actually have him come out and say he's like a runaway train. Voight and Roberts are powerful enough actors (plus they scream continuously) to cover up their trite lines—on the other hand, De Mornay gets caught. Russian émigré Andrei Konchalovsky directs the vigorous, brutal action scenes with varying degrees of success—he's hampered because he has too few major characters to kill anyone off. His best shots are those of the train charging through snow-covered Siberian-like terrain. Also with: Kyle T. Heffner, Kenneth McMillan, T. K. Carter.

RUSS MEYER'S VIXEN/VIXEN (1968) C/70m.

Landmark soft-core sex film from "King of the Nudies" Russ Meyer bypassed stag-movie circuit for long runs in major theaters. It made what was probably biggest rate of profit on investment in independent-film history until *Halloween*—playing in some theaters for over a year, and making history at one drive-in where it sold several times more tickets than the town's population. In its own way, it had impact of and paved the way for *Deep Throat*; controversial film became subject of many articles, and star Erica Gavin did the talk-show circuit, taking on the likes of Betty Friedan, who insisted Meyer had exploited Gavin. (Years later Gavin agreed.) Film was taken to court, too. Sex isn't all that explicit, but Gavin's erotically charged performance surely is on the verge of being obscene. A perfect film for swingers. Vixen, who has an insatiable sexual appetite, lives in the British wilderness with her husband, a bush pilot (Garth Pilsbury). A straight shooter, he doesn't even consider she might fool around—but she's always on the prowl. She makes love to both a man (Robert Aiken) and his wife (Vincene Wallace) whom her husband brings to the cabin for some fishing; she also has sex with her brother (John Evans). Film has stag-movie plot, except for a bizarre finale in which the small plane carrying the foul-mouthed, racist Vixen, her upstanding husband, and a black American draft dodger (Harrison Page) is hijacked by a crazed communist (Michael Donovan O'Donnell) who wants to fly to Cuba, and all four spout their political and personal philosophies ad hilarium. Meyer keeps the tone light, even when he engages in political satire for the only time in his career. Film is characterized by sexual sight gags, cartoon-like color, breakneck editing. But picture would have faded away by now if it weren't for Gavin, certainly Meyer's best heroine. As the most aggressive female of them all, she does the best job of expressing a woman in sexual heat. Particularly impressive are her facial expressions during her lesbian scene with Wallace—a sequence she was reluctant to do. Meyer also coaxed Gavin into doing a seductive dance holding a fish that she even puts into her mouth. Gavin didn't repulse anyone; in fact, she proved to be a heroine even women viewers liked—as Gavin's fan mail indicated, women weren't used to seeing cinema heroines be so confident, so aggressive, so free of sexual inhibitions. Even today Gavin's Vixen has some qualities that most female characters are reluctant to express. I bought the John Loose soundtrack album for 66 cents. I got gypped.

Ⓢ

SABRINA (1954) B&W/113m. Only in America could the daughter of a mere chauffeur be courted by not one but two millionaires and have the opportunity to marry into an established Eastern family. Sure, sure—if you happen to have the beauty and charm of Audrey Hepburn. Hepburn grows up envying the lives of the rich family for which her father (John Williams) is chauffeur. She has her eye on the Larabee brothers, older stuffy businessman Humphrey Bogart and engineer playboy William Holden, whom she adores. But they ignore her—until she comes back from France as a beautiful, refined woman. When Holden makes a play for her—despite his being virtually engaged to Martha Hyer—Bogart decides to keep her occupied so that the romance will cool. He finds himself feeling romantic urges for the first time in his life. Whom will Hepburn choose? Billy Wilder comedy from Samuel Taylor play is Hollywood fluff and will appeal to those who prefer glamour to content, actors to characters. Hepburn, of course, is ideal, once again playing a variation on Cinderella. For Bogart, cast against type but still self-sacrificing, the ending is pretty much a reversal of *Casablanca*. Also with: Marcel Dalio, Nella Walker, Francis X. Bushman, Nancy Kulp.

SAFETY LAST (1923) B&W/70m. Harold Lloyd silent classic has a splendid mix of genteel character comedy, sight gags, slapstick comic routines, and what he called "thrill" comedy. Go-getter Harold goes to the big city, promising to send for his fiancée (Mildred Davis, whom Lloyd would marry) once he starts making money. At first he is penniless; then he manages to get a low-paying salesman job at a department store. In his letters home he says he's making a lot of money and has an important position. Davis pays a surprise visit to the store. Through quick thinking and luck he manages to get her to believe he is the store's general manager, but he realizes he has to make money quick or she'll think him a failure. Offered $1,000 if he can attract thousands of people to the store, he comes up with a publicity gimmick. He hires his human-fly roommate (Bill Strothers) to climb up the side of the eight-story store. But when his pal is busy eluding a cop, Lloyd has to do the perilous climb himself. Famous daredevil climb takes up about a fourth of the film. It is most remembered for thrilling moment Lloyd hangs from the arms of a large clock, but what's most impressive is how elaborate the entire sequence is—there is a new adventure on every floor—and how cleverly it is filmed (particularly effective is that we always see the street in the distant background). There is a sensational bit where Lloyd tries to grab a hanging rope which we know is not tied to anything—he finally grabs the rope, he falls, the camera switches into building, where his friend rushes into the room and successfully dives for the rope before it disappears out the window, thereby breaking Lloyd's fall. "Thrill" sequence shouldn't make us overlook simpler comedy that takes place earlier. Watch how he hides from his rent-seeking landlady by hanging with his coat on a hook. Or grapples with rampaging women who see there's a sale at his counter: the camera pulls back from Lloyd's face, whereupon we discover that what we saw in close-up—Lloyd appearing to be having a nervous breakdown—is deceptive. An excellent introduction to Lloyd. Directed by Fred Newmeyer and Sam Taylor.

ST. ELMO'S FIRE (1985) C/110m. Seven of Hollywood's hottest young stars were brought together for this mindless, smug film about seven shallow Georgetown grads whose friendships are tested when they start becoming serious about one another. Rob Lowe, Ally Sheedy, Demi Moore, Judd Nelson, Mare Winningham, Andrew Mc-Carthy, and Emilio Estevez are saddled with a script by director Joel Schumacher and Carl Kurlander that is trite and klutzy, a beatable combination. If these seven insipid, irrelevant characters are true to life, then all those words of disappointment we heard about the college classes of the late seventies and early eighties were correct. But why make pictures about them? Film is simply structured: the friends are always rushing to help one another at the beginning, then there is antagonism between them, then they all get together when one is in trouble. Picture would probably work better if several of the characters were eliminated—I was happy to see Lowe get on a bus, but this happens too late in the picture. What few pleasures we get are not from the characters, but from talented, sensitive actors Sheedy, Winningham, McCarthy, and Estevez, whose personalities are stronger than the script. Also with: Martin Balsam, Andie MacDowall (whose kissing scene with Estevez is probably the film's highlight), Joyce Van Patten, Jenny Wright.

SAINT JACK (1979) C/112m.
A pleasant surprise from Peter Bogdanovich that changed the attitude of those of us who assumed his only goal was to make the quintessential "commercial" film. This sleeper is a unique, effective character study of American Jack Flowers (Ben Gazzara), a well-educated Korean War hero, who's a pimp and wheeler-dealer in Singapore during the early seventies. The excellent script by Howard Sackler, Paul Theroux, and Bogdanovich, adapted from Theroux's novel, begins at a time when Flowers's business success is at its peak—he is known to madams and hookers all over town, and he provides high-priced women to English-speaking foreigners—and jealous local brothel owners are out to close down his operation. In need of cash, he accepts the $25,000 offer of an American (Bogdanovich) to secretly photograph a visiting senator (George Lazenby) while he has relations with a boy prostitute. But throughout we've been given signs that in his own way Flowers is a decent, moral, even responsible man—so we don't know if he'll sink low enough to carry out Bogdanovich's scheme. Gazzara has never been better—it actually seems that he lives in Singapore—and his scenes with British businessman Denholm Elliott (at his peak also), during which friendship and respect develop, are extremely moving. I think it's appropriate that we never come to fully figure out Flowers. Bogdanovich's added triumph is his convincing evocation of a sinful Singapore during the days of the Vietnam War. Also with: James Villiers, Joss Ackland, Rodney Bewes, Lisa Lu.

SALT OF THE EARTH (1954) B&W/94m.
Remarkable, stirring political film tells the true story of a successful 13-month strike at a zinc mine in New Mexico, begun in 1953, a strike that was won because the wives of the miners took over the picket line after a Taft-Hartley injunction enjoined their husbands from picketing. The film centers on how one Mexican-American (Juan Chacon, one of the many real striking miners in the cast) must come to terms with his wife's (professional actress Rosaura Revueltas) emergence as a political activist while he takes over the housework and children-raising. Not only does this film give women proper recognition for their contribution to the labor movement, but it also anticipated the women's movement of the seventies, in that it makes an issue of equality in jobs, equality in the home, and sexual equality. This was the first American narrative film set in America that dared to have women standing with their husbands against the oppressors. Significantly, their liberation is achieved by them independently—it is not, cannot, be given them by men; their liberation is then in turn a liberating catalyst for men, who are also trapped by sex-role convention. The film's strong theme is that the liberated woman is no real threat to her man; her existence will benefit him. As Revueltas assures the scared and confused Chacon: "I want to rise. And push everything with me as I go." Film deals with many issues of importance to miners and their wives (worker safety, sanitation), but it stresses that the real villain in the continuous worker-owner dispute is discrimination. By the end of the film, when Anglos and Chicanos and men and women stick together and are a strong force for reform for *all* workers, the owner's bigotry against Mexican-Americans is blunted. Independent production was directed by Herbert Biberman, produced by Paul Jarrico, scripted by Michael Wilson, photographed by Leonard Stark and Stanley Meredith, scored by Sol Kaplan—all men who were blacklisted in Hollywood at the time. It had been called a subversive film in Congress and the *New York Times* before its release, but you'll be surprised that such concern was shown about a picture which, basically, is pro-human rather than anti-American, which makes no pitch for revolution—just solidarity against the power elite, encompassing racial brotherhood and sexual equality. Script was written with cooperation of the participants in the strike, many of whom act in the film. We are touched by the characters because they are not epic figures—only when they stand together do they take on heroic proportions. The most famous scene: imprisoned females drive the sheriff (Will Geer) batty with cries of "The formula! The formula!" for Revueltas's baby. Many scenes will cause smiles, tears, cheers. A film that lives up to the legend. Also with: David Wolfe, Melvin Williams, David Sarvis, Henrietta Williams, Ernest Velasquez, Angela Sanchez, Joe T. Morales.

SAN FRANCISCO (1936) B&W/115m.
Old-fashioned Hollywood hokum, given an amazingly elaborate M-G-M production. Employing numerous theater and saloon sets and hundreds of extras, director W. S. Van Dyke presents a properly rowdy San Francisco of 1906 (does that year worry you?). Jeanette MacDonald is the moral daughter of a country parson. She'd like to sing opera, but settles for a job singing popular tunes in the dance hall–saloon of Clark Gable, a well-meaning but roguish character. She falls in love with Gable despite his being an atheist and allowing

gambling in his joint. She worries that he wants to marry her only because her singing helps him financially. He won't allow her to pursue an opera career if they marry—he insists that she still work for him. Scripted by Anita Loos, this is one of the first films to deal with a woman experiencing a man-vs.-profession conflict. MacDonald makes a lovely lead and is in particularly fine form singing a wide variety of material. (Opera sequences are given lavish treatment.) Gable is okay playing his typical tough guy with a soft spot in his heart, but he's thoroughly unconvincing when he finally gets religion. As a priest and Gable's boyhood chum, Spencer Tracy doesn't have enough to do. Highlight is the stunning earthquake sequence, which is famous for its impressive special effects and great montage work by John Hoffman. Because of the editing and costuming (the people look like Russians), it could easily be inserted into the "Odessa Steps" sequence of *Potemkin*. Enjoyable film is almost spoiled by a silly finale, in which earthquake victims get carried away with religious fervor. Also with: Jack Holt, Shirley Ross, Edgar Kennedy, Russell Simpson.

SANDERS OF THE RIVER (BRITISH/1935) B&W/ 98m.
The opening title: "Africa . . . Tens of millions of natives under British rule, each tribe with its own chieftain, governed and protected by a handful of white men whose everyday work is an unsung saga of courage and efficiency." Zoltán Korda's tribute to English colonialism is hard to stomach—he gives the impression that black Africans are prosperous, happy, and peaceful under British rule, that there is war between tribes as soon as the British loosen the ropes, that rebellious natives need to be "punished" (as if they were children) so they will respect discipline, that they will be happy to obey chieftains who are appointed by the British. In fact, besides the location photography (in Nigeria) and some striking footage of real natives paddling downriver while star Paul Robeson sings, the only thing positive is that in the finale a white man, Leslie Banks as Commissioner Sanders, rescues a black couple—his friend, tribal chief Robeson and wife Nina Mae McKinney. Edgar Wallace's tale was adapted by Lajos Biro and Jeffrey Dell. Editing by Charles Crichton. Robeson received top billing.

SANDS OF IWO JIMA (1949) B&W/110m.
Excellent war movie directed by Allan Dwan, with John Wayne giving an Oscar-nominated performance as tough marine Sergeant Stryker. Wayne is detested by his green troops until they learn that he is strict for their own good and truly feels love and responsibility for his platoon. The hardest nut to crack is John Agar, whose father was Wayne's commanding officer and much like Wayne—Agar despises the marine mentality and wants to teach his new baby how to use his mind rather than how to use a gun. There are several trite non-combat scenes, but others are quite special: Wayne teaching a recruit how to use his bayonet by dancing with him; Wayne visiting a prostitute and helping feed her baby. But the battles of Tarawa and fire-ravaged Iwo Jima are definitely the picture's highlights. They are spectacularly directed by Dwan, who adds to the authenticity by using actual war footage with his fiction. Significantly, being a soldier in battle is shown to be terrifying. Even Stryker admits, "I'm always scared." The film shows that for men to move forward, others must sacrifice their lives: nothing in war is accomplished without casualties. Harry Brown's script deservedly won an Oscar nomination. A memorable, emotional last scene. Also with: Forrest Tucker, Arthur Franz, Richard Jaeckel, Julie Bishop, James Brown, Martin Milner.

SANJURO (JAPANESE/1962) B&W/96m.
As in Akira Kurosawa's *Yojimbo*, Toshiro Mifune plays a mercenary samurai named Sanjuro, a mysterious, aloof vagabond with unequaled skills with the sword. Yet I doubt if this film is a sequel or the character is the same, although Kurosawa reworked his script, adapted from a novel by Shugoro Yamamoto, to capitalize on the success of *Yojimbo*, even changing his hero from being a man who won fights by using his wits into one who wins primarily because of his fighting talent. This film is much funnier, it takes a stand against unnecessary violence, and it presents a hero who does care about those who need help and is affected emotionally by what transpires around him. While not as ambitious as *Yojimbo* or as impressively photographed, it is that film's equal and one of Kurosawa's greatest achievements. Plot has Sanjuro helping a group of nine naïve but virtuous young clansman who never fully understand (after all, he is neither good nor bad) or trust him. They are conspiring against the corrupt men who have kidnapped the Chamberlain (Yonosuke Ito), the uncle of the leader of this clandestine group (Yuzo Kayama). Mifune kills scores of enemy soldiers, but he would kill many more if Ito's wife (Takako Irie) and daughter (Reiko Dan) didn't insist that violence should be kept to a minimum; it is the simplistic, foolish pacifism of the women that provides the film with much of its humor—because of them, the nearby stream doesn't run red with blood but white with camellias (who ever heard of great warriors incorporating *flowers* into their schemes?). Through their influence Mifune sees that he would be a greater, purer fighter if he always kept his sword in its scabbard. We viewers also learn our lesson: we laugh as he mows down soldiers in the early fight scenes, but when he outdraws and brutally stabs the chief villain (Tatsuya Nakadai) in the chilling finale, causing blood to gush from his body, we are shocked and disturbed by the realism of this killing. So is Mifune. Also with: Takashi Shimura, Keija Kobayashi (who is funny as a captured spy who stays willingly in an unlocked closet so as not to offend the two trusting hostesses), Akihiko Hirata, Kenzo Matsui.

SANSHO, THE BAILIFF/BAILIFF, THE (JAPANESE/1954) B&W/105m–130m.
In 11th-century Japan a provincial governor is exiled because of his benevolence toward peasants. Walking alone through dangerous territories, his wife and young son and daughter are kidnapped. His wife is sent to an island, where she becomes

a courtesan. Pining for her children, she attempts to escape, but is caught. Her leg tendons are slashed, crippling her. The children are sold to the cruel Sansho, a bailiff who has many ill-treated slaves to work his manor. The devoted boy and girl spend many years under the most difficult circumstances. But even when grown they remember their mother's love and their father's progressive philosophy that stated all people are equal and all are entitled to happiness. Determined to find his mother, improve the lives of his sister and himself, and free Sansho's slaves, the young man escapes. He will have great rewards and great despair. Masterful storytelling by Kenji Mizoguchi. His sweeping epic brilliantly evokes brutal inhumanity during the period, yet also is a beautiful character piece centering on mother and children. Film shows why Mizoguchi is known for his sensitive treatment of women—it's obvious that he greatly admires the mother and daughter for their bravery, resilience, and selflessness. A great film for adults, but teenagers also might get drawn in by Japanese legend. Exquisitely photographed by Kazuo Miyagawa. With: Kinuyo Tanaka, Yoshiaki Hanayaki, Kyoko Kagawa, Eitaro Shindo, Iochiro Sugai.

SATURDAY NIGHT FEVER (1977) C/108m—119m.
John Travolta danced the disco beat to instant superstardom in this smash hit. He plays 19-year-old Tony, who lives in a lower-middle-class Catholic neighborhood in Brooklyn. Saturday nights he's top dog at the local disco. Dancing gives him his only fulfillment. But he senses that it can't last forever. Across the Bridge is Manhattan—the promised land. Classy Karen Lynn Gorney (who can't act) also wants to make it to Manhattan. Film's theme is that every person has the talent to "make it," to escape the neighborhood where there are no opportunities; all anyone needs is drive and opportunities. Travolta and Gorney, opposites who get serious about each other, see the disco's upcoming dance contest as their springboard to the big time. Film is shallow, but Travolta is electrifying, whether getting dressed in his room, wiggling down the street, trying desperately to express himself in conversation, making love, or, of course, putting on an amazing display on the dance floor. Disco score, featuring popular Bee Gees songs, is super. Stylishly, feverishly directed by John Badham, who isn't ashamed to explore Travolta's sexual appeal—most male directors concentrate only on females' physicality. Choreographed by Lester Wilson. Sylvester Stallone directed the junky sequel, *Staying Alive*. Also with: Donna Pescow (who thinks Travolta is ignoring her), Fran Drescher, Barry Miller, Joseph Cali, Monte Rock III.

SAY AMEN, SOMEBODY (1983) C/100m.
Warmhearted documentary by George T. Nierenberg about some of the pivotal figures of gospel music. It's wonderfully uplifting seeing aged gospel icons talk about what it means to sing gospel music. The music's founding father, the Reverend Thomas A. Dorsey—who's as exciting to watch as Little Richard—and semi-retired Queen of Gospel Willie Mae Ford Smith, give highly spirited performances. And

it's good to see the gospel tradition being carried on by the middle-aged Barrett Sisters and others much younger. It's also interesting to watch revealing interviews and some of the *cinéma-vérité* footage showing the performers at home (i.e., telling a surprised husband they've decided to make a tour). But the director doesn't know how to juxtapose the concert material with the chatter, and the film loses momentum and, amazingly, becomes dull. Gospel music works when the singers can transmit their emotions to their listeners (the church congregation)—but every time we really get into the swing of things and feel intoxicated by the music, Nierenberg pauses for a lot of behind-the-scenes chatter. I wish the young filmmaker had had a veteran around to help him construct this film better—because the proper footage for a stronger film is there.

SCANNERS (CANADIAN/1981) C/102m.
Flawed, confusing, yet lively science fiction from David Cronenberg. Two hundred thirty-six "scanners" were created as a result of an experimental tranquilizer given to pregnant women back in the 1940s. The scanners have the ability to read thoughts, control other people through brain waves, and cause heads to explode. Patrick McGoohan, the doctor who invented the drug, recruits scanner Stephen Lack to halt the nefarious activities of scanner Michael Ironside. Lack finds himself in a civil war between the evil Ironside's scanner army and some decent scanners whom Ironside is trying to wipe out. Film climaxes with confrontation between Lack and Ironside in which the loser literally develops a splitting headache. Dick Smith did the special effects make-up—but I find the film's urban guerrilla warfare scenes much more enjoyable than watching eyes bulging out of sockets, blood pouring out of noses, and heads exploding. McGoohan and Ironside give solid performances; Lack isn't an appealing lead. Mark Irwin did the cinematography. Also with: Jennifer O'Neill (who's part of the guerrilla band Lack helps), Robert Silverman, Adam Ludwig, Lawrence Dane, Charles Shamata.

SCARFACE (1983) C/170m.
Brian De Palma's truly ugly, disappointing remake of Howard Hawks's 1932 classic. One might guess De Palma really cared about his anti-capitalist theme: Cuban criminals, like Al Pacino's Tony Montana, are exiled (by Castro in 1980) to America—from a place with too little freedom to a country with too much freedom. But, judging from what's on screen, I'd say he was more interested in both directing *un hommage* to screen violence and working with Pacino, who, even if his Cuban accent were half decent, gives one of the most pungent (as in *stinky*), self-impressed performances in memory—snarling, swaggering, shouting, sneering, and sniffing coke up his snout ad nauseam. Story details Pacino's rise from petty drug runner to righthand man of Miami's drug emperor to emperor himself. The path is marked by bloody rub-outs, great amounts of money floating about, connections with corrupt policemen and drug suppliers in South America, and fallings out with his pretty wife (Michelle Pfeiffer), faithful

friend (Steven Bauer, who gives the one above-average performance), and decent but naïve sister (Mary Elizabeth Mastrantonio). De Palma doesn't show the development of the incestuous, overly protective feelings Pacino has for sister after they are reunited in Miami (and she has matured from kid to sexy woman)—it happens too quickly and comes across as just a writer's convenience that will cause Pacino to break with Bauer (who loves Pacino's sister). De Palma also neglects showing inner workings of Pacino's mob. Where are *all* his men and what do they do all day? We just see a few guys repeatedly making large bank deposits. They deal drugs, but, considering this is a *gangster* film, rules of the genre dictate we be able to envision Pacino's *territory*. There are many flubs. Editing is terrible—despite the picture's great length, it's obvious that footage is missing. Female costuming is a joke—it's one of few major films where it's obvious that all the well-dressed women are wearing clothes created by the same Hollywood designer. Look of film— the sun-drenched streets, orange sunsets, Art Deco architecture (it was actually shot mostly in LA)—is good, but not so impressive now that we've seen television's *Miami Vice*. Heralded violence has shock value at beginning— particularly in the famous scene in which Pacino's crime mate is dismembered with an electric buzz saw (edited to give the film an R rating)—but it later becomes as calculated for audience response as are the film's quieter, character-development scenes. Finale in which Pacino's mansion is surrounded by guerrilla-warrior types has been praised for original spectacle, but you'll find similar scenes in low-budget Ninja films. Having Pacino—a truly despicable character—so doped up that he can withstand 100 or so bullets without dropping dead may be visually interesting, but by this time viewers desire the perverse pleasure of watching him die in pain, rather than in his "sleep." Also with: Robert Loggia, Miriam Colon, F. Murray Abraham, Harris Yulin.

SCARFACE, THE SHAME OF THE NATION
(1932) B&W/90m.   The best of the early gangster films was completed by Howard Hawks in 1930 but was held up by the censors until several changes were made. The censors wanted the public to understand that the motion-picture industry was also infuriated by crime, yet it's odd they'd pick on this film, which has one of the least glamorous visions of criminals in cinema history. Paul Muni's Tony Camonte, who, like many movie gangsters, was based in part on Al Capone, is a stupid, loutish, ugly brute—his scar is his best facial feature since he's made up to resemble an apeman (he's like Fredric March's Mr. Hyde minus the fangs). Scriptwriter Ben Hecht based his crime family on the Borgias, so he had a model for the corruption, cruelty, power-lust, and decadence that exists; instead of giving Camonte the brother he has in the Armitage Trail's source novel, he gives him a sluttish sister (Ann Dvorak), patterned on Lucretia Borgia, so he can introduce an incest theme. No one who sees this film would want to emulate the lives of these criminals. Film has exciting, atmospheric cinematography by Lee Garmes; taut, inspired direction by Hawks; and a powerful script by Hecht (with additional dialogue credit going to John Lee Mahin, Seton I. Miller, and W. R. Burnett). Hawks and Hecht got ideas for several of the murder/massacre scenes from talking to actual Chicago criminals who'd participated in such crimes. In fact, coin-flipping George Raft, who pays for being Dvorak's lover, worked for the mob when Hawks hired him for this film. Highlights include the opening, in which the camera pans for several minutes across an emptying party room and ends up showing the first victim being murdered; gangster Boris Karloff being shot just as he bowls—the camera follows the ball down the lane, where it knocks over all the pins, including the king pin, which spins for a while and topples over; the finale, in which Dvorak and Muni die in a hail of police bullets. Muni, whom Hawks discovered playing an old man in a Jewish repertory theater in New York, gives one of his finest performances—it is his one character for whom you can feel no sympathy. But I think sexy Dvorak steals the film—it's surprising that the censors were so interested in the gangsters that they didn't take a close look at Dvorak's dancing, listen to her double entendres, or notice how she and Muni looked at each other. Remarkable film was withdrawn from release and didn't resurface until 1979. Capone loved the film so much that he owned his own print. Produced independently by Howard Hughes. Also with: Osgood Perkins (as Tony's boss until Tony kills him), Karen Morley (as Perkins's girlfriend, whom Tony covets almost as much as his sister), C. Henry Gordon, Vince Barnett, Edwin Maxwell, Tully Marshall, Paul Fix, Hawks, and most of the crew.

SCARLET EMPRESS, THE (1934) B&W/110m.
Josef von Sternberg's astonishing, self-described "relentless excursion into style" is the most idiosyncratic of his seven Marlene Dietrich films, and one of the most bizarre films ever to emerge from a Hollywood studio. Dietrich plays Catherine the Great of Russia. Film begins when she's still the young Princess Sophia of Anhalt-Zerbst, far away from Russia. She travels to brutal, educationally backward Russia to marry the Grand Duke Peter (Sam Jaffe), heir to the throne of his aunt, Empress Elizabeth (Louise Dresser). Peter is a cruel, cowardly half-wit, and he and Catherine (Elizabeth changed Sophia's name) hate each other and never consummate the marriage. Catherine is happy that Peter is always busy with his mistress (Ruthelma Stevens) because she has time for affairs of her own. When she bears the son Elizabeth ordered her to have, Peter is embarrassed because everyone knows he's not the father. Peter becomes emperor when Elizabeth dies, and Catherine realizes that for her *and* Russia to survive, he will have to be overthrown. Sternberg was one of the few directors to recognize and explore the link between sexual politics and political power: Catherine's coup d'état would not be possible if she hadn't won over the members of the Russian court and the military (from top to bottom) through sexual means. The film is about a woman who rejects her fate and through self-determination

achieves self-preservation. Her whole life has been spent following the life's course others set out for her. But once she dutifully gives birth to a male heir and is hurt by her lover (John Lodge), she is through being pushed around and goes on the offensive to realize her personal ambitions, using what she acknowledges to be her own "special" weapons. Until this moment we have seen Dietrich as she has never been in a Sternberg film, without her absolute control, sense of irony, air of superiority, mystery, or indifference. Suddenly, thank goodness, Dietrich is back, living by her wits, her own code and logic, manipulating men who once thought they were controlling her. Visually, the film is dazzling, the most imaginative American film of the sound era prior to *Citizen Kane*. Sternberg worked closely with Paramount's costume designer, Travis Banton; with imported Swiss artist Peter Balbusch, Hans Dreier, and Richard Kollorsz on the incredible Byzantine sets (which were meant to be "recreations" of the Russian court); and with cinematographer Bert Glennon on his masterly composed images. Other than the sequence in which Peter curses his aunt's corpse, the film's most memorable scenes have no dialogue, just music and sound effects to heighten the impact of the extraordinary images: the wedding ceremony; the wedding banquet; and the sweeping finale. Sternberg's greatest, most perverse film has still not received its due. Also with: Dietrich's daughter Maria Sieber (Sophia as a child), C. Aubrey Smith, Olive Tell (Sophia's mother), Edward Van Sloan, Jane Darwell.

SCARLET PIMPERNEL, THE (BRITISH/1935) B&W/85m—95m—98m.　One of the cinema's most enjoyable historical romances/adventures, taken from the enduring novel by Baroness Orczy. It is 1792, during the Reign of Terror in France. Thousands of aristocrats are being led to the guillotine, but the bloodthirsty French rabble is being deprived of a few more executions by a brazen British aristocrat known as "the Scarlet Pimpernel," a master of disguises who has rescued a number of potential victims. No one would believe that this heroic figure is actually Sir Percy Blakeney (Leslie Howard), who pretends to be a frivolous, foppish, clothes-conscious, poetry-reciting weakling. Even his wife, Marguerite (Merle Oberon), is fooled by Percy's act, and he is afraid to tell her the truth because he believes (wrongly) that she already has turned others over to the French authorities. Consequently, the couple drifts apart. In an attempt to save her imprisoned brother, Oberon agrees to help villainous Frenchman Raymond Massey (a devilish performance) trap "the Scarlet Pimpernel," not realizing that she is setting up her husband for capture. Film is an unabashed tribute to both the British and French aristocracy—remember Britisher Percy has no reason to rescue the French nobility other than that he admires the nobility from all countries—and a chauvinistic Britisher's attack on the French masses as well as on all those like Massey who would not only take power from his own country's nobility but then start scheming to dismantle the British nobility. Despite the bias present in Alexander Korda's film, which makes us fantasize nobleness in the nobility, his pro-

duction is marvelous in every way. Howard makes a fine and dandy hero who, refreshingly, succeeds by quick wits rather than a quick sword (which he *never* draws!); Oberon, in fancy hats and dresses that probably were selected because their tight bodices direct one's eyes to her bosom, is a stunningly beautiful heroine: when we see Howard and Oberon together in a romantic scene, we immediately know the reason movies were invented. Film has suspense, ironic wit, excellent cinematography by Harold Rosson, beautiful costumes and impressive sets. Korda no doubt helped Harold Young, a marginal talent, with the direction after Rowland Brown was fired (for one of many times in his odd career). Also with: Nigel Bruce, Joan Gardner, Walter Rilla, Melville Cooper, Anthony Bushell.

SCARLET STREET (1945) B&W/103m.　Fritz Lang reunited his *Woman in the Window* stars, Edward G. Robinson, Joan Bennett, and Dan Duryea, for this reworking of Jean Renoir's 1931 classic with Michel Simon, *La Chienne* (itself adapted from the play by Georges de la Fouchardière). Robinson plays a middle-aged, low-paid cashier, the weakling husband of a domineering nag (Rosalind Ivan) who forces him to paint, his dearest hobby, in the bathroom. By chance—most everything that happens is a long-shot occurrence—Robinson takes a different way to the Greenwich Village subway one night and meets Bennett, who says she's an actress in a play that closed that very night (actually, she's a too-lazy-to-work "working girl"). Urged on by her lowlife boyfriend, Duryea, Bennett plays Robinson for the fool, getting him to embezzle money to rent her a studio apartment—on the pretext that he can paint there. By chance, a major art critic (Jess Barker) sees Robinson's paintings (thinking they were worthless, Duryea pawned them to a street artist) and thinks them exceptional. Bennett says she painted them, and accepts large sums of money when they are sold. Masochist Robinson (reduced to painting Bennett's toenails) continues to believe she loves him. Robinson is such a pathetic man, even in his relationship with his wife, that some viewers find no enjoyment from this film. Lang delves into his familiar serious themes—a man falls for a femme fatale and falls into fate's trap, everyone becomes his enemy, an innocent man is convicted of a crime, and the startling ending is unbearably cruel. But I think scriptwriter Dudley Nichols regarded the piece as comedy, with ironic twists, witty dialogue (especially between Bennett and Duryea), and a pathetic, wimpy character who somehow turns the tables on everyone, either ruining their lives or ending them. With excellent performances. Independently made by Diana Productions: Lang, Walter Wanger, and Bennett (Wanger's wife). Also with: Margaret Lindsay, Vladimir Sokoloff, Samuel S. Hinds, Lou Lubin.

SCHOOL GIRL (1971) C/87m.　One of the best and most influential of the early hardcore porno features. It was one of the first of the genre to feature a likable, even funny, heroine who aggressively and happily pursues sex rather than being used by men to fulfill their sexual fantasies. Debbie (a pretty, spunky actress named Debra Allen, who disappeared from the genre) is a young sociology student who answers sex ads in the *Berkeley Barb* so she can write a paper about the people who are involved in the sexual underground. At the end she concludes that these people hate what they are doing, but having watched her have sex with them, we can see that this is untrue. Not nearly as raunchy as most famous porno films. The most exciting sequence has Debbie making love to a man while his wife looks on. Directed by David Reberg (Paul Gerber).

SCOUNDREL, THE/MIRACLE ON 49TH STREET (1935) B&W/78m.

Smug, smirking, cynical New York publisher Noël Coward (his first film role) takes delight in being ruthless ("I'm never nice," he brags). As if it were his duty on earth to break the spirit of optimistic people, he matter-of-factly rejects the work of needy, suicidal writers and breaks women's hearts. He steals a nice young poetess (a fine performance by little-known, beautiful Julie Haydon) away from her fiancé (Stanley Ridges), but just when she's completely devoted to him, he dumps her to chase after a woman he considers just as worthless as he is himself. Meanwhile he orders Ridges arrested for trying to shoot him. The film takes a dramatic turn when Coward's plane to Bermuda goes down in the ocean. He is killed, but there is "no rest for those who die unloved, unmourned." He has one month in which to save his soul, which can only happen if someone sheds a tear on his behalf. Since his circle of friends hasn't an ounce of emotion among them, he searches for Haydon, hoping she'll forgive him. Bizarre mix of Broadway satire and outright fantasy was written and directed by Ben Hecht and Charles MacArthur (who won an Oscar for Best Original Story). It's the best of their directorial efforts: it looks great (thanks to Lee Garmes's atmospheric cinematography) and also has exceptional dialogue, ranging from intellectual to cynical-bitchy (when the Algonquin-type writers engage in some backbiting) to romantic to emotional. What I like best is that Hecht and MacArthur didn't worry about ruining their supersophisticated script by moving into the fantasy realm or having a simple, tear-jerking ending. Also impressive is how Coward is able to make a convincing transition in the fantasy sequence from a devil figure to an emotional, unselfish *human* being (although he's dead). Also with: Lionel Stander, Rosita Moreno, Martha Sleeper, Hope Williams, Harry Davenport, Ernest Cossart, Eduardo Ciannelli, Alexander Woollcott, Hecht.

SCREAM AND SCREAM AGAIN (BRITISH/1970) C/95m.

Still undiscovered by repertory-theater owners, this is a fascinating British horror film which Fritz Lang admired because of its political subtext. Set in the near future, there are three seemingly disjointed storylines that eventually come together: a runner repeatedly wakes up in a strange hospital to discover his limbs are being removed one at a time; police trace down the "vampire killer" (Michael Gothard), who has drained the blood of young women he's murdered; a member (Peter Sallis) of the fascist government of the divided Britain keeps doing away with those superiors who question his brutal tactics when questioning political prisoners. It all has to do with the creation of "synthetic men," who make their way into high government positions. As a scientist involved in this secret experimentation, Vincent Price gets a bit hammy in the unfortunately hokey finale, which is set in his lab, but the other actors—including Christopher Lee, Peter Cushing (a mere cameo), and particularly Alfred Marks (as the droll police captain) play it straight. The direction by Gordon Hessler is clever, particularly during the long sequence in which the police chase the killer. Most interesting is that this picture, earlier than *Alien* or *Android*, advances the spooky notion that egocentric scientists will someday create "synthetic" scientists. Also with: Judy Huxtable, Christopher Mathews, Anthony Newlands.

SCREAM OF FEAR/TASTE OF FEAR (BRITISH/ 1961) B&W/81m.

Susan Strasberg is a recently crippled girl who returns home to meet her stepmother (Ann Todd) for the first time. She is told that her father is away on a trip, but she keeps finding his corpse during her nocturnal wheelchair rides around the property. But the corpse is always gone when she brings others to see it. She suspects her stepmother has killed her father and is trying to drive her insane—in the tradition of *Gaslight*—so she can gain her inheritance. Strasberg enlists the help of handsome chauffeur Ronald Lewis to find the body and prove Todd guilty. Jimmy Sangster's script is full of holes and his many plot twists have since 1961 become old-hat. But Seth Holt's direction is imaginative and there are several times when you are guaranteed to jump. Hammer Studios production is a lot of fun for terror-movie fans. Also with: Christopher Lee as the suspicious local doctor.

SEA HAWK, THE (1940) B&W/127m.

This Errol Flynn swashbuckler is as good an old-time adventure as you'll find. It has great ships, sea battles, swordplay, spies, slaves, Spaniards, even a little smooching. It has a rousing score by Erich Wolfgang Korngold (the John Williams of his day), exuberant and stylish direction by Michael Curtiz (who, as usual, makes great use of light, shadows, and space), a strong, spirited script by Howard Koch and Seton Miller, and a marvelous group of supporting actors, including Flora Robson, Claude Rains, Henry Daniell, Donald Crisp, Alan Hale, Una O'Connor, Montagu Love, Gilbert Roland, and Edgar Buchanan. And it has Flynn, the talking picture's greatest adventure hero. Again he's a pirate; again he's the champion of the underdog, in this case the England of 1585 that is being set up for conquest by Spain. How Flynn's eyes sparkle when he speaks of his beloved country, how sincerely he delivers romantic lines to Brenda Marshall. He proves that he's an excellent *movie* actor. As Queen Elizabeth, Robson is splendid, presenting her not as a man in a woman's body but as a woman of intelligence, wit, high spirits, temper, strength, and love for country and subjects; she's no prude, she just prefers ruling men to loving them. Her verbal battles with Daniell, her untrustworthy minister, and Rains, a sneaky, shrewd Spanish ambassador, are as exciting as the physical warfare Flynn engages in on the high seas. Like another Warners film, 1942's *Casablanca* (also directed by Curtiz and co-written by Koch), this is a veiled propaganda piece that attempts to get Americans solidly into the war effort. Nazi Germany is represented by Spain, imperialistic and evil in 1585 and Hitler's ally in 1940. Elizabeth starts out like Neville Chamberlain, willing to appease the aggressors rather than risk war. But when Flynn's Captain Thorpe proves Spain plans to conquer the world, beginning with England, she becomes as dogged as Winston Churchill. Finally she is ready to fight back against the aggressors, and American audiences in 1940 must have wanted to join her underdog England in battle—if not against evil 16th-century Spaniards, then against their modern-day counterparts, the fascist Axis armies that were marching across Europe and bombing England.

SEARCHERS, THE (1956) C/119m.

John Ford's epic western is a *great* film, one that has enormous scope, breathtaking physical beauty, and a fascinating, complex lead character, John Wayne's Ethan Edwards. In 1868, Ethan returns to Texas—no one has seen him since the Civil War. His brother Aaron welcomes him into his isolated home, where he lives with his wife, Martha (whom Ethan obviously has loved for many years), son Ben, and two daughters, Lucy (Pippa Scott) and young Debbie (Lana Wood). Their adopted son is young adult Marty (Jeffrey Hunter), who is part Cherokee, which keeps Indian-hater Ethan from considering him a relative. (But it was Ethan who saved young Marty when his parents were massacred by Indians—indication that Ethan recognizes the wrongness of his racism.) Ethan's *homecoming* is one of many life rituals interrupted in the film. Ethan and Marty go off with Rangers to find some stolen cattle. They return to find that Aaron, Martha, and Ben have been massacred by Comanches, and Lucy and Debbie have been kidnapped. The pre-massacre sequence, culminating with Chief Scar (Henry Brandon) standing over scared Debbie by a grave, is the most frightening scene in the western genre. Ethan, Marty, and Lucy's beau Brad (Harry Carey, Jr.) give chase. They discover Lucy was raped and killed. Brad is killed while madly attacking Indians. For five years, Ethan and Marty look for Scar and Debbie (now played by Natalie Wood). Marty would stay behind and marry Laurie (Vera Miles), but he knows that Ethan will kill Debbie if he finds her: To Ethan, alter ego Scar's name signifies that he has continuously *defiled* the once pure Debbie (actually, when we finally see Debbie, she is perfectly fine); by having intercourse with her, Scar puts a blemish (a "scar") on the name of the pure-blooded Edwards family. By killing Debbie, Ethan feels he can end his family's, and particularly Martha's, disgrace. Ethan's knightly quest for revenge is marred by *impure* motives. His fears about the mixing of the bloods—symbolically

conveyed when he almost dies from a poison arrow—dominates his life. The cleansing of Ethan's soul is central to this picture; the film is obsessed with the concept of *pure* and *impure* (symbolized by the white man's intrusion on Indian land, the building of structures, the burial of bodies in the soil). Ethan's search is not for Debbie (he finds her back in the area from which she was kidnapped); it is for himself, his attempt to find internal tranquility and purge himself of racism and of the savagery that is embodied by Scar. Once Scar is killed, Ethan is cleansed—he no longer has the urge to kill Debbie. While his racism doesn't vanish, he finally acknowledges that it is wrong. He realizes that anyone who harbors racist feelings doesn't belong in this new thing called civilization, where the races must mix, where everyone *must* live in harmony. That's why he must allow the door to shut on him in the famous last shot (perhaps Ford was influenced by the final shot in his friend Henry Hathaway's 1948 film, *Call Northside 777*). He walks away, toward the wilderness, sadly rejected by family and time. Magnificent film was adapted by Frank S. Nugent from Alan LeMay's much different novel. Winton C. Hoch did the emotionally stirring cinematography. Max Steiner composed the score. Also with: Ward Bond, John Qualen, Olive Carey, Ken Curtis (as Marty's romantic rival), Antonio Moreno, Hank Worden (as Mose Harper), Walter Coy (as Aaron), Dorothy Jordan (as Martha), Robert Lyndon (as Ben), Patrick Wayne, Jack Pennick, Frank McGrath, Terry Wilson, Mae Marsh.

SECONDS (1966) B&W/106m.

One of the most depressing science-fiction films ever made—perhaps because its premise seems credible—and one of the most provocative. If you don't detest this film, then chances are you'll greatly admire it: it does have an enormous cult following despite being difficult to see. John Randolph is a bored, middle-aged businessman who lives with his uncommunicative wife in the New York suburbs. He pays a great sum of money to a sinister secret organization that provides clients with youthful new bodies through extensive surgery and new identities. After the operation Rock Hudson plays the character. Given a new name, Hudson is resettled in a California "bohemian" beach community where *seconds* like himself reside. At first he is happy acting out the part of a successful artist, but then depression sets in when he can't lose himself in his new identity. He longs to see his wife in New York, although he knows that if the organization finds out he made such a contact—and they have spies everywhere—he will be killed. Suspense builds along with Hudson's paranoia that he's being watched at all times, and the organization realizes that he is a failure. He should have known that the experiment was doomed: the head of the organization is an *old* man (Will Geer). Anyway, a boring man in one life will be boring and without purpose if given a second chance. The acting in the film is first-rate (Randolph is particularly effective); and John Frankenheimer's direction seems appropriately audacious, if overly self-indulgent. And Lewis John Carlino's script is an improvement on David Ely's erratic novel—for one thing, he provides Hudson with a love interest (Salome Jens). But the "star" of this film is cameraman James Wong Howe, who used black-and-white photography and assorted lenses to create the most sinister-surreal-paranoid atmosphere the genre had ever known. Howe's most striking contributions were putting a camera with a wide-angle lens on a wheeled suitcase-carrier for bizarre shots of Randolph walking through Grand Central Station; and using a fish-eye lens for the horrifying final shot of Hudson's last seconds. For the original operation sequence, Howe included a segment of a real nose operation. Ironically, Howe didn't like working with Frankenheimer, who insisted on hand-held and zoom shots without specific reasons. An unusual film. Jerry Goldsmith wrote the music. Also with: Jeff Corey, Richard Anderson, Murray Hamilton.

SECRET SIX, THE (1931) B&W/83m.
Director George Hill's follow-up to *The Big House* was one of cinema's first attacks on crime and the apathetic public. Nearly a comical character, Wallace Beery is an ugly, stupid slaughter house worker who hooks up with his smalltime gangster pal Ralph Bellamy (with a facial scar) to pull of a few jobs. When Bellamy fingers him to a competing crook, Beery kills him. He then becomes bigtime criminal Lewis Stone's top man; he makes a lot of money, has his share of women, and controls politicians. Reporters Clark Gable and Johnny Mack Brown try to bring about his downfall, with the help of Brown's girlfriend, Jean Harlow, Beery's onetime moll. But it takes "The Secret Six," a group of powerful businessmen, lawyers, government officials, etc. (who look silly in their Lone Ranger masks), to really put the heat on Beery. Not as powerful as *Beast of the City*, but the cast is first-rate and Beery's portrayal is genuinely offbeat. Scene in which Gable and Brown stand next to each other and simultaneously speak on the phone to their respective newspapers while squeezing in words to Harlow, who stands at the nearby counter, may have given Howard Hawks the inspiration for his hectic overlapping-dialogue newspapermen sequences in *His Girl Friday*. Script by Frances Marion. Also with: Marjorie Rambeau, John Miljan.

SEDUCTION OF MIMI, THE (ITALIAN/1974) C/89m.
Bawdy political comedy by Lina Wertmuller, detailing how a man who considers himself a leftist ends up working for the fascists. A problem is that the less political he becomes, the less political the film becomes. Giancarlo Giannini is Mimi, a foolish married worker who loses his job at the quarry when he votes for the candidate who is opposed by the local mafia. He goes alone to another town, gets a job in a factory, and becomes an organizer. He falls in love with anarchist Mariangela Melato, who makes love with emotion and commitment that his wife (Agostina Belli) never was capable of. When he witnesses a massacre by some relatives of the mafia back home, the terrified Giannini is transferred back home, where he goes with Melato and their baby. Humiliated, Belli allows a fascist to make love to her; she becomes pregnant. Suddenly Giannini is outraged

that his wife would humiliate him in such a manner. So, in a hilarious, grotesquely filmed scene that understandably received much criticism from many—but not all—feminists, he seduces the obese wife (Elena Fiore) of the fascist, intending to get her pregnant. When an organizer, he'd considered himself a staunch leftist, but his politics went out the window when faced with more powerful forces: love, fear, honor, the need of work and money. A comedic look at a sad subject (the depoliticization of an anti-fascist and his recruitment into the fascist cause), the film's controversial and political aspects gave way to the farcical material when it was remade in America as *Which Way Is Up?* starring Richard Pryor.

SENATOR WAS INDISCREET, THE (1947) B&W/81m.
Political satire about an incompetent, foolish, benevolently corrupt old senator (William Powell looking like a snake-oil salesman) who should be put out to pasture. Party members would like him to quit, but he refuses because of his high salary and because he's too unskilled to handle any other job, other than President. Somehow Powell becomes a candidate for President. The party bigwigs don't protest because they fear he'll publish his diary, which will reveal all their illegal activities. But the night before the convention the diary is stolen. This was the only film directed by George S. Kaufman and, though there are funny bits, its look, acting style, and pace (and opening music) would be more fitting for a fifties television sitcom than the screwball comedy it sets out to be. It needs the frantic dialogue, idiosyncratic secondary characters, and political bite that characterizes Preston Sturges's films. My favorite moment has wishy-washy Powell campaigning by a sign that says he is "Against Inflation. Against Deflation. For Flation." Charles MacArthur wrote the script, Nunnally Johnson produced. Also with: Ella Raines, Peter Lind Hayes, Arleen Wheelan, Ray Collins, Hans Conried, Allen Jenkins, Norma Varden, Myrna Loy (cameo as Powell's wife).

SEPTEMBER 30, 1955 / 9/30/55 (1978)
C/101m. The death of James Dean devastates young student Jimmy J. (Richard Thomas). He becomes obsessed with properly honoring Dean and trying to reach his spirit. His friends become disgusted with his behavior. He calls his emotionally unstable ex-girlfriend (Deborah Benson), who was even more hooked on Dean. They and some other kids gather for a ritual, then decide to shake up uncaring teenagers. There are tragic results. Odd film makes for uncomfortable viewing: it's hard not to get exasperated with Jimmy J., who acts like he *wants* to go overboard with his grief (while his ex-girlfriend can't help herself); the concept of star-worship and star-identification is scary. But the acting is convincing; we get a feel for the small Arkansas town in which Jimmy J. lives; and writer-director James Bridges, who idolized Dean in the fifties, truly understands how Dean's death affected his fans. What's most striking is how the film conveys the sadness, loneliness, and frustration that a teenager feels when no one shares his emotions about

something meaningful: Jimmy J.'s friends continue to be carefree; when he tells his mother of Dean's death, she replies, "Did I know him?" A couple of comic scenes are out of place. Also with: Lisa Blount, Susan Tyrell, Collin Wilcox, Thomas Hulce, Dennis Quaid, Dennis Christopher.

SET-UP, THE (1949) B&W/72m.
A low-budget gem (based on a poem) that unforgettably portrays the sad, sleazy world of run-of-the-mill and over-the-hill boxers. A predecessor of *Fat City*. Robert Ryan (who was a boxer at Dartmouth) is terrific as the wobbly-legged Stoker Thomson, whose glory days are behind him and has, as his long-enduring wife (Audrey Totter) warns, only brain damage in his boxing future. Tonight he's to fight a crooked young hopeful in a smalltown arena. He's such a heavy underdog that when his manager (George Tobias) and trainer (Percy Helton) promise a local racketeer that he'll lose, they simply take the payoff money without bothering to tell Stoker that he's expected to take a dive. They just figure he'll get knocked out anyway and don't want to cut him in on the money. Director Robert Wise matches the 72 minutes of screen time to real time, building tension and authenticity. The world he creates—Stoker's cheap hotel room, the carnival-like street scene, the dingy, overcrowded dressing room, the hostile arena—is atmospheric and believable. You'll respect his sympathetic feelings toward fighters, who he realizes are victimized because they haven't other options in life. And you'll not soon forget his portrayal of fight fans, each more monstrous than the other. I'm sure he wanted boxing banned if only to take away the entertainment enjoyed by these sadists. That boxers go through such agony and humiliation to earn their cheers and respect is pathetic. Also with: Alan Baxter, James Edwards, Wallace Ford.

SEVEN BEAUTIES (ITALIAN/1976) C/115m.
Extremely controversial Lina Wertmuller film will give you a chance to test your viewing sensibilities. Giancarlo Giannini is an Italian soldier who deserts and is thrown into a German concentration camp, which is much like a slaughterhouse. We flash back to colorful Naples when he was a ladies' man who dallied all day while his mother and seven fat sisters slaved away. Claiming to be a "man of honor," he killed his sister's pimp (the gun accidentally went off) and actually confessed to the crime. But now he cares nothing about honor—he'll do anything to survive, even attempt to seduce the superfat and monstrous female commandant (Shirley Stoler of *The Honeymoon Killers*). The scene in which he forces himself to use his mouth on her repulsive body half makes you laugh, half makes you ill. By this time you've started to identify with Giannini. Having comic material in a movie that takes place in a concentration camp infuriated many people. But the humor never tempers the tremendous horror we witness and, significantly, by the final concentration-camp scene, in which he must participate in the execution of seven prisoners, there is no more humor—in fact, it's hard to remember at that point anything funny that transpired earlier (we do remember the tragic elements, however). Film is ambitious, daring, marvelously photographed by Tonino Delli Colli, and most certainly provocative. Its theme: men who sacrifice their honor in order to survive instantly become walking corpses. Also with: Fernando Rey, Elena Fiore.

SEVEN BRIDES FOR SEVEN BROTHERS (1954) C/103m.
Stanley Donen's joyful, colorful musical is set in Oregon in 1850, with Jane Powell playing Snow White to new husband Howard Keel and his six brothers, attempting to turn the ruffians into gentlemen. But just when Powell seems to have had a positive effect, Keel convinces his lovesick brothers to kidnap the town girls they desire and bring them home. This causes Powell to kick out Keel. The rare musical that even young boys will love: Keel is handsome and masculine enough to get away with love songs; the male dancers are extremely athletic—when doing the "Lonesome Polecat" ballet they swing axes; and Powell is the pretty blonde teacher little boys dream about—plus there's a scene in which the six shapely young women march about in their underwear. The story, based on Stephen Vincent Benét's "The Sobbin' Women"—which was inspired by Plutarch's "The Rape of the Sabine Women"—is a lot of fun, the score by Johnny Mercer and Gene DePaul has some excellent, catchy songs, and the Michael Kidd-choreographed dances are terrific: the exuberant, spectacular "barn-raising" number, during which the brothers try to outdance some rival suitors, is the show-stopper. The brothers are played by marvelous dancers: Russ Tamblyn, Jacques d'Amboise, Marc Platt, Tommy Rall, Matt Mattox, Jeff Richards. Also with: Julie Newmeyer (Newmar), Virginia Gibson, Ruta Kilmonis (Lee), Nancy Kilgas, Betty Carr, Ian Wolf, Russell Simpson.

SEVEN DAYS IN MAY (1964) B&W/118m.
John Frankenheimer's taut political thriller surely is not a favorite at Reagan's White House. After all, it presents a noble-minded President (Fredric March) who realizes that for there to be a chance for lasting peace he must sign a disarmament pact with the Soviet Union. Burt Lancaster gives a sinister portrayal as a rightwing extremist, the Chairman of the Joint Chiefs of Staff, who plans a military coup to overthrow March and bring the Russians to their knees. March and Kirk Douglas, as Lancaster's assistant, try to stop the plot. A smart, well-acted, suspenseful film; surely if it were made today it would be a lot flashier and more gimmicky—and probably March and Douglas would be made into the villains. Rod Serling wrote the liberal script, adapting a novel by Fletcher Knebel and Charles W. Bailey II. Also with: Ava Gardner, Edmond O'Brien, Martin Balsam, George Macready, Whit Bissell, Hugh Marlow.

7 FACES OF DR. LAO (1964) C/100m.
In what may be the finest performance in a fantasy film, Tony Randall (who doesn't like this film) plays the mysterious Dr. Lao *and* the seven attractions in Lao's traveling circus—the strangest show on earth. Depending on which character

he plays—the ancient Lao, the old magician Merlin, the blond soothsayer Apollonius, the Abominable Snowman, Pan, Medusa, a serpent—Randall is hilarious, wise, touching, scary, or sad; he's always unpredictable. Lao's circus magically appears in a Western town at the turn of the century. The people are about to vote on whether to abandon their homes and sell out to rich, devious Arthur O'Connell, who has told them of a forthcoming water crisis (he knows that the railroad's coming to this town). Only newspaper editor John Ericson opposes O'Connell's plan. Ericson also is preoccupied with winning over librarian Barbara Eden (a brunette!). Everyone goes to Lao's circus, meets the attractions, and is dramatically changed. Fanciful film is not just for kids. The script by Charles Beaumont (who wrote many of the best *Twilight Zone* episodes and was a super SF/horror writer), which is adapted from Charles Finney's novel, is at times surprisingly subdued, thoughtful, and philosophical. I can't figure out why this picture doesn't have more of a following. Make-up expert William Tuttle won a special Oscar. Also with: Kevin Tate, Argentina Brunetti, Noah Beery, Jr., Royal Dano, Minerva Urecal, Lee Patrick, John Qualen.

SEVEN MEN FROM NOW (1956) C/78m. The first of seven first-class "B" westerns made between 1956 and 1960 that were directed by Budd Boetticher and starred Randolph Scott. As in the later films, Scott is a loner in a West that is becoming increasingly civilized but is no less violent or corrupt. As in most of the later films, he is a revenge hero—he's after the seven men who killed his wife during a Wells Fargo hold-up. As usual, he gets hooked up with outlaws (Lee Marvin, Donald Barry) and a married woman (Gail Russell). In *Westbound* and *Comanche Station* the women are married to cripples; here, as in *The Tall T*, she has a husband (Walter Reed) who is unworthy of her—Reed is secretly transporting the stolen gold which Marvin and Barry are after. Film is not on par with the others that were scripted by Burt Kennedy, but Scott's a solid lead, and there are interesting character conflicts, good action sequences, and a shootout worth waiting for between Scott and Marvin, who looks like a skinny, gangly, young version of Scott (which is probably why he was cast). Also with: John Larch.

SEVEN SAMURAI/MAGNIFICENT SEVEN, THE (JAPANESE/1954) B&W/141m—160m—200m. A tremendous achievement by Akira Kurosawa; regarded by most everyone as one of the all-time great films. The farmers of a small 16th-century farming village know that when their crops are harvested, 40 brigands will storm down from the hills and take everything. They decide to hire samurai to lead them in battle, but, being poor, they can offer only rice. They have no luck until they come upon the noble Takashi Shimura, a wise, aging samurai who is touched that they would sacrifice their rice and be stuck eating millet. He is joined by an old friend (Daisuke Kaito), with whom he has fought many a battle, and recruits two

more samurai, Yoshio Inaba and master swordsman Seiji Miyaguchi; and Inaba, who joins because Shimura's unique personality intrigues him, recruits Minoru Chiaki because his sense of humor will more then compensate for his being just an average fighter. Shimura agrees to let two non-samurai join the group: undisciplined but fearless Toshiro Mifune (a farmer's son who talks incessantly, is more emotional than the true samurai, has boundless energy, and scratches himself as if he were a flea-infested dog) and a young apprentice, Isao Kimura. Like the others, Mifune and Kimura are less interested in the job ahead than watching the fascinating Shimura. The samurai come to the village and teach the male farmers how to fight when the brigands attack. They set up traps on three of the four ways into the village—and in the night skirmishes that soon take place in those areas, a number of brigands are killed. The samurai and the villagers prepare for the major battle when the brigands will charge into town on horseback. The battle takes place in the day during a hard rain, with the men racing back and forth through the mud to block off the road into the village and to battle the horsemen who get through the lines—it's one of the greatest action sequences in the history of the cinema! Since Kurosawa's epic (which borrows from John Ford westerns and, I suggest, *High Noon*) is peerless as action-adventure, one tends to forget that it's also a remarkably poignant human drama. It's a brilliant character study where we come to understand that each of the seven samurai takes part in the defense of the village for a personal reason—their distinct motives are what makes each interesting and sympathetic. That when they don't desert even after they discover that these same "helpless" villagers have in the past killed samurai for their armor and that these people actually despise them—in much the same way that townspeople in American westerns thought their hired guns were necessary evils who should be discarded after their jobs were done. It is, as Shimura observes, only the farmer who can benefit if the brigands are defeated—the samurai's only rewards come from the fun of fighting (and *surviving*), from fighting with the other samurai and earning their respect, and from themselves, since each has a personal code for how he should conduct his life. In addition to dealing with the samurai as individuals and as a group, Kurosawa takes time to probe the nature of farmers, as individuals and as a group. We learn that they are selfish, cruel, and cowardly, but, as Mifune points out, it is the looting, raping, enslaving samurai of Japan who have made them that way. A visual tour-de-force, epic's best known directorial element is that there is always movement within the frame. Shimura and Mifune are superb. Remade in 1960 as an American western, *The Magnificent Seven*. Also with: Kamatari Fujiwara, Keiko Tsushima (as the village girl who sleeps with Kimura).

SEVEN YEAR ITCH, THE (1955) C/105m. Billy Wilder comedy, best known for the scene in which Marilyn Monroe stands spread-legged over a subway grating and feels delight as passing trains blow her dress high up her thighs. Wilder co-scripted with George Axelrod, adapting Axelrod's play about a married New Yorker (Tom Ewell) who sends his wife (Evelyn Keyes) and little boy off on vacation and starts feeling "the seven year itch." He starts drinking, smoking, twitching, talking to himself, and taking a fancy to Monroe, a model-actress who just moved in upstairs. He keeps inviting Monroe into his apartment, but resists the temptation to attempt a seduction—Monroe seems available, yet talks about everything but hopping into bed with him. He worries both about being discovered with Monroe and about his wife having an affair while she's away. Considering its classic reputation, film is much overrated, too talky and stagy, only occasionally funny. Monroe is appealing, but Ewell's super-neurotic character, supposedly the typical husband-father, is a complete jerk—the film is less insulting to women than to men. The most ridiculous thing about this film is that we're supposed to believe that Ewell would even consider passing up an affair with Monroe, especially when his wife is dull and far away. Also with: Oscar Homolka, Sonny Tufts, Robert Strauss, Carolyn Jones, Doro Merande, Victor Moore.

SEVENTH SEAL, THE (SWEDISH/1956) B&W/96m.
Ingmar Bergman's classic deals with such familiar Bergman themes as man's loss of faith, his disillusionment about life, his inability to overcome guilt and humiliation, his self-torment, fate vs. free will, good vs. evil, and conflict in marriage. All problems of the modern man. But this film is set in an earlier apocalyptic age, the 14th century, when we had an incomprehensible Black Plague instead of an incomprehensible Bomb, and the helpless, confused common man succumbed to his fate. Swedish knight Max von Sydow returns from the Crusades with his squire, Gunnar Björnstrand. They travel toward Von Sydow's castle, where he left his wife (Inga Landgre) 10 years before. They meet up with several other travelers, a troupe of actors, which includes simple juggler Nils Poppe, his happy wife, Bibi Andersson, and their baby. All the others are religious, but Von Sydow has lost his faith. All around him are death, despair, hysteria, pestilence, and abominable acts of cruelty. He senses that if there were a God, He would not permit such misery; and that if He does allow such atrocities, then He is cruel and undeserving of man's obedience and love. And what Bergman considers perverse is how the people commit sins against each other in God's name and how the people rationalize the Plague as being their fault, their just punishment, so they can let God off the hook. As Andersson observes, the people enjoy suffering and relish their martyrdom. Von Sydow comes to realize that life isn't meaningless although it ends in meaningless death—he learns, like Bergman, that the real purpose in life is to marry and have children. Through Poppe, Andersson, and their *special* child, his faith in humanity is restored. Surely he believes that he saves them by distracting Death (Bengt Ekerot) with the famous game of chess, and that if he had left their futures up to God, they would have perished—for those who survive the Plague aren't necessarily those who have retained

their faith in Him. Their survival is a semi-optimistic ending to a pessimistic film by a frustrated modern man who realizes that, since we will never have the absolute knowledge that Von Sydow desires about the existence or non-existence of God, life can be satisfying and safe only for those simple people who have faith, no questions asked. Film is very theatrical, with roots in Shakespeare, absurdism, farce, and medieval mystery and morality plays. As in all Bergman classics, there are strong acting, stunning photography (by Gunnar Fischer), many unforgettable images (the chess match for Von Sydow's life, the burning of a witch, the final dance of Death and his victims), and questions left for us to answer for ourselves. Also with: Inga Gill, Maud Hansson, Gunnel Lindblom, Bertil Anderberg, Erik Standmark, Ake Fridell.

SEVENTH VICTIM, THE (1943) B&W/71m.
Making her screen debut in this exceptional Val Lewton thriller, Kim Hunter is a young woman who leaves school in order to search for her missing psychologically troubled older sister (Jean Brooks) in Greenwich Village. It turns out that her sister has fallen in with devil-worshippers who are trying to force her to commit suicide for having disclosed their existence to her psychiatrist (Tom Conway again plays Lewis Judd, although Judd had been killed in Lewton's *Cat People*). Hunter falls in love with Brooks's husband (Hugh Beaumont), but he won't leave his wife because he thinks she's insane and needs his help and loyalty. This spooky "*noir*" horror film, imaginatively directed by Mark Robson, is a complete original, a cult film in England way back in the forties. It features bizarre and sinister characters (i.e., a one-armed female devil-worshipper who plays piano), smart, strong-willed women, and several scary scenes. A shower sequence, though bloodless, is shot in a manner that anticipated *Psycho*. The double suicide that ends the film is perhaps the most baffling, depressing moment in all horror films. Lewton fans will best appreciate this film: existential in nature, it is full of smart dialogue between educated characters about free will vs. fate, a Lewton obsession. The John Donne quote that begins and ends the film—"I run to death and death meets me as fast, and all my pleasures are like yesterday"—was essentially the thematic inspiration for the entire Lewton horror series. Stylishly photographed by Nicholas Musuraca. The clever script was written by Charles O'Neal and DeWitt Bodeen. Also with: Erford Gage, Isabel Jewell, Ben Bard, Chef Milani, Elizabeth Russell, Lou Lubin.

7TH VOYAGE OF SINBAD, THE (1958) C/89m.
Wondrous adventure is a major source of inspiration for most of today's fantasy-film directors, who were kids when it came out and had never seen anything like it. It's the first film in which special-effects master Ray Harryhausen employed "Dynamation"/"Dynarama," whereby he could show live actors in the same frame with his animated, imaginatively designed creatures. Handsome Kerwin Mathews is the best Harryhausen hero, his best Sinbad. When the evil magician Sokurah (Torin Thatcher) shrinks

Princess Parisa (Kathryn Grant), Sinbad and his crew set sail to retrieve a piece of an egg of a giant Roc—only that can restore her to normal size. He gets help from a boy genie (Richard Eyer). It's the genie's lamp that Sokurah desires. Sinbad battles a fire-spitting dragon, a giant Cyclops, a sword-wielding skeleton. The adventure is exciting—kids will love it—and Harryhausen's work is spectacular. A buttered-popcorn movie. It's more juvenile than *Jason and the Argonauts* but just as much fun. Followed by *The Golden Voyage of Sinbad* in 1974 and *Sinbad and the Eye of the Tiger* in 1977. Directed by Nathan Juran, produced by Charles H. Schneer, photographed in Technicolor by Wilkie Cooper, scored by Bernard Herrmann. Also with: Alec Mango, Danny Green.

SEXTETTE (1978) C/91m. Mae West's final film. Making no reference to her advanced age, West struts and gyrates across the screen as newly married (to young Timothy Dalton) movie sex queen Marlo Manners, letting fly with smutty quips, remembering good and *bed* times with a string of ex-husbands, singing, and sizing up prospective lovers. Her numerous facelifts have left her looking like a baby girl with wrinkles and a hefty woman's body. She doesn't deliver her lines badly, thank goodness, and our satisfaction comes simply from the fact that she isn't really embarrassing. Picture has a cult following due to West and some offbeat humor. But it's an awful picture that, judging from the first few scenes, could have been even worse. Ken Hughes directed. I don't know anyone who owns the soundtrack album. Also with: Dom DeLuise, Tony Curtis, George Hamilton (who claims West is still married to him), Ringo Starr, Alice Cooper, Keith Moon, Walter Pidgeon, Rona Barrett, George Raft (it's good seeing him reunited with West), Regis Philbin, Keith Allison, Van McCoy.

SHADOW OF A DOUBT (1943) B&W/108m. Top-grade Alfred Hitchcock thriller that examines the thin line between the *normal* and *abnormal*, as represented by a smart, spirited *typical* young woman named Charlie (Teresa Wright) who lives with her *average* family in an *average* American town, and her insane itinerant bachelor Uncle Charlie (Joseph Cotten), whom she was named after and to whom she feels a special telepathic bond. Wright lives in Santa Rosa, California, with her mild-mannered banker father (Henry Travers), warmhearted, trusting mother (Patricia Collinge), bookworm younger sister (a funny performance by Edna May Wonacott), and young brother (Charles Bates). She hopes that Uncle Charlie's surprise visit will put a charge in her family's dull daily routine. But while mother is occupied by two men purporting to be doing a survey on *average* American families, and father and his friend (Hume Cronyn) play murder-and-detective parlor games, she puts a few clues together and is horrified to discover that Cotten is the "Merry Widow Murderer"—object of a nationwide manhunt. And so the cat-and-mouse game begins: rather than reveal her discovery to her detective boyfriend (miscast MacDonald Carey, with a laughable hairstyle) and cause a

scandal that would break her mother's heart, Wright tries to force Cotten to leave town; meanwhile he thinks up ways to kill his niece—although in his twisted mind there exists great love for her. That the two Charlies are two sides of the same person ("twins," as they call each other) is immediately obvious. After seeing her idyllic street and house, we first find Wright lying in bed facing east (*he* is in Philadelphia), bored with the world; after seeing a nearby dump and the outside of his rundown apartment building, we first find Cotten lying in bed facing west, despising the world. Cotten's going west is an aggressive, perhaps incestuous act: he arrives on a train that spouts black smoke, indication that the devil has come to town to corrupt Wright, symbol of American innocence. He is unable to corrupt this virtuous girl, although he gives her expensive jewelry—stolen—and takes her into a sleazy bar. The strange pity we feel for Cotten comes from our realization that he has many of Wright's finer qualities, and that he might have been as virtuous and happy as she if he hadn't had a concussion-causing accident as a child that suddenly made him wild, soon after caused him to run away from home, and later led to his madness. That's why we sometimes wish Wright would stop her sleuthing. In the fine cast, Wright stands out as the brave, determined, scrub-faced Charlie; Hitchcock obviously was taken with her style of walking because he films her often, from front and back, walking through the town. Thornton Wilder, who co-wrote the script, was responsible for the smalltown-America ambiance. Remade in 1958 as *Step Down to Terror*. Also with: Wallace Ford, Clarence Muse.

SHAFT (1971) C/100m. Supercool, supersexy ("a sex machine," contends Isaac Hayes's Oscar-winning theme song) black private eye John Shaft (Richard Roundtree) is hired by a rich black gang lord (Moses Gunn) to find his kidnapped daughter. He muscles his way through the black underground, comprised of angry, frustrated, tough-talking young blacks. But he finds that white Mafia men took the girl. Gordon Parks makes effective use of New York locales, but overall his direction is as unremarkable as Roundtree's performance and Ernest Tidyman's hackneyed script. But the picture has its place in film history for being the first "blaxploitation" film and the prototype for many later entries in the genre that have stud black heroes who make love to white women and battle racist white cops and criminals, black street lingo, strong violence, female nudity, exploitive sex scenes, the sexist treatment of women, low budgets, location shooting, and one nice Caucasian so they won't be accused of being anti-white. The genre was often distasteful, but it gave talented black actors needed work. Followed by *Shaft's Big Score, Shaft in Africa*, and a cleaned-up TV series. Also with: Charles Cioffi, Christopher St. John, Gwenn Mitchell, Lawrence Pressman, Arnold Johnson.

SHALL WE DANCE (1937) B&W/116m. Not great, but an enjoyable Fred Astaire and Ginger Rogers musical. Silly plot has ballet star Astaire falling in love with musical-comedy star Rogers. They are mistaken for marrieds, which is helpful to her career (although she doesn't want marriage immediately) and harmful to his (although he wants marriage). They decide that people will believe they're not married only if they get married and then divorced. Not surprisingly, the highlights are the dances to the songs of George and Ira Gershwin. Most memorable are "They All Laughed," "They Can't Take That Away From Me" (although for some reason Astaire dances the reprise not with Rogers but with Harriet Hoctor), "Let's Call the Whole Thing Off"—during which Astaire and Rogers are on roller skates—and "Shall We Dance." The team is especially joyful in their duets. Nicest non-dancing moment has Astaire and Rogers sitting on the grass chatting. Produced by Pandro S. Berman, directed by Mark Sandrich, choreographed by Hermes Pan and Harry Losee, scripted by Allan Scott and Ernest Pagano. Also with: Edward Everett Horton, Eric Blore, Jerome Cowan, Ketti Gallian.

SHANE (1953) C/118m. George Stevens's seminal western adapted from Jack Schaefer's fine novel about a former gunslinger (played with dignity and intelligence by Alan Ladd) who becomes hired hand and friend of a Wyoming homesteader (Van Heflin), shares an understood but never stated or acted-upon love with his wife (Jean Arthur), and becomes the idol of their wide-eyed young son (Brandon de Wilde)—who represented all of us boys in the fifties who dreamed of having a quick-drawing, two-fisted western hero for a pal. Shane would like to remain with his "adopted" family and give up gunfighting for a meaningful life, but, with no law in the area, he realizes he is the only one who can stand up for them and the other peaceful farmers against two violent rancher brothers and their hired gunman (Jack Palance) who are trying to keep the land for themselves. If you want to understand the form of the "classic" western, this is the picture to study. Shane fits the blueprint set forth in Robert Warshaw's famous essay "The Westerner." He is a loner who has a mysterious, violent past that he cannot escape; he would like to settle down in the civilized West, and even has found a woman he loves, but he comes to realize he has no future—he just does the task which brought him to this town and retreats back into the past, the dead (Shane rides in through a graveyard) mythological-prehistory West. The overlap of this West (embodied by gunslingers like Shane) with the beginnings of the civilized historical West is essential to classic westerns (it also forms the basis of most Clint Eastwood westerns, including *Pale Rider*, essentially a remake of *Shane*). Picture is beautifully shot (Loyal Griggs earned an Oscar), beautifully acted, has remarkable authenticity (especially believable is the town, which has only a handful of buildings). The great scene from the book, in which gunslinger and farmer spend all day together to chop down a stubborn tree trunk, is well handled, as is their victorious back-to-back fistfight with a group of bullies. The final shootout—in which Shane takes on several bad guys—is smashingly choreographed, filmed, edited. And who can forget diabolical Palance (the best

western villain?) smilingly gunning down tiny, defenseless Elisha Cook, Jr., in the mud? Best of all is the poignant relationship between Shane and the boy, who echoed all our feelings with his final words: "Shane, come back!" Also with: Ben Johnson, Edgar Buchanan, Emile Meyer, Ellen Corby, Nancy Kulp.

SHANGHAI EXPRESS (1932) B&W/80m. For *movie* fans. Josef von Sternberg directed this absurd but delectable bit of pulp perversity in which Marlene Dietrich plays "Shanghai Lily," China's most infamous prostitute. She's one of several passengers we meet on the trouble-bound Shanghai Express. Also on board is her former lover, a humorless British military doctor (Clive Brook) whose lack of faith in her years before so crushed her spirit that she withdrew from the real world and started on her wayward path. Dietrich and Brook still love each other, but he still has no faith in her. The train is waylaid by rebel leader Warner Oland, who holds Brook for a prisoner exchange to get back his righthand man. Dietrich usually plays women who sacrifice all for love, and here she accepts Oland's offer to become his mistress so he won't carry out a threat to blind Brook. Brook doesn't know the reason Dietrich gives herself to Oland and he assumes the worst; like other Dietrich women, she doesn't even attempt to defend her actions—if he doesn't have *faith* in her, that's his problem. Dietrich isn't the only fascinating woman in this film; fellow passenger Anna May Wong, who also is looked down on by men on the train, saves the day by killing Oland. Jules Furthman's script is full of sin, sadism, and sex; the relationship between Dietrich and religious zealot Lawrence Grant echoes that between Joan Crawford and Walter Huston in the same year's *Rain*. Exotic art direction was by Hans Dreier. Lee Garmes did the superb cinematography; his close-ups of Dietrich, particularly when she's smoking against the door in the train, are breathtaking. Remade in 1951 as *Peking Express*. Also with: Eugene Pallette, Gustav von Seyffertitz, Louise Closser Hale.

SHANGHAI GESTURE, THE (1941) B&W/106m. An absolutely ridiculous film—the reason that it has a cult—directed by Josef von Sternberg, who was flat on his back, lying on a cot, during most of the shooting schedule. The extremely weird, overwritten, often dull script by Jules Furthman and others—full of awkward introductions, lectures, people yelling at each other, double entendres—comes across like a clumsy first draft that was filmed only because the next 20 drafts were lost. Most of the action takes place in the gambling club of Oriental Mother Gin Sling (Ona Munson obviously had her hair done by some who had learned to tie shoelaces). She's being forced to close down and move into the Chinese district, away from the tourist trade, by a British official (Walter Huston). At a party she throws on Chinese New Year's in "honor" of Huston, Munson reveals that she was the girl he abandoned some 20 years ago, and that she is the mother of his rebellious daughter (Gene Tierney as Poppy). Performances by the entire cast—including Victor Mature as a poetry-reciting Arab—are outrageous. So is the ending. Strangest of all is than Von Sternberg didn't recognize his folly and inserted a few inspired touches along the way that might have been saved for a better picture. Much cleaner than John Colton's source work. Also with: Phyllis Brooks (as a sexy chorus girl), Maria Ouspenskaya (wearing what's almost a crew cut), bald Mike Mazurki, Albert Basserman, Ivan Lebedeff, Eric Blore, Marcel Dalio, Mikhail Rasumny, John Abbott.

SHE-BEAST, THE (ITALIAN-YUGOSLAVIAN/ 1966) C/74m.
Michael Reeves's debut film as director presents his typically harsh world where evil is the dominant force and is indestructible. In modern-day Transylvania a young woman (Barbara Steele) disappears into a lake and steps out as a hideous-looking witch with grotesque skin and long teeth. This vampirous creature had been drowned in the 18th century (in the opening sequence). Steele's husband, Ian Ogilvy (Reeves's star in three of his four films), teams up with a Van Helsing descendant (John Karlson) in an attempt to return the murderous witch to the lake and bring Steele back alive. Well, their plan *almost* goes right. Film is full of striking imagery, but its low budget and dubbing make it really hard to appreciate. Steele's appearance is too brief; but she grabs your attention, particularly in an erotic love scene. It is watched by a disgusting, lecherous hotel proprietor (Mel Welles)—he's the typical inhabitant of Reeves's godforsaken world. Also with: Jay Riley, Richard Watson.

SHE DONE HIM WRONG (1932) B&W/66m.
In her adaptation of her Broadway hit *Diamond Lil*, Mae West struts her way through Gay Nineties New York, encountering all sorts of unsavory characters. They either die or go to jail—she comes through unscathed. West's first starring picture is usually regarded as her best film. That may be true (though I prefer *I'm No Angel* and *My Little Chickadee*), but it's not the comedy masterpiece that many critics contend it to be—the sad truth is that West made no good films. At least here West got to showcase her self-assured and uninhibited pre-Legion of Decency brand of sexuality, in which she lets fly with double entendres, which usually relate to her own sexual prowess, and displays a brazen sex-is-fun attitude that only Jean Harlow shared with her. It's amazing that one moment she can look so overweight and ridiculous strapped into her tight garments that you'll find it hard to believe she was a leading lady/sex symbol; yet a second later she is mysteriously seductive as she bats her lashes and raises her eyebrows, grins knowingly, swings out a hip, and says something women are supposedly too shy to say. Highlights include her bawdy rendition of "Frankie and Johnny" and "Easy Rider" and her meetings with leading man Cary Grant (in his first major role), a cop posing as a Salvation Army worker. "You can be had," she says confidently after he refuses her first invitation to "come up and see me." By the end he is after her, trying to hold

her hand—"It ain't heavy," is her response, "I can hold it myself." Directed by Lowell Sherman. Also with: Gilbert Roland, Noah Beery, Sr., Rafaela Ottiano (as Russian Rita), Rochelle Hudson.

SHE MARRIED HER BOSS (1935) B&W/90m.
Executive secretary Claudette Colbert has worked six long years for stuffy Melvyn Douglas, who owns a chain of department stores. She loves him, but he has never approached her romantically. When he fears losing her services, he proposes. He feels betrayed when she turns out to be like other women who would rather stay at home—running his huge house, being mother to his spoiled, neglected daughter (Edith Fellows)—than continue working, especially when he needs her help at the office. She wants him to let his hair down, forget about his work, and be a loving husband. Gregory La Cava comedy has a few good scenes (Douglas proposing, Colbert getting drunk in a mannequin-filled store window) and a fine performance by Colbert, yet it's wrecked by the inconsistency of the characters, who all seem to change from scene to scene. Feminists won't be thrilled with Colbert's assertion that marriage is the ultimate career for women; but at least she proves, before her retirement, that she's capable of running a high-pressured business as well as any man, and with less anxiety—even if she feels she must dress in a non-feminine style when at the office. Also with: Michael Bartlett, Raymond Walburn, Jean Dixon.

SHE WORE A YELLOW RIBBON (1949) C/103m.
This isn't the film with which to introduce friends to John Ford westerns, but if you're already a Ford fan, you'll love the second picture of his cavalry trilogy, made between *Fort Apache* and *Rio Grande*. Story is a tribute to the old guard/old soldiers/the old cavalry, as represented by retiring Captain Nathan Brittles (John Wayne), and to young leaders, represented by Lieutenant Flint Cahill (John Agar), who carry on in Brittles's fine tradition. Brittles has one last mission prior to retirement—he must prevent a full-scale Indian war following Custer's fall at the Little Big Horn. He realizes that Cahill is not sufficiently prepared to assume the command at such a vital time. Brittles will accomplish much, but Ford and screenwriters Frank Nugent and Laurence Stallings imply that a captain's job is never done: therefore there will come a time, a crucial time, when Brittles will have to leave his post in the hands of an inexperienced officer. It is through experience that Cahill will gain the necessary experience to be a good leader. Wayne gives a fine performance, but the film's real star is cinematographer Winton C. Hoch, who captured the Remington look. Colorful film takes place in Monument Valley. There are too many false endings (Brittles keeps being called back to the fort) and a silly romantic triangle (featuring Agar, Joanne Dru, and Harry Carey, Jr.). But once the cavalry starts singing the title song, you'll get emotional (if you're a Ford fan) and forget all the film's flaws. Not as good as *Fort Apache*, but essential Ford. Based on James Warner

Bellah's story "War Party." Also with: Ben Johnson, Victor McLaglen, Mildred Natwick, George O'Brien, Arthur Shields, Francis Ford, Chief Big Tree, Noble Johnson, Jack Pennick.

SHERLOCK JUNIOR (1924) B&W/57m.

The most technically innovative feature of the silent era, Buster Keaton's dazzling, surreal comedy has finally achieved masterpiece status in the last few years. It received special attention when Woody Allen borrowed its daring premise for *The Purple Rose of Cairo*. Like Allen's film, it explores the nature of film, both as an art form and as a world to which those with wild imaginations can escape (literally speaking in both cases); it treads the fine line between dream and reality, art and life. Buster would like to be detective, but makes a meager living as a projectionist. He's in love with pretty Kathryn McGuire, but he's kicked out of her house when her father (Joe Keaton) thinks Buster stole and pawned his watch. Actually, Keaton's rival (Ward Crane) committed the crime. Keaton falls asleep in the theater and fantasizes that McGuire, Keaton, and Crane are characters in the film. Crane has stolen a necklace. In a brilliantly conceived and edited scene, Keaton dreams that he walks toward the screen and climbs into the action. At first the screen revolts, like a body rejecting a transplanted organ. He's kicked out of the screen by Crane, but returns, only to find that the backgrounds keep changing on him—as they would to Daffy Duck in Chuck Jones's cartoon masterpiece *Duck Amuck!* (which borrows from this film). Eventually the screen accepts Keaton's intrusion and he become a character in the movie, dapper master detective Sherlock Junior. His attempts to prove Crane guilty of thievery lead to many hilarious scenes, some requiring amazing stunt work by Keaton. Great moments include Keaton riding on the handlebars of a fast-moving, driverless motorcycle, playing expert pool, and, in a bit you have to see to believe, escaping during a chase sequence by diving into a small case held by a peddler woman (actually his male assistant) and apparently disappearing through her body. Action is furiously paced, inventive, stupefying. Picture is proof positive that Keaton was more in control of and in love with the film medium than Chaplin. Produced by Joseph M. Schenck.

SHINING, THE (1980) C/142m—146m.

Stanley Kubrick adaptation of what may be Stephen King's finest novel utilizes a big budget, stars Jack Nicholson, and has some amazing camera work, but comes off as being no better than a mannered version of *The Amityville Horror*. Here, too, we have a father who goes insane/becomes possessed after moving into an evil residence and tries to kill his family, just as a previous tenant had done. Nicholson is an aspiring writer who becomes caretaker for the winter at a huge, isolated Colorado hotel so that he can work on a book. So he, passive wife Shelley Duvall, and small son Danny Lloyd move into the deserted hotel. Danny has the special power, the "shining," to see things no one else can, and he begins to have visions of the children who were murdered by a previous caretaker. He sees a future in which Nicholson tries to harm him and his mother. But the film doesn't concentrate enough on the boy's primal fears, nor does it really exploit the fact that he has a special gift. In King's book, the boy's power is why the hotel wants the boy to be sacrificed to *it*, so that he'd become part of *it* (just as the house in *The Haunting* desires Julie Harris, who has extrasensory powers). In King, the hotel is the embodiment of evil, a major character, *the* major force that affects the father and son. In Kubrick, the hotel houses evil entities but is, strangely, pretty neutral. Kubrick seems so entranced by Nicholson's creation of a psychotic that he neglects much that was essential to King's book. Most importantly, he mistakenly has Nicholson act weirdly from the outset, so that he seems only a couple of writer's-block and cabin-fever days away from insanity. For us to fully grasp Danny's primal fear that his father will turn on him and his mother, it's important that the father begin the story as a sympathetic, loving father and husband. There must be a dramatic reversal in the father's personality—because that complete switch from being the child's protector to being the very monster who wants to chop off the boy's head is what is terrifying. Anyway, Nicholson's crazed performance begins to wear on one's nerves, no matter how remarkable it is at times. By picture's end, one realizes that Duvall has outacted him. There are scary things in the movie—the appearance of the dead twins, Duvall reading her husband's lengthy manuscript and discovering that it's proof positive he is insane, Nicholson chasing his son through the outdoor maze with an axe—and for a while it is both powerful and creepy. But at the moment Nicholson talks with the ghost bartender, the picture loses its grip—from then on everything comes across as absurd. The film's final shot is a terrible choice and illustrates what Stephen King said was the matter with the film as a whole: neither Kubrick nor his co-writer, Diane Johnson, was familiar enough with horror films to know what were the clichés of the genre; most every image that they figured would shock viewers had been used many times in previous films. As do all Kubrick pictures, this one (in which he employed a Steadicam) looks great—better, in fact, than all other horror films. Here, his familiar mannered, intentionally rapid dialogue (in which everyone uses the other person's first name repeatedly) does create tension. Also with: Scatman Crothers, Barry Nelson, Joe Turkell, Anne Jackson.

SHOAH (FRENCH/1985) C/573m.

The title is the Hebrew word for annihilation. The film by Claude Lanzmann presents an oral history of the systematic extermination of Jews by the Nazis in Treblinka, Auschwitz, Chelmno, and other concentration camps. Lanzmann uses no archival footage but instead takes his cameras to the concentration camp sites and surrounding areas to see what they are like today. He takes us through Auschwitz and down into the cremation chambers—it's a terrifying experience. He takes us to Treblinka, where the gas chambers stand solitarily in the wilderness like Mayan pyramids in Mexico. At Chelmno it's hard to tell a camp existed. Lanzmann interviews concentration camp survivors (their stories are horrific), who often did special work duties that kept them alive (one cut hair of women going to the gas chamber, another cleaned the crematorium, etc.). These people talk without emotion, then something snaps and they burst into tears, and Lanzmann urges them to continue. Lanzmann also speaks to former Nazis, a Polish train engineer who transported Jews to Treblinka, and the people who lived by the camps. What is most terrifying is that these people would not protest the roundup and extermination of the Jews if it happened again. In one scene that is revolting, the one survivor of Chelmno stands with his Christian "friends" outside a Roman Catholic church—the people didn't like the Nazis but still talk about how God intended Jews to be punished for what happened to Christ. The Jew stands silent, confused. And we feel Lanzmann is exploiting him, as he exploits many other survivors, forcing them to reopen old wounds for what he believed would be the definitive film about the Holocaust. Because it is not, what they go through for him isn't worth it. But we viewers do benefit from each recollection, each harrowing detail about the slaughter. And the obsessive Lanzmann insists on details: we get exact accounts of what happened, involving the amount of time prisoner trains took to reach the camps from their destinations, what the prisoners were wearing, how they were greeted by the Nazis at the camps. Interestingly, the Nazis always kept the Jews from knowing they were to be killed. First half of the film contains much unforgettable material, second half goes off on too many tangents (i.e., a long recollection about the Warsaw ghetto). And by the end you're sick of Lanzmann (who often acts like Mike Wallace at his worst) and his techniques. Important viewing, but not consistently powerful, though it should be, considering its subject. Made with the participation of the French Ministry of Culture.

SHOCK CORRIDOR (1963) B&W-C/101m. Immature, dishonest, self-serving crime reporter Peter Breck attempts to win the Pulitzer Prize by solving a murder that occurred in an insane asylum. He forces his stripper girlfriend, Constance Towers, to tell the police that Breck is her brother and that he has been making sexual advances toward her. So in this modern version of the Nellie Bly story, Breck is committed to the asylum, where he can question the three inmates who witnessed the murder: James Best, an American soldier who was a turncoat in Korea and, disgraced, has convinced himself he's a Confederate soldier; Hari Rhodes, a black man who, after failing as a guinea pig to integrate an all-white university, has convinced himself he's white and a KKK member; and Gene Evans, a onetime genius atomic scientist who now has the mentality of a small boy. Dealing with these three men and others who are equally insane, being attacked by nymphomaniacs, and fantasizing that Towers is being unfaithful cause Breck to go insane. He once said, "Ever since my voice changed

I wanted to be in the company of journalist greats." So it's fitting that he loses his voice entirely when he wins his Pulitzer. More than any other film, Sam Fuller's cult favorite treads a fine line between art and trash. The dialogue is stilted, yet every few minutes one of the characters says something more honest and brave and moving than we are used to in American cinema. The film thrives on sensationalism; all the sexual content seems solely intended to make the picture lurid. Beneath the sleaze is a mature, sad-eyed view of America, where people are encouraged to strive beyond their capacities for accomplishment and to do their country proud even if they can't accept responsibility or fame. Best, Rhodes, Evans, and now Breck couldn't withstand the pressures of "celebrity"—they have found that their one escape from the public eye is in an asylum. Shadowy cinematography by Stanley Cortez, who photographed midgets at the end of the corridor set so that it would appear to be longer than it was (Fuller shot the poorly used color footage in Japan and Africa). Also with: Larry Tucker, William Zuckert, Philip Ahn, Chuck Robertson.

SHOCK WAVES/DEATH CORPS (1977) C/ 86m. Small boat skippered by John Carradine is forced to land on seemingly deserted island. Young passengers discover huge, dilapidated house inhabited by crazed former SS officer Peter Cushing. They fight for their lives when Cushing unleashes a horde of Nazi zombies which have the ability to stay underwater indefinitely. Premise isn't promising, but low-budget chiller is well made by Ken Wiederham, who borrows from George Romero, among others. Exciting, unexpected treat for horror fans, featuring an engaging performance by little-known Brooke Adams. Also with: Fred Buch, Jack Davidson, Luke Halpin.

SHOESHINE/SCIUSCIA (ITALIAN/1946) B&W/ 93m. Classic of Italian neorealism was Vittorio de Sica's first major film and is one of the most powerful social dramas in cinema history. In his films De Sica wanted to show how postwar Italian society was insensitive to the plight of the poor. In *Umberto D* he would deal with the hardships of the indigent aged; here he calls attention to street children, who have little chance to stay out of trouble. Pasquale (Franco Interlenghi) and Giuseppe (Rinaldo Smordoni) are inseparable pals who make very little money shining the shoes of American soldiers. Wanting enough money to buy a horse, they naively become involved in black-market activities. They are sent to a brutal, corrupt reform school, where they end up betraying each other. There is an escape, but one kills the other—only to realize the great tragedy that has occurred. We feel tremendous sympathy for Pasquale and Giuseppe and understand their fears, confusion, desperation, misplaced anger, and worry about being betrayed by the only person they love (each other). They are ignored by society and are at the mercy of the times. De Sica's film is unsparingly harsh, yet it also has a tender, poetic quality. Also with: Anniello Mele, Bruno Otensi.

SHOOT (CANADIAN/1976) C/98m.

Potentially controversial anti-gun film was ignored by moviegoers and given short shrift by critics. Certainly it draws the most disturbing and believable portrait of gun addicts/hunters/nuts (in the dangerous sense of the word) there has been on film. Cliff Robertson plays an ex-combat soldier who is completely bored with wife, job, home, and civilian life. His only excitement comes from weekend hunting excursions with Ernest Borgnine, Henry Silva, and several other vets. They don't care about bagging animals; their pleasure comes from pulling their triggers (the height of masculine pleasure). One day they come upon hunters from a nearby town who stand on the other side of a frozen river. They curiously stare at each other and automatically become enemies. A shot injures one of Robertson's group; Silva returns the fire, killing one man. No one in Robertson's group goes to the authorities. Instead they prepare for a return engagement. Although they have no way of knowing if the men from the other town are also getting ready for a deadly rematch, Robertson and his buddies recruit other men from the town. Dressed as soldiers and thrilled to be returning to action, they return to the woods. They hope for combat, but get much more than they bargained for. All along we think how stupid these men are for engaging in militaristic training—but it's nothing compared to what the other side has been planning. This picture is worth a look because it is one of the few films to take a stand against National Rifle Association types—we see what they'd really be doing if they had their druthers. Most frightening is that we expect the intelligent Robertson or any of his friends to stop the madness in time—but this never happens. The unexpected ending is terrifying. Directed by Harvey Hart. Also with: James Blendick, Larry Reynolds, Les Carlson, Kate Reid, Helen Shaver.

SHOOT THE PIANO PLAYER/TIREZ SUR LE PIANISTE (FRENCH/1962) B&W/85m.

François Truffaut's second feature is one of his finest achievements, a picture that still seems excitingly original (because no director has broken cinema's rules in quite the same way) and that still deeply affects the true movie lover. Charles Aznavour gives an oddly moving performance as a meek pianist who works in a bar. Under his real name he'd been a successful concert pianist, but he'd withdrawn into anonymity when his wife (Nicole Berger) committed suicide. A waitress, she'd slept with an impresario in order to get her husband his break. When he didn't forgive her, she'd leaped from a balcony to her death. Now at the bar he falls in love with another waitress (Marie Dubois) who admires his talent. Soon he again looks out a window and sees the woman he loves lying dead, indirectly because of him. Adapted from a melodramatic crime novel, *Down There*, by American David Goodis, Truffaut's film borrows from such diverse sources as American "B" gangster pictures (the major subplot has to do with gangsters trying to get revenge on Aznavour's two adult brothers for double-crossing them after a robbery; they kidnap Aznavour and Dubois and then

his younger brother); fatalistic *noir* films made in America and France (starring Jean Gabin); Hitchcock, Renoir, Lubitsch, Guitry, Tashlin, Welles, Gance, Godard, Chaplin, and the Marx Brothers. No film better juxtaposes comedy and dark tragedy, or shows how similar are the two in our world. No film is more romantic, yet it makes a strong case for not falling in love. In Truffaut, it makes sense that murderous gangsters have clever senses of humor; or that they can run around like bumbling Keystone Kops and still break our hearts by killing someone we love. In one sense the film is a comical look at a timid man trying to sneak through life in a loud, dangerous world and, if he can muster up the courage, buy a drink for or hold hands with a pretty girl, Dubois. But on a sadder level it's about the destructiveness of love, how men treat women as sexual objects, how men's actions contradict their thoughts, and, in an existential sense, how the continuous passivity of men like Aznavour can keep them "alive" but result in all the most important people in their lives literally falling dead around them. A wonderful film, full of unforgettable moments. Cinematography by Raoul Coutard. Also with: Albert Rémy, Michèle Mercier, Daniel Boulanger.

SHOOTING, THE (1967) C/82m.

Puzzling but excellent existential western directed by Monte Hellman in the Utah desert in 1965, in conjunction with *Ride in the Whirlwind*. Hellman's unusual, interesting West is ugly, barren, and godforsaken. It's a lonely, cruel world where one's nearest neighbor lives a day's ride away; where women are as scarce as the wildlife; where most men live with male companions/work partners. Those who live here are a hard, violent people, uneducated, possessive, distrustful, humorless. For 365 days they toil in the sun without conversation to disrupt their daily routine. It's little wonder that many of these people have lost some of their faculties. Warren Oates gives a solid performance as a bounty hunter, and Will Hutchins, once TV's *Sugarfoot*, is surprisingly effective as his simple-minded companion. Two days after Oates's brother fled town after getting drunk and running down a small boy, Oates and Hutchins are hired by a mysterious woman (Millie Perkins) to escort her to another town. Perkins is soon joined by an evil Jack Palance-like gunslinger, played by Jack Nicholson (who produced this film and wrote *Whirlwind*). He keeps threatening Hutchins, but we have faith that the intelligent Oates could outwit Nicholson in a fight. The journey eventually takes the four characters so deep into the desert that it's unlikely they'll get out alive—but instead of retreating, they move forward. As in *Whirlwind*, the good guys suddenly find themselves in a predicament that is beyond their comprehension—they end up taking journeys to nowhere. While you may guess the surprise climax, you'll be hard pressed to figure out its meaning. The end may ask more questions than it answers, but the exciting journey that brings us to this point is one of the most compelling sequences in the history of westerns. This unique film deserves better distribution than it has received. A fine script by Adrien Joyce (*Five Easy Pieces*); excellent photography by Gregory Sandor.

SHOP AROUND THE CORNER, THE (1940)
B&W/97m. Enchanting Ernst Lubitsch comedy set in Budapest, involving the owner (Frank Morgan) and employees of Matuschek's, a small gift shop that specializes in leather goods. James Stewart, the kindly Morgan's top salesman, and new saleswoman Margaret Sullavan constantly squabble. Each thinks that the other can't compare to their pen pals, with whom they've been carrying on romantic correspondence but have never met. Stewart is startled to discover that he and Sullavan are each other's pen pals. But when he's about to reveal himself to Sullavan, Morgan unexpectedly fires him, mistakenly believing Stewart to be his wife's secret lover. Like most Lubitsch farces, this has to do with mistaken identity, deception, and characters masking their true selves. An early discussion about a cigarette box, which has *imitation* leather and is sold by Sullavan as a *candy* box, immediately calls our attention to the fact that nothing (not objects, not people) is what it seems to us or to the characters in the story. Stewart and Sullavan (a marvelous team!) conceal their idealistic, romantic visions of the world, life, and love; Morgan conceals the depth of his humanity behind a gruff exterior; errand boy William Tracy doesn't reveal his slick style or managerial skills until he's promoted to salesman; and social-climbing salesman Joseph Schildkraut covers his worst treachery (he's Morgan's wife's lover) with a deceitful attitude that he knows anyone can see through: indeed, this gossipy, word-twisting, back-stabbing sneak is the picture's equivalent of a war spy—he is rooted out and appropriately ostracized. Yet this is Lubitsch's gentlest, most chaste (there's only *one* kiss) comedy, one in which he was more interested in revealing the humanity of his characters (excluding Schildkraut, of course) than in sexual innuendo. And we fall in love with the people at Matuschek's, as individuals and as a family, much like the acting troupe in Lubitsch's *To Be or Not to Be*. Samson Raphaelson wrote the script, which has some of the screen's finest comedic dialogue, and some of its sweetest moments. It was loosely adapted from a play by Nikolaus Laszlo. Remade in 1949 as the Judy Garland–Van Johnson musical *In the Good Old Summertime*. Also with: Felix Bressart, Sara Haden, Inez Courtney, Edwin Maxwell.

SHOT IN THE DARK, A (1964) C/101m.
Hilarious Blake Edwards farce, with Peter Sellers establishing his prideful yet stupid, bumbling, and accident-prone Inspector Clouseau as one of the screen's all-time great comic creations. (Sellers had gotten only second billing playing Clouseau in *The Pink Panther*.) Much to the chagrin of nervous-because-of-Clouseau police chief Herbert Lom, Clouseau is assigned to an important murder case. Arriving at George Sanders's well-populated estate, he announces he suspects no one, he suspects everyone. All evidence points to maid Elke Sommer, but he doesn't believe she is guilty. He angers Lom by repeatedly letting her out of prison so he can follow her—only to be tossed in jail himself for using the wrong disguises. Meanwhile someone tries to ambush Clouseau, but accidentally murders many innocent bystanders. The storyline is fairly conventional—in fact, Edwards and William Peter Blatty adapted a play—but Sellers makes it unique. He is a joy, whether mispronouncing words like *bump* and *monkey*, getting his finger stuck in his globe, falling into water, leaning back in a chair and toppling over, engaging in brutal hand-to-hand combat with Japanese houseboy Burt Kwouk (whom he's ordered to attack him at all times), trying unsuccessfully to synchronize watches with his assistant, setting his coat on fire, or stripping so he can do some sleuthing at a nudist colony. Everything happens to Clouseau, but he emerges unscathed while bodies fall around him. Like Don Adams's Maxwell Smart, he never realizes that he's anything but a lethal, supercool detective, although everyone else sees that he's a fool. What's interesting is that everyone he meets eventually descends to his "fool" level under his influence. Followed by several sequels, beginning in 1975. Also with: Tracy Reed, Graham Stark, André Maranne.

SHOW BOAT (1936) B&W/113m.
Best screen version of Jerome Kern–Oscar Hammerstein musical, retaining soap-opera elements from Edna Ferber's novel. Picture's theme (the theme of Ferber's *Cimarron* and *Giant*)—which is expressed in several songs—is that men are invariably a disappointment to their wives, but the women never stop loving them. Reprising a role she played briefly on Broadway, Irene Dunne is the daughter of Charles Winninger and Helen Westley, the owners of a show boat. When the lead actress (Helen Morgan) in the boat's melodramas is dismissed because she's half black, Dunne takes over her friend's roles, and the male leading parts go to a handsome, shiftless gambler (Allan Jones). The two fall in love and, with their baby daughter, move to Chicago. Jones tries hard, but can't find profitable work and walks out on his family. Dunne becomes an internationally known musical star. Picture has lavish production, wonderful music, and a splendid cast. Dramatic highlights include the scene in which the play is performed on the Show Boat, and conversations between Paul Robeson and Hattie McDaniel. Musical highlights include the McDaniel–Robeson duet, Helen Morgan giving a soulful rendition of "Bill," some surprisingly effective singing by Dunne (in a role that would have been ideal for Jeanette MacDonald), and, of course, Robeson's spellbinding "Old Man River." The film's portrayal of blacks is a sticky issue. On the one hand, they fit into stereotypes. On the other, they display class, talent, strength—they are beloved friends to Dunne; significantly, the black stars are given quality screen time. Remake of 1929 film; remade in 1951. Directed by James Whale; flavorful, schmaltzy, and rewarding. Also with: Donald Cook, Eddie Anderson, Clarence Muse, Queenie Smith.

SIEGFRIED/SIEGFRIEDS TOD (GERMAN/1924) B&W/92m. Fritz Lang's monumental two-part, three-hour *Nibelungen Saga*, scripted by Thea von Harbou (Lang's wife), was based less on Wagner's opera *The Ring of the Nibelungen* and the Norse sagas that Wagner used as his sources than on a two-part play written in 1862 by Freidrich Hebbel and the 13th-century German epic *The Lay of the Nibelungs*. This first part is a marvel, one of the truly great silent films and one of the most spectacular ventures into fantasy and legend that there has ever been on the screen. It is best known for the stunning design work by Otto Hunte, Erich Kettelhut, and Karl Vollbrecht (supervised by former architect Lang), the vast sets (filmed in long shot to make them seem larger) and photography by Carl Hoffmann and Günther Rittau which, latter-day critics have pointed out, owes less to expressionism than—as we see in scenes set in the sun-filtered forest—romanticism (i.e., the paintings of Swiss Romanticist Arnold Böcklin, who also inspired the look of Skull Island in *King Kong*). But the characters are grand and the story is exciting, subtle enough for adults and magical enough for kids. The hero is Siegfried (Paul Richter), Lang's usual lone figure who wanders alone through a world that turns hostile. He travels to Burgundy to propose to Kriemhild (Margarete Schön), the sister of King Günther (Theodor Loos). On the way he kills a 70-foot dragon and becomes invincible—but for one spot on his back—from bathing in its blood; he also kills the wicked king of the dwarves (the Nibelungun) and acquires a rope helmet that can make him invisible. The treacherous Hagen (Hans Adalbert von Schlettow), Günther's half-brother, makes it clear to Siegfried that he can't marry Kriemhild until he helps Günther win the hand of Brunhild (Hanna Ralph), the Icelandic warrior queen. Siegfried uses his invisibility and great strength to help Günther defeat Brunhild in athletic competition and win her hand; then he takes the form of the King to force Brunhild's cooperation on their wedding night. When Kriemhild unwittingly brags to the snobbish Brunhild what Siegfried has done, Brunhild (who harbors a secret love for Siegfried) shows such rage that Günther agrees to let Hagen attempt to kill his friend. So we have a typical Lang hero who is doomed by one foolish act (using his special powers to deceive Brunhild); most interestingly, he is another Lang hero, this time a *super*hero, whose defeat is brought about by a combination of his own innocence and the various weaknesses (jealousy, anger, pride, disloyalty, cowardice) of the humans he encounters. Followed by the much more somber *Kriemhild's Revenge*.

SILENT PARTNER, THE (CANADIAN/1978) C/ 103m. Timid bank clerk Elliott Gould (giving his best performance since *The Long Goodbye*), the type of guy everyone underestimates, figures out that a fake Santa Claus (Christopher Plummer) outside the bank is planning a hold-up. So he arranges the money in his drawer in such a way that Plummer gets away with only a small amount—while Gould secretly stashes a huge amount in his safe-deposit box. Unfortunately, his cleaning lady loses his key, so he has to figure out how to get the money out of the bank. Meanwhile he has to play a deadly cat-and-mouse game with the sadistic and crazy Plummer, who is determined to get Gould's money. A terrific sleeper, directed by Daryl Duke. It's full of offbeat characters, plot twists, delicious surprises. Picture has wit and excitement, but the violence is *too* strong; this may be one film you'll enjoy on television in a slightly cut version. Also with: Susannah York, Celine Lomez (who almost steals the film as Plummer's sexy girl-friend who falls for Gould), Michael Kirby, Ken Pogue, John Candy.

SILVERADO (1985) C/133m. Lawrence Kasdan's expensive (the money is well spent!), expansive, epic western should have brought back the genre from the grave simply because it's a good enough movie to appeal to today's movie audience, and it shows why westerns have such special appeal to their diehard fans. As soon as a glorious landscape fills the screen (the picture was beautifully photographed by John Bailey in 70mm), or horses gallop four abreast across the foreground, or a hero displays a lightning-fast draw, a western fan will get an emotional charge because it's evident that the western has returned in good hands—director Kasdan and his co-writer brother, Mack Kasdan, obviously love the western and understand its joys, its uniqueness. Story is simple: brothers Scott Glenn (a top man with a gun) and Kevin Costner (fun-loving and reckless) join forces with ex-con Kevin Kline (a free-thinker, an idealist) and Danny Glover (a black man out to avenge his father's death) to clean up a town run by a corrupt sheriff, Brian Dennehy (who used to ride with Kline), and a murderous cattle baron. Whereas Kasdan affectionately preserves clichés that make westerns *westerns*, he expands the parameters for the genre—opening up the possibilities for other directors who want to venture into the form but were bored by the strict form of the classic western. Particularly impressive is how Kasdan gives us characters who are immediately recognizable western types (with the important exception of Kline)—who have "pasts" and specific dreams for the future—but allows them extra qualities that have been denied their predecessors: mainly, the ability to not only talk a lot but to engage in hip, witty dialogue (even the bad guys are funny). It's to Kasdan's credit that we can accept these novel characters as people who may indeed have been inhabitants of the West. Final shootout between Kline and Dennehy is proof positive that Kasdan understands genre because it is choreographed in manner to express the genre's most important theme: the former gunslinger must decide if he wants to be part of civilization or retain his savagery. The great offbeat cast includes: Linda Hunt (who lends intelligence and taste as a barmaid and Kline's soulmate), Jeff Goldblum (a snake-in-the-grass gambler), John Cleese (a conceited, dictatorial English lawman), Rosanna Arquette (sadly wasted in the minor part of a homesteader).

SIMON OF THE DESERT (MEXICAN/1965)

C/45m. Bizarre, laugh-out-loud Luis Buñuel comedy about St. Simon Stylites (Claudio Brook), whose unequaled devotion to God (in the 5th century) causes him to spend 37 years on top of a tall column in the desert preaching God's word to passersby, and supposedly attempting miraculous cures of the sick and handicapped who flock to him. At times the wild-bearded Simon comes across as a fool: he blesses everything, even the food in his teeth; his belief in God is so masochistic that at one point he decides to stand on one foot until God sends him a sign. But Buñuel does not really mock him; rather I think he pities him for being so loyal to a God who doesn't seem to care he exists. The devious devil repeatedly turns up to test and tempt him, but God is off on vacation, leaving Simon vulnerable. Equally sad is fact that the people he helps—all typically weird Buñuel characters—don't appreciate what he does for them; it's a common Buñuel theme that good, even saintly works, are wasted on ignorant, self-interested, self-professed Christians. Brief film ends with unsatisfactory jolt. Until then, parable is great fun and thought-provoking. Also with: Mortensia Santovena, Enrique Alvarez.

SIN OF HAROLD DIDDLEBOCK, THE/MAD WEDNESDAY (1947) B&W/79m—90m. Disappointing but mildly amusing Preston Sturges comedy provides Harold Lloyd with his last role, actually a reprise (but for a name change) of the character he created in his 1925 silent classic, *The Freshman*. In fact, film begins with footage of the *big* football game from that film. Because of his last-minute heroics Diddlebock is given a low level position at an ad agency. His motto is "Success is around the corner"—just as it is Sturges's favorite theme—but he stagnates in his job for 25 years, until he is fired. A lifeless figure, he says farewell to the young woman he loved from afar (Frances Ramsden). There is a trip to the bar, where he gets zonked by the house special. He wakes up on Thursday, having completely forgotten what he did on Wednesday (shades of Betty Hutton in Sturges's *The Miracle of Morgan's Creek*). In Sturges, a man's fortunes change overnight. In this case, Lloyd won money on a race and bought a down-and-out circus. Undaunted, he thinks up a scheme to unload the circus on a banker. The enthusiastic, aggressive Lloyd of the silents is once more upon us. If this Everyman (he wears glasses even when he sleeps) can succeed, then we must be optimistic. Sturges always injected slapstick into his sophisticated comedies, so how he must have loved working with a master of the form. Film's highlight finds Lloyd dangling high above city by a rope attached to the neck of a lion—it's a bit that would have fit in nicely with his daredevil antics in *Safety Last*, his silent masterpiece. Sturges's sterling cast includes: Jimmy Conlin, Raymond Walburn, Rudy Vallee, Edgar Kennedy, Arline Judge, Franklin Pangborn, Margaret Hamilton, Al Bridge.

SINBAD AND THE EYE OF THE TIGER

(BRITISH/1977) C/113m. In the third installment of special-effects expert Ray Harryhausen's *Sinbad* series, our hero (Patrick Wayne) wants to marry a beautiful princess (Jane Seymour). But their plans are put on hold when her evil stepmother (Margaret Whiting, who sounds like a *foreigner*!) turns her brother into a baboon so her own son can become caliph. Wayne, Seymour, and the baboon embark on a perilous sea journey to find a way to reverse the transformation. They are joined by a legendary magician (Patrick Thoughton) and his daughter (Taryn Power, Tyrone's beautiful daughter) and head into the frozen north in search of the "Shrine of the Four Elements." Whiting, her son, and a metal giant with a metal bull's head follow in another boat. Disappointing fantasy-adventure, lacking the imagination of the two earlier Sinbad films. Harryhausen's creations are derivative of his earlier work or are just plain dull (basketball-sized bee, a giant walrus). The script is too long and lacks excitement; surprisingly, Sinbad himself spends most of the film as a bystander. Directed by Sam Wanamaker.

SINGIN' IN THE RAIN (1952) C/103m. One of the great joys of the cinema, the most uplifting of films ("I'm laughing at clouds so dark up above"), the ultimate musical for lovers of the film medium. Not only do innovative directors Gene Kelly and Stanley Donen use "film" (color, lighting, editing, special effects, camera placement and movement, and sound) to enhance the fabulous songs and dances, but, as scripted by Adolph Green and Betty Comden, this is also one of the best, funniest, most perceptive and informative pictures ever made about the movie industry. Song-and-dance men Don Lockwood (Kelly) and Cosmo Brown (Donald O'Connor) become Hollywood stuntmen during the silent era. Conceited Don becomes obnoxious Lina Lamont's (Jean Hagen) leading man and they become romantic idols. When they have to make a sound picture, *The Dancing Cavalier*, Don's girlfriend, Kathy Selden (Debbie Reynolds)—who has cured Don of conceit—dubs the singing and talking for Lina, who has a terrible voice. But mean, jealous Lina arranges that Kathy will never get credit for her remarkable talents. However, Don and Cosmo turn the tables on Lina. Green and Comden beautifully spoof numerous Hollywood types: suicidal stuntmen who'll do anything to be in pictures; starlets with pretensions of being serious thespians who will jump out of cakes to be part of show biz; brainless gossip columnists; tough directors who think the set is a battlefield; smug diction coaches; confused producers; flaky music coordinators; cocky actors who know the importance of "image" to stardom ("Dignity—always dignity"); and stupid, conceited actresses who believe their own press. The scenes without music are delightful; the musical numbers are *all* outstanding, with Kelly, O'Connor, and Reynolds displaying amazing athletic dancing skills. Unforgettable highlights include the three dancing on furniture and singing "Good Morning"; O'Connor running up walls and flipping during "Make 'Em Laugh"; the "Broadway Rhythm" number, especially when Kelly and Cyd Charisse perform a dreamlike

ballet; and the title number, which has Kelly happily dancing through puddles (who among us hasn't copied him on rainy nights?); in the film's great moment, the camera moves directly over Kelly's beaming face for a close-up just as he sings "There's a smile on my face." The greatest movie musical has become a stage musical. Produced by Arthur Freed. Songs by Freed and Nacio Herb Brown. Also with: Millard Mitchell, Rita Moreno, Douglas Fowley, King Donovan, Madge Blake, Russ Saunders, Kathleen Freeman, Mae Clarke, Dawn Addams, Elaine Stewart, Joi Lansing.

SISTERS (1973) C/92m. A creepy, funny, visually innovative but not that satisfying suspense thriller by Brian De Palma. He not only borrows themes and scenes from Alfred Hitchcock (i.e., *Rear Window*, *Psycho*) but also has a standout score by Bernard Herrmann, Hitchcock's best composer. He also seems inspired by *The Cabinet of Dr. Caligari* and Val Lewton's *Cat People*. In a performance that recalls Simone Simon, Margot Kidder is unexpectedly sweet and vulnerable as French-Canadian Danielle Breton, a model working in New York. But even she has her bad side: Dominique, her murderous, detached Siamese twin. When reporter Grace Collier (Jennifer Salt) sees a murder committed in Danielle's apartment, she calls in the police. But since there is no body, the police don't believe her. Salt continues to investigate on her own, even hiring a private detective (Charles Durning). She discovers that Danielle had a twin, but is shocked to learn that Dominique died on the operating table when Dr. Emil Breton (Bill Finley), Danielle's ex-husband, separated them! When the strange doctor takes Danielle to his private sanitarium, Grace follows, not realizing she'll become one of the patients. Film is a bit too violent, but if it has a *major* problem, it is that the opening sequence is so technically exciting (with tracking shots, split screen, sharp cutting), witty (there's a hilarious parody of TV game shows called *Peeping Toms*), and suspenseful that it's never equaled. This sequence also takes up so much screen time that the end comes much earlier than expected, long before we've been given a sufficient number of suspense sequences. Also with: Lisle Wilson, Barnard Hughes, Dolph Sweet, Mary Davenport.

SITTING DUCKS (1980) C/90m. In Henry Jaglom's cult comedy, middle-aged, balding odd couple Michael Emil and Zack Norman run off with the Mafia's daily collection and head for Florida. Along the way they're joined by a friendly young guitar-player (Richard Romanus), who becomes their chauffeur; a neurotic, recently fired waitress (Irene Forrest), who becomes the object of Emil's affections; and a recently dumped but upbeat young woman (Patrice Townsend, wife of Jaglom), whom Norman tries to get into bed. Unorthodox comedy quickly wins you over. Philosophical, gabby Emil (who brags he's the world's best lover) and womanizer Norman (a 60-second man) are a hilarious team—you could trade Louis Malle's entire dinner with André for the five-minute conversation Emil and Norman have in a bathtub. "Family" scenes in car are really fun—

especially the one in which they all discuss masturbation; as in other scenes, characters must be ad-libbing because their interaction seems so natural. The women may be too emotional, weak, and manipulative for some, but I find them delightfully offbeat and, we discover, more than what we first thought. A true surprise! Also with: Jaglom.

SIXTEEN CANDLES (1984) C/93m. Samantha Baker (Molly Ringwald) has her sweet sixteenth birthday, but her parents and, amazingly, even her visiting grandparents have forgotten it due to the hoopla surrounding her older sister's marriage. Contributing to her torment is her unrequited love for a handsome senior (Michael Schoeffling) who's taking his beautiful blonde girlfriend (Haviland Morris) to the big dance and beer bash. It seems to her that the only person who knows she exists and sees that she's special is a gawky sophomore, The Geek (Anthony Michael Hall) near whom she doesn't want to be seen but who keeps making a play for her in public—totally humiliating her. However, during the course of this eventful day-night-following-morning, she'll discover that The Geek is a neat guy—a good friend with the same insecurities she has—and that Schoeffling also has eyes for her. Director-writer John Hughes has moderate success making a comedy out of teenage angst, pain, and insensitivity (even heroine Ringwald can be cruel—as she reveals in her insults toward Hall). There is much teenage interplay and many teenage types that you'll recognize if you have any contact with high-school kids; and Hughes also has an ear for teenage lingo. Characters who start out as smart and witty eventually become stupid and offensive—as in most teen sex comedies. Hughes's mistake is to forsake Samantha for supporting characters, for as long as Ringwald is on the screen, the film is first rate. Ringwald is absolutely fantastic, presenting a *real*, special teenager. She's especially funny when reacting through facial expressions (particularly lifting her upper lip), body language, eye movements, and voice nuances to each aggravation and disappointment. Hughes would reunite Ringwald and Hall for *The Breakfast Club* and *Pretty in Pink* (which he produced). Also with: Paul Dooley, George Watanabe, Blanche Baker, Carlin Glynn, Edward Andrews, Billie Bird, Justin Henry, John Cusack.

SLAP SHOT (1977) C/122m. Paul Newman is the middle-aged player-coach for a bad minor-league hockey team, the Charlestown Chiefs. The team looks like it will fold because of poor attendance. But then the meek players start to play like goons and as they bloody their opponents they chalk up win after win. Crowds start to come to the games, not necessarily to see the Chiefs win but to cheer their dirty tactics. I'm glad that George Roy Hill's comedy doesn't presume to attack today's hockey/sports fan for demanding that violence be part of the game, because the movie itself aims to please viewers, to make 'em laugh, by including much preposterously brutal sports action (i.e., fistfights, stick slashing, dirty body checks). Indeed, the more violent, the funnier it is; you find yourself laughing at the most ridiculous things in this film—such as the Chiefs' three bespectacled Hanson brothers (Jeff Carlson, Steve Carlson, David Hanson) taking to the ice for the first time and pulverizing the opposition with Genghis Khan tactics. Script by Nancy Dowd received much attention because it contained more profanity, sexual content, and brutality than had ever been contained in a screenplay written by a woman not in the porno field; but even more unusual are the quirkiness of her characters and the unexpected ways in which they act and converse with one another. For instance, there's nothing trite about the scene in which Newman lies in bed with bare-breasted Melinda Dillon and nuzzles on her tummy while she tells him of a lesbian affair she's having (he says he approves). Newman gives one of his most interesting performances—boy, is it strange hearing *him* use gutter language! A disappointing ending. Edited by Dede Allen. Also with: Michael Ontkean, Lindsay Crouse, Strother Martin, Jennifer Warren, Jerry Hauser, Andrew Duncan, Kathryn Walker, Swoosie Kurtz, M. Emmett Walsh, Paul Dooley.

SLAUGHTERHOUSE FIVE (1972) C/104m.
Adaptation of Kurt Vonnegut's masterpiece did poor box office, but somehow does justice to seemingly unfilmable novel. Direction by George Roy Hill, script by Stephen Geller, and cinematography by Miroslav Ondricek are all superb, contributing to give form to a wildly complex structure, and credibility to bizarre sci-fi/fantasy material. Michael Sachs is Billy Pilgrim, a middle-aged optometrist, a passive, spineless marshmallow without personality, without any comprehension of what goes on in the world. Not only was he not meant for *this* world, but he is "unstuck in time," constantly leaving the present to return to the past when he was a WWII POW in Dresden at the time Allied fire-bombings wiped out the city; or to zoom to the future when aliens whisk him into a terrarium on the planet Tralfamadore, where he can live with his faithful dog and the half-naked actress Montana Wildhack (Valerie Perrine). Scenes in present and future have a surreal quality; those in Dresden are astonishingly believable, and terrifying. The scene in which Billy's fatherly friend Derby (Eugene Roche) is killed is one of the most jarring sequences in cinema history, one that leaves your stomach queasy. Hill has him unceremoniously taken to the back of the frame, where we see a firing squad shoot him as if he were a nonentity not even deserving a final smoke. Sam Peckinpah would have had the killing done up close and personal, in slow motion, with buckets of blood put to good use—but it wouldn't have had nearly the impact, or expressed the Germans' horrifying feeling that his death was of no significance. Indeed, one of the film's most interesting aspects is this casual handling of death (which by no means makes us feel less pain), which corresponds to Vonnegut's after-death refrain "So it goes." It's no wonder that Hill was attracted to the work of John Irving and directed many tragic yet somehow ironic death scenes in *The World According to Garp*. Sharp editing by Dede Allen. Also with: Ron Leibman (as the vengeful Paul Lazzaro), Kevin Conway, Perry King, Holly Near, Sharon Gans (as Billy's overweight wife), John Dehner.

SLEEPER (1973) C/88m.
Silly but enjoyable Woody Allen satirical comedy. Woody wakes up from a minor ulcer operation to discover that it's 2173. Never before political, he is recruited by the underground to perform a mission that will bring down the totalitarian regime. But he finds it difficult to elude the fascist police; at one time he passes himself off as a servant-robot at bourgeois hedonist Diane Keaton's party. Film becomes sort of a futuristic *The 39 Steps* when Allen forces Keaton to go along with him. At first she screams her head off, but then she too joins the underground. Of course they fall in love. Lots of gags and slapstick don't work, but there's also much hilarity. Highlights include Allen's first steps after his long sleep, Allen visiting a robotic Jewish tailor, and the philosophical discussions between Allen and Keaton about such things as sex and death ("two things that come once in a lifetime"). Keaton is extremely endearing—this is the film where she really came into her own as a comedienne; but all her lines come across as Allen-written, as opposed to her lines in *Annie Hall*, which seem to come from Keaton and her character. Music by the Preservation Hall Jazz Band seems inappropriate. Co-written by Marshall Brickman. Also with: John Beck, Mary Gregory, Don Keefer.

SLEEPING BEAUTY (1959) C/75m.
An elaborate, charming animated feature by Walt Disney, adapted by Erdman Penner from Charles Perrault's version of the classic fairytale. When the Princess Aurora is born, her parents, the King and Queen, don't invite the evil fairy Maleficent to the celebration. Insulted, Maleficent puts a curse on the child, saying that on her 16th birthday she will prick her finger on a spindle and die. Good fairies Flora, Fauna, and Merry Weather—who are like three lovable, squabbling, slightly daffy maiden aunts—raise Aurora in the forest, hoping Maleficent won't know where she is when she becomes 16. On her 16th birthday Aurora meets the young man of her dreams in the forest. They fall in love. She doesn't know that he is a prince and their marriage has already been arranged. And he doesn't know that *she* is his fiancée. But the marriage is put on hold when Aurora pricks her finger and falls into a deep sleep. The three fairies try to rescue the prince from Maleficent's dungeon so he can deliver his famous kiss. Picture has been criticized for not being humorous enough or exciting enough (until the end) to please children—but I saw this with a theater full of quiet kids who were absolutely spellbound. The animation is not as flamboyant as in other Disney cartoons, but there is fine detail work and some bits in which characters and objects in the same frame move at different speeds are stunning. Maleficent is an effective villainess, Aurora is one of the sexiest and most beautiful of Disney's animated heroines—like Cinderella, she was modeled on Helene Stanley (lovely Polly in *Davy Crockett*)—and the climactic battle on Forbidden Mountain is spectacular. Clyde Geronimi was

supervising director. Voices: Mary Costa (Aurora), Bill Shirley (Prince Philip), Eleanor Audley (Maleficent), Verna Felton, Barbara Jo Allen, Barbara Luddy, Taylor Holmes, Bill Thompson, Candy Candido.

SLUMBER PARTY MASSACRE, THE (1982) C/ 77m.

Mass murderer Michael Villella (spelled Villela in the end titles) escapes from prison and goes on a murder spree with a long drill. He finds his victims at a girls' slumber party. Film has received attention because it was produced and directed by a woman, Amy Jones, and scripted by radical feminist Rita Mae Brown. But as hard as one looks, it's impossible to find a satirical-political-feminist theme that would explain why Jones or Brown would be associated with this entry into the slice-and-dice genre. They follow all conventions relating to female nudity, horny teens, too many false alarms, painful death, buckets of blood. Were they just trying to prove that they could make as tough and obscenely violent a film as young male directors, or that they could make a bloody, sexy exploitation film that would rack in the same amounts of money as the male-directed *Halloween* rip-offs have? In any case, this film is trash. Every character is stupid beyond belief. There are numerous ways in which the girls could get out of their predicament, but they haven't even the intelligence to lean out a window of the two-story house and yell for help. Instead the dense girls wait around to be murdered one by one. It is infuriating and frustrating how they are set up for slaughter. Also with: Michele Michaels, Robin Stille, Debra Deliso.

SMALL CHANGE/ARGENT DE POCHE, L'(FRENCH/1976) C/105m.

François Truffaut's glowing tribute to children, who must use all their immense, amazing resources to compensate for living in a sometimes brutal, adult-made, adult-controlled world. Leisurely plotted film is set in Thiers near the end of the school year, and most scenes take place at the school, where the children (ranging from about four to 12) are more relaxed than the students in *The 400 Blows*, and the teachers are much more enlightened than those in 1959—they care about their students, find the skillful clowning and idiosyncrasies endearing, and want to teach the kids about both school subjects and life, rather than disciplining them all the time. The kids' lives are tough enough as it is. Other scenes take place around the village and in a housing development where families and teachers live—this allows us to see how the kids relate to their parents. (Unlike in *The 400 Blows*, the kids seem to have gotten the upper hand, and the parents are full of love.) And significant scenes take place in the cinema, where the entire community gathers and there is no distinction between child and adult. The two children who share center stage are those who have the most difficult home lives. Patrick (Geory Desmouceaux) lives alone with a handicapped father—what he finds missing in his life is clear when he develops a crush on his best friend's mother. Julien (Philippe Goldman) is a victim of child abuse—a subject that in 1976 was not getting much attention in film or television. While this film is known for its humor (which the kids deliver naturally), the child-abuse theme was of extreme importance to Truffaut; he even has a teacher (Jean-François Stévenin)—he will remind some of Truffaut—lecture his class on the subject. Otherwise this is a simple film about innocent themes (a boy's first kiss, boys sneaking into a movie, boys making their own breakfast, boys spying on a nude woman)—but don't let that fool you! There are unforgettable scenes and faces, and so much is revealed about children's special, often-troubled world. Also with: Virginie Thévenéx, Sylvie Grezel, Laura Truffaut (who's the mother of the weird professional writer in the movie documentary), Eva Truffaut.

SMASH PALACE (NEW ZEALAND/1982) C/ 100m.

Bruno Lawrence runs a family garage/junkyard called Smash Palace, and spends all his spare time fixing up his car for competitions he enters. Suddenly his world is shattered when his neglected wife, Anna Jemison, says she wants out of the marriage. Faced with the prospect of losing his wife and young daughter (Greer Robson), Lawrence loses control. His attempts to gain back his family are pathetic and embarrassing—a strong man begins to act like a two-year-old. We start to dislike him and we also resent Jemison for having made him act this way. This is an incisive look at marriage gone sour, where nice people act cruelly to one another and nobody plays by rules. The film is not that original and it's part of a broken-family subgenre that I'm not that fond of because of the self-pitying nature of the male-written scripts. But I prefer it to the better-acted *Shoot the Moon* and *My First Wife* simply because it surprises us with a happy ending—those other two films are just too depressing. Strong direction by Roger Donaldson.

SMILES OF A SUMMER NIGHT (SWEDISH/ 1955) B&W/108m.

Sophisticated bedroom farce is one of Ingmar Bergman's most popular films. I see it as a tribute (from a man who has been through the battle of the sexes) to those women who are clever and brave enough to shape their own worlds despite husbands and lovers who make up the rules. The central character is male, a self-pleased, middle-aged lawyer (Gunnar Björnstrand), who is married to a 16-year-old virgin (Ulla Jacobsson). They have little in common and do not satisfy each other. So Björnstrand visits his former mistress, an actress (Eva Dahlbeck), who is in her early thirties. But Dahlbeck is now mistress of a duel-obsessed military man (Jarl Kulle), who ignores his young, unhappy wife (Margit Carlquist). Dahlbeck and Carlquist scheme so that Dahlbeck will win back Björnstrand and Carlquist will win Kulle's fidelity. Everyone gathers at the estate of Dahlbeck's mother (Naima Wifstrand), including Björnstrand's son (Björn Bjelvenstam), who loves Jacobsson, and Björnstrand's hedonistic maid (Harriet Andersson), who makes a play for the groom (Ake Fridell). Film has been compared to Lubitsch's comedies of manners and Renoir's *The Rules of the Game*; I am more reminded of the works of Max Ophüls, whose men are ruled by pride and whose women are so guided by their hearts that they become obsessed with winning men who they realize aren't worthy of them (Björnstrand, Kulle, Bjelvenstam, and Fridell are no prizes). Bergman serves as matchmaker, yet makes it clear that temporary happiness has nothing to do with whether two people are ideal for each other or, conversely, the uniting of two people who seemingly are meant for each other does not mean they'll achieve permanent happiness. Film is wise and cynical—you'll also think it hilarious if you just pay attention to the indignities Björnstrand suffers (while maintaining his composure): he falls headlong into a puddle; he must wear a ridiculous nightshirt, cap, and gown; he's seen by Kulle wearing these garments (which in fact belong to Kulle); he can't get Dahlbeck to admit that her son, who has his first name, is his child; he loses his wife to his stepson (they run away together); he is caught by Kulle just as he's about to make love to Kulle's wife; he's tricked by Kulle into firing a blank cartridge at his own temple (causing his face to be covered with black powder). Still Dahlbeck realizes that this loser is the best of a sorry male lot. Excellent acting, photography (by Gunnar Fischer), set design (by P. A. Lundgren). Adapted into musical play *A Little Night Music*. Also with: Jullan Kindahl, Gull Natorp.

SMITHEREENS (1982) C/90m.

An impressive low-budget independent film directed by Susan Seidelman. Whereas in *Desperately Seeking Susan* she would portray Greenwich Village as a glitzy, fairytale world where offbeat people keep each other happy, in this earlier film it is, realistically, an ugly, hellish, unfriendly place where offbeat characters are too stoned, crazy, and selfish to help out their kind. Susan Berman plays a young refugee from New Jersey (which Rosanna Arquette would be in *Desperately*) who is trying to break into the music business, although she probably has no talent. She also has no money, no apartment, and no friends who will help her out—most everyone has had enough of her grating personality, her lies (usually about needing no one), and her shameless taking advantage of anyone she thinks may help her. She is forced to live in a van with a nice guy (Brad Rinn) from Montana, but she keeps disappointing him with her disloyalty. He wants her to go away with him, but she's planning on going to LA with a young singer (Richard Hell of the punk band, the Voidoids)—not seeing the signs that Hell (who is broke) is using her as she uses everyone else. We keep expecting Berman to wise up so she can enjoy a little happiness—we could use a little relief as well—but Seidelman won't let her: she wanted to draw an accurate portrait of the typical Village loser. It's sad because, while Berman's actions call for her to have a sorry fate, we see glimpses—under her act, under her self-deception—that she deserves better. Film has interesting array of weird characters—only Berman seems miscast. Technically, the film is fairly polished—Seidelman composes her shots well, creating striking tableaux by situating her strangely dressed and coiffured char-

acters in the frame with colorful props (Rinn's van, for instance) and bizarrely designed or graffiti-covered walls. Her camera pan through the laundromat is particularly striking. Cinematography is by Chirine El Khadem.

SNAKE PIT, THE (1948) B&W/108m.

Still among the most famous of the mental-hospital films, but its power seems to have lessened in the wake of *One Flew Over the Cuckoo's Nest* and *Frances*. In the opening scene Olivia de Havilland (whose strong performance holds up) finds herself a patient in a mental hospital. She has had a nervous breakdown and remembers nothing of her past, including her marriage to Mark Stevens. Through therapy, hypnotism, and the use of shock treatment (which the film favors!), psychiatrist Leo Genn (who always smokes a pipe) tries to find the root cause of her illness (her insecurity, her fear of loving anyone). De Havilland's state gets much worse—they don't call it the "snake pit" for nothing—before she comes out of the darkness. Directed by Anatole Litvak. From the book by Mary Jane Ward. Also with: Celeste Holm, Glenn Langan, Leif Erickson, Beulah Bondi, Lee Patrick, Isabel Jewell, Ruth Donnelly.

SNOW WHITE AND THE SEVEN DWARFS (1938) C/82m.

Walt Disney's adaptation of the Grimm fairytale was the first animation feature and the first cartoon where characters of the same type (here, the Dwarfs) are individualized. I think it is the equal of *Pinocchio* and one of the greatest pictures of all time. The Wicked Queen is jealous of orphaned servant girl Snow White's great beauty (and, I imagine, her purity). She orders her henchman to slay her, but he allows her to escape into the forest. The frightened girl is terrified by the woods, but soon makes friends with the animals, who take her to the home of the Seven Dwarfs: leader "Doc," Sneezy, Bashful, Grumpy, Sleepy, Happy, and Dopey. While they're off at their diamond mine, she cleans their sloppy house. They're not all thrilled that Snow White has moved in with them, but she wins them over—even Grumpy. She even gets them to wash up before dinner. When the Queen finds out Snow White is still alive, she turns herself into a hag and comes to the house while the Dwarfs are away. She offers Snow White an apple. . . . Children will be dazzled by the animation (scenes in the castle, including the Queen's transformation, and in the forest with the Dwarfs and Queen are especially impressive); sing along with "Whistle While You Work," "Heigh Ho," and "Some Day My Prince Will Come"; delight in the humorous Dwarfs (and fall in love with Dopey); and be excited and terrified (this movie is very scary). While adults will enjoy the same elements as the children, those with interest in interpreting dreams and fairytales will be interested in the sexual subtext. The Queen is Satan with an apple trying to corrupt Snow White by taking away her youth and her resistance to relinquishing her virginity. In her early relationship with the Dwarfs, Snow White served as surrogate daughter and mother to these childlike old men. That she gets them to wash up before meals is indicative of her desire to keep their hands clean, and off her. Yet they begin to think of her as their dream lover and stand in line for kisses; but they literally don't measure up (at one point, one sits on another's shoulders so she'll think she's with a *man*). When they forget their cowardice and rush home to save Snow White from the apple and then chase the Queen through the forest, they finally qualify as men. This, coupled with Snow White's succumbing to temptation by tasting the apple and yielding her innocence, makes it impossible for the Dwarfs and Snow White to cohabit any longer. She is now ready for the young Prince to kiss her and take her away. Songs were by Frank Churchill, Larry Morey, Paul J. Smith, and Leigh Harline. David Hand was supervising director.

SNUFF (ARGENTINIAN-AMERICAN/1976) C/ 77m.   This wretched picture became a sensation owing to a hoax perpetrated by its distributor, Allan Shackleton. He started a false rumor that it contained footage of the real murder and dismemberment of its script girl; then he obtained a lot of publicity when he hired people to picket the theaters to protest this scene, knowing full well that women-against-pornography groups would join in. (Fake FBI agents were also hired to frequent theater lines and question patrons.) The major part of the film is a 1971 Argentinian ditty called *Slaughter*, which never played in the U.S. Its muddled story has something to do with a Charles Manson–like gang of thrill butchers who eventually kill an actress and the people at whose mansion she's staying. There are incomprehensible flashbacks and brief "smoker"-caliber lovemaking scenes. New characters appear with regularity, and from out of nowhere comes a discussion about Nazis and Jews—could we be watching the missing footage from *They Saved Hitler's Brain*? Picture's surprisingly untitillating and tame for the exploitation genre. The final scene that caused all the controversy was made by Shackleton. The special effects are terrible, so you don't worry about the script girl—but it truly is *offensive*.

SO LONG AT THE FAIR (BRITISH/1950) B&W/ 90m.   A young British woman (Jean Simmons) and her older brother (David Tomlinson) arrive in Paris for the 1889 Exposition. The next morning both he and his hotel room are missing! The staff claims that neither existed, that Simmons arrived by herself. Alone in Paris, Simmons can't get anyone to believe her story until a young man (Dirk Bogarde) gives her a hand and helps her solve the baffling mystery. Alfred Hitchcock admired this film, perhaps because its premise is a slight variation on his *The Lady Vanishes*. It's very enjoyable and suspenseful, with a clever, satisfying conclusion. Sweet, pretty Simmons and handsome Bogarde make an appealing romantic team. Directed by Terence Fisher and Anthony Darnborough. Also with: Honor Blackman.

SOLARIS (RUSSIAN/1972) C/165m.   Called the *2001* of Russian sci-fi cinema, cerebral film by Andrei Tar-kovsky is about a man (Donatis Banionis) who is sent to investigate why astronauts and scientists on a space station that is situated above the planet Solaris have suffered mental breakdowns. As he discovers, the mysterious sentient "ocean" that covers the planet is capable of either reproducing images and people from a person's past *or* causing him to fantasize that he is seeing such ghostly visions. Banionis is repeatedly visited by the image of his dead wife (Nathalya Bondarchuk), who each time comes to him young, vibrant, and full of love, but dies soon after. This meeting forces him to face up to the past events in his life, his imperfect relationship with his wife, and his guilt over her death. Of course, such brutal probing causes damage to his mind. Is the image of his wife a positive force that helps him get "in touch with himself" or is she an instrument by which some alien force can study him? Slowly paced and a bit too enigmatic, but picture has hypnotic power that keeps your eyes glued to the screen. Many visuals are startling, like nothing seen in an American sci-fi film. From the novel by Stanislaw Lem. Also with: Yuri Jarvet, Anatoli Solinitsin.

SOLDIER GIRLS (1981) C/87m.   Fascinating documentary about a platoon of young women who, having believed army recruiters' false promises, undergo rugged basic training at a base in Fort Gordon, Georgia. We see them given merciless, deeply personal hazings by the commanding officers; being subjected to countless orders-for-orders sake; learning how to bite off the heads of chickens; being instructed that if they see a nuclear flash to their left, they should look to their right; and letting their true selves shine through when they're in their cabin without officers around. There's a great deal of humor in the film; most often we laugh when the clumsy or rebellious recruits frustrate the obnoxious officers' attempts to make them into fighting machines. And we feel a sense of triumph because one recruit never loses her smart-alecky grin, which she displays when the sergeants go into foolish tirades about her bad attitude—although Joan Churchill, who co-directed with Nicholas Broomfield, says that eventually this recruit did take the sergeants seriously and fear them. Film ends with a powerful scene that finally shows a sympathetic side of one hard-nosed drill sergeant—he speaks candidly about how the Vietnam War deprived him of his humanity. On one hand, one wonders how he could prepare officers for war when he knows the sad result of being a combat soldier; yet one sees that such a man is ideal for the job of dehumanizing recruits so they'll feel even less than he did when forced to kill. Film should be shown in all high schools before army recruiters start handing out brochures about computer jobs and expenses-paid Hawaiian vacations.

SOLDIER'S STORY, A (1984) C/101m.   Setting is army base in Louisiana in 1944. Black officer Howard E. Rollins, Jr., arrives to investigate the murder of Adolph Caesar, black drill sergeant of an all-black platoon. The white command is reluctant to let a black do any probing, particularly when he'll be questioning white officers and soldiers (perhaps those with links to KKK), but he has backing of U.S. government. His trail takes him away from racist whites to black soldiers who were under Caesar's harsh command. Through flashbacks we learn that Caesar (who'll remind you of a crueler version of Jack Webb, whom he resembles, in *The DI*) had so abused an uneducated black soldier for displaying stereotypical black behavior—thus humiliating his race in the white man's eyes, in Caesar's opinion—that another of Caesar's men turned on him and killed him. Adaptation of Charles Fuller's Pulitzer Prize-winning play doesn't match the reputation of the Negro Ensemble Company's production. It comes across much like an Agatha Christie mystery without the humor or clever twists. And I find it embarrassing to think that a white director, Norman Jewison, although certainly well-intentioned, stood over all these black actors saying things like "Let's try that again, with more feeling" or "I think your character would react a little differently" when their characters are digging deep to reveal thoughts and feelings singular to the black man. In truth, content seems personal—from black to blacks—with themes that others shouldn't be privy to. The Rollins character seems to be a white man's concoction who, in fact, represents white viewers who want to snoop into blacks' psyche. Rollins, who looks like Sidney Poitier, is set up like Poitier's Mr. Tibbs in Jewison's *In the Heat of the Night*, but this character has little of the defiance or drive. The worst aspect is that one joke is repeated too often—people at the base doing double takes because a black man has come to attempt to investigate. Extremely overrated. Also with: Dennis Lipscomb, Art Evans, Denzel Washington, Larry Riley.

SOME LIKE IT HOT (1959) B&W/120m.

One of Hollywood's greatest comedies, directed by Billy Wilder, scripted by Wilder and I. A. L. Diamond, and featuring Marilyn Monroe's most delectable performance. Film begins in Chicago in 1929. Sax player Joe (Tony Curtis) and bass player Jerry (Jack Lemmon) flee Spats Columbo's (George Raft) gang after they witness a mass murder. They dress up as women—Joe becomes Josephine and Jerry becomes Daphne—and they join an all-girl jazz band that goes to Miami. Sugar Kane (Monroe) is singer and ukulele player with the band. She always falls for male sax players, but Joe won't tell her he's *male* even though he's tremendously attracted to her. He realizes that unhappy Sugar could use a female friend, Josephine. He won't take advantage of Sugar when he's in his female pose—but he's willing to do so when he pretends to be a male millionaire (who speaks like Cary Grant). Meanwhile Jerry begins to enjoy the benefits of being female—and he adores the attention paid to "Daphne" by millionaire Osgood (Joe E. Brown). In Wilder's screen world, people are identified by what they wear, carry, or own, but by film's end, characters will be identified by who they are. Interestingly, Jerry and Joe don't become silly movie females when they don women's clothing. They become tough, smart, fun-to-be-with broads who take guff

from no man and are loyal friends to other women. Significantly, they develop a female perspective. What makes the film so interesting is that it subverts sexual stereotyping. Like *Sylvia Scarlett*, its theme is that when a person lives as the other sex, he or she has the opportunity to explore previously latent aspects of the personality. Daphne and Josephine aren't the alter egos of Jerry and Joe: they are *more* (extensions) of the two men. Just as the men improve themselves by allowing their female sides to show, Sugar changes, too, by taking on male characteristics: she becomes aggressive in love, she chases after a man. Farce (which deals with deception and masquerade) is endlessly clever, often hilarious, and—with all its sexual references—daring. Monroe's plumper here than in her other films, but she was never sexier than in her Oscar-winning diaphanous gowns (they all look like negligees)—Wilder's lighting directs our eyes toward her barely concealed breasts—and never more effervescent (although she had a very difficult time making this film). Film has a great last line. Music by Adolph Deutsch; Monroe's songs (all highlights) are "Running Wild," "I Wanna Be Loved By You," and "I'm Through with Love." Also with: Pat O'Brien, Nehemiah Persoff, Joan Shawlee, Billy Gray, George E. Stone, Mike Mazurki.

SOMETHING WICKED THIS WAY COMES

(1983) C/94m. Disney production of classic Ray Bradbury novel (expanded from the short story "Black Ferns") was adapted by the author. It's set in Green Town, Illinois, at the turn of century. It's an idyllic town where everyone knows each other, and everyone seems content with their lots in life. But in reality everyone has deep regrets that happiness in some form—youth, beauty, women to love, a healthy body—has escaped them. The town librarian (Jason Robards), for instance, believes he hasn't the youth or vitality to raise his young son, Will, properly; he also regrets that he missed the one opportunity to be brave in relation to Will—because his own father hadn't taught him to swim, it was up to someone else to save Will from drowning. The despair in town attracts a weird carnival that feeds on unhappiness. The strange, satanic owner, Mr. Dark (Jonathan Pryce), grants townspeople their secret desires, but at terrible prices, including their becoming part of his traveling show. Robards's son and his inseparable best friend witness what's going on and warn Robards. Meanwhile Mr. Dark hunts down the kids. Narrated by Will as an adult (the voice of Arthur Hill) looking back, film captures the young boy's sense of wonder, the depth of his fears, and, most importantly, his need for a rewarding relationship with his father. Picture doesn't really succeed as a horror film—for one thing, some of the images are too gruesome for the type of viewers who'd appreciate the other elements of the film. But, like an Earl Hamner work, it conveys nostalgia for a bygone era, with its small towns, its people, and its innocence. And, more importantly, it is a sweet story in which a father and son finally discover each other. Vidal Peterson and Shawn Carson are the two boys. Also with: Pam Grier, Diane Ladd, James Stacy.

SOMEWHERE IN TIME (1980) C/103m. Schmaltzy fantasy-romance that recalls Mildred Cram's "unfilmable" story "Forever," which bounced around Hollywood for years. Well, it was decided that Richard Matheson's novel *Bid Time Return* was filmable, and he devised the script. Christopher Reeve is modern-day playwright who wills himself back to 1910 to be with beautiful actress Jane Seymour because he senses that somehow they were once lovers. He checks into the Grand Hotel, a luxury hotel on Michigan's Mackinac Island, where she is staying and performing. Their romance blossoms despite interference from her Svengali-like manager, Christopher Plummer. Reeve and Seymour are an undeniably appealing couple, ideal for a great romance, but the filmmakers should have scuttled the dreary plot (as it is presented here, not as in Matheson's prize-winning novel), sent all the other actors home, and just had the two stars make love in every room of the glorious hotel. Stodgy direction by Jeannot Szwarc. Also with: Teresa Wright, Bill Erwin, George Voskovec.

SON OF KONG (1933) B&W/70m. Carl Denham (Robert Armstrong) returns to Skull Island with a new woman (pert Helen Mack), in search of treasure. They discover Kong's 12-foot-tall son, who is much friendlier than his pop and has no lecherous designs on women. Bargain-basement sequel to *King Kong* is a curio devoid of the original's Freudian implications, mythic and dream elements. Kids may like Kong, Jr.'s, comical nature, but fans of the original will be disappointed in most everything but the action finale, in which the sweet ape saves Armstrong and Mack from rising waters. Picture is so rushed that one can't even savor Willis O'Brien's special effects. Most interesting element as far as Kong lore goes is that Carl Denham is very apologetic about what he felt *he* did to Kong in the original. Directed by Ernest B. Schoedsack. Also with: Victor Wong, John Marston, Frank Reicher, Lee Kohlman.

SONG REMAINS THE SAME, THE (1976) C/136m. Deadening documentary of legendary defunct British supergroup Led Zeppelin, the most influential perpetrator of the "heavy metal" sound. Directors Peter Clifton and Joe Massott juxtapose footage from a 1973 concert in Madison Square Garden; ridiculous *Spinal Tap*-like backstage glimpses (incomprehensible chatter; the roadie manager telling off MSG officials for allowing the sale of Zeppelin merchandise in the building; newspaper headlines stating that the group had more than $200,000 stolen from their hotel strongbox); and pretentious fantasy sequences featuring each member of the group. Ex-Yardbird Jimmy Page has a couple of inspired guitar breaks and John Bonham has a nifty drum solo, during which he puts down his sticks and slaps his cymbals with his hands (meanwhile we see shots of him with his wife and children at home and feel sad knowing that he'd die of asphyxiation in 1980 while on a drunken binge). I've always hated Robert Plant's singing, as Zeppelin's lead singer and now during his solo career, so I find it nearly impossible to withstand his singing number after number in this film; and I'm not crazy about watching him strut around (Roger Daltrey style) with bare belly and chest. Bassist John Paul Jones stands in the background and is inoffensive. Group does many of its big hits, including "Whole Lotta Love" and its signature tune, "Stairway to Heaven." Slow numbers never end, fast songs all sound the same; but fans in audience are mesmerized. A midnight cult hit because teenagers have joined Led Zeppelin legions.

SONS OF THE DESERT (1933) B&W/69m. The definitive Laurel and Hardy film, borrows many ideas from their silent short *Their Purple Moment*. The boys tell their wives they're going to Hawaii to cure Ollie's bad cold. But they actually sneak off to Chicago for a convention of the Sons of the Desert. They get into all kinds of trouble and must deal with obnoxious conventioneer Charlie Chase, Ollie's brother-in-law. Of course, the wives find out that their husbands are in Chicago. Film is hilarious from start to finish; it perfectly illustrates how Laurel and Hardy typically relate to each other and to their wives in their movies. This is the inspiration for the famous *Honeymooners* episode in which Ralph and Norton sneak off to a Raccoons convention. Title is used as the name of L&H's international fan club. Directed by William A. Seiter. Also with: Mae Busch, Dorothy Christy, Lucien Littlefield.

SOPHIE'S CHOICE (1982) C/157m. Alan J. Pakula directed and wrote this adaptation of William Styron's powerful novel. Meryl Streep won an Oscar as Polish-Catholic concentration-camp survivor Sophie, who suffers tremendous guilt for surviving when all her loved ones died. She lives in Brooklyn with her Jewish lover, Nathan (Kevin Kline), who is losing a battle with insanity. When calm, Nathan is a charming man who provides both the intellectual stimulation and the compassion Sophie needs to keep her mind off her tragic past and soothe her open wounds. But I suspect she needs him more for his frightful insane moments when he humiliates and punishes her in the manner she thinks she deserves for having survived the Holocaust. Into their troubled lives comes a new neighbor, our narrator, Stingo (Peter MacNicol), a young Protestant from the South, who is working on his first novel. While Stingo is anxious to enter manhood by having his first sexual experience, he undergoes another rite of passage by learning about human suffering from Sophie and Nathan. He can *feel* the tragedy he writes about. But one wonders if he can distinguish between falsehoods and truths in Sophie's stories about her past in Poland. He catches her in a couple of early lies—she claimed her father was a decent, anti-Nazi professor when in fact the opposite was true—but it's likely he believes her later, revised recollections, simply because these Pakula shows in flashbacks while he didn't make her earlier lies visual. But are these flashbacks accurate or only what she makes up for Stingo? Could it be that she had no daughter and that she chose to save *herself* rather than her son? If he was taken away to be killed (she says he was taken to the children's camp, not directly to the gas chambers), this would explain why she didn't remain in Europe to search for him or get some confirmation of his death. (It's doubtful that Styron or Pakula intended anyone to make this interpretation, but the structure of the film and portrayal of Sophia make it a possibility.) Picture has many powerful scenes, particularly those in the concentration camp. Stingo's narration sounds like it was written by Jean Shepherd or Earl Hamner, Jr., but MacNicol's timid, nervous portrayal complements the more demonstrative performances of his co-stars. Streep gives a great characterization, but it's difficult to forget she's acting and that her Polish accent is not real because Sophie is constantly struggling with the English language, stumbling over every other word. After each sentence I find myself saying, "Streep was convincing there" or "Streep's beginning to sound like Martina Navratilova." Beautifully photographed by Nestor Almendros. Also with: Rita Karin, Stephen D. Newman, Josh Mostel, Josef Sommer (narrator).

SORCERERS, THE (BRITISH/1967) C/87m.

Highly unusual horror film was the late writer-director Michael Reeves's oddest film and was just as bleak and fascinating as his other works. The most pessimistic of filmmakers, Reeves advanced his typically depressing theme that people are inherently monstrous and too weak to control their worst impulses. Once again he presented an evil world in which "good" is fighting a losing battle with "evil" and "good" people give in to (or are possessed by) evil impulses. Unlike his *The She-Beast, Castle of the Living Dead,* which he co-directed, and his classic *The Conqueror Worm,* this film is set in contemporary, mod London, which is ruled by the young, who are on a never-ending quest for excitement. But a kindly, elderly couple (Boris Karloff, Catherine Lacey) are missing this excitement. Karloff, a scientist, invents a device that will allow them to stay in their modest apartment and not only to mentally control a third *young* person as he wanders through London but also to vicariously live his experiences. Their guinea pig is Michael Roscoe (Reeves's regular star Ian Ogilvy plays the director's alter ego). He's a depressed young man who runs an antique store (this signifies that his sad obsession for the old and dull is as strong as the elderly couple's obsession for youth and excitement). They force Roscoe to do increasingly dangerous acts so they can feel the excitement. As he becomes an instrument of evil, Lacey becomes more and more diabolical and greedy—eventually she forces their subject to commit brutal murder so she can enjoy the sensation. Karloff realizes that his once-sweet wife has an insatiable lust for evil. He decides to stop the "witch" before she goes too far. Low budget hurts but film has excitement, strong black humor, and strong and interesting directorial touches. Should be seen—but it's not for the squeamish, or for those out for a happy time. Also with: Susan George, Elizabeth Ercy.

SORROW AND THE PITY, THE (FRENCH-SWISS-WEST GERMAN/1970) B&W/260m. Powerful,

eye-opening documentary by Marcel Ophuls about how the citizens of the French city of Clermont-Ferrand reacted during WWII, when under loose Vichy control, and later, when occupied by German soldiers. Interviews are conducted with people who lived through the Occupation (including Germans); their recollections are juxtaposed with archival footage that in many cases contradicts what they say. Ophuls's theme is that many French people welcomed the new, antisemitic order, that France wasn't like other occupied countries because, under Marshal Pétain, it collaborated with the Germans, vigorously supporting, even refining, Nazi policies. Film is a condemnation of collaborators; but it also questions French character—when the sanctimonious French citizenry gather around after the war to watch women who slept with Germans have their heads shaved, they are like the mobs at the guillotines during the Reign of Terror. For film fans, it's disturbing seeing how French movies became racist-propaganda pieces. And you'll see too much of Maurice Chevalier, as bubbly as ever, singing for the wrong side. Landmark film is fascinating, and it's depressing—just the type of film Woody Allen's Alvy Singer character would see repeatedly in *Annie Hall*. Produced by André Harris and Alain de Sedouy.

SOUND OF MUSIC, THE (1965) C/145m–174m.

One of the most popular films of all time—which is what it was calculated to be. You'll know you're being manipulated at every turn, that you're expected to feel a lump in your throat or laugh or cry on cue (when the music swells, when a child smiles, when a stern adult is kind), that you're expected to be as undiscriminating as the audience who sits through the show "Up with People!" But even if you become sick on the sugar, you'll find it hard not to appreciate the talents of Julie Andrews, whose exuberance is infectious, whose voice is superb (which we tend to forget today when musicals aren't being made), who is as good as Streisand at *acting* while singing a song. It's easy to see why she was the top female draw of the time. In the role that reinforced her goody-goody virgin image, Andrews is a nun-in-training in Austria who becomes a *Snow White* governess to *seven* incorrigible, love-starved children. If you thought Miss Frances of *Ding Dong School* was nice to children, then you'll adore Andrews. She teaches these kids to play, sing, and have good manners (they don't protest) and their strict widower father, Christopher Plummer, to feel love again—for the children and for her. They become one happy family—the Trapp Family Singers—just in time for the serious part of the picture, when they must escape the Nazis by fleeing over the border. The familiar Rodgers and Hammerstein songs are cheery and childish and catchy—you'll feel like a fool humming them for the rest of the day. Except when nun Peggy Wood sings "Climb Every Mountain" to Andrews, they are skillfully blended into the plot. Film won Oscars for Best Picture, Best Director (Robert Wise), Best Editing (William Reynolds), Best Scoring Adaptation (Irwin Kostal), and Best Sound. From the stage musical by Howard Lindsay and Russel Crouse;

Ernest Lehman wrote the shrewd script. Also with: Eleanor Parker, Richard Haydn, Anna Lee, Angela Cartwright.

SOUTHERN COMFORT (1981) C/106m.
An urban-based National Guard unit becomes hopelessly lost during maneuvers in a Louisiana swamp. Soon one of them loses his cool and fires on some Cajun backwoodsmen, who retaliate by picking them off one by one from the cover of the swamps. As their situation becomes increasingly desperate, discipline breaks down and some of the men go berserk from fear. This extremely intense, violent, skillfully made Walter Hill film can be seen as a metaphor for American involvement in Vietnam; we see the parallels between these initially arrogant guardsmen and those American soldiers who trespassed through Vietnamese jungles and either patronized or acted with condescension toward the illiterate peasants, and, in many cases, got blown away. The finale, in which Keith Carradine (in one of his best roles) and Powers Boothe (a powerful actor) nervously party with seemingly friendly Cajun villagers while looking over their shoulders for the vengeful backwoodsmen, is truly nerve-racking. Good score by Ry Cooder. Also with: Fred Ward, Franklyn Seales, T. K. Carter, Lewis Smith, Peter Coyote, Les Lannom.

SOUTHERNER, THE (1945) B&W/91m.
Simple, poetic film by Jean Renoir, chronicling a year in the lives of a poor family trying to grow cotton on a tenant farm in Texas. The hardships are predictable—the young boy gets sick, there are problems with a mean-hearted neighbor, a flood wipes out the cotton crop—and Renoir's treatment of his characters is a bit too precious at times. But it's a well-intentioned, tender picture in which Renoir once again expresses the need for family and neighbors to stick together through crisis; also he includes a scene that illustrates the necessity for a worker-farmer alliance. Lovely visuals; yet while Renoir obviously feels great respect for the common worker, he doesn't include enough shots of work being done. Zachary Scott, a Texan, gives his farmer quiet dignity (he is more resilient than heroic—and that's the way Renoir wants it). Betty Field was probably miscast as his wife, but her sparkling eyes alone give the picture a needed dose of kindness. The brief porch scene in which husband kisses wife strongly on the mouth is a highlight, and typical Renoir. William Faulkner (uncredited) helped Renoir adapt George Sessions Perry's *Hold Autumn in Your Hand*. Also with: Beulah Bondi (overdoing it as cantankerous Grandma), J. Carrol Naish (the neighbor), Charles Kemper, Percy Kilbride, Blanche Yurka, Norman Lloyd.

SPARTACUS (1960) C/184m–196m.
Director Stanley Kubrick was disappointed in this epic about the legendary hero (Kirk Douglas) who led a slave revolt against Rome in 71 B.C. He felt that he didn't have the freedom to develop the story as he wanted. But it has come to be regarded as the best of the historical epics. It contains a spirited, emotionally charged performance by Douglas (who also produced), a superlative supporting cast headed by Jean Simmons as the slave girl Varinia (Spartacus's lover) and Laurence Olivier as the Roman Crassus (Spartacus's mortal enemy), an *outstanding* battle sequence, a sense of time and place, and an emphasis on sex. This is one of the few epics in which we're not bored when characters are talking—the palace-baths chats between Olivier, John Gavin (as Julius Caesar), Charles Laughton, and the other shrewd Romans are amusing not only because they reveal political motives for wanting Spartacus and his memory destroyed but also because there are strong intimations of homosexuality (the reason some scenes were snipped). Still, the film's major distinction is that its script, adapted from Howard Fast's novel by Dalton Trumbo, has a genuine revolutionary spirit, reflected in Douglas's speeches to his followers; Trumbo also establishes, through Crassus, the nature of a fascist. Highlights include: Douglas being forced by his Roman captors to fight to the death with fellow slave Woody Strode; Laughton and slave dealer Peter Ustinov having a gluttonous meal together; Simmons's nude swim; the fireballs being shot at the beginning of the great battle; and the fictional final scene in which the Romans try to determine which of the captured rebels is Spartacus (they all claim to be). Russell Metty did the cinematography; Alex North composed the score. Also with: Tony Curtis (the slave who is the object of Olivier's affections), Herbert Lom, John Ireland, John Dall, John Hoyt, Charles McGraw.

SPETTERS (DUTCH/1980) C/115m.
Cult film by Paul Uerhoeven is about three young male friends (Hans van Tongeren, Toon Agterberg, Marten Spanger) from a working-class neighborhood as they go through crises with girls, fathers, ambitions, self-identities, and their own masculinity. Renee Soutendijk is the beautiful, flirtatious short-order cook with driving ambitions for a better life who arrives in town with her homosexual brother/work partner and makes a play for all three, one at a time, when she thinks they can provide her with the money and security she desires. There are many admirable things in this movie: the authentic atmosphere and working-class people; the uncensored treatment of sex; the one comedy scene in which two young couples simultaneously pretend they're having successful sex (they each do a lot of heavy breathing) so the other couple won't think less of them; Soutendijk's fascinating, sympathetic "bad" girl. But so much seems to be missing—for instance, we see the friends sharing their mutual passion, motocross racing, but we never really see the extent of their relationships (they don't seem to need each other). Film is like a drastically shortened adaptation of a long book, in that no storyline seems complete—because it only skims the surface of the individual stories, the characters all come across as hackneyed or unrealistic, despite the fine acting. The most controversial scene has one of the boys being gang-raped by some homosexuals—it's offensive that he would enjoy what's happening to him and at this point admit he's a homosexual (and become the lover of the leader, Soutendijk's brother). Also with: Marianne

Boyer, Rutger Hauer (as the conceited motocross champion whom the three friends idolize), Jeroen Krabbé.

SPIES/SPIONE (GERMAN/1928) B&W/98m.
One of Fritz Lang's less heralded German silents, it is nevertheless great fun. Also it's likely Alfred Hitchcock was influenced by the film's exciting train sequence and the finale in which the villain (who is dressed as a clown) is trapped on a stage. Working from a screenplay by his then wife, Thea von Harbou (who wrote the novel, too), Lang presents a postwar world where *everyone* seems to be either a criminal or a spy. Our hero (Willy Fritsch) is an agent who's sent to track down master criminal Haighi (Rudolf Klein-Rogge), who through his network of spies is stealing secret documents so he can control the world. He falls in love with a beautiful woman (Gerda Maurus), but is upset to learn that she is working for Haighi. But she'll come through in the clutch. Film is a mite confusing and over-plotted, but, considering its diabolical supervillain, his assorted crimes, the pulp-fiction plotline (with sex and action), and the numerous episodes that end with cliffhangers, it would have made the *perfect* serial. Also with: Lupu Pick, Fritz Rasp, Lien Deyers.

SPIRAL STAIRCASE, THE (1946) B&W/83m.
Classic gothic thriller about an insane murderer who stalks women with physical infirmities in a small town. Next on his list is young mute (Dorothy McGuire) who works as a servant at a large country estate—which, conveniently, is also where he resides. On a dark, stormy night the murderer arranges for everyone else who works or lives in the house to be out of the way so he can go after his prey. It's not hard to figure out the mystery, but Robert Siodmak's atmospheric direction keeps viewers anxious. There are some particularly eerie close-ups of the murderer's eye before he attacks his victims. Adapted from the novel *Some Must Watch*, by Ethel Lina White, this was also the inspiration for the classic *Alfred Hitchcock Presents* episode "The Unlocked Window." Remade in 1975. The fine cast includes: George Brent, Kent Smith, Ethel Barrymore, Rhonda Fleming, Gordon Oliver, Elsa Lanchester, Sara Allgood, Rhys Williams.

SPIRIT OF THE BEEHIVE, THE (SPANISH/1973) C/95m.
Haunting fable is set in a sleepy Castilian village after the Spanish Civil War. The lifeless atmosphere conveys the sense of ennui present in Spain after the victory of Franco. Republican Fernando Fernán Gómez occupies his time tending bees while his wife, Teresa Gimpera, writes letters to a lost (or imaginary) loved one (a man or child). They rarely speak and give little parental attention to their children, eight-year-old Ana Torrent and the slightly older Isabel Telleria. Spending their time in their large, loveless house or the empty countryside, the girls experience tremendous loneliness. When they see a Frankenstein film, Torrent is affected deeply by the scene in which the monster befriends a little girl. Telleria convinces her that the mon-ster's spirit is wandering through the countryside. It makes sense that this lonely, imaginative girl, who has a worrisome fascination with death, would think the spirit of the monster (made from the dead) would comfort her; it is a monster that could make her world less terrifying and traumatic. But she is chasing death. Picture could be a good companion piece to Val Lewton's *Curse of the Cat People*. Scene in which Torrent comes upon Telleria, who is pretending to be dead, is unforgettable. Torrent gives a poignant performance in a difficult role. Impressively directed by Victor Erice and photographed by Luis Cuadrado.

SPIRITS OF THE DEAD (FRENCH-ITALIAN/1969) C/117m.
A disappointing horror anthology for which three Poe tales were adapted by internationally known directors and which starred actors who usually stayed away from the genre. All three deal with decadent, mean-spirited characters who meet tragic ends befitting the way that they lived. Roger Vadim directed the ridiculously erotic "Metzenger" episode, more notable for Jane Fonda's depraved libertine's revealing costumes than her orgies or acts of cruelty. (This episode must give TV censors fits.) Louis Malle directed "William Wilson," about a sadist (Alain Delon) who keeps seeing his moral counterpart, a lookalike named William Wilson. It's poorly dubbed, unnecessarily vicious, and, surprisingly, contains no surprises. Brigitte Bardot has a small part as a cigar-smoking brunette who loses to the cheating Wilson at cards and must submit to his beating. The most praised episode is Federico Fellini's "Never Bet the Devil Your Head," starring Terence Stamp as a booze-soaked, self-loathing American actor who has come to Italy to make a moralistic western about redemption. He encounters Fellini's usual array of grotesque movie-and press-types and the devil—a little blonde girl who keeps turning up in creepy settings. Like the other two episodes, Fellini's is too long and self-consciously arty. At least its violent ending, though not unexpected, is carried out in an original manner that provides the picture's one and only shock. Also with: Peter Fonda.

SPLENDOR IN THE GRASS (1961) C/124m.
William Inge scripted and Elia Kazan directed what is still the quintessential film about young love—*first* love, true love, eternal love—which is wonderful but terribly confusing while it lasts, mercilessly cruel when it ends. This is also the first film that dared emphasize that teenagers are ruled by their sexual drives and that, because of their immaturity and inability to get practical information and advice from their parents, doctors, ministers, etc., they are unable to cope with their feelings. Story is set in 1920s in Kansas and centers on high-school couple Warren Beatty (his debut) and Natalie Wood, who love each other madly but try desperately to hold off having sex until they are married. Unfortunately, Beatty's rich, domineering father (Pat Hingle) insists that his son go off to Princeton first (although Beatty would rather just marry Wood and be a dirt farmer)—hoping Beatty will forget about the girl from the other, poorer side

of town. Beatty finds he is unable to control his sexual urges, but Wood protects her virginity, causing them to separate and Beatty to take up with the class tramp. Wood is heartbroken—and angry because, just like Beatty's father, her own parents think her relationship with Beatty was merely puppy love and not to be taken seriously—and offers herself to Beatty, only to have him reject her because she is too *good* to have pre-marital sex. Wood has a breakdown and is sent to a mental hospital—Beatty goes off to college. Their love endures. Film still has impact. Kazan has tremendous sympathy for lovers and beautifully conveys their painful sexual frustration and confusion. Just by showing Wood walk through empty school corridors (which had been full when she walked them before with Beatty) he clearly reveals the emptiness she feels inside. Film perfectly captures feelings of most who have met former lovers years later and have been disappointed (as Wood is) by person whom you once were obsessed with. Throughout film, Kazan's direction of actors is superlative. Beatty is very controlled and sympathetic in his screen debut; but film belongs to Wood, who has never been more ravishing, sexy, energetic, or revealing of her own personality. She obviously had a fix on her character—she later said she was going through feelings similar to those of the girl she played. Not only should this film have ended criticism of her acting, but Wood deserved an Oscar for her performance. Excellent, extremely moving film has devoted following. Teenagers will love it. Also with: Barbara Loden, Audrey Christie, Sean Gamson, Zohra Lampert, Phyllis Diller, Martine Bartlett, Gary Lockwood.

SPY WHO LOVED ME, THE (BRITISH-AMERICAN/1977) C/125m.
Exceptional James Bond thriller where, for once, the big budget was not wasted. Interestingly, while the sets and gimmicks were the most spectacular to date, Bond and the other characters are toned down (there is a minimum of slapstick humor) so that they are more realistic than in other Roger Moore films. Moore gives his best performance in the series. In a plot that recalls the Sean Connery Bond film *From Russia with Love* (there's even a similar fight on a train), Bond and a Russian agent, Major Anya Amasova (the alluringly garbed Barbara Bach), join forces to find out who has been snatching nuclear subs from the East and West. Anya wants to kill Bond because her lover was killed when trying to do in 007, but instead she falls for him. They are an appealing couple, equal in every way. Film is a real treat—a well-acted, smartly cast, sexy, visually impressive, lavishly produced, powerfully directed (by Lewis Gilbert) mix of a spy romance and a war-mission film. It opens with the most spectacular stunt in the entire series. Carly Simon had a hit with "Nobody Does It Better" by Marvin Hamlisch. Christopher Wood and Richard Maibaum adapted Ian Fleming's novel. Claude Renoir did the excellent photography; Lamor Boren handled the underwater photography. Richard Kiel's seven-foot-tall, metal-toothed henchman "Jaws" would appear in the next Bond film, *Moonraker*. Also with: Curt Jurgens (as villain Karl Stromberg, who wants to destroy the world and rule an underwater kingdom), Caroline Munro, Walter Gotell, Bernard Lee, Lois Maxwell, Desmond Llewellyn.

SQUIRM (1976) C/92m.
As in Sq*worm*. Effective little horror film is set in Georgia, where an electrical charge from a fallen power line causes sandworms to go on a murderous rampage through a small town. Visiting New Yorker Don Scardino (*He Knows You're Alone*) and his southern belle Patricia Pearcy try to survive onslaught. Director Jeff Lieberman balances wit and shocks: one guy will discover a worm in his chocolate egg cream; another will find a worm in his cheek (one of the film's more repulsive images). We are kept squirming. There are fun characters, clever directorial touches; but I wish there were a scene in which a fisherman tries to bait his hook with a live (angry) worm. Also with: R. A. Dow, Jean Sullivan, Peter MacLean, Fran Higgins.

STAGE DOOR (1937) B&W/92m.
One of the best films of the thirties, featuring a once-in-a-lifetime group of actresses, headed by Katharine Hepburn and Ginger Rogers and including Lucille Ball, Ann Miller, Eve Arden, Gail Patrick, and Andrea Leeds. Hepburn moves into the Footlights Club, where the others live and wait for the big break that will lead to a successful stage career. The rich, refined Hepburn and her straight-from-the-hip roommate, Rogers, don't get along and they exchange some of the snappiest insult-laden dialogue found in thirties movies. Hepburn actually likes Rogers and tries to protect her from lecherous producer Adolphe Menjou. But Rogers suspects Hepburn stole Menjou from her so she could get a part in his new play—which was the reason Rogers stole Menjou from Patrick. Hepburn gets the lead in Menjou's play, not because she sleeps with him—she's not interested—but because her father (unbeknownst to her) has financed the production, believing her failure will get acting out of her system. The other women resent Hepburn taking the role—she doesn't know that suicidal young Leeds had coveted the part and considered it her last chance to succeed. In the last 15 minutes the comedy becomes a tearjerker. Scenes between the vivacious Hepburn and the sexy Rogers are priceless; but what keeps the film from dating is the camaraderie exhibited by all the would-be actresses. Their bond—in a film in which no one is serious about a man—is based on their common need to cover up their fear that they'll never get a break. The Edna Ferber–George S. Kaufman play and the much altered Morrie Ryskind–Anthony Veiller film adaptation are tributes to all those women who starve and suffer, but don't quit, while waiting for producers like Menjou to let them show their talents. Direction by Gregory La Cava is excellent. Also with: Constance Collier, Samuel S. Hinds, Franklin Pangborn, Grady Sutton, Jack Carson, Katherine Alexander, Mary Forbes.

STAGECOACH (1939) B&W/99m.
John Ford's seminal western is the type of film you'll take for granted.

Between viewings, one forgets what a magnificent film this is. Ford kept it simple—it is a simple morality play—but directed with great feeling for the West, the time, and for his characters. And it's obvious that the actors really cared about the people they played. We may recall the action scenes—a lengthy Indian attack on the stage, John Wayne as the Ringo Kid shooting it out with three bad guys—but when watching the film, one sees that Ford is more interested in how characters respond to danger—for instance, are they worrying about themselves or others when lives are at stake?—than in the action itself. In fact, Ford often cuts away from the Indians to show the characters inside the stage, and when Wayne starts firing away at the three men, Ford cuts away to Claire Trevor, the woman who loves Wayne, who hears the shots in another part of town. Dudley Nichols's script was adapted from Ernest Haycox's story "Stage to Lordsburg"—which was based on Guy de Maupassant's "Boule de Suif" (as was Val Lewton's neglected *Mademoiselle Fifi*). Several people travel by stage to Lordsburg, passing through Indian territory. Lordsburg/civilization represents "respectability," and the wilderness (embodied by the Indians) represents man's primitive, "savage" instincts. The coach serves as an arena for a clash between those who represent society—the banker (Berton Churchill), doctor (Thomas Mitchell), pregnant married woman (Louise Platt), and whiskey salesman (Donald Meek)—and those whom society considers outsiders—gunman-outlaw-escaped-prisoner Wayne, prostitute Trevor, and gambler John Carradine. Mitchell, because he's an alcoholic (and thus flawed), Platt, because she feels a female bond with Trevor, and Meek, because he's a stranger to these parts, are won over by Wayne's bravery, Trevor's good heart, and Carradine's chivalry. Only Churchill keeps his superior attitude—and Ford and Nichols later show up his hypocrisy. Driver Andy Devine and sheriff George Bancroft, who rides shotgun, sit *outside* on the ride through the wilderness—they are neutral figures who are part of civilization but have open minds toward those who don't fit in. In future Ford westerns—*Three Godfathers* is the major exception—those who represent the wilder, primitive West are shut out of civilization; in this film, civilization is not worthy of Wayne and Trevor, who leave town as Bancroft affirms that they were "saved from the blessings of civilization." Marvelously cast film has many standout performances. In the role that made him a star (what an entrance Ford gives him!) the handsome, charismatic Wayne gives an unaffected, honest, masculine yet gentle portrayal. Trevor has never been better. A great moment has Wayne, eyes sparkling, looking at Trevor with admiration as she holds Platt's new baby. Picture, which includes Ford's first footage of Monument Valley, has a timeless feel and looks like it was shot in the twenties, yet it has sound. Cinematography by Bert Glennon is magnificent. Mitchell won a Best Supporting Actor Oscar. Film won Oscar for its score, which was adapted from American folk songs. Also with: Tim Holt, Tom Tyler, Francis Ford, Yakima Canutt (who was stuntman and did second-unit work), Jack Pennick, Chief White Horse.

STALAG 17 (1953) B&W/120m. William Holden gives a hard-edged performance as a cynical, abrasive sergeant in a German POW camp. His aloofness and off-putting personality make the other men in the barracks suspect him of letting the Germans in on their subversive activities—they think he is the reason that two men were mowed down while trying to escape. They brutally beat and ostracize him. Holden tries to find out who the real spy is: a German who is passing himself off as being American. Picture stumbles along at the beginning, as we try to adjust to the rowdy comedy that plays a major part in the film (these men need laughter in their lives), but it really gets exciting once we viewers are let in on the spy's identity. The "Johnny Comes Marching Home" sequence is quite powerful. We can't wait till Holden traps the culprit. Directed by Billy Wilder. Film was the basis for TV's *Hogan's Heroes*. From the Broadway play by Donald Bevan and Edmund Trzcinski. Also with: Otto Preminger (as the smart, ruthless Kommandant), Don Taylor, Peter Graves, Robert Strauss, Harvey Lembeck, Neville Brand, Richard Erdman, Sig Rumann.

STAR IS BORN, A (1937) C/111m. Although it's in wide circulation today, chances are you didn't see this William Wellman classic until long after George Cukor's 1954 version. It's the rare case when you can see if the original stands up to the remake. And it does. Janet Gaynor is Esther Blodgett, a young woman who leaves her small hometown to become a Hollywood actress. She has no luck at all and, broke, takes a job waitressing at a Hollywood party. There she meets Norman Maine (Fredric March), an alcoholic star whose better days are behind him. Maine gets her a screen test and she's signed to a contract by the studio head (Adolphe Menjou), who changes her name to Vicki Lester. Vicki and Maine get married. But all isn't well: Vicki's star is on the rise, but Maine becomes a self-pitying alcoholic when he is declared box-office poison. In fact March was in his prime while Gaynor was two years away from retirement. This is the film that appropriately capped Gaynor's brief but impressive career—because Gaynor's playing her, we can believe the sweetness, selflessness, and inner strength that characterize Esther/Vicki. Her delivery of the final line—"This is Mrs. Norman Maine!"—was enough to justify her getting the role. March is surprisingly and effectively subdued in a role in which other actors (i.e., John Barrymore) might have chewed up the scenery. Film has flavorful Hollywood background. Script was by Dorothy Parker, Alan Campbell, and Robert Carson. Wellman and Carson won an Oscar for Best Original Story. But it was surely influenced by 1932's *What Price Hollywood?* as well as by several true Hollywood stories. Also with: Lionel Stander (as a vicious publicist), May Robson (as Esther's indomitable grandmother), Andy Devine, Franklin Pangborn.

STAR IS BORN, A (1954) C/135m–154m–181m. George Cukor's gracefully directed epic remake of the 1937 classic has been restored (by Ron Haver) to its full length; as a result we can rediscover one of the fifties' finest films. In the role that should have won her an Oscar (she was upset by Grace Kelly), Judy Garland is small-time band singer Esther Blodgett. James Mason is fading actor Norman Maine who sees her sing and detects *greatness*. He helps her break into motion pictures and "Vicki Lester" becomes a star (ironic, since Garland was long past her own peak). They get married. His failure to find work and his consequent alcoholism cause them much grief. Garland and Mason give wonderful, deeply affecting performances. What makes this film so special and so timely is how mutually supportive Vicki and Norman are: their initial excitement about and respect for each other never fades away; he gives her the confidence and encouragement ("Don't ever forget how good you are") she needs to give up her unfulfilling singing job and strive for the big time; he never feels spiteful about her success, even when feeling self-pity; she recognizes that her success is due to him ("You gave me a look at myself I've never had before"), and won't desert him when everyone else has ("I'm just giving back the gifts he gave me"); she says that none of her success has meaning without him; she identifies with him even after death ("This is Mrs. Norman Maine"). Moss Hart wrote the cynical yet compassionate you-and-me-against-the-world (Hollywood) script. Film is very sentimental, but Cukor gives Maine's suicide scene a touch of elegance. CinemaScope picture has impressive color and lighting (Sam Levitt was cinematographer) and art direction (by Malcolm Bert). Music was by Harold Arlen, Ira Gershwin, and Leonard Gershwin; highlights include Garland's "The Man That Got Away" and the super, lengthy (now restored) "Born in a Trunk" production number. Also with: Jack Carson, Charles Bickford, Tommy Noonan, Lucy Marlow, Amanda Blake, James Brown, Dub Taylor, Mae Marsh, Frank Ferguson, Grady Sutton, Pat O'Malley, Percy Helton, Henry Kulky.

STAR TREK—THE MOTION PICTURE (1979) C/132m.
The first of the films (which come out every two years) that are derived from the cult television series. Kirk (William Shatner), Spock (Leonard Nimoy), Dr. McCoy (DeForest Kelley), Scotty (James Doohan), Sulu (George Takei), Chekov (Walter Koenig), Uhura (Nichelle Nichols) are reunited on the *Enterprise* when the galaxy is threatened by a massive force called "V'ger." Trekkies were extremely disappointed in this $40 million epic. While I think it has serious faults—the special effects seem to be from another film, there are tedious stretches, the ending is incomprehensible—I personally think that it's better than the TV series because it hasn't the phony moralism that characterized every episode; there is the sense that these characters are traveling through *space* (instead of being studio-bound) and that they understand the wonder of such an endeavor; and for once these crew members don't come across as policemen on their beat, but as pioneers and defenders of our world. Acting and dialogue are as dull as they are in

the series. Directed by Robert Wise, who came in at the last moment. Special effects were handled by Douglas Trumbull and John Dykstra, who came in after the original F/X firm flubbed its assignment. Jerry Goldsmith wrote the score. Gene Roddenberry produced. Also with: Persis Khambatta (as the bald Delton android), Stephen Collins, Majel Barrett.

STAR TREK II—THE WRATH OF KHAN (1982) C/112m.
Film did what was intended: it captured the flavor of the popular television series. In fact, it serves as the sequel to a television episode titled "Space Seed," in which Kirk (William Shatner) banished the evil Khan (Ricardo Montalban) and his family to a deserted planet. In the film Khan escapes and vows revenge on Kirk for the death of his wife. That he can obtain the proper revenge is made possible by the appearance of Kirk's "family"—his former lover, Dr. Carol Marcus (Bibi Besch), and their son, David (Merritt Buttrick). Film uses birth and death motifs throughout and centers on a Genesis Device (which Khan steals) that has the power to convert barren planets into green Edens or to destroy fertile planets (like earth). For others to live, some—like Leonard Nimoy's Spock—are willing to sacrifice their own lives. Picture has an interesting premise, more humor than the series, imaginative and impressive special effects (by George Lucas's Industrial Light and Magic), and a strong, mad performance by Montalban. It also lets Kirk open up (as in a conversation with his son) more than he has in the past. Smartly directed by Nicholas Meyer, who learned from the first film that Trekkies don't believe that bigger is better. Also with: DeForest Kelley, James Doohan, Walter Koenig, George Takei, Nichelle Nichols, Paul Winfield, Kirstie Alley (appealing as the new Vulcan science officer on the *Enterprise*), Judson Scott, Ike Eisenmann.

STAR TREK III—THE SEARCH FOR SPOCK (1984) C/105m.
Commander Kirk (William Shatner) is without his logical side, now that Spock (Leonard Nimoy) is dead. Kirk's emotional side—personified by McCoy (DeForest Kelley), who feels guilt over Spock's death and senses Spock has partly inhabited him—now has free rein. So Kirk takes drastic action to try to bring his dear friend back to life, in one form or another. With the help of his crew, he disobeys his superiors and steals away with the *Enterprise*, heading for the planet Genesis, where Spock's body is. Klingons (who reveal here personality traits that were previously hidden) and the self-destructing planet make it appear that all will die. Much better than the two earlier *Star Trek* movies, this is really a lovely science-fiction fantasy. It illustrates the excitement of space travel and adventures, and utilizes a great premise—the Genesis effect is a convincing way to bring back Spock. It contemplates man's place in the universe and, at last, makes the *Star Trek* characters figure out and articulate how they feel about each other. I was awfully tired of the characters' having sup-

pressed affection for one another for several TV seasons and two movies. Here they finally open up, touch each other, hug (there's even a kiss), cry, forget their *Enterprise* hierarchy and act as a team. They aren't soldiers, but human beings. The reason for the emphasis on feelings rather than special effects? I'd guess it's because Leonard Nimoy served as director. He also was fed up with the coldness that dominated the relationships of the characters in the past. Even McCoy now admits he likes Spock. It's about time. Also with: James Doohan, George Takei, Walter Koenig, Nichelle Nichols, Christopher Lloyd, Robin Curtis, Merritt Butrick, Mark Lenard, Judith Anderson, James B. Sikking, John Larroquette, Robert Hooks.

STAR WARS (1977) C/121m. Arguably the most influential film ever made, although one can legitimately question whether its profound effect on future movie product, in Hollywood and worldwide, has been positive. Who hasn't overdosed on special effects, toys, and intergalactic wars? The brainchild of writer-director George Lucas, it borrows from *Flash Gordon* and *Buck Rogers* serials—it begins in mid-story, as episode 4 of a 9-part story—Marvel Comics (superheroes, hardware), pulp fiction, *The Wizard of Oz*, *The Searchers*, *The Hidden Fortress*, Sergei Eisenstein, Leni Riefenstahl, "B" sci-fi movies of the '50s, and thousands of other sources. It's set a long, long time ago, in a galaxy far, far away. But the characters, and the dialogue, are modern. The main character is Luke Skywalker (Mark Hamill), who is about 18 and a "Boy Scout." Over the course of the *Star Wars* trilogy, we will watch Luke realize his great destiny and find his identity. In this episode he joins the rebellion against the Empire, whose forces are being directed by evil Darth Vader (David Prowse wears a black outfit and metallic mask; James Earl Jones provides the voice). He is taken under the wing of wise and noble Jedi warrior Ben "Obi-Wan" Kenobi (Alec Guinness), who teaches him to use a mystical "force" (the art of Zen combat). Accompanied by Luke's robots, the constantly talking, civil-tongued C-3PO (Anthony Daniels) and the tiny, round, blipping and bleeping R2-D2 (Kenny Baker), they race across the galaxy to help rescue the imperiled Princess Leia (Carrie Fisher) from Darth Vader. They pay mercenary pilot Han Solo (Harrison Ford) and his lionlike companion Chewbacca (Peter Mayhew) to help them elude Empire space fighters. Solo finds himself drawn into the rebellion, partly because of his admiration for the brave young Luke. When Luke decides to destroy the enormous Death Star, Solo will be right behind him; Leia, who rarely shows emotion, is moved by both men's bravery. Film has a medal-receiving finale that combines Leni Riefenstahl and *The Wizard of Oz*. Film makes war look like fun. Equally regrettable is the shallowness of the characters: that they're shallow isn't as annoying as knowing they were designed to be that way. Also, C-3PO gets on my nerves in this film (I like him better in the sequels), and there are too many scenes with light-flashing special effects. The film's tremendous spirit, sense of fun and adventure, excitement, hip humor, imaginative

characters, and fast-paced, uncomplicated story touched a universal nerve—it became the biggest money-maker in movie history. Film is craftily made and brilliantly cast; intelligent old pros Guinness and Jones are used to balance the young actors. You've got to give Lucas all the credit in the . . . galaxy. Oscar-winning special effects by John Dykstra, John Stears, Richard Edlund, Grant McCune, and Robert Blalack. John Mollo won an Oscar for costume design; Ben Burtt, Jr., got a special Oscar for sound effects. Film also won Oscars for Art Direction, Best Original Score (by John Williams) and editing (by Paul Hirsch, Marcia Lucas, and Richard Chew). Gilbert Taylor did the cinematography; Gary Kurtz produced. Also with: Peter Cushing.

STARDUST (BRITISH/1975) C/97m. Cult film is an ambitious sequel to *That'll Be the Day*, with Michael Apted replacing Claude Watham as director. It's now the early sixties, and David Essex is with a struggling young British rock band, the Stray Cats. Adam Faith becomes their manager. He gets them gigs and a recording contract. Essex becomes the lead singer and the group has a hit. They become teen idols. Texas millionaire Larry Hagman buys the Stray Cats' contract. As his fame increases, Essex begins to feel increasingly that he's a *product*. He learns not to trust anyone but the band members. But his ego problems cause the band to break up. Essex goes on to superstardom, but he is alone, confused, corrupted. There is isolation, drugs, tragedy. This is a vivid, cynical look at the rock business and a Beatles-like group, with Essex coming across at various time like John Lennon, Paul McCartney, and George Harrison. There are few surprises in the film, but it is extremely well done, compelling, and has credibility because real rock stars Essex (who does a solid job), Faith, Dave Edmunds, and Keith Moon play major roles. Everything has a nostalgic ring. I particularly like the early scenes when the group is playing other people's music and is zipping around, feeling excited about having waxed its first record. You feel the innocence of the era. Then you watch it shattered in America. A good score. Also with: Ines Des Longchamps, Edd Byrnes.

STARDUST MEMORIES (1980) B&W/91m. Woody Allen takes Fellini's autobiographical *8½* and applies it, one assumes, to his own life. He plays Sandy Bates, a comic actor–director who is suffering crises that are both personal and professional. His relationship with neurotic girlfriend Charlotte Rampling is over; obsessed with world suffering, he has decided to go against the wishes of his legion of fans and forsake comedies for serious films. Lonely in love and depressed because the money-conscious producers are editing his first serious picture to make it seem like a comedy, Bates agrees to be guest celebrity at a weekend film seminar being conducted by a Judith Crist-type critic at a New Jersey resort, the Stardust. There he is stampeded by adoring fans, film connoisseurs (who at nightly screenings ask pretentious questions about his work), and everyone under the sun who needs a favor. Marie-Christine Barrault leaves her husband to visit him. While she is the one woman in his life, he becomes attracted to a young violinist, Jessica Harper (a fine, low-key performance), probably because she's as much a neurotic as Rampling. Picture is daring change of pace for Allen and contains wit and insight into life and thoughts of an Allen-like filmmaker, but it's not a success. This is Allen's most mature character (how confident he is with women), one whom we can believe is much like the real Allen (we can sympathize with him as he suffers grave conflicts), but we don't really like him—I would guess the side of Allen that the director shows us is not the side Allen himself likes. Picture reaches conclusion that those who have comic gifts (Allen/Bates) should present comedy to the world (the theme of Preston Sturges's *Sullivan's Travels*), whereas others should tackle serious themes. Should certainly be funnier. Not a critical success, and many resent the way "Allen's" fans are depicted. Also with: Ann DeSalvo, Tony Roberts, Daniel Stern, Amy Wright.

STARMAN (1984) C/112m. Early in 1984, John Carpenter was executive producer of *The Philadelphia Experiment*, about a man from the past who gets help from a modern-day woman in his attempt to elude authorities. Soon after, Carpenter came back with this other couple-on-the-run sci-fi picture. It's a big improvement because Carpenter directed (he wasn't directly involved in the making of the first film) and it contains much more sympathetic characters, but the story itself is still familiar and predictable. Jeff Bridges (who got a Best Actor nomination) is most appealing as a gentle alien who, like E.T., has come to study the earth. He takes on the guise of the late husband of Karen Allen, and is most convincing and amusing as he picks up human characteristics. The frightened Allen drives him from Wisconsin to the Grand Canyon, his departure point. As they elude the police and government officials, they fall in love. This becomes still another recent film in which women decide to have the babies of men whom they'll never see again: in the past a decision by an unwed character to have a child was considered idealistic, even rebellious, but in the Reagan era such a decision is a conservative one, usually tantamount to an anti-abortion statement. (At least in *The Terminator* unwed Linda Hamilton chooses to have a baby as much for political reasons—he will grow up to be a rebel leader—as for her love of the father.) Also troublesome is the starman's conclusion, the film's theme, that earth men are at their best when things are at their worst. This is not only trite but makes no sense, considering that when Bridges says it he hasn't yet seen any evidence of this. Yet, despite my reservations about themes, this film is the first indication that Carpenter cares about the characters he helps create and wants the best for them: this is apparent in all the truly sweet scenes between Bridges and the still underrated Allen, who shows here, as she did in *Until September*, that she is more comfortable than any other contemporary actress at playing love scenes. Also with: Charles Martin Smith, Richard Jaeckel.

STARS LOOK DOWN, THE (BRITISH/1939) B&W/110m. Generally regarded as the first British film with social relevance, Carol Reed's adaptation of A. J. Cronin's novel, co-scripted by Cronin, tells of an idealistic, educated collier's son (Michael Redgrave's first significant lead role) who wants to better the perilous work conditions in the mines of his Welsh town. He'd like to run for office, but his marriage to spoiled, ambitious Margaret Lockwood forces him to concentrate on making enough money to support her. He tries his hand at teaching, but his disregard for antiquated education techniques results in his dismissal. Realizing that his wife doesn't love him—she prefers weasely huckster Emlyn Williams—he is free to fight for miners' rights, and to expose the mine owners' intentional disregard for their safety. Fine, interesting, depressing film that was one of few commercial films to get into politics/economics of mining industry; it reveals the contempt rich owners have for their underpaid employees and the distrust labor has for its union leaders. Crowd scenes have a documentary look; dramatic scenes are handled simply. Cronin's book would be ideal for a *Masterpiece Theater* series. Also with: Edward Rigby, Nancy Price, Cecil Parker, Linden Travers, Ivor Barnard.

STARSTRUCK (AUSTRALIAN/1982) C/102m. Director Gillian Armstrong's follow-up to *My Brilliant Career* is this sparkling, offbeat musical comedy about a teenage girl trying to make it in the local pop-music scene. Talented, pretty Jo Kennedy, a real "find" of Armstrong's, is most appealing in her movie debut. Particularly amusing are her scenes with Ross O'Donovan as her gangly, hooky-playing younger cousin in short pants who is her clever lyricist and her entrepreneur manager. There's some disarming personal family drama thrown in, centering on the family pub and shaky household (full of insecure people who are united by familial love). But the picture thrives when Kennedy slips into one of her weird, colorful outfits and dances and sings a New Wave-type number. Among the catchy tunes that sped up Australia's pop charts: "The Monkey in Me" and "He's Got Body," which Kennedy belts out while perched on the bar as the customers dance about. Spirited and fun—it should be seen on a large screen to get the full cheer-up effect. Also with: Pat Evison, Margo Lee, Max Cullen, John O'May.

START THE REVOLUTION WITHOUT ME (1970) C/98m. In 17th-century France a nobleman's wife and a peasant woman each have twins which get mixed up, as mismatched pairs. In 1789, the year that appears on *every* title card, two cruel noblemen, the Corsican Brothers (Gene Wilder, Donald Sutherland), are offered half of France by traitorous Count Escargot (Victor Spinetti) and Queen Marie Antoinette (Billie Whitelaw plays her as a nymphomaniac) if they will assassinate Louis XVI (Hugh Griffith is the sympathetic, bumbling king). Meanwhile French revolutionaries send two poor, cowardly, apolitical brothers (Wilder, Sutherland also)—lookalikes of the Corsicans—to the king's residence at Versailles to create a diversion in preparation for the storming of the palace and the beginning of the Revolution. Naturally, there is an identity mix-up. Absurdist cult comedy has many funny gags and a bizarre performance by Wilder as the crazed, sadistic Corsican, but it no longer seems original. Halfway through, it begins to drag, and deteriorates into a silly bedroom farce in which characters keep zipping into different chambers through doors and passageways and being confused over who is who. Ending is a terrible cop-out. The French Revolution comes across as the work of dumb clucks. Directed by Bud Yorkin, who produced with Norman Lear. Also with: Jack Mac-Gowran, Ewa Aulin (star of *Candy*), Orson Welles.

STATE OF SIEGE (FRENCH/1973) C/120m.
Engrossing political film directed by Costa-Gavras, with a script by the director and Franco Solinas (*The Battle of Algiers*, *Burn!*). It's set in an unspecified South American country, but its story about the kidnapping and execution of an American adviser (Yves Montand) by the leftist underground was based on actual events that took place in Uruguay in 1970, when Dan Mitrione was killed by the Tupamaros. What's most interesting is the film's structure. At the beginning we learn that Montand has been shot to death. We don't know anything about him, just that he was a *harmless* American—an AID (Agency for International Development) adviser, supposedly on traffic control—with a large, grieving family, and that the government and military officials who attend his funeral held him in high esteem. When we flashback and see him snatched at gunpoint by some young rebels, who drug him and, now wearing hoods, imprison him in a tiny cell, our first inclination is to be on his side and despise the kidnappers (especially since we know that they will eventually kill him). But as the hooded rebel leader interrogates Montand, we come to realize that the leftists are the good guys and he, while always civil, is a despicable character who was actually sent by AID to teach torture techniques to the police and military, as he had previously done in Brazil. We also discover that the government/military/police could have prevented Montand's death if they had wished, by making a prisoner exchange, but had decided to sacrifice him to get the upper hand in their political game; as they pick up even more political prisoners, they give the liberation movement two bad choices: either kill Montand and hurt its image with revolutionary movements elsewhere or let him go and reveal that it is weak. Picture was meant to show that neo-colonialism exists in all Third World countries to which American companies/organizations send special advisers, but it's equally persuasive at showing the nearly impossible position of the underground in fascist countries. (The sequence in which the cold-blooded police methodically round up radicals is terrifying.) While it doesn't justify kidnapping and execution (and smartly avoids getting into *terrorism*), it does

propose that insurgents need to do drastic acts in order to get anything done. But the film warns that whenever leftists end up in a bargaining situation with fascist authorities (who are protecting the interests of an imperialist nation), they don't stand a chance. Music by Mikis Theodorakis is less memorable than his work in Z. Also with: Renato Salvatori, O. E. Hasse, Jacques Webber, Jean-Luc Bideau.

STATIONMASTER'S WIFE, THE/BOLWEISER (WEST GERMAN/1977) C/111m.
Rainer Werner Fassbinder's adaptation of Bavarian pacifist Oskar Maria Graf's 1930 book *Bolweiser—Novel of a Husband* was originally a two-part 200-minute television program. Fassbinder personally cut it for theatrical distribution, trimming away much material having to do with secondary characters so that the emotional warfare between weak stationmaster Xaver Bolweiser (Kurt Raab) and his brutally manipulative wife, Hanni (Elisabeth Trissenaar), seems almost non-stop. Bolweiser is a respected man in his small town who becomes a laughingstock when Hanni has an affair with the butcher (Bernard Helfrich). A dominant figure at work, Bolweiser is pathetic at home and chooses to believe Hanni when she says she has been faithful. He even commits perjury in court when Hanni and her lover sue those who have "slandered" them. Next Hanni has an affair with her hairdresser (Udo Kier). As usual, Bolweiser's anger doesn't last and he tearfully decides to overlook Hanni's infidelity. But Helfrich is infuriated about the hairdresser and shakes things up by telling the authorities that Bolweiser committed perjury. Bolweiser, the masochist that he has become, quietly accepts his four-year prison sentence. At his lowest point Hanni (who, I'd guess, loves him but despises his character) divorces him. Slow but engrossing and erotic, the film is an attack on the spineless, hypocritical middle class in Germany, a confirmation that women can be as despicable as men, and a depressing statement about the "destructiveness of love," which was perhaps Fassbinder's most prominent theme in his movies. Film's end comes earlier and is sadder than the television version's. Also with: Volker Spengler, Karl-Heinz Von Hassell.

STEEL HELMET, THE (1950) B&W/84m.
Unusual, surprisingly powerful low-budget war film, written and directed by Samuel Fuller. Set in Korea—although filmed in LA's Griffith Park—story is about a hard-bitten sergeant (Gene Evans) whose platoon is wiped out but who survives himself because of his helmet. With the help of a Korean orphan boy (William Chun as "Short Round") who latches on to him, Evans makes it through the wilderness and hooks up with a multi-racial platoon that sets up an observation post in a Buddhist temple, where they hold a communist prisoner. Evans has doubts about the platoon commander (Steve Brodie), who follows the book—Fuller believes there should be no rules in war—but Brodie proves brave when North Koreans attack the temple. Fuller's unsentimental, deglamorized portrait of war is highly atmospheric, tense, realistic; the character relationships, particularly those be-

tween Evans and Chun and Brodie, are intriguing: it's a tragedy of war that soldiers often have time to measure a person's worth only after he has died. A solid performance by Evans in a rare lead. Also with: James Edwards, Robert Hutton, Richard Loo, Sid Melton.

STELLA DALLAS (1937) B&W/111m.

Prototypical soap opera—which would become a radio staple for several decades—was one of the first to advance the form's most important tenet: whatever a woman's faults, she will be a devoted, loving, sacrificing mother. Barbara Stanwyck is Stella, a smalltown girl who marries above her class, to a dull but kind man (John Boles). She is well-meaning but restless for the wild life, and her vulgar dress and manner in public make her a mismatch for her refined husband. She is not that upset about separating from Boles—this is one of the screen's first amiable divorces—but she can't bear not being with her teenage daughter (Anne Shirley), who gives meaning to her otherwise drab life. So Stanwyck and Shirley live together through hard times, until Stanwyck realizes she is an embarrassment to her daughter and can't give her all the things she deserves—all those benefits Shirley would have if she lived with her father and his more sophisticated second wife (Barbara O'Neil) and mingled in society. So Stanwyck resolves to give up her daughter . . . and her happiness. Thematically this picture is, of course, dated, but it's still worth watching because of its classic status, the strong and sympathetic performances by Stanwyck and Shirley, and director King Vidor's interesting portrait of smalltown America. Even considering the young snobs who naïvely make fun of Stella, this film contains some of the nicest people—even O'Neil turns out to be kind-hearted. Vidor handles scenes with women especially well—it's most touching when Stanwyck tells O'Neil that she wants her to take care of Shirley and the sensitive O'Neil can see the enormity of Stanwyck's sacrifice; and when Shirley, after overhearing her mother being insulted, climbs down from her upper train berth to sleep with her. Every soap needs such tear-jerking scenes. Remake of a 1925 silent with Belle Bennett. Also with: Alan Hale, Marjorie Main, Tim Holt.

STEVIE (BRITISH/1978) C/102m.

One of those films people like to recommend to show they have good taste. Not me. I blanked out after the first 10 minutes. Glenda Jackson is eccentric English poet Stevie Smith (1902–1971), a role she previously had played on BBC radio and on the London stage. Mona Washbourne is the likable but ditzy maiden aunt she lives with—and will undoubtedly become like. Usually looking sad, Jackson talks a lot, recites her poetry, drinks a bit. It's nearly a one-woman show, and if you're a big Jackson fan, you'll probably be impressed by her performance even if you can't really unravel what Stevie's trying to tell us about herself. Jackson won several prestigious awards for her performance. I was glad that the character didn't require Jackson to do her snippety, viper-tongued bit, even in the scene (a *touching* scene,

I admit) when she scorns her would-be husband (Alec McCowen). Directed by Robert Enders. Also with: Trevor Howard (as The Man).

STOLEN KISSES (FRENCH/1968) C/90m.

François Truffaut's witty, sad, insightful meditation on Love, encompassing passion, courtship, confusion, conflict, romance, jealousy, disloyalty, dishonesty, sex, conquest, and commitment (and second thoughts). The third cinematic episode in the life of Jean-Pierre Léaud's hopeless romantic Antoine Doinel begins with Antoine being kicked out of the army. Delighted to be a civilian again, he goes to the house of Christine (Claude Jade), the girl he loves and to whom he wrote constantly, 19 times during one week. Typical of Antoine, he gets along better with the girl's parents than with the girl: although friendly, Christine resists Antoine's kisses and then she takes to avoiding him altogether; her parents get him a job as a hotel night watchman. Although he is fired from his new job for letting a detective (Harry Max) trick him into opening the door of a room where a married woman is in bed with her lover, he is given a job with the detective agency. On an undercover assignment he goes to work in a shoestore for M. Tabard (Michel Lonsdale), who wants to find out why everyone dislikes him ("My wife laughs all the time, except when I tell a joke"). Antoine forgets about Christine when he develops a tremendous crush on Tabard's wife, Fabienne (Delphine Seyrig). Typical of Truffaut: at this point Christine becomes interested in Antoine and pursues him. Film explores one of life's ironies (and one of Truffaut's favorite themes): when a person is ready to give his/her complete, devoted love to another person, that person is off kissing someone else. Everywhere one looks in this film, there is a love triangle in which the rejected person is the one who has the most love to offer: a distraught husband finds his wife having a casual affair in the hotel where Antoine works; a gay client of the detective agency agonizes over the loss of his homosexual lover to a woman; Antoine comes to visit Christine, but she slips out the side door to meet her date; Tabard loves his wife, but she's excited about the possibilities of a one-time stand with Antoine; Christine is ready to give herself to Antoine, but he's in bed with Fabienne, whom he idealizes; when Antoine and Christine do get together, a stranger who has been following Christine throughout the entire picture approaches her and confesses his great love for her as well as his willingness to wait until her temporary relationship is over and then devote every second of his life to her. Christine thinks he's crazy, but unhappy Antoine recognizes that this man loves Christine just as obsessively as he once did when she didn't want him. Truffaut and Léaud rely heavily on improvisation; we're kept off guard, ready to be surprised by images and actions. There are countless wonderful moments, including: Truffaut's camera searches for Antoine and Christine, finding them in her bed; and the sweet proposal scene. Followed by *Bed and Board*, in which Antoine and Christine are married, and *Love on the Run*, in which they are getting divorced but are still friends.

STOP MAKING SENSE (1984) C/88m—99m.
Riveting concert film of the Talking Heads, compiled from three performances staged specifically for the movie at the Hollywood Pantages Theater. Director Jonathan Demme wisely told cameraman Jordan Cronenweth to focus exclusively on the stage, the result being that we, the movie audience, feel part of the concert audience we hear under our own applause. And what takes place on stage will make even most skeptical into Talking Heads converts. At the beginning only Talking Heads leader David Byrne appears on stage, giving a jolting performance of "Psycho Killer"; with each new song, other members of the group appear one by one. The momentum builds. Sixteen songs, including smash hits "Burning Down the House" and "Days Go By"— why only nine songs on the album, Warner Bros?—run the gamut from gospel to reggae to "political" rock. Performances are invariably exciting, Byrne's lyrics are intriguing. Byrne, his head moving rhythmically as if he just had shock treatments, is spellbinding—what a talent! But, surprisingly, the excitement doesn't let up when he's off camera, leaving the singing to the women—bassist Tina Weymouth and backup singers Edna Holt and Lynn Mabry. Byrne is known for his belief that music should be performed in an interesting, *visual* manner, and this should make him proud. See it in a theater, with as big an audience as possible.

STORM WARNING (1951) B&W/93m.
Almost forgotten film was probably first Hollywood picture since 1936's *Black Legion* to take a persuasive stand against the Ku Klux Klan. Ginger Rogers visits her sister (Doris Day), discovers that her brother-in-law (Steve Cochran) belongs to Klan-like group that keeps the small southern town in grip of fear. With the help of Ronald Reagan, who plays a liberal (!) lawyer, Rogers puts fear into Klansmen who were involved in a murder she witnessed. In a frightening sequence she finds herself captive at a Klan rally. Taut, interesting film will keep you on edge of seat. Unusually gutty performance by Rogers; Day's dramatic portrayal of her weak sister is what earned her the lead in *The Man Who Knew Too Much*. Directed by Stuart Heisler. Also with: Hugh Sanders, Lloyd Gough.

STORY OF ADÈLE H, THE/HISTOIRE D'ADÈLE H., L' (FRENCH/1975) C/97m.
François Truffaut's extremely passionate telling of the true story of Adèle Hugo (Isabelle Adjani), the younger daughter of Victor Hugo. It's a moving, fascinating, original film, beautifully photographed by Nestor Almendros, with special attention paid to period detail. The film begins when she arrives in Halifax from Guernsey. Already a bit unhinged, she has come to rekindle her romance with a young soldier (Bruce Robinson) whom her father had selected as a possible husband for her. But this playboy is no longer interested in her. Desperately in love, she can't accept rejection and does everything in her power to win him back. She fills her journal with romantic flights of fancy. She writes home that she and he are in love and getting married. The nature of her obsession becomes pathetic. She spies on him making love; she sends him prostitutes; she gives him money; she puts notes in his uniform; she tells her father that they're married; she tells her prospective father-in-law that she is bearing his son's child—it's not true but she doesn't care that's she's lying or that he'll eventually find out; she has no pride. She becomes desperately ill, sleeps in a flophouse—but she doesn't give up her quest, even when she is too insane to recognize the young soldier's face. Truffaut's characters are always driven by their hearts rather than by reason and, typically, they love those who don't love them equally or at the same time, but this is the one film where he really explores the extreme humiliation and the pain one can endure when deep love is unfulfilled. The pity is that Adèle realizes the soldier is a rat—but she gives up trying to control her heart (which acts independently of her brain). It's heartbreaking to see Adjani's beautiful face (held in close-up) with bloodshot eyes and tears starting to fall—or with eyes happy as she fabricates romantic lies for her journal. Thanks to Truffaut for having her look peaceful in last scene. Also with: Sylvia Marriott, Reubin Dorey.

STORY OF O, THE (FRENCH/1975) C/112m.
Just Jaeckin's adaptation of Pauline Reage's controversial erotic classic stars Corinne Cléry as O, the woman who willingly becomes a slave to the men she loves, happily enduring whippings, sexual subservience, and humiliation to prove that they own her. Cléry is beautiful, but I seriously doubt that her character is successful as a fantasy figure for females in audience (as Jaeckin would like her to be). It's just too hard to watch her in constant agony from brutal punishment. (Cléry seems to be in pain even when the lovemaking is "normal.") Moreover, the men in her life are debonairly repulsive, the type that wears nothing under expensive suits. Jaeckin strives for eroticism, but the slow pacing and dreamy photography make the film dull—quite an accomplishment, considering the sensational subject matter. The book, which was probably written by a man using an alias, is about how a woman is betrayed by the men to whom she sacrifices herself; it ends pessimistically with her being totally debased and abandoned. Jaeckin alters the story by adding some fashionable feminism: by withstanding all that the men can dish out, O proves herself stronger than they, conquers them, ultimately turns the tables of power on them. Picture's only humor is unintentional: assistant cameraman's name is Philippe Welt. Also with: Anthony Steel, Udo Kier (of Andy Warhol movies), Jean Gaven.

STRADA, LA (ITALIAN/1954) B&W/115m.
Along with *The Bicycle Thief*, Federico Fellini's classic is the most loved of Italy's neorealist films of the post-WWII era. In this early "road" film, Giulietta Masina is a poor, innocent simpleton whose mother sells her services to a brutish strongman (Anthony Quinn) who travels through postwar Italy doing a chain-breaking act for tips. Having no sense of self-worth to begin with, she is made to feel even more inconsequential by this insensitive brute who drinks heavily,

sleeps with other women, insults her talents (she plays a small drum while he performs), and beats her as if she were a dog. Even though she gets offers to join a circus, run off with a clown and tightrope walker, "Fool" (Richard Basehart), or stay in a convent, she becomes convinced that Quinn really does need her; perhaps he loves her. But only heartbreak awaits. Masina mugs too much, but she's captivating. With a round face, dimples, and large, expressive eyes, she has the look of a clown; she'll remind you of a cross between Harpo Marx, Charlie Chaplin, and a puppy. (No wonder all the children she comes into contact with immediately take to her.) Masina's serious scenes don't really work because her temporary switch from gamine to disgruntled adult is too swift. The result is that her performance seems inconsistent, although the real problem is with the character. Quinn's character is also a bit hard to figure out—it's true that the bigger they are, the harder they fall, but when the mighty Quinn lies in a drunken heap, what is he thinking? (We assume that he's thinking of Masina, but, ignorant lout that he is, he may go through life alone without realizing her meaning, her worth, to him.) We expect him to call her name so the last puzzle piece will fit, but he says nothing. Memorable glimpses of Italian countryside, crowded villages, excitement over rituals (weddings, religious parades, circus acts). Best Foreign Film of 1954. Nino Rota contributed lovely score.

STRAIGHT TIME (1978) C/114m.
Dustin Hoffman has one of his best screen roles as two-time loser Max Dembo, just paroled from prison. The first and more interesting part of the film shows Dembo making feeble attempts to adjust to society—getting a room, a low-paying job, a girlfriend (Theresa Russell)—but finding it impossible to relax because his venal parole officer (M. Emmett Walsh) won't get off his back. I wish they'd stuck with this novel storyline instead of switching in mid-film to more conventional material: Dembo and two old buddies (Harry Dean Stanton, Gary Busey) plan to rob a jewelry store. What's most interesting from the viewer's standpoint is how we consider Dembo to be a defenseless victim in his dealings with his parole officer, who fully intends to send him back to prison, but later discover that Dembo is a tough cookie himself. He may have a personal morality, while Walsh's character has none, but they belong in the same circle of vermin. Indeed, Dembo is not a nice guy, but if Robert De Niro had played him, with Martin Scorsese as director, we'd probably be too repulsed by him to feel any of the necessary empathy. We don't like the character Hoffman plays, but at least we can relate to his need to fit in somewhere—if he can't fit into respectable society, then at least he wants some loyal friends and a loyal girlfriend. Dembo may be a habitual criminal, but it's important for us to realize that if he really did intend to go straight come hell or high water, being an ex-con makes that a near impossibility. Famed theater director Ulu Grosbard took over the direction from Hoffman and did an excellent job with his stellar cast, particularly during intimate scenes. Russell particularly stands out as the loyal but scared girlfriend. Sleeper makes good use of LA locales; the heist is exciting. Also with: Sandy Baron, Kathy Bates, Rita Taggert.

STRANGE BEHAVIOR/DEAD KIDS (AUSTRALIAN–NEW ZEALAND/1981) C/98m–105m.
Low-budget horror film was photographed in New Zealand but is set in America's Midwest. Several brutal killings take place, and police captain Michael Murphy's trail leads to the psychology lab at the local college. Students participating in experiments are being injected (right in the eye!) with a serum that makes them do the evil bidding of Arthur Dignam and nurse Fiona Lewis. Murphy's son Dan Shor is being programmed to murder his father. Picture got surprisingly good reviews. I find the script by Bill Condon and Michael Laughlin pretty witty and inventive, but at times it's so offbeat that the film becomes confusing. Direction by Laughlin is weak—he has no sense of timing during suspense scenes. His high point is the closing titles. Picture has bad sound quality. Music by Tangerine Dream. Also with: Louise Fletcher (wasted), Dey Young (from *Rock 'n' Roll High School*), Marc McClure, Scott Brady, Charles Lane, Elizabeth Cheshire.

STRANGE BREW (1983) C/91m.
Using the old I-found-a-mouse-in-my-beer-bottle trick, the McKenzie Brothers (Dave Thomas, Rick Moranis)—last seen hosting *The Great White North* on SCTV—attempt to get several free cases of Elsinore Beer. To their delight, they end up working in the factory. They foil a plot by the evil brewmeister, Max von Sydow, to gain control of the public by drugging their beer. They also help pretty Lynn Griffin regain control of the brewery from her uncle (Paul Dooley), who helped Von Sydow murder her father. Foolish comedy drags on forever. There are a few snickers along the way—but there is nothing that will make you laugh out loud (unless you dig burping M-G-M lions and Moranis's sincere "You're real nice—if I didn't have puke breath, I'd kiss you"). I'm glad Griffin was given a lead after her unusual half-comedic role as killer in *Curtains*—but she's not given anything humorous to do. The major selling point is that film would have been much worse if Cheech & Chong had been the stars, "eh?" Directed by Thomas and Moranis with little of the sharp wit found in the SCTV routines. The slapstick seems out of place.

STRANGE CARGO (1940) B&W/105m.
Strange film. Six convicts, including Clark Gable, plus loose woman Joan Crawford, flee a penal colony by small boat. One convict making the trip is a Christlike figure (played by Ian Hunter) who brings solace, peace, and, in the case of Gable and Crawford, love into the black hearts of his fellow passengers—except for Paul Lukas, the devil figure in this religious parable. Picture begins dynamically on penal colony, with extremely good, hard-edged dialogue being exchanged by the sinful characters. The initial meetings between Gable and the hostile Crawford are gems. Gable

and Crawford sizzle throughout, but the religious mumbo-jumbo gets in way of what might have been a fascinating escape film. Every time anybody wants to do something exciting, the calm and solemn Hunter stops them, tells them the possible consequences of their actions, and gives them second thoughts. Consequently, the characters' toughness and the picture's as well are diluted. Directed by Frank Borzage, with a score by Franz Waxman. Fine cast also includes: Peter Lorre (as M'sieur Pigg), Albert Dekker, Eduardo Ciannelli.

STRANGE INVADERS (1983) C/94m. Followup to *Strange Behavior* by director-producer Michael Laughlin and his co-writer, Bill Condon, is strange sci-fi. Twenty-five years ago, aliens took over the bodies and homes of the people in Centerville, Illinois. Today Columbia University entomology professor Paul LeMat discovers that his former wife (Diana Scarwid) is an alien and that the other invaders are trying to whisk his human daughter back to their planet. With new girlfriend, *National Informer* reporter Nancy Allen, LeMat heads to Centerville. First half of film is really impressive, as script is witty (i.e., alien Fiona Lewis pretends to be the Avon Lady), direction is bizarre, characters act uniquely. The later scenes are sloppy and more conventional; unfortunately, the final bit in story virtually erases everything bad that happened earlier. A good premise, worth making into a film, but, sadly, it doesn't work. Too many disgusting shots of aliens ripping off their human skins; only Lewis and Allen seem to get into right spirit. Also with: Michael Lerner, Louise Fletcher, Kenneth Tobey, June Lockhart, Wallace Shawn, Charles Lane, Dey Young.

STRANGER, THE (1946) B&W/85m—95m—115m. One of several films in the forties in which people suspect that someone in their house isn't as innocent as s/he appears, joining such pictures as *Shadow of a Doubt*, *Gaslight*, *The Cat People*, *The Lodger*, *Suspicion*, and *The Spiral Staircase*. Orson Welles directed and stars as a Nazi war criminal, the man responsible for the policy of genocide, who hides out in a Connecticut town under an assumed identity, teaching history at a prep school. So that he'll never be tracked down (there are no pictures of him), he marries unsuspecting hometown girl Loretta Young, who's popular and the daughter of a federal judge. But when a Nazi accomplice visits him, Welles realizes that Nazi-hunter Edward G. Robinson is on his trail. He must think fast to deceive Robinson and Young, to make them think he's not the fugitive Nazi. Welles's most conventional film isn't nearly as bad as he thought it was, although it is not one of his masterpieces. Although his acting is cockeyed, Welles makes a good, slimy villain, sweating underneath his suit, spewing out one falsehood after another, often speaking in a strange pattern (where the last word in a sentence sounds as if it were the first word in the next sentence). Robinson is a good adversary for Welles, but I wish they had a couple more scenes together, sparring with words. Young's character is poorly written. She's ridiculously naïve. The story

itself is *still* interesting, as is the evocation of smalltown life, far away from the public eye. Picture lacks something, but I can't figure out what it is—perhaps it's that the Nazi is not up to any diabolical act at the time Robinson comes to town, so only at the end when Welles decides to murder Young is there any suspense. There are novel touches throughout, including the manner in which Welles is done in, and the photography by Russell Metty is atmospheric. Also with: Philip Merivale, Richard Long, Bryon Keith, Billy House (stealing the picture as the checker-playing pharmacist), Martha Wentworth.

STRANGER, THE (ITALIAN-FRENCH/1967) C/105m. Luchino Visconti's reasonably well made but philosophically shallow adaptation of Albert Camus's existential novel. Marcello Mastroianni is Meursault, a Frenchman working in an office in French-controlled Algiers in the 1930s. When his mother dies, he doesn't cry—they weren't very close. He has an affair with Anna Karina and agrees to marry her—but he admits he doesn't love her. He befriends a pimp who lives in his building and is indifferent when the pimp decides to humiliate and beat his unfaithful Arab girlfriend. When the woman's brother harasses the pimp on a beach, Meursault doesn't mix in. But later he's drawn back to the beach and without much provocation or reason shoots and kills the young Arab. He faces trial, where his guilt in the crime is determined by his lack of compassion at his mother's funeral and his atheism. Mastroianni is well cast as an alienated man whose great guilt—over his indifference as well as the murder he committed—cannot be decreased because to him God doesn't exist and the hypocritical *men* who judge him cannot forgive an atheist anything. (Was it an angry God who blinded him with a ray of sun when the dead Arab pulled a knife on him on the beach?) Sadly, Meursault does have feelings and kindness, but his contempt for the world and his meaningless existence serves to anesthetize his emotions almost entirely. (When he thinks of his mother, he doesn't even understand that he's missing her.) When he commits murder, it's almost a positive act! He has finally moved out of passivity. Impressively photographed by Giuseppe Rotunno; Visconti presents believable Algerian environment. Scenes with scabrous old man and his scabrous dog are memorable. Also with: Bernard Blier, Bruno Crémer.

STRANGER THAN PARADISE (1984) B&W/90m. A very funny, original, independent film by writer-director Jim Jarmusch. Because he was given some free film stock by Wim Wenders, he was able to complete his movie for a mere $120,000. Its formal style—Jarmusch has the actors perform in front of a strategically placed static camera; the picture fades to black at the end of each scene—was influenced by innovative European and Japanese filmmakers. Its intention is to allow viewers to watch whatever they want within the frame, instead of having cuts to close-ups that force viewers to accept what the filmmaker thinks is the most important thing happening at a particular time.

The static camera perfectly reflects the static lifestyles of the characters we watch. Willie (John Lurie) lives in a New York slum apartment. He does little but watch TV, eat, hang out with his equally dull friend, Eddie (Richard Edson). They are like *two* Ed Nortons—only they don't have Norton's gift for gab. Willie's 16-year-old cousin Eva (Eszter Balint) arrives from Hungary and stays with him before going on to live with Aunt Lottie (Cecilia Stark) in Cleveland. She quickly becomes bored. At first he gets annoyed with her—she questions why his meals are called TV dinners—but later discovers she's "hip." A year later Willie and Eddie visit Eva in Cleveland. They're happy to see each other, but still no one—no one but Aunt Lottie, that is—can carry on a conversation. They observe that Cleveland's just as drab as New York. So they drive to Florida, but this "paradise," which is undergoing bad weather, is also just as lifeless as New York—especially since they stay in an out-of-the-way motel. At first the picture is jarring because nothing happens. You won't understand why it has received such critical praise. But soon you realize the humor comes from the fact that these people are incapable of breaking free from their boredom. The dialogue manages to be funny, although the characters are completely deadpan in their delivery and say very little that is perceptive. The characters are hilarious—and real!—and the actors are terrific; I thought the elderly Stark would get an Oscar nomination.

STRANGERS ON A TRAIN (1951) B&W/101m.

One of Alfred Hitchcock's supreme thrillers; scripted by Raymond Chandler and Czenzi Ormonde from Patricia Highsmith's novel. Tennis pro Guy Haines (Farley Granger) would like to marry Ann Morton (Ruth Roman), the daughter of a senator (Leo G. Carroll), but his unreasonable, sluttish wife, Miriam (Laura Elliott), won't give him a divorce. On a train, total stranger Bruno Anthony (Robert Walker's finest role) offers to murder Miriam if Guy will do away with his rich, disciplinarian father (Jonathan Hale). Guy tokenly agrees, thinking that Bruno is joking. But Bruno murders Miriam and tries to force Guy into carrying out his part of the bargain. When it's obvious that Guy won't kill Bruno's father, Bruno acts as hurt and deserted as any spoiled child would. He spitefully rushes off to plant Guy's cigarette lighter at the site of Miriam's murder; meanwhile Guy plays aggressive tennis for the first time in his life, hoping to win quickly and head off Bruno. Bruno is the piece's protagonist, its picaresque hero, who, if it weren't for a domineering father and daffy mother (Marion Lorne), might have been a great person. He, not Guy, mocks a conservative judge for condemning men to death, is disgusted that business picks up where murders are committed, has "silly" plans to blow up the White House, and, to every viewer's approval, has the audacity to pop a little tyke's balloon. Viewers can't help believing that Miriam's death is a stroke of good fortune for Guy and the world; Hitchcock also manipulates us into believing the death of Bruno's father would be a positive development. However, since Guy has our morals, we can't expect him to kill Mr. Anthony; we just feel sorry that Bruno needs Guy's help so badly. We like this fellow Walker plays; it's as if we were under his skin, sweating his sweat. We care more about his hurt feelings than about the survival of Guy and Ann's relationship. The film has several ingenious visual moments: Bruno and Guy watch a police car from behind the bars of a fence; when Bruno strangles Miriam, we watch through her fallen glasses, so everything looks distorted, twisted like her neck; Hitchcock cuts back and forth between Guy playing tennis and Bruno desperately trying to retrieve the dropped lighter, building tension by having both men perform in front of crowds; as Guy and Bruno wrestle on the floor of the merry-go-round, Hitchcock creates a surrealistic, nightmarish effect by shooting upward toward the wooden horses, which become smirking monsters hovering over the men's heads, prancing, prancing; and in the most famous shot, as the heads of the entire tennis crowd go back and forth in unison to follow the ball, the camera focuses on Bruno who looks straight ahead at Guy. Most intriguing is how Hitchcock creates excitement by building suspense, stopping short and starting over, only to reach the climax when no one is prepared for its impact; for instance, Miriam's murder comes shortly *after* we wrongly thought she'd be killed in the Tunnel of Love and shortly *before* we next expect it to happen. The last 20 minutes, divided into several suspense sequences, perfectly illustrate Hitchcock's method. Film has flaws: the atrocious dialogue between Guy and Ann; the casting of Granger and Roman; the mistake of ignoring, except for one red-herring scene, the resemblance between Ann's sister Barbara, humorously played by Patricia Hitchcock, and Miriam. But Walker's performance and Hitchcock's vast array of tricks more than compensate for them.

STRAW DOGS (1971) C/113m–118m.

Dustin Hoffman is a mild-mannered pacifist American mathematician in sneakers who finds his manhood tested when he moves to the Cornish village of his sexy young wife, Susan George. The tough young men he hires to do repairs seem to mock and threaten him, leer at George, and even kill her cat (although no one witnesses this). The scared George pressures him to stand up to them. But his attempts are feeble, causing her to lose respect for him. When one of the men rapes her—Sam Peckinpah, of course, filmed it as if George were "asking for it"—she won't even tell Hoffman, because she senses it will do no good. However, when the men come to his house to seize and murder the retarded villager (David Warner) to whom Hoffman has given "sanctuary"—not realizing he strangled a village girl—Hoffman becomes obsessed with protecting him. Now it's George who wants him to back down. Extremely controversial meditation on violence has, understandably, never appealed to women, but men seem to get cathartic satisfaction from Hoffman's violent, sadistic final acts. Peckinpah's contentions that pacifists are really cowards who would like to express themselves violently and that violence is so exhilarating that having a woman (as sex mate or wife) is nothing in comparison (as Hoffman realizes at film's end) are very suspect. His treatment of women as sluts who goad men past their breaking points is reprehensible. Not my favorite, but it's an important film. Has excellent performance by Hoffman, and George has never been better. From novel *The Siege of Trencher's Farm* by Gordon M. Williams. Expert photography by John Coquillon, editing by Paul Davies, Roger Spottiswoode, and Tony Lawson. Also with: Peter Vaughan, T.P. McKenna, Peter Arne.

STREET SCENE (1931) B&W/75m. Elmer Rice adapted his Pulitzer-winning play about life in the New York tenements; and King Vidor directed the Samuel Goldwyn production, one of the first social dramas of the sound era. Drama centers on the numerous people who occupy one tenement building—this is probably the first film to drive home the point that America was populated by foreigners, and the first to affirm that there were already clashes between these immigrants over religion, national origin, and politics. Characters gather on the front stoop or lean out windows so they can gossip, complain about the heat, argue, and, in the case of Sylvia Sidney and William Collier, Jr., speak of a happier future, perhaps together; referring to his poem, Sidney says the *almost* immortal line: "Say it again, Sam." (To give his film some visual interest, Vidor occasionally uses bizarre camera angles or pans along the street or across a row of windows.) Major stories all involve Sidney (who was swiftly becoming the cinema's symbol of the never-give-up-hope urban poor): she wonders whether to accept an invitation by her married employer to meet his show-biz connections and move into her own apartment; she wonders whether to pursue Collier romantically—I'd recommend that she leave the wimp alone—or step aside until he finishes law school; she worries that her heavy-drinking, cold-hearted father (David Landau) will do something drastic if he discovers that her mother (Estelle Taylor) is having an affair: interestingly, we viewers are supposed to agree with Sidney that Taylor's adultery is justified because everyone deserves some happiness and kindness in his/her life. Another film in which John Qualen plays a pipe-smoking Swede. Score by Alfred Newman would be used in other urban dramas. Also with: Beulah Bondi, Walter Miller, Russell Hopton.

STREETCAR NAMED DESIRE, A (1951) B&W/122m. Vivien Leigh gives an emotionally shattering performance as Blanche Dubois, the most vulnerable, bruised, and battered of Tennessee Williams's tragic heroines. Her unhappy and humiliating past and the passing of her youth have left her on the brink of insanity. She comes to New Orleans to stay with her younger sister, Stella (Kim Hunter), and Stella's brutish, T-shirt-clad husband, Stanley Kowalski (Marlon Brando). Because his life is built around bolstering his ego, Stanley can't tolerate Blanche's intelligence/education that's evident in her speech, her constant fibbing about how glorious her past was, and her moral pretensions—actually, she is moral, but hasn't lived up to

her own moral standards (except that she has "never been deliberately cruel" to anyone). Stanley won't let her find needed escape and solace in her desperate flights into fantasy. She could set him in his place if her mind were clear and she still had sturdy legs to stand on, but he takes advantage of her weak state. In Williams, the very men who have the potential to help helpless women usually choose to destroy them instead. Piggy Stanley and, to a lesser degree, his friend Mitch (Karl Malden), who courts Blanche until he learns of her "sins," fill that role. Film is a bit theatrical—at times it looks like an old kinescope—but Elia Kazan's direction of actors was never better. Leigh, Hunter, and Malden all won Oscars, and Brando's devastating portrayal ("Stella!!!") is regarded as one of the screen's greatest characterizations. Williams and Oscar Saul adapted the play. Alex North composed the score. Ann-Margret and Treat Williams starred in the solid 1984 TV-movie version.

STREETS OF FIRE (1983) C/93m. Walter Hill's rock-music thriller was a big financial and critical bomb, but it has attained a strong cult following; it is a bit better than its reputation. Stylized film has a unique look: part futuristic, part fiftyish, part Hollywood soundstage. Rock superstar Diane Lane is kidnapped by a ruthless biker gang led by brutal Willem DaFoe, who, in a strange way, resembles the Frankenstein monster. Lane's ex-boyfriend Michael Paré and Amy Madigan are hired to rescue her. Lane's nerdy manager, Rick Moranis, goes along for the ride, providing the film's humor. Some exciting action sequences (particularly the daring rescue), impressive visuals (Andrew Laszlo was cinematographer), and a pounding rock score compensate for the familiar plot and intentionally skimpy dialogue. Unfortunately, the showdown between Paré and DaFoe, while everyone else just looks on, is anticlimactic. Inspired casting of Madigan as Paré's back-up makes up for the miscasting of Lane, who lip-synchs her songs. In good and bad ways Hill's picture is reminiscent of John Carpenter's inferior *Escape from New York*. Also with: Deborah Van Valkenburgh (Hill's *The Warriors*), Elizabeth Daly, Lee Ving, Marine Jahan, Ed Begley, Jr.

STREETWISE (1984) C/92m. Bruising *cinéma-vérité* look at street kids living in Seattle's tenderloin, most of whom get along by panhandling, selling dope, engaging in prostitution, eating out of garbage dumpsters, and living in abandoned buildings. At first the kids seem happy to be free of their parents and enjoying life on their own in festive area; they have camaraderie among themselves and other street people and are proud to be making money. But we quickly see that their lives are hellish, even if they don't realize it themselves. Theirs is a world of street brawls, drugs, perverts on the make, filth, hassles with police, frequent busts. It's amazing what these kids endure; and you think that they have the *right* to something better. A girl should be deciding about which dress to wear, not which pimp to pick. And you realize how awful their home lives must have been. We get glimpses: we see one girl's caring but alcoholic mother; another's naïve mother who doesn't understand why her daughter won't come home now that her stepfather is no longer forcing her to have sex with him; a father who appears to be kindly and loving—except that he's in prison for burglary and arson and constantly bullies his son (who committed suicide after filming was completed). In fact, all these tough kids become little children when with their parents—and it's heartbreaking that there's no way these parents and children can take the love they have for each other and use that as the foundation for good lives together. The impression we get is that there is no real solution to the sorry situation. After having seen this film you may still keep your money in your pockets when you pass bratty kids who try to con you out of some change, but you'll feel profound sympathy and frustration, and curse those parents responsible for their being on street. Directed by Martin Bell. It began as a *Life* magazine piece by Cheryl McCall and photographer Mary Ellen Mark. Music by Tom Waits.

STRIPES (1981) C/105m. Bill Murray has one of those days—he loses his car, job, girlfriend—so he and good buddy Harold Ramis join the army. They are whipped into physical shape by tough Sergeant Warren Oates (although his efforts to discipline them have far less success), have great sex with female MPs P. J. Soles and Sean Young, and become heroes when they rescue Oates and the rest of their crack(ed) platoon from behind enemy lines. There are funny scenes—Murray as a cabbie (which would have made a better movie), the platoon marching as they sing "Doo Wah Diddy," Murray leading the platoon through a spastic-but-all-in-step routine in front of military brass—and Murray's at his sarcastic, uncaring, smart-talking best. But the script (co-written by Ramis) is lazy at those precise times it should be inventive; despite some off-the-wall humor, it becomes just a standard service comedy. Because the film doesn't go the fashionable army-is-a-great-character-builder route of *Private Benjamin* and *An Officer and a Gentleman*, it isn't really about anything. Best scene has all the soldiers admit they cried when they saw *Old Yeller*. Directed by Ivan Reitman (*Meatballs*). Also with: John Candy, John Larroquette, Judge Reinhold, Joe Flaherty, Dave Thomas, Fran Ryan.

STUDENT NURSES, THE (1970) C/89m. The first of New World's R-rated "nursing cycle" is perhaps director Stephanie Rothman's most solid work, effectively blending sex, comedy, action, and drama, and advancing a strong feminist viewpoint. Karen Carlson, Elaine Griftos, Barbara Leigh, and Brioni Farrell are all convincing as third-year nursing students and roommates who have chaotic, life-changing experiences prior to graduation. These women set the pattern for future Rothman females. They help and root for each other, without petty rivalries over men or careers. They make *all* their own decisions, right and wrong. While it's true that some of the men they deal with are honorable and helpful, the women know better than to trust their fu-

tures to them. Male authority figures are the enemy. In a rare moment of female hostility toward men in Rothman's films, Farrell sums it up: "Give men a chance to play inquisitor and it's thumbs down on women every time." So, as the women guide their own lives, Rothman sets up personal and professional roadblocks for each, and makes it clear that for the women to triumph, they must earn their nursing diplomas. Film has good characters and storylines; there are sex scenes, but they are unexploitive—even bad guys are gentle lovers in Rothman's films. Harrowing abortion sequence during which Leigh relives a bad acid trip won't appeal to pro-choice groups. Also with: Reni Santoni, Richard Rust.

STUFF, THE (1985) C/88m. Immoral but efficient fired FBI agent Michael Moriarty is hired by ice-cream magnates to figure out the formula for the new product that is cutting into their business. He discovers that "The Stuff" is a living organism, found in an open pit in Georgia. Not only is it addictive, but eventually the thick white liquid drives the consumer insane and finally it "consumes" his insides. (Of course, The Stuff is meant to represent drugs.) Moriarty joins forces with the woman (Andrea Marcovicci) who conceived the Madison Avenue publicity campaign for The Stuff, a brave young boy (Scott Bloom) whose family was wiped out, and the batty right-wing leader (Paul Sorvino) of a paramilitary survival group. Writer-director Larry Cohen's horror spoof satirizes (among many, many things) how Americans automatically become hooked on all trendy ice creams, cookies, and health (diet high-energy) products. Odd film has interesting non-hero types as heroes, good offbeat performances, some genuinely funny scenes, and a premise that works. But it would be so much stronger if the production values were better; it looks sloppy and choppy (the transitions between scenes are almost nonexistent) and after a while it's hard to tell what's going on. Also with: Garrett Morris, Patrick O'Neal, Danny Aiello, Alexander Scourby, Harvey Waldman.

STUNT MAN, THE (1980) C/129m. Shellshocked, paranoid young Vietnam vet Cameron (Steve Railsback) is fleeing police because of an unwarranted manslaughter charge when he stumbles onto a movie set where a WWII film is being made. His appearance on a bridge ruins a stunt, and the stuntman, Bert, drowns. Fire-breathing, egocentric, wicked, super-intellectual director Eli Cross (Peter O'Toole) offers Cameron the stuntman job *and* Bert's identity. That way neither Eli nor Cameron will have to face police questioning. Having been living on the edge for many years, Cameron already has trouble distinguishing between illusion and reality; this confusion is intensified when working on the *war* movie, where everything is faked (through make-up, stunts, doubles, editing, selective photography) to create a sense of reality. All is seen through his eyes. He becomes frightened that the godlike Eli thinks his movie is so significant that even real death on film is justified—he thinks Eli wants to kill him in his final stunt. What we have, then, is a test where each calls the other's bluff. Eli tests Cameron to see if he'll do the final dangerous stunt despite thinking Eli wants him dead; and Cameron tests Eli to see if Eli will let him undertake the final stunt without admitting that he wouldn't allow an amateur like Cameron to put his life on the line. Neither gives in; each survives the other's challenge. Although I'm not taken with Richard Rush's cult film (I tend to dislike most illusion-vs.-reality pictures), I can understand why it has such a devoted following. It is an extremely ambitious film, beautifully structured by Lawrence B. Marcus (who moves away from Paul Brodeur's novel), endlessly imaginative, strikingly photographed by Mario Tosi, and marvelously played by O'Toole. While it is thematically confusing (perhaps it attempts too much) and at times self-consciously directed (particularly during the comical scenes), you have to admire Rush for bravely undertaking such a multi-leveled, *personal* project. Full of offbeat moments and characterizations—some work, some don't. Barbara Hershey is the actress who has a fairytale romance with Cameron. Also with: Allen Goorwitz (Garfield), Alex Rocco, Sharon Farrell, Adam Roarke (star of Rush's *The Savage Seven*), Philip Burns, Chuck Bail.

SUDDEN IMPACT (1983) C/117m. In Clint Eastwood's fourth "Dirty Harry" film, the first which he directed himself, Callahan kills so many Mafia hoods and hold-up men under suspicious circumstances—typically, he aggravates them, they try to shoot him, but he gets them first—that his superiors tell him to leave San Francisco until things quiet down. Instead of vacationing, he goes to a small California beach town, where he gets on police chief Pat Hingle's bad side by investigating a bizarre murder spree that he believes is related to a killing back home. Someone has been shooting men, first in the groin and then in the head. Callahan finds himself attracted to a successful female artist, Jennifer Spencer (Sandra Locke); he is most gratified to discover that she shares his exact sentiments about the inadequacies of the law meting out justice. But he realizes there is something mysterious about her, something troubled and dangerous. As we soon learn, Jennifer is the killer, the avenger of a gang-rape endured years before by herself and her younger sister (who has been in a catatonic state ever since). We watch her brutally gun down those who participated in the rape, one by one—until the most wicked survivor goes after her. Because we learn to sympathize with her—as we do with all leads in "vigilante" movies—we trust Harry will side with her and come to her rescue. Has Dirty Harry ever disappointed us? Film is too violent, but direction by Eastwood is remarkably assured. He makes the most of his action scenes, effectively uses color filters and light and shadows to create bleak, mysterious ambience, and gets an especially interesting performance from Locke, truly an underrated actress. Callahan is almost a second banana to Locke for two-thirds of the film, until Eastwood uses his familiar "resurrection" bit (first seen in *A Fistful of Dollars*) and Callahan seems to re-emerge from another world—he has his superhuman look, standing on the pier with gun at his side, backlit so his face and body are in shadow—to come to Jennifer's aid and gun down some more vermin. Scene in which Jennifer and Callahan discuss ugliness of court and legal handcuffs placed on cops was probably inserted just so critics would waste space figuring out Callahan's philosophy, twelve years after *Dirty Harry*. Initial courtroom scene in which criminals are let go, as usual, because of a legal technicality—Harry didn't follow the rules—seems to be set up for how Callahan would get Locke off at the end. But it appears Eastwood forgot about it by then and borrowed the ending from *Casablanca*. Picture is known for Callahan's threatening "Make my day," a line that was not original to this film. Also with: Audrie J. Neenan (as a mean, foul-mouthed lesbian), Bradford Dillman, Paul Drake, Jack Thibeau, Mack Keyloun.

SUGARLAND EXPRESS, THE (1974) C/109m. Steven Spielberg's debut film is exciting, offbeat entertainment. It has the kinetic energy and visual dynamism of Spielberg's later films, but it's far more cynical. Script by Hal Barwood and Matthew Robbins is loosely based on the true story of Bobby and Ila Faye Dent. Lou Jean Poplin (Goldie Hawn) has just served a short term in a Texas prison on a robbery charge. Learning that her baby has been handed to a foster family in Sugarland, she, as always, acts impulsively. She breaks husband Clovis (William Atherton) out of a pre-release facility. She impulsively steals a car. It crashes when young patrol officer Maxwell Slide (Michael Sachs) gives chase. When Slide pulls her from the car, she impulsively grabs his gun. They take Slide hostage and, in his car, drive toward Sugarland. Captain Tanner (Ben Johnson) mobilizes the police, who keep at a safe distance behind Slide's car. It looks like a convoy headed for Sugarland. Meanwhile, Lou Jean becomes a folk heroine, admired by people along the way because of her desperate attempt to get back her baby. Notice how Spielberg sways us into favoring Lou Jean by showing us the too-old foster mother and a baby that cries anytime she holds it. But I wouldn't want the baby to be given to Lou Jean—she is a sweet person, but she's off her rocker. People like Lou Jean and Clovis have no chance—they act impulsively and naively, never comprehending that they're taking on a force that will crush them. Tanner may feel sympathetic toward the couple, but he will take only so much of their challenging the law. The police will impersonally carry out their role in the drama—just as the government scientists will carry out their impersonal role in *E.T.* The shame is that there is no attempt to understand Lou Jean and Clovis on a personal level, so that the police could understand that Lou Jean and Clovis would never harm Slide. In fact Clovis and Slide are very similar people (Atherton and Sachs even resemble each other)—only Clovis has had bad breaks (probably because of Lou Jean). Picture has interesting characters, but Spielberg gives us no one who can be admired. Acting is solid—Hawn, in an animated but rare noncomedic role, might have gotten an Oscar nomination if she'd had a few more big scenes. Action sequences are extremely well done. Some of the stunt work (such as the men flying into a puddle from off their crashing news van) anticipates *Mad Max*. Impressive photography by Vilmos Zsigmond. Scored by John Williams. Produced by Richard D. Zanuck and David Brown.

SULLIVAN'S TRAVELS (1941) B&W/91m.

Preston Sturges's marvelous social satire stars Joel McCrea as successful but frustrated Hollywood director John L. Sullivan, who decides to stop making silly comedies during the Depression and make a picture about human suffering. He and an aspiring actress (Veronica Lake as "The Girl") dress up like hoboes and, penniless, travel across America, experiencing suffering firsthand and falling in love. Having had enough of living in flophouses and rummaging through garbage cans, Sullivan calls it quits. But he's mugged, suffers temporary amnesia, and is tossed into a Southern prison camp on a murder charge. It's there he sees that laughter is all some unfortunates have. Sullivan may conclude that filmmakers have an obligation to make comedies, but Sturges is proving that a good Hollywood film can mix outrageous comedy with a social message. We laugh at the hysterical dialogue, the farcical situations (W. C. Fields could have played some scenes), the satirical barbs against Hollywood, and the slapstick: Keystone Kops-like chases, pratfalls (Lake trips repeatedly), characters getting food dumped on them or lamps broken on their heads, characters falling into water barrels or ripping the seats of their pants. But we also pay attention to the parade of poverty's victims during Sullivan's Swiftian journey. We experience the poor's suffering, desperation, and lack of dignity. Film's dialogue has humor and rhythm. It's like a relay race, with words used like batons. The second one character finishes a sentence, another starts his; characters join in, there are no gaps, and the pace becomes frenetic. Sturges often holds his camera on his actors during long stretches of dialogue, emphasizing the importance of words to each character. He democratically gives all his characters, even his supporting players, important and wise things to say; in fact, Sullivan's butler's (Robert Greig) speech about poverty (how only the morbid rich glamorize it) is the most significant in the film. McCrea, who is well over six feet tall, and Lake at five-foot-two and 90 pounds (though she'd be eight months pregnant by the end of the filming) make a wonderful screen team. Sullivan and The Girl have sweet feelings toward each other from the beginning, and are always protective of one another. She's spunky and funny, he's enthusiastic and humble. An ideal couple. This was the picture that confirmed McCrea and Lake were versatile performers. Film has many high spots, including the scene when Sullivan and the other prisoners watch a Mickey Mouse cartoon in a black church. The other actors, many in Sturges's "stock company," include: Robert Warwick, William Demarest, Franklin Pangborn, Porter Hall, Byron Foulger, Eric Blore, Margaret Hayes, Al Bridge, Esther Howard, Almira Sessions, Jimmy Conlin, J. Farrell MacDonald.

SUMMER PLACE, A (1959) C/130m.

First-rate trash about "we've-gotta-be-*good*" young lovers Sandra Dee and Troy Donahue trying to find refuge from their mixed-up parents. Dee's father, Richard Egan, was once the lover of Donahue's mother, Dorothy McGuire. When Egan, his hateful, puritanical wife, Constance Ford, and Dee vacation at the Maine resort run by McGuire and alcoholic husband Arthur Kennedy, their romance begins again. That's what Ford hoped for—she wants a big alimony settlement. Both couples divorce, and Egan and McGuire marry. Dee and Donahue, who are sent to distant schools by Ford and Kennedy, hate all the adults. Then Dee and Donahue come to visit McGuire and Egan's Frank Lloyd Wright beach house. They are unable to control their passions. Soap opera is lots of fun—it's corny, there's a lot of emphasis on sex, there's hysteria. Dee and Donahue are a movie match made in camp heaven, and Ford is deliciously diabolical; her advice to her daughter is "You have to play a man like a fish." From the novel by Sloan Wilson. Max Steiner composed the romantic score—theme song was an enormous hit for Percy Faith. Also with: Beulah Bondi.

SUNRISE (1927) B&W/97m–110m.

A great silent film by F. W. Murnau, who, in his American debut, takes a simple, universal story and gives it startling emotional impact through breathtaking camera work. Between *The Birth of a Nation* and *Citizen Kane* there is no better example in American film of visual storytelling: expressionistic (sometimes lyrical) film (photographed by Charles Rosher, with Karl Struss) reveals the psychology of its characters from moment to moment through intricate lighting, camera movement and positioning, choice of setting, scenic design, and superimpositions (that reveal thoughts) and other special effects (i.e., those that deal with changes in the weather). A young farm couple (Janet Gaynor, George O'Brien) are happy until a temptress from the city (Margaret Livingston) bedevils O'Brien. She persuades him to drown Gaynor and run away with her to that city. At the last moment O'Brien comes to his senses, but Gaynor is heartbroken about what her husband planned to do to her. She flees. But he catches up with her in the city and there is a renewal of love between the two. They spend a happy, romantic day together. We see for the first time that they are a splendid couple and that she (who'd been passive in earlier scenes) is spunky, funny, and sexier, in her wholesome way, than Livingston. Moreover, their goodness and love are so strong that the evil city becomes warm and friendly under their influence. O'Brien and Gaynor head home and there is a tremendous storm that sweeps them overboard—only now O'Brien doesn't want his wife to drown. Picture has a European look because it was designed in Germany before Murnau came to the U.S. The "City," comprised of false-front, false-perspective buildings, was built for the film, a mile-long trolley track was constructed, and trolley cars were brought in. Adding to the film's high costs were devices built to facilitate camera movement and special lighting during tracking scenes. The picture's dis-

413

appointing box-office returns resulted in Murnau's losing autonomy on future productions. Acting is fine, with Gaynor and O'Brien showing why they were one of the era's most likable screen teams, and Livingston making a devilish *femme fatale*. The scene in which Livingston seduces O'Brien, under a full moon in the swamps—featuring Murnau's most audacious visuals—is among the most erotically intense liaisons in cinema history. Scripted by Carl Mayer, from Hermann Sudermann's story "A Trip to Tilsit." Edgar G. Ulmer served as assistant art director. Also with: J. Farrell MacDonald.

SUNSET BOULEVARD (1950) B&W/110m.

Joe Gillis (William Holden) floats face down in a swimming pool by an old Beverly Hills mansion. He narrates the events leading up to his murder. Joe was broke, having had no luck selling scripts to the studios. Fleeing finance men, he pulled into the driveway of Norma Desmond (Gloria Swanson), Paramount's greatest star during the silent era. Hoping to make some easy money, he agreed to polish a script she wrote, *Salome*, which she hoped would be her comeback effort. Norma's butler, Max (Erich von Stroheim), brought Joe's belongings. Eventually Joe and Norma became lovers. When Norma ruined his affair with a young woman (Nancy Olson), Joe threatened to move out. Norma pulled out a gun. Classic film remains the harshest indictment of Hollywood on film. Director Billy Wilder, writing partner Charles Brackett, and D. M. Marshman, Jr., attack agents, producers, directors, studio heads. More than just assaulting those who have made Hollywood a place where talent and integrity have little meaning, they concocted a funeral elegy to old-style Hollywood films, from the elegant romances and comedies of the silent era to naive backlot romances of the early sound era to adaptations of brooding gothic novels to horror films. Not only does the morbid, death-obsessed plot parallel 1936's *Dracula's Daughter*, but the film abounds in horror-movie references and imagery. What better locale for a "ghost" story—about a woman long thought dead— than Hollywood, a town built on illusions and delusions, where people grow old but remain young on celluloid, where people become has-beens before they've made it. Picture also laments the passing of *film noir*, from which it borrows several elements: fatalism; its Los Angeles backdrop; its weak, tarnished hero and his destruction by romantic entanglement with a strong, manipulative, and also doomed woman; and its first-person narration. The narration has been criticized in some circles for being overly descriptive and hyperbolic. But I think this is precisely how a hack two-story-a-week writer like Joe would talk. Joe's "B"-film-style narration—in 1950, when "B" films were outdated— tells us that Joe is as obsolete as Norma in modern Hollywood. On first viewing, the film seems to be about how pathetic Norma Desmond is and how unfortunate Joe is to have fallen into her clutches. But that's only if we go along with Joe's perspective (his cynical narration)—he tries to get our sympathy by speaking of her only in pitying terms. But Norma is the one who lowered herself to be with him.

Norma was a great star and, as her Chaplin imitation confirms, still has talent—"I *am* big," she declares, "it's the pictures that got small"—while he has never accomplished anything. Joe thinks he's giving Norma a break by staying with her, but Norma's no fool: she knows he's no more than a gigolo and that it is she who is using him. A great film with many classic scenes (including Norma's "entrance" that concludes the film) and a performance by silent queen Swanson that ranks with the best of the sound era. Photographed by John F. Seitz. Music by Franz Waxman. Also with: Fred Clark, Lloyd Gough, Jack Webb, and, as themselves, Cecil B. De Mille, Hedda Hopper, Buster Keaton, Anna Q. Nilsson, H. B. Warner, Ray Evans, Jay Livingston.

SUPERMAN (1978) C/143m–192m.

A wonderful surprise when released in 1978, blockbuster wouldn't have worked at all if unknown Christopher Reeve hadn't been the ideal choice to play the most famous comic-book hero. Reeve's Superman has the handsome, square-jawed face of a classic movie hero—but he also has sweetness and playfulness in his eyes that make him completely unintimidating (except to arch-criminals); his body is strong and straight—but it doesn't look as if he got that way from spending time in the weight room. He is as honest, kind, loyal, dependable, and moral as he looks, but what makes him interesting are his secret desires (these make him complex). He wants to be *human*—to give up protecting the world—so that he can be lover to Lois Lane (Margot Kidder); this Superman is no innocent—he is attracted to women both romantically and sexually. Epic film tells of Superman's origins, beginning on the planet Krypton on the eve of its destruction. It shows him growing up in Smallville, as Clark (Jeff East), the adopted son of the Kents (Glenn Ford, Phyllis Thaxter). Reeve makes his first appearance when the adult Clark Kent, a bumbler who wears glasses and acts fearful, arrives in Metropolis to work as a reporter on the *Daily Planet*. There he meets quirky, spirited, beguiling Lois Lane (Kidder's also ideally cast), bombastic editor Perry White (Jackie Cooper), and friendly Jimmie Olson (Marc McClure). Most everyone in the country, including Lois, is raving about Superman and his mighty deeds since he turned up (at exactly the time Clark made his first appearance). In Superman's first movie adventure he attempts to stop diabolical Lex Luthor (Gene Hackman)— unably assisted by henchman Otis (Ned Beatty) and dumb girlfriend Eve (Valerie Perrine)—from causing California to drop into the ocean so he can make a real-estate killing as owner of the new waterfront. Directed by Richard Donner and scripted by Mario Puzo, David Newman, Leslie Newman, and Robert Benton, the film smoothly mixes myth, lyricism (the Smallville scenes), comedy (mostly deadpan humor), science fiction, romance, suspense, and tragedy. I don't like the broad comedy involving Luthor and his cohorts but the one plot element that really disturbs me is Lois's death, which is painful to watch—no matter that Superman brings her back to life, because the way he does it seems like cheating. With a memorable score by John

Williams and impressive cinematography by Geoffrey Unsworth. An Alexander and Ilya Salkind production. Film won a special Oscar for its special-effects work. Also with: Marlon Brando (who got about $3 million for his brief appearance as Jor-El), Susannah York (as Lara, Superman's real mother), Trevor Howard, Jack O'Halloran, Maria Schell, Terence Stamp, Sarah Douglas, Harry Andrews.

SUPERMAN II (1980) C/127m.
In the first film, three criminals on Krypton were cast into space, locked in a time warp. When Superman (Christopher Reeve) hurls a terrorist group's H-bomb into outer space so it won't explode in Paris and kill Lois Lane (Margot Kidder) and, oh yes, millions of strangers, the explosion releases them from their prison. Evil Terence Stamp, striking-looking Sarah Douglas, and brute Jack O'Halloran arrive on earth, determined to take over. As they have superpowers, only Superman has a chance against them. But Superman has gone away to his Arctic fortress with Lois, whose feeling that Superman and Clark Kent are the same person has finally been confirmed. Superman decides to give up his immortality so he can have a sexual relationship with Lois. When the world needs him, he is not able to help. Sequel got better reviews than the original, but I don't think it quite reaches that high level. The early scenes, before Superman reveals his identity to Lois, are either awkward or James Bond–slick. But once Superman and Lois arrive at the fortress, picture exhibits some of the "magic" of the original. It's surprising that Superman and Lois make love—and it's fulfilling for us who read years of those comic books waiting for Superman/Clark and Lois to get to it. Superman's *big* decision is indeed provocative. The battles of muscles and wits between Superman and the three villains, in Manhattan and at the fortress, are spectacular. But my favorite scene has Clark returning to the snowbound bar where a tough beat him up when he didn't have his powers—now that he has regained his strength, he exacts satisfying revenge (the Superman of the comics wouldn't stoop to being so human). Directed by Richard Lester, who also helmed 1983's *Superman III*, which was doomed the minute Richard Pryor was cast (or miscast) in a pivotal role. An Alexander and Ilya Salkind production. Scripted by Mario Puzo, David Newman, and Leslie Newman; the camera work was handled by Geoffrey Unsworth and Robert Paynter. Gene Hackman, Ned Beatty, Valerie Perrine, Jackie Cooper, Susannah York, and Mark McClure reprise their roles from the original. Also with: Clifton James, E. G. Marshall.

SUSPECT, THE (1944) B&W/85m.
Charles Laughton gave one of his best but least-known performances in Robert Siodmak's outstanding melodrama. The setting is 1902 London, where the gentlemanly, married Laughton works as a tobacconist. He's fat and middle-aged, but so kindly that young Ella Raines falls in love with him. Unable to take shrewish, shrieking wife Rosalind Ivan any longer, he kills her. Detective Stanley Ridges thinks Laughton is a murderer, and in a brilliant scene he re-creates the crime; but he has no proof. Laughton marries Raines and is happy, but Henry Daniell, his wife-abusing rotter neighbor, tries blackmailing him. Laughton poisons him. It's interesting to contrast this picture with Fritz Lang's *noir* films of the '40s, particularly *Scarlet Street*. Not driven to crime by a femme fatale—Raines is a good woman—Laughton makes his own decisions rather than being controlled by fate; he's caught because of a choice he makes; he does not suffer guilt—like us, he realizes that the world is a better place now that Ivan and Daniell are dead. Laughton's a sweet soul and you have to resent the smug Ridges for wanting to arrest him, especially since Ridges takes advantage of Laughton's decency. Expert, atmospheric direction by Siodmak. Also with: Dean Harens, Molly Lamont.

SUSPICION (1941) B&W/99m.
Alfred Hitchcock suspense film is about a lonely woman (Joan Fontaine) who marries a handsome man (Cary Grant) after a whirlwind courtship, before she really gets to know him. She begins to suspect he married her only for her money, in order to pay off huge debt. Soon indications are that he's trying to kill her to cash in her insurance policy. Picture has potential to be another *Gaslight*, with major difference being that here the wife does her own investigation of her secretive husband. Though she pretty much proves his guilt, the studio (RKO) imposed a weak happy ending that clears Grant of any wrongdoing. The studio wanted Grant to play only heroes, but the altered ending makes all his character's actions throughout film illogical—if he *is* innocent of planning his wife's death, then judging him from the way he's treated her, he's a mean, irresponsible jerk who is unworthy of her. Fontaine (who won Oscar) saves picture with gutsy performance. Grant looks stiff because he must deliver every line in a manner to make it suspect. He maintains record of not playing a villain—but it wasn't worth it. Film has good scenes— Grant carrying glowing glass of milk to sick Fontaine, a dinner conversation about murder—but the disappointing resolution keeps it from being top-grade Hitchcock. Also with: Nigel Bruce (perhaps his best non–Dr. Watson role as Grant's good friend), Cedric Hardwicke, Dame May Whitty, Isabel Jeans, Heather Angel, Leo G. Carroll.

SUSPIRIA (ITALIAN/1977) C/97m.
American Jessica Harper arrives in Italy, where she has enrolled in Joan Bennett's strange ballet boarding school. That night a female student, whom Harper sees fleeing the school in great distress, is murdered. Soon after, there are two more grisly deaths. Harper investigates and discovers that the school was founded by a witch and that the faculty and staff are her coven. Dario Argento's horror film has a promising beginning, but it's done in by *too* much visual flair (at the expense of content); a trite plotline and unsatisfying conclusion; poor dubbing; and deafening music supplied by the Goblens and Argento: one begins to suspect that the unseen murderer walking about is an *avant-garde* rock musician. The deaths of the two female victims are too brutal, coming

after each already had endured torturous pain. Also with: Stefania Casini, Alida Valli, Udo Kier.

SVENGALI (1931) B&W/76m. John Barrymore gave one of his finest screen performances in this unusual adaptation of George du Maurier's classic novel *Trilby*. In heavy beard, playing a Russian who speaks with a French-German flavor and a Polish intonation—close to how Du Maurier described his voice—Barrymore's a menacing, sleazy, in-need-of-a-bath figure. He is a hypnotist who puts a spell on the beautiful young Trilby (Marian Marsh) and takes her away, turning her into a famous singer. But while he can control her mind, he can't win her heart. Film was made in the same year as *Dracula* (maybe to capitalize on that picture), and it has a villain who has comparable powers; Svengali may not literally drain the blood of his victim, but he draws the life out of her. Racy subject matter with a very sexy performance by Marsh (who should have been a bigger star). A depressing ending that may surprise viewers. British remake in 1955. Directed by Archie Mayo. Striking sets by Anton Grot. Also with: Bramwell Fletcher, Donald Crisp, Carmel Myers, Lois Allen.

SWEET SMELL OF SUCCESS (1957) B&W/96m. Adapting Ernest Lehman's story, Clifford Odets and Lehman combined to write this savage glimpse at the sleazy New York show-biz scene, where a performer's chance for success depends on that despicable duo, the gossip columnist and the press agent. It's an ugly, dark (James Wong Howe filmed in *noir* style) world full of paranoia, hatred, hustling, squirming, backbiting, lying, blackmailing, sex traded for favors, schemes, threats, broken dreams, ruined lives, money, and power. Odets often wrote about young men who sell out their scruples for money and fame and make a pact (a contract, a deal) with a heartless figure who's on an express to hell. In this case, hustling press agent Sidney Falco (Tony Curtis giving his best performance) anxiously tries to win the favors of cruel, powerful syndicated Broadway columnist J. J. Hunsecker (Burt Lancaster in spectacles). The Simon Legree of gossip columnists, Hunsecker despises the ingratiating, opportunistic Falco, but promises to let him write his column while he's away if Falco can get the musician boyfriend (Martin Milner) of Hunsecker's beloved sister (Susan Harrison) out of her life and into jail by way of a hospital. Falco does a lot of lousy deeds every night (including betraying his clients) trying to get ahead in his profession, but will he stoop so low? Sure. Crisply directed by Alexander Mackendrick, with strong emphasis placed on New York locales. A great array of characters, but Milner and Harrison seem out of place (and boring) among the vipers. Women are all victims or are oddly passive. Elmer Bernstein composed the jazz score. Also with: Sam Levene, Barbara Nichols, Emile Meyer, Chico Hamilton Quintet.

SWEET SWEETBACK'S BAAD ASSS SONG (1971) C/97m. Landmark film in which writer-director-star Melvin Van Peebles tried to infuse the black cinema with a radical black consciousness. His angry picture is dedicated to the "Brothers and Sisters who have had enough of the Man." Sweetback is a sexual performer in the parlor of a black brothel (where a whore introduced him to sex as a young boy). White cops make him accompany them on their rounds so it can look like they're hassling a black. When the cops brutally beat a black they arrest, Sweetback kills them. For the rest of the film he is chased by white cops, who kill several blacks they mistake for him. So it is that a black movie stereotype, the black stud, becomes "a black on the run," the familiar figure of black myth/history in white-run America. Film was controversial because it used certain black stereotypes that whites used in their films (the violent black, the stud, the whore) that were prevalent in Hollywood films; and it never really has Sweetback develop (or express) a heightened political consciousness as a result of his experiences. Ending of picture warns us that Sweetback will come back from Mexico to exact his revenge; yet we don't see him doing so because he wouldn't risk death again unless he understands (which is *doubtful*) that he is not just a wronged individual but a symbol of his repressed people. Technically, the film is crude yet innovative (not necessarily in a positive way); it's intentionally rough rather than slick like a Hollywood film. With music by Earth, Wind, and Fire. Also with: The Black Community, Brer Soul, Rhetta Hughes, Simon Chuckster, John Amos, Hubert Scales.

SWEPT AWAY/SWEPT AWAY...BY AN UNUSUAL DESTINY IN THE BLUE SEA OF AUGUST (ITALIAN/1974) C/116m. Constantly complaining rich fascist bitch Mariangela Melato (who has a voice that would make a cat scream) and constantly grumbling communist shiphand Giancarlo Giannini are cast adrift on a desert island. On the boat, which she'd hired for an outing for her bourgeois friends, she'd treated Giannini contemptuously. On the island he reverses their roles, making her his servant, forcing her to call him sir, slapping her about, and—get this—when she no longer can resist his charms, making her kiss his feet and beg for sex. Lina Wertmuller's attempt to blend class struggle with the battle of the sexes has understandably caused much dissent among viewers. If Giannini treated Melato rudely to teach her a lesson, we could forgive Wertmuller for his actions. But we realize that he actually enjoys Melato's debasement and, on this island, would likely treat any woman, even a communist, in precisely the same manner. That Melato is turned on by her enslavement is infuriating—if he weren't handsome and a great, animalistic lover, would she be so tolerant?—but much more objectionable is that Wertmuller has Giannini be such an expert on women that he expects this to happen. We'd have no trouble accepting what happens on the island as Giannini's fantasy (it could all turn out to be *his* dream), but perhaps Wertmuller should have told the story twice, the second time from Melato's point of view, which surely would be different. The ending, back in civilization, is too long and ambiguous. And once again Wertmuller returns her woman (who opts for a life of privilege rather than a return to the island) to villain status (perhaps she is a bit humbled, but nevertheless she breaks her promise to Giannini and deserts him): a position the controversial director cynically believes anyone who has the opportunity will take.

SWING TIME (1936) B&W/105m.
Enchanting Fred Astaire–Ginger Rogers musical, breezily directed by George Stevens. There's little to complain about. For once the stars play real—well, *almost* real—people (Rogers even has a scene with suds in her hair) and, for a happy change, their characters are civil to each other throughout. Astaire needs to make $25,000 so he can marry his longtime girlfriend, Betty Furness. He tries to make the money by dancing. Rogers, whom he meets at a dancing school, becomes his partner. They fall in love. He tries *not* to make enough money to go home. When Rogers learns he has a financée, she agrees to marry slick bandleader George Metaxa. Astaire has a refreshingly friendly parting with Furness and tries to stop the wedding. Since Astaire and Rogers are both playing appealing, unpretentious characters, we want them to succeed. There is a sweetness to their romance that can't be found in their other films; that's because both seem vulnerable. This is a film in which both stars prove to be excellent comedic actors—they seem to be having a good time together even when they're not dancing, perhaps because they like the characters they're playing, too. A great score by Jerome Kern and Dorothy Fields, with exquisite dances to "Pick Yourself Up" (what a finish!), "Bojangles of Harlem" (the highlight of Astaire's solo has him fast-tapping with three giant shadows of himself), and "Never Gonna Dance," and a lovely singing duet in the snow of "A Fine Romance." (But why no final dance??) A witty screenplay by Howard Lindsay and Allan Scott. Also with: Victor Moore and Helen Broderick (as the stars' best friends), Eric Blore, Frank Jenks.

SYLVIA SCARLETT (1936) B&W/97m.
For years George Cukor would say that this box-office flop was the one embarrassing blot on his and Katharine Hepburn's illustrious careers. But in the mid-sixties it began turning up with increasing frequency on college campuses and in repertory theaters, and a cult for the film took root. Hepburn cuts her hair and poses as a boy so father Edmund Gwenn will allow her to accompany him from France to England. On the boat they hook up with Cary Grant, who, like her father, is a petty thief. Maid Natalie Paley joins them when they form a traveling Pierrot act. Hepburn continues to pass for male, even when she meets and falls for rich artist Brian Aherne. Few pictures are so rooted in theater, and you'll feel like you're watching street theater, improvisational theater, theater-in-the round, Shakespeare in the Park. No film is more concerned with "acting" as a method (rather than a profession) for living one's life; it's populated with characters whose lives revolve around disguise and decep-

tion, pretense and play-acting. But when Sylvia pretends to be a boy (see *Yentl*), she opens up a whole new world for herself and brings out her real self. Only as a male can she control her own destiny and make her own rules. Only as a male can she get her father's respect and share his decisions. This is probably the first film that calls for elimination of sexual barriers which keep women from exploring their own personalities. "Sylvester" is not the alter ego of Sylvia, but is *more* of Sylvia. Critics of the thirties never mentioned the sexual implications in the film. It's remarkable that during this period when subjects like transvestism and bisexuality were taboo, no one mentioned the strange things that happen. We actually see Hepburn kissed on the lips by Paley, who thinks she's a boy and tries to seduce him. It may be innocent of Aherne to invite "Sylvester" to sleep with him—but how many men in their thirties are such good friends with teenage boys? Then, of course, there's Aherne's famous line to "Sylvester": "I don't know what it is that gives me a *queer* feeling when I look at you." When Sylvia reveals she's female, his love for her is so quick that we have to believe he felt more than simple friendship for "Sylvester." It's fun figuring out who might be bisexual, but film is important because it breaks numerous sexual conventions. Compton Mackenzie's novel *The Early Life and Adventures of Sylvia Scarlett* was adapted by Gladys Unger, John Collier, and Mortimer Offner. Produced by Pandro S. Berman.

TABOO (1980) C/86m.
Despite the title, this is a fairly conventional XXX-rated film. Yes, a sexual "taboo" is broken in the last few minutes, but if television soap operas occasionally have storylines dealing with incest, it shouldn't be at all shocking when a porno film attempts the same subject. Busty Kay Parker plays a woman in her late thirties who is dumped by her husband for being a dull lover. After a couple of bad dates, the horny woman seduces her sleeping college-age son (Mike Ranger); once awake, he is more than willing to reciprocate. Adult movie fans will find this the best sex scene in the film and not at all uncomfortable because Parker and Ranger look so unalike that you never once believe they are mother and son making love. First in the successful "Taboo" series. Directed with little imagination by Kirdy Stevens. Also with: Dorothy Le May, Juliet Anderson.

TAKE THE MONEY AND RUN (1969) C/95m.
Woody Allen's first film as writer-director-star is an often hilarious parody of both old-style gangster movies and character documentaries (the type that played on the Mike Wallace-hosted *Biography* back in the fifties). There's a narrator (Jackson Beck) who mixes hard-boiled commentary ("he's

wanted for murder . . .") with straight-voiced absurdity (". . . and for marrying a horse"); and there are interviews with subject Virgil Starkwell's embarrassed parents (who wear Groucho Marx disguises), his grammar-school teacher, his psychiatrist, his cello instructor, and his wife (Janet Margolin)—nobody has anything complimentary to say of him. We discover that Virgil could have had a successful life in crime if it hadn't been for hard luck and stupidity, dating back to when he got his fingers stuck in a gumball machine. Picture has less structure than Allen's later films and there's only one major scene—when he prepares for his first date with Margolin—where he gets laughs by presenting a side of his soon to be familiar "Woody Allen" character. Woody piles on the gags; the immature humor and the forced humor being far outnumbered by comic gems: Virgil playing cello in a marching band; prisoner Woody taking an experimental drug and turning into a Hasidic rabbi who explains why Jewish people eat matzo on Passover; one ventriloquist visiting another at a prison but it's their dummies who have the conversation; Virgil being foiled in one bank robbery because the tellers can't read his note correctly and in another because rival bank robbers turn up at the same time; prisoner Virgil having to spend time in the hole with an insurance salesman. The worst mistake Allen makes is not keeping Margolin's character normal—halfway through the film she becomes another loony when she attempts to feed prisoner Virgil by shoving a hard-boiled egg through the separation wire in the visitors' room, causing diced egg to fall into his hands. An auspicious debut, but nothing to prepare us for Allen's later masterpieces. Also with: Louise Lasser (a brief but effective cameo), Marcel Hillaire, Jacqueline Hyde.

TALE OF TWO CITIES, A (1935) B&W/121m.
Popular adaptation of Dickens's novel of the French Revolution, expensively produced by M-G-M. It's slow in spots and the direction by Jack Conway is too restrained during the scenes after the common people take over. I guess he found it difficult to take the victims of the first part of the movie and turn them into complete villains, but the picture is well cast, has sweep, and captures the times in which it is set. That the film builds a case for revolution in France by showing how cruelly the aristocracy treated the poor makes it more thematically tolerable than something like *The Scarlet Pimpernel*, which celebrates the upper class in France and England and presents the poor as a bloodthirsty rabble that should be oppressed. Ronald Colman is Sydney Carton, a crooked, heavy-drinking, politically apathetic English lawyer. The "far, far better thing" he does is sacrifice himself to the French guillotine to save Charles Darnay (Donald Woods), husband of the woman Carton loves, Lucie Manette (Elizabeth Allan). Basil Rathbone makes a brief but effective appearance as a heartless marquis who's upset that his horses might have been injured while trampling a peasant boy. Blanche Yurka steals the film as the vengeful revolutionary Madame Defarge—her condemnation of Dr. Manette (Henry B. Walthall) in court is a great bit of acting.

A highlight is her wrestling match with Miss Pross (Edna May Oliver). Val Lewton and Jacques Tourneur collaborated for the first time, handling the revolutionary sequences for producer David O. Selznick. Scripted by W. P. Lipscomb and S. N. Behrman. Also with: Billy Bevan, Reginald Owen, Isabel Jewell, H. B. Warner, Fritz Leiber, Tully Marshall, E. E. Clive, Lucille La Verne, Claude Gillingwater.

TALK DIRTY TO ME (1980) C/80m.
Porno film won many Erotica Film Awards and has a cult following. John Leslie is a stud who tells his adoring simpleton sidekick Richard Pacheco that he can seduce any woman. He seduces a female doctor and a female real-estate agent, Juliet Anderson ("Aunt Peg"). He then zeroes in on stranger Jessie St. James, whom he drives into frenzied sexual frustration during three days of platonic courtship. Finally he makes his conquest. Leslie's not a bad actor, but his conceited character is really obnoxious—you'll want at least one woman to reject his "dirty" come-on lines. Nevertheless, the sex scenes—all of the non-kinky variety (there's not even the expected lesbian sequence) —are pretty erotic, and I suspect that because director Anthony Spinelli directed his camera mostly at the women, they seem to be enjoying themselves immensely. 1983's *Talk Dirty to Me II* is also very popular. Also with: Aaron Stuart, Chris Cassidy, Shirley Wood, Spinelli.

TALL BLOND MAN WITH ONE BLACK SHOE, THE (FRENCH/1972) C/90m.
Harmless French farce about a dizzy musician (Pierre Richard) who a group of spies mistakenly believes works for a rival spy ring. They bug his phone, follow him around, and send a beautiful woman (Mireille Darc) to seduce him so he'll reveal vital secrets. Clumsy Richard keeps acting like a fool, but the spies think it's just a clever cover. This is the type of vehicle that—minus the sex—would have been ideal for Bob Hope or Danny Kaye. Contains some funny sight gags; biggest laugh comes when Richard first sees low, low, low-cut, backless gown Darc wears in the seduction scene. Yves Robert also directed *The Return of the Tall Blond Man With One Black Shoe*. Remade in 1985 in the U.S., as *The Man With One Red Shoe*, starring Tom Hanks. Also with: Bernard Blier, Jean Rochefort, Jean Carmet.

TALL T, THE (1957) C/77m.
An obvious influence on numerous westerns, including Anthony Mann's *Man of the West*, this is probably the quintessential Randolph Scott–Budd Boetticher film. It's beautifully shot, strong yet straightforwardly written (by Burt Kennedy, who wrote four of their seven westerns), and deals with Boetticher's primary concerns: how men act according to pride and honor, and how men choose to lead their lives in a West that is becoming increasingly civilized, yet, paradoxically, more violent and amoral. In this new West everyone wants something, be it wealth, a woman, a spread, a position of respect, notches on a gunbelt, to be regarded as a man. After many years as a ramrod, Scott (who possesses the strong sense of honor,

and of self that Boetticher's bullfighters have) has the money to buy a spread—but during the course of this story he will learn that he will be happy only if he has a woman to share it with. He meets that woman, Maureen O'Sullivan, on a stage he takes through the desert. But, afraid of being an old maid, she has just married John Hubbard, who was after her money. When the stage pulls into a deserted station, driver Arthur Hunnicutt is killed and the three passengers are held captive by villain Richard Boone and his two subordinates, Henry Silva and Skip Homeier. Hubbard blabs that O'Sullivan is rich so that Boone won't kill them but ransom them instead. As they wait for the ransom money to arrive, Boone becomes fond of Scott and does everything to match him up with O'Sullivan—including murdering her husband. Not only does he envy Scott, but the two men are set up to be mirror images of one another: their final clash results from Scott being a moral man with violent tendencies and Boone being a violent man with moral tendencies. Both men could make it in the civilized world—unlike all the other men who die in this film—but only Scott is willing to do it peacefully, the hard way. To Boetticher the growth of America had to do with loners such as Scott doing away with their violent Boone-like side, putting away their guns, and settling down with good, loyal (as we find out) women like O'Sullivan. The stability of the country was dependent on marriage, family, and property—that spread they'll share together. Produced by Harry Joe Brown.

T.A.M.I. SHOW, THE (1964) B&W/100m—117m.
Teenage Awards Music International: the answer to a tough trivia question. All-star rock 'n' roll extravaganza was taped at the Santa Monica Civic Auditorium and later transferred to film. It partly makes up for their being little extant footage from television's *Shindig* and *Hullabaloo*. It's a wonderfully nostalgic concert, with some of the most cheerful acts you've ever seen. Some of the music is great; some of the performances are campy; black group Smokey Robinson and the Miracles demonstrating "The Monkey" is embarrassing. For me the thrill is to see Lesley Gore sing "It's My Party" but *you* (not I) may enjoy James Brown's famous cape-and-crying act or Jan and Dean rolling around on skateboards. Other acts include the Rolling Stones, Chuck Berry, the Supremes, Marvin Gaye, the Barbarians, Gerry and the Pacemakers (who keep returning), and Billy J. Kramer (teenagers used to scream over this guy?) and the Dakotas. Footage of the Beach Boys was excised for the shorter version that's usually in distribution. Festive show has go-go dancers, including Teri Garr and Toni Basil. Silly, innocent fun—but as a record of the '64 music scene, it's priceless. Directed by Steve Binder.

TARGETS (1968) C/90m.
Peter Bogdanovich's debut film is remarkable not only because of the sophisticated camera work (by Laszlo Kovacs) but because it is a Hollywood picture daring enough to have both an anti-Hollywood bias and a strong social message. Not since 1956's *The Harder They Fall* called for an act of Congress to outlaw boxing has a film made in wishy-washy Hollywood struck at a specific root of violence in our country. This picture is such a strong indictment of the proliferation of guns in America's private sector that one would guess that Bogdanovich is calling for more than gun control—more likely he would like a constitutional amendment that would repeal our *right* to bear arms. (Strangely, Bogdanovich denied he wanted to make a "message" picture.) The film has two seemingly unrelated storylines that come together at the end. As horror-movie veteran Byron Orlok (Boris Karloff) prepares to make a personal appearance at a drive-in debuting his latest film, Bobby Thompson, Jr. (Tim O'Kelly), an immature gun enthusiast, goes berserk and shoots his wife and mother, then shoots highway motorists while hiding on a water tower with scores of guns, and ends up behind the screen of the drive-in showing Orlok's film, shooting people as they sit in their cars. When Bogdanovich has the sniper shoot through the screen where *The Terror*, a not very scary Roger Corman horror film starring the real Boris Karloff, is being projected, we realize that Orlok was correct when he complained earlier that "real" life is more frightening than horror films. He is also reminding us that, no matter how terrifying Bobby's actions are, it is only a movie we're watching and doesn't compare to the *real* real thing. Unique picture is full of movie references, interesting offbeat touches, frightening scenes—while we get chills watching Bobby kill his wife and gun down innocent people (who could be us!), perhaps the scariest sequence is when Bobby has such an easy time purchasing firearms. Based partly on Texas tower sniper Charles Whitman, Bobby's character in many ways anticipates Robert De Niro's Travis Bickle in *Taxi Driver*. Little-seen picture has a cult following. Also with: Bogdanovich (as a director), Nancy Hsueh, James Brown (as Bobby's dominating father), Sandy Baron, Mary Jackson, Tanya Morgan.

TARZAN AND HIS MATE (1934) B&W/92m.
Englishmen Neil Hamilton and Paul Cavanagh travel into the jungle in search of the elephant burial ground; Hamilton also hopes to convince Jane to return to London with him—when he's turned down, the shifty Cavanagh makes a play for her and attempts to kill Tarzan. The second and best of the Johnny Weissmuller–Maureen O'Sullivan Tarzan series. The original film begins with a safari arriving in Tarzan's jungle; during the rest of that picture Jane and the audience learn all about Tarzan. In this sequel, a safari arrives in Tarzan's jungle; during the rest of the picture we and the Englishmen learn about Jane—specifically, how she has adapted to life in the jungle. In future films, which were meant for family audiences, Tarzan becomes increasingly civilized and domesticated under Jane's influence (he even builds them a permanent home), but in this adult film it is the lady, Jane, who reverts to her primitive nature and goes native. Picture has a lot of action: Hamilton and Cavanagh are attacked by headhunters; gorillas hurl huge boulders at them; Tarzan fights a lion, an 18-foot crocodile, and a wild rhino; and, as usual, the elephants rush to Tarzan's aid. But

the reason for the picture's cult status is that beautiful O'-Sullivan wears one of the most revealing costumes in screen history: a tiny halter top and a loincloth that leave her thighs and hips exposed and little to the imagination. Because Jane is a *lady* from England (not Baltimore, as in Burroughs's novel) with perfect diction, etc., her wearing such a provocative outfit is particularly exciting. It's symbolic of her sexual freedom. In this pre-Hays Office film Jane also swims nude with Tarzan, is constantly pawed by him, sleeps in the nude, has a scene in which she's stranded in the jungle without clothes on (Cheetah was up to his old tricks) and is seen nude in silhouette when dressing in a well-lit tent. I'm convinced that Cavanagh is killed off by the filmmaker because he sees her change clothes when she belongs to Tarzan. That Jane and Tarzan sleep together is all the more startling by Hollywood standards because they aren't married; M-G-M still gave Jane's last name in the cast credits which is submitted to newspapers in order to emphasize that she was single and living in sin. Directed by Cedric Gibbons—the husband of Dolores Del Rio, scantily clad star of the similar *Bird of Paradise*—and Jack Conway (uncredited). Also with: Forrester Harvey, Nathan Curry.

TARZAN ESCAPES (1936) B&W/95m.
The third entry in the Johnny Weissmuller–Maureen O'Sullivan series. It marked the turning point in the series from adult fare to family entertainment. Not only was Jane expected to wear a costume several times the size of the one she wore in *Tarzan and His Mate*, but several scenes considered too horrifying for children were either reshot or eliminated (including the legendary vampire-bat sequence). Still, Tarzan fans will enjoy the film, which deals with a big-game hunter (John Buckler) who wants the King of the Jungle to be his star attraction in a circus. When Tarzan breaks out of the hunter's cage, he is good and angry. Director credit went to Richard Thorpe, who replaced Jim McKay and John Farrow (who'd marry O'Sullivan). Also with: William Henry, Benita Hume, Herbert Mundin.

TARZAN FINDS A SON (1939) B&W/90m.
The fourth entry in Metro's Johnny Weissmuller–Maureen O'Sullivan Tarzan series was supposed to be the unhappy O'Sullivan's last, so the studio decided to kill Jane off and fill the gap in Tarzan's life with a young adopted son, Boy (Johnny Sheffield). Fortunately, so much pressure was placed on the studio by Tarzan fans that Jane does not die, although the entire script most definitely leads up to her demise at the end—her recovery from a fatal injury is miraculous; given a pay raise, O'Sullivan would play Jane twice more. Interestingly, Boy's origins are similar to the origins of Burroughs's Tarzan—origins denied Weissmuller's Tarzan: his parents crash (rather than being shipwrecked) in the jungle and are killed, and the baby, nephew of Lord Greystoke and heir to a fortune, is rescued by a simian. That simian is not a gorilla but one of Cheetah's chimp pals, and the baby soon finds himself in the arms of Jane and Tarzan. Five years later a safari arrives in the jungle looking for

survivors. The relatives of the dead couple (kindly Henry Stephenson and the scheming Ian Hunter and Frieda Inescort) realize that Boy is the dead couple's child (although Jane at first denies it). Tarzan orders them from the jungle. Realizing that Boy is constantly in danger in the jungle, Jane finally agrees to help the visitors take Boy back to England, although this will mean going against Tarzan and perhaps losing his love. She doesn't know that Hunter and Inescort plan to kill Boy so they can claim his money. Film is entertaining, although there's too much footage of Tarzan and Boy swimming around and not enough intimacy between Tarzan and Jane (a bad sign that the series was becoming less adult). The wild Tarzan-elephants-and-chimps-to-the-rescue finale, set in a native village, is rushed and sloppily edited. However, it does have a stunning moment when Tarzan looks angrily at Jane and starts to walk out on her for having betrayed him. Filmed in Silver Springs, Florida. Also with: Henry Wilcoxon, Laraine Day, Morton Lowry.

TARZAN, THE APE MAN (1932) B&W/99m.
First talkie Tarzan film, which borrows elements from Edgar Rice Burroughs's first Tarzan novel, *Tarzan of the Apes*—and deletes many more (including all references to Tarzan's origins)—has lots of action and adventure, but is foremost a very erotic love story set in the primitive jungles of Africa. We meet Jane (Maureen O'Sullivan) long before Tarzan (Johnny Weissmuller) makes his first appearance. She has come to Africa to join her father (C. Aubrey Smith) and a younger man (Neil Hamilton) on an expedition in search of an elephant burial ground. Smith doesn't think she should go along, but she is obstinate. Significantly, she is a young woman who seems to be searching for excitement and (early on, we see her in a revealing slip) her first lover. Hamilton is available, but she is seeking someone with less formality, with wild, uninhibited instincts. In the jungle she is literally swept off her feet by the ape man, who takes her back to his tree lair. She is frightened by him, but her heart beats quickly (and her hand rests on his thigh) as he eyes her lustily and puts his large hands all over her. She senses that underneath the initial roughness he is tender; and she knows that, despite the childish frolicking, he is a *man*! She is glad that she can act without inhibitions. She rips off parts of her skirt to use as bandages on his forehead. She swims with him and keeps climbing into his muscular arms; she runs around barefoot. She has never been more girlish. But following their long, increasingly risqué swim and playing, they both indicate that it's time they grew up. He lifts her and, as if she were a bride, carries her up the tree to his lair. When we next see them, she acts grown up. The playmates and friends have become lovers. Tarzan wants Jane to stay with him, but she feels her father needs her—of course, now that she's met Tarzan, she no longer needs her father. He will be a victim of a dwarf tribe. Tarzan, his elephants, and Cheetah arrive at the native village in time to rescue Jane from a monster gorilla (which anticipates *King Kong*). An excellent beginning to the six-film series made by Weissmuller and O'Sullivan for M-G-M. Olympic

swimming champion Weissmuller has amazing screen presence, but so few lines that 20-year-old O'Sullivan seems to be talking nonstop at some times. Her acting would improve in subsequent films—but even here she's the "perfect" Jane. Directed with adults in mind by W. S. Van Dyke.

TARZAN'S GREATEST ADVENTURE
(BRITISH/1959) C/88m. I'm partial to the Johnny Weissmuller–Maureen O'Sullivan films, but this colorful, action-packed adventure picture is usually regarded as the best of the entire Tarzan series. Released by Paramount, it was produced on a fair-sized budget by Sy Weintraub (who bought the rights to Tarzan from Sol Lesser), filmed in CinemaScope, and made on location in Kenya by a talented British crew headed by director John Guillermin (*Sheena*). Gordon Scott, who had played the jungle hero in several low-budgeted, studio-shot films in the early and mid fifties, returned as a more introspective, human, mature (he even mentions that he's aging a bit), and articulate Tarzan than he had played before. And the villains he confronts aren't cartoon characters, but complex men with singular motivations for committing crimes. Adding to the adult nature of the film is the love interest given to Tarzan: a spoiled jet-setter (Sara Shane) who changes for the better as she accompanies him upriver while he tracks down the bad guys. (However, their kissing scene was deleted from the release print.) Anthony Quayle is the chief culprit, leader of a sweaty group of men (a pre-James Bond Sean Connery, Niall MacGinnis, Al Mulock) who have murdered natives in order to acquire explosives for their diamond mine. Tarzan and Quayle have been enemies from way back, so both look forward to their confrontation and battle to the death. Scott would make one more excellent Tarzan film, 1960's *Tarzan the Magnificent*. Also with: Scilla Gabel, as Quayle's mistress, whose death is one of the most spectacular in the film.

TARZAN'S NEW YORK ADVENTURE (1942)
B&W/71m. The last of the six Johnny Weissmuller–Maureen O'Sullivan Tarzan films produced by MGM; sadly, O'Sullivan would never again play Jane, as she would reject Sol Lesser's offer to accompany Weissmuller and Johnny Sheffield to RKO for a continuation of the series. Partly to mollify O'Sullivan, who had been growing increasingly discontented about the series becoming too juvenile, Myles Connolly and William Lipman wrote a fairly adult script that gave her a chance to wear fashionable clothes and appear in a familiar, non-exotic setting. Tarzan and Jane fly to New York in pursuit of the circus owner (Charles Bickford) who has kidnapped Boy. While Burroughs's Tarzan was equally at home in the jungle and in civilization, Weissmuller is like a bull in a china shop once he arrives in the "stone jungle." Uncomfortable in his double-breasted suit, finding modern conveniences to be ridiculous, and having trouble dealing with values of civilization and articulating his own pure philosophy, Tarzan comes across as such a

savage that he almost loses Boy in a custody battle. But once he finds his niche—at the circus, where animals (including his longtime friends, the elephants) are held captive—there's no stopping him. Enjoyable Tarzan film. Highlight is Tarzan pulling a Steve Brodie off the Brooklyn Bridge—they try to console Jane, but there's no need, because she realizes Tarzan is the one person in the world who can survive such a dive. Directed by Richard Thorpe. Also with: Paul Kelly, Virginia Grey, Chill Wills, Russell Hicks, Miles Mander.

TARZAN'S SECRET TREASURE (1941) B&W/
81m. Fifth entry in MGM's Johnny Weissmuller–Maureen O'Sullivan series has villains Tim Conway and Philip Dorn entering Tarzan's jungle domain as part of a scientific expedition. Tarzan doesn't trust them, so they try to smooth-talk Jane and Boy (Johnny Sheffield) into revealing whereabouts of gold. With gold in hand, Conway kidnaps Jane and Boy and ambushes Tarzan. But Tarzan is not dead and, in an exciting finale, swims to the rescue, fights a giant crocodile, battles cannibals, and calls on the elephants. Plot is pretty standard and a bit on the juvenile level, and budget cutbacks forced director Richard Thorpe to include action footage from *Tarzan and His Mate* and *Tarzan Escapes*. But O'Sullivan is lovely, Conway is vile, and Weissmuller is an ideal adventure hero. The most interesting aspect of the film, considering that the entire series was accused (rightly at times) of racism, is that a little black orphan boy becomes an adopted member of Tarzan's family and is right there with them at the end. Predictably, he wasn't even mentioned in the next Tarzan film. Also with: Reginald Owen, Barry Fitzgerald.

TATTOO (1981) C/103m. Tattoo artist Bruce Dern becomes obsessed with top New York fashion model Maud Adams. When she realizes that he's more than a little wacko, she rejects his advances. He kidnaps her and brings her to his family's deserted house on the New Jersey shore. There he begins to tattoo her entire body. Dern has been everybody's first choice to play insane characters, but this guy takes the cake. When he tattoos Adams against her will and the needle work is obviously his sex-act substitute, we feel terribly uncomfortable because he not only is symbolically raping her but actually altering her body. This sick, repulsive movie was written by Joyce Buñuel; like her dad, Luis, she intended to present perverse, controversial material, but director Bob Brooks couldn't give it any artistry. Only amusing sidelight is that during promotion tour Dern swore that he and Adams actually had sex during film's final sex scenes; the disgusted Adams vehemently denied this. Also with: Leonard Frey, Rikke Borge, John Getz.

TAXI DRIVER (1976) C/112m. Controversial, disturbing character study by director Martin Scorsese and writer Paul Schrader is set in an unfriendly New York where

the air is thick with paranoia, despair, hopelessness, hatred, insanity, black-white hostility. Vietnam vet Robert De Niro (as Travis Bickle) takes a job as a cabbie. Unable to sleep and suffering from terrible headaches and stomach pains, he works long shifts and goes into all parts of the city for fares. He has no friends and spends his free time sitting in rundown porno theaters or in his cell-like room, writing in his diary. He gets a crush on Cybill Shepherd, who works in the presidential campaign of handsome, liberal Leonard Harris. She walks out on him in the middle of their one date (he takes her to a porno film). His headaches growing worse, he turns his attention to getting a 12-year-old prostitute (Jodie Foster) away from her pimp (Harvey Keitel as Sport). He replaces his friendly bangs with a Mohawk cut, attaches several weapons to himself, and trains for action. He wants to assassinate Harris; when that fails, he decides to pull off a daring, gun-blazing rescue of Foster. De Niro's Travis was inspired by Arthur Bremer, the protagonist in Bresson's *Pickpocket*; by Paul Schrader himself when he was living through a particularly hellish period; and, I assume, by the mass murderer in *Targets*. Film is a reworking of John Ford's *The Searchers*, with De Niro assuming John Wayne's Ethan Edwards role. Again we have a war veteran, a social misfit, an outcast, who is obsessed with rescuing a young girl (after failing to rescue a young woman) from her long-haired lover—although she is happy where she is—in order to purify his own soul (on the pretext of purifying the girl's soul). Like Ethan, he was on the non-victorious side in what he believes was a war of liberation. That's why they are so fanatical about *liberating* young girls from foreign camps. Film remains an enormous favorite among critics and fans who are impressed by its gritty realism, orgiastic violence, standout performances, and overwhelming cynicism. But an equal number resent it because of its bleak resolution, culminating in Travis's unbelievable apotheosis. Film purports that a maniac can rid himself of inner demons (Travis becomes healthy and peaceful) and become all civilized by committing cold-blooded murder. De Niro has never been better. He is terrifying when glaring into the mirror in the classic "You talkin' to me?" sequence; his verbal sparring with Harvey Keitel is great, as we can simultaneously see aspects of the character and the actor. Unfortunately, however, too often Scorsese lets his favorite actor do a standard "De Niro bit." His schizophrenia should be represented by two sides of Travis, not one side of Travis and one side of De Niro. Film's best moments are those without violence; they're the surreal rides De Niro takes in his cab. These haunting rides, establishing that Travis is out of sync with the world around him, are beautifully shot mood pieces. No director has better captured the peculiarly wretched *feel* and *odor*, as well as the look, of the underbelly of New York. The Catholic director and Calvinist-trained screenwriter are showing us a guilt-ridden man punishing himself by immersing himself in this degrading environment. Can he cleanse his soul only by emerging from purgatory? Cinematographer Michael Chapman and composer Bernard Herrmann (whose jazzy score was completed on the day he died) make vital contributions. Also with: Peter Boyle, Albert Brooks, Joe Spinell, Scorsese.

TAXI ZUM KLO (WEST GERMAN/1982) C/ 107m. Cult film about a gay schoolteacher (Frank Ripploh) who would like a monogamous relationship but can't suppress his promiscuous urges. While his loyal lover (Bernd Broaderup) waits at home, Ripploh drives around, trying to pick up men (mostly in public bathrooms). Ripploh also directed and co-wrote this crudely made, disjointed, but intriguing autobiographical account. It is a self-indulgent work—which makes sense, since the character is egocentric—but at least Ripploh makes no apologies for his errant behavior. However, he does find the need to show that as a teacher *he* could be trusted with male pupils. Film's U.S. distributor promoted it as an outrageous comedy, but while it has humor—most of it is raunchy—I don't think it can really be classified as a comedy. More accurate: it's Ripploh's perplexed but *honest* look back at the period in his life (I can't tell if he's supposed to represent a segment of the West German gay society) when he was having his last fling as a "loose" man (in a pre-AIDS-scare world) and as a teacher (he became a filmmaker). Be warned that this film has explicit sex. Perhaps more jarring is the finale, in which Ripploh goes to his class while attired in the female garb he wore to the previous night's "Queens' Ball."

TEMPEST (1982) C/142m. John Cassavetes is a successful New York architect who has a midlife crisis. He breaks up with his actress wife, Gena Rowlands—who has an affair with his gangster client, Vittorio Gassman—and takes a vacation in Greece with their 13-year-old daughter (Molly Ringwald in her debut), who has wisdom beyond her years. There he jumps into a relationship with the free-spirited Susan Sarandon. When Rowlands and Gassman come after the girl, Cassavetes, Ringwald, and Sarandon flee to a Greek island, inhabited only by a happy-go-lucky, horny sheepherder, Raul Julia. During their stay Cassavetes keeps Julia away from his daughter and, much to Sarandon's chagrin, becomes celibate himself. As time passes, he pretty much loses his senses and the females become bored with lying in the sun. When they are discovered, Cassavetes manages to conjure up a tremendous, spectacular storm over land and sea (with the help of special-effects man Bran Ferren), causing Gassman's boat to capsize and those on board to come ashore—this includes Gassman's son (Sam Robards), who immediately is attracted to Ringwald. Paul Mazursky's updating of Shakespeare has glorious scenery, beautifully photographed by Don McAlpine. The dialogue is sophisticated and the terrific ensemble (with Ringwald more than holding her own) does a great job: there are some genuinely poignant two- and three-character scenes. But film is filled with long, self-conscious stretches that make it seem interminable. Moreover, watching Cassavetes crack up and spend much of the film in a robe is not my idea of a good time. Also with: Paul Stewart, Jackie Gayle, Paul Mazursky, Betsy Mazursky.

"10" (1979) C/122m.   Dudley Moore is a successful middle-aged songwriter living in LA. He loves singer Julie Andrews but fears that commitment to her would mean he can no longer be a ladies' man. He spots young bubblehead Bo Derek and flips for her. She gets married and goes away on a honeymoon to the Caribbean. He follows! This is a middle-aged *Heartbreak Kid*. Somehow he manages to get this embodiment of sex into bed but, even with "Bolero" playing in the background, he finds that he is no longer turned on by her. Sex has no meaning when the woman is promiscuous. He must be getting old. Blake Edwards's comedy is very funny as long as it doesn't get too wild—as when Moore tumbles down the slope by his house and tries to race back up. Moore does a good job—we can relate to his confusion about sexual identity; I really find the scene with Moore and Andrews at the piano to be touching (and mature). Derek became an international sex star as a result of this film; one can understand her being Moore's dream girl. "Bolero" became a big seller with prospective romeos. Also with: Robert Webber, Dee Wallace, Brian Dennehy, Max Showalter, Don Calfa, Nedra Volz, James Noble.

TEN COMMANDMENTS, THE (1956) C/219m.
Cecil B. DeMille's last film, his most famous epic, is not to be taken seriously, but I'm told that in some places in the world it's taken as gospel. Egyptian prince Moses (Charlton Heston), who is to be the successor to the Pharaoh (Cedric Hardwicke), learns that he was actually born to Hebrew slaves—his Egyptian mother (Nina Foch) had taken the baby Moses from a basket that floated on the Nile—and chooses to join his people. He discovers that he is to be their liberator and take them from Egypt to the Promised Land. His former rival, the new Pharaoh Rameses (Yul Brynner), realizes that his bride (Anne Baxter) still loves Moses, and jealously tries to prevent Moses from accomplishing his mighty task. I love the way all the extras jabber in the background, that Woody Strode plays two characters, that the dancing is so bad, and that everybody talks in stupid metaphors ("Are her lips dry and chafed like the desert sands or soft and moist like a pomegranate?"; "[that material] shimmers like the Nile")—the word *like* is said about a hundred times. But if none of this excites you, then there's always the parting of the Red Sea (one of the greatest special-effects sequences of all time), the Burning Bush, Moses turning the Nile blood red. Despite it seeming that *almost all* the Jews Moses frees turn out to be blasphemous ingrates, the film is a lot of fun; children will think it's great. Heston's Moses is very convincing, especially to himself. He's a handsome, imposing (and finally almost *mad*) figure. I was shocked that the charismatic Joshua, whom I loved as a kid, turned out to be played by John Derek. Cinematography by Loyal Griggs; John P. Fulton won the film's one Oscar for special effects. Also with: Edward G. Robinson (as the traitorous Jew), Yvonne De Carlo, Martha Scott (as Moses's mother), Debra Paget, Vincent Price, Judith Anderson, John Carradine, H. B. Warner, Henry Wilcoxon.

TENANT, THE (FRENCH-AMERICAN/1976) C/125m.   Disturbing psychological horror film, directed by and starring Roman Polanski. Polanski is a timid, weasly clerk who moves into an old building in Paris, into the apartment of a young woman who committed suicide by jumping out a window. He begins to suspect that her insane action was caused by the neighbors, who constantly infringe on his privacy and repeatedly complain to the stern owner (Melvyn Douglas) about the noise he's causing, and even complain to the police about him (when he doesn't sign a petition against another neighbor). Mysteriously, tenants stand for hours in the hall bathroom just staring at the wall. As pressures build up—Douglas threatens to evict him, neighbors pound on his ceiling, his apartment is burglarized, he finds a tooth in his wall, the local coffee shop keeps giving him what the suicide victim used to order—he believes that there is a conspiracy to turn him into the dead woman so he'll commit suicide. Polanski spends his nights wearing her dress; he buys women's shoes and a female wig and takes to wearing make-up. First part of the film is fascinating as Polanski's paranoia regarding the neighbors intensifies. When he starts to dress like a woman, it's a bit too unsettling and ridiculous—especially since his transition is *too* quick. Also, I'd much prefer to see what's really going on with the neighbors than to suddenly see Polanski's hallucinating fantasies (which look like Hollywood clichés)—it's much scarier when the victim is *sane* and can comprehend the magnitude of what is terrorizing him. The most interesting facet of the film is the nature of Polanski's paranoia—in fact, even before he moves in, he has a tremendous feeling of *persecution*; he's a French citizen, but because he's Polish he never feels he fits in—indeed, the police chief asks for his identification. Notice how in the first scene he repeatedly apologizes to the concierge (Shelley Winters) for disturbing her and entering her apartment (he offers to come back later)—and all through the film he keeps apologizing for something, or reassuring people that he won't be a nuisance any longer, or defending why he is just standing where he is, or lying. It is the overwhelming sense of persecution because he doesn't belong (in France, in his apartment, in the café) and because even his identity is suspect—rather than just simple paranoia—that leads to his insanity. The inspired cast includes: Isabelle Adjani (the dead girl's friend, with whom he almost has an affair), Jo Van Fleet, Bernard Fresson, Claude Dauphin.

TENDER MERCIES (1983) C/89m.   Robert Duvall won an Oscar as a country-music legend turned alcoholic (Mac Sledge is much like George Jones) who finds redemption and a second chance at life with a good Christian widow (Tess Harper) and her young son (Allan Hubbard). Bare-bones, Oscar-winning script by Horton Foote has most of the characters speaking simply, humbly, and honestly, and taking long pauses between words. The attempt at realistic dialogue between common people who aren't pretentious often comes across as pretentious. You want at least a couple of occasions in which a character smashes a hammer on a thumb and lets loose with some wild profanity. We're thankful for the brief appearances of Betty Buckley and Ellen Barkin as Duvall's less inhibited ex-wife (still a country star) and troubled daughter. Australian director Bruce Beresford gets excellent performances from his entire cast and presents an interesting vision of Texas and its people. There are many touching scenes between Duvall and Harper, Duvall and Hubbard, Harper and Hubbard, Hubbard and a young friend (to whom he admits that he likes Duvall), Duvall and some admiring musicians, and Duvall and Barkin. One could more easily believe Duvall was a country superstar if his voice were better and if Foote didn't have him pretending to forget the song he used to sing to Barkin and her believing him: she, he, or anyone else involved with country music not knowing "Wings of a Dove" is like rock-music people not having heard of "Hound Dog." Duvall wrote his own songs. Also with: Wilford Brimley.

10TH VICTIM, THE (ITALIAN/1965) C/92m.
Sci-fi sex farce set in a future when war has been abolished and the sole outlet for aggressions is the government-run "Hunt." In order to gain entry into the exclusive Tens Club, beautiful huntress Ursula Andress must kill her 10th target in the Rome Colosseum for an international television audience. Her intended victim, Marcello Mastroianni, will be attempting to kill her and make his seventh successful defense. Preoccupied by monetary and domestic problems, Marcello seems uninterested in the Hunt. Andress poses as a TV journalist who wants to pay him for an interview in the Colosseum, where she plans to reveal who she is and kill him. Naturally, they fall in love. But what can they do about his obligations to his family and to the vast television audience. Whereas Robert Sheckley's short story "The Seventh Victim" is, as he states, "a commentary on love, the need for excitement and the inevitability of self-deception," the film "points out how difficult it can be to earn a living, how tiresome family problems can get, and how romance is always threatened by the long shadow of marriage, especially in Rome." Mastroianni and Andress (who at one point wears a bra equipped to fire ammunition) make a sexy screen couple, and the look of the film and a number of directorial touches by Elio Petri are reminiscent of Fellini. But the novel sci-fi premise gives way at the end to a conventional and tired Italian sex-comedy storyline. Movie has cult, but it would be bigger if it were a bit more fun. Also with: Elsa Martinelli, Salvo Randone, Massimo Serato.

TERMINAL ISLAND (1973) C/88m.
Futuristic low-budget action adventure is usually screened today because it features an early performance by Tom Selleck, as well as his *Magnum P.I.* co-star Roger E. Mosely. But it's much more interesting because of the feminist-humanist themes of director Stephanie Rothman. The setting is a prison island off California where convicted murderers are sent on a one-way trip. There are no guards on the island, but no way to escape. The story deals with a civil war for supremacy of the island between a small band of renegade prisoners and a larger group of settlement dwellers led by a tyrannical maniac. The four women on the island (Ena Hartman, Marta Kristen, Phyllis Davis, Barbara Leigh) decide to fight with the renegades because these men will allow them equal status and sexual freedom. The settlement dwellers had demanded that they work like cattle and provide sexual services as well. Rothman's intention was to "tell a story in which a group of men and women needed each other for survival and therefore couldn't afford the luxury of stereotyped sex-role behavior." This is the most egalitarian—and "unisexual"—movie in memory: the women and men renegades are interchangeable, sharing in all the action, the danger, the plotting of war strategy; when a woman makes love or converses with one man, it could just as easily be with another man—no distinct couples form. A fascinating aspect is that when the renegades win the war, they invite their former enemies to join them in a new society. On this island of murderers, a utopian society emerges: there is peace; all material wealth is shared; power is divided equally; and women and men have equal standing. Also with: Don Marshall, Sean Kenney.

TERMINATOR, THE (1984) C/107m.
This modestly budgeted sci-fi thriller deservedly became a box-office smash, cult favorite, and a *cause célèbre* of critics who compared it to *The Road Warrior* because of its bone-crushing violence, non-stop action, unrelenting suspense, black humor, vision of bleak post-apocalyptic future, and obvious marriage between the filmmaker's gadgetry and the gadgetry/machinery that dominates the screen. Director James Cameron's screenplay (written with Gale Anne Hurd) begins in 2024, when the world is rubble because of a nuclear holocaust initiated by Machines and the lengthy, continuous war between Man and Machine. When the Machines determine they've lost to the human rebels, led by John Connor, they send a sophisticated "Terminator" cyborg (Arnold Schwarzenegger) to present-day LA, to kill Sarah Connor (appealingly played by Linda Hamilton) *before* she can give birth to the person who'd cause their defeat 40 years later. John Connor sends back a young warrior (Michael Biehn) to protect Sarah and explain to her the important role she'll play—not only giving birth to John but also teaching him how to be a warrior and leader. Since Biehn hasn't the weapons to destroy Schwarzenegger, he and Hamilton are constantly on the run, with the unstoppable Terminator hot on their trail. Cameron keeps tension high by cleverly complementing his exciting visuals with jarring sounds: tires screeching, glass shattering, guns blasting, cars crashing, trucks exploding, sirens blaring, engines revving up, objects being crushed, people screaming. Most terrifying is that the Terminator is without fear, without feelings—it kills in broad daylight, in plain view; instead of getting frustrated when its quarry escapes, it just immediately resumes the chase. With his peerless physique, "foreign" accent, and completely unsympathetic demeanor, Schwarzenegger (who refused to play Biehn's role) makes the Terminator into one

of the great cinema villains, one for our nightmares. Interestingly, Biehn has a slight build, indication that Cameron chose not to go along with recent macho-hero trend. Thematically, the film has a liberal point of view: its heroes are revolutionaries; Hamilton is a strong woman who becomes a single mother; it has an anti-nuclear bias. This is also evident in its anti-technology stance. While the Terminator is the ultimate machine of the future, constructed when machines and weapons are identical, Cameron bombards us with images of other machines to show our growing dependency on technology: cars, trucks, tractors, motorcycles, guns, elevators, answering machines, telephones, television sets, playback machines, a hydraulic drive. Still the film has appeal to the soldier-of-fortune crowd and guys who like to crush beer cans on their heads. They consider the Terminator their (fascist) hero, enjoy the spectacular gunplay, and are aware that the film is punctuated by pain. Unlike Schwarzenegger, the *humans* feel the effects of being shot, stabbed, and injured repeatedly. After a while you sense the pain they feel, so obvious is their agony. This is the film's worst aspect. Noting that this picture bears a striking resemblance to his 1964 "Soldier" script for TV's *The Outer Limits*, as well as several other of his works, Harlan Ellison threatened a plagiarism suit; there was an out-of-court settlement which awarded Ellison money plus the screen credit: "The producers wish to acknowledge the works of Harlan Ellison." Also with: Paul Winfield, Dick Miller, Lance Henrickson, Bess Motta.

TERMS OF ENDEARMENT(1983) C/130m.
The Best Picture Oscar winner of 1983 is a slice-of-life seriocomedy that chronicles the combative yet loving 30-year relationship between the infuriatingly resolute widow Aurora Greenway (Oscar-winner Shirley MacLaine based her on Martha Mitchell) and her equally indomitable daughter, Emma (Debra Winger), ending with Emma's painful death from cancer. The mix of "human" comedy, outrageous comedy, perceptive family drama, and morbidity doesn't always mesh. But no one will be disappointed in the splendid performances by the three leads (who peaked as box-office stars in three different decades). It's a special treat seeing MacLaine in a good role for a change, going toe-to-toe with Winger (they're two of the best at expressing vulnerability under tough exteriors) and belly-to-potbelly with Jack Nicholson as Garrett Breedlove, the over-the-hill astronaut with whom Aurora has her first affair in 15 years. This is not one of those pictures in which a stern parent lets her ill daughter know that she indeed loves her deeply although she never could express it. There is never any question that they love each other. Instead the film is about two different women who become close *friends* when Emma moves away with her irresponsible husband, Flap (Jeff Daniels), and two sons and they begin to lead *separate* lives. Always adversaries, they now seek out each other's advice and support. Apart, they begin leading parallel lives. Both have affairs (Winger's is with John Lithgow) at the same time and they swap confidences like giddy schoolgirls. Whereas Emma

married her "hometown sweetheart," Aurora falls in love with the 50-year-old "boy next door." Whereas Aurora had always been peeved at Emma's irrational, spontaneous decisions in life and love, she suddenly feels fortunate to have such a daughter to give her advice on her own problematic love life. In the first half of the movie all the characters count on others for their happiness—and they are disappointed not to be satisfied. But the tragedy that befalls Emma leads us to the film's reassuring theme: in a crisis, especially a life-and-death situation, even irresponsible people will come through for those they love. None of these characters, including aged astronaut Garrett, is capable of grand-scale heroics like flying to the moon, but when Emma is dying they reveal previously hidden gallantry and devotion. *They peak as human beings*. We get a unique look at what makes even the most common people special. This is a touching, tear-inducing film (surprisingly, Nicholson causes the most tears, when he returns to Aurora when she needs him most, and when he makes Emma's long-neglected son feel wanted for the first time). And the ending is wonderful: while no one, including Emma and Flap, knew how to be a good parent, Aurora and Garrett, once the unlikeliest of candidates, have through the extraordinary circumstances evolved into the ideal parents for Emma's children. Adapted from Larry McMurtry's novel by James L. Brooks, who won Oscars for writing and directing. His project was rejected by several studios because executives thought it was more appropriate for a television movie. They probably noticed how Brooks set his scenes in almost every room of the various houses (rather than exotic locations) so that viewers could further identify with his common characters. Also with: Lisa Hart Carroll, Danny DeVito.

TERROR, THE (1963) C/81m.
Roger Corman costume drama was made in three days without much of a script—and the result is a tongue-in-cheek "fake" movie using the sets from his *The Raven*. Muddled plot, set in the 1700s on the Baltic coast, has lost soldier Jack Nicholson taking refuge in the castle of crazed baron Boris Karloff, who is tortured by guilt over the death of his beautiful young wife (Sandra Knight). Both men see her spirit wanderng through the castle—Nicholson even talks to her. Nicholson tries to figure out what's going on. There are many passages of Nicholson exploring the dark castle—obviously, this is filler. There are no scares and nothing really happens until the end of the film. It's pretty boring; enjoyable only for watching Karloff (who's good) and Nicholson (who's pretty lousy) wing it, and for ridiculous plot twists which were probably inserted just to confuse us. Photography is surprisingly good. Last shot is best of film. Francis Ford Coppola and Monte Hellman worked in minor capacities. Also with: Dick Miller.

TERROR OF TINY TOWN, THE (1938) B&W/
63m. This western—"a rollickin', rootin, tootin, shootin' drama of the great outdoors"—is a staple of World's Worst Film festivals strictly because it stars an all-midget

cast. In reality, it's no worse than a lot of "B" westerns of the period, and in fact uses a script that perfectly utilizes every "B" western convention and cliché around. Admittedly, it's odd seeing your hero ride up on a white *pony*, but if you want laughs or even campy entertainment, this isn't the film you've been expecting. It's a novelty film on the order of *Bugsy Malone* (in which kids play adult gangsters)—only without the wit. In a way, you've got to admire the filmmakers for playing it straight, rather than going for easy laughs that would mock the actors' sizes. The familiar story: neighboring ranchers suspect each other of rustling their cattle; Buck (Billy Curtis), the son of one rancher, falls in love with the other's niece, Nancy (Yvonne Moray). When her uncle is killed, Buck is the logical suspect, but he uncovers the real killer (Little Billy), who is also the mystery rustler. Okay direction by Sam Newfield; Helen Gurley was the story editor. Other members of Jed Buell's Midgets include: Bill Platt, John Brambury, Joseph Hearst, Nita Krebs, Charles Baker.

TESS (FRENCH-BRITISH/1979) C/170m. If you didn't know Roman Polanski directed this adaptation of Thomas Hardy's *Tess of the D'Urbervilles*, you'd never guess it, because it seems so out of character. Nastassia Kinski, looking like a young Ingrid Bergman, is the simple but proud farm girl who tries to make something of herself when her poor family, the Durbeyfields, learns it is related to a distinguished family, the D'Urbervilles, only to discover that those with social standing play rough. Afraid to say "no," she becomes mistress to Alec (John Bett), whose family bought the D'Urberville title. Feeling guilty and violated, she returns home pregnant. Her baby lives a little while, dies—the secret (that she is not a virgin, had been an unwed mother) eats at her, makes her feel impure and unworthy. When she later reveals her secret to her beloved husband, Angel Clare (Peter Firth), he walks out on her—saying she isn't the girl he married, the one that he put on a pedestal. He comes to his senses, but too late. Polanski gives Hardy's tale a modern-day feminist perspective. Tess is terribly disappointed by all the men in her life: her drunken father (John Collin) is happy to give his daughter to Alec if he can get a new horse, and won't let the priest baptize her baby because it brought shame to his new "important" name; the priest refuses to give her baby a Christian burial; Alec expresses love for Tess but really wants to control her; and Angel punishes her for her past, although he grants that her affair wasn't her fault. "Once a victim, always a victim," she protests to Alec. But Tess does not give in; she takes what support she needs from other women (who, victimized themselves, are loyal to each other), and she revolts against all the men who did her wrong, even finally telling Angel she did nothing bad and he can't be forgiven for what he did to her. Kinski may not portray Tess with enough passion, but her portrayal is interesting and sympathetic, and she gives Tess admirable strength and intelligence. The other actors are all quite good, and credible in their parts. The 18th-century world Polanski presents is so believable that

we sense the people we see really do live in those farmhouses, shacks, country estates, and townhouses. There is wonderful period detail, and few films have been more exquisitely photographed (Geoffrey Unsworth and Ghislain Cloquet share the credit). A lovely film.

TESTAMENT (1983) C/89m. Meaningful, heartfelt film by Lynne Littman is the bleakest of all nuclear-holocaust pictures. Following the detonation of a nuclear bomb, the residents of a middle-class California town find themselves cut off from the rest of the world. Displaying old-fashioned American resilience, they get back on their feet after the disaster, organize themselves, and make plans to cope until things get better. In most nuclear-holocaust films the survivors struggle but eventually figure out the way to start a new world. But here there will be *no* future: the survivors become ill and begin to die off; the sun does not shine again, but becomes blocked out by nuclear ash. With her husband (William Devane) away and probably dead, Jane Alexander must bear her children's sufferings and deaths alone. Although their deaths are inevitable, Alexander, her teenage daughter, Roxanna Zal (who regrets having never experienced love or sex), and her eldest son, Ross Harris, reveal tremendous qualities. The tragedy is that so much potential for *good* is lost—a nuclear explosion cannot be reversed. That moment when there is a flash in the sky from the bomb should give every viewer a sick feeling in the stomach. Unpolished debut film by TV veteran Littman was financially backed by the *American Playhouse* series. Littman had been much affected by Carol Amen's story "The Last Testament," which she had John Sacret Young adapt. Also with: Lukas Haas (the youngest child), Philip Anglim, Lilia Skala, Leon Ames, Lurene Tuttle, Rebecca De Mornay, Kevin Costner, Mako.

TESTAMENT OF DR. MABUSE, THE/CRIMES OF DR. MABUSE, THE/LAST WILL OF DR. MABUSE, THE (GERMAN/1933) B&W/75m—120m. For his second sound film Fritz Lang decided to bring back Dr. Mabuse (Rudolf Klein-Rogge), the heinous genius criminal of his 1922 silent classic *Dr. Mabuse, the Gambler*. Mabuse is still in an insane asylum, but he has regained his desire to mastermind great crimes, commit terrorist acts, dominate people's wills through mind control, rule the world. He destroys the mind of the detective (Karl Meixner) who is trying to sabotage his gang's activities. He then takes over the mind of his psychiatrist, Dr. Baum (Oscar Beregi), so that when Mabuse dies, Baum *becomes* Mabuse and continues to lead the gang (whose members never actually see their boss). Lang brought back the character who tracked down Peter Lorre in *M*, Inspector Lohmann (again played by Otto Wernicke), and has him work with one of Mabuse's gang (Gustav Diessl) to figure out the villain's identity. Picture was made simultaneously in German (with Wernicke) and French versions. Goebbels seized the German version because the script (although written by Lang's Nazi wife, Thea von Harbou) drew parallels between madman Mabuse and Hitler, but Lang fled Germany (without his wife) and took the French version with him. Since then numerous versions have floated around, including the subtitled *The Last Will of Dr. Mabuse*. It's likely that the only English-language prints you'll see will be dubbed, and dubbed poorly. However, you'll still enjoy several sequences that have impressive visual elements (a high-speed car chase on a country road at night, a murder at a stoplight, Baum visualizing ghostly presences, an underwater explosion). In 1960 Lang would make *The Thousand Eyes of Dr. Mabuse*. Also with: Vera Liessem.

TEXAS CHAIN SAW MASSACRE, THE (1974) C/ 87m.
Ferocious, independently made cult horror film by Tobe Hooper, leading to his *Poltergeist* assignment in Hollywood. It's about five young Texans who encounter a deranged family of murderers who have been killing passersby and using the human meat in their special sausages. In the weird cannibalism subgenre, this is the most striking example of a picture that emphasizes the *slaughter* of human beings for "meat" rather than for outright *feast*. It can be suggested that it was made by vegetarians and animal lovers who wanted to make viewers identify with poor animals in a slaughterhouse that have their heads crushed by sledgehammers (like William Vail), are hung on meat hooks (like Teri McMinn), are put in freezers (like the alive-but-no-longer-kicking McMinn), are sliced up into little chunks by chain saws in preparation for human consumption. Film duplicated the nightmarish effect of Herschell Lewis's *Two Thousand Maniacs*, where six travelers find themselves at the mercy of villains who enjoy torture and murder—in fact, each death in this film is similar to a death in Lewis's. Hooper claimed Hitchcock influenced him greatly, but their styles are dissimilar except for their shared ability to get viewers to imagine there is more blood on the screen than is actually shown. Hitchcock builds *suspense*; Hooper prefers having one shock after another to achieve *terror*. Hitchcock reminds us we're watching a movie, Hooper strives for reality. In fact, Hooper's film is too realistic for its own good. We sense the pain the characters feel, and we also correctly sense that there was pain, blood, and turmoil on the set during production. Script by Hooper and Kim Henkel (*Last Night at the Alamo*) is filled with quirky humor, bizarre characters, including Leatherface (Gunnar Hansen), and terrifying, brutally violent sequences—everyone is shocked, then numbed by Leatherface's first appearance. Well-made but unpleasant film was based, as was *Psycho*, on the infamous Ed Gein case. Also with: topbilled Marilyn Burns (as the one survivor), Paul A. Partain (as Burns's pudgy, sadistic, wheelchair-bound brother), Edwin Neal, Jim Sledow, John Dugan (as the half-dead grandfather), Jerry Lorenz.

THAT HAMILTON WOMAN/LADY HAMILTON (1941) B&W/128m.
Winston Churchill's favorite film. He had good taste. Combination of great romance (a woman sacrifices all for the man she loves) and pro-British wartime propaganda (the woman sacrifices the man she loves for the sake of England) features Vivien Leigh's finest performance as Emma Hamilton. The wife of the English envoy to the court of Naples (Alan Mowbray), she becomes romantically involved with married British naval hero Admiral Lord Nelson, played with quiet strength by Laurence Olivier. Alexander Korda's film is a tribute to the bravery, intelligence, and resourcefulness of women—indeed, it seems to say that where there's a great man, a great woman is running interference for him—and Hamilton is given much credit for Nelson's successes in battle. Perhaps Korda is playing up to American women, whom he wants to send their men into battle against the Nazis. Of course the scandalous affair between Emma and Nelson has few equals in romantic annals, and Leigh and Olivier do it justice. Their scenes together are emotional, for them and us. He is rigid but dashing; she is radiant, alive, aware, available. One of the cinema's most impressive woman characters, Leigh's Emma is brainy, witty, flirtatious when need be, serious when she wants to be, able to handle any situation or impress any person, beautiful, optimistic, helpful, caring, passionate—we feel envious of Olivier's Nelson because he has found the "perfect date." A lavishly produced, maturely scripted, beautifully acted and directed film. Also with: Sara Allgood, Gladys Cooper, Henry Wilcoxon, Heather Angel.

THAT OBSCURE OBJECT OF DESIRE (SPANISH/FRENCH/1977) C/103m.
A distinguished-looking gentlemen (Fernando Rey) pours a bucket of water on a young woman standing on the platform of a railroad station. He tells his startled compartment mates what led him to perform such an act. He relates tale of how he fell in love with the poor beautiful Conchita, who had been his maid. She led him on, always claiming to love him but never relinquishing her virginity to him—despite constantly promising this would happen in time. She seemed to delight in his humiliation, but always insisted she loved him. Finally, when he bought her a villa, she locked him outside the gates and unveiled a young lover. Umpteenth film version of Pierre Louÿs' novel *La Femme et le Pantin* is certainly the funniest. It's funny watching Rey endure humiliation because he's never positive that he is being humiliated. She's just so convincing in her explanations. For you who have been trapped in a relationship in which you rationalize waiting "One more day" for the other person to be as you want—and end up waiting day after day after day—this is a film you'll relate to. Funny characters, including midget psychologist who gives private lessons, odd background action involving terrorists attacking pedestrians and bombing cars and stores. Strangest thing about film is that Conchita is played by both Carole Bouquet and Angela Molina—surely not to underline fact that Conchita is two-faced woman. Confusing ending—but it's appropriate that Luis Buñuel's career ended not with a bang, but a genuine explosion.

THAT'LL BE THE DAY (BRITISH/1974) C/90m.

David Essex is a working-class youth in 1959–60 whose father walked out on him and his mother when he was a boy. He harbors resentment, yet has the same fears of being rooted down as his father. Perhaps it's because his father deserted him that he feels little attachment to anyone—he looks for one-night stands (girls flock around him because he's cute and shy) and avoids commitment; he won't put himself on the line for a friend who's getting beaten up. Unhappy, stuck in dead-end jobs, he finds he can feel emotionally only toward rock 'n' roll music. But once he figures out that he wants to be a performer, which will fulfill his wanderlust, he is stuck with a woman and child—just as his father once was. The type of kitchen-sink drama Alan Sillitoe or John Osborne might have come up with if they'd been writing for the younger 1974 British audience. Somber drama is based slightly on John Lennon's early years. Essex doesn't sing, as he will in the better, more flamboyant sequel, *Stardust*. But there's a great rock sound track: the scene I can really relate to has a friend bringing over a Ritchie Valens album that Essex has been dying to hear (they play "Donna," my all-time-favorite song). Essex turns in a strong performance, playing someone audiences will feel ambivalent about. Ringo Starr does a good job as Essex's pal—and he has an interesting haircut. Directed by Claude Whatham. Also with: Rosemary Leach, James Booth, Keith Moon, Billy Fury.

THEATRE OF BLOOD (BRITISH/1973) C/104m.

In what must have been his dream role, Vincent Price hit his horror-movie peak as Edward Lionheart, a Shakespearean actor who is as hammy as Price himself. Lionheart fakes his own death so he can secretly murder all the critics whose slings and arrows have pierced his ego during his lengthy career (of course, Price was never the critics' favorite). His elaborately staged murders (involving disguises and tramp accomplices) are variations on death scenes from Shakespeare's plays. Although some of the death scenes are a bit too gory, this is a suspenseful, witty, flamboyantly stylish film; viewers should have as much fun as Price seems to be having playing Lionheart. The writing by Anthony Greville-Bell and direction by Douglas Hickox are imaginative. Diana Rigg makes one of her rare screen appearances as Price's daughter, who isn't as sweet as she appears to be. The excellent all-star cast includes: Dennis Price, Arthur Lowe, Robert Morley, Robert Coote, Madeleine Smith, Harry Andrews, Ian Hendry, Coral Browne, Milo O'Shea, Jack Hawkins, Diana Dors, Michael Hordern.

THEM! (1954) B&W/94m.

Ranks with *The Thing* and *Invasion of the Body Snatchers* as the best of the countless fifties science fiction films. Presented like a mystery, it begins with a little girl in shock, wandering through the New Mexico desert. The only thing she'll say is "Them!" Police search the desert for clues to what she's talking about. They discover that several people have been killed or are missing and that great damage has been done to property. The local cop on the case, James Whitmore, is soon joined by FBI agent James Arness and scientists Edmund Gwenn and his pretty daughter Joan Weldon. They unravel the mystery! Giant mutant ants, products of nuclear bomb-testing, are ravaging the area. If they reproduce in sufficient numbers and migrate, mankind is doomed. In an exciting sequence, Whitmore, Arness, and Weldon climb into and burn out a nest of giant ants in the desert. But some mother ants have already escaped. Our four heroes trace *them* to Los Angeles. In a thrilling finale, Whitmore and Arness search the sewer system for the ants and attempt to rescue two boys who are trapped inside. Picture has been labeled a right-wing fantasy (despite Gwenn's final anti-bomb warning) in which the ants are the Red menace and it's perfectly all right for LA to be placed under martial law and for an innocent man to be kept in a psycho ward so what he knows won't leak out. You'll also find elements of *Dragnet*, the classic fifties TV police show (also set in LA), in mystery-solving scenes of Whitmore and Arness, particularly when they question oddball witnesses such as the old man in a drunk ward ("Make me a sergeant and charge the booze!") and the excited, fast-talking Southerner in the mental ward who is played by Fess Parker (the role that won him *Davy Crockett*). Intelligent, entertaining script was written by Ted Sherdeman. Film has believable characters and a particularly fine performance by Whitmore. It's the best of director Gordon Douglas's many films. Also with: Onslow Stevens, Sandy Descher, Mary Ann Hokanson, Sean McClory, Dub Taylor, Richard Deacon.

THEODORA GOES WILD (1936) B&W/94m.

In her first lead in a comedy, Irene Dunne is a young woman from a conservative small town and respected family who secretly writes racy best-sellers for a New York publisher. The firm's art director, Melvyn Douglas, takes an interest in Dunne during her visit to the city and follows her home. So he won't reveal her secret to her maiden aunts or the many town gossips, Dunne hires him as a gardener and lets him stay in the house out back. He is determined to get her to go public with her identity. Later she follows him to New York and makes a spectacle of herself (just as he did in her hometown), trying to get him to stand up to his politician father and risk divorcing his estranged wife and causing a scandal. Film's major problem is that Douglas' character is thoroughly obnoxious (his whistling will drive you crazy). Male cinema writers (in this case, Sidney Buchman) have always presented an obnoxious man who chases after a woman who wants him to go away, pays no heed to her rejections, and doesn't care what embarrassment he's causing her, her family, or her friends; then these writers have the audacity to have the woman fall in love with their hero. When Douglas flees to New York, Dunne should let him go (after all, he's ruining the movie) rather than becoming an unbearable character herself. Most interesting aspect of film is that a woman who grew up in sexually repressive environment is bursting with sexual feelings. It's too bad the story didn't deal more with Dunne's rebellion against the bluenoses in her community (the best parts) and less with her winning an unworthy Douglas. From a story by Mary McCarthy. Director Richard Boleslawski, who arrived from Russia (he was born in Poland) only a few years earlier, convincingly depicts smalltown America. Also with: Thomas Mitchell, Thurston Hall, Rosalind Keith, Spring Byington.

THESE ARE THE DAMNED/DAMNED, THE
(BRITISH/1961) B&W/77m—96m. Not released in the U.S. until 1965, and then in a shortened version because of its controversial subject matter, Joseph Losey's somber, sobering science-fiction film has never received proper distribution or attention. It's not a great picture and it's somewhat pretentious, but it's noteworthy for combining social criticism with sci-fi, its "deviant" characters, its adult treatment of the nuclear issue, and for suggesting that the British government was capable of insidious plots (long before U.S. filmmakers felt free to depict their government in less than glowing light). American Macdonald Carey takes an interest in Shirley Anne Field during a visit to an English seaside village. But her "Teddy Boy" brother, Oliver Reed, whose feelings for his sister are obviously incestuous, objects to their budding romance. While fleeing from him, Carey and Field discover that a group of children are being kept by the government in a secret, isolated facility built in the mountains along the shore. The unhappy, lonely kids are being exposed to radiation so they will be the lone survivors of nuclear warfare. Carey and Field risk contamination when they attempt to help the children escape. Alexander Knox is effective as the duplicitous British official who heads the project. Viveca Lindfors is his friend, a lesbian *avant-garde* sculptress who becomes the cinema's first victim of a free-world government's conspiracy to cover up its own immoral, illegal acts. Evan Jones adapted H. L. Lawrence's novel *The Children of Light*. Also with: Walter Gotell, James Villiers, Nicholas Clay.

THESE THREE (1936) B&W/93m. Compelling adaptation of Lillian Hellman's play *The Children's Hour*, scripted by Hellman and directed by William Wyler. Merle Oberon and Miriam Hopkins start a girls' boarding school. It runs smoothly until an evil little girl (Bonita Granville) decides to tell lies about sexual indiscretions between Hopkins and Oberon's doctor boyfriend, Joel McCrea (the only male with a large part). Granville is forcing another young girl (Marcia Mae Jones) to back her story, threatening to reveal she stole a bracelet. Granville's wealthy, influential grandmother (Alma Kruger) informs all the parents of the other students, and all the children are withdrawn from the school. Hopkins, Oberon, and McCrea decide to sue Kruger. They are further humiliated. Their professional lives are ruined, and the three split apart because Oberon suspects there was something between McCrea and Hopkins (who secretly loves McCrea). Hellman did away with the play's lesbian theme (Hopkins would have been in love with Oberon), but the picture still seems bold. Its strength lies in its exploration of several interesting females (young, mid-

dle-aged, and old) and their relationships with one another—we can compare the friendship of Oberon and Hopkins with that of Granville and her outcast pal Jones, and the relationship between Hopkins and her daffy aunt (Catherine Doucet) with that of Granville and Kruger. Oberon gives one of her finest performances; Hopkins, Granville, McCrea, and the others match her. In 1962 Wyler directed the movie *The Children's Hour*, which utilizes the lesbian theme. Photographed by Gregg Toland. Also with: Margaret Hamilton, Walter Brennan.

THEY CAME FROM WITHIN/SHIVERS/ PARASITE MURDERS, THE (CANADIAN/1975)
C/77m—87m. The first of David Cronenberg's low-budget horror films to play in the United States; it quickly established his cult. The intriguing setting is an isolated, sterile apartment complex which is a planned, self-contained community. A mad doctor implants a parasite in his young mistress. It has the power to drive its carrier violently insane. The parasite can travel on its own from apartment to apartment through the plumbing; also, it can be transferred from its carrier through sexual contact. (Cronenberg has been criticized often for having death and disease be the result of illicit sex.) Film has some tension at the beginning when the initial people are infected. It's creepiest when the parasite crawls between unsuspecting Barbara Steele's legs while she bathes; and when she kisses her lesbian lover, we notice that something crawls from inside her throat to inside her lover's. But story, character development, and the film itself go out the window when almost everybody in the building but hero Paul Hampton becomes infected and runs through the halls looking for people to attack. Exploitation picture is too violent and crude, but the special effects (i.e., creatures moving beneath the skin) by Joe Blasco anticipated those that would appear in future big-budget SF and horror films. Also with: Joe Silver, Lynn Lowry, Alan Migicovsky, Susan Petrie, Ronald Mlodzik.

THEY MIGHT BE GIANTS (1971) C/98m.
Uplifting comedy about a brilliant man (George C. Scott) who's convinced he is Sherlock Holmes and dresses and acts the part. His brother wants to have him institutionalized so he can grab his money, so he hires a psychiatrist, Dr. Mildred Watson (Joanne Woodward) to analyze him. As Watson follows Holmes on his adventurous trail through New York City in search of his possibly imaginary Moriarty, she begins to believe that he really is Holmes. They become quite a team. And the film takes on a special dimension. It becomes irrelevant whether or not he is Holmes; we have instead the story of two lonely people who find their ideal companions, who see the grand qualities in each other that no one else is aware of, who believe in each other, who are there for each other. They can exist in a private, exciting world. James Goldman adapted the script from his play. While it runs out of steam toward the end (although the final scene is quite interesting) and has its fill of silly and pretentious moments, it is really quite touching. Also the

pairing of heavyweights Scott and Woodward is to be treasured. As Scott's one male friend, Jack Gilford also has some nice moments, particularly when the timid fellow reveals his dreams of being the Scarlet Pimpernel. The direction by Anthony Harvey (a specialist with actors) is a bit sloppy, but it's surprising the film doesn't have a larger following among cultists who crave non-comformist characters. It's also surprising that no one ever used the premise for a television series. Also with: Lester Rawlins.

THEY SAVED HITLER'S BRAIN/MADMEN OF MENDORAS (1963) B&W/74m−81m. A legitimate candidate for Worst Film Ever Made title. You'll laugh, you'll yawn, you'll scratch your head when you realize plot makes no sense. Action-filled curio looks like a crummy serial edited down to feature-film length by the dreaded madmen of Mendoras. Actually, it's a mangled mix of horribly shot footage from the early sixties and footage from an unreleased 1954 film photographed by Stanley Cortez (*The Magnificent Ambersons*); since this film wasn't released when intended (either 1963 or 1964), more footage was inserted years later. Picture starts out with shaggy-haired guy talking to overweight blonde in a miniskirt. It looks like stag-movie footage. We suspect that they are the picture's leads, but they are immediately killed. From then on, character after character whizzes by in various states of distress. Who knows what's going on? It has something to do with a kidnapped scientist and his daughter who traces him to Mendoras, where he's being forced to develop a nerve gas by Nazis who are being ordered about by Hitler's preserved brain. Too bad Woody Allen didn't use film's visuals for *What's Up, Tiger Lily? II*. Funniest scene takes place in a phone booth. Directed by David Bradley. With: Audrey Caire, Walter Stocker, Carlos Rivas, John Holland.

THIEF OF BAGDAD, THE (BRITISH/1940) C/ 106m. Spectacular special effects and colorful, imaginative sets highlight this wondrous *Arabian Nights* tale, one of the cinema's most popular fantasy films. Alexander Korda's endlessly inventive production includes most everything a young fantasy fan desires: a handsome prince (John Justin), a beautiful princess (tantalizingly clad June Duprez in a role intended for Vivien Leigh), a clever and incorrigible teenager (Sabu), a diabolical dressed-in-black villain (Conrad Veidt), a flying carpet, a giant genie (marvelously and menacingly played by Rex Ingram) in a tiny bottle, an enormous spider, a dog who was originally a boy, a flower that causes amnesia, a toy horse that can fly, fantasy lands, action and adventure. Sabu is a spirited young thief who befriends Justin in prison. Veidt, the Grand Vizier, has taken Justin's throne and attempts to steal away Duprez by keeping her in a trance. Sabu is too resourceful to be kept in jail. He and Justin escape. Later Justin is to be executed by Veidt, but, fulfilling a prophecy, Sabu rides to the rescue on a magic carpet; he is the catalyst for a full-fledged revolt. About halfway through the picture Justin and Duprez sort of fade out, but that's okay because this lets Sabu and Veidt dominate the screen. They make terrific adversaries. The film is initially slow and a bit complicated, but the pace really picks up once Sabu meets Ingram's scary Djinni. It's unusual watching a long sequence (the best in the film) in a British production that features characters played by a dark-skinned Indian boy and an American black man. Certainly many of the effects influenced Ray Harryhausen; indeed, the mechanical doll, which has moving arms, is much like a Harryhausen invention. Ludwig Berger started out as the director, but he was replaced by Michael Powell and Tim Whelan. Alexander Korda and associate producers Zoltán Korda and William Cameron Menzies also directed, without screen credit. Filming of outdoor scenes was done partly in the United States. Miklos Rozsa received an Oscar nomination for his score. Set designer Vincent Korda, cinematographer Georges Périnal (who did wonders with Technicolor), and special-effects men Lawrence Butler and Jack Whitney won Oscars. This is a very loose remake of the 1924 Douglas Fairbanks silent classic. Steve Reeves starred in a 1961 Italian version that bears little resemblance to either of its predecessors. Also with: Miles Malleson (who co-wrote the script with Lajos Biro), Morton Selten, Mary Morris.

THIEVES LIKE US (1974) C/123m. Robert Altman's masterpiece was adapted by the director with Calder Willingham and then Joan Tewkesbury from Edward Anderson's novel, which was also the source for Nicholas Ray's 1948 classic *They Live By Night*. The story takes place in rural Mississippi in the thirties, when country boy Keith Carradine escapes from prison with two bank robbers, friendly Bert Remsen and brutish John Schuck. He joins them in a robbery spree and soon all three are objects of a statewide manhunt. Carradine falls in love with simple, scrawny Shelley Duvall, who helps him when he is badly injured. She doesn't try to reform him. Terrifically acted picture has exceptional, flavorful dialogue. Altman also captures period ambience through carefully chosen sets and props, hairstyles, clothes, and cars; and by establishing a lifestyle for his characters (they listen to radio programs, have family dinners, drink Cokes by the dozen; kids play baseball and explode firecrackers; etc.) that seems perfectly credible. The sets look lived in, and we come to believe that these characters have a life of their own off the movie screen. If you don't find the film *entertaining*, that's probably because of Altman's deliberate pacing and his choice to treat the action sequences the same as the dialogue scenes, without suspense or exciting climaxes—that decision was probably based on the fact Carradine himself doesn't regard the robberies and shootouts as particularly interesting events in his life. Casting is excellent down to the bit parts. The sweet lovemaking scenes between Carradine and Duvall are quite special. Jean Boffety's cinematography adds to the film's lyricism and sense of a bygone time. Also with: Louise Fletcher, Ann Latham, Tom Skerritt.

THIN MAN, THE (1934) B&W/93m. Wildly successful blend of the murder mystery and the screwball comedy, with delectable performances by William Powell and Myrna Loy as Nick and Nora Charles. He's a former police detective who's content to laze around, walk their dog, Asta, drink, and live off his wife's money. The rich Nora, Loy's first "perfect wife," matches her husband's witticisms, snide joke for snide joke, can match his drinking if she tries, tolerates his eccentricities as he tolerates her excesses. He's the type who'll get out of bed in the middle of the night to get a drink; she's the type who'll get up (while he lies there) to answer pounding at the door. She's the thrill-seeker of the two and loves the excitement she gets from hanging around Nick and his underworld connections: "Oh, Nicky, I love you because you know such lovely people." They are a sexy married couple, a married couple who enjoy each other's company, sense of humor, conversation, who have fun. And if you don't get upset by Nick's constant imbibing, you'll have fun watching them and their dog-child. Everybody thinks Nick is investigating a murder, so he finds himself involved without intending it. At the end he gathers all the suspects (one of many party and crowd scenes) and figures out who killed "thin man" Edward Ellis. Directed by W. S. ("One-take Woody") Van Dyke, in 12 days, film has an improvisational feel, with characters moving freely in and out of the frame. Married Albert Hackett and Frances Goodrich did the breezy adaptation of Dashiell Hammett's novel. Nora was based on Hammett's lover, Lillian Hellman. Fine cinematography by James Wong Howe. The fifth sequel was made in 1947. Also with: Maureen O'Sullivan (Jane in Van Dyke's *Tarzan, the Ape Man*), Nat Pendleton, Minna Gombell, Cesar Romero, Edward Brophy, Harold Huber, Porter Hall, Natalie Moorehead.

THING, THE (1982) C/108m. John Carpenter's remake of Howard Hawks's classic more closely follows John W. Campbell, Jr.'s, source story, "Who Goes There?" but it's a tremendous disappointment, trading in the good taste that made Hawks's film so special for some of the most repellent imagery in horror-movie history. An isolated arctic compound inhabited by an all-male research team is invaded by a vicious alien from outer space who has already wiped out everyone at a neighboring compound. It has the capacity to metamorphize into whatever shape, size, or person it chooses. In order to carry out its systematic slaughter of the men, it takes over their bodies one at a time so it can wander about undetected. Not surprisingly, the men lose trust in one another, fearing that the monster lurks beneath the familiar human façade of one of their co-workers. The terrifying premise is exploited by Carpenter and special-effects genius Rob Bottin, who really comes up with some amazing concoctions. But Carpenter makes a major mistake when he has the film's suspense and horror center on the visuals, particularly the extremely gory, often repulsive ways in which the men are killed off. The real horror should be that these men are losing their identities when they are inhabited by the creature. Unfortunately, Carpenter neglected to give his

characters distinct or engaging personalities to begin with; since they are already *dehumanized* from their long stay in the wilderness, we can't be too upset seeing nonentities being taken over. (We *are* upset when watching human characters being taken over in Don Siegel's *Invasion of the Body Snatchers*.) Kurt Russell has the lead, playing the only scientist who seems to have an idea of how to combat the alien intruder. Also with: A. Wilford Brimley, Richard Masur, T. K. Carter, Richard Dysart, Donald Moffat, David Clennon.

THING (FROM ANOTHER WORLD), THE (1951) B&W/87m. The first of a handful of masterpieces that came out of the fifties sci-fi cycle, it has lost none of its class and power in 35 years. Former editor Christian Nyby is credited as director, but most believe that producer Howard Hawks was more than an adviser because the film contains numerous Hawksian elements: rapid-fire overlapping dialogue; humor in the midst of turmoil; a male universe where men respect each other's talents and rank; an intelligent, strong, funny woman (Margaret Sheridan) who's passed the test and is allowed to pal around with the boys; a strong leader type (Kenneth Tobey) who's a little befuddled by the woman pursuing him, but realizes that he needs her for his life to be complete; men working together under pressure, with each—professionals all—contributing his singular skills to get the difficult task done. The story, based loosely on John W. Campbell, Jr.'s, prize-winning "Who Goes There?" is set at an isolated arctic research station that is populated by soldiers and scientists. In a scene with a documentary feel, the men discover an alien who was frozen in the ice, maybe centuries ago. The creature (James Arness), which stands seven feet tall, has resemblance to a human being but for its monstrous features; yet it's determined that it is a member of the carrot family! It thaws out and goes on rampage, attacking dogs and men. It escapes into frozen terrain, but returns to the station to get blood. Tobey tries to figure out how to stop this seemingly indestructible alien. This is the first sci-fi film to show opposing views of the military and scientists on how to deal with aliens—army men want to shoot them, scientists want (foolishly) to communicate with them. Suspenseful picture uses horror-movie elements; the biggest jolt is when Tobey opens a door expecting to find the alien hiding in a room only to have it standing right in front of him. The sustained tension is a result of the clever timing of shocks. Film is a favorite of most contemporary sci-fi directors, but few have been able to match it. Music by Dimitri Tiomkin. Script by Charles Lederer, with an assist from Ben Hecht. Remade in 1982 by John Carpenter. Also with: Robert Cornthwaite, Douglas Spencer, Dewey Martin, George Fenneman.

THINGS TO COME (BRITISH/1936) B&W/92m—113m. Monumental, extremely ambitious, and lavish Alexander Korda production was most expensive British film at the time. The truly innovative special effects and bizarre set design and "futuristic" costumes are still of interest, but what gives fantasy special interest is that it was scripted by 70-year-old H. G. Wells, who adapted his prescient novel, *The Shape of Things to Come*. Wells's script was greatly revised by Lajos Biro and he detested the finished film. Three-part picture begins in Wells's near-future, at outbreak of world war in which everything is destroyed. The war continues for three decades until the world's landscape is covered with the remnants of civilization, and people fight out of habit. There is a plague—the Wandering Sickness—that takes further toll on lives. "Everytown" becomes a medieval-like hamlet ruled by the barbarous Boss (Ralph Richardson) who wages war on the Hill People while ignoring the misery of his subjects. Suddenly, aviator John Caball (Raymond Massey)—who in the first sequence had preached peace to his friends—lands in Everytown, saying his organization, Wings Over The World, is bringing peace and sanity and technological progress around the world. Afraid of progress, the Boss imprisons Caball, but soon the skies are filled with aircraft. Caball is rescued, the Boss is killed (by a *harmless* gas), and the people are freed. Wings Over The World initiates great technological progress, and by the year 2036 the cities are architectural wonders and the people lead a leisurely life. Oswald Caball, John's grandson, is leader of a movement to begin space travel—his daughter and her fiancé are to be launched into space by a giant space gun. Afraid of progress, artists, led by Cedric Hardwicke, try to prevent the launching. Film depicts Wellsian view that near future will be catastrophic, but in time man will build a marvelous, peaceful world. This is the rare SF film that is pro-scientific advance, pro-knowledge, pro-technology. Unfortunately, Wells's spokesman, Oswald Caball, sounds today like a lunatic when he delivers his final speech about mankind spreading out into the universe. Picture is dated and flawed in other areas (the dialogue in this last sequence is laughable). Also it's hard to go along with Wells's view that *pilots* will be mankind's saviors. But epic picture looks different from any other SF film, then or now. It presents a futuristic vision that is at once ridiculous and fascinating. Directed by famous set designer William Cameron Menzies. A score by Arthur Bliss. Also with: Maurice Braddell, Edward Chapman, Ann Todd, Margaretta Scott (who steals scenes as the Boss's woman), Derrick de Marney.

THIRD MAN, THE (BRITISH/1949) B&W/104m.
Classic of the British cinema, directed by Carol Reed and scripted by Graham Greene (with additions by Reed and co-star Orson Welles) from Greene's novel. American Holly Martins (Joseph Cotten), writer of pulp westerns, arrives in postwar Vienna, which is occupied by Allied forces. Having no money, he hopes to get work with his best friend, Harry Lime (Welles), but he learns that Lime was killed in an accident. Martins does a little snooping and begins to suspect that Lime was murdered. Then he realizes that Lime is still alive, but hiding out from authorities. British officer Trevor Howard shocks Holly by presenting proof that Lime was involved in an illegal operation that sold diluted penicillin,

resulting in the death or hospitalization of children. Although Holly has fallen for Lime's former lover (Valli), he goes against her belief that they must remain loyal to Lime and, risking her hatred, cooperates with Trevor in his plan to capture Lime. Through shots of Vienna in ruins, the extensive use of bizarre camera angles, and the presentation of a sinister-corrupt-nightmarish atmosphere, Reed conveys a world out of order, where good men do evil deeds, where the British and the Russians work side by side, where betrayal is more moral than loyalty (which I believe is the film's major theme). Film has suspense, wit, fine performances. Welles is so imposing a figure that it's hard to believe he's in the picture for only a few minutes. The first and last times we see him—with his face in close-up each time—are powerful moments that give surprising insight into Lime's character. The movie has many classic scenes— Holly being bitten by a parrot, Holly being chased by a little boy who's telling everyone within earshot that Holly's a murderer, Lime and Holly speaking while on a Ferris wheel, Lime being chased through the sewers, and, in the finale, Holly waiting for Valli as she walks toward the camera. Her reaction is one of the many surprises that make the film so enjoyable. Anton Karas's classy zither-playing gives the film a romantic, haunting quality; it's just the right extra ingredient that takes this picture to *masterwork* level. Also with: Bernard Lee, Paul Hoerbiger, Wilfrid Hyde-White, Ernest Deutsch, Siegfried Breuer, Erich Ponto.

39 STEPS, THE (BRITISH/1935) B&W/81m—
89m. Alfred Hitchcock's first undisputed masterpiece, the picture that served as model for several of his later romantic suspense thrillers. Innocent Robert Donat is wanted for the murder of a woman in his apartment that was actually committed by foreign spies. Fleeing to Scotland with both police and spies on his trail, Donat can clear his name only if he can track down the leader of the spy ring (a man with a missing finger) and discover the secret of "the 39 steps." He meets lovely Madeleine Carroll on a train, immediately kissing her so the police will think them lovers. She tries to turn him in for the well-publicized murder, but he escapes. Later she winds up handcuffed to him while he's on the run. At first she stubbornly refuses to believe he's innocent; by morning they're in love. Hitchcock builds suspense and tension in several interesting ways: every character Donat comes across—from the murdered female agent to "Mr. Memory"—is holding in either secret information or secret desires; the women he meets—the agent who invites herself to his apartment, the unhappy, lonely farmer's wife who is obviously attracted to him, and Carroll, to whom he is handcuffed and with whom he sleeps—are never allowed their needed sexual release with Donat; and every time Donat enters an interior—a train compartment, a meeting hall, a theater, his apartment, a house, a car, a pub-hotel—he finds either enemies inside with him or that there are no locks to keep them on the outside: there is *no* safe place. Working from John Buchan's novel, Charles Bennett and Alma Reville wrote the sophisticated script, which, thanks

to Donat and Carroll, contains what may be the most sexually stimulating relationship between a *gentleman* and a *lady* there has been on the screen. Full of great characters and memorable sequences—episodes which Hitchcock intended to be individual stories. Also with: Lucie Mannheim, Godfrey Tearle, Peggy Ashcroft, John Laurie, Helen Haye, Frank Cellier, Wylie Watson (as Mr. Memory).

THIS GUN FOR HIRE (1942) B&W/80m.

Exciting, compact adaptation of Graham Greene's popular pulp novel. Alan Ladd became an instant star with his portrayal of lethal hired killer Philip Raven. In a trench coat with its collar turned up, a hat pulled down to his eyes, a gun in his hand, and a deep voice, he is the coolest gunman to hit the scene since James Cagney in *The Public Enemy*. Veronica Lake had found her ideal screen partner. Handsome, blond Ladd and beautiful, buxom blonde Lake, with those dreamy eyes, a peek-a-boo hairstyle, and a husky voice to match Ladd's, are an electrifying screen couple. Ladd is hiding out from police because of a murder rap and is out to kill the evil man (Laird Cregar) who has double-crossed him. The trail leads to a plant where poison gas is made for the enemy. True-blue Veronica Lake helps him out and becomes the first person ever to touch his cold heart. Interestingly, we root for Ladd on his mission of revenge because we realize that his past was so miserable that he never had a chance to be decent, because he was exploited by Cregar, because Lake sympathizes with him, and because we sense that he isn't long for this world. But I wonder how sympathetic we'd be if he had a hairlip, his most distinguishing characteristic in the novel. Climactic scene in the plant is imaginatively handled. One of the few forties crime dramas that weren't really *noir* films. Frank Tuttle directed, from a taut script by W. R. Burnett and Albert Maltz. Robert Preston plays Lake's cop boyfriend. As Cregar's elderly, sickly boss, Tully Marshall is the vilest of villains. Also with: Mikhail Rasumny, Marc Lawrence, Victor Kilian.

THIS IS SPINAL TAP (1984) C/122m.

Riotous "rocumentary" about a fictional British heavy-metal band, Spinal Tap (comedians/musicians Michael McKean, Christopher Guest, Harry Shearer), who have arrived in America for a promotional tour for their new album, *Smell the Glove*. They begin in New York, playing such classics as "Big-Bottomed Woman" for their teenage fans in overcrowded arenas; but the tour becomes a disaster. There is a series of cancellations—manager Tony Hendra tells them not to worry about losing Boston because it's "not a college town"—and fan interest falls to such a low that they wind up playing at an army base and an amusement park, where they are second-billed to a puppet show. Director Rob Reiner plays filmmaker Marty DiBergi, who accompanies the group into humiliation and, spoofing Martin Scorsese in *The Last Waltz*, asks his idols questions and nods throughout their absurd answers (which were brilliantly improvised by the actors). Reiner's parody is not just a question-and-answer session

interspersed with performance clips and interviews with people who know them (it's not like Gary Weiss's *The Rutles*). It has a story format that allows the actors to develop distinct personalities. The emphasis is placed on the shredding relationship of McKean's David St. Hubbins and Guest's Nigel Tufnel, longtime friends. Surprisingly, you really gain affection for these guys (they are unaware of their offensive characteristics) and feel sorry for them when their tour goes sour and Tufnel feels he has to quit the group. Who would think that this film could contain a scene (David and Nigel reunite on stage) that might cause you to shed a happy tear? This is a ridiculous film on many levels (for instance, the band's drummers literally blow up), but so convincing are the three stars that some not too swift people in preview audiences wondered why Reiner had chosen to make a documentary on such a mediocre, unknown band. Also with: June Chadwick (as David's disruptive girlfriend), R. J. Parnell, David Kaff, Patrick MacNee, Fran Drescher (perfect as a record-company publicist).

THIS ISLAND EARTH (1954) C/86m.

Scientists Rex Reason, Faith Domergue, and Russell Johnson are taken to a secret laboratory in Georgia by Exeter (Jeff Morrow), an emissary from the planet Metaluna. They believe they are working on a "peace" project, but soon discover they are actually being used to supply uranium to Metaluna to help it defend itself in an interplanetary war. Metaluna is doomed and the aliens plan to relocate on earth and become the dominant race. Colorful, imaginative, gadget-laden sci-fi, from the novel by Raymond F. Jones. Many fine special effects and some impressive art design of the alien planet, to which the scientists are transported. Plus the Metaluna Mutants are around for a few moments of suspense, laughs. Although not as memorable as Michael Rennie's Klaatu from *The Day the Earth Stood Still*, Exeter is an interesting philosophical alien who learns the finer qualities of earthlings. Good direction by Joseph M. Newman. Also with: Lance Fuller, Douglas Spencer.

THOUSAND CLOWNS, A (1965) B&W/118m.

Cult following has nearly disappeared for Herb Gardner's adaptation of his Broadway play, directed by Fred Coe, of '50s live-TV fame. When made, it was one of the first films that dealt with the theme of nonconformity, rather than merely having a nonconformist lead character. Today its sellout conclusion, in which the nonconformist willingly sacrifices his way of life because of familial responsibility, doesn't sit well (see Chaplin's *The Kid* for a better resolution). Jason Robards, Jr., hasn't had a job since he quit writing for Chuckles the Chipmunk's (Gene Saks) kiddie show. He spends his time as a dropout from society roaming through New York with his twelve-year-old nephew Barry Gordon, a brilliant, funny "middle-aged" kid whom Robards is trying to mold in his image. Gordon wants him to get a job. Welfare bureau threatens to take Gordon away from Robards. Inspired by kindly welfare worker Barbara Harris (her debut)—they fall in love—Robards looks for a job so he can keep Gordon. Dated film is predictable, too chatty, and no longer funny (the scenes with unfunny Chuckles are unpleasant). But it's still a pleasure to watch the acting by Robards, Harris, and Gordon, an excellent child actor (he'd make an interesting interview). With good supporting performances by: Martin Balsam (who took an Oscar), William Daniels.

THREE COMRADES (1938) B&W/100m.
Lovely, much underrated romantic tearjerker, sensitively directed by Frank Borzage—one of the few Hollywood directors who sincerely believed in the power of love. It was adapted from Erich Maria Remarque's novel by F. Scott Fitzgerald (although, much to Fitzgerald's chagrin, producer Joseph L. Mankiewicz changed much of his dialogue). The setting is Germany after WWI: there is widespread poverty and fighting in the streets between political factions. Three disillusioned war veterans, devoted friends Robert Taylor, Franchot Tone, and Robert Young, start a taxi/auto repair shop, just barely making enough money to live on and to drink a lot. None is happy, although Young gets some fulfillment working with a pacifist organization. Then they meet beautiful Margaret Sullavan, who brings a glow to their lives. She rejects rich Lionel Atwill and marries Taylor. But she realizes that she hasn't long to live because of tuberculosis. A very moving film, not only because of the love between Taylor and Sullavan but because of the love between the men—although they, too, love Sullavan, Tone and Young are not jealous of Taylor but happy for him when he wins Sullavan's love. (Tone even persuades Sullavan to marry Taylor.) This is about how three gallant men and one woman sacrifice all for love and principle. Taylor has never been better and Young, who'd mangle his Nazi role in Borzage's 1940 film *The Mortal Storm*, gives a strong, noble performance—although it's a shame that the script keeps his politics so vague. Tone is adequate as the most *heroic* of the three men—but he should know better than to chainsmoke next to the ailing Sullavan. And Sullavan is fabulous, reaching our emotions with every expression, delivering her lines with intelligence and grace and making Fitzgerald's romantic words sound like poetry. Listening to her throaty, haunted voice, one gets the feeling that her character already has one foot in heaven. A wonderful final shot. Seeming no more like Germans than the three male leads are: Guy Kibbee, Henry Hull, Charley Grapewin, Monty Woolley, George Zucco.

THREE FACES OF EVE, THE (1957) B&W/91m.
Joanne Woodward won a deserved Oscar for her portrayal of a multiple personality. She's dowdy Eve White, a dull and passive wife and mother; but more and more a second woman, Eve Black, who's sexy and hedonistic (and unmarried), emerges. Then Jane, a third, more confident, intelligent, and calm personality steps forward. The most interesting aspect of the film is how Eve Black is presented as a manifestation of Eve White's rebellion against the sexual repression her simpleton husband (David Wayne) sub-

jects her to (how angry he gets when he discovers the sexy clothes Eve Black purchased). Today, in this age of *Sybil*, this film seems tame. But when it was released, it was like a *horror* film that scared even adults. Moreover, the film held fascination for individuals who imagined that everyone has a second personality somewhere inside (who perhaps goes out on the town when the dominant personality goes to sleep); this was similar to the fascination we felt at the time—because of the Bridey Murphy case—about the possibility of having been reincarnated. Nunnally Johnson produced, directed, and wrote the enjoyable but often silly screenplay. Most moving scene has Eve White realizing that she's fading from existence and that she has to say goodbye to her daughter for the last time—knowing that next time "another" woman will be in her body. Photographed by Stanley Cortez. Also with: Lee J. Cobb (as Eve's psychiatrist), Vince Edwards, Nancy Kulp, Alistair Cooke (narrator).

THREE GODFATHERS (1948) C/106m.
Bank robbers John Wayne, Pedro Armendariz, and Harry Carey, Jr., flee into the desert with Sheriff Ward Bond's posse in pursuit. They discover a pregnant woman who has been abandoned by her husband. They help deliver the baby boy and promise the dying woman to take it to civilization. The Bible tells them to take the child to New Jerusalem, across the desert. Minor John Ford film is, of course, a Christian parable—the Christmas story. Sentimental, funny, overly symbolic, the film suffers because of sharp changes in tone— if the final scenes are an indication, it might have worked better as a straight comedy. The story bears some resemblance to *The Searchers*, in that Wayne plays a character with a shady past who exorcises his bad qualities while returning a child to civilization—only here Wayne is welcomed (in Welcome, Arizona) with open arms by the citizens because they realize *he* has reformed and can fit into their town. The Wayne of *The Searchers* committed sacrifices without getting redemption. Nicely photographed by Winton C. Hoch. Also with: Mildred Natwick, Charles Halton, Jane Darwell, Mae Marsh, Guy Kibbee, Dorothy Ford, Ben Johnson, Hank Worden, Jack Pennick, Francis Ford.

THREE MUSKETEERS, THE (BRITISH/1975) C/105m.
An inspired, rousing, often hilarious telling of Dumas's classic, deftly directed by Richard Lester. He smoothly blends sharp satire, slapstick, and swashbuckling; and mixes lusty romance and intimate tongue-in-cheek palace intrigue with furious physical action in which even the women participate. Most wonderful of all is the period detail—the people from all classes, the costumes, the well-chosen settings, the work that keeps all the extras occupied—that really transports you back to the 17th-century France that Dumas wrote about. In his best film role, Michael York is a super-enthusiastic, caution-to-the-wind D'Artagnan, who is determined to be a Musketeer. He proves himself worthy when he and his three Musketeer friends, Richard Chamberlain, Oliver Reed, and Frank Finlay, foil

a plan by Cardinal Richelieu (Charlton Heston) and the evil Milady de Winter (Faye Dunaway) to prove to the King (Jean-Pierre Cassel) that his Queen (Geraldine Chaplin) has been unfaithful. The interplay among the characters whom Lester weaves in and out of his story is delightful—one can always sense that the thoughts behind the eyes contradict the words being said. The actors are well chosen; all inject their characters with a singular brand of pride. Made at the same time as *The Four Musketeers*, which wasn't intended to be a sequel. Also with: Raquel Welch (who almost steals the film as the Queen's bumbling confidante), Christopher Lee, Roy Kinnear (hilarious as D'Artagnan's servant), Simon Ward, Spike Milligan, Sybil Danning.

3 WOMEN (1977) C/125m.

Strange film by Robert Altman has out-of-this-world performances by Shelley Duvall (as Millie Lammoreaux) and Sissy Spacek (as Mildred "Pinky" Rose) and a fascinating story line until it gets lost in search of Ingmar Bergman (the merging of women had, of course, been the theme of Bergman's *Persona*). Until picture nose-dives into mystical mire, it has all the elements of a classic horror film (such as *The Man Who Haunted Himself*), only it's not played for thrills but for baffled laughter—ironic humor dominates the film. Millie Lammoreaux is what's known in the vernacular as a zero. She carries on with a smile, a conceited air, and a motor mouth, refusing to admit that no one pays her the slightest attention. (She's a bit like Bob Uecker.) But clown-faced Pinky Rose, who never bloomed into a person, idolizes Millie, her co-worker at a Desert Springs, California, center for geriatric invalids. Having just arrived from Texas, Pinky moves in with Millie, in the Purple Sage Apartments. There she witnesses firsthand how depressing and vapid Millie's life is. When Millie treats her badly and acts in a sluttish manner, Pinky tries to drown herself in the apartment pool. Pinky Rose is born in the water and blooms in the desert. She comes back a different person and begins to act like a rude, lewd caricature of Millie. She takes Millie's Social Security number, her car, and her lover, and even writes in her diary. Throughout the film, Altman stresses such themes as duplication and replacement (there are twins, look-alike friends, twin beds, Hugh O'Brian's double from TV's *Wyatt Earp*, and birth and rebirth). So we figure that eventually Pinky will take over Millie's identity and Millie will either disappear or be stuck as Pinky, the only person who rates less than a zero. But that's not what happens. Actually, I don't know what happens (and I'm in the majority)—but it has to do with their bonding with the third woman in the story; if Sophia Loren hadn't already made *Two Women*, then perhaps Altman could have done without Janice Rule's Willie Hart, a pregnant, angry artist/earth mother. Luckily their final scene together (even if I understood it, I wouldn't like it) doesn't ruin what is a near masterpiece. Of all the haunting moments, what sticks in memory is Pinky's dull, elderly parents in the throes of lovemaking—a sight that further disorients Millie. Also with: Robert Fortier, Ruth Nelson, John Cromwell, Dennis Christopher.

THUNDER ROAD (1958) B&W/92m.

The first and choicest of the many car-chase films in which lawmen race after moonshine runners on twisting Southern backroads. It has always been a drive-in favorite; since the late sixties, critics have been added to its large cult. Robert Mitchum (who devised the story) is the best moonshine runner in Tennessee—transporting the illegal liquor his father makes in his still. He's so successful that U.S. Treasury agent Gene Barry makes a concerted effort to stop him, consequently putting pressure on other moonshine runners. Meanwhile, big city mobster Jacques Aubuchon tries to horn in on the moonshine action by rubbing out Mitchum. With the Feds and the mob after him, Mitchum decides to make one last run. Picture has exciting scenes and offbeat touches by director Arthur Ripley, but its reputation is inflated. The low budget hurts, and picture really slows down during many long, trite conversations. Supporting actors—including Mitchum's son Jim, who plays his younger brother—are weak. In fact, Mitchum carries film alone on his massive shoulders. Highlight is his phone call to Aubuchon in which he warns him that he's coming to kill him. Interesting, if not always proper, use of music. Three tunes, including classic title song, were cowritten by Mitchum. Music during car chases may have influenced "Foggy Mountain Breakdown" in *Bonnie and Clyde*. Also with: Keely Smith, Peter Breck, Trevor Bardette, Sandra Knight, Mitch Ryan.

THUNDERBALL (BRITISH/1965) C/129m.

Fourth James Bond film takes forever to get started and has too many long underwater sequences during which it's impossible to tell what's going on. Nevertheless, it's an enjoyable entry in the Bond series. Sean Connery is particularly appealing as Bond—I think he projects more confidence than in other films in the series. Adolfo Celi makes a strong, sophisticated nemesis, Largo; SPECTRE No. 2 man has stolen some atomic bombs (naturally) in order to blow up Miami. Former Miss France Claudine Auger is a top-grade (though neglected) Bond heroine—she is Domino, Largo's mistress until she sleeps with Bond and "wakes up." Luciana Paluzzi is the gorgeous and deadly Fiona Volpe. Film has no *great* scene, but it's entertaining as long as the actors stay above water. Ian Fleming's novel was adapted by Richard Maibaum and John Hopkins. Edited by Peter Hunt. Produced by Albert R. Broccoli and Harvey Saltzman. Directed by Terence Young. Also with: Rik Van Nutter, Martine Beswick, Guy Doleman, Roland Culver, Bernard Lee, Lois Maxwell, Desmond Llewellyn.

THX 1138 (1971) C/88m.

George Lucas's feature debut was financed by Francis Ford Coppola's American Zoetrope, and its dismal box-office showing almost closed the studio down. But since then it has developed a cult following, which has increased dramatically, of course, due to *Star Wars*. An expanded version of Lucas's prize-winning short *THX 2238 4EB*, which he'd made at USC, this science fiction is set in a grim future: we have the drugs of *Brave New World* and the sexual oppression found in *1984*. The dehumanized world we discover is comprised of antiseptically clean, empty underground chambers and corridors where men and women, with their heads shaved and their uniforms as white as the walls, move about with eyes straight ahead, their mouths shut, and without expressing emotion. Robot police watch out for nonconformity; unseen monitors make sure there are no rebels. In this test-tube world, babies are born only through artificial insemination; sex is not allowed and all inhabitants are given a daily drug dose (which makes them catatonic) in order to eliminate sexual desire. THX 1138 (Robert Duvall) has his drug intake decreased by his female roommate, LUH (Maggie McOmie); she also reduces her own amount. The two make love and she becomes pregnant. But they're caught. She is eliminated and he is sent to this future world's equivalent of prison, a large white room. THX decides to risk an escape to the world above. Throughout the film Lucas's imaginative visuals continuously impress us, but by showing us how lifeless his future world is, he almost puts us to sleep—that's why we're so grateful for the lengthy, old-fashioned chase at the end. A smart film, but I wish Lucas had put a little more original thought into why sex is a threat to totalitarian societies. Huxley's world in which there is so much sex (encouraged by the government) that no one connects sex with love is perhaps more frightening than what Lucas presents. Michael Haller did the art direction; Lalo Schifrin did the score. Also with: Don Pedro Colley, Donald Pleasence, Ian Wolfe, Sid Haig, Marshal Efron, Johnny Weissmuller, Jr.

TICKET TO HEAVEN (CANADIAN/1981) C/ 107m.
A real-life horror film. A young man (Nick Mancuso) who is depressed over a failed relationship is easy prey for a Moonie-like cult. Film contains convincing, terrifying sequence where he and other recruits are systematically deprived of sleep, nutritious food, and privacy, are kept involved in silly group singalongs and confession sessions, and are barraged with religious pablum until all their defenses are broken down. Mancuso becomes a mindless puppet—one of those guys who use every trick in the book to sell flowers on the street. Luckily, he has family and friends who plan to infiltrate the cult, abduct him, and hire a ruthless ex-cult member (R. H. Thomson) to deprogram him before the police can arrest them for kidnapping. A riveting film—you leave sighing with relief. Not without humor. Also with: Saul Rubinek, Meg Foster (with those creepy green eyes of hers), Kim Cattrall (bebopping her way into *Porky's*), Jennifer Dale, Guy Boyd.

TIGHTROPE (1984) C/114m.
A bit overrated but still compelling Clint Eastwood psychological thriller, written and moodily directed by his protégé, Richard Tuggle. Eastwood's a divorced New Orleans homicide detective who investigates a series of murders of prostitutes. After years walking through the sewers of society, Eastwood is on the edge, so much so that he's no longer able to resist the advances of hookers or to control his baser instincts with these women—i.e., he always handcuffs them while having sex. When the prostitutes he questions and has sex with are murdered soon after, he realizes the killer is following him around and is privy to his sexual perversity. Eastwood's search for the killer leads to self-analysis. He tries to figure out why he can be so loving and tender to his young daughters (Alison Eastwood, Jennifer Beck) yet still handcuff his lovers. He also must define the difference between himself, a sex fantasist, and the sex murderer. This is the picture that swayed the critics of America to finally take Eastwood seriously. They were wrong to think this a rare attempt to move away from the Eastwood persona (Eastwood has played with his image in almost all his films), and wrong to think detective Wes Block is a variation on Dirty Harry. They represent antithetical attitudes toward law enforcement. Harry is a maverick cop, Block plays it by the book. Harry may be like the criminals he detests in that he enjoys killing, but he would be repulsed by Block's sexual perversity. He's also incapable of being a father with a home life. (Harry is the man he is because he has nothing to lose but his own life.) I believe Block is meant to counter Eastwood's tender-lover image. Atmospheric and suspenseful. Eastwood goes one up on Charles Bronson's *Death Wish* vigilante by *not* allowing anything to happen to his family before chasing down the killer. Geneviève Bujold is strong and appealing as Eastwood's lover, a rape-crisis therapist who gets him to confront his hostility toward women. Also with: Dan Hedaya, Marco St. John.

TIME AFTER TIME (1979) C/112m.
A very entertaining, extremely clever thriller, written and directed by Nicholas Meyer. H. G. Wells (Malcolm McDowell) travels by time machine from 1890s England to contemporary San Francisco. A sweet gentleman, he is in pursuit of Jack the Ripper (David Warner), who escaped England in an earlier trip in the time machine. Jack picks up where he left off, brutally killing women in the San Francisco area. Wells has trouble adjusting to the present, where violence runs rampant and sexual mores are so far advanced from the Victorian Era, when his advocacy of "free love" had been considered scandalous. But he falls in love with bank teller Amy (Mary Steenburgen), a modern woman. And she flips for him. He enlists her aid in capturing Jack. He convinces Amy he's really H. G. Wells by taking her a couple of days into the future—they read a newspaper stating Jack has murdered her. They return to the present to try to prevent her death. Film has enormous wit, terrific suspense, and, best of all, three outstanding lead performances. Warner is memorable as a vicious, intelligent villain; and McDowell and Steenburgen completely charm us as they fall in love (off camera as well as on)—are there other violent pictures that have such a *charming* couple? The worst, least convincing, and most frustrating scene has Wells being detained by police while Amy is in danger. With music by Miklos Rozsa. Also with: Charles Cioffi, Patti D'Arbanville, Shelley Hack.

TIME BANDITS (BRITISH/1981) C/110m—116m.
Six greedy, rapscallion dwarfs, renegades from the

Supreme Being (Ralph Richardson) because they stole his map of time holes, turn up in the bedroom of an unhappy 11-year-old (Craig Warnock). They take him along as they journey through time while trying to accumulate wealth through thievery. They come across several famous personages—only King Agamemnon (Sean Connery) is nice to the boy—and they do battle with Evil (David Warner), who is after the map. Director Terry Gilliam wrote the script with fellow *Python* alumnus Michael Palin. Yet it isn't a bizarre, *Python*-like comedy but an adventure film, a spectacle. The comedy is secondary. While it's easy to see the influence of *The Thief of Bagdad*, *Alice in Wonderland*, and, especially, *The Wizard of Oz*, Gilliam's film is totally opposite to them in theme. He told me that "it is a reaction to modern fairy tales, a reaction against kids' films which are wonderful but have no guts because they present children with false reassurance that everything will turn out all right. The boy does end up on his own, somewhat disillusioned with the world. Everything isn't lovely, and you give your characters strength by having them experience some of the nastiness. I wanted to get back to Grimm." Picture is extremely fanciful and ambitious, but it wears you out. It might have been a good idea to cut an episode. My favorite character is John Cleese's Robin Hood; his dialogue with David Rappaport's dwarf leader about poverty is a gem—it even surpasses the shipboard (the *Titanic*) proposal of Palin (who has a funny thing on his nose) to Shelley Duvall (who is cut short before she can fully admit, "I have an enormous...)". Other dwarfs: Kenny Baker (*Star Wars'* R2-D2), Jack Purvis, Mike Edmonds, Malcolm Dixon, and Tiny Ross. George Harrison and Denis O'Brien were executive producers; Harrison contributed songs. Also with: Ian Holm (Napoleon), Katherine Helmond, Peter Vaughan.

TIME MACHINE, THE (1960) C/103m. Enjoyable, colorful George Pal production of H. G. Wells's novel. Rod Taylor is George, a scientist with much faith in mankind's future. He builds a time machine and leaves the year 1900 for stops in the future, only to be bitterly disappointed that time and again there is war. Fleeing a nuclear war in 1966, he zooms far into the future, to the year 802,701. There he finds a colony of Eloi—young, blond, ignorant, apathetic, and carefree people living in an Edenic garden. When a young woman (Yvette Mimieux) almost drowns, he is appalled that he is the only person who attempts a rescue. He is repelled by how far mankind has sunk: their lack of culture, their work-free existence, and their refusal to "defend themselves" from the Morlocks, who live below. These hideous mutants of a nuclear war provide food to the Elois, but, being cannibals, use the passive Eloi for their own food. George tries to teach the Eloi to fight back. Pal, who also directed, ignores Wells's intention to set up two distinct classes, the workers (the Morlocks) and the decadent leisure/capitalist class (the Eloi), as well as Wells's application of Social Darwinism to the survivors of the nuclear war. Instead his film deals with how the Eloi make the choice not to be "cattle" raised for slaughter but to regain

human traits (to care for one another, to love, to fight for survival, to gather their own food, to work)—which are distinct from the beastly traits of the Morlocks. Film has excitement and imagination, an excellent beginning, special effects, scary-looking monster-men, and a pleasing though too innocent love affair. Time-travel sequences are especially well done. Also with: Alan Young, Sebastian Cabot, Whit Bissell.

TIMERIDER (1983) C/93m. Remember that *Twilight Zone* episode in which westerner Cliff Robertson walked out of the desert and over a hill to find himself in the present? This is pretty much that premise in reverse: present-day motorcyclist Lyle Swann (Fred Ward) zooms through the desert only to find himself back in the old West. He accidentally got hooked into a time-travel experiment scientists were conducting with a monkey. In 1983 it was daring to make a western, even if it had to contain sci-fi elements to get it produced. The western sequence isn't particularly exciting—except for the lusty Belinda Bauer (of *Winter Kills*) as Ward's love interest—but it's not standard movie fare. Film is even grittier than most westerns. If it had been only a little more inventive, it might have become a real cult favorite rather than a mildly appreciated sleeper. Former Monkee Michael Nesmith (a western-movie fan) served as executive producer, helped out with the screenplay, and composed the score—he was the person most responsible for getting the picture made. Directed by William Dear. Also with: Peter Coyote, Ed Lauter.

TIN STAR, THE (1957) B&W/93m. The typical lead characters in Anthony Mann westerns are men who were once solid citizens in the increasingly tame West, but had something terrible happen to wreck their settled lives—usually the deaths of everyone they loved, caused by people they had trusted—that sent them on crazed, savage paths of revenge throughout the West. Mann's films show how these men finally rid themselves of their inner demons, allowing the prodigal sons to be welcomed back into civilization. In this case the angry, cynical Mann "hero" is a former lawman (Henry Fonda) who became a ruthless bounty hunter after his wife and child died (when his fellow citizens would not lend him money to pay the doctor's bills). He rides into a struggling town where a young deputy (Anthony Perkins) is in over his head trying to bring about law and order. Perhaps seeing himself in Perkins, when he had been a youth with hopes, dreams, and ideals, Fonda teaches him the ropes so that he can handle any situation. Fonda also becomes attached to widow Betsy Palmer and her son (Michael Ray)—a ready-made new family. He again has something to live for. Film has a pacifist theme, unusual for a western. Mann succeeds in getting us to want a peaceful resolution, without hero-vs.-bad-guy confrontation scenes. Fittingly, there are only two killings in the film, and one takes place off screen. Fonda gives a very controlled, sensible performance—he isn't nearly as neurotic as Jimmy Stewart in his Mann films. He would play a similar role in the TV series *The Deputy*, which was loosely based on this film. Script by Dudley Nichols. Also with: Neville Brand, John McIntire, Mary Webster, Peter Baldwin, Lee Van Cleef.

TINGLER, THE (1959) B&W-C/80m–82m.

Pretty good William Castle chiller has a hammy Vincent Price playing a pathologist who has some pretty strange theories about fear. He believes that, if not tempered by a scream, fear has the power to kill. He also believes that fear manifests itself as a living creature that forms on the spine and has the ability to snap the spinal cord. He actually removes such a creature from a victim's spine—and the wiggly, lobsterlike being is one of the weirdest (though not one of the best) monsters in horror-film history. There are a couple of genuinely creepy scenes—the best involves a deaf mute (Judith Evelyn) who is incapable of screaming away her deadly fears. There's also a nifty *color* bit with a blood-filled bathtub. Castle's gimmick for this film was "Percepto," whereby, at scary moments, motors would make theater seats "tingle." Also with: Darryl Hickman, Patricia Cutts, Pamela Lincoln, Philip Coolidge.

TO BE OR NOT TO BE (1942) B&W/99m.

The title of Ernst Lubitsch's comedy-propaganda masterpiece, one of the first films to debunk the Nazi myth, refers to the existence of Poland. When the film opens, Warsaw is filled with friendly adults and children milling about, and there are family names on the small shops in the background. Later Warsaw is reduced to rubble, and unhappy, starving people wander through the debris of those shops we saw earlier. When Nazis march into Warsaw, we get angrier. But America would be reluctant to help a people who have given up—so Lubitsch presents Poles whom we would want to support: they are brave, resourceful, and have an indomitable spirit. We see that all kinds of people are putting themselves on the line in the underground movement, from humble bookstore owners to hammy actors like Jack Benny (as Joseph Tura). Benny, flirtatious wife Carole Lombard (as Maria Tura), and the idiosyncratic members of their repertory company help young Polish aviator Robert Stack (who has designs on Lombard and she on him) prevent spy Stanley Ridges from delivering names of underground members to Gestapo chief Sig Rumann ("So they call me 'Concentration Camp' Ehrhardt!"). This requires Lombard to feign a romantic interest in Ridges, Benny to pass himself off as Ridges, actor Tom Dugan (as Bronski) to disguise himself as Hitler, actor Felix Bressart (as Greenberg) to finally get the chance to deliver a speech by Shylock. The continuous deception and disguises are staples of French farce, as is the bedroom intrigue, and are typical of Lubitsch. So are the moments of screwball comedy (the infighting between Benny and Lombard), the sexual innuendo and downright naughtiness, and the flights into burlesque, slapstick, and outrageous spoof. Film was roundly criticized for being funny when it's about a serious subject—but Lubitsch strongly attacks both Hitler and his followers, never letting his humorous treatment of them make us forget they are ruthless murderers. Critics also protested that Lubitsch and screenwriter Edwin Justus Mayer had a group of ham actors outwit Nazis, but if we look closely, we see that in all of Poland not even the resistance could pull off the difficult mission—only these actors have the tremendous egos to compete with Nazis like Rumann or the talent for deceit and disguise that puts them on an equal footing with a spy like Ridges. Benny (what inspired casting!) is marvelous—his attempts at Hamlet's soliloquy are classics. Lombard never looked lovelier than in her last film—at times she has an ethereal presence. She also was never better—watch how her face responds to a character in one way (usually deceptively) while her eyes tell us what Maria is really thinking and feeling. What a great all-around actress she had become! Limply remade by Mel Brooks with Anne Bancroft. Also with: Lionel Atwill, Charles Halton, George Lynn, Henry Victor, Halliwell Hobbes, Miles Mander, Frank Reicher, Helmut Dantine.

TO HAVE AND HAVE NOT (1944) B&W/100m.

Forget the Hemingway novel on which William Faulkner and Jules Furthman supposedly based their script, because Howard Hawks's popular film is really a reworking of *Casablanca*. Our new exotic location is Martinique in 1940, setting of resistance work by the Free French against corrupt and brutal Vichy government representatives. As in *Casablanca*, Bogart's an American expatriate (Harry Morgan) who's trying to ignore the political situation. He's captain on a fishing boat, a cynical, every-man-for-himself man (although we notice he has a heart from the way he treats his aging, alcoholic shipmate, Walter Brennan). He refuses to help some resistance fighters because of the danger involved, but later accepts a fee to help a resistance leader (Walter Molnar) escape by boat. Eventually he becomes inspired by them and intolerant of the fascists in power and joins their cause, just as in *Casablanca*. Molnar's wife (Dolores Moran) was originally intended to be a part almost identical to that of Ingrid Bergman's Ilsa in *Casablanca*, but the role was trimmed so that it now seems unlikely that Bogart and Moran were once lovers—although it's apparent that if he wants her at the end, he could have her. But, like Rick Blaine, he realizes that her place is with her dedicated-revolutionary husband. Unlike Rick Blaine, Bogart's Harry Morgan has another woman to fall back on, namely Lauren Bacall's "Slim," the husky-voiced singer (Andy Williams dubbed her voice!) at the hotel-nightclub where Bogart has a room. Because she has no part in the political-action story, one wonders if "Slim" became an important character in the story only after it was decided to cut back on Moran's role. Bacall still doesn't have that much screen time in her movie debut, but she makes the most of it: she's incredibly cool just slinking around a room, in control of her sexual impulses but making it obvious what's on her mind; and each time she delivers a line, her manner is so suggestive that she turns it into a *line* ("Anybody got a match?"; "You know how to whistle, don't you?—You just put your lips together and blow . . ."). She's a dream girl who tells the leading man how much she enjoyed his kiss, and who doesn't waste time playing games: "I'm hard to get, all you have to do is ask." The film itself becomes confusing and klutzy, the ending is weak, and the secondary characters are poor substitutes for *Casablanca*'s memorable cast of heroes and villains. But every time Bogie and Bacall have a scene together, we feel the romance that was building on and off camera. With excellent dialogue. Remade in 1950 as *The Breaking Point* and in 1958 as *The Gun Runners*. Also with: Hoagy Carmichael, Dan Seymour, Marcel Dalio, Sheldon Leonard, Paul Marion, Sir Lancelot, Chef Josef Milani.

TOKYO STORY (JAPANESE/1953) B&W/ 139m.
A masterpiece by Yasujiro Ozu, in which he returns to his favorite theme, the instability of the postwar Japanese family. An elderly couple (Chishu Ryu, Chieko Higashiyama) with four grown children leave their home in the port village of Onomichi for a rare visit with two married children in Tokyo. They don't complain, but immediately recognize that their doctor son (So Yamamura) and beautician daughter (Haruko Sugimura) don't want to spend time with them or money on them so that they'll have a good time. Their disappointment in their children is heightened by their realization that their grandchildren (Yamamura's two sons) are spoiled and unaffectionate. The only one who shows concern is their widowed daughter-in-law (Setsuko Hara), who is very happy to have their company. When the couple leaves Tokyo, their two natural children think they've had a wonderful time. Last part of film takes place in Onomichi, where four children, Hara, and Ryu gather by ill Higashiyama's bedside. Film deals with transciency of life, the need to care about people when they are still alive, the city's corrosive influence on *human* qualities (which occasionally resurface when the kids return to Onomichi), loneliness, the disappointment parents feel toward their adult children (as well as the difficulty children have in meeting their parents' standards of success), and how parents avoid heartbreak by eventually concluding that their children have turned out better than most. There are lovely performances, family relationships that are universal, moments to treasure. There are many times when you feel choked up—the scene that always gets to me is when Sugimura sees the elderly couple looking at the photo of her dead husband, their son, and, thrilled to have the family connection, quickly runs to a neighbor to borrow fine cups for the occasion. By all means, see this with your children! Also with: Kyoko Kagawa (the couple's sweet schoolteacher daughter, who still lives at home), Shiro Osaka (the other son).

TOM THUMB (1958) C/98m.
This classic M-G-M production of the Grimm fairytale, directed by George Pal, is back in circulation after many years of scattered showings. Russ Tamblyn had his best role as the thumb-sized boy who becomes the adopted son of a kindly couple who'd always prayed for a child. Terry-Thomas and Peter Sellers are evil twosome who want to use Tom for their own ends; their thievery gets Tom and his father into trouble. Children's film is colorful, isn't at all schmaltzy, and has imaginatively designed sets and a spectacular musical number in which the remarkably talented Tamblyn does a great dance with Pal's puppets. But if you're an adult, you may wish you were a kid again so you could enjoy it as you once did. Songs by Peggy Lee. Also with: Alan Young, June Thorburn, Jessie Matthews, Bernard Miles, Peter Bull.

TOMB OF LIGEIA (BRITISH/1965) C/81m.
The last of Roger Corman's eight Edgar Allan Poe films is a stylish Gothic tale in which Vincent Price's marriage to Elizabeth Shepherd is ruined by the evil spirit of his "dead" wife, Ligeia. Like others in the series, it has a castle, a black cat, a fire, an unburied corpse, and a guilt-ridden, mad Vincent Price. This is the classic example of how in the Poe horror films Corman managed to disguise the fact that nothing happens until the very end. To fill time, he has many shots of a black cat scurrying about, shock images, characters walking through the castle, red herrings, and Price (when he's not wearing sunglasses) looking worried or depressed, or with tongue in cheek, sounding ominous whenever he says even the most trivial bits of dialogue. My favorite line: "About ten minutes ago I tried to kill a cat with a cabbage." The ending is lively. Scripted by Robert Towne. Also with: John Westbrook, Richard Johnson, Derek Francis.

TOMMY (BRITISH/1975) C/111m.
The Who's rock opera is brought to the screen with Roger Daltrey as the deaf, dumb, and blind English boy who is pitied, ignored, abandoned, and abused until his pinball wizardry makes him a national hero. Ann-Margret is his tormented, heavy-drinking mother. Oliver Reed is his shifty, money-hungry father. Direction by Ken Russell is ambitious, flamboyant, and at times imaginative, but eventually the succession of wild, colorful, and sometimes disgusting images wears you down: the picture's about 40 minutes too long. Another problem is that the score by Pete Townshend (with help from John Entwhistle and Keith Moon) doesn't compare to the best Who music. With cameos by: Elton John, Jack Nicholson, Tina Turner, Eric Clapton, Robert Powell, Townshend, Entwhistle, Moon.

TOMORROW (1972) B&W/103m.
Modest, moving adaptation of Faulkner story was for years many viewers' "personal discovery." Picture came out of obscurity when its star, Robert Duvall, and scriptwriter, Horton Foote, won Oscars for 1983's *Tender Mercies*. Duvall is a simple, uneducated, reticent handyman who lives alone in a shack and rarely speaks to anyone. He allows a troubled, pregnant woman (Olga Bellin), who has run away from her husband, to stay in his small cabin. He falls deeply in love with her and promises her before she dies, soon after giving birth, that he will raise the baby. The boy has a happy childhood, and Duvall has sunshine in his once drab life. But then there is heartbreak. Simplicity of film is secret to its beauty. What

we discover is that Duvall's poor sharecropper, who would impress no one who didn't look deeply at him, has the greatest capacity for love of any male character within memory. Also with: Sudie Bond, Richard McConnell, Peter Masterson, William Hawley.

TOOTSIE (1982) C/116m.
The kind of project that could have turned into a disaster, one that might have elicited "What-could-they-have-been-thinking?" responses. But it works *beautifully*. Dustin Hoffman's Michael Dorsey is a down-on-his-luck New York actor who can't get work because either he isn't the right type or he has a difficult attitude. As a last resort, he disguises himself as a woman, Dorothy Michaels, and wins a part on a daytime soap opera. Dorothy's own personality (which is different from Michael's) comes across in her character—she is caring, honest, enthusiastic, friendly, independent, confident, intelligent, outspoken, antisexist, prowoman. She becomes a cult phenomenon across America, inspiration for women who want to assert themselves. She also becomes best friend and role model to Julie (Jessica Lange won Best Supporting Actress Oscar), an actress on the show. Like everyone else, Julie (a single mother) learns to feel more secure from listening to Dorothy. Michael falls in love with Julie, but is afraid to tell her he's been deceiving her, as well as Julie's widower father (Charles Durning), who proposes to Dorothy. The scene in which they sleep together like schoolgirls—only he has other thoughts on his mind—recalls Jack Lemmon in drag sharing an upper berth with Marilyn Monroe in *Some Like It Hot*. As in that 1959 comedy, where Lemmon and Tony Curtis masquerade as women and consequently free their better *female* sides from years of repression, Michael becomes more kind, gentler, more perceptive (toward women mostly, but men also) and less inclined to blame everyone else for his failures. What's great is that when Michael plays Dorothy, he doesn't base her on famous female characters (although he uses a Blanche Dubois accent), but lets Dorothy's character have a life of its own (influenced by his male knowledge of men and their power games). That he himself becomes (sexually) politicized by Dorothy is not shown to be traumatic. Developing a social consciousness is also rewarding; he becomes an optimistic person. Film has many hilarious scenes, others touch emotions. Larry Gelbart and Murray Schisgal wrote the super script, which never panders to the audience. Hoffman and Lange are a wonderful team. Highlight has Michael coming on to his agent—played by Sydney Pollack, the film's director—while made up as Dorothy. Also with: Bill Murray (uncredited), Teri Garr, Dabney Coleman, George Gaynes, Geena Davis.

TOP HAT (1935) B&W/101m.
Exceptional Fred Astaire–Ginger Rogers Depression-escaping musical with fabulous dancing, a topflight Irving Berling score, terrific supporting players (Edward Everett Horton, Eric Blore, Helen Broderick, Erik Rhodes), spectacularly stylish Art Deco sets designed by Van Nest Polglase and Carroll Clark, and a typically preposterous plot. Astaire's a dancer hired to headline wealthy Horton's show. He makes a play for Rogers, who falls in love with him when they dance, of course. But she mistakes him for Horton, whom she has never met but knows is the husband of her friend Broderick. So she angrily leaves London with dress designer Rhodes (so great in *The Gay Divorcee*). Astaire gives chase, hoping to prevent their wedding. All the musical numbers are splendid. (Regrettably, Rogers gets no solo.) I particularly like Astaire's "No Strings," in which he taps around a hotel room, slapping the walls and kicking the props. As in his "Top Hat, White Tie and Tails," when he half runs, half dances around his cane, the emphasis is on timing. The most memorable duet is "Cheek to Cheek," one of Astaire and Rogers's supreme numbers. I love the way they dance quickly only to slow down so that we catch them in some lovely position, and the way Astaire lifts Rogers in her flowing, feathery dress, momentarily holds her aloft as the music sweeps upward, and then eases her to the ground by spinning her around him. The film ends with them spinning off the screen at full speed and it's exhilarating. Astaire sings several songs; Rogers sings only the silly "The Piccolini," and Astaire seems embarrassed listening to her as she sings, smiles, and does Shirley Temple-like gestures. They barely look at one another and for once you can feel the rumored antagonism between the two stars. Fortunately, the picture doesn't end here: soon they are back on the dance floor and in each other's arms, making screen love as only they could. Directed by Mark Sandrich. Choreography by Hermes Pan. Musical direction by Max Steiner. Produced by Pandro S. Berman. Scripted by Dwight Taylor and Allan Scott. Also with: Lucille Ball (as a flower clerk).

TOPO, EL/MOLE, THE (MEXICAN/1971) C/123m.
This became the first major midnight movie when it played at New York's Elgin Theater in January 1971. For college students, acid freaks, and those into "head" pictures (films that are confusing but mentally stimulating), this controversial film became the event picture of the year. But while it attracted repeat viewers who thought it a masterpiece and its Chilean-born director-writer-star Alexandro Jodorowsky an absolute genius, more people were irritated by its ambiguity, numbed by its graphic violence (including the killing of animals), and complained that they sat through "a goddam Jesus film." It's about an egotistical man ("I am God") who, at the urging of an ambitious woman (Mara Lorenzio), rides into the desert to kill Four Masters and prove he is "the best." Among the most narcissistic films ever made, its self-congratulatory, pretentious nature makes one overlook its few moments of cinematic brilliance. Some of the action sequences and the "sex" scenes are exciting—but too often they are gratuitous. Much of the camera work is excellent and eerily conveys the mystical, holy world Jodorowsky wanted to attain, but too many of the visuals call attention to themselves. The dialogue between El Topo and the Masters is supposed to be wise and mystical, but it's often simplistic and empty, full of aphorisms like those

on TV's kiddie show *Kung Fu*. At least amidst all the carnage and religious fervor there are bits of absurdist comedy. This film was obviously made by an intelligent, talented (at least visually) director—but the film's too unwieldy. Jodorowsky borrowed from "all the books I love," plus filmmakers such as Buñuel, Godard, Leone, Fellini, Cocteau, Von Stroheim, Peckinpah, possibly Glauber Rocha, even Buster Keaton. His style and content are also derived from numerous theater traditions—from miracle plays to mime to magic acts. He borrows from poetry; he borrows from philosophers; he borrows from the various religious texts. It's about Moses, Christ, a Zen disciple, and, to make it really confusing, about Jodorowsky. It should be an impressive film, but falls flat because it's so overloaded with references—the sum total of Jodorowsky's knowledge—that it lacks clarity. That it's beyond our comprehension doesn't make it profound. Rarely screened today. Also with: Brontis Jodorowsky, David Silva, Paula Romo, Jacqueline Luis, Robert John.

TOPPER (1937) B&W/97m.

Cary Grant and top-billed Constance Bennett are George and Marion Kerby, a couple that tries to have fun 24 hours a day ("Resting's the kind of thing you've got to work up to gradually," contends George). Zipping along in their sports car, they crash and are killed. They stick around as ghosts, needing to perform a good deed before gaining entrance to heaven. Marion decides that now's the time to liven up the mundane existence of banker Cosmo Topper (Roland Young), whose conservative wife (Billie Burke) won't even let him "swear like a gentleman." The ghosts' pranks cause a great deal of trouble for Cosmo (the only person who can see them) and embarrassment for his wife. Sleek Bennett turns in a comedic performance worthy of Lombard, the always reliable Alan Mowbray and Eugene Pallette are amusing in supporting roles, and the dialogue between George and Marion, when they're alive, is as sophisticated as that between Nick and Nora Charles in the *Thin Man* movies. But the picture's not nearly as good as its reputation. Most of the humor is silly; the special effects aren't that imaginative; Grant isn't in the picture enough, and once a ghost, he's an annoying character; and the storyline doesn't have enough surprises. In 1985 it became the first picture to undergo Colorization. Young, Bennett, and Burke returned in 1939's *Topper Takes a Trip*, also directed by Norman Z. McLeod; Joan Blondell would replace Bennett in 1941's *Topper Returns*. The basis for the fifties television series. Also with: Hedda Hopper, Arthur Lake, J. Farrell McDonald, Doodles Weaver, Ward Bond.

TOUCH OF CLASS, A (1973) C/105m.

George Segal's a married American insurance adjuster stationed in London who has an affair with fashion designer Glenda Jackson, falls in love with her, and soon starts treating her as if she were his second wife. This sorry attempt at "sophisticated" comedy was a big hit, probably among people who usually bypass the cinema for the theater. The vicious verbal battles between the perplexed Segal and the viper-tongued Jackson (who never could deliver a *civil* line) are too calculated—as if they were written for a TV sitcom. They are absolutely unbearable. That writer-director Melvin Frank assumes his script is smart and sassy is pretty infuriating. Also, it's hard to accept that Jackson won a Best Actress Oscar for her snide, nasty portrayal. Also with: Paul Sorvino, Hildegard Neil, Cec Linder.

TOUCH OF EVIL (1958) B&W/93m.

Producer Albert Zugsmith gave Orson Welles his long-awaited chance to again direct a Hollywood film. Welles also wrote the script that was very loosely based on Whit Masterson's novel *Badge of Evil*. Welles the writer turned out the sleaziest story imaginable—with seedy characters and locations, drugs, sex, corruption, murder, racism, etc. Welles the director shot it like an *artist*, employing some of the most audacious visual strokes of his career. The result of this artist directing sleaze? A masterpiece. An American bigwig and his mistress are killed by a bomb in their car while crossing into the United States from Mexico. Slovenly, cigar-smoking Welles, a respected detective, accuses a young Mexican of the murder. Moral Mexican detective Charlton Heston accuses Welles of having planted evidence—dynamite—in the young man's apartment so that Welles's partner (Joseph Calleia) would discover it. Welles tries to discredit Heston by telling the authorities that he and his American wife, Janet Leigh, are addicts. Leigh is staying at the dumpy motel owned by drug dealer Akim Tamiroff, who does whatever Welles wants. Left alone by sex-crazed, immature motel attendant Dennis Weaver—we see the roots of Leigh and Anthony Perkins in *Psycho*—she is terrorized by Tamiroff's juvenile drug dealers. She is to be framed on murder and drug charges. Welles's Detective Hank Quinlan is one of his most interesting, complex characters. He is a great detective but he thinks himself above the law: he is always correct when he accuses someone of a crime, but to assure convictions he always plants incriminating evidence himself so Calleia can find it. It's interesting that Heston's character investigates Quinlan's *past* to find out who Quinlan is *now*—this search for a great man's past, and the subsequent discovery of consistent moral corruption (the reason he was able to make it to the top in the first place) was also essential to *Citizen Kane* and *Mr. Arkadin*. Welles's characters are potentially great men but none of them act nobly on their way to the thrones of their particular worlds. This is the reason Calleia, who loves Welles's Quinlan, is so disappointed: real heroes must have pure pasts. Pay attention during the lengthy, famous opening shot. Marlene Dietrich (as the only person who understands Welles) has a memorable cameo. Leigh was never sexier—Welles was the rare director to emphasize her large chest. Impressive photography is by Russell Metty. Music is by Henry Mancini. Also with: Valentin De Vargas, Ray Collins, Joanna Moore, Mort Mills, Mercedes McCambridge, Joseph Cotten, Zsa Zsa Gabor, Joi Lansing.

TRADING PLACES (1983) C/106m. This is a very funny modern-day *Prince and the Pauper* variation—with the titanic twist being that instead of lookalikes exchanging their life's positions, a white market-analyst named Louis Winthrope III (Dan Aykroyd) and a black unemployed street hustler named Billy Ray Valentine (Eddie Murphy) make the celebrated switch. The first time we see Louis he is curled up in bed, with his manservant, Coleman (Denholm Elliott), hovering over him protectively; he is secure in the knowledge he has a fancy Philadelphia brownstone, an $80,000-a-year job working for the fabulously wealthy brokers Randall (Ralph Bellamy) and Mortimer (Don Ameche) Duke, many preppie friends, and a beautiful preppie fiancée. The first time we see Billy Ray, he's wearing bum's clothing and is down on his knees, begging for a handout. But the venal Duke brothers make a $1 wager to test whether heredity or environment has more influence on a person, using the unsuspecting Louis and Billy Ray as their guinea pigs. And soon the suddenly rich Billy Ray has taken over Louis's apartment, manservant, limo, job, and friends, and penniless Louis is down on his knees in ragged clothing, begging a kind-hearted prostitute (Jamie Lee Curtis)—someone he'd never have had anything to do with—for a handout, a place to stay, and help to make it in the suddenly cruel world. Film definitely supports environment over heredity—Billy Ray becomes a businessman par excellence; Louis becomes a suicidal drunk who is willing to break the law to regain what he lost. But it is actually about loyalty, faith, and respect within friendships—the major determining factors in how a person winds up. The bond that forms between Louis, Billy Ray, the prostitute, and Coleman is truly touching. Above all, the film is about the continuing American Revolution by this country's exploited and downtrodden, represented by our four heroes, who come up with a plan to knock the Dukes off their thrones. Featuring hilarious, controlled performances by Murphy and Aykroyd and significant support from Curtis (in a role that transformed her from "damsel in distress" to sex symbol), Elliott, Bellamy, and Ameche. John Landis has made a sweet-tempered screwball comedy in the finest tradition of those memorable social satires of the thirties and forties. He borrows from Capra (the triumph of the little man over rich, corrupt robber barons), Preston Sturges (a poor man's fortunes can change overnight), and adds a dash of absurd humor that is characteristic of his own comedies and the work of his two stars. The result is a true crowd-pleaser. Also with: Paul Gleason, Kristin Holby, Al Franken and Tom Davis, Jim Belushi.

TRASH (1970) C/103m. The first genuine commercial film by Andy Warhol, the executive producer. Like *Flesh*, in which Joe Dallesandro plays a male hustler, it was directed and photographed by Paul Morrissey, only this time he utilized a more coherent storyline, and there is sharper editing and faster pacing. But it still is intended as another Warhol "documentary" that explores the lives of real people. We are taken to a squalid basement dwelling on New York's lower East Side. This is home to two unmarried lowlifes:

Joe, a muscular, handsome, but pimply 18-year-old former stud whose heroin addiction makes it hard for him to talk clearly, much less get an erection to satisfy all the women he turns on; and girlfriend Holly (female impersonator Holly Woodlawn), a nympho who picks up teenage boys for sex because Joe can no longer satisfy her, collects furniture from trash piles, and orders Joe to shape up so they can qualify for welfare and become respectable. Like many in the counterculture, they live in a world of sex, drugs, and abject poverty. The intention of the film was to elicit audience responses to unusual images. Warhol and Morrissey give viewers the expected nudity, sex, and drug-taking, but not in the expected kinky, sensual, turn-on manner. For instance, we can't get aroused watching Holly masturbate with a beer bottle or watching rich LSD freak Andrea Feldman examine Joe's penis and discover lice. One of the pivotal scenes in all of Warhol films has Joe shooting up in front of rich marrieds Jane (Jane Forth) and Bruce (Bruce Pecheur). As we'd anticipated a sex scene between the three instead, our impulse is to turn away as the needle goes into his arm—but our attention is forced back to the screen because tricky Morrissey has the couple saying to each other, "Will you look at that! Will you look at that!" The film's importance is that it is an attempt to raise the moviegoer's level of tolerance to accommodate what had traditionally seemed too "strong" or offensive for the cinema. Film is full of hilarious characters and scenes—Holly's conversation with a welfare examiner (Michael Sklar) is a highlight—and the acting by the two leads, who improvise a lot, is at times brilliant. What's most surprising is that this weird film manages moments of poignancy, when real pain and concern are revealed in the characters. Indeed, it's touching when "macho" Joe reforms and becomes compassionate toward Holly, indication of his respect for her efforts to upgrade their relationship and standard of living. Edited by Jud Johnson, the director of *Andy Warhol's Bad*. Also with: Geri Miller (the spacy go-go dancer), Johnny Putnam, Diane Poldlewski.

TREASURE OF THE SIERRA MADRE, THE (1948) B&W/126m. Masterful storytelling by John Huston, who won Oscars for his direction and his script adaptation of B. Traven's novel. This is one of the greatest American films. Humphrey Bogart had one of his finest roles as Fred C. Dobbs, revealing the brittleness and paranoia that his '40s *heroes* felt but held in check. Dobbs is a loser, a bum, an American down on his luck in Tampico, Mexico, and begging for handouts (twice from John Huston). Dobbs meets young Curtin (Tim Holt), and fellow flophouse resident Howard (Walter Huston), an old prospector who says he knows where they can find gold in the Sierra Madre. Dobbs generously gives his lottery winnings to buy equipment for the three men to go prospecting. After a long journey, during which they have their first encounter with some Mexican bandits, led by slimy Gold Hat (Alfonso Bedoya takes his place in the cinema's *villain* pantheon). The wise, fast-talking Howard teaches his two partners about mining and soon they strike it rich. As Howard warned might happen, they become distrustful of each other. Dobbs becomes increasingly paranoid that his partners want to kill him and steal his gold. In a brilliantly played character transformation (Bogart's preparing for Captain Queeg), he nears madness. As a study of greed, this picture ranks behind only *Greed*. There are many different types of *men* in this masculine drama, but they have a common trait: they think paramountly about money. Epic has dynamic scenes in wilderness and civilization, superior dialogue, exciting action-adventure, interesting characters. What really makes this film special is that Dobbs, who proves anything but moral or heroic, is the *lead* (most emphasized) character rather than having that designation going to the moral Curtin, who, in movie storytelling terms, is the more logical choice. The one bad scene: the reading of a letter of a dead man (Bruce Bennett). Among the great scenes: Dobbs and Curtin fighting the construction boss (Barton MacLaine) who owes them money; Gold Hat and his cutthroat bandits surrounding Dobbs—Gold Hat tells him emphatically that they don't have any "stinkin' badges." Huston deservedly won a Best Supporting Actor Oscar. Ted McCord was the cinematographer; Max Steiner composed the score. Also with: A. Soto Rangel, young Bobby (Robert) Blake, Jack Holt.

TREE OF THE WOODEN CLOGS, THE (ITALIAN/1978) C/185m.
Study of peasant life in Italy at the turn of the century was directed, written, photographed, and edited by Ermanno Olmi. In order to achieve his special brand of realism, Olmi cast peasants in the lead roles and to a great extent allowed them to improvise action and dialogue. Picture, which deals with joys, sorrows, and day-to-day life of one family, won the Golden Palm at Cannes and has been called a masterpiece by many U.S. critics. While I don't find the slow pacing deadly, I think it contributes to the film's lifelessness, which is mostly the result of the family being dull (as opposed to leading dull lives). Compare these characters to the spirited, fascinating people in the films of the Taviani brothers. Entire film looks like it was filmed on misty mornings—how it could use some sunshine! Film's very pro-Catholic. With: Luigi Ornaghi, Francesca Moriggi, Omar Brignoli, Antonio Ferrari, Giuseppe Brignoli, Carlo Rotta, Pasqualini Brolis.

TRIAL, THE (FRENCH-ITALIAN-GERMAN/1962) B&W/118m—120m.
Orson Welles's baroque, ambitious telling of Franz Kafka's comic nightmare about a low-rank bureaucrat named Joseph K. (Anthony Perkins) who finds himself arrested by the police of his nameless country and ordered to stand trial—although he is never charged with a particular crime. Presenting a dark, decayed, distorted labyrinth-like world, not unlike a combination of the setting found in David Lynch's *Eraserhead* and Michael Radford's *1984*, Welles has created a visual tour-de-force that resembles no commercial films of the early sixties but rather the works of surrealists and experimental filmmakers. Appropriately, the bizarre events that transpire, all with

Joseph K. on screen, have the logic of a nightmare. It's all fascinating stuff, but you may need four or five cups of strong coffee to make it to the end. Even then you may be hopelessly confused. Certainly if Joseph K. were more like us and seemed to be disoriented by the strange people he comes across and the strange situation in which he finds himself, rather than being a major part of the zaniness—what if Alice had been as mad as the Mad Hatter?—then we could empathize more with him; we don't really know how to react because he doesn't seem too upset himself. As near as I can tell, Welles is turning Kafka's downer, in which Joseph K. realizes that he's "dying like a dog," into a triumph for Man. So Perkins's guilt-ridden, apologetic man takes on the guilt of all Man, which explains why he has guilt no matter what the crime. And so Perkins's prideful man becomes prideful of being Man, who refuses, in his final defiant act, to be crushed by a higher order that may be: the impersonal State, God, or Fate/Destiny. The pin-screen animation prologue was provided by Alexander Alexeieff and Claire Parker. Also with: Welles, Jeanne Moreau, Romy Schneider, Elsa Martinelli, Suzanne Flon, Madeleine Robinson, Akim Tamiroff.

TRISTANA (SPANISH-FRENCH-ITALIAN/1970) C/105m.
Luis Buñuel's adaptation of Benito Perez Galdos's novel moved the setting from 1890s to 1920s Toledo, perhaps to better illustrate, through the use of symbolic characters, the moral corruption of the old order. Catherine Deneuve plays the title role, an innocent young woman who is taken advantage of by her aged guardian, played by Fernando Rey. When it comes to financial (he has little money) or political matters, he is an honorable man, but when it comes to women, anything goes. Deneuve feels completely trapped by him, but since in Spain there is no work for single young women, she must stay with him. She grows to detest him (although one senses she also feels a perverse attraction toward him). Yet she comes to believe in much he taught her. She runs off with an artist (Franco Nero), but refuses to marry him. When she gets a tumor on her leg, she returns to Rey's home. But now she is in charge. Once he had said that in the ideal relationship the woman would be confined to the home with a broken leg. But even when her leg is amputated, she keeps him at bay. She marries him—he had refused to marry her years before—just so she can deny him his conjugal bliss. That he suppressed her and corrupted her comes back to haunt him. She is handicapped and married, but, as her last vengeful act in the film perfectly illustrates, she is liberated. An interesting, well-acted Buñuel film, but it lacks the devastating wit and subversive quality of his more enjoyable works. Also with: Lola Gaos (as the housekeeper), Jesús Fernández (as the housekeeper's deaf-mute son).

TRIUMPH OF THE WILL (GERMAN/1935) B&W/120m.
One of the most argued-about films ever made, Leni Riefenstahl's documentary on the 1934 Nazi Party Congress in Nuremberg was commissioned by the Party and

Hitler himself. Riefenstahl always contended that her film was art rather than propaganda. That's nonsense. In fact, Riefenstahl employed tremendous cinematic artistry to glorify Nazism and the Führer, who comes across as a Messiah (his plane descends from the clouds to open the film), hero (thousands of people line the streets as he rides past, standing in an open car and welcoming the cheers), solemn and caring father figure (he personally greets some of the people, who look at him with awe and childish gazes), military leader (he reviews the parading troops), and a respected, firm party leader (his speech wins wild applause from the Party members). Today's political media consultants no doubt study this film to learn how to project a positive image for their clients. Riefenstahl's employment of symbols (the swastika, eagle, and Nazi banners and flags), camera movement (to keep potentially dry material from seeming static), camera placement (Hitler is always shot from below to make him seem heroic), and thematic use of light and darkness is expert. Most controversial is how on occasion she filmed the people/soldiers as if they weren't human, but statues or part of Albert Speer's new architecture. Equally disturbing are images of uniformed Hitler youths having the time of their lives, looking no more dangerous than Cub Scouts as they engage in playful roughhousing—Riefenstahl pans slightly to a tent where an adult officer works, showing that Nazis such as he are very tolerant of young Nazis having a good time (which should convince other German kids to join the ranks). Film makes Germans feel comfort about future. Worth seeing, if only because of its fame. You may boycott it strictly because of its ideology, but, ironically, you've probably seen most of the footage already, in American- and British-made anti-Nazi propaganda pieces.

TRON (1982) C/96m. If you like to hang out at the local arcade, playing video games or just looking over someone's shaking shoulders for a couple of hours, then you might get a kick out of this attempt by computers (with the aide of "filmmakers") to take over the cinema. Otherwise you'll likely tire quickly of the computer-generated imagery, no matter how impressive and ambitious the visuals are. Weak storyline has computer-games whiz Jeff Bridges literally entering giant video game and battling villain David Warner and his soldiers. Bridges, Warner, Bruce Boxleitner (who plays the computer figure, Tron), and pretty Cindy Morgan themselves become computer-generated characters while in the confines of the video game. Conceived and directed by Steven Lisberger, who allowed story to be too subordinate to technique. Disney production was subject of *Time* cover story and the talk of the industry before its release. It was feared that its success would at least temporarily change the look of film and start a wave of computer-generated films. Geared to too select an audience, who had a better use for $5 worth of quarters, film flopped, saving us from such a terrible occurrence. Whatever you do, don't see this on television, where it is totally incomprehensible. Syd Mead designed the vehicles. Also with: Barnard Hughes, Dan Shor.

TROUBLE IN PARADISE (1932) B&W/83m. Sophisticated sex comedy was directed by Ernst Lubitsch and written by Samson Raphaelson and Grover Jones before the Production Code was enforced. So Lubitsch and Raphaelson could be bold: an unmarried couple live together, every line between male and female has a sexual meaning, every act—especially thievery—is a form of sexual seduction. In Lubitsch's world, you can't judge a book by its cover; in fact, who a person *is* bears little relation to who he pretends to be. A garbage man is classy because he sings opera, indigent thieves are classy because they rob people of class. In Vienna, penniless thieves Herbert Marshall and Miriam Hopkins rob each other over dinner (the seduction) and fall in love in the process. They move in together. He's extremely sophisticated; she's more down-to-earth, but wants the jewelry that would raise her status. They plot to rob rich widow Kay Francis. Marshall becomes Francis's personal secretary and hires Hopkins as his assistant. Hopkins becomes jealous when Francis gets too romantic with Marshall. Marshall will have to choose between becoming a hypocritical aristocrat or being true to his own class, where being dishonest is just a job, not a way of life. With excellent dialogue, sly performances. I don't find it as spirited as other Lubitsch comedies, but many critics regard this as his masterpiece. Also with: Charles Ruggles, Edward Everett Horton, C. Aubrey Smith.

TROUBLE WITH HARRY, THE (1955) C/99m. One of the four Alfred Hitchcock films from the fifties that were long kept out of circulation. It's an odd comedy about a dead body that turns up in the woods near a small, peaceful town. Edmund Gwenn thinks he killed Harry when out rabbit hunting; Mildred Natwick thinks she killed him with the heel of her shoe; the dead man's wife, Shirley MacLaine, thinks she may have killed him by hitting him with a milk bottle. Artist John Forsythe helps his friends out as they repeatedly bury Harry and then dig him up to show the authorities. On this day he and MacLaine and Gwenn and Natwick fall in love. Everyone who saw this film when it came out thought it funny, but today it looks like Hitchcock, stuck with a one-joke premise, made a half-hearted effort. It lacks pace, style, and, most importantly, humor. Major point of interest is the debut of young Shirley MacLaine. Her performance—the matter-of-fact delivery of lines, and the weird rhythm of her speech—is disarming. I can recall no scene in cinema that is similar to her weird initial conversation with Forsythe on her porch: she comes across much like Candy Clark. Also with: Royal Dano, Mildred Dunnock, Jerry Mathers (before *Leave It to Beaver*).

TUNNELVISION (1976) C/67m. It's 1985, David Eisenhower is President, and a congressional committee is holding hearings on the new uncensored television network that has destroyed the country's initiative—everyone just stays home all day and watches Tunnelvision. Excerpts from a day's schedule are shown and you'll never be able to figure out why anyone would stay home to see this stuff—

it's hard enough to sit through 67 minutes of it. The shows we see are not outrageous enough, and those we see promos for may make us laugh (*Animal Lawyer*, *The Last Hippies*), but there's no way they'd attract an audience (I hate to quibble, but, after all, these shows are supposed to represent what a 1985 audience would watch if it had its choice). About the only show that would certainly attract an audience (now that *The Gong Show* has gone off) is the sick *Remember When?*, in which a guy in a dress and woman wearing panties and pasties (Betty Thomas of TV's *Hill Street Blues*) win prizes by filling in details about past events in their lives (why she beat the baby, the name of the hospital in which the girl he raped and turned into a vegetable is staying, etc.). Picture also has many commercials, the best being for a room freshener that smells like five U.S. cities. In many ways this is a dry run for such television shows as *Saturday Night Live*, *SCTV*, and *Not Necessarily the News*. You'll spot Chevy Chase, Laraine Newman, John Candy, and Al Franken and Tom Davis. Directed by Brad Swirnoff and Neil Israel. Also with: Phil Proctor, Howard Hesseman, William Schallert, James Bacon (a funny bit as a movie reviewer), Gerrit Graham, Israel.

TURKISH DELIGHT (DUTCH/1973) C/100m. Paul Verhoeven's bizarre romance won nomination for Best Foreign Film, but is still relatively unknown in the U.S. It's just waiting for cultists to discover it. Rutger Hauer is an artist-sculptor whose work is sexually oriented. He spends all his free time picking up young women all over Amsterdam. He's an insensitive chauvinist pig who thinks nothing of insulting his lovers and has the audacity to keep a scrapbook of souvenirs of his sexual conquests. He seems to care about nothing, but he has one sad, serious memory. We flash back two years to an intense relationship he had with Monique Van Der Ven. Both were sexually uninhibited, carefree, volatile, rebellious, and took pride in being affronts to "respectable" society. But whereas he was simply incorrigible, she was mentally unbalanced: it turned out she had a brain tumor. At first you think you'll hate both impossible characters throughout the film, but you come to realize that their constant sex is not as artificial as the sex Hauer has with women in the opening scene but the powerful means by which they express their passionate bond. Film is erotic (there's enough frontal nudity and graphic sex to qualify it as a soft-core porno movie) and also extremely gross (you'll want to bathe after it's over) and—you'll be surprised—tender and touching. It sticks with you—in 1973 I rushed out to find Jan Wolkers's equally shocking source novel. Hauer would star in Verhoeven's *Soldier of Orange* and *Spetters*; Van Der Ven (a talent who never made it big) would star in the director's excellent subsequent film, *Keetje Toppel*. Verhoeven began his collaboration with producer Rob Houwer and screenwriter Gerard Souteman.

12 ANGRY MEN (1957) B&W/95m. Twelve men enter the jury room to reach a verdict. It seems to be an open-and-shut case against a young Puerto Rican who is accused of murdering an old man. Only Henry Fonda votes "not guilty"—not because he's convinced the boy is innocent but because he thinks the boy deserves that they talk about the case. One by one, the other jurors come over to Fonda's side. Ingenious script by Reginald Rose (who adapted his television play) has jurors questioning evidence, reenacting crime, theorizing about the witnesses' motives for accusing the young boy of murder, and getting the most resistant among them (Lee J. Cobb, Ed Begley)—the ones who steadfastly vote "guilty"—to reveal the prejudices that have influenced their verdicts. It's fascinating and exciting. Rose's belief (his faith in the jury system) is that a group of diverse Americans will make the right decision because those who are biased will be outnumbered. Sure. Most interesting aspect of the film is the concept of hero: few movie characters are more admirable than Henry Fonda, who stands fast against 11 jurors; indeed, defense lawyers use the character as an example when they select jurors. He *is* a hero—but Rose's valid point is that he can't do it alone. Film is idealistic, but it's not dated (as anyone who has recently served on a jury knows). Faultless direction by Sidney Lumet (his film debut), who immediately established himself as being expert with actors. Remarkable cast also includes: Joseph Sweeney (the old man who is the first juror to back Fonda), E. G. Marshall, Jack Warden, Martin Balsam, Edward Binns, John Fiedler, Robert Webber, George Voskovec (who makes the pro-democracy speech), Jack Klugman.

TWELVE CHAIRS, THE (1970) C/94m. Uneven but fairly enjoyable Mel Brooks comedy set in post-Revolution Russia. Exiled nobleman Ron Moody and young hustler Frank Langella join forces to look for some chairs Moody left behind when he fled the country. Moody didn't realize that his mother-in-law had sewn a fortune in jewels in one of the chair seats. Dom De Luise also searches for the booty. One of the first things they discover is that the chairs have been scattered about, and that it will be difficult to track down the various owners. But they're greedy enough to accomplish this task. For once Brooks's pacing is deliberate—he is patient enough to wait a few seconds before hitting us with his next gag. Unfortunately, the story starts to drag so much that one wishes at times he would punch it up with silly humor. We wouldn't need those gags if we truly cared about the developing relationship between Moody and Langella, but they are just too unsympathetic. Still, I much prefer Moody's performance to his counterpart in Brooks's *The Producers*, Zero Mostel, whose hamminess and scene-stealing do him in. I love watching Moody's beady eyes suddenly become uncontrollably greedy—this happens repeatedly. The scripted jokes in the picture aren't particularly funny, but I do like some of the sight gags: I laugh when frustrated Dom De Luise runs into the side of a mountain in an impulsive and immediately regretted suicide attempt—but such humor is a matter of taste. Brooks has a small part early on as Moody's ex-servant who's now a drunken, unshaven bum—too bad he didn't go along on the journey. Made in Yugoslavia, film is a sort of period remake of *It's in the Bag*.

TWENTIETH CENTURY (1934) B&W/91m.

Howard Hawks's classic was not only the first sound comedy to have the male (John Barrymore) and female leads (Carole Lombard) not only carry the brunt of the comedy instead of designating the laughs to the supporting players, but also to have their characters make absolute fools of themselves. These changes, plus the film's *frenetic* pacing, is why many critics regard it, and not the previously released *It Happened One Night* (also made at Columbia), as the first *screwball comedy*. Hawks worked with screenwriters Ben Hecht and Charles MacArthur; their original play had been based on Charles Bruce Milholland's play *Napoleon on Broadway*. Barrymore plays Oscar Jaffe, the epitome of a pretentious theater director ("the sorrows of life are the joys of art") and a shameless egomaniac. He takes a timid unknown named Mildred Plotka (Lombard), changes her name to Lily Garland, and makes her into the theater's biggest star. But his jealousy, possessiveness, and phony acts of self-pity drive her away. She goes to Hollywood and becomes a movie star; he directs one flop after another in New York. Of course, they're fated to be together and they end up on a cross-country train—the Twentieth Century—and Oscar sees his final chance to get her name on a contract. As we discover, he has no scruples. At times the script is slight, but the film itself is consistently funny because of the bravura performances by Barrymore and Lombard. Oscar and Lily's furious verbal squabbles make the legendary first round of the Hearns-Hagler fight seem tame. What's most unusual about this piece is that, instead of the two characters coming to their senses, they remain to the very end in a state verging on lunacy; instead of Lily once again becoming the sweet, unaffected Mildred Plotka, she becomes just as pretentious (she wears furs to rehearsal) as Oscar. Hecht and MacArthur's cynical point is that once the theater gets in your blood, you lose your humanity. Lily becomes like Oscar in that she can't stop *acting*, even off stage. What makes her compatible with Oscar is what makes Lombard a great partner for Barrymore: as the era's top screen comedienne, she can match his *hamminess*, while no one else, male or female, even comes close. Also with: Walter Connolly, Roscoe Karns, Charles Levison, Etienne Girardot (funny as a crazy passenger), Dale Fuller, Ralph Forbes, Edgar Kennedy, Edward Gargan.

28 UP (BRITISH/1984) B&W-C/136m.

Michael Apted's unique, fascinating documentary began as a television short called *7 Up*, made in 1963 by Granada Television. The crew interviewed 14 seven-year-old school-children about what they wanted in their futures in regard to education, occupation, money, and marriage. These pupils were again interviewed at ages 14, 21, and, lastly, at 28—an age at which the directions of the subjects' lives have pretty much been determined and we/they can see if they have fulfilled the ambitions they had for themselves when they were younger. The viewer is placed in an awkward position in that s/he becomes a *judge* as to whether these 28-year-olds have succeeded, as most contend they have, in reaching their potential happiness; and the unfortunate tendency, I believe, is to feel superior to most of these people who have lives we don't envy. For the most part, the subjects set very narrow goals for themselves to begin with, almost as if they could foresee that England in the eighties would have no place for anyone who wanted to live in a different way or work in a special profession. An exception, a male subject who had a privileged education, has found a personally though not financially rewarding career teaching at an East End school—but even he knows that his underprivileged pupils, because of their backgrounds, will have little opporunity for success of any kind in England. The "successes" we see are those subjects who have somehow achieved some freedom—the science researcher who has fled with his wife to Wisconsin, the bricklayer who is raising a family in Australia, others who have found some peace in the country. But there's a near-genius who has dropped out altogether and lives on welfare and seems in need of therapy (supposedly when this film was relased he got job offers and marriage proposals) and a cabbie who is satisfied with "freedom" he gets from his job and his close family life, but whose poor education deprived him of what a person of his natural intelligence and warmth deserves. Picture leaves you sad—but surely a documentary on any seven subjects taken over 20 years would have the same result because, let's face it, kids look happier, cuter, and more enthusiastic than adults.

20 MILLION MILES TO EARTH (1957) B&W/84m.

In an exciting, well-animated opening shot, a ship returning from a mission to Venus plummets into the Mediterranean. Lone survivor William Hopper has an egg he obtained on Venus. It hatches. The small creature it yields soon grows into an enormous monster—the first of special-effects expert Ray Harryhausen's Dynamation creations. Naturally, scientists want to study it, but when it goes on a rampage through Rome similar to Godzilla's through Tokyo, Hopper tries to figure out how to destroy it. A lively film with an impressive monster—one that would serve as model for future Harryhausen creations. Harryhausen's most exciting sequence features the monster (called Ymir) battling an elephant. Harryhausen, underrated director Nathan Juran, and producer Charles H. Schneer would team again on *The 7th Voyage of Sinbad*. Also with: Joan Taylor, Frank Puglia, John Zaremba, Thomas B. Henry.

TWILIGHT ZONE—THE MOVIE (1983)

C/102m. Since Rod Serling's classic anthology series is still seen in syndication throughout America, there was no need to make this film, particularly since three of the four episodes are remakes of old shows that hold up quite well. But one can't feel harshly toward the directors because John Landis, Steven Spielberg, Joe Dante, and Australian George Miller loved the show when they were kids and wanted to pay homage to it and its creator. But, as anyone could have predicted: while their episodes are better made than the originals, they aren't better. The "feel" of the original series is missing, as is the late Serling as host and narrator (Burgess Meredith, who appeared in several classic episodes, narrates but doesn't appear on screen). Also, the young filmmakers have slightly altered the stories, changing the themes to better fit modern times. For instance, in Spielberg's version of "Kick the Can," residents of an old-age home don't *wish* themselves permanently back to childhood—instead, old people supposedly are content to remain old and in homes if they can just *think young*. Sure. At the end of the original "It's a Good Life," a little boy with monstrous powers completely controls a town through fear—but the end of Dante's updated, liberal version states that even a boy (Jeremy Licht) capable of terrible deeds wants help, needs sincere friendship, and prefers guidance (from teacher Kathleen Quinlan) to being a spoiled brat. In the film's best episode, Miller's wild version of "Nightmare at 20,000 Feet," it is no longer necessary to have the man (John Lithgow takes over William Shatner's role) who swears he sees a creature on the airplane wing be identified as a former mental patient—it's scarier that no one will believe a *sane* man. The opener, John Landis's episode about a bigot (Vic Morrow) who himself becomes the object of bigotry, is too simplistic and moralistic but is in many ways most reminiscent of the series. Unfortunately, the tragic deaths of Morrow and two children during filming (which probably accounts for the abrupt ending) make it difficult to appreciate the episode on any level. Special praise should go to the cartoonist design in Dante's episode (the boy has created a world to correspond to what he sees in TV cartoons). Also, special-effects experts Rob Bottin and Craig Reardon should be singled out for creating some truly spectacular creatures. Best of all is Landis's truly wacky and terrifying prelude with Dan Aykroyd and Albert Brooks. Also with: Scatman Crothers, Bill Quinn, Selma Diamond, William Schallert, Billy Mumy, Abbe Lane.

TWO ENGLISH GIRLS/DEUX ANGLAISES ET LE CONTINENT, LES (FRENCH/1971) C/97m–108m.
François Truffaut's last project was to re-edit this picture and restore about 11 minutes of footage that distributors once insisted he excise. I once thought the film depressing and endless, but, having seen the restored version, I now consider it one of Truffaut's most romantic films, a heartfelt exploration of the passions, jealousies, inadequacies, and insecurities of young lovers. Set in France and Wales in WWI, film centers on young Frenchman Claude Roc (Jean-Pierre Léaud), who eventually becomes an art critic, and the lovely Brown sisters (slightly based on the Brontës), sculptress Anne (Kika Markham) and teacher Muriel (Stacey Tendeter), who is as passionate as her older sister but more sexually repressed. Truffaut's three sheltered, innocent characters take years to consummate their loves, so handicapped are they by interfering mothers, as well as by physical infirmities and cockeyed personal moralities. The relationships between Claude and each sister are mutually beneficial, no matter that he takes advantage of them and they manipulate him into filling their sexual and intellectual needs. As in *Jules and Jim* (also from a novel by Henri-Pierre Roche) and *Stolen Kisses*, lovers never love each other equally at the same time; also typical of Truffaut: his love-obsessed characters best express their passion through "art" (writing, sculpting) rather than words. As usual, Truffaut is uncomfortable when his characters enjoy physical love; here he undercuts his most intimate scenes with narration. But the *romance* comes through anyway because of cinematographer Nestor Almendros's pictorial beauty (Truffaut experimented with color for the first time), Georges Delerue's lush, haunting score, and Truffaut's singular ability to make us sense that the hearts of his characters (humans, not robots) are beating several times faster and louder than our own. Also with: Sylvia Marriott, Marie Mansart, Philippe Léotard.

TWO FOR THE ROAD (BRITISH/1967) C/112m.
This is the cult film for romantics; many have been known to become emotionally attached to it. Albert Finney (as Mark) is a successful architect and Audrey Hepburn (as Joanna) is his wife of 12 years. They bicker constantly and admit that they aren't particularly happy. They wonder how their marriage lasted so long since they remember that's how their entire life together has been. But writer Frederic Raphael and director Stanley Donen take us back in time, and we see Finney and Hepburn at various times in their relationship so we can examine their marriage from the outside. Each time, they are traveling together through Europe: we see the road-as-life and trip-as-marriage metaphors. We watch them intentionally hurt each other, suffer as individuals and as a couple, get on each other's nerves, disappoint each other, have affairs (one each), criticize each other, and squabble. That's all they remember. But we also see them laugh together, make love, appreciate and love one another. We come to like these two people more than they do themselves—and we understand why their marriage has lasted *and* will survive. They are a great couple, flaws and all; they are one of the few screen couples since William Powell and Myrna Loy who make marriage seem exciting. Even their squabbling is romantic. Finney and Hepburn are wonderful—it's too bad they never teamed up again. Raphael's script is his best: the dialogue is excellent and he smoothly blends comedy (e.g., Finney and Hepburn make love despite being sunburned), painful drama (e.g., Finney sees Hepburn's lover and Donen uses a shocking freeze-frame, Hepburn is devastated when Finney insinuates she's been a tramp), and sentimentality. Donen does a good job handling the changes in tone, except when he attempts some speeded-up slapstick during the film's least successful sequence, in which Hepburn and Finney travel with super-punctual William Daniels, his wife, Eleanor Bron, and their bratty daughter. Henry Mancini's score helps create the romantic aura. Also with: Claude Dauphin, Nadia Gray, George Descrieres (as Hepburn's lover), Gabrielle Middleton, Jackie Bisset (whose case of chicken pox gives Hepburn her chance to date Finney).

200 MOTELS (1971) C/98m. Produced in England. Cult item by Frank Zappa, founder of the Mothers of Invention, was transferred from videotape, but should have been erased instead. It's impossible to describe, but it's meant to be visualization of a Mothers tour seen through the eyes of someone (presumably Zappa) who has gone crazy from being on tour with the Mothers. The Mothers perform many boring songs, with Flo 'n' Eddie doing most of the leads, and play a lot of comedy scenes with bizarre supporting characters. Throughout, Tony Palmer's visuals are so wild and weird—to correspond to Zappa's zany direction of the actors—that this film makes Ken Russell seem conservative. Ringo Starr is funny, made up to look like Zappa (who makes only cameo appearances); and Theodore Bikel, of all people, runs around playing the devil. Dialogue (mostly about penises) and lyrics ("I get so hard I can die") is irreverent; visuals are occasionally imaginative but mostly annoying. Picture is never as witty as one would like (the Mothers are funny on *stage*) and it becomes tiresome. It's a shame that there's no film of a Mothers concert circa 1966, when they were truly an amazing live band. Also with: Keith Moon.

TWO-LANE BLACKTOP (1971) C/102m. Monte Hellman's film never lived up to pre-release publicity—in a cover story *Esquire* predicted it would be "the movie of the year," turn the youth market as only *Easy Rider* had, and lift Hellman into the bankable elite among directors. But it's a unique, thematically interesting film that has deservedly become a cult favorite. James Taylor, the singer, is The Driver and Dennis Wilson, late drummer of the Beach Boys, is The Mechanic. They race their car, a souped-up '55 gray Chevy with 454 engine and four on the floor, back and forth across America's highways and byways—going fast, but going nowhere on the metaphoric endless highway of meaningless life. In fact, the big race that dominates the film, between The Car and the GTO driven by G.T.O. (a great Warren Oates performance) never ends. Hellman spends much screen time with his camera on The Car, panning lovingly along its frame, or exploring under the hood with awe and fascination. (He directs these moments as if he were The Driver or The Mechanic.) We learn more about The Car than about the zombielike men who ride in it. Since The Driver won't talk while driving and The Mechanic won't talk while working on The Car, conversations are rare (most chatter takes place between gabby G.T.O. and his ridiculous assortment of hitchhikers). When they do talk, it is only about cars and racing. Their incomprehensible car lingo makes the film abstract. When The Girl (the late Laurie Bird) who enters their life swims nude in front of them, they reminisce about old cars, not old flames. When she eventually breaks up the bond between the two and messes up their perfect "oneness" with each other and The Car, they are unable to patch things up because they're incapable of talking about such things as women, friendship, and emotions. Better than Hopper and Fonda in *Easy Rider*, The Driver and The Mechanic epitomize the sad products of a frustration-making D.C. bureaucracy, specifically a Nixon government which is conducting a controversial war that makes complete apathy as inviting as a warm cozy bed. While other films were about the alienation of the drug culture and war protesters, Hellman's pessimistic film is about the alienation of everyone else: both those who race around the desolate, poor, conservative country and all those people inside the cubicles they pass who are just as withdrawn and isolated from the problems/horrors of their world. Film bogs down toward the end, but there's a literally mind-blowing ending. If you get the chance, see this at a drive-in. Produced by Michael S. Laughlin. Written by Rudolph Wurlitzer (who plays a hot-rod driver) and Will Corry. Also with: David Drake, Richard Ruth, Alan Vint, Jaclyn Hellman, Melissa Hellman.

TWO MULES FOR SISTER SARA (1970) C/105m. In this Don Siegel-directed comic western, adapted by Albert Maltz from a Budd Boetticher story, Clint Eastwood plays a gunfighter much like his hero in the Sergio Leone westerns. But he faces a problem that "The Man With No Name" never came across: he must deal with a woman, in this case a spirited nun played by Shirley MacLaine. This nun drinks, swears, and helps Mexican guerrillas fight the French army—she persuades Eastwood to lend his lethal hand. From this film on, Eastwood would present himself as a tough man who intimidates men but has no idea how to handle women, especially those unimpressed by his caveman tactics. As in later Eastwood films, much humor comes from his being "betwixt, speechless, and bewildered" by a woman—he often does double takes and shifts his confused eyes from side to side and then up to the heavens for guidance. MacLaine, who took the part originally intended for Elizabeth Taylor, is among the most idiosyncratic of Eastwood's women. The last shot of the two riding off into the sunset, with Eastwood wondering how he ever ended up with this strange person, is hilarious. Music by Ennio Morricone. Also with: Manolo Fabregas, Alberto Morin, Armando Silvestre, José Chávez.

2000 MANIACS (1964) B&W/75m. I don't necessarily mean this as a recommendation, but this is a goremeister Herschell Gordon Lewis's best film. Three couples driving through the South follow detour signs into the small town of Pleasant Valley. The town is having a celebration and the visitors are made the guests of honor by the cheery townspeople—but the townspeople are vengeance-bent ghosts of people who were wiped out by Northern troops in 1869. Always smiling, these Southern yokels kill off their "guests" one by one in hideous ways—in the most excruciating scene, laughing contestants line up to throw rocks at a target that will release a giant boulder which hovers over a tied-down, terrified visitor. It takes forever for her to be killed. The three other murders are just as painful—for us. And all the while the happy Pleasant Valley Boys play bluegrass. Stars Tom Mason and Connie Mason (the former *Playboy* playmate who was even worse in Lewis's *Blood Feast*) try to escape; what's frightening is that you have no confidence they will succeed, even though escape fit the conventions of the horror genre in 1964. Picture is completely unnerving because it breaks genre rules; you fear killings because you know how grisly they will be. This is a truly scary movie, a nightmare much like *The Texas Chain Saw Massacre*, which has deaths that correspond to those in this film. But this picture is terribly acted, crudely directed (although there is devilish imagination at work), and repugnant. The shock thumb-amputation is one of the most disturbing images I've ever seen in a movie. Produced by David Friedman. Also with: Jeffrey Allen, Shelby Livingston, Jerome Eden.

2001: A SPACE ODYSSEY (BRITISH/1968) C/141m–160m.

The most awesome, beautiful (the visuals and classical music), mentally stimulating, and controversial science-fiction film ever made was directed by Stanley Kubrick, adapted from Arthur C. Clarke's short story "The Sentinel" by Kubrick and Clarke, and photographed by Geoffrey Unsworth and John Alcott, and features incredible, Oscar-winning special effects by Wally Veerers, Douglas Trumbull (who supervised the miraculous star-gate sequence), Con Pederson, and Tom Howard. It begins four million years ago when a black monolithic slab appears to a family of apes. Once peaceful vegetarians, they become meat-eaters and intelligent enough to use bones as weapons to kill other animals for food and to chase other apes away from their territory. They have evolved into *apemen* and their human descendants will retain their warring instincts—progress and brutality go hand in hand—the territorial imperative, and a notion of God. It is for the viewer to decide if the superior alien intelligence that sent the monolith and caused man to evolve from the apes (instead of the neighboring tapirs!) is God as we define God. (I believe that Kubrick thinks the concept of God is so unfathomable to us that if an alien intelligence has the power over us that we always associated with God, then we might as well call it God.) Film moves from the past to 2001, when Dr. Heywood Floyd (William Sylvester), an American scientist, investigates the discovery of a monolith on the moon. The monolith sends a piercing signal (through space's vacuum?), a distant intelligence, no doubt, that man has evolved to the point where the monolith has been discovered. But man is nothing special: he is boring, untrusting (Floyd keeps the discovery secret from the Russians), nationalistic, uncommunicative; while man has made great technical advances in communication, men are incapable of meaningful, intelligent conversation, and are unworthy of their own scientific achievements. American big business has expanded: Pan Am, Bell Telephone, the Hilton chain, and Howard Johnson's are prominent at the space station. On a spaceship we see that the astronauts, Bowman (Keir Dullea) and Poole (Gary Lockwood), are completely subservient to a computer named HAL. HAL is actually more interesting than the men—they are mechanized; HAL is a neurotic. HAL represents both a Frankenstein monster turning on its human

creators (he tries to dispose of the crew) and a Big Brother which, unlike the situation in Orwell, men intentionally have set up to spy on them. There is no scarier scene than when HAL reads the lips of Bowman and Poole as they plan to dismantle this rebellious computer. In an unforgettable scene Bowman dismantles HAL. The battle between man and computer, resulting in HAL's death, releases emotions that Bowman had previously held in check: fear and sorrow. The destruction of the oppressive computer is the signal to the aliens—who may have set up the combat, if we are to believe the dualist concept of God's omnipotence and man's having free will under God's auspices—that Bowman is worthy of being *the* human being who comes to them. After traveling through space—"the ultimate trip"—Bowman finds himself in a terrarium observed by alien creatures. There he ages rapidly and becomes the first character in the film to eat at a table and the first to eat tasty food—from a plate, too. He becomes civilized man; Kubrick believes that "the missing link between the apes and civilized man is the human being—us." Lastly, Bowman dies and evolves into a star child, floating through space toward earth. The evolution of man from ape to angel is complete. Originally released in Cinerama at 160m. Peter Hyams directed the badly muddled, forgettable *2010*. Also with: Daniel Richter, Leonard Rossiter, Margaret Tyzack, Douglas Rain (voice of HAL).

UGETSU/UGETSU MONOGATARI (JAPANESE/1953) B&W/96m.

Quintessential film by Kenji Mizoguchi in that it portrays women as the victims of insensitive men, forgives women for becoming prostitutes, refutes the myth of the noble samurai, chastises men who would sacrifice familial happiness for money or glory, and blends history and legend, the real and supernatural (while showing how the dead inspire/haunt the living), and the savage and the lyrical. A kind but greedy married potter (Masayuki Mori) and his married brother-in-law (Eitaro Ozawa) go to the city to sell Mori's wares. There they both succumb to temptation: Mori becomes the lover of a beautiful lady (Machiko Kyo), not realizing that she is a ghost; Ozawa uses his money to buy a spear and armor and runs off to become a samurai. While both men indulge in their pleasures, their wives (Kinuyo Tanaka, Mitsuko Miura) are each attacked by roving bands of samurai—one becomes a prostitute, the other is killed. In Mizoguchi, for a man to rise, a woman must fall. A haunting, beautifully shot film. Among the scenes that stick in the memory are the spooky boat ride across the mist-shrouded water and Mori's strange homecoming. Tale was taken from two supernatural stories by Akinari Ueda that were included in his 1776 collection

Ugetsu Monogatari, and Guy de Maupassant's "La Déco- ration."

ULYSSES (1967) B&W/140m.

Joseph Strick's ad- aptation of James Joyce's epic novel, with Milo O'Shea as Leopold Bloom, Barbara Jefford as his adulterous wife, Molly, and Maurice Roeves as Stephen Dedalus, whose character is on screen too briefly and makes insignificant impact. College lit majors and Joyce scholars will be thank- ful that this film was made by a devotee of Joyce, but Strick proves—as he did with Henry Miller's *Tropic of Cancer*— that the source is unfilmable, as anyone who has read it (or carried the heavy thing in a bookbag) could have told him. Sleep-inducing, confusing film never sustains flavor or power of novel; it's also hard to recognize Joyce's Dublin or his colorful characters. Narration is from Joyce, but Strick's slapdash choice of images to accompany it is disconcerting. Most interesting narration is by Molly as she lies in bed with the sleeping Leopold, whose feet are by her head. Because the film was made back in 1967 when there were censorship problems, it's jarring to hear her strong lan- guage—moreover, even today it's still interesting listening to her lengthy discourse on the men in her life (she's not impressed) and their and her sexual needs. Also with: T. P. McKenna, Anna Manahan, Maureen Potter, Martin Demp- sey, Sheila O'Sullivan.

UMBERTO D (ITALIAN/1955) B&W/89m.

Vittorio De Sica's sad but beautiful postwar social drama begins with a march by elderly men through Rome streets to protest their inadequate pensions. They are routed by police—indication that these men who once were integral to the city's business community are now alienated from mainstream society, both threats to the contemporary bourgeoisie and its embarrassment. De Sica then concen- trates on an individual member of the dispossessed aged. Umberto (Carlo Battista), a retired government worker, finds that his heartless landlady (Lina Gennari) will throw him and his remarkable mongrel, Flike, out on the street unless he can pay his back rent. Too proud to ask his well-off acquaintances for a needed loan (and they never offer it) or join the growing number of beggars in the city, Umberto feels increasingly lost and tired, and would commit suicide if he didn't worry about the welfare of the dog. De Sica wisely didn't make his hero into a sweet grandfather type whom you automatically love and feel sorry for—Umberto's nice enough, but his gruff exterior and stubbornness make it difficult to see his finer qualities, which come out in his loving gestures toward his dog and his concern for the lovely unmarried young maid (Maria Pia Casilio), who is pregnant and will soon be cast into the street by the landlady. By having him come across as the type of old man who'd keep a kid's baseball if it landed in his garden, De Sica avoids sentimentality: if viewers are still upset by *his* plight, they'll have concern for all the pensioners—many nicer—whom he represents. Realistic film has many deeply moving se- quences—you won't forget Umberto sitting in his room,

which has been virtually destroyed because the landlady is having it converted into a parlor; or Umberto searching for his dog at the pound; or the maid silently going through her morning routine while obviously thinking of her unhappy future. And you'll remember the glorious final shot, which allows Umberto D, Flike, and us at least a moment of relief.

UMBRELLAS OF CHERBOURG, THE (FRENCH-GERMAN/1964) C/92m.

For all of us who occa- sionally burst into song at the dinner table, with a melodic "Will youuuu pass theeee bread, pleeeease???" Experimen- tal work by Jacques Demy is a throwback to the all-singing Hollywood musicals of the late twenties. In addition to legitimate songs, all the dialogue—even the most mundane lines—is sung. Everything is so pretty—the enchantingly colored pink-and-red-dominated sets (Cherbourg citizens al- lowed their buildings to be painted), the music by Michel Legrand, the dubbed voices, and the young faces—that you'd expect to be sickened by the whole thing. But this curious film is, surprisingly, quite pleasant to sit through. Bittersweet romance set in the late fifties. Seventeen-year- old shopgirl Catherine Deneuve (who became known from the film) loves gas-station attendant Nino Castelnuovo, but her widowed mother (Anne Vernon) says she's too young to get married. Before he is sent off to fight in the Algerian War, the two make love. Deneuve becomes pregnant. When Castelnuovo's letters stop coming—it turns out he was in a hospital with a leg injury—she agrees to marry a kind suitor (Marc Michel). Then Castelnuovo returns. Picture was extremely popular because it manages to be cheerful due to its colorful look and music, yet cynical due to the sad events that occur and Demy's lyrics. Young people in the sixties liked it because, despite its fairytale appearance, it dealt with what was important to them: premarital sex, love, pregnancy, dealing with parental figures, and war, which Demy despised because it destroys romance and re- lationships. Also with: Ellen Farner, Mireille Perrey.

UNCLE HARRY/STRANGE AFFAIR OF UNCLE HARRY, THE (1945) B&W/80m.

In this unusual lit- tle sleeper by suspense expert Robert Siodmak, George Sanders plays a dull, naïve, weak-willed, middle-aged man who lives with his squabbling unmarried sisters, Geraldine Fitzgerald and Moyna MacGill (Angela Lansbury's mother), in the family home in New Hampshire. For the first time in his life he falls in love, with pretty New Yorker Ella Raines. But his marital plans are ruined by the possessive Fitzgerald, whose obviously incestuous feelings for Sanders (she acts like the *perfect wife*) surely gave the Hays Office fits. So mild-mannered Sanders plans to poison his sister; but the results are unexpected. Interestingly, just as Sand- ers's murder plan begins, Fitzgerald becomes sympathetic for the first time and we quickly turn away from Sanders; but in Siodmak's *The Suspect*, just before Charles Laughton kills his shrewish wife (also because he loves Ella Raines), his wife is at her most despicable, so we urge on Laughton. As is characteristic of a Siodmak film, the cinematography and lighting add much to the mood (by, in fact, expressing the moods of the moody characters); much care went into set design; and the dialogue is intelligent, befitting the characters. And the acting by Sanders, Raines, and especially Fitzgerald is excellent. Film has many twists, all fine but for the horrible ending that was demanded by the censors (who probably had to be appeased for allowing the incest theme). Stephen Longstreet and Keith Winter adapted Thomas Job's play. Produced by Joan Harrison, known for her work with Alfred Hitchcock. Also with: Sara Allgood, Samuel S. Hinds, Harry Von Zell.

UNDERGROUND U.S.A. (1980) C/85m.
Cult film by Eric Mitchell has had some success as a midnight movie (particularly in New York) and has played on PBS as an example of arty/*avant-garde* independent films currently being made. Mitchell plays a bisexual Greenwich Village street hustler who latches on to a former movie actress (Patti Austen), only to discover that she has no money or friends and is weirded out from taking drugs to relieve her depression (she was not a big enough star for fans to have forgotten her, or important enough for directors to want to put up with her again). Mitchell and her loyal male housemate and companion (Rene Ricard) try to keep her spirits up. I wish that Mitchell hadn't decided to make another variation on *Sunset Boulevard*, especially since Andy Warhol had already made a pretty good counterculture version in 1972, *Heat*, because at this point the story hasn't many surprises left. From this film it's hard to tell how talented or original Mitchell is. There are some interesting scenes, use of color, and camera angles, but in general I find the characters uninvolving, the dialogue trite, and the pacing too slow—everyone seems to be sleepwalking. (To be fair, this is what Mitchell intended.) Only the last line is funny. Jim Jarmusch did the sound, and it's probable that he borrowed his static, one-camera-setup-per-scene method, used on *Stranger Than Paradise*, from Mitchell. Also with: Tim Wright, Cookie Mueller, Jackie Curtis, Terry Toye, Taylor Meade.

UNDERWORLD U.S.A. (1961) B&W/98m.
Ex-con Cliff Robertson infiltrates the mob in order to rub out the three surviving criminal bigwigs whom he saw beat his father to death years before. Only in Sam Fuller's America can a petty thief move all the way up in the organization. Once in striking range of his targets, Robertson uses the lawmen on the case to bring about their demises. He then must kill the Boss (Robert Emhardt) in order ever to lead a clean life. This unflinching crime drama—we even see a little girl run down—draws parallels between criminals and lawmen, who wage *war* against each other in the identical emotionless manner, planning their strategies in nearby buildings. Picture shows how the criminal element has ruined the fabric of our society. Fuller's sympathy lies with children who are victimized if parents are either mobsters or top-level lawmen (who are forced to accept payoffs to keep their kids alive)—or who are seduced into a world of prostitution and drugs. Repeatedly there are references to a child's loyalty to his or her criminal father—in some cases, like Robertson's, obsessive loyalty's ill-advised. The mobsters are some of our most respectable, philanthropic citizens when not involved in criminal activities—Fuller has them meet by a swimming pool to contrast their filthy personalities with clean water (the unsuspecting public perceives them as being pure). The only people who swim in the pool are the Boss and his invited guests, the city's underprivileged young, possible recruits for prostitution and drug addiction. Solid Fuller film has typical strong Fuller visuals; you'll want to wash your hands after it's over. It's unusual because our "hero" really is a bastard. Robertson gives one of his best performances. Beautiful Dolores Dorn as Robertson's prostitute girlfriend; Beatrice Kay as his surrogate mother (who is incapable of bearing kids of her own, so collects dolls); and Richard Rust as a hit man are also memorable. Also with: Larry Gates, Paul Dubov, Gerald Milton, Allan Gruener, David Kent, Peter Brocco.

UNFAITHFULLY YOURS (1948) B&W/105m.
Uncharacteristically cynical Preston Sturges comedy about the fury beneath the serene facade of supposedly happy, trusting marriages. Englishman Rex Harrison is a famous, self-assured, sharp-tongued orchestra conductor. He has a lovey-dovey relationship with his American wife, Linda Darnell, and never doubts her faithfulness. When he gets back from a trip, he discovers that, unbeknownst to him, brother-in-law Rudy Vallee had hired detectives to tail Darnell in his absence. He is infuriated with Vallee's gall and rips up the detective's report without reading it. But when he goes to tell off Edgar Kennedy's flatfoot, he hears that one night Darnell had gone to his male secretary's (Kurt Kreuger) room while wearing a negligee. Convinced that Darnell was unfaithful, Harrison becomes insanely jealous and contemplates murdering her. While conducting pieces by Rossini, Wagner, and Tchaikovsky, he has *three* fantasies: he slashes Darnell's throat and pins the murder on Kreuger; he nobly gives Darnell a check for $100,000 so she can live happily without him; he shoots himself in the head while playing Russian Roulette with Darnell and Kreuger. Following his performance, he rushes home to prepare for the murder he concocted in his first fantasy, but, in the most chaotic slapstick routine in any Sturges film, he nearly wrecks the apartment without managing to get even the simplest part of his plan to work. This picture lost money and got mixed reviews when it came out, but many modern critics regard it as a masterpiece; its reputation certainly has improved since the release of the unwatchable 1984 remake starring Dudley Moore and Nastassia Kinski. While there are some sparkling moments, I think it's the worst of Sturges's forties comedies. I find the subject itself distasteful; moreover, the throat-slashing of Darnell in the first fantasy is too gruesome for a comedy, and it's impossible to forgive Harrison after he conceives such an act (would we forgive Ralph Kramden for dreaming that he sent Alice to the moon?). Indeed, the quick shifts in tone—yes, I know that Sturges

is not taking Harrison's overly dramatic jealous response very seriously—do not work well. (Notice how, with just a few changes, the entire film could be taken as a serious melodrama.) Except for Harrison's difficulties with a recording machine, the slapstick isn't particularly funny. In fact, it's annoying. Darnell's character is given little humorous to say; but she's miscast anyway. The supporting parts aren't worthy of the fine actors who play them (Lionel Stander's stuck playing an Akim Tamiroff role) and have few of the fine lines Sturges gave his secondary characters in his earlier films. Also with: Barbara Lawrence, Alan Bridge, Robert Greig, Julius Tannen, Torben Meyer.

UNINVITED, THE (1944) B&W/98m.   Classy horror film, the cinema's first really good ghost story. Ray Milland and sister Ruth Hussey get a good deal on a large country house. But they soon discover that it is inhabited by two female apparitions. One is friendly and mournful, the other is evil and hostile. Milland falls in love with neighbor Gail Russell, who lived in the house as a baby and believes that her dead mother's ghost is trying to tell her something important. But the other ghost seems determined to kill her. Milland, Hussey, and local doctor Alan Napier attempt to solve the mystery about what happened years ago in the house so they can understand why it is haunted. Film is atmospheric, suspenseful, and witty (with a great last line); it even contains a lesbian subtext. Considering that only Val Lewton was making quality horror films at the time, it's strange that this film would be made at all, particularly at Paramount with an "A" budget. The origin of the standard "Stella by Starlight." From Dorothy Macardle's novel *Uneasy Freehold*. Directed by Lewis Allen. Also with: Donald Crisp, Cornelia Otis Skinner.

UNION CITY (1980) C/87m.   In the dull fifties a bored housewife (Deborah Harry) must cope with her boorish husband (Dennis Lipscomb). He doesn't have an inkling she's having an affair because he's so obsessed with catching red-handed the culprit (Everett McGill) who has been sneaking into their apartment building each morning and sipping their milk. When he finally does catch the vagrant, he beats him to teach him a lesson—too hard. He then hides the still body in the wall-bed of a vacant apartment, not realizing it's about to be rented. This Cornell Woolrich story is the type of twist-ending tale that used to turn up regularly on *Alfred Hitchcock Presents*. Only its offbeat direction by Mark Reichert and characters (who could be transposed to a Dostoevsky novel)—as well as the casting of rock superstars Harry and Pat Benatar—give the picture its cultish quality. More than satisfactory, but it has look and feel of just a top-grade and expanded student film. Music by Blondie's Chris Stein.

UNMARRIED WOMAN, AN (1978) C/124m. Paul Mazursky's seriocomedy about a woman in her midthirties (Jill Clayburgh) who must put her life back together after her husband (Michael Murphy) suddenly dumps her

for someone in her early twenties (who's less than 10 years older than their daughter). It was hailed as a ground-breaking feminist film, but, considering that the women's movement had been going strong for a good eight years, it was long overdue and daring only by Hollywood standards. Nevertheless, it is an interesting film, sensitively made by a male director-screenwriter who obviously feels compassion for his female lead and disappointment in the man who let her down. Clayburgh should have won an Oscar playing Erica. She makes us feel her confusion and humiliation; her initial hatred for and distrust of *all* men; her jealousy toward her teenage daughter for having a boyfriend, and her worry that her "baby" is getting too involved with someone of the heartless gender; her desperate need to pull herself out of the dark abyss when she sees a psychiatrist; her timidity around new men, curiosity about them and how she'll respond toward them sexually, and her improved self-image when she does herself proud during a one-night stand (with Cliff Gorman); her realization that she's still a desirable woman because of a wonderfully reciprocal relationship with a friendly, handsome artist (Alan Bates); and her final delighted discovery that she's truly in control of her life for the first time and that being independent and *un*married is scary but exciting. Clayburgh's character is flawed, but we forgive her and she learns to accept her imperfections (even if her *husband* could not). She's also funny, so strong-willed that she resists running off with Bates (while women in the audience were swooning over him), and so sexy that minutes after Mazursky has her throw up on screen (when her husband dumps her) we find her enticing. While this film may have gotten its landmark status by default, it is a perceptive portrait of a woman who becomes more interesting by the moment. Also with: Pat Quinn, Kelly Bishop, Lisa Lucas, Mazursky.

UNSUSPECTED, THE (1947) B&W/103m. Claude Rains is well cast as shrewd, urbane scoundrel Victor Grandison, whose job is to relate spooky murder cases on the radio, and whose pastime is murdering those who stand in the way of an inheritance. There are no box-office attractions among his co-stars: Joan Caulfield as Grandison's trusting ward, whose money he desires; Audrey Totter as his treacherous niece; Hurd Hatfield as Totter's husband, who has become a whimpering alcoholic since she stole him away from Caulfield; Constance Bennett as Grandison's producer, who suspects he was responsible for the death of his secretary (in the film's creepy opening); Michael North as the stranger who turns up claiming to be Caulfield's husband (although she doesn't remember him) and tries to get evidence against Grandison; Fred Clark as Grandison's policeman friend; and Jack Lambert as his henchman. Plot has clever twists, but there are so many of them that it becomes confusing. However, the dialogue is sharp and all the actors but the miscast North give strong, interesting characterizations, especially Rains and Totter. What makes this a really exceptional *noir* melodrama is the startling direction by Michael Curtiz. The spooky, tense atmosphere is as much the result of Curtiz's bizarre camera angles, his placement of characters (in relation to each other, the camera, and the walls and props within the frame), his thematic and dramatic use of shadows and darkness, and his camera trickery (lens distortions, shooting reflections off objects) as due to the oppressively moody, neurotic portrayals. From the *Saturday Evening Post* novelette by Charlotte Armstrong.

UP! (1976) C/84m. Ugly Russ Meyer film with sex scenes that are more graphic and repulsive than those usually found in Meyer films. Meyer humor is lacking: instead film contains a tasteless S&M sequence that involves a Hitler lookalike named Adolf Schwartz (Edward Schaaf), plus a couple of rapes—including a gang bang in a bar, much like the controversial true case in a Massachusetts fishing town, but here it's played for "laughs." It's evident that Meyer's films always contain "hicks" so he can get away with objectionable dialogue. Story centers on young couple (Janet Wood, Robert McLane) who run a smalltown diner. To make money the husband choreographs S&M sessions for Adolf Schwartz. While he's away, Wood has sexual encounters with a lady trucker (Linda Sue Ragsdale). The local sheriff (Monte Bane) takes up with a buxom beauty (Raven de la Croix) who killed her rapist. Bane gets her a job working in the diner. This happy scene is shattered when an unknown murderer bumps off Schwartz and goes after the buxom beauty. The murderer's identity is pretty easy to figure out. Picture's best scene has two surviving women running nude through the forest, trying to kill each other and simultaneously carrying on a lengthy conversation that ties up all the film's loose ends—now, this is Meyer at his most outrageous. Also with: Larry Dean, "Kitten" Navidad.

UP IN SMOKE (1978) C/117m. Screwy screen debut of Cheech and Chong trying to score marijuana so their band will be at its best during a battle of the bands at LA's Roxy. With policeman Stacy Keach and his crack team on their trail, our stoned heroes search high and low in LA and Tijuana for some good dope, and eventually cross the border in a van made out of pure marijuana. Directed by their record-producer, Lou Adler, this is by far C&C's best movie. It's terribly made, no doubt—entire scenes seem to be missing, good gags get lost among the dross, actors garble their dialogue, and one improvisational bit after another falls flat. Yet the scatological and drug-related humor I dread in contemporary comedies is surprisingly funny here (i.e., for some reason I laugh when Cheech becomes ill from a Tijuana burrito and desperately rushes to find a bathroom in an upholstery factory so noisy that he can't hear anyone's directions and finally finds it occupied by someone he deduces had the same burritos.) Chong is oblivious to everything; he's either getting high, passing out, or throwing up. Cheech, who is funnier, talks only about dope or his privates. They are stupid, lazy, and filthy but genial and you needn't worry that your kids will emulate them because they—and all other weirdos in this film—are cartoon characters. Also with: Mills Watson, Tom Skerritt, Strother Martin, Edie Adams, Zane Buzby, Anne Wharton, Rainbeaux Smith.

USED CARS (1980) C/111m. Fast-moving, eccentric, often hilarious comedy from director Robert Zemeckis and his writing partner, Bob Gale (who'd later team up for *Back to the Future*). It's a properly amoral tribute to that American institution, the shyster used-car dealer who has made a genuine *craft*—or is it an *art*?—out of fast-talking us into believing the junk he's literally put together with spit and polish (and bubble-gum) is the car of our dreams. Kurt Russell and Gerrit Graham are supersalesmen who unload lemons by hook or crook. When their boss, Jack Warden, dies from a heart attack intentionally caused by his heartless twin brother, who owns the dealership across the street, they pretend he's still alive so the brother won't take over the business. They continue to win customers away from the brother by hiring strippers and, more sneakily, interrupting *Monday Night Football* and a presidential address with raunchy car commercials. Humor is imaginative and consistently funny (although the final sequence is a bit farfetched). One of the many funny moments has Russell charming a prospective customer by telling her that her hair (black) matches the color of the car's tires. In his first really good role Russell proves to be a first-rate comic actor; and he gets great help from Graham, Warden, Frank McCrae (as the shop's loud, violent, foul-mouthed mechanic), a brilliant little pooch, and a host of fine improvisational actors. Filmmakers' attitude is revealed when Russell changes his mind about buying into a corrupt political party—there's a big difference between crooked car dealers and crooked politicians. Risqué but inoffensive; very entertaining. Also with: Deborah Harmon (as the good Warden's daughter, who becomes Russell's lover but doesn't even try to get him to mend his ways), Joseph P. Flaherty, Michael McKean and David L. Lander (Lenny and Squiggy on TV's *Laverne and Shirley*), Andrew Duncan, Betty Thomas (as a stripper), Al Lewis, Wendie Jo Sperber, Alfonso Arau.

VALLEY, THE/VALLÉE, LA (FRENCH/1972) C/100m. Most unusual, rarely screened film directed by Barbet Schroeder. Released when young people all over the world were searching for alternative lifestyles, it tells the story of a group of French men and women who journey through uncharted regions of New Guinea in search of a "mythical" valley, supposedly an Eden. In addition to being a fascinating adventure, Schroeder's work has ethnographic interest because of scenes in which the professional actors interact with primitive Mapuga tribesmen who know nothing about films or cameras. Some of the stars even participated in tribal rituals that required them to strip and don ornamental bracelets, beaded necklaces, and weird hats. One always feels that the expedition is for real, and that if the valley is not found, the actors, Schroeder, and cameraman Nestor Almendros are doomed. The picture is beautifully, hauntingly photographed. Nudity is treated casually at times, but the atmosphere is always extremely erotic. Original music is by Pink Floyd. Starring: Bulle Ogier (most appealing as a French consul's elegant wife who forgets her inhibitions), Jean-Pierre Kalfon, Michael Gothard, Valerie Lagrange.

VAMPIRE CIRCUS (BRITISH/1972) C/87m.
Very unusual Hammer horror film set in 19th-century Serbia. Vampire Count Mitterhouse (Robert Tayman) is killed by villagers and his human lover (later to be played by Adrienne Corri) is made to run the gauntlet; he swears revenge. Fifteen years later a strange circus comes to town, and people keep turning up dead, with the blood drained from their bodies. Circus people are all either vampires or humans capable of transforming into animals. When the vampires drink blood, it helps revive Count, whom Corri, the circus's owner, keeps hidden. Story gets confusing, but I think vampires are after Corri's innocent daughter (Lynne Frederick); her boyfriend (John Moulder-Brown) interferes. Film combines lurid sex and extreme violence on the part of both the vampires and the villagers—the body count is astronomical; in fact, this may be the first film since *Frankenstein* that has monsters killing children, and here it's done *on screen*. Direction by Robert Young has artistic flourishes, and he is able to give his few non-bloody scenes a genuinely sensual quality; he makes great use of religious symbolism and visuals that make us question whether we're witnessing reality or have entered a dream state. Also with: Thorley Walters, Anthony Carlan, Laurence Payne, Richard Owens, David Prowse.

VAMPIRE LOVERS, THE (BRITISH-U.S./1970) C/89m.
Hammer Studios and AIP co-produced this adaptation of Sheridan Le Fanu's Gothic horror novella *Carmilla*, the first major literary work about a female vampire. Ingrid Pitt is Carmilla Karnstein, a two-hundred-year-old vampire with a lust for young women (she usually drains blood from their breasts). She falls in love with pretty Madeleine Smith, niece of Peter Cushing. She seduces her, night after night, wanting her to be her lover for eternity. Cushing and vampire-hunter Douglas Wilmer try to prevent Smith's death. Not a bad horror film, with Pitt engaging in some really vicious attacks, but its popularity is due less to genre conventions than to the surprising amount of female nudity, the lesbian sex scenes, the unabashedly *physical* performance by Pitt, the low-cut and transparent gowns, etc. Hell-bent for physical pleasure, Pitt's Carmilla rarely displays the remorse of the novel's vampire, but there's an effective scene in which she bursts out crying upon seeing a funeral procession and realizing all will die but her. Story has been filmed several times, most memorably as Roger Vadim's

Blood and Roses and *Terror in the Crypt*. The equally sexy sequel, *Lust for a Vampire*, stars blonde Yutte Stensgaard. Directed by Roy Ward Baker. Also with: Pippa Steele, George Cole, Dawn Addams, Kate O'Mara, Jon Finch.

VAMPYR/CASTLE OF DOOM (FRENCH-GERMAN/1932) B&W/65m–70m–83m.
Carl Dreyer's classic is not like any other vampire film. It's not so much a horror film as an eerie mood piece, a dream, the visualization of the conflict between the heart and the brain for the soul. David Gray—played by the film's producer, Julian West (an alias for Baron Nicolas de Gunzburg)—is an investigator of the supernatural whose journeys take him to the village of Courtenpierre. He finds that sisters Léone (Sybille Schmitz) and Gisèle (Rena Mandel) are being threatened by a vampire-witch (Henriette Gérard) and her evil human colleagues, a doctor (Jan Hieronimko) and a peg-legged gamekeeper (Albert Bras). Léone is already deathly ill and shows signs of turning into a vampire. Most vampire films—indeed, most horror films—deal with the conflict between good and evil; but Dreyer links his vampire with Satan and makes Courtenpierre a religious battleground where believers and blasphemers wage war. Survivors David and Gisèle can leave at the end and venture into a heavenly forest. Picture is slow-paced and has no shocks, but even young horror-movie fans should be able to recognize why it is regarded as a classic of the genre. Filmed as if it were a silent film, it contains several startling visual passages (David thinking himself a corpse and seeing his own funeral, shadows dancing on the inn's wall, possessed Léone's evil face shown in close-up as she leers at her sister, a death in a flour mill). The whole film has an effectively haunting, misty look due to the use of gauze in front of the camera. Cinematographer Rudolph Maté deserves as much credit as Dreyer for this monumental work. Suggested by stories in Sheridan Le Fanu's *In a Glass Darkly*, also the basis of a much different vampire film, Roger Vadim's *Blood and Roses* (1960). Also with: Maurice Schutz, N. Babanini, Jane Mora.

VANISHING POINT (1971) C/99m.
Cult movie about a dropout from mainstream society (Barry Newman) who takes a drive-away car from Denver to San Francisco. He drives at such high speeds that police in three states become obsessed with capturing him. Along the way several people from the counterculture, including a blind black deejay, Super Soul (Cleavon Little), help him elude the cops. He becomes a symbol of freedom of the individual, who, in his Challenger, challenges authority. Director Richard Sarafian was looking for the perfect movie formula when he decided to mix an endless car chase, hallmark of the contemporary action film, into then popular existential road film where *the road* serves as a metaphor for lives that have no meaning, no direction, no beginning or end. He threw in some gorgeous Colorado-Nevada-California scenery (everyone was getting into nature in those days), a bit of nudity (a naked girl on a motorcycle in a desert?), some

acoustic and psychedelic rock music, and stereotypes from the counterculture. And the youth cult ate it up. Never mind that the picture makes little sense. There is much in the film to dislike: the dialogue is stupid ("I love your scar") and trite, particularly the pretentious aphorisms ("Only if you make war on war will you overcome it"); the women are all love objects who are willing to hop into the sack with any stranger; the only misfits who don't help Newman are homosexuals; the actors all look dog-tired in the desert heat; and because Newman commits only misdemeanors, the police will not even attempt to shoot at him. Worst of all is how Sarafian tries to manipulate everyone into liking Newman by making him a war hero who was against the war; an ex-cop who turned on other cops; who is liked by "cool" characters we would like (who in reality would not like him at all). Like Tom Laughlin's Billy Jack, he becomes (in our eyes) champion of those who don't fight back. Only this guy never does anything heroic—in fact, his driving is so dangerous I wish he'd get arrested. He drives like a tourist guide who missed his last rest stop. But at least the scenery is breathtaking and camera work from fast-moving vehicles and helicopters in conjunction with the spectacular driving and stunt work is astonishing. What I like best about the film, however, is its depiction of a coast-to-coast network of weirdos, dropouts, and misfits ready to help wayfaring strangers—this was one of the finer aspects of sixties-seventies counterculture. Cinematography by John A. Alonzo. Also with: Dean Jagger, Victoria Medlin, Paul Koslo, Bob Donner, Timothy Scott, Gilda Texter, Anthony James, Karl Swenson, Severn Darden, John Amos, Delaney and Bonnie & Friends (including Rita Coolidge).

VELVET VAMPIRE, THE/CEMETERY GIRLS (1971) C/80m.
During a trip into the desert by young marrieds Michael Blodgett and Sherry Miles, their car breaks down. Suddenly "velvet vampire" Celeste Yarnell drives up in broad daylight in a yellow dune buggy. She takes them to stay in her modern, neat, plant-filled house that sits alone in the desert. Soon Blodgett and Miles are sick of each other, but very much attracted to their mysterious hostess. Although Yarnell seduces Blodgett, she is really more interested in Miles. So he's odd man out. Although this offbeat vampire movie contains much in the classic horror tradition, it is basically about an unconventional love triangle in which one of the two women just happens to be a vampire. There is not much bloodletting; there's plenty of nudity and racy dialogue. The few critics who saw this film upon release guessed they were laughing at lines and situations that were so outrageous that they couldn't have been planned that way. But the film is most certainly a comedy. (At one point the two women argue as to who is the greater voyeur!) Stylish set design, direction by Stephanie Rothman. Its plotline and feminist perspective will remind some of *Daughters of Darkness*. My only complaint is that Rothman backs away from showing a lesbian love scene, which she could have handled well, and instead ends film with a disappointing chase sequence in LA. Also with: Jerry Daniels.

VERONIKA VOSS (WEST GERMAN/1982) B&W/105m.
The last film in Rainer Werner Fassbinder's postwar trilogy, following *The Marriage of Maria Braun* and *Lola*. Rosel Zech (who may remind you of Delphine Seyrig) plays a once famous UFA actress who has become a morphine addict. Hilmar Thate is a sportswriter who falls under Zech's spell, giving up his girlfriend to spend a night with her, giving her money to prove his devotion. In Fassbinder films, relationships are sado-masochistic power struggles in which one person becomes dominant and the other hangs around to be humiliated. Thate settles into his puppy-dog role and discovers that Zech is in his position in a relationship with a female doctor (Annemarie Düringer), who keeps middle-aged women like Zech hooked on morphine so they'll sign over their property to her. Rare uncomplicated Fassbinder picture is of interest mainly because of what Veronika Voss represents. She symbolizes both the once great, proud Germany that shrinks away in pain, guilt, and humiliation and the victims of the decadent postwar social order. Equally significant: Fassbinder, who often identified with his heroines, probably related to Veronika Voss's drug addiction since his own dependency was increasing at this time. That's Fassbinder playing a character in the opening scene, sitting in a theater near Veronika Voss, watching a film in which the actress is signing over property for a drug injection. Perhaps Fassbinder sensed his imminent demise and that it would be similar to Veronika Voss's. Shot in black and white, to show that all the glitter and glamour, blood and spirit, life and happiness have faded from Veronika Voss and Germany. Also with: Cornelia Froboess, Doris Schade, Volker Spengler.

VERTIGO (1958) C/123m.
Alfred Hitchcock's most perplexing film begins with a chase across a San Francisco roof. Police detective John "Scottie" Ferguson (James Stewart) slips and finds himself dangling from a drainpipe high above the street. A cop who tries to save him plummets to his death and suddenly Scottie develops a fear of heights, experiencing extreme vertigo when he looks downward. Although in the next scene the retired Scottie is safe, it's significant that Hitchcock never shows him being rescued—in fact, he makes it seem as if rescue is impossible. By leaving Scottie in mid-air, Hitchcock instills in us the feeling (which lasts the whole film) that Scottie has slipped into a surreal, dreamlike netherworld that exists between life and death, the present and past, the real and illusionary. Feeling guilty because a cop died in his place, Scottie is attracted to death, which is embodied by the beautiful, ethereal Madeleine (Kim Novak is well cast), the suicidal wife of Elster (Tom Helmore), one of Scottie's old school chums. Hired by Elster to follow her, Scottie jumps headlong into the deathly world through which this unhappy woman sleepwalks. They meet when he pulls her from the ocean during a suicide bid. They fall in love. But when Madeleine climbs a high tower to jump to her death, Scottie's vertigo prevents him from stopping her. (Conveniently: he never looks at the body.) Mourning for Madeleine, Scottie happens upon a

simple shopgirl, Judy Barton (also Novak), who bears a striking resemblance to his lost love. He obsessively tries to re-create Madeleine, dying Judy's red hair blond, dressing her like Madeleine and taking her to places he took Madeleine—Robert Burks's eerie camera work makes it seem as if past and present are mingling. What attracted Hitchcock to the project is that Scottie wants to indulge in necrophilia by resurrecting a dead woman and making love to her. He's also showing through Scottie how many directors can turn a simple girl like Kim Novak into a haunting screen presence. Hitchcock sets up distinctions between elegant Madeleine and Judy and between Madeleine and Midge (Barbara Bel Geddes), the pert, down-to-earth fiancée whom Scottie dumps for Madeleine. Hitchcock states that, given a choice of women, men are so weak they'll always pick the helpless over the independent, the attractive over the plain, the frigid over the accessible, and the illusionary over the real. For two thirds of the film we believe we're watching a mystery in which Scottie will uncover Elster's murder plot in which Scottie was the patsy. But suddenly the audience is let in on Judy being Madeleine, and the picture becomes an intense, psychological character study of Scottie. The structure is unique and brilliant, but I find it infuriating. I prefer the mystery unraveling to Scottie unraveling and becoming unbearably obsessive, tyrannical, and self-destructive. We come to root for the fragile Judy, despite what she did to him, and despise Scottie. That's why the tragic ending is so unsatisfying and depressing. Bernard Herrmann's score contributes a great deal to the haunting atmosphere. From *D'Entre les Morts* by Pierre Boileau and Thomas Narcejac. Also with: Henry Jones, Raymond Bailey, Ellen Corby, Konstantin Shayne.

VICE SQUAD (1982) C/97m. Sleazy sexploitation film about a Hollywood hooker (Season Hubley, who's a pretty good actress) who helps a police detective (Gary Swanson) trap the sadistic pimp (Wings Hauser) who killed her hooker friends. But she's the one who falls into a trap. Another film which gives the wrong impression that all street hookers are model types. Extremely brutal and unpleasant, particularly the finale. Even so, Hauser's scary villain is someone you'll love to hate. Directed by Gary A. Sherman. Look for MTV veejay Nina Blackwood in a small part. Also with: Pepe Serna, Beverly Todd.

VICTIM (BRITISH/1961) B&W/100m. Well-made drama in which Dirk Bogarde is a distinguished, married English barrister with a homosexual past that only his wife (Sylvia Syms) and homosexual acquaintances know about. A young man (Peter McEnery) who has been arrested for embezzlement commits suicide rather than have blackmailers expose his relationship with Bogarde. (He loved Bogarde, but while Bogarde was physically attracted to McEnery, he had rejected the boy because of his love for his wife.) Bogarde decides he must help the police solve McEnery's death, even though he knows his career will be ruined when his homosexuality is made public; he also fears

Syms will walk out on him once his name is dragged through the mud. This was the first film to be *about* homosexuality, and, fortunately, it's strongly directed by Basil Dearden and maturely and sympathetically written by Janet Green and John McCormick. In the key scene Bogarde and other middle-aged homosexuals talk about the antiquated laws dealing with homosexuality between, as they said even back then, "consenting adults." It's a discussion that no other picture would be brave enough to include for many years to come. Of interest, upon its U.S. release a critic for the respected *Films in Review* wrote: "Although the Motion Picture Association of America's Code Administration refuses its seal to practically nothing these days, it did refuse a seal to this piece of undistinguished propaganda for homosexuality. Made in England, where sexual perversion is said to now infect 4% of the population, *Victim* blatantly pleads for a change in the law which makes homosexuality a crime, on the grounds that such a law abets blackmailing. The biological, social and psychological evils resulting from homosexuality are never mentioned. The false contention that homosexuality is congenital is stressed throughout." That gives us some idea how far ahead of its time this picture was. If you see this on TV, make sure it's not the cut version in which, remarkably, homosexual references are excised; for years I had no idea what this picture was about! Also with: Dennis Price, Hilton Edwards, John Barrie, Donald Churchill.

VIDEODROME (CANADIAN/1983) C/87m. James Woods is the seedy, profit-motivated owner of a cable channel that specializes in soft-core porn and violence. A local video pirate tells him that he's hooked into a station called Videodrome that secretly broadcasts non-stop real torture, mutilations, and murder. Woods pretends interest in the snuff channel because he might be able to buy the low-cost programming for his own station, but the more he watches the weird images, the more obsessed he becomes with the S&M content. His baser feelings emerge, he slips into possible madness, his concepts of reality and illusion become blurred. But it's not really his fault. He has fallen into a trap and is under someone else's control. The images have a hallucinatory power—and a puritanical rightwinger wants to broadcast them on Woods's station in order to destroy the minds of all people who would watch such trash. David Cronenberg's horror film is ambitious and makes strong points about the hypnotic power of television and its ability to turn a mind to mush. But it becomes so cerebral that its fascinating premise is lost in a mass of confusion in the last third of the film. The special effects by Rick Baker are well done, but many of the images are both stupid and repulsive (i.e., Woods's stomach opening up and swallowing a gun, a video cassette, a hand). And when Woods starts clamoring about "The New Flesh"—where the animate, inanimate, and organic merge—then I think the film is really out of its mind. Nevertheless, Woods gives a fine performance and singer Deborah Harry is truly seductive ("Let's try a few things") as Woods's masochistic lover.

Also with: Sonja Smits (who is linked in some way to Harry), Peter Dvorsky, Les Carlson, Jack Creley, Lynne Gorman.

VIEW TO A KILL, A (1985) C/132m.

Roger Moore's last portrayal of James Bond and, despite what reviewers automatically reported, he looks trimmer and more energetic than in some of the previous efforts. British agent 007 is pitted against a master criminal, played by Christopher Walken, who intends to blow up Silicon Valley. Action takes place all over the globe, in the air, on the ground, underwater. I wish Bond had a few more of his famous gadgets on hand, but his action scenes are exciting and some of the stunt work is spectacular (although it's too easy to tell that Moore has a double). Walken's the first Bond villain who is not so much an evil person as a crazed neurotic. I find him more memorable than some of the recent Bond foes. Anyway, viewers will be more interested in his lover and righthand woman, Mayday, played by singer Grace Jones, whose exotic features and lightning-quick karate maneuvers make her an intimidating presence. Unfortunately, the filmmakers—who ruined villain Jaws by making him a nice guy in *Moonraker*—make the mistake of switching Mayday at the end from Bond's nemesis to his accomplice, depriving us of a slam-bang fight to the finish between the two. (I suppose gentleman Bond isn't allowed to kill women, even monsters like Mayday.) Leading lady Tanya Roberts must get by on beauty alone since she is stuck with a character (spunky but true blue) who is the least mysterious of Bond's women to date. Picture lacks the flamboyance of other Bond films, and has a terrible slapstick chase sequence in San Francisco (with stupid cops rather than Walken's henchmen), but overall it's fast-paced, fairly enjoyable, and a worthy entry in the series. Directed by John Glen. Also with: Patrick MacNee, Lois Maxwell, Robert Brown, Desmond Llewellyn.

VILLAGE OF THE DAMNED (BRITISH/1960) B&W/78m.

Loose adaptation of John Wyndham's novel *The Midwich Cuckoos* is top-notch horror film. A small English village is mysteriously cut off from outside world for a few hours; afterward none of the inhabitants can remember what happened, but 12 of the women are mysteriously pregnant. On the same day, they all give birth. A few years pass, and the blue-eyed, blond children display a lack of emotion and a superintellect. They can communicate with each other telephathically, read people's thoughts, and use mind control. Their survival instinct is so strong that when threatened by townspeople, they use mind control to force them to commit suicide. Scientist George Sanders, the father of one of the children (Martin Stephens) and the only earthling they respect (because of his vast knowledge), theorizes that these children were created by aliens bent on world takeover. As their instructor, he realizes that once their brainpower develops to its potential, they will be invulnerable. He devises a plan to destroy them before they can read his mind and learn his intentions. A scary, well-made movie—although it was first to exploit children-as-monsters horror potential. Blond kids with glowing eyes wreaking havoc is one of the classic horror-movie images. Indeed, film is an intelligent meditation on *intelligence* (the full use of brain's potential), a trait that has always been held in low esteem in horror movies. Impressive atmospheric direction by Wolf Rilla, who never made another important film and turned to making sleazy sex comedies. Fine sequel, *Children of the Damned*, has nothing to do with this story. Also with: Barbara Shelley (who is very good as Sanders's wife), Michael Gwynn, Laurence Naismith.

VIRIDIANA (SPANISH-MEXICAN/1961) B&W/90m.

Luis Buñuel's once scandalous religious satire was shot in Spain, but Spanish authorities considered it subversive and seized all prints in the country before it could be released. However, Buñuel had fled Franco's Spain for France and had already smuggled several copies there. After it won the Palme d'Or prize at Cannes, it received worldwide distribution from its Mexican producer. Silvia Pinal is a naïve novice nun whose Mother Superior sends her to visit her uncle Fernando Rey, on his farm before she takes her final vows. Rey's blonde, beautiful niece conjures up memories of his dead wife and he gets the urge to possess her. After he spikes her drink, he suffers such guilt that he commits suicide. As the girl is blamed for the rich man's downfall, she leaves the convent. She inherits her uncle's estate and, being a good Catholic, opens it up to the poor. But they aren't worthy of her kind gesture. In Buñuel, it doesn't pay to be a good Samaritan. Buñuel points out the hypocrisy of Spain's Catholic establishment, which, when tested, is neither moral nor Christian in attitude, and the Church's ineffectiveness in relating to its poor constituency; film also shows contempt for equally corrupt, indecent, and hypocritical human behavior. It has lost some of its satirical bite (although American conservatives will delight in how Buñuel depicts the poor as freeloading ingrates), but the perverse sexual content (including rapes, incest, transvestism, necrophilia), kooky characters, disarming deadpan humor, and its classic gluttonous-orgiastic dinner held by the poor in Pinal's house when she's away (beneath a painting of *The Last Supper*) still keep the film high on the list of weird movies. A hilarious final joke. Good performances by Pinal, Rey, and Francisco Rabal (as Rey's illegitimate adult son). Also with: Margarita Lozano, Victoria Zinny, Teresa Rabal, Luis Heredia, José Manuel Martin.

VIVA ZAPATA! (1952) B&W/113m.

Directed by Elia Kazan and scripted by John Steinbeck, this controversial film is about Mexican hero Emiliano Zapata's (Marlon Brando) rise (or is it a moral *decline*, as the film contends?) from peasant revolutionary leader to President and, following his voluntary abdication, return to the peasant movement. While it's a fairly exciting action-adventure film, it is historically inaccurate—Zapata never was President, he was not illiterate, etc.—and it is politically confusing. Kazan and Steinbeck wanted to make an anti-communist tract, equating the Mexican revolution to what happened in Russia. But while they get across their central theme that power corrupts *anybody*—when President Zapata realizes he has betrayed the revolution and become just like the overthrown Díaz (just like Stalin became as autocratic as the Czar)—they are also responsible for making viewers realize the necessity of *armed* insurrection in some countries, which is certainly a revolutionary stance for an American film. Film is depressing because, while it shows that revolution is sometimes necessary, there can never be success because the leaders of a revolution will invariably sell out their followers. While it's obvious that the filmmakers intended heartless hardliner Fernando (Joseph Wiseman) to represent turncoat Stalin—he arranges for Zapata's demise just as Stalin ordered the assassination of Trotsky—from the beginning he comes across as being apolitical, without any social conscience. It's interesting that Fernando is a writer because it confirms that Kazan and Steinbeck are contending that learned leftists will eventually consider themselves too good to be permanently associated with the masses. Similarly, when Steinbeck has Zapata ask his wife (Jean Peters) to teach him to read (on their wedding night!), he is implying that Zapata has decided he wants to be better than his uneducated followers and on even terms with Fernando—it is the educated revolutionary who will become an elitist and then a reactionary. Film's most striking scenes are those that show the peasants working together at revolutionary action. But it's annoying when Kazan presents the adult peasants as children, as if he had Díaz as his cultural adviser. By giving a surprisingly subdued performance (probably because the corners of his eyes were glued down), Brando got a Best Actor nomination; the more emotional Anthony Quinn won as Best Supporting Actor. With an excellent score by Alex North and impressive outdoor photography by Joe MacDonald. Also with: Lou Gilbert, Harold Gordon (as Madero), Alan Reed (as Pancho Villa), Margo, Henry Silva, Frank Silvera, Mildred Dunnock, Arnold Moss, Philip Van Zandt.

VIVRE SA VIE (A FILM IN TWELVE EPISODES)/ MY LIFE TO LIVE (FRENCH/1962) B&W/82m–85m.
Jean-Luc Godard's exceptional fourth film starred his then wife, Anna Karina, as a young woman who has left her husband (André-S. Labarthe) and child to make it as an actress. But she winds up a prostitute in order to pay her rent. At first she works on her own, but then hooks up with a pimp (Sady Rebbot). Eventually he tries to sell her and she is gunned down during the money transaction. Godard's approach to Karina's prostitute is detached, not because he doesn't care about Karina but because his remote style is meant to underscore the fact that this woman makes no emotional connection with the men she has sex with. Godard's point—made by the old philosopher (Brice Parain) with whom Karina converses, and proven to her by the young client she comes to love (revealingly, Godard himself dubbed Peter Kassowitz reading to Karina)—is that pleasure and fulfillment come less from the sexual act than through a stronger form of communication: talking, the interchange of words. The great tragedy of Karina's murder is that it happens directly after she has finally opened up emotionally and expressed happiness in response to Kassowitz's *speaking* to her as an equal rather than using her sexually. (She had shown happiness previously only when she danced to some loud rock music as she flirted with Kassowitz.) Final scene is shocking. As in all early Godard films, he experiments with his camera (i.e., juxtaposing abstract and real images in order to express ideas). He also makes thematic references to films, literature, music. Cinematography by Raoul Coutard. Also with: Guylaine Schlumberger.

VORTEX (1982) C/85m.
Curious cult item, written and directed by Beth B. and Seth B., underground favorites because of their experimental films in Super 8. This was their first venture into 16mm and the first time they had real money to work with (some of it provided by arts endowments). And while the film tends to be slow and confusing at times, it is quite impressive, particularly from a visual standpoint. Controversial, eccentric underground film/music superstar Lydia Lunch (writer and star of *The Right Side of My Brain*) plays a private eye who works on a murder case involving industrial espionage and computer theft. She comes across a bunch of quirky, paranoid figures, including her client, who traps her in a net, and a crippled, germ-conscious, reclusive corporation owner who's trying to sell a defense system to the military. She becomes involved— sexually, not romantically—with the recluse's temperamental, neurotic aide (James Russo), and in an exciting scene on a rooftop, this almost causes her demise. Picture is odd mix of the *film noir*, science fiction, and the experimental film. If you like alternate approaches to familiar storylines, then this film is worth a look. Lydia Lunch contributed to the solid music track; so did John Lurie, who'd later star in *Stranger Than Paradise* for director Jim Jarmusch, who worked in this film's crew. Also with: Bill Rice.

WAGES OF FEAR, THE/SALAIRE DE LA PEUR, LA (FRENCH-ITALIAN/1953) B&W/105m–156m.
Unbearably suspenseful existential classic by writer-director Henri-Georges Clouzot, who adapted Georges Arnaud's novel. A young Corsican (Yves Montand), an aging Parisian (Charles Vanel), a German who endured a labor camp (Peter Van Eyck), and a fatally ill Italian (Folco Lolli) are stranded, penniless, in a backward, godforsaken South American village, seemingly on the edge of the world and one step from hell. They are about to take that fatal final step. In order

to escape this existence, they accept an offer of $2000 each from an American-based fuel company to transport two truckloads of nitroglycerine over 300 miles of hazardous mountain roads. Any second they may be dead. Their trip is heart-stopping. *Three* unforgettable scenes—the trucks back onto rotting planks over a mountain ledge; Van Eyck uses nitro to blow up a boulder that blocks the road; Montand drives his truck through a lake of spilled oil while Vanel swims in the black liquid, trying to get out of the way—rate with the most thrilling sequences in cinema history. Clouzot's film is, in part, about how men are considered expendable. One of the angriest, most cynical filmmakers, he vigorously attacks corporations (the U.S. oil firm) which continually exploit individuals and let them risk their lives—especially non-union workers in Third World countries—so that the company profits. But he's equally disappointed in men (such as our "heroes") who are careless with their own lives. On the surface, film is about how these four men test themselves on the dangerous, death-defying drive to see if they can come through under pressure, be equal to their companions, be brave, be MEN. But in truth, brave or cowardly, resourceful or confused—it doesn't matter. Soon you have as much respect for cowardly Vanel wallowing in the oil and clearing a path as for Montand, who's doing the heroic drive through the oil. Death comes to everyone—and death is heroic for no one. A man's only solace, considering these sad facts, is the love of women and the camaraderie of men—but Clouzot's self-centered men reject human connections. William Friedkin remade film as *Sorcerer*, a disappointment in 1977. Also with: Vera Clouzot as the knocked-about barmaid who loves Montand, William Tubbs.

WALK IN THE SUN, A (1945) B&W/117m.
Solid war film was directed by Lewis Milestone, 15 years after his anti-war classic *All Quiet on the Western Front*. A platoon commanded by Dana Andrews lands in Salerno, Italy, in 1943. It has orders to march six miles to a farmhouse, although no one knows what it will find there. The script by Robert Rossen, who adapted Harry Brown's novel, includes much dialogue, so that the emphasis is less on the fighting *per se* than on how war affects the various men in the platoon (who hail from all over the U.S.). Each man responds differently. Picture is visually interesting because the men are shown in relationship to the flat landscape and wide sky, which at times is blocked out by smoke from exploded bombs and gunfire. Milestone often pans effectively over the hostile terrain. The men are attacked repeatedly by the enemy. Realistically, we *never* see the faces of the enemy, who strike from inside planes, tanks, and, finally, the farmhouse. This is a rare WWII film in which our men have second thoughts about being soldiers. The terrifying finale confirms that fighting isn't fun for Americans in WWII, just necessary. Also with: Richard Conte, Sterling Holloway, Lloyd Bridges, John Ireland, George Tyne, Norman Lloyd, Huntz Hall.

WALK ON THE WILD SIDE (1962) B&W/114m.
Brooding, once shocking adaptation of Nelson Algren's novel is set in 1930s New Orleans, where Texan Laurence Harvey has come to look for his onetime lover, Capucine. He expects that she's still a sculptress-artist, as when he last saw her three years ago, but he discovers she works in Barbara Stanwyck's bordello, The Doll House. After his initial shock he forgives her and wants to take her back but Stanwyck, who has romantic designs on Capucine herself, uses her thugs and political connections to try to scare Harvey out of town. Film is very watchable—for one thing, Harvey's hair isn't too greasy—but the actors, though good, are extremely stiff, as if they feared moving about and not being able to find the floor markers on the dark sets. Only hip-swinging Jane Fonda, as a wildcat tamed by Stanwyck's threats, projects any energy; but it's difficult to tell if her performance is correct or completely wrong since her style is so much more expressive than that of the other stars. It's unusual to see a film with four solid female parts (Anne Baxter also gets a lot of screen time as a kindly Spanish café owner who, like Capucine and Fonda, loves Harvey). But so many of their feelings—those that explain who they are—are kept bottled inside, as if the many scriptwriters (including Clifford Odets and Ben Hecht) were either afraid or incapable of expressing them or unable to because of censorship problems. Stilted look to film can be attributed to director Edward Dmytryk. Score by Elmer Bernstein. The leads were clients of agent Charles Feldman, the film's producer; Capucine was his current lover, and he insisted she wear modern-day Cardin outfits. Also with: Richard Rust, Karl Swenson, Juanita Moore.

WALKABOUT (AUSTRALIAN/1971) C/95m.
Wondrously photographed, haunting film by Nicolas Roeg, filmed in the Australian outback. English children, teenager Jenny Agutter (her movie debut) and young brother Lucien John, live with their parents in a modern Australian city. Father John Meillon drives his kids to the desert for a picnic. Crazed—probably from the dullness of his work and home life—he tries to kill them, then sets fire to the car and commits suicide. Agutter and John, wearing their school uniforms, walk through the desert in search of civilization. They nearly die before happening on a lone fruit tree and a pool of water: Eden. In the morning the pool and fruit have vanished. A young aborigine, David Gumpilil, off on his own to prove his manhood, comes upon them and guides them through the wilderness toward civilization. While John is able to communicate with Gumpilil through grunting and sign language, Agutter makes no attempt to. A strong sexual attraction develops between the teenagers (and Agutter told me that she played the role at the time of her own sexual awakening); but the girl, product of a regimented upbringing, refuses to acknowledge her blossoming feelings. Resistant to Gumpilil's mating dance, she finds it more comfortable to treat him as a servant than as a prospective lover. Only years later, when trapped as a house-

wife, does Agutter realize what Gumpilil had offered her; she thinks of paradise lost. Young and sexually repressed, she had failed to realize the potential of the journey. It should have been a journey of self-realization as well as a sexual rite of passage. One wonders whether if the boy were white, the girl would have allowed her instincts to supersede her conditioning. What the film is about is the boundary that separate two cultures (the theme of Peter Weir's later films). Neither Gumpilil nor Agutter can understand the other; the tragedy is that until it is too late, Agutter does not attempt to understand either him or herself. Mesmerizing film has unbelievably gorgeous photography (by Roeg) of the outback, its creatures, its desert sands, its stump trees. Roeg intercuts sensual images (naked skin, water, connecting tree branches) with others that are unexpectedly harsh (such as animals being killed), shots of the outback with those of impersonal civilization. Fascinating, original movie will stay with you. Contains the first of Agutter's many nude movie swims. Scripted by Edward Bond, from the novel by James Vance Marshall. Music by John Barry.

WALKING TALL (1973) C/125m.   This once controversial box-office smash is a highly fictionalized account of real-life Tennessee sheriff Buford Pusser (Joe Don Baker), a former wrestler who used club (literally) and fang tactics to clean up crime and corruption. His one-man crusade against powerful, politically influential men places him in constant danger and results in his wife (Elizabeth Hartman) being killed in an ambush. But he doesn't back down. Phil Karlson's hard-hitting action film is a throwback to old-style westerns in which well-intentioned lawmen never had to make excuses for ringing up a high body count each day. It also recalls Karlson's *Phenix City Story*, in which a crusading lawyer cleans up corruption, and vigilante-with-badges urban melodramas like *The Big Heat* and *Dirty Harry*. Initially, leftist viewers joined the rednecks in applauding Pusser's efforts, figuring he was a populist figure who hated corrupt authority figures as much as they. But in retrospect this film helped start the unfortunate Hollywood trend in which thuggish lawmen who shoot first and ask questions later are presented as appealing "rebels" because they're willing to risk their jobs and promotions by circumventing the law to make our streets safer. Nowhere to be found are the moral citizens who take a stand against vigilante justice because, unlike in these movies, innocent people are victimized too—indeed, it should be remembered that Pusser was *voted* out of office because his strong-arm tactics scared innocent people. Modestly budgeted film is crude, brutal, and manipulative. However, the powerfully built, ruddy-faced Baker is a dynamic action hero; and the Tennessee locales give the film an authentic atmosphere. Bo Svenson starred in the inferior sequels, *Part 2, Walking Tall* and *Final Chapter—Walking Tall*, and the short-lived television series. Also with: Gene Evans, Rosemary Murphy, Noah Beery, Jr., Brenda Benet, Felton Perry, Kenneth Tobey, Lurene Tuttle.

WANDA (1970) C/105m.   Regarded by most critics as an interesting failure when released, Barbara Loden's independent film—she was the writer, director, and star—is most impressive today because in the lengthy interim other filmmakers haven't come up with a more honest portrait of an American woman with an empty life. In a role for which studios would have courted Joanne Woodward, Loden is exceptional as a passive, unskilled, uneducated, unambitious woman from a mining town. That she has no feeling of self-worth is reflected in her simple lines: "I don't have anything"; "I'm stupid"; "I'm no good." In the only decision of her life, she grants her children to her husband during divorce procedures. She then goes off with small-potatoes thief Michael Higgins. It's sad watching this sensitive woman accepting the hostility, insults, and demands (in regard to sex, the way she dresses and wears her hair, etc.) of this weak loser who thinks himself so much better than she—just so she can have meaning in someone's life. Shot in 16mm, picture has the look and feel of documentary: it's hard to believe that a hidden camera didn't capture moments from the lives of real, unhappy people.

WANDERERS, THE (1979) C/113m.   Philip Kaufman directed this cult favorite set in the Bronx in 1963 and dealing with members of an Italian high-school gang called the Wanderers. Picture has individual scenes that flirt with greatness, but the changes in tone are so drastic that it lacks cohesion. Seen mostly through the eyes of handsome Ken Wahl (a star-making performance that didn't make him a star), picture deals with gang rivalries, copping feels, Italian brotherhood (which has good and bad points), macho fathers, how music reflects the energy and rebellious spirit of youth, loyalty, growing up. There is much brutality, yet this past is shown to be a time of innocence because it doesn't compare to the Vietnam years ahead. End of innocence is reflected by Kennedy's assassination, the recruitment of the Fordham Baldies into the military, graduation, boys running away to California, and Wahl's dream girlfriend, non-Italian Karen Allen, going to a Village club to hear Bob Dylan sing "The Times They Are a-Changin'." Picture has drive, humor, much nostalgia, erotic moments (e.g., Allen suggests a strip-poker game), an epic battle of the gangs, and terrifying scenes in which our guys wander into a weird gang's section of town. Excellent use of music. Photographed by Michael Chapman. From the fine novel by Richard Price. Also with: Linda Manz, John Friedrich, Toni Kalem, Alan Rosenberg, Erland van Lidthe de Jeude, Dolph Sweet, Tony Ganios, Jim Youngs, Val Avery.

WAR OF THE WORLDS, THE (1953) C/85m.   Martians invade earth and destroy people and property with deadly heat rays. Earthlings try to ward off devastation with every weapon possible, from hand guns to an atomic bomb. But nothing works. Just when it appears that the human race is doomed, the Martians keel over dead—victims of simple bacteria to which earth creatures have developed an immunity. Producer George Pal updated H.

G. Wells's SF classic from late 19th century to mid-20th century; switched the prime setting from London to Los Angeles; transformed the Martians from sea-type creatures with 16 tentacles to little, two-legged, mutant-like beings; jettisoned (at Paramount's insistence) the story of a man searching for his wife in his war-torn country for one in which a man (Gene Barry) (whose girlfriend, Ann Robinson, merely looks on, serves coffee) becomes one of the few scientists in the SF cinema to work *with* the military to rub out aliens (this time a *priest* is the one who wishes to communicate with his fellow creatures). None of the changes is as annoying as the inclusion of a lot of hokey religion. The film's narrator (Cedric Hardwicke) quotes Wells when he states that the alien-causing bacteria had been placed on earth because of "God's infinite wisdom"—implying that at the point of earth's creation He had set up a fail-safe system against alien invasion. But in the film God is *directly* responsible for the aliens' demise and the continuation of the human race—it is implied that the bacteria do their dirty work, not uncoincidentally, at the exact moment the aliens attack a *church*, probably the only building left in the city. Barry is grateful for God's kindness, but has he forgotten how much death occurred before the aliens were stopped? Rescue seems more on account of the church than of the earthlings inside—not five minutes before, we witnessed a mob scene which demonstrated the worst in human behavior, making us question whether such brutal, selfish people are worthy of redemption. In fact, film doesn't show why earth's people or their way of life should be preserved; unlike in the book, the hero doesn't reflect on places, past events, and people that he'd once taken for granted but now appreciates. Barry is a sturdy if dull hero; Robinson, who has no less than three moments of hysteria, is an embarrassment. Pal always tried to be scientifically accurate, so his depiction of an atomic-bomb explosion, during which curious onlookers stay no more than a mile away so they supposedly won't feel the effects, is creepy in that it really reflects the attitude at the time toward A-bomb testing near populated areas. The bomb doesn't work against the alien ship, but if it did, I'm curious as to whether Pal would have had the military dropping A-bombs all over the world on alien craft. Film has an enormous cult following, presumably because of the tremendous special effects, particularly evident during the scenes in which LA is set ablaze: we all feel a perverse fascination at seeing our world almost completely obliterated. Its popularity is due, certainly in part, to its being the first film in which America itself is turned into a war zone because of an invasion: it anticipates television's *V* and John Milius's *Red Dawn*. Colorful but overrated. Directed by Byron Haskin. Also with: Les Tremayne, Robert Cornthwaite, Henry Brandon, Jack Kruschen.

WARGAMES (1983) C/110m. Teenager (Matthew Broderick) interfaces his home computer with government's early-warning-missile-detecting-system computer and accidentally sets course for a Global Thermonuclear War. As U.S. officials give chase, believing him to be working for the Russians, he and his new girlfriend (Ally Sheedy) race against time to find the reclusive scientist (John Wood) who built the computer, so he can shut it down. John Badham skillfully directed this popular and provocative nail-biter. The pacing is fast and furious throughout, with liberal doses of humor tossed in along the way. The ending is dragged out a bit, but is still exciting. Broderick and Sheedy are most appealing leads. Film is in a way a tribute to the resourcefulness and ingenuity of young people, but it's a shame that their casual crime of tapping into their school's computer to alter their grades is treated humorously and condoned. Picture also got valid criticism for having all the adults be jerks; a theme should be that smart adults and smart children should be able to communicate on even terms. Badham became irritated that reporters and disturbed government spokesmen zeroed in on computer break-in angle but ignored picture's more relevant issue: no one can win a nuclear war. Film is also of note for being the first to have a computer whiz be a regular person rather than a professional programmer or scientist. Also with: Dabney Coleman, Barry Corbin, Juanin Clay.

WARRIORS, THE (1979) C/95m. Walter Hill's nifty, stylized, heart-pounding action movie is set in a surreal, fantasy New York, a playground for numerous tribes (called gangs) which stake out territories and parade around in garish identifying costumes, brandishing weapons and spray paint with which to decorate everything in their paths. It's a dream world, an enormous arena of parks and empty subway tunnels, the perfect obstacle course. The Warriors, a little known Coney Island gang, travel far uptown into the unfamiliar Bronx to attend a meeting of all city gangs. When the leader of the most revered gang in the city is assassinated by the crazed leader (David Patrick Kelly is a great, wacky villain) of the Rogues, all the gangs think the Warriors were responsible. Without their leader (who was killed in retaliation), the eight unarmed Warriors flee for their lives, with all the other gangs giving chase. Swan (Michael Beck) assumes command—all but Ajax (James Remar) follow his lead. Hill's Warriors are participants in a sporting contest analogous to a baseball game. They must, in effect, leave home (Brooklyn) and return home in order to "score points" with the other gangs of the city. The subway trains—neutral territory in Sol Yurick's much different (his gang members are stupid and undisciplined punks) source novel—are Hill's bases, safe territory. Out of the trains they do battle with four gangs, one for each baseline. The police are another tribe, the Men in Blue who serve as umpires and remove all rule breakers from the game. There is even a play-by-play announcer, a female deejay who reports the Warriors' progress. She refers to the gang as "a minor-league team." Another gang, the Baseball Furies, wear Yankee uniforms and carry bats. They are *major-league*, but the Warriors leave them in their wake. Their fight reveals that the Warriors, despite their fragile appearance, can fight anyone, and that the film is bloodless. The violence is cartoonlike, with every brutally beaten character feeling fine immediately after. The choreography of the fight scenes is first-rate. Only one person is killed on screen—a small number considering this film was the object of a huge anti-violence-in-film campaign due to some incidents in theaters in which it played. Hill gives picture great energy and drive. Music is well used. Also with: Deborah Van Valkenburgh (a street girl who becomes Beck's girlfriend), Thomas Waites, Dorsey Wright, Brian Tyler, David Harris, Tom McKitterick, Marcelino Sanchez, Perry Michos, Roger Hill, Lynn Thigpen.

WATCH ON THE RHINE (1943) B&W/114m.
Well-known German freedom fighter Paul Lukas, his American wife, Bette Davis (a *bad* performance), and their three children come from Europe to live with her mother (Lucile Watson) and brother (Donald Woods) in Washington, at the home in which Davis grew up. Lukas and Davis explain to the politically naive Watson and Woods that there is a growing fascist threat throughout the world, even in the United States. Sure enough, another houseguest (George Coulouris) is a decadent Romanian count who is in league with the Nazis at their Washington embassy. Watson and Woods see firsthand the devious nature of fascists when Coulouris, threatening to tell the local Nazis that Lukas is planning to sneak back into Germany, demands that Lukas give him money designated to help the underground. Lukas has only one option. Dashiell Hammett adapted Lillian Hellman's 1941 anti-fascist play, but it probably wasn't as stagy in the theater. Characters gather in a room and, instead of engaging in believable discussion, take turns giving high-minded speeches that express their views of the global situation—and explain how they fit in. Even the children—the type you'd consider returning to the orphanage—seem to be indoctrinated rather than speaking from the heart. Only the spirited Watson and sleazy Coulouris seem like real people. Even with all the problems, however, the picture remains unique in that its major character, a *sympathetic* character, is a professional resistance fighter—"I fight fascists" is Lukas's jarring self-definition (at a time few movies used the word *fascist*)—and he is allowed to shoot and kill an unarmed fascist without being arrested or killed himself. Lukas won a Best Actor Oscar with an uneven performance—sometimes he sounds like Bela Lugosi. Directed by Herman Shumlin. Also with: Geraldine Fitzgerald, Henry Daniell, Beulah Bondi, Janis Wilson, Donald Buka.

WATERLOO BRIDGE (1940) B&W/103m.
An extremely well-made, extremely depressing adult romance that Vivien Leigh fans—at least those who don't mind watching her suffer for 75 minutes—have long held dear. In London during WWI, Leigh is a very sweet and innocent ballet dancer who quickly falls in love with a handsome army captain (Robert Taylor does his best, although miscast in role intended for Laurence Olivier). Before they can marry, he's sent off to fight—she loses her dancing job for skipping a performance to see him off. Soon after, Leigh reads that Taylor has been killed. Sickly, suicidal, and penniless, she becomes a prostitute. Still alive, Taylor returns to London, still determined to marry Leigh. She feels too much guilt to marry him without letting him know what she'd done in his absence, and she can't bear to tell him. Robert E. Sherwood's play was sanitized quite a bit, yet it was still daring for the cinema of the day. The film may have been a warning to young women not to wander while their men are away at war; but Leigh and Virginia Field, who is really appealing as her roommate and best friend, play their prostitute roles with great empathy, so that we admire rather than look down on them. More interesting than the undying love between Taylor and Leigh are the supportive relationships among the various women. Field and Leigh's other female friends are happy when she becomes engaged, although that's what they want for themselves; Leigh and Taylor hug numerous times and truly care for one another; even Taylor's rich, socially conscious mother (Lucile Watson) is willing to forgive Leigh for her prostitution. Director Mervyn LeRoy, never known for his handling of women, directs with great sensitivity. But the picture belongs to Leigh, who is absolutely splendid, passionate as well as beautiful. Also with: C. Aubrey Smith, Maria Ouspenskaya (as a coldhearted ballet instructor who is the opposite of her kindly dance teacher in the same year's *Dance, Girl, Dance*).

WAY DOWN EAST (1920) B&W/110m—119m—150m.
Lillian Gish plays Anna Moore in D. W. Griffith's classic silent film, adapted from the popular play by Lottie Blair Parker. She's an innocent New England country girl who goes to visit rich relatives. She is duped into a false marriage by ladies' man Lennox Sanderson (Lowell Sherman). When she becomes pregnant he deserts her. The baby dies in her arms (Anna becomes a Madonna figure). Anna goes to live with a religious farm family. She becomes part of the family and falls for the son, David (Richard Barthelmess). But she worries that her past will be revealed. This is the best of Griffith's pastoral films. What's most surprising is how Griffith, who usually relishes a chance to make a woman suffer, doesn't try to milk the audience's tears. Instead, Anna is resilient in her many hardships—she steels herself while giving her dead baby a home-style baptism. Griffith (or is it Gish?) wants us to admire Anna, not pity her. Finale is which the freezing Gish walks perilously across ice floes during a blizzard is justifiably one of Griffith's most famous sequences. What Gish endured while filming the numerous takes—she was required to repeatedly put her hand into the icy water—is part of her legend. Other than *The Birth of a Nation*, this was Griffith's greatest success. Also with: Burr McIntosh, Kate Bruce, Florence Short.

WAY OUT WEST (1936) B&W/63m.
Consistently funny, well-paced Laurel-and-Hardy film finds Stan and Ollie arriving in Brushwood Gulch to deliver the

deed to a gold mine to the daughter (Rosina Lawrence) of a dead prospector. But they're swindled by a bartender (Jimmy Finlayson) into handing the deed to his wife (Sharon Lynn), who they think is the miner's daughter. Learning the truth, they try to reclaim the deed. One of the duo's best films, it's full of sight gags, slapstick, and witty verbal repartee. You'll see Laurel cry because Hardy's forcing him to eat a hat, but then enjoy its taste immensely; Hardy repeatedly almost drown in a shallow creek; and the boys do a delightful impromptu dance together and sing a couple of amusing songs. My favorite image is Laurel being outwrestled and tickled by Lynn, who wants the deed in his pocket. One of the first films to undergo Colorization. Directed by James W. Horne. Also with: Stanley Fields, Vivien Oakland.

WAY WE WERE, THE (1973) C/118m. Robert Redford and Barbra Streisand have truly amazing chemistry in this irresistible (as far as I'm concerned), deeply moving movie romance. We come to really sympathize with their characters, to understand their need for each other, to realize that the reasons they aren't totally compatible—for once a couple's problems have a political basis—can never be resolved. At college in 1937, Katie Morosky is a campus joke with her frizzy hair, fervent left-wing activism, and bad temper whenever anyone doesn't take politics seriously. She has a crush on handsome Hubbell Gardiner, a popular, apolitical athlete. She also recognizes that he has great writing talent. When she sees him seven years later in New York, a soldier asleep in a bar, she can't believe her eyes. When she later puts him to bed and makes love with him, she needs confirmation she's not dreaming. Katie falls in love with Hubbell, but finds it impossible to tolerate his frivolous friends and his steadfast refusal to get involved politically. He loves her, but finds her seriousness about politics to be overwhelming. They break up, but she is so desperate for him that she promises to cool her politics if she can stay with him. They marry and go to Hollywood, where Hubbell is to write an adaptation of his first novel. Katie finds that he sold out by allowing producer Bradford Dillman to commercialize his novel. When Hubbell sells out his good values (as many Redford characters do), we are disappointed. This attractive all-American WASP, who seemingly has everything going for him, hasn't the courage to stand by what is morally correct, while the gawky, funny-looking Jewish Katie—his accusing conscience—will sacrifice everything, including dream lover Hubbell, to follow her convictions. Characters are believable and their problems are compelling; the two stars have never been better. As in the best romances, there are laughter and tears by the bucketful—when the crying Katie (Streisand at her most lovable and vulnerable) calls Hubbell to ask him to take her back, when they break up in the hospital, when they meet years later in New York. Sydney Pollack directed. Arthur Laurents adapted his excellent novel. Marilyn and Alan Bergman and Marvin Hamlisch wrote the nostalgia-inducing Oscar-winning title song, performed by Streisand. Also with: Patrick O'Neal, Viveca Lindfors, Lois Chiles, Murray Hamilton.

WEAVERS: WASN'T THAT A TIME!, THE (1982) C/78m. Make the kids join you for this uplifting and informative documentary on the Weavers—Pete Seeger, Lee Hays, Ronnie Gilbert, Fred Hellerman—the most famous and influential folk-singing group of all time. It was made at the time they reunited for two appearances at Carnegie Hall, scene of some of their earlier triumphs. Through interviews and vintage film clips, director Jim Brown traces the career of the group, emphasizing their tremendous popularity during the forties and fifties and how their career sputtered to an almost complete halt when they were blacklisted for supporting leftwing and unionist causes. Plus it shows them warily preparing for the reunion concert, gaining confidence when their singing immediately clicks (as if they'd been singing together all those years), and performing for an informal gathering of family and friends (it's great watching the onlookers' faces). A duet between visitor Holly Near and her idol, Ronnie Gilbert, should be placed in a time capsule. The picture concludes with the Weavers' triumphant return to a sold-out Carnegie Hall for what would be the group's, and particularly the late Lee Hays's, last hurrah. As you watch them perform, you truly feel their tremendous spirit. My only objection is that there is not enough footage of the concert—in this case, there could never be too much of a good thing.

WEE WILLIE WINKIE (1937) B&W/74m—99m. While not a pivotal work in John Ford's illustrious career, this enjoyable period piece is one of Shirley Temple's finest films. If you ever wondered what qualified the adult Shirley Temple to be an ambassador, just take a look at her films in which the little girl repeatedly pacified gruff adults. In this film she tames *two* indomitable warriors and brings about peace between their warring nations. Set in the 1840s, Kipling tale has Shirley and her widowed mother (June Lang) coming to stay at a British outpost in Raipore, India, where grandfather C. Aubrey Smith is the colonel. As the isolated fort is situated in what is enemy-Indian territory, what we're seeing is a physical set-up that anticipated Ford's *Fort Apache*, which starred a much older Temple. The sweet little girl melts the cold heart of Smith and forms what is essentially a comedy team with rough but sentimental Sergeant Victor McLaglen. When McLaglen is killed and it appears that others will die in fights between the British and Indians, gutsy Shirley decides to go and see the leader (Cesar Romero) of the rebellious Indians to see if she can convince him that her grandfather will stop fighting if he does. Film has visual beauty, exciting action scenes, humor, strong characterizations. It has warmth rather than the sentimentality one usually associates with both Ford and Temple. But you'll feel choked up during picture's most memorable, beautifully directed scene: Temple unpretentiously sings "Auld Lang Syne" at McLaglen's deathbed. Also with: Michael Whelan, Gavin Muir, Jack Pennick.

WEEKEND (FRENCH-ITALIAN/1967) C/95m—103m. In one of Jean-Luc Godard's most astonishing films, he mixes Buñuel and Mao, slapstick and polemics. Bickering bourgeois couple (Mireille Darc, Jean Yanne), who both have secret lovers and plan to kill their spouses, drive into the country for a weekend visit with Darc's mother. On every road are crashed cars, Godard's symbols for bourgeois materialism (perhaps he is showing us that the capitalists are bringing about their own destruction). In what is meant to represent bourgeois hell, fires devour the wrecked autos, dead bodies line the roads, and irritating leftwingers of all types come up to our insensitive travelers to spout their radical philosophies. Yanne crashes the car (Darc is most upset about the loss of her Hermès bag), so they try to steal a car to continue their journey. When that fails, they attempt to hitch but are repeatedly turned down when they fail to answer "political" questions correctly (i.e., Yanne gets rejected when he says he'd rather sleep with Lyndon Johnson than Mao). To complete their madcap adventure, they are kidnapped by cannibalistic Maoist guerrillas, and Darc, doing an about-face that Patty Hearst would have been proud of, joins the rebels and eventually devours Yanne's corpse ravenously. Godard includes moments of political discourse, as well as references to favorite films (*Johnny Guitar*, *The Searchers*, *Gösta Berling*, etc.) and quips about the relation of art to reality, but I believe that his main goal was to make his arrogant, cruel bourgeois couple literally go through hell. He also wanted to tease his movie audience. That's apparent early on: Darc, wearing just a bra and panties, sits fetchingly on the desk of her lover-analyst and tells him of being seduced by a woman and her husband, but just when the acts she is describing have us at the height of sexual curiosity, she starts talking about the wife sitting in a bowl of the cat's milk and the husband breaking an egg on her buttocks—not the climax we wanted. In the film's most famous scene Raoul Coutard pans his camera left to right for 10 minutes as our couple drives around a traffic jam that's as ridiculous as the ones Laurel and Hardy used to get stuck in, but just when we're most amused we see the horrendous accident and dead bodies (the first we've come across) that caused the jam and are shocked out of our smiles. Film was most impressive when it was released; today the humor still has punch and the visuals are startling, but I find that the picture peters out once the guerrillas turn up—particularly upsetting are the needless shots of a pig and a chicken being slaughtered. It's not for all tastes—when I recently saw it with an audience of people who'd never heard of the New Wave, half of them left early—but it's essential Godard. Also with: Jean-Pierre Kalfon, Valerie Lagrange, Jean-Pierre Léaud.

WEEK'S VACATION, A (FRENCH/1980)
C/102m. Exceptional character piece by Bertrand Tavernier about a Lyons high-school teacher (Nathalie Baye) who suffers burn-out from trying to get through to her seemingly uninterested students. She takes a week's sick leave. Upset by her inadequacies as a teacher and her inability to establish a rapport with her students, she con-

templates giving up her career. Her problems with her students are reflected in her unwillingness to have a child with her boyfriend (Gérard Lanvin). Baye needs to get away from pressure; she visits her parents in the country. Back home, she spends an evening with the father of one of her problem students and his friend (Philippe Noiret), whose son is in prison. Her concern for children returns, as does her hope that she can make a difference. Intimate film is sensitively directed by Tavernier, exquisitely acted by Baye, who creates a real character any person with career and personal problems can relate to. The relationship she has with her boyfriend, which is full of humor, tenderness, and support, is unique and one many viewers will feel jealous toward. But film makes the point that an ideal love life doesn't fully compensate for dissatisfaction with one's productivity outside the home. The scene in which Baye moves restlessly around her apartment without release for her frustration will strike home. One of the most interesting aspects of the film is how Baye is able to study (and think about) people of *all* ages. Also with: Michel Galabru, Flore Fitzgerald, Marie-Louise Ebeli, Jean Dasté, Philippe Delaigue.

WELCOME TO LA (1977) C/106m.
Robert Altman produced Alan Rudolph's directorial debut and his influence is quite evident. The film has interweaving storylines, improvisation, social satirizing, and quick insertions of off-the-wall humor and musical numbers. But this poor man's *Nashville* falls flat on all counts. A sour look at a city, marriage, work, and romance, the film centers on a cynical songwriter (Keith Carradine with an ugly goatee) who comes to LA to work on an album. He squabbles with his millionaire father (Denver Pyle) and sleeps with numerous women. Geraldine Chaplin's unhappily married woman is the most interesting: she's a weird character with a Camille complex who spends her days in taxis and answers phone calls in the hope that they're wrong numbers. We're introduced to several other depressed, frustrated characters. Everybody fools around because of dissatisfaction at home; everybody chases dreams and dream lovers. Nothing works out. Everyone looks to the wrong people for happiness. A major problem is that we never feel we're in LA. Scenes take place in nondescript indoor settings; the unhappy people drink rather than sniff cocaine, today's LA indicator. The performances are okay—Harvey Keitel, looking unusual in a vest, is particularly effective as Chaplin's husband—but the people are dull. Perhaps Rudolph's major accomplishment is to present obnoxious characters and, finally, get us to empathize with them as their lives further deteriorate. Unfortunately, just when we get to like them a bit better, the film ends. Fine cast includes: Sissy Spacek (as a flaky maid), Sally Kellerman, Lauren Hutton, Viveca Lindfors, John Considine, Richard Baskin (who provides the mediocre music).

WEREWOLF OF LONDON, THE (1935) B&W/
75m. In an exciting, atmospheric opening, botanist Henry

464

Hull (in a rare lead) is attacked by a werewolf while in the Himalayas searching for a legendary flower. Back in London, Hull becomes a werewolf when the sun goes down and commits grisly murders. A mysterious Japanese "gentleman" (Warner Oland) pays him a visit. He is the werewolf who bit Hull and now he wants the flower, which when in bloom contains a juice that temporarily will cure a werewolf. The first werewolf movie was seriously, somberly made; it set the rule for future entries to the subgenre by having an unhappy ending. Chestnut is not a bad horror film, although it isn't particularly frightening. The acting is solid. The best scenes are the beginning and when Hull transforms into a werewolf as he walks behind some columns. (Hull's lupine look is more effective than Lon Chaney, Jr.'s, would be.) Also with: Valerie Hobson (as Hull's wife, whom he fears harming), Lester Matthews, Spring Byington, Ethel Griffies.

WEREWOLF OF WASHINGTON, THE (1973)
C/90m. Odd blend of horror and political satire, concocted during Watergate hysteria. Dean Stockwell added another peculiar role to his weird career by playing the title character, who, when he's not terrorizing DC, acts as the President's press secretary. The film is technically erratic, but there are a couple of inspired bits. My favorite scene has the werewolf trapping someone in a fallen telephone booth—the growling werewolf can't get in, the caller (or screamer) can't get out even if he wanted to. This scene is reminiscent of Marilyn Burns sitting inside an immobile locked car while a ghoul tries to shake it open in *Night of the Living Dead* and Tippi Hedren being trapped in a phone booth in *The Birds*. I also like it when Stockwell does his transformation in the President's plane—it's startling to see a U.S. president bitten by a werewolf! Directed and written by Milton Moses Ginsberg. Also with: Biff McGuire, Clifton James, Michael Dunn (as Dr. Kiss).

WESTERNER, THE (1940) B&W/100m.
Agreeable "A"-budget western directed by William Wyler and produced by Samuel Goldwyn. Gary Cooper has remarkable presence as a slow-talking, quick-thinking cowpoke who's passing through Texas on his way to California. Arrested for stealing a horse (which he actually bought from the thief), he's put on trial in the kangaroo court of Judge Roy Bean (Walter Brennan), the legendary self-proclaimed judge (and saloon owner) who was known as "The Law West of the Pecos." Brennan lets Cooper off when he's led to believe that Cooper is friend of British actress Lillie Langtry (Lillian Bond), for whom Brennan's heart is aflutter. The two men become friendly, but Cooper finally stands up to the judge after Bean orders his men to burn out some homesteaders: Brennan believes the range should be open. Film mixes standard western themes and confrontations with light comedy. Cooper's amusing when sweet-talking Doris Davenport (a surprisingly *strong* female lead) into giving him a lock of her hair—which we know he'll tell Brennan belonged to Lillie Langtry; and when he tells Brennan tall tales about Langtry. Brennan, who won a Best Supporting Actor Oscar, steals the film, playing Bean as someone who is part dictator and part spoiled child (much like a 10-year-old king) who doesn't see anything wrong with his murderous forays. For history buffs: unlike in this film, Bean did see Langtry perform, and he died of old age and too much liquor. From a story by Stuart N. Lake. Photography by Gregg Toland has exquisite composition, particularly when the sky is visible. Music by Dimitri Tiomkin. Also with: Fred Stone, Chill Wills, Forrest Tucker, Dana Andrews, Paul Hurst, Tom Tyler.

WESTWORLD (1973) C/88m.
Timid Richard Benjamin and his macho friend James Brolin vacation at a futuristic adult amusement park that is designed like the old West. (Other sections of the park are designed like other historical sites.) Among its robotic occupants, who are programmed to satisfy every whim of the park's guests, are computer-controlled saloon girls to provide sex and dressed-in-black villains to provide excitement. The villain-robots (one played by Yul Brynner) are programmed to be outdrawn by the human guests. But this film was written and directed (his debut) by Michael Crichton, so we expect this foolproof system to go haywire. The robots revolt against the computers and humans who control them. They begin to massacre employees and guests. When Brynner guns down Brolin, Benjamin finds that he must take on the seemingly invincible robot—he's like the scared John Voight character in *Deliverance* once his tough friend Burt Reynolds is incapacitated. In Crichton, man starts out working with machines, is careless, and invariably ends up pitted against them. Final battle between Benjamin and Brynner is a lot of fun, a fitting climax to witty, provocative thriller for the popcorn crowd. A surprise hit. Also with: Norman Bartold, Allan Oppenheimer, Victoria Shaw, Steven Franken.

WHAT EVER HAPPENED TO BABY JANE?
(1962) B&W/132m. A Grand Guignol, this landmark in personality-disorder horror films is often regarded as a camp classic; and it is hard not to smile a bit while Bette Davis is brutally mistreating her off-screen nemesis, Joan Crawford (especially today when we have knowledge that Crawford was a child abuser). But the violence is too ferocious, the direction by Robert Aldrich is too stylish and assured, the script by Lukas Heller (from Henry Farrell's novel) too intelligent, and the acting by Davis, Crawford (at her nicest), and Victor Buono too impressive for this film to be regarded as camp. In fact, it is a direct descendant of *Sunset Boulevard*, Billy Wilder's Hollywood horror show. Jane was a famous child star while sister Blanche (Crawford) was jealous. But in the thirties sister Blanche became a movie star while Jane flopped as an adult actress. A mysterious car accident left Blanche confined to a wheelchair. Everyone assumed Jane had tried to run down her sister—including Jane, who had been drunk that night. For 30 years Blanche kept a terrible secret. Meanwhile the sisters lived together, with Jane both taking care of and dominating her

handicapped sibling. At the point the contemporary part of the story begins, Jane (who reverts to childhood) has gone off her rocker. Realizing Blanche is selling the house, she holds her sister prisoner. Only at the end do we learn who the real villain is—although Aldrich gives us clues all along. A scary, perverse character study that explores extreme rivalry between prideful sisters, film features Davis's most flamboyant performance and one of her best. When she hires a mediocre pianist (Buono) to revive her old vaudeville act for her, we think of former screen queen Gloria Swanson hiring hack scriptwriter William Holden to revive her career in *Sunset Boulevard*. As Holden did to Swanson, Buono (memorable as a schlemiely mama's boy) leads her on for the money, mocking her talents although he has none himself and she once was great. Like Swanson, Davis is a victim of the talking picture who should be helped, not exploited and humiliated. Worst sidelight of picture is that it led to a whole slew of fright films in which humor came from looking at grotesquely made-up faces of old women (played by once beautiful actresses). Those stock characters would hold the fort until the insane Vietnam vet, another stereotype, came along. Also with: Anna Lee, Marjorie Bennett.

WHAT PRICE HOLLYWOOD? (1932) B&W/88m.
In George Cukor's classic, Constance Bennett is extremely appealing as Mary Evans, a spunky Brown Derby waitress who wants to be a Hollywood star. Director Lowell Sherman gives Bennett the break that leads to her becoming a major star, "America's Pal." Forever grateful to her friend, she is the only person who remains loyal once alcoholism ruins his career. She sacrifices much for him: her marriage to rich polo player Neil Hamilton ends because he is angry about the attention she pays to Sherman, and the gossip columnists won't leave her alone. Jane Murfin, Ben Markson, Gene Fowler, and Rowland Brown adapted a story by Adela Rogers St. John. Their sharply written depiction of Hollywood is more cynical than vicious: careers are shown to be fragile and personal lives are easily shattered, but at least the souls of good people are not destroyed. Film wavers between being highly original and very conventional (everything involving Hamilton). It's interesting watching the inner workings of a Hollywood studio, but the best part of the film is the core relationship between Bennett, whose star is on the rise, and Sherman, whose career is in a drunken tailspin—supposedly he patterned his role on brother-in-law John Barrymore—leading to suicide. Film would serve as inspiration for all three versions of *A Star Is Born* (Cukor directed the 1954 film). Slavko Vorkapich created the shocking suicide montage. Also with: Gregory Ratoff, Brooks Benedict, Louise Beavers, Eddie Anderson.

WHAT'S NEW, PUSSYCAT? (1965) C/108m.
Outrageous sex farce was written by Woody Allen. We can be thankful that he changed directions. This is tiresome, sexist, grating fluff—the best thing that can be said about it is that it's a little better than *Kiss Me, Stupid*. Peter O'Toole, who had no comic timing back then, is a Paris fashion magazine editor who finds it impossible keeping beautiful women away because "when the light hits him in a certain way, he's almost handsome." He can't be faithful to Romy Schneider when Capucine, quirky Paula Prentiss, and Ursula Andress are available. He visits long-haired and horny Viennese psychiatrist Peter Sellers ("I like thighs, do you?"), who would like to learn the "knack" of getting women from O'Toole. Wouldn't Freud have been turned on by his sex research? That's the question Allen seems to be asking. Picture becomes increasingly wild as O'Toole (another *Alfie*) dashes from woman to woman, Allen's character (his acting debut) also goes after women, and Sellers reaches hysterical heights. But no one is funny except Prentiss. Directed by Clive Donner.

WHAT'S UP, TIGER LILY? (1966) C/80m.
Woody Allen's first film as writer-director. He also appears at the beginning to explain that he has taken a Japanese spy film, *Kagi no Kag*, and had American actors dub all the dialogue with absurd comedy—he says that the only time this has been done before was with *Gone With the Wind*. Film footage is wild to begin with—it would be interesting to see the original—which is why the ridiculous inserted dialogue works. Allen's film is about several factions who are willing to kill for an egg-salad recipe. Some of Allen's lines come out of left field and are brilliant—a bad guy holds up a small piece of paper and points to a diagram of a house, saying, "He lives *here*"; the guy he's talking to asks if *he* lives on the piece of paper. Most of the film is merely amusing. The novelty wears off long before the end, and you may try substituting your own silly lines to see if they better Allen's. For some reason, the Lovin' Spoonful have a couple of musical interludes. Louise Lasser provides one of the voices.

WHEN FATHER WAS AWAY ON BUSINESS (YUGOSLAVIAN/1985) C/144m.
Disarming seriocomedy—it's full of delights, rather than being *delightful*—begins in Sarajevo in 1950, two years after Tito's break from Stalin, and concludes two years later when there is less political confusion and paranoia. Miki Manojlovic plays a minor Party official who has a pretty, loyal wife (Marijana Karanovic) and two young sons—the younger boy (Moreno D'E Bartolli), a sleepwalking, soccer-loving six-year-old, is the film's smart narrator. The family is happy and full of love (they're always hugging and kissing), yet father is incapable of being faithful. His mistress, fed up with his promises that he'll get a divorce and marry her, breaks off the relationship. Out of spite, she tells his brother-in-law, a powerful Party official, that he made indelicate comments about a political cartoon that ran in the party newspaper. Because the brother-in-law wants to steal the mistress, he has Manojlovic arrested and sent to a work camp. The boys are told that father is away on business. Manojlovic has one reunion with his wife and smallest son while he works at the camp, and months later she and the boys come live with him in a distant town while he under-

goes re-socialization. After this they return to Sarajevo. Director Emir Kusturica and poet Abdulah Sidran, the screenwriter of this memory piece, break many cinematic rules. They intrude upon serious, even tragic moments with comedy (some of it *slapstick*); humor segues into poignant drama; scenes for children become carnal; warm-hearted moments are followed by a scene that is cruel and cold. What's most interesting is how they let the boys' parents disappoint us just as they inadvertently disappoint the boys: we admire how father loves his wife and kids, yet even after he is reunited with them he risks breaking up the family with his habitual philandering; we admire how mother starts a fistfight with the mistress and refuses to forgive her brother for what he did to her husband, yet, despite her anger toward her husband for cheating on her, she too easily forgives him his infidelities, thus allowing him room to wander some more. So at film's end we find our initial feelings reversed: we're angry with the parents because they should know better, and we no longer despise the brother-in-law and mistress because they are in such a pathetic, guilt-ridden state. While the children's adult role models lie and act selfishly and pettily, the children conduct their lives with purity, are loyal to those they love, and aren't selfish when it comes to preserving the family's happiness. Along with the offbeat humor, what one remembers most about this film is the characters' love for one another and the heartbreak of those who are denied love that matches the love they offer.

WHEN WORLDS COLLIDE (1951) C/81m.
Producer George Pal's follow-up to *Desintation Moon* is an adaptation of the Philip Wylie–Edwin Balmer novel that Cecil B. DeMille had wanted to make back in the early thirties. It's a much better film than Pal's pioneer predecessor because its premise is much more exciting, encompassing no less than the destruction of earth. Finding out that two planets are heading directly for us, flyer Richard Derr and astronomer Larry Keating organize the speedy construction of a huge space ark that will take 40 passengers—drawn by lottery from the workers—to an earthlike planet. Tension mounts as the collision day draws near; and, of course, once the ship is completed, in the nick of time, new obstacles occur prior to launch, including a revolt by those workers being left behind. Selfish, evil, wheelchair-bound industrialist John Hoyt, the biggest threat to the launch, anticipated Dr. Strangelove by a decade. The Oscar-winning special effects are particularly impressive during the catastrophe-riddled climax, which, of course, includes New York being struck by a tidal wave. Is this the first picture in which earth is destroyed? Directed by Rudolph Maté. Also with: Barbara Rush (as Derr's love interest), Peter Hanson (as Derr's romantic rival), Judith Ames, Hayden Rorke, Mary Murphy, Laura Elliott.

WHERE THE BOYS ARE (1960) C/99m.
Cult favorite has college girls Dolores Hart, Paula Prentiss (who wants children), Connie Francis (who sings Neil Sedaka's title song), and naive, vulnerable, and very sexy Yvette Mimieux going to Fort Lauderdale during spring break. They have many adventures, find future husbands or heartbreak. Hart gets to see if she really believes in sex before marriage. Film is dated in many ways, but it's surprisingly more advanced than other films of the period in regard to sex. It is about sex, the dialogue about sex is frank, it's clear that our four girls are in search of boys for *sex*. The four leads are very appealing (they all have a sense of humor) and their characters are believable. It's rare to see an early film in which the girls are supportive friends, rather than rivals. Considering that Hart became a nun, it's interesting that her character startles her teacher and dean with admissions of sexual longings. An enjoyable, offbeat, interesting film, with appealing performances by the lead actresses. Remade as *Where the Boys Are '84*. From the novel by Glendon Swarthout. Directed by Henry Levin. Also with: Jim Hutton, George Hamilton (developing his tan), Frank Gorshin, Barbara Nichols, Jack Kruschen, Chill Wills (as the police chief who wages "war against higher education").

WHERE THE SIDEWALK ENDS (1950) B&W/95m.
One of Otto Preminger's best melodramas, reuniting his leads from *Laura*: Dana Andrews and Gene Tierney. Andrews, a brutal cop known for running roughshod over suspects, accidentally kills a suspect (Craig Stevens) in a murder case. Rather than face a departmental investigation, he cleverly covers up his act. But by doing so, he implicates the father of Tierney in whom he has a keen interest. He tries to get him off the hook without implicating himself. Influenced by sweet Tierney, Andrews replaces hostile feelings with a conscience. Stylish, atmospheric film has a solid script by Ben Hecht—it is marred only by a trite, overly simple ending and the fact that cops so easily convince Tierney's father that he'll be judged guilty in court. Exciting scenes have Andrews taking on mobsters Gary Merrill and his tough henchmen, including sadistic Neville Brand. Romance between leads would be more effective if Tierney were as pretty as she'd been in 1944's *Laura*. From a novel by William L. Stuart. Also with: Karl Malden, Tom Tully, Bert Freed, Ruth Donnelly, Harry Von Zell.

WHERE'S POPPA? (1970) C/87m.
A litmus test for viewers that will expose one's taste for comedy and tolerance for tastelessness. It is a successful attempt by director Carl Reiner and screenwriter Robert Klane (working from his own novel) to persuade us that as far as comedy goes, nothing is sacred. George Segal is a New York lawyer who lives with his senile mother, Ruth Gordon. She ruins his life, but he refuses to put her in a home because of a promise he made to his late father. Gordon doesn't realize that Poppa is dead and constantly asks for him; Segal tries to keep her happy by dressing up as a gorilla (she slugs him in the crotch) and feeding her six orange slices and Lucky Charms drowned in Pepsi for breakfast. Because his married brother, Ron Leibman, won't take care of Gordon, Segal hires nurses. Segal often falls for them, but after they spend

time with Gordon they flee. He now hires Trish Van Devere, although most of her patients have died. They fall in love at first sight (in the film's funniest scene) and he invites her for dinner. He warns Gordon: "If you mess this one up, I'll punch your heart out." She does mess it up when she eats off Van Devere's plate, discusses the length of her son's pecker, and yanks down his pants and kisses him on the "tush." Van Devere runs out in disgust, twice. United Artists re-releases this film periodically and I suggest that you see it with an audience rather than alone at home on a cassette. One's laughter is enhanced by the realization that all those around you—including bluenoses—are being subjected to the same embarrassing material (the minute Van Devere meets Segal she reveals that on her wedding night her naïve groom performed a definite booboo). Collective embarrassment can be fun. The haywire world we are presented is unforgettable. Cabbies pick up men in gorilla suits rather than perfectly dressed black ladies. Coaches snatch 10-year-old kids without their parents' permission. In the middle of the city is a veritable jungle (Central Park) ruled by uncivilized "tribes" (black gangs). Female prostitutes turn out to be male cops in drag—the one on whom Leibman is forced by a gang to perform a deviant act gets a crush on him (which is reason enough for viewers to have a negative response). The craziness in the apartment Segal and Gordon share is merely a reflection of the surrounding world. Even those turned off by the humor will enjoy the standout performances. Again Gordon proved that there was no one better at playing irrepressible old ladies. Old ladies in movies are usually treated with respect, but Gordon's Mrs. Hocheiser has no redeeming qualities—you don't even feel sorry for her when Segal abandons her in a home (in the novel he ends up climbing into bed with her). Nor will you pity the son she drives batty with her relentlessly obnoxious behavior. Segal is a jerk who creates his own misery. Giving a whole new meaning to the word *aggravated*, Segal gives a remarkable impression of a man who is on his last legs. Both Gordon and Segal were given much freedom and as a result gave performances that are comedic gems. For them alone, this film is worth seeing. Also with: Barnard Hughes, Vincent Gardenia, Rae Allen, Paul Sorvino, Rob Reiner, Joe Keyes, Jr.

WHILE THE CITY SLEEPS (1956) B&W/
100m. Dana Andrews is a crack reporter with a big-city newspaper that is part of a massive communications network. Helping out his editor, Thomas Mitchell, he follows leads on a case involving a homicidal maniac (John Drew Barrymore), a mama's boy who has been rubbing out young women. The slimy new editor, Vincent Price, offers a promotion to whoever of his top men—Mitchell, George Sanders, or Howard Duff—is responsible for cracking the case; he delights in watching the three opportunists competing with each other to gain his favor. Price doesn't realize that his wife, Rhonda Fleming, is having an affair with Duff. Meanwhile, in this incestuous tale Sanders is involved with ambitious woman's-page editor Ida Lupino, who at his re-

quest makes a play for Andrews—although Andrews is engaged to Sanders's secretary, Sally Forrest. Got it? Silly but diverting soap opera was directed by Fritz Lang, who puts emphasis on sleaziness of rich man Price and the unsavory backbiting of his hirelings. Mystery takes a back seat, which is just as well since the simple case should take about one minute to solve. Film has distinction of having most alcohol consumed by characters since *The Lost Weekend*. One wonders about Andrews playing a never-sober reporter because, as Andrews later disclosed, he really was an alcoholic. Also with: Mae Marsh.

WHITE HEAT (1949) B&W/114m. Director Raoul Walsh and James Cagney, who had starred in his *The Roaring Twenties*, reunited for this superb gangster film. Cody Jarrett resembles Cagney's '30s criminals in that he is more cunning, energetic, humorous, violent, suicidal, more *everything* than any of his gang members; although cynical about the world, he is optimistic about his own future: death doesn't frighten him because he believes in his own immortality. But Cagney's '30s gangsters became tough, bitter killers because of the cruel Depression Era environment in which they existed (where there were no honest jobs available). Cody's problem is that he is insane (this is the '40s, when psychiatry was a hot topic)—his criminal father died in an institution, and his shrewd Ma (who never blinks) would have trouble passing a lunacy test. Brilliantly played by Margaret Wycherley, Ma is nothing like those sweet mothers who used to try to steer Cagney of the '30s in the right direction. Cody trusts no one but Ma, the power behind his throne—not even his wife, Verna (a strong performance by Virginia Mayo), whom he treats like his child. In fact, his mother fixation is so weird—he even sits on her lap— that I'm sure the film would have run into censorship problems if Cody hadn't also had a wife. Cagney's portrayal of Cody is something to behold. He's older and paunchier than we think of Cagney the gangster, but he's still intense, his eyes are fiery, and his energy is ferocious. How terrifying he is when, with wild eyes, he half-strangles Verna for betraying him to gang member Big Ed (Steve Cochran). How pathetic he is during his headache bouts, when he staggers across the floor like a wounded animal, mewing and moaning. How terrifying, pathetic, and sympathetic he is in the classic prison-cafeteria scene when he learns that Ma is dead. It's interesting that Walsh treats the story's potential hero—undercover policeman Hank Fallon (Edmond O'Brien), who infiltrates Cody's gang and gains his trust—as the story's villain, no better than a filthy spy. Walsh obviously felt for Cody, who's at least honest where his friends are concerned. So Walsh gives Cody a "happy" ending: he dies in a refinery explosion and is blown into space, his ashes scattered in the air we breathe. Unlike previous Cagney gangsters, who die unheroically, Cody actually achieves immortality. "Made it, Ma," he smiles. "Top of the world!" Walsh's direction matches Cagney's dynamic performance: film has remarkable pacing; great touches; hard-hitting, brilliantly edited action sequences. Music by

Max Steiner. Also with: John Archer, Fred Clark, Ford Rainey.

WHITE ZOMBIE (1932) B&W/73m.
Impressive early sound shocker was directed by Victor Halperin and starred Bela Lugosi as an evil practitioner of voodoo in Haiti. A plantation owner (Robert Frazer) asks Lugosi to help halt a wedding between our hero, a Haitian banker (John Harron), and our lovely American heroine (Madge Bellamy), whom Frazer wants for himself. The film has many fairytale elements and, just as Snow White tasted the poisoned apple, Bellamy falls victim to a poisoned rose. Harron thinks her dead, but Lugosi has made her one of his zombies who roam his castle. (He has also drugged Frazer.) Just as the prince roused Sleeping Beauty in her castle, it's up to Harron to sneak into Lugosi's castle and rouse this member of the "Walking Dead." Film has marvelous visuals, some that are extremely poetic—and the lengthy non-verbal passages in which the emphasis is on character movement, set design, creating atmosphere through light and shadow, and music (there's a fine, varied score) are like something from a classic silent horror film, perhaps *Vampyr* by Carl Dreyer. The scene in which the zombies work in the sugar mill recalls the workers in *Metropolis*. Some scenes are static, others silly, but this "sleeper" is guaranteed to please the true-blue horror fan. Lugosi gives one of his best performances. An exciting last scene. Also with: Brandon Hurst, Clarence Muse, Joseph Cawthorne.

WHO'LL STOP THE RAIN? (1978) C/126m.
Soldier Nick Nolte returns from Vietnam carrying heroin for his war buddy Michael Moriarty, a onetime idealist who has become cynical due to the lunacy of the war. Nolte tries to make the drop with Moriarty's wife, Tuesday Weld, but she hasn't the money for him. They take flight when two brutal hitmen (Richard Masur, Richard Sharkey) who work for a crooked cop (Anthony Zerbe) come after the heroin. But when Moriarty returns to his Berkeley home, the bad guys grab him and submit him to torture. He helps them track down Nolte and Weld, who have become romantically involved. Zerbe offers to exchange Moriarty for the heroin—but Nolte knows he's not to be trusted. Film is based on Robert Stone's *Dog Soldiers* and, while it's not as *sordid* in its depiction of Vietnam-U.S. drug trafficking, picture still packs a wallop. It is *not* for the squeamish: characters are extremely brutal; action scenes are frightening. Characters are memorable, casting is perfect, dialogue is sharp and imaginative, and direction of actors strong. It's good to see Moriarty in a non-neurotic role; and Nolte, looking fit, is an action hero to rival Rambo. What's most rewarding is that we're made privy to a fascinating true-to-life storyline that other directors wouldn't touch because there is no "hero" fighting for what we'd think is a worthy cause. Picture has excellent, eclectic score, including Creedence Clearwater's classic from which film's title was derived. Hank Snow's "Golden Rocket" is interesting choice of background music

for big shootout. Also with: Gail Strickland, David Opatoshu, Charles Haid.

WHO'S MINDING THE MINT? (1967) C/97m.
From the *It's a Mad Mad Mad Mad World* school, only on a smaller scale. U.S. mint worker Jim Hutton accidentally destroys a lot of money. He calls on some friendly thieves to help replace the money before the loss is discovered. But the date of the mission is moved up one night so that all these men and women must "come as they are," which means they wear the most outrageous outfits imaginable. Hilarious comedy is deservedly a cult hit. Wild direction by Howard Morris. Standout cast with: Dorothy Provine, Milton Berle, Joey Bishop, Victor Buono, Jack Gilford, Walter Brennan, Jamie Farr, Jackie Joseph.

WHY SHOOT THE TEACHER (CANADIAN/1977) C/101m.
Released in the U.S. in 1982. Agreeable, unpretentious little sleeper is set in Canada in 1935. Bud Cort is a young teacher whose first assignment is a one-room school in a small family community that is feeling the effects of the Depression. Discovering that his salary is both meager and uncollectable, and that his living quarters are beneath the school, he is terribly upset. Moreover, he doesn't get much satisfaction teaching his class because of the unruly older boys and the general chaos. He can't wait till the season's conclusion and when it comes he leaves with no intention of returning—when he tells us, in his narration, that he returned the next year, we realize we were correct in assuming that he was adapting to his impoverished environment and his unusual farmers' children, for whom book learning wasn't necessarily the most important form of education. Picture achieves realism by not allowing there to be a solution to any of the problems Cort encounters—having no climaxes in the story line and no personal triumph for anyone can be disconcerting and a bit frustrating. But the point made is that it's the teacher's education that is incomplete—he's returning next season to rectify this. Episodic film contains several memorable scenes; some are amusing, others sad. Directed by Silvio Narizzano. Jim Defilice adapted Max Braithwaite's book (which I presume is a memoir). Also with: Samantha Eggar (deglamorized as a neglected farmer's wife to whom Cort is attracted), Kenneth Griffith, Chris Wiggins.

WICKER MAN, THE (BRITISH/1973) C/87m–102m.
Written for the screen by Anthony Shaffer. Now that the long-suppressed 102-minute print of this one-of-a-kind occult film is in circulation, don't bother seeing the abbreviated television version. I find this cult film to be overrated and much less profound than the few critics who saw it in 1973 contended, but it's beautifully photographed by Harry Waxman, witty, erotic, and such an unusual entry in the horror genre—particularly because of Paul Giovanni's extensive and clever use of music (bawdy ballads are sung, acoustic instruments are played throughout)—that one can understand why it would impress many viewers.

Edward Woodward, a devoutly religious, middle-aged policeman on the Scottish mainland, goes alone to Summerisle to investigate the disappearance of a teenage girl. The people are friendly, but claim the girl never existed. His investigation tells him differently. During his stay he becomes aware of preverse sexual activity all around him. A lay preacher, he has to fight being intoxicated by the aura of sexuality; he fights his attraction to the innkeeper's sexy daughter, Britt Ekland (who seduces a young boy and does an erotic nude dance—both scenes are cut from shorter prints). He discovers that everyone on the island follows the pagan teachings of their leader, Christoper Lee (as Lord Summerisle). He thinks the missing teenager is to be sacrificed at the May Day ceremony so that there won't be another crop failure on the island. He doesn't realize that she is merely the bait to lure him, a good Christian, for sacrifice in the giant Wicker Man. Film is a combination of British TV's *The Avengers* and British horror films *Doomwatch* and *Horror Hotel*, in which Lee lures victims to Salem for sacrifice in a satanic rite. This is the only Christianity (good) vs. paganism (evil) film in which both are shown to be impotent. We believe neither Woodward's contention that he'll be resurrected nor Lee's that Woodward will be reincarnated. We don't believe Lee's contention that a blood sacrifice will bring about a successful crop or Woodward's that Lee will be punished for his sin (murder). Woodward is presented as a Christ figure, a stranger in a strange land run by a fake lord. What I find fault with is not that he is killed in the shocking finale, but that the villagers' and Lee's constant mockery of him (he ends up dressed as a fool) gives the impression that Shaffer is the one mocking him, not just questioning his beliefs. The film has a cheery feel (singing, dancing, happy people, comic touches, flowers, and sunshine): only when it's too late do we and Woodward realize that paganism's cruel aspects are hidden under a shroud of joviality. With hindsight, nothing seems amusing. We realize that, as weird as these people on Summerisle are, their real-life counterparts indeed exist. Also with: Diane Cilento, Ingrid Pitt, Lindsay Kemp.

WILD ANGELS, THE (1966) C/83m—90m—93m. The first of the motorcycle-gang cycle of the sixties and early seventies was directed by Roger Corman and scripted by Charles B. Griffith. Unworthy of either man's talents, it's a despicable film that thrives on brutality, vulgarity, cheap thrills. Peter Fonda's the leader of a band of California Hell's Angels. They want freedom and to have a good time. So they spend their time riding their motorcycles, beating up people (including a priest), having orgies, gang-raping women, drinking beer, taking drugs. Bruce Dern is killed by a cop ("The Man"), so the Angels have a funeral for him, draping his coffin with a swastika. After Fonda expresses the Angels' need for freedom, the service deteriorates into a wild orgy, with rapes and beatings included. Rather than showing concern about the Hell's Angels developing into a national social problem, Corman took advantage of their existence: he was on the lookout for a surefire exploitation subject. The characters he presents are intolerable and what they do is offensive. The acting is bad, Fonda's "freedom" speech is drivel, the wild camera work only calls attention to plot deficiencies. Only good visual is of the Fonda-led funeral procession from the church to the grave. This film made a lot of money—otherwise we might have been spared the development of the motorcycle-gang genre. Peter Bogdanovich and Monte Hellman were part of the crew. Also with: Nancy Sinatra (who has very little to say in a role meant to capitalize on her then-hot recording career), Michael J. Pollard, Lou Procopio, Coby Denton, Buck Taylor, Diane Ladd, Gayle Hunnicutt, members of the Hell's Angels of Venice, California.

WILD BUNCH, THE (1969) C/127m—143m. Sam Peckinpah's violent, controversial western begins in Texas in 1913. Following a foiled bank robbery, six outlaws cross into Mexico: William Holden, the leader; loyal Ernest Borgnine; mean, always complaining brothers Ben Johnson and Warren Oates; Jaime Sanchez, an independent young Mexican; and old ex-gunslinger Edmond O'Brien. Former Wild Bunch member Robert Ryan is now leader of the murderous bounty hunters on their trail. Needing to pull off one more job before they can retire (Peckinpah and co-writer Walon Green borrow from the "caper" movie), the outlaws agree to rob an American train carrying rifles and ammunition and sell the cargo to a ruthless bandit leader (Emilio Fernandez as Mapache) who has been terrorizing Sanchez's mountain people. In Peckinpah westerns, over-the-hill losers, whom time and glory have passed by, are given a chance for redemption. What distinguishes the Wild Bunch is that they die nobly, sacrificing themselves in a battle against Fernandez's mighty forces. The way they die makes them *heroic* in our eyes, and no longer the bastards we saw in the beginning who were willing to gun down innocent people. Visually, the picture contains much that is stunning, even mesmerizing; however, the battle scenes, containing great slaughter, are what gives the film its rhythm, power, spectacle, and excitement. It is known for its bloody, slow-motion death scenes, but I find them self-consciously presented—not "realistic," as Peckinpah intended. Much more impressive are the quieter scenes: when the Wild Bunch rides majestically through Sanchez's village, proud that the people look on with respect, and that wonderful moment before the suicidal battle with Fernandez when Holden looks back and forth between his last bottle of whiskey and his last woman. Peckinpah was a tough guy, but his best screen moments were those when he allowed his romantic tendencies to slip through, when he gave his characters the dignity that means so much to them. The worst aspect of this film is that Peckinpah never establishes any camaraderie among members of the gang. He went through so much trouble creating an authentic western milieu, only to fill it with stereotypes speaking in clichés. Picture is a semi-remake of Peckinpah's *Major Dundee*; he also borrows freely from John Huston's *The Treasure of the Sierra Madre*, Buñuel, Kurosawa, and Aldrich's *The Dirty Dozen*. Peckinpah's film managed to sneak by anti-war protesters under the guise of being a western—actually, it's a war film (check out the weapons used). The controversy surrounding the film was centered on its violence; few at the time noticed the strong parallels between Peckinpah's Mexico and North Vietnam. Photographed by Lucien Ballard. Edited by Louis Lombardo. Also with: Albert Dekker, Strother Martin, L. Q. Jones, Bo Hopkins.

WILD CHILD, THE (FRENCH/1969) B&W/85m.

In 1798 a wild boy (Jean-Pierre Cargol) is discovered in a French forest. No one knows who he is, and he can't speak or hear. Director François Truffaut plays the doctor who takes him into his own house, educates him, teaches him to be a moral being (who knows the difference between right and wrong), and gives him love—which is reciprocated. True story makes for a fascinating movie premise, and the portrayals by both Cargol and Truffaut are believable. But it's not as enjoyable as one would hope—perhaps because of the absence of humor; perhaps because there are few surprises, since fictional works have covered the same subject; perhaps because we resent what the doctor is doing (even though he has good intentions); perhaps because the mystery of the boy's origins was never solved. The most interesting scenes are those in which the boy temporarily tires of civilization's restraints/rules and, like Tarzan, returns to the wilderness and his brutish state. The ending is too abrupt. Also with: Jean Dasté, Paul Ville.

WILD IN THE STREETS (1968) C/97m.

Ambitious politician Hal Holbrook sees that the only way he can win the Presidential election is to lower the voting age to 18 and get the youth vote. He enlists the help of rock singer Christopher Jones and begrudgingly endorses Jones's proposition that the voting age drop to 14. Eventually the youth of America takes over the government; old people are ousted and put in concentration camps. Film was written by Robert Thom, from his story "The Day It All Happened." Obviously, the premise seems ideal for some sharp satire, but after a promising beginning the picture goes out of control, becomes cruel, becomes repulsive. This is a vile movie, a fascist fantasy, an insult to America's politically conscious youth of 1968. What awful characters. AIP geared it for the youth market it exploited, and somehow it developed a cult. Bad, self-conscious, self-pleased direction by Barry Shear. Also with: Shelley Winters, Diane Varsi, Bert Freed, Ed Begley, Richard Pryor.

WILD ONE, THE (1954) B&W/79m.

The first and best of a terrible genre: the motorcycle film. It is the film that firmly established Marlon Brando's alienated antihero/rebel screen image, although he was to play such characters only a few times in his career. Stanley Kramer's production is based on true events: in 1947, 4,000 members of a motorcycle club gathered for a three-day convention in Hollister, California, and terrorized the town. The well-publicized incident inspired Frank Rooney's short story "The Cyclists' Raid," the source for the film. Brando plays the moody, mumbling, leather-jacketed leader of the "Black Rebels." He is a tough guy, but it's obvious he is smarter and, beneath his detached attitude, more decent than the other punks. Cyclists like Lee Marvin are just plain mean; Brando has only turned his back on society and tried to anesthetize his emotions. But when he meets sheriff's daughter Mary Murphy (star of one of my favorite bad war movies, *Beachhead*), a nerve is touched, and traces of humanity emerge. Always thinking and groping for words, he realizes that one can't be a rebel against society but *conform* to what cyclists are supposed to be like. Picture has a few exciting scenes—Brando's out-of-control riderless motorcycle, Murphy being surrounded by cyclists—and Brando is fun to watch, but film isn't particularly impressive. Probably young people respond to it because of poor judgment on the filmmakers' part—the townspeople who try to drive away the cyclists come across as being just as bad as the cyclists. Directed by Laslo Benedek. Also with: Robert Keith, Jay C. Flippen, Ray Teal, Jerry Paris, Alvy Moore.

WILD STRAWBERRIES (SWEDISH/1957) B&W/90m.

Ingmar Bergman's protagonist is Isak Borg (a captivating performance by Victor Sjöström, the legendary Swedish director from the silent era), an elderly professor-doctor who lives in Stockholm. On the night before he is about to return home to Lund to receive an honorary doctorate, he has a nightmare (filmed in a manner to recall Sjöström's spooky *The Phantom Carriage*) in which he discovers his own corpse. His drive to Lund becomes one of Bergman's "journeys of self-knowledge," in which this man who fears that death is approaching realizes that he has never *lived*. Like his mother (Naima Wifstrand) and his son (Gunnar Björnstrand), he has been one of the walking dead, completely devoid of feelings that emanate from the heart. Outsiders—the three young hitchhikers to whom he offers a ride, the gas-station owner (Max von Sydow) and his wife—consider Isak generous to a fault, but those who have known him best—his daughter-in-law, Marianne (Ingrid Thulin), his long-ago fiancée, Sara (Bibi Andersson, who also plays the teenage hitchiker), his long-dead wife (Gertrud Frud)—realized he was *cold* through and through. He stops by the lake house where he spent many years and flashbacks on his past, to when Sara betrayed him in the strawberry patch (she would marry his hot-blooded brother) and to when his wife betrayed him with another man in the woods, knowing Isak would accept the blame for her being unfaithful. It's almost as if we're with Scrooge on a look at Christmas Past. As expected, this cold man begins to thaw out. He doesn't do a complete reversal to saint as Scrooge did, but he begins to display traces of humanity and compassion—so much so that pregnant Marianne, a life force, comes to like him. He is one of Bergman's few tormented men who find peace. Bergman's classic has withstood the test of time. It is still cinematic storytelling at its best. Rather than being as intimidating as later Bergman films, it is simple enough on the surface for viewers to have the energy to dig for the inner meanings and complexities. This is one of those films that defy criticism, so great has its impact been on "art"-film lovers, film students, and filmmakers. (Still I wish I understood the last minute of the movie.) Also with: Jullan Kindahl, Folke Sundquist.

WILLY WONKA AND THE CHOCOLATE FAC-TORY (1971) C/98m.
Roald Dahl adapted his own novel *Charlie and the Chocolate Factory* and the result is one of the most bizarre children's films ever made. Charlie Bucket (Peter Ostrum) lives with his impoverished mother and four grandparents. His sad life is enlivened when he becomes one of the five lucky kids who win a tour of the dazzling factory owned by Willy Wonka (one of Gene Wilder's classic roles), the most famous confectioner in the world. He takes along Grandpa Jo (Jack Albertson). Willy Wonka turns out to be a weird, unfriendly fellow who severely punishes all the kids when they disobey his rules. He is so mean that Charlie considers selling a Gobstopper (a new, secret candy) to Wonka's chief rival so he can steal the formula. But Charlie turns out to be honest: he is the good child Willy has been looking for. As *Wonka* expert Henry Blinder astutely points out, this film improves on the novel because it has to do with more than a boy proving himself honest. It is also about a man searching for a son to whom he can leave his business and a boy looking for a surrogate father—significantly, in the book Charlie has a father. First-time viewers, especially children, have much difficulty warming to this film: the tone is dreary, Wonka is scary, the music is forgettable, the Oompa-Loompas (Wonka's helpers) are dreadful concoctions, and the kids are shown to be bratty and are treated viciously. But the picture improves with subsequent viewings (see it on TV so you can plan snack breaks): the kids, their parents, and the unpredictable Wonka suddenly seem cleverly conceived. Songs are by Leslie Bricusse and Anthony Newley. Quaker Oats helped finance this David L. Wolper production. Mel Stuart directed. Also with: Michael Bollner, Ursula Reit, Denise Nickerson, Leonard Stone, Julie Dawn Cole, Roy Kinnear.

WINCHESTER '73 (1950) B&W/92m.
Classic adult western by Anthony Mann, the first of five he directed with James Stewart. Borden Chase and Robert L. Richards's strong, adult script has Stewart riding into Dodge City with his friend Millard Mitchell. Stewart, who often plays a revenge-obsessed hero for Mann, has spent a long time tracking down his criminal brother, Stephen McNally, who killed their father. He finds McNally in Dodge, but since neither is wearing guns, their competition is limited to a shooting contest. Stewart wins, but McNally makes off with the prize, a rare Winchester '73. During the film the rifle will change owners several times, falling into the hands of a gambler and Indian trader (John McIntire), the Indian chief who kills him (Rock Hudson), the cowardly lover (Charles Drake) of dance-hall girl Shelley Winters (to whom Stewart feels a slight attraction), a crazy bad guy (Dan Duryea),

McNally again, and finally Stewart again. Film has excellent action sequences: an Indian attack, Stewart and Duryea shooting it out, the brothers fighting it out in the mountains (the preferred location for Mann's final gun battles). What makes it special are the unusual characterizations and interesting relationships. The characters have all made choices about how they want to spend their lives. There's fine, unpretentious dialogue. Photographed by William Daniels.

WINGS (1927) B&W/139m.
Grand-scale silent classic about two young men (Charles "Buddy" Rogers, Richard Arlen) from the same hometown who fulfill their lifelong passion for flying by joining American Expeditionary Forces in Europe. Although from different social brackets and in love with the same girl (Jobyna Ralston), they become great pals as well as flying aces. Only prior to the last air battle does their rivalry over Ralston surface, which is foolish because Rogers, without realizing it, actually loves the girl next door (Clara Bow). Former pilot William A. Wellman directed this epic. It is known for some truly spectacular dogfight sequences, which feature some amazing stunt work and aerial photography. I still don't know how they got some of the shots of burning planes plummeting through the clouds. (Of course, the one problem with air battle scenes is that you can't tell who's who.) Picture is beautifully filmed throughout—watch for Wellman's revolutionary boom shot at the Paris café in which his camera zooms over several tables into a close shot of the drunk Rogers and Arlen with some French trollops. Story has greatly improved by the time of the Paris sequence, because by then the boys have lost their innocence—they have learned that the war, with blood and death, is no fun after all. The sweeping final battle—on land and in air— is remarkable! Film's major problem is that, except for the vivacious and peppy Bow (whom we first see climbing over a fence), the leads have little screen presence. In fact, when Gary Cooper makes a quick appearance, the unknown actor immediately displays the magnetism that both Rogers and Arlen lack. Today the film seems a little slow—but the brutality seen in the impressive war sequences keeps it timely. Also with: Arlette Marchal, El Brendel, Henry B. Walthall, Richard Tucker.

WINTER KILLS (1979) C/97m.
Comic fantasist William Richert wrote and directed this cult film adapted from a novel by Richard Condon. Richert had worked for Ivan Passer, who would later direct *Cutter and Bone*, also starring Jeff Bridges. Here Bridges is the half-brother of President Keegan, who was assassinated in 1960. Discovering that there was a conspiracy, Bridges attempts to track down the man who ordered the murder. The circuitous trail leads him to several suspects, including his own father, John Huston (as a ruthless, rakish Joseph P. Kennedy figure). Picture has off-the-wall humor, bizarre characters, innumerable plot twists, strange moments: girlfriend Belinda Bauer talking to Bridges while sitting on the toilet; Huston

walking around in red bikini shorts; Bridges riding out of Dad's earshot to yell back, "You stink!"; loco spy-network wizard Anthony Perkins carrying on a calm conversation with Bridges although Bridges has just broken his arms; a doorman in a temper tantrum; Huston, about to die, telling Bridges to invest in South America. But there are too many loose ends and overly eccentric characters (we could do without Sterling Hayden's war-games fanatic); it seems as if none of the star actors read the whole script; scenes have little connection to one another. The tongue-in-cheek approach makes what could have been a provocative vision of the corrupt American power elite into something quite trivial. Picture was shut down before completion, and in an effort to raise additional money, Richert made *The American Success Company* with Bridges and Bauer. Revised for a 1982 re-release. Cinematography by Vilmos Zsigmond. Robert Boyle designed the weird sets. Also with: Richard Boone, Elizabeth Taylor (unbilled), Eli Wallach, Ralph Meeker, Dorothy Malone, Toshiro Mifune, Tomas Milian, Erin Gray, Candice Rialson.

WINTER SOLDIER (1971) B&W/94m. Gut-wrenching, myth-shattering documentary made by the Winterfilm collective in conjunction with Veterans Against the Vietnam War. See *Rambo*, *Missing in Action*, and all those other wrongly revisionist Vietnam War history films, but you *must* see this film to understand why so many people (including vets) protested the Vietnam War and demanded that our troops come home. Filming took place in Detroit from Jan. 31 to Feb. 2, 1971, when veterans gathered to give testimony about heinous atrocities being perpetrated by U.S. soldiers in Vietnam against South and North Vietnamese civilians as well as enemy soldiers. These men, who speak with shaky voices, cry, and express embarrassment and guilt, not only bear witness against other soldiers but willingly admit that they, too, were guilty of war crimes, so strong is their determination to end the war. Vets speak of torturing POWs, machine-gunning innocent villagers so they could brag about a high enemy body count, using poisonous gas, participating in gang rapes, stoning a 10-year-old boy who threw a rock at an army truck; and watching officers and other soldiers gun down young boys who gave them the finger, kick bound prisoners out of their helicopters (a common practice), stab and insert objects into an injured woman's vagina, cut open a dead woman from vagina to neck and pull our her entrails, cut off ears, and on and on. Crimes were committed to scare the enemy, to relieve boredom, to show off, to make a play for medals! We see photographs of smiling soldiers posing with the dead Vietnamese as their trophies and footage of villages being burned and crying, terrified villagers being herded away; we see petrified Vietnamese hiding in the rice fields from U.S. helicopters, knowing that it made little difference if they were civilians—as one vet says, when they killed a Vietnamese they automatically classified him/her as the enemy. (They literally got away with murder.) Long-haired vets who were once crew-cut young kids tell how they were brainwashed so they thought that anything they did to the "gooks" (*all* Vietnamese) was justified. They learned that our government didn't care about the South Vietnamese people, just the strategic territory; that the American policy was racist and the Vietnamese were fair *game*. (And it was a game, based on enemy body count, often inflated so our government would happily add more funds to the war effort.) One vet sums up why he is giving testimony and attempting to bring the other soldiers home: "I didn't like being an animal and seeing everyone else turn into animals." Shocking film shows how our native sons were turned into cold-blooded, racist murderers—who, as the Nazis used to say, were just doing what was expected of them. (Vietnam War protesters weren't against the U.S. soldiers who served in Southeast Asia; they just despised what these soldiers were doing in the name of freedom.) Horrifying, unforgettable, essential viewing, especially with the recent wave of every -U.S.-soldier-was-a-hero-and-the-Vietnam-War-was-moral films. That it never got its message across to Middle America or Hollywood is clear: when director Michael Winner complained that *Death Wish III* was given an X rating because it had 63 killings while the R-rated *Rambo* had 80 killings, the woman at the Ratings Board explained that most of those killed in *Rambo* are Vietnamese.

WITNESS (1985) C/114m. Traveling with his recently widowed mother, Rachel (Kelly McGillis), a young Amish boy (Lukas Haas) witnesses a brutal murder in the men's room of the Philadelphia train station. Tough but legit homicide detective John Book (Harrison Ford) gets testimony from the boy and discovers that two crooked cops were the killers. He tells his findings to his superior, who it turns out was the one who gave the orders. Book is shot and badly wounded and flees with the woman and her son, who is in great danger. She takes Book into her home and nurses him back to health. As in all Australian director Peter Weir's movies, two cultures collide: Here, Book, who lives by the gun and has survived because he has the capacity for violence and the skills to match the criminals, finds himself a resented alien in a world of pacifists. And Rachel finds herself challenging the Amish code because of her attraction to this outsider. Peter Weir's fascinating meditation on violence/peace is extremely well made. It is gorgeous to look at, very suspenseful, and contains the most delicately sensual sexual content within memory: a scene of the beautiful, radiant McGillis standing bare-breasted and unembarrassed as she exchanges stares with Book in the next room and another scene in which the two dance in the barn (while Book sings along to the radio, "Wonderful World") are as exciting as anything in *Body Heat*. However, the Amish people's protest that this film didn't present them properly seems to have foundation: we learn little about them except for their abhorrence of violence (which at times seems like a convenient plot device) and their sense of community (the film has the best communal building scene since the one in *Seven Brides for Seven Brothers*). After a while, McGillis's father-in-law (Jan Rubes) comes across like a Hollywood stereotype, rather than someone who lives according to a deeply meaningful philosophy. In fact, the major problem with the film is that it has trouble mixing commercial Hollywood elements with the mysterious elements that usually dominate Weir's films. For instance, there's something amiss when the highlights (according to audience cheers) are when Book, who finally realizes the power of nonviolence, acts violently. Weir seemed to enjoy filming the violent action sequences, and the promos for the picture emphasized the violence. With truly memorable performances by the two leads; too bad the screenwriters Earl W. Wallace and Bill Kelley didn't allow them a scene near the end where their characters actually discuss whether they should stay together—after all, if a guy could swim off with a mermaid in *Splash*, an affair with an Amish woman is at least a possibility. John Seale did the excellent cinematography. Also with: Alexander Godunov, Josef Sommer, Patti LuPone.

WITNESS FOR THE PROSECUTION (1958) C/114m.
There is no courtroom drama more enjoyable than this adaptation of Agatha Christie's play. High comedy was directed by Billy Wilder, who wrote the script with Harry Kurnitz. Charles Laughton is an aged London barrister with a heart condition who takes on a strenuous murder case, defending foppish Tyrone Power. Laughton's task is made more difficult when Power's cold German wife, Marlene Dietrich, testifies that her husband really did kill a rich lady for her money. Laughton must convince the jury that Dietrich is committing perjury, but he can't figure out her motive for turning on Power. Like all Christie stories, this has innumerable twists and a surprise ending. The most fun comes from trying to figure out if the obvious overacting by the defendant and witnesses is being done by the actors or by the characters they're portraying. The picture is well cast. Dietrich, in her last strong movie role, seems comfortable working again with Wilder. And Laughton is just marvelous, making a difficult role—one which most actors (and, you'd expect, Laughton) would have hammed up—seem easy. His comical scenes with wife Elsa Lanchester, who plays his doting nurse, are gems. Also with: John Williams, Henry Daniell, Una O'Connor, Ian Wolfe, Torin Thatcher.

WIZARD OF OZ, THE (1939) C/100m.
The effect this Hollywood classic has had on Americans cannot be overestimated. Its influence on filmmakers alone is profound: it's often joked that every film since 1939 includes some reference to it, and I'm not so sure this isn't true. We know every scene by heart, but still its annual television shows are as vital/comforting to us as birthdays and the opening day of the baseball season. This is the ultimate *family* picture. Adults can be assured that their rebellious children, like Judy Garland's Dorothy, will discover their need for home and family. Young children will be excited by its fairytale elements: a journey into a strange land, scary moments (how wonderfully frightening Margaret Hamil-

ton's Wicked Witch is!), and a dazzling assortment of characters: a wizard (Frank Morgan), a good witch (Billie Burke), Munchkins, winged monkeys, a scarecrow without a brain (Ray Bolger), a tin man without a heart (Jack Haley), and a lion without courage (Bert Lahr). In addition, there are horses of different color, catchy songs, a castle, talking apple trees with arms and lousy dispositions, and many spectacular occurrences provided by M-G-M's special-effects department. But the film has greatest meaning to teenage girls who live dull lives in drab environments and dream of escaping over a rainbow and finding a glamorous life. Kansas represents their dreary existence. Oz represents Hollywood, to which teenage girls dream of running in hopes of breaking into movies. Our travelers get a beauty treatment; later they win awards. The Emerald City is M-G-M; the Wizard is Louis B. Mayer. That teenagers subconsciously equate Oz with Hollywood isn't ridiculous when one considers that the picture was meant to showcase the best Hollywood could muster in the way of production values. Dorothy's journey can be interpreted as a young girl's last childhood experience. When she chooses to return home to Kansas at the end, she has matured into a young woman—I'm surprised that M-G-M didn't have Garland burst out of the straps that held her well-developed breasts in place (so that she'd look 11 and not 16). Of course, the film's "There's no place like home" theme is nonsense. Unlike in L. Frank Baum's book, Oz—without the Wicked Witch—is a wonderful place for Dorothy to stay. It's much preferable to sepia-colored Kansas, where she was lonely except for having Toto (who was going to be taken away) and lived with an unsupportive and elderly uncle and aunt on a very barren, gray farm. She should stay in brightly colored Oz with all her new friends! Despite the adult propaganda and a few flaws along the way, this is a wonderful film, with considerable humor and imagination, great songs and dances, characters, and, of course, the peerless Garland. We are delighted by her dynamic yet touching performance, yet grieve because we know this is the role that launched her into the world of superstardom she was never able to handle. When she so beautifully sings "Over the Rainbow," we sense that it is Garland as much as Dorothy who is seeking peace and happiness. We want to warn her to be careful once she makes it over the rainbow. Victor Fleming directed, Mervyn LeRoy produced, Harold Rosson did the cinematography, Arnold Gillespie handled the special effects, Harold Arlen contributed the music and E. Y. Harburg the lyrics. Also with: Charley Grapewin, Clara Blandick, Pat Walshe, the Singer Midgets.

WOLF MAN, THE (1941) B&W/70m.
Ranks behind only *Bride of Frankenstein* on Universal's horror parade. Intelligent, literate, fatalistic chiller is set in England. Lawrence Talbot (Lon Chaney, Jr.) returns home to his father's (Claude Rains) estate after being away for 18 years. Things look up when he meets a pretty shopgirl (Evelyn Ankers). But the old gypsy fortune teller Mariva (the definitive Maria Ouspenskaya role) spots the pentagram, the

sign of the werewolf, on his hand and warns him he's in danger. He is attacked by her werewolf son (Bela Lugosi) and, though he kills the beast with his recently purchased cane with a silver wolf's head, he is bitten. When the autumn moon is full, it doesn't matter that he's "pure in heart and says his prayers by night," because he turns into a werewolf and stalks victims. (I have never been able to figure out why he retains his human form and walks on two furry feet, while Lugosi was a full-fledged wolf.) Although tortured by what is happening, he can do nothing to prevent it. In the exciting climax, set in the misty woods, the werewolf chases Ankers while Rains, carrying the cane, tries to prevent her murder. Exciting, bloodless horror classic has an excellent cast (who play their roles seriously); fine direction by George Waggner (who knows how to use a fog machine); an atmospheric score by Frank Skinner and Hans J. Salter; and convincing werewolf makeup created by Jack Pierce. The transformation scenes are particularly effective. What made this film so popular is not only its within-every-man-there-is-a-beast theme but that Chaney's sympathetic performance is a variation on the familiar forties doomed hero—an innocent man who suddenly finds himself trapped and tortured by Fate, which causes him to commit crimes that will eventually lead to his destruction. The fine supporting cast includes: Ralph Bellamy, Warren William, Patric Knowles, Fay Helm.

WOMAN IN THE WINDOW, THE (1944) B&W/99m.
Middle-aged psychologist (Edward G. Robinson), whose wife and kids are out of town, accepts an invitation from a beautiful model (Joan Bennett, who is more fetching and sympathetic than usual), whose portrait he'd been admiring in a window, to visit her apartment. And so director Fritz Lang opens up his trap for another innocent man to fall into. A man charges into the apartment and tries to strangle Robinson in a jealous rage. Robinson kills him in self-defense. Realizing their lives will be ruined by scandal if they're linked to the death, Robinson and Bennett decide to dispose of the body. Bennett was the dead man's mistress, but didn't know his true identity. He turns out to be a millionaire whose death causes a full-scale investigation. A snappily dressed blackmailer (Dan Duryea) demands money from Bennett to keep quiet—now the two contemplate premeditated murder. Superlative melodrama, smoothly written by Nunnally Johnson. What's fascinating is how Lang masterfully builds tension. For instance: Robinson cuts his finger, he later cuts his hand on barbed wire, a poison-ivy rash develops on his hand; he is stopped by cops for not having his car lights on, the garage attendant tells him his brakes are loose, his dime for the toll falls into the street, etc. (Some tricks are Hitchcockian.) And Lang's forte: he builds on Robinson's guilt so he's almost giving himself away, and on his paranoia so he can feel the web of the law closing in on him. In Lang, it doesn't matter whether or not you're guilty of a crime—you still have to pay for it. Twist ending is hokey and familiar, but in this case it is crowd-pleasing. A fine companion piece to Lang's *Scarlet Street*, also with

terrific performances by Robinson, Bennett, and Duryea. Also with: Raymond Massey, Edmund Breon, Thomas E. Jackson, Bobby Blake, Dorothy Peterson.

WOMAN OF PARIS, A (1923) B&W/83m.
Charlie Chaplin made only a brief cameo appearance in his first feature film (he's unrecognizable as a porter). He sensed that his appearance in any major role would keep audiences from realizing that his picture was intended to be serious (with comic moments) rather than comic (with serious moments). Nevertheless, viewers were bewildered—perhaps because it was not only a serious Chaplin film, but one that was cynical as well—and it failed at the box office, influencing Chaplin to keep it out of circulation for more than 50 years. Fortunately, prints (greatly shortened from the near-two-hour original length, and with a lovely Chaplin score) are now in wide distribution. In a role that was inspired in part by Peggy Hopkins Joyce, Edna Purviance plays a young woman who lives in the country with her strict stepfather. She and her boyfriend, Carl Miller, plan to run away to Paris, but she goes alone when she thinks he's abandoned her—actually, he didn't meet her at the station because his father suffered a fatal heart attack. They meet by accident a year later in Paris. She is mistress of fabulously wealthy and carefree Adolphe Menjou, who treats her well but doesn't take her seriously and won't give her what she wants most: a family. Miller is an artist, living with his possessive mother (Lydia Knott). They still love each other and would like to marry, but can't ever reach an accord. She is attached to Menjou, he to his mother. Her desire for wealth and the easy life conflicts with his puritanical attitude and weakness in regard to his mother. Impressively acted by Purviance, Menjou (who became an instant film star), and all the supporting actresses, Chaplin's work is of particular interest because it was the rare silent film to explore the psychological reasons characters act as they do (we're always trying to figure out if what they're thinking differs from what they're saying), and to show single women for whom sex is integral to their lives and not take an accusatory stance against them. Also it was the rare Chaplin film in which the lead female character is treated with sympathy rather than being idealized. Also with: Charles K. French, Clarence Geldert, Betty Morrissey, Malvina Polo.

WOMAN OF THE YEAR (1942) B&W/112m.
The first time Spencer Tracy's sportswriter and Katharine Hepburn's political columnist lay eyes on each other, they can feel the chemistry—just as moviegoers can immediately feel the chemistry between the stars in their first scene together on the screen. And it's a special joy watching their characters get to know each other, because we're also watching the stars develop their inimitable interplay. After a whirlwind romance, average guy Tracy marries the worldly Hepburn, only to discover that she's too busy to work at being a good wife (after all, she can speak numerous languages but doesn't know how to make coffee). The relationship becomes very strained when she adopts a Greek

orphan without consulting Tracy and then hasn't the time to be a mother. Film is hurt by silly and overly sentimental plot contrivances, and because once they're married neither character is very appealing, but Tracy and Hepburn ride out the rocky road. What's most fascinating about the film is Hepburn's uninhibitedly sexual performance—you won't forget her aggressive behavior toward Tracy in a cab and then in her dark apartment (it's obvious that *she* is ready to go all the way, although they aren't married yet); her sexiness comes from how she uses her eyes, voice, body, and, more significantly, her *mind* prior to lovemaking. Directed by George Stevens. An Oscar-winning script by Ring Lardner, Jr., and Michael Kanin. Adapted into a Broadway musical starring Lauren Bacall (and later Raquel Welch). Also with: Fay Bainter, Dan Tobin, Reginald Owen, William Bendix.

WOMEN, THE (1939) B&W/132m.
Delicious adaptation (by Anita Loos) of Clare Boothe's classic stage comedy, directed by George Cukor, and starring a peerless all-female cast. The characters are like wild animals—claws and fangs bared—let out of their cages. Story centers on the stable, sensible, proud Norma Shearer, happily married mother of a young girl, who discovers that her husband has been having an affair with a golddigging shopgirl (Joan Crawford). Having too much pride to forgive her husband, although they love each other, she goes to Reno for a divorce. Soon two old friends—tongue-wagging Rosalind Russell and meek Joan Fontaine—along with new friends Paulette Goddard and much-married Mary Boland, join her to get divorces of their own. Just when Shearer decides to return to her husband, she learns he has married Crawford. But she won't lose him without a fight. Picture is ideal starting point for discussions on how women are portrayed in film. The lives of idle rich women are characterized by malicious gossip, backstabbing, snooping, bragging about how they have their own husbands under their thumbs, and giving advice on how other women should handle their husbands. They attend parties, teas, fashion shows. Men come across as ineffectual, at the mercy of women on the prowl, too timid to ask wives for forgiveness. Some find the film's portrayal of women objectionable, but these women are resilient, always pulling through when men let them down. Shearer's friends range from young to old (she also has a special relationship with her mother and daughter) and include golddiggers (Goddard), passive wives (Fontaine), those who financially support their men, those who use their husbands' money to fritter their days away, those who push men around, and those who have been dumped by their wayward husbands. It's a joy watching scenes between women who are friends—because, of course, friendships between women have traditionally been ignored by male filmmakers. Even though they often betray each other through gossip (a habit they don't wish to break), there is a camaraderie among them. They obviously care for one another, know the petty problems the others have living in a society where the men control the money. Most unique is that *all* these women have a genuine sense of humor—not solely the ability to make wisecracks; they even put up with each other's barbs. Film has broad humor, slapstick (usually involving Russell), subtle wit. Cukor obviously loves these characters. So we can forgive him for intentionally overdoing it. Watch for Shearer's "women are equal" speech and the Russell-Fontaine exercise scene. Terrific performances by everybody. Fashion show is in color. Remade in 1956 as *The Opposite Sex*. Also with: Lucile Watson, Marjorie Main, Hedda Hopper, Virginia Grey, Virginia Weidler, Phyllis Povah, Mary Beth Hughes.

WOMEN IN LOVE (BRITISH/1970) C/129m.
Ken Russell directed this visually impressive, sexually explicit adaptation of D. H. Lawrence's 1920 novel about the difficult love affairs of sisters Gudrun (Glenda Jackson) and Ursula (Jennie Linden) with Gerald (Oliver Reed) and Birkin (Alan Bates), respectively, and the male bond that forms between Gerald and Birkin. The relationship between strong, passionate, cerebral Gudrun and the hard, unloving Gerald is about the struggle for power—it is combative and self-destructive and drives them apart. Meanwhile Ursula and Birkin, who are more romantic and simpler, grow closer together. They are seemingly the perfect couple because they love each other equally and each has equal standing in the relationship—yet ultimately Linden says she is satisfied with Birkin alone, while Birkin admits he needs male companionship as well. Russell's imagery is annoyingly flamboyant where Lawrence's words are graceful and sensual, but he does manage to convey Lawrence's difficult point about people in a romance pushing and pulling each other and themselves into their correct "positions" in the relationship—just as animals in a jungle form a hierarchy based on predators and prey. These characters both symbolize nature's forces and are controlled by nature—in fact, the three deaths in the film are, in effect, "sacrifices" to nature (two by drowning, one by exposure). When the characters make love, especially outdoors, the "animal" analogy is obvious; but it's interesting to watch how Russell keeps them involved in other physical activities when they're not having sex—they spend *much* time dancing, they swim, they go sledding, they roll in the snow; there is slapping, there is fighting, some men are even knocked down by attack dogs. These people may be intelligent and philosophical, but their primitive instincts are dominant. The performances by the four leads are quite strong—Jackson won an Oscar—and they are to be commended for appearing in X-rated (not XXX) love scenes when stars of that era were reluctant to do so. But, from a director's standpoint, the nude fight scene between Birkin and Gerald and the scene in which the nude Birkin and Ursula run toward each other and Russell turns their images within the frame so that they're horizontal are shamefully pretentious. Worse still is Gudrun's improvisational outdoor dance, which is much like Jules Feiffer's dancer flying around to a ridiculous "Ode to Spring." Larry Kramer wrote and produced the film; Billy Williams did the exquisite cinematography; and Georges Delerue con-

tributed the music. Also with: Vladek Sheybal, Eleanor Bron, Alan Web, Catherine Willmer, Richard Heffer, Christopher Gable, Michael Gough.

WOODSTOCK (1970) C/184m.
More than 500,000 young people showed up for the legendary three-day rock-music concert in 1969 on a farm in upstate New York, but several times that number now claim to have been there. In truth, the whole youth-protest movement was there in spirit and took pride in how peaceful this event was. It was where the love generation's dreams came true: a beautiful communal society where everyone pulled together under difficult circumstances, where there was the sound of music instead of gunfire. This epic documentary beautifully covers this seminal cultural event, conveying that far more important than the all-star performances were the people who had gathered and lived for three days without adequate food supplies, bathroom facilities, medical supervision, or protection from the heavy rains. It turned into a successful communal experiment. Performers later admitted that they were overwhelmed by the spirit of the event and felt it a privilege to play for this audience. Superb camera work by a large crew. Footage of young people skinny-dipping and bathing and sexually frolicking earned the picture an X rating. Directed by Michael Wadleigh in *cinéma-vérité* style; at times he uses a split screen. Martin Scorsese (an editor) and Lewis Teague were on the crew. Acts include: pregnant Joan Baez, Sha Na Na, Country Joe and the Fish, Joe Cocker, Jimi Hendrix, Richie Havens, Santana, The Who, Sly and the Family Stone, the Jefferson Airplane, and the "new" group Crosby, Stills, and Nash.

WORLD OF APU, THE (INDIAN/1959) B&W/103m.
Final installment in Satyajit Ray's classic *Apu Trilogy* finds Apu (Soumitra Chatterji) dropping out of college for lack of funds; trying to finish his autobiographical novel while living in poverty. To save his best friend's family from disgrace, he makes what he believes is a noble gesture and marries a girl he doesn't know (Sharmila Tagore), taking her from a leisurely life into his roach-filled room. Surprisingly, they illuminate each other's lives, falling deeply, madly in love, and living for each other's company. As in most of Ray's films, there will be great tragedy, reflection, guilt, and, ultimately, an affirmation of life. Beautiful film has familiar plotline, but Ray presents everything in unique ways. The everything-is-equal relationship between Chatterji and Tagore differs from all our (at least, my own movie-based) preconceptions about marriage in India. Tagore, who displays intelligence and cleverness, a sense of humor and a willingness to express her love for Apu without embarrassment, is much different from the Indian women we've seen in the works of non-Indians. Ray sensitively handles the final sequence in which Apu befriends his rebellious young son (Swapan Mukherji, who, like all Ray's actors, has a remarkable face). And the final shot of them together, with the happy boy on the shoulders of his beaming father,

is the perfect reward to us for having gone through so much suffering with Apu in *Pather Panchali, Aparajito*, and this film. Ray has been criticized for failing to give a clear picture of the changing India. Here we see industrialization, get a quick view of a picket line, hear of strike-breaking, get a glimpse of a decrepit school where no education is possible and the back room of a factory where workers waste their lives "labeling" for slave wages, and, of course, see the poverty—yet even if this isn't a social document, it manages to give us insight into people (men and women, children) that few filmmakers have been able to match. For viewers, there aren't many films that are as emotionally rewarding as the *Apu* films. Music by Ravi Shankar. Also with: Alok Chakravarty.

WR—MYSTERIES OF THE ORGANISM (YUGOSLAVIAN/1971) B&W/84m.
Dušan Makavejev's controversial cult film about the correlation between sex and politics, or, more specifically, the impossibility of revolution or political freedom if there exists sexual oppression—which was the basis of the radical "free love" philosophy of Austrian-born, American-killed psychoanalyst Wilhelm Reich (the WR of the title). The director did away with a narrative or straight documentary approach for an experiment in free association; the various images in his montage often contradict those that precede or follow them. He whips up confusion by juxtaposing such diverse footage as: superficial biographical material on Reich (which, if expanded, might make a more involving film); a Yippie running around New York with a toy machine gun, scenes from the 1946 Soviet propaganda film *The Vow*, starring Stalin (who is sentimental and fatherly); hard-to-watch torture sequences from a Nazi pro-euthanasia film; an explicit lovemaking scene from a sex documentary; scenes of Reich's disciples going through vigorous therapy in which they hope to liberate their bodies so they can have fulfilling orgasms (it's hard to tell if the director is mocking them as they go into wild contortions); transvestite Jackie Curtis recalling his first sexual encounter with a male; and a long, part-satiric, part-burlesque segment, set in 1971 Belgrade, in which one of two female roommates spends all her time having sex and the other (Melina Dravic) spends her time addressing the workers, shouting Reichian philosophy about the necessity of sex in revolution. In the film's most revealing sequence the sexually liberated Yugoslavian woman is killed by a sexually repressed Russian skater after a lengthy lovemaking session—indication that fascist Russia continues simultaneously to repress sexual freedom and revisionist political thinking. Makavejev is so excited by his stylistic impositions that he barely gets this message across or the irony that Reich was persecuted in America because his "free love" philosophy was taken as proof that he was a Stalinist when in fact he detested Russia because it stifled continuing revolution by denying people sexual freedom. Interesting, but humor is distracting and film is at times so vague you'll drift off. Also with: Jagoder Kaloper, Ivica Vidovic, Tuli Kupferberg, Soran Radmilovic.

WRITTEN ON THE WIND (1956) C/99m.

Tempestuous melodrama, produced by Albert Zugsmith, adapted from Robert Wilder's novel by George Zuckerman, and directed by Douglas Sirk, the German emigré who made films about American life and family. Robert Stack is an alcoholic Texas millionaire, the son of oil tycoon Robert Keith. By flaunting his wealth, he so impresses Lauren Bacall, a secretary with the New York office, that she marries him. What's ironic about this is that Stack blames his alcoholism (his expression of self-hatred), his mixed-up sister Dorothy Malone's promiscuity (her expression of self-hatred), and all their lifelong problems on daddy's fortune. Indeed, these wealthy siblings seek out excitement in the most sordid areas of town. Malone is unhappy when Stack brings home his bride. It becomes obvious that Stack's best friend Rock Hudson, whom Malone has loved since childhood, is in love with Bacall. When Bacall becomes pregnant, Stack, thinking he's sterile, believes it's Hudson's baby. Malone adds fuel to the fire, and the drunk Stack gets out his gun. This ranks with *The Tarnished Angels* as Sirk's best work. This is also about tarnished characters—those who have money (Stack and Malone) are doomed, as if money created bad genes; those who have close contact with the wealthy (Hudson, Bacall) tend to act or think immorally because of this but can escape (they flee in the end). As in all good potboilers, the characters are driven by their passions and are surrounded by destructive forces: those characters who are destroyed also have destructive forces emanating from the inside. Strong performances, especially by an extremely sexy Malone, who won a Best Supporting Actress Oscar. Photography by Russell Metty. Alexander Golitzen and Robert Clatworthy did the art direction. Also with: Grant Williams, Harry Shannon, Robert J. Wilke, Edward C. Platt.

WRONG BOX, THE (BRITISH/1966) C/105m.

John Mills and brother Ralph Richardson are last in line for an inheritance, each hoping that the other kicks off first. Hearing Mills is on his deathbed, Richardson and wicked cousins Peter Cook and Dudley Moore greedily head for London. When Richardson is supposedly killed en route, the cousins plot to hide his body until after Mills dies so they can claim the money in Richardson's name. Of course, there are mix-ups when it turns out Richardson isn't really dead. Then who's in the coffin? Actors are funny, lines are funny, but once-popular black comedy isn't funny. Director Bryan Forbes has no sense of comedy pacing. This picture has no snap, it goes on and on without hitting any comedy peaks. Best scenes are the *Kind Hearts and Coronets*-like opening and Cook purchasing a death certificate from wacky doctor Peter Sellers. Also with: Michael Caine, Nanette Newman, Wilfrid Lawson, Tony Hancock.

WRONG MAN, THE (1956) C/105m.

Alfred Hitchcock's depiction of a real-life story about a New York musician (Henry Fonda) who is wrongly accused of committing a series of robberies, actually carried out by a lookalike. Not even his wife (Vera Miles) fully believes in his innocence, and the strain is so great she ends up in a mental hospital. First part of the picture, in which Fonda is arrested outside his home, questioned, fingerprinted, paraded in front of witnesses, and tossed into jail, is masterfully directed with a sense of precision that's even above Hitchcock's usual standards. It perfectly illustrates Hitchcock's lifelong terror of being arrested for a crime he knew nothing about. This Kafkaesque sequence is so frightening that everything that comes afterward seems anticlimactic—Miles's breakdown is bothersome rather than compelling because it takes time away from the mystery. When you first see the real killer, you'll get chills. I think this picture is of special significance because Fonda represents the most extreme example of the initially dull Hitchcockian hero whose every minute is planned out and whose life doesn't vary at all from day to day—he is the one hero without any sense of humor. Scripted by Maxwell Anderson and Angus MacPhail from Anderson's "The True Story of Emmanuel Balestrero." Photography by Robert Burks, music by Bernard Herrmann. Also with: Anthony Quayle, Harold J. Stone, Charles Cooper, John Heldabrand, Richard Robbins (the Right Man), Esther Minciotti, Nehemiah Persoff.

WUTHERING HEIGHTS (1939) B&W/103m.

Emily Brontë's harsh, haunting love story became one of the screen's classic romances, thanks to director William Wyler, producer Sam Goldwyn, cinematographer Gregg Toland, and the inspired casting of Merle Oberon as Cathy and Laurence Olivier as Heathcliff. Goldwyn was chiefly responsible for the elegance of the film (with its lush music, vast two-room sets that are lit by candles and fireplaces, lovely costuming, romantic dialogue, handsome actors, and beautiful actresses) and for reconstructing the Yorkshire moors in the Conejo Hills in California and building the Wuthering Heights manor. Together Wyler and Toland (who used deep focus and close-ups that are diffused with soft candle-lighting effects) turn the manor into a haunted house: bleak, brooding, oppressive, dark with anger and hatred. The tumultuous atmosphere—with electrical storms, heavy rains, and driving snowstorms—perfectly defines "wuthering"; but too often the atmosphere conveys characters' emotions that otherwise wouldn't be evident from the acting alone. Unlike in the book, the characters don't come across as being *forces of nature* more than human beings. There is much in the film that differs in disturbing ways from the novel (other than that it covers only half the story). To scriptwriters Ben Hecht and Charles MacArthur, Heathcliff's anger is directed toward Cathy for marrying rich Edgar Linton (David Niven), and all that he intentionally does wrong, including marrying Edgar's naive sister, Isabella (Geraldine Fitzgerald), is his way of getting revenge. In Brontë, Heathcliff's fight is with all who are civilized; it is the savage, instinctual being against the corruptive civilizing influence that degrades and oppresses those like him, and attracts those like Cathy. Hecht and MacArthur's biggest crime is to turn Cathy into the film's villain, directly responsible for all the tragedy that follows her marriage to Edgar—even that caused by Heathcliff. In the film Cathy chooses civilization over savagery: Linton, whom she doesn't love, over Heathcliff, whom she loves desperately and passionately. But Brontë's Cathy loves them both, wants them both—and can't understand why they won't go along with such an arrangement. In Brontë, Cathy's thrilled when Heathcliff returns and not unhappy when he decides to marry Isabella. Film has a polished veneer, but the issues are far more complex in the novel, as are the characters—and they are far more interesting. But there's no denying that Oberon and Olivier are a wonderful couple, and their scene in the make-believe castle on Peniston Crag—in which Cathy and Heathcliff express their love for each other, Cathy says that *inside* she'll never change, and they embrace—is one of the most romantic bits in cinema history. Significantly, it is original to Hecht and MacArthur (who wanted to *humanize* the characters and make them more likable than in Brontë). The breathtakingly beautiful Oberon is surprisingly good, and Olivier is better; his delivery has such strength that we tend to overlook those lines which make no sense. A memorable last shot. Remade in 1954 (by Luis Buñuel) and 1970. Music by Alfred Newman. Also with: Flora Robson (as housekeeper Ellen Dean), Hugh Williams (as Hindley, Cathy's brutal brother), Leo G. Carroll, Cecil Humphreys, Miles Mander, Romaine Callender, Cecil Kellaway (as Cathy's father, who adopts urchin Heathcliff), Rex Downing (Heathcliff as a child), Sarita Wooton (Cathy as a child), Douglas Scott (Hindley as a child).

"X"—THE MAN WITH X-RAY EYES (1963) C/80m.
Competent, philosophical sci-fi film, directed by Roger Corman for AIP. Ray Milland plays a scientist who devises a drug that allows him to see through objects. Of course his new power has bad side effects (light nearly blinds him) and eventually gets out of control. After accidentally killing a man, he hides out with a carnival, pretending to be a mind-reader. He tries to find an antidote, but loses out on his chance for redemption when he uses his power to win money in Las Vegas by seeing through cards. God will have retribution on this man who ventured into His domain. Story is predictable, but Milland makes a good lead—a man who's not entirely sympathetic. Corman uses color well (photography was by Floyd Crosby), and the special effects are satisfactory. Final few seconds are powerful. Also with: Diana Van Der Vlis, Harold J. Stone, Don Rickles, John Hoyt.

XICA/XICA DA SILVA (BRAZILIAN/1976) C/120m.
Popular film by Carlos Diegues tells the legendary story of a black slave woman named Xica (Zeze Motta).
In 18th-century Brazil she was slave to a bourgeois Portuguese family and sexual mistress to both father and son. Realizing that she has sexual skills that most men desire, she barges into the office of the new Royal Diamond Contractor, João Fernandes (Walmor Chages) and so startles him with a striptease (supposedly to show where she has been beaten) and brazen words that he buys her. Fernandes's wife is in Portugal, and he takes Xica for his mistress. He grants her freedom and gives her much money, some from the royal treasury. Having wealth, freedom, and power, Xica behaves in an extravagant and, as far as the poor Portuguese are concerned, arrogant manner. She spends much money on herself and to make Fernandes happy, but she also tries to make life better for the blacks in the area, building a church for them, replacing many in the mines with Portuguese workers, etc. The King sends a snooty count (José Wilker) to investigate Fernandes and his now famous mistress. In some ways Xica reminds one of Cleopatra, who also—so we've been told—used her sexual wiles on powerful men to improve her status and influence. But, as played by Motta, I can't see what Xica's attraction is; she's lusty rather than sexy—I think it's more a case of the men who desire her being weak than her being strong. Picture is colorful, like *Black Orpheus*, but not particularly interesting, especially when one considers that Xica really was something special. I never really understand what Xica is up to, particularly with the Count—we think her exotic dance and African meal for him are part of an elaborate plan to sabotage his efforts to take Fernandes back to Portugal, but they prove to be of no consequence and there doesn't even seem to be a plan. Also unsatisfying is that most things of a political nature take place *off* screen. Also with: Altair Lima, Marcus Vinicus.

YAKUZA, THE (1975) C/112m.
Interesting, intricately plotted thriller set in Japan. American Robert Mitchum returns to Japan after many years' absence to attempt the rescue of friend Brian Keith's daughter from the Yakuza, a violent underground crime organization. He looks up the Japanese woman (Kishi Keiko) he loved during the American occupation after WWII. And he enlists the help of her brother (Takakura Ken), a former Yakuza. Much bloody action counterpoints the film's solemn tone. What makes the film unusual is that is is not about the violence, but about friendship and loyalty—Mitchum comes to realize that Americans like Keith think differently about such things than Japanese like Ken. Directed by Sydney Pollack. It was perceptively written by Paul Schrader (long a student of Japanese culture) and Robert Towne. Leonard Schrader devised the original story. Also with: Herb Edelman, Richard Jordan, Okada Eiji, James Shigeta, Kyosuke Mashida.

YANKEE DOODLE DANDY (1942) B&W/ 126m.
Stirring, sentimental musical bio of an American institution, George M. Cohan, a songwriter whose unwavering devotion to friends, family, and flag made him an ideal subject for Warner Bros.' pro-war, pro-Roosevelt propaganda in 1942. Today the superpatriotic aspects of the film, which are laid on mighty thick by the end, have a diluted impact. Yet flag-waving still has an undeniable charm and the entire film is appealing. In an Oscar-winning performance James Cagney is magnificent as Cohan. He has infectious spirit, energy, and drive. And, boy, can he dance! He plays Cohan with spit and vinegar and heat. Watching him hoof across stages or on tables is delightful. Cagney's scenes with Joan Leslie, who is extremely winning as Cohan's girlfriend, then wife, are very special—it's truly moving when they sing "Mary" together. But what's even more impressive is that Cagney proves to be one of the few actors we've had who can comfortably play tender scenes with other men. Lavish production is strongly directed by Michael Curtiz. The musical numbers are particularly well done in a non–Busby Berkeley style. Lengthy camera pans are novel. Infectious songs include "Over There," "Grand Old Flag," "Give My Regards to Broadway," and the title tune, spectacularly sung and danced by Cagney. Film is odd in that almost nothing bad happens to its protagonist. Also with: Walter Huston, Rosemary DeCamp, Jeanne Cagney, Richard Whorf, S. Z. Sakall (in a scene-stealing bit as a producer who asks, "Why take *his* wife's money instead of *my* wife's money?"), Walter Catlett, Frances Langford, Eddie Foy, Jr. (as Cagney's great friend Eddie Foy), George Tobias, Minor Watson.

YEAR OF LIVING DANGEROUSLY, THE (1983) C/116m.
You'll feel you've been transported back to 1964–65 in Jakarta, Indonesia, during the final year of the Sukarno regime. That's how convincing it is. Peter Weir's re-creation of a sweltering environment is distinguished by paranoia, police action, political turbulence (instigated by the insurgent communists), poverty in the extreme, and the disconcerting presence of decadent, insensitive foreigners: rich dignitaries who throw lavish balls and members of the press who spend their time drinking heavily, whoring, and filing reports on a situation that they don't try to comprehend. Mel Gibson is ambitious but inexperienced Australian correspondent Guy Hamilton, who is taken under the wing of a half-Oriental, half-European dwarf photographer: Linda Hunt deservedly won an Oscar playing the enlightened male Billy Kwan. Because Billy believes Hamilton is more caring and trusting than all the other correspondents, he gets him many exclusive interviews. He even sets him up with his friend Jill Bryant (Sigourney Weaver), a beautiful British attaché. Hamilton has the affair with Jill that Billy probably desires himself. But that's okay with Billy. What destroys him is Hamilton jumping at the opportunity to file a story about the political situation that Jill told him in strictest confidence. This film is about mistrust, ambition, and reporters who exploit misery rather than doing something to alleviate it (Billy believes every person can spread sun-

shine). But mostly it's about *betrayal*, which Billy thinks is the greatest sin of all—Sukarno betrays his people, reporters betray their subjects, and Hamilton has betrayed both Jill and Billy. Film contains frightening violent sequences, a great deal of suspense (e.g., when Hamilton attempts to reach the airport), and some erotic romantic scenes between Hamilton and Jill. The characters are most interesting (especially Billy), as are the relationships between them. A smart, provocative, eerie film. Filming was finished in Australia after cast and crew fled the Philippines upon receiving death threats from Moslem extremists who thought the film would be anti-Moslem. From the novel by C. J. Koch, who collaborated with Weir and David Williamson on the screenplay. Also with: Michael Murphy, Noel Ferrier, Bill Kerr.

YELLOW SUBMARINE (BRITISH/1968) C/85m.
Dazzling animation feature in which the Beatles use music to defeat the Blue Meanies, invaders of Pepperland. The witty, satirical script and bizarre characters recall Lewis Carroll as well as the Beatles' live-action films; colorful animation owes inspiration to diverse sources, including Dali, Pop Art, Sunday comic strips. As directed by Britisher George Dunning and designed by German animator Heinz Edelman, the visuals are consistently imaginative, innovative, colorful, and startling. Although the emphasis is on graphics (lines more than circles) rather than characters, some of the creatures the Beatles come across are very impressive-looking. And the music—mostly from *Sergeant Pepper's Lonely Hearts Club Band*—is wonderful accompaniment to the psychedelic imagery (one of the reasons the film became a cult among acid heads). Amazingly ambitious, but it's a shame that the Beatles (who do make a cameo appearance at the end) didn't provide the voices for their cartoon figures, but had impostors fill in.

YENTL (1983) C/134m.
Barbra Streisand decided back in 1968 that she wanted to star in an adaptation of Isaac Bashevis Singer's short story "Yentl the Yeshiva Boy." A dozen years later she finally realized that for this to happen she also would have to direct, produce, and co-write the film. Many critics and moviegoers consider this film a tremendous ego trip; in Hollywood, Academy members snubbed Streisand come Oscar time (although the score won the award), pointing out that Singer himself was upset by what Streisand had done to his tale. But I find the film quite enchanting, humorous, inspiring, and extremely ambitious. Filmed in Czechoslovakia and England, the story is set in Eastern Europe at the turn of the century. Yentl is a brilliant young Jewish woman who disguises herself as a young man, "Anshel," so she can attend rabbinical school and quench her thirst for knowledge and intellectual discourse. "Anshel" impresses the professors with ideas that are much different from those of other students. "He" becomes best friends with Avigdor (Mandy Patinkin), a handsome classmate who is engaged to Hadass (Amy Irving), whose brightness is wasted because she must live the traditional dull life of a Jewish woman. Yentl falls for Avigdor and, out of fear of

seeing him go away when Hadass's parents reject him for their daughter (because his brother committed suicide), "Anshel" agrees to marry Hadass so that at least Avigdor can still visit the woman he loves. While Yentl keeps her sex a secret from her "wife," Hadass falls for "Anshel," who has given her unexpected freedom, respect, and the book-learning that she'd always been denied. Streisand mistakenly neglects to have Yentl continue to hungrily devour knowledge once she realizes her love for Avigdor, but we can appreciate how Streisand uses her unique character—who has lived as both woman and man—as a positive influence on both Avigdor and Hadass. It is through Yentl-"Anshel" that they become more enlightened in regard to how men and women should perceive and relate to one another. Sadly, once she makes each an ideal mate, she must step aside. The 12 Michel Legrand songs, with lyrics by Alan and Marilyn Bergman, are all utilized as Yentl's internal monologues. They won't appeal to everyone, but Streisand sings them with conviction and they show that this director really wanted to understand her character—the typical male director might have asked for a less introspective score. Streisand handles herself well as director, deftly moving from funny moments to tender scenes between "Anshel" and Hadass to the jolting scene in which Yentl reveals herself to Avigdor (a masterly directed and acted bit). Moreover, one shouldn't so easily dismiss the fact that this first-time director managed to get excellent performances from her two co-stars as well as the touching, humorous, very warm performance she herself gives. Also with: Nehemiah Persoff, Steven Hill.

YOJIMBO/BODYGUARD, THE (JAPANESE/ 1961) B&W/110m.
Akira Kurosawa's classic, his most financially successful film, was influenced by westerns such as *Shane* and in turn influenced a whole slew of westerns itself, most notably Sergio Leone's *A Fistful of Dollars*, which completely lifts the plot. Toshiro Mifune is a masterless samurai who, no longer restricted by a code of honor, wanders through Japan selling his sword to the highest bidder. The town Mifune wanders into represents the decay of a moral, chivalrous Japanese society. A sake dealer (Takashi Shimura) and an equally cruel silk merchant (Kamatari Fujiwara) wage a war for control of the town's gambling. Both are cowards who have hired scores of evil henchmen. Because the henchmen are also cowards, each side is afraid to make the first move. As one of the fast-action movie heroes who think before they act, Mifune devises a clever plan by which he can exploit the situation to his financial gain. He sells his bodyguard services to one side, then the other. He kills his share of men and blames his dirty work on one side or the other, causing the two sides to eliminate each other—he takes care of the leftovers, including the cocky henchman (Tatsuya Nakadai), who owns the only pistol in the territory. He leaves the town richer, and, as he says, the town is much "quieter" than when he got there. Like Leone's films, this is a *bloodbath* (the violence is ferocious) that we react to with laughter—it is a comedy where the bad guys have the misfortune to be happened upon by a *hero* who can challenge and defeat them on their own amoral terms. As in Leone's films, every death results in someone (Mifune) making a financial profit; as in Leone, when the hero acts with emotion—acts *human* for the only time—he ends up paying the price, by suffering physical punishment. As in Leone, the hero, who has nothing to lose in the first place, comes back from the dead—which is what makes the Mifune figure a *mythic* universal hero. Classic is beautifully photographed by Kazuo Miyagawa (*Rashomon*), who does a remarkable job with composition and deep focus. The most striking shot has the coffin maker hanging in the foreground, facing us; some bad guys in the middle plane, facing away from us toward the far end of town; and the "resurrected" Mifune in the distance, facing us, with myth-making dust blowing past him from our right to left. Great movie-making.

YOL (TURKISH-SWISS/1982) C/111m.
Grand Prize winner at Cannes in 1982 was scripted by director Yilmaz Guney while he was interned in a Turkish prison. Several prisoners go home to their villages while on a week's leave. A main story is about a man who finds that his family has banished him because he was responsible for his brother-in-law's death—during a robbery, he panicked and drove away, leaving the brother-in-law to face the police guns. Now he suffers guilt, humiliation, and fear of reprisal from his in-laws, but is determined to see his wife (who also is appalled by his cowardice) and children. Another prisoner discovers that his unfaithful wife has been chained in a cell for eight months; forbidden to speak, even to her young son, or to be touched; given only bread and water for sustenance; denied an opportunity to bathe; left to wallow in her own filth. He attempts to take her home to her brother, but they must cross five miles of frozen terrain. Guney's powerful theme is that, in Turkey, hostility and repression exist on every level of society: guards over prisoners, men over women, the heads of families over their relatives, the people themselves over those they consider "sinners." Film is fascinating, brutal, depressing, and confusing (because it jumps back and forth in time and between the various stories and because all the men have mustaches and resemble each other). There's an unforgettable scene on a train when a prisoner and his wife are caught trying to have sex in the bathroom and everyone on the train either hits them or threatens them with violence. With: Tarik Akan, Seref Sezer, Halil Ergun, Necmettin Cobanglu.

YOU CAN'T CHEAT AN HONEST MAN (1939) B&W/76m.
W. C. Fields is at his loudest, meanest (he throws Charlie McCarthy to the alligators), and most larcenous as a one-step-ahead-of-the-sheriff circus owner named Larson E. Whipsnade. When he's on screen—gypping customers and employees out of money, doing a terrible ventriloquism act, selling front-row seats "right next to the elephants," talking about snakes in genteel society, playing

a wild Ping-Pong match, wrestling a little girl—the film's a delight. However, too much time is given Edgar Bergen, not only for comedy bits with Charlie McCarthy and Mortimer Snerd—which are slow but funny—but also for some romance with Constance Moore, Whipsnade's surprisingly sensible daughter. One becomes impatient during Fields's absence. Fields's bits with his idiot assistant, Grady Sutton, are particularly funny. Directed by George Marshall and Eddie Cline (uncredited). Also with: James Bush, Mary Forbes, Thurston Hall, Edward Brophy, Eddie Anderson.

YOU CAN'T TAKE IT WITH YOU (1938) B&W/ 127m.
Frank Capra's adaptation of George S. Kaufman–Moss Hart stage success. It's about the idealistic son (James Stewart) of a rich, cold-hearted businessman (Edward Arnold) who wants to marry his secretary (Jean Arthur) although her nutty, carefree family will never meet his parents' social standards. Wedding plans seem to be off for good when Stewart brings his parents over for dinner—one night early—and everyone lands in jail. Grandfather Lionel Barrymore, who heads Arthur's family clan, tries to explain to Arnold that having friends, not money, is the secret to happiness and that he must become less interested in business if he's to be a good father to Stewart. Comedy won Best Picture and Best Director Oscars, but it's not among Capra's best films. There are many funny moments and the cast is great, but film is too preachy and many of the political-social points made—especially about the wonderfully peculiar character of democratic Americans—are vague or unconvincing; moreover, themes such as "the richest man is the one with the most friends" are better and more honestly conveyed in Capra's later *It's a Wonderful Life* (1946). Barrymore gives a surprisingly lifeless performance—perhaps he and Arnold should have switched roles. My favorite scenes are those in which Stewart and Arthur talk openly about families, hopes, dreams, their love for each other—these moments are surprisingly quiet and mature for a screwball comedy. Particularly effective is their scene in the park, where the camera doesn't cut away during their long conversation. Also with: Mischa Auer, Ann Miller (looking fine in simple clothes, doing continuous improvisational ballet), Spring Byington, a *young* Dub Taylor, Eddie "Rochester" Anderson, Donald Meek, Halliwell Hobbes, Samuel S. Hinds, Harry Davenport, Ian Wolfe, Frank Ferguson.

YOU ONLY LIVE ONCE (1937) B&W/86m.
Fritz Lang's second American film. Henry Fonda plays a petty criminal who's been in jail three times. Now he promises to go straight, but only his wife, Sylvia Sidney, believes him. No one will give him a break; the law expects him to return to crime. Gangsters frame him for a bank robbery and murder they committed. The police arrest him, and he is convicted by a jury that is influenced by circumstantial evidence and his previous record—they won't believe him. In Lang, the innocent are usually judged guilty. At wits' end, Fonda tries to escape to avoid execution. A priest, William Gargan, tries to tell him that they've found out he is innocent, but Fonda no longer trusts anyone—he shoots the priest. Fonda and Sidney become one of the screen's first couples on the run. They try to reach the Canadian border. Of course, you can't allow someone to kill a priest and get off scot-free at the end—but Lang makes it clear that his sympathies are with Fonda, and with Sidney, the only person to give an outcast a chance to prove good. Film is very bleak, but strongly acted (Fonda and Sidney play well together) and directed; it makes a powerful statement about American justice and the shabby treatment that people with no money or power must endure—they have no defense against the forces that take control of their lives. Ending is overly sentimental and is Hollywood-style religious—I guess only God can forgive a priest-killer. Moody cinematography by Leon Shamroy. Music by Alfred Newman. Also with: Barton MacLane, Jean Dixon, Jerome Cowan, Margaret Hamilton, Ward Bond, Jonathan Hale.

YOU ONLY LIVE TWICE (BRITISH/1967) C/ 117m.
Fifth James Bond film has Sean Connery's British agent trying to prevent a nuclear war (what else?). Someone snatched an American rocket, and the chief suspect is Russia. Bond pretends to be killed so he can do his snooping without anyone looking for him. He discovers that the culprit is SPECTRE's Blofeld (Donald Pleasence), whose headquarters and launching station are contained in a Japanese volcano. Not a bad Bond film, but it doesn't compare to its predecessors—the formula had become a little stale. It should have been about twenty minutes shorter. Lewis Gilbert directed. Roald Dahl took great liberties with Ian Fleming's novel. Freddie Young did the photography, Peter Hunt edited, John Barry composed the score, Ken Adam designed the impressive sets. Also with: Mie Hama (as Kissy Suzuki), Akiko Wakabayashi, Tetsuro Tamba, Karin Dor, Teru Shimada, Charles Gray, Tsai Chin, Bernard Lee, Lois Maxwell, Desmond Llewellyn.

YOUNG AND INNOCENT/GIRL WAS YOUNG, THE (BRITISH/1937) B&W/80m.
A very entertaining, sadly overlooked Alfred Hitchcock suspense thriller. If it doesn't reach the heights of *The 39 Steps*, which it greatly resembles, that's because the earlier film (also cowritten by Charles Bennett) has more mature characters (this film is about a young girl's maturation into womanhood), more glamorous stars in Robert Donat and Madeleine Carroll, and a couple-on-the run story in which more is at stake than just our hero proving his innocence (i.e., the country's security). Writer Derrick de Marney is arrested for the murder of an actress acquaintance. She had been strangled with the belt of his missing raincoat. De Marney escapes during his trial. Nova Pilbeam (the teenage kidnap victim in Hitchcock's 1934 version of *The Man Who Knew Too Much*), a brave and resourceful young woman he meets, *voluntarily* (unlike Carroll) helps the hero elude the police and track down the real killer, a man with a nervous eye twitch. This means that Pilbeam must go against her father (Percy Marmont) for the first time, and what makes her decision most

difficult is that Marmont is county constable. Surely the film would have been a bit more exciting if De Marney and Pilbeam (a likable screen couple) were ever in more serious danger than just being arrested. However, their search for the murderer is most entertaining. Notice how pivotal things are lost, stolen, or misplaced: the raincoat, the belt, the lawyer's glasses, the "lost" drumbeat which gives away the identity of the black-faced drummer. Film's highlight is Hitchcock's pan from high above a hotel dance floor to the bandstand and to a close-up of the drummer's twitching eyes. Adapted by Bennett and Alma Reville from Josephine Tey's novel *A Shilling for Candles*. Also with: Edward Rigby (as Old Will), Mary Clare, John Longden, George Curzon, Basil Radford.

YOUNG FRANKENSTEIN (1974) B&W/ 105m.
This spoof of Universal's 1931 version of *Frankenstein* is the only Mel Brooks film that almost everyone likes. For a change, Brooks remains tasteful throughout; keeps his actors under reasonable control (this is helped by his limiting his own appearance to a mere cameo); maintains the picture's tone by including only one "burlesque" interlude (Frankenstein and the Monster perform a hilarious rendition of "Puttin' on the Ritz") and holds that until nearly the end so it won't be intrusive; and, while the humor is outrageous, it is subtly played. Most important is that Brooks shows a knowledge and affection for both *Frankenstein* and the horror genre that he would not display for the western in *Blazing Saddles*. The use of lab props from the 1931 movie, the use of black-and-white film, and an atmospheric score by John Morris contribute greatly to Brooks's attempt to recapture the ambiance of the old Universal horror pictures. Wild-eyed Gene Wilder as the mad Baron, Peter Boyle as the Monster, Marty Feldman as the hunchbacked Igor, Madeline Kahn as the Baron's fiancée, Cloris Leachman as the weird housekeeper, and Teri Garr as a lab assistant who displays a great deal of cleavage do justice to the clever Brooks-Wilder script. The highlight is a scene in which Boyle visits bearded blind man Gene Hackman, a brilliant take-off on the memorable, maudlin scene in *Bride of Frankenstein*. Also with: Kenneth Mars, Richard Haydn.

YOUNG SHERLOCK HOLMES (1985) C/109m.
Barry Levinson directed and Steven Spielberg "presented" this amiable if weakly written tale that shows teenager Holmes (Nicholas Rowe) solving his first mystery. Several men, including Holmes's eccentric mentor, are struck by poisonous darts that cause them to experience violent hallucinations: each dies while in a state of panic. The tall, gangly, gallant Holmes and his short, chubby, courageous new classmate John Watson (Alan Cox), who adores him, come upon a clandestine Egyptian cult that is responsible for the murders and try to figure out who is the chief culprit. Since writer Chris Columbus provides only a couple of suspects, it will take viewers about half the time it takes Holmes to figure out whodunit. This is one reason we never are overly impressed by his detective work. The opening scenes are the best, not only because Levinson provides some authentic Victorian flavor when filming snowy London or the school campus, but because we can see hints of the adult Holmes in the inquisitive, cocky, maturing teenager. But later the familiar overblown Spielberg adventure spectacle—the Egyptian temple with bald, diabolical priests involved in a sacrificial ritual is something Indiana Jones would encounter—replaces mystery-solving and our hero could be any indomitable Spielberg teenager, rather than a detective extraordinaire or, specifically, Holmes. It's a shame because English actors Rowe and Cox are so well cast and play so well together. Fine performances, excellent special effects by Industrial Light and Magic. For those of you who like to find things in films that make no sense: try to figure out why the Egyptian villain would choose this particular time to read a school library book about Egypt, if not for the sole simple reason Columbus needed to provide Holmes with a piece to the puzzle he couldn't find otherwise. Photographed by Stephen Goldblatt. Also with: Sophie Ward (as Holmes's love interest), Anthony Higgins, Freddie Jones.

YOUNG TORLESS (WEST GERMAN/1967) B&W/87m.
Compelling adaptation of Robert Musil's 1906 novel, written and directed by Volker Schlöndorff. Torless (Matthieu Carrière) becomes a pupil in an upper-class boys' academy. It's not as oppressive as other boarding schools we've seen in films, but it's a cold, sterile, orderly environment that provides no intellectual stimulus. Torless and his friends Beineberg (Bernd Tischer) and Reiting (Alfred Dietz) discover that another student, Basini (Marian Seidowsky), stole money to pay off a debt. Rather than turn Basini in to the faculty, Beineberg and Reiting make Basini their slave and take to beating and humiliating him. Basini does not fight back. Torless does not participate in Basini's debasement, but watches passively. He is formulating opinions about human nature that he will express in his climactic speech to the faculty. Picture presents military academies as breeding grounds for fascists, and draws parallels between what happens in the school and the rise of Nazism in Germany in the early 1930s and victimization of Jews. But, more interestingly, it's about how similar people can, through circumstances, go in opposite directions—one becomes an oppressor and the other an outcast victim. What disturbs Torless about Basini is his masochistic acceptance of his degradation and victimization; what he detests about Beineberg and Reiting is that they intellectualize that what they're doing to Basini is an experiment in human nature (to see how much he will take)—significantly, their actions against him are systematically accomplished—when in fact they're looking for excuses for their sadism. Also with: Fritz Gehlen, Barbara Steele.

YUM-YUM GIRLS, THE (1976) C/93m.
Your reputation's on the line if you admit to having seen a film with such a title. Actually, this R-rated exploitation film about a young model-actress (Michelle Daw) who must play the "game" in order to get ahead in New York is relatively tame

as far as the sex goes. In fact, most of the memorable moments are comedic, featuring an array of funny actresses auditioning or making stupid commercials. Daw is sympathetic as the girl who is almost driven to suicide because of guilt and frustration. Nothing special, but it could have been much worse. Then unknowns Judy Landers and Tanya Roberts play small roles. Directed by Barry Rosen. Also with: Barbara Tully, Carey Poe.

Z (FRENCH-ALGERIAN/1969) C/128m. A craftily made, spellbinding political thriller that unravels like a detective novel to reveal the mechanics of rightwing conspiracies to silence the opposition. Directed by Costa-Gavras, who adapted Vassili Vassilikos's novel with Jorge Semprun (*La Guerre Est Finie*), film is fiction based on fact. Yves Montand plays a Greek pacifist leader who is clubbed on the head and killed after making a public speech. As happened in the case of his real-life counterpart, Gregorios Lambrakis (who was murdered on May 22, 1963, at Solinka), the magistrate (played by Jean-Louis Trintignant) assigned to investigate discovers that there was a conspiracy behind the assassination, involving high-level government leaders (from the political right), the military and police, and a secret anti-communist organization (known in the film as CROC), from which thugs could always be recruited to physically disrupt leftist activities. It's fascinating and truly exciting watching the conservative but honest Trintignant make discoveries that show that the top-brass witnesses have been lying about the incident and convince him that the so-called "accident" (Montand was supposedly killed by an apolitical drunk) was a skillfully planned assassination. And it's great fun (like watching Sam Ervin take on the Watergate conspirators) watching Trintignant stand up to the big boys and push forward with the case, knowing that the indictments he'll be handing out will probably cause the downfall of the government. (The upsetting part is the end, when we learn that the military coup of 1967 not only wiped out all the sentences that were meted out, but resulted in the imprisonment and death of many of those who uncovered the plot. We're told that the letter "Z," which the new government banned from usage, stands for "He Lives!" referring, of course, to Lambrakis.) This film was banned in several rightwing countries, but, interestingly, it has always received harsh criticism from the radical left because Costa-Gavras chose to take a moral rather than an ideological stance in presenting a distinctly *political* story (he said that if he made it more factual, many people would have thought Lambrakis's position—on NATO, for instance—would have justified his being eliminated) and because the director chose to ignore all the leftists in Greece who were at least as responsible as the magistrate for bringing the conspirators to justice. I think that while much of the criticism is justified, the film should at very least be praised for showing the nature of fascist conspiracies in a way that the layman can understand—whether the viewer can apply what he's learned to situations other than Greece of the sixties is another matter. Splendid cinematography by Raoul Coutard (who at times uses grainy stock to give the picture a documentary flavor), editing by Françoise Bonnet, and music by Mikis Theodorakis (who, when the picture was made, in Algiers, was under house arrest back in Greece). Extremely influential. Also with: Irene Papas, Jacques Perrin, Charles Denner, François Périer, Pierre Dux, Renato Salvatori, Marcel Bozzufi.

ZABRISKIE POINT (1970) C/112m. Michelangelo Antonioni directed this interesting failure at M-G-M. It's a myopic vision of America, full of piggy cops, flabby tourists, hungry workers, and fat cats. It's a consumer society, distinguished by billboards, television sets, Wonder Bread, Campbell's soup, refrigerators, and fast food. If this America is to be vanquished, it's imperative that white youths join black revolutionaries in the war lines. White Mark Frechette decides he is willing to die for the cause. Perhaps he is responsible for a cop's being killed at a black protest. At least, the cops think he is guilty. He steals a plane and zooms over Death Valley. He lands and meets mini-skirted Daria Halprin—her employer is businessman Rod Taylor, who's in Phoenix trying to work out a land deal. In Death Valley, Daria and Mark and several other couples who miraculously appear copulate in the sands, symbolically giving birth to . . . ? I'm not sure. But after they make love, Daria has developed Mark's political consciousness. That's why, in the stunning explosion-filled finale, she can imagine the capitalist apocalypse. Picture is politically ambiguous, terribly acted by Halprin and amateur Frechette, and stops dead with the foolish Death Valley orgy. But it has moments of interest—it still is astounding that Hollywood would make a film with a pro-revolutionary theme. Frechette was killed in prison, where he was serving a term for bank robbery (meant to be a political act). Sam Shepard was part of the writing team. A good rock score. Also with: Paul Fix, G. D. Spradlin, Kathleen Cleaver (as herself).

ZAMBIZANGA (ANGOLAN/1972) C/102m. Radical film, directed by Sarah Maldorer, French-born black feminist, and co-written by her husband, a leader in the Angolan resistance, was made "to make Europeans, who hardly know anything about Africa, conscious of the forgotten war in Angola, Mozambique, and Guinea-Bissau." Filmed in the Congo, it is set in Angola in 1961, the year Portuguese forces quelled a large-scale revolt by black nationalists. The story is about a politically naïve woman whose activist husband is whisked away by troops and sent to Luanda, the notorious torture prison. Maldorer follows the wife as she goes from prison to prison in search of her husband. As she discovers that what is happening to prisoners (including her husband) is horrific, she develops a political consciousness. Terrific, unforgettable picture reveals the horrid nature of political oppression in colonial countries where there are liberation movements. In Portuguese. Starring: Domingos Oliviera, Elisa Andrade, Dino Abeilno, Jean M'Vondo.

ZARDOZ (BRITISH/1974) C/105m.
A dizzy, big-budget sci-fi film, poorly conceived and directed by John Boorman. Looking like Pancho Villa in a red diaper, a pudgy Sean Connery plays Zed, an exterminator—the highest class and slavemasters of the primitive Brutals—in the year 2293. He sneaks into the giant flying stone head of the frightful god Zardoz to which the Brutals give all their wheat. The Zardoz head flies above the invisible shield that separates the Outlands, where the Brutals live, from the Vortex, which Zardoz always told them was heaven. Zed discovers that it is not heaven but a depressing world inhabited by a brilliant but emotionless super race, the Eternals. As the Eternals cannot die, some have become Apathetics who live as catatonics. Others became Renegades and were turned old and senile as punishment for standing against the female-controlled government. Zed is taken prisoner by the Eternals: Consuella (Charlotte Rampling) wants to execute him, but May (Sara Kestelman) wants him to breed with the women of the Vortex to give new blood to the race, as the men are all impotent. But he has other plans. Once a murderer, an avenging angel, and a truth seeker, Zed becomes a liberator ("a slave who could free his master") and Adam to Consuella's Eve. Boorman mistakenly takes too long to let us know who Zed is; because we try to learn about an alien environment and its people through a character who is alien to us, it's like doing a science experiment using *two* variables. We become hopelessly bewildered, trying to sort out Boorman's themes: too much technology will cause our senses to dissipate; the obsolescence of sex and childbirth will emancipate women and make men ineffectual; turbulent change is preferable to stagnation; death is preferable to immortality (the major theme); and the fear of death is what results in stagnation. The themes are valid, but the presentation is laughable. While Connery is doing double takes, Boorman is taking his film too seriously. It has all the characteristics of bad spectacles, from horrible costumes and cheap props to terrible direction of extras (everyone does exactly the same thing) to embarrassingly pretentious and trite scenes and dialogue. There's even an excessively brutal massacre scene. Also with: John Alderton, Sally Anne Newton, Niall Buggy.

ZATOICHI MEETS YOJIMBO (JAPANESE/1970) C/116m.
Cult film temptingly features two of Japan's most popular action heroes. Shintaro Katsu's fugitive blind swordsman appeared in a series of action films in the late sixties and early seventies; Toshiro Mifune's mercenary bodyguard made an awesome debut in Akira Kurosawa's 1961 classic, *Yojimbo*. Plot has the two men taking opposite sides in a business rivalry between a brutal young man and his rich, respectful father. The two heroes join forces to find missing gold at the center of the dispute between their employers. Once the bodies of almost everyone in town lie around them—it turned out that everybody, including the father, was corrupt—they decide to fight it out between themselves. With its broad humor, extreme violence, search for gold, uneasy alliance, and final showdown, this film was obviously influenced by Sergio Leone's *For a Few Dollars More* and *The Good, the Bad and the Ugly*. But it's not nearly as enjoyable. In fact, it's pretty slow going for about two thirds of the picture, until an assassin (he'd qualify as Leone's "Bad") arrives in the village and bloody massacres begin in earnest. Mifune spends too much time lazing about half drunk, pining for his lost love, who, deeply in debt, has given herself to the rich father. The swordsman, who looks like a plump Japanese version of Donald Pleasence, is supposed to drive other characters batty because of his astute mind and mastery of his four intact senses, but his whimpering and fake modesty get on my nerves as well. Directed by Kihachi Okamato.

ZELIG (1983) B&W-C/79m.
Bizarre one-joke satire by Woody Allen—it's the type of project he might have conceived back in his *Take the Money and Run* days, but he might have botched it back then. This is a pseudodocumentary about Leonard Zelig (Allen), an abused child of a Jewish immigrant family who becomes famous in the '20s as the Human Chameleon. He takes on the personality traits of anyone he comes into contact with. That he turns up at a Hitler rally wearing a Nazi uniform perfectly illustrates the serious theme behind all the humor: Zelig, a zero in the personality department, is the ultimate conformist, perfect material to be one of the faceless soldiers (not one an individual) who marched for Hitler. Film is consistently funny, but it never rises to a higher level. However, it is technically brilliant. We see actual newsreel footage of famous historical figures—and there in the frame with them is Leonard Zelig. How did Allen and cinematographer Gordon Willis perform such wizardry? A clever score by Dick Hyman. Brilliantly edited by Susan E. Morse. Also with: Mia Farrow (as Zelig's analyst), Stephanie Farrow, Garrett Brown, Ellen Garrison, Patrick Morgan (narrator), Mary Louise Wilson, Will Holt, John Rothman, Howard Erskine, and, in cameos, Susan Sontag, Irving Howe, Saul Bellow, Bruno Bettelheim.

ZÉRO DE CONDUITE/ZERO FOR CONDUCT (FRENCH/1933) B&W/44m.
Jean Vigo's remarkably subversive film about four young boys (one an unhappy newcomer meant to represent Vigo as a child) who not only refuse to accept the strict regimentation at their boarding school but ultimately stage a full-scale revolt on alumni day. Poetic, surreal, and wildly comical, it's a tribute to the honest spontaneity of children, their creativity, and their anarchical Marxist (as in Groucho, Chico, and Harpo) spirit that causes them to wage war against the repressive rules of the hypocritical bourgeoisie. It's a film kids will love and identify with, but it's a mature film, both cine-

matically and thematically. It's best known for the kids' wild slow-motion pillow fight (a homage to a similar scene in Abel Gance's *Napoleon*) during which feathers float about the room, but the real surge of emotion comes at the end of the sequence when the procession of smiling kids glides dreamlike toward the camera, an image that echoes the triumphant French peasants marching through Paris after the Revolution. This masterpiece greatly inspired Truffaut and other European filmmakers; it's the source for Lindsay Anderson's *if*. . . . Louis Lefèvre, Gilbert Pruchon, Gérard de Bedarieux, and Constantin Goldstein-Kehler play the four boys. Also with: Jean Dasté (the one popular teacher because he imitates Chaplin, does handstands, plays ball, chases women, and lets the kids do as they please), Robert Le Flon, Delphin (the midget principal).

ZOMBIE ISLAND MASSACRE (1984) C/87m. A group of obnoxious tourists are taken to a "voodoo island" and find themselves stranded there at night. They are knocked off one by one by something lurking in the dark. Not too bad a premise, but the production is slipshod and the scary scenes run out halfway through the film. Moreover, you gotta hate any "horror" film in which there is a rational explanation for supernatural happenings. The film's major point of interest is its star, Rita Jenrette, ex-wife of ABSCAM congressman John Jenrette. Making her screen debut, she's as good as anyone else in the cast, which isn't much of a compliment. She even does some nudity at the beginning, displaying her enormous chest *and* enormous waist and hips, too. Directed by John N. Carter. Also with: David N. Broadnax, Tom Cantrell.

Additional "Must See" Films

IN THE MAJOR PORTION OF THIS BOOK I HIGHLIGHTED 1630 "MUST-SEE" MOVIES, TAKING A STRONG CROSS SECTION OF FILMS FROM DIFFERENT GENRES, ERAS, AND COUNTRIES. THE FILMS LISTED BELOW ARE NOT "ALSO-RANS" BUT OTHER MOVIES THAT I BELIEVE ARE ESSENTIAL VIEWING FOR THE TRUE FILM LOVER. AS BEFORE, I HAVE TRIED TO CREATE A WORKLIST OF FILMS OF DIFFERENT TYPES, FROM CLASSICS TO EMBARRASSMENTS, FROM COMMERCIAL BLOCKBUSTERS TO CULT FAVORITES, FROM OSCAR-WINNERS TO SLEEPERS, FROM CEREBRAL FILMS TO THOSE THAT TRY ONLY TO ENTERTAIN.

AGAIN I AVOID A *RATING* SYSTEM BECAUSE I DON'T WANT TO DISCOURAGE YOU FROM SEEING ANY OF THE FILMS LISTED. BUT I HAVE PROVIDED A SYSTEM THAT WILL HELP YOU UNDERSTAND WHY I HAVE INCLUDED MANY TITLES.

THE KEY:
CC: CAMP CLASSIC
CM: CULT MOVIE
H: FILM HAS A PLACE IN FILM *HISTORY* OR IS A CRITICS' FAVORITE
PR: PERSONAL RECOMMENDATION
S: SLEEPER
T: TRASH (NOT ESSENTIAL VIEWING)
XXX: PORNO (NOT ESSENTIAL VIEWING)

☐ *Abraham Lincoln* (1930) d: D. W. Griffith   H

☐ *Accattone* (Italian/1961) d: Pier Paolo Pasolini   H

☐ *Accident* (British/1967) d: Joseph Losey

☐ *Across the Pacific* (1942) d: John Huston

☐ *Adolescente, L'* (French-German/ 1979) d: Jeanne Moreau   PR

☐ *Adventures of Sherlock Holmes* (1939) d: Alfred L. Werker

☐ *Advise and Consent* (1962) d: Otto Preminger

☐ *Affair to Remember, An* (1957) d: Leo McCarey   CM

☐ *Against All Odds* (1984) d: Taylor Hackford

☐ *Alambistra!* (1977) d: Robert M. Young   S PR

☐ *Alamo, The* (1960) d: John Wayne

☐ *Alex in Wonderland* (1970) d: Paul Mazursky   CM

☐ *Alfie* (British/1966) d: Lewis Gilbert

☐ *Alice in the Cities* (West German/ 1974) d: Wim Wenders   CM PR

☐ *Alice's Restaurant* (1969) d: Arthur Penn   CM PR

☐ *All Screwed Up* (Italian/1974) d: Lina Wertmuller

☐ *All That Heaven Allows* (1955) d: Douglas Sirk   S CM

☐ *All The King's Men* (1949) d: Robert Rossen   H

☐ *All the Marbles/California Dolls, The* (1981) d: Robert Aldrich   CM PR

☐ *Alvin Purple/Sex Therapist, The* (Australian/1973) d: Tim Burstall

☐ *Amanda By Night* (1981) d: Robert McCallum   XXX

☐ *Amazing Colossal Man, The* (1957) d: Bert I. Gordon

☐ *Amazing Doctor Clitterhouse, The* (1938) d: Anatole Litvak   S

☐ *Amazing Transplant, The* (1971) d: Louis Silverman   T

☐ *America, America* (1963) d: Elia Kazan   PR

☐ *American Madness* (1932) d: Frank Capra   PR

☐ *American Pop* (1981) d: Ralph Bakshi   CM

☐ *American Success Company, The/ Success* (1979) d: William Ri-chert   S CM

☐ *American Tragedy, An* (1932) d: Josef von Sternberg

☐ *Americanization of Emily, The* (1964) d: Arthur Hiller   CM

☐ *Anatahan* (1953) d: Josef von Sternberg   CM

☐ *Anatomy of a Murder, The* (1959) d: Otto Preminger   PR

☐ *And Now for Something Completely Different* (British/ 1972) d: Ian McNaughton   CM

☐ *And the Ship Sails On* (Italian/ 1984) d: Federico Fellini

☐ *Andrei Rublev* (Russian/1966) d: Andrei Tarkovsky   H CM

☐ *Angel Baby* (1961) d: Hubert Cornfield, Paul Wendkos   S CM

☐ *Angel Face* (1953) d: Otto Preminger

☐ *Angelo, My Love* (1983) d: Robert Duvall

☐ *Angels Hard As They Come* (1971) d: Joe Viola   CM

☐ *Angels in the Outfield* (1951) d: Clarence Brown   PR

☐ *Angels Over Broadway* (1940) d: Ben Hecht, Lee Garmes

☐ *Angi Vera* (Hungarian/1979) d: Pál Gabor

☐ *Animal Farm* (British/1955) d: John Halas, Joy Batchelor   PR

☐ *Anna and the King of Siam* (1946) d: John Cromwell

☐ *Anna Christie* (1930) d: Clarence Brown   H

☐ *Anna Karenina* (1935) d: Clarence Brown   H

☐ *Anniversary, The* (British/1968) d: Roy Ward Baker

☐ *Another Thin Man* (1939) d: W.S. Van Dyke

☐ *Apartment, The* (1960) d: Billy Wilder   H

☐ *Applause* (1929) d: Rouben Mamoulian   H

☐ *Apprenticeship of Duddy Kravitz, The* (Canadian/1974) d: Ted Kotcheff   PR

☐ *Arabian Nights* (Italian-French/ 1974) d: Pier Paolo Pasolini

☐ *Argent, L'* (French-Swiss/1983) d: Robert Bresson   PR

☐ *Around the World in Eighty Days* (1956) d: Michael Anderson   H

☐ *Arrowsmith* (1931) d: John Ford   H

☐ *Arthur* (1981) d: Steve Gordon

☐ *Artists and Models* (1955) d: Frank Tashlin

☐ *Asphyx, The* (British/1972) d: Peter Newbrook   S

☐ *Assassination Bureau, The* (British/1969) d: Basil Deardon   CM

☐ *At Long Last Love* (1975) d: Peter Bogdanovich   CC

☐ *At the Circus* (1939) d: Edward Buzzell

☐ *At War with the Army* (1951) d: Hal Walker   H

☐ *Atalante, L'* (French/1934) d: Jean Vigo   H PR

☐ *Attack of the Crab Monsters* (1957) d: Roger Corman   CC

☐ *Au Hasard, Balthazar* (French/ 1966) d: Robert Bresson   H PR

☐ *Avanti!* (1972) d: Billy Wilder

☐ *Awful Dr. Orloff, The* (Spanish/ 1961) d: Jess Franco

☐ *Babes in Arms* (1939) d: Busby Berkeley   H

☐ *Baby, The* (1973) d: Ted Post   CC

☐ *Baby Face* (1977) d: Alex DeRenzy   XXX

☐ *Baby Face Nelson* (1957) d: Don Siegel   H

☐ *Baby, It's You* (1983) d: John Sayles   CM PR

☐ *Baby Snakes* (1979) d: Frank Zappa   CM

☐ *Baby, the Rain Must Fall* (1965) d: Robert Mulligan   S

☐ *Bachelor Flat* (1961) d: Frank Tashlin

☐ *Back Street* (1932) d: John M. Stahl

☐ *Bad and the Beautiful, The* (1952) d: Vincente Minnelli   PR

☐ *Bad Boys* (1983) d: Rick Rosenthal   CM

☐ *Bad Company* (1972) d: Robert Benton   S CM PR

☐ *Bad Day at Black Rock* (1954) d: John Sturges   CM PR

☐ *Bad Girl* (British/1959) d: Herbert Wilcox   S

☐ *Bad News Bears, The* (1976) d: Michael Ritchie   PR

☐ *Bad Seed, The* (1956) d: Mervyn LeRoy   CM

☐ *Bad Timing/Sensual Obsession, A*

(British/1980) d: Nicolas Roeg
CM

□ *Badman's Country* (1958) d: Fred F. Sears

□ *Bait* (1954) d: Hugo Haas CC

□ *Bal, Le* (French/1982) d: Ettore Scola

□ *Balance, La* (French/1982) d: Bob Swaim

□ *Ball of Fire* (1941) d: Howard Hawks H

□ *Ballad of Gregorio Cortez, The* (1982) d: Robert M. Young

□ *Barbara Broadcast* (1977) d: Henry Paris (Radley Metzger) XXX CM

□ *Barbary Coast* (1935) d: Howard Hawks

□ *Barbed Wire Dolls* (Mexican/1979) d: Jesus Franco T

□ *Barefoot Contessa, The* (1954) d: Joseph L. Mankiewicz

□ *Barefoot in the Park* (1967) d: Gene Saks

□ *Barkleys of Broadway, The* (1949) d: Charles Walters

□ *Baron Blood* (Italian/1972) d: Mario Bava

□ *Barrier* (Polish/1966) d: Jerzy Skolimowski

□ *Barry Lyndon* (British/1975) d: Stanley Kubrick CM

□ *Battle Cry* (1955) d: Raoul Walsh

□ *Battle Hymn* (1957) d: Douglas Sirk

□ *Battle of San Pietro, The* (1945) d: John Huston H

□ *Battling Butler, The* (1926) d: Buster Keaton PR

□ *Beach Blanket Bingo* (1965) d: William Asher CC

□ *Beach Red* (1967) d: Cornel Wilde

□ *Beast with Five Fingers, The* (1946) d: Robert Florey

□ *Beat Generation, The* (1959) d: Charles Haas

□ *Beau Geste* (1939) d: William Wellman H

□ *Beau Serge, Le* (French/1958) d: Claude Chabrol H PR

□ *Beautiful Blonde from Bashful Bend, The* (1949) d: Preston Sturges

□ *Becket* (1964) d: Peter Glenville H

□ *Bed-Sitting Room, The* (British/1969) d: Richard Lester CM

□ *Bedford Incident, The* (1965) d: James B. Harris

□ *Before I Hang* (1940) d: Nick Grinde

□ *Before the Revolution* (French-Italian/1964) d: Bernardo Bertolucci PR

□ *Beggars of Life* (1928) d: William Wellman H

□ *Beginning of the End* (1957) d: Bert I. Gordon

□ *Beginning or the End, The* (1947) d: Norman Taurog

□ *Being There* (1979) d: Hal Ashby

□ *Bela Lugosi Meets the Brooklyn Gorilla* (1952) d: William Beaudine CC

□ *Belle of the Nineties* (1934) d: Leo McCarey

□ *Belles of St. Trinian's* (British/1955) d: Frank Launder

□ *Below the Belt* (1980) d: Robert Fowler S

□ *Beneath the Valley of the Ultravixens* (1979) d: Russ Meyer CM

□ *Ben-Hur* (1926) d: Fred Niblo H

□ *Benji* (1974) d: Joe Camp

□ *Berlin Express* (1948) d: Jacques Tourneur

□ *Berserk* (British/1967) d: Jim O'Connolly

□ *Best Friends* (1982) d: Norman Jewison PR

□ *Betrayal* (British/1983) d: David Jones PR

□ *Between Heaven and Hell* (1956) d: Richard Fleischer S PR

□ *Beyond a Reasonable Doubt* (1956) d: Fritz Lang

□ *Beyond the Forest* (1949) d: King Vidor

□ *Beyond the Law* (1968) d: Norman Mailer

□ *Beyond the Limit* (1983) d: John MacKenzie S

□ *Big Beat, The* (1958) d: Will Cowan CC

□ *Big Bird Cage, The* (1972) d: Jack Hill CC CM

□ *Big Brawl, The* (1980) d: Robert Clouse

□ *Big Broadcast of 1938, The* (1938) d: Mitchell Leisen PR

□ *Big Bus, The* (1976) d: James Frawley

□ *Big Clock, The* (1948) d: John Farrow

□ *Big Combo, The* (1955) d: Joseph H. Lewis CM

□ *Big Country, The* (1958) d: William Wyler

□ *Big Deal on Madonna Street* (Italian/1956) d: Mario Monicelli H

□ *Big Fix, The* (1978) d: Jeremy Paul Kagan CM

□ *Big House, The* (1930) d: George Hill H PR

□ *Big Knife, The* (1955) d: Robert Aldrich

□ *Big Parade, The* (1925) d: King Vidor H PR

□ *Big Sky, The* (1952) d: Howard Hawks

□ *Big Street, The* (1942) d: Irving Reis

□ *Big T.N.T. Show, The* (1966) d: Larry Peerce

□ *Big Trail, The* (1930) d: Raoul Walsh H

□ *Big Wednesday* (1978) d: John Milius CM

□ *Bigamist, The* (1953) d: Ida Lupino

□ *Bigger Than Life* (1956) d: Nicholas Ray PR

□ *Billion Dollar Brain* (British/1967) d: Ken Russell

□ *Billy Budd* (British-American/1962) d: Peter Ustinov

□ *Billy Jack Goes to Washington* (1977) d: Tom Laughlin CM

□ *Billy Liar* (British/1963) d: John Schlesinger

□ *Billy the Kid vs. Dracula* (1966) d: William Beaudine CC

□ *Birch Interval* (1977) d: Delbert Mann S

□ *Birdman of Alcatraz* (1962) d: John Frankenheimer

□ *Birdy* (1984) d: Alan Parker

□ *Birgit Haas Must Be Killed* (French/1981) d: Laurent Heynemann

□ *Birth of the Blues* (1941) d: Victor Schertzinger

□ *Bitch, The* (British/1979) d: Gerry O'Hara CC

□ *Bite the Bullet* (1975) d: Richard Brooks

□ *Bitter Tea of General Yen, The* (1933) d: Frank Capra H

□ *Bitter Tears of Petra Von Kant, The* (West German/1973) d: Rainer Werner Fassbinder PR

□ *Bitter Victory* (French/1958) d: Nicholas Ray

□ *Bizarre, Bizarre* (French/1937)

d: Marcel Carne

☐ *Black and White in Color* (French-West German-Ivory Coast/1977) d: Jean-Jacques Annaud

☐ *Black Belt Jones* (1974) d: Robert Clouse

☐ *Black Friday* (1940) d: Arthur Lubin

☐ *Black Fury* (1935) d: Michael Curtiz   PR

☐ *Black Girl* (1972) d: Ossie Davis

☐ *Black Legion* (1936) d: Archie Mayo   H

☐ *Black Like Me* (1946) d: Carl Lerner

☐ *Black Pirate, The* (1926) d: Albert Parker   H

☐ *Black Room, The* (1935) d: Roy William Neill

☐ *Black Sabbath* (Italian/1964) d: Mario Bava

☐ *Black Windmill, The* (British/1974) d: Don Siegel

☐ *Blackboard Jungle, The* (1955) d: Richard Brooks   H PR

☐ *Blackmail* (British/1929) d: Alfred Hitchcock   H PR

☐ *Blindman* (Italian/1972) d: Ferdinando Baldi   CM

☐ *Blonde Bombshell/Bombshell* (1933) d: Victor Fleming   PR

☐ *Blood and Black Lace* (Italian-French-German/1964) d: Mario Bava   CM

☐ *Blood and Roses* (Italian/1961) d: Roger Vadim   CM

☐ *Blood and Sand* (1922) d: Fred Niblo   H

☐ *Blood and Sand* (1940) d: Rouben Mamoulian

☐ *Blood Bath* (1966) d: Stephanie Rothman, Jack Hill

☐ *Blood from the Mummy's Tomb* (British/1972) d: Seth Holt

☐ *Blood on Satan's Claw, The* (British/1971) d: Piers Haggard   CM

☐ *Bloody Mama* (1970) d: Roger Corman   CM

☐ *Blue Dahlia, The* (1946) d: George Marshall   PR

☐ *Blue Lagoon, The* (British/1949) d: Frank Launder   H

☐ *Blue Light* (German/1932) d: Leni Riefenstahl

☐ *Blue Sunshine* (1976) d: Jeff Lieberman   CM

☐ *Blue Thunder* (1983) d: John Badham

☐ *Bluebeard* (French/1963) d: Claude Chabrol

☐ *Bluebeard's Eighth Wife* (1938) d: Ernst Lubitsch

☐ *Blues in the Night* (1941) d: Anatole Litvak

☐ *Blume in Love* (1973) d: Paul Mazursky   CM PR

☐ *Bobbie Jo and the Outlaw* (1976) d: Mark L. Lester

☐ *Bohemian Girl, The* (1936) d: James Horne, Charles R. Rogers

☐ *Bonjour Tristesse* (1958) d: Otto Preminger

☐ *Bonnie Parker Story, The* (1958) d: William Witney   CC

☐ *Boogeyman, The* (1980) d: Ulli Lommell   S

☐ *Boom Town* (1940) d: Jack Conway

☐ *Born in Flames* (1983) d: Lizzie Borden   CM

☐ *Born Losers* (1967) d: T.C. Frank (Tom Laughlin)   CM

☐ *Born to Kill* (1947) d: Robert Wise   S

☐ *Born to Win* (1971) d: Ivan Passer   S

☐ *Bostonians, The* (British/1984) d: James Ivory

☐ *Bound for Glory* (1976) d: Hal Ashby   PR

☐ *Bounty, The* (1984) d: Roger Donaldson   PR

☐ *Bowery, The* (1933) d: Raoul Walsh   H

☐ *Boxcar Bertha* (1972) d: Martin Scorsese   CM PR

☐ *Boy/Shonen* (Japanese/1969) d: Nagisa Oshima   PR

☐ *Boy Ten Feet Tall, A/Sammy Going South* (British/1963) d: Alexander Mackendrick

☐ *Boys Town* (1938) d: Norman Taurog   H

☐ *Brain from Planet Arous, The* (1958) d: Nathan Juran   CC

☐ *Bread and Chocolate* (Italian/1978) d: Franco Brusati   PR

☐ *Breaker Morant* (Australian/1979) d: Bruce Beresford   H PR

☐ *Breakin'* (1984) d: Joel Silberg   CM

☐ *Breaking Away* (1979) d: Peter Yates   PR

☐ *Breaking the Sound Barrier* (British/1952) d: David Lean   H

☐ *Breathless* (1983) d: Jim McBride

☐ *Brewster's Millions* (1945) d: Allan Dwan   H

☐ *Bride of the Gorilla* (1951) d: Curt Siodmak   CC

☐ *Bride Wore Black, The* (French/1968) d: François Truffaut   PR

☐ *Brides of Dracula, The* (British/1960) d: Terence Fisher

☐ *Bridge, The* (West German/1960) d: Bernhard Wicki   H

☐ *Bring Me the Head of Alfredo Garcia* (1974) d: Sam Peckinpah   CM

☐ *Bring on the Night* (1985) d: Michael Apted   PR

☐ *Britannia Hospital* (British/1982) d: Lindsay Anderson   CM

☐ *Broadway Melody* (1929) d: Harry Beaumont   H

☐ *Broken Arrow* (1950) d: Delmer Daves

☐ *Brontë Sisters, The* (French/1979) d: André Techine   CM

☐ *Brother Orchid* (1940) d: Lloyd Bacon

☐ *Brothers Rico, The* (1957) d: Phil Karlson

☐ *Brute Force* (1947) d: Jules Dassin   H

☐ *Brute Man* (1946) d: Jean Yarbrough   CC

☐ *Bucket of Blood, A* (1959) d: Roger Corman   CC CM

☐ *Buddies* (1985) d: Arthur Bresson   H

☐ *Buffalo Bill* (1944) d: William Wellman

☐ *Buffalo Bill and the Indians, or Sitting Bull's History Lesson* (1976) d: Robert Altman

☐ *Burglar, The* (1956) d: Paul Wendkos

☐ *Burn, Witch, Burn!/Night of the Eagle* (British/1962) d: Sidney Hayers   S PR

☐ *Burroughs* (1983) d: Howard Brookman

☐ *Butch and Sundance: The Early Years* (1979) d: Richard Lester   S PR

☐ *Bwana Devil* (1952) d: Arch Oboler

☐ *Bye Bye Brazil* (Brazilian/1980) d: Carlos Diegues

☐ *Cabin in the Cotton* (1932) d: Michael Curtiz   H

☐ *Caddyshack* (1980) d: Harold Ramis

□ *Café Express* (Italian/1981) d: Nanni Loy

□ *Caged* (1950) d: John Cromwell

□ *California Dreaming* (1979) d: John Hancock   S

□ *California Split* (1974) d: Robert Altman

□ *Call Northside 777* (1948) d: Henry Hathaway   PR

□ *Call of the Wild* (1935) d: William Wellman

□ *Calling Dr. Death* (1943) d: Reginald LeBorg

□ *Cameraman, The* (1928) d: Edward Sedgwick, Jr.   PR

□ *Camille* (1936) d: George Cukor   H   PR

□ *Camille 2000* (1969) d: Radley Metzger

□ *Can Hieronymous Merkin Ever Forget Mercy Humppe and Find True Happiness?* (British/ 1969) d: Anthony Newley   CM   PR

□ *Can She Bake a Cherry Pie?* (1983) d: Henry Jaglom   CM

□ *Canary Murder Case* (1929) d: Malcolm St. Clair   H

□ *Candidate, The* (1972) d: Michael Ritchie   PR

□ *Candy* (1968) d: Christian Marquand   CC

□ *Cannonball* (1976) d: Paul Bartel

□ *Cannonball Run, The* (1981) d: Hal Needham

□ *Canterbury Tales, The* (Italian-French/1972) d: Pier Paolo Pasolini   H

□ *Canterville Ghost, The* (1944) d: Jules Dassin

□ *Canyon Passage* (1946) d: Jacques Tourneur

□ *Capricorn One* (1978) d: Peter Hyams

□ *Captain Horatio Hornblower* (1951) d: Raoul Walsh

□ *Captains Courageous* (1937) d: Victor Fleming   H   PR

□ *Captive Wild Woman* (1943) d: Edward Dmytryk

□ *Car Wash* (1976) d: Michael Schultz

□ *Carabiniers, Les* (French/1963) d: Jean-Luc Godard   PR

□ *Carmen* (Spanish/1983) d: Carlos Saura

□ *Carmen* (French-Italian/1984) d: Francesco Rosi

□ *Carmen Jones* (1954) d: Otto Preminger   H   PR

□ *Carnival in Flanders* (French/ 1935) d: Jacques Feyder

□ *Carny* (1980) d: Robert Kaylor   CM   PR

□ *Carousel* (1956) d: Henry King

□ *Carpetbaggers, The* (1964) d: Edward Dmytryk

□ *Carrie* (1952) d: William Wyler

□ *Carry on Nurse* (British/1960) d: Gerald Thomas

□ *Cartouche* (French-Italian/1964) d: Philippe de Broca   PR

□ *Case Against Brooklyn, The* (1958) d: Paul Wendkos

□ *Casque d'Or* (French/1952) d: Jacques Becker   H

□ *Castle, The* (German-Swiss/1968) d: Rudolf Noelte   CM

□ *Castle Keep* (1969) d: Sydney Pollack

□ *Castle of the Living Dead* (Italian-French/1964) d: Herbert Wise (Luciano Ricci) and Michael Reeves

□ *Cat and the Canary, The* (1927) d: Paul Leni   H   PR

□ *Cat and the Canary, The* (1939) d: Elliott Nugent

□ *Cat Ballou* (1965) d: Elliot Silverstein

□ *Cat on a Hot Tin Roof* (1958) d: Richard Brooks

□ *Cat Women of the Moon* (1954) d: Arthur Hilton   CC

□ *Catch-22* (1970) d: Mike Nichols   CM

□ *Cat's Eye* (1985) d: Lewis Teague

□ *Cattle Annie and Little Britches* (1980) d: Lamont Johnson   CM

□ *Cattle Queen of Montana* (1954) d: Allan Dwan

□ *Caught* (1949) d: Max Ophüls   H   PR

□ *Caught in the Draft* (1941) d: David Butler

□ *Ceiling Zero* (1935) d: Howard Hawks   H   PR

□ *Ceremony, The* (Japanese/1971) d: Nagisa Oshima

□ *Champ, The* (1931) d: King Vidor   H

□ *Champagne Murders, The* (French/1967) d: Claude Chabrol   PR

□ *Chang* (1927) d: Merian C. Cooper, Ernest B. Schoedsack   H

□ *Changeling, The* (Canadian/1979) d: Peter Medak   S

□ *Chant of Jimmie Blacksmith, The* (Australian/1978) d: Fred Schepisi   CM

□ *Chapman Report, The* (1962) d: George Cukor

□ *Chappaqua* (1967) d: Conrad Rooks   CM

□ *Charade* (1963) d: Stanley Donen

□ *Charge of the Light Brigade, The* (1936) d: Michael Curtiz

□ *Chariots of Fire* (British/1981) d: Hugh Hudson   H

□ *Charles—Dead or Alive* (Swiss/ 1969) d: Alain Tanner   H   PR

□ *Charley Varrick* (1973) d: Don Siegel   S

□ *Charlie Bubbles* (1968) d: Albert Finney   CM

□ *Charlie Chan at the Opera* (1937) d: H. Bruce Humberstone

□ *Charlie Chan at Treasure Island* (1939) d: Norman Foster

□ *Chastity* (1969) d: Alessio de Paola   S

□ *Cheaper by the Dozen* (1950) d: Walter Lang

□ *Cheerleaders, The* (1973) d: Richard Lerner   CC

□ *Chelsea Girls, The* (1966) d: Andy Warhol   H

□ *Cheyenne Autumn* (1964) d: John Ford   PR

□ *Chienne, La* (French/1931) d: Jean Renoir   H   PR

□ *Child Is Waiting, A* (1963) d: John Cassavetes

□ *Child Under a Leaf* (Canadian/ 1974) d: George Bloomfield

□ *Children of the Damned* (British/ 1964) d: Antone Leader   S

□ *Children's Hour, The* (1962) d: William Wyler

□ *China Is Near* (Italian/1967) d: Marco Bellocchio

□ *China Gate* (1957) d: Samuel Fuller   CM

□ *Chinese Roulette* (West German/ 1976) d: Rainer Werner Fassbinder

□ *Chloe in the Afternoon* (French/ 1972) d: Eric Rohmer   H   PR

□ *Chosen, The* (1981) d: Jeremy Paul Kagan   PR

□ *Christ Stopped at Eboli* (Italian/ 1979) d: Francesco Rosi   H

□ *Christine Jorgensen Story, The* (1970) d: Irving Rapper   CC

□ *Christmas Holiday* (1944) d: Robert Siodmak

□ *Christmas in July* (1940) d: Preston Sturges H

□ *Christopher Strong* (1933) d: Dorothy Arzner H

□ *Cimarron* (1960) d: Anthony Mann

□ *Cinderella* (1950) d: Wilfred Jackson, Hamilton Luske, Clyde Geronimi PR

□ *Circle of Deceit* (French-German/ 1981) d: Volker Schlöndorff

□ *Circle of Iron* (1979) d: Richard Moore CM

□ *Circus of Horrors* (British/1960) d: Sidney Hayers

□ *Citadel* (British/1938) d: King Vidor

□ *City for Conquest* (1940) d: Anatole Litvak S PR

□ *City Girl* (1984) d: Martha Coolidge

□ *City of Women* (Italian/1981) d: Federico Fellini

□ *City Streets* (1931) d: Rouben Mamoulian H

□ *Claire's Knee* (French/1971) d: Eric Rohmer H PR

□ *Claudine* (1974) d: John Berry S

□ *Cleo from 5 to 7* (French/1962) d: Agnès Varda H

□ *Cleopatra* (1963) d: Joseph L. Mankiewicz S CC

□ *Cloak and Dagger* (1946) d: Fritz Lang

□ *Clockmaker, The* (French/1973) d: Bernard Tavernier H

□ *Clonus Horror, The/Parts: The Clonus Horror* (1978) d: Robert S. Fiveson

□ *Cloud Dancer* (1980) d: Barry Brown

□ *Cluny Brown* (1946) d: Ernst Lubitsch H PR

□ *Cobweb, The* (1955) d: Vincente Minnelli

□ *Cockfighter/Born to Kill* (1974) d: Monte Hellman CM

□ *Cocktail Molotov* (French/1980) d: Diane Kurys

□ *Coffy* (1973) d: Jack Hill

□ *Cold Turkey* (1971) d: Norman Lear CM

□ *Collector, The* (1965) d: William Wyler CM PR

□ *College* (1927) d: James W. Horne PR

□ *College Confidential* (1960) d: Albert Zugsmith CC

□ *Color Me Blood Red* (1965) d: Herschell Gordon Lewis CM T

□ *Colorado Territory* (1949) d: Raoul Walsh PR

□ *Colossus of New York, The* (1958) d: Eugene Lourie

□ *Come Back Africa* (American- South African/1959) d: Lionel Rogosin H PR

□ *Come Back, Little Sheba* (1952) d: Daniel Mann

□ *Comedy of Terrors, The* (1964) d: Jacques Tourneur

□ *Comes a Horseman* (1978) d: Alan J. Pakula S

□ *Coming Apart* (1969) d: Milton Moses Ginsberg CM

□ *Command, The* (1954) d: David Butler H

□ *Comperes, Les* (French/1983) d: Frances Veber

□ *Competition, The* (1980) d: Joel Oliansky

□ *Compulsion* (1959) d: Richard Fleischer PR

□ *Confession, The* (French/1970) d: Costa-Gavras H

□ *Confessions of a Nazi Spy* (1939) d: Anatole Litvak H

□ *Confessions of a Window Cleaner* (British/1974) d: Val Guest CM

□ *Confessions of an Opium Eater* (1962) d: Albert Zugsmith

□ *Confidentially Yours* (French/ 1983) d: François Truffaut S

□ *Connecticut Yankee in King Arthur's Court, A* (1949) d: Tay Garnett

□ *Connection, The* (1961) d: Shirley Clarke H PR

□ *Conqueror, The* (1956) d: Dick Powell CC

□ *Conquest* (1937) d: Clarence Brown PR

□ *Conquest of Space* (1955) d: Byron Haskin

□ *Conquest of the Planet of the Apes* (1972) d: J. Lee Thompson S PR

□ *Contest Girl* (British/1965) d: Val Guest S

□ *Continental Divide* (1981) d: Michael Apted S PR

□ *Convoy* (1978) d: Sam Peckinpah

□ *Cool and Crazy, The* (1958) d: William Witney CC S PR

□ *Cool Hand Luke* (1967) d: Stuart Rosenberg

□ *Cool World* (1964) d: Shirley Clarke H PR

□ *Cooley High* (1975) d: Michael Schultz

□ *Corn Is Green, The* (1945) d: Irving Rapper

□ *Cornbread, Earl, and Me* (1975) d: Joe Manduke S

□ *Corpse Grinders, The* (1971) d: Ted V. Mikels T

□ *Corpse Vanishes, The* (1942) d: Wallace Fox

□ *Cotton Comes to Harlem* (1970) d: Ossie Davis CM

□ *Count of Monte Cristo, The* (1934) d: Rowland V. Lee H

□ *Countdown* (1968) d: Robert Altman

□ *Countess Dracula* (British/1972) d: Peter Sasdy

□ *Countess from Hong Kong, A* (British/1967) d: Charles Chaplin CM

□ *Country* (1984) d: Richard Pearce

□ *Country Girl, The* (1954) d: George Seaton H

□ *Country Man, The* (Jamaican/ 1982) d: Dickie Jobson CM

□ *Coup de Torchon* (French/1981) d: Bertrand Tavernier H

□ *Court Jester, The* (1956) d: Norman Panama, Melvin Frank

□ *Cousin Angelica* (Spanish/1974) d: Carlos Saura

□ *Cousin, Cousine* (French/1975) d: Jean-Charles Tacchella CM

□ *Cover Girl* (1944) d: Charles Vidor

□ *Covered Wagon, The* (1923) d: James Cruze H

□ *Crack in the Mirror* (1960) d: Richard Fleischer

□ *Crack in the World* (1965) d: Andrew Marton

□ *Craig's Wife* (1936) d: Dorothy Arzner H

□ *Crazies, The/Code Name: Trixie* (1973) d: George Romero S

□ *Crazy Quilt* (1966) d: John Korty

□ *Crazylegs* (1953) d: Francis D. Lyon

□ *Creation of the Humanoids* (1962) d: Wesley E. Barrie CC CM

□ *Creature from the Haunted Sea* (1961) d: Roger Corman CC

□ *Creeper, The* (1948) d: Jean Yarbrough CC

□ *Creeping Unknown, The/ Quatermass Experiment, The* (British/1956) d: Val Guest

□ *Crime and Punishment* (1935) d: Josef von Sternberg   H

□ *Crime in the Streets* (1956) d: Don Siegel   CM

□ *Crime without Passion* (1934) d: Ben Hecht, Charles MacArthur   CM

□ *Crimes of the Future* (Canadian/ 1970) d: David Cronenberg   CM

□ *Crossfire* (1947) d: Edward Dmytryk   H

□ *Cruising* (1980) d: William Friedkin

□ *Cry of the City* (1948) d: Robert Siodmak

□ *Cry of the Hunted* (1953) d: Joseph H. Lewis

□ *Cry of the Penguins/Mr. Forbush and the Penguins* (British/1971) d: Roy Boulting, Arne Sucksdorff   PR

□ *Cry Terror* (1958) d: Andrew L. Stone

□ *Cry the Beloved Country* (British/ 1951) d: Zoltan Korda   H

□ *Cry Tough* (1959) d: Paul Stanley

□ *Cuba* (1979) d: Richard Lester   S

□ *Cuban Rebel Girls* (1959) d: Barry Mahon   CC

□ *Cul-de-Sac* (British/1966) d: Roman Polanski   CM PR

□ *Curse of the Werewolf, The* (British/1961) d: Terence Fisher

□ *Curtains* (Canadian/1983) d: Jonathan Stryker   PR

□ *Custer of the West* (American-Spanish/1968) d: Robert Siodmak

□ *Daddy Long Legs* (1955) d: Jean Negulesco

□ *Daddy's Gone A-Hunting* (1969) d: Mark Robson

□ *Daisy Kenyon* (1947) d: Otto Preminger

□ *Daisy Miller* (1974) d: Peter Bogdanovich

□ *Dames du Bois de Boulogne, Les* (French/1945) d: Robert Bresson   H PR

□ *Damned, The* (Italian-West German/1969) d: Luchino Visconti   H

□ *Dance With a Stranger* (British/

1985) d: Mike Newell   CM PR

□ *Dancing Lady* (1933) d: Robert Z. Leonard   H

□ *Dangerous* (1935) d: Alfred E. Green

□ *Dangerous Moves* (Swiss/1985) d: Richard Dembo

□ *Daniel* (1983) d: Sidney Lumet

□ *Dante's Inferno* (1935) d: Harry Lachman

□ *Danton* (Polish-French/1982) d: Andrzej Wajda

□ *Darby O'Gill and the Little People* (1959) d: Robert Stevenson

□ *Dark Command* (1940) d: Raoul Walsh   PR

□ *Dark Crystal, The* (British/1983) d: Jim Henson, Frank Oz

□ *Dark End of the Street, The* (1981) d: Jan Egleson   PR

□ *Dark Passage* (1947) d: Delmer Daves

□ *Darling* (British/1965) d: John Schlesinger

□ *Darling Lili* (1970) d: Blake Edwards

□ *Daughter of Dr. Jekyll* (1957) d: Edgar G. Ulmer   CC

□ *David and Lisa* (1963) d: Frank Perry   PR

□ *David Copperfield* (1935) d: George Cukor   H

□ *David Holzman's Diary* (1968) d: Jim McBride   H CM PR

□ *Davy Crockett, King of the Wild Frontier* (1955) d: Norman Foster   H CM PR

□ *Dawn Patrol, The* (1930) d: Howard Hawks   H PR

□ *Dawn Patrol, The* (1938) d: Edmund Goulding

□ *Day at the Races, A* (1937) d: Sam Wood   PR

□ *Day in the Country, A* (French/ 1936) d: Jean Renoir   H

□ *Day of the Dolphin, The* (1973) d: Mike Nichols

□ *Day of the Jackal, The* (British-French/1973) d: Fred Zinnemann

□ *Day of the Locust, The* (1975) d: John Schlesinger

□ *Days and Nights in the Forests* (Indian/1970) d: Satyajit Ray   PR

□ *Days of Glory* (1944) d: Jacques Tourneur

□ *Days of Wine and Roses* (1962)

d: Blake Edwards

□ *Dead and Buried* (1981) d: Gary Sherman

□ *Dead Easy* (1984) d: Bert Deling

□ *Dead Pigeon on Beethoven Street* (German/1972) d: Samuel Fuller

□ *Dead Reckoning* (1947) d: John Cromwell

□ *Deadhead Miles* (1972) d: Vernon Zimmerman   CM

□ *Deadly Companions* (1961) d: Sam Peckinpah   S

□ *Dealing: or The Berkeley-to-Boston Forty-Brick Lost-Bag Blues* (1972) d: Paul Williams   CM PR

□ *Death By Hanging* (Japanese/ 1968) d: Nagisa Oshima   PR

□ *Death in Venice* (Italian/1971) d: Luchino Visconti   H

□ *Death of a Cyclist/Age of Infidelity* (Spanish/1955) d: Juan Antonio Bardem   H

□ *Death of a Gunfighter* (1962) d: Allen Smithee (Robert Totten, Don Siegel)

□ *Death of a Salesman* (1951) d: Laslo Benedek

□ *Death Takes a Holiday* (1934) d: Mitchell Leisen   H

□ *Deathsport* (1978) d: Henry Suso, Allan Arkush

□ *Death Watch* (French-West German/1980) d: Bertrand Tavernier   CM

□ *Decline of Western Civilization* (1985) d: Penelope Spheeris   CM PR

□ *Deep Inside Annie Sprinkle* (1981) d: Annie Sprinkle   XXX

□ *Defiance* (1974) d: Armond Weston   XXX

□ *Defiant Ones, The* (1958) d: Stanley Kramer   H

□ *Delinquents, The* (1957) d: Robert Altman

□ *Demon Pond* (Japanese/1980) d: Masahiro Shinoda   H

□ *Deranged* (1974) d: Jeff Gillen, Alan Ormsby   CM

□ *Derby* (1971) d: Robert Kaylor   S

□ *Dernier Combat, Le* (French/ 1983) d: Luc Besson   CM

□ *Designing Woman* (1957) d: Vincente Minnelli

□ *Desire* (1936) d: Frank Borzage

□ *Desiree* (1954) d: Henry Koster

- Desk Set (1957) d: Walter Lang
- Despair (West German/1979) d: Rainer Werner Fassbinder CM
- Desperate Characters (1971) d: Frank D. Gilroy S PR
- Desperate Hours, The (1955) d: William Wyler
- Desperate Journey (1942) d: Raoul Walsh
- Destination Tokyo (1943) d: Delmer Daves
- Destroy All Monsters! (Japanese/ 1968) d: Inoshiro Honda CC
- Detective, The/Father Brown (1954) d: Robert Hamer
- Detective Story (1951) d: William Wyler
- Devi (Indian/1960) d: Satyajit Ray H PR
- Devil and Daniel Webster, The (1941) d: William Dieterle
- Devil and Miss Jones, The (1941) d: Sam Wood
- Devil Commands, The (1941) d: Edward Dmytryk
- Devil Doll (British/1964) d: Lindsay Shonteff S PR
- Devil's Disciple (British/1959) d: Guy Hamilton
- Devil's Doorway (1950) d: Anthony Mann CM
- Devil's Playground, The (Australian/1976) d: Fred Schepisi
- D.I., The (1957) d: Jack Webb
- Diary of a Chambermaid (1946) d: Jean Renoir H PR
- Diary of a Chambermaid (French-Italian/1964) d: Luis Buñuel H PR
- Diary of a Lost Girl (German/ 1929) d: G.W. Pabst H CM PR
- Diary of a Mad Housewife (1970) d: Frank Perry CM
- Diary of a Shinjuko Thief (Japanese/1968) d: Nagisa Oshima H
- Diary of Anne Frank, The (1959) d: George Stevens H
- Different Story, A (1978) d: Paul Aaron
- Dillinger (1945) d: Max Nosseck S
- Dillinger (1973) d: John Milius
- Dime With a Halo (1963) d: Boris Sagal S PR
- Directed by John Ford (1971) d: Peter Bogdanovich

- Dirty Little Billy (1972) d: Stan Dragoti S
- Dirty Mary Crazy Larry (1974) d: John Hough CM
- Dirty Money (French/1972) d: Jean-Pierre Melville PR
- Dishonored (1931) d: Josef von Sternberg CM
- Disorderly Orderly, The (1964) d: Frank Tashlin
- Disraeli (1929) d: Alfred E. Green H
- Divine Madness! (1980) d: Michael Ritchie CM
- Divorce, Italian Style (Italian/ 1962) d: Pietro Germi H PR
- Doc (1971) d: Frank Perry
- Docks of New York, The (1928) d: Josef von Sternberg H
- Doctor and the Devils, The (British/1985) d: Freddie Francis CM
- Dr. Bull (1933) d: John Ford
- Dr. Ehrlich's Magic Bullet (1940) d: William Dieterle H
- Doctor in the House (British/ 1954) d: Ralph Thomas
- Dr. Jekyll and Mr. Hyde (1920) d: John S. Robertson
- Dr. Jekyll and Mr. Hyde (1941) d: Victor Fleming
- Dr. Jekyll and Sister Hyde (British/1972) d: Roy Ward Baker CM
- Dr. Terror's House of Horrors (British/1965) d: Freddie Francis
- Doctor X (1932) d: Michael Curtiz H
- Doctor Zhivago (1965) d: David Lean
- Dodes'ka-den (Japanese/1970) d: Akira Kurosawa H PR
- Dodge City (1939) d: Michael Curtiz
- Dodsworth (1936) d: William Wyler H PR
- Dog Star Man (1965) d: Stan Brakhage H
- Dogs of War, The (1981) d: John Irvin
- $ (1972) d: Richard Brooks
- Doomed Love (Portuguese/1978) d: Manuel de Oliveira H CM
- Donkey Skin (French/1971) d: Jacques Demy
- Don's Party (Australian/1976) d: Bruce Beresford

- Don't Bother to Knock (1952) d: Roy Ward Baker
- Don't Knock the Rock (1957) d: Fred F. Sears CC
- Don't Look Back (1967) d: D.A. Pennebaker CM PR
- Donovan's Reef (1963) d: John Ford
- Doomwatch (British/1972) d: Peter Sasdy S
- Double Life, A (1947) d: George Cukor PR
- Double Suicide (Japanese/1969) d: Masahiro Shinoda
- Down Argentine Way (1940) d: Irving Cummings H
- Downhill Racer (1969) d: Michael Ritchie
- Dozens, The (1981) d: Christine Dall, Randall Conrad
- Dragnet (1954) d: Jack Webb H
- Dreamchild (British/1984) d: Gavin Millar S
- Dreamscape (1984) d: Joseph Ruben
- Dresser, The (British/1983) d: Peter Yates
- Drifters (British/1929) d: John Grierson H
- Drive-In (1976) d: Rod Amateau CM
- Drums (British/1938) d: Zoltan Korda H
- Drums Along the Mohawk (1939) d: John Ford H PR
- Drunken Angel (Japanese/1948) d: Akira Kurosawa H
- Duck, You Sucker/Fistful of Dynamite, A (Italian/1972) d: Sergio Leone CM PR
- Duel in the Sun (1946) d: King Vidor
- Duet for Cannibals (American-Swedish/1969) d: Susan Sontag H
- Dusty and Sweets McGee (1971) d: Floyd Mutrux CM
- Dutchman (British/1966) d: Anthony Harvey PR
- Dynamite Chicken (1971) d: Ernest Pintoff

- Each Dawn I Die (1939) d: William Keighley
- Eagle, The (1925) d: Clarence Brown
- Eagle and the Hawk, The (1933) d: Stuart Walker

□ *Early Summer* (Japanese/1951) d: Yasujiro Ozu PR

□ *Earthquake* (1974) d: Mark Robson

□ *Easy Living* (1937) d: Mitchell Leisen

□ *Easy Money* (1983) d: James Signorelli

□ *Eaten Alive* (1976) d: Tobe Hooper CM

□ *Eboli* (Italian/1979) d: Francesco Rosi

□ *Eclisse, L'/Eclipse, The* (Italian/1962) d: Michelangelo Antonioni H

□ *Edge of Darkness* (1943) d: Lewis Milestone

□ *Edge of Eternity* (1959) d: Don Siegel

□ *Edge of Hell* (1956) d: Hugo Haas CC

□ *Edge of the City* (1957) d: Martin Ritt

□ *Edvard Munch* (Norwegian/1976) d: Peter Watkins CM

□ *Edward, My Son* (British/1949) d: George Cukor

□ *Effect of Gamma Rays on Man-in-the-Moon Marigolds, The* (1972) d: Paul Newman

□ *Effi Briest* (West German/1974) d: Rainer Werner Fassbinder PR

□ *El Cid* (1961) d: Anthony Mann

□ *El Super* (1979) d: Leon Ichaso, Orlando Jimenez-Leal PR

□ *Electra* (Greek/1961) d: Michael Cacoyannis

□ *Electra Glide in Blue* (1973) d: James William Guerico CM

□ *Elephant Boy* (1937) d: Robert Flaherty, Zoltan Korda

□ *Elephant Man, The* (1980) d: David Lynch H CM

□ *Elmer Gantry* (1960) d: Richard Brooks PR

□ *Elusive Corporal, The* (French/1963) d: Jean Renoir

□ *Elvis: That's the Way It Is* (1970) d: Denis Sanders

□ *Emigrants, The* (Sweden/1971) d: Jan Troell H

□ *Empire of Passion* (Japanese/1978) d: Nagisi Oshima

□ *End of St. Petersburg, The* (Russian/1927) d: Vsevolod Pudovkin H

□ *End of the Road* (1970) d: Aram Avakian

□ *Endless Love* (1981) d: Franco Zeffirelli CC

□ *Endless Summer, The* (1966) d: Bruce Brown CM

□ *Enter Laughing* (1967) d: Carl Reiner PR

□ *Enter the Ninja* (1981) d: Menahem Golan CM

□ *Entertainer, The* (British/1960) d: Tony Richardson

□ *Entertaining Mr. Sloane* (British/1970) d: Douglas Hickox

□ *Entre Nous* (French/1983) d: Diane Kurys H CM

□ *Erendira* (Spain/1984) d: Ray Guerra

□ *Erotikon* (Swedish/1920) d: Mauritz Stiller H

□ *Errand Boy, The* (1961) d: Jerry Lewis CM PR

□ *Escape* (1940) d: Mervyn LeRoy

□ *Escape from Alcatraz* (1979) d: Don Siegel

□ *Escape to Witch Mountain* (1975) d: John Hough

□ *Eureka* (British/1984) d: Nicolas Roeg CM

□ *Europeans, The* (1979) d: James Ivory

□ *Even Dwarfs Started Small* (West German/1970) d: Werner Herzog H PR

□ *Evergreen* (British/1935) d: Victor Saville

□ *Every Man for Himself* (French-Swiss/1980) d: Jean-Luc Godard

□ *Executive Action* (1973) d: David Miller

□ *Exile, The* (1947) d: Max Ophüls

□ *Exodus* (1960) d: Otto Preminger

□ *Exorcist II: The Heretic* (1977) d: John Boorman CC

□ *Experience Preferred . . . But Not Essential* (British/1983) d: Peter Duffell

□ *Experiment in Terror* (1962) d: Blake Edwards PR

□ *Experiment Perilous* (1944) d: Jacques Tourneur

□ *Explosive Generation, The* (1961) d: Buzz Kulik

□ *Exposed* (1983) d: James Toback CM

□ *Eye for an Eye, An* (1981) d: Steve Carver CM

□ *Eye of the Needle* (1981) d: Richard Marquand PR

□ *Eyes of Laura Mars* (1978) d: Irvin Kershner

□ *Eyes Without a Face/Horror Chamber of Dr. Faustus, The/Yeux Sans Visage, Les* (French/1959) d: Georges Franju PR

□ *Eyewitness* (1981) d: Peter Yates S

□ *F for Fake* (French/1973) d: Orson Welles

□ *Fabulous Baron von Munchausen, The* (Czech/1961) d: Karel Zeman CM PR

□ *Fabulous World of Jules Verne, The* (Czech/1958) d: Karel Zeman

□ *Face Behind the Mask, The* (1941) d: Robert Florey S

□ *Face of Fire* (1959) d: Albert Band

□ *Face to Face* (Swedish/1976) d: Ingmar Bergman

□ *Faces* (1968) d: John Cassavetes H PR

□ *Falcon and the Snowman, The* (1985) d: John Schlesinger S PR

□ *Fall of the Roman Empire, The* (1964) d: Anthony Mann

□ *Fallen Angel* (1945) d: Otto Preminger

□ *Fallen Idol, The* (British/1948) d: Carol Reed

□ *Family Game, The* (Japanese/1983) d: Yusaku Matsuda

□ *Family Jewels, The* (1965) d: Jerry Lewis

□ *Family Plot* (1976) d: Alfred Hitchcock

□ *Fanny* (1961) d: Joshua Logan

□ *Fanny and Alexander* (Swedish/1983) d: Ingmar Bergman H

□ *Fantasies/And Once Upon a Love* (1981) d: John Derek

□ *Far from the Madding Crowd* (British/1967) d: John Schlesinger

□ *Far from Vietnam* (French/1967) d: Alain Resnais, William Klein, Joris Ivens, Agnès Varda, Claude Lelouch, Jean-Luc Godard

□ *Farewell, My Lovely* (1975) d: Dick Richards PR

□ *Farewell to Arms* (1932) d: Frank Borzage

□ *Farmer's Daughter, The* (1947) d: H.C. Potter

□ *Fat Man, The* (1951) d: William Castle

□ *Fata Morgana* (West German/

1971) d: Werner Herzog   H
PR

☐ *Father of the Bride* (1950) d: Vincente Minnelli

☐ *Faust* (German/1926) d: F.W. Murnau   H

☐ *Fear City* (1985) d: Abel Ferrara

☐ *Fearless Vampire Killers or: Pardon Me, But Your Teeth Are in My Neck, The* (British/1967) d: Roman Polanski   CM   PR

☐ *Fedora* (West German/1978) d: Billy Wilder

☐ *Fellini's Casanova* (Italian/1976) d: Federico Fellini

☐ *Fellini's Roma* (Italian/1972) d: Federico Fellini

☐ *Female Jungle/Hangover* (1956) d: Bruno VeSota

☐ *Femme Douce, Une* (French/1969) d: Robert Bresson   H
PR

☐ *Fiddler on the Roof* (1971) d: Norman Jewison   PR

☐ *Fiend Without a Face* (British/1958) d: Arthur Crabtree

☐ *Fifth Horseman Is Fear, The* (Czech/1965) d: Zbynek Brynych   H   PR

☐ *55 Days of Peking* (1963) d: Nicholas Ray

☐ *Fighting Mad* (1976) d: Jonathan Demme   CM

☐ *File on Thelma Jordan, The/ Thelma Jordan* (1949) d: Robert Siodmak

☐ *Fillmore* (1972) d: Richard T. Heffron

☐ *Finders Keepers* (1984) d: Richard Lester   S

☐ *Fine Madness, A* (1966) d: Irvin Kershner   S

☐ *Finian's Rainbow* (1968) d: Francis Ford Coppola

☐ *Finishing School* (1934) d: Wanda Tuchock, George Nicholls, Jr. S

☐ *Fiona on Fire* (1978) d: Kenneth Schwartz (Warren Evans) XXX

☐ *Fire Over England* (British/1937) d: William K. Howard

☐ *First Comes Courage* (1943) d: Dorothy Arzner

☐ *First Men "In" the Moon* (British/1964) d: Nathan Juran

☐ *First Name: Carmen* (French/1984) d: Jean-Luc Godard

☐ *First Time, The* (1983) d: Charlie Loventhal   S   PR

☐ *Fist in His Pocket* (Italian/1966) d: Marco Bellochio   H   PR

☐ *Five Against the House* (1955) d: Phil Karlson   PR

☐ *Five Came Back* (1939) d: John Farrow   H

☐ *Five Fingers* (1952) d: Joseph L. Mankiewicz

☐ *Five Graves to Cairo* (1943) d: Billy Wilder

☐ *Five on the Black Hand Side* (1973) d: Oscar Williams

☐ *Five Star Final* (1931) d: Mervyn LeRoy

☐ *Fixer, The* (1968) d: John Frankenheimer

☐ *Flame and the Arrow, The* (1950) d: Jacques Tourneur

☐ *Flaming Creatures* (1962) d: Jack Smith   H   CM

☐ *Flamingo Kid, The* (1984) d: Garry Marshall

☐ *Flash of Green, A* (1984) d: Victor Nunez   S

☐ *Flesh and Fantasy* (1943) d: Julien Duvivier

☐ *Flesh and the Devil* (1927) d: Clarence Brown   H

☐ *Flight for Freedom* (1943) d: Lothar Mendes   S

☐ *Flight of the Phoenix* (1966) d: Robert Aldrich   PR

☐ *Flirtation Walk* (1934) d: Frank Borzage

☐ *Floating Weeds/Drifting Weeds* (Japanese/1959) d: Yasujiro Ozu   PR

☐ *Floradora Girl, The* (1930) d: Harry Beaumont   PR

☐ *Flying Deuces, The* (1939) d: A. Edward Sutherland

☐ *Flying Leathernecks* (1951) d: Nicholas Ray

☐ *Flying Serpent, The* (1946) d: Sherman Scott (Sam Newfield) CC

☐ *Fool for Love* (1985) d: Robert Altman

☐ *Foolish Wives* (1922) d: Erich Von Stroheim   PR

☐ *Footsteps in the Fog* (British/1955) d: Arthur Lubin

☐ *For Heaven's Sake* (1926) d: Sam Taylor

☐ *For Whom the Bell Tolls* (1943) d: Sam Wood

☐ *Forbidden Zone* (1980) d: Richard Elfman   CM

☐ *Foreign Affair, A* (1948) d: Billy Wilder

☐ *Foreigner, The* (1978) d: Amos Poe   CM

☐ *Forever Amber* (1947) d: Otto Preminger

☐ *Forever and a Day* (1943) d: Rene Clair, Edmund Goulding, Cedric Hardwicke, Frank Lloyd, Victor Saville, Robert Stevenson, Herbert Wilcox

☐ *Fortune, The* (1975) d: Mike Nichols

☐ *Fortune and Men's Eyes* (Canadian-American/1971) d: Harvey Hart   H   PR

☐ *Forty Guns* (1957) d: Samuel Fuller   CM

☐ *49th Parallel, The* (British/1941) d: Michael Powell   H

☐ *Foul Play* (1978) d: Collin Higgins

☐ *Fountainhead, The* (1949) d: King Vidor   CM

☐ *Four Daughters* (1938) d: Michael Curtiz

☐ *Four Feathers, The* (British/1939) d: Michael Curtiz

☐ *Four Horsemen of the Apocalypse, The* (1921) d: Rex Ingram   H

☐ *Four Men and a Prayer* (1938) d: John Ford

☐ *Four Musketeers* (British/1975) d: Richard Lester   PR

☐ *Four Nights of a Dreamer* (French/1971) d: Robert Bresson

☐ *Four Seasons, The* (1981) d: Alan Alda

☐ *4D Man* (1959) d: Irvin S. Yeaworth, Jr.

☐ *Fox, The* (1968) d: Mark Rydell

☐ *Fox and His Friends* (West German/1975) d: Rainer Werner Fassbinder   CM

☐ *Foxy Brown* (1974) d: Jack Hill CM

☐ *Frances* (1982) d: Graeme Clifford

☐ *Frankenstein Meets the Wolf Man* (1943) d: Roy William Neill

☐ *Frankenstein's Daughter* (1959) d: Richard Cunha   CC

☐ *Fraternity Row* (1977) d: Thomas J. Tobin   S

☐ *Freaky Friday* (1977) d: Gary Nelson   S

☐ *French Cancan* (French/1955) d: Jean Renoir   H

☐ *French Lieutenant's Woman, The* (British/1981) d: Karel Reisz

□ *French Postcards* (1979) d: Willard Huyck

□ *French Quarter* (1977) d: Dennis Kane

□ *Frenzy* (British/1972) d: Alfred Hitchcock

□ *Freud* (1962) d: John Huston

□ *Friday Foster* (1975) d: Arthur Marks   CM

□ *Friendly Persuasion* (1956) d: William Wyler

□ *Friends of Eddie Coyle, The* (1973) d: Peter Yates   S   PR

□ *Fright Night* (1985) d: Tom Holland

□ *Frisco Kid, The* (1979) d: Robert Aldrich   S

□ *Frogs* (1972) d: George McGowan

□ *From Mao to Mozart: Isaac Stern in Concert* (1980) d: Murray Lerner

□ *From Noon Till Three* (1976) d: Frank D. Gilroy   S

□ *From the Earth to the Moon* (1958) d: Byron Haskin

□ *Front Page, The* (1931) d: Lewis Milestone

□ *Fugitive Kind, The* (1959) d: Sidney Lumet

□ *Full Moon High* (1981) d: Larry Cohen

□ *Funeral in Berlin* (1966) d: Guy Hamilton

□ *Funhouse, The* (1981) d: Tobe Hooper   CM

□ *Funny Face* (1957) d: Stanley Donen

□ *Funny Girl* (1968) d: William Wyler

□ *Funnyman* (1971) d: John Korty S

□ *Furies, The* (1950) d: Anthony Mann

□ *F/X* (1986) d: Robert Mandel

□ *Gabriel Over the White House* (1933) d: Gregory La Cava   CM   PR

□ *Gai Savoir, Le* (French/1967) d: Jean-Luc Godard

□ *Gambler, The* (1974) d: Karel Reisz

□ *Games* (1967) d: Curtis Harrington

□ *Ganja and Hess/Double Possession/Blood Couple* (1973) d: Bill Gunn   CM

□ *Gator Bait* (1976) d: Fred and Beverly C. Sebastian   CM

□ *Geisha, A* (Japanese/1953) d: Kenji Mizoguchi   PR

□ *General Died at Dawn, The* (1936) d: Lewis Milestone H

□ *Genevieve* (British/1953) d: Henry Cornelius   H   PR

□ *Gentleman's Agreement* (1947) d: Elia Kazan   H   PR

□ *George Raft Story, The* (1961) d: Joseph M. Newman

□ *Georgy Girl* (1966/British) d: Silvio Narizanno

□ *Gertrud* (Danish/1964) d: Carl Theodor Dreyer   H

□ *Gervaise* (French/1956) d: René Clement   H

□ *Get Carter* (British/1971) d: Mike Hodges

□ *Get Out Your Hankerchiefs* (French-Belgian/1978) d: Bertrand Blier   H   CM

□ *Get to Know Your Rabbit* (1973) d: Brian De Palma

□ *Getaway, The* (1972) d: Sam Peckinpah

□ *Getting Straight* (1970) d: Richard Rush

□ *Ghidrah, the Three-Headed Monster* (Japanese/1965) d: Inoshiro Honda   CC

□ *Ghost and Mrs. Muir, The* (1947) d: Joseph L. Mankiewicz

□ *Ghost Breakers* (1940) d: George Marshall

□ *Ghost Catchers* (1944) d: Edward F. Cline

□ *Ghost Goes West, The* (British/1936) d: Rene Clair

□ *Ghost of Frankenstein, The* (1942) d: Erle C. Kenton

□ *Ghost Ship* (1943) d: Mark Robson

□ *Ghoul, The* (British/1933) d: T. Hayes Hunter   S

□ *Giant Behemoth, The* (1959) d: Eugene Lourie

□ *Gidget* (1959) d: Paul Wendkos

□ *Girl Crazy* (1943) d: Norman Taurog

□ *Girl from Missouri, The* (1934) d: Jack Conway

□ *Girl Hunters, The* (1963) d: Roy Rowland   CM

□ *Girl in Every Port, A* (1928) d: Howard Hawks

□ *Girl on a Motorcycle/Naked Under Leather* (British-French/1968) d: Jack Cardiff   CM

□ *Girlfriends* (1978) d: Claudia Weill   S   CM

□ *Girls Town/Innocent and the Damned* (1959) d: Charles Haas CC

□ *Gizmo!* (1980) d: Howard Smith

□ *Glass Key, The* (1935) d: Frank Tuttle

□ *Glass Key, The* (1942) d: Stuart Heisler

□ *Glen and Randa* (1971) d: Jim McBride   CM

□ *Glenn Miller Story, The* (1954) d: Anthony Mann

□ *Glorifying the American Girl* (1929) d: Millard Webb

□ *Go-Between, The* (British/1971) d: Joseph Losey

□ *Go, Man, Go* (1954) d: James Wong Howe

□ *Go Masters, The* (Chinese-Japanese/1983) d: Junya Sato, Duan Jishun   CM

□ *Go West* (1925) d: Buster Keaton

□ *Go West* (1940) d: Edward Buzzell

□ *Goalie's Anxiety at the Penalty Kick, The* (West German-Austrian/1971) d: Wim Wenders

□ *God's Little Acre* (1958) d: Anthony Mann   CM

□ *Godzilla 1985* (Japanese/1985) d: Kohji Hashimoto, R.J. Kizer CC

□ *Going in Style* (1979) d: Martin Brest   CM

□ *Gold Diggers of 1935* (1935) d: Busby Berekely

□ *Gold Diggers of 1937* (1937) d: Lloyd Bacon

□ *Golden Coach, The* (French-Italian/1952) d: Jean Renoir

□ *Good Earth, The* (1937) d: Sidney Franklin   PR

□ *Good Fairy, The* (1935) d: William Wyler

□ *Good Fight, The* (1983) d: Mary Dore, Sam Sills, Noel Buckner

□ *Good Guys Wear Black* (1979) d: Ted Post   CM

□ *Good News* (1947) d: Charles Walters

□ *Good Times* (1967) d: William Friedkin

□ *Goodbye Columbus* (1969) d: Larry Peerce

□ *Goodbye Girl, The* (1977) d: Herbert Ross

□ *Goodbye, Mr. Chips* (British/1939) d: Sam Wood   H   PR

□ *Goodbye, New York* (1985) d: Amos Kollek s PR

□ *Gore Gore Gore Girls, The* (1972) d: Hershell Gordon Lewis T

□ *Gorgo* (British/1961) d: Eugene Lourie

□ *Gorgon, The* (British/1964) d: Terence Fisher

□ *Gorilla at Large* (1954) d: Harmon Jones

□ *Grandma's Boy* (1922) d: Fred Newmeyer H PR

□ *Grass Is Greener, The* (1960) d: Stanley Donen

□ *Grease* (1978) d: Randal Kleiser

□ *Greased Lightning* (1977) d: Michael Schultz

□ *Greaser's Palace* (1972) d: Robert Downey CM

□ *Great Day in the Morning* (1956) d: Jacques Tourneur

□ *Great Escape, The* (1963) d: John Sturges H PR

□ *Great Expectations* (British/1946) d: David Lean H PR

□ *Great Gabbo, The* (1929) d: James Cruze

□ *Great Gatsby, The* (1949) d: Elliott Nugent

□ *Great Gatsby, The* (1974) d: Jack Clayton

□ *Great Lie, The* (1941) d: Edmund Goulding

□ *Great Locomotive Chase, The* (1956) d: Francis D. Lyon

□ *Great Moment, The* (1944) d: Preston Sturges

□ *Great Northfield, Minnesota Raid, The* (1972) d: Philip Kaufman

□ *Great Rock and Roll Swindle, The* (British/1980) d: Julian Temple

□ *Great Santini, The* (1979) d: Lewis John Carlino CM

□ *Great Train Robbery, The* (British/1979) d: Michael Crichton

□ *Great Ziegfeld, The* (1936) d: Robert Z. Leonard H

□ *Greatest, The* (1977) d: Tom Gries

□ *Greatest Show on Earth, The* (1965) d: Cecil B. DeMille H

□ *Greatest Story Ever Told, The* (1965) d: George Stevens H

□ *Greeks Had a Word for Them, The/Three Broadway Girls* (1932) d: Lowell Sherman

□ *Green Berets, The* (1968) d: John Wayne CC

□ *Green Man, The* (British/1956) d: Robert Day

□ *Green Pastures, The* (1936) d: William Keighley, Marc Connelly

□ *Green Room, The* (French/1978) d: François Truffaut

□ *Green Slime, The* (Japanese-American/1969) d: Kenji Fukasaku CC

□ *Grey Fox, The* (Canadian/1982) d: Philip Borsos s PR

□ *Grey Gardens* (1975) d: David and Albert Maysles CM

□ *Group, The* (1966) d: Sidney Lumet CM

□ *Group Marriage* (1972) d: Stephanie Rothman CM

□ *Gruesome Twosome* (1968) d: Hershell Gordon Lewis T

□ *Guadalcanal Diary* (1943) d: Lewis Seiler H

□ *Guardsman, The* (1931) d: Sidney Franklin H

□ *Guerre Est Finie, La* (French-Swedish/1966) d: Alain Resnais PR

□ *Guess Who's Coming to Dinner* (1967) d: Stanley Kramer H

□ *Gulliver's Travels* (1939) d: Dave Fleischer

□ *Gumshoe* (British/1972) d: Stephen Fears CM

□ *Gunfight at the O.K. Corral* (1957) d: John Sturges H

□ *Gunfighter, The* (1950) d: Henry King H

□ *Gunsman's Walk* (1958) d: Phil Karlson CM

□ *Guns of Navarone, The* (1961) d: J. Lee Thompson H

□ *Gunslinger* (1956) d: Roger Corman

□ *Guys and Dolls* (1955) d: Joseph L. Mankiewicz

□ *Gypsy* (1962) d: Mervyn LeRoy

□ *Hail Hero!* (1969) d: David Miller s

□ *Hair* (1979) d: Milos Forman

□ *Halls of Montezuma* (1951) d: Lewis Milestone

□ *Hallelujah, I'm a Bum* (1933) d: Lewis Milestone H

□ *Halloween III: Season of the Witch* (1983) d: Tommy Lee Wallace s

□ *Hamlet* (British/1948) d: Laurence Olivier H PR

□ *Hammett* (1983) d: Wim Wenders CM

□ *Hand, The* (1981) d: Oliver Stone

□ *Hanging Tree, The* (1959) d: Delmer Daves

□ *Hangmen Also Die* (1943) d: Fritz Lang H

□ *Hans Christian Anderson* (1952) d: Charles Vidor

□ *Harakiri* (Japanese/1962) d: Masaki Kobayashi

□ *Hard Times* (1975) d: Walter Hill

□ *Harp of Burma* (Japanese/1956) d: Kon Ichikawa H

□ *Harper* (1966) d: Jack Smight

□ *Harriet Craig* (1950) d: Vincent Sherman

□ *Harry and Tonto* (1974) d: Paul Mazursky CM PR

□ *Harvey* (1950) d: Henry Koster CM

□ *Harvey Girls, The* (1946) d: George Sidney

□ *Has Anybody Seen My Gal?* (1952) d: Douglas Sirk s

□ *Hasty Heart, The* (British/1949) d: Vincent Sherman

□ *Hatari!* (1962) d: Howard Hawks

□ *Hatchet for a Honeymoon* (Italian-Spain/1970) d: Mario Bava

□ *Hatful of Rain, A* (1957) d: Fred Zinnemann

□ *Haunted Palace, The* (1963) d: Roger Corman

□ *Haunts* (1977) d: Herb Freed s

□ *He Ran All the Way* (1951) d: John Berry

□ *He Who Must Die* (French/1957) d: Jules Dassin

□ *H.E.A.L.T.H.* (1979) d: Robert Altman

□ *Heart of Glass* (West German/1976) d: Werner Herzog

□ *Heartaches* (Canadian/1981) d: Donald Shebib s

□ *Heartbreakers* (1985) d: Bobby Roth s

□ *Hearts of the West* (1975) d: Howard Zieff s

□ *Hearts of the World* (1918) d: D.W. Griffith

□ *Heat* (1972) d: Paul Morrissey

□ *Heat and Dust* (British/1983) d: James Ivory

□ *Heatwave* (Australian/1983) d: Phillip Noyce

☐ *Heaven Can Wait* (1978) d: Warren Beatty, Buck Henry

☐ *Heaven Knows, Mr. Allison* (1957) d: John Huston   PR

☐ *Heavy Metal* (Canadian/1981) d: Gerald Potterton   CM

☐ *Heimat* (West German/1985) d: Edgar Reitz

☐ *Heiress, The* (1949) d: William Wyler   H   PR

☐ *Helen Morgan Story, The* (1957) d: Michael Curtiz

☐ *Hell and High Water* (1954) d: Samuel Fuller

☐ *Hell in the Pacific* (1968) d: John Boorman

☐ *Hell Is for Heroes* (1962) d: Don Siegel

☐ *Hell's Angels* (1930) d: Howard Hughes   H

☐ *Hell's Angels on Wheels* (1967) d: Richard Rush   CM

☐ *Hellstrom Chronicle, The* (1971) d: Walon Green

☐ *Hellzappopin* (1941) d: H.C. Potter

☐ *Henry V* (British/1945) d: Laurence Olivier

☐ *Heroes for Sale* (1933) d: William Wellman

☐ *Herostratus* (British/1967) d: Don Levy   CM

☐ *Hester Street* (1975) d: Joan Micklin Silver   S   CM   PR

☐ *Hey Good Lookin'* (1982) d: Ralph Bakshi   CM

☐ *Hi, Mom!* (1970) d: Brian De Palma   CM   H

☐ *Hide in Plain Sight* (1980) d: James Caan

☐ *Hideous Sun Demon, The* (1959) d: Robert Clarke   CC

☐ *High and Low* (Japanese/1962) d: Akira Kurosawa   PR

☐ *High and the Mighty, The* (1954) d: William A. Wellman   H

☐ *High Anxiety* (1977) d: Mel Brooks   CM

☐ *High School* (1969) d: Frederick Wiseman   H   PR

☐ *High School Fantasies* (1974) d: Morris Deal   XXX

☐ *Hired Hand, The* (1971) d: Peter Fonda   CM

☐ *Hireling, The* (British/1973) d: Alan Bridges

☐ *History Is Made at Night* (1937) d: Frank Borzage

☐ *History of the Blue Movie* (1970) d: Alex DeRenzy   XXX   H

☐ *History of the World—Part I* (1981) d: Mel Brooks

☐ *Hit, The* (British/1984) d: Stephen Frears   CM   PR

☐ *Hitchhikers, The* (1972) d: Fred and Beverly Sebastian   CM

☐ *Hitch-Hiker, The* (1953) d: Ida Lupino

☐ *Hitler: A Film from Germany* (West German/1977) d: Hans Jurgen Syberberg   CM   H

☐ *Hitler's Children* (1942) d: Edward Dmytryk   H

☐ *Hitler's Madman* (1943) d: Douglas Sirk   H

☐ *Hobson's Choice* (British/1954) d: David Lean   H   PR

☐ *Hold Back the Dawn* (1941) d: Mitchell Leisen   PR

☐ *Hold Back Tomorrow* (1955) d: Hugo Haas   CC

☐ *Hold That Ghost* (1941) d: Arthur Lubin   PR

☐ *Hold Your Man* (1933) d: Sam Wood

☐ *Hollywood Or Bust* (1956) d: Frank Tashlin   CM   PR

☐ *Holy Matrimony* (1943) d: John M. Stahl

☐ *Holy Mountain, The* (Mexican-American/1973) d: Alexandro Jodorowsky   CM

☐ *Home and the World, The* (Indian/1984) d: Satyajit Ray   PR

☐ *Home Movies* (1979) d: Brian De Palma   CM

☐ *Home of the Brave* (1949) d: Mark Robson   H

☐ *Homecoming, The* (British/1973) d: Peter Hall

☐ *Homicidal* (1961) d: William Castle   CM   PR

☐ *Honky Tonk Freeway* (1981) d: John Schlesinger

☐ *Hoodlum Priest, The* (1961) d: Irvin Kershner

☐ *Hoppity Goes to Town/Mr. Bug Goes to Town* (1941) d: Dave Fleischer

☐ *Horn Blows at Midnight, The* (1945) d: Raoul Walsh   CM   PR

☐ *Horrible Dr. Hichcock, The* (Italian/1962) d: Robert Hampton (Riccardo Freda)   CM

☐ *Horror of Party Beach* (1964) d: Del Tenney   CC

☐ *Horse Soldiers, The* (1959) d: John Ford

☐ *Horse's Mouth, The* (British/1958) d: Ronald Neame   H   CM   PR

☐ *Hospital, The* (1971) d: Arthur Hiller   H

☐ *Hot Box, The* (1972) d: Joe Viola   CM

☐ *Hot Tomorrows* (1977) d: Martin Brest   S   PR

☐ *Hotel New Hampshire* (1984) d: Tony Richardson   S   PR

☐ *Hound-Dog Man* (1959) d: Don Siegel   CM

☐ *Hound of the Baskervilles, The* (British/1959) d: Terence Fisher

☐ *Hour of the Furnaces, The* (Argentinian/1968) d: Fernando Solanas   H   PR

☐ *Hour of the Wolf* (Sweden/1968) d: Ingmar Bergman   H

☐ *House by the River, The* (1950) d: Fritz Lang

☐ *House of Dark Shadows* (1970) d: Dan Curtis   CM

☐ *House of Dracula* (1945) d: Erle C. Kenton

☐ *House of Frankenstein* (1944) d: Erle C. Kenton

☐ *House of Strangers* (1949) d: Joseph L. Mankewicz

☐ *House on Haunted Hill* (1958) d: William Castle   CM   PR

☐ *House on 92nd Street, The* (1945) d: Henry Hathaway   H

☐ *How Green Was My Valley?* (1941) d: John Ford   H   PR

☐ *How Tasty Was My Little Frenchman* (Brazilian/1971) d: Nelson Pereira dos Santos   H   CM

☐ *How the West Was Won* (1963) d: John Ford, Henry Hathaway, George Marshal   H

☐ *How to Steal a Million* (1966) d: William Wyler

☐ *How to Stuff a Wild Bikini* (1965) d: William Asher   CC

☐ *Hucksters, The* (1947) d: Jack Conway   PR

☐ *Hud* (1963) d: Martin Ritt

☐ *Humanoids from the Deep* (1980) d: Barbara Peeters

☐ *Humoresque* (1946) d: Jean Negulesco   H

☐ *Hurricane, The* (1937) d: John Ford   H   PR

☐ *Hurry Sundown* (1967) d: Otto Preminger

☐ *Husbands* (1970) d: John Cassavetes   CM   PR

☐ *I, A Woman* (Swedish/1968) d: Mac Ahlberg

☐ *I Am a Camera* (British/1955) d: Henry Cornelius   H

☐ *I Bury the Living* (1958) d: Albert Band

☐ *I Confess* (1953) d: Alfred Hitchcock

☐ *I Could Go on Singing* (British/1963) d: Ronald Neame

☐ *I Dismember Mama* (1972) d: Paul Leder   CC   CM   T

☐ *I.F. Stone's Weekly* (1973) d: Jerry Bruck, Jr.

☐ *I Know Where I'm Going* (British/1945) d: Michael Powell

☐ *I Love You Again* (1940) d: W.S. Van Dyke II   PR

☐ *I Love You, Alice B. Toklas* (1968) d: Hy Averback   CM

☐ *I Married a Shadow* (French/1982) d: Robin Davis

☐ *I Never Sang for My Father* (1970) d: Gilbert Cates

☐ *I Remember Mama* (1948) d: George Stevens   H

☐ *I Sent a Letter to My Love* (French/1981) d: Moshe Mizrahi

☐ *I Vitelloni* (Italian/1953) d: Federico Fellini   H   PR

☐ *I Wake Up Screaming* (1941) d: H. Bruce Humberstone

☐ *I Want to Live* (1958) d: Robert Wise

☐ *I Want You* (1951) d: Mark Robson   S

☐ *I Was a Male War Bride* (1949) d: Howard Hawks   CM

☐ *Ice* (1970) d: Robert Kramer

☐ *Ice Castles* (1979) d: Donald Wrye

☐ *Iceman* (1984) d: Fred Schepisi

☐ *Iceman Cometh, The* (1973) d: John Frankenheimer   H   PR

☐ *Idiot, The* (Japanese/1951) d: Akira Kurosawa

☐ *Idolmaker, The* (1980) d: Taylor Hackford   CM

☐ *If I Were King* (1938) d: Frank Lloyd

☐ *Ilsa, Harem Keeper for the Oil Sheiks* (1976) d: Don Edmunds   CM   T

☐ *Images* (American-British/1972) d: Robert Altman   CM

☐ *Imitation of Life* (1934) d: John M. Stahl   H   PR

☐ *Immortal Sergeant, The* (1943) d: John M. Stahl

☐ *Immortal Story, The* (French/1968) d: Orson Welles

☐ *I'm No Angel* (1933) d: Wesley Ruggles   H

☐ *Importance of Being Earnest, The* (British/1952) d: Anthony Asquith

☐ *In a Year of Thirteen Moons* (West German/1978) d: Rainer Werner Fassbinder

☐ *In Cold Blood* (1967) d: Richard Brooks   H   PR

☐ *In Harm's Way* (1965) d: Otto Preminger

☐ *In-Laws, The* (1979) d: Arthur Hiller

☐ *In Name Only* (1939) d: John Cromwell

☐ *In Praise of Older Woman* (Canadian/1978) d: George Kaczender

☐ *In Search of the Castaways* (1962) d: Robert Stevenson

☐ *In the Devil's Garden/Assault/Tower of Terror* (British/1971) d: Sidney Hayers   CM

☐ *In the Heat of the Night* (1967) d: Norman Jewison   H

☐ *In the White City* (Swiss-Portuguese/1983) d: Alain Tanner   PR

☐ *In This Our Life* (1942) d: John Huston

☐ *In Which We Serve* (British/1942) d: Noel Coward, David Lean   H   PR

☐ *Incredible Journey, The* (1963) d: Fletcher Markle   PR

☐ *Incredible Shrinking Woman, The* (1981) d: Joel Schumacher

☐ *Incredible Two Headed Transplant, The* (1971) d: Anthony M. Lanza   CC

☐ *Incredibly Strange Creatures Who Stopped Living and Became Mixed-Up Zombies, The/Teenage Psycho Meets Bloody Mary* (1963) d: Ray Dennis Steckler   CC

☐ *Independence Day* (1983) d: Robert Mandel   S   PR

☐ *India Song* (French/1975) d: Marguerite Duras   H

☐ *Indiscreet* (1958) d: Stanley Donen

☐ *Indiscretion of an American Wife* (American-Italian/1953) d: Vittorio De Sica

☐ *Inferno* (Italian/1978) d: Dario Argento   CM

☐ *Informer, The* (1935) d: John Ford   H   PR

☐ *Inherit the Wind* (1960) d: Stanley Kramer   H

☐ *Inn of the Sixth Happiness, The* (1958) d: Mark Robson   PR

☐ *Innocent, The* (Italian/1979) d: Luchino Visconti

☐ *Innocents, The* (British/1961) d: Jack Clayton   CM

☐ *Inside Daisy Clover* (1965) d: Robert Mulligan   CM   PR

☐ *Inside Moves* (1965) d: Richard Donner   S

☐ *Intermezzo* (Swedish/1936) d: Gustav Molander   H

☐ *Intermezzo* (1939) d: Gregory Ratoff

☐ *International House* (1933) d: A. Edward Sutherland

☐ *Intimate Lightning* (Czech/1965) d: Ivan Passer

☐ *Intruder, The/I Hate Your Guts!/Shame* (1961) d: Roger Corman   S

☐ *Intruder in the Dust* (1949) d: Clarence Brown

☐ *Investigation of a Citizen Above Suspicion* (Italian/1970) d: Elio Petri

☐ *Invisible Boy, The* (1957) d: Herman Hoffman

☐ *Invisible Invaders* (1959) d: Edward L. Cahn   CC

☐ *Invisible Man Returns, The* (1940) d: Joe May

☐ *Invisible Ray, The* (1939) d: Lambert Hillyar

☐ *Invitation to the Dance* (1957) d: Gene Kelly

☐ *Ipcress File, The* (British/1965) d: Sidney J. Furie   H   PR

☐ *Irma La Douce* (1963) d: Billy Wilder

☐ *Irreconcilable Differences* (1984) d: Charles Shyer   S   PR

☐ *Is There Sex After Death?* (1971) d: Jeanne and Alan Abel   CM

☐ *Isadora/Loves of Isadora, The* (British/1969) d: Karel Reisz   H

☐ *It* (1927) d: Clarence Badger   H

☐ *It Came from Beneath the Sea* (1955) d: Robert Gordon

☐ *It Came from Outer Space* (1953) d: Jack Arnold   CM   PR

☐ *It Conquered the World* (1956) d: Roger Corman

☐ *It Happened Here* (British/1966) d: Kevin Brownlow, Andrew Mollo

☐ *It Happens Every Spring* (1949) d: Lloyd Bacon   PR

☐ *It Should Happen to You* (1954) d: George Cukor   H   PR

☐ *It! The Terror from Beyond Space* (1958) d: Edward L. Cahn   CC

☐ *It's a Big Country* (1951) d: Charles Vidor

☐ *It's Only Money* (1962) d: Frank Tashlin

☐ *It's a Wonderful World* (1939) d: W.S. Van Dyke II

☐ *Italian Straw Hat, The* (French/ 1927) d: René Clair   H

☐ *Ivanhoe* (1952) d: Richard Thorpe

☐ *Jabberwocky* (British/1977) d: Terry Gilliam

☐ *J'Accuse* (French/1919) d: Abel Gance   H

☐ *J'Accuse* (French/1938) d: Abel Gance   H

☐ *Jack the Giant Killer* (1962) d: Nathan Juran   S

☐ *Jackie Robinson Story, The* (1950) d: Alfred E. Green

☐ *Jack's Wife/Hungry Wives* (1971) d: George Romero   CM

☐ *Jamaica Inn* (British/1939) d: Alfred Hitchcock

☐ *James Dean Story* (1957) d: George W. George, Robert Altman

☐ *Jane Eyre* (1944) d: Robert Stevenson   H

☐ *Janis* (1975) d: Seaton Findlay, Howard Alk

☐ *Jazz on a Summer's Day* (1959) d: Bert Stern   H

☐ *Je T'Aime, Je T'Aime* (French/ 1968) d: Alain Resnais   H

☐ *Jeanne Dielman, 23 Quai du Commerce, 1080 Bruxelles* (Belgian/1975) d: Chantal Akerman   H

☐ *Jeanne Eagles* (1957) d: George Sidney

☐ *Jeremiah Johnson* (1972) d: Sydney Pollack

☐ *Jesse James* (1939) d: Henry King   H   PR

☐ *Jesse James Meets Frankenstein's Daughter* (1966) d: William Beaudine   CC

☐ *Jesus Christ, Superstar* (1973) d: Norman Jewison

☐ *Jet Pilot* (1957) d: Josef von Sternberg

☐ *Jim Thorpe, All American* (1951) d: Michael Curtiz

☐ *Jimi Plays Berkeley* (1970) d: Peter Pilafian   CM

☐ *Jitterbugs* (1943) d: Malcolm St. Clair

☐ *J-Men Forever* (1979) d: Richard Patterson, Philip Proctor, Peter Bergman   CM

☐ *Joe Hill* (Swedish/1971) d: Bo Widerberg

☐ *Johnny Belinda* (1948) d: Jean Negulesco

☐ *Joli Mai, Le* (French/1963) d: Chris Marker

☐ *Jolson Story, The* (1946) d: Alfred E. Green   H   PR

☐ *Jonah Who Will Be 25 in the Year 2000* (Swiss/1976) d: Alain Tanner   PR

☐ *Jonathan Livingston Seagull* (1973) d: Hall Bartlett

☐ *Jour de Fête* (French/1949) d: Jacques Tati   H

☐ *Journey into Fear* (1942) d: Norman Foster   S

☐ *Journey to the Center of the Earth* (1959) d: Henry Levin

☐ *Journey to the Far Side of the Sun/Doppelganger* (British/ 1969) d: Robert Parrish

☐ *Journey's End* (1930) d: James Whale   S

☐ *Journeys from Berlin* (1971) d: Yvonne Rainer   H   CM

☐ *Juarez* (1939) d: William Dieterle

☐ *Judge Priest* (1934) d: John Ford   H   PR

☐ *Judgment at Nuremberg* (1961) d: Stanley Kramer

☐ *Juggernaut* (British/1974) d: Richard Lester   S   PR

☐ *Julius Caesar* (1953) d: Joseph L. Mankiewicz

☐ *Jungle Princess, The* (1936) d: William Thiele

☐ *Junior Bonner* (1972) d: Sam Peckinpah

☐ *Just a Gigolo* (West German/ 1979) d: David Hemmings   CM

☐ *Just Imagine* (1930) d: David Butler   H

☐ *Just Tell Me What You Want* (1980) d: Sidney Lumet   S

☐ *Kameradschaft* (German-French/ 1931) d: G.W. Pabst   H

☐ *Kanchenjunga* (Indian/1962) d: Satyajit Ray

☐ *Kansas City Confidential* (1952) d: Phil Karlson

☐ *Kaos* (Italian/1986) d: Paolo and Vittorio Taviani

☐ *Keeper of the Flame* (1942) d: George Cukor

☐ *Keetje Tippel* (Dutch/1975) d: Paul Verhoeven   S

☐ *Kes* (British/1970) d: Ken Loach   H   CM

☐ *Key, The/Kagi* (Japanese/1959) d: Kon Ichikawa

☐ *Key Largo* (1948) d: John Huston   H

☐ *Kid Blue* (1973) d: James Frawley   S

☐ *Kid for Two Farthings, A* (British/1955) d: Carol Reed

☐ *Kid from Brooklyn, The* (1946) d: Norman Z. McLeod

☐ *Kid from Cleveland, The* (1949) d: Herbert Kline

☐ *Kid from Spain, The* (1932) d: Leo McCarey

☐ *Kid Galahad/Battling Bellhop, The* (1937) d: Michael Curtiz

☐ *Kid Galahad* (1962) d: Phil Karlson

☐ *Kid Millions* (1934) d: Roy Del Ruth

☐ *Killer Elite, The* (1975) d: Sam Peckinpah

☐ *Killer Shrews, The* (1959) d: Ray Kellogg   CC   S

☐ *Killing of a Chinese Bookie, The* (1976) d: John Cassavetes   CM

☐ *Killing of Sister George, The* (1968) d: Robert Aldrich   CM

☐ *King and Country* (British/1964) d: Joseph Losey   H

☐ *King and I, The* (1956) d: Walter Lang   H

☐ *King in New York, A* (British/ 1957) d: Charles Chaplin   CM

☐ *King Kong* (1976) d: John Guillerman   CC

☐ *King Kong vs. Godzilla* (Japanese/1963) d: Thomas Montgomery   CC   PR

☐ *King Lear* (British-Danish/1970) d: Peter Brook   H

☐ *King of Jazz, The* (1930) d: John Murray Anderson

☐ *King of Kings, The* (1927) d: Cecil B. DeMille   H

☐ *King of Kings* (1961) d: Nicholas Ray H PR
☐ *King of Marvin Gardens, The* (1972) d: Bob Rafelson CM
☐ *King Rat* (British/1965) d: Bryan Forbes
☐ *King Soloman's Mines* (British/1937) d: Robert Stevenson
☐ *King Soloman's Mines* (1950) d: Compton Bennett
☐ *King Steps Out, The* (1936) d: Josef von Sternberg
☐ *Kings of the Road* (West German/1976) d: Wim Wenders CM
☐ *King's Row* (1941) d: Sam Wood H
☐ *Kipps* (British/1941) d: Carol Reed
☐ *Kirlian Witness, The* (1978) d: Jonathan Sarno CM
☐ *Kiss Before Dying, A* (1956) d: Gerd Oswald S
☐ *Kiss Before the Mirror, The* (1933) d: James Whale
☐ *Kiss Me Kate* (1953) d: George Sidney
☐ *Kiss Me, Stupid* (1964) d: Billy Wilder CM
☐ *Kiss of the Vampire* (British/1963) d: Don Sharp
☐ *Kitten with a Whip* (1964) d: Douglas Heyes S
☐ *Kitty Foyle* (1940) d: Sam Wood H PR
☐ *Klondike Annie* (1936) d: Raoul Walsh
☐ *Knack, and How to Get It, The* (British/1965) d: Richard Lester
☐ *Knife in the Head* (West German/1978) d: Reinhard Hauff
☐ *Knightriders* (1981) d: George A. Romero S CM PR
☐ *Knock on Wood* (1954) d: Norman Panama, Melvin Frank
☐ *Knute Rockne—All American* (1940) d: Lloyd Bacon
☐ *Koko—A Talking Gorilla* (1978) d: Barbet Schroeder
☐ *Kongo* (1932) d: William Cowan
☐ *Kon-Tiki* (1951) d: Thor Heyerdahl H PR
☐ *Kremlin Letter, The* (1970) d: John Huston
☐ *Kronos* (1957) d: Kurt Neumann
☐ *Kwaidan* (Japanese/1964) d: Masaki Kobayashi H

☐ *Lacombe, Lucien* (French/1973) d: Louis Malle H PR

☐ *Ladies of Leisure* (1930) d: Frank Capra H
☐ *Lady and the Monster, The* (1944) d: George Sherman H
☐ *Lady for a Day* (1933) d: Frank Capra H PR
☐ *Lady in the Lake* (1946) d: Robert Montgomery H PR
☐ *Lady of Burlesque* (1943) d: William Wellman
☐ *Lady Sings the Blues* (1972) d: Sidney J. Furie
☐ *Lady Takes a Chance, A* (1943) d: William A. Seiter
☐ *Lady Windermere's Fan* (1925) d: Ernst Lubitsch H
☐ *Lady with the Dog, The* (Russian/1960) d: Josef Heifitz
☐ *Ladykillers, The* (British/1955) d: Alexander Mackendrick
☐ *Lancelot of the Lake* (French/1974) d: Robert Bresson CM
☐ *Landlord, The* (1970) d: Hal Ashby
☐ *Las Vegas Hillbillys/Country Music, U.S.A.* (1966) d: Arthur C. Pearce
☐ *Last Angry Man, The* (1959) d: Daniel Mann
☐ *Last Command, The* (1928) d: Josef von Sternberg H
☐ *Last Command, The* (1955) d: Frank Lloyd S PR
☐ *Last Days of Man on Earth, The/Final Programme, The* (British/1973) d: Robert Fuest CM
☐ *Last Days of Pompeii, The* (1935) d: Ernest B. Schoedsack H
☐ *Last Frontier, The* (1955) d: Anthony Mann
☐ *Last Gangster, The* (1937) d: Edward Ludwig
☐ *Last Holiday* (British/1950) d: Henry Cass
☐ *Last Hurrah, The* (1958) d: John Ford PR
☐ *Last Man on Earth, The* (American-Italian/1964) d: Sidney Salkow
☐ *Last Metro, The* (French/1980) d: François Truffaut H
☐ *Last of Shiela, The* (1973) d: Herbert Ross
☐ *Last of the Mohicans, The* (1936) d: George B. Seitz
☐ *Last Starfighter, The* (1984) d: Nick Castle
☐ *Last Summer* (1969) d: Frank Perry

☐ *Last Sunset, The* (1961) d: Robert Aldrich
☐ *Last Tycoon, The* (1976) d: Elia Kazan
☐ *Last Valley, The* (British/1971) d: James Clavell S
☐ *Last Voyage, The* (1960) d: Andrew L. Stone
☐ *Last Woman, The* (French/1976) d: Marco Ferreri
☐ *Last Year at Marienbad* (French/1962) d: Alain Resnais H
☐ *Late Chrysanthemums* (Japanese/1954) d: Mikio Naruse H PR
☐ *Late Show, The* (1977) d: Robert Benton
☐ *Latino* (1985) d: Haskell Wexler
☐ *Laughter* (1930) d: Harry D'Arrast H
☐ *Lavender Hill Mob, The* (British/1950) d: Charles Crichton
☐ *Law and Disorder* (1974) d: Ivan Passer
☐ *Law and Order* (1932) d: Edward L. Cahn H PR
☐ *Law and Order* (1969) d: Frederick Wiseman
☐ *Lawless Breed, The* (1952) d: Raoul Walsh
☐ *Lawrence of Arabia* (British/1962) d: David Lean H
☐ *Leadbelly* (1976) d: Gordon Parks S
☐ *Learning Tree, The* (1969) d: Gordon Parks
☐ *Leather Boys, The* (British/1966) d: Sidney J. Furie
☐ *Leave Her to Heaven* (1945) d: John M. Stahl
☐ *Left-Handed Woman, The* (West German/1978) d: Peter Handke
☐ *Legend of Hell House, The* (British/1973) d: John Hough
☐ *Legend of Lylah Clare, The* (1968) d: Robert Aldrich CM
☐ *Legend of the Lost* (1957) d: Henry Hathaway
☐ *Lemora, the Lady Dracula* (1974) d: Richard Blackburn S
☐ *Leo the Last* (British/1970) d: John Boorman
☐ *Let It Be* (British/1970) d: Michael Lindsay-Hogg CM
☐ *Let's Do It Again* (1975) d: Sidney Poitier
☐ *Let's Make Love* (1960) d: George Cukor
☐ *Let's Scare Jessica to Death*

(1971) d: John Hancock S PR

☐ *Letter to Jane* (French/1972) d: Jean-Luc Godard, Jean-Pierre Gorin

☐ *Liaisons Dangereuses, Les* (French/1959) d: Roger Vadim

☐ *Liberation of L.B. Jones, The* (1970) d: William Wyler

☐ *Lickerish Quartet, The* (1970) d: Radley Metzger CM

☐ *Life and Death of Colonel Blimp, The* (British/1943) d: Michael Powell, Emeric Pressburger H CM PR

☐ *Life and Times of Rosie the Riveter, The* (1980) d: Connie Field

☐ *Life Is a Bed of Roses* (French/1983) d: Alain Resnais

☐ *Life of Brian, The/Monty Python's The Life of Brian* (British/1979) d: Terry Jones CM

☐ *Life of Emile Zola, The* (1937) d: William Dieterle PR

☐ *Life with Father* (1947) d: Michael Curtiz

☐ *Lifeguard* (1976) d: Daniel Petrie S

☐ *Light That Failed, The* (1939) d: William A. Wellman

☐ *Light Years Away* (Swiss-French/1981) d: Alain Tanner

☐ *Lili Marleen* (West German/1981) d: Rainer Werner Fassbinder

☐ *Lilies of the Field* (1963) d: Ralph Nelson

☐ *Lilith* (1964) d: Robert Rossen H CM

☐ *Lineup, The* (1958) d: Don Siegel

☐ *Lion and the Horse, The* (1952) d: Louis King S

☐ *Lion Is in the Streets, A* (1953) d: Raoul Walsh

☐ *Lion in Winter, The* (British/1968) d: Anthony Harvey H

☐ *List of Adrian Messenger, The* (1963) d: John Huston

☐ *Lisztomania* (British/1975) d: Ken Russell CM

☐ *Little Big Horn* (1951) d: Charles Marquis Warren S

☐ *Little Foxes, The* (1941) d: William Wyler H PR

☐ *Little Giant, The* (1933) d: Roy Del Ruth

☐ *Little Giant* (1946) d: William A. Seiter

☐ *Little Kidnappers, The* (British/

1953) d: Philip Leacock

☐ *Little Laura & Big John* (1973) d: Luke Moberly, Bob Woodburn

☐ *Little Lord Fauntleroy* (1936) d: John Cromwell

☐ *Little Miss Marker* (1934) d: Alexander Hall

☐ *Little Murders* (1971) d: Alan Arkin

☐ *Little Romance, A* (1979) d: George Roy Hill

☐ *Little Theatre of Jean Renoir, The* (French/1970) d: Jean Renoir

☐ *Little Women* (1933) d: George Cukor H PR

☐ *Lives of the Bengal Lancer* (1935) d: Henry Hathaway H

☐ *Living Desert, The* (1953) d: James Algar H

☐ *Living in a Big Way* (1947) d: Gregory La Cava

☐ *Living Nightmare/Nazi Love Camp #27* (1979) d: William Hawkins T

☐ *Lizzie* (1957) d: Hugo Haas

☐ *Lodger, The* (British/1926) d: Alfred Hitchcock H PR

☐ *Logan's Run* (1976) d: Michael Anderson

☐ *Lola* (French/1962) d: Jacques Demy

☐ *Lone Wolf McQuade* (1983) d: Steve Carver

☐ *Lonely Hearts* (Australian/1981) d: Paul Cox PR

☐ *Long Day's Journey Into Night* (1962) d: Sidney Lumet H PR

☐ *Long Gray Line, The* (1955) d: John Ford

☐ *Long, Hot Summer, The* (1958) d: Martin Ritt

☐ *Long Pants* (1927) d: Frank Capra H PR

☐ *Long Voyage Home, The* (1940) d: John Ford S PR

☐ *Longest Day, The* (1962) d: Ken Annakin, Andrew Marton, Bernard Wicki H

☐ *Longest Yard, The* (1974) d: Robert Aldrich

☐ *Look Back in Anger* (British/1958) d: Tony Richardson

☐ *Looking for Mr. Goodbar* (1977) d: Richard Brooks

☐ *Lord Jim* (1965) d: Richard Brooks

☐ *Lord of the Flies* (British/1963) d:

Peter Brook H PR

☐ *Lord of the Rings, The* (1978) d: Ralph Bakshi CM

☐ *Losin' It* (1983) d: Curtis Hanson S

☐ *Loss of Innocence* (British/1961) d: Lewis Gilbert

☐ *Lost Honor of Katherina Blum, The* (West German/1975) d: Volker Schlöndorff H PR

☐ *Lost World, The* (1925) d: Harry Hoyt H

☐ *Lost World, The* (1960) d: Irwin Allen

☐ *Louisiana Purchase* (1941) d: Irving Cummings

☐ *Loulou* (French/1980) d: Maurice Pialat

☐ *Love* (1927) d: Edmund Goulding H

☐ *Love Affair* (1939) d: Leo McCarey

☐ *Love and Money* (1982) d: James Toback

☐ *Love at Twenty* (French-Italian-Japanese-Polish-West German/1962) d: François Truffaut, Renzo Rossellini, Shintaro Ishihara, Marcel Ophüls, Andrzej Wajda

☐ *Love Bug, The* (1969) d: Robert Stevenson

☐ *Love Finds Andy Hardy* (1938) d: George B. Seitz H

☐ *Love Happy* (1949) d: David Miller

☐ *Love in the Afternoon* (1957) d: Billy Wilder H

☐ *Love Letters* (1945) d: William Dieterle

☐ *Love Me or Leave Me* (1955) d: Charles Vidor

☐ *Love Me Tender* (1956) d: Robert D. Webb CM

☐ *Love Me Tonight* (1932) d: Rouben Mamoulian H PR

☐ *Love of Jeanne Ney, The* (German/1927) d: G.W. Pabst H

☐ *Love with the Proper Stranger* (1963) d: Robert Mulligan S

☐ *Lover Come Back* (1961) d: Delbert Mann

☐ *Lovers and Other Strangers* (1970) d: Cy Howard S

☐ *Loves of a Blonde* (Czech/1965) d: Milos Forman CM

☐ *Loving* (1970) d: Irvin Kershner S

☐ *Loving You* (1957) d: Hal Kanter

☐ *Lower Depths, The/Bas-Fonds, Les* (French/1936) d: Jean Renoir

☐ *Lower Depths, The* (Japanese/1957) d: Akira Kurosawa

☐ *L-Shaped Room, The* (British/1962) d: Bryan Forbes   H PR

☐ *Luck of Ginger Coffey, The* (Canadian/1964) d: Irvin Kershner

☐ *Lumiere* (French/1976) d: Jeanne Moreau

☐ *Luna* (1979) d: Bernardo Bertolucci

☐ *Lured* (1947) d: Douglas Sirk

☐ *Lust for a Vampire/To Love a Vampire* (British/1971) d: Jimmy Sangster   CM

☐ *Lust for Life* (1956) d: Vincente Minnelli

☐ *Macabre* (1958) d: William Castle

☐ *Macao* (1952) d: Josef von Sternberg

☐ *Machine Gun Kelly* (1958) d: Roger Corman

☐ *Macomber Affair, The* (1947) d: Zoltan Korda   S PR

☐ *Mad Bomber, The* (1972) d: Bert I. Gordon

☐ *Mad Dog Coll* (1961) d: Burt Balaban

☐ *Mad Dog Morgan* (Australian/1976) d: Philippe Mora

☐ *Mad Genius, The* (1931) d: Michael Curtiz

☐ *Mad Ghoul, The* (1943) d: James Hogan

☐ *Madame Bovary* (French/1934) d: Jean Renoir   H PR

☐ *Madame Bovary* (1949) d: Vincente Minnelli

☐ *Madame Curie* (1943) d: Mervyn LeRoy

☐ *Madame Rosa* (French/1977) d: Moshe Mizrahi   S PR

☐ *Madame X* (1966) d: David Lowell Rich

☐ *Made in U.S.A.* (French-Italian/1966) d: Jean-Luc Godard   H

☐ *Mademoiselle Fifi* (1944) d: Robert Wise   S

☐ *Mafu Cage, The* (1978) d: Karen Arthur   S

☐ *Magic Box, The* (British/1951) d: John Boulting

☐ *Magic Christian, The* (British/1970) d: Joseph McGrath   CM

☐ *Magic Flute, The* (Swedish/1974) d: Ingmar Bergman

☐ *Magic Garden of Stanley Sweetheart, The* (1970) d: Leonard Horn

☐ *Magician, The* (Swedish/1959) d: Ingmar Bergman   H PR

☐ *Magnificent Matador, The* (1955) d: Budd Boetticher

☐ *Magnificent Obsession, The* (1935) d: John M. Stahl   H PR

☐ *Magnificent Seven, The* (1960) d: John Sturges   CM

☐ *Mahler* (British/1974) d: Ken Russell   CM

☐ *Maidstone* (1971) d: Norman Mailer

☐ *Maisie* (1939) d: Edwin L. Marin

☐ *Major and the Minor, The* (1942) d: Billy Wilder   H PR

☐ *Major Barbara* (British/1941) d: Gabriel Pascal   H

☐ *Male and Female* (1919) d: Cecil B. DeMille   H

☐ *Male Animal, The* (1942) d: Elliott Nugent   PR

☐ *Maltese Falcon, The* (1931) d: Roy Del Ruth   H PR

☐ *Man, The* (1972) d: Joseph Sargent

☐ *Man Between, The* (British/1953) d: Carol Reed

☐ *Man Called Horse, A* (1970) d: Elliott Silverstein

☐ *Man for All Seasons, A* (British/1966) d: Fred Zinnemann   H

☐ *Man from Snowy River, The* (Australian/1982) d: George Miller

☐ *Man from the Alamo, The* (1953) d: Budd Boetticher

☐ *Man Hunt* (1941) d: Fritz Lang

☐ *Man in the Iron Mask, The* (1939) d: James Whale   S PR

☐ *Man of a Thousand Faces* (1957) d: Joseph Pevney

☐ *Man of Aran* (British/1934) d: Robert Flaherty   H PR

☐ *Man of Iron* (Polish/1980) d: Andrzej Wajda   H PR

☐ *Man of Marble* (Polish/1977) d: Andrzej Wajda   H PR

☐ *Man on the Roof* (Swedish/1977) d: Bo Widerberg

☐ *Man They Could Not Hang, The* (1939) d: Nick Grinde

☐ *Man Who Came to Dinner, The* (1941) d: William Keighley

☐ *Man Who Could Work Miracles, The* (British/1937) d: Lothar Mendes   H PR

☐ *Man Who Laughs, The* (1928) d: Paul Leni   H PR

☐ *Man Who Loved Women, The* (French/1977) d: François Truffaut

☐ *Man Who Reclaimed His Head, The* (1934) d: Edward Ludwig   S PR

☐ *Man With a Movie Camera, The* (Russian/1929) d: Dziga Vertov

☐ *Man With Bogart's Face, The* (1980) d: Robert Day   S CM PR

☐ *Man's Favorite Sport?* (1964) d: Howard Hawks   CM

☐ *Manchurian Candidate, The* (1962) d: John Frankenheimer   CM

☐ *Mandabi* (Senegalese/1968) d: Ousmane Sembene   H PR

☐ *Manhattan Melodrama* (1934) d: W.S. Van Dyke II   H PR

☐ *Mannequin* (1937) d: Frank Borzage

☐ *Marat/Sade* (British/1967) d: Peter Brook   H PR

☐ *Marjoe* (1972) d: Howard Smith

☐ *Mark, The* (British/1961) d: Guy Green

☐ *Mark of the Devil* (British-West German/1970) d: Michael Armstrong   T

☐ *Mark of the Vampire* (1935) d: Tod Browning   H

☐ *Mark of Zorro* (1920) d: Fred Niblo   H

☐ *Mark of Zorro, The* (1940) d: Rouben Mamoulian   H PR

☐ *Marlowe* (1969) d: Paul Bogart

☐ *Marquise of O, The* (French-West German/1976) d: Eric Rohmer   H

☐ *Marriage Circle, The* (1924) d: Ernst Lubitsch

☐ *Marriage, Italian Style* (Italian/1964) d: Vittorio De Sica

☐ *Married Woman, The* (French/1964) d: Jean-Luc Godard   H

☐ *Marseillaise, La* (French/1937) d: Jean Renoir

☐ *Marty* (1955) d: Delbert Mann   H

☐ *Mask* (1985) d: Peter Bogdanovich   S PR

- *Mask, The/Eyes of Hell, The* (Canadian/1961) d: Julian Roffman CM
- *Mask of Demitrious, The* (1944) d: Jean Negulesco
- *Mask of Fu Manchu, The* (1932) d: Charles Brabin H PR
- *Massacre* (1933) d: Alan Crosland S PR
- *Master Gunfighter, The* (1975) d: Frank Laughlin
- *Master of the World* (1961) d: William Witney
- *Max Havelaar* (Dutch/1976) d: Föns Rademakers CM
- *Mayerling* (French/1936) d: Anatole Litvak
- *Maze, The* (1953) d: William Cameron Menzies S
- *McVicar* (British/1980) d: Tom Clegg CM
- *Me and the Colonel* (British/ 1958) d: Peter Glenville
- *Melanie* (Canadian/1982) d: Rick Bromfield S
- *Member of the Wedding, The* (1953) d: Fred Zinnemann
- *Memories Within Miss Aggie* (1974) d: Gerard Damiano XXX
- *Men, The* (1950) d: Fred Zinnemann H
- *Mephisto* (Hungarian/1981) d: Istvan Szabo H
- *Mephisto Waltz, The* (1971) d: Paul Wendkos
- *Mercenary, The* (Italian/1970) d: Sergio Corbucci
- *Merchant of Four Seasons* (West German/1971) d: Rainer Werner Fassbinder
- *Mermaids of Tiburon, The* (1962) d: John Lamb CC
- *Merrill's Marauders* (1962) d: Samuel Fuller CM PR
- *Merrily We Go to Hell* (1932) d: Dorothy Arzner
- *Merry Christmas, Mr. Lawrence* (British-Japanese/1983) d: Nagisa Oshima CM PR
- *Merry Widow, The* (1934) d: Ernst Lubitsch H PR
- *Message from Space* (Japanese/ 1978) d: Kinji Fukasaku CC CM
- *Mickey One* (1965) d: Arthur Penn CM
- *Micki & Maude* (1984) d: Blake Edwards
- *Middle of the World, The* (Swiss/ 1974) d: Alain Tanner
- *Midnight* (1939) d: Mitchell Leisen
- *Midsummer Night's Dream, A* (1935) d: Max Reinhardt H
- *Midsummer Night's Sex Comedy, A* (1982) d: Woody Allen
- *Mike's Murder* (1984) d: James Bridges
- *Mikey and Nicky* (1976) d: Elaine May CM PR
- *Milestones* (1975) d: Robert Kramer, John Douglas
- *Milky Way, The* (1936) d: Leo McCarey
- *Milky Way, The* (French/1970) d: Luis Buñuel
- *Millhouse: A White Comedy* (1967) d: Emile de Antonio
- *Million Dollar Legs* (1932) d: Edward Cline CM PR
- *Mind of Mr. Soames, The* (British/1970) d: Alan Cooke S
- *Minnie and Moskovitz* (1971) d: John Cassavetes CM
- *Miracle, The* (Italian/1948) d: Roberto Rossellini H
- *Miracle in Milan* (Italian/1951) d: Vittorio De Sica H
- *Miracle Woman, The* (1931) d: Frank Capra H
- *Miserables, Les* (1935) d: Richard Boleslawski H
- *Mishima* (American-Japanese/ 1985) d: Paul Schrader CM
- *Miss Julie* (Swedish/1950) d: Alf Sjöberg H
- *Mission to Moscow* (1943) d: Michael Curtiz H
- *Mississippi* (1935) d: A. Edward Sutherland H
- *Mississippi Mermaid* (French/ 1970) d: François Truffaut PR
- *Missouri Breaks, The* (1976) d: Arthur Penn CM
- *Mr. and Mrs. Smith* (1941) d: Alfred Hitchcock
- *Mr. Blandings Builds His Dream House* (1948) d: H.C. Potter PR
- *Mr. Klein* (French/1977) d: Joseph Losey
- *Mr. Peabody and the Mermaid* (1948) d: Irving Pichel
- *Mister Roberts* (1955) d: John Ford, Mervyn LeRoy H PR
- *Mr. Rock and Roll* (1957) d: Charles Dubin CC
- *Mr. Skeffington* (1944) d: Vincent Sherman
- *Mrs. Wiggs of the Cabbage Patch* (1934) d: Norman Taurog
- *Moana* (1926) d: Robert Flaherty H PR
- *Moby Dick* (1956) d: John Huston
- *Modesty Blaise* (British/1966) d: Joseph Losey
- *Mogambo* (1953) d: John Ford
- *Molly Maguires, The* (1970) d: Martin Ritt S
- *Moment By Moment* (1978) d: Jane Wagner CC
- *Monitors, The* (1969) d: Jack Shea
- *Monkey Business* (1952) d: Howard Hawks PR
- *Monsieur Beaucaire* (1946) d: George Marshall PR
- *Monsieur Vincent* (French/1947) d: Maurice Cloche H
- *Monster Club, The* (British/1980) d: Roy Ward Baker S
- *Monster on the Campus* (1958) d: Jack Arnold
- *Montenegro* (Swedish-British/ 1981) d: Dusan Makavejev CM
- *Monty Python Live at the Hollywood Bowl* (British/1982) d: Terry Hughes
- *Monty Python's the Meaning of Life* (British/1983) d: Terry Jones CM PR
- *Moon and Sixpence, The* (1942) d: Albert Lewin
- *Moon Is Blue, The* (1953) d: Otto Preminger
- *Moon Over Miami* (1941) d: Walter Lang
- *Moonshine County Express* (1977) d: Gus Trikonis CM PR
- *More American Graffiti* (1979) d: B.W.L. Norton S
- *Morgan the Pirate* (Italian/1961) d: Andre de Toth
- *Morning Glory* (1933) d: Lowell Sherman
- *Morons from Outer Space* (British/1985) d: Griffen Rhys- Jones S CM
- *Moscow Does Not Believe in Tears* (Russian/1980) d: Vladmir Menshov
- *Most Dangerous Man Alive, The* (1961) d: Allan Dwan
- *Mother, Jugs & Speed* (1976) d:

Peter Yates   s

☐ *Mother Wore Tights* (1947) d:
Walter Lang

☐ *Mothra* (Japanese/1962) d:
Inoshiro Honda

☐ *Mother and the Whore, The*
(French/1973) d: Jean Eustache
CM   PR

☐ *Mother Küsters Goes to Heaven*
(West German/1975) d: Rainer
Werner Fassbinder   CM   PR

☐ *Mouchette* (French/1967) d:
Robert Bresson   H   PR

☐ *Moulin Rouge* (1952) d: John
Huston

☐ *Mouse on the Moon* (British/
1963) d: Richard Lester   PR

☐ *Mouse That Roared, The* (British/
1959) d: Jack Arnold   H
PR

☐ *Movie Crazy* (1932) d: Clyde
Bruckman

☐ *Muddy River* (Japanese/1981) d:
Kohei Oguri

☐ *Muppet Movie, The* (1979) d:
James Frawley   PR

☐ *Muppets Take Manhattan, The*
(1984) d: Frank Oz

☐ *Murder at the Gallop* (British/
1963) d: George Pollock

☐ *Murder by Contract* (1958) d:
Irving Lerner

☐ *Murder by Decree* (Canadian-
British/1979) d: Bob Clark
S   PR

☐ *Murder, He Says* (1945) d:
George Marshall   s

☐ *Murder Inc.* (1960) d: Burt
Balaban, Stuart Rosenberg

☐ *Murder on the Orient Express*
(British/1974) d: Sidney Lumet

☐ *Murderers Among Us* (German/
1946) d: Wolfgang Staudte
H   S

☐ *Murders in the Zoo* (1933) d: A.
Edward Sutherland   s

☐ *Muriel* (French-Italian/1963) d:
Alain Resnais

☐ *Music Lovers, The* (British/1971)
d: Ken Russell   CM

☐ *Music Man, The* (1962) d:
Morton Da Costa

☐ *Music Room, The* (Indian/1958)
d: Satyajit Ray   H   PR

☐ *Mustang Country* (1976) d: John
Champion   s

☐ *Mutations, The* (British/1973) d:
Jack Cardiff   CM

☐ *Mutiny on the Bounty* (1962) d:
Lewis Milestone

☐ *My Beautiful Laundrette* (British/
1985) d: Stephen Frears   CM
PR

☐ *My Bodyguard* (1980) d: Tony
Bill

☐ *My Cousin Rachel* (1952) d:
Henry Koster

☐ *My Favorite Blonde* (1942) d:
Sidney Lanfield

☐ *My Favorite Brunette* (1947) d:
Elliott Nugent

☐ *My Favorite Spy* (1951) d:
Norman Z. McLeod

☐ *My Foolish Heart* (1951) d: Mark
Robson   s

☐ *My Sister Eileen* (1955) d:
Richard Quine   PR

☐ *My Son John* (1952) d: Leo
McCarey   CC

☐ *My Uncle Antoine* (Canadian/
1971) d: Claude Jutra

☐ *Myra Breckinridge* (1970) d:
Michael Sarne   CC

☐ *Mysterious Island* (British/1961)
d: Cy Enfield

☐ *Mystery of Edwin Drood* (1935)
d: Stuart Walker

☐ *Mystery of Picasso, The* (French/
1955) d: Henri-Georges Clouzot

☐ *Naked and the Dead, The* (1958)
d: Raoul Walsh

☐ *Naked Came the Stranger* (1975)
d: Henry Paris (Radley
Metzger)   XXX

☐ *Naked City, The* (1948) d: Jules
Dassin   H

☐ *Naked Dawn, The* (1955) d:
Edgar G. Ulmer   CM   PR

☐ *Naked Night, The/Sawdust and
Tinsel* (Swedish/1953) d:
Ingmar Bergman   H

☐ *Nana* (1934) d: Dorothy Arzner

☐ *Narrow Margin, The* (1952) d:
Richard Fleischer

☐ *National Velvet* (1944) d:
Clarence Brown

☐ *Naughty Marietta* (1935) d: W.S.
Van Dyke II   H   PR

☐ *Navy vs. the Night Monsters, The*
(1966) d: Michael Hoey   CC

☐ *Nazarin* (Spanish/1961) d: Luis
Buñuel

☐ *Ned Kelly* (British/1970) d: Tony
Richardson

☐ *Negatives* (British/1968) d: Peter
Medak   CM

☐ *Nell Gwyn* (British/1934) d:
Herbert Wilcox   H

☐ *New Land, The* (Swedish/1972)
d: Jan Troell

☐ *New Leaf, A* (1971) d: Elaine
May   CM   PR

☐ *Newsfront* (Australian/1978) d:
Philip Noyce   CM   PR

☐ *Next Voice You Hear, The* (1950)
d: William Wellman

☐ *Nicholas and Alexandra* (British/
1971) d: Franklin Schaffner

☐ *Nicholas Nickleby* (British/1947)
d: Alberto Cavalcanti

☐ *Nick Carter—Master Detective*
(1939) d: Jacques Tourneur

☐ *Nickelodeon* (1976) d: Peter
Bogdanovich

☐ *Night and Day* (1946) d: Michael
Curtiz

☐ *Night and Fog in Japan*
(Japanese/1960) d: Nagasi
Oshima   H   PR

☐ *Night and the City* (1950) d: Jules
Dassin   S   PR

☐ *Night Caller from Outer Space/
Blood Beast from Outer Space*
(British/1965) d: John Gilling
S   PR

☐ *Night Games* (1980) d: Roger
Vadim   CM

☐ *Night Has a Thousand Eyes*
(1948) d: John Farrow

☐ *Night Monster, The* (1942) d:
Ford Beebe

☐ *Night Moves* (1975) d: Arthur
Penn   CM   PR

☐ *Night Must Fall* (1937) d:
Richard Thorpe

☐ *Night Nurse* (1931) d: William
Wellman

☐ *Night of the Iguana, The* (1964)
d: John Huston

☐ *Night Passage* (1957) d: James
Neilson

☐ *Night Porter, The* (Italian/1974)
d: Liliana Cavani   CM

☐ *Night Shift* (1982) d: Ron Howard
S

☐ *Night They Raided Minsky's, The*
(1968) d: William Friedkin

☐ *Night to Remember, A* (British/
1958) d: Roy Ward Baker

☐ *Night Train/Night Train to
Munich* (British/1940) d: Carol
Reed

☐ *Nightcomers, The* (British/1972)
d: Michael Winner

☐ *Nightfall* (1956) d: Jacques
Tourneur

☐ *Nighthawks* (British/1979) d: Ron
Peck, Paul Hallam   H   PR

□ *Nighthawks* (1981) d: Bruce Malmuth

□ *9 to 5* (1980) d: Colin Higgins

□ *1984* (British/1956) d: Michael Anderson

□ *92 in the Shade* (1975) d: Thomas McGuane   CM

□ *No Highway in the Sky* (British/1951) d: Henry Koster

□ *No Nukes* (1980) d: Julian Schlossberg

□ *No Sad Songs for Me* (1950) d: Rudolph Maté

□ *No Way Out* (1950) d: Joseph L. Mankiewicz

□ *No Way to Treat a Lady* (1968) d: Jack Smight   PR

□ *Noah's Ark* (1929) d: Michael Curtiz   H

□ *Nobody Waved Goodbye* (Canadian/1965) d: Don Owen

□ *None But the Lonely Heart* (1944) d: Clifford Odets

□ *Non-Stop New York* (British/1937) d: Robert Stevenson   S

□ *Norman . . . Is That You?* (1976) d: George Schlatter   CM

□ *North Star, The* (1943) d: Lewis Milestone

□ *Northern Lights* (1979) d: John Hanson   S

□ *Northwest Mounted Police* (1940) d: Cecil B. DeMille

□ *Northwest Passage* (1940) d: King Vidor

□ *Nostalghia* (Russian-Italian/1983) d: Andrei Tarkovsky

□ *Not of This Earth* (1956) d: Roger Corman

□ *Nothing But a Man* (1964) d: Michael Roemer   S   PR

□ *Notte, La* (Italian/1961) d: Michelangelo Antonioni

□ *Nude Bomb, The/Return of Maxwell Smart, The* (1980) d: Clive Donner

□ *Nuit de Varennes, La* (French-Italian/1983) d: Ettore Scola   PR

□ *Number Seventeen* (British/1932) d: Alfred Hitchcock

□ *Numero Deux* (French/1975) d: Jean-Luc Godard

□ *Nun's Story, The* (1959) d: Fred Zinnemann   H

□ *Nurse Sherri/Beyond the Living* (1978) d: Al Adamson   T

□ *Oblomov* (Russian/1980) d: Nikita Mikhalkov

□ *Oblong Box, The* (British/1968) d: Gordon Hessler

□ *Obsession* (1976) d: Brian De Palma   CM

□ *Octagon, The* (1980) d: Eric Karson   CM

□ *October Man, The* (British/1947) d: Roy Ward Baker

□ *Odd Couple, The* (1968) d: Gene Saks

□ *Ode to Billy Joe, The* (1976) d: Max Baer   S   PR

□ *Odette* (British/1950) d: Herbert Wilcox

□ *Of Mice and Men* (1939) d: Lewis Milestone   H

□ *Oh, God!* (1977) d: Carl Reiner

□ *Oklahoma!* (1955) d: Fred Zinnemann

□ *Oklahoma Kid, The* (1939) d: Lloyd Bacon

□ *Old Boyfriends* (1979) d: Joan Tewkesbury

□ *Old Enough* (1984) d: Marisa Silver   S

□ *Old-Fashioned Way, The* (1934) d: William Beaudine   H   PR

□ *Old Ironsides* (1926) d: James Cruze   H   PR

□ *Old Man and the Sea, The* (1958) d: John Sturges   H

□ *On Approval* (British/1943) d: Clive Brook   H

□ *On the Nickel* (1980) d: Ralph Waite   S

□ *On the Yard* (1979) d: Raphael D. Silver   S   PR

□ *One from the Heart* (1982) d: Francis Coppola   S

□ *One Hour with You* (1932) d: Ernst Lubitsch, George Cukor

□ *One Hundred Men and a Girl* (1937) d: Henry Koster

□ *One Is a Lonely Number* (1972) d: Mel Stuart   S

□ *One Million, B.C.* (1940) d: Hal Roach, Hal Roach, Jr., D.W. Griffith (uncredited)   H

□ *One Night of Love* (1934) d: Victor Schertzinger   H

□ *One of Our Aircraft Is Missing* (British/1941) d: Michael Powell, Emeric Pressburger   H

□ *One on One* (1977) d: Lamont Johnson   S

□ *One Potato, Two Potato* (1964) d: Larry Peerce

□ *One Sings, the Other Doesn't* (French-Belgian/1977) d: Agnès Varda   H

□ *One Trick Pony* (1980) d: Robert M. Young

□ *One, Two, Three* (1961) d: Billy Wilder

□ *One Way Passage* (1932) d: Tay Garnett   H   PR

□ *Onion Field, The* (1979) d: Harold Becker   S   PR

□ *Only Angels Have Wings* (1940) d: Howard Hawks

□ *Only Game in Town, The* (1970) d: George Stevens

□ *Opening Night* (1978) d: John Cassavetes   S

□ *Operation Petticoat* (1959) d: Blake Edwards

□ *Orchestra Rehearsal* (Italian/1979) d: Federico Fellini

□ *Organizer, The* (Italian/1963) d: Mario Monicelli   H   PR

□ *Orgy of the Dead* (1965) d: A.C. Stephen   CC

□ *Ossessione* (Italian/1942) d: Luchino Visconti   H   PR

□ *Osterman Weekend, The* (1983) d: Sam Peckinpah

□ *Othello* (Italian/1955) d: Orson Welles

□ *Othello* (British/1955) d: Laurence Olivier   H   PR

□ *Other, The* (1972) d: Robert Mulligan   S   PR

□ *Other Side of the Mountain, The* (1975) d: Larry Peerce   PR

□ *Our Daily Bread/City Girl* (1930) d: F.W. Murnau   H   PR

□ *Our Dancing Daughters* (1928) d: Harry Beaumont   H

□ *Our Hospitality* (1923) d: Buster Keaton, Jack G. Blystone   H   PR

□ *Our Man in Havana* (British/1960) d: Carol Reed

□ *Our Mother's House* (British/1967) d: Jack Clayton

□ *Our Relations* (1936) d: Harry Lachman   H   PR

□ *Our Time/Death of Her Innocence* (1974) d: Peter Hyams

□ *Our Town* (1940) d: Sam Wood

□ *Our Vines Have Tender Grapes* (1945) d: Roy Rowland   PR

□ *Out of Towners, The* (1970) d: Arthur Hiller

□ *Outback/Wake in Fright* (Australian/1971) d: Ted Kotcheff   CM   PR

□ *Outcast of the Islands* (British/1951) d: Carol Reed

- *Outlaw Blues* (1977) d: Richard T. Heffron S
- *Outlaws Is Coming, The* (1965) d: Norman Maurer
- *Outsiders, The* (1983) d: Francis Coppola CM
- *Owl and the Pussycat, The* (1970) d: Herbert Ross

- *Paisan* (Italian/1946) d: Roberto Rossellini H PR
- *Pajama Game, The* (1957) d: George Abbott, Stanley Donen
- *Pandora and the Flying Dutchman* (British/1951) d: Albert Lewin
- *Panic in Needle Park, The* (1971) d: Jerry Schatzberg
- *Panic in the Streets* (1950) d: Elia Kazan H PR
- *Panic in the Year Zero* (1962) d: Ray Milland
- *Panique* (French/1947) d: Julien Duvivier
- *Paper Chase, The* (1973) d: James Bridges
- *Paper Moon* (1973) d: Peter Bogdanovich
- *Papillon* (1973) d: Franklin Schaffner
- *Paradine Case, The* (1948) d: Alfred Hitchcock
- *Paradise Alley* (1978) d: Sylvester Stallone S
- *Paranoiac* (British/1963) d: Freddie Francis
- *Pardon My Sarong* (1942) d: Erle C. Kenton
- *Parents Terribles, Les* (French/1949) d: Jean Cocteau H PR
- *Park Row* (1952) d: Samuel Fuller CM
- *Parting Glances* (1986) d: Bill Sherwood
- *Party Girl* (1958) d: Nicholas Ray CM
- *Passion* (French-Swiss/1982) d: Jean-Luc Godard
- *Passion of Anna, The* (Swedish/1969) d: Ingmar Bergman H PR
- *Passport to Pimlico* (British/1948) d: Henry Cornelius
- *Pat and Mike* (1952) d: George Cukor
- *Pat Garrett and Billy the Kid* (1973) d: Sam Peckinpah
- *Patsy, The* (1964) d: Jerry Lewis

- *Patton* (1970) d: Franklin Schaffner
- *Pauline at the Beach* (French/1983) d: Eric Rohmer
- *Pawnbroker, The* (1965) d: Sidney Lumet
- *Pearl, The* (1948) d: Emilio Fernandez
- *Pedestrian, The* (West German/1974) d: Maximilian Schell
- *Penitentiary* (1979) d: James Fanaka
- *Penthouse* (1933) d: W.S. Van Dyke II
- *People Will Talk* (1951) d: Joseph L. Mankiewicz
- *Peppermint Soda* (French/1977) d: Diane Kurys S PR
- *Perceval* (French/1978) d: Eric Rohmer CM
- *Perfect Couple, A* (1979) d: Robert Altman
- *Period of Adjustment* (1962) d: George Roy Hill
- *Permanent Vacation* (1980) d: Jim Jarmusch CM
- *Pete Kelly's Blues* (1955) d: Jack Webb
- *Pete's Dragon* (1977) d: Don Chaffey
- *Peter Pan* (1953) d: Hamilton Luske, Clyde Geronimi, Wilfred Jackson
- *Petit Soldat, Le* (French/1963) d: Jean-Luc Godard H
- *Peyton Place* (1957) d: Mark Robson S
- *Phantasm* (1979) d: Don Coscarelli S PR
- *Phantom Carriage, The* (Swedish/1921) d: Victor Sjöstrom H PR
- *Phantom India* (Indian/1967–68) d: Louis Malle H PR
- *Phantom Lady* (1944) d: Robert Siodmak CM PR
- *Phantom of Liberty, The* (French/1974) d: Luis Buñuel H PR
- *Phantom of the Opera, The* (1943) d: Arthur Lubin
- *Phantom of the Rue Morgue* (1954) d: Roy Del Ruth
- *Phantom Tollbooth, The* (1969) d: Chuck Jones PR
- *Phase IV* (1974) d: Saul Bass CM
- *Phenix City Story, The* (1955) d: Phil Karlson CM PR
- *Phffft!* (1954) d: Mark Robson

- *Pickpocket* (French/1959) d: Robert Bresson H PR
- *Pickup* (1951) d: Hugo Haas CC
- *Pickup on South Street* (1953) d: Samuel Fuller CM
- *Picnic on the Grass* (French/1959) d: Jean Renoir H
- *Pied Piper, The* (1942) d: Irving Pichel S PR
- *Pigpen* (Italian/1969) d: Pier Paolo Pasolini
- *Pilgrimage* (1933) d: John Ford
- *Pinky* (1949) d: Elia Kazan H
- *Pirate, The* (1948) d: Vincente Minnelli
- *Pirates of Penzance, The* (1983) d: Wilford Leach
- *Pit and the Pendulum, The* (1961) d: Roger Corman
- *Plague of the Zombies, The* (British/1966) d: John Gilling
- *Plainsman, The* (1936) d: Cecil B. DeMille
- *Planet of Blood/Queen of Blood* (1966) d: Curtis Harrington CM
- *Planet of the Vampires* (Italian/1965) d: Mario Bava CM
- *Plantinum Blonde* (1931) d: Frank Capra
- *Platinum High School* (1960) d: Charles Haas CC
- *Play It As It Lays* (1972) d: Frank Perry
- *Playtime* (French/1967) d: Jacques Tati H CM
- *Pleasure Garden, The* (British/1925) d: Alfred Hitchcock
- *Ploughman's Lunch, The* (British/1983) d: Richard Eyre S PR
- *Plumber, The* (Australian/1980) d: Peter Weir S PR
- *Pocketful of Miracles* (1961) d: Frank Capra
- *Pollyanna* (1960) d: David Swift
- *Poor Little Rich Girl* (1936) d: Irving Cummings
- *Pope of Greenwich Village, The* (1984) d: Stuart Rosenberg
- *Popeye* (1980) d: Robert Altman S
- *Poppy* (1936) d: A. Edward Sutherland PR
- *Porgy and Bess* (1959) d: Otto Preminger
- *Pork Chop Hill* (1959) d: Lewis Milestone
- *Portrait of Jason* (1967) d: Shirley Clarke H PR

□ *Portrait of Jennie* (1949) d: William Dieterle

□ *Portrait of Teresa* (Cuban/1979) d: Pastor Vega

□ *Posse* (1975) d: Kirk Douglas

□ *Postman Always Rings Twice, The* (1946) d: Tay Garnett   H   PR

□ *Postman Always Rings Twice, The* (1981) d: Bob Rafelson

□ *Power, The* (1968) d: Byron Haskin

□ *Power and the Glory, The* (1933) d: William K. Howard   H

□ *Prelude to War* (1942) d: Frank Capra   H

□ *Pretty Boy Floyd* (1960) d: Herbert J. Leder

□ *Pretty in Pink* (1986) d: Howard Deutch

□ *Pride and Prejudice* (1940) d: Robert Z. Leonard   H   PR

□ *Pride of St. Louis, The* (1952) d: Harmon Jones

□ *Pride of the Marines* (1945) d: Delmer Daves

□ *Pride of the Yankees* (1942) d: Sam Wood   H   CM

□ *Prime Cut* (1972) d: Michael Ritchie   CM

□ *Prime of Miss Jean Brodie, The* (British/1969) d: Ronald Neame

□ *Prince and the Showgirl, The* (1957) d: Laurence Olivier

□ *Prince of the City* (1981) d: Sidney Lumet

□ *Princess and the Pirate, The* (1944) d: David Butler

□ *Prisoner of Shark Island, The* (1936) d: John Ford

□ *Private Affairs of Bel Ami, The* (1947) d: Albert Lewin

□ *Private Afternoons of Pamela Mann, The* (1975) d: Henry Paris (Radley Metzger)   xxx

□ *Private Files of J. Edgar Hoover, The* (1977) d: Larry Cohen   CM

□ *Private Hell 36* (1954) d: Don Siegel

□ *Private Lessons* (1981) d: Alan Myerson

□ *Private Life of Sherlock Holmes, The* (1970) d: Billy Wilder   S   PR

□ *Private Lives of Elizabeth and Essex, The* (1939) d: Michael Curtiz

□ *Privates on Parade* (British/1982) d: Michael Blakemore

□ *Prizefighter and the Lady, The* (1933) d: W.S. Van Dyke II

□ *Professionals, The* (1966) d: Richard Brooks

□ *Projectionist, The* (1971) d: Harry Hurwitz   S

□ *Prom Night* (Canadian/1980) d: Paul Lynch

□ *Promises! Promises!* (1963) d: King Donovan

□ *Proud Valley, The* (British/1940) d: Pen Tennyson

□ *Providence* (French-British-Swiss/1977) d: Alain Resnais

□ *Prowler, The* (1951) d: Joseph Losey

□ *Psycho II* (1983) d: Richard Franklin   S   PR

□ *Puberty Blues* (Australian/1981) d: Bruce Beresford   S

□ *Pumpkin Eater, The* (British/1964) d: Jack Clayton

□ *Purple Heart, The* (French/1960) d: Lewis Milestone

□ *Purple Noon* (French/1960) d: René Clement

□ *Purple Plain, The* (British/1955) d: Robert Parrish

□ *Pursuit of Happiness, The* (1971) d: Robert Mulligan   S

□ *Puzzle of a Downfall Child* (1970) d: Jerry Schatzberg   S

□ *Pygmalion* (British/1938) d: Anthony Asquith   H

□ *Pyx, The* (Canadian/1973) d: Harvey Hart   S

□ *Quality Street* (1937) d: George Stevens

□ *Quartet* (British/1949) d: Ken Annakin   H   PR

□ *Quatermass Conclusion* (British/1980) d: Piers Haggard

□ *Queen, The* (1968) d: Frank Simon   CM

□ *Queen Kelly* (1928) d: Erich von Stroheim   H   CM

□ *Quest for Fire* (French-Canadian/1981) d: Jean-Jacques Annaud   CM

□ *Quick Millions* (1931) d: Rowland Brown

□ *Quiet American, The* (1958) d: Joseph L. Mankiewicz

□ *Quintet* (1979) d: Robert Altman

□ *Quo Vadis?* (Italian/1912) d: Enrico Guazzoni   H

□ *Quo Vadis?* (1951) d: Mervyn LeRoy

□ *Rabbit Test* (1978) d: Joan Rivers

□ *Racing With the Moon* (1984) d: Richard Benjamin

□ *Racket, The* (1928) d: Lewis Milestone   H

□ *Rafferty and the Gold Dust Twins* (1975) d: Dick Richards   S

□ *Raggedy Ann and Andy* (1977) d: Richard Williams

□ *Ragtime* (1981) d: Milos Forman

□ *Rain* (1932) d: Lewis Milestone   H

□ *Rainmaker, The* (1956) d: Joseph Anthony

□ *Raintree County* (1957) d: Edward Dmytryk

□ *Raisin in the Sun, A* (1961) d: Daniel Petrie

□ *Ramparts of Clay* (French-Algerian/1971) d: Jean-Louis Bertucelli   H   PR

□ *Ramrod* (1947) d: Andre de Toth   S

□ *Random Harvest* (1942) d: Mervyn LeRoy

□ *Rasputin and the Empress* (1932) d: Richard Boleslawski   H

□ *Raven, The* (1963) d: Roger Corman

□ *Raven's End* (Swedish/1963) d: Bo Widerberg

□ *Raw Deal* (1948) d: Anthony Mann

□ *Razor's Edge, The* (1946) d: Edmund Goulding   H

□ *Rebel Rousers* (1967) d: Martin B. Cohen

□ *Reckless Moment, The* (1949) d: Max Ophüls   PR

□ *Red and the Black* (French/1954) d: Claude Autant-Lara

□ *Red Badge of Courage, The* (1951) d: John Huston   H

□ *Red Desert* (Italian-French/1964) d: Michelangelo Antonioni   H   PR

□ *Red Line 7000* (1965) d: Howard Hawks

□ *Red Planet Mars* (1952) d: Harry Horner

□ *Red Pony, The* (1949) d: Lewis Milestone

□ *Red Sky at Morning* (1970) d: James Goldstone   S   PR

□ *Red Sonja* (1985) d: Richard Fleischer

□ *Red Tent, The* (Russian-Italian/1971) d: Mikhail K. Kalatozov

□ *Reflections in a Golden Eye* (1967) d: John Huston

- [ ] *Reign of Terror* (1949) d: Anthony Mann
- [ ] *Reivers, The* (1969) d: Mark Rydell
- [ ] *Rembrandt* (British/1936) d: Alexander Korda
- [ ] *Remember My Name* (1978) d: Alan Rudolph
- [ ] *Renaldo and Clara* (1978) d: Bob Dylan   CM
- [ ] *Requiem for a Heavyweight* (1962) d: Ralph Nelson
- [ ] *Restless Breed, The* (1957) d: Allan Dwan
- [ ] *Return of Count Yorga* (1971) d: Bob Kelljan
- [ ] *Return of Dr. X, The* (1939) d: Vincent Sherman   CC
- [ ] *Return of Martin Guerre, The* (French/1982) d: Daniel Vigne   PR
- [ ] *Return of the Soldier* (British/1983) d: Alan Bridges
- [ ] *Return to Oz* (1985) d: Walter Murch   S
- [ ] *Revenge of the Creature* (1955) d: Jack Arnold
- [ ] *Revolutionary, The* (1970) d: Paul Williams   S PR
- [ ] *Rhapsody in Blue* (1945) d: Irving Rapper
- [ ] *Rich and Strange/East of Shanghai* (British/1932) d: Alfred Hitchcock
- [ ] *Rich Kids* (1979) d: Robert M. Young
- [ ] *Richard Pryor Here and Now* (1983) d: Richard Pryor
- [ ] *Richard III* (British/1956) d: Laurence Olivier   H PR
- [ ] *Ride the Pink Horse* (1947) d: Robert Montgomery   PR
- [ ] *Rider on the Rain* (French/1970) d: René Clement
- [ ] *Riders of the Purple Sage* (1925) d: Lynn Reynolds   H
- [ ] *Rio Grande* (1950) d: John Ford
- [ ] *Riot in Cell Block 11* (1954) d: Don Siegel   CM PR
- [ ] *Rise and Fall of Legs Diamond, The* (1960) d: Budd Boetticher   CM PR
- [ ] *River of No Return* (1954) d: Otto Preminger
- [ ] *River's Edge, The* (1957) d: Allan Dwan
- [ ] *Road to Glory* (1936) d: Howard Hawks
- [ ] *Road to Hong Kong, The* (1962) d: Norman Panama

- [ ] *Road to Morocco, The* (1942) d: David Butler   CM
- [ ] *Road to Rio, The* (1947) d: Norman Z. McLeod   CM
- [ ] *Road to Utopia, The* (1945) d: Hal Walker   CM
- [ ] *Road to Zanzibar, The* (1941) d: Victor Schertzinger   CM
- [ ] *Roadie* (1980) d: Alan Rudolph
- [ ] *Robe, The* (1953) d: Henry Koster
- [ ] *Robin and Marian* (British/1976) d: Richard Lester   S PR
- [ ] *Robinson Crusoe on Mars* (1964) d: Byron Haskin
- [ ] *Rocco and His Brothers* (Italian-French/1960) d: Luchino Visconti   H PR
- [ ] *Rockers* (Jamaican/1978) d: Theodoros Bafaloukos   CM
- [ ] *Roman Holiday* (1953) d: William Wyler   H
- [ ] *Roman Scandals* (1933) d: Frank Tuttle   PR
- [ ] *Roman Spring of Mrs. Stone, The* (1961) d: Jose Quintero   CM
- [ ] *Romance of a Horse Thief* (American-Yugoslavian/1971) d: Abraham Polonsky
- [ ] *Romance on the High Seas* (1948) d: Michael Curtiz
- [ ] *Romantic Englishwoman* (British/1975) d: Joseph Losey   CM
- [ ] *Romeo and Juliet* (1936) d: George Cukor   H
- [ ] *Romeo and Juliet* (British-Italian/1966) d: Franco Zeffirelli   PR
- [ ] *Room at the Top* (British/1959) d: Jack Clayton   H PR
- [ ] *Room for One More* (1952) d: Norman Taurog
- [ ] *Rose Marie* (1936) d: W.S. Van Dyke II   H
- [ ] *Rose Tattoo, The* (1955) d: Daniel Mann   PR
- [ ] *Roseland* (1977) d: James Ivory   CM
- [ ] *Round-Up, The* (Yugoslavian/1966) d: Miklós Jancsó
- [ ] *Roxie Hart* (1942) d: William Wellman
- [ ] *Royal Wedding* (1951) d: Stanley Donen
- [ ] *Ruby Gentry* (1952) d: King Vidor   PR
- [ ] *Rude Boy* (British/1980) d: Jack Hazan, David Mingay   CM
- [ ] *Ruling Class, The* (British/1972) d: Peter Medak   CM

- [ ] *Rumble Fish* (1983) d: Francis Coppola
- [ ] *Run for Cover* (1955) d: Nicholas Ray
- [ ] *Run of the Arrow* (1957) d: Samuel Fuller   CM
- [ ] *Rush to Judgment* (1967) d: Emile de Antonio
- [ ] *Rust Never Sleeps* (1979) d: Bernard Shakey (Neil Young)   CM
- [ ] *Rustler's Rhapsody* (1985) d: Hugh Wilson
- [ ] *Ruthless* (1948) d: Edgar G. Ulmer
- [ ] *Ryan's Daughter* (British/1970) d: David Lean

- [ ] *Sabotage* (British/1936) d: Alfred Hitchcock
- [ ] *Saboteur* (1942) d: Alfred Hitchcock
- [ ] *Sad Sack, The* (1957) d: George Marshall
- [ ] *Safe Place, A* (1971) d: Henry Jaglom   CM
- [ ] *Sahara* (1943) d: Zoltan Korda   PR
- [ ] *Sailor Who Fell from Grace With the Sea, The* (British/1976) d: Lewis John Carlino   CM
- [ ] *Saint Joan* (1957) d: Otto Preminger
- [ ] *St. Louis Blues* (1958) d: Allen Reisner
- [ ] *St. Martin's Lane/Sidewalks of London* (British/1938) d: Tim Whelan   S
- [ ] *St. Valentine's Day Massacre, The* (1967) d: Roger Corman   CM
- [ ] *Salamandre, La* (Swiss/1971) d: Alain Tanner   S PR
- [ ] *Salesman* (1969) d: Albert and David Maysles
- [ ] *Sally of the Sawdust* (1925) d: D.W. Griffith
- [ ] *Salvador* (1986) d: Oliver Stone   S PR
- [ ] *Samson and Delilah* (1949) d: Cecil B. DeMille
- [ ] *Sanctuary* (1961) d: Tony Richardson
- [ ] *Sand Pebbles, The* (1966) d: Robert Wise
- [ ] *Sands of the Kalahari* (British/1965) d: Cy Endfield   S
- [ ] *Sans Soleil* (French/1982) d: Chris Marker

Santa Claus Conquers the Martians (1964) d: Nicholas Webster CC

Santa Fe Trail (1940) d: Michael Curtiz

Saps at Sea (1940) d: Gordon Douglas

Saratoga (1937) d: Jack Conway

Satan Bug, The (1965) d: John Sturges

Satan Met a Lady (1936) d: William Dieterle

Satan's Sadists (1969) d: Al Adamson T

Saturday Night and Sunday Morning (British/1960) d: Karel Reisz H PR

Savage Eye, The (1960) d: Ben Maddow CM

Savage Innocents, The (British-French-Italian/1959) d: Nicholas Ray CM

Savage Messiah (British/1972) d: Ken Russell CM

Savage Seven, The (1968) d: Richard Rush CM

Savages (1972) d: James Ivory CM

Saxon Charm, The (1948) d: Robert Montgomery

Sayonara (1957) d: Joshua Logan

Scandal in Paris/Thieves' Holiday (1946) d: Douglas Sirk S

Scandal Sheet (1952) d: Phil Karlson

Scared Stiff (1953) d: George Marshall

Scarlet Claw, The (1944) d: Roy William Neill PR

Scarlet Letter, The (1926) d: Victor Seastrom H

Scars of Dracula (British/1971) d: Roy Ward Baker

Scenes from a Marriage (Swedish/1973) d: Ingmar Bergman H PR

Schizo (British/1977) d: Pete Walker CM

Schlock (1971) d: John Landis S CM PR

School for Scoundrels (British/1960) d: Robert Hamer PR

Screaming Mimi (1958) d: Gerd Oswald CM

Sea Wife (British/1957) d: Bob McNaught

Sea Wolf, The (1941) d: Michael Curtiz PR

Séance on a Wet Afternoon (British/1964) d: Bryan Forbes

Search, The (1948) d: Fred Zinnemann

Search for Bridey Murphy, The (1956) d: Noel Langley

Secret Agent (British/1936) d: Alfred Hitchcock

Secret Ceremony (British/1968) d: Joseph Losey CM

Secret Honor (1984) d: Robert Altman CM

Secret Life of Walter Mitty, The (1947) d: Norman Z. McLeod

Secret of NIMH, The (1982) d: Don Bluth

Secret Places (Australian/1985) d: Zelda Barron S

Secret Policeman's Other Ball, The (British/1982) d: Julian Temple, Roger Graef

Seduced and Abandoned (Italian/1964) d: Pietro Germi

Seeing Red: Stories of American Communists (1983) d: Julia Reichert

Seizure (Canadian/1974) d: Oliver Stone

Senso (Italian/1954) d: Luchino Visconti H

Sensuous Nurse, The (Italian/1976) d: Nello Rossati

Separate Tables (1958) d: Delbert Mann

Sergeant Rutledge (1960) d: John Ford

Sergeant York (1941) d: Howard Hawks H

Serial (1980) d: Bill Persky

Serpico (1973) d: Sidney Lumet

Servant, The (British/1963) d: Joseph Losey H CM PR

Seven Chances (1925) d: Buster Keaton H PR

Seven Days to Noon (British/1950) d: John and Roy Boulting

Seven Little Foys, The (1955) d: Melville Shavelson

Seven Percent Solution, The (1976) d: Herbert Ross

Seven Women (1966) d: John Ford CM

1776 (1972) d: Peter H. Hunt

Seventh Cross, The (1944) d: Fred Zinnemann

Seventh Heaven (1927) d: Frank Borzage H

Seventh Veil, The (British/1945) d: Compton Bennett

Sex Kittens Go to College/Beauty and the Robot, The (1960) d: Albert Zugsmith CC

Sex World (1978) d: Anthony Spinelli XXX

Shack Out on 101 (1955) d: Edward Dein CC CM

Shadows (1960) d: John Cassavetes H CM PR

Shadows of Forgotten Ancestors/Wild Horses of Fire (Russian/1964) d: Sergei Paradzhanov

Shaggy Dog, The (1959) d: Charles Barton

Shake Hands with the Devil (1959) d: Michael Anderson

Shakespeare Wallah (Indian/1965) d: James Ivory

Shame (Swedish/1968) d: Ingmar Bergman H PR

Shameless Old Lady, The (French/1965) d: René Allio

Shampoo (1975) d: Hal Ashby

Shanks (1974) d: William Castle S

Sharky's Machine (1981) d: Burt Reynolds S

She (1935) d: Irving Pichel, Lansing D. Holden

She (British/1965) d: Robert Day

Sheba Baby (1975) d: William Girdler

Sheer Madness (West German/1985) d: Margarethe Von Trotta

Sheik, The (1921) d: George Melford H

Sherlock Holmes (1932) d: William K. Howard

Shining Victory (1941) d: Irving Rapper

Ship of Fools (1965) d: Stanley Kramer

Shock Treatment (1981) d: Jim Sharman CM

Shogun Assassin (Japanese/1980) d: Kenji Misumi, Robert Houston CM

Shoot the Moon (1982) d: Alan Parker

Shooting Party, The (British/1985) d: Alan Bridges

Shootist, The (1976) d: Don Siegel S

Shop on Main Street, The (Czech/1964) d: Jan Kadar

Short Eyes (1977) d: Robert M. Young S PR

Shout, The (British/1979) d: Jerzy Skolomowski CM

Show Boat (1951) d: George Sidney

Siberiade (Russian/1979) d:

Andrei-Mikhalov Konchalovsky

- *Siddhartha* (1973) d: Conrad Rooks
- *Signal 7* (1983) d: Rob Nilsson
- *Silence, The* (Swedish/1963) d: Ingmar Bergman
- *Silencers, The* (1966) d: Phil Karlson
- *Silent Movie* (1976) d: Mel Brooks
- *Silent Night, Bloody Night* (1973) d: Theodore Gershuny
- *Silent Running* (1971) d: Douglas Trumbull   CM
- *Silent Scream* (1980) d: Denny Harris
- *Silent World, The* (French/1955) d: Jacques-Yves Cousteau   PR
- *Silk Stockings* (1957) d: Rouben Mamoulian
- *Silkwood* (1983) d: Mike Nichols
- *Silver Chalice, The* (1954) d: Victor Saville   CC
- *Silver Lode* (1954) d: Allan Dwan
- *Silver Streak* (1976) d: Arthur Hiller
- *Simon* (1980) d: Marshall Brickman
- *Since You Went Away* (1944) d: John Cromwell
- *Sitting Pretty* (1948) d: Walter Lang   PR
- *Six of a Kind* (1934) d: Leo McCarey
- *Skidoo* (1969) d: Otto Preminger
- *Skin Game* (1971) d: Paul Bogart
- *Skippy* (1931) d: Norman Taurog
- *Sky Above, the Mud Below, The* (French/1959) d: Pierre-Dominique Gaisseau   H   PR
- *Skyline* (Spanish/1983) d: Fernando Colomo
- *Slave of the Cannibal God* (Italian/1978) d: Sergio Martino   CC
- *Sleeping Car Murders, The* (French/1966) d: Costa-Gavras
- *Sleeping Dogs* (New Zealand/1977) d: Roger Donaldson   S
- *Sleuth* (1972) d: Joseph L. Mankiewicz   H
- *Slight Case of Murder, A* (1938) d: Lloyd Bacon
- *Slime People, The* (1962) d: Robert Hutton   CC
- *Slither* (1973) d: Howard Zieff
- *Slumber Party '57* (1976) d: William A. Levey   CM
- *Smallest Show on Earth, The* (British/1957) d: Basil Dearden   S
- *Smile* (1975) d: Michael Ritchie   PR
- *Smokey and the Bandit* (1977) d: Hal Needham
- *Smooth Talk* (1985) d: Joyce Chopra   S
- *Sniper, The* (1952) d: Edward Dmytryk
- *So Dark the Night* (1946) d: Joseph H. Lewis   S
- *S.O.B.* (1981) d: Blake Edwards
- *Sodom and Gomorrah* (Italian/1963) d: Robert Aldrich, Sergio Leone
- *Soft Skin, The* (French/1964) d: François Truffaut
- *Soldier Blue* (1970) d: Ralph Nelson
- *Soldier in the Rain* (1963) d: Ralph Nelson
- *Soldier of Orange* (Dutch/1979) d: Paul Verhoeven   CM   PR
- *Solid Gold Cadillac, The* (1956) d: Richard Quine
- *Some Came Running* (1958) d: Vincente Minnelli
- *Somebody Up There Likes Me* (1956) d: Robert Wise
- *Son of Dracula* (1943) d: Robert Siodmak
- *Son of Frankenstein* (1939) d: Rowland V. Lee
- *Son of Fury* (1942) d: John Cromwell   PR
- *Son of Paleface* (1952) d: Frank Tashlin
- *Son of the Sheik* (1926) d: George Fitzmaurice   H
- *Song is Born, A* (1948) d: Howard Hawks
- *Song of Bernadette, The* (1943) d: Henry Hathaway
- *Song of Songs* (1933) d: Rouben Mamoulian
- *Song of the South* (1946) d: Wilfred Jackson, Harve Foster   H
- *Songwriter* (1985) d: Alan Rudolph
- *Sons and Lovers* (British/1960) d: Jack Cardiff
- *Sounder* (1972) d: Martin Ritt
- *Soup for One* (1982) d: Jonathan Kaufer
- *South Pacific* (1958) d: Joshua Logan
- *Sparkle* (1976) d: Sam O'Steen   S
- *Sparrows* (1926) d: William Beaudine   H   PR
- *Specter of the Rose* (1946) d: Ben Hecht
- *Speedy* (1928) d: Ted Wilde
- *Spellbound* (1945) d: Alfred Hitchcock
- *Spermula* (French/1975) d: Charles Matton
- *Spider's Strategem, The* (Italian/1970) d: Bernardo Bertolucci
- *Spirit of St. Louis, The* (1957) d: Billy Wilder
- *Spite Marriage* (1929) d: Edward Sedgwick, Jr.
- *Spoilers, The* (1942) d: Ray Enright
- *Spook Who Sat By the Door, The* (1973) d: Ivan Dixon
- *Spy Who Came in from the Cold* (1965) d: Martin Ritt
- *Stage Fright* (1950) d: Alfred Hitchcock
- *Stairway to Heaven/Matter of Life and Death, A* (British/1946) d: Michael Powell, Emeric Pressburger
- *Stalker* (Russian/1980) d: Andrei Tarkovsky   CM   PR
- *Star, The* (1953) d: Stuart Heisler
- *Star Is Born, A* (1976) d: Frank Pierson
- *Stars in My Crown* (1950) d: Jacques Tourneur   S   PR
- *Starting Over* (1979) d: Alan J. Pakula
- *State of the Union* (1948) d: Frank Capra
- *State of Things* (West German/1982) d: Wim Wenders
- *Station-Six Sahara* (British/1964) d: Seth Holt
- *Stavisky* (French/1974) d: Alain Resnais
- *Stay Hungry* (1976) d: Bob Rafelson   CM
- *Steamboat Bill, Jr.* (1928) d: Charles F. Reisner   H   PR
- *Steamboat 'Round the Bend* (1935) d: John Ford
- *Steelyard Blues* (1973) d: Alan Myerson   CM
- *Stepford Wives, The* (1975) d: Bryan Forbes
- *Steppenwolf* (1974) d: Fred Haines   CM
- *Sterile Cuckoo, The* (1969) d: Alan J. Pakula
- *Still of the Night/Stab* (1982) d: Robert Benton   S

- [ ] *Sting, The* (1973) d: George Roy Hill H
- [ ] *Stir Crazy* (1980) d: Sidney Poitier
- [ ] *Storm Over Asia/Heir of Genghis Khan, The* (Russian/1928) d: V. I. Pudovkin H
- [ ] *Story of a Three Day Pass, The* (French/1967) d: Melvin Van Peebles
- [ ] *Story of Alexander Graham Bell, The* (1939) d: Irving Cummings
- [ ] *Story of G.I. Joe, The* (1945) d: William Wellman H
- [ ] *Story of Joanna, The* (1975) d: Gerard Damiano XXX
- [ ] *Story of Louis Pasteur, The* (1936) d: William Dieterle
- [ ] *Story of Mankind, The* (1957) d: Irwin Allen CC
- [ ] *Story of Vernon and Irene Castle, The* (1939) d: H.C. Potter
- [ ] *Straight Shooting* (1917) d: John Ford
- [ ] *Strait-Jacket* (1964) d: William Castle
- [ ] *Strange One, The* (1957) d: Jack Garfein
- [ ] *Stranger and the Gunfighter, The* (Italian/1976) d: Anthony Dawson
- [ ] *Stranger on Horseback* (1955) d: Jacques Tourneur
- [ ] *Stranger on the Third Floor, The* (1940) d: Boris Ingster S
- [ ] *Strangler, The* (1964) d: Burt Topper
- [ ] *Strangler of the Swamp* (1945) d: Frank Wisbar S CM PR
- [ ] *Stranglers of Bombay, The* (British/1959) d: Terence Fisher
- [ ] *Strategic Air Command* (1955) d: Anthony Mann
- [ ] *Stratton Story, The* (1949) d: Sam Wood
- [ ] *Strawberry Blonde, The* (1941) d: Raoul Walsh
- [ ] *Strawberry Statement, The* (1970) d: Stuart Hagmann
- [ ] *Stray Dog* (Japanese/1949) d: Akira Kurosawa
- [ ] *Streamers* (1983) d: Robert Altman S
- [ ] *Street Fighter, The* (Hong Kong/1975) d: Shigehiro Ozawa
- [ ] *Street Love/Scarred* (1983) d: Rose-Marie Turko CM
- [ ] *Street of Shame* (Japanese/1955) d: Kenji Mizoguchi H PR
- [ ] *Strike* (Russian/1924) d: Sergei M. Eisenstein H PR
- [ ] *Strike Me Pink* (1936) d: Norman Taurog PR
- [ ] *Stripper, The* (1963) d: Franklin Schaffner
- [ ] *Stromboli* (Italian/1949) d: Roberto Rossellini H
- [ ] *Strong Man, The* (1926) d: Frank Capra H PR
- [ ] *Strong Medicine* (1980) d: Richard Foreman CM
- [ ] *Stroszek* (West German/1977) d: Werner Herzog
- [ ] *Student Bodies* (1981) d: Mickey Rose S PR
- [ ] *Student of Prague, The* (German/1913) d: Stellan Rye H
- [ ] *Student Teachers, The* (1973) d: Jonathan Kaplin CM
- [ ] *Study in Terror, A* (British/1965) d: James Hill
- [ ] *Subject Was Roses, The* (1968) d: Ulu Grosbard
- [ ] *Subway* (French/1986) d: Luc Besson
- [ ] *Suburbia* (1984) d: Penelope Spheeris
- [ ] *Such a Gorgeous Kid Like Me* (French/1973) d: François Truffaut
- [ ] *Such Good Friends* (1971) d: Otto Preminger
- [ ] *Suddenly* (1954) d: Lewis Allen S
- [ ] *Suddenly, Last Summer* (1959) d: Joseph L. Mankiewicz
- [ ] *Sugar Cane Alley* (Martinique/1983) d: Euzhan Palcy S PR
- [ ] *Sugarbaby* (West German/1985) d: Percy Adlon
- [ ] *Sullivans, The/Fighting Sullivans, The* (1944) d: Lloyd Bacon
- [ ] *Summer and Smoke* (1961) d: Peter Glenville
- [ ] *Summer of '42* (1971) d: Robert Mulligan
- [ ] *Summer Stock* (1950) d: Charles Walters
- [ ] *Summer Storm* (1944) d: Douglas Sirk
- [ ] *Sun Also Rises, The* (1957) d: Henry King
- [ ] *Sun Never Sets, The* (1939) d: Rowland V. Lee
- [ ] *Sun Shines Bright, The* (1953) d: John Ford CM PR
- [ ] *Sunday, Bloody Sunday* (British/1971) d: John Schlesinger
- [ ] *Sundays and Cybèle* (French/1962) d: Serge Bourguignon
- [ ] *Sundowners, The* (1960) d: Fred Zinnemann PR
- [ ] *Sunshine Boys, The* (1975) d: Herbert Ross
- [ ] *Super, El* (1979) d: Leon Ichaso, Orlando Jimenez-Leal S PR
- [ ] *Superfly* (1972) d: Gordon Parks, Jr. CM
- [ ] *Supergirl* (1984) d: Jeannot Szwarc
- [ ] *Superman III* (1983) d: Richard Lester
- [ ] *Supervixens* (1975) d: Russ Meyer
- [ ] *Support Your Local Sheriff* (1969) d: Burt Kennedy
- [ ] *Sure Thing, The* (1985) d: Rob Reiner S PR
- [ ] *Surrender* (1927) d: Edward Sloman S
- [ ] *Susan and God* (1940) d: George Cukor
- [ ] *Swamp Thing* (1982) d: Wes Craven
- [ ] *Swamp Water* (1941) d: Jean Renoir
- [ ] *Swamp Women* (1955) d: Roger Corman
- [ ] *Swarm, The* (1978) d: Irwin Allen CC
- [ ] *Swann in Love* (West German-French/1984) d: Volker Schlöndorff
- [ ] *Sweet Bird of Youth* (1962) d: Richard Brooks
- [ ] *Sweet Charity* (1969) d: Bob Fosse PR
- [ ] *Sweet Hours* (Spanish/1982) d: Carlos Saura
- [ ] *Sweet Movie* (French-Canadian/1974) d: Dusan Makavejev CM
- [ ] *Sweet Sugar* (1972) d: Michel Levesque CM
- [ ] *Swimmer, The* (1968) d: Frank Perry CM
- [ ] *Swing Shift* (1984) d: Jonathan Demme
- [ ] *Swiss Family Robinson* (1960) d: Ken Annakin
- [ ] *Swiss Miss* (1938) d: John W. Blystone
- [ ] *Sympathy for the Devil/One Plus One* (French/1970) d: Jean-Luc Godard

- [ ] *Tabu* (1931) d: Robert Flaherty, F.W. Murnau H PR

□ *Take Me Out to the Ball Game* (1949) d: Busby Berkeley

□ *Taking of Pelham One Two Three, The* (1974) d: Joseph Sargent

□ *Taking Off* (1971) d: Milos Forman   CM

□ *Tales of Hoffmann* (British/1951) d: Michael Powell, Emeric Pressburger   H

□ *Tales of Manhattan* (1942) d: Julien Duvivier

□ *Tales of Ordinary Madness* (Italian/1983) d: Marco Ferreri   CM

□ *Tales of Terror* (1962) d: Roger Corman

□ *Talk Dirty to Me II* (1983) d: Tim McDonald   XXX   CM

□ *Talk of the Town, The* (1942) d: George Stevens

□ *Tall Target, The* (1951) d: Anthony Mann

□ *Tamango* (French/1957) d: John Berry

□ *Tamarind Seed, The* (1974) d: Blake Edwards   S

□ *Tanya's Island* (Canadian/1980) d: Alfred Sole

□ *Tarantula* (1955) d: Jack Arnold

□ *Tarnished Angels, The* (1958) d: Douglas Sirk   CM   PR

□ *Tarzan, the Ape Man* (1981) d: John Derek   CC

□ *Tarzan the Fearless* (1933) d: Robert Hill

□ *Tarzan the Magnificent* (British/1960) d: Robert Day

□ *Taste of Honey, A* (British/1961) d: Tony Richardson

□ *Tattered Dress, The* (1957) d: Jack Arnold

□ *Teahouse of the August Moon, The* (1956) d: Daniel Mann

□ *Teenage Cheerleader* (1974) d: none listed   XXX   PR

□ *Tell Me a Riddle* (1980) d: Lee Grant   S   PR

□ *Tell Me That You Love Me, Junie Moon* (1970) d: Otto Preminger

□ *Tell Them Willie Boy Was Here* (1969) d: Abraham Polonsky

□ *Ten From Your Show of Shows* (1973) d: Max Leibman   PR

□ *Teorema* (Italian/1968) d: Pier Paolo Pasolini   CM

□ *Terminal Man, The* (1974) d: Mike Hodges

□ *Terra Trema, La* (Italian/1948) d: Luchino Visconti   H

□ *Terror in a Texas Town* (1958) d: Joseph H. Lewis

□ *Terror Train* (Canadian/1980) d: Roger Spottiswoode

□ *Testament of Orpheus, The* (French/1959) d: Jean Cocteau   H

□ *That Cold Day in the Park* (1969) d: Robert Altman   CM

□ *That Lady in Ermine* (1948) d: Ernst Lubitsch, Otto Preminger

□ *That Man from Rio* (French/1964) d: Philippe de Broca   PR

□ *That Sinking Feeling* (Scottish/1979) d: Bill Forsythe   S

□ *Themroc* (French/1973) d: Claude Faraldi   S

□ *There's No Business Like Show Business* (1954) d: Walter Lang

□ *Therese and Isabelle* (1968) d: Radley Metzger

□ *Thérèse Desqueyroux* (French/1962) d: Georges Franju

□ *They All Laughed* (1981) d: Peter Bogdanovich

□ *They Call Me Trinity* (Italian/1971) d: E.B. Clucher

□ *They Died With Their Boots On* (1941) d: Raoul Walsh   H   CM   PR

□ *They Drive By Night* (1940) d: Raoul Walsh

□ *They Knew What They Wanted* (1940) d: Garson Kanin

□ *They Live By Night* (1949) d: Nicholas Ray   CM   PR

□ *They Made Me a Criminal* (1939) d: Busby Berkeley

□ *They Shoot Horses, Don't They?* d: Sydney Pollack   H   CM   PR

□ *They Were Expendable* (1945) d: John Ford   S   PR

□ *Thief* (1981) d: Michael Mann

□ *Thieves Highway* (1949) d: Jules Dassin

□ *Third Generation, The* (West German/1979) d: Rainer Werner Fassbinder

□ *13 Frightened Girls* (1963) d: William Castle

□ *13 Ghosts* (1960) d: William Castle   CM

□ *Thirty Seconds Over Tokyo* (1944) d: Mervyn LeRoy

□ *36 Hours* (1964) d: George Seaton   S

□ *This Is Elvis* (1981) d: Malcolm Leo, Andrew Salt

□ *This Man Must Die* (French/1970) d: Claude Chabrol   H   PR

□ *This Property Is Condemned* (1966) d: Sydney Pollack

□ *This Sporting Life* (British/1963) d: Lindsay Anderson   H   PR

□ *Thomas the Imposter* (French/1965) d: Georges Franju

□ *1000 Eyes of Dr. Mabuse, The* (West German-French-Italian/1960) d: Fritz Lang

□ *Three Ages, The* (1923) d: Buster Keaton, Eddie Cline

□ *Three Bad Men* (1926) d: John Ford

□ *Three Caballeros, The* (1945) d: Norman Ferguson

□ *Three Days of the Condor* (1975) d: Sydney Pollack

□ *Three in an Attic* (1968) d: Richard Wilson   CM

□ *3 Men and a Cradle* (French/1985) d: Coline Serreau

□ *Three Musketeers, The* (1939) d: Allan Dwan

□ *Three Musketeers, The* (1948) d: George Sidney

□ *Three on a Match* (1932) d: Mervyn LeRoy

□ *Three on a Meathook* (1973) d: William Girdler   T

□ *Three Sisters* (British/1970) d: Laurence Olivier

□ *Three Smart Girls* (1937) d: Henry Koster

□ *Three Strangers* (1946) d: Jean Negulesco

□ *3:10 to Yuma* (1957) d: Delmer Daves

□ *Three Worlds of Gulliver, The* (British/1960) d: Jack Sher

□ *Threepenny Opera, The* (German/1931) d: G.W. Pabst   H   PR

□ *Threshold* (Canadian/1981) d: Richard Pearce   S

□ *Throne of Blood* (Japanese/1957) d: Akira Kurosawa

□ *Through a Glass Darkly* (Swedish/1962) d: Ingmar Bergman   H

□ *Thunder Bay* (1953) d: Anthony Mann

□ *Thunderbolt and Lightfoot* (1974) d: Michael Cimino

□ *Thundercrack* (1976) d: Curt McDowell   CM

□ *Tiger Bay* (British/1959) d: J. Lee Thompson   PR

☐ *Tiger Makes Out, The* (1967) d: Arthur Hiller S
☐ *Tiger Shark* (1932) d: Howard Hawks
☐ *Tight Little Island/Whisky Galore* (British/1949) d: Alexander Mackendrick
☐ *Tight Spot* (1955) d: Phil Karlson
☐ *Tillie and Gus* (1933) d: Francis Martin
☐ *Tillie's Punctured Romance* (1914) d: Mack Sennett
☐ *Time for Dying, A* (1969) d: Budd Boetticher CM
☐ *Time of Their Lives, The* (1946) d: Charles Barton
☐ *Time of Your Life, The* (1948) d: H.C. Potter
☐ *Time Stands Still* (Hungarian/1981) d: Peter Gothar
☐ *Time to Live and a Time to Die, A* (1958) d: Douglas Sirk
☐ *Times of Harvey Milk, The* (1984) d: Robert Epstein
☐ *Tin Drum, The* (West German/1979) d: Volker Schlöndorff
☐ *Tin Pan Alley* (1940) d: Walter Lang
☐ *Titanic* (1953) d: Jean Negulesco
☐ *Titicut Follies* (1967) d: Frederick Wiseman
☐ *T-Men* (1947) d: Anthony Mann
☐ *To Catch a Thief* (1955) d: Alfred Hitchcock
☐ *To Die in Madrid* (French/1965) d: Frederic Rossif
☐ *To Die of Love* (French/1972) d: Andre Cayatte
☐ *To Hell and Back* (1955) d: Jesse Hibbs
☐ *To Kill a Mockingbird* (1962) d: Robert Mulligan
☐ *To Live and Die in L.A.* (1985) d: William Friedkin CM
☐ *To the Ends of the Earth* (1948) d: Robert Stevenson
☐ *Tobacco Road* (1941) d: John Ford
☐ *Tol'able David* (1921) d: Henry King H PR
☐ *Tom Brown's School Days* (British/1951) d: Gordon Parry
☐ *Tom, Dick, and Harry* (1941) d: Garson Kanin
☐ *Tom Jones* (British/1963) d: Tony Richardson H
☐ *Toni* (French/1935) d: Jean Renoir H
☐ *Too Late the Hero* (1970) d: Robert Aldrich

☐ *Toolbox Murders, The* (1978) d: Dennis Donnelly T
☐ *Topkapi!* (1964) d: Jules Dassin
☐ *Topper Returns* (1941) d: Roy Del Ruth
☐ *Topper Takes a Trip* (1939) d: Norman Z. Mcleod
☐ *Tora! Tora! Tora!* (American-Japanese/1970) d: Richard Fleischer, Toshio Masuda, Kinji Fakasaku
☐ *Torment* (Swedish/1947) d: Alf Sjöberg H PR
☐ *Torn Curtain* (1966) d: Alfred Hitchcock
☐ *Tortilla Flat* (1942) d: Victor Fleming
☐ *Tous Va Bien* (French/1972) d: Jean-Luc Godard
☐ *Tower of London* (1939) d: Rowland V. Lee
☐ *Tracks* (1977) d: Henry Jaglom CM
☐ *Trader Horn* (1931) d: W.S. Van Dyke II H
☐ *Traffic* (French/1972) d: Jacques Tati
☐ *Train, The* (1965) d: John Frankenheimer CM
☐ *Tramp, Tramp, Tramp* (1926) d: Harry Edwards
☐ *Transatlantic Tunnel/Tunnel, The* (British/1935) d: Maurice Elvey H
☐ *Traviata, La* (Italian/1982) d: Franco Zefferelli
☐ *T.R. Baskin* (1971) d: Herbert Ross
☐ *Treasure Island* (1934) d: Victor Fleming
☐ *Treasure Island* (1950) d: Byron Haskin
☐ *Tree Grows in Brooklyn, A* (1945) d: Elia Kazan
☐ *Trial of Billy Jack, The* (1974) d: Frank Laughlin
☐ *Trip, The* (1967) d: Roger Corman
☐ *Trip to Bountiful, The* (1985) d: Peter Masterson
☐ *Tropic of Cancer* (1970) d: Joseph Strick CM
☐ *Trouble in Mind* (1985) d: Alan Rudolph CM S
☐ *Trouble with Girls, The/Chautauqua* (1969) d: Peter Tewksbury S PR
☐ *Troublemaker, The* (1964) d: Theodore J. Flicker
☐ *Truck Stop Women* (1974) d:

Mark Lester CM
☐ *True Confessions* (1981) d: Ulu Grosbard
☐ *True Grit* (1969) d: Henry Hathaway H
☐ *True Heart Susie* (1919) d: D.W. Griffith H
☐ *Try and Get Me/Sound of Fury, The* (1951) d: Cyril Endfield S PR
☐ *True Story of Jesse James, The* (1957) d: Nicholas Ray
☐ *Tumbleweeds* (1925) d: King Baggot
☐ *Tunes of Glory* (British/1960) d: Ronald Neame
☐ *Turning Point, The* (1977) d: Herbert Ross
☐ *Twelve O'Clock High* (1949) d: Henry King
☐ *27th Day, The* (1957) d: William Asher
☐ *20,000 Leagues Under the Sea* (1954) d: Richard Fleischer
☐ *Twice in a Lifetime* (1985) d: Bud Yorkin S
☐ *Twice Upon a Time* (1983) d: John Korty S
☐ *Twinkle Twinkle, Killer Kane/Ninth Configuration, The* (1980) d: William Peter Blatty CM
☐ *Twins of Evil* (British/1972) d: John Hough
☐ *Twitch of the Death Nerve/Last House on the Left Part II* (Italian/1972) d: Mario Bava CM PR
☐ *Two-Faced Woman* (1941) d: George Cukor
☐ *Two for the Seesaw* (1962) d: Robert Wise PR
☐ *Two of Us, The* (French/1967) d: Claude Berri
☐ *Two or Three Things That I Know About Her* (French/1967) d: Jean-Luc Godard PR
☐ *Two Rode Together* (1961) d: John Ford
☐ *Two Weeks in Another Town* (1962) d: Vincente Minnelli
☐ *Two Women* (Italian/1961) d: Vittorio De Sica H TR
☐ *Twonky, The* (1953) d: Arch Oboler CM

☐ *UFOria* (1980) d: John Binder S
☐ *Ugly American, The* (1963) d: George Englund

☐ *Ulysses* (Italian/1955) d: Mario Camerini

☐ *Ulzana's Raid* (1972) d: Robert Aldrich   CM   PR

☐ *Unconquered* (1947) d: Cecil B. DeMille

☐ *Undead, The* (1957) d: Roger Corman

☐ *Under Capricorn* (British/1949) d: Alfred Hitchcock

☐ *Under Fire* (1983) d: Roger Spottiswoode   PR

☐ *Under Milk Wood* (British/1973) d: Andrew Sinclair

☐ *Under the Volcano* (1984) d: John Huston

☐ *Under Two Flags* (1936) d: Frank Lloyd

☐ *Undercover Man, The* (1949) d: Joseph H. Lewis

☐ *Undertaker and His Pals, The* (1967) d: T.L.P. Twicegood   T

☐ *Underworld* (1927) d: Josef von Sternberg   H   PR

☐ *Undying Monster, The* (1942) d: John Brahm

☐ *Unforgiven, The* (1960) d: John Huston

☐ *Unholy Rollers* (1972) d: Vernon Zimmerman   CM

☐ *Unholy Three, The* (1925) d: Tod Browning   H

☐ *Unholy Three, The* (1930) d: Jack Conway   H

☐ *Union Maids* (1976) d: Julia Reichert

☐ *Union Pacific* (1939) d: Cecil B. DeMille

☐ *Unman, Wittering, and Zigo* (British/1971) d: John MacKenzie   S

☐ *Untamed Youth* (1957) d: Howard W. Koch

☐ *Up the River* (1930) d: John Ford

☐ *Uptown Saturday Night* (1974) d: Sidney Poitier

☐ *Urban Cowboy* (1980) d: James Bridges   PR

☐ *Valentino* (1977) d: Ken Russell   CM

☐ *Valley Girl* (1983) d: Martha Coolidge

☐ *Valley of Gwangi, The* (1969) d: James O'Connolly

☐ *Valley of the Dolls* (1967) d: Mark Robson   CC

☐ *Variety* (German/1925) d: E.A. Dupont   H

☐ *Variety* (1985) d: Bette Gordon   S

☐ *Variety Lights* (Italian/1951) d: Federico Fellini   H

☐ *Vengeance Is Mine* (Japanese/1979) d: Shohei Imamura   H   PR

☐ *Vera Cruz* (1954) d: Robert Aldrich   CM

☐ *Verboten!* (1959) d: Samuel Fuller

☐ *Verdict, The* (1946) d: Don Siegel

☐ *Verdict, The* (1982) d: Sidney Lumet   PR

☐ *Very Curious Girl, A* (French/1969) d: Nelly Kaplan   PR

☐ *Victor/Victoria* (1982) d: Blake Edwards   CM

☐ *View from the Bridge, A* (American-French-Italian/1962) d: Sidney Lumet   PR

☐ *Vigil in the Night* (1940) d: George Stevens   PR

☐ *Vikings, The* (1958) d: Richard Fleischer

☐ *Village of the Giants* (1965) d: Wolf Rilla   CC

☐ *Violons du Bal, Les* (French/1974) d: Michel Drach   PR

☐ *Violette* (French/1978) d: Claude Chabrol   H   PR

☐ *Virgin and the Gypsy, The* (British/1970) d: Christopher Miles

☐ *Virgin Spring, The* (Swedish/1959) d: Ingmar Bergman   H

☐ *Virginia City* (1940) d: Michael Curtiz

☐ *Virginian, The* (1929) d: Victor Fleming   H

☐ *Vision Quest* (1985) d: Harold Becker

☐ *Vitelloni, I/Young and the Passionate, The* (Italian/1953) d: Federico Fellini   H   PR

☐ *Viva La Muerte* (French-Tunisian/1971) d: Arrabal   H   PR

☐ *Viva Las Vegas* (1964) d: George Sidney

☐ *Viva Maria!* (French/1965) d: Louis Malle

☐ *Viva Villa!* (1934) d: Jack Conway, Howard Hawks

☐ *Vivacious Lady* (1938) d: George Stevens

☐ *Voice in the Wind, A* (1944) d: Arthur Ripley   S   CM

☐ *Voices* (1979) d: Robert Markowitz   S   PR

☐ *Voyage en Douce* (French/1980) d: Michel Deville

☐ *Voyage to Italy, The* (Italian/1953) d: Roberto Rossellini

☐ *Voyage to the Bottom of the Sea* (1961) d: Irwin Allen

☐ *Voyage to the Planet of Prehistoric Women* (1968) d: Derek Thomas (Peter Bogdanovich)   CC

☐ *Wagonmaster* (1950) d: John Ford   S   PR

☐ *Wait 'Til the Sun Shines, Nellie* (1952) d: Henry King   S

☐ *Wait Until Dark* (1967) d: Terence Young

☐ *Waitress!* (1982) d: Samuel Weil, Michael Hertz

☐ *Wake Island* (1942) d: John Farrow

☐ *Walk, Don't Run* (1966) d: Charles Walters

☐ *Walk With Love and Death, A* (1969) d: John Huston

☐ *Walking Dead, The* (1936) d: Michael Curtiz

☐ *Wanda Whips Wall Street* (1982) d: Larry Revenc   XXX

☐ *War and Peace* (American-Italian/1956) d: King Vidor

☐ *War and Peace* (Russian/1968) d: Sergei Bondarchuk   H

☐ *War Game, The* (British/1967) d: Peter Watkins   H   CM   PR

☐ *War Hunt* (1962) d: Denis Sanders   S

☐ *War Lord, The* (1965) d: Franklin Schaffner

☐ *War Wagon, The* (1967) d: Burt Kennedy

☐ *Warkill* (1968) d: Ferde Gofre, Jr.   S

☐ *Watermelon Man* (1970) d: Melvin Van Peebles

☐ *Watership Down* (British/1978) d: Martin Rose   S   PR

☐ *Wavelength* (Canadian/1967) d: Michael Snow   H

☐ *Waxworks* (German/1924) d: Paul Leni   H   PR

☐ *Way to the Stars, The/Johnny in the Clouds* (British/1945) d: Anthony Asquith

☐ *Wayward Bus, The* (1957) d: Victor Vicas   S

☐ *We All Loved Each Other So Much* (Italian/1977) d: Ettore Scola   S

☐ *We Are All Murderers* (French/1957) d: Andre Cayatte   H

519

□ *We Are Not Alone* (1939) d:
Edmund Goulding

□ *Wedding, A* (1968) d: Robert
Altman

□ *Wedding in Blood* (French-Italian/
1973) d: Claude Chabrol   H
PR

□ *Wedding in White* (Canadian/
1972) d: William Fruet   S
PR

□ *Wedding March, The* (1926) d:
Erich von Stroheim   H   PR

□ *Wedding Party, The* (1969) d:
Cynthia Munroe, Brian De
Palma   CM

□ *Wee Geordie* (British/1956) d:
Frank Launder

□ *Weird Woman* (1944) d: Reginald
LeBorg

□ *Welcome to Arrow Beach/Tender
Flesh* (1974) d: Laurence
Harvey

□ *Welcome to Hard Times* (1967) d:
Burt Kennedy

□ *Wells Fargo* (1937) d: Frank
Lloyd

□ *West of Zanzibar* (1928) d: Tod
Browning   H

□ *West Side Story* (1961) d: Robert
Wise, Jerome Robbins   H

□ *Westbound* (1959) d: Budd
Boetticher

□ *Western Union* (1941) d: Fritz
Lang

□ *Westward the Women* (1951) d:
William Wellman   S

□ *Wet Parade*, The (1932) d: Victor
Fleming

□ *Wetherby* (British/1985) d: David
Hare

□ *What?* (Italian/1973) d: Roman
Polanski

□ *What Have I Done to Deserve
This?* (Spanish/1984) d: Pedro
Almodovar

□ *What Price Glory?* (1926) d:
Raoul Walsh

□ *What Price Glory?* (1952) d:
John Ford

□ *What's the Matter with Helen?*
(1971) d: Curtis Harrington

□ *What's Up, Doc?* (1972) d: Peter
Bogdanovich

□ *When Dinosaurs Ruled the Earth*
(British/1970) d: Val Guest

□ *When The Legends Die* (1972) d:
Stuart Millar   S

□ *Where the Green Ants Dream*
(West German/1985) d: Werner
Herzog   S   PR

□ *Where the Lillies Bloom* (1974) d:
William A. Graham   S

□ *Where's Charley?* (1952) d:
David Butler

□ *Which Way Is Up?* (1977) d:
Michael Schultz

□ *Whirlpool* (1949) d: Otto
Preminger

□ *Whistle Down the Wind* (British/
1961) d: Bryan Forbes   H
PR

□ *Whistler, The* (1944) d: William
Castle

□ *White Cargo* (1942) d: Richard
Thorpe

□ *White Christmas* (1954) d:
Michael Curtiz

□ *White Dawn, The* (1974) d: Philip
Kaufman   CM

□ *White Dog* (1982) d: Samuel
Fuller   CM

□ *White Line Fever* (1975) d:
Jonathan Kaplan   CM

□ *White Rose, The* (West German/
1985) d: Michael Verhoeven

□ *White Sheik, The* (Italian/1951) d:
Federico Fellini   H

□ *Who?* (British/1974) d: Jack Gold
S

□ *Who Is Killing the Great Chefs of
Europe?* (1978) d: Ted Kotcheff

□ *Who Killed Mary What's' ername?*
(1971) d: Ernie Pintoff

□ *Who Killed Teddy Bear?* (1965)
d: Joseph Cates

□ *Who Slew Auntie Roo?* (1971) d:
Curtis Harrington

□ *Whole Town's Talking, The*
(1935) d: John Ford

□ *Whoopee* (1930) d: Thornton
Freeland

□ *Who's Afraid of Virginia Woolf?*
(1966) d: Mike Nichols   CM
PR

□ *Who's That Knocking on My
Door?* (1968) d: Martin
Scorsese   CM

□ *Why Worry?* (1923) d: Fred
Newmeyer, Sam Taylor   H
PR

□ *Wichita* (1955) d: Jacques
Tourneur

□ *Wild Boys of the Road* (1933) d:
William Wellman   S   PR

□ *Wild in the Country* (1961) d:
Philip Dunne   S   PR

□ *Wild River* (1960) d: Elia Kazan
S

□ *Wild Wild World of Jayne
Mansfield, The* (1968) d:

Arthur Knight   CM

□ *Wild Women of Wongo* (1958) d:
James Wolcott   CC   CM

□ *Wildrose* (1984) d: John Hanson
S

□ *Will Penny* (1968) d: Tom Gries
S

□ *Will Success Spoil Rock Hunter?*
(1957) d: Frank Tashlin   CM

□ *Willie and Phil* (1980) d: Paul
Mazursky   CM

□ *Wind, The* (1927) d: Victor
Sjostrom (Seastrom)   H   PR

□ *Wind Across the Everglades*
(1958) d: Nicholas Ray

□ *Window, The* (1949) d: Ted
Tetzlaff

□ *Windy City* (1984) d: Armyan
Bernstein

□ *Wings of Eagles, The* (1957) d:
John Ford

□ *Winning Team, The* (1952) d:
Lewis Seiler

□ *Winter Light* (Swedish/1962) d:
Ingmar Bergman   H

□ *Wise Blood* (1979) d: John
Huston   CM   PR

□ *Witchcraft Through the Ages/
Haxan* (Swedish/1920) d:
Benjamin Christensen   H
CM

□ *Without a Trace* (1983) d: Stanley
R. Jaffe   S

□ *Without Warning/It Came Without
Warning*(1980) d: Greydon
Clark   S

□ *Wizard of Gore, The* (1970) d:
Herschell Gordon Lewis   T
CM

□ *Wobblies, The* (1979) d: Stewart
Bird, Deborah Shaffer

□ *Wolfen* (1981) d: Michael
Wadleigh

□ *Woman in Flames, A* (West
German/1982) d: Robert Van
Ackeren

□ *Woman in the Dunes* (Japanese/
1964) d: Hiroshi Teshigahara
H   PR

□ *Woman Is a Woman, A* (French/
1960) d: Jean-Luc Godard   H

□ *Woman Next Door, The* (French/
1981) d: François Truffaut

□ *Woman on the Beach, The* (1947)
d: Jean Renoir

□ *Woman Rebels, A* (1936) d: Mark
Sandrich

□ *Woman Under the Influence, A*
(1974) d: John Cassavetes
CM   PR

☐ *Woman's Face, A* (1941) d: George Cukor

☐ *Woman's Secret, A* (1949) d: Nicholas Ray

☐ *Woman's Vengeance, A* (1947) d: Zoltan Korda

☐ *Women in Cages* (1972) d: Gerry De Leon   CM

☐ *Women in Revolt* (1972) d: Andy Warhol   CM   PR

☐ *Wonderful World of the Brothers Grimm, The* (1962) d: Henry Levin

☐ *Working Girls, The* (1973) d: Stephanie Rothman   S

☐ *World According to Garp, The* (1982) d: George Roy Hill   CM   PR

☐ *World of Henry Orient, The* (1964) d: George Roy Hill   PR

☐ *World, the Flesh, and the Devil, The* (1959) d: Ranald MacDougall

☐ *Woyzeck* (West German/1979) d: Werner Herzog   CM

☐ *Wrestling Women vs. the Aztec Mummy, The* (Mexican/1965) d: Rene Cardona   CC

☐ *Wuthering Heights* (Mexican/1954) d: Luis Buñuel

☐ *Wuthering Heights* (British/1970) d: Robert Fuest

☐ *Xala* (Senegalese/1974) d: Ousmane Sembene   H   PR

☐ *Yanks* (1979) d: John Schlesinger   PR

☐ *Yearling, The* (1946) d: Clarence Brown

☐ *Yesterday, Today, and Tomorrow* (Italian/1964) d: Vittorio De Sica

☐ *You Were Never Lovelier* (1942) d: William A. Seiter

☐ *You'll Never Get Rich* (1941) d: Sidney Lanfield

☐ *Young Cassidy* (1965) d: John Ford, Jack Cardiff

☐ *Young Girls at Rochefort, The* (French/1968) d: Jacques Demy

☐ *Young Lions, The* (1958) d: Edward Dmytryk

☐ *Young Mr. Lincoln* (1939) d: John Ford   H   PR

☐ *Young Savages, The* (1961) d: John Frankenheimer

☐ *Your Cheatin' Heart* (1964) d: Gene Nelson   S

☐ *Your Past Is Showing* (British/1957) d: Mario Zampa

☐ *Your Three Minutes Are Up* (1973) d: Douglas N. Schwartz   S

☐ *You're a Big Boy Now* (1966) d: Francis Ford Coppola   CM

☐ *You're Telling Me* (1934) d: Erle C. Kenton

☐ *Youth Runs Wild* (1944) d: Mark Robson   S

☐ *Zachariah* (1971) d: George Englund   CM

☐ *Zazie/Zazie dans le Metro* (French/1960) d: Louis Malle   H   CM

☐ *Zenobia* (1939) d: Gordon Douglas

☐ *Ziegfeld Follies* (1946) d: Vincente Minnelli

☐ *Ziegfeld Girl* (1941) d: Robert Z. Leonard

☐ *Zoo in Budapest* (1933) d: Rowland V. Lee   S   PR

☐ *Zoot Suit* (1981) d: Luis Valdez   S   PR

☐ *Zorba the Greek* (1964) d: Michael Cacoyannis   H   PR

☐ *Zorro, the Gay Blade* (1981) d: Peter Medak   S

☐ *Zulu* (British/1964) d: Cyril Endfield

About the Author

DANNY PEARY IS A FILM AND TELEVISION CRITIC, SPORTSWRITER, AND SCRIPTWRITER. HE HAS A B.A. IN HISTORY FROM THE UNIVERSITY OF WISCONSIN AND AN M.A. IN CINEMA FROM THE UNIVERSITY OF SOUTHERN CALIFORNIA. HE CURRENTLY WRITES FOR *TV GUIDE-CANADA*, *VIDEO TIMES*, AND THE UNITED STATIONS RADIO NETWORK. HIS PREVIOUS BOOKS ARE *CLOSE-UPS: THE MOVIE STAR BOOK* (EDITOR), *THE AMERICAN ANIMATED CARTOON: A CRITICAL ANTHOLOGY* (COEDITOR WITH GERALD PEARY), *CULT MOVIES*, *CULT MOVIES 2*, AND *SCREEN FLIGHTS/SCREEN FANTASIES: THE FUTURE ACCORDING TO THE SCIENCE FICTION CINEMA* (EDITOR). HE LIVES IN NEW YORK CITY WITH HIS WIFE, SUZANNE, AND DAUGHTER, ZOË.